Neate: Bank Confidentiality

Fourth Edition

Neate: Bank Confidentiality

Fourth Edition

Tottel
publishing

the global voice of
the legal profession

TOTTEL PUBLISHING, MAXWELTON HOUSE, 41–43 BOLTRO ROAD, HAYWARDS HEATH, WEST SUSSEX, RH16 1BJ

A CIP Catalogue record for this book is available from the British Library.

ISBN 13 978 1 84592 236 8

ISBN 10 1 84592 236 0

Typeset by Phoenix Photosetting, Chatham, Kent
Printed and bound in Great Britain by Antony Rowe, Chippenham, Wilts

PREFACE

Once again I have had the pleasure of editing a new edition of Neate on Bank Confidentiality.

In the early eighteenth century William Congreve remarked 'I know that's a secret for it's whispered everywhere'. However, as the first edition of this book demonstrated, in many jurisdictions there was a very real duty of secrecy or confidentiality owed by a banker to its customer.

The next two editions resulted from sessions at International Bar Association Conferences which illustrated gradual erosions of the duty. However, the impetus for this new edition was a perception that recently there have been more rapid changes leading to greater transparency in relation to banks' dealings with their customers, backed by the force of law. Now no 'whisperings' are necessary in many circumstances to find out a customer's position.

Since many of these changes have arisen from international initiatives aimed at preventing money-laundering, the opportunity has been taken to add a general chapter dealing with that topic.

The contributors to the previous edition have updated their own jurisdictional chapters and new chapters have been added to deal with the position in the Cayman Islands and China. They are all up to date as at 30 April 2006.

As before, many of the contributors are members of the Banking Committee, which now forms part of the Legal Practice Division of the International Bar Association. We are fortunate to have a new introduction from the original editor, Francis Neate, who is currently President of the International Bar Association. He reflects on some of the changes which have occurred.

As ever, my thanks are due to all those who have participated in this project. They have worked very hard to produce an interesting comparative study of an increasingly complex subject.

It only remains for me to thank my own colleagues at Barlow Lyde & Gilbert for their support in relation to the updating of the English chapter and Cliff Godfrey for his invaluable assistance on the editorial aspects of my role. My thanks are also due to Paul Crick at the International Bar Association and Andy Hill and his colleagues at Tottel Publishing who have been unfailingly efficient and helpful in bringing this new edition to fruition.

Gwendoline Griffiths
July 2006

INTRODUCTION TO THE 4TH EDITION OF BANK CONFIDENTIALITY

Sensible as I hope I always am, the first thing I did upon being invited to write this introduction to the fourth edition of Bank Confidentiality, was to re-read my Introductions to the first and second editions. This was a great mistake, because it left me with the feeling that there was nothing left to add. In the Introduction to the first edition, I claimed to detect a number of trends indicating the erosion of both the legal and the moral basis of banking secrecy; in the preface to the second edition I declared it dead and buried. What more is there now to say?

These statements were, of course, an exaggeration. A bank's duty to keep its customers' affairs confidential still exists and, almost certainly, will continue to exist. But the tendency of governments to impose exceptions will undoubtedly also continue to exist and, I would guess, to expand. The result, of course, will be more and more, increasingly complicated laws. With the financial services industry leading the globalisation of business activity, the need for cross-border co-operation between regulators will increase. International crime will not go away, nor will international money laundering.

None of this is bad news for lawyers, though I am sure many would say that it is bad news for their clients. I venture to disagree. Over ten years ago, I was consulted by a client who had just discovered that he had been defrauded of a large sum of money. Finding and recovering the money, or at the least some of it, was the first priority, a long way ahead of finding and prosecuting the perpetrator. (The police's priorities were, of course, the opposite, a cause of some frustration). We never recovered a penny by using the orthodox legal processes. They were too slow and cumbersome. The money went first, of course, to Switzerland, then promptly onwards. We did recover some of it by less orthodox means.

This experience contributed to my own developing scepticism about the importance of the principle of confidentiality. Every lawyer who has had to advise on whether or not a fact is material for disclosure – whether in a prospectus or in any other document – knows that the more anxious the client is to avoid disclosure, the more certain it is that it ought to be disclosed, even if he (the lawyer) is not sure that he knows the reason why. This test extends well beyond the legal sphere – to many business decisions and to many ethical issues. The questions are always the same: why do you not want people to know? Would you do whatever it is you intend to do if people did know? It is as good a test as I know for judging the propriety of many of the more difficult decisions that arise in the course of a legal, or a business, or a political, or even a private life.

Transparency is one of the current buzz-words for describing the principles which should govern the conduct of public life. When I first heard it used, I was dismissive, instinctively sceptical. I was brought up in another age – the age of the 'Establishment'. The Establishment was at the heart of the City of London. There were few rules, certainly few that were written down. 'My word is my bond'. Few outside the City understood what the City did or how it did it. It was not written down and nobody explained it. This was one of the ways in which the Establishment maintained its power and position. Insider dealing was merely one aspect of the lack of transparency. Confidentiality can hide a multitude of sins. The Establishment thrived on it.

I started my professional life over 40 years ago as a member of the Establishment and a firm believer in the importance of the principle of confidentiality – as I explained at some length in my Introduction to the first edition. 40 years of professional experience have lead to a complete reversal of my attitude. I am now deeply suspicious of anyone who seeks to resist or control disclosure of anything they regard as sensitive. To take a recent, controversial example: if the leaders of our armed forces, or the UK Cabinet, or indeed the public at large, had known the detail of the Attorney-General's original advice about the legality of the proposed invasion of Iraq, is there anyone who seriously believes that the invasion would still have taken place (or if it did, that the UK would still have been a part of it)?

I am not suggesting that there should never be a duty to keep a confidence. Clearly, business is entitled to keep its secrets from its competitors; those who confess to their priest, those who consult their lawyers, whistle-blowers, those who give information to a journalist in confidence, all are entitled to have their confidence protected. However, I am not convinced that customers of banks are in the same category. There are other, equally important, conflicting considerations and the law will continue to struggle to balance them in a coherent, constructive way. I have little doubt, therefore, that the law governing confidentiality will continue to develop and will become increasingly complex. This will occur in more and more countries as the process of globalisation continues, particularly in the financial sector, and it seems to me very likely that further editions of this book will be needed, possibly at decreasing intervals. The Banking Committee of the Legal Practice Division of the International Bar Association is perfectly positioned to undertake this task. Its members comprise many of the leading practitioners in the financial centres of the world. I welcome the addition of yet more countries whose laws are covered in this edition. This is a subject which will not lose its importance or its worldwide relevance. I congratulate the contributors and especially the editor, Gwen Griffiths, and thank them for undertaking a valuable task. I hope their enthusiasm will not be blunted for updating this edition yet again in a few years' time.

Francis Neate
July 2006

CONTENTS

Contents

INTERNATIONAL BAR ASSOCIATION

The global voice of the legal profession

In its role as a dual membership organisation, comprising 30,000 individual lawyers and over 195 Bar Associations and Law Societies, the International Bar Association (IBA) influences the development of international law reform and shapes the future of the legal profession. Its Member Organisations cover all continents and include the American Bar Association, the German Federal Bar, the Japan Federation of Bar Associations, the Law Society of Zimbabwe and the Mexican Bar Association.

Grouped into two Divisions – the Legal Practice Division and the Public and Professional Interest Division – the Association covers all practice areas and professional interests. It provides members with access to leading experts and up-to-date information as well as top-level professional development and network-building opportunities through high quality publications and world-class Conferences. The IBA's Bar Issues Commission provides its Member Organisations with substantive programmes and social activities in and between meetings and the IBA's Human Rights Institute works across the Association, helping to promote, protect and enforce human rights under a just rule of law, and to preserve the independence of the judiciary and the legal profession worldwide.

Banking Law Committee

The Banking Law Committee provides a worldwide forum for banking lawyers and other legal professionals within the banking community to address all sorts of practical and legal issues arising in commercial and regulatory activities in this context.

For further information please visit the IBA website at *www.ibanet.org*

Further Information

Contact: International Bar Association, 10th Floor, 1 Stephen Street, London, W1T 1AT, United Kingdom. Tel: +44 (0)20 7691 6868. Fax: +44 (0)20 7691 5544.

E-mail: *member@int-bar.org*. Website: *www.ibanet.org*

CONTRIBUTORS

Argentina – Rafael La Porta Drago

The contributor is from Allende & Brea.

Rafael La Porta Drago specialises in banking, capital markets, M&A and international transactions. He joined the firm after graduating from the University of Buenos Aires Law School (1960). He is currently a member of the Ethics Tribunal of the Buenos Aires Bar Association and is a visiting professor in Finance at the Universidad de San Andrés. He is also a contibutor to the Banking and Finance Chapter of the Argentine Legislation Digest, a project sponsored by the Ministry of Justice to compile the current legislation.

Email: *rlp@allendebrea.com.ar*

Australia – Ros Grady and Sandra Zivcic

Ros Grady is a Partner in the Melbourne office of Mallesons Stephen Jaques where she specialises in financial services, privacy, anti-money laundering and commercial transactions involving financial institutions. Her experience includes advising major financial institutions and industry bodies on financial services regulation and product development, privacy laws, anti-money laundering and counter terrorism financing laws, consumer credit laws, electronic banking and payment systems, financial service provider acquisitions, bank/non-bank financial service agreements and loyalty card schemes. Ros drafted the Code of Banking Practice for the Australian Bankers' Association and has extensive experience in advising on its terms and related compliance systems. Ros has spoken at numerous industry conferences, and published widely, in her fields of expertise.

Email: *ros.grady@mallesons.com*

Sandra Zivcic is a senior associate in the Melbourne office of Mallesons Stephen Jaques, practising mainly in financial services regulation. Her experience includes advising banks and other financial institutions on privacy, anti-money laundering, financial services and consumer credit legislation. Prior to her role at Mallesons, Sandra was a senior lawyer at the Australian Securities and Investments Commission and was heavily involved in the implementation of the Financial Services Reform Act including the development of administrative policy and as a delegate on exemption applications.

Email: *sandra.zivcic@mallesons.com*

Austria – Stefan Tiefenthaler and Klemens Keferböck

Stefan Tiefenthaler is partner of Binder Grösswang Rechtsanwälte, one of the leading law firms in Austria and advises Austrian and international banks and corporates in banking law matters and finance transactions, in particular banking regulatory law, structured finance and project finance. He further focuses on private international and jurisdiction law. He holds the degree of a doctor of law of the

University of Innsbruck and a master degree in European law of the University of Saarbrücken. He is author of numerous publications on finance and banking law and co-author of the Austrian commentary on European jurisdiction and enforcement law (Orac-LexisNexis, 2nd edition 2003).

Email: *tiefenthaler@bgnet.at*

Klemens Keferböck is junior partner of Binder Grösswang Rechtsanwälte and part of the firm's banking and finance team with an emphasis on banking regulatory law and structured finance. He holds the degree of a doctor of law of the University of Vienna and a master degree in American law of the Wake Forest University School of Law. He is author of several publications on finance and banking law.

Email: *keferboeck@bgnet.at*

Belgium – Jacques Richelle and David Verroken

The contributors are from Linklaters De Bandt.

Jacques Richelle graduated from Brussels University Law School (1988) and received an LLM from Southern Methodist University School of Law (1989). After working for the Belgian Minister for Europe, he was called to the Brussels Bar in 1990 and joined De Bandt, van Hecke & Lagae (1992). A partner since 1998, he mainly practises banking law (transactional and regulatory aspects) and general financial law.

Email: *jacques.richelle@linklaters.com*

David Verroken graduated from the Universities of Kortrijk and Leuven (2002), having spent one year (2000-2001) at King's College, London. He received an LL.M. from the University of Chicago, Law School (2003). Thereafter, he was called to the Brussels Bar. He joined Linklaters De Bandt in 2003 where he mainly practices banking and financial law.

Email: *david.verroken@linklaters.com*

Brazil – Jorge Nemr

Educational Background: LLB from University of São Paulo; Post-Graduation from FGV-SP; specialization courses in Public Law, Commercial, and International Law.

Personal History/Titles: Enrolled with the OAB under N. 117.256, State of SP; Member of the OAB Law Firms' Committee, State of São Paulo; Member of the Committee of Competition Law and International Trade of the IASP (São Paulo Lawyers Institute); Member and advisor of the ICLA (International Criminal Law Association); Member of the IBA (International Bar Association) as a Latin American Chair of the Committee 10 (Practice Management and Technology); Member of the Legislation, Telecommunications, and Environmental Committees of the American Chamber of Commerce and of the CESA's Support Committee of Exportation. He has published several articles in specialized magazines and collaborates with the American Magazine IELR (International Enforcement Law Reporter).

Areas of Practice: Specialist in International.

Languages: Portuguese and English.

E-mail: *jorgen@tostoadv.com*

Canada – Karl Delwaide and Nicolas Leblanc

Karl Delwaide is a senior partner at the Montreal office of Fasken Martineau DuMoulin LLP. He acts as legal counsel as well as a litigator, particularly in public and government regulation matters. He has expertise in issues relating to privacy, including the protection of information held or managed by a company as well as the protection of personal information and its use on the Internet. He has extensive experience of courts and tribunals in this field. He is one of the founders of the National Protection of Information and Privacy Practice Group of Fasken Martineau and its current Chair. He is also the "Chief Privacy Officer" of Fasken Martineau. His diversified practice also includes advising companies in the natural resources industry and professional societies, as well as advising on various business regulation matters.

Email: *kdelwaide@mtl.fasken.com*

Nicolas Leblanc is a B.C.L./LL.B. student at the Faculty of Law of McGill University and a Student-at-Law at the Montréal office of Fasken Martineau DuMoulin LLP.

Email: *nleblanc@mtl.fasken.com*

Cayman Islands – Julian Black, Virginia Czarnocki and Wayne Panton

Viriginia Czarnocki worked for the Scottish law firm Dundas & Wilson, as Regional Director of one of the largest engineering companies in the world in their PPP consultancy practice and as a partner in the projects and corporate team of another Scottish law firm before joining Walkers. She is a member of the Corporate and International Finance department where she works on asset financing and a broad range of corporate and commercial matters.

Email: *virginia.czarnocki@walkersglobal.com*

Julian Black qualified as an English solicitor in 1994 and before joining Walkers worked for Clifford Chance in London working on Eurobonds, bond repackagings and securitisation and in the Structured Finance team at Freshfields. He specialises in structured finance transactions, including securitisations, CBOs/CLOs, secured note programmes, alternative risk transfer and project bonds.

Email: *julian.black@walkersglobal.com*

Wayne Panton obtained his law degree from University of Liverpool and did his professional training at Walkers. Most recently he has worked in the areas of capital markets and structured finance as well as general corporate law and asset finance. He is also a member of Walkers' Shipping and E-commerce groups and co-heads the firm's Capital Markets and Structured Finance team.

Email: *wayne.panton@walkersglobal.com*

China – Ji Jianfeng

Ji Jianfeng qualified in 1988 and joined China Global Law Office, where he became Head of Finance in March 1990. In 1995, he left China Global Law Office and set up Summit Law Office, where he is the Managing Partner. His practice involves banking and corporate finance, project finance and development, mergers and acquisitions, capital markets and investments. He has represented international lenders, multinational corporations and investment vehicles in connection with their business, joint venture and direct investment activities in China. He also has substantial experience in project finance and M&A, representing both international lenders and developers in connection with infrastructure (power, toll roads, tunnels and bridges, water treatment and gas) projects. He speaks Chinese and English.

Email: *jerry_ji@summitlawoffice.com*

Czech Republic – Pavla Henzlová

Pavla Henzlová received a doctorate in law from Charles University, Prague in 1980. Prior to being called to the Bar, she worked as an in-house lawyer and a legal consultant. She gained a wide range of experience from a three-year co-operation with a British law firm where she ran her own legal practice. After spending 10 years with prominent Czech law firms, she joined Squire, Sanders & Dempsey, Prague office in 2004. She has had a wealth of experience in many aspects of corporate and commercial law, advising Czech and international clients on investments in the Czech Republic in connection with mergers and acquisitions, securities transactions and banking.

Email: *PHenzlova@ssd.com*

Denmark – Herman D Federspiel

He graduated with a law degree from Copenhagen University Law School in 1966 followed by European law studies at the University of Paris. He was a lecturer in public international law at the University of Copenhagen from 1967–1968 and was a member of the Danish Ministry of Justice's Committee on Legislation for Commercial Agents. He was an associate with the law firm of Dragsted, Kromann, Nørregaard, Friis in Copenhagen from 1967–1972. He became a partner in the law firm of Per Federspiel (now Gorrissen Federspiel Kierkegaard) in 1974. His areas of practice include banking and finance, insolvency and general corporate work. He is a member of the IBA's Banking Committee and of the Danish Bar Association's Educational Committee. He is the author of various articles on banking subjects in the Danish Weekly Journal of Law (*Ugeskrift for Retsvæsen*).

Email: *HF@gfklaw.dk*

England – Gwendoline Griffiths and Simon Robert-Tissot

Having graduated from St Anne's College, Oxford in 1977 Gwendoline Griffiths trained and was admitted as an English solicitor in 1979. Her specialisation is banking law, dealing mainly with transactional matters and related regulatory issues. She has worked mainly in London but also in Singapore from 1984-1986. She was seconded to Citicorp Investment Bank (1983-1984). She is currently a Consultant in the Banking and Finance group at Barlow Lyde & Gilbert and a Visiting Lecturer at the College of Law. Her previous published works include the English chapter of the *EACT Technical Guide to International Cash Management* (2004) and the English chapter, and the editorship, of *International Acquisition Finance: Law and Practice* (IBA and OUP, 2006). She is an officer of the IBA's Banking Law Committee and Co-chair of its Legal Opinions sub-committee having previously been the Committee's Publications Officer and Vice-chair.

Email: *ggriffiths@blg.co.uk*

Simon Robert-Tissot is a commercial litigation partner at Barlow Lyde & Gilbert. He graduated from Magdalene College, Cambridge and then practiced as a barrister in London. He became an English solicitor and Higher Court Advocate practicing in Hong Kong from 1988 to 1991 and subsequently in London. He specialises in High Court Litigation and Arbitration and contentious FSA regulatory matters. Many of his cases involve claims against financial institutions or professionals. He has advised upon many high profile cases including the demerger of British Gas, i-21 Germany v Federal Republic of Germany in ECJ, and FSA investigations into Sportsworld Media Group and Shell's Proved Reserves. In 1997 he was a Compliance Manager and in house Counsel at the London Metal Exchange. He is a member of FOA, ICC and LCIA.

Email: *srtissot@blg.co.uk*

Finland – Lauri Peltola and Helena Sallila

Lauri Peltola joined Waselius & Wist, one of the leading commercial law firms in Finland, as a partner in 2002. He graduated from the law faculty of Helsinki University in 1974 and was admitted to the Finnish Bar in 1978. Before joining Waselius & Wist, he worked for the Ministry of Trade and Industry, Competition Bureau (1975–1976), Procopé & Hornborg (1976–1992) (partner 1980, head of London Branch 1984, secondment S.G. Archibald, Paris 1980) and for Roschier Holmberg (1993–2002) (head of London Branch 1993, partner 1995). He has extensive experience in the area of banking and capital markets as well as cross-border M&A work. He regularly acts for a large number of public and private Finnish and international companies and financial institutions, including private equity and hedge funds.

Email: *lauri.peltola@ww.fi*

Helena Sallila joined Waselius & Wist in 2000 as an associate. She obtained her LL.M. from the University of Helsinki in 1996. In 2000, she obtained a LL.M.Eur from the Law Department of the Europa-Institut at the University of Saarland and was admitted to the Finnish Bar in 2002. Prior to joining Waselius & Wist, she worked as a trainee in the Amt der Steiermärkischen Landesregierung in Graz (1995), as a trainee in the Anwaltssozietät Dr. Kohl & Gernert in Trier (1996) and as a Legal Advisor at the Finnish Consumers' Association (1996-1998). Her main areas of practice include capital markets and banking law.

Email: *helena.sallila@ww.fi*

France – Jean-François Adelle

Jean-François Adelle, born in 1958, is a French qualified Avocat and a Partner of JeantetAssociés. He graduated from the law schools of Nancy and Paris Assas, the Paris Institute of Comparative Law (magna cum laude), and the University of

Pennsylvania (LL.M). Admitted to the Bar in 1979, he gained his experience in foreign international and French law firms. He chaired the European Alliance of Commercial Law Affiliates (now Meritas) in 2000-2001.

He has developed a specialist practice as counsel in banking and financial law. He focuses primarily on structured finance transactions (acquisition, project, infrastructure financings, asset based lending, international cash pooling) for an extensive French and foreign clientele including arrangers. He also handles regulatory matters in banking law and asset management, litigation and arbitration.

Jean-François Adelle has authored many articles in the field of banking and finance and speaks regularly at International Conferences on financial law issues. He chairs the Security Interest Committee of the Financial Law group of Paris Europlace.

Email: *jfadelle@jeantet.fr*

Germany – Thomas Schulz and Torsten Fett

The contributors are from Nörr Stiefenhofer Lutz.

Dr Thomas Schulz is a partner in the Munich office and Co-Head of the corporate department. He graduated from the University of Munich and Georgetown University Washington DC (LLM). He is a German attorney-at-law and a New York attorney and counsellor-at-law. He was counsel at the European Bank for Reconstruction and Development in London from 1996-1997. He specialises in corporate law, M&A, project and structured finance.

Email: *thomas.schulz@noerr.com*

Dr Torsten Fett graduated from the University of Bielefeld. He completed his postgraduate studies at the Humboldt-University of Berlin where he worked as an assistant at the Institute for Banking and Capital Markets Law (1998-2001). He joined the firm's Berlin office in 2001. In 2004, he was seconded to Macfarlanes, London. He specialises in corporate law, capital markets, banking compliance and regulatory advice.

Email: *Torsten.Fett@noerr.com*

Greece – Marios Bahas

Marios Bahas, born, Athens, Greece, 1944, graduated from the University of Athens, Law School (LL.B.), 1967, he has followed post graduate studies (LL.M.) in the University of London, 1969, admitted in the Supreme Court of Greece, 1979. Mr. Bahas, leads the law firm's Company/ Commercial and Banking/ Finance practice and has been the principal senior litigate for major clients of the firm for many years. He regularly advises on company and commercial issues on the context of mergers and acquisitions as well as litigation. In recent years, he has represented a number of boards of directors and companies. Mr. Bahas, is a member of the Athens Bar Association, the International Bar Association and he is a correspondent of Tax Letter Europe of the European Law Press. Author: "Bank Confidentiality in Greece", 1989. Mr. Bahas at present serves also as Senior Legal Advisor of the Egnatia Bank in Greece. Mr. Bahas speaks Greek, English and French.

Email: *law-firm@bahagram.com*

Hungary – Péter Köves and Gábor Felsen

The contributors are from Köves Clifford Chance, Budapest and both are registered members of the Hungarian Bar.

Dr. Köves is a Senior Partner and the head of the Banking & Finance Practice. He obtained a diploma in law with distinction (summa cum laude) in the Faculty of Law and Politics at the University Eötvös Loránd in 1983 and is a doctor of law. He has extensive experience in advising financial institutions on all aspects of their operation and on complex structured finance transactions in several sectors, and in litigation. He advises leading Hungarian and international companies, banks, advisory firms and government institutions.

Dr. Köves has received an award from the Minister of Economy and Transport for his contribution to the introduction of PPP techniques in Hungary. He was also awarded the "Eötvös Prize" by the Hungarian Bar Association for his professional achievement. He is Second Vice President of the Council of Bars and Law Societies of Europe, prospective president in 2008. Councillor for Hungary in the International Bar Association.

Email: *Peter.Koves@CliffordChance.com*

Dr. Felsen is a senior associate in the Banking & Finance practice. He graduated from the Faculty of Law and Politics at the University Eötvös Loránd with distinction (summa cum laude) in 1997, is a doctor of law and holds a diploma in banking law (1993-1994). He specialises in the area of finance law, with emphasis on structured financial products, derivatives and securitisation, as well as project finance transactions in the energy and other infrastructure sectors. Dr. Köves, as team leader and Dr. Felsen acted for the Ministry of Economy and Transport during the M5 PPP motorway transaction (Project Finance International Deal of the Year award for 2004), and also acted for the consortium of banks in connection with the financing of the M6 PPP motorway project. They recently participated the first ever secured bond issue in Hungary (and the first for 5 years in the CEE) in respect of the refinancing of the M6 PPP motorway project.

Email: *Gabor.Felsen@CliffordChance.com*

Ireland – William Johnston

William Johnston is a partner at the law firm of Arthur Cox in Dublin, where he is head of the Banking Law Department. An economics graduate of Trinity College Dublin, William has extensive experience advising banks on regulation and financing facilities as well as debt capital market transactions. He is chairman of the Law Society's Business Law Committee, a member of the Company Law Review Group and Publications Officer (and Newsletter Editor) of the International Bar Association's Banking Law Committee. He is author of the first published book on Irish banking law, *Banking and Security Law in Ireland (Butterworths 1998)*, co-author of *Structuring Company Lending after the Company Law Enforcement Act 2001 (Butterworths 2001)*, co-editor of the IBA's *Set-off Law and Practice – An International Handbook (Oxford University Press 2006)* and author of several other chapters and articles.

Email: *William.Johnston@arthurcox.com*

Italy – Marcello Gioscia and Giuseppe de Falco

Marcello Gioscia is the senior partner of Ughi & Nunziante and head of the banking and financial department, also specializing in M&A and privatisation. He graduated in law at University of Genoa and took the LLM at the Columbia University School of Law.

He was Co-chairman of the Banking Committee of the IBA and is member of the Council of the *Association Européenne pour le Droit Bancaire et Financier* (AEDBF). He is the author of several publications in Italian, English and French.

Email: *m.gioscia@unlaw.it*

Giuseppe de Falco is a partner of Ughi e Nunziante involved in banking, finance, corporate and privatisation matters. He graduated in law and specialized in commercial law at the University of Naples and took the LLM in Banking and Financial Law at the London School of Economics. He was awarded a scholarship for a PhD concerning Regulation of the Securities Market and is the author of several publications in Italian and English.

Email: *g.defalco@unlaw.it*

Luxembourg – Pit Reckinger

He graduated from the University of Paris I (Panthéon-Sorbonne) with a maitrise en droit and received a postgraduate diploma in business law from the University of Paris I (Diplôme d'Etudes Approfondies en droit des affaires). He was called to the Luxembourg Bar in 1990. He joined Linklaters and Paines, solicitors in London, for a year before becoming a partner in the corporate, banking and financing group at Elvinger, Hoss & Prussen in 1994. He advises banks, large corporates and private equity funds in corporate and capital market transactions as well as on a continuous basis for corporate housekeeping and compliance matters. His areas and expertise focus specifically on mergers and acquisition, shareholders agreements and financing documents, bond and equity listings, bank secrecy, aspects of money laundering and compliance issues for banks. He has also been advising on securitisations and SICARs.

Email: *pitreckinger@ehp.lu*

Mexico – Thomas S Heather

Before joining the Mexico City office White & Case in May 2005, he was Senior Partner at Ritch, Heather y Mueller. His practice includes securities, banking and acquisitions, in addition to arbitration and cross border insolvency. He was legal advisor to the financial services coordinator for the Mexican Businessmen Council in regard to the NAFTA negotiations; he has acted as arbitrator for the International Court of Arbitration, ICC, Paris. Mr. Heather has a law degree from the *Escuela Libre de Derecho* and a LLM from the University of Texas at Austin. Mr. Heather chaired the Mexican Mediation Institute through 2005 and currently chairs the Financial Law Section of the Mexican Bar. He is a member of the board of directors of Scotiabank Inverlat, and acted as the insolvency administrator in the successful cross border restructuring of Satmex, the Mexican satellite system.

Email: *theather@whitecase.com*

The Netherlands – Victor P G de Serière

Victor de Serière graduated from Leyden University in 1972, and obtained an LLB at Cambridge University in 1974. He joined the law firm of Loeff Claeys Verbeke in 1976, and became a partner in 1980. He is now a partner in the banking and finance department of the Amsterdam office of Allen & Overy. He mainly works on structured finance transactions, securitisations, leveraged finance deals, restructurings and regulatory advice.

Email: *Victor.deSeriere@Amsterdam.AllenOvery.com*

Norway – Terje Sommer and Vibeke K Svendsby

Terje Sommer is a partner in Bugge, Arentz-Hansen & Rasmussen, a leading Norwegian law firm. He was born in Norway and obtained a law degree from Oslo University in 1969. He became an Advokat in 1973. From 1969 to 1989, he worked with Bergen Bank (now known as Dnb NOR Bank) in Oslo holding various positions including General Counsel. From 1989 to 1991 he was General Manager of the bank's London branch. From 1991 to 2000, he was Resident Partner of Bugge, Arentz-Hansen & Rasmussen in London, returning to Oslo in 2000 to become a partner within the firm's Finance and Transaction Group of which he is also head of.

Email: *tso@bahr.no*

Vibeke K. Svendsby is a senior associate in Bugge, Arentz-Hansen & Rasmussen, a leading Norwegian law firm. She obtained a law degree from the University of Oslo in 1998 and became an Advokat in 2001. Vibeke K. Svendsby is a member of Bugge, Arentz-Hansen & Rasmussen's Financial Markets Group.

Email: *vks@bahr.no*

Panama – Carlos Ivan Sucre

Carlos Ivan Sucre is a partner at Sucre Arias & Reyes, where he specializes in Banking and Financial Law, Corporate Law and Trust Law, and manages SAR Trust Services, the firm's trust company. Born in 1970, he studied at Santa María La Antigua University, School of Law (LL.B., 1994); and Tulane University Law School (LL.M., International Trade and Finance, 1995). Admitted in Panama, 1995. He is a member of the Panamanian Bar Association, STEP (Panama Branch), the Panamanian Association of International Lawyers, and the American Chamber of Commerce.

Email: *carlosivan@sucre.net*

Poland – Tomasz Wardyński, Michał Steinhagen and Katarzyna Petruczenko

Tomasz Wardyński CBE, advocate, founding partner of Wardyński & Partners.

A specialist in international project financing, privatisation and restructuring of state-owned enterprises, he has a breadth of knowledge of all matters concerning the financing of investment projects. He is experienced in advising parties to credit agreements and has directed numerous undertakings involving the participation of international financial institutions. He has taken part in many privatisation projects, resolving questions of commercial law, and supervising the drafting of agreements to finance projects. He is experienced in negotiations regarding large public projects and in arbitration proceedings.

A graduate of the Law Faculty at Warsaw University (1970), the College of Europe, Bruges, Belgium (1973) and the Institute of European Studies and Law Faculty, University of Strasbourg, France (1974-75). He is a Honorary Commander of the Civil Division of Most Excellent Order of the British Empire (2001). Since 1986, he has been a honorary legal adviser to her Britannic Majesty's Ambassador in Poland.

Email: *tomasz.wardynski@wardynski.com.pl*

Michał Steinhagen graduated from Law Faculty at Warsaw University, Poland (2000) and the College of Europe, Bruges, Belgium (2001). He is an associate at Wardyński & Partners in the Bankruptcy and Restructuring Practice Group. He is advocate trainee at the Polish Bar Association in Warsaw. He specialises in litigation, arbitration, bankruptcy law, corporate law, contract law and EU law.

Email: *michal.steinhagen@wardynski.com.pl*

Katarzyna Petruczenko, graduated from Law Faculty at Warsaw University, Poland (2005). She is an associate at Wardyński & Partners in the Dispute Resolution and Arbitration Practice Group. She is legal advisor trainee at the National Council of Legal Advisers in Warsaw. She specialises in litigation, and has written several publications relating to competition law and bankruptcy law.

Email: *katarzyna.petruczenko@wardynski.com.pl*

Portugal – Manuel P Barrocas and Teresa Baptista

Manuel P. Barrocas graduated from the University of Lisbon Law School, and was admitted to the Portuguese Bar in 1968. He is a founding and senior partner of Barrocas Sarmento Neves in Lisbon and is also a member of the council of the IBA-SBL, the Union Internationale des Advocats, the American Bar Association, (section on international law and practice), the Law Society of England and Wales (Solicitors European Group), Association Européene d'Études Juridiques et Fiscales, and the Center for American and International Law.

He was a Professor of Commercial Law at the Lisbon Business School from 1970 to 1978 and has been recommended as a leading Portuguese lawyer in international directories and publications.

Manuel P. Barrocas is the author of a number of publications both in Portugal and abroad and has participated as speaker and moderator at several national and international conferences on the following practice areas: corporate law, banking and finance, corporate finance law, mergers and acquisitions and commercial contracts. His experience includes transactional and advisory work in mergers and acquisitions, private and public equity, corporate tax, insurance and investment funds with particular experience in acquisitions, disposals, mergers, flotations, takeovers, security issues and corporate tax.

E-mail: *mpbarrocas@barrocas.com.pt*

Teresa Baptista graduated from the Catholic University of Lisbon Law School, and was admitted to the Portuguese Bar in 1998. She has a Master Degree – LL.M. in Transnational Business Practice, Mcgeorge School of Law, University of the Pacific (Sacramento, Californa, USA) and post-graduation courses in Contentious Community Law (EU), Catholic University of Lisbon, Law School, and Contentious Public Law and Tax, University of Lisbon, Law School.

Teresa Baptista's experience includes transactional and advisory work in banking and finance, project finance, PPP / PFI and corporate and commercial law.

E-mail: *tbaptista@barrocas.com.pt*

Singapore – Alvin Yeo and Joy Tan

The contributors are from WongPartnership.

Alvin Yeo is Managing Partner of WongPartnership and is also Joint Managing Director of Clifford Chance Wong, the Singapore joint venture law firm between Clifford Chance and WongPartnership. His main areas of practice are banking and corporate disputes, and insolvency and restructuring matters. A graduate of King's College, London University, he was admitted to the English Bar (1987) and the Singapore Bar (1988). He was appointed Senior Counsel (2000), and is a member of the Council of the Law Society of Singapore and the Appeals Advisory Panel of the Monetary Authority of Singapore (2003). He is also a Member of Parliament.

Email: *alvin.yeo@wongpartnership.com.sg*

Joy Tan graduated from Cambridge University (1991) with first class honours. She was admitted to the English Bar (1992) with an award from the UK Council of Legal Education, and the Singapore Bar (1993). Her main areas of practice are banking, corporate and commercial litigation and dispute resolution. She is a member of the Disciplinary Committee of the Law Society appointed by the Chief Justice under the Legal Profession Act.

Email: *joy.tan@wongpartnership.com.sg*

South Africa – Angela Itzikowitz

Angela Itzikowitz is the Nedcor Professor of Banking Law at the University of Witwatersland, Johannesburg, where she teaches negotiable instruments, banking and financial markets law. She is also a professorial fellow at Queen Mary College, University of London, and a member of the Board of International Scholars, Banking and Finance Law Unit and the London Institute of Banking, Finance and Development Law (University of London). She is also a Founder Member of the Association of Banking Lawyers of Southern Africa (ABLASA). She is a partner at Edward Nathan (Pty) Ltd, where she heads the Financial Markets Division. Her specialisation includes, securitisation and all regulatory aspects of banking and financial markets.

Email: *aitzikowitz@edwardnathan.com*

Spain – Carlos Paredes

Carlos Paredes is a partner in the Madrid office of Uría Menéndez, where he begun his career in 1995 after obtaining his degrees in Law and Business Administration.

His practice focuses on commercial and company law, mergers and acquisitions, corporate governance, banking and securities law.

He was an International associate of Simpson Thacher & Bartlett in New York from 1999 to 2000 and between 2001 and 2002 he headed the firm's office in Lima (Peru), thereby acquiring first-hand experience in Latin America.

He is currently a professor at the San Pablo CEU University and the Instituto de Empresa Business School as well as a regular speaker and commentator at law seminars and conferences relevant to his areas of practice.

Email: *cpg@uria.com*

Sweden – André Andersson and Daniel Jönsson

André Andersson graduated from the University of Lund in 1986 (LLM and MBA), and attended Christ Church College, Oxford (Diploma in Legal Studies) in 1987. He joined the Swedish law firm Mannheimer Swartling in 1987 and was made a partner in 1994. He is currently a member of the board of the firm, chairman of the Financial Institutions industry group as well as of the Banking and Insurance practice group. He specialises in lending and structured financing, including securitisation and leasing. His work also includes advice on clearing and settlement rules, supervisory issues relating to financial institutions and other regulatory matters.

Email: *aa@msa.se*

Daniel Jönsson graduated from the School of Business, Economics and Law, Göteborg University, and attended Università degli Studi di Ferrara. He joined Mannheimer Swartling in 2005.

Email: *daj@msa.se*

Switzerland – Stefan Breitenstein

Stefan Breitenstein graduated from the Law School of the University of Zurich and continued his legal education at the College of Europe in Brussels where he received the "Diplôme des Hautes Etudes Européennes". After his admission to the Zurich Bar he completed his postgraduate studies at the University of Zurich with a Dr iur and received an LL.M. from Harvard Law School in 1988. He returned to Lenz & Staehelin in Zurich where he became a partner in 1994. He practises in the corporate and financial law and he is head of the banking practice group of Lenz & Staehelin in Zurich. He is Co-Chair of the Banking Committee of the Zurich Bar Association and was Co-Chair of the Sub-Committee on Banking Regulation of the IBA.

Email: *stefan.breitenstein@lenzstaehelin.com*

USA – Danforth Newcomb

Danforth Newcomb is a litigation partner in the New York Office of Shearman & Sterling LLP. His practice covers civil, administrative and criminal proceedings often acting for financial institutions in Europe, Asia, the Middle East and Latin America. He is the author of articles on bank secrecy, trans-border fraud, terrorist financing and money laundering. He received his JD degree from Columbia University in 1968.

Email: *DNewcomb@Shearman.com*

International Anti-Money Laundering Initiatives –
Chris McNeil and Stephen Revell

Chris McNeil is a lawyer at Freshfields Bruckhaus Deringer specialising in anti-money laundering law and regulation. Chris was educated at the University of Sydney and admitted as a Legal Practitioner in 1996. Previously, Chris worked in house at Deutsche Bank, London focusing on international money laundering issues. He is consulted and advises clients from a variety of Business Sectors on money laundering issues. Chris is also a visiting lecturer at the CASS Business School's Masters in Financial Crime program.

Email: *chris.mcneil@freshfields.com*

Stephen Revell became a partner of Freshfields Bruckhaus Deringer in 1987 and from 1998-2002 was based in the New York office as US managing partner. Stephen was educated at Christ's College, Cambridge. Stephen's specialisations include privatisations, debt and equity securities offerings and market regulation. His sector experience includes banking and financial services, pharmaceuticals, leisure and energy. He is co-author of a variety of books and a regular speaker on market regulation including in particular the Prospectus Directive and the Transparency Directive. Through his work on various City of London committees, Stephen is an acknowledged expert on the Prospectus Directive, the new UKLA rules and the Transparency Obligations Directive. He is active in the IBA both as an SBL Council member and in its Capital Markets Forum. He heads the IBA's '*Anti-Money Laundering Legislation Implementation Group*' and in this role has been actively participating in the debate surrounding the lawyer's role and responsibilities following the application of anti-money laundering legislation to lawyers around the world.

Email: *stephen.revell@freshfields.com*

PREFACE TO THE 3RD EDITION (2003)

This publication represents one aspect of the activities of the Banking Committee (Committee E) of the Section on Business Law of the International Bar Association (IBA). Its past history is set out in the following introduction to the 1990 edition and the preface to the 1997 edition, which were both edited by Francis Neate. This new edition is the result of a session on Banking Secrecy and the Treatment of Information chaired by him at the IBA's Business Law International Conference in Cancun in November 2001. There was a good deal of lively debate and interest in what had become a topical matter.

It became apparent that there had been a number of developments in the field which merited the new edition to update the 24 existing chapters. The opportunity has been taken to add five new chapters by some of the participants at the conference whose jurisdictions had not been covered previously (Argentina, Brazil, Mexico, Panama and South Africa). Francis Neate asked me to edit this third edition. I am grateful to him for the opportunity to undertake such an interesting project and for his wise counsel on the process.

The revisions to the chapters which appeared in the 1997 edition illustrate the way in which the law is constantly and rapidly evolving in this area on a global basis. Both the existing chapters and the new chapters had to be amended further in the course of production. They are up to date as at 30 April 2003. Several contributors have mentioned forthcoming developments. In most jurisdictions, these continuing changes seem to be the result of a number of similar factors.

The erosion of banking secrecy detected by Francis Neate continues to gain momentum. Here the main factor seems to be the international effort to prevent the laundering of the proceeds of crime and the use of funds by terrorist organisations. Developments such as the provision of banking services on the Internet are thought to have made the banking system more vulnerable to abuse. The events of 11 September 2001 prompted further international initiatives, which are reflected in a plethora of new laws and regulations in many jurisdictions.

However, this is not always the overwhelming trend, since in some jurisdictions there is an attempt to preserve, or even promote, bank confidentiality by appropriate laws and regulations. There is a view that consumers should be protected against disclosure of their personal data to the maximum extent possible. The provision of banking services on the Internet is also relevant here, since there are concerns about the security of information passed between banks and their customers. The tendency for banks to outsource administrative functions, sometimes to service providers in different jurisdictions, also gives rise to concerns about the disclosure of information to third parties.

The result is that banks and financial institutions face a complex mixture of rights and obligations in dealing with information on their customers. They have to strike a proper balance between the rights of customers to privacy and their duties to law enforcement agencies and regulators. In most jurisdictions, this seems to be an area where sound and wide-ranging legal and regulatory knowledge needs to be coupled with practical and constructive advice.

Perhaps this is just one reflection of the increasingly 'global' business community in which bankers and their advisers work. In any event, this publication should prove to be a useful tool in understanding the issues involved in the relevant jurisdictions and working out appropriate solutions.

My thanks are due to all the contributors, who have spent a good deal of time on this project. They have responded courteously and efficiently to the various deadlines and comments and queries. Without their dedication this edition would not have been possible. I am sure that there are also a number of other members of their own law firms to whom thanks are due for their support.

For my own part, I have been most appreciative of the comments of Ashley Booker and the research of my colleague, Wendie Mensah, in relation to my chapter on England. Cliff Godfrey has provided invaluable advice and support, particularly in his review of the other contributions. My secretary, Yvonne Chandler, deserves a special word of thanks for her calm efficiency in co-ordinating the project. Finally, Ruth Eldon of the IBA has been unfailingly helpful and constructive throughout.

Gwendoline Griffiths
June 2003

PREFACE TO THE 2ND EDITION (1997)

Almost all the papers in this publication were first presented in May 1997 at the Annual International Financial and Banking Law Seminar of the Section on Business Law of the International Bar Association. Some of the papers were revised in the light of the discussion at the seminar. However, the reader should not assume that they take account of any changes in law occurring after May 1997.

This is the second edition of this publication, but it is the third occasion upon which members of the Banking Committee (Committee E) of the Section on Business Law of the International Bar Association have combined to publish a set of papers on this subject. The prior history was explained in my introduction to the previous edition in 1990, which is reproduced verbatim in this edition. It is reproduced not merely to explain the history, but more importantly because in that introduction I claimed to detect a number of trends in this area of the law, all of which I can now claim to be clear and unambiguous. In 1990, I detected the erosion of banking secrecy; in 1997 we can declare it dead and buried. In particular, the introduction throughout the European Union of money laundering legislation now means that no one can any longer feel confident that he can hide his money away in his bank safe from the prying eyes of government. Recent revelations about the alleged liberties which the Swiss banks have taken with Jewish money over the years have demoralised the Swiss and demolished the moral authority with which they once defended the principle of banking secrecy against all-comers. Whether or not we should welcome these trends is a different question. They are now clearly established and will not be easily reversed.

We have expanded the present edition to include papers not only from all countries of the European Union, but also from three countries on the eastern edge of the European Union, as well as papers from the other jurisdictions which were represented in the previous edition and a paper from Singapore which also covers Malaysia. Maybe, in the next edition, if time and energy permit, we will be able to expand still further to cover yet more jurisdictions.

The burden of editorial responsibility for the previous edition was shared by my friend, Roger McCormick, of Freshfields. He has recently become Chairman of the Banking Committee of the Section on Business Law and this has meant that he has not been able to take on an editorial role in connection with this edition, so this time the editorial responsibility has been entirely mine. I have greatly missed his constructive and efficient assistance.

My thanks are also due to all the contributors. Without their courteous and usually prompt and efficient co-operation, my task as editor would have been impossible. In fact, they made it very easy for me. Those with experience of organising a group of international business lawyers to contribute to a publication of this nature will not believe me when I say that almost all the contributors delivered their papers on time and responded to my requests promptly on almost every occasion. That is nevertheless true and I am very grateful to each and every one of them. I am also extremely grateful to my secretary, Eleanor Carter, and to Deborah Roberts of the IBA staff, who between them kept track of the papers and organised both the papers and me with their usual calm patience and efficiency.

Francis Neate
September 1997

xxix

INTRODUCTION TO THE 1ST EDITION (1990)

In September 1979 at the Biennial Conference of the Section on Business Law of the International Bar Association, the Banking Committee (Committee E) conducted a comparative survey of the laws relating to banking confidentiality in a wide variety of jurisdictions. A large number of papers were read and subsequently published[1]. Switzerland, of course, led, followed by Austria, Germany and a number of other continental European jurisdictions. Then came the US, a stark contrast to Switzerland. The common law countries—England, Australia, New Zealand, Canada—brought up the rear. It was an interesting exercise. I delivered the English law paper at that conference. I emerged from the conference with a recollection of two striking contrasts.

The first contrast was the one between those countries, notably Switzerland, also Austria, in which breach of the banker's duty of confidence was enforced by the criminal law, and those where it was merely a civil obligation. In the former, enforcing the duty seemed to be straightforward. Everything was nicely cut and dried. One does not, after all, hesitate long when the choice is between performing one's duty and going to gaol. In the latter jurisdictions, by way of contrast, much doubt and uncertainty seemed to exist in some of the grey areas thrown up by the increasing internationalisation of banking business: to take one example, how should the branches or subsidiaries of a bank in one country respond to demands for information from the supervisory authorities in another country? There was an attractive simplicity to the certainty engendered by the harsh Swiss approach to these issues. On the other hand, it also seemed to encourage a rigidity which did not always make a lot of sense; whereas the greater flexibility permitted by those laws which provided merely for a civil duty appeared to me to permit a more pragmatic approach. After all, is serious harm likely to result to customers (unless they are criminals) from the disclosure of information to responsible supervisory authorities? Or, as an alternative way of looking at the problem, is there not greater risk overall to customers in general if the supervisory authorities are unable to do their job properly because of their failure to obtain information which is withheld in the interests of the few who might be damaged by its disclosure?

The second contrast lay in the extreme isolation of the US from most of the other countries. One of the principal causes of this was the very considerable resentment engendered in other countries by the recurring US tendency to extend its jurisdiction beyond its shores. The US representatives were themselves so sensitive to this resentment that one heard them apologising on more than one occasion for their authorities' behaviour; indeed, I cannot recall anyone during the 1979 conference trying to defend the US approach to the issue of jurisdiction.

However, another strong element contributing to the US isolation was the strong European feeling that the US banking and securities industries were overregulated. The US Securities and Exchange Commission was the body we all loved to hate. The European view seemed to be that our longer history had enabled us to develop systems of regulation and supervision which allowed for pragmatism and greater flexibility for sensible bankers and securities firms to conduct sensible business

1 'Banking Secrecy' published by the International Bar Association in January 1980.

efficiently and quickly, without being trammelled by detailed regulations or the necessity of having a lawyer at their side every step of the way. In the English context, after the Financial Services Act and the 'Guinness' and 'Blue Arrow' scandals (among others) of the last decade, one might view this attitude with some amusement; alternatively, one might hark back to the 1970s, when this attitude was prevalent, with nostalgia for a golden age. But there is no doubt that such an attitude was widespread and was encouraged by many of the US bankers, lawyers and others then operating in Europe. It was natural enough for the US lawyer in private practice to look upon the SEC (or, in the case of banks, the Comptroller of the Currency) as the organisation primarily responsible for making his and his clients' lives so difficult; and to contrast this with the apparent freedom in Europe. In addition, he must have been worn down by the chore of endlessly explaining to his European counterparts the detailed ramifications of the activities of powerful regulatory organisations of which they had no experience and knew no equivalents. As to the US bankers and securities dealers, the experience of coming to Europe in the 1970s was a culture shock which many found liberating. I can remember many questions from US bankers in the early 1970s as to whether there was any fundamental legal impediment to the transaction being proposed; to which often the reply would be— why should there be? What do you have in mind? In consequence, there were few articulate defendants of the US approach to whom Europeans were exposed; rather, they were encouraged in their faith in their own systems by the majority of US practitioners in Europe. Scandals such as the IOS affair were conveniently forgotten.

One wonders also how far this divergence in attitude was reinforced by more deep-rooted historical and cultural attitudes. Certainly, it is a commonplace assertion that to declare an act a criminal offence is to reinforce the underlying belief that it constitutes a moral wrong. Everyone knows the historical reasons why Switzerland takes so seriously the banker's duty of confidence and treats breach of it as a criminal offence. In the paper on Swiss law delivered in 1979, these reasons were stated proudly and unequivocally. It may be a sign of the times that, in the equivalent paper in this publication, the statement is more muted. There can be no doubt that in 1979 the stringency of Swiss law on this subject was highly respected and the reasons for it well understood. In a sense, Switzerland was regarded as the acme of banking rectitude.

No doubt, there was (as there still is) a strong competitive element also. There always has been and always will be a huge quantity of international money, owing allegiance to no particular country, looking for a home where secrecy is guaranteed. Switzerland's assumed success in attracting a large proportion of this money has long been regarded with envy by bankers in other countries.

There may also have been an element of assertion of cultural superiority by the old world over the new, a recurring tendency in many parts of Europe after (if not also before) the Second World War.

Many of these factors were contributing to the apparent isolation, during the 1970s, of US attitudes to banking regulation and banking secrecy from the European attitude. Certainly, this isolation was apparent from the papers delivered and views expressed at the conference in 1979. Yet, even then, the discerning observer might have perceived the beginnings of a convergence in those attitudes. The most concrete indication was, perhaps, the Treaty of 25 May 1973 between Switzerland and the US concerning mutual assistance in criminal matters, which was mentioned in almost apologetic terms by the Swiss speaker at the 1979 conference as a minor tear in the enveloping fabric of Swiss banking secrecy, yet to some appeared to drive a coach and horses through the principle. In the United Kingdom, the Banking Act 1979 was strengthening the powers of the banking supervisors; legislation against insider trading was also mooted. This first came into effect in the Companies Act 1980.

Ten years later, one can see that a distinct shift in European attitudes has taken place. There appear to be several reasons for this. First, and perhaps foremost, the increasing globalisation of the banking and securities businesses presents a whole new range of problems to the domestic supervisors. It has become clear to them that the traditional concept of jurisdiction limited by territorial boundaries is wholly inadequate in the context of the developing global market. Simultaneously, there has been an increasing recognition of and determination to tackle the money laundering which is an inherent feature of international and organised crime. Finally, there has been a growing appreciation and acceptance, in the securities industry, of the principle of the 'integrity' of the market; in other words, that confidence in financial markets can only be preserved by the provision of simultaneous and, where possible, instantaneous access for all to all relevant information. The principal source of all these ideas has been the US. It is no longer isolated.

In the United Kingdom, the legal effect has been dramatic. As already mentioned, insider trading became a criminal offence in 1980. The attack on organised crime (particularly drug- or terrorist-related) has been stepped up to such an extent that, in one case today, a bank which merely suspects that it is handling the proceeds of crime itself commits a criminal offence if it fails to report its suspicion[2]. The investigatory powers of the authorities have been strengthened or, in the case of inquiries instituted by the Department of Trade under the Companies Acts, utilised to an extent never seen before. Market practices which, in the past, might have been considered dubious but would certainly have gone unpunished, if not undetected, have been ruthlessly stamped on. Finally, 'Big Bang'—presented as the 'deregulation' of the securities industry—has been accompanied by the Financial Services Act, under which the securities industry is now regulated to an extent it has never known before.

Although the United Kingdom would, no doubt, claim that it has worked out (and is still working out) its own solutions, the similarities between the approach of the United Kingdom and that of the US are far more striking than the differences. No doubt many reasons can be offered for this convergence of attitudes, but I will limit myself to suggesting two. The first is obvious: the much-trumpeted 'victory' of the philosophy of the free market. There is no need to enter the debate over whether or not the philosophy is right, or whether it has been victorious over competing ideologies. It is sufficient to acknowledge that in the United Kingdom, in the last decade, this philosophy has been dominant and that the one field of activity to which its principles have been applied most vigorously has been the financial sector. This is not to say that the financial sector has been opened to unrestricted free enterprise. Rather, as already noted, it has been subjected to greater regulation than ever before. There have been substantial borrowings from the longer US experience of running an economy dedicated to the free enterprise principle. The paradox is that maintenance of the free market appears to require the strictest regulation of the market participants.

The second reason is more complex, but also represents a borrowing, albeit less conscious, from US experience. The increasing internationalisation of the banking

2 Drug Trafficking Offences Act 1986.

and securities industries is rapidly eroding the cultural homogeneity of local financial markets. In the United Kingdom this process is already almost complete. Twenty years ago, the financial system in the United Kingdom was the preserve of the middle class 'establishment'. This is not to say that it was a closed shop. Many successful careers in the City of London started at the level of 'office boy' or the like. But the values of the City and its (unwritten) codes of conduct were those of the establishment and even those who did not 'belong' when they started aspired to join. The cynic would, of course, say that one reason why this way of doing things endured for so long was that, as with any system organised and run by and for the establishment, abuses of the system were ignored—at least until one section of the establishment began to disapprove of the activities of another, as happened in the insurance market at Lloyd's in the late 1970s. But that was not the whole story. The system enabled financial business to be conducted quickly and efficiently, with the minimum of regulation and relatively modest paper-work, because it was based to a considerable extent upon trust between the majority of participants engendered by shared standards and mutual understanding. However, much of this has been lost as a result of the internationalisation of the City of London which has been taking place over the last 20 years, considerably accelerated by 'Big Bang'.

Once again, one has to look to the US for the longest experience of organising a society comprising a mix of widely different cultures. Once again, one finds that the solution lies in the promulgation of regulations spelling out in great detail what behaviour is and is not permitted. When there are no shared assumptions, written rules are the only recourse; alternatively, if the only common understanding is that what is not forbidden is permitted, then a detailed list of what is forbidden must be provided.

All these factors have been at work in the United Kingdom over the last ten years and all have contributed to a very substantial shift in attitudes towards regulation of the banking and financial industries, which have been reflected in legislation. To return to the narrower scope of this book—the banker's duty of confidence—the same trend has occurred. In the paper on English law on this subject which I delivered to the conference in 1979, I said that the basic principle of English law was that the law will not permit you to keep your secrets by hiding them in a bank. At the time, this seemed to be a bold over-statement. Today, it is clearly right.

It was because I believed that there had been, over the last ten years, so clear a convergence of attitudes between the United Kingdom and the US, that I thought it would be interesting, in 1989, to revisit the subject of banking secrecy on a comparative basis, if only to discover to what extent a similar convergence might be found in other countries. Accordingly, at the Sixth Annual International Financial and Banking Law Seminar of the Section on Business Law of the International Bar Association, held in Copenhagen in May 1989, a session was devoted to this subject. A number of panellists, mainly but not exclusively from European jurisdictions, were invited to submit papers and a variety of case studies were discussed. The title of the topic was changed—from 'Banking Secrecy' to 'Use and Abuse of Confidential Information'. This change was deliberate, in order to ensure that two topics were dealt with which had scarcely featured in the 1979 papers. The first was insider trading. The second was the subject of conflict of interests. It is ironic that the principal reform associated with 'Big Bang'—the removal of enforced dual capacity in securities dealing—has introduced a whole league of new problems of this nature. Today, you may well find your trusted broker, whom you have instructed to buy shares for you, selling you his own at a considerable profit. In the banking context, the most interesting field in which these problems have started to arise is in the context of take-over bids. Target companies have been alarmed to find their own bank representing, or lending money to, the bidder. The Takeover Panel has addressed this kind of problem but, if the law also has a role to play, it seems likely that this will be found in the law relating to abuse of confidence. Similarly, the new fashion among banks and others of offering a 'one stop' service to customers, ranging from traditional banking to estate agency, stockbroking, merchant banking, equipment leasing, etc has introduced the temptation to weaken the duties of confidentiality traditionally owed by commercial banks in order to maximise 'cross-marketing' opportunities within the enlarged group of which the commercial bank forms part. It is relatively easy for banks to include standard terms in documentation with their customers in order to achieve this; if this practice is to be curbed, legislation will be required and the matter becomes one of public policy.

Insider trading, of course, has been given wide coverage in the media during the last decade. Some still see it as a 'victimless crime' or as merely 'an Anglo-Saxon obsession'. Many complain that, although laws have been enacted in various jurisdictions, they are not applied with much rigour. Indeed, insider trading is a classic example of the inherent weakness in 'harmonisation' measures in the international community. Legislative bodies do not actually catch international criminals by passing sophisticated new laws: it is how the laws are applied that matters.

The quality of the papers and of the discussion at the seminar in 1989 was uniformly excellent and it seemed worth while to repeat the 1979 experiment by producing a publication. A number of other contributors were, therefore, also approached and the original contributors revised their papers in the light of the discussion at the seminar. The results are contained in the following chapters. All European jurisdictions are covered except Sweden, together with the other leading common law jurisdictions: Australia and Canada, and, of course, the US.

It is for the reader to judge whether, and to what extent, the trends suggested above can be seen to be more widespread. I write merely from a United Kingdom perspective. Certainly, the jurisdictions covered in the following chapters vary considerably in their experience of the problems and the level of sophistication with which they have so far been addressed, and this is reflected to some extent in the papers in question. I would suggest, however, that the trends suggested above can be discerned in many of the countries in question; and further that, if the factors underlying and compelling those trends continue to exist, each country will eventually be forced to choose. One option will be to join the global market; in which case one would expect increasingly rigorous supervision of the financial industry, coupled with more exchanges of information and standardisation of supervisory criteria among the supervisors; an ever more vigorous attack on the money laundering activities of international crime; and ever more detailed rules designed to preserve the 'integrity' of the financial markets. Insider dealing will be made a criminal offence (if it is not already) and more strenuous efforts made to catch the offenders. The alternative is to join the 'off-shore haven' club, among whose members, no doubt, the concept of banking secrecy will be elevated to an ever higher moral plane. Members of the European Community will all have to make the same choice and it seems clear that this will be for the first option.

Francis Neate
March 1990

Table of Cases

xxxvii

Table of cases

Table of cases

Table of National Legislation

Table of European and International Legislation

1 Argentina

Rafael La Porta Drago

GENERAL OVERVIEW

[1.1] Argentine law has traditionally recognised a principle of bank secrecy consisting of both a bank's right to protect the privacy of its records and proprietary commercial information and a customer's right to privacy.

Until 1969, when it was specifically addressed by statute for the first time, a bank's duty of confidentiality was construed on the basis of the customers' constitutional right of privacy provided by s 18 of the Argentine constitution and a combination of various other provisions of the Civil Code, the Criminal Code and the Civil and Commercial Procedural Code.

Some scholars construed that this duty was an implied term in all contracts entered into between a bank and its customers resulting from commercial usage and the parties' broader duty of good faith. An analogy was also drawn with a bailee's duty to maintain the confidentiality of the property delivered in bailment (Civil Code, s 2207). Based on this 'implied contract term' theory, if a bank disclosed information provided by a customer, the customer was said to be entitled to compensation for breach of contract not only during the life of the contract, but also before entering into it and following its termination. A bank's breach of this duty of secrecy was also construed as a tort, ie an illicit act giving rise to a customer's right to compensation for damages. In addition, s 1071 bis of the Civil Code, which prohibits the 'arbitrary disturbance' of another person's privacy – a term broad enough to cover a bank's indiscretion – may also apply.

In further support, s 156 of the Criminal Code prohibits those entrusted with a secret as a result of their job or profession from disclosing it and s 444 of the Civil and Commercial Procedural Code allows a witness to refuse to disclose information considered as 'privileged communication'.

FINANCIAL ENTITIES LAW

[1.2] In 1969, Law 18,061, which regulated the activities of banks and other financial institutions, specifically established for the first time a general duty of confidentiality applicable to banks, subject to certain exceptions. Although the spirit of the law was to protect customers' privacy, it did not exclude the banks' right to protect their proprietary information. Law 18,061 was later replaced by Law 21,526 (the Financial Entities Law, 'FEL'), which addressed the duty of confidentiality in s 39. Section 39 underwent a number of amendments over time that gradually limited the scope of this duty and broadened its exceptions. Further exceptions have been recently introduced under international conventions to counter money laundering, terrorism and corruption, as discussed below.

1

The FEL governs all entities (governmental or private) which regularly intermediate in the supply and demand of financial resources in Argentina, such as commercial banks, investment banks, mortgage banks, financial companies, savings and loan co-operatives, etc. The Argentine central bank is the regulatory authority charged with applying the provisions of the FEL, issuing regulations and supervising the activities of banks and other financial entities.

While, in its original version, the FEL protected all banking transactions and customer data received by banks, bank secrecy today is confined to deposits and other banks' liabilities.[1] This confidentiality duty does not apply when the disclosure is requested by:

1 a court in a judicial proceeding;
2 the Argentine central bank within the scope of its authority;
3 the tax authorities; and
4 other banks and financial institutions (with the central bank's prior authorisation).

In addition, bank secrecy does not apply to requests for information made in the course of investigations of money laundering activities, as discussed below.

In 1981, the Supreme Court concluded that s 39 of the FEL is not only applicable to banks, but also to individuals and companies handling confidential information delegated to them by a bank.[2] The case involved a credit card processing company which refused to provide the tax authorities with certain information which had been furnished to it by the banks (and was at that time protected by the banks' duty of confidentiality). This ruling is particularly applicable to the outsourcing of services and has become emphasised by the Habeas Data Law (discussed below), which makes the transferor of personal data jointly and severally liable with the transferee for any breach of confidentiality concerning personal information.

Bank secrecy is limited to deposits and other banks' liabilities

[1.3] As mentioned above, s 39 of the FEL, as amended, only applies to what is accounted for as deposits and other banks' liabilities ('confidential transactions'). This means that it does not apply to loans and other bank transactions accounted for as assets, nor to account memoranda, which reflect a broad range of transactions that are not reflected in the liabilities side of a bank's balance sheet. This limitation is aimed at allowing banks to share information on the credit rating of customers and prospective customers for the purposes of protecting loans. As part of this policy, all banks are required to supply information on their loans to the central bank on a monthly basis. Under Communication A 3360, these reports include:

1 information identifying the borrower (name, tax identification number, domicile, credit rating, whether or not the customer is deemed to be an insider of the bank, etc);
2 information relating to the debt (type of loan facility, loss reserves made by the bank, etc);
3 information as to whether or not the borrower is part of an economic group;

---

1 This limitation reflects a criterion previously suggested by the Argentine Supreme Court in *Re Banco de Londres y América del Sud*, Fallos 302-1116 (1980).
2 *Argencard SA v Gobierno Nacional (Tribunal Fiscal de la Nación)*, LL 1982-B 462 (1981).

4   additional information on 'significant borrowers' (those who meet certain standards set by the central bank, such as principal activity aggregate outstanding with the financial system, etc); and
5   certain aggregate statistical information.

This data is processed by the central bank, which in turn publishes certain parts of it (a list of borrowers, their credit rating and type and amount of their indebtedness – so-called 'public information') on the Internet. Banks and financial institutions also have access to information relating to the average interest rates and remaining life of the loans. Pursuant to Communication A 3360, banks and other financial institutions may not directly supply to third parties any information other than public information. Thus, although lending transactions are not protected by the duty of confidentiality, access to the information relating to such transactions is restricted.

Note that under the last sentence of s 39, bank personnel are prohibited from disclosing any information about the bank's customers and transactions, whether relating to confidential transactions or not. Disclosures made in breach of this provision may give rise to administrative penalties imposed by the central bank and might subject the person or institution who disclosed the information to civil liability or, in certain cases, criminal prosecution (see 'Remedies' below).

Exceptions

Court order

[1.4]   Pursuant to s 39(a) of the FEL, a court may request a bank's report on otherwise confidential information in the context of a judicial procedure.

Other than in criminal procedures, a bank's duty to disclose confidential information in response to a court order is limited by general rules of civil procedure providing that:

1   the court's request must refer to concrete facts, clearly identified and at issue during the trial; and
2   the bank's report must be drawn from its accounting records, documents and files (Civil and Commercial Procedural Code, ss 364 and 396, respectively).

Thus, during a trial, a court will assess the admissibility of the request to obtain information from a bank and, if appropriate, will issue a subpoena ordering the bank to disclose such information in writing directly to the court. In general, the courts have interpreted this exception restrictively (at least in cases involving litigation between private parties). Thus, for instance, they have dismissed a subpoena for a bank to report whether an individual does have an account with it[3] and have resolved that the statement of assets filed by a customer when opening a bank account is protected by bank secrecy.[4] Note that the general rule contained in s 39 of the FEL, prohibiting the bank's personnel from disclosing any information about the bank's customers and transactions, together with s 444 of the Civil and Commercial Procedural Code, which permits a witness to refuse to disclose information considered as 'privileged information', may prevent a court from requiring a bank employee to provide testimony about a bank's customer.

---

3 *Sociedad Mixta Siderurgia Argentina v Luis y Raúl Zecchin SA*, C Nac Civil y Com Fed Sala 2ª, 7 June 2000.
4 *Rossi Eduardo v Sanguinetti, Guillermo*, C Nac Com, Sala B, 9 February 1987; *Banco Argenfé SA v Payaslian, Martin*, C Nac Com Sala E, 31 March 1987.

3

These principles do not apply to criminal procedures, which are of an inquisitive nature. Thus, at any stage of a criminal procedure, a bank may be required by a judge or public prosecutor to disclose otherwise confidential information about one of its customers, without even giving notice to the customer.

As to foreign court orders, any request for information – whether confidential information or not – is to be made through a letter rogatory addressed to a local court and processed through diplomatic channels. In civil and commercial matters, Argentina is a party to the 1957 Hague Convention on Civil Procedure and the 1976 Hague Convention on the Taking of Evidence Abroad in Civil and Commercial Matters, whereby it undertakes to process and give full force and effect to letters rogatory from other parties to the Convention. These Conventions regulate in great detail the requirements to process letters rogatory among member countries. Otherwise, foreign letters rogatory are subject to the soft law resulting from the 'international committee' which requires the offering of reciprocity. In general, we may say that, to the extent that reciprocity is offered and that the letter rogatory states reasonable grounds for lifting bank confidentiality, a letter rogatory requesting information from a bank will be answered by the Argentine courts even if it is issued by a judge sitting in a jurisdiction which is not a party to the Hague Conventions referred to above.

The same rules applies in criminal matters. Argentina is a party to several bilateral treaties of mutual assistance on criminal matters.[5] In such absence, Law 24,767 applies (Law on the International Assistance on Criminal Matters) which provides that Argentina will render such assistance even if the offence being investigated by the foreign court is not punishable under the laws of the requested country, provided the requested action does not involve, among others, the seizure of assets or the interception of private correspondence.

A special note should be made when it comes to money laundering, terrorism and corruption investigations as, under the international conventions discussed below, Argentina is committed to render judicial mutual assistance to other parties to the conventions in the investigation and prosecution of such activities and has specifically waived the invoking of bank confidentiality in that regard.

Central bank

[1.5] Section 39(b) of the FEL provides that information 'required by the central bank within its competence' is excluded from the banks' duty of confidentiality. All information received by the central bank is in turn protected by s 40 of the FEL which requires the central bank, its personnel and any external auditors to maintain the confidentiality of all information gathered in the course or in the occasion of their duties.

The language in s 39(b) has become important within the context of a conflict between local banks and two Congress committees created to investigate the flight of capital which occurred in Argentina in 2001. In July 2002, the central bank requested general information on certain operations from all Argentine banks for the purpose of submitting such information to the Congress committees. Although the banks spontaneously responded to such request providing non-confidential information,

---

5 Treaties with Canada, Colombia, Chile, El Salvador, Spain, Italy, Mexico, Peru, USA and members of the Mercosur (Bolivia, Brazil, Paraguay and Uruguay).

they refused to submit information subject to confidentiality. Their main argument was that the central bank's request was made for the purposes of providing a response to the Congress committees, which is not within the scope of its authority. In other words, the central bank's responsibility is to supervise the correct functioning of financial institutions and the financial market and not to serve as an 'access door' to other governmental organisations not included in the exceptions to s 39. State-owned banks requested the opinion of the Attorney for the Treasury, who upheld the lifting of bank secrecy maintaining that, although the law does not expressly include committees among those who are entitled to access confidential information, the Congress resolution whereby Congress committees were created authorised them to request all kinds of information. In another debatable part of his opinion, the Attorney for the Treasury held that bank secrecy is 'relative in nature and must bow to senior principles or interests, as is the case of public policy'. Other banks have brought legal actions seeking to avoid having to give such information. Final judgment on these cases is still pending at the time of writing.

Tax authorities

[1.6]   Initially, s 39(c) of the FEL set out a limited exception to the general principle of banks' secrecy for the exclusive benefit of Argentina's national tax authorities (the National Tax Bureau). With the purpose of guaranteeing the taxpayers' right to due process, this exception was generally limited by the following requirements:

1   that the requested information refers to a particular taxpayer;
2   that such taxpayer is then subject to a tax audit; and
3   that a prior written notification be made.

The scope of this exception was gradually broadened in the succeeding years. First, to benefit provincial and municipal tax authorities as well and then to exclude the application of points 1 and 2 above when the request is made by the National Tax Bureau.

As a result, today, the National Tax Bureau has very broad powers to request otherwise confidential information from banks. However, as in the central bank's case, the National Tax Bureau is limited by (i) the scope of its own competence (ie it may not request information other than for purposes of pursuing tax collections or investigating tax evasion) and (ii) its own duty of confidentiality towards the taxpayer.[6]

Pursuant to such broad powers, under resolution 160/98 of the National Tax Bureau, banks and other financial institutions are required to report monthly to such agency: (i) all bank accounts opened and (ii) bank accounts that are credited during such month with 8,000 pesos (approximately US$2,800 at the time of writing) or more in aggregate. In addition, banks and exchange houses are also required to report certain incoming foreign exchange transfers in excess of US$50,000 per month [7]

Other banks

[1.7]   Section 39(d) of the FEL refers to information requested by 'other financial institutions with the prior express authorisation of the central bank'. This exception

---

6 Law 11,683, s 101.
7 Resolution 1926.

was never implemented and has now become redundant since its main objective – to facilitate the sharing of information on creditworthiness – has been accomplished directly by the central bank through the reception and redistribution of information on loans.

OTHER EXCEPTIONS TO BANK SECRECY
Consent
[1.8] Even within the limited scope of s 39 of the FEL, it is generally agreed that disclosure made with the affected customer's consent does not constitute a breach of the bank's duty of secrecy.

As a particular application of this principle, the Argentine courts have decided that a bank cannot refuse to respond to a request made by the holder of a cheque returned unpaid to be provided with information that helps to identify and locate the issuer of such cheque. It is understood that a customer who issues a cheque has consented to such disclosure of information, the purpose of which is to allow the cheque's beneficiary to enforce his rights.[8]

A similar conclusion must be reached when a bank and its customer are opposing parties during a trial: the latter is assumed to have consented to the bank's disclosure of confidential information within the limited scope of the trial.

Another example is the previous consent given by borrowers of a loan secured by a mortgage for the purposes of securitisation of a loan portfolio by the bank acting as lender. Such consent is usually contained in the mortgage deed and relieves the bank from the obligation of notifying the borrowers of the assignment of their loans and it is also interpreted as a release of the confidentiality obligation regarding the credit record of the borrower.

In addition, as a general practice, Argentine subsidiaries and branches of foreign banks generally include in their printed forms a customer's consent to the sharing of information between subsidiaries and branches, their parent institutions and other affiliates. However, a word of caution should be given as consent must be given in an 'express, free and informed manner'.[9] A clause whereby a client is deemed to have given his consent to a bank using its customers' database for marketing purposes and credit risk evaluations, unless the client expressly signs a clause to the contrary, was declared null by the court.[10]

Illegal drugs
[1.9] Argentina is a party to the UN Convention Against the Illicit Traffic of Narcotic Drugs and Psychotropic Substances (the Vienna Convention of 1988). As a party to this Convention, in 1989, the Argentine Congress passed Law 23,737 which deals with drug-related crimes. Section 26 specifically provides that, during the investigation of any such crimes, no bank secrecy may limit the task of the judge in charge of such investigation. This language suggests that, within the scope of this statute, a criminal judge may order any bank to submit generic information otherwise

---

8 *San Sebastián SA v Toro, Ximena*, E LL 1984-C 485 (1984).
9 Law 25,326, s 5.
10 *Union de Usuarios y Consumidores v Citibank NA*, CN Com Sala E, 12 May 2006, el Dial AA 34A0.

protected by the bank's duty of secrecy. However, the Money Laundering Law (referred to below) has superseded this statute in all matters relating to bank secrecy.

Money laundering

[1.10]   Pursuant to its commitment as a member of the Financial Action Task Force ('FATF'), in May 2000, Argentina enacted Law 25,246 (the Money Laundering Law, 'MLL') aimed at preventing and punishing the laundering of assets connected with the illegal trafficking of drugs and arms, racial or political terrorist organisations, government corruption, organised crime, child prostitution and pornography and increasing the punishment for aiding and abetting such crimes.

Under ss 20 and 21 of the MLL, banks and other financial institutions, as well as their officers and employees, are obliged to report to the Financial Information Unit ('FIU') any transaction which is either (i) unusual in the light of commercial usage of the industry involved, (ii) without economic or legal justification or (iii) of an uncommon or unwarranted complexity, either in an isolated or repeated fashion in each case. However, note that the FIU regulations apply the FATF guidelines for detecting what should be deemed to be a suspicious transaction ('ST').

The FIU has broad powers to request information from any public or private entity. However, under the original text of the MLL, while banks and other financial institutions were requested to report any ST spontaneously, when it came to answering a request for confidential information from the FIU, a court subpoena was required. This requirement caused delays in answering some of the requests for information made by the FIU to the banks, which could have even compromised their investigations. Following this experience and acting upon a mutual evaluation report conducted by the FATF in 2003, on 29 March 2006, the MLL was amended to remove the need to obtain a subpoena to have any bank secrecy lifted when answering a request for information made by the FIU, provided such request is made in the course of the investigation of a suspicious transaction report ('STR').[11] Thus, as from the second quarter of 2006, there are no instances where – either from a legal or practical point of view – Argentine rules for banking or financial secrecy would prevail over the FATF recommendations.

Section 22 of the MLL imposes on FIU personnel (and all persons required to provide information to it, ie banks and their personnel) the obligation to keep strict secrecy of all information and reports. They are also obliged to refrain from 'tipping off' any client or third party of an STR.

The failure to report an ST to the FIU is penalised with a fine ranging from one to ten times the aggregate value of the unreported ST, provided such failure does not involve a more serious offence. If the value of the ST cannot be determined, the applicable fine ranges from 10,000–100,000 pesos (approximately US$3,000–30,000 at the time of writing). The fine is imposed on the bank and on each of the officers or employees who failed to comply with the reporting obligation.

The FATF conducts evaluations on Argentina's compliance with its recommendations on an annual basis. Findings on the 2005 mutual evaluation will be published on the FIU's webpage (www.uif.gov.ar) in the second half of 2006.

---

11 Law 26,087.

Terrorism

[1.11]   Financial and exchange entities are obliged to report to a special intelligence unit of the central bank any transaction made or attempted to be made by an individual or legal entity included in the lists prepared by the UN Security Board within the framework of resolution 1267 and to freeze the funds or assets owned directly or indirectly by such persons. Financial and exchange entities are also obliged to report to this special unit any transaction suspected of being related to terrorism financing following the detecting standards set out by the central bank and the international community.[12]

In 2005, Argentina ratified the International Convention for the Suppression of the Financing of Terrorism[13] adopted by the UN on 9 December 1999, which, in s 12, provides that state parties 'shall not dismiss a petition for reciprocal judicial assistance under the protection of bank secrecy', but has not yet categorised the crimes listed in s 2 of this Convention in its domestic criminal law.

Corruption

[1.12]   On 10 May 2006, Argentina ratified the UN Convention Against Corruption.[14] Section 40 of this Convention obliges member countries to 'ensure that, in the case of criminal investigation of offences established in accordance with this Convention, there are appropriate mechanisms available within its domestic legal system to overcome obstacles that may arise out of the application of bank secrecy laws'. Similarly, s 46 provides that member countries 'shall not decline to render mutual legal assistance on the grounds of bank secrecy' in the investigations, prosecutions and judicial proceedings in relation to the offences covered by this Convention.

Argentina has not yet defined the crimes under chapter III of the Convention. Thus, for the moment, the lifting of bank secrecy in cases of international judicial assistance only applies to acts of corruption categorised as crimes by domestic laws.

REGULATION OF SECURITY MARKETS

[1.13]   Pursuant to Law 17,811, securities markets come under the supervision of the National Securities Commission ('NSC'). The NSC has broad powers to investigate and request information from securities markets, dealers and brokers and also to bring administrative or criminal actions. However, except in the course of an STR, the NSC needs a court subpoena to lift bank secrecy. Stock exchanges and self-regulated securities markets (eg the electronic open market) can also inspect and audit their brokers and agents.

All information gathered by the NSC, stock exchanges and self-regulated securities markets is to remain secret and can only be disclosed by a court subpoena issued in the course of a criminal investigation directly related to the facts at issue in such investigation (s 8, Law 17,811).

Brokers and other security agents are bound to keep confidential all transactions conducted on behalf of third parties. Any information related to such transactions can

---

12 Communication A 4384 of the central bank, Decree 1235/2001.
13 Law 26,024.
14 Law 26,097.

only be disclosed to (i) the NSC, (ii) the respective stock exchange or self-regulated market, (iii) the tax authorities or (iv) upon a criminal court subpoena, as described above.

The secrecy imposed by s 8 does not apply to information to be reported to the FIU. Further, note that, under the MLL, stock exchanges, self-regulated securities markets, stockbrokers and all intermediaries in securities, futures or options, as well as mutual fund managers and custodians, are expressly included among those who are subject to the obligation spontaneously to report any ST and to answer a request for information issued by the FIU in the course of an investigation of an STR.

Insider trading

[1.14]   Although there is almost no case law related to the subject, insider trading is extensively regulated by the NSC as a serious offence against the transparency of the securities markets.[15]

Insiders (as defined below) are bound never directly or indirectly to (i) participate in any market transaction related to the securities, futures or options ('securities') in respect of which they have acquired inside information (as defined below), (ii) disclose such inside information to any third parties (except for the performance of his or her duties) or (iii) make any recommendation to a third party for the purchase or sale of securities based on inside information.

Insiders are defined as anyone who, by reason of his or her duties, has information relating to an issuer or a securities market which is not public and, had it been made public, may affect the placement or trading of a security ('inside information').[16]

Further, all participants in the securities markets and individuals or entities that, by reason of their duties, have access to confidential information are bound (i) to prevent such information from being disclosed to their employees or any third party, (ii) eventually remedy the consequences of any leakage and (iii) report to the NSC any conduct that is likely to result in a breach of the duty of confidentiality or the use of inside information. Thus, to the extent the management has taken adequate safeguards against any leakage of information, Chinese Walls are permitted.

REMEDIES
Damages

[1.15]   A customer is entitled to recover damages caused by any illegitimate disclosure of information made by his bank. The extent of compensation depends on whether the claim is based on tort or breach of contract. Most scholars predicate the first alternative, which results in the bank being liable for both direct and indirect damages. Alternatively, if a customer sues for breach of contract, indirect damages are only imposed if the bank has acted with malice.

However, note that the client has the burden of proving the actual economic damage suffered as a consequence of the illegal disclosure of the confidential information, which in most cases becomes an insurmountable barrier for success in this kind of

---

15 *Díaz, Pedro v Banco Rio*, CN Com Sala D, 26 April 2003, LexisNexis Jurisprudencia Argentina no 0003/9676.
16 Decree 677/01 and NSC Regulations, chapter XXI.

action. A good example of how strict the demonstration of economic damage actually suffered by the client could be is a recent case where, in the middle of a divorce, a bank provided the wife with a copy of her husband's statement of account. The husband sued the bank arguing that, on the basis of such disclosure, his wife was able to obtain an increase in her alimony and had tried to obtain a greater portion of the community property. The complaint was allowed by the judge, but was dismissed on appeal on the grounds that, all in all, the assets the wife had discovered through the leak of the statement belonged to the community property and, thus, no actual damage had been caused to the husband.[17]

In addition to compensation for economic damage, a customer is entitled to compensation for 'moral damage'. However, note that in the imposition of moral damages, a court will mainly take into account the customer's 'affliction' caused by the arbitrary disclosure of financial information and not the bank's inappropriate conduct; moral damage is not equivalent to 'punitive damages'.

Because Argentine law does not contemplate punitive damages and the Civil Code's system strongly relies on a strict demonstration of actual damage, there are very few precedents of claims filed by customers harmed by their banks' breach of confidentiality. However, we can see a trend toward awarding moral damages even in the absence of conclusive evidence as to the actual economic damage caused by such breach,[18] particularly in cases resulting from wrong information supplied to databases regarding the credit rating of a client (see 'Habeas Data Law' below).

It is not usual to include a clause limiting the bank's responsibility for disclosure in the documentation signed between a bank and its clients (ie an application for opening a bank account) in Argentina. A probable explanation for this is that, given the low level of litigation in the industry, such a provision might reflect poorly on the bank's image without any noticeable benefit. In any event, any such provision should take into consideration that mandatory principles of Argentine law prohibit waiving in advance the wilful misconduct of the other party to a contract (that is, the limitation could only apply to negligent disclosures). Additionally, a court of law could disregard such limitation if it found the agreed maximum liability amount to be unreasonably low, particularly taking into account the fact that bank agreements are usually on pre-printed forms in which the client has little or no possibility of negotiating terms and conditions.

---

17 Chapter XXI, s 15 of the NSC Regulations specifically lists as insiders: (i) members of the board of the issuer, managers, auditors, members of the supervisory committee, controlling shareholders and professionals employed or retained by the issuer, (ii) executives, officers and employees of rating agencies, of private controlling entities, securities exchanges and self-regulated markets, (iii) officers and employees of public controlling agencies, including the NSC and (iv) any person who, by reason of being temporarily or accidentally related to the issuer or by reason of being a social acquaintance or relative of the controlling shareholders or of any of the individuals listed above, may have access to inside information.

18 For instance, in a case where the bank provided a third party with a copy of a loan application, the bank was ordered to pay moral damages in spite of the fact that the application had never actually been pursued by the prospective borrower. The bank argued that, under such circumstances, the plaintiff could not be deemed to be a customer and further that s 39 only covers transactions accounted for as liabilities. Again, the plaintiff failed to prove actual economic damage, but the court awarded moral damages on the grounds of the breach of the plaintiff's right to privacy (*PDR v Banco de Formosa*, Corte Superior de Justicia de Formosa, 2 April 2003, LLLitoral 2003 (August) 833).

Habeas Data Law

[1.16]   The 1994 amendment to the Argentine constitution granted every person the right to access any public – or, if it is for the purpose of providing information to third parties, private – databases or files that include personal data about the person and the right to demand the deletion, rectification, confidential treatment or updating of any false or discriminatory piece of data, as applicable (s 43).

In November 2000, s 43 of the Argentine constitution was regulated by the Habeas Data Law (Law 25,326) aimed at protecting personal data contained in public or private databases. Section 10 of the Habeas Data Law provides that any person or company handling personal data must maintain its confidentiality even after the termination of such person or company's relationship with the owner of such data.

Further, under s 16, a person is entitled to file a habeas data claim requiring the holder of a database to maintain the confidentiality of his or her personal information if such confidentiality is applicable. This section, combined with the FEL, allows a customer expeditiously to compel a bank to maintain the confidentiality of any personal information protected by the duty of secrecy. A preliminary injunction preventing a bank from disclosing information until the habeas data claim is solved adds efficiency to this proceeding.

A person harmed by wrong information available from a public database has a course of action for damages against the provider of the information. Actually, there are numerous claims against banks for giving wrong credit rating data about individuals to public databases. Again, plaintiffs generally do not succeed in proving economic damage caused by such wrong information, but nevertheless they are usually awarded moral damages.[19]

Unless appropriate consent, as defined above, has been given by the client, the transfer of personal data abroad is forbidden. Exceptions to this rule include when the transfer is made pursuant to (i) international treaties, (ii) international judicial assistance, (iii) international co-operation among intelligence agencies for the campaign against organised crime, terrorism or the illegal trafficking of drugs, (iv) a money or securities transfer to the extent needed or (v) when the transfer is made to a country or international organisation that provides the data so transferred with an 'adequate level of protection'.[20]

Administrative penalties

[1.17]   A bank's breach of its duty of secrecy constitutes a breach of the FEL, regardless of whether or not it has caused any actual damage. This breach is subject to administrative sanctions imposed by the central bank on the bank in default and any of its responsible employees. These penalties include a formal warning, fines and

---

19 *Dominguez Alvaro, Eloy v Banco Río de La Plata SA*, CNC SB, 30 December 2002, elDial.com AA14F3; *Mazza, Miriam Elizabeth v Citibank NA*, CNC SD, 20 November 2001; *Derderían Carlos v Citibank NA*, CNC SB, 12 September 2002, elDial.com AA1334; *Sosa Marcelo v Citibank NA*, CNC SH, 4 June 2002, R 339970, elDial.com AA135C; *Rebagliati, María Dolores v Banco Meridian SA*, CNC SG, 22 March 2006, elDial AA3377; *Santi Daniel Oscar v Banco de la Nación Argentina*, CNC y Com Fed S III, 28 April 2005, elDial AA2A0C; *Maderas y Servicios SA v BankBoston NA*, CNC SA, 11 May 2005, elDial AA2AA9; *Travieso Vitales, Roberto Sellivan v Lloyds TSB Bank plc*, elDial AE1F70.
20 Defined as when such protection is 'provided directly under the law, self-imposed regulation or contractual clause' (s 12 of the Regulation approved by Decree 1558/2001).

temporary or permanent disqualification from being a member of the board, manager, auditor or shareholder of a bank or other financial institution, as the central bank may deem appropriate. Sanctions imposed by the central bank are subject to appeal in the courts.

Breaches of securities regulations

[1.18]   A breach of the duty of confidentiality imposed on individuals and entities subject to Law 17,811 will make them liable for damages, as described above in regard to the breach of bank secrecy. In addition, any such breach would make the party responsible liable to administrative sanctions, which range from admonishment to fines up to 1.5 million pesos (approximately US$500,000 at the time of writing). These may be coupled with disqualification of up to five years from being a member of the board, manager, member of the supervisory committee or auditor of any issuer, rating agency, mutual fund, manager or depository broker or securities agent and prohibition or suspension from placing or working with securities.

Insider trading is more severely sanctioned, as fines may be increased by up to five times the benefit obtained or the damage caused. Further, the issuer may seek redress of the difference between any purchase and sale transaction (or from any sale and purchase transaction, as the case may be) made by the insider in respect of any securities of the issuer within a period of six months of the illegal trade. If the issuer does not seek redress within 60 days of being requested to do so, any shareholder may bring the action on behalf of the issuer. The action for redress is cumulative with the action provided for in s 276 of the Law of Corporations, whereby the directors and managers are jointly and severally liable for any breach of their duties.

CONCLUSION

[1.19]   The principle of bank secrecy is protected by the Argentine constitution and expressly regulated by the FEL. However, many exceptions to it have significantly limited its scope. First, as a general rule, bank confidentiality does not apply to loans and other similar bank transactions accounted for on the asset side or in memorandum accounts of the banks' balance sheet. Secondly, subject to certain procedures, the courts, the central bank, the tax authorities and the FIU are empowered to request disclosure of otherwise confidential information. Furthermore, banks are even requested regularly to report certain ordinary transactions to the tax authorities, as well as spontaneously to report to the FIU whatever they may consider an ST. As time goes by, there is a clear trend emerging by both the authorities and public opinion to prioritise the 'public interest' over individual rights and thus we may expect that even more restrictive legislation and legal interpretation of the duty of bank confidentiality will occur.

2   Australia

Ros Grady
Sandra Zivcic

INTRODUCTION

[2.1]   Australia is a federation of six states and two territories, together with a federal (Commonwealth) government. The Australian constitution gives the federal government the power to legislate throughout Australia with respect to banking.[1] Each of the states and territories can also legislate where there is a connection with its geographic area, subject to the supremacy of Commonwealth law where there is inconsistency.[2]

Whilst each of these nine governments has the power to legislate in respect of the banker's duty of confidence, there is no legislation in Australia which codifies the duty. There are many federal and state statutes which are relevant, but these mainly allow disclosure in certain circumstances and hence represent exceptions to the duty.

In the absence of legislation, the basis for the duty in Australia rests in common law and equity. The principles set out in the leading English case of *Tournier v National Provincial and Union Bank of England*,[3] discussed in depth in Chapter 11, England, still succinctly summarise for Australian law purposes the principal scope of the duty and the category of exceptions to it.[4]

TOURNIER v NATIONAL PROVINCIAL AND UNION BANK OF ENGLAND[5]

[2.2]   The principles expressed in *Tournier* apply to banks. They are not usually regarded as having an application to building societies, credit unions or other financial institutions.[6]

However, the principles from *Tournier* have been reflected in the Code of Banking Practice. Both building societies and credit unions also have codes of practice. Section 12 of the Credit Union Code of Conduct is very similar to the provisions in s 22 of the Code of Banking Practice. Section 11 of the Building Society Code is less

---

1   Other than 'state banking', which covers the business of banking engaged in by a state itself as banker which is currently of little importance as all the state banks have been privatised.
2   Commonwealth constitution, s 109.
3   [1924] 1 KB 461. The principles in *Tournier* have been reaffirmed recently in, amongst other cases, *Christofi v Barclays Bank plc* [1998] All ER 484.
4   See 'Further Duties of Confidence in Australia' below.
5   *Tournier v National Provincial and Union Bank of England* [1924] 1 KB 461.
6   *The Laws of Australia*, para 124, Division 5, Part D of chapter 4.

similar to s 22 of the Code of Banking Practice, but still imposes duties of confidentiality. Alan Tyree concludes that *Tournier* would apply to building societies and credit unions on the basis that the judgment in *Tournier* was not limited strictly to the bank–customer relationship.[7]

REMEDIES FOR BREACH

[2.3]   As the common law duty lies in contract in Australia, normal contractual remedies exist for breach of contract.[8] Further, equitable remedies may exist on the basis of a breach of confidence or breach of fiduciary duty such as an injunction or damages.[9] There is also the possibility of bringing a claim under the tort of defamation, which depends entirely on the nature of the disclosure. Finally, there are statutory provisions in some cases. An example is the Privacy Act 1988. Section 36(1) provides (subject to s 36(1A)) that an individual may complain to the Privacy Commissioner about an act or practice that may be an interference with the privacy of the individual. Under s 36(1A), s 36(1) does not apply if the complaint is about an act or practice of an organisation that is bound by a privacy code approved by the Privacy Commissioner that contains a procedure for making and dealing with complaints to an adjudicator in relation to acts or practices that may be an interference with privacy and that is relevant to the complained act or practice.

Section 52(1)(b)(iii) provides that, after investigating a complaint, the Commissioner may find the complaint substantiated and make a determination, including a declaration that the complainant is entitled to a specified amount to compensate for any loss or damage. Such loss or damage includes injury to the complainant's feelings or humiliation suffered. The Privacy Commissioner, however, has in place a procedure of mediation and its success has resulted in only two determinations under s 52(1)(b)(iii) to date.

DISCLOSURE UNDER COMPULSION OF LAW

[2.4]   This is the first of the exceptions to the bank's duty of non-disclosure.

Confidentiality is not of itself sufficient to deny a request to produce information. Indeed, confidentiality may sometimes have to defer to a higher public interest which may be served by disclosure.[10] In *Sankey v Whitlam*,[11] Gibbs ACJ said: 'confidentiality is not a separate head of privilege, but may be a material consideration to bear in mind when privilege is claimed on the ground of public interest.'[12] He then went on to comment:

> 'The court will of course examine the question with especial care, giving full weight to the reasons for preserving the secrecy of documents of this class, but it will not treat all such documents as entitled to the same measure of protection –

---

7 Tyree 'Does Tournier apply to building societies?' (1995) 6 J Banking and Finance Law and Practice 206.

8 *Federal Comr of Taxation v Australia and New Zealand Banking Group Ltd* (1979) 143 CLR 499 at 522.

9 See 'Further Duties of Confidence in Australia' below.

10 *Campbell v Tameside Metropolitan Borough Council* [1982] 3 WLR 74. The principles in *Campbell* were more recently applied in *M v L* [1997] 3 NZLR 424.

11 *Sankey v Whitlam* (1978) 142 CLR 1.

12 (1978) 142 CLR 1 at 42–43.

the extent of protection required will depend to some extent on the general subject matter with which the documents are concerned.'[13]

The decision of whether there should be disclosure involves a balance between the public interest in protecting the confidence and the public interest in having all relevant material available for the determination of a dispute.[14] In *Trade Practices Commission v Queensland Aggregates Pty Ltd (No 2)*,[15] Justice Shepherd referred to the judgment of Lord Kilbrandon in *D v National Society for the Prevention of Cruelty to Children*[16] in which Lord Kilbrandon stated that, in civil proceedings, a judge generally has no discretion to direct a party not to disclose information that has passed in the context of a confidential relationship. However, if the disclosure would be in breach of an ethical or social value involving the public interest, his honour went on to say that a court has a discretion to uphold a refusal to disclose evidence where, on balance, the public interest would be better served by excluding such evidence. In doing so, the question will be whether the subject matter is clearly of public interest so that to break the seal of confidentiality would endanger that interest. While his honour noted that disclosure of all evidence relevant to the trial of an issue is a matter of considerable public interest, the question to be determined is whether it is clear that the public interest would be better served by excluding evidence despite its relevance. In summary, it was concluded that if, on balance, the matter is left in doubt, disclosure should be ordered.[17]

These principles were considered in the criminal context in the state of Victoria in *Falconer v Australian Broadcasting Commission*.[18] Vlado Rajicic had been a police informer and was given a new identity known only to a small group of police officers. The defendant proposed to broadcast photographs, identified as photographs of Vlado Rajicic. The plaintiff, a senior police officer, sought an interlocutory injunction to restrain publication. Justice Ashley undertook the balancing process and decided that the public policy considerations against disclosure of Rajicic's present identity were material to the exercise of his discretion and tended in favour of the interlocutory relief.

This approach was reiterated, again in a criminal context, in the state of South Australia in *R v Richard Edward Mason*.[19]

Subpoena

Requirements of the law

[2.5]   The courts do not give banking secrecy preferential protection over other types of confidential information. In court proceedings where evidence concerning a person's banking arrangement is relevant, that evidence can be obtained by subpoena. For example, in the state of Victoria, order 42 of the Supreme Court (General Civil Procedure) Rules 2005 provides that a subpoena can be filed for production of a document or item for evidence or an order to attend for the purpose

---

13 (1978) 142 CLR 1 at 43.
14 *Campbell v Tameside Metropolitan Borough Council* [1982] 3 WLR 74. See also *National Tertiary Education Industry Union v Commonwealth of Australia* (2001) 111 FCR 583.
15 (1981) 51 FLR 364.
16 [1978] AC 171.
17 [1978] AC 171 at 245–246.
18 [1992] 1 VR 662.
19 (2000) 74 SASR 105.

of giving evidence. The information requested in the subpoena is to be delivered to the court that issued the subpoena and not to the issuing party or its solicitors. In the absence of a reasonable excuse, failure to comply with a properly issued and served subpoena may constitute a contempt of court or a statutory offence.[20]

The principles in relation to setting aside subpoenas were discussed by Justice Beach in *Re ACI International Ltd.*[21] The fact that documents are confidential is usually not a ground for having the subpoena set aside, but is relevant to issues such as inspection and access.[22]

Effects on banker's duty of confidentiality

[2.6]   In *Robertson v Canadian Imperial Bank of Commerce*,[23] the Privy Council considered issues relevant to a bank complying with a subpoena. Lord Nolan said, on disclosing the existence of the subpoena to a customer, that it should be done 'if only as a matter of courtesy and good business practice'.[24] Lord Nolan declined to place an express duty on a bank to inform a customer. Respected Australian writer Weaver observes that the practice in Australia is not to tell the customer or to tell the customer at the last minute.[25] Lord Nolan, however, in the *Robertson* case, suggested that it would be prudent to tell the customer of the existence of the subpoena at least to give the customer the opportunity of pursuing any available remedies.

The other issue of interest from the *Robertson* case was what information the bank should disclose. For example, a bank statement may show relevant deposits, but may also show several other payments. One would expect that bank statements, if provided, should black out every other transaction aside from those which are relevant to the subpoena. The *Robertson* case held no firm view on the exact nature of the disclosure. A court and a customer would expect a bank to be extremely careful when answering a subpoena not to disclose information that is not required and is of a particularly sensitive nature. However, in this process, it is for the bank to form its own opinion about each item of information and whether it comes within the terms of the subpoena.

In practice, the importance of the bank delivering the documents to the court, and not to the party that issued the subpoena, is critical for two reasons. First, to fall within the exception of compulsion of law, the bank must comply with the law and the law only requires production to the court. Secondly, confidentiality will be a material factor in deciding issues of inspection and reproduction of the documents. If the documents are produced to a third party, then the party issuing the subpoena will not have to seek leave of the court to inspect and the court will not have an opportunity to consider the issue of confidentiality.[26]

In relation to orders of foreign courts and foreign authorities, see 'International Requests for Information' below.

---

20 *Halsbury's Laws of Australia*, para 105-315.
21 (1986) 11 ACLR 240.
22 (1986) 11 ACLR 240 at 243.
23 [1995] 1 All ER 824.
24 [1995] 1 All ER 824 at 830.
25 This is on the basis that there is no legal duty to inform the customer and there is little a customer can do to intervene.
26 Particularly, where there are several parties to the litigation, the court may limit inspection to the party that issued the subpoena.

Search warrants

Requirements of the law

[2.7] The leading authority on search warrants is the decision of the full court of the High Court of Australia in *George v Rockett*.[27] The court acknowledged that at a search warrant authorises an invasion of premises without the occupier's consent. State and Commonwealth statutes provide several mechanisms by which to obtain search warrants.[28]

Effects on banker's duty of confidentiality

[2.8] The statutes do not provide an exception for a bank's confidential information. However, the decision to issue a search warrant is a reviewable decision for the purposes of the Administrative Decisions (Judicial Review) Act 1977 (Cth). Further, in *R v Tillett*,[29] the court held that the fact that a search warrant had been executed did not preclude relief by way of *certiorari*.[30]

Subject to any express requirements of law,[31] a bank in receipt of a search warrant in relation to one of its customers should be careful to exercise caution in assisting an officer's request. The possibility exists, although it is unlikely in relation to documents held by a bank, that the customer may make a claim for legal professional privilege in relation to documents which are the subject of a search warrant.[32] This may be relevant, for example, where a customer keeps highly confidential files (which would have to be within the ambit of the legal professional privilege test) in a safe deposit box at the bank. As the privilege is that of the customer, the bank must not do anything which inadvertently amounts to a waiver of the customer's privilege. Therefore, it is always sensible to involve the customer at the outset.

Prudence would also suggest that a bank, from a legal and commercial perspective, should inform a customer when it receives a search warrant in order to allow the customer to avail himself of all possible remedies, notwithstanding the bank's public duty to assist law enforcement officers in their investigations. This factor is important because search warrants generally precede criminal prosecution.

A bank officer should also request time to check the validity of the warrant and, in particular, ensure that the people named on the warrant are authorised to execute it and that they are the only people seeking to exercise it.

---

27 (1990) 170 CLR 104. The principles in *George v Rockett* have been recently applied in *Adler v Gardiner* (2002) 43 ACSR at 24.
28 As an example of a typical legislative prescription, see s 3E(1) of the Crimes Act 1914 (Cth) which provides: 'an issuing officer may issue a warrant to search premises if the officer is satisfied by information on oath that there are reasonable grounds for suspecting that there is, or there will be within the next 72 hours, any evidential material at the premises'.
29 (1969) 14 FLR 101.
30 *Certiorari* is an administrative remedy issued by a superior court exercising its supervisory jurisdiction. It is only available after the inferior court has made a decision and it results (if awarded) in the quashing of the decision. For an introductory discussion, see Margaret Allars *Introduction to Australian Administrative Law* (1990) paras 6.103–6.113.
31 For example, the National Crime Authority Act 1984, s 29B which makes it an offence to disclose the existence of a summons from the National Crime Authority.
32 *Baker v Campbell* (1981) 153 CLR 52.

Corporations Act 2001 (Cth)

Requirements of the law

[2.9] The principal function of corporate regulation is contained in the Corporations Act 2001 (Cth).[33] The provisions that are most relevant to the banker's duty of confidentiality, however, are contained in other statutory prescriptions which confer investigative powers upon certain corporate regulators.[34] Nonetheless, there are some sections in the Corporations Act which are relevant.

Section 983C provides that, where a court makes an order under s 983A to restrain dealings in respect of specified accounts with financial institutions that a person holds or maintains (whether in Australia or elsewhere), there is a duty on the financial institution where the order is directed to disclose to the Australian Securities and Investments Commission ('ASIC') every account kept by the institution in the name of the person to whom the order relates and any account that the institution reasonably suspects is held or kept for the benefit of that person. Further, the financial institution must permit the ASIC to make a copy of, or to take an extract from, any account of the person or any of its books relating to that person.

Effects on banker's duty of confidentiality

[2.10] These sections specifically apply to financial institutions. One difficulty is that the institution is required to form a judgment as to any account that it reasonably suspects is held for the benefit of that person. This is analogous to the difficulties with s 16 of the Financial Transaction Reports Act 1988 (Cth).[35] It raises the difficult issue of having to form a judgment on what is 'reasonable suspicion'.

Some indication as to the meaning of 'reasonable suspicion' may be drawn from the High Court case of *George v Rockett*[36] where the full court quoted with approval the following statement of Justice Kitto in *Queensland Bacon Pty Ltd v Rees*:[37]

> 'A suspicion that something exists is more than a mere idle wondering whether it exists or not; it is a positive feeling of actual apprehension or mistrust, amounting to "a slight opinion, but without sufficient evidence", as *Chamber's Dictionary* expresses it. Consequently, a reason to suspect that a fact exists is more than a reason to consider or look into the possibility of its existence.'[38]

Income Tax Assessment Act 1936 (Cth)

Requirements of the law – s 263

[2.11] Section 263 of the Income Tax Assessment Act 1936 (Cth) ('ITAA') gives the Commissioner of Taxation (or any authorised officer),[39] at all times, full and free

---

33 The Corporations Act is an Act of the federal government enacted, in part, on the basis of a referral of legislative powers by the states to the Commonwealth.
34 See the Australian Securities and Investments Commission and Australian Crime Commission investigations below.
35 See 'Disclosure of Cash Transactions Under the Financial Transaction Reports Act 1988' below.
36 (1990) 170 CLR 104.
37 (1966) 115 CLR 266.
38 (1966) 115 CLR 266 at 303.
39 Or any officer authorised by him.

access to all buildings, places, books, documents and other papers for any of the purposes of the ITAA and the power to make extracts from, or copies of, any such books, documents or papers. Section 263(2) provides that an officer is not entitled to enter or remain on or in any building or place if, on being requested by the occupier for proof of authority, the officer does not produce an authority in writing signed by the Commissioner stating that the officer is authorised to exercise powers under s 263.[40] Section 263(3) places an obligation on the occupier of a building or place entered, or proposed to be entered, under sub-s (1) to provide the Commissioner or the officer with all reasonable facilities and assistance.

In *Simionato Holdings Pty Ltd v Federal Comr of Taxation (No 2)*,[41] it was assumed that s 263 powers could be used to obtain documents from a bank for use in proceedings to recover unpaid tax.

It is an offence for a person to hinder or obstruct an Australian Taxation Office ('ATO') officer exercising his right of access under s 263.

The requirements of s 263(3) mean that an officer should be able to make reasonable use of, for example, office space and facilities to extract information stored on computer.[42] The officer is also entitled to reasonable assistance in the form of advice and access to where relevant documents are located. An occupier who fails to provide the necessary facilities or assistance is liable to a fine of up to $3,300, if an individual, and up to $16,500, if a corporation.

Effects on banker's duty of confidentiality

[2.12]   A bank does not have any special protection from the provisions in s 263. Further, an authorised officer is entitled to take all reasonable and necessary steps to remove any physical obstruction to access, but should not act in an excessive manner. This was illustrated in *Kerrison v Federal Comr of Taxation*[43] where the bank refused to open a safe deposit box or supply a key. The officer was entitled to attempt to open the box and, as that failed, to break open the box by the use of 'not excessive force'.

The ATO officers have been issued with guidelines on how they should exercise their powers of access.[44] The guidelines state, among others, that:

1   access requests should be avoided without prior notice unless there are exceptional circumstances;
2   officers should grant a request by the occupier to delay the search temporarily to enable professional advice to be obtained;
3   where it is expected that some of the records sought will be subject to legal professional privilege, the custodian should be given the opportunity to make a privilege claim (the doctrine of legal professional privilege protects communications made between a lawyer and his client for the predominant

---

40 In practice, the Australian Taxation Office officers carry identification cards with the ss 263 and 264 powers outlined on the back.
41 (1995) 60 FCR 375.
42 See *Australian Master Tax Guide* (2006) para 25-220.
43 (1995) ATC 4720.
44 *Australian Taxation Office Guidelines: Access and Information Gathering Powers* published by the Australian Taxation Office. The working title of the guidelines is 'Access and Information Gathering Manual' and it is one volume of approximately 1,000 pp. See, in particular, para 2.11.1 in chapter 2 on notices.

purpose of giving or receiving legal advice or for use in existing or anticipated litigation);[45]

4   where access is temporarily delayed to enable professional advice to be obtained, arrangements should be made to ensure there is no tampering with the records;

5   when acting under an access provision, answers can only be demanded to questions that are incidental to the exercise of the right of access (for example, the location of records); and

6   access to documents includes access to hard disks, CD-ROMs, magnetic tapes or other storage of electronic information.

It may be possible to request a delay to an s 263 search so that legal advice can be taken on the issues of the validity of the notice and legal professional privilege. This will not amount to an obstruction.[46] In *FCT v Citibank Ltd*, it was held that the access powers in s 263 are restricted by the doctrine of legal professional privilege.[47] The validity of this proposition has been questioned in *Re Questions of Law Reserved (No 1 of 1998)*.[48] The doctrine of legal professional privilege protects communications made between a lawyer and his client for the predominant purpose of giving or receiving legal advice or for use in existing or anticipated litigation.[49]

It is also possible that the decision to use s 263 is reviewable under the Administrative Decisions (Judicial Review) Act 1977 (Cth). *Simionato Holdings Pty Ltd v Federal Comr of Taxation (No 2)*[50] is an example of a case where an application was made to seek orders of review under the 1977 Act of decisions and conduct of the Commissioner of Taxation in making a decision under s 263 of the ITAA. Importantly, under the 1977 Act, a person who makes a decision to which the Act applies is required to furnish a person who is aggrieved by the decision with a statement in writing setting out the findings on material questions of fact, referring to the evidence or other material on which those findings were based and giving the reasons for the decision.[51]

Requirements of the law – s 264

[2.13]   Section 264 of the ITAA provides:

'The Commissioner may by notice in writing require any person, whether a taxpayer or not . . . —

(a)   to furnish him with such information as he may require; and

(b)   to attend and give evidence before him or before any officer authorised by him in that behalf concerning his or any other person's income or assessment, and may require him to produce all books, documents and

---

45   *Federal Comr of Taxation v Citibank Ltd* (1989) 20 FCR 403.
46   Note that Division 149 of the Schedule to the Criminal Code Act 1995 imposes a penalty for obstructing a tax officer of $2,000 or six months' imprisonment.
47   *Federal Comr of Taxation v Citibank Ltd* (1989) 20 FCR 403.
48   *Re Question of Law Reserved (No 1 of 1998)* (1998) 70 SASR 281.
49   A 'dominant purpose' test applies for evidentiary purposes in federal proceedings pursuant to ss 118 and 119 of the Evidence Act 1995 (Cth) and to a claim for legal professional privilege in relation to discovered documents on the basis of the High Court's decision in *Esso Australia Resources Ltd v Comr of Taxation* (1999) 201 CLR 49.
50   (1995) 60 FCR 375.
51   Administrative Decisions (Judicial Review) Act 1977, s 13(1), provided there is not an express exemption from complying with s 13(1) in the relevant Act.

other papers whatever in his custody or under his control relating thereto.'[52]

Section 264 cannot be used by the Commissioner to compel the production of documents subject to legal professional privilege.[53] The Commissioner can only require a person to produce documents where these documents are in the custody of, or under the control of, that person.[54] This includes persons who have the physical ability to produce the documents. This is relevant to a bank because of the High Court decision in *Comr of Taxation v Australia and New Zealand Banking Group Ltd (Smorgon case).*[55] That decision found that a bank has custody or control of the contents of a safe deposit box kept on its premises and can therefore be compelled to produce its contents.[56]

A decision by the Commissioner to issue a notice under s 264 is reviewable under the Administrative Decisions (Judicial Review) Act 1977 (Cth).[57]

Again, the sanction for failure to comply with an s 264 notice is the risk that the person may be guilty of an offence. Both the ATO officer conducting the examination and the person being examined are entitled to have legal counsel[58] present at the examination to advise on legal issues such as legal professional privilege.[59]

The comments of Justice Mason in the *Smorgon* case,[60] as quoted in *Industrial Equity Ltd v Deputy Comr of Taxation,*[61] are a good illustration of the breadth of the powers in this regard. He said:

> 'The strong reasons which inhibit the use of curial processes for the purposes of a "fishing expedition" have no application to the administrative process of assessing a taxpayer to income tax. It is the function of the Commissioner to ascertain the taxpayer's taxable income. To ascertain this he may need to make wide-ranging inquiries and to make them long before any issue of fact arises between him and the taxpayer. Such an issue will in general, if not always, only arise after the process of assessment has been completed. It is to the process of investigation before assessment that s 264 is principally, if not exclusively, directed.'[62]

---

52 Section 264 also applies by operation of s 128Q to Division 11A, which deals with dividends, interest and royalties paid to non-residents and to certain other persons.
53 *Baker v Campbell* (1983) 153 CLR 52.
54 On this subject, see *Simionato Holdings Pty Ltd v Federal Comr of Taxation (No 2)* (1995) 60 FCR 375.
55 (1979) 143 CLR 499.
56 The Commissioner's powers to require production of documents do not extend to authorising him to require persons to make copies of documents: *Perron Investments Pty Ltd v DCT* (1989) 25 FCR 187.
57 *Industrial Equity Ltd v Federal Comr of Taxation* (1990) 21 ATR 934. See, in particular, the majority judgment.
58 *Dunkel v Deputy Comr of Taxation (NSW)* (1990) 91 ATC 4142.
59 Note the comment by Weerasooria in his book *Banking Law and the Financial System in Australia* (5th edn, 2000) p 491, n 10 that, in view of the decision of the High Court in *Corporate Affairs Commission (NSW) v Yuill* (1991) 172 CLR 319, Australian decisions prior to 1991 on legal professional privilege may be affected by the 3:2 majority that held that the power conferred by s 295(1) of the Companies (NSW) Code in power and production of documents was not subject to legal professional privilege. See also *Daniels Corpn International Pty Ltd v Australian Competition and Consumer Comr* (2002) 213 CLR 543. Here, the High Court held unanimously that the ACCC powers in s 155 of the Trade Practices Act 1974 are subject to legal professional privilege.
60 (1979) 143 CLR 499.
61 (1990) 21 ATR 934 at 939.
62 (1990) 21 ATR 934 at 939.

Effects on banker's duty of confidentiality

[2.14]   Section 264 of the ITAA is a further example of where a bank can be compelled by law to override its common law duty of confidentiality to a client.[63]

Bankers' books evidence provisions

Requirements of the law

[2.15]   Specific provisions relating to the use of bankers' books in legal proceedings exist in all Australian jurisdictions except New South Wales, Tasmania and the Commonwealth of Australia.[64] These provisions provide an expeditious method of receiving the contents of bankers' books into evidence. The provisions do not mean that the information does not have to be provided, but rather allow it to be provided in a more convenient manner. The statutes include provisions relating to a banker's role in any legal proceeding to which their bank is not a party where it cannot be compelled to produce books of accounts.

The Evidence Acts of New South Wales, Tasmania and the Commonwealth of Australia contain provisions that apply generally to the production of documents. The effect of these provisions is that, instead of producing the books themselves, the bank may produce verified copies of entries in books.[65]

Effects on banker's duty of confidentiality

[2.16]   The sections provide uniformly (except for New South Wales, Tasmania and the Commonwealth) that a banker shall not be compellable to produce any bankers' book, the contents of which can be proved under the Act in question. Further, the banker shall not be compellable to appear as a witness to prove the matters, transactions and accounts recorded in the bankers' books unless by order of a judge. The object of the statutes is to save the time of bankers and protect them from the inconvenience of producing the originals of their books.[66]

The courts have adopted a wide interpretation of the concept of a bankers' book, including, for example, computer print outs.[67]

The provisions apply to both civil and criminal matters. Clearly, if a bank is subject to a court order to produce its books, this will be an exception to the bank's duty of

---

63 Section 218 of the ITAA is also relevant to a bank; it is where the Commissioner may collect tax from a person owing money to a taxpayer. Such a direction could be forwarded to a bank under s 218(1)(b). Importantly for a bank, s 218(4) provides that any person making any payment in pursuance of this section shall be deemed to have been acting under the authority of the taxpayer and of all other persons concerned and is indemnified in respect of such payment.

64 Queensland: Evidence Act 1977, ss 83–91 (books of account of any business); Victoria: Evidence Act 1958, ss 58A–58J (books of account of any business); South Australia: Evidence Act 1929, ss 46–51; Western Australia: Evidence Act 1906, ss 89–96; Northern Territory: Evidence Act 1939, ss 43–47; Australian Capital Territory: Evidence Act 1971.

65 New South Wales: Evidence Act 1995, Parts 2.2 and 4.3; Tasmania: Evidence Act 2001, Part 2 of Chapter 2 and Part 3 of Chapter 4; Commonwealth of Australia: Parts 2.2 and 4.3.

66 However, from the perspective of the duty of confidentiality, it is irrelevant whether the original or a copy of a document is produced.

67 See, for example, *ANZ Banking Group Ltd v Griffins* (1990) ACLD 577.

confidentiality to its customer. The bank is, however, entitled to rely on the special rules outlined in the various bankers' books provisions in the different jurisdictions in order to avoid unnecessary inconvenience or cost.[68]

Disclosure of cash transactions under the Financial Transaction Reports Act 1988 (Cth)[69]

Requirements of the law

[2.17]   The principal legislation that places obligations on financial institutions in relation to anti-money laundering is the Financial Transaction Reports Act 1988 ('FTRA'). The FTRA was enacted on the basis that cash transactions are used in the evasion of tax and for other illicit purposes. It applies to cash dealers, defined to include a financial institution, which in turn is defined to include a bank.[70] The FTRA is divided into three reporting divisions.

Division 1 of Part II requires a cash dealer to report any 'significant cash transaction' to the Australian Transaction Reports and Analysis Centre ('AUSTRAC'). A significant cash transaction is defined as a cash transaction involving the transfer of currency of not less than $10,000 in value.[71] The transaction must be reported regardless of whether it is suspicious.

Division 2 of Part II, in particular s 16, requires that, where a cash dealer is a party to a transaction and the cash dealer has 'reasonable grounds to suspect' that information that the cash dealer has concerning the transaction may be relevant to an investigation into tax evasion, prosecution of a person for an offence against a law of the Commonwealth or a territory, may be of assistance in enforcement of the Proceeds of Crimes Act 1987 (Cth) or may be relevant to the investigation of, or prosecution of a person for, the financing of a terrorism offence (an offence under

---

68 See the comments by Weerasooria, n 59 above, for further detail.
69 The Financial Transaction Reports Amendment Bill 1996 received royal assent on 17 April 1997. The principal object of this amendment was to give effect to several recommendations of 'Checking the cash: a report on the effectiveness of the Financial Transaction Reports Act 1988', a report of the Senate Standing Committee on Legal and Constitutional Affairs 1993. The recommendations that have been given legislative effect are access to financial transactions reports, information by state and territory revenue authorities, definition of transactions, inadmissibility of suspect transaction report information, increase in the reporting threshold for imported and exported currency and definition of the point at which currency transferred is considered to have been exported. The other features of the Bill were the introduction of significant cash transaction reporting by solicitors, consolidation of the powers and inspection of the AUSTRAC to access and examine the records and record keeping systems of persons required to keep records under the Act, updating of the penalty provisions of the Act in accordance with current drafting practices and to align the quantum and expression of penalties with those in other Commonwealth statutes, updating other specific provisions that contain superseded terminology or are otherwise in need of modernising and the making of minor technical amendments to correct minor drafting errors.
    The Financial Transactions Reports Act 1988 was amended in 2002 by the Suppression of the Financing of Terrorism Act 2002 (Cth) to provide for the reporting by cash dealers of transactions that they suspect are 'preparatory to the commission of a financing of terrorism offence' or if information concerning the transaction 'may be relevant to investigation of, or prosecution of a person for, a financing of terrorism offence'; see s 16(1A).
70 FTRA, s 3.
71 FTRA, ss 3(1) and 7(1).

s 103.1 of the Criminal Code[72] or ss 20 or 21 of the Charter of the United Nations Act 1945[73]), then the cash dealer must, as soon as practicable after forming that suspicion, prepare a report of the transaction and communicate the information contained in the report to the AUSTRAC. Failure to report is an offence under s 28 and, if the offender is a body corporate, there is potential liability for a fine not exceeding $55,500. Some protection is afforded in s 16(5), which provides that a

---

72 Section 103.1 of the Criminal Code provides that:
'(1) A person commits an offence if:
    (a) the person provides or collects funds; and
    (b) the person is reckless as to whether the funds will be used to facilitate or engage in a terrorist act.
Penalty: Imprisonment for life.
(2) A person commits an offence under subsection (1) even if the terrorist act does not occur.
(3) Section 15.4 (extended geographical jurisdiction – category D) applies to an offence against subsection (1).'
'Terrorist act' is defined in s 100.1(1) to mean 'an action or threat of action where:
    (a) the action falls within subsection (2) and does not fall within subsection (2A); and
    (b) the action is done or the threat is made with the intention of advancing a political, religious or ideological cause; and
    (c) the action is done or the threat is made with the intention of:
        (i) coercing, or influencing by intimidation, the government of the Commonwealth or a state, territory or foreign country, or of part of a state, territory or foreign country; or
        (ii) intimidating the public or a section of the public.'
Section 100.1(2) provides that 'action falls within this subsection if it:
    (a) causes serious harm that is physical harm to a person; or
    (b) causes serious damage to property; or
    (ba) causes a person's death; or
    (c) endangers a person's life, other than a life of the person taking the action; or
    (d) creates a serious risk to the health or safety of the public or a section of the public; or
    (e) seriously interferes with, seriously disrupts, or destroys, an electronic system including, but not limited to:
        (i) an information system; or
        (ii) a telecommunications system; or
        (iii) a financial system; or
        (iv) a system used for the delivery of essential government services; or
        (v) a system used for, or by, an essential public utility; or
        (vi) a system used for, or by, a transport system.'
Section 100.1(2A) provides that 'action falls within this subsection if it:
    (a) is advocacy, protest, dissent or industrial action; and
    (b) is not intended:
        (i) to cause serious harm that is physical harm to a person; or
        (ii) to cause a person's death; or
        (iii) to endanger the life of a person, other than the person taking the action; or
        (iv) to create a serious risk to the health or safety of the public or a section of the public.'
73 Under s 20 of the Charter of the United Nations Act 1945:
'(1) A person commits an offence if:
    (a) the person holds an asset; and
    (b) the person:
        (i) uses or deals with the asset; or
        (ii) allows the asset to be used or dealt with; or
        (iii) facilitates the use of the asset or dealing with the asset; and
    (c) the asset is a freezable asset; and
    (d) the use or dealing is not in accordance with a notice under s 22.
Penalty: Imprisonment for five years.
(2) Strict liability applies to the circumstances that the use or dealing with the asset is not in accordance with a notice under s 22 (authorised dealing).
(3) It is a defence if the person proves that the use or dealing was solely for the purpose of preserving the value of the asset.
(4) Section 15.1 of the Criminal Code (extended geographical jurisdiction – category A) applies to an offence against subsection (1).'

legal action does not lie against a cash dealer in relation to any action taken by the cash dealer under s 16 or in the mistaken belief that such action was required under the section.

Division 3 of Part II requires a cash dealer to prepare a report to the AUSTRAC if the cash dealer is the sender or recipient of an international funds transfer instruction.[74] One of the following conditions must also apply: the cash dealer is acting on behalf of, or at the request of, another person who is not a bank or the cash dealer is not a bank.[75] All international funds transfer instructions have to be reported regardless of the amount involved.

Effects on banker's duty of confidentiality

[2.18]   A cash dealer is prohibited from informing a client that the cash dealer has formed a suspicion, or that information has been communicated to the AUSTRAC, or from giving the client any other information from which the client could reasonably be expected to infer that a suspicion has been formed or that information has been so communicated.[76] A cash dealer who contravenes this section is guilty of an offence punishable on conviction by a fine not exceeding $11,100 or imprisonment for a term not exceeding two years or both. The fine for a corporation is up to $55,500.

The AUSTRAC guideline no 1 (suspect transaction reporting) provides detailed information about reporting procedures. A suspect transaction report is filed on AUSTRAC form 16 and all pertinent details are required. In relation to the principle of 'know your customer', this guideline states:

> '… branches of financial institutions are encouraged to "know their customers" and where possible be able to judge whether the amount of cash or other moneys going through accounts are consistent with the line of business or occupation being undertaken by the customer. The Act also requires the identification of new signatories to accounts and where customers try to avoid that requirement it might give rise to a suspicion of tax evasion or other illegal conduct.'[77]

The principle of 'know your customer' is one foundation of the FTRA.

The FTRA is a clear exception to the banker's duty of confidentiality. Section 16(5) has been seen as a reinforcement of the exception of disclosure of information under

---

Section 21 of the Charter of the United Nations Act 1945 provides that:
'(1) A person commits an offence if:
    (a) the person, directly or indirectly, makes an asset available to a person or entity; and
    (b) the person or entity to whom the asset is made available is a proscribed person or entity; and
    (c) the making available of the asset is not in accordance with a notice under s 22.
Penalty: Imprisonment for five years.
(2) Strict liability applies to the circumstance that the making available of the asset is not in accordance with a notice under s 22 (authorised dealings).
(3) Section 15.1 of the Criminal Code (extended geographical jurisdiction – category A) applies to an offence against subsection (1).'
74 FTRA, s 17B(1)(a).
75 FTRA, s 17B(1)(b).
76 FTRA, s 16(5A).
77 AUSTRAC guideline no 1: (suspect transaction reporting), p 15.

compulsion of law.[78] An important provision in terms of gathering further information is s 16(4) of the FTRA. It provides that where a cash dealer communicates information to the AUSTRAC under s 16(1) or (1A), the cash dealer shall, if requested to do so by either the director of the AUSTRAC, the relevant authority[79] or an investigating officer who is carrying out an investigation arising from a report, give such further information as is specified in the request to the extent to which the cash dealer has that information.

Section 16(4) has the potential to have a substantial effect on the banker's duty of confidentiality in terms of the amount of information which is disclosed. It is not difficult to see how this section may be manipulated by an investigative agency. If an investigative agency were to indicate to a bank that a certain customer of the bank had been arrested on drug charges, the bank would then have reasonable grounds to suspect that information in relation to the customer's account may be relevant for an investigation or prosecution of the customer for an offence against a law of the Commonwealth and would then be in the position of having to report under s 16(1) or (1A). On the basis of that report, an investigative agency could use s 16(4) to obtain whatever further information it may require from the bank.

Section 17 provides that a dealer who fulfils the s 16 duty shall be taken, for the purposes of Division 400 of the Criminal Code, not to have been in possession of the information at any time.[80] Division 400 sets out the offences of money laundering. The money laundering offences previously appeared in ss 81 and 82 of the Proceeds of Crime Act 1987.

The main offences are those in ss 400.3 to 400.8. The distinction between each offence turns on the value of the money or property constituting the proceeds of the crime. The greater the value, the greater the penalty. The main offences occur when a person deals with money or other property in circumstances where:

1   the money or property is, and the person believes it to be, or is reckless or negligent as to whether it is, proceeds of crime; or
2   the person intends that the money or property will become an instrument of crime.

The maximum prescribed penalty applies in respect of an offence under s 400.3 where the value of the money or property is in excess of $1 million. The penalty in this situation is a fine of up to $165,000 and/or 25 years' imprisonment when the offender is a natural person and $825,000 where the offender is a body corporate. The lesser offence, which is not dependent on the value of the money or property, is described in s 400.8 and carries a maximum penalty of up to $6,600 and/or 12 months' imprisonment for a natural person and $33,000 for a body corporate.

Section 400.9 sets out a further money laundering offence where a person engages in certain acts in relation to proceeds of crime and it is reasonable to suspect that the money or property is proceeds of crime.

The intention of s 17 is to protect a bank from exposure under Division 400 of the Criminal Code. This may influence a bank to make a report. The comments, however, of Walter and Erlich are poignant:

---

78 Tyree 'The Cash Transaction Reports Act 1988' (April 1990) J Banking and Finance Law and Practice 57.
79 A relevant authority is defined to include the Commissioner of the Australian Federal Police, the Chairperson of the NCA, the Commissioner of Taxation and the Comptroller-General of Customs.
80 FTRA, s 17.

'It must be pointed out that bankers are not trained to carry out the function of detecting crimes and that s 16 is drafted in wide and woolly terms; what do the expressions "reasonable grounds" and "suspect" mean?'[81]

Walter and Erlich highlight that the section is forcing the banker to make a judgment on what is suspicious behaviour. The difficulty for the bank is that a disclosure which is not sanctioned will leave the bank open to an action by its customer for a breach of confidentiality.[82]

The provisions, in particular s 17, have sustained further criticism from Weerasooria, who concludes that s 17 'says something alarming'.[83] It enacts that:

'Where a cash dealer, or a person who is an officer, employee or agent of a cash dealer commutes or gives information under s 16, the cash dealer or person shall be taken, for the purposes of ss 81 and 82 of the Proceeds of Crime Act 1987 not to have been in possession of that information at any time.'[84]

Therefore, the statute enacts that a bank is protected from committing an offence under the Criminal Code.[85]

The 2004–05 annual report of the AUSTRAC reveals that the number of suspicious transactions reported has increased from 7,247 in 2000–01 to 17,212 in 2004–05. Reports lodged by the banking sector continued to provide most suspicious financial activity reported to the AUSTRAC.[86]

Legislative reform

[2.19]   On 13 July 2006, the Minister for Justice and Customs released the second draft of the Anti-Money Laundering and Counter Terrorism Financing Bill 2005 ('AML Bill') for public consultation. The AML Bill is the centrepiece of current regulatory reforms that will ultimately replace the FTRA. The purpose of the AML Bill is to give effect to the international standards on anti-money laundering and counter terrorism financing issued by the Financial Action Task Force on Money Laundering.

Part 3 of the AML Bill sets out the reporting obligations of banks and other financial service providers that are caught by the AML Bill. If enacted in its present form, Division 3 of Part 3 of the AML Bill extends the current reporting obligation of banks to specified transactions involving cash or 'e-currency' of $10,000 or more (or the foreign equivalent). 'E-currency' is defined in clause 6 of the AML Bill as:

'An Internet-based, electronic means of exchange that is:

(a) known as:
    (i)   e-currency; or
    (ii) e-money; or
    (iii) digital currency; and

---

81 Walter and Erlich 'Confidences – bankers and customers: powers of banks to maintain secrecy and confidentiality' (1989) 63 AU 413.
82 Walter and Erlich, n 81 above.
83 Weerasooria 'Tournier Turns 70' (December 1993) Australian Banker 314.
84 FTRA, s 17.
85 Weerasooria, n 83 above.
86 AUSTRAC 2004–05 annual report.

(b) backed either directly or indirectly by:
   (i)   precious metal; or
   (ii)   bullion; or
   (iii) a thing of a kind prescribed by the AML/CTF Rules; and
(c) not issued by or under the authority of a government body.'

The 'AML/CTF Rules' is short for 'Anti-Money Laundering/Counter Terrorism Financing Rules' that will be issued by the AUSTRAC and form part of the overall regulatory framework.

Division 2 of Part 3 will require banks to make suspicious transaction reports to the AUSTRAC where they have reasonable grounds to suspect that the transaction may be related to money laundering or terrorism financing activities. Reports will also be required in relation to suspicions concerning tax evasion or offences against Commonwealth, state and territory and foreign laws.

Further, under Division 4 of Part 3 of the AML Bill, if a bank provides a customer with certain specified services that relate to an international funds transfer instruction, the bank will need to provide the AUSTRAC with a report about the provision of the service.

Each of these reports will require disclosure to the AUSTRAC of information about relevant customers and their transactions.

Clause 95 of the AML Bill prohibits a person from making a disclosure to any person (which would, for example, include a related body corporate or any sort of adviser and would certainly include the customer in question) about the filing of a suspicious matter report with the AUSTRAC or about any information relating to the relevant suspicion or report. In this way, the AML Bill restricts the disclosure of customer information, although the underlying rationale for prohibiting disclosure of the information is not to protect the confidentiality of the customer's information for the benefit of the customer, but to reduce the likelihood that the customer will discover that a suspicious transaction report has been made or that the relevant suspicion has been formed.

At this stage, it is expected that the new AML Bill will be passed in late 2006 and that the obligations will commence, with a transition period, in 2008.

Information gathering under the FTRA

Requirements of the law

[2.20]   The Proceeds of Crime Act 1987 gives various information gathering powers to Commonwealth and state enforcement agencies which may be used to search or obtain property in the possession of a financial institution. Further to this, Part 3 of the FTRA provides that a bank must retain each essential customer generated financial transaction document for the minimum retention period, which is seven years after the day on which the account is closed. This includes documents that relate to the opening or closing by a person of an account, the operation by a person of an account and the transmission of funds using the person's account in its original form.

Effects on banker's duty of confidentiality

[2.21]   The mere keeping of these records as required by the FTRA does not override the banker's duty of confidentiality, but it does indicate that a bank may be required, in order to comply with the FTRA, to maintain the confidential material for up to seven years after an account is closed. Therefore, it cannot avoid disclosing documentation by putting in place a system of document destruction. These prescriptions merely ensure that the information in relation to customers' accounts is available to be examined in the event that an appropriate order is made by a court.

Disclosure under trade practices legislation

Requirements of the law

[2.22] Section 155 of the Trade Practices Act 1974 (Cth) ('TPA') provides that if the Australian Competition and Consumer Commission ('ACCC')[87] has reason to believe that a person is capable of furnishing information, producing documents or giving evidence relating to a matter that constitutes, or may constitute, a contravention of the TPA or is relevant to the making of a decision in relation to exclusive dealing, a member of the ACCC may, by notice in writing served on that person, require that person to furnish to the ACCC any such information in writing or to produce to the ACCC any such documents or to appear before the ACCC to give evidence.[88]

Effects on banker's duty of confidentiality

[2.23] There is no exemption for a bank from the operation of s 155. If a bank is in receipt of a notice under it, then a bank will be required to comply unless some proper ground of challenge to the issue or form of the notice can be established.

ASIC investigations

Requirements of the law

[2.24] The ASIC is a federal government agency established by the Australian Securities and Investments Commission Act 2001 ('ASIC Act'). The function of the ASIC is primarily to administer the Corporations Act 2001 (Cth). The ASIC also provides administrative support to various boards such as the Australian Accounting Standards Board and has a role to play in advising on law reform.

Part 3 of the ASIC Act is entitled 'investigations and information gathering'. Division 3 of Part 3 relates to the inspection of books and provides, in s 30, that the ASIC may give to a body corporate a notice to produce books about the affairs of a body corporate. These powers are mirrored in ss 31 and 33 in relation to securities and futures contracts and in s 32A in relation to the provision of financial services. Investigations conducted by the ASIC may lead to the issue of a search warrant pursuant to the ASIC Act.[89] Failure to comply with the notice requiring production is a prerequisite for the issue of the search warrant. Therefore, the procedure is only

---

87 Or the Chairperson or Deputy Chairperson of the ACCC.
88 Some exceptions do exist in s 155(2A), none of which is relevant to this discussion.
89 Sections 35 and 36.

available where the ASIC's interest in particular documentation has already been revealed.[90]

Division 2 (s 19) provides mechanisms for the examination of persons on oath. These powers can only be exercised if the ASIC holds reasonable grounds for suspecting or believing that the person can provide information 'relevant to a matter' under investigation and serves a written notice on the person in a prescribed form. The ASIC may also require any person who is involved in the compilation or production of documents to explain any matter about them or to which any of them relate: s 37(a). In addition, the ASIC may require a person to state where the documents may be found and the identity and whereabouts of the person who last had possession of them (to the best of their knowledge or belief): s 38.

A breach of any of the above sections without reasonable excuse is an offence under s 63 and the offender is liable to a penalty of $11,000 or imprisonment for two years or both.[91] A corporation can be fined up to $55,000 for breach.

Effects on banker's duty of confidentiality

[2.25] In *Australian Securities Commission v Zarro*,[92] the Federal Court of Australia held that the bank's obligation of confidentiality was no reasonable excuse for non-compliance with a notice to produce documents in its possession. The decision in *Zarro* confirms that the requirements of the ASIC Act are an exception to the banker's duty of confidentiality. There is, however, some comfort in s 92 of the ASIC Act, which provides that a person complying with the ASIC Act 'is neither liable to a proceeding, nor subject to a liability, merely because the person has complied, or proposes to comply, with a requirement made, or purporting to have been made, under this Part'.[93]

Australian Crime Commission

Requirements of the law

[2.26] The Australian Crime Commission ('ACC') was established by the Australian Crime Commission Act 2002 (Cth) ('ACCA').[94] Although created by federal legislation, it is also empowered by state and territory legislation.[95] (The Australian Crime Commission replaces the National Crime Authority established by the National Crime Authority Act 1984 (Cth).) The ACC can apply to a judge of the Federal Court or a court of a state or territory for the issue of a warrant where there are reasonable grounds for believing that there is in specified premises a thing connected with 'a special ACC operation/investigation' (referred to as 'things of the

---

90 *The Laws of Australia*, n 6 above, paras 11.2 and 17.

91 There is also the power in s 70 of the Australian Securities and Investments Commission Act 2001 to apply for a court order forcing a person to comply with Part 3.

92 (1991) 105 ALR 227. See also, for example, *Insurance & Superannuation Commission v Glaser* (1997) 79 FCR 505.

93 Australian Securities and Investments Commission Act 2001 (Cth), s 92.

94 Australian Crime Commission Act 2002 (Cth), s 7.

95 See *The Laws of Australia*, n 6 above, para 11.2. The reference in this chapter to the National Crime Authority Act 1984 and the National Crime Authority should now be read as a reference to the Australian Crime Commission Act 2002 and the Australian Crime Commission, respectively. See also the Australian Crime Commission Establishment Act 2002 (Cth).

relevant kind') and that there could be a risk of concealment or destruction of that thing.[96] The issued warrant authorises entry for the purposes of search and seizure.

Section 28 of the ACCA gives a member of the ACC the power to summon witnesses and to take evidence. Section 29 gives a member of the ACC the power, by notice in writing served on a person, to require that person to produce a specified document or thing specified in a notice which is relevant to an investigation that the ACC is conducting in performance of its special functions. Importantly, s 29A provides that a summons or notice issued under ss 28 or 29 may provide that disclosure of information about the summons or notice, or any connected official matter, is prohibited, except in the circumstances, if any, specified in the notation. Section 29B provides that any person served with, or otherwise given, a summons or notice containing such a notation must not disclose the existence of the summons or notice or any information about it. If a disclosure is made, the maximum penalty is $2,200 or imprisonment for one year.[97] For a corporation, the fine is a maximum of $11,000.

Effects on banker's duty of confidentiality

[2.27] There is no special treatment afforded to confidential information in the possession of a bank. A bank in receipt of an ACC warrant or notice properly issued and served will be required to comply with it regardless of the common law duty of confidentiality. Further, s 29A would clearly prevent a bank advising an affected customer of the issue of a s 28 summons or a s 29 notice.

Commonwealth bankruptcy legislation

Requirements of the law

[2.28] The Bankruptcy Act 1966 (Cth) provides a number of methods for a trustee in bankruptcy to obtain documents. Where information is sought in relation to a bankrupt's account, the trustee in effect is acting as the bankrupt. One example is if a bank is the subject of a written direction of the 'official receiver' under the Bankruptcy Act. The 'official receiver' will be entitled at all reasonable times to full and free access to all premises and books which are the subject of the written direction.[98] Considerations that are relevant when faced with court orders to disclose information are also relevant in this context.[99]

Section 77A of the Bankruptcy Act provides a 'bankruptcy investigator', who is conducting an investigation under s 19AA in relation to a person, the power to require a person to produce, at a specified time and place, specified books or classes of books. The purpose of this section is to extend the investigatory powers of the trustee as recommended by the Costigan Royal Commission.[100]

Another example is s 125 of the Bankruptcy Act, which is specifically directed at the situation where a prescribed organisation[101] (which includes a bank) has ascertained

---

96 National Crime Authority Act 1984 (Cth), s 22.
97 Section 29B(2) provides certain circumstances in which a person is entitled to make a disclosure, including, in para (b), disclosure to a legal practitioner for the purposes of obtaining legal advice or representation relating to the summons.
98 See the Bankruptcy Act 1966, s 77AA in regard to the official receiver's powers.
99 See the discussion under 'Disclosure Under Compulsion of Law' above.
100 See McDonald *Bankruptcy Law and Practice*, p 3607.
101 Prescribed organisation is defined to include a bank in s 125(3).

that an account holder is an undischarged bankrupt. In that case, unless the prescribed organisation is satisfied that the account is on behalf of some other person, it must inform the trustee in bankruptcy, in writing, of the existence of the account. Further, payments out of the account are prohibited, except under an order of the court. If, within one month from the date on which the prescribed organisation informed the trustee of the existence of the account, a copy of the court order has not been served on the prescribed organisation and it has not received written instructions from the trustee, the prescribed organisation is entitled to act without regard to any claim or right the trustee may have in respect of the account.

Effects on banker's duty of confidentiality

[2.29]   There is no specific exemption for banks from the operation and effect of these provisions and, therefore, they are another example of the compulsion of law exception.

The Privacy Commissioner has, however, publicly released advice as to the need for credit providers to make sure they are legally bound to release information requested in purported reliance on the Bankruptcy Act to avoid breaches of s 18N of the Privacy Act.[102]

Miscellaneous statutory provisions

[2.30]   Instances exist of the protection of the principles in *Tournier*,[103] for example, s 18N(1)(d) of the Privacy Act limits (subject to some exceptions) disclosure by credit providers of personal information contained in reports relating to matters such as a customer's creditworthiness.[104]

State and Commonwealth legislation may also detract from the principles in *Tournier*. In most cases, this arises out of reporting obligations to regulatory authorities or the power of regulatory authorities to enter and search premises and to compel the production of documents. Relevant Commonwealth legislation includes the Banking Act 1919, Life Insurance Act 1995, Privacy Act 1988 and the Trade Practices Act 1974. Examples of state legislation include the Estate Agents Act 1980 (Vic), Legal Practice Act 1996 (Vic) and the New South Wales Crime Commission Act 1985 (NSW).[105]

In *Johns v Australian Securities Commission*,[106] the High Court considered the issue of regulators disclosing information obtained from a person or company to another regulator. On this subject, Justice Brennan commented:

'A statute which confers a power to obtain information for a purpose defines, expressly or impliedly, the purpose for which the information when obtained can be used or disclosed. The statute imposes on the person who obtains information

---

102   See the credit reporting advice summaries released by the Privacy Commissioner. See below for a brief discussion of such summaries.

103   *Tournier v National Provincial and Union Bank of England* [1924] 1 KB 461.

104   Examples of situations where the disclosure of a report or information is permitted include to a credit reporting agency for the purpose of being included in the relevant individual's credit information file (s 18N(1)(a)) or where the individual has consented (s 18N(1)(b)) or the disclosure is to a guarantor (s 18N(1)(ba)).

105   Statutes from Victoria and New South Wales are chosen as an illustration of legislation which exists at a state level.

106   (1993) 178 CLR 408.

in exercise of the power a duty not to disclose the information obtained except for that purpose ... The person obtaining information in exercise of such a statutory power must therefore treat the information obtained as confidential whether or not the information is otherwise of a confidential nature.'

See, however, as an illustration, the ACCA, in particular ss 19A and 20. which give the ACC powers to seek information from Commonwealth agencies, and s 59, which gives the ACC power to disclose information it has obtained to other regulators.

DISCLOSURE IN THE PUBLIC INTEREST

[2.31]   This is the second exception to the bankers' duty of confidentiality in *Tournier*.[107]

Weerasooria, in *Banking Law and the Financial System in Australia*,[108] concludes:

'While the right to disclose under this exception should not be lightly assumed, it would appear that it would apply in the following cases:

- during time of war where the customer's dealings indicate that he is trading with the enemy;
- during time of national emergency where a customer is reasonably suspected of treasonable activities against the state;
- to prevent the perpetration or aid in the detection of serious frauds and crimes.'[109]

The decision of Justice Staughton in *Libyan Arab Foreign Bank v Banker's Trust Co*[110] is worthy of note in relation to this exception. In the context of the order of the US President on 8 January 1986 blocking all trade with Libya, Bankers Trust Co in New York was the subject of a claim (amongst others) of breach of confidence for disclosures to the US Federal Reserve Bank. The claim was defended on the basis that the bank was acting pursuant to a higher public duty. Justice Staughton stated:

'... it seems to me that the Federal Reserve Board, as the central banking system in the United States, may have a public duty to perform in obtaining information from banks ... I am prepared to reach a tentative conclusion that the exception applied in this case ... I need not reach a final conclusion on that point, because I am convinced that any breach of confidence there may have been caused the Libyan bank no loss.'[111]

Australian courts have not resolved any of the uncertainty regarding this exception. In *Allied Mills Pty Ltd v Trade Practices Commission (No 1)*,[112] Justice Sheppard, when considering the balance between disclosure of private and confidential information and the public interest in the disclosure of iniquity, commented:

---

107 *Tournier v National Provincial and Union Bank of England* [1924] 1 KB 461.

108 Weerasooria, n 83 above.

109 Weerasooria, n 83 above.

110 [1989] QB 728.

111 [1989] QB 728.

112 (1981) 34 ALR 105. The issues enunciated by Justice Sheppard in *Allied Mills* were considered recently by Justice Moore in *King v AG Australia Holdings Ltd (formerly GIO Australia Holdings Ltd)* [2002] FCA 151.

'The authorities establish that the public interest in the disclosure [sic] (to the appropriate authority or perhaps the press) of iniquity will always outweigh the public interest in the preservation of private and confidential information.'[113]

A bank, therefore, has to establish first whether the conduct amounts to 'iniquity'. After reviewing the authorities, Justice Sheppard concluded that iniquity is wider than a crime or misdemeanour.[114] In *Allied Mills*, a breach of the TPA, liability for which was only civil, amounted to iniquity because Justice Sheppard found Parliament had taken a serious view of the importance of the legislation from the standpoint of the public interest.[115]

Walter and Erlich suggest that, where bankers are involved, the judiciary may develop a test to weigh up whether the disclosure was justified. Walter and Erlich consider the following factors would be relevant to such an assessment:

1   whether the facts in front of the court display a situation a reasonable banker would understand to be one that would be in the public interest to disclose;
2   whether clear, real and extensive danger to the public exists;
3   whether the sole purpose for releasing the information was in the public interest and not a collateral purpose;
4   whether the bank has carefully considered whether its action would be constructive and in the public interest;
5   whether there is a lack of options for the bank to pursue; and
6   whether the bank weighed up and balanced the harm that might flow from the disclosure, directly and indirectly.[116]

Weaver and Craigie suggest that, in the absence of any clear authority on this exception, the warning given by Sir John Paget in relation to the use of this exception remains as valid today as it was when he delivered it in 1924: 'it would be inadvisable for a banker to exercise his private judgment in such matters at the expense of the customer'.[117]

DISCLOSURE IN THE INTERESTS OF THE BANK

[2.32]   Traditionally, this exception has been considered relevant where the bank issues civil proceedings against a customer of the bank or in defence of civil proceedings. It is also relevant where the bank wishes to make a disclosure to a potential guarantor of a customer.[118] There has not been a reported case directly under this exception in Australia.

The English case of *Sunderland v Barclays Bank Ltd*[119] is an example of a reported case under this exception, but it has not been judicially considered in Australia.[120] In *Sunderland*, it was held to be in the bank's interest for the bank to disclose confidential information in reply to a demand for an explanation of what appeared to be discourteous behaviour. Further details of this case are given in Chapter 11, England, in the section which deals with disclosure in the interests of the bank.

113 (1981) 34 ALR 105 at 141.
114 (1981) 34 ALR 105 at 141.
115 (1981) 34 ALR 105 at 142.
116 Walter and Erlich, n 81 above, at 416.
117 Weaver and Craigie *Banker and Customer*, p 2647.
118 See 'Guarantees' below. In relation to responses in general to inquiries by guarantors, see *Commercial Bank of Australia Ltd v Amadio* (1983) 151 CLR 447.
119 (1938) 5 LDAB 163.

The only sensible basis for the decision in *Sunderland* is that Mrs Sunderland consented to the disclosure. Otherwise, we are left with the absurd position that a bank may disclose one customer's interests to another because the inquirer wants to know and will be offended if the bank does not disclose. The proper course for the bank to take would have been to show the inquirer that the dishonour was justified by reason of insufficient funds.

Bank of Tokyo Ltd v Karoon[121] is an example of where a bank sought to argue that it was in the interests of the bank to pass information between a parent company and a subsidiary in relation to a customer of the bank. The bank argued there had been no disclosure because the parent and subsidiary were part of one corporate group and, if there were disclosure, that it was in the interests of the bank. The court treated the parent and subsidiary as separate entities and therefore held that there had been a disclosure. The purpose for the disclosure was to assist the parent in its interpleader to the court in England. The argument in relation to the disclosure being in the interests of the bank was found to be an issue that was more appropriate for the New York court to decide.

In Australia, the effect of *Bank of Tokyo Ltd v Karoon* was previously limited by the application of the Code of Banking Practice.[122] Section 12.2(a) of the Code of Banking Practice previously provided that a bank could disclose to a related entity information necessary to enable an assessment to be made of the total liabilities (present and prospective) of the customer to the bank and the related entity.[123] Further, a bank was permitted to disclose to a related entity of the bank, which provided related or ancillary financial services to those provided by the bank, information concerning the customer. This was unless the customer had instructed the bank not to.[124]

However, s 12.2(a) has been deleted from the Code of Banking Practice, thereby leaving open the question of the effect, in Australia, of *Karoon*. Nevertheless, Part IIIA of the Privacy Act 1988 permits a bank, in its capacity as a credit provider, to disclose to a related corporation certain consumer credit information relating to an individual.[125] Such a disclosure would accordingly seem to be 'authorised by or under law' and hence occur within the s 18N(1)(g) exemption in the Privacy Act 1988 and be permissible notwithstanding that it is not clearly within one of the *Tournier*[126] exceptions.

Disclosure by express or implied consent

[2.33]   It will usually be clear when a bank is entitled to disclose under the exception of express consent. A more difficult issue is where a bank seeks to rely on the exception of the implied consent of the customer.

---

120 For a discussion of *Sunderland v Barclays Bank Ltd*, see Walter and Erlich, n 81 above, at 416.
121 [1987] 1 AC 45.
122 See the discussion under 'Code of Banking Practice' below.
123 Where the Code of Banking Practice seeks to alter the agreement between the bank and the customer (relying on s 1.3(b)) in a way that could disadvantage the customer (ie s 12.2(a)), then the bank will have to rely on a term in the original contract to the effect that it can change the terms of the contract at any time without consideration.
124 Section 12.2(b) of the Code of Banking Practice.
125 Section 18N(1)(d).
126 *Tournier v National Provincial and Union Bank of England* [1924] 1 KB 461.

It has been argued by some commentators[127] that the information a bank can disclose to a guarantor or prospective guarantor is an example of an exception of express or implied consent.[128] The other area where this exception has traditionally been discussed is the giving of bankers' opinions.[129]

It is a well-established practice that banks give opinions concerning their customers' creditworthiness. Some debate has taken place on whether the practice of giving bankers' opinions has reached a level whereby it is a trade custom of which the customer is, or should be, aware and to which the customer gives implied consent. However, some commentators believe that the giving of bankers' opinions is not well known amongst customers and, accordingly, an implied consent to the giving of bankers' opinions cannot be drawn from the custom of bankers.[130]

The position on bankers' opinions has been resolved by the Credit Reporting Code of Conduct (which has statutory force under ss 18A and 18B of the Privacy Act). The Credit Reporting Code of Conduct provides:

'A credit provider which is a bank may not disclose to another bank a "banker's opinion" relating to an individual's consumer creditworthiness, unless that individual's specific agreement to the disclosure of such information for a particular purpose has been obtained.'

Paragraph 71 of the explanatory notes to the Code further provides that:

'The provision by banks of opinions relating to an individual's commercial creditworthiness is unaffected by the provisions of the Code of Conduct or the Privacy Act.'

GUARANTEES
Disclosure to guarantors

[2.34]   There has been some confusion about what a bank can disclose to a guarantor or prospective guarantor. In *Ross v Bank of New South Wales*,[131] Chief Justice Harvey found that a guarantor of a customer's loan account with a bank is not entitled to demand from the bank a copy of the loan account, but is entitled to information as to the balance then owing, the rate of interest charged and the amount, if any, realised by the bank in respect of collateral securities.[132] A guarantor is the guarantor of the loan obligations of the borrower and this does not entitle a guarantor to information in relation to accounts held by the borrower in his capacity as a customer of the bank. Chief Justice Harvey commented:

'So far as the plaintiff is concerned, I think her rights must be determined in exactly the same way as if the mortgagee creditor was not a bank at all, but was an ordinary mortgagee.'[133]

---

127 See Walter and Erlich, n 81 above, at 416.
128 See the discussion under 'Guarantees' below.
129 See the discussion of the Privacy Act 1988 below.
130 Walter and Erlich, n 81 above, at 419.
131 (1928) SR (NSW) 539.
132 (1928) SR (NSW) 539 at 542.
133 (1928) SR (NSW) 539 at 541.

Arguably, when disclosing to a guarantor, the bank could fall under the exception of the disclosure either being in the interests of the bank or with express or implied consent.

The argument that disclosure to a guarantor is in the bank's interest could be justified on the basis that there has been considerable development in the law relating to guarantees and guarantors, particularly since the decision of the High Court in *Amadio*.[134] Therefore, a higher duty has been placed on banks to ensure that guarantors are aware of their obligations and hence it is more likely to be accepted by a court that it was in the interests of the bank to provide information to a potential guarantor. This is particularly the case given the High Court's decision in *Garcia v National Australia Bank Ltd*[135] that a creditor may have a positive duty to take steps to explain a transaction to a guarantor.

The difficulty with this argument is that, in the vast majority of cases, there will be a simple alternative, namely, to advise customers that they must give consent for the disclosure of information to the guarantor if the loan facility is to be made available.

The effect of the Code of Banking Practice on guarantees

Requirements of the Code

[2.35] Section 28 of the Code of Banking Practice applies to each guarantee and indemnity obtained from a third party who is an individual for the purpose of securing any financial accommodation or facility provided by a bank to another individual or a small business.[136]

Section 28.4(a) sets out a number of things which the bank must do before it takes a guarantee. These include giving the prospective guarantor a prominent notice advising (amongst other things) that the guarantor can request information about the transaction or facility to be guaranteed (including any facility with the bank to be refinanced by the facility to be guaranteed). Under s 28.4(b)(i), the bank must also tell the prospective guarantor about:

1   certain notices of demand made by the bank on the debtor and excesses, overdrawings or dishonours in relation to any facility the debtor has, or has had, with the bank within a specified time; and
2   if any existing facility the bank has given the debtor will be cancelled or if the facility to be guaranteed will not be provided if the guarantee is not provided.

Before accepting the guarantee under s 28.4, the bank has to provide a prospective guarantor with:

1   a copy of any related credit contract or security contract;
2   the final letter of offer provided to the borrower by the bank, together with details of any conditions in an earlier version of that letter of offer that were satisfied before the final letter of offer was issued;

---

134 (1983) 151 CLR 447.
135 (1998) 194 CLR 395.
136 'Small business' is defined for these purposes in s 40 of the Code of Banking Practice to mean a business employing:
    (a) fewer than 100 full-time (or equivalent) employees if the business is or includes the manufacture of goods; or
    (b) in any other case, fewer than 20 full-time (or equivalent) people.

3   any related credit report from a credit reporting agency;

4   any current related credit insurance contract in the bank's possession;

5   any financial accounts or statement of financial position given to the bank relevant to the facility to be guaranteed (and any other statement in the last two years relating to a facility the debtor has, or has had, with the bank where there has been a notice of demand issued and any excess, overdrawing or dishonour);

6   certain statements of account relating to the facility; and

7   any notice previously given to the borrower relevant to the facility to be guaranteed with which the borrower has not complied.

The bank must also give the guarantor other relevant information (including any facility to be refinanced by the new facility) that the guarantor reasonably requests (but the bank does not have to give the guarantor its legal opinions). The guarantor must be given until at least the next day to consider the information unless the person has received independent legal advice.[137]

Effects on banker's duty of confidentiality

[2.36]   The provisions of the new Code of Banking Practice relating to guarantees would seem to have little direct effect on the banker's duty of confidentiality. If the bank cannot obtain the borrower's consent to provide the required information, then the banker will not be able to take the guarantee.

The effect of the Consumer Credit Code on guarantees

Requirements of the law

[2.37]   Section 34(1) of the Consumer Credit Code provides that a credit provider must, at the request of a debtor or guarantor, provide a statement of the current balance of the debtor's account, any amounts credited or debited during the period specified in the request, any amounts overdue and when each such amount became due and any amount payable on the date it became due. There are also provisions in s 34(2) in relation to the time within which the statement must be provided.

Section 51(1) further provides that, before the obligations under a credit contract are secured by guarantee, the credit provider must give to the prospective guarantor a copy of the contract document of the credit contract or proposed credit contract and a document in the form prescribed by the regulations explaining the rights and obligations of the guarantor. Failure to do so renders the guarantee unenforceable.[138]

Section 163(1) also provides that other contracts and documents must be provided to a guarantor on request. These include any credit related insurance contract in the credit provider's possession and any notice previously given to the debtor under this Code.

Effects on banker's duty of confidentiality

[2.38]   Unlike the provisions of the Code of Banking Practice, the provisions in the Consumer Credit Code require disclosure under compulsion of law with statutory

---

137 Code of Banking Practice, clause 28.5.
138 Section 51(2).

force. It may be a defence to a claim for wrongful disclosure to a guarantor under the provisions of the Consumer Credit Code that disclosure was made under compulsion of law. However, to avoid any doubt on this issue, banks may wish to obtain an express consent to the relevant disclosures from the potential borrower as part of the loan application process.

ASIC ACT 2001, S 12DA – EFFECT ON BANKER'S DUTY OF CONFIDENTIALITY[139]

[2.39]   Section 12DA of the ASIC Act imposes an obligation on a financial corporation to refrain from misleading or deceptive conduct in trade or commerce. One potential difficulty is that, under certain conditions, silence itself may be construed as misleading conduct. The general approach was formulated by Justice French in *Kimberley NZI Finance Ltd v Torero Pty Ltd*[140] in relation to s 52 of the TPA as being:

'. . . unless the circumstances are such as to give rise to the reasonable expectation that if some relevant fact exists it would be disclosed, it is difficult to see how mere silence could support the inference that the fact does not exist . . .'[141]

In *Kabwand Pty Ltd v National Australia Bank Ltd*,[142] this issue arose in relation to a bank. A banker acted as banker for both the vendor and purchaser of a business. The banker told the purchaser the business had 'an excellent cash flow situation'. The business, however, was unprofitable and the bank manager deliberately refrained from telling the purchasers. Did s 52 place an obligation on the manager to disclose that overrode the manager's duty of confidentiality? The court found there was no duty of disclosure since the bank was under a contractual duty of secrecy to its customer. The reasoning has been criticised by Alan Tyree on the basis that it is circular:

'There is no duty of secrecy if disclosure is under compulsion of law. There is compulsion if there is a reasonable expectation, but according to *Kabwand*, there is no reasonable expectation because there is a duty of secrecy.'[143]

It is important to note that in *Kabwand* the applicants did not plead a case that, once the banker had made the statement about the excellent cash flow of the business, s 52 imposed upon the banker an obligation to go on and give the true picture in relation to the business. Had that been done, the result might have been different.

---

139 For developments in relation to silence amounting to a breach of s 52 (which predated s 12DA of the ASIC Act), see Warren Pengilley 'Section 52: can the blind mislead the blind?' (March 1997) 5 Trade Practices LJ.
140 (1989) 11 ATPR 46-054.
141 (1989) 11 ATPR 46-054 at 53 and 195. This approach has been applied recently in *Hadid v Lenfest Communications Inc* [1999] FCA 1798.
142 (1989) 11 ATPR 40-950. In *Winterton Construction Pty Ltd v Hambros Australia Ltd* (1992) 39 FCR 97, Justice Hill endorsed the court's view in *Kabwand* of a bank's duty of confidence for a merchant bank.
143 Tyree 'Section 52 and the Banker's Duty of Confidentiality' (June 1990) J Banking and Finance Law and Practice 144. In Daniel Clough's article 'Misleading and deceptive silence: Section 52, Confidentiality and the General Law' (1994) 2 Trade Practices LJ 76 at 93, see the section entitled 'The Financier's Duty of Confidentiality: does it take precedence over section 52'.

CODES OF PRACTICE

[2.40] There are a number of duties of confidentiality imposed by various Codes of Practice in Australia. For example:

1 the Code of Banking Practice, Building Society Code of Practice, Credit Union Code of Conduct and the Electronic Funds Transfer Codes of Conduct each contain a duty of confidentiality;
2 the Internet Industry Codes of Practice (first released in May 2002 and revised in May 2005) only deal with privacy issues in very broad terms, for example, there is a requirement that the privacy of users' details obtained by Code subscribers in the course of business will be respected;
3 the Australian Direct Marketing Association ('ADMA') Code of Practice (November 2001) sets out specific standards of conduct for ADMA members who are participants in the direct marketing industry. Privacy principles similar to the national privacy principles in the Privacy Act 1988 are an integral part of this Code.

The most important code in the bank–customer relationship is the Code of Banking Practice.

Code of Banking Practice

[2.41] As a result of the November 1991 House of Representatives Standing Committee on Finance and Public Administration[144] report entitled 'A Pocket Full of Change',[145] the Code of Banking Practice was formulated. Since then, the Code has been revised to apply to all banking facilities provided in s 40 of the Code and to each bank that has publicly announced that it has adopted the Code.[146] Since November 1996, as part of the movement towards the development and implementation of the Consumer Credit Code,[147] Australian banks have been advertising their adoption of the Code of Banking Practice and it is now growing in terms of its legal enforceability.

Once adopted, the terms of the Code become an express part of the contract between the bank and its customer. The Code applies to dealings between customers of a bank who are individuals or a small business, including any individual from whom the bank obtains a guarantee. A breach of the Code is a breach of contract and normal contractual remedies will be available.[148]

The intention of the Code is that it should not impose obligations on banks relating to privacy and confidentiality in addition to their existing obligations under the Privacy Act 1988 and their general duty of confidentiality.

Under s 22 of the Code, a bank acknowledges that, in addition to the bank's duties under the Privacy Act 1988, the bank has a general duty of confidentiality towards its customer, except in the following circumstances:

1 where disclosure is compelled by law;

---

144 The Martin Committee.
145 AGPS (1991).
146 There is also provision for a bank to adopt the Code by incorporating its terms into a contract with a customer: see clause 10.3 of the Code.
147 The Consumer Credit Code provides for consumer protection regulation. It regulates the provision of credit for personal, domestic or household purposes.
148 See the discussion under 'Remedies for Breach' above.

2   where there is a duty to the public to disclose;

3   where it is in the bank's interests to require disclosure; or

4   where disclosure is made with the customer's express or implied consent.

Consumer Credit Code

[2.42]   The Consumer Credit Code provides for substantially uniform consumer credit regulation throughout Australia. It provides for the regulation of the provision of credit to individuals for domestic, personal or household use. Several provisions of the Consumer Credit Code impinge upon the banker's duty of confidentiality. See, in particular, the discussion in relation to guarantees above.

PRIVACY ACT 1988

[2.43]   The Privacy Act 1988 (Cth) (incorporating the amendments made to it by the Privacy Amendment (Private Sector) Act 2000) applies to the private sector in relation to all dealings with the personal information of individuals. The national privacy principles ('NPPs') in the Privacy Act set out how private sector organisations (including banks) should collect, use and disclose, keep secure and provide access to personal information.[149] The principles also give individuals the right to know what information an organisation holds about them and a right to correct that information if it is wrong.

The Federal Privacy Commission has written guidelines to the NPPs to assist private sector organisations to meet their obligations in the handling of personal information. A series of information sheets has also been developed and provides more detailed explanations and good practice or compliance tips on various aspects of the NPPs and the private sector provisions.

Part IIIA of the Privacy Act governs credit reporting and the use and disclosure of credit-sensitive information. It is these two areas which are of particular interest in the present context. Part IIIA will clearly apply to a 'bank' given that the definition of a 'credit provider' in s 11B(1)(a) specifically refers to a bank.

Part IIIA only regulates consumer credit information, ie information relating to a 'loan'[150] to an individual to be used wholly or primarily for domestic, family or household purposes. These provisions, by definition, do not apply to data relating to any person other than an individual (ie they would not apply to information concerning an incorporated company), aggregate bank data or data which does not identify an individual.

Broadly, Part IIIA, as far as it relates to credit providers, regulates:

1   the accuracy and security of credit reports;[151]

2   access to, and alteration of, credit reports held by credit providers by customers;[152]

---

149 Principle 1 – Collection, Principle 2 – Use and disclosure, Principle 3 – Data quality, Principle 4 – Data security, Principle 5 – Openness, Principle 6 – Access and correction, Principle 7 – Identifiers, Principle 8 – Anonymity, Principle 9 – Transborder data flows and Principle 10 – Sensitive information.

150 A 'loan' is broadly defined in s 6(1) of the Privacy Act to cover, in effect, any debt deferral arrangement.

151 Section 18G.

152 Sections 18H and 18J.

3   the purpose for which credit providers can use credit reports;[153]
4   the information which must be provided to an applicant where a credit application is refused wholly or partly on the grounds of a credit report in relation to the applicant;[154] and
5   disclosure by credit providers of a 'report' or personal information derived from a 'report'.[155]

The restrictions in the Privacy Act on disclosures of a 'report' or personal information derived from a 'report' are of particular relevance to a banker's duty of confidentiality. In summary, s 18N prohibits the disclosure of such information for any purpose unless one of the various specified exceptions applies.

A 'report' is broadly defined to include:

1   any 'record' (which is in turn defined in s 6(1) to include a document, database or any pictorial representation of a person, subject to certain exceptions);
2   a 'credit report'; and
3   any other record or information, in any form, that has any bearing on an individual's creditworthiness, credit standing, credit history or credit capacity, other than publicly available information.[156]

A 'credit report' is essentially a report on creditworthiness obtained from a credit reporting agency, such as the Baycorp Advantage Business Information Services Ltd.[157]

The exceptions provided for in s 18N(1) relate to disclosures:

1   to a credit reporting agency for specified purposes;
2   with the specific agreement of the individual, to another credit provider for a particular purpose;
3   to a guarantor of a loan for enforcement purposes;
4   to a mortgage insurer for specified purposes;
5   to a dispute resolution authority;
6   to a minister, department or authority in a state or territory whose functions include the giving of mortgage credit, the management or supervision of schemes or arrangements involving mortgage credit;
7   to a supplier for the purpose of allowing the supplier to determine whether to accept payment by means of a credit card or electronic transfer of funds;
8   to potential assignees;
9   to debt collectors;
10   to persons who manage loans for the credit provider;
11   to related corporations;
12   where disclosure for the particular purpose is required or authorised by or under law;
13   to the individual themselves or a person authorised in writing by the individual to seek access to the relevant report or information;
14   to a person authorised to operate an account maintained by the person; and
15   in a case where there has been a serious credit infringement and the disclosure is made to another credit provider or a law enforcement authority.

---

153 Section 18L.
154 Section 18M.
155 Section 18N.
156 Section 18N(9).
157 Section 6(1).

The exceptions to the rule in *Tournier* differ somewhat from the circumstances where disclosure is authorised under Part IIIA and the NPPs. In some respects, Part IIIA expands the scope of disclosure by permitting disclosure on the basis that it is 'authorised' by law. The question is whether a disclosure 'authorised' by law for the purposes of Part IIIA is permissible in derogation from the common law duty not to disclose. Where there is an express intention on the part of the legislature to override the common law, this issue is not problematic, for example, the Privacy Act itself expressly allows disclosures between related corporations.[158] Such a disclosure would accordingly seem to be 'authorised by or under law' and hence be within the s 18N(1)(g) exception and be permissible notwithstanding that it is clearly not within one of the exceptions to *Tournier*.[159] Many statutes 'authorise' (as opposed to 'require') disclosure, however, in vague terms. In such instances, it is still arguable that Part IIIA will still authorise disclosure on the basis of the s 18N(1)(g) exception.

The Part IIIA provisions sit together with the NPPs in relation to banks' collection, use and disclosure of customer information. If a bank wants to disclose credit information, it must, after first establishing that the disclosure is permitted under Part IIIA, confirm that the disclosure is also allowed under the NPPs. NPP 1 provides that an organisation (including a bank):

1   must not collect personal information unless the information is necessary for one of its functions or activities;
2   must only collect personal information by lawful and fair means and not in an unreasonably intrusive way;
3   must, at or before the time (or as soon as practicable thereafter) it collects personal information about an individual from the individual, take reasonable steps to ensure that the individual is aware of the identity of the organisation and how to contact it, the fact that he can gain access to it, the purposes for which the information is collected, the organisations (or types of organisations) to which the organisations usually disclose information of that kind, any law which requires the particular information to be collected and the main consequences (if any) to the individual if any or part of the information is not provided.

In addition, NPP 1.4 provides that, where it is reasonable and practicable to do so, an organisation must only collect personal information about an individual from that individual. Under NPP 1.5, if the information is collected from someone else, the organisation must take reasonable steps to make sure that the individual whose information it is is aware of the matters set out in NPP 1.3 except to the extent this would pose a serious threat to their life or health.

Under NPP 2.1, a bank must not use or disclose personal information (including credit information) about an individual for a purpose ('secondary purpose') other than the primary purpose of collection unless:

1   the secondary purpose is related to the primary purpose of collection and, if the personal information is sensitive information, directly related to the primary purpose of collection and the individual would reasonably expect the organisation to use or disclose the information for the secondary purpose;
2   the individual has consented to the use or disclosure; or

---

158 Privacy Act, s 18N(1)(d).
159 See the discussion of *Bank of Tokyo Ltd v Karoon* [1987] 1 AC 45 under 'Disclosure in the Interests of the Bank' above.

3   if the information is not sensitive information and the use of the information is for the secondary purpose of direct marketing:

      (a)   it is impracticable for the organisation to seek the individual's consent before that particular use, and

      (b)   the organisation will not charge the individual for giving effect to a request by the individual to the organisation not to receive direct marketing communications, and

      (c)   the individual has not made a request to the organisation not to receive direct marketing communications, and

      (d)   in each direct marketing communication with the individual, the organisation draws to the individual's attention, or prominently displays a notice, that he or she may express a wish not to receive any further direct marketing communications, and

      (e)   each written direct marketing communication by the organisation with the individual (up to and including the communication that involves the use) sets out the organisation's business address and telephone number and, if the communication with the individual is make by fax, telex or other electronic means, a number or address at which the organisation can be directly contacted electronically; or

4   one of the other provisions in NPP 2.1(d)–(h) apply, including the use or disclosure of the personal information as required or authorised by or under law (NPP 2.1(g)).

Under the NPPs, an organisation must also:

1   take reasonable steps to make sure that the personal information it collects, uses or discloses is accurate, complete and up to date (NPP 3);

2   take reasonable steps to protect the personal information it holds from misuse and loss and from unauthorised access, modification or disclosure (NPP 4.1);

3   take reasonable steps to destroy or permanently anonymise personal information if it is no longer needed for any purpose for which the information may be used or disclosed under NPP 2 (NPP 4);

4   set out in a document clearly expressed policies on its management of personal information on request (NPP 5.1); and

5   on request by a person, take reasonable steps to let the person know, generally, what sort of personal information it holds, for what purposes and how it collects, holds, uses and discloses that information (NPP 5.2).

If an organisation holds personal information about an individual, it must provide the individual with access to it on request subject to certain exceptions (including if the denial of access is authorised or required by law (NPP 6.1(h) and NPP 6.1)). However, where providing access would reveal information that is the result of an exercise of judgment or an evaluation process (termed 'evaluative information' in the Privacy Act) generated within the organisation in connection with a commercially sensitive decision-making process, the organisation may, under NPP 6.2, give the individual an explanation for the commercially sensitive decision rather than direct access to the information.

NPP 9 sets out the conditions under which an organisation in Australia or an external territory may transfer personal information about an individual to someone (other than the organisation or the individual) who is in a foreign country. Such transfers are only authorised if:

1   the organisation reasonably believes that the recipient is subject to a law, binding scheme or contract which effectively upholds principles for fair handling of the information that are substantially similar to the NPPs;

2   the individual consents to the transfer;

3   the transfer is necessary for the performance of a contract between the individual and the organisation or for the implementation of pre-contractual measures taken in response to the individual's request;

4   the transfer is necessary for the conclusion or performance of a contract concluded in the interest of the individual between the organisation and the third party;

5   all of the following apply:

    (a) the transfer is for the benefit of the individual,

    (b) it is impracticable to obtain the consent of the individual to that transfer, and

    (c) if it were practicable to obtain such consent, the individual would be likely to give it; or

6   the organisation has taken reasonable steps to ensure that the information which is transferred will not be held, used or disclosed by the recipient of the information inconsistently with the NPPs.

Credit Reporting Code of Conduct

[2.44]   The Privacy Act's rules applicable to credit providers must be read in conjunction with the Credit Reporting Code of Conduct ('Credit Reporting Code') which has been issued by the Privacy Commissioner under s 18A of the Privacy Act. The Credit Reporting Code has statutory force by virtue of s 18B of the Act. The Credit Reporting Code, like Part III of the Act, only applies to consumer credit information and supplements Part IIIA.

Among other things, the Credit Reporting Code requires credit providers (including banks) and credit reporting agencies:

1   to deal promptly with individual requests for access and amendment of personal credit information;

2   to ensure that only permitted and accurate information is included in an individual's credit information file;

3   to keep adequate records in regard to any disclosure of personal credit information;

4   to adopt specific procedures in settling credit reporting disputes; and

5   to provide staff training on the requirements of the Privacy Act.

Credit reporting advice summaries

[2.45]   Part IIIA of the Privacy Act (and the NPPs as relevant) must also be read in conjunction with the credit reporting advice summaries issued by the Privacy Commissioner. These advice summaries do not have force of law, but nevertheless clarify the Privacy Commissioner's view of many of the ambiguities inherent in s 18N(1). By way of example, the Privacy Commissioner is apparently of the view that a disclosure by a credit provider to certain service providers (such as lawyers, accountants, authors, consultants and mailing companies) in connection with the management of loans provided by the credit provider may be regarded as a permitted 'use' of information rather than as a prohibited 'disclosure', provided the credit provider maintains control of the information and there are appropriate confidentiality provisions.[160] Such explanations of s 18N(1) are useful, but they do

---

160 Paragraph 10.24 of the credit reporting advice summaries issued by the Privacy Commissioner.

not have the force of law and consequently there must be some uncertainty in relying on them.

Interaction between the Privacy Act 1988 and the *Tournier* case

[2.46] Part IIIA of the Privacy Act bears on the banker's common law duty of confidentiality as established by the *Tournier* case, for example, the *Tournier* duty of confidentiality attaches at the commencement of the bank–customer relationship, commensurate with its contractual nature, and terminates when the relationship comes to an end.

The Privacy Act, in contrast, operates with statutory force in relation to personal information, including certain consumer credit personal information. It is not affected by the commencement or cessation of the bank–customer relationship. Hence, the Privacy Act imposes obligations on credit providers (including banks) in a wider set of circumstances than *Tournier* does.

Furthermore, the rule in *Tournier* applies in respect of information, such as account information, concerning the conduct by the bank of the customer's business, irrespective of its source and purpose of collection. Part IIIA and the NPPs regulate, however, credit providers in respect of all information that comes within the broad definition of a 'report'. This latter class of information is clearly broader than the class of information in respect of which the *Tournier* duty of confidentiality attaches.

Many other aspects of Part IIIA and the NPPs exceed the *Tournier* duty of bank confidentiality, for example, the obligations concerning the collection of personal information, accuracy and security safeguards, restrictions on internal use of credit reports and permitted customer access are not represented at common law. In contrast, the *Tournier* duty is confined to disclosure (and, to some degree, use).

The common law duty of non-disclosure also differs, however, from its counterpart provisions in Part IIIA and NPP 2. The best way to specify the differences is to examine the impact of Part IIIA and NPP 2 upon the four exceptions to the common law rule.

Disclosure under compulsion of law

[2.47] An example at common law is where a bank is required to give evidence concerning a customer's account in civil or criminal proceedings.

Under Part IIIA of the Privacy Act[161] and NPP 2.1(g), the disclosure of a credit report by a credit provider is permitted if it is 'required or authorised by or under law'. 'Required' connotes compulsion such as mandatory legislation[162] or court order. An example is the Financial Transaction Reports Act 1988 (Cth) which requires 'cash dealers', among others, to supply reports of any transactions that they suspect on reasonable grounds may be relevant to the investigation of tax evasion or a federal offence.

---

161 Privacy Act, s 18N(1)(g).
162 For example, the Income Tax Assessment Act 1936 (Cth), ss 263 and 264 (power to inspect and seize documents and to require disclosure of income and assets for use as evidence).

'Authorised' indicates a right or entitlement, such as the right to disclose information under the Proceeds of Crime Act 1987 (Cth) (for example, the right under s 46 of the Act to adduce evidence in relation to a proposed restraining order on property where the person appearing has an interest in the property) or the right to disclose confidential legal information under the common law exceptions to legal professional privilege. The 'compulsion of law' exception to *Tournier* would not appear to allow disclosure on this basis.

The Credit Reporting Code contains the following explanation by the Privacy Commissioner of this exception which indicates it should be broadly interpreted and, in particular, that it should cover any disclosure allowed by *Tournier* (except to the extent that one of the other specific exceptions in s 18N indicates to the contrary):

> '. . . where the disclosure is required or authorised by or under law. This applies to both statute law and common law. It is not limited to Commonwealth law but applies also to state law, and laws of other Australian jurisdictions to which credit providers may be subject. It also includes statutory provisions authorising warrants and other instruments for searching premises, obtaining information, etc.'[163]

Disclosure in the public interest

[2.48]   Part IIIA of the Privacy Act contains no general public interest exception to its disclosure rules, but it does permit disclosure in circumstances where, on reasonable grounds, a credit provider believes than an individual has committed a serious credit infringement. A 'serious credit infringement' is defined in s 6(1) of the Privacy Act to mean:

> 'an act done by a person:
>
> (a) that involves fraudulently obtaining credit, or attempting fraudulently to obtain credit; or
> (b) that involves fraudulently evading the person's obligations in relation to credit, or attempting fraudulently to evade those obligations; or
> (c) that a reasonable person would consider indicates an intention, on the part of the first-mentioned person, no longer to comply with the first-mentioned person's obligations in relation to credit.'

In such a case, information may be passed on to another credit provider or to a law enforcement agency.[164]

NPP 2.1(e), (f) and (h) provide clear general public interest exceptions to the disclosure rules otherwise set out in NPP 2.1. Under NPP 2.1(e), an organisation may use and disclose personal information about an individual other than for the primary purpose of collection where it reasonably believes that the use or disclosure is necessary to lessen or prevent:

1   a serious and imminent threat to an individual's life, health or safety; or
2   a serious threat to public health or public safety.

NPP 2.1(f) provides for use and disclosure of personal information by an organisation where there is reason to suspect that unlawful activity has been, is being

---

163 Paragraph 74 of the explanatory notes to the Credit Reporting Code.
164 Privacy Act, s 18N.

or may be engaged in and the organisation uses or discloses the personal information as a necessary part of its investigation of the matter or in reporting its concerns to relevant persons or authorities.

NPP 2.1(h) provides for use and disclosure of personal information by an organisation where it reasonably believes that the use or disclosure is reasonably necessary for one or more of the following by or on behalf of an enforcement body:

1   the prevention, detection, investigation, prosecution or punishment of a criminal offence, breaches of a law imposing a penalty or sanction or breaches of a prescribed law;

2   the enforcement of laws relating to the confiscation of the proceeds of crime;

3   the protection of the public revenue;

4   the prevention, detection, investigation or remedying of seriously improper conduct or prescribed conduct; and

5   the preparation for, or conduct of, proceedings before any court or tribunal or implementation of the orders of a court or tribunal.

Disclosure in the interests of the bank

[2.49]   The counterpart of this exception in Part IIIA of the Privacy Act is narrower. It permits disclosure to a person recognised and accepted in the community as being appointed for the purpose of settling disputes between credit providers and customers for the purpose of settling such a dispute.[165]

Disclosure by consent

[2.50]   At common law, there is scope for implying consent in certain circumstances. As far as individual consent goes, Part IIIA of the Privacy Act should probably only be regarded as recognising express consent to disclosure.[166]

In particular, Part IIIA affects the giving of 'bankers' opinions'. It requires the specific consent of the individual to be given before a credit report or information may be disclosed by one credit provider to another.[167] This clearly covers the giving of bankers' opinions. It could be argued that, if at common law banks do have the implied consent of their customers to give opinions (which in itself may be debated),[168] then the practice of giving opinions is 'authorised' by law.[169] On this view, it should not be necessary to rely on the s 18N(1)(b) exception. Instead, there could be reliance on the s 18N(1)(g) exception for disclosures which are 'authorised' by law. However, it would be anomalous to regard Part IIIA otherwise than as being intended to prevent the giving of bankers' opinions without consent. This is so notwithstanding the wide view expressed by the Privacy Commissioner as to what 'authorised' by law means.

The position is made clear by the Credit Reporting Code, which provides that 'a credit provider which is a bank may not disclose to another bank a "banker's opinion" relating to an individual's consumer creditworthiness unless that

---

165   Privacy Act, s 18N(1)(bc).
166   Privacy Act, s 18N(1)(b).
167   Privacy Act, s 18N(1)(b).
168   See the discussion on bankers' opinions above.
169   Privacy Act, s 18N(1)(g).

individual's specific agreement to the disclosure of such information for the particular purpose has been obtained'.[170]

This conclusion is supported by the provision in NPP 2.1(b) for the use or disclosure of personal information by consent of the individual concerned. Any implied consent for these purposes ideally should be asked within the Privacy Commissioner's guidelines. The safest position to adopt is to act on a customer's proactive response to a consent question. However, the value of a 'yes' answer to a consent question which relates to personal information which may be gathered over a long period may diminish over time if no steps are taken to 'refresh' the consent.

State privacy legislation

[2.51]   The following state privacy legislation may also be relevant to the banker's duty of confidentiality.

Fair Trading Act 1987 (South Australia)

[2.52]   Part 5 of the Fair Trading Act 1987 (South Australia), which deals with fair reporting, is broad in scope and is not confined to credit. It applies to any communication made to a trader by a reporting agent or another trader of any information relating to a person, except where the person concerned is aware of the communication and the information. Such a communication is a 'prescribed report'.

A reporting agency is generally defined to mean a person that carries on the business of providing prescribed reports. A trader is a person who, in the course of a business, supplies, or offers to supply, goods or services. It is arguable that the provision of credit constitutes the supply of services.

A trader is required to notify an individual of certain information, including the name and address of a relevant credit reporting agency, where the trader:

1   denies a prescribed benefit sought by the individual or grants a prescribed benefit sought by the individual on less favourable terms compared with other persons to whom the trader has granted prescribed benefits; and
2   has obtained a prescribed report on the individual in the last six months.

A prescribed benefit includes a benefit of a commercial nature.

The legislation also deals with a person's right to gain access to information held by a reporting agency and a person's right to dispute the accuracy of that information. It may apply where a credit provider uses a prescribed report in respect of commercial credit. However, where a bank issues a banker's opinion (in respect of consumer or commercial credit), then it arguably could be caught by the legislation as a reporting agency.

---

170 Credit Reporting Code, clause 2.16. See the discussion on bankers' opinions above. The same would apply in respect of information relating to a prospective guarantor's creditworthiness where the purpose for which the borrowing was made is not relevant to the question of whether the opinion may be sought. What is relevant is the kind of information sought in respect of the guarantor. His prior consent may only be required if the information relates to the guarantor's consumer creditworthiness. Paragraph 71 of the explanatory notes to the Credit Reporting Code of Conduct confirms this view and states that '[t]he provision by banks of opinions relating to an individual's commercial creditworthiness is unaffected by the provisions of the Code of Conduct or the Privacy Act'.

Credit Reporting Act 1978 (Victoria)

[2.53] The Credit Reporting Act 1978 (Victoria) only deals with credit reporting. However, it is not limited to consumer credit. It also applies to commercial credit and may apply to companies as well as individuals despite its apparent restriction to 'consumers'. That is because a 'consumer' is defined as 'any person with respect to whom a credit report is made or with respect to whom any information is held by a "credit reporting agent"'.[171] A 'credit report' is in turn broadly defined in s 2 as:

> 'Any written, oral, or other communication with respect to the creditworthiness, credit standing, or credit capacity of a person but does not include a report containing information solely as to transactions or experiences between the person making the report and the person who is the subject of the report.'

The Act primarily deals with the notification by a user of a credit report, to an individual, of the refusal of credit and the individual's subsequent rights to obtain access to information held by the relevant 'credit reporting agent' (a person who engages in the practice of providing credit reports)[172] and to dispute the accuracy of that information.

A 'credit reporting agent' has the following further obligations (amongst others):

1. to give an affected consumer access to information compiled by the agent and the right to request corrections;[173]
2. to advise an affected consumer where amendments are made to relevant credit information and to advise the consumer and any or all persons who have been supplied with information concerning the consumer in the previous six months and any other person requested by the consumer.[174]

Interrelationship between the Privacy Act 1988 and state legislation

[2.54] Section 3 of the Privacy Act provides that the Act is not to affect the operation of a state or territory law that:

> '... makes provision with respect to the collection, holding, use, correction, disclosure or transfer of personal information (including such a law relating to credit reporting or the use of information held in connection with credit reporting) and is capable of operating concurrently with this Act.'

The Commonwealth therefore does not purport to cover the field in relation to credit reporting. Accordingly, if there is no inconsistency with the Commonwealth Act, the relevant provision of the state law should be complied with, otherwise the Privacy Act prevails.

INTERNATIONAL REQUESTS FOR INFORMATION

[2.55] Whether a bank is permitted to transfer information that is subject to the duty of confidentiality will largely depend on the application of the exceptions to the

---

171 Section 2.
172 See s 2 definitions.
173 Section 6(1) and (2).
174 Section 6(3).

duty that permit disclosure. It will also depend on the application of the Privacy Act (which contains provisions that restrict the disclosure of personal information and its transfer to a foreign country) and Australia's anti-money laundering legislation.

Hypothetical example[175]

[2.56] The branch[176] of a bank in the UK is approached by the Financial Services Authority ('FSA') in relation to various transactions which are thought to have been improper. They do not give rise to criminal liability, but are suspected to have been undertaken by various customers of the bank in London possibly with the connivance of officers of the bank. The FSA wishes the bank to make available all its records to its investigators. All these records are held in Australia by the head office of the bank.

Application of legal principles to the hypothetical example[177]

[2.57] The bank's duty not to disclose information about a customer to a third party applies even when the third party is a wholly-owned subsidiary of the bank and operates, in practice, as a part of the bank.[178] Each foreign branch of the bank is regarded as independent of its parent body.[179] Therefore, care must be taken in the transfer of information between branches.[180] Consent to the transfer of information to another office of the same bank in the ordinary course of the banking business may readily be implied in the contract between the bank and its customer. However, consent to the forwarding of customer details to another branch in another country in response to an order of a foreign court, or to bring information within the jurisdiction of a foreign authority, would rarely be implied.[181]

First exception: disclosure under compulsion of law

[2.58] One qualification to the *Tournier* case is disclosure under compulsion of law. Where there is a statutory duty to disclose information, any contractual duty owed by a bank to the depositor is overridden by the statutory duty.[182]

The first issue in the hypothetical example is the appropriate law governing the contract. Normally, the law in force in the place where the account is held by the

---

175 In relation to cross-border issues, one should bear in mind the power of the Australian Taxation Office to issue offshore information notices pursuant to s 264A.
176 If the branch is in fact a subsidiary, it will be treated as a separate legal entity and the issue of which documents are in its control or possession will be assessed on that basis.
177 Australian law would not prevent the disclosure of information to the subsidiary if the information did not identify particular customers. However, it is assumed for the purposes of the hypothetical example that customer-specific information may be disclosed and that the FSA is operating under legislative (not court) powers.
178 *Bank of Tokyo Ltd v Karoon* [1987] 1 AC 45.
179 *Power Curber International Ltd v National Bank of Kuwait SAK* [1981] 3 All ER 607.
180 See the discussion under the Privacy Act 1988 above.
181 *FDC Co Ltd v Chase Manhattan Bank NA* [1990] 1 HKLR 277 at 283–284. This case has been considered in *Bank of Valetta plc v National Crime Authority* (1999) 164 ALR 45.
182 *Federal Comr of Taxation v Australian and New Zealand Banking Group Ltd* (1979) 143 CLR 499 at 521.

customer will govern the obligations under it.[183] Therefore, in the hypothetical example, the account would be governed by the principles in *Tournier*, as well as any applicable legislation in England.

The consequences of this may be seen in *X AG v A Bank*,[184] in which an injunction was sought by a customer in London to prevent the London branch of the bank from answering a subpoena served upon its New York headquarters by the US Justice Department. It was held that English law governed the banking contract, that insufficient reason had been demonstrated for failing to uphold the confidentiality of the documents and that the binding legal obligation in England would probably be an adequate excuse to any contempt proceedings prosecuted in the US for the failure to produce the documents.[185] In the hypothetical example, the accounts are held in London and, therefore, it is likely that English law will be the law governing the obligation to disclose.

Compulsion of law – relevant authorities

[2.59]   There is no Australian decision on what amounts to compulsion of law in an international context. However, English and Hong Kong cases provide that the compulsion of law exception does not include an order directed by a foreign court requiring the production of documents of a branch overseas.[186] In *FDC Co Ltd v Chase Manhattan Bank NA*, Huggins VP said that it was never within the contemplation of the judges in *Tournier* that disclosure under compulsion of law included an order of a foreign court to produce documents which are in Hong Kong. Huggins VP expressed the view that such a construction of the exception 'would not be reasonable'.[187]

In *Power Curber International Ltd v National Bank of Kuwait SAK*,[188] Lord Denning MR stated:

> 'Each branch has to be licenced by the country in which it operates. Each branch is treated in that country as independent of its parent body. The branch is subject to the orders of the courts of the country in which it operates; but not to the orders of the courts where its head office is situate.'[189]

In *MacKinnon v Donaldson*,[190] Justice Hoffmann considered the situation where a plaintiff, under the bankers' books provisions in England, had obtained an ex parte order against a US bank, which required the US bank to produce books and other papers held at its head office in New York in the English court. The plaintiff then issued a subpoena *duces tecum* against an officer of the bank at its London office. Justice Hoffmann held in discharging the order and the subpoena:

---

183 *Libyan Arab Foreign Bank v Bankers Trust Co* [1989] QB 728 at 746, per Justice Staughton.
184 [1983] 2 All ER 464.
185 Lee Aitken 'The bank's duty of confidence in transnational proceedings' (June 1994) J Banking and Finance Law and Practice 109 at 111.
186 *FDC Co Ltd v Chase Manhattan Bank NA* [1990] 1 HKLR 277.
187 [1990] 1 HKLR 277 at 283.
188 [1981] 3 All ER 607.
189 [1981] 3 All ER 607.
190 [1986] Ch 482.
191 *MacKinnon v Donaldson* [1986] Ch 482 at 493. The principle in *MacKinnon* was applied by Justice Habersberger in *Gao v Zhu* [2002] VSC 64.

'In principle and on authority, it seems to me that the court should not, save in exceptional circumstances, impose such a requirement upon a foreigner, and, in particular, upon a foreign bank. The principle is that a state should refrain from demanding obedience to its sovereign authority by foreigners *in respect of their conduct outside the jurisdiction*' (emphasis added).[191]

Justice Hoffmann considered it relevant that in the case there were two other methods by which the documents could have been obtained without infringing US sovereignty and without Citibank losing the protection of a New York court order. First, the plaintiff could have applied directly to a court in New York under provisions of US or New York legislation. Secondly, the plaintiff could have applied to a master under the English Rules of the Supreme Court for the issue of letters of request to the courts of New York specifying the documents required to be produced.[192]

X AG v A Bank is also relevant (as mentioned above and in the consideration of subpoenas from other jurisdictions in the section on extra-territorial aspects of compulsion of law in chapter 11).

Application of the relevant authorities to the hypothetical example

[2.60]   In considering the application of these cases to the hypothetical example and assuming that English law applies because the account is held in London, the following facts will be important:

1   whether the documents sought by the FSA relate to conduct of the Australian bank in England or outside England; and
2   whether there are other methods available to obtain the documents.

If the relevant activities took place in England, then, on the authority of *MacKinnon v Donaldson*, the court is likely to take the view that it is a legitimate exercise of the subject matter jurisdiction of the English court and therefore appropriate. In such a case, it should not matter where the documents are physically held at the time of the request for production. If the bank is trading in England and the activities to which the request for production relates occurred in England, it would appear not to infringe any principle of sovereignty for the English authorities to require the branch trading in its jurisdiction to produce documents relating to that trading provided that those documents remain within its control. It would be an all too easy device for foreign branches trading in a foreign jurisdiction to escape regulatory scrutiny merely by moving the documents offshore.

However, the position would appear to be different if the relevant activity took place outside the jurisdiction. In these circumstances, it is likely the court would take the view that it is an illegitimate exercise of English subject matter jurisdiction in effect to use a compulsory process such as a subpoena to obtain documents situated abroad relating to transactions conducted abroad.[193] Significantly, a Memorandum of Understanding exists between the ASIC and the FSA for mutual assistance in relation

---

192 This is on the basis that the US and UK are both parties to the Hague Convention on the taking of evidence abroad in civil or commercial matters and, subject to any questions of privilege or public policy under New York law, the English court is entitled under the Convention to the assistance of the New York courts in obtaining evidence for the purposes of any pending action.
193 *MacKinnon v Donaldson* [1986] Ch 482.

to the provision of documents to each other. Legislative provision to enable the ASIC to honour its obligations under the Memorandum of Understanding is provided in the Mutual Assistance in Business Regulation Act 1992 (Cth). Section 5(1) provides:

> 'The object of this Act is to enable Commonwealth regulators to render assistance to foreign regulators in their administration or enforcement of foreign business laws by obtaining from persons relevant information, documents and evidence and transmitting such information and evidence and copies of such documents to foreign regulators.'

The existence of this alternative would be a relevant factor for the court to take into account in considering the position.

The position may also be different depending on the source of the power to compel the production of the documents. If the source of the power is legislative, then the position may well turn on the proper interpretation of the legislative provisions.

A bank finding itself in these circumstances should consider notifying its customer of the existence of the court order and of its intention to comply (bearing in mind that a refusal to comply may cause adverse consequences on the client's branch in London). The bank should request that the customer consents to the disclosure of the information.[194] If the customer objected to the disclosure, then the customer could seek an injunction and, in those injunctive proceedings, the bank could bring to the attention of the court all relevant factors.[195]

Second exception: disclosure in the public interest

[2.61] It is unlikely that a bank could claim an exception to its duty of confidentiality on the basis that there is a duty to the public to disclose the information to the foreign authority. It is difficult to see what the duty to the public is in this context.[196]

Third exception: disclosure in the interests of the bank

[2.62] The possibility of relying on the third exception to the banker's duty of confidentiality, where the interests of the bank require disclosure, has been limited by the decision in *Libyan Arab Foreign Bank v Bankers Trust Co*,[197] where Justice Staughton rejected out of hand the argument that disclosure to the US authorities was required in Bankers Trust's own interest on the basis of this exception.

Fourth exception: disclosure with the customer's consent

[2.63] The possibility of relying on the customer's express or implied consent will naturally be limited in situations where the customer itself is the subject of the investigation. However, a customer may be willing to give its express consent to the disclosure of information to a foreign authority where the customer is particularly concerned with its role as a corporate citizen or acutely aware of its public duty.[198]

---

194 On occasions, the terms of the production order may prohibit such disclosure.
195 *X AG v A Bank* [1983] 2 All ER 464.
196 See the discussion under 'Disclosure in the Public Interest' above.
197 [1989] QB 728.
198 See Justice Staughton's comments on this exception in *Libyan Arab Foreign Bank v Bankers Trust Co* [1989] QB 728 at 770–771.

Effect of the Privacy Act 1988 (Cth)

[2.64] The Privacy Act restricts the manner in which banks may deal with information about a natural person. The Privacy Act does not restrict the bank from disclosing:

1 data in respect of companies and other incorporated bodies;
2 aggregate bank data; or
3 data with respect to specific transactions or credits which do not identify the customer.

Further, the Privacy Act does not prevent disclosure if the disclosure and use of personal information is required or authorised by or under law[199] or the use of the report or information for that purpose is required or authorised by or under law.[200] Other exceptions are discussed above.

The key issue is whether 'authorised by or under law' is only a reference to Australian law or whether it is wide enough to be interpreted to mean laws of a foreign jurisdiction as well. However, given the decisions in *Federal Comr of Taxation v Australian and New Zealand Banking Group Ltd*,[201] *FDC Co Ltd v Chase Manhattan Bank NA*[202] and *Power Curber International Ltd v National Bank of Kuwait SAK*,[203] the most likely conclusion is that it would be interpreted as meaning Australian law only.

Note clause 10.40 of the credit reporting advice summaries released by the Privacy Commissioner, where, in relation to this subject, it was commented:

> 'It is important to note that the disclosure by the credit provider must itself be authorised or required. That is, s 18N(1)(g) and NPP 2.1(g) may not necessarily be satisfied if the request is made by a person or body who is performing functions which are authorised by law. Credit providers who have been requested to disclose information under law should therefore request some evidence of the particular authority under which disclosure by the credit provider is required or authorised.'[204]

It is also important to note that any cross-border data flow of personal information must be in accordance with NPP 9 requirements. NPP 9 authorises the transfer of personal information about an individual to someone who is in a foreign country subject to prescribed conditions, including the recipient of the information being subject to a law, binding scheme or contract which effectively upholds principles for fair handling of the information in a way substantially similar to the NPPs (NPP 9(a)) or the disclosing organisation taking reasonable steps to ensure that the transferred information will not be held, used or disclosed by the recipient inconsistently with the NPPs (NPP 9(f)).

---

199 Privacy Act, s 18N(1)(g). See also NPP 2.1, in particular NPP 2.1(g) and 9.
200 Privacy Act, s 18L(1)(e). See also NPP 2.1
201 (1979) 143 CLR 499, in particular, the comments of Gibbs ACJ at 521.
202 [1990] 1 HKLR 277, in particular, the comments of Huggins VP at 281.
203 [1981] 1 WLR 1233, in particular, the comments of Lord Denning at 1241.
204 The credit reporting advice summaries do not cover the issue of foreign courts or foreign authorities.

Effect of the Proceeds of Crime Act 1987 and Financial Transaction Reports Act 1988

[2.65] The disclosure obligations under the Proceeds of Crime Act 1987 and Financial Transaction Reports Act 1988 only require disclosure to Australian authorities. Neither Act authorises disclosure by the bank to authorities of non-Australian governments. However, s 27(1)(d) of the Financial Transaction Reports Act 1988 provides that the Director of the AUSTRAC may, in writing, authorise the Commissioner of the Australian Federal Police ('AFP Commissioner') to have access to information obtained by the Director under Part II of the 1988 Act for the purposes of communicating the information to a foreign law enforcement agency. The AFP Commissioner may communicate that information to a foreign law enforcement agency if the Commissioner is satisfied that the agency has given appropriate undertakings as to the protection of the confidentiality of the information and its use.

Effect of the Foreign Proceedings (Excess of Jurisdiction) Act 1984

[2.66] Even if disclosure fell within one of the exceptions discussed above, disclosure may still be prohibited by the Attorney General. Under s 7 of the Foreign Proceedings (Excess of Jurisdiction) Act 1984, the Commonwealth Attorney General may, by order in writing, prohibit, among other things, the production of a document which is in Australia in a foreign court. This is based on the assumption that, in the hypothetical example above, the FSA obtained a court order.

The Attorney General may only make an order under s 7 if he or she is satisfied that:

1. the making of an order is desirable for the protection of the national interest;
2. the assumption of jurisdiction by the foreign court, or the manner of exercise by the foreign court, is contrary to international law or is inconsistent with international comity or international practice; or
3. the taking of that action by an authority, or the manner of taking that action, is contrary to international law or is inconsistent with international comity or international practice.[205]

BANKER'S DUTY OF CONFIDENTIALITY AND INSIDER TRADING

[2.67] In Australia, the prohibitions against insider trading are set out in Division 3 of Part 7.10 of the Corporations Act. There are two forms of the prohibition. The first applies in respect of *dealings* in securities, derivatives, managed investment products, superannuation products and any other financial products that are able to be traded on a financial market. The second applies to the *communication* of inside information where the relevant financial products are able to be traded on a financial market that is operated in Australia.

The prohibitions apply if:

1. a person (the insider) possesses information that is not generally available;

---

205 Foreign Proceedings (Excess of Jurisdiction) Act 1984, s 6.

2   a reasonable person would expect that information to have a material effect on the price or value of particular financial products if that information were generally available; and

3   the person knows, or ought reasonably to know, that the information is not generally available and that, if it were generally available, a reasonable person would expect it to have a material effect on the price or value of the particular financial products.[206]

In other words, to be an 'insider' within the meaning of Division 3 in relation to, for example, securities of a particular company, one does not need to be connected in any way with the company and the source of the relevant information is immaterial. One becomes an 'insider' simply by virtue of being in possession of information that is not 'generally available'.

An insider that holds inside information must not:

1   deal directly in the relevant financial products by applying for, acquiring or disposing of the financial products or entering into an agreement to do so;[207]

2   deal indirectly by procuring another person to deal in the relevant financial products (for example, inciting, inducing or encouraging another person to deal directly);[208] or

3   if the securities are listed on the Australian stock exchange or any other financial market operating in Australia, directly or indirectly communicating that information to another person or cause that information to be communicated to that other person if the insider knows, or ought reasonably to know, that the other person would, or would be likely to, deal directly or indirectly in the relevant financial products.[209]

Section 1042G of the Corporations Act provides, for the purposes of Division 3, that:

'(a) a body corporate is taken to possess any information which an officer of the body corporate possesses and which came into his or her possession in the course of the performance of duties as such an officer; and

(b) if an officer of a body corporate knows or ought reasonably to know any matter or thing because he or she is an officer of the body corporate, it is to be presumed that the body corporate knows or ought reasonably to know that matter or thing.'

It will be readily seen that the effect of s 1042G is to make a bank an insider in relation to most, if not all, of its corporate customers by virtue of information about the customer in the possession of one or more of its officers that is not 'generally available'.

There are two factors that in practice substantially mitigate the potential effect of s 1042G on a bank. First, the definition of 'debenture' in s 9 of the Corporations Act generally excludes normal bank securities for financial accommodation. In other words, an issue to a bank by its customer of a document acknowledging a debt or a security for a debt does not amount to the subscription or purchase of 'securities' for the purposes of Division 3. That exemption will not, however, apply to a facility for the subscription by a bank of equity capital in a customer, such facilities having been recently permitted in Australia as the result of a change of policy by the Reserve

---

206 Section 1043A of the Corporations Act.
207 Section 1043A(1)(c) of the Corporations Act.
208 Section 1043A(1)(d) of the Corporations Act.
209 Section 1043A(2) of the Corporations Act.

Bank of Australia. For such a facility, a bank may well need to take advantage of the second factor which is Chinese Walls. The Chinese Wall exception is in s 1043F of the Corporations Act. This exception provides that a body corporate does not contravene s 1042G(1) by entering into a transaction or agreement at any time merely because of information in the possession of an officer of the body corporate if:

1   the decision to enter into the transaction or agreement was taken on its behalf by a person other than that officer; and
2   it had in operation at that time arrangements that could reasonably be expected to ensure that the information was not communicated to the person who made the decision and that no advice with respect to the transaction or agreement was given to that person by a person in possession of the information; and
3   the information was not so communicated and no such advice was so given.

Notwithstanding the wide scope of Division 3, it is doubtful whether in practice it involves an extension of the banker's duty of confidentiality; misuse by a banker of information in contravention of Division 3 would almost certainly also involve a breach of the duty of confidentiality. Nevertheless, whereas a breach of the duty of confidentiality generally only gives rise to a civil action for damages, a contravention of Division 3 involves criminal as well as civil liability.

BANKER'S DUTY OF CONFIDENTIALITY AND CHINESE WALLS

[2.68]   Chinese Walls is a practice that emanates from the United States of America, having been devised by investment banks in their attempt to justify representation of conflicting interests. A Chinese Wall is intended to restrict the passing of information between employees or departments of a bank, for example, and typically involves policies and procedures to limit the dissemination of information and possibly physical separation of documents.

Modern banking is multi-functional and multi-divisional, particularly following partial deregulation of the Australian financial system. Whether the bank–customer relationship is seen in a narrow traditional sense or as including information gained through any service provided by a bank for a customer is a moot issue. A bank is placed in an invidious position. A bank, as a matter of contract, could attempt to obtain authorisation. It is likely, however, that such authorisations will be treated with the same rigorous scrutiny and narrow construction as exemption clauses have received at the hands of the courts. However, even that position is unsatisfactory since a bank may not realise in advance that a particular transaction will generate a potential conflict until it is well into the transaction, when to withdraw from the transaction may expose it to a significant liability.

It has been suggested that the best a bank can hope for, apart from wise liability insurance and a sophisticated conflict monitoring programme, is to construct Chinese Walls which will not inhibit the sensible commercial interchange of information (that, at the same time, look credible) and, where possible, to write into investment advice and other contracts the right to withdraw if, in the bank's opinion, a conflict situation is developing and without telling the customer the specific reason.[210] While

210   Burton and Jamieson 'Modern Banking Services – Rights and Liabilities' (September 1989) Australian Law Journal, vol 63, 604.

Australian[211] and United Kingdom[212] courts have been sceptical about the effectiveness of Chinese Walls, such structures are a recognised defence to the insider trading provisions of the Corporations Act[213] and are a well established part of corporate practice.

FURTHER DUTIES OF CONFIDENCE IN AUSTRALIA

[2.69] It is well established that the banker's duty of confidence principally arises out of the contractual relationship with the customer. There is also a duty of confidentiality that arises in equity and the possibility of a fiduciary relationship. Further, there may also be an express term in the contract between a banker and a corporate customer in relation to confidentiality.

Equitable duty of confidence

[2.70] The equitable duty of confidence was considered and recognised by the High Court in *Commonwealth v John Fairfax & Sons Ltd*.[214] The duty consists of two elements:[215] the information is of its nature confidential and it is imparted in circumstances where the recipient could reasonably expect to have realised that it was under an obligation to keep the information confidential.[216] The test to apply was discussed in *Castrol Australia Pty Ltd v Emtech Associates Pty Ltd*.[217] In the context of the bank–customer relationship, the test may apply as follows: if a bank received information from a customer in the course of the bank–customer relationship and the bank knew or ought to have known that it was receiving the information in confidence and a reasonable banker would consider that that information should only be used for the purpose for which it was supplied, the bank would be unable to use the information for an unrelated purpose. Therefore, the equitable duty of confidence applies to use of confidential information, as well as disclosure. An equitable duty of confidence can exist concurrently with a contractual obligation.[218]

Concurrency of contractual rights and equitable principles

[2.71] The concurrency of contractual rights and the underlying equitable principles based on breach of confidence give more substance to the duty.[219] This allows it to withstand legislative attempts to narrow the duty. It is also relevant where a court has resisted a foreign court's attempts to require disclosure on the basis that the protection under local law of the duty of confidence has been seen in the public interest and not merely as the protection of a private right.

---

211 *Mallesons Stephen Jaques v KPMG Peat Marwick* (1990) 4 WAR 357.
212 *David Lee & Co Ltd v Howard Chance* [1990] 3 WLR 1278.
213 Section 1043G of the Corporations Act.
214 (1980) 147 CLR 39. The equitable duty of confidence has been discussed by the High Court in *Australian Broadcasting Corpn v Lenah Game Meats Pty Ltd* (2001) 208 CLR 199.
215 There is some doubt over whether there is a third element which is an unauthorised use causing detriment to the claimant. See the discussion in Meagher, Gummow and Lehane *Equity Doctrines and Remedies* (3rd edn) para 4109.
216 See Meagher, Gummow and Lehane, n 215 above, para 4109 and chapter 41 in general on confidential information.
217 (1980) 33 ALR 31.
218 *Stephens Travel Service International Pty Ltd, Receivers and Managers Appointed v Qantas Airways Ltd* (1988) 13 NSWLR 331 and *A-G v Guardian Newspapers Ltd (No 2)* [1988] WLR 776.
219 See Francis Neate and Roger McCormick *Bank Confidentiality* (1st edn, 1990).

The further importance of the concurrency of the equitable duty is that it fills the position prior to a contract forming between a bank and a prospective customer and, as expressed by Walter and Erlich, continues 'hovering' over the contractual obligation throughout the life of the contract and continues to exist after the life of the contract.[220]

Fiduciary relationship[221]

[2.72] Further substance is added to the bank–customer relationship by the possibility of a fiduciary duty being owed where the bank gives financial advice, for example, when the bank takes on the role of investment adviser or provides a service where the customer is relying upon the bank's advice.[222]

The possibility of a fiduciary relationship, namely a relationship of trust or confidence, existing between a banker and a customer will depend to a large extent on the character of the customer. As Chief Justice Gibbs said in *Hospital Products Ltd v United States Surgical Corpn Ltd*:

> '. . . the fact that the arrangement between the parties was of a purely commercial kind and that they had dealt at arm's length and on an equal footing has consistently been regarded by this court as important, if not decisive, in indicating that no fiduciary duty arose . . .'[223]

Justice Mason said in his judgment:

> 'True it is that a promise or a contractual term may be so precise in its regulation of what a party can do that there is no relevant area of discretion remaining and therefore no scope for the creation of fiduciary duty . . .'[224]

In the joint judgment of Justices Woodward, Northrop and Sheppard in the Federal Court in *Paul Dainty Corpn Pty Ltd v National Tennis Centre Trust*,[225] in reliance on the High Court's decision in *Hospital Products Ltd v United States Surgical Corpn Ltd*, their honours in *Paul Dainty* considered that the authorities made it clear that equity will not impose fiduciary obligations on parties who have entered into ordinary and arm's length commercial relationships, which fully prescribe the respective powers and duties of the parties. This is particularly so when the parties involved are substantial corporations having equal bargaining power and they agree to limit the scope of the contract.[226]

Remedies for breach of fiduciary obligations

[2.73] The scope for different fiduciary relationships calls for a wide variety of remedies. A fiduciary may of course be restrained by injunction from breaching his

---

220 Walter and Erlich, n 81 above.
221 On fiduciary relationship in a commercial matrix, see Lehane 'Fiduciaries in a commercial context' in Finn (ed) *Essays in Equity* (1985).
222 *Commonwealth Bank of Australia v Smith* (1991) 42 FCR 390 and *Hospital Products Ltd v United States Surgical Corpn* (1984) 156 CLR 41. On fiduciary relationship in a commercial matrix, see Lehane 'Fiduciaries in a commercial context' in Finn (ed) *Essays in Equity* (1985).
223 (1984) 156 CLR 41 at 70.
224 *Hospital Products Ltd v United States Surgical Corpn* (1984) 156 CLR 41 at 98.
225 (1990) 22 FCR 495.
226 (1990) 22 FCR 495 at 515–516.

fiduciary duty. A fiduciary who profits from a breach of duty is liable to account for that profit. Where the profit can be traced into identifiable property in the hands of the defaulting fiduciary, proprietary remedies may be appropriate. Where the breach of duty by a fiduciary causes loss to his or her principal, it is well established that compensation is available in the exclusive jurisdiction of equity to make good the loss. Finally, a fiduciary relationship may co-exist with contract and a fiduciary may owe his or her principal duties, breach of which results in damages in tort or gives rise to other common law remedies.[227]

CONTRACTING OUT OF DUTIES OF CONFIDENCE

[2.74] If a financial institution were to seek to contract out of its duties of confidence or to exercise a broad contractual discretion to avoid them, its conduct may, depending on the character of the relevant transaction, be held to be unconscionable conduct under ss 12CA, 12CB and 12CC of the ASIC Act or s 51AC of the TPA.

Section 12AC of the ASIC Act prohibits a person in trade or commerce from engaging in conduct in relation to financial services if the conduct is unconscionable within the meaning of the unwritten law. (The conduct prohibited by s 12CB of the ASIC Act is excluded from the application of s 12AC.) Section 12CB(1) of the Act prohibits conduct that is, in all the circumstances, unconscionable in connection with the supply or possible supply of financial services to a person. 'Financial services' is defined by s 12CB(5) for these purposes as 'a reference to financial services of a kind ordinarily acquired for personal, domestic or household use'.

Section 12CC of the ASIC Act prohibits any person (in trade or commerce) from engaging in conduct that is, in all the circumstances, unconscionable:

'… in connection with:

(a) the supply or possible supply of financial services to another person (other than a listed public company); or
(b) the acquisition or possible acquisition of financial services from a person (other than a listed public company).'

Under s 12AC(1) of the ASIC Act, the above provisions extend to:

'… the engaging in conduct outside Australia by:

(a) bodies corporate incorporated or carrying on business outside Australia;
(b) Australian citizens; or
(c) persons ordinarily resident in Australia.'

Section 51AC(3) of the TPA mirrors, for a corporation's supply or possible supply of goods or services to a person in trade or commerce, the same prohibition of unconscionable conduct as s 12CC of the ASIC Act provides for the supply of financial services.

---

227 See Meagher, Gummow and Lehane, n 215 above, paras 547–554.

3   Austria

Stefan Tiefenthaler
Klemens Keferböck

BANK'S DUTY OF CONFIDENTIALITY
Introduction

[3.1] Austrian law expressly recognises and protects a bank's duty of confidentiality (sometimes referred to as 'bank secrecy') with respect to information received by or relating to its customers. This duty is primarily governed by s 38(1) to (4) (scope and exceptions) and s 101 (criminal liability) of the Austrian Banking Act ('BWG') and supplemented by several provisions of a procedural nature such as the Revenues Penal Act ('FinStrG') and the Criminal Procedure Code ('StPC').

Section 38(5) of the BWG, a provision of constitutional law, affords special protection to the provisions of s 38(1) to (4) of the BWG by stipulating that an amendment of these provisions requires – similar to an amendment of a provision of constitutional law – a quorum of at least 50% and a majority of two-thirds of the deputies to the National Council (*Nationalrat*, the more powerful of Austria's two Houses of Parliament).[1]

Since 1 January 1994, the provisions on bank secrecy were partly amended, in particular with regard to money laundering, as Austrian law and banking practice initially principally permitted the opening of anonymous accounts. By amendment of s 40 of the BWG, with effect from 1 November 2000, the potential to open anonymous accounts was abolished (BWG, s 40(1), no 1). This was supplemented by a new s 40(6), according to which no payments may be made on existing savings accounts unless the identity of the holder was registered by the bank. As of 30 June 2002, savings accounts of unidentified holders need to be particularly labelled by the bank and no payments into and no withdrawals from such accounts are permissible unless the holder has been identified.

Council Directive 2003/48/EC on Taxation of Savings Income in the Form of Interest Payments does not affect Austria's rules on bank confidentiality as Austria is exempted from the Directive's principle of automatic exchange of information.[2] According to this principle, certain interest payments made or secured by economic operators established in one (EU) member state to or for the benefit of beneficial owners who are individuals resident in another member state are to be automatically

---

1 With regard to the predecessor provision of s 38(5) of the BWG, s 23a of the KWG, see the criticism by Jabornegg *Neues zum Bankgeheimnis* (1990) WBl at 30 and 61.
2 Only if Switzerland, Monaco, Andorra and San Marino abolish their laws on bank confidentiality with regard to interest payments affected by the directive would Austria, after 1 July 2011, have to switch to the Directive's principle of automatic exchange of information.

notified to the competent (tax) authorities of such individuals' member state. Instead of such automatic exchange of information and in order to protect its bank confidentiality laws, Austria will apply a withholding tax to the interest payments covered by the Directive.[3]

THE BANK'S DUTY OF CONFIDENTIALITY

[3.2] Section 38(1) of the BWG reads:

'The credit institutions, their shareholders, organ members, employees, as well as persons otherwise becoming active for the credit institutions, are prohibited from disclosing or exploiting secrets which were entrusted to, or to which access was made available for, them on the basis of the business relationship with clients or on the basis of s 75(3)[4] hereof exclusively ("Bank Secrecy"). If, in the conduct of their official activities, organs of public authorities or of the Austrian National Bank receive information which is subject to the Bank Secrecy, they shall maintain the Bank Secrecy as an official secret from which they may be released only in one of the cases set out in s 38(2). The duty of confidentiality applies without limit as to time.'

The provisions contained in the BWG, s 38 contain elements of public administrative law.[5] The expressly stipulated confidentiality obligation on the part of public authorities which gain access to information which is subject to bank secrecy or the supervision of the banks' compliance with the provisions on bank secrecy within the framework of the general supervision of banks certainly constitute such elements. The BWG, s 38 further defines the scope of a duty which forms part of every contractual relationship between a bank and its customers. Views are split on whether or not the duties imposed by statutory bank secrecy can be contracted away in whole or in part.[6]

---

3 As of 1 July 2005, the withholding tax amounts to 15%; as from 1 July 2008, the withholding tax will amount to 20% and, as from 1 July 2011, the withholding tax will amount to 35%. See also Höllinger *Ab 1. Juli wird's ernst: Die neue EU-Zinsrichtlinie* (2005) VWT at 48; Gläser *EU-Zinsenbesteuerung – Vermeidung der Doppelbesteuerung* (2005) SWI at 325; Kirchmayr/Schwarz *EU-ZinsRL in Kraft – Europa nimmt den Kampf gegen Steuersünder aus der Schwarzveranlagung auf!* (2005) taxlex at 257; Bendlinger/Walch *Steuerabzug bei Zahlungen ins Ausland* (2005) VWT at 28.

4 Section 75 of the BWG provides that credit institutions and finance institutions, as well as contract insurance businesses, have to provide certain data (name and address of the borrower and the amount borrowed) on large borrowings (more than 350,000 euros) to the Austrian National Bank which collects them and (according to para 3) has to provide the Austrian Financial Market Authority with the collected data and to pass them on to other credit and finance institutions, to contract insurance businesses and deposit protection facilities (et al) upon request. The BWG, s 38(1) to (3) also applies to finance institutions and contract insurance businesses in respect of information received pursuant to the BWG, s 75(3) (see the BWG, s 38(4)). The BWG, s 38(4) was last amended on 1 May 1999 extending the application of the provisions on bank secrecy and the exceptions to guarantee schemes, except for the co-operation required by the BWG, ss 93 to 93b with other guarantee schemes, deposit guarantee schemes and investor compensation schemes.

5 See Arnold *Das Bankgeheimnis* ZGV Service 1/1981, p 20; Avancini, Iro and Koziol *Österreichisches Bankvertragsrecht* (1987) vol I, p 103ff; Frotz *Die Bankauskunft nach österreichischem Recht* in Hadding and Schneider (ed) *Bankgeheimnis und Bankauskunft in der Bundesrepublik Deutschland und in ausländischen Rechtsordnungen* (1986) p 257; Jabornegg, Strasser and Floretta *Das Bankgeheimnis* (1985) p 31ff; Laurer *Das Bankgeheimnis in der Entwicklung von Lehre und Rechtsprechung* (1986) ÖJZ at 385.

6 See Arnold, n 5 above, p 20; Arnold *Zum Bankgeheimnis, Anmerkungen zu einer kontroversiell diskutierten Rechtsthematik – zugleich eine Buchbesprechung* (1986) ÖBA 359 at 360; Avancini, Iro and Koziol, n 5 above, vol I, p 104; for a mandatory nature, see Jabornegg, Strasser and Floretta, n 5 above, p 34ff.

The elements contained in the above s 38(1) of the BWG can be described as follows:

1   the BWG, s 1(1) defines as a credit institution (hereafter 'bank') whoever is authorised to conduct banking transactions (explicitly enumerated and defined in s 1(1) of the BWG) on the basis of the BWG or any other provision of federal law. Views are split on whether bank secrecy also applies to institutions which conduct banking transactions without authorisation, ie which have not received the necessary banking licence.[7] The Austrian National Bank is not subject to the bank secrecy provisions of the BWG, but to its own provisions. Finance institutions, ie institutions authorised to conduct specific finance transactions as defined in s 1(2) of the BWG without qualifying as credit institutions, as well as contract insurance businesses, are principally also not subject to bank secrecy;[8]

2   it is the prevailing view that the term 'shareholders' as used in s 38 of the BWG means all shareholders of a bank to the extent such shareholders gain access to confidential information by virtue of their position as shareholder.[9] 'Organ members' are the holders of offices which are provided for in the applicable corporate law. A trustee in bankruptcy is deemed an organ member of the bank.

'Persons otherwise becoming active for the banks' are physical and other persons who are not integrated into the banks' internal organisation, including their outside counsel and other experts, as well as other banks employed for the accomplishment of banking transactions.[10]

Physical persons may be simultaneously shareholders, organ members, employees of, or persons otherwise becoming active for, the same bank;

3   'secrets' are facts, proceedings and conditions of a factual or legal nature which are known to a limited group of persons only and to which other interested persons cannot gain access at all or can only gain access with difficulty. Further, an objective interest to keep the facts in question secret is required, but regularly presumed on the part of the clients;[11]

4   'clients' are persons who deal with the banks in the context of banking transactions. It is not necessary that such transactions actually close.[12] Since bank secrecy is unlimited in time, it continues to exist after termination of the contractual relationship and even after the death (or liquidation) of the client. If a bank gains access to a secret relating to a client in a manner other than through the business relationship, there is no duty of confidentiality upon the bank pursuant to bank secrecy.[13] Non-clients, and therefore not directly entitled to bank secrecy, are third parties with respect to which the banks receive confidential information from clients. The banks are nevertheless obliged

---

7   Avancini, Iro and Koziol, n 5 above, vol I, p 106; Jabornegg, Strasser and Floretta, n 5 above, p 55; for banks with concession only, see Arnold, n 5 above, p 4; Frotz, n 5 above, p 257.

8   An exception contained in the BWG, s 38(4) with regard to the information passed on according to the BWG, s 75(3); see n 4 above. In respect of finance institutions, however, the statutory language is not very clear as to the question of whether bank secrecy applies even beyond the BWG, s 75(3); for a broader application, see Laurer in Fremuth, Laurer, Linc, Pötzelberger and Strobl *Kommentar zum Bankwesengesetz* (1999) p 476; compare with Klippl *Geldwäscherei* (1994) p 31.

9   Arnold, n 5 above, p 5; Avancini, Iro and Koziol, n 5 above, vol I, p 108; Jabornegg, Strasser and Floretta, n 5 above, p 56ff; Kastner *Kreditwesengesetz und Gesellschaftsrecht* (1980) JBl 62 at 70.

10 Avancini, Iro and Koziol, n 5 above, vol I, p 110ff; Jabornegg, Strasser and Floretta, n 5 above, p 65ff.

11 Arnold, n 5 above, p 8; Burgstaller *Der strafrechtliche Schutz wirtschaltlicher Geheimnisse* in Ruppe (Hrsg) *Geheimnisschutz im Wirtschaftsleben* (1980) p 13; Frotz, n 5 above, p 237; Jabornegg, Strasser and Floretta, n 5 above, p 37; the required interest might become very weak after a long period of time, see Laurer, n 8 above, p 458.

12 Laurer, n 8 above, p 458.

13 Exception: the BWG, s 75(3), see n 4 above.

towards their clients not to disclose secrets relating to third parties which they learn from clients;[14]

5 'disclosing' a bank secret generally means making it known (or allowing it to become known by refraining from taking reasonable action to prevent disclosure) to somebody who did not know it before. There is quite a dispute about the scope of those persons to whom bank secrets may be disclosed on the ground that such persons would also be subject to bank secrecy with respect to the relevant information (for example, other bank employees, etc). One view holds that a bank secret may only be disclosed to those others within the same organisation (bank) with reasonable grounds for learning about the secret in question, such grounds depending on the relevant internal organisation.[15] The opposite view advocates that bank secrets may be freely passed on within the same organisation (bank), only provided that the recipients of the information themselves are strictly bound by bank secrecy as well.[16] Another controversial question is whether bank secrecy shall prevail over the (bank's) supervisory board's or the shareholders' right to information;[17]

6 'exploiting' a bank secret is generally interpreted as an economic exploitation of a bank secret to the detriment of the bank's client in question.[18] One of the leading commentaries holds that a bank is entitled to use clients' secrets for its own business dispositions, provided such use does not adversely affect the clients in question, further its own dispositions towards the clients even if that affected them adversely and, finally, for its usual counselling of other clients, provided that the secret is thereby not indirectly disclosed or that the clients in question are not otherwise adversely affected;[19]

7 bank secrets disclosed to the courts or other public authorities become official secrets[20] and generally must not be disclosed to other courts or public authorities or exploited by the latter as a basis for the initiation of proceedings of any kind. To this extent, (transformed) bank secrecy prevails over the general duty of public authorities to mutual assistance.[21] Furthermore, official secrecy is lifted once a trial has commenced.[22]

---

14 Arnold, n 5 above, p 8; Avancini, Iro and Koziol, n 5 above, vol I, p 114ff; Haushofer, Schinnerer and Ulrich *Die österreichischen Kreditwesengesetze* (1980) s 23/16; Jabornegg, Strasser and Floretta, n 5 above, p 40ff; Laurer, n 8 above, p 457.

15 Avancini, Iro and Koziol, n 5 above, vol I, p 125; Jabornegg, Strasser and Floretta, n 5 above, p 137ff; Bzoch and Bittner *Bankwesengesetz 1993* (1995) s 38-5, by referring to a decision of the OGH in 1991 (OGH 4 Ob 114/91), according to which bank secrecy was breached as secrets were disclosed to other bank employees within the same bank who themselves were obliged by the bank's duty of confidentiality, even though they had no dealings with the client's affairs. Note, however, that the decisive ground for the holding of this decision was the abuse of information for reasons of unfair competition.

16 Laurer, n 5 above, at 389 and n 8 above, p 456.

17 See Greiter *Das Auskunftsrecht des Aktionärs und des Partizipanten gemäß § 112 AktG* (1989) ÖJZ 524 at 526 and 528.

18 Avancini, Iro and Koziol, n 5 above, vol I, p 125ff; Haushofer, Schinnerer and Ulrich, n 14 above, s 23/7; Jabornegg, Strasser and Floretta, n 5 above, p 86; Schinnerer *Zur Problematik einer gesetzlichen Regelung des börslichen Insider-Geschäftes in Österreich* (1985) ÖBA at 271.

19 Avancini, Iro and Koziol, n 5 above, vol I, p 126.

20 A release from the duty of non-disclosure of official secrets shall be limited to the grounds of the BWG, s 38(2); according to Laurer, n 8 above, p 458, this shall also be applied to the information duties under the Act on Information Duties (against, however, the Austrian Administrative Court (VwGH) 89/17/0028 (1992) ÖBA at 89).

21 Avancini, Iro and Koziol, n 5 above, vol I, p 127; Jabornegg, Strasser and Floretta, n 5 above, pp 69ff, 124ff.

22 Avancini, Iro and Koziol, n 5 above, vol I, p 127; Liebscher *Das Bankgeheimnis im In- und Ausland* (1984) ÖJZ 253 at 255.

CUSTOMERS' REMEDIES FOR BREACH OF CONFIDENCE

Injunction

[3.3] If a breach of bank secrecy is threatened, the client may seek injunctive relief and also, in rare cases, removal (*Beseitigung*) of the breach, for example, by making a bank recall passed on information. For a client's claim to an injunction or removal, no fault is required on the part of the person against whom such remedy is sought.[23]

Damages

[3.4] A client who suffers damages through a breach of bank secrecy is entitled to reimbursement in accordance with the general principles of tort. The client will generally be entitled to reimbursement of pecuniary damages which have been caused by such breach through the fault of a tortfeasor. If the party in breach is a bank (or one of those for whom a bank is liable), pecuniary damages will include lost profit; if the tortfeasor is one of the other persons subject to bank secrecy, this will often, but not always, be the case.[24] Such right to claim damages might not exist if the pecuniary 'damage' is caused by a breach of bank secrecy revealing tax evasion towards the tax authorities.[25]

It is the prevailing view that the right to damages may be contracted away in respect of a tortfeasor's lower levels of fault (at least for slight negligence) and that provisions to that effect contained in the bank's general conditions are valid if such conditions have become a part of the contractual relationship between the bank and the client.[26] A bank will be liable for all its agents and other personnel, whether employed or not, who inflict damage upon clients through a (faulty) breach of bank secrecy. On the other hand, such agents and other personnel will also be protected by the above disclaimer as to lower degrees of negligence.[27]

If breaches of bank secrecy cause damage to third parties (other clients or non-clients), the Austrian Supreme Court ('OGH') has held that third parties (in this case another client) are not entitled to damages from the bank in cases where they breach bank secrecy towards another client.[28]

Termination of business relationship

[3.5] A client who is the victim of a breach of bank secrecy by a bank or tortfeasor whose actions are attributed to such bank will be entitled to terminate the contractual relationship with the bank with immediate effect.[29]

---

23 Avancini, Iro and Koziol, n 5 above, vol I, p 163ff; Jabornegg, Strasser and Floretta, n 5 above, p 160ff.

24 Arnold, n 5 above, p 20; Avancini, Iro and Koziol, n 5 above, vol I, p 164ff; Jabornegg, Strasser and Floretta, n 5 above, p 162ff.

25 Schauer *Geheimnisbruch und Steuerschaden* (2004) RdW at 297.

26 Avancini, Iro and Koziol, n 5 above, vol I, p 165ff; Frotz, n 5 above, p 267ff; compare with Jabornegg, Strasser and Floretta, n 5 above, p 163.

27 Avancini, Iro and Koziol, n 5 above, vol I, p 165ff.

28 OGH 27.2.2002 (2002) ecolex at 194.

29 Avancini, Iro and Koziol, n 5 above, vol I, p 168; Jabornegg, Strasser and Floretta, n 5 above, p 164.

Criminal punishment

[3.6] A physical person who discloses or exploits facts which are subject to bank secrecy with the intent to enrich himself, a third party or to affect another party adversely is subject to criminal punishment (imprisonment for up to one year or a fine), but shall only be prosecuted upon application of the person whose interest in confidentiality was impaired (BWG, s 101). Public officials in breach of bank secrecy may be subject to (even more serious) criminal punishment for the offence constituted by a breach of the official secret.

Action by bank regulatory authorities

[3.7] The bank regulatory authority, the Austrian Financial Market Authority (*Finanzmarktaufsichtsbehörde*, 'FMA')[30] has to intervene in cases of breaches of bank secrecy attributable to a bank (BWG, s 70(4)). The most severe consequence is the withdrawal of the bank's banking licence.[31]

EXCEPTIONS TO THE GENERAL DUTY OF NON-DISCLOSURE

[3.8] Section 38(2) of the BWG provides for nine exceptions to bank secrecy. It is the general consensus that this list is not exhaustive.[32] The following text describes those exceptions set out in the BWG, s 38(2), as well as those which are based on other provisions or principles of the law.

Customer's consent

[3.9] There is no bank secrecy if the client 'expressly consents in writing' to the disclosure or exploitation of a secret (BWG, s 38(2), no 5). A valid consent must be clearly formulated in writing and signed by the client. If a secret relates to non-clients, the waiver nevertheless has to be issued by the client who passed the secret onto the bank. It is not clear how precisely the waived secrets have to be defined in the declaration of consent. The OGH has held that a reasonably defined waiver, by signing the application form for the opening of a bank account which contains a corresponding clause, was valid.[33] A waiver of bank secrecy in general terms and conditions or without limit as to time (in particular, the future) or scope could be

---

30 With effect from 1 April 2002, the FMA is the supervisory authority for banks, securities and capital markets, insurance companies and pension funds.
31 Avancini, Iro and Koziol, n 5 above, vol I, p 170ff; Jabornegg, Strasser and Floretta, n 5 above, p 165ff.
32 Arnold, n 5 above, pp 12, 18ff; Avancini, Iro and Koziol, n 5 above, vol I, p 129; Jabornegg, Strasser and Floretta, n 5 above, p 93; restrictively, Laurer, n 8 above, p 454, according to whom additional exceptions (ie information duties, eg under the General Civil Code or the Act on Foreign Exchange Control) could only prevail over bank secrecy if enacted as a provision of constitutional law or as an exception based upon a provision of judicial criminal law.
33 OGH 29.1.1997 (1997) ecolex at 498; this decision was criticised by Wilhelm *Formularmäßige Entbindung vom Bankgeheimnis* (1997) ecolex at 490.

qualified as invalid.[34] It is not clear whether or not a waiver of bank secrecy can be revoked at any time.[35]

Litigation between bank and client

[3.10] There is no bank secrecy if the disclosure is 'necessary for the resolution of legal issues arising out of the relationship between banks and clients' (BWG, s 38(2), no 7). This exception only relates to litigation between the bank and its client.

General information on a customer's economic situation

[3.11] There is no bank secrecy for 'generally phrased information on the economic situation of a business', as usually given by banks, unless the former expressly objects (BWG, s 38(2), no 6). This exception only applies to business clients as opposed to private customers. The bank will have to balance the interests of the clients and those of the recipients of the bank's information. It may only give a general picture of their clients' state of affairs without directly or indirectly disclosing exact data.

Balancing of interest

[3.12] This exception is not set out in statutory law. It has been argued in legal literature that no bank secrecy probably exists if, upon balancing the client's interest in confidentiality with conflicting interests of the bank or third parties, the bank's or such third parties' interests appear to be significantly overriding.[36] After all, the expressly codified exceptions to bank secrecy are provisions on special conflict of interest situations in which the law stipulates that other interests prevail over bank secrecy. Therefore, the balancing of interests in cases not statutorily provided for must result in a clear preponderance of those interests which conflict with bank secrecy. Accordingly, the OGH, in confirming this view, held in one decision that in principle a bank is not bound to maintain bank secrecy if an overriding interest in the disclosure exists.[37]

Typical cases are those in which the bank or its employees would incur (criminal) punishment by non-disclosure of bank secrets or civil litigation in cases with third parties who themselves are under the bank's duty of confidentiality.

---

34 Laurer, n 8 above, p 464; Arnold, n 5 above, p 17; Avancini, Iro and Koziol, n 5 above, vol I, p 131ff; Frotz, n 5 above, p 244ff; Jabornegg, Strasser and Floretta, n 5 above, p 99ff. A waiver contained in general terms and conditions is invalid towards consumers: OGH 19.11.2002 4 Ob 179/02f.

35 Against a revocation at any time: Laurer *Bankgeheimnis* 386 FN 19; and Laurer, n 8 above, p 465. In favour of a revocation at any time: Arnold, n 5 above, p 17; Avancini, Iro and Koziol, n 5 above, vol I, p 139; Frotz, n 5 above, p 245; Jabornegg, Strasser and Floretta, n 5 above, p 103

36 See Arnold, n 5 above, p 19; Avancini *Der Auskunftsanspruch des Bürgen gegenüber dem Gläubiger – Zugleich ein Beitrag zum Bankgeheimnis* (1985) JBl 193 at 204ff; Avancini, Iro and Koziol, n 5 above, vol I, p 161ff; Frotz, n 5 above, p 254ff; Jabornegg, Strasser and Floretta, n 5 above, p 142ff; Steiner *Zur Aufklärungspflicht der Kreditunternehmung bei Wechseldiskontgeschäften* (1983) JBl 189.

37 OGH 29.1.1997 (1997) ecolex at 491.

Payment of another's debt or surety

[3.13] There is probably no bank secrecy if the bank is asked by a surety or a person who has actually posted or is contemplating posting security for an obligation by a bank's client towards such bank for information on such debtor's financial state.[38]

The OGH held in various decisions that bank secrecy had to be lifted for third parties who have paid a client's debt to the bank, for which debt such third parties were personally liable or have posted other security. Such third parties are assignees of the (bank) creditor's rights by operation of law. Such third parties are further entitled, inter alia, to delivery of all other security posted for the debt in question and of such other documents or information (namely the underlying credit agreements, other suretyship agreements, drafts and correspondence executed by the other sureties or the debtor and relating to the debtor's credit account, but not the internal memoranda and correspondence signed by the bank) as are necessary for the payers to pursue their right of recourse against the debtor and against others who have posted security for such debt.[39] The OGH also expanded this exception to the pledgee's right of information about the pledgor's financial state in order to evaluate whether or not to claim for an additional pledge by the pledgor.[40]

Criminal proceedings

[3.14] There is no bank secrecy in Austrian penal courts in connection with initiated judicial criminal proceedings nor to Austrian fiscal penal authorities (*Finanzstrafbehörden*) in connection with initiated penal proceedings because of intentional fiscal offences (*vorsätzliche Finanzvergehen*) except for fiscal irregularities (ie fiscal offences of a lesser degree, *Finanzordnungswidrigkeiten*) (BWG, s 38(2), no 1).

Criminal proceedings are proceedings with respect to such crimes or offences (including certain crimes and offences of a fiscal nature) as shall be conducted by the regular court system. Fiscal offences are certain offences provided for in the FinStrG (for example, tax fraud and smuggling) and other fiscal offences defined as such in other statutes. Fiscal offences are offences against the federal tax system; they may be subject to judicial criminal punishment or to administrative (fiscal) penal punishment. Fiscal penal authorities are administrative agencies.

Whether or not courts or fiscal penal authorities may request the disclosure of bank secrets depends mainly on whether or not a relevant proceeding is deemed 'initiated' and whether or not there is (sufficient) 'connection' between the proceeding and the requested disclosure. A resolution of these issues must take the generally advocated principle into consideration that the exception to bank secrecy in connection with criminal and certain administrative penal proceedings shall not enable the prosecution to gather information for potential crimes or offences ('fishing expeditions'), but only to corroborate (or dispel) well-founded and reasonably defined suspicions of such crimes or offences.[41]

---

38 See Avancini, n 36 above, at 193ff; Steiner, n 36 above, at 189ff; against: Laurer, n 8 above, p 454.
39 OGH 2.2.1984 (1984) SZ 57/29; OGH 29.4.1986 (1986) JBl at 511; Avancini, Iro and Koziol, n 5 above, vol I, p 157; Frotz, n 5 above, p 252ff; Jabornegg, Strasser and Floretta, n 5 above, p 151ff.
40 OGH 7.11.1991 (1992) ÖBA at 654, which is, however, disputed by two major commentators (Jabornegg (1997) ÖBA at 655ff; Laurer, n 8 above, p 454).
41 Arnold *Entscheidungsanmerkung* (1986) AnwBl at 417; Avancini, Iro and Koziol, n 5 above, vol I, p 141; see also Jabornegg, Strasser and Floretta, n 5 above, p 110ff.

'Initiated' criminal proceedings

[3.15] Under Austrian law, a criminal proceeding is normally conducted in three stages. The initial stage is the preliminary inquiry (*Vorerhebung*) conducted under the guidance of the public prosecution, which in turn employs the police or the courts for the actual inquiry. The next phase is the preliminary investigation (*Voruntersuchung*) in which a judge is in charge. This is followed by the trial as the last stage. A preliminary investigation can only be directed against one or more identified persons, whereas a preliminary inquiry may also be directed against unknown perpetrators.

Whether a criminal proceeding should be deemed initiated upon the commencement of preliminary inquiries or only upon the opening of a formal preliminary investigation was resolved by a decision of the OGH,[42] which held that the taking of any measures against known or unknown perpetrators in the course of criminal proceedings, including the stage of preliminary inquiries, constituted the initiation of criminal proceedings.

'Initiated' fiscal penal proceedings

[3.16] Fiscal penal proceedings are formally initiated by a decree pursuant to the FinStrG, ss 82 and 83, subject to appeal. The suspect must receive notice of such initiation. A fiscal penal proceeding is to be initiated if there is suspicion of a fiscal offence unless the offence is unlikely to be proven. Suspected facts do not constitute a fiscal offence or the suspect has not committed the offence or cannot be prosecuted or punished for it.

Sufficient 'connection'

[3.17] There is a sufficient connection between proceedings and bank secrets if there is an objectively ascertainable relevance for the requested information to the proceedings in question. This is a question of degree and there are only a few court decisions on the point.[43] It is, however, the prevailing view that such relevance may also exist for the bank secrets of one party in relation to a crime or fiscal offence of a third party in which the former did not participate.[44]

Search and seizure

[3.18] In the context of fiscal penal proceedings, s 89(4) of the FinStrG provides that such evidence which is in the custody of banks and which concerns secrets within the meaning of the BWG, s 38(1) may only be seized if it is 'directly connected' with the intentional fiscal offence(s) (not just fiscal irregularities) for which bank secrecy is (already) lifted pursuant to the BWG, s 38(2), no 1.

This limitation applies not only for the benefit of the party whose suspected fiscal offence formed the basis of the initial search order, but also for the benefit of third parties. The direct connection between the originally suspected fiscal offence and one on the part of such third party which comes into the open in the course of a search

---

42 OGH 18.1.1989 (1989) JBl at 454; see also Weber *Das Bankgeheimnis bei eingeleiteten gerichtlichen Strafverfahren* (1990) RdW 435.
43 See eg OGH 11 Os 171/86; VwGH 15.4.1997, 93/14/0080.
44 Avancini, Iro and Koziol, n 5 above, vol I, pp 141, 144; Jabornegg, Strasser and Floretta n 5 above, p 108ff; Liebscher, n 22 above, at 254. Against a lifting of bank secrecy, see Arnold, n 5 above, p 13.

and seizure is probably only present if it turns out that the third party is a direct accessory to the original suspect's fiscal offence. A closely related but formally separate fiscal offence, a crime or other contravention of law will probably not suffice.[45]

If the bank formally alleges that information was seized in breach of bank secrecy, such information must be sealed and a formal decision on the legality of the seizure must be issued, which is subject to appeal.

Finally, s 98(4) of the FinStrG provides that evidence seized in breach of the above must not be used for the rendering of the decision (punishment order) to the detriment of the accused or an accessory. This provision is interpreted to mean (in addition) that the fiscal authorities must not use such evidence in an initiated proceeding and no court or other public authority may use it to commence proceedings whatsoever against those involved.[46]

There is probably one exception to the above: the fiscal authorities which receive such privileged information may use it for an assessment (or reassessment) of the original suspect's taxes.[47]

The corollary to s 89(4) of the FinStrG is s 145a of the StPO. Under this provision, banks (and persons acting for banks) are under a duty to hand over all documents concerning the type and scope of the business relationship with the client, as well as business transactions and other related operations, to the authorities if, based upon specific facts, it must be assumed that the business relationship of a client with a bank is connected to the rendering of a criminal act (crimes or offences). Such context must also be assumed if the business relationship is used for the transfer of an economic benefit which was derived from or received for a criminal act or which is under the disposition of a criminal organisation. Under the same prerequisites, persons acting for banks are under a duty to testify as witnesses on such business operations. The existence of this duty of a bank (or persons acting for a bank) must be ascertained by way of a decision of the judge presiding over the preliminary investigation, which needs to contain the facts giving rise to the connection between the business relationship and the subject matter of the preliminary investigation, as well as a description of the documents to be handed over by the bank. Section 145(2) of the StPO affords the bank the right to request a sealing of the seized documents. In such a case, a panel of three judges decides whether the documents may be searched or whether they must be returned to the bank. Their ruling cannot be appealed. In the case of a seizure of objects beyond the limitations set by s 145a of the StPO, a criminal judgment rendered on the basis of such evidence could be appealed as void.

Foreign legal proceedings

International treaties

European Convention on Mutual Assistance in Criminal Matters of 20 April 1959

[3.19]   Austria is a party to the European Convention on Mutual Assistance in Criminal Matters of 20 April 1959 (the 'European Mutual Assistance Convention').

---

45 Arnold *Die Finanzstrafgesetznovelle 1985* (1986) ZGV at 7; Avancini, Iro and Koziol, n 5 above, vol I, p 146.

46 Arnold, n 45 above, at 9; Avancini *Neueste gesetzliche Regelungen zum Bankgeheimnis* (1986) RdW at 299; Avancini, Iro and Koziol, n 5 above, vol I, p 146.

47 Avancini, n 46 above, at 299; Avancini, Iro and Koziol, n 5 above, vol I, p 147.

The main requirements for and exceptions to Austria's duty to render legal assistance under it are:

1 legal assistance will only be granted for offences which are subject to judicial criminal punishment in the requesting country and in Austria (art 1(1) and the Austrian reservation);

2 legal assistance will not be granted in respect of political or fiscal offences (Austrian reservation to art 2a);

3 legal assistance will not be granted if it impairs Austria's sovereignty, security, *ordre public* or other essential interests (art 2b; Austria has made a reservation to art 2b declaring that it understood as 'other essential interests', in particular, respecting the duties of confidentiality provided for by Austrian law);

4 'Austria will only comply with requests for search or seizure if such search or seizure is in accordance with Austrian law' (Austrian reservation to art 5(1)).

In 1983, Austria, by ratifying the Additional Protocol to the European Mutual Assistance Convention (the 'Additional Protocol'), waived the exception as to fiscal offences for breaches of revenue, tax and customs laws. Upon ratification of the Additional Protocol, Austria made a declaration in which it stated that it would grant legal assistance in criminal proceedings relating to revenue, tax and customs laws subject to the condition that, in accordance with the duties of confidentiality provided for by Austrian law, information and evidence received by way of legal assistance will only be used in the criminal proceeding for which legal assistance was requested and in revenue, tax or customs proceedings directly connected to such proceeding.

In an additional unilateral declaration, Austria withdrew the reservation it made to art 2a with respect to those parties to the European Mutual Assistance Convention which had not become parties to the Additional Protocol and announced that it would henceforth apply art 2a of the European Mutual Assistance Convention in accordance with domestic law, ie the Act on Extradition and Legal Assistance in Matters of Criminal Law described below.[48]

Consequently, there now seem to be two groups of parties to the European Mutual Assistance Convention: those who are parties to the Additional Protocol and to whom legal assistance will be granted in criminal proceedings of a fiscal nature and those who are not parties to the Additional Protocol and to whom such assistance will, in the absence of further bilateral treaties, not be granted. We believe that the above-mentioned special requirements and limits under which bank secrecy may be lifted in a domestic proceeding will apply likewise to the grant of legal assistance under the Convention (to either group) in view of the above reservation to art 2b and the declaration on duties of confidentiality made in connection with the ratification of the Additional Protocol.[49, 50]

---

48 For a detailed description of the above, see Laurer, n 5 above, at 391ff; Schütz *Die Anfechtung des Bankgeheimnisses aufgrund eines ausländischen Amtshilfeersuchens in Strafsachen* (1996) JBl at 502ff and OGH 9.3.1995 (1996) JBl at 532.

49 Avancini, Iro and Koziol, n 5 above, vol I, p 149.

50 On 8 November 2001, the Council of Europe passed a Second Additional Protocol to the European Convention on Mutual Assistance in Criminal Matters. Under the new art 1(3) of the European Convention on Mutual Assistance in Criminal Matters, 'mutual assistance may also be afforded in proceedings brought by the administrative authorities in respect of acts which are punishable under the national law of the requesting or the requested party by virtue of being infringements of the rules of law, where the decision may give rise to proceedings before a court having jurisdiction in particular criminal matters'. To date (April 2006), the Second Additional Protocol has not yet come into force.

Convention on Mutual Assistance in Criminal Matters of 29 May 2000

[3.20] On 29 May 2000, the Council of the European Union established the Convention on Mutual Assistance in Criminal Matters between member states of the EU (2000/C197/01) which aims at supplementing the provisions and facilitating the application between the EU member states of, inter alia, the European Mutual Assistance Convention and the Additional Protocol.

Under art 3, mutual assistance shall also be afforded in proceedings brought by the administrative authorities in respect of acts which are punishable under the national law of the requesting or requested member state, or both, by virtue of being infringements of the rules of law and where the decision (by administrative authorities) may give rise to proceedings before a court having jurisdiction in particular criminal matters. In addition, mutual assistance shall also be afforded in connection with proceedings which relate to offences or infringements for which a legal person may be held liable in the requesting member state.

Further, on 16 October 2001 the Council of the European Union established the Protocol to the Convention on Mutual Assistance in Criminal Matters between member states of the EU (2001/C326/01) which forms an integral part of the Convention. It details member states' duties with regard to requests for information by other member states on bank accounts, banking transactions and for the monitoring of banking transactions. Pursuant to art 7, a member state shall not invoke banking secrecy as a reason for refusing any co-operation regarding a request for mutual assistance from another member state. In Austria, both the Convention and its Protocol came into force on 3 July 2005.[51]

The most important provisions of the Protocol provide as follows:

1 according to art 1, each member state shall take the measures necessary to determine, in answer to a request sent by another member state, whether a natural or legal person who is the subject of a criminal investigation holds or controls one or more accounts in any bank located in its territory and, if so, provide all the details of the identified accounts. This obligation shall only apply if the investigation concerns (i) an offence punishable by a penalty involving imprisonment of a maximum period of at least four years in the requesting member state and at least two years in the requested member state, or (ii) an offence referred to in art 2 of the 1995 Europol Convention or in the Annex to that Convention, as amended, or (iii) to the extent that it may not be covered by the Europol Convention, an offence referred to in the 1995 Convention on the Protection of the European Communities' Financial Interests (or its protocols);

2 according to art 2, on request by the requesting member state and in connection with a criminal investigation, the requested member state shall provide the particulars of specified bank accounts and of banking operations which have been carried out during a specified period through one or more accounts specified in the request, including the particulars of any sending or recipient account;

3 according to art 3, each member state shall undertake to ensure that, at the request of another member state and in connection with a criminal investigation, it is able to monitor, during a specified period, the banking operations that are being carried out through one or more accounts specified in the request and communicate the results to the requesting member state.

---

51 BGBl (Federal Gazette) III no 65/2005, 66/2005.

Austria made the execution of a request under art 1, as well as under art 2, dependent on the same conditions as they apply in respect of requests for search and seizure (see art 1, para 5 and art 2, para 4). Accordingly, Austria in particular may only follow any request under arts 1 or 2 in case of the compliance of such request with national law (which includes the provisions of bank secrecy and its exceptions as described above).

Austria's obligations under arts 1 to 3 of the Protocol are incorporated into national legislation by s 145a of the StPO described above. Thus, a judge has to decide upon the application on any request in accordance with the Protocol.

Bilateral treaties

[3.21]   In addition to the above, Austria has entered into a number of bilateral treaties, some of which supplement the European Mutual Assistance Conventions.

Act on Extradition and Legal Assistance in Matters of Criminal Law

[3.22]   In the absence of applicable treaties, legal assistance to foreign authorities is governed by the Act on Extradition and Legal Assistance in Matters of Criminal Law ('ARHG'). Pursuant to the ARHG, s 50, legal assistance may be granted by or through the Austrian courts to foreign courts, foreign public prosecutors and foreign prison authorities provided there is reciprocity. Legal assistance shall not be granted if, inter alia:

1   the offence on which the request for legal assistance is based is:
   (a)   not subject to criminal punishment under Austrian law,
   (b)   of a political nature,
   (c)   of a military nature, or
   (d)   a breach of revenues, monopolies or customs laws or a breach of exchange control, rationing, import or export control laws;
2   the request is made by a country which does not meet certain human rights standards regarding its criminal procedure and enforcement system;
3   the special requirements under Austrian law for certain measures (in particular, seizure and opening of post or telephone tapping) are not met;
4   the legal assistance would lead to a breach of Austrian law providing for duties of confidentiality which shall be maintained with regard to penal courts as well; or
5   the compliance with the request for legal assistance would be contrary to the public policy or other essential interests of the Republic of Austria.

It is the prevailing view[52] that legal assistance shall be granted on the basis of the ARHG if its conditions are met and the special requirements and limits under which bank secrecy may be lifted in purely domestic proceedings are fulfilled.

Summary

[3.23]   Austrian authorities will not render legal assistance to foreign authorities in civil matters if such assistance is contrary to bank secrecy. Austria will render legal

---

52   OGH 16.12.1993 (1994) ÖBA at 728; OGH 9.3.1995 (1996) JBl at 532; Avancini, Iro and Koziol, n 5 above, vol I, p 149; Jabornegg, Strasser and Floretta, n 5 above, p 156; Laurer, n 5 above, at 393.

assistance in criminal matters in accordance with applicable treaties or the ARHG even if that requires a lifting of bank secrecy, provided the requirements for and the limits to a lifting of bank secrecy are fulfilled. If provided for in applicable treaties, such (foreign) criminal matters may include fiscal offences and both requesting authorities and authorities rendering legal assistance may be administrative agencies as well.

Money laundering and financing of terrorism

[3.24] According to a report of the IMF in 2004, Austria has a high level of observance of internationally accepted standards in the area of anti-money laundering. Accordingly, there is no bank secrecy in connection with a founded suspicion of money laundering or financing of terrorism due to a duty to disclosure under s 41(1) and (2) of the BWG (BWG, s 38(2), no 2). Basically, s 41 provides as follows:

1   if there is reasonable suspicion (i) that a transaction, which has already occurred, is in progress or is about to occur, serves the purpose of money laundering (generally speaking, the underlying criminal offences considered to give rise to money laundering offences are those punishable by more than three years' imprisonment; however, certain other offences punishable by lesser penalties, such as bribery, are also considered to give rise to money laundering offences), or (ii) that a client has breached its duty to disclose fiduciary relationships pursuant to the BWG, s 40(2), or (iii) that a client is a member of a terrorist organisation or a transaction serves the purpose of financing terrorism, banks (including financial institutions) shall, without delay, inform the relevant authority (to be determined according to the Austrian Security Police Act) and shall, until the case has been solved, stop any further execution of the transaction unless there is danger that a delay in the transaction would complicate or obstruct the investigation of the case;

2   banks shall, without undue delay, inform the authority of all requests by customers to withdraw saving deposits if such requests are made after 30 June 2002, the identity of the account holder has not yet been established (according to s 40(1) of the BWG) and the payment is made from a savings deposit with a balance of at least 15,000 euros. Such payouts may only be effected seven days after the customer's request;

3   banks (including financial institutions) shall, upon request, provide the authority with all information which the latter deems necessary to prevent or prosecute money laundering (in this respect, the BWG does not refer to the financing of terrorism);

4   the authority is entitled to request that a transaction already in progress or about to occur with respect to which there is reasonable suspicion that it may serve the purpose of money laundering (in this respect, the BWG does not refer to the financing of terrorism) shall not be carried out or shall be provisionally delayed and that requests by a client to withdraw funds may only be carried out by the bank with the authority's approval. The bank's client may appeal against any such requests of the competent authority to a tribunal;

5   the banks (including financial institutions) shall keep secret towards their clients and third parties all proceedings designed to implement these provisions at least until a request as described in the preceding paragraph has been made by the competent authority;

6   a fine of up to 20,000 euros may be imposed on responsible persons

(*Verantwortliche*) within the meaning of Austrian law who do not comply with these duties under the BWG if, generally speaking, such non-compliance does not infringe provisions of the Austrian Criminal Code (such as aiding and abetting money laundering; in this case, since 1 January 2006, the bank concerned might under certain circumstances also be held responsible). Further, with respect to any bank infringing the rules described above, the FMA may avail itself of its rights as supervisory authority and, accordingly, request the bank to comply with the Austrian Banking Act's rules, bar the management of the respective bank from conducting the bank's business or even withdraw the bank's concession.

In order to fulfil the duties described above, banks are under an obligation to request disclosure of the identity of their clients (i) when entering into a continuous business relationship, (ii) in all other transactions involving a total amount of at least 15,000 euros (irrespective of whether the transaction is carried out in a single operation or in several operations which are obviously closely linked to each other), (iii) if there is founded suspicion that the client is a member of a terrorist organisation or (even unknowingly) participates in transactions that serve the purpose of money laundering or the purpose of financing terrorism or (iv) if, after 31 October 2000, payments to saving accounts and, as from 30 June 2002, withdrawals from saving accounts are carried out and the amount paid in or withdrawn exceeds 15,000 euros (BWG, s 40(1)). Moreover, banks shall request the customer to declare whether it intends to execute the continuous business relationship or the other transaction for its own or for someone else's account and the customer shall comply with that request. If the customer declares that it acts for someone else's account, it must disclose the beneficiary's identity to the bank (BWG, s 40(2)). If certain prerequisites are met, a client's identity to be disclosed due to the reasons set out in (i) or (ii) above may be determined without such client appearing in person (BWG, s 40(8)). Further, exceptions may apply if a bank's client is itself a credit or finance institution (BWG, s 40(9)).[53]

Enforcement proceedings

[3.25]   There is no bank secrecy with respect to requests for information on a person's claims against banks (as garnishees) which were attached in enforcement proceedings.[54]

Guardianship court

[3.26]   There is no bank secrecy towards a guardianship court where the client is a minor or a ward (BWG, s 38(2), no 4). This provision complements the guardianship court's right and duty regularly to examine whether a minor's or a ward's property held in trust are invested as statutorily determined.

Inventories of estates by the probate court

[3.27]   There is no bank secrecy towards the probate court and its aides, ie notaries public fulfilling court functions during probate proceedings, in the case of a client's

---

53 See also Kreisl *Die Identifikation des Kunden nach der BWG-Novelle 2003/35* (2003) ecolex at 950.
54 Laurer, n 8 above, p 454; Arnold, n 5 above, p 22; Avancini, Iro and Koziol, n 5 above, vol I, p 158; Jabornegg, Strasser and Floretta, n 5 above, p 153ff.

death, namely in connection with compiling of inventories or other determination of the assets and obligations which belong to the estate of a deceased person (BWG, s 38(2), no 3). Even though the exception pursuant to s 38(2), no 3 principally only applies to requests for information by Austrian probate courts in Austrian probate proceedings, requests by (competent) foreign probate courts in foreign probate proceedings must be deemed to be Austrian probate proceedings and must therefore be complied with by the Austrian probate court in accordance with the laws of Austria if the foreign court has its jurisdiction within a member state of the Hague Convention on Civil Procedure or any other (bilateral) international convention.[55]

Tax liabilities of deceased persons

[3.28]   There is no bank secrecy in respect of the banks' duty according to s 25(1) of the Inheritance and Gift Tax Act to 'give notice to the fiscal authorities of assets belonging to or deposited with them for the disposition of a deceased person' (ie assets which were held in deposit or administered for the deceased in the course of the banks' business) within one month from the death becoming known to the banks (BWG, s 38(2), no 8).

Assessment of banks' taxes

[3.29]   There is no bank secrecy to the extent that a disclosure of bank secrets is necessary for the assessment of taxes to be paid by the banks themselves (BWG, s 38(3)). Certainly, bank secrets obtained by the (fiscal) authorities in such manner are subject to official secrecy and must not be passed on to other public authorities or used in whatever manner with regard to third parties to which such bank secrets relate.

Exchange control, income tax, the FMA, deposit protection facilities, bank auditors, Ombudsman, Audit Office, trustee in bankruptcy

[3.30]   Furthermore, there is no bank secrecy with respect to the Austrian National Bank's right to certain information in matters of exchange control,[56] with respect to certain notice requirements under the Income Tax Act or other revenue laws, further, with regard to the right to information of, and the duty of disclosure to, the FMA in its function as bank regulatory authority (BWG, s 69ff) and as securities supervisory authority (BWG, s 38(2), no 9),[57] deposit protection facilities (BWG, s 38(2), no 2 in connection with ss 93 and 93a), bank auditors (BWG, s 38(2), no 2 in connection with s 61(1)), the Audit Office (*Rechnungshof*), the Ombudsman (*Volksanwalt*) and towards the trustee in bankruptcy in bankruptcy or reorganisation proceedings.

---

55 Laurer, n 8 above, p 475ff; OGH 1.12.1998 (1999) EvBl at 100.
56 VwGH 28.10.1994 (1995) WBl at 256.
57 It should be noted that upon the establishment of the FMA, the BWG, s 38(2) no 9 has not been amended accordingly. Therefore, it still mentions its predecessor, the Federal Securities Supervisory Authority (*Bundes-Wertpapieraufsicht*), as the authority towards which bank secrecy shall be lifted. It is disputed whether this non-amendment has the consequence that no exception to the duty of bank confidentiality shall exist towards the new FMA in its function as securities supervisory authority. See Brandl and Wolfbauer (2002) ecolex at 294ff, according to whom bank secrecy shall not be lifted towards the FMA as securities supervisory authority. Against: see Painz and Tauböck (2002) ecolex at 132ff.

Foreign bank regulatory authorities

[3.31]   Pursuant to s 77 of the BWG, the FMA may give official information to foreign competent authorities provided:

1   public policy (*ordre public*), other essential interests of the Republic of Austria, bank secrecy and the revenue law duty of confidentiality are not breached;
2   there is reciprocity; and
3   a similar request for information made by the FMA would be in accordance with the purposes of the BWG.

The FMA may only provide official information if s 77(5) to (7) of the BWG (specifying the countries to whose authorities official information may be transferred and the tasks under which such transfer is permissible) or applicable treaties do not provide to the contrary. At present, there is no such treaty; in particular, Austria has not ratified the Convention on International Assistance in Administrative Matters. Section 77 of the BWG does not grant to foreign bank regulatory authorities a specific right to request information, but definitely specifies the limits of the FMA upon granting international legal assistance.

Furthermore, the FMA may give information on large borrowings in the sense of s 75(3) of the BWG to the relevant authorities of any member state of the EU upon its request (BWG, s 75(5)) provided:

1   the requesting member state maintains a similar register on large borrowings;
2   there is reciprocity;
3   the data will only be used for bank regulatory purposes; and
4   the information given is subject to professional secrecy pursuant to art 30 of Council Directive 2000/12/EC.

CONFLICTS OF INTEREST AND FIDUCIARY DUTIES

[3.32]   Conflicts of interest might occur both between the interests of the bank and its client and between the interests of two or more clients of the same bank. As a matter of general contract law, the contractual relationship between the bank and its client entails certain mutual fiduciary duties and duties of care (*Schutz- und Sorgfaltspflichten*).[58] Particularly with respect to securities transactions, the bank's contractual duties also entail the duty to inform and advise the client (*Aufklärungs- und Beratungspflichten*) properly.[59]

The duty of confidence pursuant to bank secrecy might conflict with the bank's duty to inform and advise its clients. There is the prevailing view that the interest of another client of the bank in being informed and advised properly does not constitute an exception to bank secrecy. Consequently, the bank may – without the client's express and written consent – only provide general information on the economic situation of such a client, even if the other client seems to need further information with regard to a proper investment decision.[60] This view was confirmed by the OGH, which held that a financing bank, if under a duty to inform the private investor about the undertaking to be financed, must either refrain from the contemplated transaction or, prior to the information of the client about its concerns, obtain the undertaking's

---

58 Avancini, Iro and Koziol, n 5 above, vol I, p 42ff.
59 Avancini, Iro and Koziol, n 5 above, vol II, p 588ff.
60 Avancini, Iro and Koziol, n 5 above, vol II, p 614ff.

consent (provided that general information on the undertaking's economic situation would not have been sufficient) in order to comply with bank secrecy.[61]

The conflict of interest problems may gain particular relevance in situations where a bank gains access to inside information, for example, because it assists an issuer of securities or because an executive board member of the bank or a bank employee serves as a member of the supervisory board of another company at the same time.[62] Such conflict might arise both in *nostro* transactions of the bank itself and in transactions of other clients to whom the bank gives advice (for example, with regard to the sale or purchase of securities or the granting of credits or loans to other bank clients). According to the rules on insider trading (which are dealt with in detail below), both the trading in, and the recommendation of, securities by a bank having inside information as to these securities, as well as the disclosure of inside information, constitutes a criminal offence. Thus, a bank is not only prohibited from exploiting information obtained from one of its clients in its own transactions, but also is neither entitled nor obliged to pass on inside information to any other of its clients.[63] In this respect, Chinese Walls may be used in order to mitigate the risk of infringing those rules.

BANK CONFIDENTIALITY AND INSIDER TRADING

[3.33] Insider trading is, in accordance with ss 48ff of the Stock Exchange Act ('BörseG'), subject to both criminal and administrative punishment.[64] The respective provisions are complemented by supporting measures for the prevention of insider trading. However, the Austrian law on insider trading does not contain an explicit provision that creates a statutory basis for claims under civil law in situations involving insider trading.[65] Under the BörseG, the FMA is not only the responsible supervising authority with respect to insider trading situations, but is granted certain rights in the case of criminal proceedings before Austrian courts.

Criminal offence

[3.34] The core of the provisions on insider trading is s 48b of the BörseG, a provision of criminal law which covers both primary insiders '(insiders') and secondary insiders ('tippees').[66]

According to s 48b of the BörseG, it is a criminal offence (punishable by imprisonment for up to five years or a fine) if a person who, qualifying as an insider, exploits inside information in the course of trading with financial instruments with the intention of obtaining an economic advantage for himself or a third person, provided such person (the insider) (i) either buys, sells or recommends the sale or

---

61 OGH (1995) ÖBA at 627ff; OGH (1998) ÖBA at 733.
62 For details see Koziol *Pflichtenkollisionen im Wertpapiergeschäft bei Übernahme von Aufsichtsratsmandaten durch Mitarbeiter der Bank* in Enzinger, Hügel and Dillenz *Aktuelle Probleme des Unternehmensrechts* (1993) p 351ff.
63 See eg OGH (2002) RdW at 341.
64 See also Noll/Klimscha *Über die Sinnhaftigkeit der Bestrafung von Insidergeschäften* (2005) ÖJZ at 38.
65 Of course, it might be possible to have recourse to statutory provisions of a more general nature to find a legal basis for such claims: see Hausmanninger *Insider Trading* (1997) p 408ff.
66 See also Raschauer *Neues zum materiell-rechtlichen Insiderstraftatbestand* (2004) RdW at 525.

purchase of such financial instruments to a third party or (ii) discloses such information to a third party without being obliged to.

In addition, a person who does not qualify as an insider (a tippee) is subject to criminal punishment (by imprisonment for up to three years or a fine) if he knowingly exploits inside information that was communicated to him or which he learned otherwise with the same intent as set out above, provided such person (the tippee) exploits inside information by either buying, selling or recommending financial instruments or disclosing information as set out in the preceding paragraph.

Lastly, a person who is either an insider or a tippee is subject to criminal punishment (by imprisonment for up to six months or a fine) if he knowingly or grossly negligently unknowingly exploits inside information by either buying, selling or recommending financial instruments or disclosing information as set out above, however, without the intention of obtaining an economic advantage for himself or a third person.

The most important elements contained in these provisions are defined in the BörseG as follows:

1   'insider' is deemed to be any person having access to inside information due to his profession, occupation, task or participation in the share capital of the issuer. This definition does not only cover the issuer of financial instruments (including its organ members, employees and shareholders who hold any direct or indirect participation in the issuer that enables them to have access to inside information of the issuer and the organ members of such shareholders), but also persons receiving inside information due to a temporary contractual relationship with the issuer (for example, the issuer's attorneys, accountants, public relations advisers and other consultants), further institutional investors, market makers, brokers, journalists and, in particular, banks. Persons who receive inside information due to a criminal act are also deemed to be insiders. Lastly, insiders are also representatives of a legal entity who decided to make a (financial instruments) transaction for the account of such legal entity;

2   the qualification as a 'secondary insider' does not necessarily require that the secondary insider was aware of whether or not the received information was – directly or indirectly – communicated to it by a (primary) insider. Thus, a secondary insider is any person who learns or knows of any inside information, irrespective of the source of the information and the means of how it learned of the inside information, only provided it does not qualify as a primary insider;

3   'inside information' is generally any information about a certain confidential (ie not known to the general public) fact (as opposed to rumours or opinions) which is either connected to financial instruments or to the issuer of financial instruments and which could have a material impact on the price of the financial instruments if the fact became known to the public;

4   'financial instruments' are particularly securities within the meaning of Council Directive 93/22/EC, money market instruments, financial futures, swaps, equity swaps, forward rate agreements, options, derivatives and all other instruments which are admitted for trading on a regulated market of a (EU) member state or regarding which an application for such admission to a regulated market has been filed.

As described above, particularly in the course of an initiated judicial criminal proceeding with respect to an alleged insider trading, a bank's confidentiality obligation under the BWG may be lifted.

Ancillary measures, Compliance Code and disclosure of inside information

[3.35]   In addition to the criminal sanctions set out above, Austrian law requires the establishment of organisational measures in order to prevent the abuse and passing on of inside information. Section 82(5) of the BörseG imposes the duty on any issuer for the purpose of preventing insider transactions:

1   to notify its employees and any other persons actively involved with the issuer of the prohibition of abuse of inside information;
2   to establish, and supervise the compliance with, internal guidelines for the passing on of information within the enterprise; and
3   to adopt appropriate organisational measures to prevent any abuse or passing on of inside information.

In addition to the issuer, these duties are also imposed on banks and institutional investors (contractual insurance companies and pension funds) (BörseG, s 48s), on all members of the stock exchange (BörseG, s 18, no 5) and stock exchange dealers (BörseG, s 36(6)). Breach of these duties is subject to administrative penalties (by fines of up to 20,000 euros) and disciplinary sanctions (by elimination or suspension from participation in the stock exchange). In addition, the Act on the Supervision of Investment Services in the Securities Field (*Wertpapieraufsichtsgesetz*) contains further compliance provisions for banks engaged in investment services relating to securities which also aim to prevent and track insider transactions.

Section 82(5a) of the BörseG authorises the FMA to issue a regulation setting out principles for the passing on of information within the enterprise pursuant to 1 above, as well as for the establishment of organisational measures pursuant to 3 above. These principles shall, in particular, preclude the possible creation, and assist in tracing, of situations involving insider trading. In this regard, the FMA has issued a Compliance Code (*Emmittenten-Compliance-Verordnung*) for issuers of financial instruments admitted to a regulated market in Austria.[67]

Finally, s 48d of the BörseG principally requires any issuer of financial instruments to disclose without undue delay any inside information. Prior to such notification to the public, the issuer must file a notification of these facts to the FMA and the stock exchange (BörseG, s 82(7)).

---

67 BGBl (Federal Gazette) II no 108/2005; see also Khol/Kozak *Reform der Director's Dealing Meldungen – zu § 48d Abs 4 BörseG sowie zu den Entwürfen der ECV und VMV* (2005) ecolex at 336; Kapfer *Die Marktmissbrauchsverordnungen der FMA* (2006) ecolex at 71.

4 Belgium

Jacques Richelle
David Verroken

INTRODUCTION

[4.1] Banks' duty of confidentiality (or 'duty of discretion' as referred to by the Belgian Supreme Court (*Cour de Cassation/Hof van Cassatie*)) is a long-established concept under Belgian law, even though its principle has never been embodied in a statutory provision. Case law is scarce in this matter and has not been of much help in determining the scope of banks' obligations and the remedies available to clients in case of breach. The main decision in this area was rendered on 25 October 1978 by the Supreme Court,[1] which held that a breach of a bank's duty of confidentiality is not a criminal offence.

Exceptions to the confidentiality rule can be found in general statutory provisions applicable not only to banks such as the Judicial Code or the Code of Criminal Procedure. Other exceptions are specific to banks and can be found in statutes such as the various Tax Codes, the laws on consumer credit and the law on money laundering.

Since the 1990s, the scope of these specific exceptions has been extended in several areas. The most important examples are to be found in the Income Tax Code, the legislation on consumer credit (including the specific law on mortgage credit) and the law on money laundering.

NATURE OF THE DUTY OF CONFIDENTIALITY
The duty of confidentiality as a civil law concept
Contractual and other grounds

[4.2] A bank may be liable for damages incurred by its clients due to the breach of its duty of confidentiality. The nature of this duty and its resulting liability depend on the circumstances.

When a bank and its client reach an agreement, the duty of confidentiality arises out of the contract itself. Whether expressly provided for in the agreement or, as in most cases, merely implied, this duty is undoubtedly contractual. The nature of the duty of confidentiality is not so clear, however, in the absence of a contract, for example, during the negotiation process or when a person cashes a bank cheque as a one-off

---

1 Cass, 25 October 1978, Pas 1979, I, 237 and JT 1979, 371–378, note A Bruyneel.

operation. Legal authors have put forward many legal grounds on which to enforce a bank's duty of confidentiality in such circumstances:

1   in tort, under art 1382 of the Civil Code;[2]
2   on the basis of an implied pre-contractual agreement;
3   on the basis of a *sui generis* contract; and
4   on the basis of the *culpa in contrahendo* doctrine.

It seems that, in most cases, liability could be based on an implied agreement of confidentiality, independent from any subsequent formal contract. If evidence of such an agreement cannot be provided, however, art 1382 of the Civil Code is always applicable.

Client's remedies

[4.3]   If the duty of confidentiality is contractual, the client may claim damages for breach of contract (arts 1142 and 1145 of the Civil Code).

As far as tortious liability is concerned, pursuant to art 1382 of the Civil Code, the client may be awarded damages if he can establish (i) that there has been a breach of the duty of confidentiality, (ii) damage and (iii) a causal link between the two.

A judgment of 25 February 2000 by the Court of First Instance of Brussels[3] (*Tribunal de Première Instance/Rechtbank van Eerste Aanleg*) awarded moral damages to a client whose bank had mistakenly communicated information regarding the client's financial situation beyond what had been asked by the auditor to whom the information was communicated. The court was of the opinion that both material and moral damage can be suffered when a bank breaches its duty of confidentiality. The moral damage consists not only of the broken relationship of confidence between the bank and its client, but also of the fact that private information has been communicated to a third party, which has offended the client.

Scope of the duty of confidentiality

[4.4]   The scope of banks' duty of confidentiality is very broad. It may be approached from three different angles.

Type of operations

[4.5]   The duty of confidentiality applies to banking operations in the broad sense: deposit taking, credit, transfer of funds, foreign exchange, financial advice, the rental of a safety deposit box, letter of credit, etc. Such duty would not apply to activities unrelated to banking, such as the operating of a travel agency.

Origin of the information

[4.6]   The duty of confidentiality extends to all facts a banker comes across in the course of his business relationship with his client. This includes information released directly by the client himself, as well as that known by the banker from any other

---

2 Article 1382 of the Civil Code provides, freely translated, that any act of a person causing harm to another brings with it the obligation for the person responsible for the harm caused to compensate such harm.
3 Civ Bruxelles, 25 February 2000, RDC 2001, 860, note J Buyle and M Deliernieux.

source (for example, the banker's own investigation, client blacklists, etc). Mere hints or facts suspected by the banker are also included.

Some legal authors have suggested that (i) facts known by the banker in another capacity (for example, as a friend) and (ii) facts discovered by the banker by a mere coincidence are not included in the scope of the duty of confidentiality because they do not come to the banker's attention 'in the course of his business relationship with the client'. Such drawing of a fine line must be handled very carefully.

Type of information

[4.7]   The duty of confidentiality applies to various types of information. including:

1   facts about the client himself, for example, financial situation, commercial practices or strategy, etc;
2   types of banking operations, for example, the opening of an account or line of credit, transfer of funds, receipt of funds, etc; and
3   the amounts involved, account balances, etc.

It must be added that the mere disclosure of the existence of a business relationship does not seem to constitute a breach of a bank's duty of confidentiality under Belgian law.

Breach of the duty of confidentiality does not constitute a criminal offence

[4.8]   In its decision of 25 October 1978, the Belgian Supreme Court[4] clearly held that a breach of the bankers' duty of confidentiality does not constitute a criminal offence. The issue before the court was whether bankers should come under the scope of application of art 458 of the Criminal Code, which provides that doctors, surgeons, health officers, pharmacists and all other persons who, because of their status or profession, are confided secrets will be, subject to certain exceptions, fined and/or imprisoned if they reveal these secrets.

The court held that this article does not apply to bankers because they are merely held to a duty of 'discretion'. The court added that neither the nature of their duties nor any statutory provision makes them subject to art 458 of the Criminal Code.

The judgment of 25 October 1978 is very short. Hints as to the court's reasoning can be found in previous decisions and in the comments of legal authors:[5]

1   bankers do not have any legal monopoly as is the case with the professions mentioned in art 458;
2   entering into a relationship with a banker does not necessarily involve confiding secrets in him; at least, it is not the banker's primary function;
3   it is not deemed as socially important for a banker to keep the secrets he is told as it is for a lawyer or a doctor; the latter have a much more intimate relationship with their clients, whose trust is essential to their function; patrimonial interests, such as property and goods, are seen as less worthy of legal protection than personal interests, such as life and physical integrity.

---

4 See n 1.
5 See eg A Bruyneel *Le secret bancaire en Belgique après l'arrêt du 25 octobre 1978*, JT 1979, 371–378.

These arguments have been the subject of controversy among legal authors. Whatever the underlying reasoning, however, the rule of law is clear: bankers are not criminally liable for revealing secrets confided to them by their clients.

EXCEPTIONS TO THE DUTY OF CONFIDENTIALITY

Introduction

[4.9]   Exceptions to the rule of confidentiality are based on either general law concepts applied by legal scholars, general procedural rules applicable to any party in civil or criminal proceedings or specific statutory provisions.

Client's consent

[4.10]   The client can relieve the bank of its duty of confidentiality, either expressly or implicitly. The underlying reasoning for this rule is that the bank's duty only protects its client's private material interests, not any larger public interest.

Interest of the bank

[4.11]   A bank is allowed to release information about its client when its own material interest is at stake. Whether or not such disclosure is limited to judicial proceedings to which the bank is a party is the subject of controversy among legal authors.

Information to persons within the sphere of confidentiality

[4.12]   Certain persons may require information from the bank because of their special relationship with the client. Such persons may be those associated with, or those that have taken over, the management of the client's assets and are, therefore, included within the sphere of confidentiality. These situations should not be considered as real exceptions, but rather as flexible applications of the rule of confidentiality.

The following categories can be drawn up:

1   persons representing the client, including representatives of persons lacking legal capacity, the client's agents (for example, the directors of a corporation), the trustee of a bankrupt company or person, the company's liquidator, etc;
2   persons continuing the client's legal status after his death, for example, the legal heir or the heir by will having accepted the estate as a whole (*légataire universel/algemene legataris*);
3   persons having the same right as the client to assets in the bank's possession, for example, the spouse under certain circumstances. The bank must advise the client's spouse of the opening of any account or renting of a safety deposit box (art 218 of the Civil Code). The spouse may request information from the banker as to the client's assets provided he or she can show evidence that such money or property is jointly owned by the couple.

Criminal proceedings

Introduction

[4.13]   A bank can be compelled to disclose information about its client's operations at various stages of criminal proceedings, ie during the investigation process and by the court at the trial hearings. In these cases, its duty of confidentiality is irrelevant; the bank must testify through its representatives or accept a search, just like any other person.

The same rules apply if the bank is itself under investigation or on trial. In that case, however, its fundamental right to remain silent supersedes any duty of disclosure. Therefore, the bank cannot be forced to testify.

Investigation stage

[4.14]   The judge leading the investigation (*juge d'instruction*/*onderzoeksrechter*) has the power:

1   to compel the bank to disclose confidential information about its client (art 71ff of the Code of Criminal Procedure – *Code d'Instruction Criminelle*/*Wetboek van Strafvordering*, 'CCP').

   The judge may request the public prosecutor (*procureur du roi*/*procureur des konings* and his *substituts*/*substituten*) or the federal police (*police fédérale*/*federale politie*) to interrogate the banker. If the banker refuses to testify before the judge leading the investigation, he can be fined and forced to appear (CCP, art 80).

   At this stage, false testimony is not a criminal offence. The witness can modify his testimony up until the close of the trial. However, this traditional rule has been called into question by some legal authors and courts;[6]

2   to order a search (*perquisition*/*opzoeking*) at the bank (CCP, art 87).

   This is the judge's most effective alternative, since the bank may not oppose the search. The banker may, however, include his own written comments in the official minutes of the search. He will do so when:

   (a) a procedural rule has been broken, for example, if the judge lacks territorial jurisdiction, or

   (b) the search is unrelated to the charges brought against the person under investigation.

   This may lead the trial court eventually to reject as evidence any material found during the search.

It is important for the banker to distinguish the official, formal investigation described above from an unofficial investigation led by the public prosecutor. When serious indications exist that the investigated crimes could carry a sentence of over one year in prison, a public prosecutor can compel a bank to disclose all bank accounts linked to a suspect (as owner, attorney or identified beneficiary) and any past or present movements on any of those bank accounts (CCP, art 46 quater). Failure to co-operate carries criminal sanctions (imprisonment and fines) Outside of these limited circumstances, however, as there is no legal obligation for the banker to answer any questions, the banker's duty of confidentiality should keep him from disclosing any confidential information.

---

6 See eg A Bruyneel *Le secret bancaire en Belgique après l'arrêt du 25 octobre 1978*, JT 1979, 375.

Trial stage

[4.15]   At the trial hearings, the trial court may order a banker, in the same manner as for any other person, to testify (CCP, arts 153, 190 and 315). A refusal to testify then leads to the same consequences as at the investigation stage (CCP, arts 157, 189 and 355).

Spontaneous disclosure

[4.16]   The CCP, art 30 provides that anyone who witnesses an attempt to commit a crime against 'public safety' or the life or property of an individual must advise the public prosecutor. Faced with such situation, the banker would not be liable to the client for disclosing information evidencing the attempted crime.

Subpoenas from foreign jurisdictions

[4.17]   Belgium is a party to the European Convention on Mutual Assistance in Criminal Matters, signed in Strasbourg on 20 April 1959, supplemented by the Council Act of 29 May 2000, and to various other bilateral and multilateral treaties. Under the European Convention, a subpoena from a signatory state must be executed by the judicial authorities of the receiving state in accordance with the latter's own procedural rules. Therefore, once the subpoena is accepted by the Belgian authorities, the banker finds himself in the same situation as when faced with a subpoena from a Belgian judge.

In the absence of an international treaty, the foreign subpoena must be authorised by the Belgian Minister of Justice (art 873 of the Judicial Code).

A specific procedure for foreign subpoenas ordering searches or the production of documents is set out in art 11 of the Law of 15 March 1874 on extradition.

Conclusion

[4.18]   A banker faced with criminal proceedings has very little room within which to manoeuvre. In most cases, in order to avoid criminal sanctions, he will have no other options than to disclose information about his client or undergo a search.

In these circumstances, the bank will not be liable to its client for breach of the duty of confidentiality provided that it stays within the general limits of disclosure. This would require the bank, for instance, to limit its answers to the specific questions asked during the testimony and to mention any procedural irregularities related to the search of which it is aware. The bank will never be liable to its client if the latter is eventually convicted of the charges pending at the time of the investigation or trial.

Civil proceedings

Banks' testimonies and production of documents

[4.19]   The rules relating to evidence in Belgian civil proceedings are based on two principles:

1   litigants and third parties must co-operate in the search for the truth; and
2   the court has the power to force them to do so.

The court has the power to compel litigants (arts 871 and 877 of the Judicial Code –

Code Judiciaire/Gerechtelijk Wetboek, 'JC') and third parties (JC, arts 877 and 878) to produce documents. If they fail to comply with the court's order, they may have to pay damages to the party to whom their conduct has caused damage (JC, art 882). Similar rules apply to testimonies (JC, arts 915 and 916). In addition to possible damages, a refusal to testify may also lead to criminal penalties. including imprisonment (art 495 bis of the Criminal Code; see also art 495).

In a judgment of 29 June 1995,[7] the Commercial Court of Namur held that this duty of disclosure does not entail an obligation of the bank to *comment* on the disclosed documents.

As in criminal proceedings, the banker, despite his duty of confidentiality, is subject to the same rules of disclosure as any other person. This broad duty of disclosure is, however, qualified by two sets of rules.

The court's subpoena must be valid

[4.20]   This rule is laid down in the JC, art 929, which, by its terms, only applies to testimony. It is widely accepted, however, that the same rules apply to the production of documents (see the JC, arts 878 and 882 and the Van Reepinghen Report,[8] on which the 1967 enactment of the Judicial Code was based).

The JC, art 929 provides that:

1   witnesses may request the court to be relieved of their duty to testify because of a legitimate reason (*motif légitime/wettige reden*);
2   professional secrecy, among other things, is to be deemed a legitimate reason; and
3   the court must hear the witness and the (other) parties before reaching a decision as to this request.

Bankers' duty of confidentiality is not generally deemed a duty of professional secrecy within the meaning of the JC, art 929. In specific circumstances, however, such duty of confidentiality can constitute a legitimate reason for not testifying or producing documents. Therefore, the judge would have to take the bank's request into consideration and balance the bank's duty of confidentiality with the requirements of the search for the truth. Legal authors agree that such request by the bank is not likely to succeed as the courts would construe the 'legitimate reason' concept narrowly.

The subpoena may be opposed for a 'legitimate reason'

[4.21]   The tests of such legitimacy are laid down in the JC, arts 877 (production of documents), 915 (testimony at the request of the litigant) and 916 (testimony at the request of the court). They can be summarised as follows, the first test applying to both testimony and presentation of documents, the following two only to the latter:

1   the subpoena must present the evidence of a relevant and specific fact; requests which are too broad (for example, 'all documents in your possession') or too vague (for example, 'any relevant document available') do not meet this test;

---

7 Comm Namur, 29 June 1995, JT 1996, 328.
8 Charles Van Reepinghen, Ministerie van justitie *Verslag over de gerechtelijke hervorming*, Belgisch staatsblad, 1964 (two volumes: 842 and 543pp).

2   there must be specific and serious presumptions that the document is in the hands of the person requested to produce it; a mere suspicion of the possession of the document is therefore not enough; and

3   the document must exist at the time of the request; a demand to draft a new document will be rejected.

With regard to subpoenas from foreign jurisdictions, Belgium is party to many bilateral or multilateral treaties, including the International Convention on Civil Proceedings signed in The Hague on 1 March 1954. As in criminal proceedings, the general principle of execution of the subpoena in accordance with the procedural rules of the party requested to produce a document is applied.

In the absence of an international treaty, the foreign subpoena must be authorised by the Belgian Minister of Justice (JC, art 873).

In conclusion, as in criminal proceedings, the bank does not have many options when requested to testify or produce documents regarding its clients. It will not be liable to its client for breach of its duty of confidentiality provided it has verified the validity of the subpoena, raised any available legitimate reason to oppose disclosure and stayed within the general limits of its duty of disclosure.

Garnishee orders

Introduction

[4.22]   A creditor of a bank's client may have the bank garnished as a third party owing money or property to the client debtor. The garnishment order may be either a mere sequestration pending the outcome of litigation (*saisie-arrêt conservatoire/bewarend beslag onder derden*) or a step in the execution of a judgment (*saisie-arrêt exécution/uitvoerend beslag onder derden*). The procedures are strictly regulated by the JC, art 1386ff.

Garnishment obviously entails disclosure of information by the garnishee, ie the bank.

The bank must be the client's debtor – specific problems

[4.23]   In order for the garnishment procedure to be valid, the bank must be the client's debtor for a particular amount of money or property which corresponds to the garnishee order. Questions which arise concern what is to be considered as a debt in a bank–client relationship.

THE BANK'S SAFE

[4.24]   If the client leaves property to be kept by the bank in the bank's safe, the bank has the duty to deliver it back to the client at his request. The bank is thus the client's debtor. If the client rents a private safety deposit box at the bank, however, the bank is a mere lessor and is not a debtor with regard to any of the property contained in it.

LINE OF CREDIT

[4.25]   This issue is not yet settled in Belgian law. A decision by the attachment judge (*juge des saisies/beslagrechter*) of Brussels has declared valid the application of the garnishment procedure to a line of credit,[9] but case law to the contrary also exists and some legal authors disagree.[10] The practical significance of such garnishee order in this case, however, is limited as the bank can, in principle, revoke the line of credit as a result of loss of confidence vis-à-vis its client at the time it receives the notice of the order.

PENDING OPERATIONS

[4.26]   The amount of the debt is equal to the credit balance of an account at the time notice of the order is given to the bank. Some operations prior to that date, but affecting the balance at a later stage, must also be taken into account. Such is the case for cheques signed by the account holder, but not yet presented for payment at the bank. Such is not the case, however, for transfers of funds ordered prior to the garnishee order, but not yet executed by the bank.

Operations taking place after the notice is given do not affect the amount of the debt subject to the order.

Banks' duty to disclose

[4.27]   Upon receipt of notice of a garnishee order relating to one of its clients, a bank must disclose to the creditor (with a copy for the client), within a 15-day period, the following information (JC, arts 1452–1456):

1   in the case where the bank is currently the client's debtor:
    (a)   the origin of the debt, ie type of account or other banking operation from which the debt derives,
    (b)   the amount of the debt,
    (c)   the terms of payment, if any, and
    (d)   the specific conditions of the debt, if any;
2   in the case where it has never been the client's debtor, the bank may simply so declare;
3   in the case where it is no longer a debtor, the bank must state when and how the debt was paid off and produce any relevant document evidencing such fact.

The bank must also disclose prior orders of which it received notice. It is not clear whether the bank must inform the creditor of accounts with a debit balance. The bank may always turn to the attachment judge for information regarding the extent of the required disclosure.

Failure to issue such statement within the 15-day period or any misrepresentation of facts may result in the bank being held liable for part or all of its client's debts. Fraud, bad faith or negligence can constitute possible grounds for a such measure, but it is left entirely up to the attachment judge whether and to what extent such a penalty will be imposed. For instance, a short delay for technical reasons or which causes the client's creditor no harm will normally not be penalised by the attachment judge.

Conclusion

[4.28]   In view of the penalty at stake, the bank must be careful to adhere strictly to the requirements of the garnishee order. Its role is not to protect its client, who has at

---

9   Tribunal de première instance Bruxelles, chambre des saisies, 10 April 1986, Saisie – Saisie-arrêt conservatoire (unpublished).
10   See eg Bruxelles, 16 June 1989, JLMB 1989, 802, note G De Leval.

his disposal various means of opposing wrongful or abusive garnishments by his creditors. The bank is not expected, for instance, to oppose an order relating to amounts much greater than the client's debt. Many banks seem, however, to overreact in the other direction and have the habit of disclosing and blocking any increase in the client's credit balance after notice of the garnishee order is given until the credit equals the client's debt to his creditor. Such a practice is overly cautious and lacking in any legal grounds.

Information to the tax authorities

Introduction

[4.29] A distinction must be drawn between:

1 income tax; and
2 registration, inheritance and value added taxes.

Specific statutory provisions as to bank confidentiality, ie limits to a Tax Administration's powers of investigation into bank records with respect to their clients, only apply to income tax. It is important to note that these provisions were amended by Royal Decree of 20 December 1996 (published in the Belgian State Gazette of 31 December 1996) limiting banks' rights to invoke their duty of confidentiality in order to oppose the Income Tax Administration's investigations.

Income tax

[4.30] The Income Tax Administration may request from any individual or corporation information and relevant material necessary to determine the tax liability of that party or any third party (art 315ff of the Income Tax Code 1992 – *Code des Impôts sur les Revenus* 1992/*Wetboek van de Inkomstenbelastingen* 1992, 'ITC').

As far as banks are concerned, this broad duty of disclosure is qualified by the ITC, art 318(1), which provides that the Income Tax Administration may not check banks' books or records in order to determine their clients' tax liability. Some case law has complemented this rule by rendering it illegal for the Income Tax Administration to request banks to disclose information about clients that the Administration itself is not allowed to seek out in the bank's records.

However, if, in the course of an inquiry related to a bank's own tax situation, the Administration discovers relevant information leading to a suspicion that a mechanism exists or is being prepared by which the client is trying to avoid the taxation of his income illegally (*mécanisme de fraude fiscale/mechanisme van belastingontduiking*), then the Administration is allowed to investigate into the bank's records in order to determine the client's tax liability (ITC, art 318(2)). This article does not require the bank's involvement in the fraudulent mechanism, as was the case before.

Furthermore, if a tax investigation leads to a criminal investigation, the specific duty of confidentiality provided for in the ITC, art 318(1) is no longer relevant as the general rules on criminal proceedings will apply (see above). In addition, if the Banking, Finance and Insurance Commission, whose responsibility includes the supervision of banks and investment firms, discovers special mechanisms (*mécanismes particuliers/bijzondere mechanismen*) having as their purpose or as a consequence the promotion of fiscal fraud by third parties and put in place by banks (or investment firms) and where the Banking, Finance and Insurance Commission has knowledge that these special mechanisms constitute a tax offence punishable by criminal sanctions for the banks (or investment firms) themselves, it must advise the judicial authorities and not just the Income Tax Administration, as was the case until 1999 (art 46 of the Law of 2 August 2002).

In a judgment of 23 October 2001,[11] the Antwerp Court of Appeal (*Cour d'Appel/Hof van Beroep*) has clarified the scope of the fiscal banking secrecy rules laid out in the ITC, art 318 with regard to Banksys, the operator of the electronic payment system in Belgium and provider of ATMs and bank card payment terminals (for example, in shops). The Tax Administration had asked Banksys to provide it with information regarding electronic payments made through a terminal placed by Banksys in the taxpayer's shop and obtained such information. The taxpayer claimed that the Tax Administration had breached the fiscal banking secrecy rule as laid out in the ITC, art 318 by obtaining the information in such a way. The Tax Administration claimed that Banksys is not a bank. The court held that Banksys is indeed not a bank, but only a system-operating intermediary which rents or sells payment terminals linked to a central computer. The prohibition on seeking out bank records laid out in the ITC, art 318(1) is as such not directly applicable to Banksys, but the court held that the Tax Administration had nonetheless breached the banking secrecy rule by attempting to bypass the prohibition laid out in the ITC, art 318 by trying to obtain the same information from Banksys, which is, moreover, not the owner of the electronic data which is processed through its installations.

The ITC, arts 335 and 336 provide that information discovered by one Tax Administration may be used by another to determine another category of tax. It seems, however, that the Income Tax Administration may not use this provision as a basis for requesting other Tax Administrations to obtain from a bank the information the Income Tax Administration needs regarding one of the bank's clients. Such a construction of the ITC would render meaningless the limits to the Income Tax Administration's power of investigation. The ITC, art 318 was enacted in 1980, over 40 years after the ITC, arts 335 and 336, and it should be understood as limiting the rule of co-operation among the various Tax Administrations. Some legal authors have, however, identified this co-operation among Tax Administrations as presenting a potential risk to banking confidentiality.[12]

When a taxpayer contests the taxation of his income, the Income Tax Administration may require information from his bank in order to investigate the validity of the complaint (ITC, art 374). It is accepted, however, that the taxpayer may forbid his bank from disclosing any information, even though such attitude will obviously greatly undermine his chances of a successful complaint. Banks often spontaneously refuse to release information that could reveal the identity of other clients.

Registration tax

[4.31]   Various types of operations, such as the sale of real estate, are subject to registration and payment of a tax to the Registration Administration (*Administration de l'Enregistrement et des Domaines/Administratie der Registratie en Domeinen*).

---

11 Antwerpen, 23 October 2001, RW 2002–2003, afl 1, 27.
12 See eg E De Baenst *La protection de la confidentialité en matière fiscale*, JDF 1991, 193 (quoted in D Mareels and M Bihain *Le secret bancaire en droit fiscal belge*, JDF 1996, 193–240) and I Quinet and L Herve *Préparation à un contrôle fiscal: droits et devoirs de l'administration fiscale*, Pacioli n 50, 15 March 1999.

Banks may be compelled by this Administration's controllers (acting by virtue of an authorisation of a high ranking official) to disclose any information and documents deemed relevant to the determination of the exact amount of tax to be paid when the bank or one of its clients is subject to such taxation (art 183 of the Registration Tax Code – *Code des Droits d'Enregistrement/Wetboek Registratierechten*).

Inheritance tax

[4.32]   The following rules of disclosure only apply when the deceased is a Belgian resident. Non-residents are not subject to Belgian inheritance taxes, except with regard to real estate, which is irrelevant in a bank–client relationship.

Banks have a passive duty of disclosure similar to the one related to registration taxes. The Registration Administration (which is also in charge of the collection of inheritance taxes) may request information from banks related to any operation of the deceased, his or her spouse or heir, or any third party that took place before or after the death and that may affect the taxation of the inheritance (art 100 of the Inheritance Tax Code – *Code des Droits de Succession/Wetboek Successierechten*).

In addition, banks must maintain a record of all clients depositing sealed envelopes or parcels or renting safety deposit boxes, along with the identity of their spouses. They must also maintain a list of signatures of all of a client's mandatees or co-lessees who request to have access to the envelope, parcel or safety deposit box. These records are transmitted to the Registration Administration (art 102-1 of the Inheritance Tax Code). The following disclosures occur in the event of the death of a client or his or her spouse:

1   the banker must transmit to the Registration Administration a list of all of the client's funds, securities or other properties in the bank's possession before paying or delivering them back to the estate (art 97 of the Inheritance Tax Code);
2   if the banker is in possession of sealed envelopes or parcels or if the client has rented a safety deposit box, the banker must:
    (a)   notify the Registration Administration of the intended opening of the envelope, parcel or safety deposit box at least five days in advance, and
    (b)   transmit a list of the contents of the envelope, parcel or safety deposit box at the time it is opened. The Registration Administration may send one of its agents to witness such opening (arts 98 and 101 of the Inheritance Tax Code).

Value added tax

[4.33]   Banks, like any other party subject to VAT, must list, in regular VAT returns, all operations with clients who are themselves subject to VAT.

Banks also have a positive duty of disclosure. If the bank is itself subject to an investigation from the VAT Administration, it must supply the VAT controllers, at their request, with all the registers and documents the bank, like any other party subject to VAT, is required to maintain pursuant to the VAT Code, as well as any other information (arts 61, §1 and 62, §2 of the VAT Code). If the investigation targets third parties (whether or not clients), the bank is under the same duty to disclose such other information provided the request is authorised by a high ranking official (art 62 bis of the VAT Code).

Disclosure of bank accounts abroad

[4.34]   It must be noted that the Royal Decree of 20 December 1996 amended the ITC, art 307, §1 and introduced the obligation for Belgian individuals to list in their income tax return all their bank accounts with banks abroad. This obligation is being contested on various grounds by legal authors, but has nevertheless been applicable to tax returns filed since 1997.

This provision is complemented by the new art 315(2) of the ITC, according to which the Income Tax Administration may request from individuals all documents relating to their foreign bank accounts.

Supervision by the Banking, Finance and Insurance Commission

[4.35]   The Banking, Finance and Insurance Commission ('CBFA') supervises banks directly and through accredited statutory auditors (Law of 22 March 1993 on the Legal Status and Supervision of Credit Institutions and Law of 2 August 2002 on the Supervision of the Financial Sector and Financial Services). Neither auditors nor members of the CBFA may reveal any information they come across in the course of their supervisory activities, subject to certain exceptions, such as:

1   criminal proceedings;
2   the filing of a complaint by the CBFA with the public prosecutor's office with regard to discovered offences; and
3   the communication of information to foreign supervisory authorities, to the extent such authorities are bound by similar secrecy rules.

A breach of this rule leads to the criminal sanctions provided for in art 458 of the Criminal Code (arts 7 and 8 of Royal Decree no 185 of 9 July 1935, as amended by the Law of 22 March 1993, and art 74ff of the Law of 2 August 2002).

The CBFA may enter into reciprocal agreements with foreign supervisory authorities in order to organise exchanges of information and supervision abroad (art 77 of the Law of 2 August 2002). Such agreements (Memoranda of Understanding) have already been entered into with most other EU member states' supervisory authorities.

Outsourcing

[4.36]   Banks wishing to outsource a certain number of services (for example, IT services) will have to make sure that the appropriate technical and organisational measures are taken to ensure that confidential information is not used by the outsourcer nor disclosed to third parties. Data protection rules will have to be complied with as well. If a disclosure of confidential information occurs as a consequence of the outsourcing, the bank may be held liable for damages. The CBFA, which should be informed of any proposed outsourcing by banks, will examine the scope of any proposed outsourcing project and evaluate whether the limits of the outsourcing are clearly defined and whether the outsourcing meets the prudential requirements regarding the proper organisation and functioning of the bank.

Communication of information among banks

Information to the Belgian National Bank (Consumer Credits Centre)

[4.37]   Two types of credit information must be notified by banks to the Belgian National Bank, which operates the Consumer Credits Centre established by the Law of 10 August 2001 on the Consumer Credits Centre (as implemented by the Royal Decree of 7 July 2002). This Centre replaces the formerly separate positive and negative databases. The National Bank has the task of registering in the Consumer Credits Centre:

1   consumer credit agreements;
2   mortgage loan credit agreements (covered by the Law of 4 August 1992); and
3   default payments under consumer credit and mortgage loan credits.

The Consumer Credits Centre comprises a positive and negative section.

Positive section

[4.38]   Banks are compelled to notify the National Bank of any grant (or acquisition) of a credit or loan, irrespective of the amount. The information registered includes personal data regarding the credit recipient, the name and address of the creditor (or the assignee), the type of credit, the amount of the credit, the amount actually drawn down, the period of the credit and specific additional information depending on the type of credit. The positive section of the Consumer Credits Centre basically contains all credit information, whether or not the client has defaulted. Notification must be made within two business days after the conclusion of the agreement (or repayment of the credit).

Negative section

[4.39]   All defaults under consumer credits and mortgage loan credits must be reported to the negative section of the Consumer Credits Centre provided that certain criteria are met, depending on the type of credit (for example, when an amount due under a mortgage credit loan has not been paid within three months after the maturity date). Defaults have to be notified to the Consumer Credits Centre within eight business days of their being ascertained. Regularisations of defaults also have to be reported to the Centre. Such regularisations of defaults may consist of, inter alia, (i) full repayment of all sums due under a credit, (ii) full remedy of the relevant default and continuation of the credit relationship under the original terms and conditions of the credit or (iii) successful termination of a court-imposed debt repayment scheme (*règlement collectif de dette/collectieve schuldenregeling*).

Consultation

[4.40]   Consultation of the Consumer Credits Centre (both positive and negative sections) is mandatory for banks prior to any offer of credit to a consumer (20 or 15 calendar days prior to a consumer credit or a mortgage credit loan respectively). The information disclosed is basically the same as the information which has to be registered in the Consumer Credits Centre excluding, however, the name of the creditor or assignee and the number and language of the credit agreement(s).

Credit recipients have the right to access their file in the Consumer Credits Centre and can request rectification or removal of incorrect information.

Private databases

[4.41]   The Law of 12 June 1991 on Consumer Credit allows, under specific conditions, the setting up of private databases on consumers and their credit details. The Law determines the type of information that may be included in the databases, as well as the categories of persons to whom, and the purpose for which, the information may be disclosed.

A consumer must be informed of his initial inclusion in such a database. Consumers involved are entitled to have access to the information at all times and have the right to request that false or irrelevant data be amended or omitted.

Prior to the Law of 12 June 1991, private organisations had already set up databases to gather information for their members regarding their clients, especially in case of defaults or fraud. Such private blacklists are not necessarily limited to information on consumers. An example of such private blacklist is the one organised by the *Union Professionnelle du Crédit/Beroepsvereniging van het Krediet.*

Some legal authors seem to agree that such private blacklists are legal, whether they are 'positive' or only 'negative'. This exception to banks' duty of confidentiality is accepted on the following grounds:

1   disclosure is made to other banks; their duty of discretion prevents information from being leaked to the general public;
2   such disclosure is justified by a higher social and economic interest, which means safer and healthier credit for the public as a whole; and
3   the system only affects 'bad' clients, ie those who do not accurately disclose the existence of other credits to their bankers and those who have defaulted on previous credits.

On 5 June 1991, the Court of Appeal of Liège held a Belgian bank and the *Union Professionnelle du Crédit* liable for damages to a client for keeping outdated information on a blacklist.[13] The client's default was partly due to technical problems and had soon been cleared. The default was still mentioned on the blacklist, however. Notwithstanding the absence of evidence that the client had been refused other credits because of the incorrect data, the court nevertheless held that the burden of the investigation undertaken by the client to discover the existence of the blacklist constituted recoverable damages. The court held that the plaintiff's right to privacy had been breached because the blacklist was secret and did not allow amendments to the data in the case of a subsequent change in the debtor's situation, for example, the reimbursement of his debt or a judicial decision declaring the debt to be null and void.

The court seems to agree that blacklists are lawful provided they meet certain tests regarding disclosure and updating. These tests are similar to those established in the Law of 12 June 1991 on Consumer Credit.

In addition to the specific provisions of the Law of 12 June 1991 and for information on individuals not related to consumer credits, such databases must be operated in accordance with the Law of 8 December 1992 on the Protection of Privacy, which imposes obligations on the manager of a database with respect to the inputting of

---

13 Liège, 5 June 1991, JT 1992, 36.

information, the information to be provided to individuals, its internal treatment and its disclosure to third parties.

By a decision of 15 September 1994,[14] the president of the Commercial Court of Brussels held that a bank which had used data found on transfer forms (used by its clients to transfer funds to another bank) to approach these clients for a specific marketing campaign had breached the Law of 14 July 1991 on Trade Practices. Part of the unlawful practice spotted by the president of the court was the use of data handled in breach of the provisions of the Law of 8 December 1992 on the Protection of Privacy.

Money laundering

Applicable laws and CBFA circulars

[4.42]   The Law of 11 January 1993 (the 'Money Laundering Law') implemented EEC Council Directive of 10 June 1991 on the prevention of the use of the financial system for money laundering purposes in Belgium.[15] The Money Laundering Law has been amended on several occasions to extend its scope of application and the notion of 'illegal origin' of the funds which is included in the definition of money laundering. The events of 11 September 2001 have led to a number of legislative initiatives in order to widen the scope of the existing legislation further.

The CBFA issued circulars for the credit institutions under its supervision to specify the practical measures to be taken in order to comply with the Money Laundering Law. A circular was also sent to banks' auditors requesting them to comment in their reports on the implementation of the Money Laundering Law by the banks.

Definition of money laundering

[4.43]   According to art 3 of the Money Laundering Law, the concept of money laundering includes certain types of transactions (listed in the Money Laundering Law) aimed at acquiring, holding, using, converting, transferring, etc goods or funds having an illegal origin. These goods or funds are considered as having an illegal origin if they derive from certain offences (listed in the Money Laundering Law) linked with terrorism, organised crime, drug dealing, illegal arms trading, people trafficking, exploitation of prostitution, illegal use or trafficking of hormones, illegal trade in human organs or tissues, 'serious and organised tax fraud' involving complex mechanisms or international schemes, corruption and embezzlement, counterfeiting currency, piracy of products, environmental crime, insider trading and market manipulation, fraudulent bankruptcy, robbery and theft, etc. Since the Law of 12 January 2004, the financing of terrorism is explicitly included in this list of offences.

Measures to be taken by banks

[4.44]   In addition to a general duty to take all necessary measures to implement its provisions, the Money Laundering Law imposes the following obligations upon banks in order to prevent the use of such institutions by persons trying to launder money:

---

14 Prés Comm Bruxelles, 15 September 1994, DAOR 1995, liv 34, 85.
15 Council Directive 91/308/EEC.

1   properly identifying clients and other persons involved in any financial operation;
2   the maintaining of records related to the identification of clients (and of these other persons) for a period of five years after the end of the relationship;
3   the heightening of employees' awareness of the Money Laundering Law;
4   the designating of one or more employees responsible for the implementation of the Money Laundering Law within the financial institution; and
5   the declaring of money laundering operations, or their suspicion, to the Committee for the Handling of Financial Information.

Also, a suspicious transaction report has to be issued to the Committee for the Handling of Financial Information (see below) when the bank knows or suspects that funds are linked to money laundering. Sanctions for non-compliance with this obligation, or with any decisions issued under the Money Laundering Law, range from publication by the CBFA of its decisions to administrative fines of up to 1.25 million euros.

'Tipping off' a client when a declaration is made to the Committee for the Handling of Financial Information is forbidden.

Banks must prepare certain documents and check the identity of both regular and occasional clients. As soon as a client enters into a relationship, pursuant to which he will become a regular client, the identification should be made by means of documentary evidence, a copy of which needs to be retained. It is not necessary for a client to have an account with the bank to be considered 'regular'. Occasional clients must be identified:

1   where they wish to carry out a transaction involving 10,000 euros or more, even if this amount is spread over different operations between which there seems to be a link; and
2   each time a client wants to carry out a transaction which is suspected of being a money laundering operation, even if the amount involved is below 10,000 euros.

Client identification is not required if the client is (i) a credit institution, (ii) a financial institution, (iii) itself subject to the identification and other obligations imposed by the Money Laundering Law or (iv) a life insurance company and the amount of premiums is limited.

Reporting certain transactions could lead to a breach of the bank's duty of confidentiality (for example, when a 'clean' transaction is mistakenly reported). Therefore, the Money Laundering Law provides immunity against criminal or civil proceedings to banks which have reported a transaction in good faith even if, in retrospect, there was no reason for suspicion (art 20 of the Money Laundering Law).

The Money Laundering Law applies in principle to all banks (and other agents) having their head or branch office in Belgium. The international context has, however, shown that money laundering criminals are increasingly looking for countries and regions with absolute banking secrecy. The Money Laundering Law was amended by a Law of 3 May 2002, which has added the possibility of extending by Royal Decree the duty to report all transactions and facts (irrespective of the amount) involving natural or legal persons domiciled, registered or having their residence in a state or region, the legislation of which is regarded as inadequate by a competent international institution (ie the Financial Action Task Force on Money Laundering, 'FATF') or which does not co-operate in the fight against money laundering (art 14 ter of the Money Laundering Law). A direct link between the transaction or facts and the state or region concerned is required. Extensions to a number of states and regions by Royal Decree are to be expected.

Committee for the Handling of Financial Information

[4.45]   The Money Laundering Law set up a Committee for the Handling of Financial Information. Its tasks include following up declarations made by banks on money laundering operations. When faced with serious indications of money laundering, the Committee must forward the information to the public prosecutor's office. It should be noted that the Committee for the Handling of Financial Information is itself bound by a strict duty of secrecy, subject to certain exceptions comparable to those for the CBFA mentioned above (for example, testimonies before court, in the framework of the international fight against fraud and money laundering, etc).

FATF evaluation report for Belgium

[4.46]   In June 2005, the FATF published an evaluation report on the status of Belgian anti-money laundering rules and regulations compared with the recommendations published by the FATF. There were no important omissions reported, although on some issues (such as the application of certain anti-money laundering rules to non-financial entities, the identification of ownership and control in legal entities or the freezing of certain terrorist assets) the FATF is of the opinion that there is need for further action.

Brokerage in transferable securities

[4.47]   The Law of 2 August 2002 has centralised supervision over operations carried out by brokers, including banks, on transferable securities with the CBFA. The CBFA may request any information from brokers in order to ensure compliance with the relevant laws and regulations. It has far-reaching investigative powers, including the right to conduct on-site inspections (art 34), and it can impose penalties, including fines, on any person in relation to the orders issued by it.

Specific rules and more extensive investigative powers apply in case the CBFA suspects that insider trading is occurring or that the price of listed securities is being manipulated by fraudulent means.Also, banks are not subject to specific Chinese Walls requirements, but a general duty to avoid conflicts of interest applies with respect to the provision of investment services.

CONCLUSION

[4.48]   This description of banks' duty of confidentiality has placed much more emphasis on the exceptions to the rule, which are more specific to Belgian law, than on the duty itself.

In many circumstances, the banker will not be allowed to use his duty of discretion to oppose requests for disclosure. It must be recalled, however, that the rule of confidentiality, in its principle and scope, and the potential liability in case of a breach of such rule are clearly established in Belgium. Therefore, a bank, if required to disclose information to the public authorities or private persons regarding its clients' operations, must not depart from its traditional cautious conduct; it must ensure that procedural rules have not been breached and limit the release of information or documents to the minimum required.

5 Brazil

Jorge Nemr

INTRODUCTION

[5.1]   The legal duty of bank secrecy in Brazil was formerly ruled by art 38 of Law no 4,595, of 31 December 1964, for almost 40 years. Bank secrecy is currently ruled by Complementary Law no 105, of 10 January 2001, regulated, on the same date, by Decree no 3,724, one of several measures recently adopted by the Union with the purpose of intensifying the campaign against tax evasion.

When it was created, the legal duty of bank secrecy caused great controversy, mainly in questions involving public power. Developments over the last few years have not been sufficient to clarify the matter considering that legislative changes, the new constitution of 1988 and several other new situations have contributed to the continuous raising of doubts in connection with this matter.

Bank secrecy is currently a worldwide practice. It emerged in view of the ethical and moral requirements of certain professional categories. With social evolution, values were established, among them trust and discretion. Such ethical requirements changed into moral rules, then into technical rules and finally into legal rules.

It is worth noting that bank secrecy appeared as a variant of professional secrecy. It developed as a means of protection for private interests, but with society's approval, as bankers were acquainted with businesses, assets and even family secrets.

BANK SECRECY UNDER BRAZILIAN LAW

[5.2]   After the arrival of the Portuguese Royal Family in Brazil in the nineteenth century, Banco do Brasil, the first Brazilian bank, was created. This bank was liquidated in 1829 as a result of the excessive expenses of the Crown, the return of the Royal Family to Lisbon, Brazil's gaining of independence and the struggle for political consolidation in the new empire.

With the creation of new banks, several laws were enacted to regulate banking operations clearly evidencing the concern of the government with the appropriate functioning of the system. The enactment of the Brazilian Commercial Code of 1850 provided bank secrecy with a certain legal protection as mercantile secrecy could also be applied to banks and their transactions. Based on this rule, the banks refused to supply information on their transactions and their clients, even in response to judicial requests.

In 1940, with the enactment of the current Criminal Code, the breach of professional secrecy was typified among crimes against the inviolability of secrets. The purpose was to protect the privacy of the citizen against a possible betrayal of confidence.

Despite the fact that no express reference was made to bankers and professionals in the area, legal writing and case law placed them among the persons covered by the norm. At that time, breach of bank secrecy was made a crime with a penalty of imprisonment or fines.

Little by little, public power, particularly in judicial or tax-related matters, started to reduce the strictness of compliance with bank secrecy rules. Some decisions of the courts supported the unconditional character of bank secrecy, while others defied such character. The conservative legal writing of that time insisted on the inviolability of secrecy. However, this view did not prevail and bank secrecy, absolute in origin, became relative with limits expressly set out in law.

REGULATION OF THE SUBJECT

[5.3]   Law no 4,595, of 31 December 1964, was enacted to reorganise the banking system. Article 38 of this Law, which provided for bank secrecy, was revoked by Complementary Law no 105, of 10 January 2001, regulated, on the same date, by Decree no 3,724.

In contrast to the preceding provision, it is now provided that a breach of secrecy may be ordered when it is necessary for the investigation of any illicit act in any phase of the inquiry or judicial proceedings, especially in cases of terrorism, illicit trafficking of narcotics or similar drugs, contraband or trafficking of weapons, ammunition or material designed for their production, extortion from kidnapping, crimes against the national financial system, public administration, tax regime and social security, money laundering or hiding criminal assets or crimes practiced by a criminal organisation (art 1, para 4 of Complementary Law no 105/2001).

Among the measures adopted by the Union to intensify the campaign against tax evasion, an important measure is the potential for the tax authorities and agents of the Union, states, federal district and municipalities to breach the bank secrecy of taxpayers without prior authorisation from the judiciary. Such power, as mentioned above, was granted to the tax authority by means of Complementary Law no 105/2001 regulated, on the same date, by Decree no 3,724/2001. According to art 6 of this Law, provided an administrative procedure has been commenced or a tax proceeding is in progress, the administrative authority and tax agents may request information in documents, books and registers of financial institutions, including taxpayers' deposit accounts and investments. Note that there is permission for the breach of bank secrecy even before the commencement of the administrative procedure as the law mentions 'an inspection proceeding in progress', ie during the inspection itself.

Leaving aside the arguments relating to the material constitutionality of the law in question, it is worth mentioning that the breach of bank secrecy is an extremely controversial issue in Brazil as this may involve the breach of privacy and intimacy, assured as a fundamental right by item X of art 5 of the federal constitution. The individual rights and guarantees are included in the so-called 'immutable clauses', the abolition of which is not allowed under art 60, para 4 of the federal constitution.

DEFINITION OF BANK SECRECY

[5.4]   Several scholars have defined 'bank secrecy'. We may cite a few, such as, for example, Malagarriga, who defines bank secrecy as 'the obligation imposed on the banks of not revealing to third parties, without a justified cause, information relating to their clients to which they may have knowledge as a consequence of the legal relations which bind them'.[1]

According to Sichtermann, bank secrecy is the 'right corresponding to the obligation of the bank of not providing any information whatsoever, whether on the accounts of its clients, whether on subsequent facts to which it may have knowledge in view of its relations with clients'.[2]

Finally, in accordance with the concept of Sérgio Carlos Covello, a Brazilian scholar, bank secrecy may be defined as 'the obligation which the banks have of not revealing, except for just cause, the information they may obtain by virtue of their professional activity'.[3]

LEGAL NATURE

[5.5]   Over time, the ethical duty which bankers had to maintain the secrecy of their clients' banking transactions was changed into an obligation of a mandatory nature. Therefore, the single moral duty, the breach of which could simply produce disapproval, became a legal duty with criminal sanctions for those who had the duty of maintaining secrecy.

It should be noted that the legal duty continues even after the ending of the relationship between the financial institution and the client. Besides persisting in time, it is an *erga omnes* obligation, as the duty of non-disclosure of the information by the bank applies to any person, except as provided by law.

THE RELATIVITY OF BANK SECRECY

[5.6]   The right to bank secrecy, just like other rights, is not absolute. According to the teachings of Ariel Dotti:

> ' ... all rights, since the most fundamental one which is life, are subject to privations and limitations: death and imprisonment penalties, patrimonial sanctions, confinement, banishment, searches and seizures, expropriations, seizures under legal process and so many other measures in progress with the purpose of satisfying collective or individual interests are examples. Such limitations result from the imposition of life in society in its most diversified expressions.'[4]

In order to avoid contraventions of other general rights, society must restrict certain rights in some circumstances. In certain circumstances, there is a conflict of interests between intimacy, which is a private interest of the individual, and the information which may be relevant to the state or to other citizens.

As already mentioned, on 10 January 2001, Complementary Law no 105 was enacted, which regulates the secrecy of transactions of financial institutions and makes up part of the governmental package in its campaign against tax evasion and avoidance.

---

1 Malagarriga, Juan Carlos *El Segreto Bancário*, Buenos Aires, Abeledo-Perot, 1970.
2 Covello, Sérgio Carlos *O Sigilo Bancário*, Leud, 2001.
3 Covello, Sérgio Carlos *O Sigilo Bancário*, Leud, 2001.
4 Dotti, René Ariel *Proteção da Vida Privada e Liberdade de informação*, São Paulo, Editora RT, 1980.

A heated debate took place in connection with art 6 of this legal rule, which provides for the possibility of a breach of bank secrecy by the tax authorities and agents of the Union, states, federal district and municipalities without the necessity of prior judicial authorisation. In order to regulate this legal provision, the federal government enacted Decree no 3,724/2001 providing for the breach of bank secrecy by tax agents and defining that such measure shall only be possible when an inspection proceeding is in progress and provided that it occurs in one of 11 situations where bank verification is deemed indispensable by the competent authority.[5]

Under this scenario, it is extremely important to analyse the question of the breach of bank secrecy without judicial authorisation in view of the fundamental rights relating to private life and data secrecy set out in items X and XII of art 5 of the federal constitution, respectively.

As stated by Professor Pedro Luís Piedade Novaes,[6] the Universal Declaration of Human Rights, signed by Brazil on 10 December 1948, provides, in art XII, that:

' . . . no one shall be subjected to arbitrary interference with his privacy, family, home or correspondence, nor to attacks upon his honour and reputation. Everyone has the right to the protection of the law against such interference or attacks.'

This is also the wording of art 11, item 2 of the American Convention of Human Rights ratified by Brazil on 25 September 1992.

Bank secrecy, therefore, is a fundamental right protected by the constitution of 1988 as an immutable clause, which may not be abolished or limited even by a constitutional amendment as provided by art 60, para 4, item IV of the federal constitution. However, legal writing and case law in Brazil state that no private liberty is absolute and that, therefore, there will be situations where two or more fundamental rights are in conflict with each other.

In order to resolve this tension between constitutional principles, one may resort to the principle of proportionality, imported from German law, which provides that, there being two constitutional principles in conflict, one must place on them an imaginary balance in order to sacrifice that of lesser social relevance. In the instant case, we find precisely such a conflict of rules: on the one hand, the individual right to bank secrecy and, on the other, the public interest, which is represented by the intent of the tax authorities to investigate a possible tax evasion or crime. One must, therefore, assess both rights in order to decide which of them shall prevail.

Initially, it is worth mentioning that the present matter is not new, there being decisions rendered by the High Court of Justice and by the federal Supreme Court, which define the rules to be followed for the breach of tax secrecy under the federal constitution of 1988.[7] The federal Supreme Court, in this regard, has already stated that the breach of bank secrecy is legal when there is a relevant public interest, such

---

5 See the appendix, Decree no 3,724, of 10 January 2001, art 3, items I–XI.
6 Professor Pedro Luis Piedade Novaes *O Sigilo Bancário e a Lei Complementar no 105/2001*, Brazilian Institute of Tax Planning Studies of the IBPT, 2001.
7 HCJ Special Appeal (1997/0075348-4), DJU 15 December 1997/Appeal in Writ of Mandamus (1988/0098502-6), Justice Fernando Gonçalves FSC (decision rendered by Justice Sepúlveda Peretende in IC no 901-6-DF, DJU 23 February 1995/Writ of Mandamus 23964-DF, reporting Justice Celso de Mello, DJU 21 June 2002).

as that of an investigation based on a reasonable suspicion of a criminal offence, provided it is duly ordered by the judiciary.[8]

Following this rationale, Celso Bastos clarifies that:

' ... the breaching of bank secrecy is only admissible when based on sound reasons, when there is a relevant public interest, such as that of a criminal investigation or criminal procedural finding of facts or by virtue of the exceptionality of the motive, provided that a judicial authorisation is rendered.'

Likewise, the High Court of Justice has decided that:

' ... the legal order authorises the breaching of bank secrecy under exceptional situations. Should it imply, however, a restraint on the citizen's privacy rights, assured by the constitutional principle, it is indispensable to evidence the necessity of the information requested with the strict compliance of the authorising legal conditions.'

According to the unanimous understanding of the federal Supreme Court, even before the enactment of Complementary Law no 105/2001, a breach of bank secrecy may only take place in two cases: (i) under a Parliamentary Inquiry Committee and (ii) upon a judicial order, provided that both situations are justified. In this regard, art 6 of Complementary Law no 105/2001, by allowing a breach of bank secrecy without judicial authorisation, diverges from the present understanding of the federal Supreme Court. For this reason, it may not be admitted to Brazil's legal system as it breaches art 5, items X and XII of the federal constitution.

For discussion purposes only, even if Complementary Law no 105/2001 provided for the breach of bank secrecy upon judicial authorisation, such rule would only be valid for an investigation of tax crimes and not in the case of administrative proceedings aimed at ascertaining tax credits in favour of the Treasury. This is because, applying the principle of proportionality, bank secrecy must only be breached for the investigation of crimes as this public interest is deemed to be more important than the privacy rights of the individual or legal entity.

It is worth pointing out that governmental assurances that a breach of bank secrecy shall be carried out prudently, responsibly and under the rules set out by Decree no 3,724/2001 are not convincing and do not have the power to change art 6 of Complementary Law no 105/2001 into a provision protected by the constitution.

In Brazil's legal system, it is widely accepted that a breach of bank secrecy may only be decreed by a judicial order or in cases (within limits) where other bodies are, by express mention of the federal constitution, held equivalent to the judiciary, as is the case of Parliamentary Inquiry Committees (art 58, para 3 of the federal constitution). It should be noted that the federal constitution does not, in any of its articles, grant to the federal Revenue Office the status of a body equivalent to the judiciary. For this reason, a breach of bank secrecy, as provided by art 6 of Complementary Law no 105/2001, is invalid without the authorisation of the judiciary, otherwise the preparation of a law regulating the breach of bank secrecy would not be necessary as the federal Revenue Office already has the means to catch tax evaders by way of a joint action with the Public Prosecution which would require the disclosure of bank

---

8 FSC, Writ of Mandamus no 21.729-4 DF, DJU 19 October 2001.

secrets in court. This would not be unconstitutional as it is in agreement with the current understanding of the federal Supreme Court regarding bank secrecy.

In short, if the government intends to adopt measures aimed at fighting tax evasion, it must first respect the federal constitution, otherwise it will be at risk of being worse than the persons it is investigating. While tax evaders are breaking the law, the government (including the legislative and executive powers) would be breaching the federal constitution and international treaties ratified by Brazil.

Unless the federal Supreme Court drastically changes its understanding, which was confirmed by nine out of the 11 justices constituting part of its present plenary composition, a breach of bank secrecy without judicial authorisation must be declared unconstitutional as it breaches items X and XII of art 5 of the federal constitution.

LEGAL LIMITS

[5.7]   In Brazil, there are several limitations on the public decree for lifting bank secrecy. When there was not any express law on the matter, information on the personal and private life of citizens was not provided. Compulsory disclosure was only admitted in special cases and with due care.

The limits of bank secrecy may only be established by a complementary law of the Union and, therefore, only another complementary law of the Union may provide for their exceptions, in addition to those already in existence. Municipal or state laws may not regulate this matter. A law which admits exceptions to general rules, or restricts rights, only covers the cases it specifies. Hence, banks may only provide public authorities with the information permitted by law, in the manner provided by such law, under penalty of breach of the obligation and consequent imposition of sanctions.

The legal restrictions on bank secrecy may not be used for the purpose of carrying out an investigation into a citizen's private life. The breach of secrecy, when so ordered, must be restricted to the period which is being investigated. This is because the public interest which is being protected by the decree of breach of secrecy may not breach human dignity, which is fundamental to the maintenance of the state and to society.

The state, in the exercise of its jurisdictional function, very often needs to investigate facts in order to render a just solution to the case under analysis. However, such facts may, time and again, be covered by bank secrecy, thus preventing the solution of the case by the judiciary. For such reason, the legislation in force requires banks to provide information to the judiciary. Bank secrecy may only cover the just and legitimate interests of the client. Any illicit interest would represent an injury to third parties and, therefore, legal conscience may not protect it under the veil of secrecy.

With the enactment of Complementary Law no 105/2001, the authorities and tax agents of the Union, state, federal district and municipalities may only examine documents, books and registrations of financial institutions, including those relating to deposit accounts and investments, when an administrative procedure is commenced or a tax proceeding is in progress and when such examinations are considered to be indispensable by the competent administrative authority.

The result of the examinations, information and documents referred to by this article shall be kept secret with due regard to the tax legislation (art 6 and sole paragraph of

Complementary Law no 105/2001). According to Decree no 3,724/2001, which regulates art 6 of Complementary Law no 105/2001, the examination of the information breaching bank secrecy may only take place when there is an inspection proceeding in progress and when such examinations are deemed absolutely necessary.

The inspection proceeding will only commence by virtue of an express order contained in a writ of tax proceeding by a tax auditor of the federal Revenue Office. However, in cases of obvious breach of tax legislation which may jeopardise the interests of the Treasury, the inspection proceeding must be commenced immediately and, within five days of the date of commencement, a special writ of tax proceeding shall be issued and the investigated party shall be officially informed. According to Professor Gilberto Marques Bruno,[9] such provisions render taxpayers vulnerable to the inspection proceeding, which allows public agents to examine financial transactions.

Even if we take into account the fact that a breach of secrecy in financial institutions' transactions helps the federal government fight tax evasion, we may question the admissibility of a complementary law granting the tax authorities powers of verification of secret data and information, which, hitherto, could only be disclosed upon the intervention and approval of the judiciary, with the appearance of a total breach of the Principle of Inviolability of Data Secrecy, consecrated by item X of art 5 of the federal constitution, as mentioned above. More than simply a governmental instrument designed to fight tax evasion, the authority contained in Complementary Law no 105/2001 and regulated by Decree no 3,724/2001 may become a mechanism to satisfy the requirements of the tax authorities resulting in a real invasion of taxpayers' privacy.

NATURAL LIMITS

[5.8] The natural limits of bank secrecy arise either from the wishes of the holder of the secrets or from the nature of banking transactions, or, in addition, from the rules of civil law. They indicate to what extent a bank is authorised to disclose the secrets without breaching its duty.

The natural limits must be sought mainly in the rules of civil law. If there is any doubt, the obligation of secrecy must prevail. For financial institutions, it is preferable to deny the information and let the interested party go to the courts to obtain the information, rather than to inform and risk breaching the secrecy and then becoming subject to criminal, administrative and civil penalties.

Without breaching bank secrecy, the bank may and must supply to the client information regarding his current account, such as balance, credits and debts, copies of cheques drawn, name of the person who paid an instrument of credit to his benefit with the establishment, etc. However, the bank must not disclose more than is necessary for compliance with its power. This means that it must not disclose facts which do not concern its obligation, under penalty of breaching the privacy of a third party and thus being held liable.

In the event of representatives or attorneys of the client, it is necessary that the bank analyses, on a case-by-case basis, the powers granted in the power of attorney to the

---

9 Professor Bruno *Quebra do Sigilo Bancário*, Estudos IBPT, Instituto Brasileiro de Planejamento Tributário, 2001.

attorney-in-fact. For example, if the attorney-in-fact was only given powers to open a current account, there would be no reason for giving him access to subsequent business information concerning the client. In relation to legal entities, only those vested with representation powers may share the secret information. In Brazilian law, partners do not have access to secret information and any wish to exercise their right to such information must proceed in accordance with the provision of art 18 of the Commercial Code.

In the case of heirs and successors, they may have access to information protected by bank secrecy as they may need such information in order to carry on the business and safeguard their own interests. However, such access must be limited to strictly patrimonial information. Information that is not necessary to safeguard the patrimonial interests of the heirs must not be undisclosed.

The client of the bank may authorise it to supply information to third parties and the bank may not decline to do so. This is due to the fact that the obligation of secrecy exists in order to preserve the privacy of the client and it would not be reasonable that it reached the point of imposing itself against the will of the protected party. Only the protected party may select the information which must remain secret. There are circumstances where a client may have reason to disclose certain information about his banking transactions (such as the number of transactions, dates, balance in current account, etc) in order to evidence his financial standing.

With regard to marital relationships, bank secrecy applies to spouses, even if the information is necessary to proceed with a conjugal separation. In such cases, the interested party must resort to the judiciary.

Bank accounts in Brazil may also be 'joint' (where several persons hold an account). In such cases, each holder has the right to be informed of the patrimonial character relative to the operation of the bank account because each act practiced by a holder affects the others. The bank must inform each holder of the balance of the current account, cheques drawn, withdrawals and deposits made, etc. However, personal information of a holder which does not relate to the operation of the current account must not be supplied to the other holder without due authorisation.

Finally, in litigation between a bank and its client, the financial institution may disclose any and all information regarding the client with the purpose of avoiding harm or damage. However, the bank may only disclose facts strictly necessary to the defence of its rights and must not disclose those facts of which it has knowledge and which do not benefit the bank and cause harm to the client.

BANKING INFORMATION

[5.9]   Banks hold important information concerning the private and patrimonial profile of a person and which may contribute to the regularisation of the financial system. However, they have the right to be silent by virtue of the secrecy which they are committed to respect. The supply of information may conflict with the obligation of secrecy. Information requested by third parties and by other banking establishments may only be supplied upon authorisation of the client; without authorisation, the bank must deny information to whomsoever is requesting it. If the financial institution has filed a lawsuit against the client or declared an instrument of credit representing a debt, this becomes public knowledge and, therefore, the bank may state that a client is in default. With the exception of this case, the bank has the duty to be silent, given that one of its main virtues is discretion.

With regard to the issue of secrecy, there is an interesting question: with respect to the central bank, would such prohibition be valid, taking into account that the banks' obligation of secrecy extends to all and may only be disclosed upon a judicial order? The answer is 'yes'. According to art 2 of Complementary Law no 105/2001, the duty of secrecy applies to the central bank in relation to the transactions it carries out and to the information it obtains in the exercise of its functions.

The secrecy, including information regarding deposit accounts and investments held with financial institutions, may not be detrimental to the central bank in the performance of its functions of inspection encompassing the investigation of illegal acts by controlling parties, administrators, members of boards, managers, attorneys and representatives of financial institutions, not even while proceeding to an inquiry into a financial investigation submitted to a special regime (art 2, para 1 of Complementary Law no 105/2001).

The commissions charged with the inquiries may examine any documents relative to the assets, rights and obligations of financial institutions, its controlling parties, administrators, members of boards, attorneys, managers and representatives, including current accounts and transactions with other financial institutions.

The bank has the obligation to inform the central bank of the amount of its transactions, assets, liabilities, etc. However, this is related to the inspection power held by the central bank. It does not have the power to breach bank secrecy, which is a rule of public order. Allowing the central bank to obtain any and all information from the financial institutions would mean granting the state, by means of a supervision body, the permission to investigate in full the private transactions of banks' clients. Therefore, there is bank secrecy before the central bank, which, being a financial institution itself, must comply with such legal provision.

MONEY LAUNDERING

[5.10] Criminal offences taken into consideration which characterise money laundering are the hiding and/or disguising of the nature, origin, location, handling, disposal or ownership of the assets, rights or values directly or indirectly arising from drug trafficking, terrorism, extortion from kidnapping, smuggling or gun running, crimes against the public administration as a whole – including the state, private/public companies, foundations, etc – and crimes against the financial system, as well as those performed by criminal organisations. Likewise, the conversion of such assets, rights or values into legitimate assets, their acquisition, receipt, exchange, safeguarding, deposit, handling or transfer is also considered to be a criminal offence characterising money laundering. The import or export of goods with a false value constitutes money laundering, as well as the use of assets, values or rights which knowingly originate from any of the above-mentioned crimes.

It is important to emphasise that, on the basis of the current money laundering legislation, there is no typification of money laundering crime without the so-called 'precedent' crimes, which are those listed above. However, in order to cover this gap left by the law, the National Congress is examining a federal Bill stating that major criminal activities with serious ramifications, such as tax fraud and human trafficking, among others, may be deemed indicative of money laundering. This is different from what currently happens when only the crimes provided in art 1 of Law no 9,613/1998 constitute money laundering offences. Following the approval of the referred federal Bill, any serious crime may also be indicative of money laundering.

Law no 9,613, of 3 March 1998 (the Money Laundering Law), defined the crime of money laundering and created the Council of Financial Activities ('COAF') with the function of gathering information on illegal transactions. The circumstances and obligations which give rise to a suspicious transaction report by legal entities exercising activity related to the investment of financial resources, such as financial institutions, stock exchanges, commodities and forwards exchanges, insurers and insurance brokers, credit card companies, etc listed by the National Law of Money Laundering Prevention (Law no 9,613/1998), are those which may constitute serious indications of the crimes in the above-mentioned law, are reasonably grounded and based on investigations made by the competent authorities (the federal and civil police and the General Attorney Office). Such legal entities, in addition to identifying their clients and maintaining updated records, shall notify, without telling their clients, the relevant authorities (which, in this case, is the COAF) of all transactions in local or foreign currency, securities, credit securities, metals or any assets capable of being converted into cash which exceed R$100,000, such limit being determined by the COAF.

Should the legal entities fail to comply with their obligations and not report such suspicious transactions, under the terms of the current legislation, the competent authorities will impose the following penalties: (i) a summons, (ii) a variable fine or (iii) temporary disqualification of the legal entities as determined by the National Law of Money Laundering Prevention.

Such information, besides breaching bank secrecy, disregards the general right to privacy set out by art 5, item X of the federal constitution and makes banks subject to civil liability, in addition to other penalties. In the present writer's view, the administrative regime of passing on information (without being submitted to the approval of the judiciary), which the Money Laundering Law intended to create, is unconstitutional. Specifically, there has been no kind of challenge or judicial action against the money laundering legislation since its enactment in mid-1998. After research in the High Courts, we have found no legal suit challenging the legality or constitutionality of the National Law of Money Laundering Prevention. Specific actions, filed by individuals and/or legal entities, challenged the classification of their behaviour as money laundering without, however, discussing the validity of the legislation against money laundering itself.

GAFI/FATF

[5.11] On its tenth anniversary, in June 1999, the GAFI/Financial Action Task Force ('FATF') invited three Latin American countries to join the group, one of which was Brazil. In order to do so, however, such countries would have to commit themselves to follow the 40 recommendations of the GAFI/FATF, actively perform a regional leadership role and be subject to a mutual evaluation process. The evaluation process in Brazil involved, initially, the completion of a detailed questionnaire on the country's action on preventing money laundering. The second step consisted of a visit by the GAFI/FATF experts to the cities of Brasília, São Paulo and Rio de Janeiro in 2000 to examine in detail the money laundering prevention policies and measures effectively implemented in the country. In June 2000, a final report was officially submitted to the GAFI/FATF headquarters in Paris concerning the evaluation of Brazil and the approval of the country.

Brazil is currently an active participant of the Work Group on terrorism finance, the Europe and Americas Review Group for non-co-operative countries and territories, the Review Group of the 40 recommendations and presides over the ad hoc Americas Group of the GAFI/FATF. The work developed by Brazil is widely recognised by the international community in money laundering prevention, the GAFI/FATF having acknowledged in their annual reports of 2001 and 2002 the conformity of Brazil with its 40 recommendations, which attest to the good image of the country in that regard. However, in spite of observing the official recommendations of the GAFI/FATF, Brazil still shows some deficiencies in preventing money laundering, such as corruption in public and private institutions, which hinders the action of the relevant authorities and honest people who aim to remove the blemish of money laundering from the country.

Recommendation 4 of the GAFI/FATF states that countries shall ensure that their rules on bank/financial secrecy do not hinder the imposition of the GAFI'FATF's 40 recommendations. From such provision (recommendation 4), it is evident that the National Law of Money Laundering Prevention does not, at any time, create obstacles to the GAFI/FATF recommendations because, having been enacted after publication of the recommendations, Law no 9,613/1998 was prepared specifically to ensure observance with the 40 recommendations and not to challenge or prevail over them. However, in spite of this noble intention of the legislature, it seems that, in trying to adopt the GAFI/FATF recommendations as soon as possible, certain rules modifying the money laundering legislation have breached constitutional provisions in clear disregard of the federal constitution.

LEGAL GUARANTEE

[5.12]   A legal rule usually provides, in principle, for a penalty previously established for cases of non-compliance. Such penalty is imposed on the person or on their assets and has the purpose of remedying the injury caused by non-compliance with the duty. The penalty brings the external force and coercion necessary for the effectiveness of the right. It is the extreme method to which the state has to resort in order to obtain due regard to the rules of behaviour. The penalty also works psychologically on the public as, generally, people comply with the obligation in order to avoid the penalty.

Penalties can be criminal or civil. Criminal penalties have a repressive or punitive character and civil penalties are for the purpose of reparation, but both have a preventive nature, since ordinary people do not wish the imposition of penalties of a restrictive nature on their personal or patrimonial freedom.

With regard to bank secrecy, the law provides for a criminal and administrative penalty in the event of non-compliance. The breach is punished with a penalty of imprisonment from one to four years and a fine of up to 200 times the highest minimum wage in force in Brazil.

PREVENTIVE RELIEF

[5.13]   Avoiding the breach is the best protection that can be given to bank secrecy. The trouble caused by the breach of an interest is a wrong which the legal system can hardly reinstate satisfactorily. Preventive relief is the most efficient protection of personal rights and especially the right to privacy, which, as any right, exists to be exercised. In Brazilian law, there is no specific measure for the preventive protection of privacy, nor of bank secrecy.

However, in Brazil's legal system, there are writs of prevention with the purpose of ensuring the efficacy of executive measures provisionally supporting a right which, in principle, seems unquestionable until the merits are finally decided. The writ of prevention has the purpose of ensuring the proper progress of the main lawsuit which was filed or will be filed ensuring its function of settlement of the litigation or of satisfaction of the credit. Therefore, the writ of prevention is a legal instrument used in order to avoid an injury.

The Brazilian Code of Civil Procedure allows a judge to determine the writs of prevention or provisional measures which he deems proper in order to maintain the entire and unassailable juridical right intended by the parties when there is a fair and justified fear that one of the parties will cause, prior to the final decision, severe harm to the other party's right, which is difficult to be repaired.

There are two indispensable requisites of the writs of prevention: the *periculum in mora* and the *fumus boni iuris*. The first is the possibility of damage resulting from the delay in the final judgment of the issue and the second is the probability of the existence of the right by the claimant. As a rule, both requisites are present in the case of a breach of bank secrecy. The breach of bank secrecy represents severe harm as it offends one of the most valuable personal rights. Such harm is difficult to remedy, mainly in relation to moral damage, and for this reason it is preferable to prevent than to compensate. The writ of prevention seeks the preventive defence of the right protected by bank secrecy, both in its patrimonial and in its exclusively moral aspects. However, in order to prevent injury by means of a writ of prevention, the party wishing to preserve the secrecy should also file a main lawsuit, which may be an indemnification or a merely declaratory lawsuit.

REPARATION OF DAMAGE

[5.14]   Article 186 of the New Civil Code protects any and all subjective rights and imposes the obligation of indemnification by a party which caused damages to third parties. By imposing civil liability on the person responsible, the legislator protects bank secrecy, not only for the right of reparation assured to the injured party, but also for the unfavourable situation imposed on the person responsible, as he is required to remedy the damage. Such an obligation holds back the person responsible from committing the breach again and discourages others from committing the same breach. Civil liability repairs the damage or, at least, attempts to mitigate the consequences.

In order to define the illicit behaviour justifying a penalty, one must verify what the breach consists of. Breaching is the action of disclosing the information under secrecy, thus causing an undue invasion of a party's privacy. With the breach of bank secrecy, privacy, which is a protected juridical right, is damaged due to the acknowledgement or disclosure of protected information and facts. The disclosure may be made directly or indirectly, in writing, orally or even by gestures.

However, not every disclosure made by a bank is a breach of bank secrecy as there may be reasons that justify it. In order to render the bank liable, the disclosure must be against the law, ie must be in absolute non-compliance with the legal system. Otherwise, such behaviour is legal and does not imply the burden of indemnification. Its liability shall only be excepted upon evidence that the damage occurred by virtue of *force majeure*, legitimate self-defence or by virtue of strict compliance with a legal duty.

Upon the occurrence of damage, the relevant indemnification, for which the re-establishment of a state or situation under the law is intended, must be provided for, with the purpose of erasing the effects of the illegal behaviour. It must be sufficiently wide to cover the whole damage arising from non-compliance with the obligation.

We may define 'damage' as any harm to a juridical right, which may mean goods, provisions, features of the person and products of the mind. With regard to the breach of bank secrecy, the indemnification must cover the material damage, as well as extra-patrimonial damage.

Material damages are relatively easy to ascertain, whether upon comparison with other goods of the same type or upon evaluation made by experts on the matter. On the other hand, in the event of non-material damages, the indemnification is at the judge's discretion, which may be significant to the extent of being symbolic, and therefore inefficient, or excessive, causing an unlawful enrichment. Alternatively, extra-patrimonial damages, especially those arising from a breach of the right to privacy, honour and image, are assured by art 5 of Brazil's constitution. Due to the difficulty in evaluating the extent of such types of damage in order to establish an indemnification, such compensation, under Brazilian law, is fixed by arbitration based on the judge's criteria.

Under Brazilian law, it is not necessary to evidence moral damages. The judge is likely to presume them, ie to consider their occurrence until there is evidence to the contrary. The burden of proof, in the event of a breach of bank secrecy, rests with the offender, who must show the non-existence of damage, thus reversing the presumption.

The indemnification lawsuit for the occurrence of breach of bank secrecy may only be filed by the client of the bank or by an authorised third party. Being a private interest, the compensation of the damage caused may not be claimed by members of the Public Prosecution or determined by the judge's own initiative. In cases where the breach of bank secrecy applies to more than one person (a plausible situation), each holder has the right to claim reparation of the damage individually suffered. Therefore, the compensations are distinct and may be claimed in independent lawsuits.

CONCLUSION

[5.15] The Brazilian legal system has established that breaching bank secrecy may only be decreed by a judicial decision (within the limits already mentioned) and where other bodies, by express reference of the federal constitution, are held equivalent to the judiciary, such as Parliamentary Inquiry Committees (art 58, para 3 of the federal constitution.)

An example which corroborates this is the amendment to Decree no 4,489, of 28 November 2002, after a great deal of pressure from both lawyers and the public, as provided by Decree no 4,545, of 26 December 2002. The first Decree (no 4,498/2002), which complemented the regulation of the utilisation of information covered by bank secrecy for the purposes of inspection by the federal Revenue Office, allowed indiscriminate access by the federal Revenue Office to information regarding the financial operations of all clients involving, within a one-month period, amounts in excess of R$5,000 (for individuals) and R$10,000 (for legal entities). Financial institutions were obliged to send such information to the tax authorities on a monthly basis from 1 January 2003.

Displeased with the content of this Decree, the Brazilian Bar Association issued an opinion pointing out the defaults of legality and unconstitutionality of the first Decree, which contributed to the enactment of a new Decree (no 4,545/2002) revoking the first one and excluded the financial institutions' obligation to send information on their clients to the tax authorities.

Notwithstanding the enactment of the new Decree, the federal Revenue Office may still have access to financial institutions' clients, however, without the facility granted by Decree no 4,489/2002, as it must request such information from the financial institutions by means of a filing of the relevant administrative or tax procedure.

Finally, it is worth mentioning again that, being an extremely invasive action, a breach of bank secrecy may not take place without the approval of the judiciary. The unjustified investigation into someone's private life is incompatible with the fundamental rights assured by the federal constitution. It remains clear, therefore, that the measure under discussion may only be justified on the grounds of strong evidence or clearly-defined indications of irregularities capable of giving good reason for the adoption of such extreme measures.

The Appendix below contains relevant extracts from Brazilian legislation.

APPENDIX

Complementary Law no 105, of 10 January 2001

On the secrecy of transactions of financial institutions and other matters

[5.16]

THE PRESIDENT OF THE REPUBLIC

I hereby state that the National Congress has decreed and I sign the following Complementary Law:

Article 1. The financial institutions shall maintain the secrecy of their active and passive transactions and services rendered.

Paragraph 1 – For the purposes of this Complementary Law, the following are considered financial institutions:

I   banks of any kind;
II   distributors of securities;
III   exchange and securities brokers;
IV   companies of credit, financing and investments;
V   companies of real estate credit;
VI   administrators of credit cards;
VII   leasing companies;
VIII   administrators of the over-the-counter organised market;
IX   credit unions;
X   associations of savings and loans;
XI   stock exchanges and futures and commodities exchanges;
XII   entities of liquidation and clearance;
XIII   other companies which, by virtue of the nature of their transactions, may be so
       considered by the National Monetary Council.

Paragraph 2 – Companies of commercial stimulation or factoring, for the purposes of this Complementary Law, shall comply with the rules applicable to the financial institutions set out in paragraph 1.

Paragraph 3 – The following do not represent a breach of the duty of secrecy:

I   the exchange of information between and among financial institutions, for records purposes, including classification of risk, in compliance with the rules enacted by the National Monetary Council and the Central Bank of Brazil;

II the supply of information mentioned in registrations of drawers of bad cheques and debtors in default, to entities of credit protection, in compliance with the rules enacted by the National Monetary Council and the Central Bank of Brazil;

III the supply of the information referred to in paragraph 2, article 11 of Law no 9,311, of 24 October 1996;

IV the information, to the competent authorities, of the practice of criminal or administrative breaches, encompassing the supply of information on transactions which involve funds arising from any criminal action;

V   the disclosure of secret information with the express consent of the interested parties;

VI the provision of information in the terms and conditions set out in articles 2, 3, 4, 5, 6, 7 and 9 of this Complementary Law.

Paragraph 4 – The breaching of secrecy may be decreed when necessary for the investigation or the occurrence of any illicit act, in any phase of the inquiry or judicial procedure, and especially in the following crimes:

I   terrorism;
II   illicit trafficking of narcotics or similar drugs;
III contraband or trafficking of weapons, ammunition or material designed for their production;
IV   extortion from kidnapping;
V   against the national financial system;
VI   against the public administration;
VII against the tax regime and social security;
VIII laundering of money or the disguising of goods, rights and values;
IX   practices by a criminal organisation.

Article 2. The duty of secrecy is extended to the Central Bank of Brazil in relation to the transactions it carries out and to the information it obtains in the exercise of its functions.

Paragraph 1 –Secrecy, including deposit accounts and investments held with financial institutions, may not be opposed to the Central Bank of Brazil:

I   in the performance of its functions of inspection, encompassing the investigation, at any time, of illegal acts practiced by controlling parties, administrators, members of boards, managers, attorneys and representatives of financial institutions;

II while proceeding to an inquiry in a financial investigation submitted to special regime.

Paragraph 2 – The commissions charged with the inquiries mentioned by item II of paragraph 1 may examine any documents relative to the assets, rights and obligations of financial institutions, of its controlling parties, administrators, members of boards, managers, attorneys and representatives, including current accounts and transactions with other financial institutions.

Paragraph 3 – The provision of this article applies to the Securities and Exchange Commission in cases of inspection of transactions and services in the securities market, including financial institutions which are listed companies.

Paragraph 4 – The Central Bank of Brazil and the Securities and Exchange Commission, in their areas of competence, may execute conventions:

I   with other public bodies monitoring financial institutions, with the purpose of carrying out joint inspections in compliance with their respective responsibilities;
II   with central banks or inspection entities of other countries, seeking:
     a)   the inspection of branches and subsidiaries of foreign financial institutions operating in Brazil and branches and subsidiaries abroad of Brazilian financial institutions;
     b)   the mutual co-operation and exchange of information for the investigation of activities or transactions which imply the investment, negotiation, disguising or transfer of financial assets and securities in connection with the practice of illicit acts.

Paragraph 5 – The duty of secrecy provided by this Complementary Law shall be extended to the inspection entities mentioned in paragraph 4 and their agents.

Paragraph 6 – The Central Bank of Brazil, the Securities and Exchange Commission and the other inspection entities, in their areas of competence, shall provide to the Council of Financial Activities (COAF) mentioned in article 14 of Law no 9,613, of 3 March 1998, information on the registration and operation of amounts relative to the transactions set out in item I, article 11 of the mentioned Law.

Article 3. The Central Bank of Brazil, the Securities and Exchange Commission and the financial institutions shall provide information required by the judiciary, preserving their secret character by means of restricting access by the parties, which may not use them for purposes foreign to the proceeding.

Paragraph 1 – The providing of information and supply of secret documents requested by a commission of administrative inquiry destined to ascertain the liability of a public servant for breaches committed in the exercise of their functions, or which is connected to the functions of their office, is dependent upon on the prior authorisation of the judiciary.

Paragraph 2 – In the cases in paragraph 1, the requirement of breaching secrecy does not depend on the existence of a judicial procedure in progress.

Paragraph 3 – In addition to the cases set out in this article, the Central Bank of Brazil and the Securities and Exchange Commission shall provide to the Attorney General of the Union the information and documents necessary to the defence of the Union in lawsuits in which it is involved.

Article 4. The Central Bank of Brazil and the Securities and Exchange Commission, in their areas of responsibility, and the financial institution shall provide to the federal legislature the secret information which is necessary to the exercise of their respective constitutional and legal functions.

Paragraph 1 – The Parliamentary Inquiry Committees, in the exercise of their constitutional and legal responsibility of investigation, shall obtain the secret information and documents which they need, directly from the financial institutions, or through the intermediation of the Central Bank of Brazil or the Securities and Exchange Commission.

Paragraph 2 – The requests mentioned in this article must be previously approved by the Plenary Session of the Deputies Chamber, of the federal Senate, or of the plenary of their respective Parliamentary Inquiry Committees.

Article 5. The executive power shall regulate, including the timing and limits of amount, the criteria according to which the financial institutions shall inform the tax administration of the Union the financial transactions carried out by the users of their services.

Paragraph 1 – For the purposes of this article, the following are considered financial transactions:

I   deposits in cash and on credit, including in savings accounts;
II   payments made in currency or cheques;
III   issuance of orders of credit or similar documents;
IV   redemptions in accounts of deposits in cash or on credit, including savings;
V   loan agreements;
VI   cashing trade acceptance bills, promissory notes and other credit instruments;
VII   purchases and sales of fixed-income/variable-income securities;
VIII   investment funds;
IX   purchases of foreign currency;
X   conversions of foreign currency into national currency;
XI   transfers abroad of currency and other assets;
XII   transactions with gold as a financial asset;
XIII   transactions with credit cards;
XIV   transactions of leasing; and
XV   any other transactions of a similar nature which may be authorised by the Central Bank of Brazil, Securities and Exchange Commission or other competent body.

Paragraph 2 – The information transferred as provided in the caput of this article shall be restricted to data related to the identification of the makers of the transactions and the aggregate amounts operated monthly, it being forbidden for the insertion of any element which allows the identification of their origin or the nature of the expenses made.

Paragraph 3 – Financial transactions carried out by the direct and indirect administrations of the Union, of the states, of the federal district and of the municipalities are not included in the information referred to in this article.

Paragraph 4 – Upon receipt of the information referred to in this article, should any indications of falsification, omission or tax breaches be detected, the interested authority may request the information and documents it may need, as well as carry out an inspection or audit for a proper investigation of the facts.

Paragraph 5 – The information referred to in this article shall be maintained under tax secrecy, as provided by the legislation in force.

Article 6. The authorities and tax agents of the Union, state, federal district and municipalities may only examine documents, books and registrations of financial institutions, including those relating to deposit accounts and financial investments, when an administrative procedure has commenced or a tax proceeding is in progress and when such examinations are considered necessary by the competent administrative authority.

Sole Paragraph – The result of the examinations, information and documents referred to by this article shall be kept secret, with due regard to the tax legislation.

Article 7. Without prejudice to the provision of paragraph 3 of article 2, the Securities and Exchange Commission, upon the commencement of an administrative inquiry, may request from the competent judiciary authority the disclosure, from financial institutions, of information and documents relating to assets, rights and obligations of an individual or legal entity submitted to its regulatory power.

Sole Paragraph – The Central Bank of Brazil and the Securities and Exchange Commission shall maintain a permanent exchange of information on the results of the inspections they carry out, the inquiries they make and the penalties they impose, whenever the information is necessary for the performance of their activities.

Article 8. Compliance with the requirements and formalities set out in articles 4, 6 and 7 shall be expressly declared by the competent authorities in the requests addressed to the Central Bank of Brazil, the Securities and Exchange Commission or the financial institutions.

Article 9. Whenever the Central Bank of Brazil and the Securities and Exchange Commission, in the exercise of their functions, verify the occurrence of a crime defined by law, or indications of the practice of such crimes, they shall inform the Public Prosecution, adding to the communication the documents necessary to the investigation or evidencing the facts.

Paragraph 1 – The communication mentioned in this article shall be made by the Presidents of the Central Bank of Brazil and the Securities and Exchange Commission, the delegation of competence being admitted, within a maximum term of 15 days from the receipt of the procedure, with the opinion of the respective legal departments.

Paragraph 2 – Regardless of the provision of the caput of this article, the Central Bank of Brazil and the Securities and Exchange Commission shall inform the competent public bodies of the irregularities and administrative illicit acts of which they have knowledge, or indications of their practice, enclosing the relevant documents.

Article 10. Breaching secrecy, with the exception of the cases authorised in this Complementary Law, constitutes a crime and makes those responsible liable to imprisonment, from one to four years, and a fine, with the application of the Criminal Code, as the case may be, without prejudice to other applicable penalties.

Sole Paragraph – All who omit, unreasonably delay or unlawfully render information required in the terms of this Complementary Law are subject to the same penalties.

Article 11. A public servant who utilises or causes the utilisation of any information obtained as a consequence of breaching secrecy provided by this Complementary Law is personally and directly liable for the consequent damages, without prejudice to the objective liability of the public entity, should it be evidenced that the servant acted in an official capacity.

Article 12. This Complementary Law shall become effective as of the date of its publication.

Article 13. Article 38 of Law no 4,595, of 31 December 1964, is hereby revoked.

Brasilia, 10 January 2001; 180th of the Independence and 113th of the Republic.
FERNANDO HENRIQUE CARDOSO
José Gregori; Pedro Malan; Martus Tavares

Decree no 3,724, of 10 January 2001

Regulates article 6 of Complementary Law no 105, of 10 January 2001, relative to the request, access and utilisation, by the federal Revenue Office, of information regarding transactions and services of financial institutions and equivalent entities

[5.17]

THE PRESIDENT OF THE REPUBLIC, empowered by item IV of the constitution, and in view of the provision of Complementary Law no 105, of 10 January 2001, decrees:

Article 1. This Decree provides, in the terms of article 6 of Complementary Law no 105, of 10 January 2001, for the request, access and utilisation, by the federal Revenue Office, of information regarding transactions and services of financial institutions and entities held equivalent thereto, in compliance with article 1, paragraphs 1 and 2 of the mentioned Law, as well as establishes procedures to preserve the secrecy of the information obtained.

Article 2. The federal Revenue Office, through a servant holding the function of tax auditor of the federal Revenue, may only examine information relative to third parties, mentioned in documents, books and registrations of financial institutions and of entities held equivalent thereto, including those relating to accounts of deposits and financial investments, when an inspection proceeding is in progress and when such examinations are considered necessary.

Paragraph 1 – An inspection proceeding shall be deemed to be the method of tax proceeding referred to by articles 7 and so on of Decree no 70,235, of 6 March 1972, which provides for the tax administrative procedure.

Paragraph 2 – The inspection proceeding shall only commence by virtue of a specific order called a Writ of Tax Proceeding (MPF), instituted by an act of the federal Revenue Office, with the exception of the provisions of paragraphs 3 and 4 of this article.

Paragraph 3 – In obvious cases of contraband, improper clearance or any other breach of the tax legislation, where the delay of the beginning of the tax proceeding may jeopardise the interests of the national Treasury, due to the possibility of the destruction of the evidence, the tax auditor of the federal Revenue shall immediately commence an inspection proceeding and, within five days from the date of commencement, a special MPF shall be issued, by means of which the investigated party shall be officially informed.

Paragraph 4 – The MPF shall not be required in cases of inspection proceedings which are:

I   carried out during customs clearance;
II   internal (customs review);
III   relating to contraband and improper clearance, carried out in an extensive operation;
IV   relating to tax returns (tax inspections).

Paragraph 5 – For the purposes of this article, the MPF must comply with the following:

I   the competent tax authority issuing the MPF shall be the holder of the office of

General Co-ordinator, Superintendent, Delegate or Inspector or member of the federal Revenue Office;

II it shall contain, at a minimum, the following information:
  a) the amount of the tax or contribution relating to the inspection proceeding, as well as the corresponding period of assessment;
  b) the term of the inspection proceeding, extendable at the discretion of the authority which issued the MPF;
  c) name and enrolment number of the tax auditors of the federal Revenue responsible for the performance of the MPF;
  d) name, telephone number and office address of the chief of the tax auditors of the federal Revenue mentioned in the previous indent;
  e) name, enrolment number and signature of the authority which issued the MPF;
  f) internet access code which shall allow the investigated subject, target of the inspection proceeding, to identify the MPF.

Paragraph 6 – The examination referred to in the caput shall not apply to the inspection proceeding mentioned in item IV of paragraph 4 of this article.

Article 3. The examinations referred to in the caput of the previous article shall only be considered necessary in the following cases:

I   undervaluation of the amounts of transactions, including foreign trade, purchase or sale of goods or rights, based on corresponding market prices;
II   obtaining of loans from non-financial legal entities or individuals, when the investigated subject fails to provide proof of the resources;
III transactions with individuals or legal entities resident or domiciled in a country which meets the conditions set out in article 24 of Law no 9,430, of 27 December 1996;
IV   omission of net revenue or gains arising from financial investments of fixed or variable income;
V   amounts or investments in excess of available revenue;
VI   remittance abroad, for any reason, by means of a non-resident account, of amounts incompatible with declared revenue;
VII cases set out in article 33 of Law no 9,430, of 1996;
VIII legal entities classified, under the National Corporate Taxpayers' Register, in the register as:
  a) cancelled;
  b) unqualified, in the cases set out in article 81 of Law no 9,430, of 1996;
IX   individual not enrolled with the Individual Taxpayers' Register (CPF) or whose registration was cancelled;
X   denial, by the lawful holder of an account, of the actual holding or of responsibility for its operation;
XI   indication that the lawful holder is a representative of the actual holder.

Paragraph 1 – The provisions of items I to IV shall not apply when the differences assessed do not exceed ten per cent of the market or declared prices, as the case may be.

Paragraph 2 – It shall be deemed an indication of being a representative, for the purposes of item XI of this article, when:

I   the information relating to the investigated subject indicates a financial operation ten times in excess of declared revenue or, in the absence of an income tax return, the annual amount of the operation exceeds the limit established in item II, paragraph 3, article 42 of Law no 9,430, of 1996;

II   the record of the investigated subject with the financial institution, or entity held equivalent thereto, contains:
    a)   false information as to address, revenue or net worth; or
    b)   revenue lower than ten per cent of the annual amount of the operation.

Article 4. The information mentioned in the caput of article 2 may be requested by the competent authorities to issue the MPF.

Paragraph 1 – The request mentioned in this article shall be formalised by a document called a Request of Information on Financial Operation (RMF) and shall be addressed, as the case may be, to:

I   the President of the Central Bank of Brazil or the representative thereof;
II   the President of the Securities and Exchange Commission or the representative thereof;
III the president of the financial institution, or entity held equivalent thereto, or the representative thereof;
IV the manager of the bank branch.

Paragraph 2 – The RMF shall be preceded by a service of process on the investigated subject for the rendering of their financial information, necessary to the accomplishment of the MPF.

Paragraph 3 – The investigated subject is liable for the veracity and integrity of the information rendered, with due regard to the applicable criminal legislation.

Paragraph 4 – The information rendered by the investigated subject may be in corroboration with the institutions mentioned by article 1, including through the Central Bank of Brazil or the Securities and Exchange Commission, as well as a comparison with other information available at the federal Revenue Office.

Paragraph 5 – The RMF shall be issued based on a circumstantiated report, prepared by the tax auditor of the federal Revenue in charge of the execution of the MPF or by their immediate chief.

Paragraph 6 – In the report cited in the previous paragraph, the reason for the proposal of the issuance of the RMF must be given, which evidences, precisely and clearly, that this is a situation covered by the necessary requirement set out in the previous article, with due regard to the principle of reasonableness.

Paragraph 7 – In the RMF, at a minimum, the following must be given:

I   name or corporate name of the investigated subject, address and number of enrolment with the CPF or CNPJ;
II   identification number of the MPF to which it relates;
III the information requested and the period which the request concerns;
IV name, enrolment number and signature of the authority which issued the request;
V   name, enrolment number and office address of the tax auditors of the federal Revenue in charge of the execution of the MPF;
VI manner of presentation of the information (in paper or electronic means);
VII deadline for delivery of the information, as provided by the applicable legislation;
VIII internet access code which allows the requested institution to identify the RMF.

Paragraph 8 – The issuance of the RMF presumes the necessity of the information requested, as provided by this Decree.

Article 5. The information requested as provided by the previous article:

I   encompasses:
  - a)   data on the records of the investigated subject;
  - b)   individual amounts of debits and credits made within the period;

II   shall:
  - a)   be presented, before the deadline established in the RMF, to the authority which issued it or to the tax auditors of the federal Revenue responsible for the execution of the MPF;
  - b)   substitute the investigation proceeding in progress, with due regard to the provision of article 42 of Law no 9,430, of 1996;
  - c)   begin part of the tax administrative procedure, when it pertains to the evidence of voluntary assessment.

Paragraph 1 – The documents regarding debits and credits, in the cases set out in items VII to XI of article 3, may only be requested by means of certified copies.

Paragraph 2 – Information not used in the tax administrative procedure, in the terms of an act by the federal Revenue Office, must be returned to the investigated subject, destroyed or obliterated.

Paragraph 3 – All who omit, unreasonably delay or falsely provide to the federal Revenue Office information referred to by this article shall be liable to the penalties established by article 10, caput, of Complementary Law no 105, of 2001, without prejudice to the penalties applicable according to the tax or regulatory legislation, as the case may be.

Article 6. In compliance with the provision of article 9 of Complementary Law no 105, of 2001, the Central Bank of Brazil and the Securities and Exchange Commission, through their respective Presidents or servants delegated for a specific purpose, shall voluntarily inform the federal Revenue Office, within a maximum of 15 days, any irregularities and illicit acts of which they have knowledge, or indications of the practice thereof, enclosing the relevant documents, whenever such facts may imply a breach of the federal tax legislation.

Sole Paragraph – Non-compliance with the provision of this article constitutes an administrative and disciplinary breach by the manager or servant responsible, without prejudice to the application of the provision of article 10, caput, of Complementary Law no 105, of 2001, and other applicable civil and criminal penalties.

Article 7. The information, results of the tax examination and documents obtained by virtue of the provision of this Decree shall be kept secret, as provided by the pertinent legislation.

Paragraph 1 – The federal Revenue Office shall control access to the tax administrative procedure and, in the event of any circulation of information, a receipt shall be recorded at all times.

Paragraph 2 – In the issuance and handling of the information, the following must be complied with:

I   the information shall be sent in two sealed envelopes:
  - a)   one external, which shall contain only the name or function of the addressee and its address, without any indication of the degree of secrecy of the contents;
  - b)   one internal, on which the name and function of the addressee, its address,

the number of the MPF or the tax administrative procedure must be inscribed, and a note which clearly indicates that it deals with a secret matter;

II the internal envelope shall be sealed and its sending shall be evidenced by a receipt;

III the receipt sent to the controller of the custody of the information shall contain details of the sender, the addressee and the number of the MPF or the tax administrative procedure.

Paragraph 3 – It is incumbent upon the persons responsible for the receipt of secret documents:

I to verify and register, as the case may be, indications of any breach or irregularity in the correspondence received, informing such fact to the addressee, who shall inform the sender;

II to sign and date the receipt, as the case may be;

III to provide for the registration of the document and for the control of the handling thereof.

Paragraph 4 – The internal envelope may only be opened by the addressee or its authorised representative.

Paragraph 5 – The addressee of the secret document shall inform the sender of any indication of breach, such as erasures, errors of printing or pagination.

Paragraph 6 – Secret documents shall be stored under special conditions of safety.

Paragraph 7 – Information sent by electronic means shall of necessity be encrypted.

Article 8. The servant who utilises or allows the utilisation of any information obtained under this Decree, for a purpose or case different from that set out by law, regulation or administrative act, shall be liable for non-compliance with the official duty of complying with the legal or regulatory rules, referred to by article 116, item III of Law no 8,112, of 11 December 1990, if the facts do not imply a serious breach, without prejudice to their liability in the appropriate action of recovery and of applicable criminal liability.

Article 9. The servant who divulges, discloses or facilitates the disclosure of any information dealt with by this Decree, stored by information technology systems, records of documents or files of procedures protected by tax secrecy, which breaches the provision of article 198 of Law no 5,172, of 25 October 1966 (National Tax Code), or of article 116, item VIII of Law no 8,112, of 1990, shall be subject to the penalty of dismissal, set out by article 132, item IX of Law no 8,112, without prejudice to the applicable civil and criminal penalties.

Article 10. The servant who allows or facilitates, by the disclosure, supply or loan of a password, access by unauthorised persons to information systems, data banks, records or files of procedures which contain the information mentioned in this Decree, shall be liable, as provided by the specific legislation, without prejudice to the applicable civil and criminal penalties.

Sole Paragraph – The provision of this article also applies should the servant unduly use the restricted access.

Article 11. It is a breach by the servant of the official duties of exercising the functions of office and of compliance with legal and regulatory rules, as provided by article 116, items I and III of Law no 8,112, of 1990, without prejudice to the applicable criminal and civil liability, as provided by articles 121 to 125 of such Law, if the facts do not imply a more serious breach:

I   a failure to take due care in the storage and utilisation of their password, or lending it to another servant, however qualified they may be;
II   to access unjustifiably information systems of the federal Revenue Office, records of documents or files of procedures, which contain information protected by tax secrecy.

Article 12. The investigated subject who has suffered damage by the unlawful utilisation of the information requested, in the terms of this Decree, or for the abuse of the requiring authority, may address a petition to the General Magistrate of the federal Revenue Office, with a view to investigating the fact and, as the case may be, to imposing the applicable penalties on the servant responsible for the breach.

Article 13. The federal Revenue Office shall issue instructions necessary for the execution of the provisions of this Decree.

Article 14. This Decree shall become effective as of the date of its publication.

Brasilia, 10 January 2001; 180th of the Independence and 113th of the Republic.
FERNANDO HENRIQUE CARDOSO
Pedro Malan

Federal constitution of 1988

[5.18]

Article 5. All persons are equal before the law, without any distinction, Brazilians and foreigners residing in the country being assured of inviolability of the right to life, to liberty, to equality, to security and to property, under the following terms:

(. . .)
X   the privacy, private life, honour and image of persons are inviolable, and the right to compensation for property or moral damages resulting from their breach is ensured;
(. . .)
XII   the secrecy of correspondence and of telegraphic, data and telephone communications is inviolable, except, in the latter case, by court order, in the cases and in the manner prescribed by law for the purposes of criminal investigation or criminal procedural finding of facts.

Article 60. The constitution may be amended on the proposal of:

(. . .)

§ 4. No proposal of amendment shall be considered which is aimed at abolishing:

(. . .)

IV   individual rights and guarantees.

Law no 9,613, of 3 March 1998 (the Law on Money Laundering)

Chapter VI Customer identification and record keeping

[5.19]

Article 10. The legal entities referred to in section 9 shall:

I   identify their customers and maintain an updated record in compliance with the provisions set out by the competent authorities;
II   keep an up-to-date record of all transactions, in national and foreign currency, involving securities, bonds, credit instruments, metals, or any asset that may be converted into cash, and that exceeds an amount set by the competent authorities and in accordance with the requirements they may issue;
III comply with notices sent by the Council established under section 14, within the time period stipulated by the competent judicial authority. The judicial proceedings pertaining to such matters shall be conducted in a confidential manner.

Paragraph 1 – In the event that the customer is a legal entity, the identification mentioned in item I of this section shall include the individuals who are legally authorised to represent it, as well as its owners.

Paragraph 2 – The reference files and records mentioned in items I and II of this section shall be kept for a minimum period of five years, counted from the date the account is closed or the date the transaction is concluded. The competent authorities may decide, at their own discretion, to extend this period of time.

Paragraph 3 – The registration under item II of this section shall also be made whenever an individual or legal entity, or their associates execute, during the same calendar month, transactions with the same individual, legal entity, conglomerate or group that exceed, in the aggregate, the limit set out by the competent authorities.

(. . .)

Section 14. The Council for Financial Activities Control (COAF) is hereby instituted, under the jurisdiction of the Ministry of Finance, for the purpose of regulating, applying administrative sanctions, receiving pertinent information, examining and identifying any suspicious occurrence of illicit activities set out in this Law. The actions of COAF shall not conflict with the jurisdiction of other agencies.

Paragraph 1 – COAF shall be the agency responsible for issuing the instructions set out in section 10 to the legal entities specified in section 9 that are not subject to any specific regulatory or surveillance agency. In these cases, COAF shall also be responsible for defining the entities and applying the sanctions set out in section 12.

Paragraph 2 – COAF shall also be responsible for co-ordinating and advancing suggestions for the adoption of systems of co-operation and exchange of information designed to enable rapid and efficient responses in the campaign against the practice of concealment or disguise of assets, rights and values.

Section 15. COAF shall notify the competent authorities whenever it finds evidence of the existence of crimes defined in this Law, of clear indications of the occurrence of such crimes, or of any other illicit activity, so as to enable such authorities to take the appropriate measures.

Section 16. The members of COAF shall be civil servants of outstanding reputation and capability, named by act of the Minister of Finance and chosen from the career personnel of the Central Bank of Brazil, the Securities and Exchange Commission, the Superintendence of Private Insurance, the General Attorney Office for the National Treasury, the Secretariat of Federal Revenue, the Brazilian Agency of Intelligence, the Federal Police Department, and the Ministry of Foreign Affairs. In the last three cases, the Ministers having jurisdiction over each such entity shall nominate the members.

Paragraph 1 – The Chairperson of the Council shall be appointed by the President of the Republic, acting on a recommendation of the Minister of Finance.

Paragraph 2 – The decisions of COAF regarding the application of administrative sanctions may be appealed to the Minister of Finance.

Section 17. COAF's internal organisation and mode of operation shall be set out in bylaws to be approved by a decree of the executive branch.

(. . .)

Law no 10,701, of 9 July 2003

Modifies and adds provisions to Law no 9,613, of 3 March 1998, concerning money laundering

[5.20]

THE PRESIDENT OF THE REPUBLIC

The National Congress decrees and I approve the following Law:

Article 1. Article 1 of Law no 9,613, of 3 March 1998, will now contain the following alterations:

II   from terrorism and its financing;
VIII (forbidden).

Article 2. The only paragraph of article 9 of Law no 9,613, of 3 March 1998, will now contain the following clause XII:

XII   the natural persons or legal entities that sell luxury or high-value goods or that perform an activity that involves a large volume of cash.

Article 3. Law no 9,613, of 3 March 1998, will now contain the following article 10A:

Article 10A. The Central Bank shall maintain a centralised registry making the general register of account holders and clients of the financial institutions, even though from their mandatory.

Article 4. Article 11 of Law no 9,613, of 3 March 1998, will now contain the following alteration:

II a) all the transactions consisting of paragraph II from article 10 that exceed the limit fixed by the same authority and according to the conditions established by it, must be amended to the identification, which refers to paragraph I from the same article.

Article 5. Article 14 of Law no 9,613, of 3 March 1998, will now contain the following paragraph:

§ 3. The COAF can require from the public administration agencies banking and financial information of people involved in illegal activities.

Article 6. This Law will take effect on the date of its publication.

Brasilia, 9 July 2003
LUIZ INÁCIO LULA DA SILVA
Márcio Thomaz Bastos

Law no 10,467, of 11 June 2002

Adds Chapter II-A to Title XI of Decree Law no 2,848, of 7 December 1940 – Criminal Code, and a provision to Law no 9,613, of 3 March 1998

[5.21]

THE PRESIDENT OF THE REPUBLIC

I hereby state that the National Congress has decreed and I sign the following Law:

Article 1. The purpose of this Law is to give effectiveness to Decree no 3,678, of 30 November 2000, which enacts the Convention on the Campaign Against the Corruption of Foreign Public Servants in Commercial Transactions concluded in Paris on 17 December 1997.

Article 2. Title XI of Decree Law no 2,848, of 7 December 1940 – Criminal Code, will now contain the following Chapter II-A:

Chapter II-A Crimes practiced by an individual against a foreign public administration

CORRUPTION IN INTERNATIONAL COMMERCIAL TRANSACTIONS

Article 337-B. To promise, offer or give, directly or indirectly, an undue advantage to a foreign public servant, or to a third party, in order to cause them to practice, omit or delay an official act in connection with an international commercial transaction.

Penalty – Imprisonment from one (1) to eight (8) years and a fine.

Sole Paragraph – The penalty shall be increased by a third if, by virtue of the advantage or promise, the foreign public servant delays or omits an official act, or practices it in breach of an official duty.

INFLUENCES IN INTERNATIONAL COMMERCIAL TRANSACTIONS

Article 337-C. To request, demand, collect or obtain, for oneself or a third party, directly or indirectly, an advantage or promise of advantage with the purpose of affecting an act practiced by a foreign public servant in the exercise of their functions, in connection with an international commercial transaction.

Penalty – Imprisonment from two (2) to five (5) years and a fine.

Sole Paragraph – The penalty shall be increased by a half if the agent alleges or suggests that the advantage is for a foreign public servant.

FOREIGN PUBLIC SERVANT

Article 337-D. For criminal purposes, a foreign public servant is deemed to be any person who, even if on a temporary basis or without remuneration, exercises a public office, employment or function in state entities or in diplomatic representations of a foreign country.

Sole Paragraph – A person who exercises an office, employment or function in companies controlled directly or indirectly by the public power of a foreign country or in international public organisations shall be held equivalent to a foreign public servant.

Article 3. Article 1 of Law no 9,613, of 3 March 1998, will now contain the following item VIII:

VIII practiced by an individual against a foreign public administration (articles 337-B, 337-C and 337-D of Decree Law no 2,848, of 7 December 1940 – Criminal Code).

Article 4. This Law shall become effective as of the date of its publication.

Brasilia, 11 June 2002; 181st of the Independence and 114th of the Republic.
FERNANDO HENRIQUE CARDOSO
Miguel Reale Júnior

Law no 10,406, of 10 January 2002 (new Civil Code)

Title III Illicit acts

[5.22]

Article 186. A person who, due to a voluntary action or omission, negligence or imprudence, breaches a right and causes damage to a third party, even of an exclusively moral nature, commits an illicit act.

6   Canada

Karl Delwaide
Nicolas Leblanc[1]

INTRODUCTION

[6.1]   This chapter examines Canadian legal aspects of the management of information and its confidentiality in the relationship between a bank and its customers. The analysis has become more complicated and the implications potentially more significant as a result of increasingly aggressive and innovative efforts by Canadian banks to diversify into new areas of financial services, assisted by a sweeping reform of the financial sector legislation in 1992 which blurred some of the distinctions between the so-called 'four pillars' of the Canadian financial system: banking, insurance, trust companies and the securities industry. These factors have also been influenced by the apparent willingness of Canadian courts to impose responsibilities and obligations upon banks which reflect their new powers and activities and which go beyond those which banks have traditionally assumed.

The relationship between a bank and its customers has always been multifaceted, but, in the past, relatively straightforward in regard to each facet. It is one of debtor and creditor as regards the money in the customer's account, but is better characterised as one of agent and principal with respect to the bank's obligations to pay the customer's cheques. Canadian courts have held, however, that under the appropriate circumstances, a bank may be held to be a fiduciary in relation to its customer.[2] In addition to judicial development, there are increasing statutory responsibilities, some expanded by recent legislative initiatives, that apply in new areas of activities for Canadian banks, such as securities dealing and investment banking.

Moreover, concerns about the 'dirty' money of crime have recently led to the adoption, at the federal level, of fairly recent money laundering legislation under which banks have mandatory reporting obligations for prescribed and suspicious transactions, as well as for cross-border movements of large amounts of currency. In parallel, customer concerns regarding the potential abuse of personal information have resulted in 2000 in the introduction of a federal privacy statute regulating private entities. This statute was gradually brought into force and came into full effect on 1 January 2004. At the provincial level, two provinces, British Columbia and Alberta, followed suit in the adoption of private sector privacy regimes, an initiative that had already been implemented in 1994 in the province of Quebec. The

---

1   The text of this chapter was originally written by James E Fordyce and Elizabeth Shriver of Osler, Hoskin & Harcourt and revised in 2003 by Karl Delwaide and Isabelle Durand of Fasken Martineau DuMoulin.
2   D Waters, 'Banks, Fiduciary Obligations and Unconscionable Transactions' (1986) 65 Can BR 37.

federal Personal Information Protection and Electronic Documents Act[3] ('PIPEDA') also imposes new duties on banks, not only with respect to their customers, but also with respect to their own employees, as they now have to state the purpose for which they collect or gather any personal information and the use they will make of it. Consequently, Canadian banks now have to take into consideration accrued confidentiality requirements for the personal information of their customers and the newly-enacted obligatory disclosure of transactions that meet given standards of either importance or dubiousness.

These developments and the ongoing administration and regulation of these activities are complicated by the Canadian constitutional structure, which is a federal system that places banks under the overlapping jurisdictions of the federal and provincial governments. While banking per se is a federal matter governed by the federal Bank Act,[4] other financial transactions in which banks or their subsidiaries are involved, such as securities matters, are primarily under provincial jurisdiction. Moreover, to the extent not specifically dealt with by federal banking legislation, matters such as contract law and agency are governed by the laws (common law and statutory) of each province.[5] A good example of this somewhat complicated pattern can be illustrated by the statutes regulating privacy in the private sector which have been enacted both at the federal and the provincial levels. Pursuant to a provision in the federal statute, the government may grant an exemption for the statutes' application to organisations doing business within provinces that have enacted similar legislation. The implications of these exemptions as they relate to the concurrent application of provincial and federal statutes are discussed later in the chapter. So far, however, the exemption orders that have been granted provide for the continued application of the federal statute to the operations of a Federal Work, Undertaking or Business ('FWUB'), which includes banks. While the British Columbia private sector privacy statute is expressly stated not to apply where the federal PIPEDA applies (thus to FWUB),[6] the Alberta statute contains no such provision, but is understood by the Privacy Commissioners of Canada and Alberta not to apply to FWUB.[7] Apart from a recent decision which is currently pending

---

3 SC 2000, c 5.
4 RSC 1991, c 46. Although banks in Canada are governed by federal law and may (and normally do) carry on business through branches in one or more provinces, ss 461 and 462 of the Bank Act, SC 1991, c 46, provide, in essence, for a 'branch of account' for each deposit account of a customer, which is the *situs* of the debt owing by the bank to the customer in respect of that account and also provide that notices of process or assignment and the like relating to an account only bind the bank if served on the branch of account. Apart from providing relief to banks with many branches in different provinces (up to 1,000 or more), these provisions codify and refine the common law as to the *situs* of the contract of confidentiality between a bank and its customer and hence the governing law of such contract.
   It should also be noted that the Bank Act, SC 1991, c 46, applies to foreign banks carrying on the business of banking in Canada.
5 While there may be some variation between the laws of the Canadian common law provinces, mainly as a result of statutory provisions, it may in general be said that laws applicable to commercial operations are similar in each of those provinces. In addition, the laws in the province of Quebec are based on the French civil law system, which, although often similar in result to that found in the common law provinces, nevertheless further complicates the regulatory system.
6 BC Personal Information Protection Act, SBC 2003, c 63, s 3(2)(c).
7 Alta Personal Information Protection Act, SA 2003, c P-6.5 ('Alta PIPA'). See the Privacy Commissioner of Canada, Annual Report 2004, online: http://www.privcom.gc.ca/information/ar/200405/2004_pipeda_e.pdf at 22; Alta Privacy Commissioner, 'Guide to the Personal Information Protection Act', online: http://www.oipc.ab.ca/ims/client/upload/PIPAbrochure.pdf; Alta Privacy Commissioner, 'A Guide for Businesses and Organisations', online: http://www.oipc.ab.ca/ims/client/upload/PIPAGuidev4.pdf at 17. See 'Alberta's Personal Information Protection Act' below.

appeal, Quebec's legislation has generally been found applicable to FWUB, including banks, doing business in the province.

THE BANK'S DUTY OF CONFIDENTIALITY

[6.2] Confidentiality is fundamental to the relationship between a bank and its customers. In Canada, as in the other Commonwealth jurisdictions, the bank's legal duty of confidentiality is founded in the common law and consists of an implied contractual duty (subject to certain exceptions) not to divulge information about its customers' accounts to third parties without the consent of the customer, as laid down in the leading English case of *Tournier v National Provincial and Union Bank of England*.[8] Although the principle is easy to state, its ultimate scope continues to evolve such that its potential breadth always remains somewhat unclear. The exceptions to the confidentiality principle, as discussed below, have been further refined by the courts, but the main spur to development of the law in this area has come from statutory enactments that delimit the bank's obligations of secrecy and clarify the circumstances under which a bank is entitled or even bound to disclose what would otherwise be confidential information.

Exceptions to the duty of confidentiality

[6.3] While the *Tournier* case is more fully discussed in the chapter relating to English law, we can state briefly the four exceptions to the bank's duty of confidentiality that are outlined in the case:

1 the bank may disclose information when the customer consents to the disclosure expressly or by necessary implication;
2 disclosure may be made when it is necessary to the bank's interests;
3 the bank must disclose confidential customer information when it is so compelled by law; and
4 disclosure is permitted where there is a public duty to do so.

These exceptions are discussed in light of relevant developments in Canadian law.

Disclosure with express/implied consent of the customer

[6.4] As a general principle, no disclosure is authorised beyond what is necessary by implication in order to carry out the customer's instructions. Thus, as indicated in *Tournier*, it is clearly permissible to disclose customer account information when the bank has been asked to give a credit reference. However, consent is not to be implied simply because the banker believes disclosure to be in the customer's best interest, particularly if it is possible to contact the customer to ascertain directly whether permission would be given. In addition, the information which may be disclosed in a credit reference without express consent is limited.[9]

---

8 [1924] 1 KB 461, CA [*Tournier*].
9 In the Ontario case of *Hull v Childs & Huron and Erie Mortgage Corpn* [1951] OWN 116, Ont HCJ, where the customer had signed a series of blank cheques, the financial institution was held liable for breach of its duty of secrecy because it disclosed to the bearer of the cheques the total amount of money in the account so as to enable him to withdraw it all. The High Court held that it was unwarranted for the bank to infer that the customer intended all of his funds to be withdrawn by virtue of his having given someone blank cheques.

Disclosure in the bank's own interest

[6.5] In *Tournier*, this exception was discussed as referring to cases where a bank brings an action against its customer for payment of a debt owed. Obviously, it is necessary under such circumstances to disclose the amount owed even though this would otherwise be in breach of the bank's duty of confidentiality.[10] This exception does not apply, however, to cases where the bank is a third party to a proceeding. In addition, when courts do interpret this exception, by necessity, they will construe it narrowly, as Taylor JA noted in *Canadian Imperial Bank of Commerce v Sayani* (discussed below):

> 'The scope of [the bank's own interest] exception must, of course, be a limited one, for if the bank could make disclosure of its customer's confidential information whenever this served its interests, the duty of confidentiality would have little meaning …'[11]

In *Rodaro v Royal Bank of Canada*,[12] it was recognised that the 'bank's own interest' exception covers disclosure of information that is necessary for the exercise of a right that the bank has. The Ontario Court of Appeal noted that 'in the context of a proposed assignment, it was very much in the interest of RBC to make full disclosure of all of this information to a potential assignee. Failure to disclose relevant information could leave the bank open to a subsequent action by the assignee'.[13] The Court of Appeal reasoned that a bank's 'unqualified right to assign its benefits under [an] agreement … implied the right to make such disclosures as are essential to the exercise of that right'.[14] Also in that case, the Court of Appeal rejected the distinction between 'business information' and 'account information' that the trial judge had made in coming to his conclusion that some information had been improperly disclosed. However, it should be noted that the bank had a contractual right, pursuant to the assignment clause, to disclose any information it deemed necessary for the purpose of such assignment. The trial judge, however, had not considered this clause in his reasons and the Court of Appeal did not make a final determination on this issue.[15]

In the context of a bank holding a security interest in its customer's property, it was held that disclosure of information in an attempt by the bank to protect its security interest was a permitted disclosure under the 'bank's own interest' exception.[16] Subsequently, it was held that by granting a security interest to the bank, the grantor 'impliedly authorises the grantee to inform those persons who have some involvement in the assets so secured of the grantee's interest'.[17] Thus, the bank may rely on the 'consent' exception, presumably in addition to the 'bank's own interest' exception, to disclose information relating to a security interest. The information so disclosed, however, will have to fall within the scope of consent or be necessary for the protection of the bank's interests.

In some cases, an exchange of information in the bank's own interest is supported by

---

10 Cases invoking this exception are relatively rare, however, the exception was recently reaffirmed by the British Columbia Supreme Court in *Royal Bank of Canada v Vincenzi*, [1994] BCJ No 772, BCSC (QL) [*Vincenzi*].

11 (1993), 83 BCLR (2d) 167 at 176, BCCA [*Sayani*].

12 (2002), 59 OR (3d) 74, Ont CA [*Rodaro*].

13 *Rodaro* (2002), 59 OR (3d) 74, Ont CA, para 44.

14 *Rodaro* (2002), 59 OR (3d) 74, Ont CA, para 45.

15 *Rodaro* (2002), 59 OR (3d) 74, Ont CA, para 46.

16 *Royal Bank of Canada v Brattberg*, [1993] 8 WWR 139, 11 Alta LR (3d) 190, Alta QB.

17 *Vincenzi*, [1994] BCJ No 772, BCSC (QL), para 17.

a statutory provision. For example, the federal Competition Act[18] contains express provisions setting out conditions under which banks are permitted to have agreements or arrangements with one another which might otherwise be considered as anti-competitive. Among the permitted arrangements are those for the exchange of credit information. As noted above, the exchange of customer information or 'networking' among banking and certain non-banking members of a bank group has been restricted, but, in Canada, the debate over whether such a restriction is appropriate has turned more on whether the ability to 'network' would provide an unfair advantage to bank-owned insurance companies over independent insurance companies than on issues of confidentiality.

Compulsion of law

[6.6] In keeping with increased legislation relating to the bank's duty to keep customer information confidential, the bank's duty to disclose confidential information under compulsion of law is defined primarily by an ever-increasing web of statutory provisions.

Disclosure in the course of legal proceedings

[6.7] Parties to legal proceedings often seek to require banks that are not named in the proceedings to disclose information about their customers through a subpoena *duces tecum* or a summons. The banker's duty of confidentiality will not prevent disclosure of the information as the duty is not a recognised privilege at law, but rather an implied contractual term.[19] Disclosure that is effected pursuant to a valid order of a competent court will be permitted under the compulsion of law exception referred to in *Tournier*.

First, the compulsion of information from banks through subpoenas is regulated in Canada by the Bank Act.[20] Section 462(2) provides that:

> 'Any notification sent to a bank with respect to a customer of the bank ... constitutes notice to the bank and fixes the bank with knowledge of its contents only if sent to and received at the branch of the bank that is the branch of account of an account held in the name of that customer.'

Section 461(1) defines 'branch of account'. A subpoena that is not notified in accordance with these provisions will not constitute notice to the bank of the order. A seizure effected pursuant to such defective procedure would be invalid and declared null by a court.[21]

In any event, banks must remain careful to ensure that the production of evidence is validly compelled. A subpoena (now a summons in Ontario and New Brunswick) is first and foremost a document requiring the person concerned to attend in court, often with certain documents. Lower courts in Canada have sometimes held that a subpoena is not an order of a court sufficient to compel disclosure under *Tournier*'s 'compulsion of law' exception. The witness subpoenaed would have to present

---

18 RSC 1985, c C-34, as amended, s 49.
19 Manes & Silver, *The Law of Confidential Communications in Canada* (Toronto: Butterworths, 1996) p 77.
20 SC 1991, c 46.
21 *ICI Cheque v Travel Currency Inc,* JE 2005-708, 3 March 2005, 500-17-024364-054, Que Sup Ct, leave to appeal refused, 6 April 2005, 500-09-015425-051, Que CA.

himself in court and specifically ask for the court to order him to disclose the information sought. This was directly decided in a case called *Haughton*,[22] where the witness bank manager sought to refuse to comply with a subpoena seeking disclosure of information and documents pertaining to the bank's client, the defendant. The Superior Court agreed with the witness' counsel that a subpoena is not what was meant in *Tournier* when the Privy Council stated 'the banker will not divulge [information] … unless the banker is compelled to do so by order of a court'.[23] The Superior Court held that 'the witness was within his right to refuse to answer the questions until either the consent of the customer or a court order was obtained'.[24]

The subsequent case of *Art's Welding*[25] interpreted the 'compulsion of law' exception to permit disclosure of information relating to a person not party to the litigation pursuant to an order of the court. Master Breitkreuz in *Art's Welding* would have been prepared to go so far as to recognise a fifth exception, namely disclosure in the interests of justice, should disclosure by an order of a court not fall within the compulsion of law exception. Although he does not explicitly state this, Master Breitkreuz seems to understand an 'order of court' as not including a simple subpoena.

More recently, the *Robertson* case dealt with this issue.[26] In this Commonwealth case of St Vincent and the Grenadines, both the High Court of Justice[27] and the Court of Appeal,[28] citing *Haughton*, held that a subpoena was not a 'court order' sufficient to compel disclosure.[29] The Privy Council decision, however, did not address this issue directly.[30] For a discussion of other issues in *Robertson*, see 'Common Law Developments Limiting Disclosure' below.

Although the issue of whether a subpoena is a sufficient form of compulsion of law to warrant disclosure of information without the client's consent is not fully answered by the courts, the issue has been settled in all Canadian provinces but two.[31] Legislation relating to evidence provides that a financial institution is not, in any legal proceeding to which it is not a party, compellable to produce any books or record or appear as witness to prove the matters, transactions and accounts therein recorded, unless an order of the court made for special cause orders such production or testimony.[32]

22 *Haughton v Haughton*, [1965] 1 OR 481, Ont SC, Assistant Master Saunders [*Haughton*].
23 *Tournier*, cited in *Haughton*, [1965] 1 OR 481, Ont SC, para 7.
24 *Haughton*, [1965] 1 OR 481, Ont SC, para 8.
25 *Royal Bank of Canada v Art's Welding & Machine Shop (1980)*, [1989] AJ No 491, Alta QB, Master Breitkreuz (QL).
26 *Robertson v Canadian Imperial Bank of Commerce*, [1995] 1 All ER 824, [1994] 1 WLR 1493, PC [*Robertson*].
27 *Robertson v Canadian Imperial Bank of Commerce* (unreported, 1988), St Vincent and the Grenadines HCJ, no 340.
28 *Robertson v Canadian Imperial Bank of Commerce* (unreported, 1990), Eastern Caribbean CA, St Vincent and the Grenadines, Civil Appeal no 4.
29 E K Rowan-Legg, 'New Developments in Bank's Duty of Confidentiality' (1995) 26 Can Bus LJ 455, 456–457.
30 *Robertson*, [1995] 1 All ER 824, [1994] 1 WLR 1493, PC.
31 Que and Nfld.
32 Alta Alberta Evidence Act, RSA 2000, c A-18, s 41(5); BC Evidence Act, RSBC 1996, c 134, s 34(5); Can Canada Evidence Act, RSC 1985 c C-5, s 29(5); Man Manitoba Evidence Act, CCSM c E150, s 48(4); NB Evidence Act, RSNB 1973, c E-11, s 46(3); NWT Evidence Act, RSNWT 1988, c E-8, s 51(3); NS Evidence Act, RSNS 1989, c 154, s 21(3); Nu Consolidation of Evidence Act, RSNWT 1988, c E-8, s 51(3); Ont Evidence Act, RSO 1990, c E-23, s 33(4); PEI Evidence Act, RSPEI 1988, c E-11, s 30(4); Sask Saskatchewan Evidence Act, RSS 1978, c S-16, s 28(4); YT Evidence Act, RSY 2002, c 78, s 45(3).

Before there can be a valid court order compelling disclosure of information, a subpoena must first be correctly issued. Every province has legislation setting out the requirements for the valid issuance of a subpoena.[33] A subpoena that is issued pursuant to a provincial authority is only valid within the jurisdiction of such authority, which cannot extend beyond the province's territory. If a subpoena is issued in a province, in order to compel testimony or the production of documents by a person in another province, the subpoena must be enforced in that other province pursuant to the relevant legislation.[34] This legislation stipulates that the court of the province or territory in which the witness is present will adopt the subpoena that is issued by the court of another province or territory if it is accompanied by a certificate signed by a judge of a superior court, county or district court of the issuing province and impressed with the seal of that court signifying that the judge is satisfied that the attendance in the issuing province of the person subpoenaed is necessary for the due adjudication of the proceeding, is reasonable and, in relation to the nature and importance of the cause or proceeding, is essential to the due administration of justice in the province and that the subpoena is accompanied by witness fees and travelling expenses.[35]

Every interprovincial subpoena legislation requires that the province compelling attendance of the witness has a provision ensuring that the person that is the subject of the subpoena be deemed not to have submitted to the issuing province's jurisdiction other than as a witness in the proceedings to which the subpoena relates and be immune from 'seizure of goods, service of process, execution of judgment, garnishment, imprisonment or molestation of any kind relating to a legal or judicial right, cause, action, proceeding or process' except for proceedings that relate to events occurring during or after the required attendance in the issuing province.[36]

A line of argument supports the proposition according to which the issuance and service of a subpoena in contravention of the requirements set out in the interprovincial subpoena legislation amounts to an abuse of process. Macaulay and Sprague argue, in the context of proceedings before administrative agencies, that for an adjudicative body to issue a subpoena to compel the attendance of a witness that is outside the agency's jurisdiction in the hopes that the person concerned 'might be misled as to his or her obligations and respond under the mistaken belief that he or she must do so' is an abuse of process.[37]

---

33 Alta Rules of Court, Alta Reg 390/68 (Court of Queen's Bench Act, RSA 2000, c C-31), r 293; BC Rules of Court, CB Reg 221/90 (Court Rules Act, RSBC 1996, c 90), r 40(39); Can Federal Court Rules, SOR/98-106 as am, r 41; Man Queen's Bench Rules, Man Reg 553/88 (Court of Queen's Bench Act, CCSM c C280) r 53.04; NB Rules of Court, NB Reg 82-73 (Judicature Act, RSNB 1973, c J-2), r 55.03; Nfld Rules of the Supreme Court, SNL 1986 c 42, Sch D (Judicature Act, RSNL 1990, c J-4), r 46.23; NWT Supreme Court Rules, R-010-96 (Judicature Act, RSNWT 1988, c J-1), r 364; NS Civil Procedure Rules, (Judicature Act, RSNS 1989, c 240), r 31.24; Nu follows NWT; Ont Rules of Civil Procedure, RRO 1990, Reg 194 (Courts of Justice Act, RSO 1990, c C-43), r 53.04; Que CCP, RSQ c C-25, art 280; Sask Queen's Bench Rules, (LS 1998, c Q-1.01) r 306; YT follows BC.

34 Interprovincial Subpoena Act, RSA 2000, c I-9; Subpoena (Interprovincial) Act, RSBC 1996, c 442; Interprovincial Subpoena Act, CCSM c S212; Interprovincial Subpoena Act, SNB 1979, c I-13.1; Interprovincial Subpoena Act, RSNL 1990, c I-20; Interprovincial Subpoena Act, SNS 1996, c 1; Interprovincial Subpoenas Act, RSNWT 1988, c I-9; Interprovincial Subpoenas Act (Nunavut), RSNWT 1988, c I-9; Interprovincial Summonses Act, RSO 1990, c I.12; Interprovincial Subpoena Act, RSPEI 1988, c I-9; Special Procedure Act, RSQ, c P-27, s 9; Interprovincial Subpoena Act, RSS 1978 (Supp), c I-12.1; Interprovincial Subpoena Act, RSY 2002, c 126.

35 Interprovincial Summonses Act, RSO 1990, c I.12, s 2.

36 Interprovincial Summonses Act, RSO 1990, c I.12, s 6(2).

37 Macaulay & Sprague, *Practice and Procedure Before Administrative Tribunals* (looseleaf, 2nd edn, Toronto: Carswell), 12-90.9.

Once a bank has received a valid order compelling it to attend legal proceedings for the purpose of disclosing information that is subject to the banker's duty of confidentiality, it should be mindful of further restrictions that have been developed through later jurisprudence. In particular, the bank must be mindful of the need generally to notify its customer of the receipt of a subpoena, as well as of restrictions on the extent to which information can be validly disclosed under the 'compulsion of law' exception. These qualifications are discussed under the heading 'Common Law Developments Limiting Disclosure' below.

Legislation relating to evidence

[6.8] There are federal and provincial statutes that generally provide that a bank must disclose records in its possession where they could serve as evidence in the course of civil, criminal or arbitral proceedings not involving the bank. However, a court order is usually required before the bank can be compelled either to appear as a witness or to produce a customer's records.[38]

Tax legislation

[6.9] Under the Income Tax Act,[39] Revenue Canada may examine a third party's records if they relate to a taxpayer and the third party must answer any relevant questions. Therefore, a bank may be required to provide for inspection to Revenue Canada a customer's bank records and respond to inquiries on the customer's transactions. These provisions have been interpreted to mean that a bank can be required to disclose records of transactions even if the result would mean disclosing private information of the bank's customers who are not themselves under investigation.[40]

Securities and corporate law

[6.10] The provincial securities acts provide broad powers of investigation, search and seizure which Securities Commission staff utilise in investigating securities law matters. These are frequently used to investigate a wide range of securities-related activities such as allegations or suspicions of insider trading or other misuse of confidential information.[41]

---

38 Eg see the Canada Evidence Act, RSC 1985, c C-5 and provisions listed at note 26AB. The provisions in the Evidence Act ensure that bank records are not seized every time one of its customers is in litigation and they take precedence over the Criminal Code provisions, RSC 1985, c C-46, which permits seizure of records where there are reasonable grounds to believe the records will afford evidence of the commission of an offence: *R v Mowat, ex p Toronto-Dominion Bank* (1968), 1 OR 179, HCJ. In general terms, these provisions are not dissimilar to those of the Bankers' Books Evidence Act 1879 which has been widely adopted in British Commonwealth jurisdictions.

39 RSC 1985, 5th Supp, s 231.2. Revenue Canada must obtain authorisation for such third party disclosure through ex parte application to a judge. With effect from 20 June 1996, the Income Tax Act was amended to repeal requirements that a judge must be satisfied that: (i) there was a reasonable expectation that the third party has failed or would fail to comply with the Act and (ii) that the information was not otherwise readily available. This amendment dramatically increases the power of Revenue Canada to embark upon judicially authorised 'fishing expeditions'.

40 *Canadian Bank of Commerce v A-G of Canada* (1962), 35 DLR (2nd) 49, SCC.

41 Eg see the Ontario Securities Act, RSO 1990, c S-5, as amended. There are also powers that can be granted to inspectors under the corporate law statutes. See eg the Ontario Business Corporations Act, RSO 1990, c B-16, Pt XIII. In the Canadian context, these latter powers are used less frequently than in some other jurisdictions given the broad powers and responsibilities of securities regulators. Investigations under the powers of the corporate statutes tend to focus on internal matters involving the corporation and its directors or holders of its securities.

Money laundering and terrorism legislation
PROCEEDS OF CRIME (MONEY LAUNDERING) AND TERRORIST FINANCING ACT

[6.11]   By virtue of the Proceeds of Crime (Money Laundering) and Terrorist Financing Act[42] ('PCMLTFA') and its recent amendments and regulations, banks conducting business in Canada now find themselves faced with a series of new reporting obligations.

In essence, the PCMLTFA and its subsequent regulations establish a mandatory reporting system for prescribed and suspicious transactions as defined by the Act and regulations (see below), as well as for cross-border movement of large amounts of currency or monetary instruments. This system applies to a broad range of individuals and entities operating in Canada, including domestic and foreign banks, trust and loan companies and other intermediaries, as well as lawyers, accountants, real estate brokers and certain Crown-owned entities. Where circumstances warrant, these entities are now required to identify their clients, create and maintain records and report financial transactions and/or the cross-border movement of funds. An organisation may not escape its reporting requirement except pursuant to the exceptions expressly set out in the PCMLTFA or its associated regulations. In addition, these entities are required to develop and implement policies aimed at ensuring compliance with the PCMLTFA and its regulations. The objective of the PCMLTFA is to implement specific measures to detect and deter money laundering and the financing of terrorist activities and to facilitate the investigation and prosecution of money laundering offences.

The PCMLTFA requires a committee of Parliament to commence the process of revising the Act within five years of its enactment.[43] The Ministry of Finance has produced a consultation paper[44] setting out the proposed scope for the upcoming review. The changes that are to be brought to the PCMLTFA seek to address the Financial Action Task Force's ('FATF')[45] revised 40 recommendations,[46] as well as the Auditor General's audit of the National Initiatives to Combat Money Laundering.[47] Amongst the proposed changes, some are of particular interest to the banking community, including:

1   enhanced customer due diligence standards;
2   the extension of reporting obligations to suspicious attempted transactions (including a reasonable effort obligation to obtain the names and addresses of the individual undertaking the transactions);
3   the introduction of a new administrative and monetary penalties regime to deal with entities that fail to comply with the requirements of the Act (including provisions for greater co-operation between Canadian and foreign entities that have similar compliance functions, which would be effected through Memorandums of Understanding ('MOUs')); and
4   the establishment of an anti-money laundering/anti-terrorist financing advisory committee composed of senior representatives from the public and private sectors.

---

42 SC 2000, c 17.
43 SC 2000, c 17, s 72.
44 'Enhancing Canada's Anti-Money Laundering and Anti-Terrorism Financing Regime', consultation paper, June 2005, online: http://www.fin.gc.ca/toce/2005/enhancing_e.html.
45 The FATF is an inter-governmental body whose purpose is to develop and promote national and international policies to combat money laundering and terrorist financing.
46 FATF Annual Report 2002–2003, online: http://www.fatf-gafi.org/dataoecd/13/0/34328221.pdf.
47 Online: http://www.oag-bvg.gc.ca/domino/reports.nsf/html/20041102ce.html/$file/20041102ce.pdf.

In addition to those specific proposals, the government will be reviewing some of the existing regime's provisions, such as the CDN$10,000 reporting threshold for electronic fund transfers and the requirements that apply to financial services provided over the Internet. Yet other proposals seek to clarify or modify existing requirements under the PCMLTFA, including the explicit application of the Act to foreign branches, an explicit requirement for reporting entities to have compliance regimes in place, an extension to five years of the time bar for summary conviction proceedings of non-compliance offences (currently one year) and the establishment of criminal penalties for non-reporting under Part 2 (Reporting of Currency and Monetary Instruments) of the PCMLTFA.

THE FINANCIAL TRANSACTIONS AND REPORTS ANALYSIS CENTRE OF CANADA

[6.12] To help meet its objective, the Act establishes the Financial Transactions and Reports Analysis Centre of Canada ('FINTRAC').[48] FINTRAC's principal role is to collect, analyse, assess and disclose information in order to assist in the detection, prevention and deterrence of money laundering and of the financing of terrorist activities, as well as acting at arm's length with law enforcement agencies and other entities to which it is authorised to disclose information.[49] It is therefore to FINTRAC which the banks must report the financial transaction information requiring disclosure pursuant to the Act.

TRANSACTIONS WHICH A BANK MUST REPORT

[6.13] *Suspicious transactions.* Banks must report to FINTRAC, in the prescribed form and manner, every suspicious transaction. That is, banks must report every financial transaction that has occurred in the course of their activities and in respect of which there are reasonable grounds to suspect that the transaction is related to the laundering of money or the financing of a terrorist activity.[50] More precisely, the bank activities which may trigger this obligation to report include the remitting or transmitting of funds and the issuing or redeeming of money orders, travellers' cheques or other similar negotiable instruments, except cheques payable to a *named person or entity*.[51]

[6.14] *Prescribed transactions.* Banks must also report certain 'prescribed' transactions. A prescribed transaction is a cash transaction or electronic fund transfer of CDN$10,000 or more.[52] Also considered to be prescribed transactions are two or more transfers or transactions made within 24 hours that together total CDN$10,000 or more.[53]

[6.15] *Import/export of currency or monetary instruments.* The PCMLTFA further requires the reporting to an officer[54] of the 'importation or exportation of currency or monetary instruments'[55] of a value greater than or equal to CDN$10,000.[56] It is the

---

48 SC 2000, c 17, s 40.
49 SC 2000, c 17, s 40.
50 SC 2000, c 17, s 7.
51 Proceeds of Crime (Money Laundering) and Terrorist Financing Suspicious Transaction Reporting Regulations, SOR/2001-317, s 4.
52 Proceeds of Crime (Money Laundering) and Terrorist Financing Regulations, SOR/2002-184, s 12.
53 Proceeds of Crime (Money Laundering) and Terrorist Financing Regulations, SOR/2002-184, s 3.
54 The PCMLTFA definition at s 2 refers to s 2(1) of the Customs Act, RS, 1985, c 1 (2nd Supp), which reads: 'a person employed in the administration or enforcement of this Act, the Customs Tariff or the Special Import Measures Act and includes any member of the Royal Canadian Mounted Police'.
55 PCMLTFA, SC 2000, c 17, s 12.
56 Cross-Border Currency and Monetary Instruments Reporting Regulations, SOR/2002-412, s 2(1).

person in charge of the conveyance, the importer or exporter, or the person on whose behalf the importation or exportation is effected who has the obligation of reporting.[57] Monetary instruments are defined as a closed list of instruments 'in bearer form or in such other form as title to them passes on delivery' and do not include 'securities or negotiable instruments that bear restrictive endorsements or a stamp for the purposes of clearing or are made payable to a named person and have not been endorsed'.[58] A reporting person is required to 'answer truthfully any question that the officer asks with respect to information required to be contained in the report'.[59]

Where a person or entity indicates to an officer[60] that they have currency or monetary instruments to report, but that the report has not yet been completed, the officer may, after giving the prescribed notice, retain the currency or monetary instruments for seven days after the notice is given or sent or 30 days in the case of importation or exportation by courier or post.[61] The currency or monetary instruments may not be detained once they have been reported or if the importer or exporter advises the officer that they have decided not to proceed further with the importation or exportation.[62] If the person who has the obligation to report the importation or exportation of currency or monetary instruments fails to do so by the expiry of the prescribed period of retention, the currency or monetary instruments are forfeited to Her Majesty in Right of Canada.[63]

The regulations provide for exemptions to the reporting requirement in cases of importation of instruments where, subject to the conditions set out in the regulations, the instruments are imported into Canada, but have as their destination a place outside of Canada and are not removed from the conveyance (the means of transport by which the instrument is imported) while in Canada.[64]

INFORMATION TO BE PROVIDED IN REPORT TO FINTRAC

[6.16] The information which must be included in a report to FINTRAC is lengthy and includes elements such as the identity of the parties and accounts involved and the sum of the transaction. In the event that the bank does not possess certain elements of such information, it must make all 'reasonable efforts' to obtain it and provide it to FINTRAC.[65]

PROHIBITION AGAINST 'TIPPING OFF'

[6.17] A person or entity is prohibited from disclosing that a report of suspicious transactions has been made or from disclosing the content of such report with the intent of prejudicing a criminal investigation.[66]

---

57 PCMLTFA, SC 2000, c 17, s 12(3).
58 Cross-Border Currency and Monetary Instruments Reporting Regulations, SOR/2002-412, s 1(1).
59 PCMLTFA, SC 2000, c 17, s 12(4)(a).
60 The PCMLTFA definition at s 2 refers to s 2(1) of the Customs Act, RS, 1985, c 1 (2nd Supp), which reads: 'a person employed in the administration or enforcement of this Act, the Customs Tariff or the Special Import Measures Act and includes any member of the Royal Canadian Mounted Police'.
61 Cross-Border Currency and Monetary Instruments Reporting Regulations, SOR/2002-412, s 17.
62 PCMLTFA, SC 2000, c 17, s 14(3).
63 PCMLTFA, SC 2000, c 17, s 14(5).
64 Cross-Border Currency and Monetary Instruments Reporting Regulations, SOR/2002-412, s 9.
65 Proceeds of Crime (Money Laundering) and Terrorist Financing Regulations, SOR/2002-184, s 53.
66 SC 2000, c 17, s 8.

PENALTIES

[6.18] Breach of any of the provisions of the PCMLTFA or its regulations is punishable by fines ranging from CDN$50,000 to CDN$2 million and/or imprisonment up to a maximum of five years.[67]

MONEY LAUNDERING AND FINANCING TERRORIST ACTIVITY OFFENCES

[6.19] Money laundering is an offence under the Criminal Code.[68] It involves the use, transfer, disposition or otherwise dealing with of any property or its proceeds with intent to conceal or convert that property, knowing or believing that the property was obtained or derived directly or indirectly as a result of the commission of a designated offence or as a result of an act which, if it had occurred in Canada, would have constituted a designated offence. A designated offence is any indictable offence under any Act of Parliament, other than excluded offences.[69]

Mutatis mutandis, providing, collecting, making available, using or possessing property or financial services with the intent that it be used or knowing that it will be used, in whole or in part, for the purpose of carrying out or facilitating a terrorist activity or any act or omission intended to cause death or serious bodily harm to a civilian or for the purpose of benefiting any person who is doing so, is an offence.[70] Terrorist activity is defined as one of the following. First, an act or omission that is committed in or outside Canada that, if it were committed in Canada, would be one of the listed offences (which are offences referred to in various international treaties and conventions). Secondly, an act or omission that (i) is committed 'in whole or in part for a political, religious or ideological purpose, objective or cause' and that is committed, in whole or in part, with intent to intimidate the public or a segment of it with regard to its security (including economic security) or with intent to compel a person or government or international organisation, whether inside or outside Canada, to do or refrain from doing any act and (ii) that intentionally causes death or serious bodily harm through the use of violence, endangers life, causes risk to public safety or health, causes substantial property damage or causes interference with essential services. It excludes acts or omissions committed during armed conflict in accordance with applicable international customary or conventional law.[71]

Knowingly participating in or contributing to, directly or indirectly, any activity of a terrorist group for the purpose of enhancing the ability of such group to facilitate or carry out a terrorist activity is an offence.[72] A terrorist group is either an entity that has as one of its purposes or activity facilitating or carrying out any terrorist activity, or a listed entity.[73]

ISSUES WITH THE PCMLTFA

[6.20] So far, it does not appear that Canada has been the subject of an FATF Mutual Evaluation Report.[74]

---

67 SC 2000, c 17, ss 74–77.
68 RSC 1985, c C-46, s 462.31 ['Cr C'].
69 Cr C, RSC 1985, c C-46, s 462.3(1), see Regulations Excluding Certain Indictable Offences from the Definition of 'Designated Offence', SOR/2002-63.
70 Cr C, RSC 1985, c C-46, ss 83.02, 83.03 and 83.04.
71 Cr C, RSC 1985, c C-46, s 83.01.
72 Cr C, RSC 1985, c C-46, s 83.18.
73 Cr C, RSC 1985, c C-46, s 83.01.
74 FATF Mutual Evaluation Reports 2005–2006, online: http://www.fatf-gafi.org/document/32/0,2340,en_32250379_32236982_35128416_1_1_1_1,00.html.

There exist certain constitutional issues with regard to a provision of the PCMLTFA which purports to grant immunity from civil or penal proceedings in case of bona fide reporting under the Act.[75] Commentators have noted that the effectiveness of this protection in civil proceedings is questionable. As a matter of constitutional law, the power to legislate over 'Property and Civil Rights' is within the exclusive competence of Provincial Legislatures. The immunity provided by the federal statute could, arguably, be sustained by Parliament's powers of 'Trade and Commerce' and 'Peace, Order and Good Government', as well as through their various heads of power over certain reporting entities (mainly FWUB), the postal system, criminal matters and matters of national security.[76] The validity of this provision has not been challenged so far.

The Federation of Law Societies has, however, challenged the validity of certain other provisions of the Act, mainly on the ground that those provisions would displace the solicitor–client privilege. As a result, changes have been made to the Suspicious Transaction Reporting Regulations[77] repealing reference to 'legal firms' in the regulations, thus subtracting them from the application of Part 1 of the PCMLTFA.[78] The PCMLTFA also expressly provides that its requirements do not require legal counsels to disclose any communication that is subject to solicitor–client privilege.[79]

Other legislation

[6.21] In addition to the foregoing, there are many other statutes in Canada, ranging from bankruptcy to public inquiries statutes, which can also apply as exceptions to the duty of confidentiality.[80]

Compulsion of foreign legislation

[6.22] Disclosure of information to foreign authorities pursuant to foreign legislation may also be a valid exercise of the 'compulsion of law' exception to the bank's duty of confidentiality. In *Park v Bank of Montréal*,[81] a Korean branch of a Canadian bank disclosed, of its own volition, but pursuant to requirements of Korean legislation, information to Korean authorities regarding the illegal cross-border movement of currency from Korea. In a lawsuit in Canada, the British Columbia

---

75 PCMLTFA, SC 2000, c 17, s 10.

76 Manzer, *A Guide to Canadian Money Laundering Legislation* (2005 edn, Markham, Ont: Butterworths, 2004) p 61.

77 Proceeds of Crime (Money Laundering) and Terrorist Financing Suspicious Transaction Reporting Regulations, SOR/2001-317.

78 PCMLTFA, SC 2000, c 17, s 5(j).

79 PCMLTFA, SC 2000, c 17, s 11.

80 Bankruptcy and Insolvency Act, RSC 1985, c B-3: the Act imposes on the bank an affirmative duty to inform the trustee in bankruptcy if the bank discovers that its customer is an undischarged bankrupt. In addition, banks may be ordered by the court to produce the records or accounts of a company winding up under the provisions of the Winding-Up and Restructuring Act, RSC 1985, c W-10.

Inquiries Act, RSC 1985, c I-13: banks can also be subject to the Inquiries Act which provides that, in the course of an inquiry, any person can be subpoenaed to appear, testify and produce any documents in his possession which relate to the subject matter of the inquiry. This provision is particularly far reaching since there are at least 47 federal statutes which confer powers of inquiry by reference to the Inquiries Act and hence any of these statutes could be used to impose a duty of disclosure. See R Regan, 'You Don't Say' (1982), 89 Canadian Banker 32 at 34.

81 [1997] BCJ No 787, BCSC (CanLII) [*Park*].

Supreme Court accepted the bank's argument that it had been validly compelled by a provision of Korean law to divulge the information. The disclosure made under these circumstances was thus held not to be a breach of the bank's duty of confidentiality. The converse issue, that is the effect of foreign legislation preventing disclosure on the compellability of foreign banks in domestic proceedings, is discussed later in the chapter under the 'Domestic Proceedings to Obtain Information from Foreign Banks or Branches' heading.

Public duty to disclose

[6.23]   This rarely-used exception was referred to in *Tournier* in the context of preventing acts that might present a danger to the state. The decision seemed to imply that there would be a wide range of circumstances in which this exception might apply.

In a sense, the primary 'public duty' obligations come under specific legislation such as the traditional evidence legislation or the new money laundering provisions. The legislated duty in these situations relieves the bank of having to decide whether a sufficiently high public good would be served by disclosure so as to supersede the private duty to maintain confidentiality. This difficult judgment, combined with the ever-broadening legislative requirements, may explain why this has been a little-used exception.[82]

Common law developments limiting disclosure

[6.24]   As previously indicated, subsequent common law developments have further qualified the four *Tournier* exceptions, in particular, the 'compulsion of law' exception and the steps that banks are expected to take when disclosing information without its customer's consent pursuant to those exceptions. The Privy Council appears to have expanded the scope of a bank's obligation to its customer when the bank is presented with a legally enforceable demand by a third party for information about the customer. In *Robertson v Canadian Imperial Bank of Commerce*,[83] a case in which the original action was heard by the High Court of Justice of St Vincent and the Grenadines, the Privy Council held that a bank has the following additional obligations in such a situation:

1   when a bank receives a demand for information about a customer from a third party, the bank must use its best efforts to inform the customer of the demand,

---

82 In *Canadian Imperial Bank of Commerce v Sayani* (1993), 83 BCLR (2d) 167, BCCA, the Court of Appeal held that a bank's disclosure of a customer's indebtedness to the bank to prevent a trust company's reliance on the customer's misrepresentation of its indebtedness was a valid exercise of the public duty exception. In *Murano v Bank of Montreal* (1995), 31 CBR (3d), 20 BLR (2d) 61, Ont HCJ, affd (1998), 41 OR (3d) 222, 163 DLR (4th) 21, 41 BLR (2d) 10, 5 CBR (4th) 57, 111 OAC 242, Ont CA, disclosure by a bank to its customer's other creditors that the customer was 'dishonest' was held to fall outside of the 'public duty to disclose' exception.

In *BMP Global Distribution Inc v Bank of Nova Scotia*, [2005] BCJ No 1662, BCSC, appeal pending as of 13 March 2005, the bank had collected a counterfeit cheque for its customers. Because the cheque had been settled by the drawee bank, the Supreme Court held that the collecting bank was never at a loss position and thus could not invoke the 'bank's own interest' exception to divulge information about its customers in a grid warning to other financial institutions. It further held that because its customers were never under investigation for fraud, it could not claim protection of the 'public duty to disclose' exception either.

83 [1995] 1 All ER 824, [1994] 1 WLR 1493, PC.

unless the legal authorities have requested that the bank refrain from such notification; and

2   a bank must exercise care to give only that information that is specifically required by and relevant to the inquiry.

The factual background of the case involved a previous collection action, in which a subpoena *duces tecum* was issued to the Canadian Imperial Bank of Commerce ('CIBC') with respect to the accounts of a customer in order to show that a cheque had been deposited to the customer's account. The manager of the CIBC branch attended in court with a monthly statement of the customer's account, which showed numerous other transactions, including an overdraft, that were not relevant to the action. Following the collection action, the customer sued CIBC for breach of contract and negligence in disclosing the information about his account without his consent.

At the trial court level,[84] the judge held that a subpoena is not a court order to disclose in breach of a contractual duty of confidentiality and that CIBC therefore had a duty either to secure its customer's consent or ask the court to order it to testify and to produce the documents in question. As CIBC had done neither, it had breached its duty to its client. The Eastern Caribbean Court of Appeal[85] agreed that the subpoena was not a court order, but rejected the finding that CIBC had a duty to seek to avoid the disclosure, citing *Barclays Bank*[86] as authority for the proposition that the duty to maintain confidentiality does not exist within the four *Tournier* exceptions.

The Privy Council, however, ruled that the 'compulsion of law' exception in *Tournier* did not take away CIBC's obligation to advise its customer of the receipt of the subpoena. The obligation, however, was not an 'absolute duty' because the bank may either be unable to contact the customer or because the bank may, in certain situations, be entitled or compelled by public duty not to inform the customer. The major example cited by the Privy Council in this regard was an instance where the legal authorities requesting the information also requested that the disclosure remain confidential from the customer. *Robertson* indicates that banks must not view the legal compulsion exception as absolving them of the duty to the customer. To the contrary, the ruling places additional responsibility on banks to ensure that the fiduciary duty of confidentiality remains paramount and instils in the bank the responsibility, where appropriate, to narrow the intrusion by the legal authorities as much as possible.[87]

Canadian courts have explored the requirement of a duty to warn the customer since the Privy Council's decision in *Robertson*. In *Foundation Co*,[88] Justice Farley of the Ontario Court of Justice's Commercial List, after granting an ex parte application for an injunction enjoining the defendant's bank to freeze its client's assets, also known

---

84 *Robertson v Canadian Imperial Bank of Commerce* (unreported, 1988), St Vincent and the Grenadines HCJ, no 340.

85 *Robertson v Canadian Imperial Bank of Commerce* (unreported, 1990), Eastern Caribbean CA, St Vincent and the Grenadines, Civil Appeal no 4.

86 *Barclays Bank plc (trading as Barclaycard) v Taylor,* [1989] 3 All ER 563, [1989] 1 WLR 1066, CA [*Barclays Bank*].

87 For a more complete discussion of *Robertson*, see the commentary by E K Rowan-Legg, 'New Developments in Bank's Duty of Confidentiality' (1995) 26 Can Bus LJ 455.

88 *Foundation Co of Canada Ltd v Dhillon,* [1995] OJ 3211, Ont Ct J (Gen Div), (QL) [*Foundation Co*].

as a 'Mareva' injunction,[89] indicated, referring to *Robertson*, that 'under normal circumstances it would be quite proper for the bank to notify its client', but that in the circumstances of the case, where the defendant customer had allegedly breached a trust, committed fraud and accepted secret commissions, no such duty existed.[90] The following year, again referring to *Robertson*, the Court of Justice in *Budzisch*[91] hinted that there may well be such a duty in Canadian law, this time with regard to disclosure by a bank of the plaintiff's information to Revenue Canada pursuant to the Income Tax Act.[92] However, this second decision granted the defendant bank's motion to dismiss the plaintiff's action, holding, amongst other things, that even if there were such a duty and the defendant bank had breached it, the plaintiff had failed to establish any damages flowing from that alleged breach.[93]

The British Columbia Supreme Court decision in *Park* recognised that *Robertson* and *Foundation Co* established that 'ordinarily, where a bank is compelled by law to breach confidentiality in circumstances where the customer is not alleged to have been involved in criminal activity, it should use its best efforts to warn the customer of what it is about to do'.[94] Justice Henderson went on to apply *Barclay's Bank* in saying that:

> 'There is no implied term in the agreement between the bank and [the defendant] that the bank would warn him before disclosing to [the] authorities what it considered, on reasonable grounds, to be criminal conduct by him... [as it] could do significant damage to an ongoing criminal investigation without, however, in any way adding to the business efficacy of the banker–customer contract.'[95]

An interesting interpretation was placed on the public duty exception in *Canada Deposit Insurance Corpn v Canadian Commercial Bank*.[96] There, the plaintiff deposit insurance corporation (an agency of the federal government) brought an action against a bank which had gone into receivership in order to obtain access to the bank's records directly, rather than by way of discovery. Such access would enable it more effectively to seek recovery of funds it had paid out to the bank's depositors. The Alberta Court of Queen's Bench held that this case fell under *Tournier*'s public duty exception and that the public interest required that disclosure be made in this more efficient way.

Statutory limitations on disclosure

[6.25]   For many years, Canadian legislators had not seen fit to disturb the common law traditions as the foundation of the confidential relationship. Currently, however, the parameters of permissible disclosure of customer information by a bank are statutorily defined at the federal level and provincial governments have also implemented similar legislation.

---

89 After *Mareva Compania Naviera SA v International Bulk Carriers SA, The Mareva (1975)*, [1980] 1 All ER 213n, [1975] 2 Lloyd's Rep 509, CA; see generally Berryman, *The Law of Equitable Remedies* (Toronto: Irwin, 2000) p 60.
90 *Foundation Co*, [1995] OJ 3211, Ont Ct J (Gen Div), 26 October 1995, Appendix A (QL).
91 *Budzisch v Toronto Dominion Bank*, [1996] 2 CTC 278, Ont Ct J (Gen Div) [*Budzisch*].
92 RSC 1985, 5th Supp, s 231.2.
93 *Budzisch*, [1996] 2 CTC 278, Ont Ct J (Gen Div).
94 *Park v Bank of Montreal*, [1997] BCJ No 787, BCSC (CanLII), para 127.
95 *Park*, [1997] BCJ No 787, BCSC (CanLII), para 130.
96 [1989] AJ No 44, no 8503-23319, Alta QB.

Federal private sector privacy legislation

The Personal Information Protection and Electronic Documents Act

[6.26]   In April 2000, the federal government adopted the Personal Information Protection and Electronic Documents Act ('PIPEDA').[97] This new Act literally incorporates in its Sch 1 the principles of the Canadian Standards Association ('CSA') Model Code for the Protection of Personal Information,[98] which was itself based on the 1980 Guidelines on the Protection of Privacy and Transborder Flows of Personal Data of the Organisation for Economic Co-operation and Development.

Some Canadian provinces[99] have also enacted private sector privacy regimes. For a discussion of the issues that arise in connection with the interaction of federal and provincial law, see 'Concurrent Application of Federal and Provincial Privacy Legislation' below.

Application of PIPEDA

[6.27]   PIPEDA gradually came into force starting on 1 January 2001 and took full force and effect on 1 January 2004. PIPEDA applies to:

> 'every organisation in respect of personal information that the organisation collects, uses or discloses in the course of commercial activities; or is about an employee of the organisation and that the organisation collects, uses or discloses in connection with the operation of a Federal Work, Undertaking or Business.'[100]

'Commercial activities' means any transaction that is of a commercial character.[101] PIPEDA applies to commercial activities irrespective of whether (or not) these are provincial or extra-provincial activities. It also applies to any organisation, whether federally or provincially regulated. Secondly, PIPEDA applies in respect of personal information that is about an employee of an organisation that is a Federal Work, Undertaking or Business ('FWUB'). This refers solely to personal information held in relation to the management of human resources of FWUB.

'Personal information' is defined in PIPEDA to mean information about an identifiable individual, with the exception of the name, title or business address or telephone number of an employee of an organisation.[102]

There are exceptions to the application of PIPEDA.[103] The exceptions provide that PIPEDA does not apply to personal information that is collected, used or disclosed by an organisation for journalistic purposes[104] or by an individual for domestic purposes[105] and PIPEDA does not apply where the Privacy Act[106] applies.[107]

---

97   SC 2000, c 5.
98   CAN/CSA-Q 830-96.
99   Specifically, Quebec, Alberta and British Columbia.
100   PIPEDA, SC 2000, c 5, s 4(1).
101   See the definition of 'commercial activity', PIPEDA, SC 2000, c 5, s 2(1).
102   PIPEDA, SC 2000, c 5, s 2(1).
103   PIPEDA, SC 2000, c 5, s 4(2).
104   PIPEDA, SC 2000, c 5, s 4(2)(c).
105   PIPEDA, SC 2000, c 5, s 4(2)(b).
106   RSC 1985, c P-21.
107   PIPEDA, SC 2000, c 5, s 4(2)(a).

As of 1 January 2004, s 30, which for three years suspended the application of PIPEDA to organisations dealing with personal information within a province other than in connection with a FWUB, ceased to have effect.

PIPEDA also contains provisions for a review of the Act every five years by a parliamentary committee.[108] In her Annual Report to Parliament 2004 – 'Report on the Personal Information and Electronic Documents Act'[109] – the Privacy Commissioner of Canada has identified issues to address in the upcoming 2006 review. Amongst the issues to be addressed, the Commissioner suggests the review of the scope of PIPEDA's application with respect to employee information and to certain business information that is currently not excluded from the definition of personal information and the clarification of the distinction, if any, between 'commercial' activity and 'professional' services. The Commissioner further proposes to discuss the possible inclusion of a business transaction exception, as in the British Columbia and Alberta Acts (discussed below), as well as the possibility of granting enforcement powers to the Privacy Commissioner of Canada.

Principles

[6.28] The principle underlying PIPEDA is that personal information should not be collected, used or disclosed without the prior knowledge and consent of the individual concerned, subject to limited exceptions in the Act,[110] a principle that is also part of the CSA Model Code.[111] Other principles include the accountability of the organisation gathering the information,[112] the necessity of identifying the purposes of the collection,[113] the limitation of the collection, use and disclosure of the information to the identified purposes[114] and the necessity for the information to be maintained accurately.[115]

The consent of the concerned individual can be either express or implied under PIPEDA and the express character of the consent relates directly to the sensitivity of the information implied. It should be noted, however, that health and financial information is almost always considered sensitive.[116] Banks should therefore seek the express consent of the individuals whose personal information they gather. Moreover, the Act provides that the consent must be given for specific purposes, which implies that the individual must be aware, at the time of his consent, of the use that will be made of the personal information he provides. This gives rise to a delicate situation, where the object of the collection of personal information must be clearly stated for the organisation validly to use the collected information, but must not be too broadly worded or a court may hold that the person who agreed could not

---

108 PIPEDA, SC 2000, c 5, s 29.
109 Online: http://www.privcom.gc.ca/information/ar/200405/2004_pipeda_e.pdf ['PIPEDA 2004 Report'].
110 Eg see PIPEDA, SC 2000, c 5, s 7(3)b) and c) for situations where the communication of personal information without a consent is allowed (for the purpose of collecting a debt owed by the individual to the organisation or for disclosure made to a governmental entity that made a request for the information).
111 PIPEDA, SC 2000, c 5, Sch I, s 4.3; principle 3 of the CSA Model Code.
112 PIPEDA, SC 2000, c 5, Sch I, s 4.1; principle 1 of the CSA Model Code.
113 PIPEDA, SC 2000, c 5, Sch I, s 4.2; principle 2 of the CSA Model Code.
114 PIPEDA, SC 2000, c 5, Sch I, ss 4.4 and 4.5; principles 4 and 5 of the CSA Model Code.
115 PIPEDA, SC 2000, c 5, Sch I, s 4.6; principle 6 of the CSA Model Code.
116 The form of consent will vary depending on the sensitivity of the information involved: see PIPEDA, SC 2000, c 5, Sch I, s 4.3.4.

know all the implications of the consent. A detailed and complete description of the motives for which the information is gathered, the use that will be made of it and the people to whom it may be communicated is therefore advised. Moreover, the Act provides individuals with a right to access their personal information file retained by an organisation and to make corrections to incorrect or false information. [17]

The Privacy Commissioner, who is in charge of the application of PIPEDA, has already proceeded with numerous inquiries relating to complaints from individuals. Banks are prime targets for such inquiries and the cases are numerous where they were ordered to provide individuals with specific information. For instance, a bank was ordered to provide an individual with the personal information on which it had based its refusal to issue him a credit card and banks were also ordered to provide individuals with personal information regarding their credit rating when required to do so by the individuals. [118]

Provincial private sector privacy legislation

[6.29] It is relevant to consider provincial legislation since, as explained in more details under 'Concurrent Application of Federal and Provincial Privacy Legislation' below, under the Canadian constitutional system, it is likely that the provincial statutes will be found applicable concurrently to PIPEDA and that organisations located in provinces where privacy protecting statutes have been adopted will have to comply with both. So far, the decisions rendered generally recognised the applicability of Quebec's Act Respecting the Protection of Personal Information in the Private Sector ('PPIA')[119] to federal undertakings. Where both PIPEDA and the PPIA stem from the same Model Code and principles, they do, however, suffer some differences, especially the exceptions they allow to the necessity of consent for the collection, use and disclosure of personal information, as well as the cases where communication of personal information can be refused to an individual. In 2004, private sector privacy Acts also came into force in the western provinces of Alberta[120] and British Columbia.[121] The structure of these two Acts is also very similar, although the two regimes are not identical. Interestingly, the two western provinces' private sector privacy acts provide for a 'business transaction' exception to the limitation on the collection, use and disclosure of personal information.

Quebec's Act Respecting the Protection of Personal Information in the Private Sector

[6.30] Among the provinces, Quebec has taken the lead in legislating privacy protection. In 1994 (partly in January and partly in July), the PPIA came into effect making Quebec the first Canadian province to enact privacy legislation concerning the private sector. The Act applies to any personal information, whatever the nature of its medium and whatever the form in which it is accessible, whether written, graphic, taped, filmed, computerised or other.[122] 'Personal information' is defined to be 'any information which relates to a natural person and allows that person to be

---

117 PIPEDA, SC 2000, c 5, Sch I, s 4.8; principle 8 of the CSA Model Code.
118 Decisions rendered on 29 and 30 April 2002, for instance, available on the site of the Privacy Commissioner at www.privcom.gc.ca, the names of the parties are kept confidential.
119 RSQ, c P-39.1.
120 Alta Personal Information Protection Act, SA 2003, c P-6.5 ['Alta PIPA'].
121 BC Personal Information Protection Act, SBC 2003, c 63 ['BC PIPA'].
122 PPIA, RSQ, c P-39.1, s 1.

identified'[123] and therefore cannot relate to a legal person or a corporation as only personal information relating to individuals is covered by the Act. The Act is based on the same principle as the federal Act and the consent of an individual must be obtained in order to collect, use or disclose his personal information. This consent must always be express. Indeed, the Act states that 'consent to the communication or use of personal information must be manifest, free, enlightened and must be given for specific purposes'.[124] A consent that does not meet these four conditions is therefore deemed to be null. As for the 'specific purposes', it involves the same necessity for cautious drafting as the federal Act requires, as the description of the purposes for which the individual consents must be broad enough to allow for proper use of information, but must not be too general in order to qualify as 'specific'.

Interestingly, the Act provides, under s 17, that a:

> 'person carrying on an enterprise in Quebec who communicates, outside Quebec, information relating to persons residing in Quebec ... must take all reasonable steps to ensure that the information will not be used for purposes not relevant to the object of the file or communicated to third persons without the consent of the persons concerned and, in the case of nominative lists, that the persons concerned have a valid opportunity to refuse that personal information concerning them be used for purposes of commercial or philanthropic prospection and, if need be, to have such information deleted from the list.'

Companies operating in Quebec, such as banks, that communicate personal information outside the province should take steps to ensure that this provision is respected. If the receiving country or location does not have a legislative system ensuring the same protection of personal information, contractual provisions should be drafted to that effect.

It should be noted, moreover, that the fact of a company communicating personal information pertaining to Quebec residents outside the province is covered by the Act, even if this company does not have an office in Quebec.[125] The notion of 'carrying on an enterprise' does not relate to a specific location, but to the question of whether or not juridical acts involving personal information took place. Personal information stored electronically on a server that is not located in Quebec would therefore be covered as well.

In 2004, the Privacy Commissioner of Canada solicited Karl Delwaide and Antoine Aylwin to prepare a review of the jurisprudence developed under Quebec's PPIA during its ten years of application. The document, which is available in both English and French, may be found on the Commissioner's website.[126]

British Columbia's Personal Information Protection Act

[6.31]   Unlike Quebec's personal information protection legislation, the western province's legislation does not apply to organisations subject to the federal PIPEDA.

---

123 PPIA, RSQ, c P-39.1, s 2.
124 PPIA, RSQ, c P-39.1, s 14.
125 *Institut de l'Assurance Canadien v Guay,* [1998] CAI 431, Que CQ.
126 Delwaide & Aylwin, *Learning from a Decade of Experience; Quebec's Private Sector Privacy Act/Leçons tirées de dix ans d'expérience: la Loi sur la protection des renseignements personnels dans le secteur privé du Quebec*; Privacy Commissioner of Canada, 2005, online: http://www.privcom.gc.ca/information/pub/dec_050816_e.pdf.

This is stated explicitly in British Columbia's legislation. Most banks, as FWUB, remain subject to the application of PIPEDA[127] as the exemption order specifically states that FWUB are not exempt from the application of PIPEDA.[128] As such, they are exempt from the application of BC's PIPA. However, certain financial entities, such as credit unions, might be regulated by provincial law such that the federal legislation is inapplicable to them regarding the collection, use and disclosure of personal information within the province as per the exemption order discussed under 'Concurrent Application of Federal and Provincial Privacy Legislation' below.

The purpose of BC's PIPA[129] is essentially similar to the federal PIPEDA's.[130] The PIPA applies to every 'organisation'.[131] It does not apply, however, to certain activities, including 'the collection, use or disclosure or personal information if the federal Act [PIPEDA] applies to the collection, use or disclosure of the personal information'[132] and 'the collection of personal information that has been collected on or before this Act comes into force'.[133] The provisions of the PIPA prevail over conflicting provisions of other provincial enactments unless such enactment expressly provides otherwise.

'Personal information' is defined to mean 'information about an identifiable individual and includes employee personal information, but does not include (i) contact information or (ii) work product information'.[134]

An individual's consent is generally required before personal information regarding the individual may be collected, used or disclosed.[135] Consent must be informed and must be provided in accordance with the provisions of the Act, that is after having received the required information as to the purpose of the collecting organisation, in the absence of false, misleading or deceptive practices by the organisation.[136] An individual may not be required to consent to the collection, use or disclosure of personal information beyond what is necessary to provide a product or service.[137] The Commissioner has held that 'necessary' does not mean 'indispensable', such that information may be necessary even if it is not strictly impossible to provide a product or service without it.[138] Consent is deemed to have been given for a purpose where, at the time consent is deemed to be given, that purpose would be considered obvious to a reasonable person or if the individual voluntarily provides personal information for that purpose.[139] Consent may be withdrawn at any time, subject to limitations that the withdrawal does not frustrate the performance of a legal obligation or to limitations that apply for consent given to credit reporting agencies.[140]

---

127 BC PIPA, SBC 2003, c 63, s 4(1).
128 See Order in Council SOR/2004-220, 12 October 2004, Canada Gazette, vol 138, no 22, 3 November 2004.
129 BC PIPA, SBC 2003, c 63, s 2.
130 PIPEDA, SC 2000, c 5, s 3.
131 BC PIPA, SBC 2003, c 63, s 1: a defined term including a person, unincorporated association, trade union, trust or not-for-profit organisation.
132 BC PIPA, SBC 2003, c 63, s 3(2)(c); see the definition of 'federal Act' at s 1.
133 BC PIPA, SBC 2003, c 63, s 3(2)(i).
134 BC PIPA, SBC 2003, c 63, s 1.
135 BC PIPA, SBC 2003, c 63, s 6.
136 BC PIPA, SBC 2003, c 63, s 7(1).
137 BC PIPA, SBC 2003, c 63, s 7(2).
138 Order P05-01, paras 77–78 and 91.
139 BC PIPA, SBC 2003, c 63, s 8(1).
140 BC PIPA, SBC 2003, c 63, s 9.

Organisations may only collect personal information after disclosing the purpose of such collection to the individual and that purpose must be one that a reasonable person would consider appropriate in the circumstances.[141] The collection, use or disclosure of information without consent is allowed where collection with consent would compromise the availability or accuracy of the personal information and the collection is reasonable for an investigation or proceedings, where the collection is required or authorised by law, where the collection is necessary to facilitate the collection or payment of a debt owed to or by the organisation or where the information was disclosed to the organisation in circumstances where consent was not required for the disclosure.[142] Disclosure is further permitted without consent where such disclosure is in accordance with the provision of a treaty requiring or authorising it, is for the purpose of complying with a 'subpoena, warrant or order issue or made by a court, person or body with jurisdiction to compel the production of personal information', is made to a public body or law enforcement agency in the context of an investigation relating to an offence or is made to a lawyer representing the organisation.[143]

Moreover, the Act contains a provision that allows the disclosure of personal information in the context of a business transaction defined in the Act to mean 'the purchase, sale, merger or amalgamation or any other type of acquisition, disposal, or financing of an organisation or a portion of an organisation or of any of the business or assets of the organisation'.[144] The application of the exception is limited to business transactions involving substantial assets of the organisation other than the personal information.[145]

With regard to such a transaction, the BC Act provides that an organisation may disclose personal information about its employees, customers, directors, officers or shareholders without their consent to a prospective party if the personal information is necessary to decide whether to proceed with the transaction and the parties to the transaction have entered into an agreement limiting the use and disclosure of the personal information solely for purposes related to the prospective business transaction.[146] Once the organisation proceeds with the transaction, it may disclose information about the same class of persons if the party to whom the information is disclosed only uses or discloses the information for the purposes for which the information was originally collected, used or disclosed by the organisation, if the disclosure relates directly to a business transaction and if the individuals are notified that the transaction has taken place and that the information has been disclosed.[147] Should the transaction not be completed, the prospective party must destroy or return personal information it has collected.[148]

The Act also provides for mechanisms enabling individuals to access and correct personal information. It further assigns responsibility to organisations for the care of personal information in their custody or control. Finally, the PIPA provides for offences and penalties for failure to respect the provisions of the Act.

---

141 BC PIPA, SBC 2003, c 63, ss 10 and 11.
142 BC PIPA, SBC 2003, c 63, s 12(1)(c), (h), (i) and (j); s 15(1)(c), (h), (i) and (j); s 18(1)(c), (g) and (o).
143 BC PIPA, SBC 2003, c 63, s 18(1)(h), (i), (j) and (m).
144 BC PIPA, SBC 2003, c 63, s 20(1).
145 BC PIPA, SBC 2003, c 63, s 20(7).
146 BC PIPA, SBC 2003, c 63, s 20(2).
147 BC PIPA, SBC 2003, c 63, s 20(4).
148 BC PIPA, SBC 2003, c 63, s 20(6).

Alberta's Personal Information Protection Act

[6.32]   Although there is no provision expressly stating that the Alberta PIPA does not apply to organisations subject to PIPEDA, both the Privacy Commissioners of Canada and Alberta have expressed the view that it does not.[149] However, because the federal Act is applicable to such organisations in any event,[150] one presumes that the Albertan legislature perceives these organisations to be federally regulated and thus outside the province's field of influence.

The purpose of Alberta's PIPA[151] is also similar to BC's PIPA and the federal PIPEDA's. Alberta's PIPA applies to every organisation[152] in respect of all personal information.[153] Information acquired prior to the PIPA's coming into force is deemed to have been collected with consent and may be used and disclosed by the organisation for the purposes for which the information was collected.[154] The provisions of the PIPA take precedence over the provisions of another provincial enactment where there is inconsistency or conflict between the two unless the latter expressly provides otherwise or is the Freedom of Information and Protection of Privacy Act;[155] they are also of public order.[156] Personal information is defined to mean 'information about an identifiable individual'.[157]

An organisation is responsible for the personal information that is in its custody or control.[158] An organisation must obtain an individual's consent prior to collecting, using or disclosing their personal information.[159] An organisation may only collect, use or disclose personal information for purposes that are reasonable.[160] The PIPA defines reasonableness for the purposes of its application as 'what a reasonable person would consider appropriate in the circumstances'.[161]

---

149 See Privacy Commissioner of Canada, Annual Report 2004, online: http://www.privcom.gc.ca/information/ar/200405/2004_pipeda_e.pdf at 22 (Commissioner states that the statutes of Alberta and BC apply to 'all organisations within the two provinces, except for (a) those covered by other provincial privacy legislation and (b) federal works, undertakings or businesses covered by PIPEDA'); Alta Privacy Commissioner, 'Guide to the Personal Information Protection Act', online: http://www.oipc.ab.ca/ims/client/upload/PIPAbrochure.pdf (Commissioner states that PIPA does not apply to 'a federally-regulated organisation that is already covered by the federal Personal Information Protection and Electronic Documents Act (eg banks, airlines, telecommunications, inter-provincial transportation and radio and television broadcasting companies)'); Alta Privacy Commissioner, 'A Guide for Businesses and Organisations', online: http://www.oipc.ab.ca/ims/client/upload/PIPAGuidev4.pdf at 17 (Commissioner states that PIPA applies 'to provincially-regulated private businesses, non-profit organisations, trade unions and self-governing professions doing business inside Alberta. However, PIPEDA still applies to these organisations when carrying out commercial activities involving personal information that crosses Alberta's borders. PIPEDA continues to apply to federally-regulated industries located in Alberta').
150 See Exemption Order: Order in Council SOR/2004-219, 12 October 2004, Canada Gazette, vol 138, no 22, 3 November 2004.
151 Alta PIPA, SA 2003, c P-6.5, s 3.
152 A defined term including corporation, unincorporated association, a trade union, partnership and individual.
153 Alta PIPA, SA 2003, c P-6.5, s 4(1) with the exception of certain listed instances at s 4(3).
154 Alta PIPA, SA 2003, c P-6.5, s 4(4).
155 RSA 2000, c F-25.
156 Alta PIPA, SA 2003, c P-6.5, s 4(6) and (7).
157 Alta PIPA, SA 2003, c P-6.5, s 1(j).
158 Alta PIPA, SA 2003, c P-6.5, s 5(1).
159 Alta PIPA, SA 2003, c P-6.5, s 7.
160 Alta PIPA, SA 2003, c P-6.5, ss 11, 16 and 19.
161 Alta PIPA, SA 2003, c P-6.5, s 2.

An organisation may collect, use or disclose information without consent in circumstances listed in the PIPA.[162] Of particular interest to banks, an organisation may, without consent, collect, use or disclose information if it is done pursuant to a statute or regulation of Alberta or Canada that authorises or requires the same.[163] It may collect, use or disclose, without consent, information necessary to collect a debt owed to it or repay a sum owed by it[164] and it may use information without consent where the information may be disclosed by an organisation without consent.[165] It may disclose information without consent where disclosure is to a public body that is authorised or required by an enactment of Alberta or Canada to collect the information from the organisation,[166] or where disclosure is in accordance with a provision of a treaty that authorises or requires its disclosure and is made under an enactment of Alberta or Canada,[167] or where disclosure 'is for the purpose of complying with a subpoena, warrant or order issued or made by a court, person or body having jurisdiction to compel the production of information or with a rule of court that relates to the production of information',[168] or where disclosure is made to a public body or law enforcement agency in Canada to assist in an investigation either undertaken with a view to a law enforcement proceeding or from which a law enforcement proceeding is likely to result,[169] or where disclosure is reasonable for the purposes of an investigation or legal proceeding,[170] or where disclosure is for the purposes of protecting against, or for prevention, detection or suppression of, fraud, market manipulation or unfair trading practices and the disclosing organisation or the organisation to which the information is being disclosed is qualified to carry out such purposes.[171]

Alberta's PIPA provides an exception for business transactions. Section 22 provides for the collection, use and disclosure of personal information for the purposes of a business transaction[172] between an organisation and one or more other organisations if such collection, use or disclosure is effected in accordance with the section.[173] Thus, organisations that are parties to a business transaction may, during the period leading up to and including completion, if any, of the business transaction, collect, use or disclose personal information without consent if the parties have entered into an agreement restricting such collection, use or disclosure to the purposes that relate to the business transaction and the information is necessary to determine whether to proceed with the business transaction or to carry out and complete the business transaction. Moreover, after completion of the business transaction, the parties may collect, use or disclose personal information without consent if the parties have entered into an agreement which restricts such collection, use or disclosure to the purposes for which the information was initially collected and the information relates solely to the carrying on of the business or activity or the carrying out of the objects for which the transaction took place. Should the business transaction not take place,

---

162 Alta PIPA, SA 2003, c P-6.5, ss 14, 17 and 20.
163 Alta PIPA, SA 2003, c P-6.5, ss 14(b), 17(b) and 20(b).
164 Alta PIPA, SA 2003, c P-6.5, ss 14(i), 17(j) and 20(i).
165 Alta PIPA, SA 2003, c P-6.5, s 17(h).
166 Alta PIPA, SA 2003, c P-6.5, s 20(c).
167 Alta PIPA, SA 2003, c P-6.5, s 20(d).
168 Alta PIPA, SA 2003, c P-6.5, s 20(e).
169 Alta PIPA, SA 2003, c P-6.5, s 20(f).
170 Alta PIPA, SA 2003, c P-6.5, s 20(m).
171 Alta PIPA, SA 2003, c P-6.5, s 20(n).
172 Defined at Alta PIPA, SA 2003, c P-6.5, s 20(1)(a).
173 Section 22, Alta PIPA, SA 2003, c P-6.5, does not apply to transactions whose primary purpose is the transfer of personal information (Alta PIPA, SA 2003, c P-6.5, s 22(6)).

the party to whom the information was disclosed must either destroy it or return it to the party that disclosed it.

Note that Alberta's business transaction exception is wider than BC's as it covers any personal information, not just information relating to employees, customers, directors, officers or shareholders.

The PIPA also provides for whistleblower protection for employees of organisations who disclose possible contravention of the PIPA to the provincial Privacy Commissioner. The PIPA also provides for offences, penalties and damages for breach of the Act.

Concurrent application of federal and provincial privacy legislation

[6.33] It should be noted that, under the currently prevailing interpretation of private sector privacy legislation, there are circumstances where activities relating to personal information could be subject to more than one privacy regime.

The Governor in Council has the power to exempt an organisation, a class of organisations, an activity or a class of activities from the application of Part 1 of PIPEDA with respect to the collection, use or disclosure of personal information that occurs in a province if the Governor in Council is satisfied that the legislature of that province has implemented legislation that is 'substantially similar' to Part 1. So far, Quebec's PPIA[174] and the PIPA of Alberta[175] and British Columbia[176] have been deemed substantially similar. The exemption orders apply to organisations that are subject to one of the provincial privacy statutes in respect of the collection, use and disclosure of personal information that occurs within the province. The exemption orders specifically provide that they do not apply to organisations that are a FWUB, which remain subject to PIPEDA.

According to the Privacy Commissioner of Canada, some intra-provincial activities of exempt organisations could remain subject to PIPEDA.[177] This would occur when a type of personal information is not covered by the substantially similar provincial legislation. She gives the example of personal health information in Alberta. Health information is excluded from the scope of Alberta's PIPA[178] and the Health Information Act[179] does not apply to practitioners in private practice. Thus, she says, private practitioners would be subject to PIPEDA.[180] Should there be other situations where personal information is not covered by a provincial statute, PIPEDA would continue to apply to it.

Secondly, PIPEDA applies when the collection, use or disclosure by an exempt organisation includes an extra-provincial component. Moreover, the flow of

---

174 RSQ, c P-39.1; Order in Council SOR/2003-374, 19 November 2003, in Canada Gazette, vol 137, no 25, 3 December 2003.
175 SA 2003, c P-6.5; Order in Council SOR/2004-219, 12 October 2004, Canada Gazette, vol 138, no 22, 3 November 2004.
176 SBC 2003, c 63; Order in Council SOR/2004-220, 12 October 2004, Canada Gazette, vol 138, no 22, 3 November 2004.
177 PIPEDA 2004 Report, online: http://www.privcom.gc.ca/information/ar/200405/2004_pipeda_e.pdf at 24.
178 Alta PIPA, SA 2003, c P-6.5, s 3(f).
179 RSA 2000, c H-5.
180 PIPEDA 2004 Report, online: http://www.privcom.gc.ca/information/ar/200405/2004_pipeda_e.pdf at 24.

information across provincial boundaries remains subject to PIPEDA. If an exempt organisation, let us say in Alberta, discloses information outside the province to an organisation in Saskatchewan for instance, then the interprovincial transaction is subject to PIPEDA. Alternatively, an individual could complain about the disclosure to the Privacy Commissioner of Alberta under Alberta's PIPA or about the corollary collection of information to the Privacy Commissioner of Canada as Saskatchewan does not have a private sector privacy regime.[181] Thus, an organisation which operates in more than one province will often be subject to the federal and provincial regimes.

As discussed above, the federal PIPEDA applies to all FWUB throughout Canada. Under the terms of the BC PIPA[182] and the interpretation given to Alberta's PIPA by the Privacy Commissioners of Canada and Alberta,[183] such FWUB are exempt from the application of the provincial statutes. Such FWUB, however, remain subject to the Quebec PPIA. Indeed, Quebec's PPIA does not restrict its application as regards federally-regulated organisations. The *Commission d'accès à l'information* has held that organisations subject to federal jurisdiction are subject to the application of the PPIA in their dealings with Quebec individuals;[184] this includes banks.[185] A 2003 Superior Court decision,[186] however, might reverse this trend. In *Air Canada*, the Superior Court held that the provincial privacy legislation is inapplicable to certain core aspects of federally-regulated enterprises, in this case, personal information relating to the hiring of flight attendants of an airline.

The Superior Court found that the pith and substance of Quebec's PPIA was the 'creation, management and access to records of an enterprise'.[187] It went on to decide that the hiring of flight personnel was part of the specifically federal nature of the jurisdiction to which the organisation is subject. As such, the Superior Court held that the effect of the provincial statute was to regulate a vital part of the management and operation of the federally-regulated organisation because it sought to regulate part of the airline's hiring process.

'Thus, according to [*Bell Canada v Quebec (Commission de la santé et de la sécurité du travail)*, [1988] 1 SCR 749], as soon as we come to the conclusion that the impugned legislation overlaps on a domain that is within the exclusive competence of Parliament, as the management of a federal enterprise or a vital or

---

181 PIPEDA 2004 Report, online: http://www.privcom.gc.ca/information/ar/200405/2004_pipeda_e.pdf at 24.
182 BC PIPA, SBC 2003, c 63, s 3(2)(c).
183 PIPEDA 2004 Report, online: http://www.privcom.gc.ca/information/ar/200405/2004_pipeda_e.pdf at 22; Alta Privacy Commissioner, 'Guide to the Personal Information Protection Act', online: http://www.oipc.ab.ca/ims/client/upload/PIPAbrochure.pdf; Alta Privacy Commissioner, 'A Guide for Businesses and Organisations', online: http://www.oipc.ab.ca/ims/client/upload/PIPAGuidev4.pdf at 17. See 'Alberta's Personal Information Protection Act' above.
184 *Pierre v Federal Express Canada Ltee,* [2003] CAI 129; *Rioux v Recyclage Kebec Inc,* [2000] CAI 117; *Jabre v Middle East Airlines–AirLiban SAL,* [1998] CAI 404; *DeBellefeuille v Canpar Transport Ltee,* [1998] CAI 178; *Laperrière v Air Canada,* [1997] CAI 167, review granted for other reasons 8 October 1997, Que Sup Ct, appeal rejected 20 April 2000, Que CA.
185 *Lamarre v Banque Laurentienne,* CAI 99 09 63, AZ-50144774, 21 August 2002, Commissioners D Boissinot, M Laporte and J Stoddart.
186 *Air Canada v Constant,* 2003 IIJCan 1018, [2003] CAI 710, JE 2003-1799, AZ-50191009, 500-05-074681-022, Que Sup Ct (cited to IIJCan); appeal pending as of 8 March 2006, 500-09-013818-034, Que CA [*Air Canada*].
187 *Air Canada,* 2003 IIJCan 1018, Que Sup Ct, para 28, authors' translation.

essential element of the specifically federal nature of its jurisdiction, the provincial law is, for this reason, inapplicable to federal enterprises.'[188]

The provincial private sector privacy legislation seeks to regulate enterprises directly.[189] In doing so, the PPIA 'touches or affects the management or operation of Air Canada and, in the instant case, an essential or vital element of the specifically federal nature of the jurisdiction over Air Canada, which is sufficient to render [the PPIA] inapplicable towards [Air Canada]'.[190]

Moreover, the Superior Court remarked that 'in other words, it seems that if the [PPIA] was applicable [to Air Canada], Air Canada would [since the coming into force of PIPEDA] be faced with two statutes, one federal, the other provincial, having the same object'.[191] Because of its decision on the inapplicability of the legislation, however, the Superior Court held that it was unnecessary for it to decide what the impact of the co-extensive application of both regimes would be.

It should be noted that the government of Quebec has since asked the Quebec Court of Appeal to rule on whether Part 1 of PIPEDA is intra vires of the Parliament of Canada.[192]

FWUB doing business in Quebec and elsewhere should be careful to ensure that they comply with the PPIA. Unless the personal information at issue is within the specifically federal nature of the organisation, it appears that the PPIA's provision will be applicable to FWUB. See 'Application of PIPEDA' above for other instances where PIPEDA could apply to exempt organisations.

Private sector privacy developments in other provinces

[6.34]   As for the other Canadian provinces, they all have a privacy legislation dealing with the public (governmental) sector, but have not, so far, adopted any Act similar to existing provincial statutes with regards to the private sector. At the time of writing, Bill 207 the Personal Information Protection and Identity Theft Prevention Act is before the Manitoba legislature. Manitoba has, however, enacted the Personal Health Information Act.[193] Saskatchewan has also enacted legislation to deal with health information[194] and so has Ontario.[195] Ontario's Act has been deemed substantially similar to Part 1 of PIPEDA as regards personal health information.[196] Further developments could see the expansion of privacy legislation in the private sector in other Canadian provinces.

Provincial consumer reporting legislation, such as the Consumer Reporting Act in Ontario,[197] governs the operations of credit bureaux. The legislation does not require explicit consent before a bank or other credit granting agency can give a credit reference. It does, however, differentiate between 'credit' information and 'personal'

---

188 *Air Canada*, 2003 IIJCan 1018, Que Sup Ct, para 112, authors' translation.
189 *Air Canada*, 2003 IIJCan 1018, Que Sup Ct, para 121.
190 *Air Canada*, 2003 IIJCan 1018, Que Sup Ct, para 140, authors' translation.
191 *Air Canada*, 2003 IIJCan 1018, Que Sup Ct, para 147, authors' translation.
192 Order in Council 1368-2003, 17 December 2003, Official Gazette, no 2, 14 January 2004.
193 CCSM, c P33.5.
194 Health Information Protection Act, SS 1999, c H-0.021.
195 Personal Health Information Protection Act, SO 2004, c 3, Sch A.
196 Exemption Order: Order in Council SOR/2005-399, 28 November 2005, Canada Gazette, vol 139, no 25, 14 December 2005.
197 RSO 1990, c C-33.

information. If personal information is to be supplied or if a report is to be requested from a credit bureau regarding a customer, the customer must be notified in a prescribed manner prior to making a request for a credit report or providing such personal information. As a matter of routine, however, this notification is incorporated into standard forms, such as applications for loans used by banks, and credit reports are routinely given and obtained by Canadian banks on their customers through independent credit reporting agencies, as well as by way of direct reports to other banks. Normally, a bank will not knowingly give a credit report other than to another financial institution or a bona fide credit reporting agency.

Outsourcing

[6.35] Canadian privacy legislation also imposes constraints on financial institutions' ability to enter into outsourcing arrangements that involve the transfer of personal information that is within their custody. Principle 4.1.3 of the CSA[198] provides that an organisation is responsible for information in its possession or custody that has been transferred to a third party for processing. It specifically requires that the organisation uses contractual or other means to ensure an equivalent level of protection of the information while it is being processed. However, the feasibility of ensuring similar levels of protection is problematic when the third party is subject to foreign legislation. Should a Canadian organisation outsource some data processing function to a foreign entity, that entity would most likely be subject to foreign legislation that could compel disclosure to third parties, such as governmental agencies.

The Assistant Privacy Commissioner of Canada has had the opportunity to review the application of this principle in a recent ruling under PIPEDA.[199] Case 313 concerned the outsourcing by a Canadian bank of its credit card service to a service provider located in the US. In particular, concerns stemmed from that service provider's obligations under the USA PATRIOT Act.[200] The Commissioner held that PIPEDA does not prohibit the use of foreign-based third party service providers, but does oblige Canadian organisations using those providers to have provisions in place to ensure a comparable level of protection. She held that no contractual provision, however, could override the laws of the foreign-based service provider's jurisdiction and information disclosed to that provider would be subject to those laws. However, the risk of disclosure of information to foreign authorities is a comparable legal risk to that of disclosure to Canadian authorities. The Commissioner held that an organisation should notify its customers of the risk of disclosure of information to US authorities, but that it was not required to obtain its customers' consent to outsource its data processing operations.

The Commissioner noted that PIPEDA cannot prevent US authorities from lawfully accessing personal information held by Canadian organisations in Canada or in the US, nor can it force Canadian organisations to stop outsourcing to foreign-based service providers. Further, she noted that PIPEDA demands that 'organisations be transparent about their personal information handling practices and protect customer personal information in the hands of foreign-based third party service providers to the extent possible by contractual means'.[201] Organisations, she added:

---

198 PIPEDA, SC 2000, c 5, Sch 1.
199 Case summary 313, online: http://www.privcom.gc.ca/cf-dc/2005/313_20051019_e.asp.
200 Uniting and Strengthening America by Providing Appropriate Tools Required to Intercept and Obstruct Terrorism Act 2001, Pub L No 107-56, 115 Stat 272.
201 Case summary 313, online: http://www.privcom.gc.ca/cf-dc/2005/313_20051019_e.asp.

'are not required to provide customers with the choice of opting out where the third party service provider is offering services directly related to the primary purposes for which the personal information was collected. A customer provides consent to the primary uses of personal information when he or she initially signs the application form or when he or she continues to use the service after being advised of substantive changes to the service agreement.'[202]

Organisations are not required to obtain their customers' consent before outsourcing their data processing activities to the US. The Office of the Privacy Commissioner has taken the position that organisations are not required to provide customers with the choice of opting out where the third party service provider is offering services directly related to the primary purposes for which the personal information was collected.

What matters is 'transparency': the organisation must notify customers of the risk that their personal information could be lawfully accessed by US authorities because of where it is processed. This could signal the creation of an independent 'duty of transparency'.

In a more recent ruling, the Assistant Privacy Commissioner held that an organisation is allowed to transfer its data management operations to its affiliate from Canada to the US.[203] Although the principles embodied in this decision borrow from those of ruling 313 discussed above, the newer decision includes a very interesting statement:

'Principle 4.1.3 demands that an organisation uses contractual or other means to provide a comparable level of protection when information is transferred to a third party for processing. As this is an example of information sharing between a parent company and an affiliate, a separate contract between the two parties is not necessary. What is required is that both companies adhere to the same levels of data protection.'[204]

Although the Assistant Privacy Commissioner applies principles that are very similar or identical to those underlying provincial privacy legislation, all organisations should be careful to check whether the most recent ruling is applicable in the context of provincial privacy legislation, which may not be the case. For instance, although the letter of the law in Quebec is very similar in substance, the Quebec *Commission d'accès à l'information*, the administrative body charged with the supervision of the Quebec Private Sector Act, has given an interpretation which is different from that adopted in the Assistant Privacy Commissioner's most recent ruling. Section 20 of the Quebec PPIA reads as follows:

'**20.** In the carrying on of an enterprise, authorised employees, mandataries or agents may have access to personal information without the consent of the person concerned only if the information is needed for the performance of their duties or the execution of their mandates.'[205]

This section is drafted as an exception to the principle of consent. When third parties such as mandataries or agents are involved, the *Commission d'accès à l'information*

---

202 Case summary 313, online: http://www.privcom.gc.ca/cf-dc/2005/313_20051019_e.asp.
203 The summary of findings of this ruling is unreported at the time of writing.
204 At p 5 of the Assistant Privacy Commissioner's reasons.
205 PPIA, RSQ, c P-39.1, s 20.

has, through its decision-making power,[206] imposed some specific requirements adding to the text of s 20 of the Act. When an enterprise transfers information to a third party (mandatary or agent),[207] the *Commission* requires that it be accomplished through a written contract covering the following items and specifying:

1   the scope of the mandate;
2   the purposes for which the mandatary (or agent) wants to use the information in light of the objects or purposes of the file;
3   the category of individuals who would have access to the information; and
4   the obligation to keep the information confidential.

In light of s 17 of the PPIA, it is important to insist that such a written contract be entered into.

> '**17.** Every person carrying on an enterprise in Quebec who communicates, outside Quebec, information relating to persons residing in Quebec or entrusts a person outside Quebec with the task of holding, using or communicating such information on his behalf must take all reasonable steps to ensure
>
> > (1) that the information will not be used for purposes not relevant to the object of the file or communicated to third persons without the consent of the persons concerned, except in cases similar to those described in ss 18 and 23;
> > (2) in the case of nominative lists, that the persons concerned have a valid opportunity to refuse that personal information concerning them be used for purposes of commercial or philanthropic prospection and, if need be, to have such information deleted from the list.'[208]

Thus, when a person carrying on an enterprise in Quebec communicates, outside Quebec, personal information on a Quebec resident,[209] that person must make sure that the receiving organisation will take comparable protection measures to the ones set out in the PPIA. This can be achieved either by ensuring that a comparable privacy regime is in place in the receiving jurisdiction or through a contractual undertaking.

Electronic documents legislation

Electronic evidence

[6.36]   When it adopted PIPEDA, Parliament also modified the Canada Evidence Act to provide for the use of electronic evidence.[210] Most Canadian provinces have followed suit in the enactment of legislation dealing with the use of electronic evidence.[211] These statutes are based on the Uniform Law Conference of Canada

---

206 See *Deschesnes v Groupe Jean Coutu,* [2000] CAI 216.
207 Bill 86, 2nd Sess, 37th Leg, Quebec, 2005, which, at the time of writing, is pending before the Quebec National Assembly, proposes to extend this exception to other third party service providers (contract for services).
208 PPIA, RSQ, c P-39.1, s 17.
209 Bill 86, 2nd Sess, 37th Leg, Quebec, 2005, proposes to rescind this requirement relating to Quebec residents.
210 Canada Evidence Act, RSC 1985, c C-5, ss 31.1 to 31.8.
211 Alberta Evidence Act, RSA 2000, c A-18, ss 41.1 to 41.8; Manitoba Evidence Act, CCSM, c E150, ss 51.1 to 51.8; Evidence Act, RSNB 1973, c E-11, ss 47.1 and 47.2; Evidence Act, RSNS 1989, c 154, ss 23A to 23H; Evidence Act, RSO 1990, c E.23, s 34.1; Electronic Evidence Act, RSPEI 1988, c E-4.3; An Act to Establish a Legal Framework for Information Technology, RSQ c C-1.1; Saskatchewan Evidence Act, RSS 1978, c S-16, ss 29.1 to 29.6; Electronic Evidence Act, RSY 2002, c 67; BC, Nfld, NWT and Nu have not enacted such modifications.

('ULCC')'s Uniform Electronic Evidence Act ('UEEA').[212] This model legislation does not seek to displace statutory or common law rules of evidence, except rules relating to best evidence.[213] The Act seeks to permit the use of electronic documents as evidence in legal proceedings where the integrity of such records can be demonstrated with regards to the electronic record system in or by which the data is recorded or stored.[214] This integrity is presumed where there is evidence that the system was at all material times operating properly (or, if it was not, that the integrity of the electronic record was not affected) and that there are no other reasonable grounds to doubt the integrity of the electronic record system. It is also presumed where the record is recorded or stored in the usual course of business by a person not party to the proceedings and not under the control of the party seeking to adduce the record.[215]

Electronic documents and records

[6.37]   Using the principles of the ULCC's UEEA, Parliament and the Legislatures of all provinces and the Yukon Territory enacted legislation to provide a framework for the use of electronic documents in commerce.[216] These statutes regulate the form and validity of electronic documents and signatures.

The reach of the federal legislation only extends to federal governmental institutions, which renders the obligations of the Act of little interest for private entities such as banks. As for the provincial Acts which apply to private entities, their purpose is generally to ensure that electronic documents have a legal status equivalent to the one of paper-based documents, thus permitting the use of electronic-based documents as evidence and enabling enterprises and companies to convert their paper documents into more convenient electronic files.

THE QUEBEC EXAMPLE

[6.38]   The Quebec Act to Establish a Legal Framework for Information Technology[217] is one of these statutes. It details the parameters under which organisations may validly transfer paper-based documents to an electronic support. The Act also provides for protection measures with regard to confidential information (which is broader than personal information, since it covers any information that has been declared by law to be confidential) and therefore imposes an additional obligation on entities that employ electronic means to communicate or process their information and data. Just like all the other provincial statutes dealing with electronic documents, it also requires that the technology used to create, access or communicate electronic-based documents allows for the integrity of such documents to be maintained.

---

212 Online: http://www.ulcc.ca/en/us/index.cfm?sec=1&sub=1u2.
213 UEEA, online: http://www.ulcc.ca/en/us/index.cfm?sec=1&sub=1u2, s 2.
214 UEEA, online: http://www.ulcc.ca/en/us/index.cfm?sec=1&sub=1u2, s 4.
215 UEEA, online: http://www.ulcc.ca/en/us/index.cfm?sec=1&sub=1u2, s 5.
216 Electronic Transactions Act, SA 2001, c E-5.5; Electronic Transactions Act, SBC 2001, c 10; Personal Information Protection and Electronic Documents Act, SC 2000, c 5, Part II; Electronic Commerce and Information Act, CCSM, c E55; Electronic Transactions Act, SNB 2001, c E-5.5; Electronic Commerce Act, SNS 2000, c 26; Electronic Commerce Act, SNL 2001, c E-5.2; Electronic Commerce Act, 2000, SO 2000, c 17; Electronic Commerce Act, RSPEI 1988, c E-4.1; An Act to Establish a Legal Framework for Information Technology, RSQ, c C-1.1; Electronic Information and Documents Act, 2000, SS 2000, c E-7.22; Electronic Commerce Act, RSY 2002, c 66.
217 RSQ, c C-1.1.

The Act applies to both governmental and private entities and therefore to banks (with the exception of constitutional incompatibilities). The Act states that when the information contained in a document is declared by law to be confidential, its confidentiality must be protected by means appropriate to the mode of transmission, including on a communication network.[218] The person who is responsible for access to such a document must therefore ensure that its confidentiality is protected by controlling access to this document through a restricted view technique or any other technique that prevents unauthorised persons from accessing the confidential information or from otherwise accessing the document or the components providing access to the document.[219] The Act is silent as to which specific technologies would be considered appropriate and banks must therefore ensure that the above-listed criteria are fulfilled by electronic services such as online banking or e-mail communications that contain confidential information. Moreover, the Act requires that a link be established between an electronic document and a person to give full legal effect to the document.[220] To do so, any technology may be used to the extent that it allows the identity and location of the communicating person to be confirmed, as well as that person's link to the document, and that it allows for the document to be identified and its destination and origin to be determined at any given time. The Act also requires that documents containing confidential information remain unmodified and sets, in s 6, the standard as follows:

'the integrity of a document is ensured if it is possible to verify that the information it contains has not been altered and has been maintained in its entirety, and that the medium used provides stability and the required perennity to the information.'

Once again, no specified technology is required and banks who store information that is confidential on electronic documents must therefore ensure that their technological means meet those standards.

THE ONTARIO EXAMPLE

[6.39] The Electronic Commerce Act 2000 does not require a person to use, provide or accept information or documents in electronic form, it merely sets out a framework that allows such document to meet legal requirements of 'writings' if a person consents to its use.[221] Thus, a provision of law or statute which requires the use of writing will be satisfied if the requirements of the Act are met. The Act also allows a document to be retained, provided or examined in electronic form if there are reliable assurances of the integrity of the document and, if the electronic document is to be provided to a person, that document is accessible so as to be usable for subsequent references and capable of being retained by that person.[222] Documents so retained, whether their original was created, sent or received in written or electronic form, must be in the same format or in a format which accurately represents the information in the original document, they must be available for subsequent reference and, in the case of retention of documents originally sent or received in electronic form, they must preserve the information, if any, that identifies

---

218 RSQ, c C-1.1, s 34.
219 RSQ, c C-1.1, s 25.
220 RSQ, c C-1.1, s 38.
221 Electronic Commerce Act, 2000, SO 2000, c 17, ss 3–7.
222 Electronic Commerce Act, 2000, SO 2000, c 17, s 8.

the document's origin, destination and the date and time at which it was sent or received.[223]

Apart from specifying that a document is not provided to a person if it is merely made available for access by that person (for example, on a website),[224] the Act does not require the use of any particular technology to satisfy its requirements. Any technology that provides the requisite reliable assurances of integrity will be sufficient. The system must allow the document to remain 'complete and unaltered, apart from the introduction of any changes that arise in the normal course of communication, storage and display'.[225] Whether there are sufficiently reliable assurances of that depends on the circumstances and the purpose for which the document was created.[226] The Act also sets out criteria for the valid use of electronic signatures as defined under the Act.[227]

The Act further establishes a framework for electronic transactions and agents. It sets out rules relating to the electronic expression and transmission of offers and acceptances, for the validity of contracts in electronic form, the enforceability of such contracts in circumstances where the individual makes a material error and the time and place of formation of the contract.[228]

The Act specifically does not apply to permit the use of biometric information as electronic signatures, nor does its provisions apply to wills, documents creating interests in land, negotiable instruments, documents of title and other prescribed documents.[229] Other statutes may still validly limit the use of electronic information.[230]

ELECTRONIC RECORDS SYSTEMS

[6.40] Statutes dealing with electronic documents provide for a general framework, but do not specify the technical standards that an organisation should follow in setting up an electronic records system. The Canadian General Standards Board has recently published its 'Electronic Records as Documentary Evidence' standard.[231] The standard, which is meant to apply to private and public sector activities involving electronic records, aims to 'ensure reliability, integrity and authenticity' of electronic records, as well as to 'maximise the admissibility and the weight of electronic records as evidence in legal proceedings'.[232]

Limitations on networking

[6.41] As mentioned above, one of the critical concerns posed by the efforts of financial institutions to bridge the gaps between the 'four pillars' of the Canadian financial services industry for marketing purposes – those efforts are sometimes referred to as 'networking' – is the protection of confidential customer information.

---

223 Electronic Commerce Act, 2000, SO 2000, c 17, s 12.
224 Electronic Commerce Act, 2000, SO 2000, c 17, s 10.
225 Electronic Commerce Act, 2000, SO 2000, c 17, s 8(2)(a).
226 Electronic Commerce Act, 2000, SO 2000, c 17, s 8(2)(b).
227 Electronic Commerce Act, 2000, SO 2000, c 17, s 11.
228 Electronic Commerce Act, 2000, SO 2000, c 17, ss 19–22.
229 Electronic Commerce Act, 2000, SO 2000, c 17, ss 29 and 31.
230 Electronic Commerce Act, 2000, SO 2000, c 17, s 26.
231 CAN/CGSB-72.34 (2005).
232 CAN/CGSB-72.34 (2005), s 1.1; in O'Shea, *Records Retention Law and Practice*, vol 1 (looseleaf) (Toronto: Carswell, 2006) 17–34.

In the Canadian context, insurance companies and financial intermediaries are among the largest private sector collectors and users of personal information. The customer information which insurance companies possess is ideal for the target marketing of non-insurance products, while the very large branch networks of Canadian banks, with financial data relating to enormous numbers of bank customers, is very fertile ground for targetting sales of insurance products.

The federal government has attempted to deal with the threat to customer confidentiality by imposing a regulatory regime[233] designed to restrict the networking of insurance products by deposit-taking institutions, including banks, factoring corporations, financial leasing corporations, information services corporations, investment counselling and portfolio corporations and mutual fund corporations, amongst others. Generally speaking, the regime prohibits banks and their subsidiaries from providing, directly or indirectly, customer or employee information to an insurance entity. Banks and trust and loan companies are also prohibited from providing a telecommunications device that links their customers to an insurance entity if it is primarily for the use of customers in Canada. The regulations also require that such deposit-taking institutions must ensure that their customers are aware that the premises of any insurance entity adjacent to a bank or trust and loan branch are clearly separate and distinct. Lobbying efforts by banks to change these limitations have been multiplied in recent years in anticipation of the mandatory review of the Bank Act[234] which is set to take place in 2006. So far, there have been no firm commitments by the government to accede to those demands.

As noted above, in the development of these restrictions, more attention appears to have been paid to the concerns of the independent insurance companies about competition from the banks than to issues of confidentiality of bank customer information.

International aspects

[6.42]   Canadian banks have always operated in the international arena and the nature and scope of these activities have developed and expanded along with the general trend of globalisation of the financial services sector. The interaction of rules of different jurisdictions in connection with these activities can result in a conflict of legislative goals and, therefore, courts and legislators have attempted to deal with banks or others caught between conflicting rules. While Canada, like many other countries, has enacted legislation which may contribute to such dilemmas faced by banks, the actual use of power under such rules has been very sparing since governments no doubt wish to avoid disturbance of international comity.

Provisions to restrict demands for information

Federal legislation

[6.43]   As an example of such a rule, when Canadian banks are subpoenaed by foreign courts to provide information regarding customer accounts, they may be protected from having to breach their customers' confidence by virtue of the blocking

---

233   See the Insurance Business (Bank) Regulations SOR/92–330, ss 8–10 and the Insurance Business (Trust and Loan Companies) Regulations SOR/92-331, ss 8–10. The two regulations are substantially identical.
234   SC 1991, c 46.

legislation in the Foreign Extraterritorial Measures Act ('FEMA').[235] This statute provides that the Attorney General of Canada can block the production, disclosure or identification of any records in the possession or control of a Canadian citizen or a person resident in Canada if he believes that significant Canadian interests in international trade will be adversely affected. Such an order can be made in response to an order by a foreign tribunal, foreign court judgment or measures taken by a foreign state. The term 'records' is defined very broadly so as to include virtually any stored or recorded information. If the Attorney General makes such an order and believes that it may not be complied with, he may apply to a superior court to seize the records in question for safe keeping. Contravention of a blocking order by the Attorney General is an indictable offence, even if it is committed outside Canada, and is punishable by a fine of up to CDN$10,000 or a prison term of up to five years. There are, however, no reported cases where this legislation has been used to prevent disclosure of confidential customer records by a Canadian bank. In practice, as noted above, because Canadian courts and governments generally follow principles of international comity, the FEMA's blocking powers have been invoked very rarely and only when there is a political or foreign policy rationale behind the making of a blocking order.

The Competition Act may also be used to block the implementation of foreign judgments, decrees, orders or other processes in Canada if the Competition Tribunal finds that their effect would be detrimental to competition, trade or industry in Canada without providing compensating advantages. These blocking provisions generally parallel those of the FEMA and do not appear ever to have been invoked.

Provincial legislation

[6.44] Provincial legislation such as Quebec's Business Concerns Records Act[236] and Ontario's Business Records Protection Act[237] may also be used to prevent disclosure of documents to recipients outside of the province.

The Quebec Act prevents anyone from removing or sending from a place in Quebec to a place outside of Quebec any document relating to any concern pursuant to or under a requirement of any legislative, judicial or administrative authority outside Quebec.[238] A document is defined as 'any account, balance sheet, statement of receipts and expenditure, profit and loss statement, statement of assets and liabilities, inventory, report and any other writing or material forming part of the records or archives of a business concern'.[239] The prohibition has four exceptions: two of those relate to securities, one allows such removal where authorised by any law of Quebec or of the Parliament of Canada and the fourth allows such removal and sending 'by an agency, branch, company or firm carrying on business in Quebec, to a principal, head office, affiliated company or firm, agency or branch situated outside Quebec, in the ordinary course of their business'.[240] The Attorney General of Quebec or any person having an interest in a concern may petition a Court of Quebec judge to issue an order requiring any person to furnish an undertaking or security ensuring such

---

235 RSC 1985, c F-29.
236 RSQ, c D-12.
237 RSO 1990, c B-19.
238 RSQ, c D-12, s 2.
239 RSQ, c D-12, s 1.
240 RSQ, c D-12, s 3(a)

document will not be removed or sent out of Quebec under pain of contempt of court.[241] The Ontario Act is essentially similar to the Quebec Act.

However, the Canadian Supreme Court in *Hunt* has declared Quebec's Act to be constitutionally inapplicable to requests for the production of documents of other Canadian courts.[242] In that case, the Supreme Court felt it was unnecessary to consider whether the statute was wholly unconstitutional on the ground that it relates to a matter that arguably is outside the province. Thus, a bank would be unable to prevent disclosure of information if the disclosure was ordered by another Canadian court, but might be able to prevent it if the disclosure was ordered by a foreign court.

In Quebec, the Court of Appeal in *Unit Structures*[243] held that a request for the examination of witnesses and the production of documents under s 9 of the Special Procedure Act[244] was properly barred by the application of s 2 of the Business Concerns Records Act.[245]

Section 9 of the Special Procedure Act reads:

> '**9.** When, upon petition to that effect, it is shown to the Superior Court or to one of the judges thereof, charged with the administration of justice in the district, that a court of any other Province of Canada, or of any other British possession, or of a foreign country, before which any civil or commercial case is pending, desires to have the evidence of any party or witness in the district, such court or judge may order that such party or witness may be examined under oath, either by means of question in writing or otherwise, before any person mentioned in the said order, and may summon, by the same or by a subsequent order, such party or witness to appear for examination, and may order him to produce any writing or document mentioned in the order, or any other writing or document relating to the matter, and which may be in his possession.
>
> The same rule applies, with the necessary modifications, when an inquiry commission instituted by the Governor General in Council or by the Lieutenant-Governor in Council of another Province of Canada desires to have the evidence of a witness.'[246]

Decisions of the turn of the century of the Superior Court and the Court of Quebec decisions confirm this view.[247]

The Court of Appeal of Ontario in *De Havilland*,[248] in relation to Ontario's Business Records Protection Act[249] and the Canada Evidence Act,[250] has come to the opposite conclusion. Section 46 of the Canada Evidence Act provides that:

> '**46.** (1) If, on an application for that purpose, it is made to appear to any court or judge that any court or tribunal outside Canada, before which any civil,

---

241 RSQ, c D-12, ss 4, 5 and 6.
242 *Hunt v T & N plc*, [1993] 4 SCR 289, SCC [*Hunt*].
243 *Unit Structures Inc v Koppers Co Inc*, [1990] RDJ 330, Que CA [*Unit Structures*].
244 RSQ, c P-27.
245 RSQ, c D-12.
246 RSQ, c P-27, s 9.
247 *Polaris Industries Inc v Rasidescu*, [1999] JQ no 126, Que Sup Ct; *Trottier v Matrox Graphic Inc*, [2000] JQ no 155, Que CQ.
248 *Republic of France v De Havilland Aircraft of Canada Ltd and Byron-Exarcos* (1991), 3 OR (3d) 705, Ont CA [*De Havilland*].
249 RSO 1990, c B-19.
250 RSC, 1985, c C-5.

commercial or criminal matter is pending, is desirous of obtaining the testimony in relation to that matter of a party or witness within the jurisdiction of the first mentioned court, of the court to which the judge belongs or of the judge, the court or judge may, in its or their discretion, order the examination on oath on interrogatories, or otherwise, before any person or persons named in the order, of that party or witness accordingly, and by the same or any subsequent order may command the attendance of that party or witness for the purpose of being examined, and for the production of any writings or other documents mentioned in the order and of any other writings or documents relating to the matter in question that are in the possession or power of that party or witness.'[251]

In *De Havilland*, an application had been made to an Ontario judge pursuant to s 46 to require the taking of evidence. Section 1 of the Business Records Protection Act essentially provides that an order of a foreign court may not compel the production of documents in Ontario. However, the Court of Appeal held that an order of an Ontario court pursuant to s 46 is not an 'order, direction or subpoena emanating from a jurisdiction outside of Ontario' even if the order is issued further to a request of a foreign authority.[252] In other words, the Court of Appeal held that the order of a foreign court, by application pursuant to s 46, is transformed into an Ontarian order. This implies that the making of an application pursuant to s 46 is not an indirect way of enforcing an order of a foreign court or, at any rate, is not offensive to the Business Records Protection Act. Thus, the communication of documents pursuant to the order of a foreign court could not be blocked by the application of the Ontario Act. The Court of Appeal was also of the view that the removal of a document pursuant to the Canada Evidence Act would, at any rate, be a removal pursuant to a 'law of Ontario or of the Parliament of Canada'.[253]

Given the Supreme Court decision in *Hunt* and the conflicting jurisprudence regarding the application of Ontario and Quebec's business records Acts, banks should be wary of the effectiveness of such protection against foreign orders compelling disclosure of documents. A foreign order could be submitted in Canada in a provincial jurisdiction amiable to the enforceability of such orders, which, following the reasoning in *De Havilland*, would make it an order of a Canadian court. This order could then be enforced in Quebec in reliance on *Hunt*.

Procedures for agreed exchange of information

[6.45] Although Canadian legislators have attempted to ensure there would not be inappropriate compulsion of information by tribunals, they have also co-operated to facilitate exchange in appropriate circumstances. A good example is the Memorandum of Understanding ('MOU') executed in January 1988 between several Canadian provincial securities regulators and the US Securities and Exchange Commission. These MOUs provide for a broad exchange of information in the interest of regulating securities markets which are increasingly international in scope. When combined with the broad powers of search and seizure provided to provincial securities regulators, the MOUs increase the potential for confidential information being distributed to an even wider group.

251 RSC, 1985, c C-5, s 46.
252 *De Havilland* (1991), 3 OR (3d) 705, Ont CA, 719.
253 Business Records Protection Act, RSO 1990, c B-19, s 1(d); *De Havilland* (1991), 3 OR (3d) 705, Ont CA, 719.

Domestic proceedings to obtain information from foreign banks or branches

[6.46]   Although there is Canadian legislation to block information going abroad in circumstances where it would be contrary to Canadian policy, the same can occur in reverse where a Canadian court attempts to overcome restrictions on disclosure in a foreign jurisdiction. The conditions under which Canadian courts will insist on disclosure of records from a foreign bank have been explored in *Frischke v Royal Bank of Canada*[254] and *Re Spencer and the Queen*.[255]

Frischke involved an appeal from a court order requiring Royal Bank employees in Panama to give evidence about certain customers' accounts in breach of Panamanian law. The Court of Appeal, in allowing the appeal, refused to use its jurisdiction over the Royal Bank to order to compel its Panamanian employees to break their own country's laws.

Frischke was distinguished in *Re Spencer*, however. There, the Crown sought to call an employee of the Royal Bank as a witness on charges against a customer of the bank under the Income Tax Act. While a subpoena of this kind would present no problems in the normal case, the employee was at the material time manager of the Royal Bank's Bahamian branch and was being asked to give evidence regarding transactions which had been made in the Bahamas contrary to bank confidentiality provisions of Bahamian law. The Ontario Court of Appeal held that the compellability of a witness was a matter for the *lex fori* and that in Canada this witness was compellable. He was not being forced to give any evidence in contravention of Canadian laws even though he might be exposed to liability in another jurisdiction.

On appeal to the Supreme Court of Canada, the Court of Appeal decision was upheld on the grounds that even if the giving of evidence in Canada constituted a crime in the Bahamas, the courts and the public have a right to the evidence. To permit a witness to refuse to testify would be to permit a foreign country to frustrate the administration of justice in Canada with regard to a Canadian citizen. It was suggested by Justice Estey, however, that comity would require that the witness be allowed to make an application to that foreign jurisdiction to permit disclosure before the court compels him to do so.

To date, there has been no decision by a Canadian court that resolves the conflicting jurisprudence found in *Frischke* and *Spencer*. The recent trend, however, appears to indicate that bank secrecy laws of a foreign jurisdiction will generally not be a sufficient bar to the production of evidence if the action falls properly under the jurisdiction of the Canadian court and the bank is a party to the action. Most recently, in *Arab Bank v Coopers & Lybrand*,[256] Justice Halperin of the Quebec Superior Court held that representatives of four plaintiff banks should be compelled to testify regardless of bank secrecy laws in their home jurisdictions of Germany and Switzerland. The judge took the position that, the plaintiff banks having chosen to litigate in a forum where the law did not adhere to the same rigid rules of banking secrecy as found in their own jurisdictions, they should be required to comply with the rule of Canadian law as regards compellability of testimony.

---

254 (1977), 80 DLR (3d) 393, Ont CA.
255 (1983), 145 DLR (3d) 344, Ont CA, affd (1985), 21 DLR (4th) 756, SCC.
256 Cited as [1996] JQ no 1436, no 500-05-002564-936, Que Sup Ct.

Similarly, in the Ontario case of *Comaplex Resources International v Schaffhauser Kantonalbank*,[257] the issue considered was whether Swiss banking secrecy laws, which apparently prohibited disclosure by the defendant bank of such documents and information, could form a valid basis for the defendant bank's refusal to answer questions and produce the documents in Canada. Master Sandler of the Ontario High Court of Justice decided that neither *Frischke* nor *Spencer* applied to the *Comaplex* case and instead based his decision on US cases which have held that, procedurally, a person should not be permitted to invoke foreign law prohibitions against the disclosure of information in an application to compel the disclosure. Rather, the objection should only be raised at the time the court is considering sanctions for breach of an order to disclose.

CONFIDENTIALITY IN THE CONTEXT OF A FIDUCIARY RELATIONSHIP

[6.47] As noted above, although the traditional bank–customer relationship is normally one of debtor and creditor or principal and agent, under the appropriate circumstances, it can become a fiduciary relationship. Such a relationship goes beyond confidentiality and may impose additional duties upon a bank. In Canada, a fiduciary relationship has been found to arise when a bank steps outside of its conventional relationship and gives advice to a customer, upon which the customer relies (to the bank's knowledge) and from which the bank stands to receive a benefit or, alternatively, when the bank misuses information obtained from a customer. Although it is possible that such a relationship arises in circumstances where a bank is confining itself to more traditional banking activities, the circumstances in which it may be created are being expanded as banks move into the securities dealing and investment banking fields and take a broader and more active role in areas such as trading, investment management, takeovers and mergers and acquisitions.

Establishment of fiduciary relationship

[6.48] The leading Canadian case dealing specifically with a bank's fiduciary duties towards its customers continues to be *Standard Investments Ltd v Canadian Imperial Bank of Commerce*.[258] In this case, the plaintiffs attempted to acquire control of a publicly quoted trust company. They sought the advice and assistance of the bank's president, who agreed to help them. Unbeknown to the president, however, the bank's chairman had already decided to have the bank purchase for its own account just under 10% of the shares of the trust company in order to thwart an anticipated takeover attempt, which some speculated was to be made by the plaintiffs. An outside director of the bank was also a director of the trust company and controlled or influenced significant shareholdings in the trust company. Both this director and the trust company were important customers of the bank. In addition, when it became clear there was a fight for control, the bank subsequently assisted another of its customers in the purchase of a 44% interest in the trust company which, together with the bank's 10% interest (which it subsequently sold to that other customer), effectively prevented the plaintiffs' takeover from being successful.

---

257 (1989), 42 CPC (2d) 230, Ont HCJ.
258 (1985), 52 OR (2d) 473, Ont CA.

It was held by the Court of Appeal that a fiduciary relationship had been created. The plaintiffs had 'bared their souls' to the bank by providing it with confidential information regarding their takeover plans. In addition, the plaintiffs relied on the advice and assistance of the bank in their endeavour and the bank was aware of that reliance. Finally, the bank itself had obtained a benefit through the increased business that resulted from the plaintiffs' relationship with the bank as a result of their previously transferring accounts to the bank. Thus, all the criteria for the establishment of a fiduciary relationship were satisfied. As a result, the Court of Appeal held that the bank had a duty to disclose its conflict of interest.

It might be noted that there were actually two conflicts at play in this case. First, there was a conflict between the bank's interests and those of its customers, the plaintiffs. Secondly, there was the conflict between the interests of the plaintiffs and those of the bank's other customers who, to the knowledge of the bank, wanted to prevent the takeover from occurring. The Court of Appeal acknowledged that the bank probably had a legal obligation not to disclose the second conflict. However, the Court of Appeal said that if the bank was either unwilling or unable to disclose the nature of the conflicts, it should have said that it was unable to advise the plaintiffs due to existing conflicts of interest. Alternatively, if the bank was unwilling or felt unable to disclose to a customer that a conflict existed, the bank should simply have refused to advise the plaintiffs on the matter. In fact, the Court of Appeal found the bank did neither of these things, but rather allowed the plaintiffs to believe, over the course of seven years, that their takeover bid had a chance of success. The bank was, therefore, held to be in breach of its duties to them. Damages were assessed at the amount of the plaintiffs' purchase price of the trust company shares, plus the interest lost from what would have been safe investments, minus the amount received in dividends and ultimate proceeds from the plaintiffs' sale of the shares (which fell substantially in value when the third party was able to acquire control).

A recent case, although not involving financial institutions, suggests that courts might be prepared to widen the ambit of what must be disclosed to the beneficiary of the fiduciary obligation. More than ten years ago already, the Supreme Court of Canada indicated that the obligations imposed on the fiduciary will be 'tailored to the legal and practical incidents of a particular relationship'.[259] In *Xerex Exploration Ltd v Petro-Canada*,[260] Petro-Canada had acquired information on its own about the value of drilling rights owned by Xerex. It contacted Xerex to arrange for an agreement by which Petro-Canada acquired Xerex's rights in exchange for a percentage of the revenues derived from those rights. The Court of Appeal found that Petro-Canada owed fiduciary obligations to Xerex. Resting its decision on the passage of Justice LaForest's reasons in *Hodgkinson* (discussed below), the Court of Appeal in *Xerex* held that the fiduciary had the obligation to disclose to the beneficiary the information it had acquired on its own about the beneficiary's assets (its drilling rights) in negotiating an agreement with the beneficiary.[261] The Court of Appeal, however, stressed that its findings were based on the specific circumstances of the particular relationship between the parties and refrained from commenting on any of the questions raised by its finding, including whether the fiduciary should

---

259 *Hodgkinson v Simms,* [1994] 3 SCR 377, [1994] 9 WWR 609, SCC [*Hodgkinson* cited to WWR] 632, La Forest J; for a discussion of *Hodgkinson*, see 'Provision of Special Skills' below.
260 *Xerex Exploration Ltd v Petro-Canada,* [2005] AJ No 774, 2005 ABCA 224 (CanLII), Alta CA [*Xerex* cited to CanLII].
261 *Xerex*, 2005 ABCA 224 (CanLII), Alta CA, para 80.

disclose an investigation that yields no useful results, or results which the fiduciary does not intend to use or whether the fiduciary could refrain from entering into a fiduciary relationship with the beneficiary and attempt to profit from the results of its investigation some other way.[262]

The *Xerex* decision is an illustration that, in the context of a fiduciary relationship, organisations, such as banks, cannot hide behind the fact that they gathered the information (or that they 'own' the information) to avoid disclosing it to the client concerned. The obligation to deal with information in a certain way, whether to disclose it or not and to whom, depends upon the relationship between parties, whether fiduciary or otherwise; the 'ownership' interest of one party cannot supplant that party's obligation to divulge to its counterpart or to maintain confidentiality with regard to third parties.[263] For example, when a bank is found to be in a fiduciary relationship vis-à-vis its client, it may have the obligation to disclose to the client information about the client, regardless of where the information was obtained in the first place. One must distinguish between that scenario and the case where the information relates to a third party. In that second example, the bank should not have the obligation to disclose information about a third party to the client, even though the information might be of interest to the client. What remains unsettled is whether a bank should disclose to the client information that concerns both the client and a third party. So far, it appears that no tribunal has tackled this issue directly.

Although the courts have been careful to point out that the question of whether a fiduciary relationship will be found to exist depends on all of the circumstances of a given case, there appear to be some common threads. For example, where the bank goes further than simply to explain the nature and effect of a transaction and advises on its merit, it may be held to have 'crossed the line' from a normal debtor–creditor relationship into one involving fiduciary duties.[264]

Reliance by customer

[6.49] It would appear, however, that in order for a fiduciary relationship to be established, there must also be an element of special reliance or confidence placed in the bank by the customer, either by virtue of communication of particular knowledge or by reason of ignorance or infirmity of the customer. In either case, the bank must either know, or be in circumstances where it ought to know, of the reliance being placed upon it. Once that reliance is found, then a fiduciary relationship may be said to exist and the breach thereof, by misuse of information provided or by permitting the bank's own interests to conflict with those of the customer, is actionable.

Standard Investments provides an illustration of a finding of reliance by reason of the customer having provided particular information, notwithstanding that the customer's principals were experienced businessmen. An example of reliance found by reason of the circumstances of the customer (a more common situation) is *Hayward v Bank of Nova Scotia*,[265] where the trial judge found a fiduciary

---

262 *Xerex*, 2005 ABCA 224 (CanLII), Alta CA, para 81.
263 See generally *Lac Minerals Ltd v International Corona Resources Ltd,* [1989] 2 SCR 574, SCC, where it is not the fact that the information belongs to a party that matters, but the fact that it was communicated in circumstances giving rise to a duty of confidence and a fiduciary duty; *R v Stewart,* [1988] 1 SCR 963, SCC, para 24.
264 Waters, 'Banks, Fiduciary Obligations and Unconscionable Transactions' (1986) 65 Can BR 37 at 58.
265 (1984), 45 OR (2d) 542, Ont HCJ, affd 510 OR (2d) 193, Ont CA.

relationship to exist where a highly respected small-town bank manager undertook to advise a farm widow in modest circumstances on investments in exotic cattle, for which she was proposing to borrow from the bank against the security of the family farm. Through dealings with the promoter of the investment (who was also heavily indebted to the bank and behind in his obligations in respect of that debt), the bank manager had gained considerable knowledge of the exotic cow business. His enthusiasm for the business was not shared to the same extent by his superiors, although their doubts were not fully communicated to the bank manager.

At trial, the case turned on the naivety of the customer and the faulty advice provided by the bank manager coupled with the inequality of bargaining position. Little, if anything, was said about where the proceeds of the investment were to go. Presumably, they went to pay down the promoter's loans, which would, of course, be of advantage to the bank since he was behind in his payments. The Court of Appeal reluctantly affirmed the trial decision disapproving, however, the trial judge's reliance on the inequality of bargaining position as being relevant to the breach of fiduciary duty as opposed to the creation of the fiduciary relationship. However, the Court of Appeal again made no clear reference to what appeared to be a direct conflict between the bank's interest in having support for the cow business and its obligation to provide appropriate advice to the widow. In both judgments, the courts appeared to rely upon the decision of the English Court of Appeal in *Lloyds Bank Ltd v Bundy*.[266] The reasons of the Court of Appeal in *Hayward*, however, also referred to the later decision of the House of Lords in *National Westminster Bank plc v Morgan*,[267] quoting from Lord Scarman's speech,[268] to the effect that the presumption of undue influence cannot arise from the evidence of the relationship of the parties without there also being evidence that the transaction itself is wrongful, in that it constitutes an advantage taken of the party subjected to the influence. Thus, the notion that a fiduciary relationship can be established by reason of inequality of bargaining power alone was rejected.

Provision of special skills

[6.50] More recently, the Supreme Court of Canada has articulated more precisely the required components of a fiduciary relationship in *Hodgkinson v Simms*.[269] The case, while dealing with an accounting firm, not a bank, has clear implications for the potential liabilities of which banks must be cognisant as they enter into non-traditional financial services areas, such as dealing in securities. The case is notable as well for its finding of a fiduciary duty even though the plaintiff investor was a relatively sophisticated individual familiar with the investment markets.

In *Hodgkinson*, the plaintiff, a 30-year-old stockbroker, sought the defendant accountant's advice to shelter some of his income in conservative investments. The accountant advised the plaintiff to invest his money in some real estate ventures in which, unbeknown to the plaintiff, the accountant also had an interest. When the real estate market collapsed, the plaintiff lost most of his investment and sued the defendant for breach of fiduciary duty and breach of contract.

---

266 [1974] 3 All ER 757.
267 [1985] All ER 821.
268 [1985] All ER 821 at 827.
269 [1994] 3 SCR 377, [1994] 9 WWR 609, SCC.

While the trial court found for the plaintiff in both claims, the British Columbia Court of Appeal found a breach of contract, but held there was no fiduciary duty to the investor because the choice to invest was entirely his. On appeal, a majority of the Supreme Court of Canada overturned the Court of Appeal's ruling and found that a fiduciary duty did exist, despite the apparent lack of 'vulnerability' of the plaintiff.

Two elements were crucial to the Supreme Court's decision. The first was the finding that a 'power dependency relationship' existed between the parties. The Supreme Court noted that for this type of relationship to exist there must be more than a simple undertaking by one party to provide information and execute orders for the other, as in most everyday transactions between a bank customer and a banker. However, it may exist when the complexity and/or importance of the subject matter make it reasonable for the customer or adviser to expect that the adviser or banker is exercising his special skills in the customer's best interest.[270] The second element was the Supreme Court's ruling that the existence of the fiduciary relationship flows not from the plaintiff's ability to protect himself from harm, but from the nature of the parties' reasonable expectations of the relationship. The case, although not dealing specifically with a bank's fiduciary duty to a customer, thus suggests the need for banks to use caution when providing advice or special services beyond routine banking transactions, regardless of the level of sophistication of the customer.

Standard Investments and cases such as *Hayward*, which were decided in the early and mid-1980s, indicated that the courts were becoming more willing to find the existence of a fiduciary relationship. A strand of case law from the late 1980s gave some indication that the courts were again becoming less inclined to superimpose a fiduciary relationship on the dealings between a bank and its customers, particularly if the plaintiffs are themselves knowledgeable business people.[271] It remains to be seen, however, whether these more recent cases will really assist the bank in circumstances such as contested takeovers where the parties do have a significant degree of investment experience and sophistication. *Hodgkinson* and the cases which have subsequently followed it, however, reinforce the concept that a bank may not assume that a fiduciary duty is unlikely to be found simply because the bank is dealing with a 'sophisticated' customer.

CONFLICTS OF INTEREST AND CONFIDENTIALITY

[6.51]   As mentioned in the preceding discussion, banks have duties of confidentiality in the normal course of a banking relationship. Where the relationship can be characterised as fiduciary, a bank may have, amongst other obligations, an affirmative duty to disclose a conflict of interest or at least not to act in a transaction if to do so would result in a conflict of interest. As the range of activities in which banks and their affiliates are engaged has increased, so has the potential for such conflicts.

Internal conflicts

[6.52]   Perhaps the most straightforward conflict is the situation where a director or officer of the bank is considered to have an interest in a transaction to which the bank

270 [1994] 3 SCR 377, [1994] 9 WWR 609, SCC, 629–630.
271 Eg see *Continental Bank of Canada v Hunter*, Alta CA, 6 November 1986 and *Sugar v Peat Marwick Ltd* (1989), 66 OR (2d) 766, Ont SC.

is a party. Prior to the 1992 reform of Canadian financial institutions legislation, the Bank Act took a conventional corporate law approach and provided that, except under specified circumstances, a director could not attend or vote at a board or committee meeting at which the bank is considering whether to advance funds to him, to a firm of which he was a member or a corporation of which he was a director. In addition, the old Bank Act set out certain restrictions on loans to officers, employees and directors of a bank and to entities in which officers or directors of a bank have interests.[272]

The 1992 revisions of the Bank Act, as amended by the new financial institutions legislation noted above, instituted a much more comprehensive regime to restrict such transactions. The rationale for this change stemmed partly from the concern over self-dealing in the context of the failures of financial institutions in Canada and abroad and partly from the widening scope of operations, investments and affiliations that banks have acquired under the revised legislation. This restrictive code regulates transactions between a bank and related parties that might be in a position to exert influence over the bank's decision making. Such related parties include senior officers, shareholders and directors of the bank, their spouses and minor children, and entities controlled by those individuals. The Bank Act also empowers the Superintendent of Financial Institutions to designate related parties at its discretion. Any person whose interest in the bank, or relationship with either the bank or a related party, might reasonably be expected to influence the exercise of the best judgment of the bank in respect of a transaction – for example, a major creditor or debtor of the bank – may be designated a related party.

In addition, the Bank Act stipulates that every bank must institute an independent conduct review committee consisting of a majority of directors not affiliated with the bank. The committee is charged with monitoring the bank's procedures for complying with the self-dealing regime.

These provisions are potentially more significant than may first appear because in Canada there is a relatively small number of major banks, all of which tend to have large boards of directors, coupled with a significant and increasing concentration of ownership in Canadian business.

External conflicts

[6.53]   A more frequent and increasing occurrence is that of conflicts of interest resulting from transactions involving customers of the same bank. In the field of hostile takeovers, the interaction of the concentration of ownership of Canadian business and the relatively small number of large Canadian banks can make such conflicts particularly problematic. As in the US, most Canadian bids are financed with a significant amount of debt. In a major takeover bid in Canada, it is not uncommon to find that most of the major Canadian banks hold significant amounts of debt of the target. As a result, in order to preclude any claim of conflict, the acquirer may seek to finance the acquisition debt completely from non-Canadian bank sources, although this can raise other problems such as withholding tax. At the very least, the target's 'relationship' banks would be expected to preclude themselves from financing a hostile takeover bid.

Conflicts can also arise between the interests of the bank and those of its customers as exemplified in *Standard Investments Ltd v Canadian Imperial Bank of*

272 Bank Act, SC 1991, c 46, ss 418 and 491.

Commerce,[273] where the bank purchased shares in the target trust company for its own account while simultaneously 'assisting' the plaintiff customers in their takeover bid and also keeping the plaintiffs' important banking business. As noted above, the Court of Appeal held that the bank could have resolved the conflict by either disclosing to the customers the nature of the conflict or by simply refusing to advise them on their takeover plans.

Securities dealings

[6.54] The potential for conflict may now also arise between banks' lending activities and the underwriting and selling activities of their new securities affiliates. When banks were permitted to enter the securities business, the securities regulators expressed concern about the potential for conflict if a securities firm was underwriting and distributing debt or equity securities of a third party issuer in circumstances where that issuer was significantly indebted to, or otherwise connected in a material way with, the securities dealer's bank affiliate. Accordingly, a complex set of regulations is now in place to attempt to meet these concerns.[274]

Under these regulations, the bank's securities affiliate must prepare a statement of policies outlining how it will deal with the securities of connected issuers and must send the policy to the regulators and to customers. If a third party issuer is considered 'connected' to the bank, then any prospectus of the issuer in which the securities affiliate is an underwriter must disclose the existence and nature of the relationship in bold print on the cover of the prospectus, with a more detailed description in the body of the prospectus. The interpretation and application of these provisions is made difficult by the subjective nature of their application.

An issuer is considered 'connected' to a bank when:

1   the level of indebtedness or other relationship of the issuer with the bank is such as to lead a potential purchaser of securities to question the independence of the issuer from the bank; or
2   there is a reasonable likelihood such investor would consider such indebtedness or other relationship important in his investment decision.

In addition to the disclosure requirements, there are certain prohibited activities in respect of connected issuers. As an example, the securities affiliate is not permitted to underwrite securities of any connected issuer or those of its bank affiliate unless an independent dealer underwrites at least the same proportion as the bank's securities affiliate.

The concern about conflicts between banks and their securities affiliates has also been noted by the federal banking regulators. At the time that Canadian banks were first authorised by the federal authorities to acquire securities dealers, guidelines were set up outlining procedures for federally-regulated financial institutions, such as banks, to obtain approval for the acquisition of more than a 10% interest in a Canadian corporation, such as a securities firm.[275] Among other things, the guidelines require the applicant to outline specifically their policies and procedures 'for

273 (1985), 52 OR (2d) 473, Ont CA.
274 See Pt XIII of the regulations, RRO 1990, reg 1015 to the Ontario Securities Act, RSC 1990, c S-5.
275 Office of the Superintendent of Financial Institutions of Canada, 'Guideline 18 Re Shareholdings by Federally-Regulated Financial Institutions in Securities Dealers', 27 July 1989.

effective handling of any conflicts of interest that may arise between the bank and the securities firm'.

COMBATING MISUSE OF CONFIDENTIAL INFORMATION

[6.55]   The entry by Canadian banks into the field of securities activities has also increased the potential for misuse of confidential information. In the context of the new multi-service approach of contemporary Canadian banking, this problem can arise more often as a result of the bank's obligations to different clients in its various areas of business. For example, problems could arise if confidential information moved between a bank's commercial lending operations and its securities sales or trading functions or related activities. Information held by one department or affiliate could materially affect the decisions made in the other if that information were available to it.

Segregation of information

[6.56]   To date, the methods which have been utilised to deal with these potential concerns have evolved, or been derived, primarily from the North American securities experience and practice. The principal approach is to rely on concepts such as Chinese Walls or other systems which are intended to provide for segregation of information within separate areas and departments so as to allow financial institutions to conduct activities in all areas of the financial services sector without improper use of information.

As discussed further below, most banks and other financial institutions active in a range of financial services have instituted procedures to avoid potential conflicts of interest by preventing the transmission of information among departments or to subsidiaries. In addition to Chinese Walls, restricted securities lists such as so-called 'grey' or 'watch' lists which prevent or restrict trading by employees or departments in specified securities are now commonly employed.[276]

The additional responsibilities and the steps taken to deal with them have not arisen solely by virtue of expanding the banks' areas of permitted activity. At the same time as the restrictions on the activities of banks and other financial institutions have been reduced, securities legislators have also been introducing expanded rules relating to insider trading or other misuse of confidential information.

Regulation of insider trading

[6.57]   Regulation of insider trading is considered within the legislative competence of both levels of government. The federal government (through the

---

276 A 'grey' list refers to a list of companies for which a dealer has been retained on a matter which represents, or makes the dealer otherwise aware of, material undisclosed information in respect of a public company. As the information is not public, only certain senior officers of the dealer would be aware of the companies on the grey list and would be responsible to ensure the dealer undertook no trading or other improper activity. A 'restricted' list is broadly circulated within the dealer and used for companies for which the dealer will not trade due to the activities of the dealer or the issuer. At this stage, the nature of the dealer's activities have been disclosed publicly, but the restriction on trading continues.

Bank Act[277] and the Canada Business Corporations Act[278]) and the provinces (through securities statutes) have enacted legislation dealing with insider trading. The legislation typically precludes trading on the knowledge of a material fact or a material change concerning a public company which has not been generally disclosed.[279] It also precludes informing or 'tipping' anyone about such information, except in the necessary course of business. In either case, in order for the trading or tipping to be an offence, the party in question must be in a special relationship with the public company. The term 'special relationship' is broadly defined, however, and includes any party that engages or proposes to engage in a business or professional activity on behalf of a party such as a prospective bidder. As a result, a bank which proposes to fund or advise a bidder is in a special relationship and subject to the legislation and can only disclose material information to the extent it can conclude it is in the necessary course of business to do so.

Tightened standards

[6.58]   In certain provinces, insider trading legislation has become increasingly stringent both in scope of application and potential fines. For example, previously, it was possible to defend a charge of insider trading by showing that, although the vendor or purchaser of securities was *aware* of material undisclosed information, it *did not make use* of it in making the trade. Therefore, if material undisclosed information was known by persons in different departments in a financial group, it did not preclude trading so long as the party did not make use of the information in trading. The regulators became increasingly concerned that it would be difficult to prove whether or not a party made use of the information and, accordingly, the regulators have removed the exception. The vendor or purchaser must show that persons who participated in the decision to implement the trade *did not have access* to the information.

This change has had an impact on the methods by which certain financial institutions conduct their activities. For instance, in the past, it would not have been unusual for one or more members of senior management of a bank to have knowledge of the major activities of, or developments in, more than one department. They could have had knowledge of undisclosed negative information about an issuer emanating from the corporate lending department and at the same time been aware of principal trading, research or underwriting in securities of the issuer in other departments. Under the previous test, mere knowledge alone was not a sufficient base for a case of improper trading, the issue was whether the bank made use of such information in any securities dealings. Under the new and more restricted exception, the information must now be kept separate from all persons who may be considered to participate in trading decisions.

Mandatory policies for confidential information

[6.59]   At the same time as they narrowed the exception, securities regulators have introduced provisions which provide that the existence and maintenance of policies relating to confidential information will be a factor in discharging the burden of proof

277 SC 1991, c 46.
278 See the Bank Act, Pt IV, Div H and regulations; the Canada Business Corporations Act, RSC 1985 c C-44, Pt XI and the Ontario Securities Act, RSC 1990, c S-5, s 74.
279 Ontario Securities Act, RSO 1990, c S-5, s 76.

in any action for breach of the rules.[280] Some other jurisdictions have questioned whether segregating or compartmentalising information, through Chinese Walls or otherwise, can ever solve these concerns. In the new provisions, however, the Canadian securities regulators have specifically endorsed the concept of Chinese Walls. In fact, they have gone further and implemented a policy to serve as a guideline for establishing a Chinese Wall.[281]

The provisions acknowledge that the particular procedures that are appropriate for a given company or industry will vary and require that parties dealing with confidential market-sensitive information must set out their policies in writing. The policy outlines suggested procedures in the areas of employee education, containment of information, restriction of transactions and compliance. The policy is drafted primarily for dealers in securities, but also states that financial institutions in general should consider how they might implement procedures to protect themselves from allegations of insider trading. In fact, the policy has found the support of the Canadian Bankers Association.[282]

It is reasonable to conclude that in determining an appropriate standard, whether in litigation or in order to prevent it, the guidelines prescribed by the securities regulators, and the steps taken by others to attempt to follow them, are likely to be a standard against which activity will be tested.

Effectiveness of Chinese Walls – the courts' view

[6.60] Although the regulators have endorsed the concept of Chinese Walls, there may be some question as to how the Canadian courts will react. In addition to the issue of fiduciary duties, the *Standard Investments* case[283] discussed above also considered the problem of the bank's responsibility for the conflicting acts and intentions of two or more responsible officers, in that case, the president and chairman. The Court of Appeal's solution was to extend a doctrine of 'identification' for corporate responsibility which had previously been enunciated by the Supreme Court of Canada[284] in the context of criminal actions and apply it to civil actions regarding corporate breaches of fiduciary duties.[285]

Under this extension of the 'identification' doctrine, the Court of Appeal in *Standard Investments* held that it is possible for a corporation to have more than one directing mind in the same field of operations and that one person's lack of knowledge about the actions of the other will not serve to protect the corporation from liability for the actions of either or the combined effect of both. It commented that:

'In civil cases, where the element of mens rea is not applicable, when there are two or more directing minds *operating within the same field assigned to both* of

---

280 Ontario Securities Act, RSO 1990, c S-5, s 76, regulations, s 175(3).
281 OSC, 'Policy 10.2 Guidelines for the Establishment of Procedures in Relation to Confidential Information' (1989) 12 OSCB 2387.
282 Regulations, RRO 1990, reg 1015 to the Ontario Securities Act, RSO 1990, c S-5, s 175.
283 *Standard Investments Ltd v Canadian Imperial Bank of Commerce* (1985), 52 OR (2d) 473, Ont CA.
284 *Canadian Dredge and Dock Co Ltd v The Queen* (1985), 19 DLR (4th) 314, SCC.
285 The test for establishing that an employee's actions can be attributed to the corporation involves showing that the action: (i) was within the field of operation assigned to him, (ii) was not to defraud the company and (iii) was by design or result partly for the benefit of the company.

them, the knowledge, intention and acts of each becomes together the total knowledge, intention and acts of the corporation which they represent.[286]

It could be argued that the Court of Appeal was, in effect, implying that a company could not in some way keep separate the knowledge it has within separate departments. Although this case can be distinguished on its unusual facts and although there has been legislative action by the securities regulators supporting Chinese Walls, these judicial comments may be used to question the appropriateness and effectiveness of Chinese Walls from a judicial perspective. It is likely, however, that where a Chinese Wall is sufficiently effective so as to preclude a finding that the directing minds of the corporation are operating in the same field, courts may well accept the effectiveness of the Chinese Wall.

CONCLUSION

[6.61] In the last few years, the Canadian financial industry has undergone unprecedented change in both the domestic regulatory environment and the international market for financial services. The broader powers Canadian banks now possess, many as a result of their own requests, have unquestionably opened up new opportunities for them. It is clear, however, that banks must be mindful that Canadian courts and regulators are prepared to impress these new powers with new duties and responsibilities. While there has been some legislative encroachment on the general rule of bank confidentiality, particularly in the tax and money laundering areas, these initiatives have been accepted in Canada as representing intrusions for justifiable public policy reasons. Moreover, these incursions to some extent are counterbalanced as legislators begin to take a proactive role in protecting the privacy of personal information and in dealing with potential conflicts of interest that inevitably arise as the scope of activities undertaken by banks increases.

---

286 (1985), 52 OR (2d) 473, Ont CA, 494.

7   Cayman Islands

Virginia Czarnocki
Sara Collins

INTRODUCTION

[7.1]   The Cayman Islands is a British Overseas Territory whose constitution is derived from the United Kingdom. However, most matters, save for defence and foreign policy, are devolved to a locally elected government. In general terms, Cayman Islands law is derived from English common law, equity and certain English statutes (which either are considered to have been accepted as part of the law of the Cayman Islands through past general usage or which have been expressly extended to the Cayman Islands by statutory instrument), together with local legislation enacted by the Cayman Islands Legislative Assembly.

The Cayman Islands is a tax-free jurisdiction and neither companies nor individuals operating in and from the Islands are subject to direct taxation. With a vibrant economy, it is essential that the Cayman Islands demonstrate to the outside world its desire to comply with international standards to avoid it becoming subject to financial crime.

This chapter sets out to demonstrate the laws and other procedures in place to maintain confidentiality for businesses and individuals operating in the Cayman Islands, whilst addressing the Islands' desire to combat financial crime.

BANK CONFIDENTIALITY
Common law duty of confidence

[7.2]   Confidentiality of business transactions is governed by both the common law and statute. As one of the world's leading banking centres, the Cayman Islands legislature has had to achieve a balance between the need for transparency in its dealings with other countries in an attempt to combat financial crime, together with a need to respect the privacy and duty of confidentiality owed to customers of its many financial institutions.

As is the case under English law, a bank owes a common law duty of confidence to its customers. This duty may arise expressly or impliedly. Further, information communicated to a bank by or on behalf of its customers and whether orally or in writing may be subject to an implied duty of confidence depending on the nature of the information and the manner in which it was communicated.[1]

---

1   The English case of *Tournier v National Provincial and Union Bank of England* [1924] 1 KB 461 would apply in the Cayman Islands.

In general terms, breach of the duty would give rise to a claim by the customer for damages. What loss or damage would be suffered would depend on the circumstances of each disclosure. Under common law, it is permissible to disclose otherwise confidential information with the express or implied consent of the customer.

The Confidential Relationships (Preservation) Law (1995 Revision)

[7.3]   The most important piece of legislation in the Cayman Islands regulating the disclosure of confidential information is the Confidential Relationships (Preservation) Law[2] ('CRPL'). The CRPL was first introduced in 1976 and makes it a criminal offence to divulge confidential information, as defined therein.

The CRPL was enacted with a view to protecting business activities by documenting (i) what constitutes confidential information, (ii) the circumstances in which such information could lawfully be disclosed and (iii) prescribing penalties for unlawfully disclosing confidential information. The law recognises the duty of bankers, accountants, financial professionals and lawyers to maintain confidentiality as to the identity and business of their clients.

Section 5(1) of the CRPL makes it a criminal offence to 'divulge' or 'attempt, offer or threaten to divulge' confidential information.

The term 'confidential information' is widely defined as including 'information concerning any property which the recipient thereof is not, otherwise than in the normal course of business, authorised by the principal to divulge'. 'Property' includes 'every present, contingent and future interest or claim direct or indirect, legal or equitable, positive or negative, in any money, moneys, realty or personality, moveable or immoveable, rights and securities there over and all documents and things evidencing or relating thereto'.

'Normal course of business' means 'the ordinary and necessary routine involved in the efficient carrying out of the instructions of a principal including compliance with such laws and legal process as arises out of and in connection therewith and the routine exchange of information between licensees'.

'Principal' is defined as 'a person who has imparted to another confidential information in the course of transaction of business of a professional nature'.

Thus, the CRPL extends to cover a bank which gives a credit reference in relation to a customer. If the bank does so without first receiving the authorisation of the customer, it is guilty of an offence in terms of the CRPL.

The CRPL purports to have extra-territorial effect and is said to apply to all confidential information with respect to any business of a professional nature which arises in or is brought into the Cayman Islands and to all persons coming into possession of such information at any time, whether they be within or outside the jurisdiction. Business of a professional nature is defined as including 'the relationship between a professional person and a principal, however the latter may be

---

2 Confidential Relationships (Preservation) Law (1995 Revision).

described'. 'Professional person' is also very widely defined.[3] The wide definitions leave some doubt as the precise scope of the law and this section. The official record of the Cayman Islands Legislative Assembly would suggest that the law was intended to ensure confidentiality with respect to the operation of the financial services industry and that 'professional person' was intended to mean people involved in the operation of the financial services industry in the Islands.

There are several exceptions set out in s 3(2), which outlines the circumstances in which confidential information may be disclosed, including:

1   where information is given to a court, tribunal or other authority in connection with any proceeding, whether within or outside the Cayman Islands, and directions have been obtained from the Grand Court of the Cayman Islands authorising such disclosure;[4]
2   where information is given by or to a professional person acting in the normal course of business;
3   where the information is given with the express or implied consent of the principal;
4   where disclosure is made by or to a constable (in the Cayman Islands Police) of the rank of Inspector or above;
5   where disclosure is made by or to the Financial Secretary of the Cayman Islands or, in relation to particular information specified by the Governor of the Cayman Islands, such other person as the Governor may authorise;
6   where disclosure is made by a bank in any proceedings, cause or matter, and to the extent reasonably necessary, to protect the bank's interest either against its customers or against third parties in respect of transactions of the bank for or with its customers;
7   where disclosure is made by or to the relevant professional person with the approval of the Financial Secretary when necessary for the protection of himself or any other person against crime.

Unless one of the exceptions applies, confidential information cannot be disclosed.

In relation to the first exception set out above, the CRPL provides for information to be disclosed in a court, tribunal or other authority where such information is to be given in evidence in proceedings where the person intending to make the disclosure has first obtained the permission of the Grand Court of the Cayman Islands. Pursuant to s 4(1) of the CRPL, any person who is required or who intends to give evidence in proceedings before any court, tribunal or other authority and regardless of whether these proceedings are within the Cayman Islands or not, must apply for directions from the Grand Court of the Cayman Islands before disclosing any confidential information. The court can rule either that (i) the evidence may be given, (ii) the evidence may not be given or (iii) the evidence may be given subject to conditions. These conditions could be, for example, that the confidential information may only be disclosed to certain identified individuals and/or with certain information redacted.

---

3   At s 3(1). The term 'professional person' is defined as including 'a public or government official, a bank, trust company, an attorney-at-law, an estate agent, an insurer, a broker and every kind of commercial agent and advisor whether or not answering to the above descriptions and whether or not licensed or authorised to act in that capacity and every person subordinate to or in the employ or control of such person for the purpose of his professional activities'.
4   As is the position under English law, the courts of the Cayman Islands can compel a bank to disclose information by subpoena.

An application under s 4 is made by way of summons which must be supported by an affidavit sworn on behalf of the applicant stating:

1   the circumstances in which evidence is to be given;
2   identifying the principal of the information and the basis of the confidential relationship;
3   the nature of the evidence and an explanation of why it constitutes confidential information; and
4   the grounds on which the principal objects to the proposed disclosure.

The application is heard by a judge sitting alone and in camera (in chambers). In making any determination, the judge of the Grand Court will consider:[5]

1   the interests of justice (in a criminal case) and public policy;
2   any offer of compensation or indemnity; and
3   whether an order would operate as a denial of the rights of any person in the enforcement of a first claim.

In the decision of the Cayman Islands Grand Court in *Re Ansbacher*,[6] the court explained that:

> '[On an s 4 application,[7]] the court is called upon to weigh the competing interests and decide, in the exercise of its discretion, whether and if so how [confidential information should be disclosed in evidence] having regard to the requirements of the administration of justice in the proceedings to which the application relates.'

The court also held that it had no jurisdiction to award the costs of contesting an s 4 application to a principal who successfully challenged the disclosure of his confidential information as an application under s 4 is not to be considered 'proceedings' in which one party would be considered to be successful (the court drew on the definition of 'successful' in the Cayman Islands Judicature Law (1995 Revision) which essentially means the winning party).

In another case, *Re W*,[8] decided in 2005, it was held that the court has no jurisdiction under s 4 to make a positive injunctive order restraining a person from disclosing confidential information, but only to give directions as to whether or not, and if so and on what conditions, confidential information might be given in evidence. In this case, the court also held, as it had in *Re Ansbacher* (above), that it had no jurisdiction to award the costs of contesting an s 4 application.

It is open to a party seeking to restrain the disclosure of confidential information to apply for injunctive relief. However, when the proposed disclosure is in order to give the information in evidence in proceedings before a court, tribunal or other authority, it appears that the courts will prefer to deal with the matter under the terms of the CRPL and will weigh the various considerations in the balance in determining whether to permit disclosure and, if so, under what conditions. The court would consider, inter alia, whether names and other terminology could be redacted, whether names could be given by alphabetical reference, whether the court could direct that information only be disclosed to certain identified individuals in controlled circumstances and whether evidence could be given in camera (meaning in chambers and in private).

5 Section 4(6).
6 *Re Ansbacher (Cayman) Ltd* [2001] CILR 214.
7 CRPL.
8 [2004–2005] CILR 554.

On an application for injunctive relief, the position is similar to that in England, in that the applicant must apply for the injunction before the information reaches the public domain. The initial hurdle is to satisfy the court that the information is likely to be disclosed and to demonstrate what loss or damage will be suffered if it is disclosed.

It is a criminal offence to 'divulge' in any way or attempt, offer or threaten to divulge confidential information. It is also a criminal offence wilfully to obtain or attempt to obtain confidential information for whatever purpose. Generally, the penalty for an offence pursuant to the CRPL is a fine[9] and imprisonment for up to two years. It is also an offence to solicit confidential information either for yourself or the benefit of another with the purpose of using the information to obtain a reward. The penalty for the latter offence is a fine equal to the reward received, together with forfeiture of the reward.

A professional person who commits any of these offences, namely, (i) divulging, attempting, offering or threatening to divulge or wilfully obtaining or attempting to obtain confidential information, (ii) receiving or soliciting information for himself or another for the purpose of receiving a reward or (iii) using any confidential information for his own purposes and is found guilty of any of the offences, is liable to double the penalties set out above.[10]

Recent developments in case law in respect of the CRPL

[7.4] There are few reported cases under the CRPL involving banks. In *Re Ansbacher*,[11] a case referred to above, the applicant, a Cayman Islands bank, applied to the court for directions under s 4 of the CRPL allowing it to disclose confidential information in proceedings in Ireland. The applicant had been served with an order of the Irish High Court authorising an investigation into allegations that its affairs had been conducted with intent to defraud its clients' creditors by tax evasion. The order authorised the court's inspectors to examine the business activities of Ansbacher in Ireland. The applicant wished to assist in this investigation by disclosing confidential information which would include some of its clients' identities and applied to the court for directions permitting it to release such information. Some of Ansbacher's clients objected to the application on the basis that such disclosure would be an invasion of their privacy and, accordingly, a breach of the duty of confidentiality owed to them by the bank. The Attorney General submitted that, inter alia, the public interest would be secured by assisting the Irish inspectors with their inquiry since the Irish inspectors had been appointed to carry out duties similar to those of the Cayman Islands Monetary Authority. It was held that the applicant, having shown a sufficient interest to protect, would be directed to disclose the requested information subject to the condition that clients' identities be concealed. Any questions the inspectors required the individual clients to address should be issued to those clients in writing and those clients could respond anonymously. It was also held that since an order of directions under s 4(3) of the CRPL was mandatory, the bank would have no liability to its clients for a purported breach of confidentiality.

---

9 CI$5,000.
10 CI$10,000 and imprisonment for four years.
11 [2001] CILR 214.

In *UBS (Bahamas) Ltd v Weybridge and Barclays Bank plc*,[12] the court held that it would not make an order for discovery conferring on the recipient a discretion to use disclosed material in any foreign proceedings to pursue a related claim. It was held that such an order would override the implied duty not to use discovered information for purposes other than the proceedings at hand and would conflict with the principle that the court has no automatic remit over matters outside of its jurisdiction. The court must be satisfied that such further use is warranted. When an application is made under the CRPL in response to the order, the court will require an express undertaking from the respondent not to use the information abroad without leave before it will permit any disclosure.

In *Re K, B (E) and B (P)*,[13] the Grand Court confirmed that it would not permit the use of information obtained from a bank in breach of the CRPL as evidence in proceedings overseas. The court stated that to permit further use of it would not only have the effect of furthering an illegal transaction, but would also cause the person who received the information to be in breach of the CRPL as the holder of the confidential information would be making use of it without the consent of the principal. The court ordered the return of the documents to the bank and the destruction of copies held by the person who had received them.

The various decided cases have established guidelines as to what will be considered by the court when determining whether to order disclosure of confidential information under the CRPL:

1   public policy – in *Re H*,[14] the Grand Court held that it would be against public policy to allow disclosure by a trustee of information about the trust's assets in compliance with a subpoena issued by a grand jury in the United States whilst a legal challenge to the validity of the trust existed. To do so would be in breach of the trustee's duties if the trust was valid and, if it was not, the US authorities would have access to the information without having to issue a subpoena against the trustee. The court also remarked that it was not obliged, as a matter of comity, to assist a United States grand jury and that not only did the subpoena lack the clear endorsement of the relevant state court, but it purported to have extra-territorial effect in breach of Cayman Islands law;

2   the court could also consider whether the information could be obtained by alternative means, ie could disclosure be compelled under another statute?

3   the court will often conduct a balancing exercise – in *Re Ansbacher*, the court held that it was appropriate to weigh the bank's interest in disclosure against the client's right to privacy. The English authority of *Tournier v National Provincial and Union Bank of England*[15] was applied in that case.

The Cayman Islands has significant legislation in place under which confidential information can be disclosed to law enforcement authorities both within and outside the Islands and also to foreign regulatory bodies. This legislation will be considered throughout the chapter, but it includes the Proceeds of Criminal Conduct Law, the Mutual Legal Assistance (United States of America) Law (1999 Revision) and the Monetary Authority Law 2004. The anti-money laundering and anti-terrorism legislation require the disclosure of information by banks where there are reasonable grounds to believe that the customer is engaged in specified offences (suspicious

---

12   24 September 1998, Grand Court (Smellie J).
13   24 November 1997, Grand Court (Smellie J).
14   8 October 1997 (N9), Grand Court (Smellie J).
15   [1924] 1 KB 461.

circumstances). This conflicts with the common law position as evidenced by the *Tournier* decision where it was held that a general duty of confidentiality exists.

Disclosure by compulsion of law

[7.5]   As is the position under English law, it is under this heading that most inroads have been made in relation to the duty of confidence. The duty is penetrated by court orders, as well as statutory requirements.

Compulsion by order of court

[7.6]   If a court considers the production of a document to be necessary for the purpose of proceedings before it, it may order any person to attend any proceedings in a cause or matter and produce any document to be specified or described in that order. It should be noted that no person shall be compelled to produce any document at the proceedings which he could not be compelled to produce at the trial of that cause or matter.[16] Documents include any device by means of which information is recorded or stored.[17]

An order may also be sought under s 8 of the Evidence Law (2004 Revision) which states that, on the application of any party to a legal proceeding, the court may order that such party be at liberty to inspect and take copies of any matter in a banker's book for the purpose of such proceeding and an order under this section may be made with or without summoning the bank or any other party. Compliance with such an order shall be deemed to be giving in evidence of the matter in the banker's book to be inspected. Section 7(2) provides that a copy of an entry in a banker's book will not be received in evidence unless it is first established that the book was, when the entry was made, one of the ordinary books of the bank and the entry was made in the normal and ordinary course of business and that the book is in the custody and control of the bank.

The provision of entries in a banker's book is subject to the general provision of the CRPL requiring the bank to obtain directions from the Grand Court in relation to any confidential information to be provided pursuant to an order obtained under s 8 of the Evidence Law.

Compulsion by statute

[7.7]   There are fewer statutory provisions available in the Cayman Islands than in England to compel banks to produce information on their customers. In England, for example, the Inland Revenue has wide-ranging statutory powers to investigate the activities of any national. There are no such taxing authorities in the Cayman Islands. Companies in the Cayman Islands have no requirements to file their official records for public consumption. Whilst companies are required to make filings with the Registrar of Companies, this information will only be disclosed if authorised by the company (normally in writing). It is not, therefore, necessarily possible to check director, shareholder or other details, nor is it possible to check financial status.

---

16 Order 38, r 13(1) and (2) of the Cayman Islands Grand Court Rules 1995.
17 Evidence Law (2004 Revision).

A court has extraordinary powers in relation to the winding up of a company. In terms of s 127(1):[18]

> 'The court may summon before it any person whom the court may think capable of giving information concerning the trade, dealings, estate or effects of the company; and the court may require any such person (to include any officer of the company) to produce any books, papers, deeds, writings or other documents in his custody or power and relating to the company.'

The court has the power to apprehend persons who fail, without lawful impediment, to appear before the court when summoned. Further, the court may 'examine upon oath, either orally or upon written interrogatories, any person appearing or brought before it concerning the affairs, dealings, estate or effects of the company' and may put the answers in writing and compel their subscription.

Police and other enforcement bodies

[7.8] The Financial Crime Unit of the Royal Cayman Islands Police Force was actively involved in an investigation of financial crime which led to the recent prosecution of an individual who was fined US$1 million.[19] The individual was found guilty of four money laundering offences between August 1998 and April 1999 involving some US$6 million. The individual was found guilty on two counts of assisting another to retain the benefit of criminal activities and two counts of concealing or transferring proceeds belonging to another (knowing these proceeds to be derived from criminal conduct).

Pursuant to s 192(1) of the Criminal Procedure Code (2005 Revision):

> 'Any court may order the seizure of any property which there is reason to believe it has been obtained by or is the proceeds of any offence, or into which the proceeds of any offence have been converted, and may direct that the same shall be kept or sold and that the same, or the proceeds thereof if sold, shall be held as such court directs until some person establishes a right thereto to the satisfaction of the court.'

If no such right is established within 12 months of the date of the seizure, then the property or proceeds shall vest in the Financial Secretary for the use of the Cayman Islands.

INTERNATIONAL MONEY LAUNDERING INITIATIVES

Overview

[7.9] The Cayman Islands has framed its regulatory system pursuant to anti-money laundering in accordance with international standards. As a leading offshore jurisdiction, is it essential for the Cayman Islands to comply, and be seen to be complying, with recognised standards and demonstrating an active campaign against financial crime.

---

18 Companies Law (2004 Revision).
19 Unreported at the time of writing.

The 1988 Basle Committee set out banking principles to deal with money laundering. The Committee's principles were endorsed by the Cayman Islands Monetary Authority ('CIMA') on its inception and a statement was circulated by CIMA to all banking institutions in the Cayman Islands. The statement or guidance made recommendations in relation to:

1   customer identification – it was recommended that all banking institutions should ensure that they are aware of the true identity of their client;
2   record keeping and systems to enforce adequate anti-money laundering procedures; and
3   compliance with anti-money laundering procedures without breaching client confidentiality.

In 1989, the heads of government of the G7 countries established the Financial Action Task Force ('FATF'). In June 1990, 15 Caribbean states and five members of the FATF met in Aruba and produced 21 recommendations, 19 of which were adopted as Caribbean Financial Action Task Force recommendations. In June 1992, a second meeting was held and further recommendations were made which were subsequently presented at a ministerial meeting convened in Kingston, Jamaica in November 1992. Twenty Caribbean states participated, together with representatives from the FATF. The result of this meeting was the Kingston Declaration on money laundering endorsing the implementation of the 1988 United Nations Vienna Convention, the Organisation of American States Model Regulations, the 40 FATF recommendations and the 19 regional specific objectives.

The International Monetary Fund ('IMF') carried out a review of the Cayman Islands in March 2005. This report was prepared following a request by the Cayman Islands. The IMF compared the procedures adopted in the Cayman Islands against other recognised international standards such as the Basle Core Principles for Effective Banking Supervision and the FATF methodology. The IMF suggested a number of improvements, but generally concluded that there was a comprehensive regulatory system in place. CIMA is currently considering the IMF's recommendations.

The Cayman Islands Monetary Authority

[7.10]   CIMA has a pivotal role in the campaign against financial crime. CIMA came into being by virtue of the Monetary Authority Law 1996 and was formed by the merging of the Currency Board and the Financial Services Supervision Department.

CIMA is an independent regulatory body. Its objectives are to promote and maintain a sound financial system in the Cayman Islands. It also seeks to reduce the possibility of the Cayman Islands financial services businesses being used to launder or to assist in the perpetration of other crimes. CIMA has the task of understanding international standards for combating financial crime and then implementing these standards, so far as is practical, in the Cayman Islands.

CIMA has five regulatory divisions: banking, insurance, investments, securities and fiduciary services, all of which are supported by legal and compliance divisions. The regulatory functions include:

1   regulating and supervising financial services business carried on in or from the Cayman Islands;
2   monitoring compliance with the Money Laundering Regulations; and
3   performing any other regulatory or supervisory duties that may be imposed on CIMA by any other law.

CIMA is obliged to review its regulatory laws and to establish working groups to make recommendations in connection with existing laws. The working groups are made up of senior CIMA staff and recognised representatives from industries in the Cayman Islands. These groups are established to focus on the various types of financial business conducted within the Cayman Islands and the types of business conducted are in part regulated by the type of licence provided to the business in question by CIMA.

Relevant legislation

[7.11]   The legislation relating to money laundering in the Cayman Islands is principally contained in the Proceeds of Criminal Conduct Law (2005 Revision), the Proceeds of Criminal Conduct Law – Money Laundering Regulations (2006 Revision), the Misuse of Drugs Law, the Terrorism (UN Measures) (Overseas Territories) Order and the Terrorism Law, together with related regulations. Guidance on complying with the Money Laundering Regulations is set out in the 'Guidance Notes on the Prevention and Detection of Money Laundering in the Cayman Islands' published by CIMA.

The Money Laundering Regulations are mandatory and they require all those engaged in the activities of a 'relevant financial business' to have in place proper systems and training to prevent money laundering.

'Relevant financial business' is defined in reg 4 of the Regulations as including 'banking or trust businesses, building societies, co-operative societies, insurance businesses, mutual fund administration and company management businesses'. The activities are set out in Sch 2 of the Regulations, which include any business which accepts deposits, lends, acts in financial leasing, is involved in money transmission services, issues and administers means of payment (credit notes or bankers' drafts), is involved with guarantees and commitments, trades on its own account or for the account of customers in, for example, money market instruments, foreign exchange, financial futures exchange and interest rate instruments and transferable securities, participation in securities issues and advice on capital structures and industrial strategy.

These 'relevant financial businesses' are required by the Regulations to maintain the following procedures:

1   procedures for establishing the identity of clients and customers;
2   procedures relative to record keeping to record the transactions carried out by each client/customer;
3   internal reporting procedures to ensure that employees have a contact to report suspicious activities;
4   procedures to ensure that employees involved in any relevant business are aware of the procedures, relevant laws and regulations and what is required of them; and
5   training systems and procedures for employees.

Proceeds of Criminal Conduct Law

The offences

[7.12]   Money laundering offences are set out in the Proceeds of Criminal Conduct Law (2005 Revision). These offences are:

1   assisting another to retain the benefit of criminal conduct;
2   the acquisition, possession and use of property representing the proceeds of criminal conduct;
3   concealing or transferring the proceeds of criminal conduct;
4   'tipping off'; and
5   failure to disclose knowledge or suspicion of money laundering.

Assisting another to retain the benefit of criminal conduct

[7.13] It is a criminal offence to assist another ('A') in any arrangement which assists, in whatever way, that other party retaining or controlling any property which is the proceeds of his criminal conduct. The crime is also committed by concealing property, removing property from the Cayman Islands and/or transferring the property to another party. The level of participation need not be direct and it can involve actions in relation to part of the property, as well as the whole of the property.

To be guilty of such an offence, it must be established that the culpable party had knowledge or suspicion of the fact that A is a person who is or has been engaged in criminal conduct. It is not an offence under the CRPL to disclose actual knowledge or a suspicion in accordance with these provisions to a relevant person.

Acquiring, possessing or using property

[7.14] It is an offence to acquire, possess or use property with the knowledge that it represents another person's proceeds of criminal conduct. Possession, even if that possession is only temporary, is sufficient to constitute an offence.

The crime is committed where the person acquires the property for a value less than the actual value of the property. Accordingly, it is a defence to show that the property was acquired for adequate consideration.

Concealing or transferring the proceeds of criminal conduct

[7.15] It is a criminal offence to conceal or disguise property which (either in whole or in part) represents the proceeds of criminal conduct. It is also an offence to convert or transfer that property in whatever manner or remove the property from the Cayman Islands.

It is also an offence to assist another in the foregoing either knowingly or where it can be shown that that person had reasonable grounds to suspect that the offence was being committed. Possession, even if temporary, is sufficient to constitute an offence.

'Tipping off'

[7.16] Tipping off is the disclosing to any other person of information or any other matter which is used to prejudice an investigation or potential investigation into money laundering.

Failure to disclose knowledge or suspicion of money laundering

[7.17] A person is guilty of an offence if he:

1   knows or suspects that another is engaged in money laundering;

2   gains that information or knowledge through the course of his trade, profession, business or employment; and

3   fails to disclose the information or suspicion as soon as reasonably practicable after it came to his attention or knowledge.

Defences

[7.18]   There are a number of possible defences to the crimes set out above. It is a defence if:

1   the person charged did not know or suspect that the arrangement related to the proceeds of a person's criminal conduct;

2   the person charged with the offence can establish that he acquired the property for adequate consideration. This means that the property must have been acquired for value;

3   the person charged did not know or suspect that any property was obtained through criminal means;

4   a person in employment discloses the relevant information to the appropriate person in accordance with his employer's anti-money laundering procedures;

5   the person can establish that he intended to disclose his knowledge or suspicion, but had a reasonable excuse for not so doing. It should be noted that 'reasonable' excuse is not defined and, accordingly, it will be for the courts to determine what this means.

No prosecution may be brought without the consent of the Attorney General.

Financial Reporting Authority

[7.19]   The Proceeds of Criminal Conduct Law provided for the establishment of the Financial Reporting Authority (the 'Authority'). The Authority, also known as the 'Financial Reporting Unit', consists of two people appointed by the Governor of the Cayman Islands. Disclosure of information to the Financial Reporting Unit will not be treated as a breach of any statutory or other confidentiality obligation.

This Authority is responsible for receiving, in certain cases, requesting, analysing and distributing disclosures of financial information relating to the proceeds or suspected proceeds of criminal conduct, money laundering, terrorism or the financing of terrorism.

Anyone who fails to provide information to the Authority upon a written request by it is guilty of an offence. The penalty for such an offence is a fine of CI$50,000 and imprisonment for two years.

It should be noted that the Authority cannot insist that, for example, information in the hands of a professional legal adviser in privileged circumstances is disclosed. 'Privileged circumstances' means information communicated to the adviser by a client or a representative of a client in connection with the rendering by the legal adviser of legal advice to the client or by a representative of a person seeking legal advice from an adviser or by any person in contemplation of, or in connection with, legal proceedings and for the purpose of these proceedings. However, this does not mean that a legal adviser should not inform the Authority if he suspects that a money laundering offence is being committed. The legal adviser will be guilty of an offence in these circumstances.

Information disclosed to the Authority will not be further disclosed without the consent of the Attorney General, who must take into consideration the purpose of the further disclosure and the information of third parties except when the information is being disclosed to law enforcement agencies on the Islands, to CIMA or to any overseas financial intelligence unit.

Employees of the Authority who disclose information obtained by the Authority (except in the circumstances permitted by the law) are guilty of an offence and liable, on summary conviction, to a fine of CI$5,000 and up to two years' imprisonment or, on conviction on indictment, to a fine and imprisonment for up to 14 years.

How to identify a potential money laundering activity

[7.20]   There are certain exempted categories in relation to which verification of identity may not necessarily be required unless suspicion or knowledge of a crime exists.

Exempted categories

[7.21]

1   a 'one-off transaction'. This is a transaction other than a transaction carried on in the course of an established business relationship formed by a person acting in the course of a relevant financial business; or
2   an 'exempted one-off transaction'. This means a one-off transaction (whether a single transaction or a series of related transactions) where the total amount is less than CI$15,000. The guidance notes issued by CIMA recommend that the figure should be the sum of transactions carried out in a 12-month period.

Verification of identity will not necessarily be required for exemption 2 above, unless the circumstances surrounding the transaction appear unusual, in which event, identity should be verified. If the circumstances remain suspicious, a report should be made irrespective of the value of the transaction.

It is unnecessary to obtain verification of identification where:

1   the customer is bound by the provisions of the Money Laundering Regulations;
2   the customer is acting in the course of business regulated by an overseas regulatory authority and is subject to the laws of a territory specified in the Money Laundering Regulations; and
3   in the case of a one-off transaction, where the introducing agent is bound by the regulations of a recognised territory and that introducing agent confirms that he has carried out the necessary checks.

Record keeping procedures

[7.22]   It is a mandatory requirement to (i) keep evidence of a client's identification and (ii) keep records of the details of all transactions carried out by a client in the course of a relevant business.

Records must be kept for five years from the date any client business is completed or where the client has become insolvent or insolvency is suspected and steps are taken to recover debts payable for a period of five years from the date when debt recovery proceedings commenced.

Reporting procedures for suspicious entities

[7.23] The Money Laundering Regulations require internal reporting procedures to be maintained which must include the following:

1 provisions identifying a specific individual to be the money laundering reporting officer ('MLRO') to whom internal reports are to be made by employees of information giving rise to a knowledge or suspicion of money laundering;

2 provisions requiring any such internal report to be considered by the MLRO having regard to all other relevant information in order to determine whether the information passed on gives rise to a knowledge or suspicion of money laundering;

3 provisions to enable the MLRO (or other designated individual(s)) to have reasonable access to any other information which may be of assistance to him/them in considering any such internal report;

4 provisions to ensure that information contained in any such internal report is disclosed to the Authority if the information concerned is considered to give rise to a knowledge or suspicion of money laundering.

Other procedures for internal control and communication

[7.24] The Money Laundering Regulations require relevant financial businesses to maintain such other systems of internal controls and communications as may be appropriate for the purposes of forestalling and preventing money laundering. This will require detailed consideration of what other internal procedures are appropriate for the particular type of business, the laying down of clear guidelines, lines of communication and regular review.

All relevant businesses conducting financial services are required to maintain manuals for their staff detailing the procedures to be adopted in the event that a suspicious entity is identified and guidance notes detailing what the staff should be made aware of and what type of behaviour constitutes suspicious activities. The guidance notes identify such activities as: unusual financial activities, unusual transactions, unusual method of settlement, unwillingness to provide information requested, an unusual or disadvantageous early redemption of an investment product or the unusual employment of an intermediary in the course of a normal business transaction.

A suitably qualified individual should be identified as the business's MLRO. If he is satisfied that an activity is suspicious, he is obliged to report it to the Authority.

Recent cases

[7.25] The recent confirmation by the Cayman Islands Court of Appeal[20] of the conviction of an individual for his role in the 'Cash4Titles' money laundering scheme demonstrates that the Cayman Islands is seriously fighting financial crime. That individual is currently serving a three-year sentence for money laundering offences (the maximum sentence is 14 years), the sentence apparently being light in view of the individual's age. This case is the first successful prosecution in the Cayman Islands for money laundering offences.

---

20 *R v Rowe and Tibbetts* [2004–2005] CILR 183.

There were two defendants in the action charged with various offences involving the fraudulent use of investors' funds. The defendants were owners and directors of two companies. Both companies were inspected by officers of CIMA. As a result of their findings, the companies were placed in controllership. When the proceedings were commenced, the defendants challenged the admissibility of evidence given by them in interviews with the inspector and the controller. The evidence was held to be admissible as it was voluntarily given. One defendant was found guilty of assisting another to retain the proceeds of criminal conduct.

The other major money laundering case, the *Euro Bank* case,[21] which collapsed on the basis that the United Kingdom (specifically MI6) had interfered with evidence, deals with issues of disclosure.

The liquidators of a bank applied for directions concerning their duty to disclose material to the Crown Court for the purpose of criminal prosecutions against former employees and account holders. The defendants were charged with conspiracy and related money laundering offences. It was held that, inter alia, disclosure would be required not only if the material were relevant to the offence charged, but also if it had some bearing on the surrounding circumstances. It was held in the same case that the bank had benefited from its alleged offences to the full extent of the funds restrained (the court restrained funds of the defendants) since the meaning of 'benefit', for the purposes of s 5(3) of the Proceeds of Criminal Conduct Law, was not confined to the profit it had obtained, but to the whole funds. The proceeds of the fraud paid into the account had become the bank's property. Accordingly, the whole amount so obtained was to be regarded as property obtained as a result of or in connection with alleged money laundering offences and was liable to confiscation.

Terrorism Law

[7.26] Anti-money laundering and combating financial crime is also regulated through the Misuse of Drugs Law, the Proceeds of Criminal Conduct Law, the Terrorism (United Nations Measures) (Overseas Terrorism) Order and the Terrorism Law 2003, together with their regulations and the CIMA guidance notes referred to above, which are similar, if not virtually identical, to the guidance notes issued by the Joint Money Laundering Steering Group of the UK.

Terrorism means 'the use or threat of action ... designed to influence the government or intimidate the public ... for the purpose of canvassing a political, religious or ideological cause'. The law is very similar to the UK Terrorism Act 2003 and, for example, deals specifically with money laundering. Section 22(1) states:

'A person commits an offence if he enters into or becomes concerned in an arrangement which facilitates the retention or control by or on behalf of another person of terrorist property by concealment, by removal from the jurisdiction or by transfer to nominees.'

A person commits an offence by not disclosing a suspicion as soon as he becomes aware of the offence (subject to the suspicion being reported as soon as reasonably practicable).

The Terrorism Law applies extra-territorially. Where it is neither prohibited by law, subject to the provisions of other laws governing disclosure procedures, nor

---

21 *A-G v Euro Bank Group* [2002] CILR 334.

prejudicial to national security or public policy, the Authority and the Commissioner of Police may, on a request made by the appropriate authority of a foreign state, disclose to that authority information in its possession concerning terrorist groups and acts.

There are certain designated protected disclosures pursuant to the Terrorism Law. Schedule 1, para 2 states 'that the information or other matter disclosed came to the person making the disclosure in the course of a business in the regulated sector'. The 'regulated sector' includes banks, building societies and trust companies. 'The second condition is that the information ... causes the discloser to know ... or suspect' that a person has committed an offence under the Terrorism Law and, thirdly, 'the disclosure is to a nominated officer in the course of his business'. The Law authorises forfeiture orders and restraint orders at Sch 2. A forfeiture order shall not come into force until there is no further possibility of it being varied or set aside. A restraint order comes into place where proceedings have been instituted, but not yet concluded. Essentially, the restraint order operates to prevent any applicable property being transferred or removed from the Cayman Islands.

Overall, a failure to report under this Law is punishable by a fine and imprisonment for up to five years.

The Terrorism (United Nations Measures) Order 2001 applies in the Cayman Islands under the guise of the Terrorism (United Nations Measures) (Overseas Territories) Order 2001: 'any person who invites another to provide funds, and intends that they should be used, or knows that they may be used, for the purposes of terrorism, is guilty of an offence under this order', as is 'any person who makes funds available' without the authority of a licence granted by the Governor of the Cayman Islands:

> 'The Governor may direct any person to furnish to him any information in his possession or control, or to produce to him any document in his possession or control, which he may require for the purpose of securing compliance with or detecting evasion of this order.'

The Cayman Islands operates strict 'know your client' procedures and, when the regulations were enacted, the requirements for identifying customers were made retrospective so that all existing clients of banks, for example, were required to be vetted. The deadline for having complied with the CIMA requirement was 2004 and the Cayman Islands now operates on the basis that all of its banking customers have been vetted. The Cayman Islands has no reported terrorist cases under any guise.

In relation to the Misuse of Drug Law, the only reported prosecutions relate to use, possession and supply, as opposed to the trafficking of proceeds of the offences and money laundering.

OBTAINING EVIDENCE FOR USE IN FOREIGN PROCEEDINGS

[7.27]   The terms of the UK Evidence (Proceedings in other Jurisdictions) Act 1995 have been implemented in the Cayman Islands by virtue of the Evidence (Proceedings in other Jurisdictions) (Cayman Islands) Order 1978, which came into effect on 10 January 1979.

Civil proceedings

[7.28]   Where an application is made to the Grand Court for an order for evidence to be obtained in the Cayman Islands, the court may make provision for, among others, examination of witnesses,[22] either orally or in writing,[23] for the production of documents and for the inspection,[24] photographing, custody or detention of any property:

> 'An order under this section shall not require any particular steps to be taken unless they are steps which can be required to be taken by way of obtaining evidence for the purposes of civil proceedings in the court making the order.'

An order cannot compel a person to provide or disclose evidence which he would not be required to disclose in civil proceedings instituted before a Cayman Islands court.

Criminal proceedings

[7.29]   The law in the Cayman Islands relating to the discovery and production of evidence in the criminal courts is very similar to that in England, on which it is based.

An order for evidence can also be made by the court in criminal proceedings, again by virtue of an application to the Grand Court pursuant to the Grand Court Rules. An order can only relate to the provision for examination of witnesses, either orally or in writing, and for the production of documents. The order extends to evidence to be produced in relation to international proceedings, such as proceedings before the International Court of Justice, in which event the Governor of the Cayman Islands may direct that the provisions of the order shall have effect.

Sections 26–28 of the Criminal Procedure Code (2005 Revision) relate to the issue and execution of search warrants. A court, if satisfied by information on oath that there is reasonable suspicion that an offence has been committed, may issue a search warrant. Such a warrant empowers a search of any place for 'anything' necessary pursuant to the conduct of an investigation. Anything found will be seized and brought before the court.

Sections 37–42 of the same law allow for the issue of witness summonses. A summons allows a court to require a person to attend court and to produce all documents 'in his possession or power'. If the witness fails to attend, the court can ultimately order that such a person be arrested and brought before the court.

Also, under s 143 of the same law, the court can, during a trial and in certain circumstances, call a witness of its own volition.

Mutual Legal Assistance (United States of America) Law (1999 Revision)

[7.30]   Under the Mutual Legal Assistance Law ('MLA'), the government of the Cayman Islands has legislated to provide assistance to the United States federal authorities in relation to serious crime. The MLA (in its earlier form, the Mutual

---

22 Section 2(a).
23 Section 2(b).
24 Section 2(c).

Legal Assistance (USA) Law 1986) implements the Mutual Legal Assistance Treaty between the USA, the UK and the Cayman Islands. The purpose of the MLA is to codify the principles for the provision of mutual assistance for the investigation, prosecution and suppression of criminal offences and civil and administrative proceedings.

The MLA does not apply to individuals and does not confer on an individual any right to obtain, suppress or exclude any evidence or to impede the execution of a request. Under the MLA, all requests for information from the USA must be submitted to the Mutual Legal Assistance Authority ('MLAA') (the Chief Justice of the Cayman Islands) for consideration. Where the execution of a request requires the issue under the law of the Cayman Islands of a subpoena, search warrant, order for the seizure of any article or other necessary order by a magistrate, justice of the peace or officer of a court, a certificate given by the MLAA that the issue of any such document or order is required for the purposes of a request to which the MLA relates shall be sufficient authority for the issue or making of such subpoena, warrant or order without further enquiry. The MLA does not permit assistance to be given in respect of pure tax offences and only applies where there are suspicions of a serious crime.

The MLA provides that where assistance is being given in terms of this order, the statutory duty of confidence contained in the CRPL will not apply.

SUMMARY

[7.31]   Confidentiality of business transactions in the Cayman Islands is strictly observed, but only in so far as the business activities are bona fide. The CRPL makes the divulging of confidential information (unless authorised) a criminal offence. Where there is any attempt to commit any financial crime or where there are merely grounds for suspicion that a business may be committing a financial crime, the Cayman Islands has sought to implement every necessary law and procedure to investigate these crimes and bring the perpetrators to court. The Cayman Islands has also brought into force procedures for restraining and confiscating the proceeds of criminal conduct.

8 China

Ji Jianfeng

THE BASIC POSITION

[8.1]   Bank confidentiality is a contractual obligation of a bank under the laws and regulations of the People's Republic of China ('PRC'). First, banking is a service to the public and does not normally require a particular contract or contractual term regarding confidentiality between a bank and its customer and it would be most unlikely that a customer would raise the particular issue of bank confidentiality. Secondly, a customer is usually fully confident that a bank will, as a responsible public financial institution, assume its confidentiality obligations according to generally-accepted rules, as well as the duties and responsibilities of a bank, even though no specific requirement of bank confidentiality is raised. Thirdly, the relationship between a bank and its customer is a contractual one and the bank, as a party to a contract, must comply with its confidentiality obligations based upon the nature and objective of the contract and the general practice of the particular transaction as expressly provided in art 60 of the Contract Law. In this regard, a bank is obliged to perform its contractual confidentiality obligations on the basis of its factual and contractual relationship with its customer irrespective of whether such relationship concerns savings and loan transactions or agency.

Bank confidentiality is also a statutory obligation for a bank. The Law on Commercial Banks, which was promulgated on 1 July 1995 and amended on 27 December 2003, expressly provides in clause 1 of art 29 that a commercial bank must adhere to the principle of keeping depositors' information confidential when handling their saving accounts. The Law also requires the staff of a bank not to disclose any state or business secrets they may discover during their employment (art 53). The Regulations for Individuals' Saving Accounts on a Real Name Basis, promulgated on 1 April 2000, contain a provision that a financial institution and its staff must assume the obligation of confidentiality with regard to any information concerning individuals' saving accounts. Furthermore, according to art 23 of the General Rules for Loan Transactions promulgated on 28 June 1996, a lender is obliged to keep confidential the information concerning any debts, operation and financial circumstances of the borrower. Therefore, it can clearly be seen that bank confidentiality is expressly stipulated in many specific areas, including savings, loans, account operation, e-banking and e-payments.

THE SCOPE OF CONFIDENTIAL INFORMATION

[8.2]   Information covered by bank confidentiality consists of its customers' business secrets and personal privacy. The bank's confidentiality obligation on business secrets is expressly provided in art 53 of the Law on Commercial Banks.

Pursuant to clause 3 of art 10 of the Law on Anti-Unfair Competition promulgated in 1993, business secrets refer to utilised technical and business information which is unknown to the public and which may constitute business interests or profits for its owners and is kept secret by them. However, there is no express definition in the laws and regulations of the PRC of technical and business information, although the Certain Provisions on Prohibition of Acts Infringing Upon Business Secrets promulgated by the State Administration for Industry and Commerce on 23 November 1995 only list technical and business information as including design matters, product formulae, manufacturing techniques and methods, management secrets, client lists, supply of goods information, production and marketing strategies, bid prices and the contents of bid documents.

On 18 August 2005, the People's Bank of China ('PBOC'), the central bank of the PRC, published the Provisional Regulations on the Administration of a Basic Database for Individual Credit Information, pursuant to which individual credit information covered by bank confidentiality means basic personal information, individual credit transaction details and other information regarding personal creditworthiness. 'Basic personal information' refers to such information as the identification, profession and domicile of a natural person, 'individual credit transaction details' refer to the track record of a natural person's transactions in credit-related activities, including personal loans, credit cards and security arrangements, and 'other information regarding personal creditworthiness' refers to any other relevant information concerning personal creditworthiness other than individual credit transaction details.

EXCEPTIONS TO BANK CONFIDENTIALITY

[8.3]   Bank confidentiality is a principle under the laws and regulations of the PRC, although certain exceptions are allowed. Articles 29 and 30 of the Law on Commercial Banks authorise a bank to refuse to answer any inquiries into an individual's saving deposits, except where otherwise provided for by law.

Pursuant to the Regulations for Individuals' Saving Accounts on a Real Name Basis, financial institutions may not provide information about an individual's saving account to any entity or individual and have the right to refuse to answer any inquiries and refuse to freeze and deduct an individual's saving deposits as made or requested by any entity or individual, except where otherwise provided for by law.

Those organisations authorised by the laws and regulations of the PRC to make inquiries into an account of an individual or entity and other related information mainly include the public security bureau, the people's prosecutor, the people's court, the customs office, the tax bureau and the PBOC.

CONFLICT OF BANK CONFIDENTIALITY WITH THE DISCLOSURE OBLIGATION

[8.4]   As a public service institution, a bank maintains a business relationship with its customers. It would obviously be unfair if the bank refused to disclose any necessary information to a customer under certain special circumstances since it is in a more favourable position to acquire information than the customer. In this regard, bank confidentiality is not only confined by law, but is also in conflict with its disclosure obligation.

PRC law is silent on the bank's disclosure obligation towards its customer, which often places the bank in a dilemma. In this regard, the Law on Commercial Banks needs to be amended to include detailed provisions that will ensure the priority of the bank's information disclosure obligation under certain special circumstances, whereby the bank must fully disclose the customer's information and the customer is precluded from claiming against the bank for breaching its confidentiality obligation. The priority of the bank's disclosure obligation under certain special circumstances does not necessarily conflict with the importance of the bank's confidentiality obligation since these two obligations are of a different nature: confidentiality is a general obligation, while disclosure is a special obligation. Another important reason for such priority is mainly that these two obligations will have different effects on the parties concerned. Comparatively speaking, the bank's disclosure obligation might cause a direct and material effect on the safety and success of a third party's transaction, while the confidentiality obligation would generally not have a material effect on the parties concerned. Conversely, an absolute confidentiality obligation for a bank would hardly be conducive to the public interest.

ANTI-MONEY LAUNDERING

[8.5]   The Rules for Financial Institutions on Anti-Money Laundering are the first systematic rules governing money laundering, which was formulated by the PBOC and became effective on 1 March 2003. Money laundering is defined as any action which attempts to disguise the source and nature of illegal revenue arising from criminal activities such as drug trafficking, organised crime, terrorist acts or smuggling. The PBOC and the State Administration of Foreign Exchange promulgated the Rules on Administration of Reporting Large Value and Suspicious RMB Payment Transactions and the Rules on Administration of the Reporting by Financial Institutions of Large Value and Suspicious Foreign Exchange Transactions respectively, both of which became effective on 1 March 2003. These Rules contain specific provisions relating to large value and suspicious RMB payment and foreign exchange transactions and set out the system of recording, analysing and reporting such transactions. All these Rules demonstrate the first step of the PRC's legal framework on anti-money laundering.

Under the above Rules, the administration and supervision of anti-money laundering will be targetted at various financial institutions, including banking and non-banking financial institutions, credit co-operatives, postal savings institutions and foreign-funded financial institutions.

Financial institutions in the PRC are required to establish four major systems on anti-money laundering. The first is to identify the customer and record his/her information based upon his/her valid identification or other reliable personal information presented by the customer with whom the financial institution establishes its business relationship or conducts its transactions. The second major system is the reporting of large value transactions whereby financial institutions must report to the PBOC or the State Administration of Foreign Exchange all transactions exceeding a specified value (whether normal or otherwise). The third major system is the reporting of suspicious transactions whereby financial institutions must promptly report to the PBOC or the State Administration of Foreign Exchange transactions which are suspected to originate from criminal activities. The fourth major system is the obligation on financial institutions to keep account information and transaction records of its customers for a certain period of time.

The implementation of the above four systems does not constitute a breach by financial institutions of their confidentiality obligations towards their customers or result in any infringement of their customers' rights. On the one hand, financial institutions must generally assume their confidentiality obligations towards their customers (both individuals and entities) pursuant to the constitution of the PRC, the Law on Commercial Banks, the Regulations on Administration of Savings, the Regulations for Individuals' Saving Accounts on a Real Name Basis and other relevant regulations. Financial institutions will not contravene the relevant provisions which protect the legitimate rights and interests of their customers when they perform their duties and responsibilities with regard to anti-money laundering. Financial institutions will also not be considered to breach their confidentiality obligations towards their customers in the event that they report large value and suspicious transactions and keep any related account information and transaction records because the authorities (to whom financial institutions must report) will keep the information strictly confidential in accordance with the relevant regulations and neither the authorities nor financial institutions will disclose such information to the public or any unauthorised person.

In recent years, there has been an increasing number of cases of illegal capital transfers from smuggling, drug dealing, bribery and corruption. Consequently, money laundering has become an important issue which could not only upset the nation's financial order, but also cause serious damage to its economic well being and social stability. As legislation on anti-money laundering became more urgent and important, the PRC started to work on the draft of the Law on Anti-Money Laundering in March 2004. After a repeated review and solicitation of comments on the draft over the past two years, the Law on Anti-Money Laundering is now in its final draft form and will, it is hoped, be adopted and promulgated soon.

With the economic globalisation and internationalisation of floating capital, money laundering has spread significantly from developed to developing countries and has become more and more of a cross-border issue. Since money laundering cannot be tackled by one country alone, international co-operation on anti-money laundering is of critical importance. The incorporation of international co-operation in the draft Law on Anti-Money Laundering has clearly demonstrated the high value attached by the PRC to the role of international co-operation in anti-money laundering, as well as the PRC's determination to fight money laundering by strengthening international co-operation between member states. Until now, the PRC has acceded to the United Nations Convention Against Illicit Traffic in Narcotic Drugs and Psychotropic Substances, the United Nations Convention Against Transnational Organised Crime, the United Nations Convention Against Corruption and the International Convention for the Suppression of Financing of Terrorism.

LEGAL CONSEQUENCES ARISING FROM BREACH OF CONFIDENTIALITY OBLIGATIONS

[8.6]   There are express provisions under the PRC laws and regulations regarding the legal consequences arising from breaching confidentiality obligations not only by employees of a commercial bank, but also by employees of the PBOC and the banking regulatory authority. For example, disciplinary measures must be taken against those employees of a commercial bank who disclose state or business secrets they discover during their employment and prosecution will follow where such acts constitute a criminal offence (art 87 of the Law on Commercial Banks). The Law on the People's Bank of China, promulgated on 18 March 1995 and amended on 27 December 2003, expressly provides in art 50 that any employee of the PBOC who divulges state or commercial secrets will be liable to prosecution if the case constitutes a criminal offence or to administrative sanctions if the matter is less serious. Furthermore, art 42 of the Law on Banking Regulation and Supervision expressly provides that any of the banking regulatory authority's employees who divulge state or commercial secrets will, if the case constitutes a criminal offence, be subject to prosecution, while administrative sanctions will be imposed in less serious matters.

The Provisional Regulations on Administration of the Basic Database for Individual Credit Information contain specific provisions relating to the legal consequences arising from unauthorised access to, and disclosure of, individual information. For example, in the case of acts like unauthorised access to the individual credit information database, use of individual credit information for purposes other than those specified in the Regulations and breach of the requirements on security management set out in the Regulations, the PBOC may impose a fine of RMB10,000–30,000 yuan and will pass on the case to the judicial authorities if any criminal offences are committed (art 39). So far as such acts are concerned the PBOC may also recommend the commercial bank takes disciplinary sanctions against the directors, senior managers and other staff immediately accountable for the misconduct and will have the case transferred to the judicial authorities if any criminal offences are committed (art 40). In cases where any staff of the Credit Information Centre breach the Regulations by altering, destroying, disclosing or illegally using individual credit information or providing a false credit report by collaborating with other parties, including natural persons, legal persons and other institutions, the PBOC will impose administrative sanctions upon such staff and will pass on the case to the judicial authorities if any criminal offences are committed (art 41).

Finally, in the case of a loan transaction, disciplinary sanctions and fines will be imposed on the staff of a lender responsible for a breach of the bank's confidentiality obligations as laid down by the General Rules for Loan Transactions. Any such person will be removed from his/her position or dismissed in the case of serious or repeated misconduct and will be subject to prosecution if such misconduct results in material economic losses or constitutes a criminal offence (art 65 of the General Rules for Loan Transactions).

CONCLUSION

[8.7] Although there is as yet no specific PRC law or regulation governing bank confidentiality, more and more importance has been attached to such confidentiality by the regulatory authorities, as well as the commercial banks of the PRC. Particularly in the past decade, the PRC has been formulating and introducing a great number of laws and regulations on different business areas of the financial services industry, many of which relate to bank confidentiality. With the deepening of the PRC's economic reforms, the continuous innovation of financial products and the strengthening of international co-operation, there is now great urgency to place bank confidentiality at the top of the agenda. Therefore, a specific law or regulation on bank confidentiality is expected to be in place in the PRC within a short period of time which will expressly provide for the rights and obligations of a bank and its customers with regard to bank confidentiality and solve the possible conflict between a bank's confidentiality and information disclosure obligations.

9 Czech Republic

Pavla Henzlová

INTRODUCTION

[9.1] In general terms, the principle of confidentiality has always existed in all spheres of law in the legal system of the Czech Republic and the bank confidentiality principle is, in fact, only a modification of this, although perhaps one of the most sensitive. Regardless of continuous discussions concerning the definition, content and practical application of bank confidentiality, the relevant legal regulation of banking has created a new foundation for the further development of the whole banking system, including, inter alia, bank confidentiality aspects. In addition, the legislation of the Czech Republic has been through significant changes and development since the publication of the third edition of this book in 2003 in consequence of the entry of the Czech Republic into the European Union on 1 May 2004 and, quite logically, implementation of EU directives and regulations.

The purpose of this chapter is not to provide an extensive jurisprudential essay, but to outline the basic principles of bank confidentiality under the law of the Czech Republic and to stress potential problems which might occur in connection with the application, protection and breach of bank confidentiality in the Czech Republic.

It should be noted that a bank under the law of the Czech Republic does not mean only a 'bank' in its limited sense, but any legal entity established in the form of a joint stock company which obtained a licence from the Czech National Bank to accept deposits from, and to provide loans to, the general public.

THE BASIC RULE OF CONFIDENTIALITY
The source of confidentiality

[9.2] The general provisions on bank confidentiality under Czech law have been incorporated, quite logically, into the Act on Banks (no 21/1992 Coll, as amended), the Act on the Czech National Bank (no 6/1993 Coll, as amended) and the Decree of the Czech National Bank on Requirements for a Licence to Operate as a Bank (no 166/2002 Coll).

In addition to these Acts being the main sources of bank confidentiality, which in general terms apply to both banks established and registered in the Czech Republic as joint stock companies and branches of foreign banks, a number of other Acts and legal rules exist which regulate, deal with or affect bank confidentiality, for example, the Foreign Exchange Act (no 219/1995 Coll, as amended), the Act on Provisions Against the Legalisation of Profits from Criminal Activity (no 61/1996 Coll, as amended, the 'Money Laundering Act') and the Act on Protection of Personal Data (no 101/2000 Coll, as amended, the 'Personal Data Protection Act'), as well as the provisions in the double taxation treaties between the Czech Republic and foreign countries (since there might also be an international aspect under certain circumstances).

Bank confidentiality rules, which are common to all banks registered and operating in the Czech Republic and also apply to all branches of foreign banks operating as banks in the Czech Republic, are clear: all banking transactions and banking financial services, including the state of bank accounts and deposits, are subject to bank confidentiality. There is, however, one unclear 'detail': none of the provisions on bank confidentiality defines the contents of bank confidentiality, which, unfortunately, brings some uncertainty into the whole issue.

Since the banks, as legal entities, are bound by bank confidentiality, employees of the bank (including members of the board of directors, who must always be employees of the bank), members of its supervisory board and persons providing bank supervision are also obliged to keep all matters relating to the interests of the bank and its clients confidential. This obligation to maintain professional confidentiality remains in existence even after the termination of an employment or similar relationship.

It is also important to stress that the relevant provision of the Act on Banks imposes this obligation not only on employees and other representatives of Czech banks, but that the same rules also apply to employees and representatives of the branches of foreign banks. Therefore, if it is not explicitly stressed otherwise, references to a bank include also a branch of a foreign bank.

A foreign bank having its registered office out of the EU, which applies for a banking licence for its branch in the Czech Republic, must in addition provide the Czech National Bank, which is a licensing authority, with a written covenant by the banking supervisory authority in its own country to inform the Czech National Bank of any changes to the concept and application of the principles of bank confidentiality in that country, in particular, as they affect the branches of banks established abroad. On the other hand, in accordance with the Act on Banks, a regime of granting a banking licence to a branch of a foreign bank having its registered office within the EU and being duly licensed in the country of its domicile has been simplified. The whole process has been limited to only an exchange of the relevant information between the supervising authorities of the respective EU country and the Czech Republic. Such a foreign bank is then authorised to carry out almost all of its activities in the Czech Republic through its branch without a special licence from the Czech National Bank.

The confidentiality rules appear not only in the abstract sphere of rights and obligations to be observed from a legal point of view, but the accent is also placed on the technical, administrative and organisational provision and protection of data and information to be secured by the bank or by the branch of a foreign bank. Specification and details of the data protection system constitute mandatory requirements of an application for a banking licence.

The same confidentiality requirements, as applied to the bank, are also imposed on supervisory, regulatory and other bodies of state administration or courts if they dispose of bank information by virtue of law. The same principle applies to the employees and representatives of such bodies and authorities as regards professional confidentiality.

The nature and extent of bank confidentiality

[9.3]   Bank confidentiality can be viewed from different aspects according to the different legal relations in which it applies and according to the different positions of the entities or natural persons involved. The three basic legal aspects of bank confidentiality will be dealt with in more detail below. This section summarises the general concepts of the different views on this issue.

The activities of banks and branches of foreign banks are subject to bank supervision by the Czech National Bank. The Czech National Bank acts vis-a-vis banks as a general licensing, supervisory and regulatory authority (together with the Ministry of Finance, under certain circumstances). The Czech National Bank performs supervision as regards observance of the law and of the regulations which it issues and imposes remedies and measures, which will be specified below, if it discovers any breach or shortcoming in the activities of a bank or a branch of a foreign bank as set out in the Act on Banks. All persons involved in the provision of bank supervision by the Czech National Bank vis-a-vis banks are subject to the obligation to keep all information obtained during the supervision confidential. By virtue of law, such persons are entitled to disclose such information to the authorities supervising the financial market and financial institutions in the Czech Republic and also to similar authorities abroad, as well as to the relevant EU bodies in connection with fulfilment of international treaties.

All measures and actions taken under the Act on Banks against a bank or a branch of a foreign bank which has breached any of its mandatory obligations or the law (in general) are of an administrative law nature. The consequences of such a breach are regulated and specified in the Act on the Czech National Bank and the Act on Banks. Measures and remedies ordered and taken by the Czech National Bank are of an administrative law character, which means that the procedure against the bank or the branch of a foreign bank which breached bank confidentiality would be governed by the Administrative Procedure Act (no 500/2004 Coll, as amended). The Czech National Bank would act in the procedure as the administrative body. With the exception of the Act on Banks, Czech law in general does not define a breach of bank confidentiality as a particular title for a remedy or recourse, either under civil law or under criminal law. This does not mean, however, that the person or entity affected by the breach might not seek a civil law remedy or that the relevant employee or representative of the bank or the branch of the foreign bank who disclosed the confidential bank information would not, under certain circumstances, be accused of a criminal offence as follows.

Any bank customer (a legal entity or a natural person) may apply to a civil court for damages or a satisfaction (for instance, a reasonable public apology or public retraction of the statement, a removal of consequences of unjustified interference with personal integrity, etc) or for another remedy in the event that he or it has sustained damage in connection with a breach of bank confidentiality. Under the law of the Czech Republic, a liability for damage cannot be limited or even excluded by an agreement between a bank and its customer.

In some cases, a breach of bank confidentiality might be classified under criminal law, although the Criminal Code (no 140/1961 Coll, as amended) does not specify a breach of bank confidentiality as a separate criminal offence. In the event that an employee, representative or other person involved in banking operations discloses or misuses confidential bank information and fulfils the factual substance of a specific criminal offence, he will be responsible under criminal law. Further details are given in the next section.

Recourse against breach of bank confidentiality

[9.4]   It has been mentioned above that responsibility for a breach of bank confidentiality is reflected in three spheres of law: administrative, civil and criminal, although the level of protection provided by each of these is not always equal and adequate.

Administrative law concept

[9.5]   As discussed above, the Czech National Bank carries out and executes the supervision of banks, including branches of foreign banks, as regards their observance of the law and regulations issued by the Czech National Bank. In the event that the Czech National Bank discovers a shortcoming, a breach of the law or any other activity on the part of the bank breaching the interests of its customers, it will be authorised to take the measures and actions specified in the Act on Banks and set out below. A bank activity which breaches the interests of its customers is determined by the Act to be, in particular:

1   breach of the terms of a banking licence;
2   breach of the Act, special laws, legal regulations and measures issued by the Czech National Bank;
3   conduct of transactions in a manner which is detrimental to the depositor's interests or which jeopardises the reliability and stability of the banking system;
4   conduct of a bank by persons having insufficient ability or credibility; or
5   breach of laws of a foreign country where a branch of a bank has been established in consequence of a business activity of a bank.

In accordance with the Act, the Czech National Bank is authorised to take the following measures and actions:

1   to request that adequate redress be made by the bank or the branch of a foreign bank or that the bank or the branch of a foreign bank restrains the relevant unauthorised activities or provides for personnel changes;
2   to change the bank licence by elimination or restriction of some of the licensed activities;
3   to impose a receivership on the bank (this may not apply to a branch of a foreign bank);
4   to impose a penalty of up to 50 million Czech crowns;
5   to reduce the registered capital of the bank under certain conditions; and
6   to prohibit or restrict a provision of banking operations by persons who are closely connected with a bank or who are a part of the same consolidated unit with a bank.

The measures specified under 3 and 6 above shall not apply to a branch of a foreign bank.

Despite quite a wide range of administrative remedies under the Act on Banks, apparently only the remedies specified under 1 above would apply in the event of a breach of bank confidentiality and remedies under 2 and 4 if the remedy under 1 is not complied with or in cases of some urgency.

In addition to the remedies listed above which might be imposed by the Czech National Bank, the Act on Banks also provides that the bank licence may be withdrawn from a bank or a branch of a foreign bank by the Czech National Bank in agreement with the Ministry of Finance. Such a remedy would apply in the event that serious shortcomings or breaches persist in the conduct of a bank or a branch.

In any case, the remedy or recourse in the event of the disclosure of confidential information may only apply on the basis of an administrative procedure in which proper and sufficient evidence of a breach of confidentiality has been presented, which might in many cases be the most difficult issue.

In addition, the administrative remedy is directed against the bank only and therefore does not provide a direct recourse to the customer affected by the breach of confidentiality.

Civil law concept

[9.6]   Under general civil law principles, a customer may take a civil law action against the bank or a foreign bank through its branch either for damages, satisfaction (for instance, a reasonable public apology or public retraction of the statement, a removal of consequences of unjustified interference with personal integrity, etc), a restraint of disclosure of information or for removal of the consequences of a breach of bank confidentiality. The civil law procedure would be based on and would follow the Civil Proceedings Code (no 99/1963 Coll, as amended), which stipulates the conditions and rules governing the conduct of civil law proceedings, including the court's decisions and remedies.

The legal action for damages or for satisfaction would probably be very problematic since the customer would have to determine the damage he or it sustained in connection with a breach of bank confidentiality or to estimate the satisfaction he or it considers appropriate.

A claim for removal of the consequences of a breach of bank confidentiality would also be more likely to raise questions as to its practicability than to provide some positive compensation to the customer and a potential recourse against the bank in the form of an injunction to restrain the disclosure of confidential information may not be regarded as an adequate remedy.

The length of the civil law process unfortunately adds a further argument in support of this sceptical viewpoint. Czech law does not prescribe any period in which the court would be obliged to issue its injunction and, although Czech law provides for the institution of preliminary measures which may be imposed by the court in order to achieve a rapid and effective preliminary solution of a current situation before the proceedings are completed and the injunction is issued, it would not be advisable to rely on this since it is always at the discretion of the court and, according to general practice, the courts are rather reluctant to award preliminary measures. Should, however, a preliminary measure be awarded, then the court is obliged to do so within seven days following the submission of the relevant petition by the claimant (customer).

Although the customer affected by a breach of bank confidentiality may claim a remedy through civil law proceedings, under present conditions a civil law action (an event where the injunction satisfies the customer's claim) probably cannot be regarded in most cases as a sufficient and adequate recourse and protection for bank customers.

Criminal law concept

[9.7]   A breach of confidential bank information by employees or representatives of a bank or a branch of a foreign bank might also be classified as a criminal offence under the Criminal Code, in which case such a breach might fall into one of the following categories of criminal offences:

1   *the unauthorised disclosure of personal data*: in accordance with the definition of this criminal offence, any person who discloses or makes available confidential data and information which he obtained in connection with his employment or other position where he was obliged to maintain professional confidentiality will be sentenced to imprisonment for up to three years (or five years if he has caused substantial damage by this criminal offence or if he has officially published such confidential information) or he will be subject to a financial penalty or a ban on his professional activity;

2   *the misuse or damage to records of a data system*: in accordance with the definition of this criminal offence, any person who, in pursuit of unauthorised financial profit, gains access to a data system and misuses or damages the data it contains will be sentenced to imprisonment for up to one year (or up to five years if he has caused extensive damage) or he will be subject to a financial penalty or a ban on his professional activity;

3   *the misuse of information in the conduct of business (insider dealing)*: in accordance with the definition of this criminal offence, any person who, in pursuit of unauthorised profit, misuses confidential information which he gained through his employment or other position in a business operation or in the course of the trading of goods or securities will be sentenced to imprisonment for up to three years (or up to 12 years if he gained extensive profit) or he will be subject to a financial penalty or a ban on his professional activity.

The above three are examples of the most typical criminal offences which occur in the event of the unauthorised disposal and disclosure of confidential information directed against employees and other representatives of banks and branches of foreign banks. Although the Criminal Code sets out quite severe punishments and penal sentences, the question arises as to whether such measures represent any real prevention of a breach of professional confidentiality since the success of criminal proceedings will always be dependent upon the production of sufficient evidence. Given the sophisticated methods used by potential offenders, this could be hard to achieve and could prove to be a weak point in the whole concept of criminal responsibility in this area.

The provisions and rules summarised above would also reasonably apply to branches of foreign banks.

EXCEPTIONS TO THE BASIC RULE OF CONFIDENTIALITY

[9.8]   The obligation on the part of the banks and their employees and representatives to keep bank information confidential is not absolute. The Act on Banks sets out circumstances under which a bank is either authorised or even obliged to disclose confidential information.

The disclosure of confidential information with a customer's consent

[9.9]   Except for the cases specified in the Act on Banks, the bank may disclose only confidential information with the customer's consent. Although the Act does not specify the form of such consent, for the sake of the protection of both the bank and the customer, it should always be in written form and duly signed by the customer or a statutory representative of the customer, provided that the customer is a legal entity. The consent should also specify the extent and purpose of the disclosure of confidential information.

Basic rules on disclosure of confidential information in the interests of the bank and the public

[9.10] In all cases, release from the obligation to keep information confidential on grounds of public interest or in the interests of the bank must be based upon the general provisions of the Act on Banks, under which a bank will be entitled or obliged to disclose confidential information by virtue of the law. In addition to the cases mentioned below, the Act on Banks implements rules under which the bank is authorised to disclose confidential information either in its own interests or in the public interest.

Under these rules, the bank is entitled to exchange information on customers' bank accounts and solvency and credibility with another bank. Such information may also be exchanged between the banks through an entity which is not a bank. Nevertheless, the ownership interests in such an entity may be held only by banks. Further, the bank is permitted to inform other banks, any third party or even the general public of the name of any client who is in default with fulfilment of their obligations vis-a-vis the bank for the period exceeding 60 days.

The disclosure of information on the customer and their business in connection with criminal information made by the bank, which is a general obligation where a suspicion of a criminal offence exists, will not be regarded as a breach of bank confidentiality, ie in the event that the information gives rise to criminal proceedings.

The same rule applies in the event that the bank fulfils its obligations under the Money Laundering Act. Under this Act, the bank is obliged to report to the Ministry of Finance any 'suspicious business' carried out by its customers. The Act defines 'suspicious business' as a business which is carried out under circumstances raising suspicion of an attempt to legalise profits or suspicion that the funds used in the transaction are intended for the financing of terrorism. The legalisation of profits under the Act means 'an activity intended to hide an illegal origin of profits from such activity with a view to raise an appearance that the profits have been gained in accordance with law', regardless of whether or not such an activity has taken place in the Czech Republic. The legalisation of profits within the above-mentioned definition under the Act means, in particular:

1   an exchange or a transfer of property originating from a criminal activity in order to hide such property or to help a person who committed a criminal act to avoid the legal consequences of such activity;
2   a concealment of a real nature, source or placement of a property and handling therewith with the knowledge that such property originates from a criminal activity;
3   an acquisition or a use of or a handling with a property with the knowledge that it originates from a criminal activity;
4   a criminal conspiracy in order to carry out activities mentioned under 1, 2 or 3 above.

The following activities may be regarded as suspicious business under the Act:

1 cash deposits followed by their immediate withdrawals or transfers to other bank accounts;
2 an opening of bank accounts by a client, provided that the number of such bank accounts is disproportionate to the scope of business or financial position of such a client;
3 transactions at accounts of a client, provided that the transactions are disproportionate to the scope of business or financial position of such a client;
4 the number of turnovers at a bank account during one day or within the following days does not correspond with the usual financial transactions of a client;
5 the transactions are apparently without an economic reason;
6 a participant to a transaction is, directly or indirectly, a legal entity or a physical person against which international sanctions are applied by the Czech Republic under special laws;
7 the objects of the business are sanctioned goods or services provided to a sanctioned subject or sanctioned entity;
8 the transactions are targetted at a country which does not apply or insufficiently applies measures against money laundering.

In the event that the bank discovers such 'suspicious business', it shall inform the Ministry of Finance forthwith, within five days at the latest, of the discovery of such 'suspicious business'.

In the event of disclosure of confidential information under the law, the statutory body of the bank will release the relevant employees, members of the supervisory board and other persons providing banking supervision from their obligations to keep professional information confidential in order to provide the necessary information and to allow co-operation with the relevant authorities. Such a release will always be in writing, and will also be delivered to the relevant authority that has requested the information.

Disclosure of information

[9.11] Whilst the above dealt with the general principles of the authorised disclosure of confidential information and, in particular, with the instances when confidential information is disclosed in an action to be taken at the bank's discretion, the following specifies cases when the bank, and also a branch of a foreign bank, is requested by the relevant authorities to disclose confidential information.

Authorities which may request information

[9.12] Under the Act on Banks, the bank (and therefore, obviously, also a foreign bank through its branch) shall disclose confidential information without the consent of the customer on the written request of and to:

1 the body of bank supervision, ie the Czech National Bank (and the Ministry of Finance under certain circumstances);
2 the courts for the purposes of civil law proceedings;
3 the authorities involved in criminal proceedings;
4 the tax authorities for the purpose of tax proceedings;
5 the Ministry of Finance and the Securities Commission for the purposes of its supervisory activities;
6 the Ministry of Finance under conditions stipulated in the Money Laundering Act;

7   the social security and health insurance authorities;
8   the court executives authorised to carry out executions in respect of the customer;
9   the labour office in connection with a return of funds obtained from the state budget; and
10 the National Security Office, intelligence services or the Ministry of Interior.

The basic characteristics of the obligations to disclose bank information

[9.13]   The characteristic features set out below show the basic and typical situations in which the bank may be approached by the relevant authorities (see above) in order to disclose confidential information.

The Czech National Bank in its supervisory capacity

[9.14]   Under the Act on the Czech National Bank, the bank is obliged to inform the Czech National Bank, at its request, of any matter which is subject to bank confidentiality, such as, for example, bank transactions, banking services, the state of bank accounts and deposits, in order that the Czech National Bank may supervise and review the bank's compliance with generally binding legal regulations when performing its activities and operations. In the course of this supervision, the Czech National Bank may impose on the bank the administrative law remedies and measures specified above at 'Administrative Law Concept' under items 1 to 5.

The courts for the purposes of civil law proceedings

[9.15]   A civil court's request for confidential information would be based on the Civil Proceedings Code. The purposes behind a request for the disclosure of bank information can vary. A bankruptcy proceeding may serve as a typical example. However, the power of the court is not unlimited. For instance, some problems might occur if, for example, the civil court ordered the enforcement of a judgment through an assignment of money from the bank account of the debtor on the request of the creditor. The creditor should specify in his request the number of the relevant account. In the event that he does not know the number of the account, he may request the court to obtain this information, but the only possibility given to the court is to ask the debtor. If the debtor ignores the request of the court, the only remedy available is to impose on the debtor a fine of up to 50,000 Czech crowns. This means that the principle of statutory exemptions from the obligation to maintain bank confidentiality is not unconditional and, especially in the event of civil proceedings, will probably always depend on the particular issue.

Authorities involved in criminal proceedings

[9.16]   Under the Criminal Procedure Code (no 141/1961 Coll, as amended), the courts, state attorneys, investigators and the police (the relevant branch) are authorised to request confidential information from the bank under the following conditions:

1   the request is made in relation to criminal proceedings in progress; and
2   the requested information is necessary for the clarification of a criminal offence or for the estimation of the personal financial standing of the accused or for the purpose of enforcing a judgment.

On being approached by the authorities involved in the criminal proceedings, the bank is not entitled to consider whether the above conditions have been met.

The amendment to the Criminal Code brought a new provision to Czech criminal proceedings, that is the 'freezing' of bank deposits in an account. Under the relevant provision of the Criminal Code, the chairman of the criminal court senate, the state attorney, the investigator or the relevant police authority may issue an order to the bank requesting that it blocks its customer's deposits in the event of a suspicion that:

1   the deposits have been designated for the commitment of a criminal offence;
2   the deposits have been used for the commitment of a criminal offence; or
3   the deposits have resulted from a criminal offence.

In comparison with the position of the civil court, which is rather unclear vis-a-vis the bank, the position of the criminal court and the other authorities involved in criminal proceedings is undisputable, in that it has been strengthened even further by the adoption of the new provision (mentioned above) on the 'freezing' of deposits.

Tax authorities

[9.17]   The tax authorities, ie in most cases the relevant finance offices, may request the disclosure of bank information for the purpose of a tax assessment during tax proceedings, in accordance with the Act on Administration of Taxes and Fees (no 337/1992 Coll, as amended). The tax authorities may approach the bank in the event that a suspicion exists of the concealment of the customer's income or if the customer does not co-operate with the tax authority or if any other suspicion exists of a breach of tax law by the customer.

The Ministry of Finance and the Securities Commission as supervisory bodies

[9.18]   A typical example of involvement on the part of the Ministry of Finance and the Securities Commission with bank confidentiality is the statutory supervision exercised by the Ministry and the Securities Commission in relation to a bond (in particular to a mortgage bond) issued under the Act on Bonds (no 190/2004 Coll, as amended). From their positions as licensing and regulatory bodies in relation to bond issues, the Ministry of Finance and the Securities Commission may request confidential bank information in the event that the issuer of the bonds (a bank in the case of mortgage bonds) is suspected of a breach of the Act on Bonds or any other obligation related to the relevant bond issue. Also, in accordance with the Act on Trading in Securities Markets (no 256/2004 Coll, as amended), a securities dealer, including a dealer being a bank, has an information duty vis-a-vis the Securities Commission in respect of business transactions carried out within the preceding calendar quarter. Such information duty includes, inter alia, details of kinds and extent of all investment services provided and all business transactions carried out within the relevant calendar quarter and information on a volume of property of its customers entrusted by them in connection with investment services provided by a securities dealer.

The Ministry of Finance in relation to the Money Laundering Act

[9.19]   Some aspects of this issue have already been dealt with in connection with the bank's obligation to inform the Ministry of Finance under the Money Laundering Act (see above). In addition to the bank's obligation, the Ministry of

Finance is authorised to perform its own investigation regarding a suspicious business transaction' and to request the bank to present the Ministry with all information and documents on 'suspicious businesses' or to allow the employees of the Ministry access to relevant information and documents and to request information on all persons involved in such 'suspicious businesses'. Furthermore, the Ministry may order that the bank postpones the performance of the customer's instruction, which is subject to review by the Ministry, for a period of 24 to 72 hours from the time that the Ministry obtained information on the suspicious business' from the bank.

In the event that the bank does not fulfil its obligation to advise the Ministry or to provide it with the requested evidence and documents under this Act, the Ministry may impose a penalty of up to 10 million Czech crowns (or up to 50 million Czech crowns if the bank repeatedly fails to comply with its obligation or fails to fulfil its obligation for a 12-month period). The statutory barred period for a penalty to be imposed by the Ministry for the non-fulfilment of the obligations under this Act is two years from the end of the year in which the 'suspicious business' occurred.

All of the above authorities are obliged to observe the confidentiality of bank information obtained from the bank. They may only disclose such information under the same conditions and for the same reasons as those applying to the bank. The consequences of a breach of bank confidentiality by the relevant authorities would probably be the same as above. The same applies to their employees and representatives as regards their observance of professional confidentiality.

The social security and health insurance authorities

[9.20]   The social security and health insurance authorities may request the disclosure of bank information for the purpose of proceedings related to mandatory social security and health insurance contributions, in accordance with the Act on Social Security (no 100/1988 Coll, as amended) and the Act on Health Insurance (no 48/1997 Coll, as amended). The relevant authorities may approach the bank in the event that the customer does not pay the contributions or for the purpose of the execution of the due contributions.

The court executive

[9.21]   The court executive may request the disclosure of bank information for the purpose of execution of an effective court judgment against the customer to be carried out under the Executory Rules (no 120/2001 Coll, as amended) in the event that the execution is to be provided by payment from the customer's bank accounts.

The National Security Office, intelligence services and the Ministry of Interior

[9.22]   Pursuant to the Act on Protection of Secret Information and on Security Qualification (no 412/2005 Coll), the bank shall provide the information on a client at the request of the National Security Office, intelligence services or the Ministry of Interior within security proceedings for the purposes of either an issuance of a security certificate or for the purposes of an access to secret information. Such proceedings may be commenced upon a request of a natural person seeking a proof of their integrity and also upon a request of the relevant EU authority in respect of a citizen of the Czech Republic.

DISCLOSURE OF CONFIDENTIAL INFORMATION IN RELATION TO FOREIGN AUTHORITIES

[9.23] Rules similar to those which apply to the observance or compulsory disclosure of confidential information in the Czech Republic will probably apply in other countries. However, the 'exchange' of banking information might be rather problematic. Although Czech law makes a distinction between rendering information in the course of providing legal assistance or, in general, on the request of a judicial authority (ie the courts) and rendering information on the request of another authority (ie the banking or administrative authority), the procedure in both situations will be very similar.

Disclosure of confidential information at a court's request

[9.24] Under principles of Czech law, legal assistance in relation to foreign countries may be provided either on the basis of generally applicable EU regulations and directives within the EU countries or in accordance with an international treaty or upon a reciprocity principle if an international treaty with the relevant country does not exist. Basically, legal relations between countries with different jurisdictions are regulated by the Act on International Private and Proceedings Law (no 97/1963 Coll, as amended), which, inter alia, sets out basic principles of international legal assistance. In addition to this Act, a number of treaties on legal assistance exist between the Czech Republic and other countries. In addition to the generally applicable EU regulations and directives, the Czech Republic is also a signatory of some multilateral international treaties, for instance, the European Treaty on Legal Assistance in Criminal Matters.

In principle, a foreign court may approach a bank in the Czech Republic, when seeking confidential information, only after complying with certain requirements stipulated either by the Act on International Private and Proceedings Law or by the relevant EU regulation or international treaty.

The treaties on legal assistance also usually designate the authorities of the relevant countries involved, which will be authorised to mediate between contacts in the provision of legal assistance. If a treaty does not exist or if the treaty does not designate the relevant authority, the procedure of the provision of the legal assistance and the relevant authorities involved are regulated by the Instruction of the Ministry of Justice no 56/2004 in respect of civil law matters and commercial law matters and the Instruction of the Ministry of Justice no 131/1997 and the General Instruction no 1/2005 of the Supreme State Attorney in respect of criminal law matters.

In any case, different regimes apply depending on whether or not the provision of confidential information is requested by the courts or other judicial authorities within the EU or out of the EU and also whether or not an international treaty between the Czech Republic and the relevant country exists.

Examples of procedure in connection with the disclosure of confidential information at a court's request

[9.25] In order to clarify this, some typical examples are as follows:

1   the relatively easiest procedure applies in the event that the requesting court is of the EU member state. In such a case, the courts may, within the relevant EU

regulations, contact the courts in other EU member states either directly or through the consulates of the relevant state;

2   if, however, a court in a country outside of the EU with which the Czech Republic has not entered into any treaty on legal assistance requests confidential information, the request of the court or other judicial authority must be submitted to the relevant country's Ministry of Justice (or a similar authority). The ministry will pass this request to the Ministry of Foreign Affairs (or a similar authority). The Ministry of Foreign Affairs will then forward the request to the Ministry of Foreign Affairs of the Czech Republic and this ministry will pass the request to the Ministry of Justice of the Czech Republic, which will eventually serve the request on the relevant court for a settlement, ie depending on other circumstances mentioned below, the court may request the bank to provide it with confidential information;

3   in the event that a treaty on legal assistance exists, the procedure would depend on the regulation of the mutual contacts between the relevant authorities of the two countries. Provided that the contacts are at ministerial level, the requests of the courts or other judicial authorities are delivered by the Ministry of Justice (or by an authority with a similar capacity) of the relevant country to the Ministry of Justice of the Czech Republic. The Ministry of Justice will then serve the request on the relevant court;

4   in the event that the mutual contacts between the two countries are at a consular level, the Ministry of Justice or a similar authority of the relevant foreign country will forward the request to the Ministry of Foreign Affairs (or a similar authority) and this ministry will pass the request to the consulate of the relevant country in the Czech Republic. The consulate will then serve the request directly on the court in the Czech Republic. Depending upon the other circumstances, the court may request that the bank provide confidential information

The same procedure will apply in reverse when a court in the Czech Republic requests confidential information from a bank abroad.

Therefore, the whole procedure regarding the means of delivering the request to the relevant court in the Czech Republic depends on:

(a) whether or not the relevant court is that of an EU member state,

(b) whether a treaty on mutual legal assistance exists and also whether the treaty covers the spheres of both civil and criminal law or only one of these, and

(c) how the contacts between the two countries have been regulated, ie which state authorities have to be involved in the delivery process.

The delivery of the request, however, forms only a part of the total of all legal steps to be taken and considered in connection with the provision of confidential bank information to a foreign court.

Provided that all of the procedures for delivery of the request as described above have been duly completed, a Czech court will provide legal assistance on the request of a foreign judicial authority only on condition that (i) the relevant EU regulation exists within the EU member states or (ii) reciprocity exists between the Czech Republic and the relevant country. Reciprocity may be based either on a treaty on mutual legal assistance or, in the event that such a treaty does not exist or that the existing treaty does not regulate reciprocity, on mutual practice between the two countries.

Disclosure of confidential information at the request of another foreign authority

[9.26]   A similar situation will then occur if another foreign authority, other than the courts, requests confidential bank information.

In the event that the request falls within the capacity of the state administrative body of the Czech Republic and not the Ministry of Justice, the request will be forwarded to the relevant state administrative body, which in this case might be the Czech National Bank or the Ministry of Finance. The Czech National Bank or the Ministry of Finance (as the case may be) would then follow a similar procedure to that of a court, ie they might at their discretion and depending on other circumstances request the confidential information from the bank.

The requested legal assistance will always be based on the laws of the Czech Republic, including generally applicable EU regulations within the EU member states, which means that the Czech court, the Czech National Bank or the Ministry of Finance (as the case may be) will only approach the bank with a request to provide confidential information when the disclosure of such information is in compliance with the law. Otherwise, the requested authority will refuse to provide the assistance sought. Obviously, the bank would only be obliged to provide the confidential information under the conditions and circumstances set out in the Act on Banks, as explained above.

It has been mentioned above that the procedure similar to that when a court requests confidential information would apply in the event that an administrative body requests such information. For instance, if the banking supervisory authority in the foreign country outside of the EU requires information from a Czech bank (which might also be a wholly-owned subsidiary of a foreign bank), such a request would have to go through the Czech Ministry of Foreign Affairs, which means that the requesting authority would have to forward its request to the relevant state administrative authority of its country first and the request would then be passed by this authority to the Ministry of Foreign Affairs of the Czech Republic. The Ministry would then serve the request on the relevant state administrative body, ie the Czech National Bank or the Ministry of Finance, which would then approach the bank.

The provision of confidential information would therefore be based on the same principles as in the case of the provision of information on the request of a court, ie information would be provided in accordance with (i) the relevant EU regulations between EU members states, (ii) an international treaty, if it exists, and (iii) otherwise under the general principles of Czech law as described above.

The situation does not seem to be any less complicated where an international treaty exists between the Czech Republic and a relevant foreign country. For instance, the double taxation treaties presume an exchange of information between the relevant tax authorities of the two countries. However, at the same time, some of the treaties stipulate that such a provision shall not apply to any confidential information, including bank confidential information (the treaty with Switzerland, for example), or stipulate that the requested party is not obliged to disclose any confidential information.

This means that if the relevant authority from a foreign country insists that the Czech bank make confidential information available, regardless of whether an international treaty exists, the authority would have to pass the whole procedure through the state administrative bodies.

It is doubtless unnecessary to stress that the relevant Czech administrative authority could approach the bank with a request to disclose confidential information and that the bank could only do so in the event that reciprocity in exchange of information between the Czech Republic and the relevant foreign country has been established and that such a disclosure was not contrary to Czech law. This means that the information might only be made available if its disclosure fell within the cases, specified by the Act on Banks, in which a bank may provide confidential information.

Disclosure of confidential information maintained by a branch of a foreign bank

[9.27] It is necessary to emphasise that the above provisions and procedure would apply in the event that the confidential information was requested from a bank being a Czech legal entity, ie a bank incorporated under Czech laws as a joint stock company or a state monetary institution and registered in the commercial register in the Czech Republic. As far as branches of foreign banks are concerned, they are not regarded as Czech legal entities. Therefore, in the event of a Czech court or a state administrative body requesting information from a foreign bank with its branch office in the Czech Republic, it should approach the foreign bank, since the Act on Banks does not enable the Czech courts or state administrative bodies to request confidential information directly from the branch.

The whole concept of bank confidentiality as applied to the branch of a foreign bank would then be based on the Act on Banks, as explained above. That is to say, when the head office of a foreign bank in a foreign country is affected by a civil, criminal or administrative investigation in the Czech Republic through its branch office, it would be obliged, in respect of the activities of the branch, to keep confidential all banking information obtained and collected by the branch and only to disclose it on the legal basis stipulated by the Act on Banks. If the head office of a foreign bank refused to provide the information requested, although all statutory requirements had been met, it would be exposed to the risk that relevant measures might be imposed on it by the Czech National Bank.

The same rules then apply in the case of a branch of a Czech bank abroad, subject to potential differences in the concept of a branch of a foreign bank in some countries. For example, if a court in England requests that all account records of the customer of a Czech bank be made available, it will have to follow the procedure applicable to banks domiciled in the EU countries.

The same rules apply in the event that the information is required by a state administrative body or by a banking supervisory authority.

PROCESS OF TRACING OF FUNDS

[9.28] In the process of tracing funds which have been the subject of a criminal offence or any illegal disposal, all the procedures and measures which have been dealt with above might apply in general. This means that the elements of banking supervision by the Czech National Bank and of interference executed by the Ministry of Finance, as well as the elements of criminal law and also of the civil law would appear at various stages of such a process. There would, however, be differences depending upon whether the funds could be traced in the Czech Republic or whether they disappeared abroad.

Tracing of funds in local banks

[9.29] The process of tracing funds will always face the barrier of bank confidentiality and the rather strict rules on the possibility of compelling banks to disclose confidential information. Although the process of tracing funds has two basic legal aspects, the administrative law aspect and the criminal law aspect, in the whole concept of the law of the Czech Republic, only certain authorities involved in criminal proceedings are authorised to carry out effective interference with such a process.

Moreover, even if it were suspected that funds resulting from an illegal business or criminal activity were deposited in banks, only the courts would have the power to compel the bank to make available the confidential information about such funds. The reasons for, and examples of, the court's interference have been set out above.

An example of tracing funds might be as follows: if the customer of a bank were defrauded by its employee, who illegally transferred the money to other bank accounts in other banks in the Czech Republic, the customer may report a criminal information charge against the employee to the relevant body involved in criminal proceedings and the investigator would commence a criminal investigation.

In accordance with the Criminal Proceedings Code, only the chairman of the criminal senate, the state attorney, the investigator or a relevant police body within criminal proceedings may issue an order to block the deposits in a bank account, provided a justified suspicion exists that the money is connected with a criminal offence. The authority ordering a block on the deposits must also state in its order all the details related to the relevant account.

In the event that details of such a bank account are not available or that the customer and the authorities referred to above do not have sufficient information as to where the funds have been transferred, after the criminal proceedings have been commenced against the employee, the state attorney or the chairman of a criminal senate will approach the customer's bank with the request that the bank provides all information about the movements and disposal of funds in the customer's accounts. Under such circumstances, the bank shall be obliged to disclose the confidential information, as explained above.

The Money Laundering Act also signifies a substantial contribution towards greater transparency of banking transactions. The basic provisions and obligations imposed on banks in the Czech Republic, in the event of the appearance of 'suspicious business', are dealt with above. Under this Act, the Ministry of Finance would be obliged to inform the competent bodies involved in criminal proceedings in the case of any suspicion of a criminal offence.

The Ministry of Finance may also interfere with the banking operations to a certain extent, provided that it has been informed by the bank that a suspicion exists that the relevant deposits were the result of criminal activity. In such a case, the Ministry may order a suspension of the banking operation for a period of 24 to 72 hours from the time it has been notified by the bank.

In its supervisory capacity, the Czech National Bank also plays a role in the process of tracing funds. It is, however, necessary to stress that the Czech National Bank, in its position as a supervisory authority, would probably only be involved in the investigation and measurement of frauds or similar fraudulent actions having an effect on a large number of people or of very wide scope (for instance, frauds in investment funds, which are quite frequent). In such situations, the bank would also be obliged to disclose all confidential information in relation to the fraud and the offenders.

It follows from the examples given that, despite all the above-mentioned instruments which might help to trace and identify funds which resulted from or were the subject of a criminal offence, its practical application does not seem to be very efficient. Under current legal regulations, none of the authorities, ie neither the Ministry of Finance and the Czech National Bank nor the authorities involved in criminal proceedings, can execute its powers to stop any movements of money quickly and with immediate effect, as the obligatory procedural steps to be taken are in practice so complicated and lengthy that the authorities are unable to compete with all the possible fraudulent actions which may be taken by offenders.

Tracing of funds abroad

[9.30] As indicated above, tracing funds which have disappeared on being transferred to Czech bank accounts is likely to be very difficult, lengthy and of uncertain outcome. The chances of succeeding in tracing funds which have disappeared abroad are minimal, despite the fact that transfers of money abroad are regulated by law and, moreover, that the bank must always be involved in such transfers. (The obligations of the banks in cases where criminal activity is suspected have been described above.)

The rules of foreign exchange control, including those dealing with transfers of money abroad, are set out in the Foreign Exchange Act. Some of the basic principles of the Foreign Exchange Act are as follows.

Under this Act:

1   any no-cash transfers abroad or any trading in foreign currency may only be made through a bank or a branch of a foreign bank which is authorised by a foreign exchange licence issued by the Czech National Bank to carry out foreign exchange transactions;
2   a Czech legal entity or a natural person may open an account abroad without a foreign exchange permission. He or it is only obliged to inform the Czech National Bank of such an account – the same applies to any deposit of money into a bank account abroad;
3   a Czech legal entity or a natural person may also fulfil its or his financial obligations towards a foreign entity or a foreign natural person without a foreign exchange licence;
4   a foreign legal entity or a foreign natural person may transfer foreign currency abroad without any restrictions or without the need to obtain foreign exchange permission; and
5   the bank shall be obliged to inform the Ministry of Finance and the Czech National Bank of any breach of foreign exchange rules it discovers.

These provisions of the Foreign Exchange Act have been included here in order to demonstrate that, although foreign exchange control may interfere to a limited extent with the free disposal of money by Czech legal entities and physical persons, there is, on the other hand, quite a large range of possibilities for legally transferring money abroad. Moreover, despite the fact that the Foreign Exchange Act imposes the obligation to obtain foreign exchange permission for certain operations, the avoidance of which might result in a fine under the Act (the maximum fine may be up to 50 million Czech crowns) or even by a punishment under the Criminal Code in serious cases, which states that any person who, in contradiction of the foreign exchange regulations, disposes of Czech crowns or foreign currencies will be sentenced to imprisonment for up to three years (or up to six years if he committed the offence as a member of an organised group or if he committed the criminal offence in breach of his professional obligations) or will be subject to a ban on his professional activity or to a financial penalty, a potential criminal is probably not very likely to observe the foreign exchange rules.

In addition, as already noted, neither the Ministry of Finance nor the Czech National Bank can execute its authority to stop or restrict a transfer of funds. The Ministry of Finance may only order the suspension of a bank transaction for up to 72 hours in the event of the suspicion of money laundering (under the Money Laundering Act).

The only means of tracing funds exists at the moment through criminal proceedings initiated in the Czech Republic when the funds are actually transferred abroad, but even if the criminal court obtains confidential information from a Czech bank as to where the funds have been transferred abroad, further steps towards banks abroad would have to be taken through the complicated procedure described above. In addition, such a procedure would only be successful where the money was actually deposited in a bank account abroad if the concept of bank confidentiality in the country in question permitted disclosure of confidential information at the request of the relevant court in such country and if reciprocity existed in provisions of legal assistance with the Czech Republic.

MISCELLANEOUS
Insider dealing

[9.31] Insider dealing, even if it is not specifically defined, is to a certain extent regulated by the Act on Banks. It is possible to say that, in general terms, the prevention of insider dealing has been incorporated into the principle of the maintenance of professional confidentiality by all employees and representatives of banks, who are obliged to keep confidential all information obtained in the course of their employment or functions at the bank and related to the interests of the bank and its customers. This rule also applies to the employees and representatives of a foreign bank who work or perform their activities in a branch of the relevant bank in the Czech Republic.

The Act on Banks also stipulates that the bank may not do business with persons with whom the bank has a special relationship if such a transaction would not be made with other clients because of the nature, purpose or risk of such business. For the purposes of the Act on Banks, the following persons shall be regarded as having a special relationship with a bank:

1   members of the bank's statutory body and directors of the bank;
2   members of the bank supervisory board;
3   legal entities holding a controlling interest in the bank;
4   persons close to the persons and entities mentioned under 1, 2 and 3 above (ie family members and relatives in general);
5   legal entities in which any of the persons listed under 1, 2 and 3 above hold an ownership interest in the registered capital which exceeds 10% of the total amount of that capital;
6   major shareholders of the bank and any legal entity under their control;
7   members of the Banking Board of the Czech National Bank; and
8   persons controlled by the bank.

Any bank breaching the relevant provision of the Act on Banks, under which it may not do business with the persons listed above, would be exposed to an administrative penalty by the Czech National Bank.

Certain preventive measures against insider dealing might also be found in the regulation of employment matters in the Czech Republic. Most banks insist on a provision in a contract of employment in respect of the members of its management and other employees above a certain level in the bank's hierarchy, under which the employees in question are forbidden to deal in information learnt in the course of their functions within the bank.

Taking into account the aforementioned consequences of a breach of bank confidentiality and the fact that, under Czech law, insider dealing would only be a modified version of a misuse of confidential information, insider dealing might be subject to:

1   a civil law action – in respect of the potential damage sustained by the customer;
2   a criminal action – in respect of unauthorised dealing with personal data and misuse of information in doing business (both criminal offences have been dealt with above); or
3   a labour law penalty – dismissal, demotion or payment of damages.

However, the basic condition of any penalty which might be applied to an unauthorised 'dealer' in confidential information will always be that there is sufficient evidence of such dealing and a credible valuation of the potential damage or profit the 'dealer' gained, which will always be a crucial issue in any relevant proceedings. Therefore, the question of insider dealing will always depend to a large extent upon the moral principles of those who have access to confidential information.

Personal Data Protection Act

[9.32]   The Personal Data Protection Act provides, in general, for the protection of data concerning natural persons. At the moment, no similar Act exists which would provide data protection for legal entities.

Although the current legal banking regulations do not define or determine the contents of the term 'bank confidentiality' or 'professional confidentiality', based on the definition of 'personal data', 'collection of personal data' and 'processing of personal data', the provisions of the Personal Data Protection Act would apply to a bank information system which collects and processes bank information regarding the bank's customers as natural persons. The reason for this assumption is the general and broad application of the Data Protection Act and, at the same time, the requirement set out in the Act on the Czech National Bank and in the Act on Banks that the Czech National Bank co-ordinates and develops a banking information system based on data systems of all entries regarding its customers, their bank operations and bank accounts operated and maintained by a bank (including data of natural persons).

In accordance with the definition set out in the Personal Data Protection Act, 'collection of personal data' means a systematic collection of data for the purposes of their processing and 'processing of personal data' means any operation regarding any storing, disposals, records, use, classification and maintenance of personal data.

The personal data in banking systems may only be operated and used in accordance with the Act on Banks or with the consent of the relevant natural person. The Act on Banks and the Act on the Czech National Bank specify not only the obligation of the bank to meet the requirements of a data system, but also set out the conditions under which the data may be disclosed.

The principle of 'know your customer'

[9.33] The principle of 'know your customer', which might eliminate potential problems between the bank and its customers and vice versa, is not specifically regulated in any of the banking-related Acts. However, it is possible to trace certain indications of this rule in some of the Acts which have already been dealt with above. An attempt to control the nature of customers appears in the Decree on Requirements for a Licence to Operate as a Bank. For instance, when the founders of a bank apply to the Czech National Bank for a banking licence, they must present the main intentions of the bank regarding the granting of loans and taking deposits, in particular as regards the nature of its future customers, ie whether the bank will concentrate on natural persons or commercial companies, from which of the main sectors of the economy the customers will be drawn, etc. This is not a typical example of the 'know your customer' principle. Nevertheless, the requirement may eliminate in advance the situation where the bank faces problems with customers, which would otherwise be unacceptable from the point of view of the banking sector as a whole. In the event that the Czech National Bank traces any potential problems, it will either refuse to issue a banking licence or it may persuade the applicant to change its type of customers. This rule applies to local applicants for a banking licence, as well as to foreign banks intending to set up branches in the Czech Republic.

Rules which relate to the 'know your customer' principle are mainly contained in the Money Laundering Act. Under the provisions of this Act, the bank must carry out a so-called 'customer's identification' in the event that the customer makes a banking transaction which exceeds 15,000 euros. Identification means the verification of the full name, personal number or date of birth and permanent address (for natural persons) and the verification of the business name, registered offices, identification number and identification of the representative (for legal entities).

In addition to the general obligation to identify transactions exceeding 15,000 euros, the following transactions are also subject to the identification duty:

1 any suspicious transaction;
2 opening a bank account or concluding a contract on a deposit;
3 the rental of a safety deposit box;
4 conclusion of a life insurance policy, provided that the aggregate insurance premium exceeds 1,000 euros per year;
5 purchase of items having a cultural value; or
6 acceptance of pledges (but the duty to identify does not apply to other types of security).

The bank is obliged to keep all customer identification data for a period of ten years following the completion of the relevant banking transaction.

Other than by the special provisions of the Money Laundering Act, the most natural way of getting information about a customer is through the formalities connected with any opening of a bank account or, to a greater extent, any granting of a bank loan, as stipulated by the Act on Banks.

On opening a bank account, the customer must disclose to the bank all data as mentioned above in connection with the identification duty. Such data must be supported by relevant documentation. The Act on Banks also states that the bank is obliged to request proof of identity (ie personal data supported by relevant documents in the case of natural persons or an extract from the Commercial Register in the case of a legal entity) in the event of any transaction exceeding 100.000 Czech crowns (approximately 3,500 euros).

The arrangements between the bank and the customer regarding a bank loan are in addition based on the requirement that the customer will only be entitled to use the loan for the purposes precisely specified in the loan agreement. The bank usually requests that a security be provided by the customer. As a result of all these formalities, the bank might be in a position to estimate the nature and legal status of the customer, at least to some extent.

Regardless of attempts to rate and estimate the standing and probity of customers, as implemented by the rules mentioned above, the main responsibility for getting to know its customers and the prevention of potential risks will always lie with the bank and, in particular, with its employees and representatives.

Conflicts of interest

[9.34] Under the present legal regulation of the banking system in the Czech Republic, no provision exists which would prevent the bank from providing both the usual commercial services for its customers and, at the same time, offering advisory services and assistance in investments. However, the relevant provisions of the Act on Banks stipulates that the bank, as well as a branch of a foreign bank, is obliged (i) not to use the information obtained in connection with investment transactions for the purposes of credit transactions and vice versa and (ii) not to use the information obtained in connection with investment transactions of customers for the purposes of its own investment transactions.

In order to comply with the above obligations, the bank is required to implement relevant measures in its organisational, operation and control system to secure the separation of investment transactions and credit transactions. The compliance of the bank with the above-mentioned obligations must be already proved when the bank applies for the banking licence under the Decree on Requirements for a Licence to Operate as a Bank, where the bank must specify precisely its technical, organisational and operational prerequisites for the separation of investment transactions and credit transactions.

In addition, a principle of 'statutory collision' exists and is applicable under the laws of the Czech Republic. This is where a bank is obliged to refuse to act for a customer in the same matter in which it acts for another customer if the interests of the two customers are in conflict. This is a basic principle of professional ethics which appears in general in the Czech legal system. In other cases, for instance, if the bank acts for clients whose interests might be in conflict under other circumstances, though not in the matter in question, some sort of Chinese Wall would probably be created, depending on the internal arrangements and rules of each bank.

SUMMARY

[9.35] The information contained in this chapter seems to indicate that the bank confidentiality concept in the Czech Republic still faces some problems and that some gaps continue to appear, in particular, as regards the tracing of funds and the prompt and effective intervention in connection with money laundering or other criminal actions in the banking sphere.

9.35 *Czech Republic*

Nevertheless, although some legal institutions still do not operate as intended, nor with the desired result, some positive progress has already been achieved in this area. We can only hope that the membership of the Czech Republic of the EU and the adoption of the relevant EU regulations and directives will contribute to further development of banking in the Czech Republic and will bring more transparency and certainty to this entire issue.

10   Denmark

Herman D Federspiel

INTRODUCTION

[10.1]   Danish law recognises a duty of confidentiality owed by a bank with regard to the affairs of its customers, both to private third parties and to public authorities. The original motive for banks to observe confidentiality was that it served the bank's business interests; a client was only likely to entrust its business to a bank which treated their affairs as confidential. While it originally was a right for the banks, it subsequently became an obligation which clients could invoke as part of the contractual relationship between the bank and its customers. Bank secrecy is statutorily regulated and since 1990 breaches have been subject to criminal liability.

THE BANK'S DUTY OF CONFIDENCE
Source of the obligation

[10.2]   The individual's right to privacy is an important principle of Danish law, deriving some authority both from international treaties like the UN Convention on Civil and Political Rights (art 17) and the European Convention on Human Rights (art 8),[1] as well as from the Danish constitution (art 72). On a more commercial level, s 19 of the Danish Act on Marketing[2] prohibits a person who is an employee or has a contractual relationship with a particular business enterprise from obtaining or trying to obtain 'by improper means' knowledge of its business secrets. If the person has lawfully acquired knowledge or possession of business secrets, the person may not disclose or make use of such secrets if such disclosure or use has not been authorised. Similarly, a recipient of such information is unauthorised to use the information if it has been obtained in contravention of s 19. Section 19 of the Danish Act on Marketing is sanctionable both by civil and criminal remedies. Chapter 27 of the Danish Criminal Code[3] makes it a criminal offence to obtain unauthorised access to another person's data or business secrets. Other legislation expresses this principle as well. In consequence, bank confidentiality has developed in parallel with these legal developments.

In Denmark, there has not been much discussion about the legal qualification of bank confidentiality. For a long time, bank confidentiality (or secrecy) was only based on custom and usage, which gradually obtained the force of 'customary' law. Under

---

1 Incorporated into Danish law by Act no 285 of 29 April 1992, now Consolidated Act no 750 of 19 October 1998, as last amended by Act no 538 of 8 June 2006.
2 Consolidated Act no 1389 of 21 December 2005, as last amended by Act no 538 of 8 June 2006.
3 Consolidated Act no 909 of 27 September 2005, as last amended by Act no 542 of 8 June 2006.

Danish law, customary law means a practice generally followed for a considerable period and considered by those concerned to have become legally binding. The obligation of confidentiality can now also be said to be an implied term in the contractual relationship between the bank and its customer which can be waived by the customer. By Act no 306 of 16 May 1990, the Danish Bank Act was amended 'codifying' the banks' duty of confidentiality. The Danish Bank Act has been repealed and the codification of the duty of confidentiality can now be found in the Danish Act on Financial Business (the 'Financial Business Act'),[4] which applies to all regulated financial undertakings.[5, 6] The first sentence of s 117(1) of the Financial Business Act states in the unofficial translation provided by the Danish Financial Supervisory Authority (the 'Danish FSA'):

> 'Members of boards of directors, members of local boards of directors or similar organs, members of the committee of shareholders in a financial undertaking other than a savings bank, auditors and inspectors and their deputies, founders, valuation officers, liquidators, managing directors, responsible actuaries, general agents and administrators in an insurance company and other employees shall not without due cause disclose or use confidential information obtained during the performance of their duties.'

Section 117(2) of the Financial Business Act provides for the following:

> 'Any person receiving information pursuant to subsection (1) hereof shall fall within the scope of the duty of silence [duty of confidentiality] specified in said subsection (1).'

Section 373(1) of the Financial Business Act provides that a breach of s 117(1) shall be punishable by a fine or imprisonment for up to four months, unless a more severe penalty is incurred under other legislation.

Thus, these sections of the Financial Business Act make it a criminal offence for the bank and its employees to transmit or utilise, without due cause, confidential information with which they have become acquainted during the performance of their functions. The statute has two purposes:

1   protection against disclosure of confidential information about the bank itself, for instance, accounts, engagements in particular credits, exposures, strategies, general and particular dispositions and what in general are considered business secrets; and

2   protection of the bank's customers against transmission of or disclosure of confidential information which the customer has entrusted to the bank. The Financial Business Act thus complements the general rules contained in the Danish Act on Data Protection (the 'Data Protection Act').[7]

Pursuant to s 123 of the Financial Business Act, information on purely private affairs may not be passed on without obtaining prior written consent from the customer, unless such disclosure is justified under ss 117(1) or 118(2). What constitutes 'purely

---

4 Consolidated Act no 286 of 4 April 2006, as amended by Act no 527 of 7 June 2006.
5 Financial undertakings are defined as (i) investment companies, (ii) insurance companies (including lateral pension funds), (iii) banks, (iv) mortgage credit institutions and (v) investment management companies.
6 The Danish FSA has issued a guidance letter on the rules of confidentiality of financial undertakings published on 25 October 2002 on the official website of the Danish FSA at www.ftnet.dk.
7 Act no 429 of 31 May 2000, as last amended by Act no 158 of 9 March 2006.

private affairs' is not defined in the Act, however, the term is likely to apply to information on the customer's religious beliefs, race and ethnic origin. Further, s 122 of the Financial Business Act provides that all banks must establish and publish guidelines for the transfer of customer data and once a year the bank must inform its customers of which type of information may be disclosed with the customer's consent, the purpose or purposes for which such disclosure may take place and the recipients of the information; cf s 123(3). Secrets relating to the bank's own affairs are also protected by the general rules in s 19 of the Danish Act on Marketing and s 160 of the Danish Companies Act,[8] which make it a criminal offence for directors, registered managers, auditors and certain others to disclose confidential information of a company. The Financial Business Act goes further as it also includes employees and information on customers.

It is irrelevant to the application of the provisions on confidentiality in the Financial Business Act whether the disclosure of information is conducted by electronic or non-electronic means.

Definition and extent of bank confidentiality

[10.3]   Danish banking law does not have a definition of 'confidential information'. The term is interpreted widely as including everything which the customer has told the bank about his affairs and which is not public knowledge. Even information that a particular person is a client of the bank is confidential. Information supplied by a third party or information which the bank has collected elsewhere or in connection with its dealings with the client is protected as well. In the following text, no distinction will be made between information supplied by the customer or a third party.

The duty of confidentiality has two aspects. One is that the information may only be passed on or disclosed with due cause. The Danish FSA has stated in a decision that a bank is entitled to pass confidential information on to an IT company in connection with outsourcing of the bank's IT functions if such IT company has an acceptable security level.[9] If the IT company breaches the duty of confidentiality, the bank is not subject to any statutory (criminal) liability as the IT company, in connection with the outsourcing, undertakes on behalf of the bank the duty of confidentiality. However, the bank may be liable for damages to its client for any losses suffered.

The other is that it may not be utilised for purposes other than those for which it was acquired. For instance, confidential information may only be disclosed to such other persons or departments within the bank which have a business reason to obtain the information. The Danish FSA has held that the auditor's minute book, which could contain confidential customer information, could not be passed on to a bank's shareholders' committee as there was no business reason to disclose the matter to the committee.[10] On the other hand, the Danish FSA has held that confidential customer information may be passed to another bank in connection with a transfer of loan portfolios for business reasons under circumstances where the bank sold its entire

---

8 Consolidated Act no 649 of 15 June 2006 consolidating the amendments to Act no 1001 of 8 October 2004.

9 Decision of the Danish FSA of 26 July 2005 published on the official website of the Danish FSA at www.ftnet.dk.

10 Decision of the Danish FSA of 22 February 1995 mentioned in the annotated edition of the Bank Act by C Boye Jacobsen et al (1996) p 391.

loan portfolio of a certain kind to another bank.[11] The obligation of confidentiality or secrecy is not absolute. The statute only extends to disclosure 'without due cause'. If the information is publicly available, there is no duty of confidentiality. For instance, this is the case where the bank has obtained judgments over its customer or where expedited proceedings have been initiated in the Bailiff's Court, in which case the bank may report such information to credit rating agencies. Information which may be obtained publicly with the Danish Commerce and Companies Agency, in a land registration book or similar public registers may also be disclosed by a bank without consent.

The duty of confidentiality continues after the termination of the client relationship. In a ruling in 1995, the Danish FSA held that in principle a bank could not deliver its historical records from the middle of the nineteenth century to a local museum, but in each case would have to examine whether the records transmitted could be considered confidential, in which connection, of course, the length of time and other circumstances could be taken into consideration.[12]

REMEDIES FOR BREACH OF CONFIDENCE

[10.4]   The customer has several remedies in case of breach of confidence, not only under criminal and civil law, but also under administrative law.

Administrative law

[10.5]   In Denmark, it is most likely that a customer fearing disclosure without due cause of information subject to bank confidentiality or having been exposed to such disclosure will file a complaint with the Danish FSA. The Danish FSA will then be obliged to take action in its capacity as the administrative authority supervising compliance with the banking laws. In most cases, a letter from the Danish FSA will determine the matter. The decision can be brought before the Danish Commerce and Companies Appeal Board and the ordinary courts.

Criminal sanctions

[10.6]   As the Financial Business Act makes it a criminal offence for the bank or its employees to breach bank confidentiality, the customer – or the Danish FSA – may ask the prosecuting authorities to initiate criminal proceedings against the bank and/or the disclosing employee for any breach of confidence. The sanctions are fines and, in the case of physical persons and very serious cases of breach, could be imprisonment.

Civil remedies

[10.7]   An effective remedy under civil law for a customer appears to be the right to obtain an injunction against the bank under Chapter 57 of the Danish Administration of Justice Act.[13] An injunction is an order by the Bailiff's Court prohibiting the bank

11 Decision of the Danish FSA of 5 July 2005 published on the official website of the Danish FSA at www.ftnet.dk.
12 Decision of the Danish FSA of 5 April 1995 published on the official website of the Danish FSA at www.ftnet.dk.
13 Consolidated Act no 910 of 27 September 2005, as last amended by Act no 542 of 8 June 2006.

from making disclosure and will require a subsequent affirmation by an ordinary court under ss 634–639 of the Danish Administration of Justice Act. It is a preliminary legal measure granted by the court at short notice and after summary proceedings. Failure to comply with the order will constitute a criminal offence. An injunction would only make sense if it can be obtained before disclosure or to stop continuing disclosures.

If the bank breaches bank secrecy, the client will always be entitled to initiate civil proceedings before the ordinary courts requesting a so-called 'declaratory' judgment that the bank was not justified in the disclosure and/or claiming damages for any losses suffered. In most cases, this may not be an adequate remedy as the Danish courts will only award damages to the extent that the claimant can show an actual loss suffered as a result of the breach of the bank secrecy. Normally, it would be difficult, if not impossible, to prove a loss in such situation. Danish law does not recognise punitive damages. Should a customer be able to show an actual loss, it is unlikely that the bank would be able to limit the amount of claims for damages a customer may try to seek from the bank in the event of breach of confidentiality subject to their standard terms and conditions. It is not customary for Danish banks to include such a limitation in their standard terms and conditions. It follows from general principles of Danish law that disclaimers limiting the liability of a bank would not be upheld in a Danish court of law if the loss was caused by the bank's wilful misconduct or gross negligence.

Another action is the disciplinary sanction which the bank may invoke against employees who have acted in breach of bank confidentiality. A case of clear breach of bank confidentiality may entitle the bank to dismiss the employee by termination of the employment contract without notice and the bank would be entitled to claim damages from the employee for losses suffered; cf s 4 of the Danish Act on the Legal Relationship between Employers and Employees.[14]

EXCEPTIONS TO THE DUTY OF CONFIDENCE
Express and implied consent

[10.8]   The customer is the master of the information that has been submitted to the bank. The customer's consent therefore releases the bank from its duty of confidentiality. The consent must be obtained voluntarily and be specific and be informed. Under s 123 of the Financial Business Act, the consent must be given in writing. The consent must state which information may be disclosed, who may receive the information and for what purpose the information may be disclosed.[15] Consent cannot be given in advance in the bank's general terms and conditions. The consent requirements in the Financial Business Act should be construed in accordance with the similar provisions in the Data Protection Act. Examples of express consents are where, for instance, the customer asks the bank to confirm the customer's creditworthiness to the customer's trade creditors, providers of credit facilities or credit card companies.

One of the oldest examples of exceptions to bank confidentiality has been the custom of banks giving information on a confidential basis about customers' creditworthiness without specific consent. It was unclear whether the giving of this

---

14 Consolidated Act no 68 of 21 January 2005, as last amended by Act no 566 of 9 June 2006.
15 See the guidance letter by the Danish FSA; cf n 6 above.

information was an exemption from bank confidentiality based on customary law or whether it was based on an implied consent from customers on the grounds that it was generally in their interest.

This area has now been regulated by the Ministry of Justice's Executive Order no 531 of 15 June 2000. The Danish Bankers' Association has issued supplementary guidelines. The information may only be given to the bank's own business customers, non-Danish businesses,[16] Dankort A/S (the company which handles a charge card known as 'Dankort' on behalf of Danish banks), businesses within the PBS Group (the Payment Business Services Group), Danish and non-Danish banks, public institutions, Danish or non-Danish credit rating agencies, foreign embassies and, subject to the customer's express consent, to others. The bank passing on the information must be convinced that the inquiring bank has an acceptable commercial reason for obtaining the information and that the inquiring bank will treat the information confidentially. Furthermore, no specific information may be passed on, for instance, the amount of any bank balances, credits, cheques returned unpaid, arrears, etc, but only information in general terms, for example, whether the customer is considered good for a certain credit, ownership, management, its line of business, capital, turnover and earnings in general terms, account relation, liquidity and any special risk issues. However, specific financial information which cannot be obtained from the Danish Commerce and Companies Agency may not be passed on without the consent of the customer. Disclosure in respect of private customers may only be given in the case of guarantees and then only to the bank benefiting from the guarantee. If the customer's consent has been obtained, information may furthermore be given in connection with the application for a charge card or in connection with the purchase of real estate. Finally, information may be given if the customer has explicitly requested it be given in writing. Information that is especially sensitive, such as that on race, colour, criminal records, health, etc or of a purely private nature, such as that on family affairs and significant social problems, may not be passed on.

The bank is obliged to inform its customer within four weeks from the first time that it has disclosed information and the customer is entitled to see the disclosure upon request, although not the name of the addressee. In any event, the customer may specifically request the bank not to pass on information, in which case any subsequent disclosure is unauthorised.

An implied consent from the customer is also supposed to apply in cases of a bank disclosing certain information to its customer's guarantor, such as, for example, the balance on the credit or loan. If the guarantor has had to repay the loan, he is entitled to be informed of any securities given by the customer in respect of which the guarantor has a right to subrogate. The bank may also disclose to a guarantor if certain property or assets which the customer has given as security are put up for sale.[17]

In published decisions, the Danish courts have not had the opportunity to take any position as to the validity or non-validity of so-called 'consent directives' issued under US practices. Consent directives are understood to be documents whereby a

---

16 Information about a customer's creditworthiness may only be passed on to businesses outside the EU/EEA if the member state in question has a sufficient level of protection. A list of secure countries may be found at the official website of the Data Protection Agency at www.datatilsynet.dk.
17 R Jørgensen *Fagskrift for Bankvæsen, marts* (1981), p 73.

customer or former customer of the bank authorises or directs the bank to disclose certain information concerning his dealings with the bank to the US authorities. A person can, by a court order, be compelled to sign the consent under the threat of fines or imprisonment for failure to sign.

The extent of the duty of confidentiality owed by a Danish bank is governed by Danish law and any consents to disclosure must be in accordance with Danish law. It is doubtful whether a Danish court would consider a consent directive as fulfilling the requirement to consent which must be freely given. There is no published court decision containing any guidance.

Disclosure in the interests of the bank

Legal proceedings involving the bank as a party

[10.9]   For the purpose of protecting its own interest as a party in legal proceedings which take place in public, it is generally held that a bank may submit in court confidential information about its affairs with the counterparty, whether the bank is the claimant or defendant. The right of disclosure must be limited to what is relevant and necessary for the particular case.

Legal proceedings involving third parties

[10.10]   The bank may also be involved in cases where a third party is in legal proceedings with a client of the bank regarding a particular asset in respect of which the bank has an interest. The bank is entitled in court to disclose to the third party any security interests, rights of set-off and other preferential rights. For instance, in the case of a forced sale requested by a third party of a piece of real estate owned by the client of a bank, the bank may disclose its claims and any such further information necessary for the courts and other lien holders to determine the amount of the bank's claim. The Danish FSA has further ruled that a bank is entitled to disclose to a third party who has levied execution or has taken a second priority interest in an asset in which the bank has a first security interest the amount of the bank's claim on the pledgor (the bank's customer).[18]

A special situation has arisen in connection with the Danish Financial Services Complaints Board, which is an institution to resolve disputes between banks and consumers and in certain business matters. The Board consists of a chairman and two deputy chairmen, appointed by the Danish Consumer Council and the Danish Bankers' Association, who must all meet the requirements for the appointment as a High Court judge. The Danish FSA has held that it is not in breach of the confidentiality obligation if the bank, in its defence of a complaint, reveals confidential information about a third party if this is necessary for the bank's defence.[19] The Danish FSA noted in its decision that the members of the Danish Financial Services Complaints Board were bound by a duty of confidentiality as laid down in the constitutive documents of the Board.

---

18 Decision of the Danish FSA of 6 May 1996, referred to in the Annual Report 1996 of the Danish FSA, p 134; O Simonsen UFR 1980 B, p 246; Jørgensen, n 17 above, p 73 and G Wenning UFR 1996 B, p 49ff.
19 Annual Report 1987 of the Danish FSA, p 60.

DISCLOSURE FOR THE PERFORMANCE OF ADMINISTRATIVE TASKS

[10.11] A bank may disclose 'usual' customer information for the performance of administrative tasks as part of outsourcing; cf s 118(1) of the Financial Business Act. The Danish FSA has stated in a decision that a bank is entitled to outsource its handling of ordinary post, such as the storage and scanning of postal items, if the bank has a practical need for having this function outsourced to a third party.[20] Information of this type may be passed on to group companies, as well as non-group companies. What constitutes 'administrative tasks' is not defined in the Financial Business Act, but, according to the preparatory works, the term should be interpreted broadly. Examples of administrative tasks are the joint preparation and distribution of account statements and insurance summaries, as well as reporting of other companies' information to the tax authorities, etc. In a decision, the Danish FSA has stated that the disclosure of usual customer information to an opinion poll institute was in accordance with s 118(1) as the conduct of a customer satisfaction study could be characterised as an administrative task.[21] However, the information may not be passed on for marketing or advisory purposes and only information necessary for the performance of the administrative task may be passed on.

Further, according to s 118(2), information may be disclosed to a limited company owned wholly by the Labour Market Supplementary Pension Scheme, to the Labour Market Supplementary Pension Scheme and the administrative company of a joint administrative organisation under the Danish Insurance Business Act for the performance of administrative tasks. Again, information may only be passed on for the performance of administrative tasks. However, under s 119, information of a purely private nature may also be passed on if necessary for the performance of administrative tasks. According to s 118(3), any person or company to whom information is transmitted pursuant to subsection (1) and (2) shall be bound by the duty of confidentiality laid down in s 117(1). The bank passing on the information is obliged to ensure that the recipient is aware of this duty of confidentiality.

'Usual' customer information is defined in Executive Order no 1075 of 17 December 2001 issued pursuant to the Financial Business Act and includes general information such as name, sex, address, occupation, trade category, organisation of business and certain financial information such as customer category, number of accounts, etc, but not specific information on customer affairs, such as arrears, income figures, etc. Further, specifically for bank customers and customers of investment companies, usual information is also information on the buyer and seller in securities trades, the quota code, information in respect of the security and/or the underlying asset, instrument name, spot/term/repo pricing, etc. The Executive Order is exhaustive and information not listed in the Executive Order cannot be considered as usual customer information.

Disclosure within the banking group

[10.12] Section 120(1) of the Financial Business Act provides that information may be disclosed to a bank's parent company for the purpose of risk management of

---

20 Decision of the Danish FSA of 6 February 2006 published on the official website of the Danish FSA at www.ftnet.dk.
21 Decision of 17 April 2002 published on the official website of the Danish FSA at www.ftnet.dk.

undertakings within the group if the parent company is a financial undertaking or a financial holding company.[22] This does not apply to information on purely private affairs. Further, information on private customers may not be disclosed for the purpose of risk management unless information on a private customer concerns commitments which are or may become significant in size; cf s 118(2). The information may only be passed on to a foreign company if such company is subject to a duty of confidentiality comparable to the duty of confidentiality stipulated in s 117(1) of the Financial Business Act.

According to s 120a(1) of the Financial Business Act, information on commercial customers may be exchanged between banks and mortgage credit institutions within the same group for the purposes of risk management, including credit rating and credit administration. The same shall apply to exchanges of information with the financial holding companies and subsidiary companies of the undertakings. Information may only be exchanged with subsidiary companies that grant loans or carry out leasing activities. Section 120a(2) provides that the provision in subsection (1) shall also apply to exchanges of information between jointly owned banks and mortgage credit institutions and owners of holdings in the relevant bank or mortgage credit institutions when the owners mentioned are banks or mortgage credit institutions and they jointly own more than 80% of the holdings. The same shall apply to exchanges of information with these subsidiary companies of the jointly owned undertakings that grant loans or carry out leasing activities. Disclosure under s 120a(1) and (2) shall not cover information on purely private affairs; cf s 120a(3).

Disclosure for marketing and advisory purposes

[10.13]   Pursuant to s 121(1) of the Financial Business Act, information regarding private customers may not be disclosed for marketing or advisory purposes unless such private customer has consented in writing. However, general customer information on private customers may be disclosed to group undertakings[23] without the consent of the customer under three conditions:

1   the information is general customer information forming the basis for separation of customer categories;
2   such disclosure is necessary to enable the undertaking receiving such information to pursue justifiable interests and regard for the customer does not override such interests; and
3   the group undertaking to which the information is disclosed must be subject to a duty of confidentiality as set out in s 117(1) (s 121(2)).

---

22 For the purpose of the Danish Financial Business Act, a financial holding company is a parent company whose exclusive or principal activity is ownership of capital interests in subsidiaries which are financial undertakings or finance institutions and where at least one subsidiary is a financial undertaking. Branches of Danish financial undertakings in other EU/EEA member states are subject to the provisions of the Danish Financial Business Act in accordance with the principle of 'home state supervision'. Further, as a rule, the provisions of the Act apply to branches of financial undertakings in countries outside the EU and countries with which the EU has entered into an agreement.

23 For the purpose of the Danish Financial Business Act, a 'group' is defined as a parent company and its subsidiaries. A 'parent company' is defined as an undertaking which (i) holds the majority of the voting rights of an undertaking, (ii) is a shareholder and entitled to appoint or remove the board of directors, management board or similar, (iii) exercises a controlling influence on an undertaking or (iv) commands the majority of the voting rights within the undertaking.

Examples of usual customer information are, according to the preparatory works, name, address, sex and age. Further, information on whether the customer owns real estate, a car or similar information is usual customer information. However, more detailed information of a personal or financial nature and information which reveals purely private matters may not be disclosed; cf ss 119, 120 and 121(1). Usual customer information on business customers may be disclosed for marketing or advisory purposes to a financial undertaking under a duty of confidentiality as specified in s 117(1). The provisions complement the general rules of the Data Protection Act which apply to financial undertakings, as well as to other undertakings. As a rule, the Data Protection Act only applies to the processing of data on individuals. Consequently, information may only be passed on without the consent of the customer pursuant to s 121(2) if the customer has not objected under s 36 of the Data Protection Act.

Facilitation of securitisations

[10.14]   In Denmark, no legislation has been passed to ensure that questions of bank confidentiality do not impede the use of a bank's assets in securitisations, nor is such legislation contemplated.[24] The Danish FSA has previously taken a very restrictive view that sales of loans would be a breach of bank confidentiality pursuant to s 117 of the Financial Business Act, but the decision referred to above (note 11) may signal a more positive attitude.

Where disclosure is by compulsion of law

Compulsion by order of court

Duty to testify

[10.15]   Employees of banks are in general subject to the same duty to testify in court as other persons; cf s 168 of the Danish Administration of Justice Act. The rules do not exempt bank employees, as is the case in respect of certain professions such as lawyers, clergymen, doctors and certain other individuals. However, the court may rule under s 170(3) that evidence should not be given with respect to matters where, according to statutory law, the witness is subject to a duty of confidentiality and such duty has a substantial importance. When deciding whether this exemption should apply, the court will have to weigh, on the one hand, the general interest in the protection of confidentiality between a bank and its client and, on the other, the interests of the court in having the appropriate relevant information and evidence to ensure that justice is done. The court will attach importance as to whether the party requesting the bank officer to give evidence could obtain the requested information by other means. A court ruled in 1979 that a bank employee was compelled to give evidence in the Bailiff's Court about a customer's bank balances in a case concerning a creditor levying execution on the assets of the customer on the grounds that the

---

24 Further, see the decision by the Danish FSA of 25 May 2000 concerning a credit swap agreement entered into by a bank and a third party. The Danish FSA assumed that the customer was not informed of the credit swap agreement. Under the agreement, the third party would acquire engagements from a defined loan portfolio when certain credit 'events' occurred. When such events occurred, the third party would be informed of the bank customer's name and, at a minimum, be informed that the bank customer's engagement was failing. The Danish FSA found such credit swap agreement to be a breach of the bank secrecy obligation.

customer himself would have been compelled to disclose this.[25] The rules of testifying apply in civil as well as in criminal cases.

Duty to submit documents

[10.16] Although Danish law does not recognise the concept of pre-trial discovery rights, during legal proceedings a party may require the court to impose on the other party to the litigation the duty to submit certain documents in accordance with rules of disclosure; cf s 298 of the Danish Administration of Justice Act. No 'fishing expeditions' are allowed as the party requesting a particular document to be disclosed must indicate the circumstances which should be proved by the document. The court may dismiss such a request on the same grounds as testifying may be exempted, namely, accepting that such documents should be covered by the duty of confidentiality under the Financial Business Act. In 2002, the Supreme Court ruled that a bank must make anonymous and submit transcripts of its board minutes and its recommendations to the board in respect of negotiations concerning a share issue.[26] During legal proceedings, the court may also, upon request by a party, impose on a third party the obligation to show or submit documents which may be of importance to the case; cf s 299 of the Danish Administration of Justice Act. Again, the court may dismiss such a request on the same grounds as testifying may be exempted; cf s 170(3) of the Danish Administration of Justice Act.

Arbitration proceedings

[10.17] In arbitration proceedings, a court of arbitration does not have the power to force persons to testify. However, under the Danish Act on Arbitration, s 27,[27] the court of arbitration may seek assistance from the ordinary courts and thereby compel persons to testify. Through these means, confidential information could be disclosed in an arbitration court in the same manner as in proceedings before the ordinary courts.

Bankruptcy

[10.18] According to s 240 of the Danish Bankruptcy Act,[28] the Bankruptcy Court is entitled to summon before it any person the court thinks capable of giving information on the business or affairs of the bankrupt. The general obligation of testifying will apply as set out in the Danish Administration of Justice Act, ss 169–172. On the same grounds, the court may as mentioned earlier exempt a bank officer from testifying.

Bank confidentiality continues while a bank is under insolvency proceedings or bankruptcy, although the bankruptcy proceedings may justify some wider entitlement to disclosure.[29] The liquidator is entitled to all information necessary to administer and realise the assets and wind up the estate and the bank must release such information. Creditors of a bank under bankruptcy do not have any access to confidential information.

---

25 UFR 1979, p 216 VLK.
26 UFR 2002, p 1734 H.
27 Act no 553 of 24 June 2005, as amended by Act no 909 of 27 September 2005.
28 Consolidated Act no 118 of 4 February 1997, as last amended by Act no 538 of 8 June 2006.
29 Ruling by the Danish FSA, as upheld in a decision by the Ministry of Business Appeal Board of 10 August 1995.

Compulsion by statute

The Danish Tax Control Act

[10.19]   It is reasonable to conclude from the Danish Tax Control Act[30] which, inter alia, regulates the obligations of banks (and others) to provide information, that there is hardly any bank secrecy vis-à-vis the tax authorities. However, the situation is no different in relation to other types of business or profession. The Act distinguishes between three types of disclosure requirements: a reporting obligation upon request; a reporting obligation upon inspection in the bank and automatic reporting. The obligation to report automatically without request has, in particular, increased significantly in recent years. It is worth mentioning that the statutory powers of the tax authorities are continuously being vested on lower levels within the tax authorities to require disclosure and are aimed at an increasingly wider range of persons.

It follows from s 8D of the Danish Tax Control Act that banks must upon request provide the tax authorities with such information as is deemed by the authorities to be of substantial importance for tax assessment. The statute does not contain any details as to the extent of this obligation on the bank or, in other words, what documentation can be required to be submitted or how far back information can be requested. It must be assumed that the authorities, as far as possible, must first request the information from the taxpayer himself.

Section 8G(2) of the Tax Control Act gives the tax authorities the right to undertake inspections in banks in order to carry out spot examinations of accounting records, agreements and other documents.

The Danish Tax Control Act further provides a substantial number of instances where banks are now required annually and without request to provide certain information regarding their customers. The requirements comprise, inter alia, pension arrangements (s 8F), deposits and accrued interest (s 8H), loans and accrued interest (s 8P), information on balances and accrued interest on mortgage deeds in real estate in custody (s 8Q), redeemed interest coupons, interest on bonds and value at year end (s 10A), dividends from unit trusts, etc (s 10A), information on transfer of bonds and interest coupons (s 10B), agreements on transfer of forward contracts and certain other assets (s 10B).

The reporting requirements only extend to banks subject to Danish jurisdiction. However, private individual taxpayers who have deposits or securities held in custody by non-resident banks (or other non-resident institutions) are required to agree with the relevant foreign bank or institution that it annually without request advises the Danish tax authorities of the size of deposits, securities deposited, interest accrued and the relevant balances at year end. In addition, the Danish resident taxpayer must provide the tax authorities with a power of attorney authorising the Danish tax authorities to obtain information directly from the account; cf the Danish Tax Control Act, s 11A and 11B. Presumably, this is an attempt by the tax authorities to obtain the taxpayer's consent, thus releasing the foreign bank of its duty of confidentiality. If the foreign bank or institution by law is prohibited from such disclosure or does not wish to undertake it, dispensation can be obtained in certain cases.

---

30   Consolidated Act no 1126 of 24 November 2005, as last amended by Act no 515 of 7 June 2006.

Value added tax and social legislation

[10.20] According to s 75(3) of the Danish Value Added Tax Act,[31] banks must upon request give the VAT authorities any information about their financial relationship with named registered enterprises. Various legislation on social pensions and unemployment insurance provide the authorities with similar rights to obtain certain information upon request.

Foreign tax authorities

[10.21] Denmark has ratified and acceded to a number of international treaties and conventions concerning mutual assistance in tax matters, both regarding administrative assistance and assistance in the recovery of tax claims. These treaties and conventions affect the disclosure obligations of banks. Among the most wide reaching is the EEC Council Directive of 19 December 1977,[32] as amended, implemented by Act no 1016 of 24 October 2005, as amended. Also applicable is the Council of Europe and OECD Convention on Mutual Administrative Assistance in Tax Matters implemented by Act no 132 of 26 February 1992 and the Nordic Tax Treaty (Denmark, Sweden, Norway, Finland, Iceland, Greenland and the Faroe Islands) of 7 December 1989, as supplemented, on assistance in tax matters.

The treaties impose on the Danish tax authorities the obligation to assist foreign tax authorities with information on residents subject to Danish jurisdiction. This may involve passing on such information which the tax authorities already have on their own files, either upon request or, sometimes, spontaneously. They also require the Danish tax authorities upon request to 'take all relevant measures to provide the applicant state with the information requested'; cf art 5 of the Council of Europe/OECD Convention. This authorises the Danish tax authorities to pass on information otherwise subject to bank confidentiality, although member states are permitted not to provide assistance if this would involve disclosing information subject to 'professional secrecy', such as, inter alia, bank secrecy; cf art 21. The Danish tax authorities may assist if (i) permitted to do so under the provisions of the Danish Tax Control Act in similar circumstances involving Danish resident taxpayers and (ii) if the applicant tax authority, under its domestic laws, would be entitled to demand the requested information.

The Nordic Tax Treaty provides for the automatic exchange of certain relevant bank information, for example, on annual accrued interest on deposits and balances at year end and value of securities at year end, including coupons redeemed during the year.

Many bilateral double taxation treaties which Denmark has concluded also include provisions on mutual assistance, although often not as specific as provided under the above-mentioned treaties. It must be assumed that, in cases where the Danish tax authorities are required to disclose information otherwise subject to bank secrecy, the customer cannot raise any objections based on the bank's duty of confidentiality.[33] It should be noted that if criminal proceedings have been initiated, whether in Denmark or abroad, the tax authorities are not entitled to pass on information administratively, but only by compulsion of court.

---

31 Consolidated Act no 966 of 14 October 2005, as last amended by Act no 518 of 7 June 2006.
32 Council Directive 77/799/EEC.
33 See also the commentaries to art 26 of the OECD Model Tax Convention.

Competition Council and Consumer Ombudsman

[10.22]   According to s 17 of the Danish Act on Competition,[34] the Danish Competition Council is entitled to demand all information which is deemed necessary for its affairs or to decide whether a certain matter comes within the law. This entitlement to information also relates to customer information with a bank if the Danish Competition Council deems it appropriate. It is possible to demand that confidential customer information is not released for circulation among the members of the Danish Competition Council. There are certain other restrictions as to this information.

The Consumer Ombudsman is also entitled to demand all information which is deemed necessary for the performance of his duties, unless it is the Consumer Ombudsman's intention to institute criminal proceedings against a bank.

Police and criminal investigations

[10.23]   The police have no right as part of their investigations to require bank officers to disclose or pass on confidential customer information, nor to demand submission of particular records or invoke other legal measures unless sanctioned by the court. In criminal matters, employees of banks are subject to the same duty to testify in court as in civil matters, which means that testimony must be given unless the court rules under s 170(3) of the Danish Administration of Justice Act that evidence should not be given due to the duty of confidentiality. Sections 801 and 803 of the Danish Administration of Justice Act provide for the court to authorise documents to be disclosed or assets (bank accounts) to be confiscated. In addition, in special cases, the court may sanction searches of records, bank balances or documents to be undertaken by the police under s 793 of the Danish Administration of Justice Act. Under very extraordinary circumstances, banks are permitted to disclose confidential customer information prior to a court order, especially if otherwise the prevention or investigation of a crime would seriously suffer, against an undertaking from the police to obtain a subsequent court order.

If the police know which bank is in possession of the information requested, the court order of disclosure will, of course, be directed to that bank. If the police do not know which bank is holding the account, the courts have authorised a procedure whereby all banks, through the Danish Bankers' Association, are ordered by the court to notify the police if they have an account in the accused person's name. Thereafter, a specific order of disclosure will be requested from the court in respect of the particular bank, but subject to a prior opportunity for the bank to question the basis on which the order is sought.[35]

In cases of disclosure, the police must show that the documents or records may be of importance as proof in connection with an identified crime. As in the case of oral testimony, the bank may invoke s 170(3) of the Danish Administration of Justice Act that the records should not be disclosed due to the duty of confidentiality. Unless the bank can show that the police, by other means and without prejudicing the purpose of the request, may obtain the same information, the court will normally give effect to the police request.

---

34 Consolidated Act no 785 of 8 August 2005.
35 UFR 1995, p 333 Ø.

Money laundering and financing of terrorism – legislation

[10.24]   There is one exception where confidential customer information may be passed on and must be offered voluntarily without either customer consent or a court order and this is in connection with the Money Laundering and Terrorist Financing Directive,[36] as implemented by Danish Act no 348 of 9 June 1993, now Consolidated Danish Act no 117 of 27 February 2006, which came into force on 1 March 2006.[37] The statute provides rules for the banking and financial services business to put in place various systems and control functions to identify customers and report suspicious transactions to the police. The Act also applies to lawyers, accountants and tax advisors, real estate brokers, insurance brokers and certain others.

Money laundering is defined as including conversion, transfer, acquisition, possession or application of monetary assets or concealment, or attempted concealment, of their form, origin, localisation, movements or ownership with knowledge or suspicion that the money is derived from a breach of the Danish Criminal Code. Terrorism is defined in s 114 of the Danish Criminal Code as the commitment of manslaughter, extreme violence, false imprisonment, obstruction of road safety and unlawful interference with the operation of ordinary means of communication or vandalism where such crimes are committed in such a way as to endanger human life or cause significant financial loss, hijacking transportation, serious breaches of the Danish Arms Act (*Våbenloven*)[38] and arson for the purpose of scaring people or unlawfully forcing public authorities or international organisations to act or not to act or destabilising or damaging basic political, constitutional, financial or social structures of a country or international organisation when the act, due to its character or the connection in which it appears, may seriously damage a country or international organisation.

It follows from s 10 and 10a of the Danish Money Laundering and Terrorist Financing Act that if there is a suspicion that a transaction is associated with money laundering or financing of terrorism, there is an obligation for the bank to examine the transaction further. This can be done by, for instance, an examination of the background to the transaction, by telephone calls to other institutions involved, checks of the civil register and surveillance of the transaction over a period of time. If the suspicion cannot be dispelled, the transaction must be put on hold until the Public Prosecutor has been notified. In the case of suspicion of money laundering, if it is not possible to avoid carrying out the transaction or the suspicion would be revealed, the transaction can be continued and the police notified immediately afterwards. The police are then entitled to demand further information from the bank, production of documents, etc which can be demanded under a 'normal' criminal investigation, ie a court order. In the case of suspicion of financing of terrorism, transactions with respect to the specific account or person may only be carried out pursuant to agreement with the Public Prosecutor. The Danish Money Laundering and Terrorist Financing Act specifically states that information disclosed to the police in good faith cannot be considered a breach of the duty of confidentiality. The bank and its employees are bound by a duty of confidentiality not to disclose the fact that the police have been informed about suspicions of money laundering.

---

36 Council Directives 91/308, 2001/97 and 2005/60 have been implemented into Danish law.
37 The new Act entails that Danish banks shall observe their customers and, more importantly, notify the police in cases of suspicious transactions.
38 Consolidated Act no 918 of 10 September 2004, as last amended by Act no 542 of 8 June 2006.

Extra-territorial aspects of compulsion of law

Obtaining information from Danish banks for use in foreign civil proceedings

[10.25]   Foreign court orders requesting Danish banks or their employees to give information or testify abroad are not enforceable in Denmark. However, in accordance with the provisions of s 347 of the Danish Administration of Justice Act and applicable treaties, the Danish courts may render judicial assistance following requests from foreign courts on the taking of evidence or the undertaking of other judicial acts.

Denmark has ratified the Hague Convention on Civil Procedure of 1 March 1954 and the Convention on the Taking of Evidence Abroad in Civil or Commercial Matters of 18 March 1970.[39] In addition, Denmark has concluded a Civil Procedures Convention[40] with the UK and an Inter-Nordic Convention on Evidence with the Nordic countries.[41] Accordingly, persons subject to Danish jurisdiction may be compelled to give evidence before a Danish judge in accordance with the request from the foreign judicial authority and the courts shall apply the appropriate measures of compulsion to the same extent as provided by Danish law. According to art 11 of the Convention on the Taking of Evidence Abroad, the person concerned may refuse to give evidence in so far as he has a privilege or duty to refuse to give evidence under Danish law or under the law of the state which has requested the evidence. This means that Danish procedural rules are applicable and may in the circumstances be invoked so that the Danish court may deny a testimony, if necessary, to protect bank confidentiality: s 170(3) of the Danish Administration of Justice Act or where this is provided under foreign law. Denmark has exercised its rights under art 23 of the Convention to declare that it will not execute requests issued for the purpose of obtaining pre-trial discovery of documents.

In cases where the request originates from countries that are not members of the various treaties, the assistance of the Danish courts may be rendered nonetheless upon request by a foreign judicial authority and the Danish courts will, based on the principle of comity, normally comply with the request as provided under s 7 of Act no 161 of 18 December 1897.

Obtaining evidence abroad for use in Danish proceedings

[10.26]   Where a claimant before a Danish court wishes to obtain evidence from a foreign bank, application must be made to the Danish court for permission to obtain such evidence in accordance with s 342 of the Danish Administration of Justice Act. A Danish court is not likely to issue any subpoenas or orders for disclosure, but will request the information in accordance with the aforementioned Hague Convention on Civil Procedure and the Convention on the Taking of Evidence Abroad in Civil or Commercial Matters and certain bilateral conventions.

Whether the foreign court will assist is a matter of local law.

Enforcement of preliminary legal measures

[10.27]   It may be relevant to seek to enforce in Denmark foreign preliminary measures such as, for example, the freezing of assets in the form of an arrest or an

---

39 Executive Order no 117C of 7 December 1973.
40 Convention of 29 November 1932; cf Executive Order no 206 of 24 May 1933.
41 Convention of 28 April 1974; cf Executive Order no 100 of 15 September 1975.

injunction against moving assets, for instance, money from an identified person's account with a certain bank. Article 25 of the Brussels Convention 1968 also applies to preliminary legal measures.[42] In many cases, the wish could be to have a simultaneous 'surprise effect' in different states in order to increase the possibility of recovering losses as a result of a fraud. In *Denilauer v SNC Couchet Frères* (125/1979),[43] the European Court of Justice held that ex parte interim measures are not covered by art 25. The other party must have been notified about the court hearing where the preliminary measure was adopted. No surprise effect is therefore possible, but the Danish courts will otherwise give effect to preliminary measures if the other party has been duly notified.

International judicial assistance in criminal matters

[10.28]   The general principle is that the executive authorities of foreign states cannot operate in Denmark nor are foreign court orders on criminal matters enforceable. However, Denmark has ratified the European Convention of 20 April 1959 on Mutual Assistance in Criminal Matters with supplements and, accordingly, Denmark shall execute, in the manner provided for under Danish law, any letters rogatory relating to a criminal matter and must grant the necessary assistance for the purpose of procuring evidence and transmitting records or documents. Search and seizure of property or documents can also be effected, but assistance may be refused if Denmark considers that the request relates to a political or fiscal offence or if it is likely to prejudice *ordre public* or other essential national interests.

In connection with its signature, Denmark has reserved its rights to make the execution of judicial assistance concerning search or seizure of property dependent on the offence being related to acts punishable under both the law of the requesting country and Danish law and that the offence motivating the request is an extraditable offence and, furthermore, that the execution of the request for assistance is consistent with Danish law.

There are no provisions under Danish law that provide coercive measures to force a witness to appear in proceedings held abroad. If a Danish bank official were to appear voluntarily before a foreign court which has ordered him to testify in respect of confidential customer information protected under Danish law, he would be in breach of s 117 of the Financial Business Act and thus subject to criminal liability. It is possible that any punishment by a Danish court will be reduced as provided by s 83 of the Danish Criminal Code. In the reverse situation, where a foreign bank officer is testifying in a Danish court on matters in respect of which he is bound by bank confidentiality rules in his home state, Danish law does not offer any relief. In determining whether the officer in question were to give evidence, the court may be guided by s 170(3) of the Danish Administration of Justice Act, under which the officer could be exempted from testifying if the duty of confidentiality imposed by his home country is deemed to outweigh the interest of clarifying the factual issues of the Danish case.

The Danish courts have also agreed to provide assistance to the authorities of non-treaty countries based on a principle of comity, although they are not bound to do so.

---

42 Executive Order no 724 of 22 October 1986, as last amended by Executive Order no 833 of 24 November 1998.
43 [1980] ECR 1553, [1981] 1 CMLR 62.

The media

[10.29] It has been discussed[44] whether a bank may in certain cases be entitled to disclose confidential information about its customers to the media in order to correct false information detrimental to the bank's interests. In general, the answer is no. In the circumstances, it may be permissible for a bank to disclose information of an expected loss on a certain client, for instance, if it is deemed necessary to refute exaggerated rumours about the size of the loss and its importance to the bank's reputation. If, in the media, the bank has been accused of certain actions or inactions, for instance, in the termination of credit with resultant insolvency or bankruptcy for large enterprises, the bank is probably prevented from presenting its views or correcting information to the extent that this would affect its duty of confidentiality. This situation could be different if the customer itself has submitted incorrect information to the public in order to place the bank in an unfavourable light. There are no published judgments or rulings from the Danish FSA defining this area, but one has to assume that the bank's duty of confidentiality is rather strict.

REGULATION OF FINANCIAL MARKETS

Powers of regulatory bodies to require the disclosure of information

Financial Supervisory Authority

[10.30] Under s 347 of the Financial Business Act, banks are obliged to provide information on a regular basis to the Danish FSA, which is also entitled to request such information both about the general affairs of the bank, as well as particular information on identified customers. The Danish FSA is entitled to carry out inspections in the bank and to demand access to all papers, contracts, etc.

Other EU supervisory authorities are also entitled to carry out inspections in Danish branches of EU banks: s 346(4) of the Financial Business Act. The staff are presumably entitled to give such information to the foreign supervisory authority which the Danish FSA may demand from banks subject to the supervision of the Danish authorities on the grounds that the foreign supervisory authority can request the host authorities to undertake the inspections; cf arts 29(2) and 56(7) of the Directive of 20 March 2000 on the taking up and pursuit of business of credit institutions.[45] Branches established in Denmark by virtue of the European 'passport' are presumably not bound by the statutory confidentiality provisions of the Financial Business Act, but are subject to similar provisions of their home country legislation, in addition, of course, to any contractually agreed terms.

According to s 354 of the Financial Business Act, employees of the Danish FSA are obliged under criminal law to keep secret all knowledge obtained during the course of their activities. According to s 152 of the Criminal Code, the penalty for any breach could be up to two years' imprisonment.

The Second Banking Directive[46] and the so-called 'BCCI' Directive[47] resulted in substantial amendments to the then Danish Bank Act concerning the right of the

---

44 R Jørgensen, n 17 above, p 74.
45 Council Directive 2000/12/EC.
46 Council Directive 1989/646/EC.
47 Council Directive 1977/780/EC.

Danish FSA to pass on confidential information it has obtained during the performance of its duties. Of particular interest is the right under the now s 347(5); cf s 354(5), nos 14–15 of the Financial Business Act to pass on confidential information to other supervisory authorities within the EU and also to similar institutions outside the EU on the basis of an international co-operation agreement, provided such information in the relevant country outside the EU is subject to, at a minimum, the same statutory duty of confidentiality as the Danish FSA and such passing on is required for the recipients to perform their duties. Further, confidential information originating from within the EU may only be passed on to such country outside the EU if the authority disclosing the information has expressly given its permission and the information may only be used for the purposes specified in the permission. In certain limited circumstances, the Danish FSA is also entitled to pass on confidential information to standing committees of the Danish Parliament and the relevant government minister.

Central bank requirements

[10.31]   Pursuant to the Danish Ministry of Industry's Executive Order on Foreign Exchange Regulations no 658 of 11 July 1994, Danmarks Nationalbank (the central bank) may also request information relating to foreign exchange transactions by physical or legal entities in Denmark for statistical reasons. Danmarks Nationalbank is an independent institution governed by a statute dating from 1936 and employees of the bank are bound by special duties of confidentiality, breaches of which are subject to penalties under the Criminal Code.

Insider trading and insiders' disclosure requirements

Source of regulation

[10.32]   The prohibition on insider trading is provided in ss 34–37 of the Danish Act on Securities Trading[48] which make insider trading a criminal offence. The prohibition applies not only to any person buying, selling or otherwise dealing in listed securities while in possession of inside information, but also to the passing on of such information. Further, defined insiders are under an obligation to notify the issuing company of their shareholdings and the issuing company must publish the net change in the total insiders' shareholdings through the stock exchange on a daily basis.

Which securities

[10.33]   The prohibition relates to all securities listed on or dealt with on a stock exchange, authorised marketplace or similar regulated market for securities. The securities may be issued by companies organised within or outside Denmark. Also included are non-quoted instruments which are linked to one or more securities listed on a stock exchange or dealt with on an authorised marketplace, as well as units in investment associations, special purpose associations and similar foreign investment institutes.

---

48 Act no 479 of 1 June 2006.

Inside information

[10.34]   Section 34(2) of the Danish Act on Securities Trading defines inside information as information of a precise nature, which has not been made public, relating to issuers of securities or to securities or market conditions with respect to such securities and which, if it were made public, would be likely to have a significant effect on the prices of those securities. Information shall be considered made public when a relevant and general conveyance of such information has been made to the market. Information submitted to a stock exchange, an authorised marketplace or a similar regulated market shall be considered made public when the stock exchange, authorised marketplace or similar regulated market has disseminated such information. According to s 34(3), 'information of a precise nature' shall mean information which indicates a set of circumstances which exists or may reasonably be expected to come into existence or an event which has occurred or may reasonably be expected to do so and is specific enough to enable a conclusion to be drawn as to the possible effect of that set of circumstances or event on the prices of the relevant securities. 'Information which would be likely to have a significant effect on the prices of one or more securities' shall mean such information which a reasonable investor would be likely to use as part of the basis of investment decisions.

Applicable persons

[10.35]   The prohibition applies to any physical or legal person who has inside information. It is therefore irrelevant whether the insider has a corporate or contractual association with the issuer or whether he is just a 'tippee' or the taxi driver who unintentionally overhears a discussion on a price-sensitive issue. The factual possession of inside information deprives the person of the entitlement to deal. The prohibition will also exclude two persons with the same inside information from dealing with each other. In order to constitute a criminal offence, it must be proved that the insider knew or ought to have known that it concerned inside information.

Security traders, for example, banks, are not prohibited from executing customary orders from customers or performing functions as market makers (s 35(3)) even though they are in possession of inside information, but if the bank has knowledge or suspicion that the buyer or seller has inside information, the bank is prohibited from executing any trade (s 35(2)).

Passing on of inside information

[10.36]   The Danish Act on Securities Trading also includes a prohibition against passing on inside information unless the passing on or disclosure takes place in connection with the insider's occupation, trade or function; cf s 36(1). It is irrelevant how the person acquired the inside information, whether as part of his occupation or by accident. It is difficult to interpret the exemption in s 36(1). Clear cases are statutory disclosure obligations to public authorities and obligations to testify in court as provided under the rules of the Danish Administration of Justice Act. In the largest insider case in Danish history, the so-called 'Midtbank case', the Danish Supreme Court ruled in 2005 that four members of the board of directors of Midtbank were not guilty of insider trading. Prior to the acquisition of Midtbank by Handelsbanken, the four board members had bought 125,000 Midtbank shares, but there was no evidence that the board members used inside knowledge to buy back the Midtbank shares from Danske Bank.

Disclosure requirements

[10.37]   Pursuant to s 37(2) of the Danish Act on Securities Trading, defined insiders in listed companies are under an obligation to notify the issuing company of their shareholdings. For the purpose of the rules, insiders are, inter alia: (i) members of the board of directors and the board of management in the listed company and its parent company, (ii) staff who, due to their position within the issuing company or its parent company, may be expected to have access to inside knowledge, for instance, managerial staff referring directly to the supervisory board or the board of management and internal auditors, (iii) the auditors of the issuing company and its parent company and (iv) certain other categories having access to inside information.

The issuing company must make a list of all insiders and notify the individual insider when he is added to the list. Insiders must notify the issuing company of their shareholdings and, further, notify the company of any change in their shareholdings. Such notification must take place immediately, ie on the same trading day. In addition to shares owned personally by the insider, shares in the issuing company held by certain other connected persons and companies must also be reported.

It should be noted that the insiders' disclosure requirements under these rules are towards the issuing company only and not directly to the stock exchange. The general shareholder disclosure requirements, however, continue to apply.

Further, the issuing company must publish the net change in the total insiders' shareholdings during the previous trading day through the stock exchange on a daily basis, unless the net change is less than 5000 euros in value and, on a quarterly basis, the issuing company is further required to publish the total shareholdings of the insiders.

Securities dealers and the employees of these undertakings carrying out transactions with securities, shall, without undue delay, inform the Danish FSA if it is reasonable to assume that a transaction constitutes a breach of s 35(1). However, this shall only apply if the transaction was carried out as part of a valid execution of a customer's order. Such notification which a securities dealer or its employees carries out for a good reason shall not be considered a breach of regulations regarding duty of confidentiality, irrespective of whether such regulations are laid down by an act, executive order or a contract.

The Danish FSA has issued Executive Order no 126 of 28 February 2005 pursuant to s 37.

Chinese Walls, etc

[10.38]   The prohibition against insider trading applies to companies and other legal persons. In accordance with the theory of the unity of a legal person when members of the management have inside information, the company as such must be considered as being in possession. This principle also applies in respect of other employees who take part in the decision-making process concerning securities or who, as a result of their position in the company, may bind the company. The consequence is that not only the persons who in actual fact are in possession of inside information are prevented from trading on behalf of the company, but also other persons without knowledge are prevented from trading on behalf of the company in affected securities.

This strict theoretical point of view creates difficulties for banks and financial institutions. The internal segregation of information between departments of a bank ('Chinese Wall') is seen as a practical way for a bank to prevent misuse of information which is the basis for the offence of insider trading. Whether a bank in the establishment of Chinese Walls can protect itself against the offence of insider trading must be decided on a case-by-case basis and the courts have not had the opportunity to express any views.

Each case will have to be decided on its own merits and with particular reference to the facts. Accordingly, even though a bank may be able to demonstrate that there has been no misuse of confidential information, the Danish FSA and/or the courts may find the circumstances to be such that the bank should be precluded from acting in a particular capacity.

DATA PROTECTION LEGISLATION

[10.39]   From 1978 to 2000, Denmark had a legal framework regarding electronic data processing, storage and passing on of private data based on two separate Acts, the Danish Private Registers Act and the Danish Public Authorities Registers Act. In 2000, the Data Protection Act,[49] which implements the EC Data Protection Directive,[50] came into force. The Data Protection Act applies to financial undertakings and, thus, complements the rules set out in the Financial Business Act. Thus, in cases of discrepancy, the Financial Business Act prevails. This Act affects banks both as regards storage of confidential customer (and other) information, as well as their rights to disclose such information. The Data Protection Act applies to all personal data, regardless of whether the data is kept in manual or electronic form. The Act generally regulates the systematic processing of personal data about individuals and non-legal persons, but, under certain circumstances, also applies to data concerning organisations, ie when processing is carried out for credit information agencies or to warn third parties against business or employment relations is involved. The collection of data may only be undertaken for specified, explicit and legitimate purposes and all data must be processed in accordance with good data processing practice as determined by the Danish Data Protection Agency. Further, the personal data must be relevant, sufficient and not excessive in relation to the purposes for which it is collected and processed. The data must be kept up to date, the bank must implement controls to ensure that it does not process inaccurate or misleading data and the bank may not store personal information so that identification of the data subject is permitted for a longer period of time than is necessary for the purpose of processing the data.

The processing of personal data (other than sensitive data or data of a purely private nature) is permitted if:

1   the data subject has consented to the data processing;
2   the data processing is necessary for the data subject's performance of a contract or in order to take steps as requested by the data subject prior to entering into a contract;

---

49 Act no 429 of 31 May 2000, as last amended by Act no 280 of 24 June 2005.
50 Council Directive 95/46/EC.

3   the processing is necessary for the data controller to comply with a legal obligation;
4   the processing is necessary to protect the vital interests of the data subject;
5   the processing is necessary to carry out a task which is in the public interest;
6   the processing is necessary to perform a task carried out in the exercise of official authority vested in the controller or a third party to whom the data is disclosed; or
7   processing is necessary for the purpose of legitimate interests pursued by the controller or by a third party to whom the data is disclosed and such interests are not outweighed by the data subject's interests (s 6).

Sensitive data, defined as data on racial or ethnic origin, political opinions, religious or philosophical beliefs, trade union membership and data concerning health or sex life, may only be processed if: (i) the data subject has given its explicit consent to such processing, (ii) the processing is necessary in order to protect the vital interests of the data subject or a third party and the data subject is physically or legally unable to give his consent, (iii) the processing is in respect of information which has been made public by the data subject or (iv) the processing is necessary for the establishment, exercise or defence of legal claims (s 7). Data of a purely private nature is defined as data regarding criminal matters, serious social problems and other matters which are considered as purely private. Such purely private data may only be disclosed if: (i) the data subject has given its explicit consent to such disclosure, (ii) the disclosure of the data is necessary in order to protect a legitimate interest and the interest clearly outweighs the consideration to the data subject, (iii) the disclosure is necessary for the performance of an authority's activities or the disclosure is needed in order for an authority to make a decision or (iv) the disclosure is required so that a person or company may perform tasks for an official authority. When undertaking data processing, the bank is under no obligation to notify the Danish Data Protection Agency unless the processing will involve the processing of sensitive data and data of a purely private nature. If, however, the bank undertakes data processing of sensitive or purely private data, the permission of the Danish Data Protection Agency must be obtained beforehand.

The Data Protection Act does not specifically regulate the transfer of personal data to countries within the EU or to countries which have entered into an agreement with the EU which contains provisions equivalent to those of the Data Protection Directive. Thus, transfer to those countries must only comply with the general rules regarding processing and the specific rules on disclosure of personal data set out in the Data Protection Act. Data may in general only be transferred to a third country if such country ensures an adequate level of protection.

Special rules apply to, among others, cash cards and payment cards associated with specific holders pursuant to the Danish Act on Certain Payment Instruments[51] which complements the Data Protection Act in respect of such cards. Pursuant to s 13 of the Act on Certain Payment Instruments, information showing where and how cardholders have used their cards may only be processed where (i) it is necessary for the completion or correction of payment transactions or other functions, (ii) it is necessary for law enforcement, (iii) it is necessary to prevent abuse or (iv) it is authorised by law. Further, information showing where cardholders have used their cards may be processed where (i) it is necessary for the issuer in order to counsel the cardholder to ensure appropriate use of the payment instrument and the information

51 Act no 1501 of 20 December 2004, as last amended by Act no 538 of 8 June 2006.

only concerns the type of payment transactions carried out by the cardholder or (ii) the issuer needs to process the information in order to adapt payment systems to ensure that such systems are safe, efficient and up to date and no information is generated at cardholder level.

SUMMARY

[10.40]   Under Danish law, bank confidentiality (secrecy) is statutorily regulated and breaches are subject to criminal sanctions, but there do not appear to be any published judgments where sanctions have been imposed. Most issues are determined administratively by the Danish FSA. Bank confidentiality in its more traditional form is under attack to the extent that it is felt to conflict with public interests. This is evidenced most significantly in tax and anti-money laundering legislation. The size of banks, their customers and their respective importance to the national economy has led to a demand and pressure on banks to disclose information on customers to an ever-increasing number of regulatory and public authorities. It must, however, be assumed that the principles of privacy which are important in Denmark will maintain a core of confidence between a bank and its customer. On the other hand, banks' commercial interests in administering their assets and operations in an efficient manner requiring transfer and disclosure of certain customer information must also be acknowledged. The observance of these widely diverging interests has led to a legislative system of extraordinary – and one may add – unnecessary complexity.

11 England

Gwendoline Griffiths
Simon Robert-Tissot

INTRODUCTION

[11.1]   Under English law, a bank owes a duty of confidence to its customer. The right to confidence is that of the customer, not of the bank (so that where a customer can be compelled to disclose his secrets, his bank can be compelled to do so as well). There is no precise definition of the scope of this basic duty. There are also numerous exceptions to the duty, both statutory and at common law, which are often as imprecise as the duty itself.

Banking confidence was considered by the Jack Committee Report on Banking Services Law in February 1989. It recommended that the statutory exceptions should be codified in a single statute. It found that they constituted a 'massive erosion' of the duty of confidence.

However, the UK government rejected the concept of a single statute. It preferred a voluntary Code of Banking Practice to deal with this and other issues raised by the Jack Committee. A Banking Code was drawn up by the British Bankers' Association ('BBA'), the Building Societies Association and the Association for Payment Clearing Services ('APACS'). Its seventh edition came into effect on 1 March 2005. Most, though not all, banks and building societies have adopted the Code, which applies to personal customers in the UK. The BBA and APACS have also developed a Business Banking Code for banks and building societies to follow when dealing with certain business customers (generally with turnovers under £1 million) in the UK. Its most recent edition came into force on 1 March 2005 and it deals with confidentiality in a similar way to the Banking Code. There is no code applicable to other types of business customers.

The government also denied that there had been a 'massive erosion' of the duty. They considered that the statutory exceptions only operated where public policy overrode the need to preserve confidence (such as the international attempt to prevent the laundering of proceeds of crime and the funding of terrorism).

The number of statutory exceptions has increased since then in line with the weight of regulation, particularly following the events of 11 September 2001. The burden on banks has also increased because of the nature of their statutory obligations, some of which require banks to disclose information voluntarily on suspicion of the commission of certain offences, failure to disclose itself being a criminal offence. Overall, there has now been a substantial erosion of the duty of confidence.

Conversely, banks and most other UK businesses are subject to legislation designed to protect individuals with regard to the processing and transfer of personal data. The first EU-wide directive was passed in 1995[1] and was implemented in the UK by the Data Protection Act 1998. The increasing use of electronic communications and the transfer of data for processing to other jurisdictions as part of outsourcing arrangements have resulted in significant interest from individuals, regulators and banks in privacy issues.

At the same time, the rise of Internet banking has changed the way that the relationship between banks and that class of customer operates and, in particular, the way that information is passed across and stored. The legal obligations upon banks remain broadly the same, but the medium does affect the way that they are implemented and some additional requirements arise. Regulatory and legal requirements are placing different obligations on banks to request and retain some information on the one hand and, at the same time, not to keep or misuse information. Among the principles of the Data Protection Act 1998 are the principles only to use information for the purpose that it was provided and not to keep it longer than necessary for the purpose for which it was collected.

Accordingly, banks have to try to reconcile a number of different rights and obligations in their day-to-day dealings with their customers. This chapter considers the implications for banks operating in the twenty-first century of the various ways in which the duty arises and the exceptions to it. It also looks at related issues which arise in relation to the regulation of the financial and securities markets.

THE BASIC DUTY OF CONFIDENCE

[11.2]　Under English law, the contract between a bank and its customer is governed by the laws of the place where the account is kept, in the absence of agreement to the contrary. The duty of a bank to keep its customer's affairs confidential is often merely an implied term of the contract between bank and customer. The duty is subject to an increasing number of exceptions, but otherwise extends to all information which the bank has about its customer.

The starting point is *Tournier v National Provincial and Union Bank of England.*[2] Tournier was a customer of the defendant bank. A cheque was drawn by another customer of the defendant in favour of Tournier who endorsed it to a third person with an account at another bank. On the return of the cheque to the defendant, its manager inquired of the other bank to whom it had been endorsed and was told it was a bookmaker. The defendant disclosed that information to third persons.

Tournier brought an action for breach of an implied term of the contract that the defendant would not disclose to third persons the state of his account or any related transactions. Atkin LJ described the duty of confidence in his judgment:

> 'It clearly goes beyond the state of the account, that is, whether there is a debit or a credit balance, and the amount of the balance. It must extend at least to all the transactions that go through the account, and to the securities, if any, given in respect of the account; and in respect of such matters it must, I think, extend beyond the period when the account is closed, or ceases to be an active account …
> I further think that the obligation extends to information obtained from other sources than the customer's actual account, if the occasion upon which the

---

1 Directive 95/46/EC of the European Parliament and of the Council of 24 October 1995.
2 [1924] 1 KB 461.

information was obtained arose out of the banking relations of the bank and its customers, for example, with a view to assisting the bank in coming to decisions as to its treatment of its customers … In this case, however, I should not extend the obligation to information as to the customer obtained after he had ceased to be a customer.'

This was confirmed as the correct position by May LJ in *Lipkin Gorman v Karpnale Ltd*,[3] who stated that 'the correctness of the principles of law stated by the majority in *Tournier's* case has not been doubted since the case was decided'.

Where a customer fears that his bank is about to breach, or has already breached, its obligation of confidence, he has two remedies available to him. He may sue for damages after disclosure or for an injunction to restrain disclosure or a repetition of a previous disclosure. In *Jackson v Royal Bank of Scotland*,[4] the customer obtained damages when the bank inadvertently disclosed its customer's mark up leading to the loss of a line of business. The bank was ordered to pay the lost profit that the customer could prove resulted.

Before granting an injunction, the court will require to be satisfied that an award of damages will not be an adequate remedy. In practice, damages will rarely be an adequate remedy. Once disclosure has taken place, the damage is done and, in many cases, it is difficult to measure the customer's loss in monetary terms. Exemplary or punitive damages are not normally awarded by English courts.

Accordingly, the main protection for the customer is his ability to obtain an injunction restraining the bank from making disclosure. Failure to comply with such an order would, in most circumstances, constitute a contempt of court. However, the court will not grant an injunction without some evidence that a disclosure is threatened and damages will not be adequate. The customer can face a dilemma because disclosure can very easily take place before he knows about it.

SCOPE OF THE DUTY AND OTHER CONFIDENTIALITY REQUIREMENTS

[11.3] *Tournier's* case[5] applies to all types of customers. However, it gives only limited guidance about the scope of the basic duty or the information subject to it. Bankes LJ summarised the position:

'The duty is a legal one arising out of contract . . . it is not absolute, but qualified. It is not possible to frame any exhaustive definition of the duty. The most that can be done is to classify the qualifications and to indicate its limits.'

Where a bank or other financial institution adopts the Banking Code and/or the Business Banking Code, the duty of confidence owed to the relevant types of customer is reinforced by express statements about treating information as private and confidential. The Banking Codes provide customers with a complaints procedure for breaches which is ultimately covered by the Financial Ombudsman Service.

---

3 [1989] 1 WLR 1340 (reversed on different grounds [1991] 2 AC 548).
4 [2005] UK HL 3. The judgment contains an indication of the way the court will assess the damage caused to the customer.
5 *Tournier v National Provincial and Union Bank of England* [1924] 1 KB 461.

Finally, banks may enter into confidentiality agreements or undertakings with customers under which express contractual obligations arise. Such a contractual duty of confidentiality was considered by the Court of Appeal in *United Pan-Europe Communications NV v Deutsche Bank AG*.[6] There, the bank had given the claimant company confidentiality undertakings in relation to the preparation of information memoranda for syndicated loan facilities. The bank had subsequently competed with the claimant and acquired a target company. The court held that the bank had breached its duty of confidence (amongst other things) and as a result granted an injunction to prevent it selling on the shares which it had acquired pending a subsequent trial.

Where a customer is an individual, the processing of personal data will also be subject to the Data Protection Act 1998. This basically requires data to be processed in accordance with eight principles, key amongst which is the requirement for fair and lawful processing. This requires a bank to satisfy certain prescribed conditions for processing and to ensure that an individual knows why its data is collected, by whom and for what purpose the data is to be processed. The requirement that the processing is lawful requires compliance with English common law and statutes, as well as art 8 of the European Convention on Human Rights (the right to respect for private and family life). Other data protection principles require that data processing is undertaken in an environment which incorporates appropriate technical and organisational security measures and that data may not be sent to destinations outside the EEA unless the relevant country has an adequate data protection legislation regime in place (the 'transfer principle'). 'Adequacy' may be established by the following means:

1   participation in the 'safe harbour' arrangements agreed between the European Commission and the US Department of Commerce;[7] or
2   a formal finding of adequacy by the European Commission.[8]

There are certain exemptions to the transfer principle,[9] in particular, where the transfer is made on approved terms. Such terms have been approved both at EU level and within the UK and many transfers take place on the basis of such terms.

EXCEPTIONS, LIMITS AND QUALIFICATIONS

[11.4]   There are various exceptions, limits and qualifications to the common law duty of confidence (which are reflected in the Banking Codes) and there are usually express exceptions in contractual confidentiality undertakings.

The case of *Christofi v Barclays Bank plc*[10] illustrates the fact that the limits of the *Tournier* duty are to be ascertained in accordance with common sense. There, it was held that it was neither sensible nor necessary to impose a duty on a bank to withhold information from a person who the bank would expect to be already in possession of it under a statutory scheme.

Tournier's case[11] also set out the following qualifications:

---

6   [2000] EWCA Civ 166, [2000] 2 BCLC 461.
7   See www.export.gov/safeharbor.
8   Under art 31(2) of the Data Protection Directive (see n 1).
9   8th Schedule.
10   [1999] 4 All ER 437, CA.
11   See n 5.

1   where the disclosure is made with the express or implied consent of the customer;
2   where the interests of the bank require disclosure;
3   where disclosure is under compulsion of law; and
4   where there is a duty to the public to disclose.

Some of these also apply to the confidentiality requirements, other than *Tournier*, mentioned above. The qualifications are considered in more detail below

THE QUALIFICATIONS TO THE DUTY
Express or implied consent of the customer
Express consent

[11.5]   If a bank notifies a customer that it proposes or is entitled to disclose specified information and the reason and actually receives consent (preferably in writing) from the customer, there will be no breach of duty. However, if notice is given to a customer by the bank and the customer does not reply, the bank will not necessarily be entitled to assume implied consent.

Under EU Directive 95/46, consent from individuals should be freely given, specific and informed if the data is 'sensitive' (which includes details of racial or ethnic origin, medical history and criminal convictions), although under the Data Protection Act 1998 explicit consent is only required for sensitive data and implied consent is sufficient for other data. As a practical matter, consent can be difficult to prove and may easily be withdrawn. In some relationships with individuals, such as the employment relationship, consent can never be 'freely given'.

Whilst the Banking Codes generally reflect *Tournier's* case[12] and its qualifications, they only provide for express (and not implied) consent. They refer to the customer asking the bank to reveal information or giving it permission (which in the case of a banker's reference must be in writing). The customer's permission is also required before disclosure of information to a third party giving a guarantee or security in respect of the customer.

Express provisions consenting to disclosure of information can be important in documentation for larger transactions such as syndicated loans where lenders may wish to transfer their interests in the future, in documentation for transactions which may later be the subject of securitisation and in inter-creditor deeds where banks with separate relationships may want to share information on a customer.

Implied consent

[11.6]   There is little decided case law on what constitutes implied consent. There had been a well-established practice of banks giving references on customers to other banks on the basis of implied consent. However, *Turner v Royal Bank of Scotland plc*[13] held that the practice was not sufficiently notorious to constitute an implied term of the banker–customer contract.

---

12   See n 5.
13   [2001] 1 All ER (Comm) 1057.

The question of implied consent arises in relation to the US practice of consent directives. Under these, a customer or former customer authorises or directs its bank to disclose information to the US authorities. A person can be compelled to sign the consent under the threat of fines or imprisonment. It is not clear that a consent directive amounts to a consent sufficient to justify disclosure of information in England and there is no English authority on this. The preferred view is that a consent obtained by compulsion of law in another jurisdiction cannot operate in effect retrospectively to support a claim that consent be implied as a term of the contract between banker and customer under English law.

Some guidance may be obtained from the attitude of the English courts towards other orders from foreign jurisdictions purporting to have extra-territorial effect. These are dealt with below in the section on the extra-territorial aspects of compulsion of law. However, the conflict between the attempt by a court in one jurisdiction to assert extra-territorial jurisdiction on the one hand and the duty of confidence owed by a bank in another jurisdiction to its customers on the other is something which has yet to be resolved satisfactorily.

The Cayman Islands courts have considered the question of 'consents' given under the order of a foreign court and their effect on a bank's duty of confidence. In *Re ABC Ltd*,[14] the applicant bank applied to the Grand Court, Cayman Islands, for a direction as to whether it would be entitled under the relevant Cayman Islands law to disclose confidential information pursuant to a 'consent' signed by its client under a US court order. The court held that the applicant bank would not be entitled to disclose in such circumstances. Summerfield CJ stated:

> 'In the absence of other direct authority in England, this decision, which applies the principles in *Tournier*, may assist in considering the position in English law. Arguably, "consent" under this *Tournier* exception is consent "voluntarily and freely given in the exercise of an independent and uncoerced judgment". This exception is dependent on the customer's consent being maintained at the time the bank makes disclosure. A practical solution may be to require a letter from the customer giving his express consent to the disclosure of the relevant information. Conversely, if the customer withdraws his consent prior to the bank making disclosure, the bank would probably be breaching its duty of confidence if it complied with the consent directive.'

Disclosure in the interests of the bank

[11.7]   This exception was illustrated in *Tournier*'s case by an example of a bank issuing a writ claiming payment of an overdraft stating on the face of it the amount of the overdraft.

Another example arose in *Sunderland v Barclays Bank Ltd*.[15] The bank dishonoured the plaintiff's cheque because she was betting. The plaintiff telephoned the bank to complain. The husband interrupted the conversation to take up his wife's case and was informed that most cheques passing through the wife's account were in favour of bookmakers. Du Parcq LJ thought that, in the circumstances, the interests of the bank required disclosure since it was being forced to give a reason for the policy it

---

14 [1985] FLR 159.
15 (1938) 5 LDAB 163.

adopted. However, it was also noted that since the husband joined the conversation, the bank had the customer's implied consent to disclose the information to him.

More recently, the interpretation of this exception has been considered in the cases of *XAG v A Bank*[16] in the High Court in London and *FDC & Co Ltd v Chase Manhattan Bank NA*[17] in the Hong Kong Court of Appeal. In both cases, customers obtained interlocutory injunctions to restrain their banks from disclosing information in order to comply with subpoenas of US courts. The banks argued that it was in their interest to disclose because otherwise they would be in contempt of court in the US. These arguments were rejected on the ground that the banks' 'interest' in disclosure was of a different character from that contemplated in *Tournier*. The court was not willing to assist the efficacy of the US courts' orders which would have extra-territorial effect.

Where disclosure is made under this exception, it must be limited strictly to information necessary to protect the bank's interest. Disclosure will be necessary and permissible under this exception if there is litigation between the bank and its customer or if the bank brings an action against a guarantor. The Banking Codes also give the prevention of fraud as a relevant example.

Since *Tournier*'s case, two major areas of concern have arisen in relation to this exception.

Other group companies

[11.8]   Whilst a bank may think it appropriate to release confidential information about its customers without their consent to other companies within its group, some of which may be non-banking subsidiaries, the English courts have taken a different view. In *Bank of Tokyo Ltd v Karoon*,[18] it was held that, for confidence purposes, each corporate entity within the banking group must be viewed as separate.

The Jack Committee recommended that to enable a banking group to be run in a cost effective way, the law should allow confidential information to be passed between the holding company, being a bank, and its banking subsidiaries without the need for customer consent. The government took the view that disclosure should only be allowed where the purpose of the disclosure is to protect against loss. However, the Banking Codes just provide that this exception will not be used to give information to anyone else, including companies in the same group, for marketing purposes.

Credit reference agencies

[11.9]   Credit reference agencies collect information on the creditworthiness of individuals (from various public sources, banks and other providers of credit) and then sell it to subscribers, normally potential lenders. There is some doubt as to which exception is applicable (if any): 'consent of the customer', 'duty to the public' or 'interests of the bank'.

The government's response to the Jack Committee proposals on the disclosure of 'black' information (about customers in default) was that banks must be able to continue to make such disclosures since shared information provides the best means of ensuring that borrowers are creditworthy and prevents the average consumer from

---

16 [1983] 2 All ER 464.
17 Civil Appeal no 65 1984.
18 [1987] AC 45.

having to bear the costs of bad debts through higher charges. However, if a bank wishes to pass on any 'white' information (about customers not in default), it must seek the customer's consent.

The Banking Codes provide that a bank may give information to credit reference agencies about undisputed personal debts which are in default and in respect of which no satisfactory proposals for repayment have been received following a formal demand if it has given at least 28 days' notice of its intention to do so to the customer. This notice period is designed to allow the customer to remedy the position before the agencies are notified.

It is unclear whether those in favour of disclosing 'white' information to agencies without the customer's express consent would seek to justify it under one of the exceptions to *Tournier*. It is also unclear what view the courts would take. However, the Banking Codes do provide that, as part of the account opening process, a customer should be told whether account details will be passed to credit reference agencies or checks made with them.

Banks should also bear in mind the data protection implications of maintaining 'black' and 'white' lists and of participating in any industry-wide initiatives. These practices are subject to the Data Protection Act 1998 in the UK. Under this legislation, an individual may request access to all personal information held by an organisation (for example, a bank) about them.

Disclosure by compulsion of law

[11.10] It is under this exception that the most inroads have been made into the duty of confidence and the other confidentiality requirements. The Jack Committee identified at least 19 statutory exceptions in 1987. Its list was not exhaustive and there has been a number of new statutes and regulations since then. This exception arises as a result of court orders, as well as statutes. Its extra-territorial aspects are also dealt with below.

Compulsion by order of court

Where the bank is a party to civil litigation or arbitration proceedings

[11.11] Banks are subject to the rules of disclosure if they are parties to litigation or arbitration proceedings, just like any other party. If a bank is involved in court proceedings in England, the disclosure rules are contained in Part 31 of the Civil Procedure Rules ('CPR'). If the bank is involved in arbitration proceedings, the order will be made by the tribunal in its discretion and subject to the arbitration rules in operation. The local court may be prepared to exercise its coercive powers in support of the arbitrators' order.

Under Part 31 of the CPR, a bank has a duty to disclose relevant documents which are or have been under its control. 'Documents' include films, tape recordings and electronic records in any format. The court will make an order confirming the proper scope of disclosure, as appropriate, and may also make orders requiring disclosure to be provided before the proceedings have even been started.

Parties are not required to disclose documents that are subject to legal professional privilege or public interest immunity, although the circumstances in which the latter arises are narrow. They only have to disclose documents that are relevant to the issues in dispute following a disclosure search that is no more arduous than that proportionate to the issues at stake. However, the fact that information is confidential to a client or protected by a bank's duty of confidentiality owed to a client is no defence to an order for disclosure. Disclosure will be ordered if necessary to try the case fairly. There are some practical steps that can be taken to protect the confidentiality of material dependent on its degree of confidentiality. Parts of a document may be masked, some parts of the document may be anonymised (such as names) or the persons given access to the material may be limited (such as to counsel only). However, this will only be ordered at the discretion of the court or tribunal. The starting point will be that relevant material should be disclosed. Once disclosed, the information should only be used by the recipients for the purposes of those proceedings and should not be used for other purposes or disclosed beyond the parties to the proceedings.

Generally, once a document has been referred to in open court by a party in the course of making submissions or in examining a witness it becomes public information. Under Part 31.22(2) of the CPR, in an appropriate case, the court can make an order restricting or prohibiting the use of information potentially exposed in this way. This is not a usual order. Specific grounds justifying it should be set out in advance of the information being exposed.

The obligation to provide disclosure is generally only on the group company who is a party to the proceedings. It will only extend to documents held by other group companies if they are regarded as within the control of the bank party because that other group company is acting as agent for the bank party in that respect or because the other group company is entirely subservient to the will of the bank party.[19] The latter is unlikely in a modern banking group, however, it is not unusual for documents to be created by one group company while acting on the instructions of the bank party and those documents will effectively fall within the sphere of control of the bank party and therefore can be disclosed.

Witness summons

[11.12]   The court also has the power to order non-parties to litigation to provide evidence to the court, whether it be oral testimony or documentary evidence, if it is relevant to the issues that the court has to resolve. If the proceedings are arbitration proceedings, the tribunal will have to rely on the coercive powers of the court with power over the witness. Once more, legal professional privilege and public interest immunity will be protected. The court will be sensitive to commercial and client confidentiality and will be prepared in an appropriate case to introduce measures to protect it. However, if the evidence is relevant to the issues and necessary for a fair determination of the dispute, an order for its disclosure will be made.

A party to the litigation must apply to the court for an order that an individual or a category of individual gives evidence or that documents held by a third party be produced to the court either at the trial or in advance. Different procedures are provided by the court depending on what is sought.[20] The applicant for the order must set out with reasonable particularity the documents or identifiable categories of documents to be produced.

In *Omar v Omar*,[21] the Court of Appeal confirmed that the documents to be produced should be identified either individually or compendiously and that each document

---

19 *Lonrho Ltd v Shell Petroleum Co Ltd* [1980] QB 358.
20 CPR, Parts 31.17 and 34.
21 (11 October 1996, unreported), CA.

should be shown to be likely to exist, to be relevant to some issue in the proceedings and to be admissible evidence in respect of that issue, as well as to be necessary for fairly disposing of the action. The witness summons may be refused or set aside if the request is irrelevant, 'fishing', speculative or oppressive.

Witness summonses cannot be used to obtain generalised disclosure from a third party or as a means of enquiring whether a bank has documentation that may be relevant.

Where an order for disclosure is made against a bank, disclosure will be within an exception to the duty of confidentiality set out in *Tournier*. As a matter of good practice and courtesy, a bank should inform its customer of the order that has been made prior to disclosing the information. However, that is not an absolute requirement and, where it is unable do so, the bank is required to comply with the order and will not be in breach of duty to its customer.[22]

Particularly difficult issues have arisen where witness summonses have been issued by courts overseas purporting to have extra-territorial effect. This is discussed in 'Extra-Territorial Witness Summonses and Disclosure Orders' below.

Bankers' Books Evidence Act 1879

[11.13]   An alternative route to obtain disclosure of bankers' books in legal proceedings is to apply for an order under s 7 of the Bankers' Books Evidence Act 1879. Section 7 provides that 'on the application of any party to a legal proceeding a court or judge may order that such party be at liberty to inspect and take copies of any entries in a banker's book for any of the purposes of such proceedings'. The Act was originally introduced to make it more convenient for banks to produce documents for court proceedings.

The Act defines 'legal proceedings' to mean 'any civil or criminal proceedings or enquiry in which evidence is or may be given, and includes an arbitration'. 'Bankers' books' are defined to include 'ledgers, day books, cash books, account books, and all other books used in the ordinary business of the bank', whether these records are in written form or on microfilm, magnetic tape or any other form of mechanical or electronic data retrieval mechanism. However, letters in a correspondence file and records of conversations or meetings between bank employees and the customer are not included.[23]

Section 3 provides that 'a copy of any entry in a banker's book shall in all legal proceedings be received as prima facie evidence of such entry, and of the matters transactions and accounts therein recorded'. The Act follows the principle that if a customer is involved in civil or criminal proceedings, he subjects himself to the necessity of disclosure and this will apply equally to his bank.

There are distinctions between civil and criminal proceedings in the application of s 7. In criminal proceedings, the position is as stated in *Williams v Summerfield*:[24]

'... in criminal proceedings, justices should warn themselves of the importance of the step which they are taking in making an order under s 7; should always recognise the care with which the jurisdiction should be exercised; should take

22 *Robertson v Canadian Imperial Bank of Commerce* [1994] 1 WLR 1493.
23 *Re Howglen Ltd* [2001] 1 All ER 376.
24 [1972] 3 WLR 131.

into account among other things whether there is other evidence in the possession of the prosecution to support the charge . . .'

The judge warned against 'fishing expeditions' such as when 'a police officer seeking to make investigations of a suspect bank account started legal proceedings for that purpose and no other'.

In civil proceedings, the statutory power to order inspection should not be inconsistent with, and not overreach, the general law of disclosure.[25] Bankers' books relating to an account of the party to litigation will be ordered to be disclosed if they are relevant to, and necessary for, the litigation and are not privileged.

In very specific circumstances, the court can authorise the inspection of a bank account of a person who is not a party to the proceedings. In *DB Deniz Nckliyati TAS v Yugopetrol*,[26] it was said that the party seeking inspection must show:

'that the bank account of the third party is in substance the account of a party to the litigation or is one in which that person is so much concerned that items in it would be admissible evidence material to the question of his liability and that there are very strong grounds, almost amounting to certainty, that there are material items in the account relevant to the matters in issue.'

Disclosure orders

[11.14] There are other circumstances where the common law provides that a bank may be required to provide disclosure of information that it holds. In *Norwich Pharmacal Co v Customs & Excise Comrs*,[27] the House of Lords established the principle that 'if, through no fault of his own, a person gets mixed up in the tortious acts of others so as to facilitate their wrongdoing, he may incur no personal liability, but he comes under a duty to assist the person who has been wronged by giving him full information and disclosing the identity of the wrongdoers'. It can apply whenever a person has become involved in wrongful conduct which infringes another's legal rights.

An order pursuant to this jurisdiction will not be made where the evidence can be sought in due course under a witness summons. Its purpose is to enable a claimant to obtain information which will enable the claim to be brought where otherwise that would not be possible. It may be allowed so as to ensure that a claim can be properly pleaded. It even extends to the case where, prior to the information being provided, the claimant does not know whether he has been legally wronged.[28] The claimant seeking the order will have to pay the blameless person's expenses in providing the information.

The jurisdiction was extended by the Court of Appeal in *Bankers Trust Co v Shapira*.[29] It was held that the court's power to order disclosure of information at the earliest stages of an action to give effect to a defrauded claimant's equitable right to trace and recover property may be used to order a bank to disclose a wide variety of

---

25 See *Parnell v Wood* [1892] P 137; *South Staffordshire Tramways Co v Ebbsmith* [1895] 2 QB 669; *Pollock v Garle* [1898] 1 Ch 1; *Waterhouse v Barker* [1924] 2 KB 759.
26 [1992] 1 All ER 205.
27 [1974] AC 133.
28 *P v T Ltd* [1997] 4 All ER 200.
29 [1980] 1 WLR 1274.

documents and correspondence relating to the account of a customer who is prima facie guilty of fraud, even though such material would normally be subject to the banker–customer obligation of confidence. In *Arab Monetary Fund v Hashim (No 5)*,[30] the court considered the exercise of discretion and limits were placed on this. It was held that the claimant must demonstrate that the information sought may lead to the location or preservation of assets to which the claimant is entitled. General disclosure will not be ordered.

The claimant is required to pay the bank's expenses of complying with the order. In two other cases, the courts have also permitted the use of confidential information disclosed pursuant to a court order for purposes which fell outside the strict terms of the order.

In *Bank of Crete SA v Koskotas (No 2)*,[31] it was alleged that the former chief executive of the claimant bank had misappropriated bank funds. The London branches of certain banks were ordered to disclose information relating to certain customers in proceedings for the recovery of funds. The order stipulated that the information could only be used for the purposes of the claimant's action. However, the Governor of the Bank of Greece established an investigation team to look into the whereabouts of the missing funds. The investigation team wanted to use the material disclosed pursuant to the English court's order for the purposes of the report (which would then have to be disclosed to the Bank of Greece under Greek law). The bank faced a dilemma between complying with an English court order and complying with Greek law. The judge said that these were exceptional circumstances and disclosure to the Greek investigatory team was ordered.

In *Omar v Omar*,[32] the claimants were seeking to recover funds allegedly misappropriated from their father's estate. They obtained an order for the disclosure of information from the London bank of one of the defendants. After the bank had supplied the information, the claimants sought leave to amend their statement of claim to include claims based on the disclosed information and to add two personal claims against certain of the defendants. They also sought disclosure of further information. It was held that the proposed 'other' purposes were entirely legitimate within the framework of the main tracing claim and their application was allowed.

Compulsion by statute

[11.15]   Most of the statutory provisions entitle the relevant body to compel a bank to produce information relevant to any matter which it is authorised to investigate. Other provisions require a bank to disclose information to the appropriate authority of its own volition on suspicion of the commission of certain criminal offences. Banks are also required to carry out inquiries as to the identity and suitability of a potential customer and to consider the source of funds and, in particular, whether they are derived from illegal activities. The penalties for failure to comply are set out in each statute. The following list of statutory provisions is not exhaustive, but deals with the more important provisions.

Once disclosure has been made to an authority, the information disclosed becomes subject to different degrees of protection in the hands of that body. This is established either by the applicable statutory provisions or case law. For example, information

---

30 [1992] 2 All ER 911.
31 [1993] 1 All ER 748.
32 [1995] 3 All ER 571.

provided to the Financial Services Authority ('FSA') pursuant to their statutory powers is subject to a strict code on its disclosure, making improper disclosure a criminal offence. Information provided to insolvency practitioners, on the other hand, is much more loosely protected. When a bank is required to disclose information, it is worth considering the degree of protection of the information in the hands of the recipient.

However, when considering information in the hands of a public authority such as the FSA or the Department of Trade and Industry, the Freedom of Information Act 2000 must be taken into account. Under the Act, a person has the power to request and be provided with information. Information provided to a public authority protected by statute (such as the Financial Services and Markets Act 2000) or provided in confidence is exempt from the requirement to disclose. The Information Commissioner is conservative in allowing the confidence exemption. It must be clear that the information is really confidential and the ambit of the claim to confidence can be no wider. It is therefore advisable to make sure that any information provided to a public authority is specifically provided in circumstances imposing obligations of confidentiality. There are other circumstances, such as the prejudice to commercial interests, that provide a qualified exemption, in which case the authority must justify the application of the exemption on the basis that the public interest in maintaining the exemption overrides the public interest in disclosing the information. Privilege also only qualifies for a qualified exemption, but the Information Commissioner or the Information Tribunal would be reluctant to override it. The protection afforded by legal privilege has been described by the courts as a fundamental human right.

Income and Corporation Taxes Act 1988 and Taxes Management Act 1970

[11.16]   Section 745 of the Income and Corporation Taxes Act 1988 ('ICTA') gives HM Revenue & Customs ('HMRC') wide investigatory powers if it suspects non-compliance with the provisions in ss 739 or 740 of ICTA. These provisions concern the avoidance of UK income tax by individuals ordinarily resident in the UK which arises through or in connection with the transfer of assets outside the UK. In *Clinch v IRC*,[33] the court considered a notice served by the Commissioners under s 481 of ICTA 1970 (the predecessor to s 745 of ICTA) on a person (Mr Clinch) who had acted as the London representative of a Bermudan bank. The notice required Mr Clinch to provide the Inland Revenue (as it then was) with lengthy details (including the names and addresses of customers and agents and transaction details) concerning transactions involving UK customers and Bermudan entities which Mr Clinch had acted on over several years. Mr Clinch maintained that the notice was void because it was merely a 'fishing expedition' and did not sufficiently identify the customers or transactions in which the Revenue was interested. Alternatively, it was invalid because it was unduly oppressive or burdensome. The court held that, in the circumstances, the notice was valid, although the court could intervene if such a notice went substantially beyond that required to enable the Revenue to decide whether or not in their opinion tax had been evaded. The burden of proving oppression is a heavy one. Such a notice can only be served on someone in England in relation to documents and files in England.

HMRC also has other powers under the Taxes Management Act 1970 ('TMA') to oblige third parties, including banks, to disclose documents. Notices served on a

33 [1973] 3 WLR 862.

bank under s 20(3) of the TMA were considered in *R v IRC, ex p Banque Internationale à Luxembourg SA*.[34] (The court also considered further notices issued under s 767C of ICTA.) The Inland Revenue (as it then was) was investigating large-scale tax avoidance schemes which had been financed by the bank. At the instigation of its customers, the bank challenged the validity of the notices on various grounds, including their impingement on the privacy and right to confidentiality of the bank and its customers in breach of art 8 of the European Convention on Human Rights. The court held that the notices were valid. As far as art 8 was concerned, the court held that there was ample justification for the impingement, as required by art 8(2) of the Convention, on the basis that the notices were issued according to law, in pursuit of a legitimate aim and necessary in a democratic society for the protection of the taxation system and revenue.

More recently, applications by HMRC have been upheld by the Special Commissioners where s 20 (of the TMA) notices were to be served on an investment bank in respect of UK customers who were thought to be conducting share transactions via a British Virgin Islands company and on a financial institution in respect of customers with UK addresses holding non-UK bank accounts.[35] Of particular interest in these cases is the fact that HMRC was able to issue the s 20 notice without being able to name the taxpayer(s).

Insolvency Act 1986 and other insolvency matters

[11.17] Section 236 of the Insolvency Act 1986 applies where an administration order is made in relation to a company, an administrative receiver is appointed, a company goes into voluntary liquidation, a provisional liquidator is appointed or a winding-up order has been made by the court. The court has the power to summon before it any person whom the court thinks capable of giving information concerning the promotion, formation, business, dealings, affairs or property of the company. The courts have given a wide interpretation to the powers under the section allowing it to be used to enable an office holder to discover the true circumstances of the affairs of the company as cheaply and efficiently as possible.[36] There is no express recognition of the right to withhold documents protected by legal professional privilege.

Under s 236(3), the court, on the application of the office holder, can require any person who satisfies the test to submit an affidavit to the court containing an account of his dealings with the company and produce any books, papers or other records in his possession or under his control relating to the company. Failure to comply with the order could result in a warrant being issued for that person's arrest and the seizure of any books, papers, etc. This section has been used against banks and is wide ranging and potentially penal in effect. It has even been used in relation to documents held abroad.[37]

Section 426 of the Insolvency Act 1986 provides for co-operation on insolvency matters between the English courts and other courts in the UK and other relevant countries and territories (mainly in the Commonwealth). Pursuant to that section, a

---

34 [2000] STC 708.
35 For decisions on share transactions, see SpC533 (2006) and SpC537 (2006) and for the decisions on offshore bank accounts and credit cards, see SpC517 (2006) and SpC536 (2006).
36 *Re British & Commonwealth Holdings plc (Joint Administrators)* [1993] AC 426; *Re Rolls Razor Ltd (No 1)* [1968] 3 All ER 698.
37 *Re Mid East Trading Ltd* [1998] 1 All ER 577.

letter of request for assistance and documents was made by the Supreme Court of South Australia in *Re JN Taylor Pty Ltd*.[38] The request for production of documents was granted since there was no serious risk that it would result in claims against the bank by third parties for breach of confidentiality. However, the request for examination of certain bank officers was not granted since, had s 236 of the Act applied, it would almost certainly have been refused.

More recently, cross-border co-operation on insolvency matters has been further extended by the EU regulation on insolvency proceedings (which is in force in all EU member states except Denmark) and the implementation in the UK (except Northern Ireland) of the UNCITRAL Model Law by means of the Cross-Border Insolvency Regulations 2006.[39]

Police and other criminal investigations

[11.18]   Recent years have seen a spate of new legislation in this area. Notably, anti-money laundering and anti-terrorism legislation requires banks to disclose confidential information if there are reasonable grounds to believe that a customer is engaged in any one of a number of specified offences or upon suspicion of money laundering. This directly conflicts with the view in *Tournier*'s case that the giving of information to the police with regard to a customer suspected of a crime would be unwarranted.

Problems can then be caused for banks (and others) by their related statutory obligations not to pay out moneys pursuant to their client's instructions pending authorisation from the authorities and not to 'tip off' individuals whom they suspect of such offences. In *Bank of Scotland v A Ltd, B & C*,[40] the bank faced a dilemma as it had reported a suspected fraud to the authorities, but then was instructed by its customer to pay out the relevant moneys. The bank could not then defend any action against it by the customer for non-payment without 'tipping off' the customer. The Court of Appeal gave guidance on ways in which the bank could have minimised its problems by discussing the position with the Serious Fraud Office and if necessary applying to the court for directions as to what could be disclosed. However, the bank would have been unlikely to be able to recover its legal costs of obtaining direction from the court, which would have had to be accepted as another cost of doing business.

There is a further complication arising out of the interaction between the Data Protection Act 1998 and legislation dealing particularly with anti-money laundering and anti-terrorism. Here, the tension arises from an individual's right of access to his personal data as opposed to the bank's or other financial institution's obligations not to 'tip off' an individual about whom suspicions have arisen. This led HM Treasury to issue 'The UK's Anti-Money Laundering Legislation and the Data Protection Act 1998: Guidance Notes for the Financial Sector' in April 2002. This offers advice on how to deal with a 'subject access request' under the Act in such circumstances. Although it is not legally binding, the Information Commissioner has been consulted and supports the approach taken. The Guidance Notes and other useful information are available on HM Treasury's website.[41]

---

38 [1998] BPIR 347.
39 EC no 1346/2000 of 29 May 2000 and SI 2006/1030.
40 [2001] 3 All ER 58.
41 www.hm-treasury.gov.uk/mediastore/otherfiles/money_laundering.pdf.

11.18 *England*

The following is a summary of some of the legislation relating to criminal investigations. The police authorities have other powers to obtain documents or information and search premises as part of their evidence gathering powers to investigate crime.

Police and Criminal Evidence Act 1984

[11.19] Section 9 of the Police and Criminal Evidence Act 1984 provides that a constable may obtain access to 'special procedure material' for the purposes of a criminal investigation by making an application under Sch 1 to the Act. 'Special procedure material' is defined as 'material other than items subject to legal privilege and excluded material, in the possession of a person who acquired or created it in the course of any trade, business, profession or other occupation and holds it subject to an express or implied undertaking to hold it in confidence'. This would include a bank. 'Excluded material' means personal records, human tissue and tissue fluid and journalistic material held in confidence. The police can apply for such an order at any stage if they believe that the special procedure material will assist their investigation of a serious arrestable offence.

Barclays Bank plc v Taylor and Trustee Savings Bank of Wales and Border Counties[42] made clear that where the police have obtained an order under s 9(1) a bank is obliged to comply with it, is not in breach of the duty of confidence by so doing and is under no obligation to oppose the application, probe the evidence given in respect of it or give notice to its customer of the application being made.

Criminal Justice Act 1987

[11.20] The Criminal Justice Act 1987 empowers the Director of the Serious Fraud Office ('SFO') to investigate any suspected offence which appears to involve serious or complex fraud (s 1(3)). Under s 2, any person can be required to answer questions, furnish information or produce documents. Section 2(10) provides that a person cannot be required to do so if:

> 'he owes an obligation of confidence by virtue of carrying on any banking business unless —
>
> (a) the person to whom the obligation of confidence is owed consents to the disclosure or production; or
>
> (b) the Director has authorised the making of the requirement or ... a designated member of the Serious Fraud Office ... has done so.'

By s 2(1), the Director can make such a requirement for the purpose of an investigation under s 1 if it appears to him that there is good reason to do so. There are no specific provisions in the Act which allow the Director's authority to be questioned, save that material covered by legal professional privilege is protected. Section 2(13) provides that any person who, without reasonable excuse, fails to comply with a requirement shall, on summary conviction, be guilty of an offence punishable by imprisonment or a fine. Judicial review of the Director's power of investigation was unsuccessfully sought in *R v Director of the Serious Fraud Office, ex p Saunders*.[43] The court rejected the argument that the power under s 2 lapsed once

---

42 [1989] 1 WLR 1066.
43 [1988] Crim LR 837.

264

a suspect had been charged. It was said, strictly obiter, that the SFO was entitled to obtain self-incriminating material in the possession of a third party, including material arising out of civil proceedings (although the court expressed a reservation as to the extent to which this could be required in view of the subject's rights against self-incrimination). Subsequently, in *Saunders v United Kingdom*,[44] the European Court of Human Rights ('ECHR') held that Mr Saunders' right to a fair trial had been breached because statements he had made under legal compulsion to that statutory inspector had been disclosed in criminal proceedings against him. However, in *R v Morrissey; R v Staines*,[45] on the use of similar compulsory powers under another Act, it was held that the ECHR could not repeal, even partially, an English statute on the basis of its ruling in *Saunders* so that the court should not exclude evidence obtained in that way. The use of such material in a prosecution has now been limited by statute.

There is little helpful authority on what would constitute a 'reasonable excuse' under s 2(13) for failure to comply with a requirement for information. It is unlikely that a bank receiving such a requirement would be able to question the decision of the Director to authorise it. However, in *Saunders*, the court said that an undertaking given by the third party to the Vice-Chancellor not to disclose the documents concerned to any person without leave of the court was a reasonable excuse.

Competition Act 1998

[11.21] By s 26 of the Competition Act 1998, the Office of Fair Trading ('OFT') is empowered to require any person to produce documents or information to it for the purposes of an investigation of an infringement under Chapters I or II under s 25 of the Act. The OFT can apply to the court for a warrant to enter premises and search for documents under ss 26 or 27 of the Act. The 1998 Act applies to agreements entered into and the practices of businesses, but the information gathering powers apply in respect of both companies and individuals. Similar powers exist under the Enterprise Act 2002, which imposes criminal law sanctions on individuals who participate in cartels.

Financial Services and Markets Act 2000

[11.22] Part XI of this Act gives the Financial Services Authority information gathering and investigatory powers. These are dealt with below in the section on the regulation of the financial markets.

Anti-money laundering and anti-terrorism

Background

[11.23] The obligations introduced into English law arising from the international commitments discussed in Chapter 32 have extended the requirements to combat money laundering to cover the proceeds of all crimes. The regime applies not only to the financial sector, but also to other non-financial activities and professions (including lawyers) which are vulnerable to misuse by money launderers.

---

44 (1996) 23 EHRR 313.
45 [1997] Crim App R 426.

Post 11 September 2001, there were further legislative changes in the UK to focus, inter alia, on the financial arrangements of terrorist organisations. Before then, the UK anti-money laundering regime was contained in three statutes: the Criminal Justice Act 1993 ('CJA'), the Drug Trafficking Act 1994 ('DTA') and the Terrorism Act 2000 and one statutory instrument, the Money Laundering Regulations 1993.[46] Now, the regime has been consolidated and expanded so that banks (and others in the regulated sector) face a complex set of obligations with corresponding offences and penalties which can apply to individual officers and employees, as well as the institutions themselves. The current position is reflected below.

Proceeds of Crime Act 2002

[11.24]   Part 7 of the Proceeds of Crime Act 2002 ('POCA') deals with money laundering and came into force on 24 February 2003. It replaces and expands the earlier anti-money laundering legislation (CJA and DTA), with the exception of the terrorism legislation which had already been strengthened (as mentioned below).

Under the POCA, it is a criminal offence:

1   to conceal, disguise, convert, transfer or remove criminal property from the UK (s 327);
2   to become concerned in an arrangement which a person knows or suspects facilitates the use or control of criminal property (s 328); and
3   to acquire, use or have possession of criminal property (s 329). There is no distinction between the original criminal and a later recipient of the proceeds of crime.

Criminal property is property wherever situated which is or represents a person's benefit from criminal conduct and the alleged offender knows or suspects that it constitutes or represents such a benefit (s 340(3)). No offence is committed if the value of the criminal property concerned is less than £250.

Criminal conduct is conduct which is a criminal offence in any part of the UK or would be an offence in the UK if it occurred there (s 340(2)). This has been amended to remove from the definition conduct reasonably believed not to be criminal in the country where it took place.[47] Accordingly, the UK has taken a sweeping view of the extent of money laundering criminalising dealing with the proceeds of all crime over the minimal threshold.

The POCA also creates three criminal offences of failure to disclose information as required:

1   persons in the regulated sector (which include bank employees) who obtain information in the course of business which gives reasonable grounds for suspecting money laundering commit an offence if they fail to make a report (s 330);
2   a money laundering reporting officer ('MLRO') in the regulated sector commits an offence if an employee makes a report to the MLRO that gives reasonable grounds for suspicion, but the MLRO does not make an onward suspicious transaction report ('STR') to the National Crime Intelligence Service ('NCIS')[48] (s 331);

---

46 SI 1993/1933.
47 SI 2006/1070.
48 The Serious Organised Crime Agency assumed the functions of the NCIS on 1 April 2006; see www.soca.gov.uk.

3   MLROs not in the regulated sector also commit an offence if they do not make an STR when they know or suspect as a result of a disclosure to them that a person is engaged in money laundering (s 332).

The UK has therefore followed the international expectation suggested by the Financial Action Task Force of reporting reasonable suspicion of money laundering. There is no direct UK authority on what amounts to 'suspicion' for these purposes. There is authority that suspicion amounts to no more than a 'state of conjecture' that arises as the starting point of an investigation which concludes with prima facie proof. This would mean a low threshold on the requirement to report and exposure to the criminal offences. However, an individual will have a defence if there is a reasonable excuse for his non-disclosure or he has not been provided with appropriate anti-money laundering training by his employer. The court will also consider whether any appropriate guidance was followed.

Section 333 deals with tipping off. A person commits an offence if:

1   he knows or suspects that a disclosure has been made under the POCA; and
2   he makes any disclosure which is likely to prejudice any resulting investigation.

There is a further offence under s 342 of making a disclosure that is likely to prejudice an investigation when the bank knows or suspects that a money laundering investigation is being or is about to be conducted. This is applicable where no authorised disclosure has taken place.

The offences carry penalties of a fine and/or imprisonment (up to a maximum of 14 years under ss 327, 328 and 329 and of five years under ss 330, 331, 332 and 333).

The NCIS may give permission to carry out a prohibited act under ss 327, 328 or 329. Under s 335, a person must be treated as having the appropriate consent if a disclosure is made to the NCIS and he does not receive a notice of refusal within seven working days after the date of disclosure. Even if a notice of refusal is received in that period, a person will be treated as having the appropriate consent if a further 31 calendar days elapse after the notice of refusal. Note the mixed used of working and calendar days. Whilst these provisions are helpful, the speed of banking transactions may still mean that a bank faces difficulties in dealing with its customer after a disclosure has been made if the customer is providing the bank with instructions to transfer moneys. The bank will not be able to do so until consent is received or deemed to be received, nor will it be able to explain the reason to its customer due to the anti-tipping off provisions. This position was upheld in *Squirrell Ltd v National Westminster Bank plc*[49] where the court refused to unblock a customer's account in such circumstances.

There are also helpful provisions on disclosures in ss 337 and 339. A disclosure which satisfies the conditions of s 337(1) or which includes additional information required by a form specified under s 339 is not to be taken to breach any restriction on the disclosure of information (however imposed). As a result, there will be no breach of any duty of confidence or other similar requirement. By contrast, information should not be disclosed if protected by legal professional privilege which, in addition to those in the legal profession, has been statutorily extended to include professionals such as accountants, auditors and tax advisers.[50] A court has

---

49 [2005] EWHC 664, Ch, [2006] 1 WLR 637.
50 *Bowman v Fels* [2005] EWCA Civ 226, [2005] Fam 326, [2005] 2 WLR 953; s 330(6) of the Proceeds of Crime Act 2002, as amended by the Serious Organised Crime and Police Act 2005 and SI 2006/308.

held that where a disclosure is required by statute there is no implied contractual term obliging the bank to give notice of the disclosure to the customer. Such a term would undermine the statutory framework.

Money Laundering Regulations 2003

[11.25]   The Money Laundering Regulations 2003[51] support the provisions of the relevant statutes. The regulations provide guidelines for those involved, inter alia, in the banking or financial services business and again there are criminal penalties for non-compliance. They relate to various matters, including the setting up of systems and training to prevent money laundering such as identification procedures ('know your customer'), internal reporting procedures and external reporting requirements.

As far as disclosure of information is concerned, internal reporting procedures have to satisfy certain requirements under reg 7. They must identify an 'appropriate person' (the MLRO) to whom a report can be made of knowledge or suspicion of money laundering. Any such report must be considered in the light of all other relevant information to determine whether there is such knowledge or suspicion. The MLRO must have reasonable access to other information in possession of the firm which may assist. Finally, there must be a mechanism for the MLRO to disclose the information to the NCIS if he knows or suspects that the person the subject of the report is engaged in money laundering.

Joint Money Laundering Steering Group Guidance Notes

[11.26]   The Joint Money Laundering Steering Group ('JMLSG') is made up of the leading UK trade associations in the financial services industry (including the British Bankers' Association). Its aim has been to promulgate good practice in countering money laundering and to give practical assistance in interpreting the legislative regime. Since the early 1990s, it has issued Guidance Notes which have been approved by HM Treasury and are not mandatory. They provide an indication of what is expected and, when tailored to a bank or other firm's own risk base, they can provide a safe harbour. The most recent revision to their Guidance Notes (approved by the Chancellor of the Exchequer on 3 March 2006) takes a risk-based approach and also places an onus on senior management responsibility.

Compliance

[11.27]   The Financial Services Authority is the prime regulator of the financial services industry. Combating financial crime is one of its statutory objectives. It supervises compliance with the money laundering regime and is a prosecuting authority for the money laundering criminal offences. It has issued general principles with which it expects the financial services industry to comply, with similar emphasis on identifying and responding to the risk of money laundering and the responsibility of senior management to ensure compliance. It will also have regard to the statutory regime and the JMLSG Guidance Notes and can take enforcement action under its own procedures if a bank (or any other firm) is in breach.

Since the position of the legislature is paramount in the UK, no challenge to the money laundering legislation is possible before the courts. The concern of the court

---

51   SI 2003/3075.

is to apply the law as set out in the statute by Parliament. The decisions that have been given have highlighted two aspects. First, the court has sought to narrow the scope of the obligation to report so as not to require a report based on information protected by legal professional privilege. However, it is long established that legal professional privilege cannot be used to protect criminal conduct. So if in fact the conduct is criminal, the information will not be protected by privilege and the obligation to report will arise. Secondly, as mentioned above, the courts have started to grapple with the difficulty for a bank or professional firm of being prevented by the legislation from honouring its obligations to its customer after a report to the NCIS has been made, but before it has been given authority to proceed and the time limit has not yet elapsed.

Anti-terrorism

[11.28]   The Terrorism Act 2000 (which replaced the previous Prevention of Terrorism Acts) remains in force. It defines terrorism as 'the use or threat of action … designed to influence the government or to intimidate the public … made for the purposes of advancing a political, religious or ideological cause'. This is wider than the previous definition and covers acts both within and outside the UK. The 2000 Act contains a comprehensive set of provisions to address terrorist money laundering. It deals with money or property likely to be used for terrorism (including lawful money donated to terrorists), as well as the proceeds of terrorist acts (such as kidnapping). It includes a money laundering offence (s 18), as well as a reporting requirement, with an offence of failure to report (s 19) and a tipping off offence (s 39).

On 13 December 2001, the Anti-Terrorism Crime and Security Act 2001 came into force with a wide range of provisions, some of which deal with terrorist money laundering in a similar way to the POCA (which at the time was a bill in Parliament). They include the addition of a new s 21A to the 2000 Act, which creates a new offence of 'failure to disclose' for banks and others in the regulated sector, which sits alongside the s 19 offence of failure to report for the wider public in the UK. The key difference is that s 21A applies not just to a failure to report any actual knowledge or suspicion, but also a failure by an institution or person to identify and report 'reasonable grounds for knowing or suspecting money laundering'. This introduced an objective test for liability. The penalty for failing to report is a fine and/or up to five years' imprisonment.

The 2001 Act also strengthened the powers of the police in investigations into terrorist money laundering. The 2000 Act allows the police to obtain disclosure orders, however, under the 2001 Act, they may obtain account monitoring orders requiring financial institutions to provide information about named account holders. These new orders will make the obligations of banks and other financial institutions much clearer and make it easier to pass on information without any fear of breaching confidentiality obligations. The police also have powers of seizure and restraint (to freeze funds during investigations), as well as eventual forfeiture.

Finally, the government has introduced a series of sanctions to give effect to decisions of the UN Security Council and the EU Council of Ministers. For example, the Terrorism (United Nations Measures) Order 2001[52] makes it an offence to make funds or finances or related services available to terrorists (without a licence from the Treasury) or to contravene a decision to freeze funds and creates related tipping off

---

52 SI 2001/3365.

offences. The Bank of England publishes lists of terrorist suspects and banks and financial institutions are obliged to check if they hold any accounts for them. If so, they must freeze the account and report it to the Bank of England, as well as the NCIS. The Bank of England's notices are available on its website.[53] Again, a bank can face a dilemma, since little assistance is given on identifying a terrorist suspect. As a result, it can be potentially faced with notifying and freezing the assets of an individual who may be innocent or breaching sanctions by allowing a terrorist suspect to slip through the net.

Extra-territorial aspects of compulsion of law

[11.29] Two particular aspects will be considered. An attempt by an overseas claimant to obtain confidential information from a bank in England and the reverse situation where the claimant is in England seeking information from a bank overseas. The position varies depending on whether the proceedings are civil or criminal and is dependent upon what international treaties or conventions apply. In cross-border insolvencies, other matters may be relevant as well (see 'Insolvency Act 1986 and Other Insolvency Matters' above).

Obtaining evidence in England for use in foreign civil proceedings

[11.30] Provision is made for claimants to obtain information from banks in England for use in foreign proceedings by the issue of a letter of request to the High Court in England. The English court will normally give effect to such a request so far as proper and practical and so far as permissible under English law. Difficulties arise where the principles of international comity are not respected by the foreign court, in which case the English court will not generally assist.

LETTERS OF REQUEST FROM OTHER JURISDICTIONS

[11.31] 'Letters of request' or 'letters rogatory' involve a request for evidence made by the foreign court to the court in the country where the person who can give such evidence is based or records are maintained. Such a request of the recipient court does not infringe that country's sovereignty either directly or indirectly because it relies upon the recipient state and its court's authority.

The response to such letters from outside the EU (save Denmark) by the English court is regulated by the Evidence (Proceedings in Other Jurisdictions) Act 1975 which provides a comprehensive statutory code for obtaining evidence in England for use in proceedings in foreign courts. For requests from courts in regulation states, being EU member states other than Denmark, a separate statutory regime has been introduced. Between regulation states, a requesting court issues a request to a designated court in another regulation state. The objective is to provide for requests to be made and honoured directly between courts of regulation states.

Under the 1975 Act, an English court may make an order for the obtaining of evidence for civil proceedings in other courts or tribunals upon a request from that court or tribunal if the evidence requested relates to proceedings 'which either have been instituted ... or whose institution ... is contemplated' (s 1(b)). The orders the court may make are wide ranging and include providing for a witness to be examined

---

[53] www.bankofengland.co.uk/publications/financialsanctions/index.html.

orally or in writing, for the production of documents, for the inspection or sampling of property, etc.

However, there are also safeguards for the person subject to the order. General disclosure will not be ordered and the documents to be produced must be specified in the request. The order will respect privilege arising under English law or the law of the requesting state.

The 1975 Act was considered by the House of Lords in *Re Westinghouse Uranium Contract*,[54] where Westinghouse was the defendant in proceedings for a breach of contract in the US. Part of its defence was an allegation of a cartel which included RTZ, an English company. The US court for the District of Virginia issued letters rogatory to the English High Court seeking orders for representatives of RTZ to attend for oral examination in London. RTZ claimed privilege which was upheld by the English Court of Appeal. The US federal judge upheld a claim by witnesses to privilege under the US Fifth Amendment. The US Department of Justice then intervened and applied for an order in the US court compelling testimony in return for the provision of immunity on the grounds that it was required for a grand jury investigation into breaches of the US anti-trust laws and with a view to issuing criminal proceedings.

The House of Lords upheld RTZ's claim of privilege and also held that the provisions of the 1975 Act did not enable an English court to make an order to provide evidence to be used for investigatory purposes such as grand jury proceedings. The Act is limited to proceedings which have been instituted. Grand jury proceedings were held not to be criminal proceedings which had been instituted; rather, they were an investigatory process prior to the institution of proceedings. Consequently, the English courts would not recognise or assist such an investigation.

The issues at stake in the *Westinghouse* case were considered so important that the Attorney General intervened to bring to the notice of the House of Lords the government's opposition to extra-territorial recognition of the US investigatory jurisdiction (at least in relation to English companies or persons).

More recently, letters of request were considered in *First American Corpn v Sheik Al-Nahyan*,[55] where it was held that, where appropriate, the court should accede to a letter of request, particularly where the litigation arose out of fraud practiced on an international scale. However, in that case, the court had to bear in mind the need to protect intended witnesses from an oppressive request.

SUBPOENAS FROM OTHER JURISDICTIONS

[11.32] Foreign courts have sought to ignore issues of international comity by serving subpoenas on local offices of international banks in order to obtain information coming from their overseas branches. Often, the bank is placed in the position of refusing to comply and being held in contempt of court or obeying and then infringing the secrecy laws of the country in which the information is maintained.

What to do in the face of such a foreign subpoena was considered in the case of *XAG v A Bank*.[56] There, the London branch of an American bank was injuncted from

---

54 [1978] 2 WLR 81.
55 [1998] 4 All ER 439, CA.
56 [1983] 2 All ER 464.

producing documents relating to accounts held in London which were required by a New York District Court order. As the accounts were opened and maintained in London, it was held that the banker–customer relationship was centred in London and governed by English law. The English court had to determine the balance of convenience with regard to:

1   the fact that the order of the New York court would take effect in London in breach of both a private interest (the banker–customer contract) and the public interest (the obligation of confidence);

2   the effect of the subpoena and the fact that, under the US doctrine of foreign government compulsion, the New York court would not hold the bank liable in contempt for complying with the injunction of the English court which had jurisdiction over the branch where the documents were located; and

3   the fact that although the court would not be 'enforcing' a foreign revenue or penal law, by permitting the subpoena to be enforced in London, the mere fact of not impeding it would involve a measure of assistance and approbation of a breach of the obligation of confidence which the court would normally, in the public interest, maintain.

Leggatt J summarised the balance of convenience thus:

> 'On the one hand, there is involved in a continuation of the injunction impeding the exercise by the US court in London of powers which, by English statutes, would be regarded as excessive, without in so doing causing detriment to the bank; on the other hand, the refusal of the injunctions, or the non-continuation of them, would cause potentially very considerable harm to the [group], which cannot be disputed, by suffering the bank to act for its own purposes in breach of the duty of confidence admittedly owed to its customers.'

A similar view was taken by the Hong Kong Court of Appeal in *FDC Co Ltd, Vanguard International Manufacturing Ltd Inc and Garpeg v Chase Manhattan Bank NA.*[57] The Hong Kong court refused to treat the fact that the bank had been exposed to considerable financial penalties and possible loss of banking licence in the US as a ground for allowing a breach of banking confidence. The majority of the Court of Appeal were of the opinion that, for the purpose of this case, the Hong Kong branch of Chase Manhattan should be considered as an entirely different entity, separate from the New York branch. This view has since been confirmed in the English decision of *Bank of Tokyo Ltd v Karoon.*[58]

Finally, the balancing test has also been applied in relation to letters rogatory. In *Re State of Norway's Application,*[59] Kerr LJ regarded as significant factors to weigh in the balance the nature, scope, quality and effect of a foreign court order or request.

Obtaining evidence abroad for use in English civil proceedings

[11.33]   A party that has brought proceedings in England may wish to obtain evidence from foreign banks which are not a party to the proceedings. Most commonly, this situation arises where funds have been misappropriated and transferred through various (unwitting) banks. In such circumstances, there are four

---

57 [1984] HKCA 245 and [1984] HKCA 248.
58 [1987] AC 45.
59 [1986] 3 WLR 453.

principal avenues to consider: letters rogatory, witness summonses, court orders for disclosure and applications to the court in the country in which the relevant bank is situated.

LETTERS OF REQUEST TO FOREIGN COURTS

[11.34] An English court can make a letter of request to obtain information from parties abroad. The reception that such a request receives from the foreign court is largely dependent on whether the country concerned is a regulation state or a party to a convention or treaty in force with the UK. Such a convention may be bilateral or multilateral (such as the Hague Convention on the Taking of Evidence Abroad in Civil and Commercial Matters 1970). Some countries are not party to any such convention, in which case their response will depend upon the provisions of their own law.

Where the evidence is sought from another regulation state (being members of the EU save for Denmark), application is made to the English court to issue a request to a designated court in the other regulation state and it should be complied with by that court under the regulation.

The procedure for obtaining information is also relatively straightforward between countries party to a multilateral convention where it has been brought into force. The principal difference between bilateral conventions and the Hague Convention is that the former usually only apply to willing witnesses. So, if a bank based in such a country refused to provide information, it could not be compelled to do so. Where a witness is willing to provide information or where, as in some circumstances under the Hague Convention, he can be compelled to do so, the information is not confined to purely oral evidence. The letter of request can seek the production of documents as well. In *Panayiotou v Sony Music*,[60] the court rejected a contention that a party could not issue a letter of request that sought the production of documents alone.

If a witness is based in a non-convention country, a letter of request can be issued by the English court. However, the receiving court is not under any obligation to compel the witness to attend to give evidence or to produce documents. Whether the foreign court will assist is a matter of local law.

EXTRA-TERRITORIAL WITNESS SUMMONSES AND DISCLOSURE ORDERS

[11.35] The English courts have adopted a restrictive approach when faced with the question of whether a foreign bank can be compelled to disclose information by subpoena, an order under s 7 of the Bankers' Books Evidence Act 1879 or an order pursuant to the principles set out in *Bankers Trust Co v Shapira*[61] (which have been considered above in relation to banks operating in England).

For example, in the criminal case of *R v Grossman*,[62] the Court of Appeal refused an order under s 7 which would have required disclosure in England of a bank's books held in the Isle of Man relating to an account there. One of the grounds for refusal was that the account concerned was outside the jurisdiction and conflict of jurisdictions should be avoided. The overseas branch of the bank should be considered as a different entity from its head office in another jurisdiction.

---

60 [1994] Ch 142.
61 [1980] 1 WLR 1274.
62 (1981) 73 Cr App Rep 302.

The case of *Mackinnon v Donaldson, Lufkin and Jenrette Securities Corpn*[63] concerned an ex parte order under s 7 obtained by the plaintiff against a US bank (which was not a party to the litigation). The plaintiff was alleging fraud against a certain company and individual defendants. The order required the bank to produce books and other papers held at its head office in New York which related to an account of one of the defendants. In addition, the plaintiff issued a subpoena against an officer of the London branch of the bank. Hoffmann J, in discharging the order and the subpoena, said that, on principle, the court should not, save in exceptional circumstances, impose a requirement on a foreigner and, in particular, a foreign bank (which would owe a duty of confidence to its customer regulated by the law of the country where the customer's account was kept) to produce documents outside the jurisdiction concerning business transacted outside the jurisdiction. He said that the need to exercise the court's jurisdiction with due regard to the sovereignty of others is particularly important in the case of banks, who are in a special position because their documents are concerned not only with their own business, but with that of their customers.

The English courts' approach to jurisdictional conflicts of this nature is therefore different from that of the US courts (as discussed above). Apart from exceptional circumstances, the English courts will voluntarily restrict their own jurisdiction within their own territorial limits and, in the interests, inter alia, of international comity, leave matters outside those territorial limits to the courts of the relevant jurisdiction. It is also interesting to note that in a decision of the New York Federal District Court in *Laker Airways v Pan American World Airways*,[64] Brieant J quashed a subpoena served on two English banks at their New York offices requiring them to produce documents held in England which related to transactions which took place in England. Brieant J was apparently of the view that the subpoena was 'inappropriate' and constituted 'an end run around the Hague Convention'.

APPLICATIONS TO THE FOREIGN COURT

[11.36] However, there is nothing to prevent a claimant who has brought proceedings in England from bringing proceedings for disclosure of documents in the courts of the country in which the bank in question is based. Whether the foreign court will grant such an order will depend on local law. However, the English courts have indicated that there is nothing improper in obtaining evidence in this manner and using it in England. In *South Carolina Insurance Co v Assurantie Maatschappij 'De Zeven Provinciein'*,[65] the plaintiff, having commenced proceedings in England, applied to the US court for an order for pre-trial discovery against a non-party. The court refused to grant an injunction in favour of the defendants restraining the plaintiff from taking any further steps in the US proceedings.

INJUNCTIONS OR DISCLOSURE ORDERS IN AID OF FOREIGN PROCEEDINGS: BRUSSELS AND LUGANO CONVENTIONS

[11.37] In *Republic of Haiti v Duvalier*,[66] the plaintiffs had commenced proceedings in France for the recovery of funds allegedly embezzled by the defendants. They also made an application in the English courts to restrain the

---

63 [1986] Ch 482.
64 607 F Supp 324 (SDNY 1985).
65 [1987] AC 24.
66 [1990] 1 QB 202.

defendants from dealing with their assets wherever situated and compelling them to disclose information relating to their assets. Staughton LJ said, at 216–217:

> 'It is beyond question that the injunction . . . was a most unusual measure, such as should very rarely be granted, but this case is most unusual.
>
> It is not the nature or the strength of the Republic's cause of action which puts it in that category. What, to my mind, is determinative is the plain and admitted intention of the defendants to move their assets out of the reach of the courts of law, coupled with the resources they have obtained and the skill they have hitherto shown in doing that, and the vast amount of money involved [\$120 million]. This case demands international co-operation between all nations. As the judge said, if ever there was a case for the exercise of the court's powers, this must be it. Or to quote Kerr LJ in the *Babanaft* case,[67] at p 33D–E: "some situations . . . cry out – as a matter of justice to the plaintiffs – for disclosure orders and Mareva-type injunctions covering foreign assets of defendants even before judgment" and I think that this is such a case.'

Whilst the disclosure order was granted against the defendant and not a third party bank, at least one commentator cites the *Duvalier* case to support the proposition that such disclosure can be ordered against a third party bank.

Originally, the Civil Jurisdiction and Judgments Act 1982 only allowed an English court to grant interim or protective relief in aid of substantive proceedings in a state which had ratified the Brussels Convention (a 'Brussels state') or in a state which had ratified the Lugano Convention (a 'Lugano state'). However, the Civil Jurisdiction and Judgments Act 1982 (Interim Relief) Order 1997[68] extended the English court's power so that it may now grant interim relief (including disclosure orders) in support of proceedings in foreign countries other than Brussels or Lugano states.

Obtaining evidence in England for use in foreign criminal proceedings

[11.38] The Crime (International Co-operation) Act 2003 makes provision for the obtaining of evidence in England by foreign authorities for use in criminal proceedings. The 2003 Act replaced the Criminal Justice (International Co-operation) Act 1990.

Section 15 of the 2003 Act enables the Secretary of State, when requested to do so by a foreign criminal court or prosecuting authority or international criminal authority, to nominate an English court to receive such of the evidence requested as appears to him to be appropriate. He must be satisfied that:

1 an offence under the relevant law has been committed or there are reasonable grounds for suspecting that one has been committed; and
2 proceedings in respect of that offence have been instituted there or the offence is being investigated.

For the purpose of satisfying himself, the Secretary of State shall regard a certificate issued by the foreign court or appropriate authority to that effect as conclusive.

Additionally, where the offence concerned is a 'fiscal offence', the Secretary of State shall not make provision for the taking of evidence unless:

---

67 *Babanaft International Co SA v Bassatne* [1989] 1 All ER 433.
68 SI 1997/302.

1 the request emanates from a Commonwealth country or is made under a treaty to which the UK is party; or
2 he is satisfied that the conduct constituting the offence would constitute a similar offence if it had been committed in the UK.

If it appears to the Secretary of State that the request relates to serious or complex fraud, he may refer the request for evidence to the Director of the Serious Fraud Office for the Director to obtain evidence which appears to him to be appropriate. The evidence provided pursuant to a request may include documents and other articles, as well as oral evidence of a witness. The UK has reserved the right to refuse to assist, inter alia, in circumstances in which UK law recognises privilege, non-comparability or another exemption from giving evidence.

Assistance is potentially available to any foreign country, though in some circumstances it may be more readily available to European and Commonwealth countries.

It is clear that the Secretary of State retains an overriding discretion to refuse to provide assistance. A factor which will be considered in deciding whether evidence should be provided will be banking confidence, but it will be overridden where that seems justified by its relevance to the investigation.

Obtaining evidence abroad for use in English criminal proceedings

[11.39] Section 7 of the 2003 Act provides that a judge or magistrate can issue a letter requesting assistance from another state to obtain evidence outside the UK where it appears that:

1 an offence has been committed or there are reasonable grounds to suspect that one has been committed; and
2 proceedings in respect of that offence have been instituted or the offence is being investigated.

The application can be made by a prosecuting authority (for example, the Attorney General, the Director of Public Prosecutions, any Crown prosecutor or the Director of the Serious Fraud Office) or by any defendant charged in the proceedings. Additionally, a prosecuting authority designated by the Secretary of State can issue a letter of request without making an application to the court.

If the request is for information on banking transactions, the request must state the grounds on which the person making the request considers the evidence specified in it to be relevant for the purposes of the investigation.

Application can also be made to the High Court in England for the issue of a letter of request to the judicial authorities of the state where the holder of the evidence is based asking for the provision of evidence for the purposes of recovering the proceeds of crime.

Duty to the public to disclose

[11.40] With regard to this final exception in *Tournier*, Bankes LJ said that many instances might be given where a bank is justified in disclosing its customers' affairs on the grounds that there is a duty to the public to do so. However, he did not give any. Scrutton LJ said that a bank 'may disclose the customer's account and affairs . . . to prevent frauds or crimes' and Atkin LJ considered that the right to disclose exists 'to the extent to which it is reasonably necessary . . . to protect the bank, or persons interested, or the public, against fraud or crime'.

As mentioned above, since *Tournier*, the passing of various statutes has imposed duties of disclosure. Thus, the 'disclosure under compulsion of law' exception in *Tournier* now includes cases where a duty to the public to disclose has been recognised and imposed by statute. One has to assume that these statutory intrusions into the bank's obligation of confidence have taken place because disclosure by the banks would not otherwise have taken place.

However, this public duty exception is not yet completely moribund. The case of *Libyan Arab Foreign Bank v Bankers Trust Co*[69] concerned the US Presidential Order of 8 January 1986 freezing Libyan assets under the control, inter alia, of overseas branches of US banks. One of the claims made by the claimants involved the scope of this exception. Staughton J said:

> 'But presuming (as I must) that New York law on this point is the same as English law, it seems to me that the Federal Reserve Board, as the central banking system in the United States, may have a public duty to perform in obtaining information from banks. I accept the argument that higher public duty is one of the exceptions to a banker's duty of confidence and I am prepared to reach a tentative conclusion that the exception applied in this case.'

More recently, in *Price Waterhouse v BCCI Holdings (Luxembourg) SA*[70] Millet J accepted in principle that the public interest exception could be relied on to justify the disclosure of confidential information to an inquiry set up to review the Bank of England's performance of its statutory functions.

However, in *Pharaon v BCCI SA (in liquidation)*,[71] Rattee J held that whilst a greater public interest in making documents available in relation to proceedings relating to fraud overrode the public interest in upholding the duty of confidence, the disclosure should be limited to what was reasonably necessary to achieve the purpose of the public interest in disclosure.

REGULATION OF FINANCIAL MARKETS

[11.41] Dealings in the financial and securities markets in the UK and their regulation also raise confidentiality issues for banks (and others) in terms of the requirement to guard information and the consequences where information leaks out or is abused and in terms of the obligations to disclose information to the regulatory authorities.

For many years, the City of London conducted a system of self-regulation which relied on an unwritten code of fair play between those operating in the financial markets. Under governmental pressure, the system expanded with the establishment of the City Panel on Takeovers and Mergers as the main supervisory body. However, in the 1980s, there was a radical overhaul of the system, which is now supported by a considerable volume of statutory regulation. Some regulatory measures were contained in the Company Securities (Insider Dealing) Act 1985 (now to be found in the Criminal Justice Act 1993) and the Companies Act 1985. The principal statute

---

69 [1989] QB 728.
70 [1992] BCLC 583.
71 [1998] 4 All ER 455.

was the Financial Services Act 1986, which has now been effectively replaced by the Financial Services and Markets Act 2000 ('FSMA'). The FSMA set up the Financial Services Authority ('FSA') as the regulator with wide ranging powers.

The functions of the previous self-regulatory organisations (such as IMRO, the PIA and the SFA), as well as the supervisory functions of other bodies, such as the Bank of England and the Building Societies Commission, have been transferred to the FSA. As a result, the regulation of banking, securities, insurance and other financial services has been brought under one roof.

Information gathering by the FSA

[11.42]   The FSMA requires the FSA to monitor firms (that is, banks and the other types of financial services organisations which it regulates) so as to achieve its various statutory functions and to ensure that firms comply with the requirements of the FSMA. The FSA is also required to take certain steps to co-operate with other regulators (such as the Takeover Panel and foreign regulators), including, where appropriate, to supply information to them. For example, the FSA and the US SEC have informal arrangements to exchange information regarding the oversight of financial services firms. The most recent 2006 Memorandum of Understanding between them even permits the SEC to conduct on-site visits in the UK.

For these purposes, the FSA needs to have access to a broad range of information. The FSA receives notifications and reports from firms themselves and one of the requirements on regulated firms is to be open and co-operative with the regulator. The FSA has statutory powers to require the provision of information to it (FSMA, s 165) or to require a report to be prepared (s 166) where reasonably required by the FSA in exercise of its functions. It also has powers to investigate and require the provision of information or documents under ss 167 and 168 of the FSMA. The FSA may require information to be provided to it or investigate at the request of an overseas regulator.

There are certain limitations on its powers. However, it may require the disclosure of information subject to banking confidentiality to its investigators in certain circumstances (FSMA, s 175(5)). Failure to comply with the FSA requirements without reasonable excuse can lead to the defaulter being treated as if he were in contempt of court (FSMA, s 177).

The FSA will not itself disclose confidential information without lawful authority, but there are circumstances when onward disclosure may be made, for example, under an applicable exception in the Financial Services and Markets Act 2000 (Disclosure of Confidential Information) Regulations 2001[72] or with the consent of the person from whom that information was received and (if different) to whom the information relates (FSMA, s 348(1)). Under s 348(4) of the FSMA, information is not confidential information if it has already been made available to the public in a way not precluded by that section or it is summarised so that information relating to a particular person cannot be ascertained.

In *Barings plc (in liquidation) v Coopers & Lybrand*,[73] the Court of Appeal took the view that transcripts of evidence given during an inquiry into the collapse of Barings were subject to similar restrictions on disclosure in s 82 of the Banking Act 1987 (the

---

72 SI 2001/2188.
73 [2000] 3 All ER 910.

predecessor to s 348(4) of the FSMA. This disapproved dicta in a previous case relating to the BCCI inquiry and reinforced the view that maintaining confidentiality encourages voluntary disclosure from banks which facilitates effective supervision. However, as the transcripts had been exhibited to affidavits sworn in the course of other proceedings, it was also held that they had been made available to the public and so could be disclosed.

If a firm enters into a material outsourcing arrangement, it must ensure that its suppliers deal in a co-operative way with the FSA as far as access and the provision of information are concerned. Outsourcing cannot act as a barrier to a firm in carrying out its regulatory obligations.

Insider dealing and market abuse

[11.43]   Insider dealing and market abuse can occur if confidential information is not sufficiently protected or leaks out. Banks may be holding inside or confidential information and so may be exposed if that information is subsequently abused.

Insider dealing in corporate securities involves the utilisation of unpublished price-sensitive information obtained through a privileged relationship to make a profit or avoid a loss by dealing in securities, the price of which could be materially affected by public disclosure of that information.

Section 52 of the Criminal Justice Act 1993 ('CJA') makes it a criminal offence for an individual who has information as an 'insider' to deal in securities to which the information relates. It is also an offence to encourage another person to deal in such securities or to disclose the information other than in the course of the individual's profession or employment. Information acquired by virtue of the insider's connection with his own company or by virtue of his employment gives rise to primary insider dealing.

Of more importance to banks is the prohibition on secondary insider dealing or 'tippee' trading. Sections 52 and 57(2)(b) deal with the situation where a person (perhaps within a bank) *obtains* inside information from an individual who is a director, shareholder, etc (a primary insider) of a company. If the 'tippee' then uses that information and deals on the stock exchange or investment exchange, he may be guilty of an offence (subject to certain defences). The information may be obtained directly from the person connected with the company or indirectly through any number of people forming a chain between the 'tippee' and the insider.

There has been a paucity of case law dealing with secondary insiders. The first case in which a prosecution was brought against a 'tippee' (under the earlier provisions of the 1985 Act) was *Re A-G's Reference (No 1 of 1988)*.[74] The Attorney General referred the issue of the passive receipt of information to the Court of Appeal. In its view (subsequently upheld by the House of Lords), a recipient of price-sensitive information, who dealt in the relevant securities, had 'obtained' the information, whether he had procured it or came to it without any positive action on his part. This would clearly catch a bank employee overhearing a conversation in the lift at work and, realising that what he was hearing was price sensitive, dealing in securities on the strength of it.

The FSMA introduced a new civil market abuse regime which is set out in the FSA's Code of Market Conduct. Amongst other things, it supplements the existing criminal

74 [1989] 1 All ER 321.

offence of insider dealing. Market abuse (FSMA, s 118) covers a number of different types of behaviour in relation to a qualifying investment as described. Prohibited behaviour includes broadly misusing information, or giving a false or misleading impression of the market or distorting the market.

As well as this primary offence, there is a secondary offence of requiring or encouraging another person to act so that the market is abused under s 123 of the FSMA. The FSA has power to impose penalties under the FSMA, as well as to enforce the CJA. There is a further criminal offence of market manipulation under s 397 of the FSMA.

Chinese Walls

[11.44]   The FSMA provides for two types of safe harbour from the offence of market abuse. The FSA can recognise in its Code of Market Conduct compliance with specific provisions of the City Code on Takeovers and Mergers (FSMA, s 122). Safe harbour status has also been given where information has been guarded in accordance with r 2.4 of the FSA Conduct of Business ('COB') on Chinese Walls, which applies to all firms (including banks) conducting designated investment business.

Chinese Walls are also important for a number of other reasons. They enable the bank to restrict the access to client confidential information within the bank so limiting the chance of it being wrongly disclosed or the bank becoming subject to a contractual duty to another customer either to disclose or use that information for the benefit of the other customer. Establishing a Chinese Wall is also one of the methods which can be used by a firm to manage a conflict of interest fairly.

COB, r 2.4 sets out the circumstances when the FSA would consider it appropriate for a firm to withhold or not use information which it would otherwise have to disclose to, or use for the benefit of, a client. It is also the only information rule made so far under s 147 of the FSMA. COB, r 2.4.4 provides:

> '(1)when a firm establishes and maintains a Chinese Wall (that is an arrangement that requires information held by a person . . . carrying on one part of its business, to be withheld from . . . persons . . . for whom it acts . . . in another part of its business), it may:
> (a)   withhold or not use the information held; and
> (b)   . . . permit persons employed in the first part of its business to withhold information . . . from those employed in that other part . . .'

but only to the extent that the business of one of them involves designated investment business or related activities.

Information may be withheld or not used when required by an established arrangement maintained between different parts of the business in the same group. A Chinese Wall arrangement has to be monitored to ensure it is effective. Chinese Walls are recognised by the FSA, but there is no direct authority from an English court as to whether Chinese Walls within banks are effective to prevent conflicts of interest as a matter of law. However, there is a line of reported cases relating to conflicts of interest arising in firms of solicitors and accountants.

The courts are now applying the principles in *Prince Jefri Bolkiah v KPMG*.[75] There, the issue was whether accountants which had provided litigation support services to

75   [1999] 2 WLR 215.

a former client and possessed information confidential to him could undertake work for another client with an adverse interest. The House of Lords held that the duty was not to disclose or misuse confidential information. For the court to intervene, there must be a real risk of disclosure and not merely a theoretical or fanciful risk. If there was, it was up to the firm to show that even so there was no risk that the information would come into the possession of those acting for the second client. The court should restrain the firm from acting unless it was satisfied that effective measures had been taken to ensure that no disclosure would occur. The court considered that an effective Chinese Wall needed to be an established part of the organisational structure of a firm and not created ad hoc.

These principles were considered in *Young v Robson Rhodes*[76] in the context of a proposed merger of two accountancy firms. Whilst a risk of disclosure was considered to be real, the court held that, in that case, ad hoc Chinese Wall arrangements would be sufficient. More recently, in *Koch Shipping Inc v Richards Butler*,[77] which involved a solicitors firm, the court again held that the proper test was whether there was a real risk of disclosure and that, in that case, there was no such risk given that undertakings had been given by the relevant solicitor not to discuss the information with anyone. It was held that the court should take a 'robust view' in such cases and not be persuaded that there was a real risk when it was no more than fanciful or theoretical.

Accordingly, whilst for many years the courts appeared reluctant to accept that Chinese Walls are effective, this now appears to be changing. Additionally, banks may be able to distinguish the management of conflicts within solicitors' firms (where client information is usually privileged as well as confidential) from arrangements within banks. It is also arguable that a Chinese Wall which complies with the FSA COB rules and is supported by trade practice has been shown to be more effective than the ad hoc segregation of information used within a firm of solicitors or accountants.

It is now open to a bank to argue that the regulatory framework that exists for banks in relation to Chinese Walls can be relied upon to prevent the informal flow of information within an organisation; accordingly, that it sets the standard of behaviour which customers are entitled to expect from their banks and which the courts should enforce as one of the accepted terms of the banker–customer relationship. The bank could also argue by implication that so long as the confidential information remained protected within the bank behind its Chinese Wall, it had fulfilled its contractual duty to the client.

Even so, there could be customers who will not be persuaded that Chinese Walls are completely effective in ensuring confidentiality. A substantial customer has the option of moving its business away from its bank. The consequences of a substantial customer removing its business may be a factor in a bank's decision whether it or a member of its group agrees to act for that customer's competitor. However, that sanction would not be available to a past customer, nor perhaps to a less substantial customer, who would be left with having to seek redress in the courts by restraining a concern for the misuse of confidential information or breach of duty by an injunction or by claiming damages in the event of breach.

As an injunction is a discretionary equitable relief, the court, when considering an application for an interlocutory injunction founded upon an arguable claim, would

---

76 [1999] 3 All ER 524.
77 [2002] EWCA Civ 1280, [2002] 2 All ER (Comm) 957.

apply a test as to where the balance of convenience lies, namely, which party would suffer more if an injunction were to be granted or refused. In assessing that, the court would take account of whether damages would be an adequate remedy. A fundamental point would be whether the Chinese Walls erected by the bank were sufficiently effective to make a breach of confidentiality unlikely so as not to justify the grant of an interlocutory injunction and affect the terms of the banker–customer relationship.

CONCLUSION

[11.45]   In England, banks face an increasingly difficult task in balancing and reconciling their various duties and obligations with regard to information on their customers and its confidentiality. Whilst customers may have greater expectations about the preservation of banking confidentiality (given the Banking Codes and such measures as the Data Protection Act 1998), banks find themselves facing a number of dilemmas, particularly given the statutory erosions to the duty of confidence. Ultimately, the public interest may well result in bank confidentiality being no longer the rule, but the exception, in England.

12 Finland

Lauri Peltola
Helena Sallila

THE BASIC POSITION
The nature of the duty of non-disclosure

[12.1] Bank confidentiality is one of the fundamental elements of the banking business in Finland; persons depositing funds, as well as other customers of banks operating in Finland, must be able to rely that information regarding their dealings with the bank or, indeed, themselves or their businesses will not be disclosed to third parties (except in circumstances as permitted by law and as explained below). Lack of trust in the maintenance of a high degree of confidentiality in the Finnish banking industry would certainly lead to, among other things, funds being directed to countries where confidentiality regulation would be more adequate. On the other hand, bank confidentiality cannot be absolute and there are circumstances where the disclosure by a bank of confidential information is allowed and an unwilling bank may even be compelled by law to disclose such information. Somewhat paradoxically, in certain special circumstances, the failure by a bank to disclose information may even constitute a criminal offence in itself.

Bank confidentiality, ie the bank's duty of non-disclosure of information applies to all information that the bank has received in a customer relationship or otherwise in connection with carrying on the banking business and which information is not public knowledge. There are no set time limits for the extinction of the duty of non-disclosure and, thus, such duty does not end at the termination of a customer relationship, for example.

The scope of bank confidentiality was in certain respects considered in connection with civil and criminal litigation, which was prompted by the very severe crisis of the Finnish banking industry in the first half of the 1990s. In the interests of maintaining bank confidentiality, some of the proceedings were conducted either entirely or partly behind closed doors and certain evidence involving information subject to bank confidentiality was declared partly or wholly secret for a fixed period of time (under law, however, a maximum of 40 years). Such consequence of the bank confidentiality provisions is, naturally, very much in conflict with the leading principle under the Finnish Procedural Code of court proceedings being open to the public and it certainly has been difficult sometimes for the courts to find a fair balance to resolve the conflict between these two principles in a satisfactory manner.

In court proceedings involving a bank, the bank may – and in many cases it should for the purposes of maintaining confidentiality – request that any material containing information subject to bank confidentiality presented to the court be declared secret.

However, the Finnish courts have wide powers to consider and decide upon the matter independently.

The above shows the difficulties which the banks are facing in dealing with bank confidentiality matters in a way which appropriately satisfies the sometimes very much conflicting interests of the various parties involved in the matter, including society in general.

Legal framework

[12.2]   The principal statute governing matters regarding Finnish banking business is the Act on Credit Institutions 1993 (the 'Credit Institutions Act'). The Credit Institutions Act includes specific provisions on the duty of non-disclosure which apply to credit institutions and companies belonging to the same consolidation group with the credit institution, their agents and other companies representing the credit institution, as well as to collectives of credit institutions (including, for example, guarantee and investor protection funds and the Finnish Bankers' Association). Companies belonging to the same consolidation group with the credit institution comprise Finnish and foreign financial holding companies of the credit institution (ie financial institutions whose subsidiaries are mainly credit or financial institutions where at least one of these subsidiaries is a credit institution), as well as Finnish or foreign credit institutions, financial institutions and ancillary banking services undertakings (i) over which the credit institution or its financial holding company exercises control, (ii) which has joint management with the credit institution, its financial holding company or their subsidiary or (iii) which is managed on a unified basis with the credit institution, its financial holding company or their subsidiary. All the above entities will be (on most occasions) referred to here, for the sake of simplicity, as the 'bank'. Furthermore, the term 'bank' used here may also include, inter alia, Finnish investment firms and Finnish asset management companies for collective investment funds, as well as branch offices in Finland of foreign credit institutions or investment firms.

Prior to the Credit Institutions Act, the confidentiality obligations of the banks were regulated by various banking statutes dating from the 1970s. Prior to those statutes, bank confidentiality was considered as an essential principle of banking business established by custom. The scope of the confidentiality obligation in the Credit Institutions Act to a large extent corresponds to that of the former specific legislation and that established by practice.

Pursuant to the Act on Operations in Finland of a Foreign Credit and Financial Institution 1993, the provisions on bank confidentiality included in the Credit Institutions Act also apply, as applicable, to branches and representative offices in Finland of foreign credit and financial institutions.

In addition to s 94 of the Credit Institutions Act, the focal provision concerning bank confidentiality, similar provisions on the confidentiality obligation are included in, inter alia, the Securities Market Act 1989, the Act on Book Entry System 1991 and the Investment Funds Act 1999, as well as in the Act on Investment Firms 1996, which implements the EC Investment Services Directive (93/22/EEC) in Finland and applies to the provision in or into Finland of investment services. In addition, the Act on Supervision of Finance and Insurance Conglomerates 2004, which sets out requirements for the operations and supervision of finance and insurance conglomerates and the entities belonging to such conglomerates, such as credit institutions, investment firms, Finnish asset management companies for collective investment funds and comparable foreign entities and insurance companies, includes a similar rule of confidentiality.

Pursuant to the Act on Unfair Business Practices 1978, which also applies to banks, no person may unlawfully acquire or try to acquire information on a trade secret, nor may such trade secret be used or disclosed. Anyone employed by or carrying out a task for the entity must not use information on such trade secret for his own benefit or disclose such trade secret to gain benefit for himself or to the detriment of another person.

Further statutes that can be relevant when assessing the bank's confidentiality obligation include, inter alia, the Personal Data Act 1999 and the Act on Preventing and Clearing Money Laundering 1998 (the 'Money Laundering Act') which provides the banks with an obligation to identify their customers and report suspicious transactions. The Act on Publicity of the Operations of Public Authorities 1999 contains exemptions from the authorities' general obligation to keep confidential documents that have been ordered as confidential or include information which is confidential under law. Moreover, several statutes include specific provisions providing the authorities with a right to disclose confidential information to other authorities.

In addition to the above, in 2003, the Finnish Bankers' Association issued the 'Instructions on Bank Confidentiality', which include the rules of interpretation of the bank confidentiality provisions as understood by the Finnish banks. These instructions are currently expected to be updated by the beginning of 2007. In 2004, the Finnish Bankers' Association also issued the 'Policy of the Banks Operating in Finland with Regard to Preventing and Clearing Money Laundering and Financing of Terrorism'.

SCOPE OF BASIC POSITION
Definition and extent of bank confidentiality

[12.3]   According to s 94 of the Credit Institutions Act, an employee or an officer, including any member or a deputy member of any statutory body of a bank, such as a member of the supervisory board of the bank (ie a credit institution or company belonging to the same consolidation group as the credit institution, an agent of the credit institution or other company representing the credit institution or a collective of credit institutions) must not disclose information concerning the financial standing or private circumstances or the business or trade secret of a customer of the bank or of some other (non-customer) person related to the bank's activities. Such other (non-customer) person can be, for instance, a person who has been in negotiations with a bank and has revealed confidential information to the bank, but no customer relationship was established. Bank confidentiality covers all information that the customer wishes to keep secret and which is not public knowledge or has not become publicly known. As a general rule, even information that a particular person is a customer of the bank is confidential. The duty of non-disclosure applies not only to an employee or officer of the bank, but also to any other person who is carrying out a service or assignment for the bank, for instance, a person carrying out ADP, posting or cleaning services for the bank. The duty of non-disclosure continues even after the employment/assignment has ended.

The Credit Institutions Act expressly provides that confidential information may not be disclosed at the general meeting of shareholders of the bank.

By law, a bank is under an obligation to disclose to the public information on its activities and financial standing. However, the information to be so disclosed by the bank must be compiled in the way that the disclosure of an individual person's confidential matters is excluded.

EXCEPTIONS, LIMITATIONS AND QUALIFICATIONS TO BASIC POSITION

[12.4]   The interests of society require that there are circumstances where an absolute bank confidentiality must be overruled. Such circumstances are covered by various specific statutes by virtue of which confidential information can or must be released by the bank to various authorities and also to certain private entities, such as, for instance, credit reference agencies. The interpretation of such exemptions allowing the disclosure is, owing to the nature of such provisions, however, generally restrictive.

This section deals with some of the most important exceptions to the confidentiality obligation.

Customer consent

[12.5]   The consent given by the customer (in this context and later in this chapter, 'customer' also means any person other than a customer of the bank on whom confidential information is held by the bank) to the bank to make a disclosure, naturally, allows the bank to do so. Section 94 of the Credit Institutions Act contains an express reference to customer consent as a ground for legitimate disclosure of information by the bank.

The Credit Institutions Act does not specify the form of the customer consent required, ie whether the consent has to be express or whether an implied consent would be sufficient. Nevertheless, it would seem logical, as the non-disclosure of information is always presumed, that (except for, possibly, in certain rather special circumstances) only on the basis of an express consent by the customer, whether written or oral, is the bank allowed to disclose information regarding the customer. For the purposes of avoiding problems of proof, it is also certainly prudent for the bank to obtain the consent from the customer in writing. The agreement between the bank and the customer may contain provisions allowing the disclosure by the bank of otherwise confidential information without specific consent being obtained each time.

Obviously, the term 'consent by the customer' opens a variety of – often very difficult – further issues, such as whether, in the case of a joint account, consent by one account holder or both is required, whether a consent given not by the holder of the account, but by someone authorised by the account holder to operate the account is acceptable, or, indeed, whether the bank may accept a 'consent' given by the customer in circumstances where the customer faces a prison sentence or may have been exposed to some other type of mental duress of which the bank possibly was or should have been aware.

Some of these difficult situations may be covered by the contractual terms between the customer and the bank. In some cases, the general principles of law or an established banking practice or the 'Instructions on Bank Confidentiality' issued by the Finnish Bankers' Association may provide guidance. The bank may, however, find itself in a very uncomfortable position in certain cases where claims for disclosure are made on the basis of customer consent, whereas some other party is insisting on the confidentiality being maintained basing his view on 'defects' in such a consent or the bank itself is aware of the existence of such 'defects'. Maintaining confidentiality in circumstances where disclosure should have been made can lead to claims for damages against the bank, whereas an unjustified disclosure can also lead, in addition to damages, to criminal sanctions.

An implied 'consent' for disclosure may be construed in circumstances where the customer himself has made an inquiry or complaint to the authorities on the bank's dealings with him. Such a request by the customer should allow the bank concerned to disclose to the authorities all information which is relevant to address the issues raised by the customer.

Interests of the bank

[12.6] For the purposes of customer services, marketing and risk management, a bank may disclose confidential information to a Finnish or foreign entity belonging to the same group, consolidation group or finance and insurance conglomerate provided that such entity is subject to the above or similar confidentiality obligation. The disclosed information may, however, not include data which the Personal Data Act defines as sensitive or data based on registered information on payments between a customer and an entity not belonging to the same group, consolidation group or finance and insurance conglomerate. The above registered information that cannot be disclosed includes, inter alia, bank account details which give information on the financial standing of the relevant customer.

The Personal Data Act contains strict rules regarding processing of sensitive data, such as information on race or ethnic origin, criminal record, state of health, sexual orientation or social welfare needs, as well as political or religious affiliation or trade union membership. Sensitive data may only be disclosed by express consent of the person concerned or on certain other grounds, as specified in the Personal Data Act.

Furthermore, a bank may disclose confidential information contained in its customer register which is necessary for the purposes of customer services and marketing, except for sensitive data, to a Finnish or foreign entity belonging to the same financial consortium as the bank, provided that such consortium is subject to the above or has similar confidentiality obligations. For example, the name and contact details of a particular customer of the bank may be disclosed, whereas the bank account details which give information on the financial standing of the customer must not. The Credit Institutions Act does not include a definition of 'entity belonging to the same financial consortium'. The right of a bank to disclose information to such entity is to be determined on a case-by-case basis, taking into consideration such issues as mutual ownership, commercial interdependence and the nature of co-operation between the entities in question. However, because the recipient of confidential information is required to be subject to the statutory confidentiality obligation, the disclosure of confidential information is in practice limited to, inter alia, credit institutions, investment firms, insurance companies and asset management companies for collective investment funds, as well as to corresponding foreign entities subject to similar confidentiality obligations.

Interests of the banking system

[12.7] A disclosure of certain confidential information is justified in the interests of securing the operation of the banking system. The 'Instructions on Bank

Confidentiality', issued by the Finnish Bankers' Association, deal with some of these circumstances.

It is considered that, generally, when a credit or debit card is presented for the purposes of making a payment, the bank is allowed to disclose to the recipient of the payment whether there is sufficient balance/credit limit available to cover the payment, although the actual amount of the balance/credit limit must not be disclosed. Disclosure of the name and address of the holder of the account is allowed where there is no sufficient balance/credit limit, provided that the bank has ensured that the receipt is duly signed. The same rights to obtain information are enjoyed by the drawee of a cheque. However, cheques are no longer used for domestic payments in Finland.

Similarly, in connection with electronic money transfers between banks, certain information which is necessary for implementing the transfer may be exchanged. If a transfer has gone astray, certain information may be disclosed for tracing the funds and directing them to the correct recipient.

Interests of financial markets

[**12.8**]   The Credit Institutions Act provides that a credit institution is entitled to disclose confidential information to, inter alia, a Finnish stock exchange (such as the Helsinki stock exchanges), a Finnish options exchange or to corresponding foreign entities operating in the countries belonging to the European Economic Area ('EEA') provided that the confidential information concerned is necessary for ensuring the supervisory functions prescribed for such entities. A similar provision is included in the Act on Investment Firms.

Credit reference agencies and personal data protection

[**12.9**]   Pursuant to the Credit Institutions Act, a credit institution may carry on credit reference services as part of its business. Credit information is primarily to be collected and recorded for the bank's own use.

However, the Credit Institutions Act expressly provides that a bank has the right to disclose certain information to external credit reference agencies. Such right has been deemed appropriate because lenders are, generally, responsible for controlling, as far as possible, the capability of the borrowers to service their loans. In this respect, the possibility of lenders obtaining information for the evaluation of the creditworthiness of a potential customer is most helpful, if not often mandatory. In addition, third party interests (such as the interests of the guarantor of a loan) benefit from the possibility of obtaining credit reference information on the solvency of the borrower or on any previous defaults.

Although the operation of a credit reference agency is not subject to a licence, dealing with information passed on to a credit reference agency is subject to restrictions as set out in the Personal Data Act.

The provisions of the Personal Data Act regulate, for instance, the extent of the registration and release of information contained in credit reference registers. The Personal Data Act only applies to information on private persons, including personal credit information, and thus the registration and release of information on legal entities by credit reference registers is unregulated by law. As regards information on such legal entities, a bank has a certain discretion in deciding to which credit reference agencies information is released by the bank. With regard to credit information on private persons, in addition to the name and the contact information, information on defaults in payments or performances may be stored in a credit reference register, as specified in the Personal Data Act. In addition, information may be recorded in a credit reference register, inter alia, on the entries contained in the register of debt administration, on the placement of a person under guardianship and on the appointment of a trustee to administer the financial affairs of a person.

The Personal Data Act expressly provides that personal credit information may only be disclosed to a credit reference agency and to an entity which needs the information for the purposes of granting credit or credit monitoring or for another comparable purpose. Furthermore, the Personal Data Act includes special provisions, inter alia, on the deletion of information from a credit reference register, notifying a registered person of the information recorded in the credit reference register, a registered person's right of access to the information on him in the credit reference register and secrecy obligation. A breach of the provisions of the Personal Data Act may constitute a criminal act which is punishable by a fine and/or imprisonment, generally for a maximum period of one year.

The authorities supervising the maintenance of appropriate data protection are entitled to obtain information from, or inspect the records of, the banks with regard to matters related to data protection, the registers and their use. As the Personal Data Act only applies to information on private persons, registers containing information on legal entities do not fall under the supervision of the data protection authorities.

Furthermore, under the provisions of the Act on Guarantees and Third Party Collateral 1999, a lender (for example, a bank) must provide a private guarantor or third party pledgor of collateral with information on debts and related costs falling within the scope of the guarantee or collateral in question and the conditions on the basis of which the guarantor's or pledgor's performance may be demanded, as well as with other information that essentially affects the position of the guarantor or pledgor. Private guarantors and pledgors must also be provided with information on the commitments and financial standing of the underlying borrower which may be relevant to the guarantor or pledgor. Such information is considered to include, inter alia, details of income, property, employment and any defaults relating to other credits granted. A lender must also comply with certain continuing obligations to provide the guarantor and pledgor with certain information. Moreover, certain information must be provided upon request by the guarantor or pledgor.

Scientific research

[12.10]   Despite the duty of non-disclosure, a bank may disclose confidential information for the purposes of scientific research, provided that the disclosed documents are at least 60 years old. In addition, the recipient of confidential information must assure in writing that the information will not be used to harm the persons or infringe the rights of persons affected by such documents.

Legal proceedings

Legal proceedings involving the bank as a party

[12.11]   Despite the duty of non-disclosure, a bank may disclose to the court confidential information in connection with legal proceedings conducted by the customer against the bank or initiated by the bank against the customer (for instance, proceedings for collecting moneys owed by the customer to the bank). However, the disclosure is only allowed to the extent necessary in respect of each particular case.

If the bank litigates against its customer, the employee or official of the bank may, without the consent of such customer, disclose confidential information relating to such customer as a witness. In addition, other information subject to bank confidentiality may be disclosed if it is necessary for solving the matter.

Legal proceedings involving third parties

[12.12]   In addition, a bank may be involved in legal proceedings, for example, where the customers of the bank or a third party and the customer of the bank are parties to such proceedings.

The Procedural Code provides that a witness, such as an employee of the bank, has the right to refuse to disclose information to the court in connection with civil or criminal proceedings if such disclosure may lead to prosecution against the witness himself or persons close to him, as specified in the Procedural Code. The Procedural Code further provides that a witness has a right to refuse to disclose information related to a business or trade secret unless 'fundamentally significant reasons' require such disclosure. In practice, such fundamentally significant reasons may be deemed to exist in cases where, for example, an innocent person would be convicted for a crime without disclosure of such information. Thus, it is unlikely that the witness's right to refuse to disclose a business or trade secret would be overridden in civil proceedings by application of such 'fundamentally significant reasons' test. Furthermore, the witness is entitled to disclose confidential information if the customer has consented. Before giving testimony, the witness must declare that he is under the bank confidentiality obligation.

Under the Procedural Code, if a witness refuses to make the disclosure as described above, he must give pertinent grounds for the refusal. However, this may sometimes mean that, when explaining the reasons for the refusal, the witness would then release confidential information.

If the court orders the witness to disclose confidential information, it may decide that the witness shall be heard behind closed doors. In such a case, the court may declare that the trial documents which contain confidential information shall be kept secret for a fixed period of time.

The above also applies in cases where a confidential document is to be presented to the court or the employee or official of the bank is to be heard as an expert in court proceedings.

Arbitration proceedings

[12.13]   Under the Act on Arbitration Proceedings 1992, arbitrators can hear the parties, witnesses and experts (however, without taking an oath) and receive documents that may have relevance as evidence in arbitration proceedings. Nevertheless, the arbitrators are not vested with the power to impose conditional fines or use coercive measures in order to force the persons to testify or present evidence. The court of arbitration may, however, seek assistance from the ordinary courts. Where the parties, witnesses or experts are heard or evidence is presented before the ordinary courts in connection with arbitration proceedings, the above general rules that apply to the disclosure of confidential information in ordinary court proceedings also apply to the disclosure in arbitration proceedings.

Disclosure to authorities

Tax authorities

[12.14] According to the provisions of the Act on Taxation Procedure 1995, the Finnish tax authorities enjoy extensive rights to obtain, for the purposes of assessing taxes, confidential information on payments or transfers made by a person and the adjustments made to such payments or transfers, the identity of the recipient of such payments and transfers and the grounds for such payments and transfers. Specific disclosure provisions apply, inter alia, to securities intermediaries as to the trades made and the derivative contracts concluded, to credit and financial institutions as to loans granted and interest paid and to asset management companies for collective investment funds as to units owned by a person and the units redeemed.

Furthermore, the obligation to disclose information applies, generally, to third parties, like banks, as regards such information which may be relevant for tax assessment or dealing with a tax appeal and which information can be identified on the basis of a name, bank account details, an identified banking transaction or other similar means of identification. This obligation is based on a specified request made by the tax authorities and covers all such information which is in the possession of or otherwise known to a person, except for such information which the person is not entitled to disclose under the provisions of the Procedural Code.

In addition, a number of provisions in various specific tax statutes further specify the right of the tax authorities to obtain information. The scope of the information to be disclosed may thus depend on the particular tax statute which is applied to the individual case. However, information may only be disclosed to the extent necessary for the tax authorities to discharge their duties in connection with the taxation under the specific tax statute.

The tax authorities must make the request for the information in writing and the bank must not give any information orally. The request must be signed by the authority which is authorised to do so under the provisions of the relevant tax statute.

In certain circumstances the bank is obliged to refuse the disclosure of information to various authorities. This duty of refusal applies to the customer's business and trade secrets, unless special circumstances require the disclosure of such information. Such special circumstances could, for instance, involve reasonable suspicion of criminal conduct in relation to tax or bookkeeping matters in which the tax authority needs the information for the purposes of proof. Information on the financial standing of a customer must, nevertheless, always be given to the tax authorities upon request.

The tax authorities can also, pursuant to specific provisions in various tax statutes, obtain information by using the right to inspect documents controlled or in the possession of the bank that may contain the information required. Such right to inspect documents can be the only means of obtaining information and thus it is not necessary that the tax authorities request the disclosure of the information by the bank first. The tax authorities must, however, present their authorisation for the inspection of the documents, as well as identify the object and extent of the inspection in each case.

Certain provisions in various tax statutes entitle the tax authorities to carry out an inspection of documents solely for the purpose of collecting information which is to be used for comparing a person or entity with other persons or entities in connection with taxation. However, such inspection for the purposes of comparison cannot be carried out in respect of information held by a licensed credit institution or a branch in Finland of a foreign credit institution. Nevertheless, if a tax inspection has been carried out on a credit institution or a branch of a credit institution, information so received can be used in connection with the taxation of another person or entity.

The information to be disclosed by the bank must cover as long a period as the tax authority requests, provided that the bank still has the access to such information. As a rule, the bank has no right to refuse to disclose the information on the grounds, inter alia, that the time limit for the assessment of that particular taxation has lapsed.

Police and other criminal investigation authorities

[12.15] Under the provisions of the Credit Institutions Act, a bank is obliged to disclose confidential information to the public prosecutor, police authorities and other pre-trial investigation authorities, such as Finnish Customs and the Finnish Border Guard Service, for the purposes of solving a crime.

The request by the police and other pre-trial investigation authorities to the bank must be in writing and signed by such person who is authorised to do so by law. The request must be specified, including the grounds for, and the extent of, the request.

If a person employed by a bank or otherwise subject to bank confidentiality obligations is being questioned as a witness in a pre-trial investigation, this person must declare that he is under the confidentiality obligation. Such witness has the right to refuse to give information on a business or trade secret of a customer unless special circumstances otherwise require and he must give pertinent grounds for the refusal.

According to the Police Act 1995, the police authorities are entitled to obtain confidential information for the purposes of crime investigation and prevention. The request for information must also be in writing and signed by the police official who is authorised to do so under the Police Act and Police Decree. Such request must include the same information as described above.

The Police Act also provides that the police authorities are entitled to obtain confidential information in connection with a non-criminal investigation carried out by the police (for instance, locating a missing person) if an important public or private interest so requires. Again, the request must fulfil the same requirements as described above.

In addition, the prosecuting, police, customs and border guard authorities have the right to receive information on the book entry accounts from the Finnish Central Securities Depository plc. In cases where the information requested is not available, the Depository directs the request to the relevant bank.

In connection with a criminal investigation, funds and assets of a suspect person may be seized for the purposes of, inter alia, securing the payment of damages and the collection of profits from the criminal act which are to be confiscated. Additionally, documents may be seized to prevent such documents being lost or destroyed.

Supervisory and regulatory authorities

[12.16]   The supervisory and regulatory authorities of the banking industry enjoy very wide powers to receive from a bank (whose definition in this chapter is very wide indeed) information that is necessary for the authority to discharge its supervisory duties. According to the Act on Financial Supervision Authority 2003, the Financial Supervision Authority (the 'FSA'), the supervisory authority for the Finnish financial and banking markets, is thus entitled to obtain from banks all information, as well as to inspect and to receive copies of any necessary documents concerning the relevant bank and its customers, including information systems held by banks, which it deems necessary for the fulfilment of its supervisory duties. In addition to a bank, the managing director and any member of the board of directors or the supervisory board of the bank should, without undue delay, provide the FSA with information requested by it.

Further, the FSA is entitled to obtain information from any entity which is controlled by the bank, including a foreign branch or subsidiary (ie a branch located outside Finland) of a Finnish bank under its supervision or any entity which controls the Finnish bank. Such an authority can, naturally, lead to a conflict if, under local laws, such foreign branch of a Finnish bank would not be in a position to disclose the information requested by the FSA.

In connection with the implementation of the Market Abuse Directive on 1 July 2005, the Act on Financial Supervision Authority was supplemented to include specific provisions providing the FSA with a right to obtain certain specified information for the purposes of discharging its supervisory powers relating to market abuse.

Notwithstanding the confidentiality obligation referred to in the Act on Publicity of the Operations of Public Authorities, the FSA is, under the Act on Financial Supervision Authority, entitled to disclose information on the financial standing or business or trade secrets of a person or entity or on the private circumstances of a person to another supervisory authority of the financial markets and to a foreign authority or institution which, by virtue of law in its home country, performs a duty and is subject to a confidentiality obligation similar to that of the FSA. Furthermore, the FSA may disclose information to, inter alia, the pre-trial and prosecuting authorities for the purposes of solving a crime, as well as to other authorities as specified in the Act on Financial Supervision Authority.

A bank must also disclose to the Bank of Finland, upon request, all information and documents which are necessary for the carrying out by the Bank of Finland of its responsibilities as the central bank or for statistical purposes.

Execution/enforcement officials

[12.17]   Under the Execution/Enforcement Act, the execution/enforcement officials (bailiffs) have the right to obtain information on the debtor from a third party, including banks, in areas such as, for example, whether:

1   the third party possesses property belonging to the debtor and the nature of such property;
2   the third party has a receivable from the debtor (and vice versa) and the grounds and amount of such receivable, as well as certain additional related information; and

3   the third party has made an agreement or arrangement with or for the benefit of the debtor that may be significant when tracing the property of the debtor and the contents of such an agreement or arrangement.

The execution/enforcement officials may, if necessary, oblige the third party to disclose such information subject to a fine in cases of non-compliance.

The execution/enforcement officials are also entitled to receive information from other authorities on, inter alia, the financial standing of the debtor. Furthermore, the execution/enforcement officials are entitled to obtain information on the book entry accounts from the Finnish Central Securities Depository plc. In cases where the information requested is not available, the Depository directs the request to the relevant bank.

Further, the Execution/Enforcement Act includes detailed provisions providing the execution/enforcement officials with the right to disclose confidential information in certain cases. Confidential information may be disclosed, inter alia, to other execution/enforcement authorities and also, if there is any reason to suspect that the debtor may have committed a crime, to the prosecuting and pre-trial authorities. The Execution/Enforcement Act also includes provisions concerning the processing of information included in the register of enforcements, as well as the publicity and transferability of such information.

Other authorities

[12.18]   Various specific statutes in Finnish law entitle certain other authorities to obtain confidential information from the banks. For instance, in connection with the supervision of bankrupt estates, the supervisory authority for bankruptcies has rights similar to those of the debtor of the bankrupt estate to receive information with respect to such bankrupt estate.

Under the provisions of the Consumer Protection Act 1978, the consumer protection authorities have a right to obtain certain information from the banks. Furthermore, competition authorities and, for instance, social security authorities have certain rights to obtain information as well.

MONEY LAUNDERING AND FINANCING OF TERRORISM

[12.19]   The focal statute containing the provisions on the prevention and clearing of money laundering and financing of terrorism is the Money Laundering Act. The provisions of the Money Laundering Act have been specified by a 'Decree on Preventing and Clearing Money Laundering' issued by the Ministry of the Interior in 2003 and the regulations and guidelines included in the standard (no 2.4) on identifying and knowing customers, as well as preventing money laundering, financing of terrorism and market abuse, issued by the FSA in 2005. Furthermore, money laundering and financing of terrorism constitute criminal acts under the Penal Code. The Finnish rules and regulations are based, generally, on the EC Anti-Money Laundering Directives (91/308/EEC and 2001/97/EC) and the recommendations by the Financial Action Task Force on Money Laundering ('FATF') (ie the recommendations in force prior to the FATF 40 recommendations of 2003).

The objective of the Money Laundering Act is to prevent money laundering and financing of terrorism and to enhance their uncovering and investigation, as well as to strengthen the tracing and recovery of benefits gained from criminal activity. The Money Laundering Act introduces a mechanism for reporting suspicious transactions and concentrates the investigation of all suspected money laundering/financing of terrorism cases to a single authority, a special unit of the Central Criminal Police called the Money Laundering Clearing House (the 'Clearing House'). The Money Laundering Act includes provisions on, inter alia, customer identification, duty to keep records, detection and reporting of unusual or suspicious business transactions, due diligence to be observed and procedures to be applied to protect the financial system against criminal abuse. In addition to the banks, a large number of entities are subject to, inter alia, the identification and reporting obligations contained in the Money Laundering Act.

The Money Laundering Act sets out a requirement for a bank to verify, unless an exemption applies, the identity of its regular customers or, where such customer acts on behalf of a third party, the identity of such third party. The expression 'regular customer' refers to a customer with a long-term business relationship (for example, opening an account or entering into a loan agreement). The identity of a non-regular customer must be verified if the total value of a single transaction or several connected transactions exceeds the equivalent of 15,000 euros. However, the identity of a customer, whether regular or not, must always be verified if there is any reason to suspect the lawful origin of the funds or other property in the transaction or the use of such funds or other property to finance (or attempt to finance) terrorism. Further provisions concerning customer identification are included, inter alia, in the Credit Institutions Act, the Act on Investment Firms and the Investment Funds Act, as well as in the above standard issued by the FSA. The Credit Institutions Act provides that the banks must be familiar with the nature of their customers' business operations and the reasons for the customers' need for services provided by the banks. Similar duty to exercise due diligence is laid down in the Money Laundering Act.

As regards exemptions from the identification obligation, there is no need to verify the identity if the customer is a credit or financial institution, an investment firm or a life insurance company licensed in a member state of the EEA or a branch office located within the EEA of a credit or financial institution, an investment firm or a life insurance company not licensed in a member state of the EEA. Furthermore, customer identification is not necessary if the customer is a credit or financial institution, an investment firm or a life insurance company licensed in such a country outside the EEA, the legislative and administrative systems for preventing and clearing money laundering and financing of terrorism of which fulfil international standards, or a branch office located in such a country of a credit or financial institution, an investment firm or a life insurance company licensed elsewhere.

Banks must keep records of customer identification data in a reliable manner for a period of at least five years after the termination of each business transaction or business relationship.

If there is a reason to believe that the funds or other property used in a transaction have an unlawful origin or will be used to finance terrorism, the bank shall either discontinue the transaction for further investigation or refuse to undertake it and inform the Clearing House. The bank must assess, on a case-by-case basis, when a transaction is to be considered unusual or suspicious, based on overall experiences in the financial sector. The Clearing House will thereafter investigate the matter if deemed necessary. The Clearing House may also order the relevant entity not to complete the transaction for a period not exceeding five banking days if necessary for carrying out the investigation. The filing of the report may not be tipped off to the suspected customer, nor to any other parties.

Under the Money Laundering Act, a person who wilfully or through negligence breaches, inter alia, his reporting obligation, obligation to identify customers or to keep records, or unlawfully tips off the filing of the report with the Clearing House, will be sanctioned with a fine.

On the other hand, in the case of an unfounded reporting to the Clearing House, suspension of a business transaction or refusal to effect a business transaction, a bank may become liable to compensate for the possible financial loss incurred by the customer. Liability for the loss does not arise if the bank or its employee has exercised reasonable diligence before taking the measures in question.

Under the Penal Code, the underlying criminal offences which may give raise to the money laundering offence are described by reference to any offence and thus are not linked to either a category of seriousness of the offences or minimum penalty of imprisonment applicable to the underlying offences, nor to any specific underlying offences. The maximum penalty for a money laundering offence is imprisonment for six years or, if the act is minor, the penalty may be a fine. The maximum penalty for an offence of financing of terrorism is imprisonment for up to eight years. Attempting to carry out these offences is also a crime. It is also clearly stated in the Penal Code that, in addition to individuals, corporate entities may also be charged with these offences.

The Finnish anti-money laundering legislation is due to be extensively reformed by the end of 2007 in connection with the implementation of the Third Anti-Money Laundering Directive (2005/60/EC), which incorporates into EU law the 2003 revision of the 40 recommendations of the FATF. The Finnish Ministry of Home Affairs has appointed a working group to prepare a proposal for the amendments to Finnish legislation to implement this Directive. Currently, the Money Laundering Act only includes certain elements of the 40 recommendations of 2003, but the recommendations are intended to be incorporated into Finnish legislation in connection with the above reform. For example, provisions concerning customer due diligence need to be amended.

Based on information received from the FSA, in 2007, the FATF will carry out an evaluation in Finland which will set out Finland's levels of compliance with the 40 recommendations of 2003. Unfortunately, it seems that the reform of the relevant Finnish legislation will not have been implemented by such evaluation.

SANCTIONS FOR CUSTOMERS

[12.20]   A breach by a person of the confidentiality obligation contained in the Credit Institutions Act (or, inter alia, the Act on Investment Firms or the Securities Market Act) is a criminal act. Sanctions include a fine and/or imprisonment for a maximum period of one year, unless the breach is of minor importance or more severe sanctions apply under other legislation. In addition, under the general principles of criminal law, profit made from criminal activity may be confiscated.

Pursuant to the provisions of the Act on Torts 1974, a breach of the confidentiality provisions may lead to the obligation to compensate any damage or loss caused by the breach. The Securities Market Act, the Credit Institutions Act, the Act on Investment Firms and the Act on Supervision of Finance and Insurance

Conglomerates include specific provisions on the liability to compensate for loss or damage in the case of a breach of the provisions in these Acts, including the confidentiality provisions.

Under Finnish law, monetary damages are the general remedy available for a person who has suffered financial loss or damage to property as a consequence of another person's negligent action. In the case of a breach of the confidentiality provisions, damages are often not a very adequate remedy, as the very disclosure of the confidential information in breach of the confidentiality obligations may in itself be the most damaging injury caused. The injured party may also find it difficult to quantify such damage/loss in monetary terms. Exemplary or punitive damages are, however, not available under Finnish law. On the other hand, disclosure of confidential information may often take place without the advance knowledge of the person concerned so that no remedy other than damages can be applied.

However, should the person become aware of the danger of an unauthorised disclosure by a bank, he may file an application for an injunction by the District Court having jurisdiction in the matter. Such an injunction can be given, initially, as an interim measure without hearing the party against which the injunction is to be addressed, ie the bank. According to the Procedural Code, injunction proceedings are to be dealt with expeditiously by the court.

If a bank in its operations fundamentally breaches any banking acts, decrees or regulations given by the authorities by virtue of such acts or decrees, including non-disclosure obligations, the licence of the bank may be revoked by the Ministry of Finance upon the proposal of the FSA or the operations of the bank may be restricted for a certain period of time.

As regards the operations of foreign banks in Finland, the FSA (or in the case of a non-EEA bank, the Ministry of Finance) may order a branch or representative office of a foreign bank in Finland to discontinue its operations in Finland if such branch or representative office is fundamentally or repeatedly in breach of Finnish banking legislation or regulations. Alternatively, the operations of the branch may be restricted for a certain period of time. Furthermore, if the branch has not complied with the relevant laws, regulations and byelaws, the branch may be dismissed from the membership of the Finnish Investor Protection Fund.

CROSS-BORDER/EXTRA-TERRITORIAL ISSUES
Foreign supervisory bodies

[12.21] The Act on Operations in Finland of a Foreign Credit and Financial Institution provides that, despite the duty of non-disclosure set out in the Credit Institutions Act, a branch or representative office in Finland of a foreign credit or financial institution has the right to disclose to the supervisory or other authorities or auditors of the credit or financial institution of the relevant home country such information which, in accordance with the home country statute or pursuant to an appropriate home country order, is to be disclosed.

Under the Act on Financial Supervision Authority, a supervisory authority of a country within the EEA is, subject to a prior notification to the FSA, entitled to carry out (or have a third party to carry out on its behalf) an inspection in a branch in Finland of a credit or financial institution, an investment firm or an asset management company for collective investment funds of that EEA country if such inspection is necessary for the supervision of the relevant credit or financial institution, investment firm or asset management company for collective investment funds. Upon request by a supervisory authority of an EEA country, the FSA may within its competence carry out an inspection in a branch in Finland of a credit or financial institution, an investment firm or an asset management company for collective investment funds from such EEA country or otherwise supervise or inspect such branch.

The Act on Financial Supervision Authority also includes provisions concerning co-operation between the FSA and a foreign authority relating to the inspections in, and the right to receive information from, a Finnish company belonging to a consolidation group of a foreign credit institution or investment firm or to certain foreign financial and insurance conglomerates.

Foreign tax authorities

[12.22]   A bank in Finland is not generally obliged to disclose any information to the authorities for the purposes of taxation in a country other than Finland. However, Finland is a party to a number of multilateral and bilateral tax conventions and treaties regarding mutual exchange of information and provision of assistance by the tax authorities of the convention/treaty countries.

Under a convention between the Nordic countries concluded in 1989 and effected in Finland in 1991, tax authorities in the Nordic countries (ie Finland, Sweden, Denmark, Norway and Iceland) have agreed to assist each other in obtaining information. Such assistance to other Nordic tax authorities will be provided by the Finnish tax authorities in accordance with the provisions regulating the right by the Finnish tax authorities to obtain such information for domestic purposes. Further, in April 1995, Finland entered into a Convention on Mutual Administrative Assistance in Tax Matters between OECD and EC member states concluded in 1988. Currently, the member states to the OECD/EC Convention are, in addition to Finland, Azerbaijan, Belgium, Denmark, France, Iceland, Italy, Norway, Poland, Sweden, the Netherlands and the USA. A request by the relevant authority of a member state shall always be delivered to the relevant Finnish authority and will then be addressed to the relevant bank by the Finnish authority.

Under the OECD/EC Convention, the member states agreed to provide exchange of information and administrative assistance to each other in tax matters. A member state must, upon request, provide another member state with information concerning a particular person or transaction. If the information available in the tax files of the requested state is not sufficient to enable it to comply with the request for information, that state must take all relevant measures to provide the applicant state with the information requested. However, the member state is not under an obligation to carry out such measures which would not be allowed under its own laws or administrative practice or such measures which it considers to be contrary to public policy or essential interests. Further, any trade, business, industrial, commercial or professional secrets need not be disclosed. This list of secrets does not, basically, cover bank confidentiality. Rather, it is at the discretion of a member state to determine whether to provide information subject to bank confidentiality. It is, however, to be assessed whether there is, in an individual case, a need to protect the interests of the relevant person liable to tax in Finland.

Furthermore, Finland has concluded a number of bilateral tax treaties which, typically, contain provisions on exchange of information and mutual assistance in tax matters. However, matters covered by bank secrecy may have been excluded in some bilateral treaties.

Mutual assistance in criminal matters

[12.23] Finland has ratified the European Convention on Mutual Assistance in Criminal Matters 1959 subject, however, to a reservation which may exclude assistance in circumstances where the subject crime is under investigation in Finland or in a third country, the person who is prosecuted in the country requesting assistance has been convicted or acquitted or is currently being prosecuted in Finland or in a third country, prosecution or investigation against the person has been dropped or suspended in Finland or in a third country or the prosecution of the crime or the enforcement of the sentence would be time barred under Finnish law.

In addition, the Act on International Assistance in Criminal Matters 1994 deals with assistance to be provided, generally, by the Finnish authorities in criminal matters. Pursuant to the Act, Finland may provide assistance to foreign authorities for various purposes like hearing of witnesses, production of documents or securing the enforcement of confiscation orders. The relevant authority to deal with requests for assistance is the Ministry of Justice to whom any requests should be addressed by the relevant foreign authority. A properly compiled and presented request should lead to assistance being provided in accordance with, and subject to, the restrictions of Finnish law. Assistance should be provided 'without delay' and, if possible, by observing the time terms expressed in the request, as stated in the Act.

However, assistance must be refused if the assistance would breach the sovereignty or would endanger the security of Finland or her essential interests. Assistance must also be refused if such assistance would be contrary to the principles of human or civil rights or the principles of Finnish law. Furthermore, assistance may be refused, inter alia, if the underlying criminal act is a political or military offence and if, pursuant to provisions of Finnish criminal law, no prosecution could be mounted because of time bar or other similar circumstances, the matter is pending before the pre-trial investigators, prosecutor or a court in Finland or in a third country or if the costs for the assistance in relation to the offence concerned would be unreasonable.

When hearing a witness for the purposes of providing assistance to authorities in a foreign country, the witness shall enjoy the rights to refuse to disclose the information as enjoyed under Finnish law or under the laws of the country requesting assistance. Furthermore, despite the duty of non-disclosure provided by Finnish law, confidential documents may be transferred for the purposes of proof in foreign criminal proceedings unless Finnish law prohibits or restricts the use of confidential information or document as proof or the transfer of confidential information or document to a foreign country.

The Act on the Execution in the European Union of Orders Freezing Property or Evidence, with effect from 2 August 2005, implements the Council Framework Decision of 22 July 2003 of the same name in Finland. The purpose of the Framework Decision is to establish the rules under which an EU member state shall recognise and execute in its territory a freezing order relating to such property that could be subject to confiscation or evidence issued by a juridical authority of another EU member state in connection with criminal proceedings (in Finland, the above freezing orders include prohibition of disposal, seizure and confiscation as security ordered by a court or prosecutor).

Mutual assistance in civil matters

[12.24] Finland has ratified a number of multilateral conventions to facilitate legal proceedings of an international character, including the Hague Convention on the Taking of Evidence Abroad in Civil and Commercial Matters 1970. However, when incorporated in Finnish law, the application of the pre-trial discovery of documents procedure, as set out in art 23 of the Convention, was excluded to the extent that such procedure would oblige someone to identify the documents in his possession which are relevant to the subject matter or to deliver documents, other than those expressly named in the request, which can be assumed, with reason, to be in his possession.

The authority in Finland which deals with requests by foreign authorities under the Convention is the Ministry of Justice. The Convention contains, in art 12, the grounds on which a formally appropriate request for assistance may be refused. There are only two grounds for such refusal, ie the measure for which assistance is requested is beyond the powers of the authority in Finland and Finland considers that the requested measure would be a breach against her sovereignty or security.

Similarly, Finland has also ratified, inter alia, the Hague Conventions 1954 and 1965, although the earlier conventions have been largely replaced by the 1970 Convention.

A convention between the Nordic countries which covers, inter alia, assistance in obtaining testimony or other evidence was entered into in 1974 and became law in Finland in 1975.

An Act on the Co-operation between Finnish and Foreign Authorities in Court Proceedings and Enforcement of Judgments in Certain Cases was enacted in 1921.

Enforcement of foreign judgments and arbitral awards

[12.25] As a rule, a foreign judgment is not enforceable in Finland unless a specific EU regulation or a bilateral or multilateral treaty or convention provides otherwise.

Enforcement in Finland of a foreign judgment or an arbitral award may also involve a bank confidentiality dimension if, for example, a customer of a Finnish bank obtains a court judgment or arbitral award outside Finland which orders the bank to release a document to the customer.

In the case of a judgment given by a foreign court in an EU or EEA state, such judgment may be enforceable under the provisions and subject to the restrictions of the Lugano Convention, the Brussels Convention or the EC regulation on jurisdiction and the recognition and enforcement of judgments in civil and commercial matters (44/2001/EC). Further, the provisions of the Convention Between the Nordic Countries on the Recognition and Enforcement of Judgments in Civil Matters and the bilateral Convention Between Finland and Austria on the Recognition and Enforcement of Judgments in Civil Matters may be relied on in relation to matters to which the above council regulation does not apply. The EC regulation on co-operation between the courts of the member states in the taking of evidence in civil or commercial matters (1206/2001/EC), which has been in force since 1 July 2001, became fully applicable on 1 July 2004.

Foreign arbitral awards are recognised and enforceable in Finland under the provisions of the Act on Arbitration Proceedings and the New York Convention 1958.

REGULATION OF FINANCIAL MARKETS
Market abuse

[12.26] As of 1 July 2005, the provisions on insider dealing and market manipulation based on the Market Abuse Directive (2003/6/EC) are contained in the Securities Market Act and the Penal Code. Misuse of inside information and market manipulation is prohibited and sanctioned pursuant to two alternative systems. Offences committed deliberately with the intention of obtaining benefit and, in the case of misuse of inside information, also by gross negligence, constitute criminal offences under the Penal Code. However, prohibitions against the use of inside information and market manipulation are also included in the Securities Market Act. A breach of the prohibitions set out in the Securities Market Act is subject to administrative proceedings, whilst a breach of the prohibitions set out in the Penal Code is subject to criminal proceedings.

Insider dealing

[12.27] The Securities Market Act defines inside information as information of a precise nature relating to a security which is subject to public trade or traded on an alternative trading system, as specified in the Securities Market Act, which information has not been made public or has otherwise been unavailable to the market and is likely to have a material effect on the value of the security. The Securities Market Act provides that inside information may not be used to acquire or dispose of, directly or indirectly, for one's own account or for the account of another, a security to which inside information relates, or directly or indirectly to advise another in their trade. The Securities Market Act also prohibits unauthorised dissemination of inside information.

Pursuant to the Penal Code, a person who wilfully or through gross negligence makes use of inside information relating to a security which is subject to public trade or an alternative trading system in order to acquire material benefit for himself or for another (i) by disposing of or acquiring such security for himself or on behalf of another or (ii) by directly or indirectly advising another in their trade, will be sanctioned for misuse of inside information with a fine or imprisonment for a maximum period of two years or, in the case of gross misuse, four years. In addition, an attempt to misuse inside information constitutes a criminal offence. In the case of an offence committed by a legal entity, such as a bank, criminal sanctions may be imposed on the physical persons that have acted on behalf of the legal entity. In addition, corporate fines may be imposed on the legal entity. Further, both legal entities and physical persons may incur civil liability for any loss or damage caused and any profit made may be confiscated.

As to the disclosure requirements, the holding of shares and other securities entitling to such shares which are subject to public trade and other securities entitling to such securities, as well as securities the value of which is based on the above securities, must be disclosed where the owner is a statutory insider listed in the Securities Market Act. On 1 July 2005, the scope of the rules on statutory insiders included in the Securities Market Act was widened to include, in addition to the management of a Finnish listed company, for instance, persons in a managerial position who regularly have access to inside information, as well as persons closely related to insiders. The Securities Market Act includes detailed provisions on the information that must be disclosed.

Further, the provisions of the Securities Market Act on insider registers oblige an issuer of listed securities to maintain a public insider register containing information on statutory insiders' securities portfolios. An issuer of listed securities is also required to publish on its website up to date information on statutory insiders' securities portfolios and any changes in that regard for a 12-month period. In addition, an issuer of listed securities is under an obligation to prepare a company-specific non-public insider register with respect to employees and persons who regularly, or in connection with specific projects, have access to inside information. Such an obligation is also extended to entities acting for or on behalf of the issuer. In preparing a company-specific insider register, (i) employees who have access to inside information on a regular basis due to their position or duties with the issuer shall be registered and (ii) other persons otherwise having access to inside information must also be registered.

Market manipulation

[12.28]   New provisions defining and prohibiting market manipulation are contained in the Securities Market Act. Market manipulation is defined to be:

1   a misleading offer to sell or buy, a fictitious trade in, or another act of bad faith concerning, a security which is subject to public trade or traded on an alternative trading system;
2   business or other activities that provide false or misleading information on the supply, demand or price of a security which is subject to public trade or traded on an alternative trading system;
3   business or other activities by means of which one or more persons co-operating with each other place the price of a security which is subject to public trade or traded on an alternative trading system at an unusual or artificial level; or
4   the publishing or other distribution of false or misleading information concerning a security which is subject to public trade or traded on an alternative trading system if the publisher or distributor of the information knew or ought to have known the information to be false or misleading.

There are exemptions from the above prohibition of market manipulation concerning, for example, market making and securities dealing services offered by a securities intermediary.

Market manipulation is sanctioned under the Penal Code. The Penal Code provides that a person who manipulates the price of a security which is subject to public trade or an alternative trading system, in order to acquire material benefit for himself or for another, will be sanctioned for market manipulation with a fine or imprisonment for a maximum period of two years or, for serious misuse, four years.

Requirement to report suspicious securities transactions

[12.29]   Following the implementation of the Market Abuse Directive on 1 July 2005, the Securities Market Act provides that a bank, when having reason to suspect that misuse of inside information or market manipulation, as referred to in the Securities Market Act or the Penal Code, may relate to a business activity, is obliged, without delay, to report such a suspicious transaction to the FSA. The bank is not allowed to reveal the filing of the report to the party subject to suspicion nor to anyone else. In 2005, the FSA issued a standard (no RA2.1) on notifying the FSA of suspicious securities transactions and other suspect transactions.

Chinese Walls/information barriers and their effect

[12.30] A bank operating in Finland may often find itself in a difficult and, indeed, delicate situation as confidential information is continuously obtained by the various departments/subsidiaries of the bank. For example, a department/subsidiary of the bank may be advising on a contemplated merger of a company, whilst another department/subsidiary of the bank is simultaneously providing broker–dealer services on the securities issued by the company, or perhaps asset management services involving shares in the company or, indeed, the bank may be carrying out proprietary trades in the shares. Considering the relatively small number of commercial banks and investment banks operating in Finland (although, especially, London and New York-based commercial banks and investment banks are also often engaged in mergers and acquisitions and capital market transactions involving Finnish companies), situations with a potential conflict aspect are not rare for the banks.

Questions relating to the segregation of securities business functions, ie the so-called 'Chinese Wall', have not been expressly regulated in Finnish law. However, guidance may be sought in the conduct of business rules which a securities intermediary (whose definition for the purposes of this chapter is equivalent to the definition of the bank used here) must observe, as well as in the 'Guideline on Segregation of Securities Business Functions' issued by the FSA in 1998

According to the conduct of business rules included in the Securities Market Act, a securities intermediary is under an obligation to execute the orders diligently, in the interests of the customer and without undue delay. Furthermore, a securities intermediary must aim at avoiding conflicts of interest and, in case they occur, treat its customers fairly and equally. The own interests of the securities intermediary or the interests of a customer or an issuer must not affect the advice given by the securities intermediary to another customer or the way of effecting the order. Accordingly, a potential conflict situation may arise not only between the bank and the customer, but also between the customers of the bank.

The 'Guideline on Segregation of Securities Business Functions' is applicable to credit institutions and investment firms licensed in Finland or having a branch in Finland. According to the guideline, due segregation of functions presupposes measures to be taken to limit the transmission of information relating to financial instruments and customers within the firm or the group. The purpose of arranging business functions in a segregated manner is, according to the guideline, to allow the firm to engage in several business activities without giving rise to conflicts of interest between the firm and its customers or between the customers. Further, the segregation of functions serves to prevent misuse of inside information.

The guideline provides that firms shall obtain a confidentiality undertaking to be signed by all individuals with access to confidential information and that those undertakings be renewed at appropriate intervals. In conjunction with renewals of such confidentiality undertakings, the personnel shall be appraised of the applicable statutes and legal sanctions concerning breaches of secrecy. Furthermore, access to parts of internal computer networks should be limited so that only individuals handling securities functions on behalf of customers have access to the relevant customer files.

The guideline requires that at least the following functions be segregated

1   any activities dealing with inside information, such as investment banking and financial advice services;

2   asset management functions;
3   proprietary trading on the bank's own account (including market making);
4   intermediary trading on behalf of customers; and
5   safe custody and the maintenance of a book entry register.

The solution applied by the Finnish banks to deal with the above requirements has been, primarily, separation (on physical, organisational and personnel levels) of those operations where the cross-distribution/access of confidential information obtained by the bank could endanger a customer's interests in relation to the bank or to another customer of the bank or could expose the bank to allegations of insider dealing, ie a Chinese Wall arrangement. Such measures may have meant, in practice, restricted access by the members of the staff to premises or to IT systems of the bank other than those required for their duties, clear definitions of the areas of responsibility for the managers and directors of the bank and also, generally, advising, training and supervising staff in the relevant matters.

Some banks have transferred their investment banking, securities intermediation, asset management and proprietary trading operations into separate subsidiary companies with their own personnel, which companies may also operate from premises entirely separate from the banking premises. In certain cases, the potential problem may be avoidable by a disclosure to the customer of the existence of the potential conflict. By obtaining the customer's consent, the bank can conduct the business as disclosed.

FURTHER REGULATIONS
Data protection

[12.31]   The processing of files comprising personal data is regulated by the Personal Data Act, which implements the EC Data Protection Directive (95/46/EC) in Finland. The scope of application of the Personal Data Act is limited to the processing of personal data in cases where the 'controller' of files is established in Finland or otherwise is subject to Finnish law. A controller is defined as a person or body for the use of whom a personal data file is set up and that is entitled to determine on the use of the file.

Under the Personal Data Act, personal data is defined to mean any personal information or any information on personal characteristics or personal circumstances based on which an individual person (the data subject) or the members of the family or the household of the data subject can be identified. The processing of personal data is defined as, inter alia, collection, recording, storage, use, combination and transfer of personal data.

The personal data to be collected and recorded must be limited to such data that is relevant for the operations of the collector (the connection requirement) and necessary for the purpose of the file in question (the necessity requirement). In the absence of the explicit consent of the data subject, under the connection requirement, personal data may only be collected and recorded provided that a relevant connection based on a customer, service, membership or other similar relationship exists between the data subject and the operations of the collector. Strict rules apply to the processing of personal identity numbers and sensitive personal data.

The personal data may be disclosed if the data subject has unambiguously consented to the disclosure. In the absence of the explicit consent of the data subject, under the above connection requirement, personal data may only be disclosed if such disclosure is a regular feature of the operations concerned and if the purpose for which the data is disclosed is not incompatible with the purposes of the processing and if it can be assumed that the data subject is aware of such disclosure. Furthermore, personal data may only be transferred to a country outside the EU or EEA in specific cases, inter alia, if the data subject has unambiguously consented to the transfer of his personal data or if the country in question guarantees an adequate level of data protection, as from time to time resolved by the European Commission.

According to the Personal Data Act, furthermore, a controller is under an obligation to compile a description of the personal data file indicating, inter alia, the controller's contact information, the purpose of the processing of the personal data, a description of the group of persons the data of which shall be recorded, including a description of the information to be collected, the regular destinations of disclosed data and whether data is transferred to countries outside the EU or the EEA and a description of the principles in accordance to which the data file has been secured. As a general rule, the above description must be submitted to the Finnish Data Protection Ombudsman and also be kept publicly available.

CURRENT STATUS OF BANK CONFIDENTIALITY

[12.32]   During the last decade, a number of legislative reforms concerning bank confidentiality were implemented in Finland. In addition, market developments such as the internationalisation and increasing cross-border nature of the banking industry, the EU legislation, the consolidation of the banking industry, the litigations during the 1990s and the expansion of information technology, including Internet banking, have had an impact on bank confidentiality. This trend has taken the direction of restricting the scope of bank confidentiality and it is to be expected that this trend will also continue in the future.

13   France

Jean-François Adelle

THE NATURE AND EXTENT OF THE BANKER'S DUTY OF CONFIDENTIALITY

Source

[13.1]   The banker's duty of confidentiality has had a long evolution, starting as early as 1810 with art 378 of the Penal Code which imposed sanctions upon people, such as doctors, who disclosed confidential information.

For more than a century, even though a tendency grew in favour of the application of the duty of confidentiality, it remained doubtful whether this provision could apply to bankers. In 1922, it was considered that this provision applied to stockbrokers. A step forward was then made in 1973 by the law on the Banque de France, which specified that their agents and employees were bound by a duty of confidentiality and that the sanctions of art 378 of the Penal Code would apply in the event of a breach of such duty.

In 1984, when the entire organisation of banks in France was revised, it was made clear that art 378 applied to 'any member of a board of directors and, if any, of a supervisory board and any person who in whatever capacity takes part in the management or operation of a bank or is employed by a bank' (art 511-33 of the Monetary and Financial Code, 'MFC'). It should be noted that, in 1994, art 378 of the Penal Code was replaced by art 226-13 of the New Penal Code, but the new wording of this article does not entail any modification of the definition of the offence. However, the applicable penalties have been increased.

The duty of confidentiality is justified by the protection of private life and patrimonial interests of clients and also by the protection of the financial markets and security of transactions because the disclosure of confidential information may result in insider dealing and affect the trust of investors. Therefore, the duty of confidentiality regulates both the disclosure and abuse of confidential information.

The banker's duty of confidentiality has been limited by a number of exemptions defined by case law or statute. In particular, it is limited by powers of the supervising authorities and, since 1990, legislation against money laundering.

It should be noted that the Law of 2 July 1996, which implemented the EC Directive on investment services,[1] requires credit establishments and investment enterprises to provide for obligations regarding the circulation of confidential information in internal regulations. However, the notion of confidential information referred to in

---

1 Council Directive 93/22/EEC.

the Law is not the same as the duty of confidentiality which applies exclusively to banks.

The scope of the duty of confidentiality

With respect to the information

[13.2]   The duty of confidentiality applies to non-public information confided to the bank by its client or a third party or which the bank has knowledge of in the course of its professional activity. However, it does not apply to all information which banks may receive.

Although the law does not distinguish, it appears that only information relating to bank operations is subject to the duty of confidentiality. The following are considered bank operations: the receipt of funds, the granting of loans and the management of means of payment. However, it is unclear whether information relating to ancillary operations (such as exchange, custody or distribution of securities, assistance and advice in portfolio management and financial engineering) are covered by the banker's duty of confidentiality. The criminal courts tend to consider such information to be subject to the bank's duty of confidentiality,[2] but a commercial judge considered information disclosed with respect to a company to a potential purchaser as not being of a banking nature.

Furthermore, according to French law, the duty of confidentiality of banks only covers specific information with respect to the amount shown by an account, transactions carried out by the client or the client's financial statements, as opposed to general information relating to the client's solvency (for example, regular payments, protests, non-compliance with maturity dates, cheques returned unpaid, etc). In accordance with bank usage, banks may therefore provide general information to clients or other banks asking for 'references' with respect to the financial situation of a company with which one is intending to do business, but they have no obligation to respond. However, the bank could be held liable if it does not communicate information in accordance with the reservation, objectivity and the rules in usage in the profession (in particular, the banker would be liable if he negligently communicated inaccurate information).

The communication of a list of clients with their names, addresses and account numbers could be seen as a breach of the duty of confidentiality.[3]

With respect to the persons subject to the confidentiality obligation

[13.3]   The confidentiality obligation applies to members of the board or supervisory board of a financial institution or to any person involved in any respect in the direction or management of a financial institution or employed by such a person.

With respect to the persons entitled to confidential information

[13.4]   The banker's duty of confidentiality aims to protect the client against disclosure of confidential information. Therefore, the client is admitted to share

2 Cass Crim, 25 January 1977.
3 Rennes, 13 January 1992.

confidential information. He is entitled to receive all information regarding transactions carried out with the bank. However, as regards cheques, banks may refuse to disclose information on the back of the cheque which contains details of the presenting bank and the account number of the payee. Neither the members of the client's family (including a spouse) nor his creditors have access to such information.

However, by way of an exception to the above-mentioned rule, a few other persons are allowed to share the confidential information confided by a client to his banker:

1   when the client is an individual:
    (a)   the heirs of such individual,
    (b)   the legal guardian, and
    (c)   the co-holders of a joint bank account;
2   when the client is a legal entity:
    (a)   its legal representative,
    (b)   the members of the board of directors or of the managing board and the supervisory board. However, it is generally considered that they should act jointly. Nevertheless, some authors deny them any right to share confidential information because they do not represent the company,
    (c)   the statutory auditors, and
    (d)   shareholders having unlimited liability for corporate debts. Such shareholders are entitled to receive information on the corporation's financial situation. Shareholders with limited liability have no right to share confidential information.

The company administrator will have the same rights as the legal representative if the court decision appointing him entrusts him with management powers. During the observation phase of bankruptcy proceedings, the receiver in bankruptcy (*administrateur judiciaire*) does not represent the company, but if the bankruptcy court orders the liquidation, the liquidator represents the company.

Moreover, there is no breach of the duty of confidentiality when the information is disclosed to a person who is bound by a duty of confidentiality such as another banker (according to art L 513-33 of the MFC, any officer of the board of directors, the managing board and the supervisory board and any other person who by reason of his office participates in the administration or management of the bank or is employed by it) or an employee of a supervisory authority such as the Banque de France.[4]

On the other hand, when the information is disclosed to a person outside the bank, there is breach of the duty of confidentiality.

Criminal sanctions

[13.5]   Article 226-13 of the New Penal Code now sets out the sanctions applicable to the breach of the duty of confidentiality formerly provided for by art 378 of the Penal Code. Accordingly, the breach by a bank of its duty of confidentiality is a criminal offence and may be punished by a year's imprisonment and a fine of up to 15,000 euros.

There are very few examples of criminal proceedings having been initiated against bankers.

---

4   Thus, a bank who reports fraudulent cheques to the Banque de France in compliance with art L 333-4 of the Consumer Code does not breach its duty of confidentiality.

Remedies

[13.6]   Should the breach of the duty of confidentiality cause the claimant to suffer a loss, the latter may claim damages. The general rules of tortious liability provided for in art 1382 of the Civil Code would apply. Accordingly, the claimant would have to establish that there has been fault, damage and a causal link between the two.

EXCEPTIONS TO THE BANKER'S DUTY OF CONFIDENTIALITY

[13.7]   There are several exceptions to the banker's duty of confidentiality and of various kinds.

The client's consent

[13.8]   While the criminal courts still seem to refuse to admit that a professional may be released from his duty of confidentiality by his client, the civil courts have adopted diverging views on this issue and held that the banker's duty of confidentiality was only aimed at the client's protection and that, accordingly, the client could waive such protection.

Most often, the issue arises in connection with actions brought by a court-appointed receiver of a bankrupt company before the President of a Commercial Court on the basis of art 145 of the New Code of Civil Procedure – which allows measures to be ordered to obtain various documents from third parties prior to any trial – to obtain from banks the disclosure of documents relating to the granting of loans to the debtor (for instance, balance sheet analysis and minutes of credit board meetings) in order to establish that the bank unduly and irregularly sustained its ailing client.

Until a Commercial Chamber of the Supreme Court (*Cour de Cassation*) 1995 precedent, disclosure could be ordered in favour of the court-appointed creditors' representative.[5] However, that solution was reversed by a 2002 decision of the Plenary Chamber of the Commercial Court, which held that the notion of the client consenting to the disclosure must be construed strictly in the context of a bankruptcy proceeding and does not benefit the sale plan commissioner (*commissaire à l'exécution du plan*) who represents the general interests of creditors.[6] As a result, banks are released from their duty of confidentiality only vis-à-vis the administrator (*administrateur judiciaire*) and the liquidator (*liquidateur judiciaire*) who represent the bankrupt debtor.

Compulsion of law

Criminal and civil proceedings

[13.9]   A banker may not invoke his duty of confidentiality when requested to provide evidence before a criminal court, including requests made by investigating magistrates or by police officers acting upon the instructions of such magistrates[7] (see art L 132-22 of the Criminal Code). However, when a banker appears before a

---

5 Cass Com, 11 April 1995.
6 Cass Com, 10 December 2002.
7 Cass Com, 27 April 1994.

civil or commercial court, a distinction must be made between whether the banker is requested to testify either as a witness or a party to the trial.

Before a civil or commercial court, a banker may, as a witness, only testify or disclose documents concerning his client, if his client agrees. However, there are three exceptions to this rule:

1   in the case of liquidation of matrimonial property (art 259-3 of the Civil Code);
2   in the case of conciliation, insolvency or bankruptcy proceedings, the commercial court or supervising judge (*juge commissiaire*) may request information from banks on the financial situation of the debtor (arts L 611-3 and L 621-55 of the Commercial Code). Upon instructions from the commercial court, the supervising judge may request similar information on the patrimony situation of the managers of the debtor. In the case of an insolvent individual, the Over-Indebted Individuals Commission (*Commission de surendettement des particuliers*) may also request information from banks on the financial situation of the debtor (art L 331-3, para 8 of the Consumer Code);
3   in the case of the attachment of an account (*saisie-attribution* or *saisie conservatoire*) by a client's creditor, where the bank is bound to declare the amount of money in the client's account on the day when the attachment is carried out (art 44 of Law n 91-650 of 9 July 1991) and cannot raise its duty of confidentiality.[8]

On the contrary, when a banker is a party to a trial before a civil or commercial court, he may testify or disclose information to the extent that such information is likely to be helpful for his defence. However, he may not rely on his duty of confidentiality for his own benefit as an excuse for refusing to provide information.[9]

Regulatory authorities

[13.10]   The banker's duty of confidentiality will not prevail either against inquiries from the *Commission Bancaire*, which is the regulatory authority for banking institutions, the Banque de France (art 511-33 of the MFC), the *Comité des Etablissements de Crédit et des Entreprises d'Investissement* ('CECEI'), which is competent to approve and strike from the list investment companies, credit institutions and to take individual decisions), or the Financial Markets Authority (*Autorité des Marchés Financiers*, 'AMF'), which assumes the previous powers of the *Conseil des Marchés Financiers* and the *Commission des Opérations de Bourse*.[10]

The AMF has access to all accounting documents, including particulars of any client's account. The fact that the information relates to an account held outside France is irrelevant provided that the information is available in France.

The agents of the AMF are themselves subject to a duty of confidentiality vis-à-vis the judicial authority acting in the course of criminal proceedings, the European

---

8 Cass 2nd Civ, 1 July 1999. Note that the creditor who has obtained an enforceable judgment and needs to know the names and addresses of the banks where accounts have been opened in the debtor's name in order to carry out the attachment of those accounts may ask the Public Prosecutor to obtain such information from the relevant banks.

9 Cass Com, 19 June 1990.

10 The *Autorité des Marchés Financiers*, established by the Financial Security Act of 1 August 2003, was formed from the merger of the *Commission des Opérations de Bourse*, the *Conseil des Marchés Financiers* and the *Conseil de Discipline de la Gestion Financière*.

Commission, foreign authorities subject to reciprocity and to their being bound by confidentiality obligations, Parliament and investigation commissions speakers, certain courts and other regulatory authorities.

The Competition Council (*Conseil de la Concurrence*) has access to all books, accounts and professional documents. However, banks are not authorised to disclose confidential information unless a visit by Competition Council agents has been authorised by the President of the Civil Court.

The National Institute for Statistics and Economic Studies (*Institut National des Statistiques et des Etudes Economiques*) and the National Commission of Computer Sciences and Liberties (*Commission Nationale Informatique et Libertés*) also have access to banks' information. However, they cannot obtain precise data on clients' accounts or operations.

Certain supervisory authorities are expressly authorised to communicate to each other all information necessary for the accomplishment of their duties: the Banque de France, the CECEI, the *Commission Bancaire*, the Insurance Control Commission (*Commission de contrôle des assurances*), the AMF, the Social Security Control Commission, the Deposits Guarantee Fund, the Insurance Guarantee Fund, market enterprises and clearance companies. All data so transmitted is subject to a duty of confidentiality under the conditions applicable both to the provider and recipient of the information.

Tax and customs authorities

[13.11]   Bankers have to declare to the authorities the opening and closing of accounts of any nature (art 1649A of the French Tax Code) and the date and amount of sums transferred outside France by individuals, associations and non-commercial companies. Furthermore, the French tax authorities have a right of access to the banks' books.

Customs authorities enjoy similar rights provided, however, the documents requested relate to the current or exceptional powers of the customs authorities.[11] However, the French social security administration has no right to banks' confidential information.

Police and other criminal investigators

[13.12]   Prior to the Banking Law 1984, police officers were not entitled to conduct investigations within banks. Article L 511-33 of the MFC states that the duty of confidentiality will not justify non-disclosure to 'the judicial authority acting in the course of criminal proceedings'.

The question therefore arose as to whether police officers may be regarded as a judicial authority. Article 75 of the Code of Criminal Procedure provides that officers and agents of the *police judiciaire* (who are defined in art 20 of the Code of Criminal Procedure) are authorised to conduct preliminary investigations either upon the Public Prosecutor's instructions or upon their own initiative. Such investigations are, in both cases, conducted under the control of the Public Prosecutor, who is a judicial authority.

11 Cass Crim, 3 May 2001.

The view is thus taken by some legal commentators that police officers are now authorised to request information from banks. Others think that police officers may only be regarded as a 'judicial authority' when acting on the Public Prosecutor's instructions. In practice, it is advisable for a bank to request the officer or agent to sign a declaration specifying his role and whether or not he is acting on the Public Prosecutor's instructions. Deputy police agents are not regarded as judicial authorities.

The fight against money laundering

[13.13]   The most recent exceptions to the banker's duty of confidentiality are related to the fight against organised crime, drug trafficking and terrorism. French rules applicable to money laundering are set out in Law n 90-614 of 12 July 1990 on the 'participation of financial institutions in the fight against money laundering and drug trafficking', subsequently amended by Law n 93-122 of 29 January 1993 on 'the prevention of corruption and the transparency of economic life and public proceedings', Law n 96-392 of 13 May 1996 on the 'fight against money laundering and drug trafficking and international co-operation relating to attachments and the confiscation of proceeds of crime', Law n 2001-420 of 15 May 2001 on 'new economic regulations', Law n 2001-1062 of 15 November 2001 on 'daily safety', as well as in the decrees of 13 February 1991, 25 September 2001, 2 February 2002 and 22 March 2002, Law n 2004-130 of 11 February 2004 (Official Journal of 12 February 2004) and Act n 2004-204 of 9 March 2004 adapting the judicial system to the evolution of crime (Official Journal of 10 March 2004 with effect from 1 October 2004). All such texts are codified under Book VI of the MFC.

The participation of banks in the fight against money laundering takes three forms:

1   the declaration of suspicions;
2   the duty of vigilance; and
3   the duty to check the identity of clients and keep information relating to them.

A bank may be subject to disciplinary sanctions if, following a gross lack of vigilance or non-compliance with its internal control procedures, it fails to meet its obligations.[12]

The declaration of suspicions

[13.14]   Article L 562-2 of the MFC compels banks to disclose any sum or transaction which may result from drug trafficking or organised crime, as well as any transactions carried out where the identity of the operator or beneficiary remains doubtful despite the care taken under art 563-3 of the MFC (see 'The Banker's Duty of Vigilance' below) or transactions effected with individuals or legal entities, including their subsidiaries or branches, acting as or on behalf of fiduciary funds or any management entity of a trust (*patrimoine d'affectation*) when the identity of the persons setting up the trust or beneficiary is unknown.

The provisions laid down in art L 562-2 of the MFC are extended to cover fraud against the financial interests of the European Communities, corruption and to money or transactions which might contribute to the financing of terrorism.[13] This

---

12 Cass 1st Civ, 2 November 2005.
13 Act n 2004-130 of 11 February 2004, art 70III and Act n 2004-204 of 9 March 2004, art 33VII I.

declaration is made to a department placed under the authority of the Ministry of Economy – called the 'TRACFIN' (*Traitement du renseignement et action contre les circuits financiers clandestins*) – set up in 1990 and composed of civil servants duly authorised by the minister.

Article L 562-1 of the MFC lists the institutions that are required to declare suspicions to the TRACFIN. Accordingly, the TRACFIN systematically informs the state prosecutor when there is evidence of organised criminal activity, corruption, defrauding European Community interests, drug trafficking and financing terrorism.[14]

The TRACFIN collects and assesses all relevant data and information contained in the declarations[15] and requests financial institutions to forward statements of the accounts of the relevant persons. If the information is likely to reveal money laundering activities, the TRACFIN will provide such information to the Public Prosecutor. The declarations may be oral and the identity of their author is not recorded in the file.

Any information likely to change the decision made by the TRACFIN or the bank at the time of the declaration must be disclosed immediately to the TRACFIN (art L 562-3 of the MFC).

Unauthorised disclosure of a declaration of suspicion to the person concerned is punishable by a fine (22,500 euros).[16] Moreover, it is forbidden for a banker to disclose to his client any information deriving from legal proceedings initiated against him and related to a declaration of suspicion.[17] However, lawyers at the *Conseil d'Etat*, the *Cour de Cassation* and the Court of Appeal are authorised to reveal to their clients (the owner of the sums or the initiator of one of the transactions referred to in art L 562-2 of the MFC) the existence of the declaration made to the department instituted by art L 562-4 or to divulge any information concerning the likely consequences.

The banker's duty of vigilance

[13.15]   French banks are at the forefront in the fight against money laundering as financial institutions are often used to launder dirty funds that derive from criminal activities. Therefore, it is significant to note that a major proportion of suspicious declarations come from banks (77.83%).[18]

Pursuant to art 563-3 of the MFC, the bank has a duty to check carefully any transaction which, although it may not seem to come from drug trafficking or organised crime, cumulatively meets the following three tests: (i) the transaction is

---

14 Article L 562-4 of the MFC.
15 The most recent data provided by the TRACFIN reveals an impressive increase in the number of declarations of suspicions:
 1,244 declarations of suspicions were made in 1998;
 1,655 declarations of suspicions were made in 1999;
 2,537 declarations of suspicions were made in 2000;
 3,598 declarations of suspicions were made in 2001;
 8,719 declarations of suspicions were made in 2002;
 9,019 declarations of suspicions were made in 2003;
 10,842 declarations of suspicions were made in 2004.
16 Article L 574-1 of the MFC, as amended.
17 Cass Com, 10 December 2003.
18 See the TRACFIN report on http://www.minefi.gouv.fr/tracfin/ressources/raptracfin2004.pdf.

for more than 150,000 euros and exceeds the amount of transactions usually carried out by the client, (ii) the transaction appears to be unusually complex and (iii) appears not to be economically grounded or have a lawful purpose.

The bank must request from its client the details of the origin and destination of these funds, as well as the purpose of the transaction and the identity of the beneficiary. The banks then records the details of the transaction to forward, upon request, either to the TRACFIN or the control authority.

In a decision of 5 March 2002,[19] the Paris Court of Appeal ruled that the unusual complexity must be assessed in practical terms. Sarl Moon had stolen a letter sent by another company to the tax authorities which included a cheque for FRF1,559,909 payable to the tax authorities and then withdrew FRF700,000 in several bank cheques. The court considered that the presentation of a cheque for FRF1,559,909 and the withdrawal of FRF700,000 in one day by means of bank cheques was unusually complex and without economic justification because Sarl Moon's account had never recorded any deposit or debit in excess of FRF100,000 and the company had never requested any bank cheques. The court therefore ordered Crédit Lyonnais to indemnify the company which had issued the stolen cheque. Thus, by ruling as it did, the Paris Court of Appeal disregarded the provisions of art L 563-3 of the MFC.

This decision was quashed by the High Court[20] (*Cour de Cassation*) on the ground that the duty of vigilance imposed upon banks and financial institutions (according to art L 563-3 of the MFC) was aimed at detecting transactions that may result from drug trafficking or organised crime.

Pursuant to arts L 563-5 and 563-6 of the MFC, the bank incurs administrative and disciplinary responsibility as a result of either a serious lack of diligence or a failure in the organisation of its internal verification procedures.

Only the TRACFIN and the bank supervisory authority are empowered to collect and assemble all the information needed to establish the origin of the sums or nature of the transaction which have been the subject of the declaration of suspicion. As a result, this information cannot be used for different purposes from those mentioned above. Consequently, the victim of such a fraud cannot rely on the non-compliance with these provisions to sue a bank for damages.

The banker's duty to know his clients

[13.16]   The duty of client confidentiality is one of the pillars of the banking sector. However, the movement towards transparency in the international business community is imposing new duties upon bankers to report to the relevant authorities suspicious transactions made by their clients.

The bank has an obligation to:

1   check the identity of its existing or new clients and keep a copy of an official document (such as the client's national identity card or passport);
2   check the identity of its clients or prospective clients who wish to remain anonymous who wish to carry out transactions exceeding 8,000 euros or wish to rent safety deposit boxes;

19 CA Paris 15, no 2001/03509, *SA Crédit Lyonnais v Sarl Moon*.
20 Cass Com, 28 April 2004, *SA Crédit Lyonnais v Sarl Moon*.

3   inquire about the identity of persons who are the beneficiaries of transactions when individuals do not seem to act on their own behalf (except when the transaction is effected through another financial institution). This includes not only French and EU institutions, but also those in countries outside the EU whose status raises questions.[21]

In order to promote the fight against money laundering, banks are also required to keep any documents relating to the identity of their existing or new clients for a period of five years from either the closing date of the client's account or the date of termination of their relationship.

The TRACFIN, as well as the supervisory authority, may (at any time and independently) require the disclosure of any documents which are likely to help in analysing a transaction which is declared as being suspicious pursuant to art L 562-2 or carefully checked pursuant to art L 563-3 of the MFC so as to determine whether this transaction is lawful.

By a decision of 12 October 2004, the Amiens Court of Appeal[22] judged that the failure of the banker to comply with art 563-3 of the MFC constituted the money laundering offence as defined in art 324-1 of the Criminal Code. Thus, a bank has a duty to check carefully any major transaction involving sums greater than 150,000 euros and which, without coming within the scope of art L 562-2, is subject to unusually complex conditions and does not appear to have any economic justification or lawful purpose. In such cases, the financial institution or person referred to in art L 562-1 must make inquiries of the client as to the origin and destination of those sums, the purpose of the transaction and the identity of the beneficiary.

A client who refuses to inform the bank about a significant deposit exceeding the amount established in art L 563-3 of the MFC is guilty of an offence. Therefore, should the client refuse to give details about his deposit, the bank is entitled to cease or break its contract with its client in order to avoid any subsequent criminal liability.

Banks which participate in the fight against money laundering benefit from double protection. Provided they have acted in good faith, they may not:

1   be prosecuted in the criminal courts on the basis of art 226-13 of the New Penal Code;
2   be held liable before a civil or commercial court for a breach of their duty of confidentiality. This means that should a client suffer a loss, the bank will not have to indemnify the client and it is the government who is liable for indemnification; nor
3   be subject to professional sanctions.

Should a banker fail to comply with his duty of vigilance, he is liable to professional and administrative sanctions according to art L 562-7 of the MFC. The banker, having knowledge of a felony, the consequences of which it is still possible to prevent or limit, or the perpetrators of which are liable to commit new felonies which could be prevented, is also bound by the provision of art 434-1 of the Criminal Code to inform the administrative or judicial authorities. The omission to do so is punishable by three years' imprisonment and a fine of 45,000 euros.

---

21 Note that the EU parliamentary conference of 7–8 February 2002 envisaged a systematic declaration with the TRACFIN of transactions carried out with fiduciary or assimilated funds in case the economic beneficiary cannot be identified.
22 *Cour d'appel d'Amiens, chambre économique*, 12 October 2004, *SA BNP Paribas v Naaijer*.

The bank's clients also benefit from protection. Thus, the rights of disclosure developed for the benefit of the TRACFIN may not be used for the benefit of any other administration, such as the tax authorities (art L 563-5 of the MFC). Such provision is very important in that it tends to protect clients and safeguard the mutual confidence which constitutes the basis of the banker–client relationship.

On 17 June 2004, the Orléans Court of Appeal ruled that the principle of non-interference in the client's business precludes a banker from systematically checking the regularity and legality of any financial transactions placed under his responsibility, nor to proceed with any investigations when the running of the account is without incident. However, this principle is mitigated by the duty of vigilance as provided in art L 563-3 of the MFC. However, the duty of vigilance is not a general one. It is limited to certain types of situations and aimed at detecting money that comes from crime or the financing of terrorism.

The invasion of banking privacy was mitigated by Act n 2003-706 of 1 August 2003 about financial security which reaffirms the important prohibition of communicating or transmitting private information to third parties who are not legally entitled to receive it. Under this legislation, French banks are able to maintain a satisfactory balance between the need to co-operate with the judicial authorities in combating money laundering, whilst ensuring that customer privacy is protected. This is all the more important as there is no banking secrecy per se in France. Therefore, banks cannot deny access to their client database by the judicial authorities or the TRACFIN.

EXTRA-TERRITORIAL ASPECTS

[13.17] French law provides for the co-operation between various control authorities for the exchange of all information necessary for the enforcement of their decisions. The rules outlined above are those provided for by French domestic law. However, rules of international law will have to be taken into account if, for example, a foreign authority seeks to obtain information or if, conversely, a French authority seeks to obtain information outside France.

Foreign authorities seeking information in France

Information sought from a bank

[13.18] The professional duty of confidentiality may override claims from a foreign authority, except possibly if such authority relies on an international treaty, such as a bilateral tax treaty, or the Hague Convention 1970 on the obtaining of evidence abroad. The Hague Convention provides that evidence may be obtained either through diplomatic or consular agents, who do not, however, have any power of compulsion, or through the French Ministry of Foreign Affairs (which conveys the request to the Ministry of Justice, which itself conveys the request to the Public Prosecutor, who, in turn, conveys it to the competent French court), but even in this case, it is doubtful whether a French judge would accept evidence where this would constitute a breach of a professional duty of confidentiality under French law.

In addition to the professional duty of confidentiality, a banker may invoke the provisions of art 1 or 1 bis of Law n 68-678 of 26 July 1968 with respect to modified disclosure of economic, commercial, industrial, financial or technical documents and information to foreign individuals or legal entities.

Article 1 states that the act of providing economic, commercial, industrial, financial or technical information to foreign public authorities is a misdemeanour where the communication of such information could interfere with the sovereignty, security or essential economic interests of France or with French public order. This applies to any individuals of French nationality or residing in France, as well as to any managers, representatives, agents or employees of a corporation having its registered office or a branch in France. This provision would therefore apply to all managers or employees of foreign banks having a branch in France.

Article 1 bis provides that when commercial or financial information is requested from any person with a view to producing evidence for any judicial or administrative proceedings abroad, the request and communication of such information are misdemeanours.

The prohibition applies to 'any person'. Therefore, if a French national who resides in France visits a foreign country and discloses information for the purpose of judicial proceedings in that country, Law n 68-678 would probably apply if the information was obtained in France.[23]

Both articles apply subject to international treaties and therefore may not be invoked if the procedure provided for by the Hague Convention 1970 is followed.

Information sought from a supervisory authority

[13.19] A foreign authority seeking information in France may request its French counterpart to provide it with such information. For instance, the American Federal Bank Examiners or the SEC could request the French *Commission Bancaire*, the Banque de France or the AMF to provide it with information concerning a US bank having a branch in France. The AMF, the *Commission Bancaire* or the Banque de France may obtain such information, notwithstanding any duty of confidentiality to which the bank may be subject (arts L 621-21 and L 632-1 of the MFC).

the question arises as to whether the French authority may be in breach of its own duty of confidentiality when providing the information to the foreign authority. As regards the *Commission Bancaire* and the Banque de France, the information may be given to the foreign authorities in charge of the surveillance of credit establishments provided that reciprocity exists and subject to the condition that these authorities are themselves bound by a professional duty of confidentiality with the same guarantees as in France. As regards the AMF (arts L 621-21 and L 632-1 of the MFC), it may provide information to either any analogous authority of another member state of the EU or of the EEA which is bound by a professional duty of confidentiality or to any analogous body of a foreign state provided that reciprocity exists and that the foreign authority is bound by a professional duty of confidentiality with the same guarantees as in France.

Article L 621-21 of the MFC restricts the forwarding of information to foreign authorities by providing that the AMF must refuse to provide the information to the foreign analogous authority if the conveyance of such information is likely to interfere with the sovereignty, security, essential economic interests or public order in France, when any criminal proceedings have been instituted in France on the basis of the same facts and against the same persons or when these persons have already been subject to a final judgment on the same facts.

---

23 Response to written question no 4356, Official Journal, Senate debate, 4 June 1987, p 390.

French authorities seeking information from a bank outside France

[13.20]   It should be pointed out that in France, at least in non-criminal matters, the courts do not play an active part in the process of producing evidence. As a consequence, issues which arise in some countries as regards, for instance, subpoenas and contempt of court are not relevant in France.

When criminal proceedings have been initiated, the investigating judge (*juge d'instruction*) may issue letters rogatory by virtue of the Hague Convention or a bilateral treaty on judicial assistance.

Finally, French supervisory authorities may obtain information through foreign analogous authorities relying on EU rules. In addition, the AMF is entitled to enter into agreements with foreign analogous entities.

REGULATED MARKETS

Regulatory authorities

[13.21]   In France, the main regulatory authority for regulated markets is the AMF. The function of the AMF is to protect savings, investments and information on investors, as well as the sound operation of regulated markets. In order to carry out such a mission, the AMF has broad powers (ie to investigate transactions, issue injunctions to stop practices which are contrary to the *Commission des Opérations de Bourse* regulations and issue sanctions). The objective of the AMF also includes a disciplinary role over market enterprises and investment services providers.

Insider dealing

[13.22]   Employees or managers of banks or financial institutions can be tempted to use information they collect to their own benefit or to the benefit of related persons.

Insider dealing may be punished by both criminal and administrative sanctions. The criminal offence of insider dealing is governed by arts L 465-1 to 465-3 of the MFC. The administrative breach of privileged information is governed by art 611-1 of the AMF which replaces the previous *Commission des Opérations de Bourse* regulation n 90-08 related to the use of privileged information. It has a much larger scope than the penal law.

The criminal offence of insider dealing

[13.23]

It has been a criminal offence since 1970 for the managers of a company or persons who obtain information with respect to a company in the course of their profession to use such information before it has become public in order to carry out transactions for their own benefit. This was extended to all persons by Law n 2001-1062 of 15 November 2001. Law n 2003-706 of 1 August 2003 concerning financial security strengthens the regime of this criminal offence.

By virtue of art L 621-15-1 of the MFC, the exchange of information between the Public Prosecutor and the AMF is far better than it used to be.

13.23   *France*

We will examine in turn:

1   the persons who may be liable;
2   the nature of the relevant information;
3   what is meant by the 'abuse' of such information;
4   the intention which must be established; and
5   the sanctions imposed on offenders.

Persons who may be liable

[13.24]   Law n 2001-1062 of 15 November 2001 and Law n 2003-239 of 18 March 2003 on domestic security, which implement the European Directive on market abuse[24] and amend art L 465-1 of the MFC, enlarge the scope of insider dealing as to the persons who may be liable. Insider dealing used to be aimed at 'persons finding themselves in possession of privileged information in the course of their profession or duties'. It was therefore necessary that the information be obtained by reason of the exercise of their profession or duties and not by mere luck or through friendly or family relationships. Since the Law of 15 November 2001, 'any person that is in possession of inside information, even if it is not in the course of his profession or duties, may also be sentenced for using or revealing such information'.

Bank managers and employees are obviously in a privileged position to obtain information with respect to the transactions that their clients contemplate and there are many examples of bank managers using such information for their own benefit. In 1978, a bank manager, who was in charge of the supervision of the personal bank account of a client, became aware of the fact that the client intended to take over a company if the results of the parliamentary elections were what he expected. For his own account, the bank manager bought 90 shares of the company after meeting the client and 155 shares of the company on the day following the elections. He was sentenced to three months' imprisonment with a remission of sentence and a fine of FRF20,000 (3,049 euros).[25]

The nature of the information

[13.25]   Article L 465-1 of the MFC does not set out any particular conditions as to the accuracy of the information. The contents of the information have been very broadly defined by case law as 'any information relating to the forecast or circumstances of an issuer or on the likelihood of a change in securities or a futures contract'. The Supreme Court has ruled that the privileged nature of information must be assessed on an objective basis.[26]

Article L 621-1 provides that the relevant inside information is of a precise nature that has not been made public, relating directly or indirectly to one or more issuers of financial instruments or to one or more financial instruments and which, if it were made public, would be likely to have a significant effect on the prices of the relevant instruments or related financial instruments.

Information is deemed to be precise if it indicates a set of circumstances or event that has occurred or is likely to occur and a conclusion may be drawn as to the possible

---

24   See now Council Directive 2003/6/EC.
25   *Tribunal Correctionnel*, Paris, 13 January 1978.
26   Paris 9th Ch, 12 March 1993.

effect of such set of circumstances or event on the prices of financial instruments or related financial instruments.

Information which, if it were made public, would be likely to have a significant effect on the prices of financial instruments or related financial instruments is information that a reasonable investor would be likely to use as part of the basis of his investment decisions.

'Abuse' of the information

[13.26] The abuse must take the form of a transaction completed on the market. Therefore, if a bank advised and led a lending syndicate for a company purporting to make a takeover bid for one of the bank's clients, there will be no offence of insider dealing, although there may be a breach of the duty of confidentiality.

The offence of insider dealing is, however, defined broadly in that (i) it is not necessary to establish a causal link between the information and the transaction completed and (ii) it is an offence for a person in possession of privileged information not only to complete a transaction directly or through an intermediary, but also to enable a third party to complete a transaction.

The prohibited transactions may be carried out by the privileged person directly or, more often, through a 'dummy' who is often a non-resident company (often located in a tax haven). The AMF has therefore called for the conclusion of international treaties.

Co-operation between the appropriate national authorities is obviously necessary, although confidentiality should be ensured. The AMF is at present authorised to provide information to its EC counterparts and also to foreign authorities outside the EC provided that the assistance is reciprocal and the foreign authority is subject to a duty of confidentiality with the same guarantees as in France. Similar provisions apply to the *Commission Bancaire* and the Banque de France.

We have seen that it is an offence for a privileged person to enable a third party to complete a transaction. This 'third party' may be a client or an employee of the same financial institution. Thus, a bank manager having privileged information regarding a company who advises its client to deal on such company's securities or who uses this information when managing its clients' securities will be liable. Similarly, a bank employee dealing with the account of a client who passes some information onto another employee dealing with the management of securities accounts falls within the ambit of arts L 465-1 to 465-3 of the MFC.

Intention

[13.27] Where the person in possession of privileged information completes a deal himself or through an intermediary, such person will be liable if he was aware of the fact that the information had not yet been disclosed to the public. Where the information is passed on by the privileged person to a third party, it must be established that the informer knew that the third party would act upon it.

The Supreme Court considers that there is insider dealing if the manager of a company uses the privileged information for a compelling reason dictated by corporate interest. It is unclear as to how the banker may benefit from the corporate interest.

Sanctions

[13.28] The penalties provided for by art L 465-1 of the MFC differ according to whether:

1 the person in possession of confidential information, whether or not obtained in the course of his profession or duties, carried out, or knowingly allowed the realisation, either directly or through an intermediary, of one or several transactions before the information was brought to the knowledge of the public; or

2 the person in possession of confidential information disclosed such information to a third party outside the usual course of his profession or duties.

In the first case, offenders may be sentenced to two years' imprisonment and a fine of up to 500,000 euros. However, the fine may not be for an amount less than the profit made and may be up to ten times the amount of such profit. In the second case, offenders may be sentenced to one year's imprisonment and a fine of up to 150,000 euros.

Note that, pursuant to arts L 465-1 and 465-3 of the MFC, legal entities may now also be subject to sanctions in compliance with the conditions set out in art 121-2 of the New Penal Code for the offences defined in art L 465-3 of the MFC.

Article 421-1 of the Penal Code, as modified by the Law of 15 November 2001, provides that the offence of insider dealing can be considered a terrorist act if the offence is committed intentionally in relation to an individual or collective enterprise aimed at disturbing public order through the means of intimidation or terror. In such case, the procedure and penalties are different. This amendment was enacted in reaction to the terrorist attacks of 11 September 2001.

Criminal sanctions are cumulative, with administrative sanctions applied by the AMF.

According to art L 621-16 of the MFC, when a prosecution is instituted pursuant to arts L 465-1 and 465-2 (the offence of insider dealing), the AMF may bring an independent action for damages. However, it cannot, with regard to the same person and the same facts, concurrently exercise the disciplinary powers it holds by virtue of the present Code and the right to take civil action.

According to art 622-1 of the MFC, 'the persons referred to in art 622-2 shall refrain from using inside information when acquiring or selling, for their own account or on behalf of others, either directly or indirectly, the financial instruments to which that information pertains or related financial instruments…'

Article 622-2 of the MFC provides that:

'the abstention requirements provided for in art 622-1 apply to any person holding inside information by virtue of:

1 his membership of the administrative, management or supervisory bodies of the issuer;

2 his holding in the issuer's capital;

3 his access to such information through the exercise of his employment, profession or duties, as well as his participation in the preparation or execution of a corporate finance transaction;

4 his activities that may be characterised as criminal offences.

These abstention requirements also apply to any person who holds inside information and who knows, or should know, that it is inside information.

Where the person referred to here is a legal person, these abstention requirements shall also apply to natural persons taking part in the decision to effect the transaction on behalf of the legal person.'

Professional rules of conduct

[13.29]   Large financial institutions raise a specific problem which is partly due to the variety of services they now provide, including dealing with securities owned by their clients. Moreover, they often carry out transactions on their own behalf and so do their employees. Conflicts of interests may therefore arise between several clients, as well as between the financial institution itself and its clients.

A working committee looked into the matter at the end of the 1980s (*Commission Brac de la Perrière* 1989 and *Commission sur la déontologie boursière* chaired by Mr Pfeiffer) whose purpose was to make recommendations for professional rules that should be included in ethical norms for the financial markets. These rules and codes aimed to go further and do better than the law. They are typical of the period in which the state disengaged and left the professionals with a duty to draft the codes. However, the responsibility for the implementation of the rules belonged to the government. For example, art 622-1 and 622-2 of the AMF provides that issuers of securities traded on a regulated market and financial intermediaries must take all appropriate measures to avoid the undue circulation of privileged information.

The implementation of the Investment Services Directive,[27] which includes certain professional rules, brought about codification. Most of the rules are codified by art 533-4 of the MFC, which applies to all investment services providers, including investment and credit establishments. These rules pursue several goals, including the protection of market integrity and the prevention of undue circulation of confidential information in every investment services provider.

Investment services providers must ensure that all employees abide by the following rules, set out by art 533-6 of the MFC. These internal regulations must provide for:

1   conditions under which employees make negotiations on financial instruments for their own account;
2   conditions under which employees must, in such case, inform their employer; and
3   obligations to avoid the undue circulation of confidential information.

The general regulation of the AMF authorises investment services providers to restrict the potential for employees performing sensitive functions to complete transactions for their own account. Sensitive functions include those exposed to the holding of confidential information, responsibility for the arrangement of financial transactions, counselling, trading on markets, financial analysis, transactions on capital structure, industrial strategy and mergers and acquisitions. Employees who have information on financial instruments must not act as traders and must not complete any transaction on the financial instruments.

Finally, compliance with professional rules of conduct is entrusted to a compliance officer. The compliance officer's functions are exclusive. He controls transactions completed by employees for their own account and establishes a surveillance list of financial instruments on which the investment services provider or its employees have sensitive information. He also establishes a prohibition list, which lists all

27 Council Directive 93/22/EEC.

financial instruments on which the employee must abstain from negotiating for his own account, distributing financial analysis or recommending negotiation to clients. Such list is disclosed to all employees.

Article 321-29 of the General Regulation of the AMF, which replaced the previous art 3-1-6 of the General Regulation of the CMF (1998), has imposed the implementation of the 'Chinese Wall' principle in order to ensure that confidential and privileged information remains secret. In practice, this procedure allows the separation of activities that are likely to create conflicts of interests in the financial institution's premises. This procedure is also used in order to provide for the conditions under which the compliance officer can authorise the transmission of confidential information from one department to another or the assignment of an employee to a department different from the one to which he belongs.

APPENDIX

[13.30] The legislation set out here constitutes the main legal framework of the banker's duty of confidentiality in France. Banks are subject to various pieces of legislation that can be found in the Penal Code, the MFC and the Commercial Code.

Legal provisions

New Penal Code

Article 226-13

[13.31] The disclosure of any secret information by any person who, by reason of his or her status or profession or temporary duties or mission, holds secret information, shall be sentenced to one year's imprisonment and a fine of 15,000 euros.

Monetary and Financial Code

Article L 142-9

[13.32] The agents of the Banque de France are bound by a professional duty of confidentiality. They may not acquire or receive any participation or interest or remuneration whatsoever in consideration of either work or advice in private, public, industrial, commercial or financial companies, unless otherwise authorised by the governor. The provisions do not apply to the production of scientific, literary or artistic works.

Article L 465-1

[13.33] The managers of any company referred to in art L 225-109 of the French Commercial Code and the persons who, by reason of their professional activities or duties, are in possession of privileged information in relation to the forecasts or to the circumstances of an issuer, whose securities are traded on a regulated market, or to the changes in a financial instrument listed on a regulated market, and who carry out or knowingly allow the carrying out, either directly or through a nominee, of one or several transactions prior to the information being made available to the public, shall be sentenced to two years' imprisonment and a fine of 1,500,000 euros, the total amount of which may be increased up to ten times the amount of the profit, if any, possibly earned, without the fine being lower than the amount of the profit.

Any person who, by reason of his or her professional activities or his or her duties, is in possession of confidential information in relation to the likely change in or to the circumstances of an issuer, whose securities are negotiated on a regulated market, or to the forecast of a financial instrument listed on a regulated market and who discloses such information to a third party beyond the scope of his or her usual professional activities or duties, shall be sentenced to one year's imprisonment and a fine of 150,000 euros.

Any person, other than those referred to in the two paragraphs above, who possesses in full knowledge inside information related to the forecasts or to the circumstances of an issuer, whose securities are traded on a regulated market, or to the change of a financial instrument listed on a regulated market, and who carries out or knowingly allows the carrying out, either directly or through a nominee, of a transaction, or who communicates the information to a third party prior to the information being made available to the public, shall be sentenced to one year's imprisonment and a fine of 150,000 euros, the total amount of which may be increased up to ten times the amount of the profit, if any, possibly made, the fine not to be lower than the amount of the profit. When the information at stake pertains to the perpetration of a crime or an offence, the sanction incurred will be increased up to seven years' imprisonment and a fine of 1,500,000 euros, if the amount of the profit earned is lower than the sum.

Any person who, by any process or means whatsoever, knowingly forwards false or misleading information related to the likely change in or to the circumstances of an issuer, whose securities are negotiated on a regulated market, or to the forecast of a financial instrument listed on a regulated market, which is likely to influence listings, shall be sentenced to the same penalties as those provided for in para 1.

Article L 465-2

[13.34] Any persons who carry out or attempt to carry out, directly or through an intermediary, steps aimed at affecting the due operation of a market or financial instruments by misleading a third party, shall be punished by the sanctions provided for in the first paragraph of art L 465-1.

Article L 465-3

[13.35] Legal entities may be held criminally liable under the conditions provided for in art 121.2 of the New Penal Code for any offence defined in art L 465-1 and 465-2.

Penalties incurred by legal entities include:

1   fines pursuant to the terms and conditions provided for in art 131.38 of the French Penal Code;
2   the penalties mentioned in art 131.39 of the French Penal Code.

The prohibition provided for in para 2 of art 131.39 of the French Penal Code refers to the activity in the course of which the offence was committed.

Article L 511-33

[13.36] All officers of a board of directors and, as the case may be, of a supervisory board (*conseil de surveillance*) and all other persons who, by reason of their office, participate in the administration or management of a credit establishment or are employed by the credit establishment, are bound by a professional duty of confidentiality under the conditions and the penalties provided for in art L 571-4.

Article L 561-1

[13.37] Persons others than those specified in art L 562-1 who, in the conduct of their business, execute, monitor or give advice on transactions resulting in capital movements, must report to the Public Prosecutor (*Procureur de la République*) transactions of which they are aware and which involve sums that they know derive from one of the offences provided for in art L 562-2.

Having made such a report in good faith, the persons shall benefit from the provisions of art L 562-8 of the Law. They must comply with the obligations provided for in art L 574-1. The Public Prosecutor shall inform the department stated in art L 562-4, which shall provide him with all relevant information.

Article L 562-1

[13.38] The provisions of this chapter apply to:

1 undertakings, institutions and departments governed by the provisions of title I of this section;
2 the Banque de France, the *Institut d'émission des départements d'outre-mer* and the *Institut d'émission d'outre-mer*;
3 undertakings referred to in art L 310-1 of the French Insurance Code and insurance and reinsurance brokers;
4 bodies which fall within the scope of art L 111-1 of the French Mutuality Code;
5 investment companies, members of regulated markets of financial instruments and legal entities mentioned in arts L 421-8 and L 442-2;
6 money changers;
7 persons which carry out, supervise or advise transactions on the purchase, sale, transfer or rental of real estate properties;
8 legal representatives and managers in charge of casinos; the legal representatives and managers responsible for casinos, groups, clubs and companies which organise games of chance, lotteries, betting and sporting or racing tips;
9 persons whose usual activity is commercial in nature or who organise the sale of precious stones or materials, antiquities and works of art;
10 companies entitled to the exemption provided for in title II of art L 511-7;
11 accountants and auditors;
12 notaries, bailiffs, receivers and court-appointed administrators, as well as advocates of the *Conseil d'Etat* and the *Cour de Cassation*, and counsel of the Courts of Appeal, as determined in art L 562-2-1;
13 court-appointed auctioneers and valuers and companies effecting voluntary sales of furniture at public auctions.

For the purposes of this section, persons mentioned in arts 1 to 6 shall be referred to as 'financial undertakings'.

Article L 562-2

[13.39] The financial undertakings and persons referred to in art L 562-1 must report to the department mentioned in art L 562-4 under the conditions specified by this section:

1   deposits of funds in their books which may result from drug trafficking from organised crime, from fraud against the financial interests of the European Communities, from corruption or from organised crime, or which might contribute to the financing of terrorism;

2   transactions involving funds which may result from drug trafficking or from organised crime, from fraud against the financial interests of the European Communities, from corruption or from organised crime, or which might contribute to the financing of terrorism.

Financial undertakings must also report to the department:

1   transactions in which the identity of the operator or beneficiary remains uncertain, in spite of the care carried out in compliance with art L 563-1;

2   operations carried out by financial undertakings on their behalf or on behalf of third parties, both individuals and legal entities, including their subsidiaries or entities.

Financial organisations are also compelled to declare to the above-mentioned service:

1   all transactions in which the instructing parties' identity or the beneficiary's identity remains doubtful, in spite of the precautions carried out pursuant to art L 563-1;

2   all operations carried out by financial organisations on their behalf or on behalf of third parties with natural or legal persons, including with the subsidiaries and establishments of the legal persons, acting under the form or on behalf of trust funds or of any instruments of management of allocation estate in which the identity of constituents or beneficiaries is unknown.

A decree may extend the obligation of declaration provided for in the first paragraph to the transactions carried out on one's own behalf or on behalf of third parties and carried out by financial organisations with individuals or legal entities, including the subsidiaries or establishments of the legal entities and domiciled, registered or established in any of the states or territories, the legislation of which is recognised as insufficient, or the practices of which are considered as being an obstacle to the fight against money laundering carried out by international consultation and co-ordination regarding the fight against money laundering. The decree shall provide for the minimum amount of operations subject to declaration.

Article L 562-2-1

[13.40]   The persons referred to in item 12 of art L 562-1 are required to make the declaration stipulated in art L 562-2 when, in the context of their professional activity, they execute for and on behalf of their customer any financial or real property transaction or when they participate by assisting their customer with the preparation or execution of transactions relating to:

1   the buying and selling of real property or business concerns;
2   the management of funds, securities or other assets belonging to the customer;
3   the opening of current accounts, savings accounts or securities accounts;
4   the organisation of the contributions required to create companies;
5   the formation, administration or management of companies;
6   the formation, administration or management of foreign law trusts or any similar structure.

The persons referred to in item 12 of art L 562-1, when they are engaged in activities relating to the transactions referred to above, and accountants when they give legal advice pursuant to the provisions of art 22 of order no 45-2138 of 19 September 1945 which instituted the Order of Accountants and regulates the title and profession of the accountant, are not required to make the declaration stipulated in art L 562-2 when the information was received from one of their clients, or obtained on one of them, within the scope of a legal consultation, unless it took place for money laundering purposes, or if those persons proceeded knowing that their client wished to obtain legal advice for money laundering purposes, or when they provide their professional services in the interest of that client in connection with judicial proceedings, whether that information was received or obtained before, during or after those proceedings, including advice given in relation to the means of initiating or avoiding such proceedings. Notwithstanding art L 562-2, advocates of the *Conseil d'Etat* and of the *Cour de Cassation*, and legal counsel of the Courts of Appeal, send their declarations, as applicable, to the president of the Order of Advocates of the *Conseil d'Etat* and of the *Cour de Cassation*, to the president of the order to which the advocate belongs or to the president of the professional body to which the counsel belongs. Those authorities send the declarations sent to them by the advocate or the counsel to the department instituted by art L 562-4, unless they consider that the suspicion of money laundering is unfounded.

In which case, the president of the Order of Advocates of the *Conseil d'Etat* and of the *Cour de Cassation*, or the president of the order to which the advocate belongs or the president of the professional body to which the counsel belongs informs the advocate or the counsel of the reasons why he believed he should not forward the information that he had sent to him. The president of the order or of the professional body who has received a declaration which he has not forwarded to the department instituted by art L 562-4 sends the information contained in that declaration to the president of the National Bar Chamber or to the president of the National Chamber of Legal Counsel. The information thus forwarded does not contain any references to the identity of the persons. Under the same conditions, the president of the Order of Advocates of the *Conseil d'Etat* and of the *Cour de Cassation*, the president of the National Bar Chamber and the president of the National Chamber of Legal Counsel send a report to the Minister of Justice on the situations which did not give rise to communication of the declarations within a time limit set in a *Conseil d'Etat* decree.

The department instituted by art L 562-4 receives that information from the Minister of Justice.

The provisions of the present article are applicable in New Caledonia, the Overseas Territories and Mayotte.

Article L 562-4

[13.41]   A department placed under the authority of the Minister for Economic Affairs and Finance must receive the report provided for in art L 562-2. The department consists of the state civil servants that the Minister endows with specific powers, under the conditions established by a decree approved by the *Conseil d'Etat*. The department collects and compiles all information, which helps determine the origin of funds or the types of transactions covered in the report. As soon as the information received evidences funds likely to result from drug trafficking or from organised criminal activity or the financing of terrorism, the department shall submit it to the Public Prosecutor and shall inform him, where applicable, that the matter has been referred to the customs authority, so that the latter may initiate an investigation to establish an offence pursuant to art 415 of the French Customs Code.

Article L 562-5

[13.42] Without prejudice to the provisions of art L 562-6, the department established pursuant to art L 562-4 shall acknowledge receipt of the aforementioned report. The acknowledgement of receipt, which may be accompanied by an injunction, shall be issued prior to the deadline for execution of the transaction.

The injunction forces execution to be delayed for up to 12 hours at the most. If the acknowledgement of receipt is not accompanied by an injunction, or if the financial undertaking or the person referred to in art L 562-1 has not obtained any decision from the president (presiding judge) of the *Tribunal de Grande Instance* of Paris or, where appropriate, from the investigations magistrate (*juge d'instruction*), it may execute the transaction at the end of the period to which the injunction applies.

The report shall deal with transactions already completed if delaying execution proves impossible, which is also the case if it has become obvious, upon execution of the transaction, that the sums appear to result from drug trafficking or from organised criminal activity or the financing of terrorism. The department established pursuant to art L 562-4 shall acknowledge receipt of the reports.

Upon consultation with the Public Prosecutor of the *Tribunal de Grande Instance* of Paris, the presiding judge of the *Tribunal de Grande Instance* of Paris may, upon request of the department established pursuant to art L 562-4, extend the period provided for in the first paragraph of this article or order temporary sequestration of funds, accounts or securities covered by the report. The Public Prosecutor of the *Tribunal de Grande Instance* of Paris may present a request for the purpose. The order, which accedes to the request, shall be immediately enforceable against the person concerned to whom the report is notified.

Article L 562-6

[13.43] The report may be oral or written. The undertaking may request that the department established pursuant to art L 562-1 does not acknowledge receipt of the report. In the event that the department refers the matter to the Public Prosecutor, the report drawn to his attention shall not be contained in the summary.

The declaration may be either written or oral. The financial organisation or the person provided for in art L 562-1 may request that the department established pursuant to art L 562-4 does not acknowledge receipt of the declaration. In the event that the department should refer the matter to the Public Prosecutor, the declaration, of which the latter is informed, shall not appear in the file of the procedure.

The department established pursuant to art L 562-4 may, upon request of the financial organisation or of the person having carried out a declaration in compliance with arts L 562-2, L 563-1, L 563-1-1 and L 563-4, indicate whether it has referred the matter to the Public Prosecutor on the grounds of the declaration.

Article L 562-7

[13.44] If, either as a consequence of a serious lack of vigilance or a shortcoming in the organisation of its internal procedures of control, a financial undertaking or person referred to in art L 562-1 fails to make a report as provided for in this section, the disciplinary authority in charge shall initiate proceedings on the grounds of professional or administrative rules and regulations and inform the Public Prosecutor.

Article L 562-8

[13.45] With respect to sums or transactions covered by the report referred to in art L 562-2, no proceedings under art 226-13 and 226-14 of the French Penal Code shall be initiated against managers or employees or any persons referred to in art L 562-1 against financial undertakings who carry out the report in good faith.

No proceedings under civil law shall be instituted, nor shall any professional sanctions be imposed against a financial undertaking, its managers or employees or any person referred to in art L 562-1, which carry out the report referred to in art L 562-2 in good faith. Should such a report entail any direct damage, the state shall be liable for the damage suffered.

The provisions of this article shall be applicable even if no evidence has been provided that the nature of the facts on which the report is founded is that of a criminal offence or if the facts have resulted in a *nolle prosequi* order, discharge or acquittal.

If the transaction is executed as provided for in art L 562-5 and unless there is collusion with the owner of the funds or the initiator of the transaction, the financial undertaking shall be relieved from any liabilities and, in such event, no penal proceedings may be initiated against its managers or employees under arts 222-34 to 222-41, 321-1, 321-2, 321-3 and 324-1 of the French Penal Code or art 415 of the French Customs Code. The other persons referred to in art L 562-1 shall also be relieved from all liabilities.

Article L 563-1

[13.46] Before opening an account, financial undertakings as referred to in art L 562-1 must determine the true identity of the account holder by obtaining evidence in writing. The financial undertaking shall apply the same conditions so as to determine the identity of occasional clients who request the financial undertaking to carry out transactions of a nature and threshold amount specified in a decree.

They shall ascertain the true identity of the persons for whom an account is opened or a transaction executed, when it appears to them that the persons asking for an account to be opened or a transaction to be carried out might not be acting on their own behalf.

Article L 563-1-1

[13.47] To ensure application of the recommendations made by the international authority for consultation and co-ordination in regard to the fight against money laundering, the government may, for public order reasons and as determined in a *Conseil d'Etat* decree, make some or all of the transactions executed for their own account or on behalf of third parties by financial institutions established in France or with natural persons or legal entities referred to in the sixth paragraph of art L 562-2, or domiciled, registered or holding an account with an institution located in a state or territory referred to in the seventh paragraph of that article, subject to specific conditions, or restrict or prohibit them.

Article L 563-2

[13.48] The provisions of art L 563-1 shall be applicable to the assets and securities referred to in art 990A of the French Tax Code. The tax status of the assets and securities shall be maintained.

The provisions of the second paragraph of art 537 of the French Tax Code shall not preclude the application of art L 563-1. Nevertheless, the information to which the article refers shall be recorded in a register separate from that established pursuant to art 537 of the French Tax Code.

Once a client has declined to authorise the financial undertaking to disclose his identity and his domicile provided, for tax purposes, to the tax authorities, the right to forward information pursuant to arts L 83, L 85, L 87 and L 89 of the Tax Procedures Manual shall apply neither to the register thus established by the present article nor to the documents evidencing identity, as referred to in the first paragraph of art L 563-1 presented for the transactions in bills, securities and assets referred to in art 990A and in the second paragraph of art 537 of the French Tax Code.

Article L 563-3

[13.49] Any large-scale transaction involving sums which, individually or in total, exceed a threshold prescribed by a decree approved by the *Conseil d'Etat* and which, without being covered by art L 562-2, occurs under complex and unusual conditions and which has no apparent economic or visible lawful purpose, must give rise to a special investigation conducted by the financial undertaking. In such case, the financial undertaking shall question the client with respect to the origin and destination of the funds, as well as to the purpose of the transaction and the payee's identity.

The particulars of the transaction shall be written down and the records kept by the financial undertaking under the conditions provided for in art L 563-4. Only the department established pursuant to art L 562-4 and the supervisory authority may be provided with the relevant documents.

Financial undertakings must ensure that the obligations specified in the preceding paragraph are applied both by its foreign branches and subsidiaries, unless precluded by local law, in which case it shall inform the department established pursuant to art L 562-4.

Article L 563-4

[13.50] Without prejudice to the provisions requiring more strict measures, financial undertakings shall keep records relating to the identity of their usual or occasional clients for a period of at least five years upon closing of the clients' accounts or upon termination of their business relations. They shall also retain documents relating to transactions made by the above clients for a period of five years further to the execution of transactions.

For purposes of the present section, the department established pursuant to art L 562-4 and the supervisory authority may request that the documents be forwarded to them for the purpose of reconstructing, in their entirety, the transactions carried out by an individual or legal entity and in connection with a transaction dealt with in a report referred to in art L 562-2 or with a special investigation provided for in art L 563-3, with the aim of providing information to the departments of other states having similar skills under the conditions provided for in art L 564-2.

Article L 563-5

[13.51] Without prejudice to the application of art 40 of the French Code of Penal Procedure, the information obtained by the department established pursuant to art L 562-4 and by the supervisory authorities in accordance with arts L 562-2 and L 563-2 to 563-4 must not be used for purposes other than those provided for by this section.

Disclosure of the information is prohibited. Except where this information is related to the facts referred to in art L 562-2, the department established pursuant to art L 562-4 is authorised to forward the information it has collected to officers of the Criminal Investigation Department (*police judiciaire*) which is appointed by the Minister of the Interior under the conditions specified by a decree approved by the *Conseil d'Etat*, as well as to the supervisory authorities. It may also transmit the information to customs. It is also authorised to obtain the information it requires, with a view to the carrying out of its tasks, from officers of the Criminal Investigation Department and from the supervisory authorities.

Article L 563-6

[13.52] If, either as a consequence of a serious lack of vigilance or default in the organisation of its internal procedures of control, a financial undertaking has failed to meet the obligations imposed under this chapter, the authority having disciplinary power may act on its own initiative under the conditions provided for in professional or administrative rules and regulations.

Article L 574-1

[13.53] Without prejudice to the application of the penalties incurred with respect to one of the offences provided for in art 222-34 to 222-41 of the French Penal Code and art 415 of the French Customs Code, the managers or employees of financial undertakings or any persons referred to in art L 562-1, which knowingly inform the owner of the funds or the initiator of one of the transactions referred to in art L 562-2 of this Law, of the existence of the report made to the department established pursuant to art L 562-4, or transmit confidential information related to any proceedings initiated on the basis of the report, may be punished by a fine of 22,500 euros.

Article L 613-20

[13.54]

1   any persons who participate or have participated in the control of the persons mentioned in art L 613-1, 613-2 and 613-10, under the conditions provided for in this chapter, are bound by a professional duty of confidentiality, subject to the penalties provided for in art 226-13 of the French Penal Code;

2   the duty may not be invoked against the judicial authority acting in the course of criminal proceedings. It may not be invoked in the event of a hearing within the context of a committee of inquiry, in the conditions provided for in the fourth paragraph of s II of art 6 of ordinance no 58-1100 of 17 November 1958 relating to the running of parliamentary assemblies;

3   notwithstanding the provisions of Law n 68-678 of 26 July 1968, the banking committee (*Commission Bancaire*) may provide information to the authorities in charge of the persons, mentioned in s I, in other countries, provided that reciprocity exists and that the authorities are themselves bound by a professional duty of confidentiality with the same guarantees as in France.

Article L 621-10

[13.55]   In order to ensure the performance of its mission, the commission for stock market transactions (*Commission des Opérations de Bourse*) may act through agents whose powers are granted by its chairman, in accordance with a decree approved by the *Conseil d'Etat*.

The agents may obtain any documents, under any form whatsoever (Law n 2001-1276 of 28 December 2001), 'including data files kept and processed by telecommunications operators within the scope of art L 32-3-1 of the *Code des postes et télécommunications* and by service providers mentioned in arts 43-7 and 43 of Law n 86-1067 of 30 September 1986 on the freedom of communication , and may obtain a copy. They may convene and interview any persons in possession of information. They have access to all professional premises.

Article L 621-11

[13.56]   Any persons summoned to appear before the Commission are entitled to be assisted by a counsel of their choice. The terms of this summons and the conditions under which such right is exercised is determined by decree. (Decree no 71-615 of 23 July 1971, art 4: 'These summons are addressed to the relevant person concerned by registered letter no later than eight days prior to the hearing. If the person summoned wishes to be assisted by a legal counsel, he must provide the counsel's identity and position to the *Commission des Opérations de Bourse* no later than eight days prior to the holding of the hearing'.) Except for judicial auxiliaries, no one may invoke a professional duty of confidentiality against agents of the Commission.

The officers and agents of the Commission are bound by a professional duty of confidentiality in respect of the facts, acts and information that they may have obtained because of their functions, under the conditions and penalties set out in art 378 of the Penal Code.

Article L 621-21

[13.57]   The Commission may, under the same conditions, procedures and sanctions as those provided for in the code, with a view to the performance of its mission, conduct investigations upon request of foreign authorities performing analogous powers, provided that reciprocity exists, except in the event of a request made by an authority of a member state of the European Communities, or by any other member state to the Treaty on the European Economic Area.

The professional duty of confidentiality provided for in art L 621-11 does not prevent the *Commission des Opérations de Bourse* from conveying the information that it has in its possession or that it has obtained upon request from authorities of other member states of the European Communities (or from any other member state to the Treaty on the European Economic Area performing analogous powers and bound by the same professional duty of confidentiality) to the authorities.

The *Commission des Opérations de Bourse* may also convey information that it has in its possession or that it has obtained upon request of authorities of other states performing analogous functions, to the authorities, provided that reciprocity exists that such foreign authorities are bound by a professional duty of confidentiality with the same guarantees as in France.

The assistance requested by a foreign authority performing analogous functions with a view to the procedures of investigation, or the disclosure of information that the Commission has or has obtained, shall be refused by the Commission when the performance of the request may interfere with France's sovereignty, security, essential economic interests or public order, or when any penal proceeding has been initiated in France on the basis of the same facts and against the same persons, or when the latter have already been subject to a final judgment on the same facts.

The *Commission des Opérations de Bourse* may, in order to comply with the foregoing paragraphs, enter into agreements organising its relations with foreign authorities performing analogous functions.

The Commission must approve the agreements under the terms and conditions provided for in art L 621-3. They are published in the *Journal Officiel* (Official Journal).

Commercial Code

Article L 621-55

[13.58] The supervising judge (*juge commissaire*) may, notwithstanding any contrary legal or regulatory provisions, obtain any information allowing him to set out accurately the debtors' economic and financial situation from the statutory auditors, the members and representatives of personnel, from public administrations and organisations, social security and state insurance organisations and credit establishments, as well as from departments in charge of centralising banking risks and defaults in payments.

14 Germany

Thomas Schulz
Torsten Fett

SOURCE OF THE SECRECY OBLIGATION

[14.1] Current German law does not define the obligation of secrecy incumbent on banks in any statute, although the concept has a very long tradition and has been subject to public regulation. For example, a decree by Friedrich the Great stated in 1756 that all banks had to maintain secrecy on the wealth of their customers and had to take that information to the grave with them.[1] Despite the long tradition, the source of the secrecy obligation has not been clarified.

Constitution

[14.2] In particular, it is still uncertain whether, as some authors argue,[2] bank confidentiality as such is guaranteed by the German constitution (*Grundgesetz*, 'GG') and, if so, to what extent.

The right to determine the use of one's personal data is part of the right of privacy[3] which is laid down in art 1, para 1 and art 2, para 1 of the GG. Since this right covers all personal data, it covers information that is subject to the secrecy obligation as well. In this respect, the secrecy obligation shares the constitutional protection of the customer's right to determine the use of his personal data. However, the bank does not participate in this protection, but it enjoys the protection of its right to choose and perform its profession as guaranteed in art 12, para 1 of the GG.[4]

The protection offered by those provisions is relatively weak, since in most cases the information on a customer will not be of a private or intimate nature. The constitution allows a number of limitations to the secrecy obligations if the limitations pursue a legitimate public interest, are based on a statute and respect the principle of appropriateness. Thus, the practical relevance of the question whether or not the constitution guarantees bank secrecy is pretty low.

Clause 2 of the General Business Conditions

[14.3] Bank confidentiality derives from contractual origins. The highest German court in civil matters, the *Bundesgerichtshof* ('BGH'), held as early as 1953 that the

---

1 *Art 19 des Reglements der Königlichen Giro- und Lehn-Banco* quoted in Claussen *Bank- und Börsenrecht* (3rd edn, 2002) p 150.
2 Overview given by Bruchner in Schimansky, Bunte and Lwowski *Bankrechts-Handbuch* 2nd edn, 2001 vol. 1) p 742.
3 Koberstein-Windpassinger *Wahrung des Bankgeheimnisses bei Asset-Backed-Securities-Transaktionen* (1999) WM, p 473 at 475.
4 Kümpel *Bank- und Kapitalmarktrecht* (3rd edn, 2003) p 60.

secrecy obligation was an implied contractual duty of the bank due to the special relationship between a bank and its customer which requires (and is therefore particularly shaped by) mutual trust.[5] Hence, there is no need for any particular agreement between bank and client on a secrecy obligation.

Since 1 January 1993, this has also been expressly provided for in clause 2 of the General Business Conditions of German banks, which apply to all orders of a bank customer, whether single or multiple, during a contractual relationship between the bank and its customer. Those general conditions are used by virtually all banks doing business in Germany and, as regards the secrecy obligation, they have taken over the development that bank confidentiality has undergone so far. Therefore, the scope and limits of the secrecy obligations can be shown by referring to clause 2 of the General Business Conditions.

Protected persons

[14.4]   The first person to be protected is the customer, ie every person with whom a bank enters into a contractual relationship.[6] As, in principle, a contract does not need to be in a certain form according to German civil law, the contract is formed when bank and customer have exchanged offer and acceptance.

Under certain circumstances, even third parties – for example, spouses or the customer's company – who are not party to a banking contract can benefit from the secrecy obligation. This is the case when the third party is affected by the bank's performance of its contractual duties.

Information subject to the secrecy obligation

[14.5]   Clause 2, para 1 of the General Business Conditions states that the bank has to maintain secrecy about any customer-related information and that no differentiation is to be made between factual information and evaluations by the bank. The obligation regarding evaluations is not limited to those based on information that is known only to the bank. However, the bank must have obtained knowledge of the information during the contractual relationship. Through which channels the bank acquired the knowledge is irrelevant.[7]

Of course, the secrecy obligation only exists if the person wants the information to remain secret. The customer's wishes prevail, even if contrary to his own interests or common sense. If his wishes are not known to the bank and cannot be established, the bank has to deduce them from all circumstances that may give indications concerning his actual wishes.[8]

Duration of secrecy obligation

[14.6]   Bank confidentiality covers all phases of the contractual relationship between bank and customer from the start of negotiations throughout the duration of the contract. Even after termination of the contractual relationship, the bank will be bound by its contractual duty not to reveal the protected information – as laid down in the decree issued by Friedrich the Great.

---

5 BGH in BB 1953, p 993.
6 Bruchner, n 2 above, p 745.
7 Kümpel, n 4 above, p 62.
8 Bruchner, n 2 above, p 744.

Limitations

[14.7] Clause 2 of the General Business Conditions also shows the limitations on bank confidentiality: information may be disclosed if it is required by law, if the customer has consented or if the bank is authorised to disclose banking affairs. The latter is more clearly defined in clause 2, paras 2, 3 and 4 and is an instrument of information exchange between banks which was established to allow the creditworthiness of a business partner to be verified. Under what prerequisites one of these three exceptions limits the secrecy obligation will be discussed in further detail in 'Exceptions to the Secrecy Obligation' below.

Remedies for breach of secrecy obligation

[14.8] If certain information falls within the scope of the secrecy obligation and none of the limitations allows disclosure, then the bank is obliged not to pass that information to third parties outside the bank or to employees of the bank whose knowledge of the information is unnecessary for the purpose of fulfilling the customer's orders.[9] Should the bank reveal the information in breach of the secrecy obligation, this may lead to the following legal consequences.

Damages

[14.9] In the first instance, the disclosure constitutes a breach of contract which will entitle the customer to claim damages if the bank acted deliberately or negligently. Any fault on the part of employees or the bank's executive organs will be attributed to the bank. The damages that may be claimed cover the loss caused by the breach; German civil law does not allow for punitive damages. There is no causation where a customer has to pay taxes after a discovery of tax evasion, since he was already obliged to pay those before the breach was committed.

The most prominent case on damages has just been decided. Deutsche Bank AG was in principle held liable by the Federal Court of Justice (*Bundesgerichtshof*) to pay damages because its manager, Mr Breuer, expressed doubts about the creditworthiness of Kirch Group.[10] In an interview on an American television station, he said that one could read and hear everywhere that the financial sector was not willing to provide Kirch Group with further equity or credit capital. With this action, he disclosed facts that were protected by the secrecy obligation without being entitled to and, hence, breached the contractual relationship of the bank with one of the Kirch companies.

Under special circumstances, a customer may also claim damages in tort, but the provisions of tort law are unfavourable to the customer since the burden of proof regarding the bank's fault – contrary to damages deriving from breach of contract – lies with the customer and the attribution of the employee's fault may be excluded.

Injunction: s 935 of the Civil Procedure Code

[14.10] If a customer learns that his bank is about to disclose information, he may apply for an injunction. The client has to substantiate that the bank is under a

---

9 Claussen, n 1 above, p 161 et seq.
10 BGH in ZIP 2006, p 317.

contractual obligation not to reveal the information and that the passing on of information is imminent.

Termination of the banking relationship

[14.11]   Since the customer relies on the bank keeping his information secret, a breach of that obligation constitutes an important reason, according to clause 18, para 2 of the General Business Conditions, entitling the customer to terminate the banking contract with immediate effect.

Legal consequences regarding employees

[14.12]   The bank's employees are under a contractual obligation, deriving both from their individual employment contract and from collective agreements, to maintain bank confidentiality and to protect their employer's interests. This holds true even after the employment is terminated. In case of a breach, the bank may claim damages and, in serious cases, terminate the employment.

Criminal law

[14.13]   There is no criminal law provision regarding the breach of bank confidentiality except in some cases of limited scope, for instance, s 93 of the Stock Corporation Act applying to board members and s 203 of the German Criminal Code applying to organs of banks incorporated according to public law. The reason for the culpability of these organs lies with the special demands for employees working in public companies. On the contrary, employees of private banks are not subject to this criminal law provision. If s 203, para 2 of the Criminal Code were interpreted in a manner as also to include banks incorporated according to civil law,[11] this would not be compatible with the clear wording of that provision. It is forbidden to expand a clear wording of a Criminal Code provision in order to establish a new culpability as this needs to be done by the legislator. Otherwise, this would constitute an infringement of the principle *nullum crimen sine lege* guaranteed in art 103, para 2 of the GG.

Privacy of data

[14.14]   The law on protection of data privacy is a corresponding field with a scope similar to bank confidentiality and has evolved very rapidly over the last few years, reflecting the growing concern for privacy of data. In order to understand how these two matters influence each other, it is necessary to establish how they are related. It will be shown that the bank has primarily to respect the provisions of the obligation of secrecy and only apply the provisions of the Federal Data Protection Act ('BDSG') when the rules of bank confidentiality fail to ensure a minimum standard.

Scope of the Federal Data Protection Act

[14.15]   In s 1, para 1 of the BDSG, the aim of the statute is defined as being the protection of the right of privacy, which is identical to the individual's right to

---

11 Schünemann in *StGB – Leipziger Kommentar* (11th edn, 2001) s 203, no 71.

determine the use of his personal data,[12] ie the right to decide when and to what extent his personal information is made known to others.[13] This reveals one fundamental difference: while the secrecy obligation aims at ensuring confidentiality towards third parties, the BDSG aims at protecting a customer against other kinds of improper use of personal data through the customer's bank.

In keeping with the nature of the right of privacy, the BDSG only provides for the protection of natural persons and not of legal entities (s 3, para 1). However, the protection of legal entities is granted when information permits conclusions to be drawn regarding personal data on the people constituting the entity.[14]

According to s 1, para 2, n 3 of the BDSG, inquiries regarding personal data, as well as processing and use of such data for professional purposes, are subject to the provisions of the Act. Section 3, para 1 gives the definition of personal data: information about personal and factual circumstances relating to a determinable person. As with clause 2 of the General Business Conditions, this includes both factual information and evaluations; information that is already generally known falls under both definitions. However, there is a difference regarding the processing of data: non-public legal entities have to comply with the provisions of the BDSG if they use methods of automated data processing, which also covers methods of more traditional record keeping.[15]

Having partially the same scope as other obligations of secrecy, s 1, para 3, sentence 2 of the BDSG states that special obligations of secrecy are left unaltered. This includes bank confidentiality,[16] while the BDSG ensures the minimum standard of data protection. Therefore, a bank has to ensure that it meets not only the requirements under the contractual secrecy obligation, but must also check whether in a given case the standards set by the BDSG are met. The latter holds especially true for the use of personal data within a bank.

Limitations on the protection of data

[14.16] The basic principle for the treatment of personal data is laid down in s 4, para 1 of the BDSG: it allows inquiries for data processing and use of data in accordance with the provisions of any statute, including the BDSG, or if the person to whom the data relates has consented to the treatment. The first exception to data protection is identical to the limitation on the secrecy obligation. Section 28, paras 1, 2 and 3 of the BDSG allows certain uses of data in non-governmental entities for professional purposes, the protection of the entity's legitimate interests and assisting in a criminal prosecution. These provisions correspond for the most part with the limitations on bank confidentiality.

However, a difference exists regarding the customer's consent. There is no obligation for the consent relating to the bank's secrecy obligation to be given expressly, since an implied consent would suffice; the BDSG requires express consent in written form allowing for only a few exceptions (s 4a). This means that the protection provided by the secrecy obligation is weaker than that under the BDSG; therefore – applying the principle of s 1, para 2 of the BDSG – the contractual provisions should be overruled.

---

12 Gola in Gola and Schomerus *Bundesdatenschutzgesetz* (8th edn, 2005) s 1, no 6, BVerfGE 65, p 1ff.
13 Gola, n 12 above, s 1, no 7.
14 Gola, n 12 above, s 3, no 11.
15 Gola, n 12 above, s 3, no 15.
16 Gola, n 12 above, s 1, no 25.

However, even implied consent is possible[17] since the bank pursues a legitimate interest of its own when fulfilling its obligation under the contract in providing the service the client requested and thus acting in the interest of the client as well.

Finally, it remains to be stated that the practical consequences of differences between secrecy obligations and the law of data protection are of little importance. Nevertheless, the bank has to ensure that the provisions of the BDSG are followed, since breach may constitute a criminal or administrative offence under ss 43 and 44 of the BDSG.

EXCEPTIONS TO THE SECRECY OBLIGATION

[14.17]   As stated above, clause 2, para 1 of the General Business Conditions lays down three main exceptions to the bank's secrecy obligation: a customer's consent, request for banking information and disclosure that is required or permitted by law.

Customer's consent

[14.18]   Since the actual wish of the bank's client is decisive with regard to what information shall be kept secret, he is obviously free to release the bank from its secrecy obligation. He may do so for a particular case or may grant the release generally in advance; the release may be complete or restricted to certain types of information. Whether the consent has been given to the bank directly or to a third party is of no importance. Even an implicit release which can be deduced from the customer's behaviour will suffice.

If the customer did not consent expressly or where the bank has no knowledge of circumstances giving indications regarding the customer's actual wish, the bank may assume that the customer's actual wish corresponds to the hypothetical wish of a reasonable average customer.[18]

In the particular case of outsourcing of data processing work or other tasks to third parties, it is advisable to obtain the customer's consent in advance. The applicability of ss 11 and 27 of the BDSG, which generally allows for the transfer of data processing and processing tasks without the customer's consent, is hotly disputed in its details.[19]

Another particular case in which the customer's consent has been generally given in advance concerns the so-called 'SCHUFA'. The SCHUFA is an entity set up by banks and other enterprises that regularly give credit to their customers. From its partners and public registers, the SCHUFA collects information regarding people's creditworthiness. The partners are obliged to transmit information about their customers to the SCHUFA in a standard format containing factual information about the customer relationship. The information given to and received by the SCHUFA does not contain any information about the financial circumstances of a person or an evaluation of his creditworthiness. The SCHUFA passes on information relating to a certain person if the partner who requested it has demonstrated a legitimate interest

---

17 Koberstein-Windpassinger, n 3 above, at pp 477 and 481.
18 Bruchner, n 2 above, p 747 et seq.
19 Steding and Meyer *Outsourcing von Bankdienstleistungen: Bank- und datenschutzrechtliche Probleme der Aufgabenverlagerung von Kreditinstituten auf Tochtergesellschaften und sonstige Dritte* (2001) BB, p 1693.

in that information and the person has agreed to the collection of this information. The customer of a bank will generally be asked to declare his consent to that procedure in advance when, for example, a banking contract is concluded.

Banking information

Definition

[14.19] Banking information is an instrument that has been developed between banks to share reliable information about the creditworthiness of their business partners. According to the contract, a bank must furnish to another true and complete information it possesses about its clients.[20] A bank will be liable for damages if it negligently breaches this duty. It is important to state that, according to clause 2, para 4 of the General Business Conditions, banking information will be provided not only to other banks, but also to clients of a bank.

Clause 2, para 2 of the General Business Conditions defines what kind of information may be provided. The rule covers general statements and comments as to the financial circumstances of the bank's customer. Unlike the SCHUFA system, the information here will not contain specific data, but comprises comments on the banking relationship, bank account movements and an evaluation of creditworthiness. The only exception to this rule is when a bank possesses information concerning cheques returned unpaid and complaints about bills.[21]

The bank is only obliged to transmit information currently available; a duty to conduct further investigation does not exist. When passing on information, the bank has to do so concisely, revealing no unnecessary information.

Preconditions of disclosure

[14.20] Clause 2, para 2 of the General Business Conditions lays down different requirements for two types of bank clients: business persons and others. Business persons are all legal entities and natural persons registered in the Commercial Register and their banking relationship can be attributed to the professional sector. Regarding these customers, banking information is considered a trade custom; business persons are assumed to know of, and to have consented to, the disclosure through implied conduct. However, a business person might prove the contrary and will then be treated as a non-business person.

Release of information about non-business persons always requires their express consent, which may generally be given in advance. For both types of clients, the requirements are the existence of a credible legitimate interest in the information and the assumption that no legitimate interest of the customer against disclosure exists. An example of an interest of the bank requesting information may be to avoid the risk of entering into business relations with insolvent debtors, while, on the customer side, banking information itself limits his legitimate interest in keeping financial information secret. Therefore, the bank has the obligation to apply a balancing test to consider which interest prevails. Should the outcome of that test not clearly favour disclosure, it is advisable to seek the specific consent of the customer concerned.

---

20 BGH in ZIP 1999, p 275.
21 Bruchner, n 2 above, p 792.

Statutory exceptions

[14.21] Generally speaking, statutory exceptions can regularly be found when state authorities require banks to furnish information necessary for the achievement of public functions, for example, in a broad variety of administrative procedures, but under certain circumstances disclosure of confidential information is also allowed when statutory provisions govern the resolution of conflicts between private persons.

Tax proceedings

[14.22] Confidentiality in tax proceedings is one of the most controversial issues since the provision acknowledging the existence of secrecy obligations (s 30a of the Tax Procedure Act) is widely considered to be unconstitutional. During the normal procedure of tax assessment, such an issue has no practical impact – only the Federal Constitutional Court may decide on the unconstitutionality of a statute – but it gives rise to problems regarding investigations of tax evasion.

Tax assessment

[14.23] In principle, banks must furnish information to the competent tax authorities about their customers and produce the relevant documents as if the secrecy obligation did not exist (s 93, para 1 and s 97, para 1 of the Tax Procedure Act) and, in fact, bank confidentiality is not a professional secret in the sense of s 102 of the Tax Procedure Act. However, banks are considered a 'special kind of information source'[22] and therefore s 30a of the Tax Procedure Act has been introduced to demonstrate the respect for the particular relationship between the bank and its customer, as s 30a, para 1 makes clear.

According to s 30a of the Tax Procedure Act, information from a bank may not be required for the purposes of general supervision, merely a repetition of the principle of due course of law,[23] according to which investigations commenced out of the blue are unlawful. While paras 3 and 4 do not apply to the procedure of tax assessment, para 5, sentence 1 states the applicability of s 93 of the Tax Procedure Act where, in para 1, sentence 3, the principle of subsidiarity is laid down. Consequently, information may only be requested from a bank if it cannot be obtained from the taxpayer himself. Furthermore, the request has to be both necessary and appropriate with respect to the assessment of taxes.[24] Such information, and the scope in which it is requested, must be stated in detail.

In practice, the tax authorities assume that the taxpayer's declaration of income is true and complete.[25] Lack of personnel prevents them from requesting information from banks even where it would be possible.[26] Therefore, further investigation will only take place in the presence of aggravating circumstances when, for instance, systematic or large-scale tax evasion and active collaboration by the bank is suspected.

---

22 Carl and Klos *Bankgeheimnis und Quellensteuer im Vergleich internationaler Finanzmärkte* (1993), p 33.
23 Metzner in Beermann *Steuerliches Verfahrensrecht – AO, FGO, Nebengesetze – Kommentar*, AO, s 30a, no 41.
24 Carl and Klos, n 22 above, p 34.
25 Metzner, n 23 above, AO, s 30a, no 38.
26 Ehrhardt-Rauch and Rauch *Ist der Schutz von Bankkunden nach §30a AO auch künftig noch haltbar? – Neue Wege bei der europäischen Zinsbesteuerung* (2002) DStR, p 57 at 58.

When the bank receives a request from the tax authorities, it is obliged to verify whether the requirements for a lawful request have been satisfied, otherwise the bank must refuse to disclose the information as an unlawful request does not release the bank from its secrecy obligations. If the request is lawful, the bank has to provide the requested information honestly and completely.

Where the lawfulness of the request is in doubt, both bank and customer may file a petition for administrative review and if the petition is denied they may initiate proceedings before a fiscal court. Bank employees are obliged to testify before a fiscal court: s 84 of the Fiscal Procedure Act and s 102 of the Tax Procedure Act.

In addition, the tax authorities may demand information to discover tax-related facts if the tax authorities have tried to obtain information from the taxpayer without success (s 93, paras 7 and 8 and s 93b of the Tax Procedure Act). Thus, the same principle of subsidiarity applies as with regard to s 93, para 1, sentence 3 of the Tax Procedure Act. The tax authorities can require access to all German bank accounts via the interface that German banks had to implement under s 24c of the Banking Act (see 'Supervision of the German Banking System' below). The banks must establish this interface to their data in a way that allows the tax authorities to access the data without their knowledge. Thus, neither the bank nor the taxpayers know when the tax authorities check their data. Legal commentators still debate whether this extensive access to customer data is in line with the above-mentioned rules of the German constitution regarding the secrecy of customers' data and which might prevail.[27] However, with this new instrument established in April 2005, the tax authorities are in a position to prevent tax evasion at a very early stage. Some politicians have argued that this further reduction in the former high standards of the bank secrecy obligation may discipline taxpayers when filing their tax returns.

Finally, even with respect to foreign authorities, the secrecy obligation proves too weak: a request for information made by a foreign authority will be fulfilled by its German counterpart provided that the requirements of the Tax Procedure Act are met.[28]

Investigation in respect of tax evasion

[14.24]   The investigation of financial fraud has a different objective (s 208 of the Tax Procedure Act covers tax evasion and the investigation of cases where taxes have not yet been assessed), but it is conducted by the same authorities and basically follows the same rules.

According to s 208, para 1, sentence 3 of the Tax Procedure Act, the principle of subsidiarity of s 93, para 1, sentence 3 of the Act is not generally applicable to the investigation procedure, thus enlarging the competence of the tax authorities, but s 30a, para 5, sentence 2 of the Tax Procedure Act re-establishes the applicability of that principle. Furthermore, s 30a, paras 2 and 3 of the Act limit the powers of the tax authorities. Therefore, the protection of confidential information depends on whether or not the provision of s 30a is constitutional.

Prior to the introduction of s 30a of the Tax Procedure Act, the tax authorities based their activities on a regulatory order with almost identical contents; it was declared

---

27 Schmidt *Das neue Kontenabrufverfahren auf dem Prüfstand* (2005) BB, p 2155.
28 Carl and Klos, n 22 above, p 70.

unconstitutional by the Federal Constitutional Court in 1991.[29] Instead of creating the potential to assess taxes equally and abolishing s 30a of the Tax Procedure Act, the legislator raised the tax-free allowance tenfold, ensuring equal taxation of all capital gains within that allowance.

A PRAGMATIC SOLUTION

[14.25]   The fact that s 30a of the Tax Procedure Act still constituted an obstacle to investigations was no longer considered a problem, although the provision itself was not brought before the Federal Constitutional Court.

In 1999, the allowance was cut by 50% and constitutional concerns are growing once more.[30] Moreover, in 1997, the eighth senate of the Federal Fiscal Court held that the provision had to be construed along the guidelines set out by the verdict of the Federal Constitutional Court and could therefore be saved from unconstitutionality.[31] Contrary to this, the seventh senate of the Federal Fiscal Court held in 2000 that the eighth senate's interpretation of s 30a of the Tax Procedure Act was compatible neither with the wording of that provision nor with the will of the legislator. The seventh senate made clear that it considered the provision unconstitutional, but was unable to submit the question to the Federal Constitutional Court for procedural reasons. The practical consequences were, according to the first opinion, a tax inspector inspecting a bank may pass on information to other authorities regarding customers of that bank if he reaches the conclusion (based on fact) that taxes might not have been assessed correctly, while, according to the second opinion, the protection of the secrecy obligation would prevail. The question remains open.

On the horizon, the next challenge is already visible – the EU is currently elaborating a directive aiming at the harmonisation of taxes on capital gains.[32] In January 2003, 12 member states, including Germany, decided to set up a systematic exchange of information between the tax authorities of all member states of the EU. Under this system, banks in Germany would be obliged to transmit information about non-German customers to the German tax authorities, which would then pass on the information to the competent tax authority abroad. That system could leave s 30a of the Tax Procedure Act unaltered since it applies to German taxpayers, but the question automatically arises whether such provision is compatible with the prohibition against discrimination of European citizens and with the guarantees of free movement of services and capital within the European single market.[33] While a reasonable justification for the discrimination of taxpayers is conceivable, the provisions regarding the single market could be breached by leaving s 30a unchanged.[34] In any case, it is desirable that German legislation acts with more sense of responsibility and far-sightedness than in the past.

Penal proceedings for tax offences

[14.26]   A prosecution can be carried out either by the tax authorities themselves or by the office of public prosecution. Both have the same powers based on the Criminal

---

29 BVerfG in ZIP 1991, p 1123.
30 Blesinger *Materielle Steuerpflicht von Zinseinkünften nach § 20 I Nr 7 EStG und Ermittlungsbefugnisse der Finanzbehörden* (2001) NJW, p 1459 at 1460.
31 BFH in NJW 1997, p 2067.
32 Blesinger, n 30 above, at p 1463.
33 Ehrhardt-Rauch and Rauch, n 26 above, at p 63.
34 Ehrhardt-Rauch and Rauch, n 26 above, at p 64.

Procedure Act, instead of the Tax Procedure Act, and therefore problems regarding s 30a of the Tax Procedure Act will not occur. Against such measures, both the bank and the customer may file a complaint before a court of ordinary jurisdiction (s 23 of the Introductory Act to the System of Judicature Act).

Special information duties

[14.27] According to s 45d of the Income Tax Act, banks are obliged to disclose to the tax authorities to what extent a single customer has made use of his tax-free allowance of capital gains.

Section 33 of the Inheritance Tax Act imposes on banks the duty to inform the tax authorities regarding all goods of deceased customers which the bank holds in its possession, as well as all claims.

Both rules are special regulations in relation to s 30a of the Tax Procedure Act and this is why s 30a of the Tax Procedure Act is never applicable in these circumstances.[35]

Criminal proceedings

No right to refuse to give evidence

[14.28] Section 53 of the Criminal Procedure Act enumerates the professional secrets enjoying protection in criminal proceedings. Unlike auditors, banks and their employees are not included in the list. Interpretation enlarging the scope of the provision is universally rejected both by the courts and commentators[36] based on the argument that even the legislator has to respect certain limits in order to maintain the efficiency of criminal proceedings.

Preliminary investigation

[14.29] The secrecy obligation is not protected during a preliminary investigation, but no person is obliged to make any statements concerning the subject of the investigation unless he is being questioned by a district attorney (s 161a, para 1, sentence 1 of the Criminal Procedure Act).

If factual information gives reason to believe the bank might be in possession of objects that could be seized according to s 94, para 1 of the Criminal Procedure Act because they constitute evidence, the office of public prosecution has the power to search the bank (s 103, para 1, sentence 1 of the Criminal Procedure Act). General experience or mere speculation are not sufficient.[37] For example, the Federal Constitutional Court upheld the constitutionality of measures against several subsidiaries of a bank based on the suspicion that one subsidiary had helped its customers evade taxes.[38] The judgments have been widely criticised, but, so far, courts regard similar searches as lawful.[39]

---

35 Metzner, n 23 above, AO, s 30a, no 8, 73.
36 Dahs in Löwe and Rosenberg *Die Strafprozessordnung und das Gerichtsverfassungsgesetz* (25th edn, 1999) s 53, no 4.
37 Kleinknecht and Meyer-Goßner *Strafprozessordnung* (48th edn, 2005) s 94, no 8, s 152, no 4.
38 BVerfG in WM 1994, p 691; BVerfG in WM 1995, p 234.
39 LG Bielefeld in WM 2000, p 239.

If the bank has no right to refuse to provide evidence, the bank also has no right to object to the seizure of documents or objects according to s 97, para 1 of the Criminal Procedure Act. Evidence regarding further criminal acts that was found by chance may be seized as well, but prosecutors are not competent to search for anything that is not covered by the objectives of the search order.

In principle, search orders have to be issued by a judge of proper jurisdiction (s 105 of the Criminal Procedure Act) and it is only in rare cases of emergency (for example, a bank employee being suspected of having aided in the criminal act) that a search order issued by the office of public prosecution will suffice. The search order must specifically name the investigated offence and may only be carried out during the hours of daylight unless there are particular circumstances (s 104 of the Criminal Procedure Act).

Often, the public prosecutor will specifically ask the bank to provide the information requested, thus rendering a search and seizure of documents superfluous. Of course, the bank is not obliged to hold back the information for as long as possible and as long as the formal requirements are not avoided, it may pass on the information, but it is important to emphasise that unless all requirements are met (including the search order issued by a judge), the bank is not obliged to produce any documents. Therefore, the bank is also obliged to check whether or not the request for information is lawful. To protect itself and its customers' interests, it may request the decision of a judge when the search has been conducted by virtue of an order from the office of public prosecution issued in an emergency or it may file a complaint against the judicial order.

International co-operation in criminal matters

[14.30]   The application of the Act on International Assistance in Criminal Matters ('IRG') is broad, 'assistance' meaning every part of the criminal proceedings from preliminary investigation to execution of a sentence, irrespective of whether the assistance is requested by a foreign court or other authority (s 59, para 2 of the IRG).

Sections 59ff of the IRG, in particular, interfere with the bank's secrecy obligation as they allow assistance basically in accordance with the German provisions on investigative measures and criminal proceedings (s 59, para 3 of the IRG). That means that the same requirements as stated in ss 94ff and 103ff of the Criminal Procedure Act for seizure of documents and searches of bank premises must be met[40] if the German authorities are to lend assistance to foreign authorities.[41]

Within the field of application of the European Convention on Mutual Assistance in Criminal Matters – provided Germany and the country of the requesting authority have both ratified the Convention – international co-operation differs only slightly from the IRG's provisions since Germany has declared a reservation regarding art 5, para 1, letters a and c of the Convention establishing the prerequisite that the crime investigated be punishable in both countries and the investigation is compatible with German law.

---

40 Lagodny in Schomburg and Lagodny *Internationale Rechtshilfe in Strafsachen* (3th edn, 1998), p 208.
41 Lagodny, n 40 above, p 318.

The ratification of the Convention on Money Laundering, Search, Seizure and Confiscation of the Proceeds of Crime on behalf of Germany has brought no changes to the previously existing legal situation.

Other proceedings

Civil and other judicial proceedings

[14.31] Contrary to the situation during criminal proceedings, the secrecy obligation is protected according to s 383, para 1, n 6 of the Civil Procedure Act and the bank's employees are obliged under the banking contract with their customer to refuse to give evidence.[42] However, the customer may release the bank from this obligation; bank employees are then obliged to testify, as are all normal witnesses (s 385, para 2 of the Civil Procedure Act).

The bank is entitled to refuse to testify if giving evidence would lead to financial losses (s 384, nn 1 and 3 of the Civil Procedure Act), for example, giving rise to liability on the part of the bank for damages for a breach of its secrecy obligation.[43] The customer's consent will not overrule the right to refuse to testify, but excludes the possibility of liability for damages.

Both provisions may be invoked where German judicial organs act upon a request by foreign courts within the scope of the Hague Convention on the Taking of Evidence Abroad in Civil and Commercial Matters (art 11, para 1, letter a). Furthermore, they apply before labour courts, in insolvency proceedings (s 4 of the Insolvency Code), in proceedings of voluntary jurisdiction (s 15 of the Code of Voluntary Judgments) and in proceedings before administrative (s 98 of the Administrative Procedure Code) and social courts (s 118, para 1 of the Social Procedure Code).

Declaration of third party debtor

[14.32] A judgment against a bank's customer might be enforced by attaching the customer's claims against the bank, such as his bank account. In these cases, the bank is obliged – just like any other third party debtor – to give the declaration of a third party debtor according to s 840, para 1 of the Civil Procedure Act. The declaration comprises the statement as to whether the bank recognises the claim and whether other creditors have already claimed or attached it. No further information regarding other claims of the customer or private facts is to be revealed.

Administrative procedure

[14.33] Participants in administrative procedures are not generally obliged to reveal information, but some special regulations do apply concerning social welfare law. For instance, if a bank's customer has applied for unemployment benefits, the bank is under a duty to pass on information about the financial situation not only of the applicant, but also of his spouse or partner if that information cannot be obtained otherwise, in particular, where the statements made by the applicant are not credible.

If a customer has requested public welfare, the bank itself is not obliged to disclose information, but s 60, para 1, n 1 of the General Social Code imposes a requirement to release the bank from its secrecy obligation.

---

42 Greger in Zöller *Zivilprozessordnung* (25th edn, 2004) s 383, no 20.

Since the second edition of this book, the number of contracting parties to the European Convention on Mutual Assistance in Administrative Matters has risen to six, so the Convention is still of only little practical importance.

Supervision of security exchanges

[14.34] The trade of securities in Germany is subject to special supervision aimed at preserving the integrity of the financial market, first, through control of the institutions participating in the exchange and, secondly, through control of the trade itself, with particular respect to insider trading. The secrecy obligation may come under the provisions regarding insider trading in two instances: the bank may be requested by the competent supervision authority (Federal Financial Supervisory Authority, *Bundesanstalt für Finanzdienstleistungsaufsicht*, 'BaFin') to supply information or the bank might be tempted to use inside information to their own or their clients' advantage.

OBLIGATIONS OF DISCLOSURE REGARDING INSIDER TRADING AND COMPLIANCE ORGANISATIONS

[14.35] The competence of supervision is limited by the definitions of 'insider', 'inside information' and 'inside securities'.[44] The latter covers stocks, bonds, stock options and others (s 2, paras 1 and 1a and s 12, sentence 1 of the Securities Trading Act), while inside information is concrete information about non-publicly known circumstances relating to the issuer or the securities themselves and capable of influencing the price of the security if publicly known. It is evident that the secrecy obligation covers more protected information than the prohibition of insider trading; in other words, not all information falling under bank confidentiality is inside information. Section 14, para 1 of the Securities Trading Act prohibits insiders from trading in securities on the basis of their inside knowledge, to pass on the inside information and to recommend the purchase or sale to third parties.

Due to the risks that may arise out of the misuse of inside information, banks and investment service companies must have sufficient compliance organisations (s 33, para 1 of the Securities Trading Act and s 25a, para 1 of the Banking Act). These organisations strive to prevent the abuse of inside information or the appearance of conflicts of interest which may lead to a disadvantage for customers (for example, if a bank acts in a transaction as investment bank and lender). A compliance organisation includes the establishment of so-called 'Chinese Walls' or 'areas of confidentiality' which have the function of keeping confidential information with the departments of the bank that need this information to render the service to the client (the 'need to know' principle). The compliance officers supervise the effectiveness of Chinese Walls via 'watch lists' and 'restricted lists'. Bank staff have to notify their internal compliance officers about all potential inside information. The compliance officers then decide whether the inside information should lead to a ban on trading of the securities related to the inside information or if trading of these securities should only be supervised. If they decide to prohibit trading, they put the relevant securities on the 'restricted list' which is publicly available within the bank for all employees. If they just decide to supervise whether the employees comply with the insider

---

43 Geger, n 42 above, s 384, no 7.
44 Assmann/Schneider *Wertpapierhandelsgesetz* (3rd edn, 2006) pre s 12, no 14.

trading restriction, they put the relevant securities on the confidential 'watch list'. By controlling all trading operations within the bank (regardless of whether they are carried out on behalf of the bank or on their own account) and comparing the results with the entries on these lists, they are able to detect any kind of prohibited insider trading at a very early stage.[45]

In addition to the aforementioned self-regulation of banks, the BaFin has been given certain powers to ensure that the prohibitions of the Securities Exchange Act are respected. First, s 9, para 1 of the Securities Trading Act obliges all institutions offering services relating to the exchange of securities to furnish particular information on every single exchange made by them. This information comprises data to identify the securities traded, date and time of sale, price and number of traded securities and – added by the fourth Financial Market Promotion Act – distinguishing marks for the depot holder and principal. If this information gives reason to believe that a breach of the regulations on insider trading has been committed, the BaFin may require the bank to give detailed information about the trading, including the information necessary to identify the principal, as well as the production of documents relating to the trading. Finally, in such cases, the bank has to acquiesce to a search of its premises (s 4 of the Securities Trading Act).[46]

The information obtained in this manner may be communicated by the BaFin to similar authorities in other member states of the EU according to s 7 of the Securities Trading Act; refusal of transmission is only permitted in very few cases (s 7, para 2 of the Securities Trading Act).

ADVISING INVESTORS

[14.36]   Without the slightest doubt, the bank is prohibited from using any inside information it has obtained in the course of a banking relationship with a client for its own sale and acquisition of securities, but when a bank advises one of its customers regarding his investments, it is obliged to provide complete and true information regarding the investment, as well as to render competent services.[47] Does this contractual duty exempt the bank from the prohibition on disclosing inside information and not to recommend transactions based on such information? It does not because a contractual provision cannot constitute grounds sufficient to justify a breach of a statutory provision.[48] Therefore, information subject to the secrecy obligation which, at the same time, amounts to inside information may not be disclosed to other customers of the bank. Whether this also holds true for information not falling under the definition of inside information remains to be seen (see 'Conflict of Duties' below).

MARKET MANIPULATION

[14.37]   The Securities Trading Act includes a ban on price manipulation (s 20a). Under s 20b, the BaFin may request information as to manipulation in the sense of s 20a from banks and institutions offering services relating to security trading. The rules are based on the European Market Abuse Directive 2004/72/EC and are accompanied by the BaFin's regulation on market manipulation (from March 2005).

---

45 Assmann/Schneider n 44 above, s 33, no 31 et seq.
46 Assmann/Schneider, n 44 above, pre s 12, no 28.
47 Assmann *Insiderrecht und Kreditwirtschaft* (1996) WM, p 1337 at 1352.
48 Assmann, n 47 above, at p 1351.

Supervision of the German banking system

[14.38]   The supervision of banks and similar institutions aims to prevent damage to the banking structure and – being a key function[49] – to the economy as a whole, as well as to avoid losses to individual customers.[50] The BaFin was established in 2002 and now centralises all supervisory competence regarding financial services and also exercises control both of the inner structure of banks and their business practices. To accomplish these tasks, the BaFin is authorised to request information from all banks and similar institutions (defined in s 1, para 1 of the Banking Act) on every part of their business and without any special cause (s 44 of the Banking Act),[51] for example, on the development of income and expenditure, large loans and even information regarding a single customer relationship. However, it is not entitled to request information incompatible with the control of structure and conduct of business and, furthermore, the request must be both necessary and appropriate to the accomplishment of its tasks.[52]

If those requirements are met, the authority also has the power to request documentation from the bank and carry out an audit. According to s 44a of the Banking Act, the BaFin assists foreign authorities in the supervision of German banks when the principles mentioned above are met.

Section 24c of the Banking Act obliges banks to create the facilities enabling online access (interface) by the BaFin to the banks' data.[53] The online access will release the authority from the necessity to issue an individual request to each of the nearly 3000 banks in Germany and will enable the BaFin to control 'with which institutions a certain person or a certain organisation maintains banking relationships'.[54] Even more than the desire of the authorities that banks screen their customers' data, this provision is bound to impair the trust of customers in bank confidentiality since the authority may pass on the data collected (bank account number, date of opening and closure, name and date of birth) to other authorities enumerated in s 24c, para 3 of the Banking Act if it is required for their purposes.[55] In addition, the tax authorities have access to this data (see 'Tax Assessment' above).

Section 25b of the Banking Act requires banks and similar institutions to collect data on the identity, bank account number and address of customers wishing to transfer money to a country other than a member state of the EU. It must also transmit the information to the bank receiving the transferred funds.

Criminal law and money laundering[56]

Section 261 of the Criminal Code

[14.39]   The purpose of this long and complicated provision is to combat money laundering, ie the introduction of money or goods deriving from criminal acts, such as tax evasion, theft, burglary and dealing in illegal drugs, into the legal circulation

---

49   Fülbier, in Boos/Fischer/Schulte-Mattler *Kreditwesengesetz* (2nd edn, 2004) Introduction, no 61 et seq.

50   Begründung zum KWG in BT Drs. III/(2563) as quoted in Boos, n 49 above, Introduction, no 61.

51   Braun, in Boos/Fischer/Schulte-Mattler, n 49 above, s 44, no 6 et seq.

52   Braun, in Boos/Fischer/Schulte-Mattler, n 49 above, s 44, no 42.

53   Stein, in Boos/Fischer/Schulte-Mattler, n 49 above, s 24c, no 2.

54   Federal Ministry of Finance, press release, 19 June 2002.

55   Escher *Bankaufsichtsrechtliche Änderungen im KWG durch das Vierte Finanzmarktförderungsgesetz* (2002) BKR, p 652 at 658.

of money. It punishes the concealment of such goods and covering up their origin, as well as acquiring or keeping such goods for someone else. This criterion is fulfilled when a bank accepts money on deposit or to transfer it. According to s 261, para 5 of the Criminal Code, the recklessness of the person accepting the proceeds from crime is sufficient to commit the offence. Obviously, according to principles of the rule of law, a bank employee is not obliged to incriminate himself if he fears that he has committed the offence of money laundering, but such self-incrimination does constitute grounds for mitigation of sentence (s 261, paras 9 and 10 of the Criminal Code), thus exercising considerable pressure on bank employees to do so.

The Act on the Detection of Proceeds from Serious Crimes

[14.40] This Act (the so-called 'Anti-Money Laundering Act', 'AML') contains provisions in order to obtain information on money laundering from banks and is therefore an implementation law with regard to s 261 of the Criminal Code. It imposes on banks duties to identify their customers thoroughly, to report any suspicious movement of money and to keep records of transactions. If a bank breaches these duties, it may constitute negligent conduct in the sense of s 261, para 5 of the Criminal Code. It always constitutes a minor offence (s 17 of the AML).

The current version of the AML, as amended on 15 December 2003, is based on the Second European Money Laundering Directive 2001/09/EC. The German Ministry of Finance announced that Germany aims to implement the Third European Money Laundering Directive 2005/60/EC by the end of 2006. Germany follows the recommendations of the Financial Action Task Force on Money Laundering ('FATF'). In its annual report 1993/94, the organisation attested that Germany follows the FATF's objectives in an exemplary manner. Further, the FATF carried out evaluations and examinations in Germany in 1997 as to whether Germany had complied with the FATF recommendations. Again, the report showed that the anti-money laundering measures taken by the German government were seen as highly commendable.[57]

The obligation to identify a customer comes into existence when the customer requires a transaction exceeding certain limits (ss 2 to 5 of the AML). According to s 11 of the AML, if a bank notices suspicious behaviour by its clients, it is under a duty to give notice of this suspicion to the competent prosecution authorities. The obligation requires that all information leading to the suspicion that a certain transaction amounts to money laundering be disclosed. The suspicion may be based on striking details of a certain transaction or on deviations from normal conduct. It is not necessary for the bank to suspect that the money originates from a criminal act.

In contrast to s 261 of the Criminal Code, which lays down the punishments for individuals, s 11 of the AML imposes the duty on the bank itself. The bank is required to ensure it complies with the provisions of the AML through measures such as the appointment of a money laundering officer and the adoption of procedures for the detection of money laundering. The pressure put on individual bank employees is therefore lessened because if a bank employee reports a suspicion to the competent officer he will not be punishable for negligence. In addition, s 14, para 2, n 2 of the AML requires the development of internal principles and the adoption of appropriate

---

56 Langweg, in Fülbier/Aepfelbach/Langweg *Geldwäschegesetz* (5th edn, 2006) s 14, no 185.
57 Fülbier, in Fülbier/Aepfelbach/Langweg, n 56 above, Introduction, no 59.

security measures relating to transactions and clients to prevent money laundering and the financing of terrorist groups. The method proposed by the BaFin is to analyse the patterns of money laundering, to gather the available information on every customer relationship and to search that data for circumstances similar to the patterns of money laundering. If this so-called 'screening' leads to a suspicion that there might be a case of money laundering (ie a breach of s 261 of the Criminal Code), the bank is obliged under s 11 of the AML to notify the authorities. Section 11, para 5 of the AML expressly prohibits the bank from disclosing to its clients or to other authorities of foreign countries that it has notified the competent authorities ('tipping off'); an infringement of this rule constitutes a minor offence (s 17, para 2, no 2 of the AML). The AML does not include a specific sanction with regard to the failure to comply with the notification requirement. However, if a bank fails to report a suspicious transaction, the employees involved are in danger of breaching s 261 of the Criminal Code themselves. By stating the potential culpability of omitting to notify the authorities, German legislation already complies with the requirement set out in art 39 of the Third European Money Laundering Directive 2005/60/EC.[58]

If a bank is forced to disclose customer data with regard to suspicious transactions, this disclosure would not be construed as an infringement of the secrecy obligation. Even if a bank wants to disclose facts without being obliged to do so, it may be authorised to breach the secrecy obligation (for example, if employees of a bank may otherwise incur a penalty in the context of a money laundering transaction by the bank's client).[59]

Civil law

Cheques, bill of exchanges and debit entry

[14.41]   Before making a demand for payment, the payee usually asks the bank if it deems the cheque payable. The positive answer is that the bank considers the drawer's bank account sufficient to the payment on the cheque. The bank is entitled to reveal this information since drawing a cheque implies that the drawer reveals both the existence of a bank account and a certain sum in its bank account.

If the bank does not pay the cheque, the bank is entitled to disclose any information on the drawer necessary for the collection of the debt. That is grounded on the assumption that the drawer has tacitly consented to disclosure guaranteeing smooth processing of his cheques.[60]

On the other hand, permission to perform debit entries does not include an implied consent to answer a request on the bank account. While the cheque has been drawn for a certain sum, permission to perform debit entries is generally given for several debit entries in advance and furthermore depends on the submissions of accounts prior to the transaction.[61]

Guarantees and other third party sureties

[14.42]   If a third party guarantees a bank's claim against a bank customer, the bank may in particular circumstances be obliged to furnish information regarding the

58 Fülbier, n 57 above, s 11, no 49.
59 Fülbier, n 57 above, s 10, no 59 et seq.
60 Bruchner, n 2 above, p 749.
61 Bruchner, n 2 above, p 750.

customer to the guarantor, for example, if the bank has learned that the customer is not creditworthy, if it was plain to the bank that the guarantor acted erroneously or the customer himself caused the guarantor to bind itself.[62]

After a guarantor has satisfied the obligation, the claim against the debtor is automatically transferred to him (s 774 of the Civil Code). According to ss 412 and 402 of the Civil Code, the guarantor is then entitled to obtain all information necessary for collection of the debt, but does this right release the bank from its secrecy obligation? Since s 402 of the Civil Code only covers the legal relationship between assignee and the bank, in this case, it may not justify the breach of a third party interest.[63] Therefore, in principle, the bank has to keep its customer's information secret. There are various solutions to this problem: the bank may decide not to pass on information relating to the client and to work as a service agent collecting the debt for the assignee or it may seek the consent of the client to disclosure of information. Regarding certain types of assignments, the consent is presumed, for instance, when the assignment forms part of a structure to share the risk originating from the claim or generally if the claim is assigned to another bank that itself is subject to a secrecy obligation.[64] Commentators argue that the consent of a customer to sureties by third parties always contains the implied release of the bank from its secrecy obligation as far as information relating to the secured claims is concerned.[65]

If the bank reveals information, it will be facts such as the identity of the debtor, the amount of the claim and the delivery of existing deeds. Information irrelevant to the collection has to be made illegible.

Assignment of claims and execution of other sureties

[14.43]   This category applies to cases where the customer has assigned a claim to his bank – the assignment itself does not have to be disclosed to the debtor. On the contrary, very often, the client will expressly wish the assignment to be kept confidential. If payment of the assigned claim is delayed, the bank may disclose the assignment in order to try to collect the debt. Usually, this will be provided for expressly in the contract underlying the assignment, especially when an instalment plan exists. The extent to which information may be disclosed is again determined by the necessities of debt collection.

Asset-backed securities

[14.44]   Asset-backed securities transactions involve the assignment of a bank's claim against its customer to a legal entity (a so-called 'special purpose vehicle') which has been created to issue securities to investors using the assigned claims as a back up. Those transactions are undertaken by banks to limit their need for proprietary capital.[66] Regarding bank confidentiality, two problems occur: the bank is obliged to furnish information about the debtor (its customer) to the assignee

---

62 Bruchner, n 2 above, p 750.
63 Koberstein-Windpassinger, n 3 above, at p 478.
64 Früh *Abtretungen, Verpfändungen, Unterbeteiligungen, Verbriefungen und Derivate bei Kreditforderungen vor dem Hintergrund von Bankgeheimnis und Datenschutz* (2000) WM, p 497 at 503ff.
65 OLG Oldenburg in WM 1985, p 748.
66 Koberstein-Windpassinger, n 3 above, at p 473.

(according to s 402 of the Civil Code) and the investors of the special purpose vehicle will want to examine the financial reliability of the claims backing their investment. To ensure the success of asset-backed securities transactions, investors must be granted the opportunity to scrutinise the financial standing of the special purpose vehicle and, in particular, the assigned claims. Therefore, they must also have knowledge of information that relates to individual customers.

As explained above, s 402 of the Civil Code does not hinder the assignment of claims.[67] However, according to a recent decision by the Higher Regional Court (*Oberlandesgericht*) of Frankfurt, clause 2, para 1 of the General Business Conditions (see above for clause 2 of the General Business Conditions) included a prohibition on assignment of claims. Thus, the court held an assignment in the context of an asset-backed securities transaction null and void.[68] Legal scholars and other regional courts disagreed with this decision. They argued that disclosing information in the context of an asset-backed securities transaction does not breach the secrecy obligation due to the lack of secrecy obligations concerning the assignment. It was consequent that s 402 of the Civil Code also gave the right to receive information about the borrower of the loan even if performance is satisfactory.[69] Further, the customer on the other side did not have an interest in protection which would prevail over the interest of disclosure. In cases of unjustified disclosure, customers may claim damages against the bank on grounds of breach of the secrecy obligation, which is held to provide sufficient customer protection.[70] Advanced by the decision of the court in Frankfurt and in order to strengthen the German finance sector, the German legislator has implemented a so-called 'refinancing register' for true sale asset-backed securities transactions in s 22a ff of the Banking Act. These rules include the implied statement of the German legislator that bank secrecy does not hinder the assignment of claims for true sale asset-backed securities transactions (see s 22j, para 2, sentence 6 and s 22d, para 4 of the Banking Act).[71]

Insolvency proceedings

[14.45] Upon appointment of an administrator in insolvency, a legal entity or natural person loses his power of disposal to the administrator. Consequently, the administrator is entitled to obtain all information about the financial situation from the bank as long as the information concerns the insolvency procedure. The secrecy obligation prevails over other information such as facts from the private sector.

Inheritance

[14.46] The heirs of a deceased bank customer automatically step into the banking relationship. As the new customer of the bank, the heir is entitled to all information relating to the banking relationship, such as the existence of bank accounts, deposits, claims and so on. However, the courts have set up a barrier to the disclosure of

---

67 BGH in NJW 1982, pp 2768, 2770.
68 OLG Frankfurt in NJW 2004, p 3266.
69 OLG Köln in ZIP 2005, p 1773; LG Frankfurt in WM 2005, p 1120; LG Koblenz in WM 2005, p 30; Büchler *Zur Abtretung von Bankforderungen*, EWiR 2006, p 41.
70 BGH in NJW 1982, p 2768; LG Frankfurt in WM 2005, p 1120; Buchner, n 2 above, p 752.
71 Tollmann, *Refinanzierungsregister für Asset Backed Securities* (2005) ZHR 169, pp 594, 618.

information regarded as a personal secret of the deceased protecting his right to privacy[72] and even subsisting after the death of a person.

Persons entitled to a compulsory portion of the inheritance and legatees are not entitled to receive information from the bank – they may only invoke such right against the heir (s 2314 of the Civil Code).

Escrow accounts

[14.47]   Banks set up accounts for certain professions, such as notaries, lawyers and auditors, that accept money in a third party's name, administrate the money and transfer it to the third party. Regarding this type of account, only the trustee has power of disposal and is solely entitled to information. Therefore, a bank is not obliged to answer a request by the beneficiary and if it did so, it would be liable to the trustee. Not even the aforementioned principle of the inclusion of a person in close relation to the bank's customer applies since the contracts regarding escrow accounts expressly exclude such protection.[73]

Self-defence

[14.48]   Under s 227 of the Civil Code, a bank is entitled to disclose information if disclosure is necessary to prevent any damage arising from illegal acts committed by the bank itself or other people (such as employees, customers and other third parties). Refusal to pay will not amount to unlawful conduct, which has to interfere with a particularly protected interest of the bank or third person. Furthermore, self-defence is only an appropriate measure when the unlawful act is either about to begin or continues and has not been completed.

Conflict of duties

[14.49]   This exception designates a very broad category of which only individual cases have been expressly laid down in statutory provisions (such as s 227 of the Civil Code). It applies in cases where a bank is under contractual duties towards two (or more) customers and those duties conflict, ie the fulfilment of one duty excludes the fulfilment of the other. A typical example is when a secrecy obligation conflicts with the bank's duty to warn a second customer of risks relating to business with the first customer. In these cases, the principle that a bank is not obliged to warn customers about the risks relating to their business partners is universally recognised.[74] The situation changes though when a bank learns that one client is attempting to deceive the other. Whether the duty to warn prevails over the secrecy obligation is a question the bank has to consider very carefully; it has to perform a balancing test similar to the one mentioned regarding banking information in order to find out which of the interests involved proves stronger.[75]

Pursuit of legitimate interests

[14.50]   Where interests of customers may conflict, a conflict of a customer's interests with the interests of the bank is also conceivable. The justification of a

---

72 OLG Stuttgart in MDR 1983, p 236.
73 Bruchner, n 2 above, p 755.
74 BGH in WM 1978, p 1038; WM 1987, p 1546; WM 1989, p 1409.
75 BGH in WM 1991, p 85.

disclosure by overriding interests of the bank would be the general principle underlying self-defence in the sense of s 227 of the Civil Code. However, the applicability of that principle has only been recognised relating to the setting up of the SCHUFA system (see 'Customer's Consent' above).[76] General applicability to other cases must be denied since then the respect of the secrecy obligation would merely depend on a balancing test carried out by a bank knowing its own interest is at stake.[77] Exceptions to this principle may be made in single cases where a customer has acted contrary to loyalty and good faith causing damage to the bank, for instance, a customer may not invoke the secrecy obligation in a lawsuit against the bank.

76 BGH in WM 1978, p 999.
77 Bruchner, n 2 above, p 757.

15   Greece

Marios Bahas

INTRODUCTION

[15.1]   This chapter deals with the issues relating to bank secrecy and confidentiality under Greek law. Such rules are included in the Greek constitution of 1975, the Penal Code and statutes regulating the pertinent issues.

The statutes in question address, in particular, the nature of the obligation of confidentiality and remedies for their breach, as well as for breaches of bank secrecy, the exceptions to, and the scope of, the rules and the question of how foreign investigatory and supervisory bodies can gain access to confidential information.

Following this line of thought, this chapter will examine some practical examples related to such access and address the pertinent questions arising. Subsequently, examples concerning the tracing of funds both in Greece and abroad are discussed. The last part of the chapter addresses various areas of the law that are worthy of examination, such as insider dealing, cross-selling, the use of information stored as data and its protection. Finally, examples relating to conflict of interest and takeovers are discussed in the light of existing Greek legislation. In the latter case, a differentiation is made between financing through public subscription and private placement and the role of the bank is clarified accordingly.

OVERVIEW OF BANK SECRECY LAW

[15.2]   The rules of Greek law relating to bank secrecy are included in the Greek constitution, the Penal Code and statutes. A brief analysis of the relevant rules is therefore necessary.

Greek constitution

[15.3]   Article 19 of the constitution of 1975 stipulates the principle of protection of communication and correspondence. Such protection also embraces foreign persons as, according to art 4, both Greek citizens and foreign nationals enjoy the same civil rights. Consequently, the constitutional protection in question includes both bank secrecy and the duty of confidentiality for Greek and foreign nationals alike.

Penal Code

[15.4]   Article 371, para 1 of the Penal Code provides that the penalties of a fine or up to a year's imprisonment be imposed upon doctors, lawyers, notaries and other persons (such as bankers and bank officials) and their assistants entrusted with

357

private secrets in the exercise of their profession who reveal such secrets to third parties in any manner whatsoever. The article in question embraces both Greek and foreign persons without distinction.

Article 371, para 2 provides that criminal proceedings are not suspended in the case of the death of the person entrusted with such a secret and that proceedings continue against the person who acquires possession of the documents and any related notes.

Article 371, para 3 stipulates that an act is justified and should not be punishable if the person responsible is aiming to fulfil a duty or the protection of a lawful or otherwise justified substantial interest, either public, his own or of a third party, that could not be otherwise protected.

THE BANKS' DUTY OF CONFIDENCE
Banks

[15.5]   Article 1 of LD 1059/1971 provides that all deposits with Greek banks are secret, thereby excluding foreign banks from its ambit of protection. However, the controversy surrounding this was settled by art 10 of L 1858/1989, which has substituted the term 'Greek banks' with the broader term 'financial institutions', thereby embracing foreign banks as well.

The principle of the secrecy of bank deposits includes deposits of any kind, for example, deposits in money and claims deriving from bonds, bank transfers and the like. Therefore, the disclosure by a bank of any information in any way regarding deposits made is prohibited.

Remedies

[15.6]   Where there is a breach of bank secrecy and confidentiality as laid down in art 1 of LD 1059/1971, the liability is both criminal, as mentioned above, and civil.

Civil liability is based on art 914 of the Civil Code, which provides that 'whoever unlawfully and intentionally has caused damage to another is liable to pay compensation'. Particularly in the case of the breach of bank secrecy, the act in question is unlawful because it infringes art 914 of the Civil Code. However, the damage, the unlawfulness of the act, the intention and the adequate connection between the act and the damage must be proven.

The person liable is obliged to redress the damage and pay compensation that includes both positive damage and loss of profits.

Finally, an injunction to restrain publication is a remedy available under art 682ff of the Code of Civil Procedures to any person having a lawful interest.

THE EXCEPTIONS TO THE DUTY OF NON-DISCLOSURE

[15.7]   Article 2, para 2 of LD 1059/1971 provides that the consent of the person protected by the secrecy does not change the criminal character of the offence. This is a literal translation of the law, which seems to suggest that a criminal offence is committed even when the customer consents.

An exception, however, is one dictated by reasons of public interest. In particular, art 3 of LD 1059/1971 provides that the disclosure of information concerning bank deposits is lawful subject to the following requirements:

1. it must result from a duly reasoned order or application or decision of an investigating organ or judgment of a Greek court; and
2. such information must be absolutely necessary for the identification and punishment of actions characterised either as crimes committed in Greece or breaches of the national currency legislation.

Greek courts hold the view that, among other cases, the secrecy is inapplicable to the case of a bankruptcy receiver of a foreign company lawfully established in Greece who seeks relevant information from a bank.

Other exceptions have been introduced by statutes and administrative decisions. In particular:

1. Article 2 of L 1325/1972 waives bank secrecy in cases of cheques returned unpaid.
2. Decisions 213/19-1-1983 and 1132/1-9-1987 of the Governor of the Bank of Greece (being the central bank) establish the right of control of auditors appointed by the Bank of Greece.
3. Article 40 of L 1806/1988 waives bank secrecy as regards some persons appointed by the Bank of Greece in the exercise of its powers related to the supervision and control of the banking system.
4. Article 27, paras 1 and 2, sub-paras a and b of L 1868/1989 waive bank secrecy as regards crimes classified as felonies vis-á-vis the Bank of Greece.
5. Article 38 of L 1828/1989 waives the right of bank secrecy vis-á-vis the Bank of Greece in the case of the appointment of a commissioner to a bank by the Governor of the Bank of Greece.
6. Article 44 of L 2065/1992 provides that bank secrecy is waived:
   (a) in cases of tax evasion where the difference in the taxable amount exceeds 300 million drachmae, and
   (b) in cases where an amount exceeding 50 million drachmae deriving from deducted taxes, duties and contributions has not been rendered to the Greek state.
7. Article 25, para 1 of L 2214/1994 waives bank secrecy and stipulates that there exists an obligation to furnish the requested information to the director of the competent tax authority. Compliance with this obligation cannot be evaded by the invocation on the part of the interested party of the secrecy of bank deposits that is waived for the facilitation of tax control. However, for such a waiver, a joint decision of the tax authority inspector and of the director of the tax authority is necessary. Moreover, bank secrecy is waived as regards cheques issued in favour of the Greek state provided they exceed 1 million drachmae.
8. Article 66, para 1 of L 2238/1994 stipulates that bank secrecy can only be waived by means of a decision of the appropriate tax authority carrying out an audit or by a joint decision of the director of the competent tax authority and the director of the Internal Revenue Service. However, in cases of identified tax evasion, the waiver of bank secrecy also embraces those deposits kept in the name of the president and the managing director, as well as those kept in the name of the administrators of limited liability companies or general partnerships, in addition to the blocking of deposits kept in the name of the company.
9. Articles 4, 5, 7 and 8 of L 2331/1995 and Circular 2/1997 of the Governor of the

Bank of Greece regulate cases related to money laundering. Credit institutions are required to ask for evidence relating to the identity of the person in question for every transaction of 15,000 euros or more. Moreover, credit institutions should not make transactions for which they know or have valid suspicions that transactions are related to the legalisation of proceeds deriving from criminal activity, unless the immediate realisation of the transaction is urgently required, as well as in cases where the non-realisation of the action is likely to make difficult the disclosure of evidence or persons involved in the legalisation of such proceeds. Where an investigation is carried out with regard to the legalisation of proceeds deriving from criminal activity, the investigator, after a concurrent opinion of the prosecutor, may prohibit the use of the accounts, provided that valid suspicions exist that the accounts in question contain moneys deriving from the legalisation of proceeds related to criminal activity. The disclosure of information in such cases is allowed, provided it is made in good faith, and may be used in court. Finally, the committee established by art 7 accepts, evaluates and investigates any information related to transactions for the legalisation of proceeds deriving from criminal activities and transmitted to it by foreign agencies with which it co-operates for the provision of possible assistance.

10 Article 14 of L 2523/1997, as amended by virtue of L 2992/2002, reiterates, completes and explains with more clarity the process of implementation of the measures set by the dispositions of art 92 of L 2.238/1994 and more specifically:

(a) paragraph 1 provides that:

 a in cases of detected tax infringements concerning non-payment to the tax authorities of sums more than 150,000 euros, then:

  a.a with respect to the public sector, bank confidentiality of deposits, accounts, joint accounts, safe deposits, etc of the taxpayer is suspended,

  a.b 50% of the above-mentioned amount is blocked,

 b the above measures may also apply against the following:

  b.a in the case of Greek SAs, against the chairmen of the board of directors, the managing directors or the authorised directors, the governors, the general directors, the directors and any person authorised to the management of the SA,

  b.b in the case of partnership or joint stock companies, against the partners or their managers,

  b.c in the case of limited liability companies, against their managers,

  b.d in the case of co-operatives, against their presidents, secretaries or their treasurers or managers,

  b.e in the case of joint ventures, societies, civil, participating or sleeping companies, against their representatives,

  b.f in the case of foreign businesses and organisations, against their directors, representatives or agents in Greece,

(b) paragraph 2 provides procedural matters,

(c) paragraph 3 determines that, within a month from the notification of the above-mentioned persons, these persons may request the removal of the prohibitive measures after a petition to the Minister of Finance,

(d) paragraph 4 determines the process of obligatory removal of the above-mentioned prohibitive measures when the liable taxpayer pays 100% of the sum owing.

11 Article 2 of L 2713/1999:

(a) paragraph 2 provides:

a.a that the dispositions of art 3 of LD 1059/1971 apply to crimes of corruption of police officers determined in this law,

a.b the process of removal of confidentiality (mentioned above) regarding the removal of confidentiality of bank accounts,

(b) paragraph 2 also provides:

b.a the process and conditions that pertain to prohibition of use of the accounts or the safe deposits,

b.b that the public sector is entitled to proceed with the confiscation of any property belonging to police officers if the acquisition of this property is a result of the perpetration of crimes described in this law.

12 Article 24 of L 2915/2001 provides that:

'The confidentiality of any kind of accounts ... is not valid against the creditor who has the right to confiscate the property of the beneficiary of the account. The confidentiality may only be removed with respect to the amount that is required in order to satisfy the creditor.'

CONFIDENTIAL INFORMATION

[15.8]   As regards the issue of the access of foreign investigatory bodies and foreign supervisory bodies to confidential information in Greece, some distinctions may be drawn. First, branches of foreign banks established in Greece are governed by Greek law. In order, however, for such bodies to have access to information in Greece, it must be inquired whether a bilateral treaty of judicial assistance is in force between the two states involved (for example, cases between the governments of the US and the UK on the one hand and the government of Greece on the other). If no such treaty is in force between the two states involved (for example, US–Greece, UK–Greece), art 3 of LD 1079/1971 applies which, as stated above, requires a duly reasoned order or application or decision of the investigating organ or judgment of a Greek court and that such information must be absolutely necessary for the identification and punishment of actions characterised either as crimes committed in Greece or breaches of the national currency legislation.

Indeed, such bilateral treaties of judicial assistance have been signed between Greece and the US and between Greece and the UK and have been ratified by L 5554/1932 and L Delta-Lambda-Alpha/1912 respectively. Therefore, the provisions of these two treaties shall be applicable in cases where the disclosure of confidential information is requested by the chief executive officer of the bank in the US in the first example and the Financial Services Authority in the second.

The issue of whether the Greek criminal or supervisory authorities who are undertaking the investigation and trying to compel the bank established in Greece to disclose information held by a branch or wholly-owned subsidiary in the UK are entitled to do so shall be decided on the basis of whether a bilateral treaty of judicial assistance is in force between Greece and the UK. In the contrary case, English law shall be the applicable one. However, as mentioned above, a bilateral treaty of judicial assistance is in force between the two states and, therefore, the provisions of the treaty shall apply to the case in question.

As regards the process of tracing funds, we shall address first the case where a client in Greece has been defrauded of large sums of money by some of its employees who have vanished. Assume that the funds have been traced from our client's bank account to various other accounts of banks in Greece. Recipient banks can be compelled to disclose whether or not they still hold the funds on the basis of art 5, para 5 of the Brussels Convention on International Jurisdiction and Execution of Judgments in Greece providing that: 'a person domiciled in the territory of a contracting party may be sued in another contracting state ... as regards disputes related to the exploitation of a branch, agency or any other kind of establishment, before the court of their seat.' In view of the fact that the US and the UK, on the one hand, and Greece, on the other, have signed the Convention, its provisions apply and, therefore, the recipient banks may be compelled to disclose whether they still hold the funds and whether they sent them to any party having a lawful interest on the basis of the procedure related to injunctions: art 682ff of the Code of Civil Procedures.

Assume that orders have been obtained obliging the banks to disclose where the money went and that the banks report that the funds have been transferred abroad to other banks which they name, in countries which again they name, for the account of named customers or to numbered accounts. In such a case, the banks of such foreign destinations cannot be compelled to help our client to trace the funds further because the foreign law of the country of final destination shall be the applicable one. The position would not be different if the foreign bank were a branch or a subsidiary of one of the banks against whom the tracing order had been obtained in Greece. Again, the foreign law of the home country would apply.

If one reverses the facts and assumes that the foreign lawyer or client has obtained orders in his own country revealing that the stolen funds have reached a particular bank in Greece, the provisions of the Brussels Convention mentioned above would apply.

REGULATION OF FINANCIAL MARKETS
Insider dealing

[15.9]   Insider dealing is assimilated to fraud pursuant to art 386 of the Penal Code. The elements of the offence are:

1   the damage to another person's property;
2   an unlawful benefit at the expense of another person's property;
3   intention;
4   intentional presentation of untrue facts as true or unlawful concealment; and
5   persuasion of another person to an act, omission or tolerance.

Moreover, civil liability against the person responsible may be established on the basis of arts 914 ff of the Civil Code.

In Greece, the inter-bank network, TEIRESIAS, serves the needs of the banks for information related to cheques and bills of exchange. However, for bank secrecy to be waived, a duly reasoned court decision would be the necessary condition as mentioned above.

Cross-selling

[15.10]   Cross-selling between companies which are members of the same group does not give rise to liability, criminal or civil. Banks are also allowed to pass each other credit information about customers, but not to their client companies because they would breach the provisions of Greek law mentioned above related to bank secrecy and confidentiality.

Data protection

[15.11]   The collection and use of personal data is governed by L 2472/1997 (the Data Protection Act) on the Protection of Individuals with Regard to the Processing of Personal Data, as amended by Laws 2819/2000 and 2915/2001, which came into force on 9 April 1997 and which implemented the Data Protection Directive. The law only applies as far as data regarding natural persons is concerned and it does not refer to legal entities. According to the law, the transfer of personal data, which is undergoing processing or is intended for processing after the transfer, shall only be permitted following a permit granted by the Authority for the Protection of Personal Data. However, even if such permit could be obtained, it would not apply in the case of data regarding bank accounts or depositions because, by virtue of LD 1059/1971, the transfer of such data would still constitute a criminal offence.

Moreover, art 42 of L 2121/1993 allows the reproduction, translation, adaptation or any other change of a computer program without a licence in order for the program to run properly. Article 43 of the same law specifies that reverse engineering, decompilation and disassembly are only allowed to the licensee in order to enable the latter to collect the necessary information and secure the networking of an independently created computer program with other programs, provided that such information is not easily and quickly accessible to the licensee and is restricted to the parts of the original program necessary for the accomplishment of its networking.

Conflicts of interest

[15.12]   Where a bank or one of its subsidiaries has financial information about a customer as a result of acting as its banker, it is not entitled to advise other customers in the stockbroking business on the benefits of buying or selling its customer's shares, nor is the bank itself entitled to deal in the customer's shares, even if it separates the two businesses. This is because, in acting in such a way, the bank breaches its duty of confidentiality and commits the offence mentioned in art 371 of the Penal Code as discussed above.

If the bank knows that its customer is in financial difficulties, while another department of the bank is simultaneously advising its clients to buy the same customer's shares, the bank again breaches its confidentiality duty in the sense that it is knowingly misguiding its clients, while a civil liability pursuant to the provisions of art 914ff of the Civil Code related to tortuous liability cannot be ruled out in the sense that such behaviour on the bank's behalf could fall within the scope of art 914 of the Civil Code, which provides that 'a person who through his fault has caused in a manner contrary to the law prejudice to another shall be liable for compensation'.

Takeovers

[15.13]   Where a bank organises financing for a takeover bid, some distinctions must be drawn. First, such financing is governed by Decision 1955/2-7-91 of the Governor of the Bank of Greece, as amended, which stipulates that financing for the purchase of shares is allowed in cases where the borrower maintains or increases his shareholding in the undertaking in whose share capital the participation is effected.

If the increase of the share capital is effected by means of a public subscription, the underwriter, the borrower and the bank in question are involved. However, the bank, as a lender, is only responsible to check the details pertaining to the financing, creditworthiness and viability of the project and to approve the loan following an approval of the share capital increase by means of a public subscription by the Capital Market Committee. Liability only arises for the underwriter in cases where the information related to the share price included in the prospectus is inaccurate, where the issuing company and the underwriter are jointly liable.

Where the increase of the share capital of the borrower company is effected by means of a private placement of shares, the bank acts simply as an intermediary for the financing and therefore no liability of the bank arises.

MONEY LAUNDERING

[15.14]   Money laundering is prohibited by virtue of L 2331/1995 (the Money Laundering Act) as amended by L 3424/2005, which implemented the respective European legislation. According to this law, money laundering means the following conduct when committed intentionally:

1   the conversion or transfer of property, knowing that such property is derived from criminal activity or from an act of participation in such activity, for the purpose of concealing or disguising the illicit origin of the property or of assisting any person who is involved in the commission of such activity to evade the legal consequences of his action;

2   the concealment or disguise of the true nature, source, location, disposition, movement, rights with respect to, or ownership of, property, knowing that such property is derived from criminal activity or from an act of participation in such activity;

3   the acquisition, possession or use of property, knowing, at the time of receipt, that such property was derived from criminal activity or from an act of participation in such activity;

4   participation in, association to commit, attempts to commit and aiding, abetting, facilitating and counselling the commission of any criminal activity.

Property means assets of every kind, whether corporeal or incorporeal, movable or immovable, tangible or intangible, and legal documents or instruments evidencing title to or interests in such assets.

The Money Laundering Act provides that the persons and/or entities having the described obligations are:

1   credit institutions;
2   financial organisations;
3   leasing companies;
4   business fund companies;
5   auditors, accountants and auditing firms;
6   tax advisors and tax advising firms;
7   casinos, internet casinos and booking agencies;
8   auction houses;
9   merchants of assets of great value and auctioneers if the transaction exceeds 15,000 euros;
10   public notaries and lawyers when they are offering their services in order for their client to buy or sell real estate or companies, manage stocks, open bank accounts or carry out any other financial transaction. The non-disclosure privilege continues to apply with the exception where the legal advisor counsels

the client in order to conduct money laundering or the legal advisor knows that his client intends to conduct money laundering;

11   postal companies, but only when intermediating in fund transferring.

Credit and financial institutions must require identification of their customers by means of supporting evidence when entering into business relations, particularly when opening an account or savings accounts or when offering safe custody facilities. The identification requirement also applies for any transaction with customers involving a sum amounting to 15,000 euros or more, whether the transaction is carried out in a single operation or in several operations which seem to be linked. Where the sum is not known at the time when the transaction is undertaken, the institution concerned shall proceed with identification as soon as it is appraised of the sum and establishes that the threshold has been reached. In the event of doubt as to whether the customers are acting on their own behalf or where it is certain that they are not acting on their own behalf, the credit and financial institutions shall take reasonable measures to obtain information as to the real identity of the persons on whose behalf those customers are acting. Credit and financial institutions shall carry out such identification, even where the amount of the transaction is lower than the threshold laid down, wherever there is a suspicion of money laundering.

Credit and financial institutions must keep the following for use as evidence in any investigation into money laundering:

1   in the case of identification, a copy or the references of the evidence required for a period of at least five years after the relationship with their customer has ended;
2   in the case of transactions, the supporting evidence and records, consisting of the original documents or copies admissible in court proceedings under the applicable national legislation for a period of at least five years following execution of the transactions.

Credit and financial institutions must especially examine any transaction which they regard as particularly likely, by its nature, to be related to money laundering.

Credit and financial institutions and their directors and employees must co-operate fully with the authorities responsible for combating money laundering:

1   by informing those authorities, on their own initiative, of any fact which might be an indication of money laundering;
2   by furnishing those authorities, at their request, with all necessary information in accordance with the procedures established by the applicable legislation. Such information shall be forwarded to the authorities and may only be used in connection with the combating of money laundering.

Credit and financial institutions shall refrain from carrying out transactions which they know or suspect to be related to money laundering until they have informed the authorities, which may give instructions not to execute the operation. Where such a transaction is suspected of giving rise to money laundering and where to refrain in such manner is impossible or is likely to frustrate efforts to pursue the beneficiaries of a suspected money laundering operation, the institutions concerned shall inform the authorities immediately afterwards.

Credit and financial institutions and their directors and employees shall not disclose to the customer concerned nor to other third persons that information has been transmitted to the authorities or that a money laundering investigation is being carried out.

The law provides for certain criminal offences, which are considered to give rise to money laundering:

1   forming a crime syndicate (art 187 of the Penal Code);
2   terrorist activity (art 187A of the Penal Code);
3   financing of terrorists (art 187A of the Penal Code);
4   bribery (art 235 of the Penal Code);
5   white slave trade (art 323A of the Penal Code);
6   computer fraud (art 386A of the Penal Code);
7   procuring prostitutes (art 351 of the Penal Code);
8   trafficking in drugs (L 1729/1987);
9   use and circulation of weapons, explosives and ammunition (L 2168/1993);
10   illegal trading of antiquities and works of art (L 3028/2002);
11   exposing other persons to ionised radiation (L 181/1974);
12   facilitation of illegal immigrants (L 3386/2005);
13   abuse of a dominant position in the market or abuse of preferential information (L 3340/2005);
14   any other criminal activity punishable by imprisonment of more than six months and by means of which proceeds of more than 15,000 euros are derived.

All persons that conduct or try to conduct a money laundering offence may be imprisoned for up to ten years. Any state employee that facilitates money laundering may also be imprisoned for up to ten years and/or fined. Any private employee that fails to comply with the provisions of the Money Laundering Act may be imprisoned for up to two years. Finally, any credit or financial institution that facilitates money laundering or fails to report suspicious transactions made known to it in any way whatsoever may be fined by the Bank of Greece and, in extreme cases of corruption, its permit may be revoked.

A World Bank evaluation has been carried out through the Bank of Greece, which has the findings and failings report. The Bank of Greece considers such information to be strictly confidential.

The anti-money laundering legislation in Greece has not yet been challenged. According to Greek legislation, internal laws always prevail over recommendations by international organisations or institutions, which are not considered to be compulsory. Therefore, Greek bank secrecy law provisions always prevail over the FATF recommendations. Of course, the Money Laundering Act states that a credit or financial institution cannot deny informing the competent authorities of suspicious transactions by relying upon bank secrecy privileges.

CONCLUSION

[15.15]   Bank secrecy cannot be waived except in cases specified in the statutes addressing the issue, in particular in cases of tax evasion, facilitation of the control exercised by the Bank of Greece by way of its supervisory role assigned to it under Greek law, in the direction of establishing anti-money laundering initiatives or in cases of crimes committed in Greece and classified as felonies.

16   Hungary

Péter Köves
Gábor Felsen

THE BASIC POSITION

[16.1]   It is generally true to say that, with respect to the regulation of banking secrecy, the fundamental conflict is one between the personal interests or rights of the client of the bank and the public interest of society as a whole. Banking is a relationship based on mutual trust and confidence and this generates the need for banking secrecy.

In Hungary, as a general rule, all information concerning clients and their bank accounts is confidential and may only be disclosed by the bank or financial institution in well-defined circumstances.

Until the beginning of the 1990s, banking secrecy in Hungary was strictly, but not clearly, regulated. The State Finances Act of 1979 provided that: '…the employees of a financial institution shall keep and maintain all banking secrets that they become aware of during the course of their work. An exemption may be granted as to this confidentiality by a statute or the person (institution) to whom the secret related.'

However, there were no general regulations defining banking secrets or the consequences of an unauthorised disclosure of such banking secrets. Confidential information was determined on an individual case-by-case basis. Until 1991, Hungarian financial institutions, in line with general banking practice, only disclosed information of any kind with the authorisation of the client.

The commencement of the reform process, with privatisations and the demands of a growing number of multinational companies, brought to light the lack of available banking information regarding the situation and solvency of Hungarian companies.

As a general rule, Hungarian banks have been fairly conservative and have always sought to protect themselves in the event that a dispute were to arise and consequently, in the absence of clear regulations, have always tended to adopt a cautious approach and, officially at least, maintain tight banking secrecy.

The roots of the current regulatory regime go back to the 1991 Banking Act. In order both to increase the confidence that clients had in banks and to provide information required for the smooth operation of the market economy, the 1991 Banking Act contained detailed provisions regulating bank secrecy. The 1991 Banking Act stipulated the scope of banking secrets and regulated the obligation to keep banking secrets, extending the obligation to keep and maintain banking secrets to all persons who acquired confidential information in the course of their work or activity and reinforce the protection of banking secrets.

However, the 1991 Banking Act recognised the need for there to be clearly regulated exceptions to the doctrine of banking secrecy with recognition of the legitimate interests of those engaged in business and those organisations 'acting in the interest of society'.

The regulation of banking secrecy under the 1991 Banking Act was widely criticised in Hungary, principally because it was felt that it was too restrictive and that, in certain key areas, it did not allow for the assertion of justifiable economic and other public interests.

Act CXII of 1993 sought to rebalance the rights and interests of individuals with those of the society as a whole and reflect international practice in this area. At the same time, Act XCII of 1993 also amended the Criminal Code and a person found to be breaching the banking secrecy regulations could be held criminally liable.

One of the prerequisites for Hungary joining the OECD in 1996 was the requirement to amend the regulations governing banking secrecy. These amendments were carried out in the first half of 1996 by way of Act XII of 1996. The overall effect of these amendments was to increase the ease with which Hungarian state institutions entrusted with the collection of taxes and other public contributions can gather information necessary to facilitate such collection.

The main legal source of the regulation of bank secrecy in Hungary is currently Act CXII of 1996 on Credit Institutions and Financial Enterprises (the 'Banking Act'), which came into force on 1 January 1997. The Banking Act regulates bank secrecy in a detailed and accurate way. The Banking Act has been modified several times since 1996; it was complemented by provisions concerning issues such as the central credit information system, the conflict of interests and insider trading.

According to the Banking Act, a 'banking secret' is any fact, information, solution or data at the disposal of a financial institution, which relates to the clients' personal details, data, property status, business activity, economic administration, owner's or business connections, as well as to the accounts (balance and turnover) maintained by a financial institution and contracts concluded between clients and a financial institution, ie a fairly wide and comprehensive definition. In addition, the Banking Act provides that any person receiving financial services from financial institutions is to be considered to be a 'client' of a financial institution.

All who become aware of business or banking secrets in the course of performing their duties or performing an assignment are obliged, without time limitation, to keep all business and bank secrets confidential, not use them outside their scope of activity or disclose them to third persons unless the Banking Act so authorises them. The Banking Act strictly prohibits the disclosure of business information to third parties or the use of it personally in order to gain business advantage and/or the use of it to the detriment of the financial institution or the clients of the financial institution.

One can conclude that, over the last 15 years, a dominant trend in Hungarian law and regulation has been a move from strict banking secrecy towards limited access to confidential banking information in specific circumstances. The principal reasons for this trend include the growing demand to fight international money laundering effectively and the desire of Hungary to adopt a legal and regulatory regime compatible with that of the European Union.

Exceptions, limitations and qualifications to basic position

[**16.2**]   The Banking Act (as amended) defines four cases where a financial institution is allowed to disclose confidential information to third parties:

1   where the client of a financial institution, his/its legal representative so requires or gives authorisation to that end. Such authorisation has to identify precisely (if the authorisation is not part of the contract concluded with the financial institution, in a document executed in a notarial deed or in a private document with full legal effect) the scope of the bank secret that may be disclosed to third parties;

2   where the interest of a financial institution itself necessitates the use of the relevant information, for the purpose of selling its claim arising under an arrangement with a client or for the recovery of its overdue claim;

3   where the Banking Act expressly grants exemption from the obligation of non-disclosure of banking secrets. These exemptions are listed in para 51, s 2 of the Banking Act and therefore financial institutions may disclose banking secrets to:

   (a)   the National Deposit Insurance Fund, the National Bank of Hungary, the State Audit Office, the Office of Economic Competition, the Hungarian Financial Supervisory Authority ('Supervisory Authority'), the voluntary institutions for protection and deposit insurance funds when discharging their functions, the Government Control Office in monitoring the lawful and expedient use of central budgetary funds and the OLAF (the European Anti-Fraud Office) in monitoring the lawful use of European Union subsidies,

   (b)   the notary public when acting in inheritance proceedings and the public guardianship authority when discharging its functions,

   (c)   the receiver, liquidator, bailiff, financial guardian or financial accountant acting in bankruptcy proceedings, winding up proceedings, court execution procedures, debt settlement proceedings of self-governing bodies or final accounts proceedings,

   (d)   the investigating authority (ie the police) and/or the Public Prosecution Office in respect of criminal proceedings,

   (e)   the court in criminal proceedings, civil actions proceedings concerning bankruptcy or winding up and in proceedings of debt settlement of self-governing bodies,

   (f)   the bodies authorised to use intelligence service tools and collect secret information, in which case the disclosure of banking secrets are subject to conditions specified under Act CXXV of 1995 on the National Intelligence Services,

   (g)   the national intelligence service discharging its functions subject to the authorisation in each instance of the general director,

   (h)   the Minister of Interior and the Minister of Finance in the case of targetted subsidy and appropriation to local self-governing bodies,

   (i)   the tax authority, the customs authority and the social security body in proceedings concerning the examination of compliance with obligations with respect to taxation, customs and social security, as well as in proceedings related to the enforcement of an enforceable document establishing such debts,

   (j)   the bailiff in judicial or administration execution proceedings and to the Treasury Property Directorate joining a judicial execution proceedings in compliance with the provisions of a government decree on housing state subsidies,

(k) the tax authority and the Supervisory Authority when fulfilling the written request of a foreign authority pursuant to the provisions of an international treaty provided that the request contains a confidentiality clause signed by the foreign authority,

(l) the financial institution when disclosing data in connection with inheritance proceedings pursuant to the provisions of Act XCII of 2003 on the Rules of Taxation,

(m) Hungarian authorities, including the National Police Headquarters, when proceeding with cases connected to money laundering, involved in criminal proceedings when fulfilling the written request of a foreign authority or a foreign Financial Information Unit involved in criminal proceedings pursuant to the provisions of an international treaty provided that the request contains a confidentiality clause signed by the foreign authority,

(n) the Supervisory Authority and the National Bank of Hungary in the course of supervision made according to statutory regulations, and

(o) the financial institution when informing the Ministry of Finance of the respective measures it has taken on the basis of (i) regulations adopted under art 60 of the Treaty establishing the European Community on the restrictive measures to be applied relating to liquid assets, other financial interests and economic resources or on the basis of regulations or decisions adopted under the authorisation by these regulations and (ii) common positions adopted under art 15 of the Treaty establishing the European Union on the restrictive measures to be applied relating to liquid assets, other financial interests and economic resources.

In addition, there is a specific regulation designed to prevent the Hungarian financial system from being used for the purposes of money laundering which complies with the EC Council Directive 91/308. The effect of this regulation is to make it easier to obtain an exemption from the rules of bank secrecy where information comes to light to the effect that a bank account or bank transaction is related to drug trafficking, terrorism, illegal arms trading, money laundering or organised crime. In such a case, the financial institution must not inform the client concerned of the request or of the transfer of data. There is no obligation on a financial institution to report to its client the request for information or the transfer of such information in cases of criminal proceedings, data collection carried out with the help of intelligence service tools and proceedings carried out by the National Security Service. In all other cases, the client must be notified by the financial institution of the request for data. The Banking Act includes several guarantees as to the means of disclosing such confidential information, for example, the financial institution must be referred to in writing, the client must be identified together with the bank account concerned and the type of information requested and the purpose of the request must also be specified.

Joining the international efforts against money laundering and the financing of terrorist activities, the Hungarian Parliament has ratified the International Convention for the Suppression of the Financing of Terrorism (the 'Convention') adopted by the General Assembly of the United Nations on 9 December 1999.

The Banking Act lists those cases which are not considered to be a breach of banking secrecy and where disclosure of certain classes of information is permitted. Consequently, it is not a breach of bank secrecy:

1 to supply aggregate data from which the personal or business data of individual clients cannot be identified;

2 to supply data concerning the name and number of the current account of the

client (subject to the restrictions set out in data protection laws in case of natural persons);

3 for financial institutions (engaged in either credit or loan operations, financial leasing, the issuance of electronic money and cash substitute payment instruments, or providing surety bonds and bank guarantees) and for legal entities (exclusively underwriting guarantee and suretyship) ('Credit Data Providers') to supply data to the central credit information system, established and operated by them or from that system to the financial institution, in accordance with the rules of the system;

4 to provide data to an auditor, a legal or other expert authorised by the financial institution, as well as to an insurance company providing insurance coverage for a financial institution to the extent necessary for discharging an insurance contract;

5 to provide data, at the written consent of the Board of Directors of a financial institution, to an owner with a qualifying holding in that financial institution, with such data being made available to a person (company) intending to acquire such holding (or to the auditor, legal or other expert authorised by such owner or prospective owner);

6 to present the sample of signatures, on request of a Hungarian court, of those having the right of disposal over the bank account of a party to the legal action;

7 to provide data suitable for individual identification of credit institutions supplied by the Supervisory Authority – with respect to the rules concerning bank secrecy – to the Central Statistical Office for the purposes of statistics or the Ministry of Finance for the purpose of the analysis of the processes of the national economy and the planning of the central budget;

8 for a financial institution to disclose data to a foreign financial institution provided that the client has previously consented in writing and the foreign financial institution's (data receiver) procedure complies with the requirements of the Hungarian statutory regulations concerning data management and the foreign country has adequate statutory regulations on data protection;

9 to disclose data to the supervisory authority of a foreign financial institution necessary for its supervision according to the provisions of the co-operation agreement between the supervisory authorities providing the confidential management and usage of the information and the Supervisory Authority's consent to the processing of data to foreign authorities involved in criminal proceedings;

10 to disclose data to a business association discharging outsourced activity;

11 to disclose data in connection with the compliance with the rules set out in the Banking Act, the Capital Markets Act and the Insurance Act regarding the supervision of the respective entities on a consolidated basis (in respect of groups the members of which conduct financial and/or insurance and/or investment services) and supplemental supervision;

12 to disclose data suitable for individual identification of credit institutions supplied by the Supervisory Authority to the Economic Competition Office when performing its functions;

13 to disclose data by the National Deposit Insurance Fund to foreign deposit insurance schemes and to foreign supervisory authorities under the co-operation agreement if they guarantee equivalent or better legal protection for the processing and utilisation of such data with the protection afforded under Hungarian law;

14 to disclose data in connection with the amount and maturity of a claim of a third party relating to the financial institution's exposures covered by such third party; and

15 to disclose data regarding the client's account number to a foreign financial institution in connection with providing correspondent banking services.

Legal consequences of breach of bank secrecy obligation

Civil law

[16.3] Breaching bank confidentiality constitutes an infringement of personal rights. These rights (and the remedy) can only be exercised or enforced personally. According to Act IV of 1959 on the Civil Code ('Civil Code'), there are a number of remedies available to the injured party. It may submit a claim to the relevant court requesting for:

1 a declaration of the infringement;
2 the cessation of the infringement and ordering the other party to restrain from further infringement;
3 a remedy in the form of a statement or by other adequate means;
4 the cessation of the injurious status and the restoration of the previous status; and
5 damages under general provisions of the Civil Code.

In relation to subsection 5, we note that, in order to obtain damages, the burden of proof lies with the client to prove that he suffered a loss or detriment as a consequence of the breach of bank secrecy (eg unlawful disclosure). In the absence of damages, the court can only make a declaration as to the unlawful conduct, the infringement of rights and restraint.

Concerning the banks' ability to limit claims for breach of confidentiality, Hungarian regulation is based on both the specific regulation of the Banking Act dealing with bank secrecy and the general rules on liability of the Civil Code.

As we have already discussed, the persons acquiring any business or bank secrets must keep them confidential without any time limitation. As the protection of consumers' interests is of utmost importance under Hungarian legislation, the obligation of keeping business or bank secrets confidential is based on law and is usually also referred to in banking contracts. According to the Civil Code, as a general rule, the liability of a bank for a breach of contract cannot be excluded or restricted.

Criminal law

[16.4] Act IV of 1978 on the Criminal Code penalises the infringement of economic secrets (including, among others, bank, securities and insurance secrets). Any person who is obliged to keep an economic secret and discloses the bank secrets to any third party (unless duly authorised) with the intent of acquiring an unjustified advantage or to cause detriment to any person, commits a misdemeanour and can be sentenced to up to three years' imprisonment.

Administrative law

[16.5] In the event of the breach of any of the provisions set out in legal regulations concerning financial and auxiliary financial services (including the breach of bank secrecy), the Supervisory Authority can impose fines and penalties (along with other measures in serious cases).

Cross-border/extra-territorial issues

[16.6]   In addition to the cross-border aspects of bank secrecy already discussed under clauses 3(k) and (m) above, sanctions may be imposed on financial institutions domiciled outside of Hungary, pursuant to the provisions of the Banking Act.

If a foreign financial institution providing cross-border services in Hungary breaches the Hungarian regulations applicable to it or if insufficiencies are detected in its operations, the Supervisory Authority is empowered to request the financial institution to rectify the problem in compliance with such regulations In cases where the financial institution does not rectify the insufficiency or the unlawful operation, the Supervisory Authority can notify the relevant foreign Financial Supervisory Authority of the financial institution, requesting it to take appropriate measures.

Regulation of financial markets

[16.7]   Financial markets in Hungary are regulated by the Banking Act, which defines the financial services and the requirements of obtaining a licence to conduct such services. The Banking Act deals with the supervision of the financial institutions and sets out the rules of bank secrecy, as well as the rules of business secrecy. On the other hand, capital markets are regulated by a separate piece of law, in particular the Capital Markets Act. The Capital Markets Act regulates the investment services and deals with securities secrecy. The insider dealings and market abuse provisions of the Capital Markets Act are in compliance with the Market Abuse Directive and the other relevant pieces of European Union law.

Insider trading and market manipulation

[16.8]   The Capital Markets Act has recently implemented the European Union legislation on insider trading and market manipulation. Insider trading was previously regulated by the Banking Act. The present regulation in the Capital Markets Act reflects the respective European Union law and the introduction of insider trading under the Criminal Code as a criminal offence.

As one might expect with a new piece of legislation, in practice, there is a lack of application and interpretation of the new provisions of the Capital Markets Act dealing with insider trading and market abuse in Hungary.

Conflicts of interests

[16.9]   The Banking Act implemented an important regulation in connection with the management of conflict of interests in a credit institution ('Chinese Wall' legislation). Credit institutions providing investment and auxiliary investment services besides financial services must guarantee in their internal rules that the two units are separated in order not to influence the transactions between their clients, the credit institution divisions, the credit institutions and other participants. The internal rules must determine precisely the way data is conveyed between the units and bank secrets should be available exclusively for those who need them for performing their tasks. The internal rules have to be submitted to the Supervisory Authority.

MONEY LAUNDERING

Background

[16.10]   Hungary was among the first countries in Europe which adopted laws in order strictly and effectively to prohibit money laundering. Besides the Criminal Code, in 2003 a new act (the 'Money Laundering Act') became effective replacing Act XXVI of 1994 on the Prevention of Money Laundering, which already had stricter provisions than most of the countries in Europe. Hungary is a party to the Strasbourg Convention on Laundering, Search, Seizure and Confiscation of the Proceeds from Crime. Hungary is not a member country of the Financial Action Task Force on Money Laundering (the 'FATF'), although this did not deter the Hungarian legislators from adopting the fundamental elements of the FATF recommendations. Hungary also implemented EEC Directive 91/308 on the Prevention of the Use of the Financial System for the Purpose of Money Laundering and EC Directive 2001/97 on the amendment of EEC Directive 308/91.

The current position

[16.11]   The scope of the Money Laundering Act, in compliance with the implemented European Union laws, extends to the following natural persons and legal entities providing their services in the territory of the Republic of Hungary (referred to as 'Service Providers'):

1   financial institutions;
2   investment service providers;
3   insurance companies;
4   entities conducting postal financial intermediation services, postal money transfers, accepting and delivering domestic and international postal money orders;
5   commodity exchanges;
6   real estate agencies;
7   auditors and audit companies;
8   accountants and entities providing accountancy services, persons and entities providing tax consulting services;
9   casinos;
10 persons and entities trading in precious metals, cultural assets or selling such goods at auctions or on consignment;
11 voluntary mutual insurance funds;
12 legal counsels and notaries; and
13 customers of the above listed persons and entities.

In addition to the above, any person who enters Hungary carrying cash in Hungarian forints or any other currency, travellers' cheques, international money orders, negotiable securities or financial market instruments worth 1 million forints or more is obliged to declare it to the customs authority in writing.

The Service Providers have to comply with two important duties under the Money Laundering Act.

Identification obligation

[16.12]   Service Providers must identify each customer when entering into a business relationship. Moreover, Service Providers may carry out a transaction involving a sum amounting to 2 million forints or more only if the respective customer has been positively identified. In certain cases, the Service Provider does not need to perform the identification procedure provided that the Service Provider has already established the identity of the respective customer, the personal identification documents have been checked for the transaction and there are no changes in the customer's data. In addition, the Service Provider does not need to perform the identification procedure if its customer is a financial institution registered in the territory of the European Union. The Money Laundering Act lists certain exceptions from the identification obligation with regard to specific services.

Reporting obligation

[16.13] As a general rule, in the event of becoming aware of any information, fact or circumstance that raises suspicion of money laundering, the directors, managers and employees of Service Providers and their immediate family members must, without delay, file a report to the person authorised by the Service Provider to forward such report to the National Police Headquarters. The Money Laundering Act expressly stipulates that such reporting is not regarded to be a breach of bank, securities, insurance, pension fund or business secrets or the breach of restrictions on the disclosure of data or information pursuant to either a legal regulation or a contract.

The Money Laundering Act does not specify the information, facts or circumstances that may suggest money laundering, however, a directive issued by the Ministry of Finance lists some examples in this regard. According to the directive, the following could be regarded as information, facts or circumstances suggesting money laundering:

1   the customer provided false information on their personal data, the owner or certain economic events;
2   the issuance or acceptance of documents relating to false economic events or transactions;
3   the issuance or acceptance of documents relating to false economic events of unidentifiable companies;
4   transactions performed without any legal title;
5   a large amount of income has been accrued against which there are no proportionate expenses;
6   unusual and unjustified large capital increases;
7   manipulation or falsification of documents;
8   high amount of valuation surplus or deficit without a proper explanation of its cause;
9   large investment by a company with minimum share capital without the use of a credit line; and
10   the obligations of the customer are regularly fulfilled by a third person.

It is essential that Service Providers employing ten or more persons must operate an internal control and information system facilitating the identification of customers in order to prevent business relations and transactions that enable or constitute money laundering. In addition, adhering to the responsibilities prescribed in the Money Laundering Act, the Service Providers must adopt internal regulations (the 'Regulations') to be approved by the organ exercising state and professional supervision over the respective Service Providers.

Sanctions

[16.14]   If the findings of any inspection under the Money Laundering Act reveal any breach of regulations or any discrepancy, the National Police Headquarters may order the respective Service Provider to restore lawful operations and eliminate the discrepancies and/or to adopt the Regulations or make revisions in the Regulations in accordance with the statutory requirements. If a Service Provider repeatedly breaches the obligations set out in the Money Laundering Act, it shall be subject to a fine (between 10,000 and 100,000 forints) unless the infringement merits a more severe punishment under the relevant laws.

The Criminal Code imposes strict penalties with regard to money laundering and the omission of the reporting obligation under the Money Laundering Act. Accordingly, if any person omits to fulfil their reporting obligations, they could be punished with imprisonment for a maximum of three years. If such person acts negligently, the punishment is a maximum of two years' imprisonment, community service or a fine.

MISCELLANEOUS

Data of public interest

[16.15]   Public information (information of public interest) means any data managed by a public authority or agency, government or local and other bodies attending to public duties specified by law. State or local public authorities are obliged to provide the general public with accurate and updated information concerning the matters under their competence, such as the budgets of the central government and local municipalities, the management of assets controlled by the central government and by local municipalities, the appropriation of public funds and special and exclusive rights conferred upon market participants, private organisations or individuals. Consequently, public accessibility to data of public interest may not be restricted by reasons of bank secrecy in cases where such data is directly connected to financial services and auxiliary financial services in relation to the following:

1   suretyship or other guarantee undertaken by the central budget;
2   target subsidy and appropriation (from the state budget) to the local self-governing bodies; and
3   the budget of central or local government bodies.

The central credit information system

[16.16]   The central credit information system was established by an amendment of the Banking Act as of 1 January 2001. The provisions regarding the central credit information system have been significantly amended in 2005. The central credit information system retains data obtained from the Credit Data Providers on their clients. The central credit information system aims at setting up a database regarding defaulted debtors. It implemented a different mechanism for natural persons and corporate entities.

Natural persons

[16.17]   The central credit information system collects and manages key data relating to specific debtors who failed to fulfil their respective contractual obligations under a certain financial agreement (such as a credit agreement or a financial lease agreement) or a certain agreement relating to investment services (such as lending securities) and regulated by the Capital Markets Act for more than 90 days after the due date. Such overdue obligation has to exceed the applicable minimum wage amount in order for a debtor to be listed in the database. Data about such a debtor will include personal details and details of the default of the credit agreement.

The central credit information system also collects and manages key data relating to those debtors who used forged documents or disclosed false information in connection with the conclusion of the respective financial contract, provided that these facts could be evidenced by documents.

The central credit information system collects and manages key data (including personal details and details of the nature and the breach of the respective obligation) concerning credit card holders or cheque holders in the following cases:

1   where the credit card holder uses his credit card following the report to the financial institution that the instrument was lost, stolen or the code necessary for the use of such instrument has become known to a third party;
2   where the credit card user uses a code or other data belonging to another person without proper authorisation from that person; and
3   criminal proceedings in connection with the credit card.

The central credit information system cannot retain or manage any identifying data for more than five years after the debt has been paid in full.

Corporate entities

[16.18]   The central credit information system manages key data of corporate entities who have a list of payments of at least 1 million forints to be debited from a bank account for more than 30 days after the due date.

The central credit information system also manages key data of those corporate entities who have breached their obligations under a contract relating to the provision of cash equivalent instruments (eg a credit card) and, as a consequence, the Credit Data Provider has terminated the respective contract.

Jurisdictional issues in relation to electronic payment and information systems

[16.19]   In line with the relevant recommendation of the Supervisory Authority, credit institutions and financial enterprises are required to adhere to general data protection and bank confidentiality laws in the process of setting up the contractual framework and settlement of electronic payments. The service providers may not take advantage of the specific features of electronic payment to hide their relevant company information from their customers or to evade consumer protection regulations.

Outsourcing

[16.20]   The outsourcing of certain administrative activities of credit institutions and financial enterprises, where data handling, processing or filing is carried out, is strictly regulated. Outsourcing some of these activities is subject to the approval of the Supervisory Authority, which must be requested at least 30 days before the execution of the outsourcing agreement. Credit institutions must attach to such request a certification proving that the legislative rules on data protection have been adhered to and the credit institution's statement that the supplier undertaking to perform the outsourced activities fulfils the criteria set by the internal control of the credit institution. The supplier, if carrying out activities for more than one credit institution in parallel, is very strictly obliged to protect and handle all the data and information received from the individual credit institutions separately from each other.

Confidentiality in the process of securitisation

[16.21] In the process of transfer of a loan portfolio of a credit institution, confidential information relating to the borrowers will also be transferred to the transferee. The Banking Act allows such disclosure of confidential information by the transferor (ie originator) if (i) the borrower of the underlying loan consents to the transfer of its loan or (ii) the interest of the transferor so requires. It is practice in the consumer loan market that credit institutions reserve the right in their credit agreements to assign their claims which are consented to and accepted by the borrower in the agreement.

CONCLUSION

[16.22] The Hungarian financial markets have, in recent years, undergone rapid growth and evolution. Now that Hungary is a member of the OECD and the European Union and has been accorded an investment grade rating by the major rating agencies, the rapid pace of change is ongoing and looks unlikely to slow in the foreseeable future.

Hungary is a civil law jurisdiction and it should be noted that, generally speaking, save for certain decisions of the Hungarian Supreme Court, a court decision in the Hungarian lower courts is not binding on subsequent courts. Unlike common law jurisdictions, Hungarian courts base their decisions predominantly on written law rather than case law. Case law precedents (especially decisions of the Supreme Court) may nevertheless have an influence on court rulings. This means that it can sometimes be difficult to advise on areas of Hungarian law and regulation that are innovative and/or contentious.

So far as banking confidentiality, insider trading and market abuse are concerned, the bad news is that, in relative terms, the regulatory framework is more or less new and as yet untested. The good news is that:

1   the legal and regulatory framework is based on the model adopted by the European Union;
2   the evolutionary process of Hungarian law governing banking secrecy, insider trading and market abuse demonstrates the focus placed on this issue by the legislators; and
3   as Hungary continues its integration into the various international bodies, such as the OECD and the European Union, the pace of legislation is likely to continue along the right lines.

The challenge for lawyers in Hungary will be to guide banking clients sensibly and practically through the potential legal and regulatory pitfalls that are inevitable where laws are evolving and frequently being amended or reinterpreted.

17   Ireland

William Johnston

THE BASIC POSITION
Introduction

[17.1]   Irish law imposes a duty of confidentiality on a bank in relation to dealings with its customers. This obligation derives, for the most part, from the common law which implies a duty of confidentiality on the bank in a contract which governs the relationship between a bank and its customer, unless the terms of the contract otherwise provide. The parameters of the common law duty of confidentiality are unclear in many respects. In addition, there is no substantial body of Irish case law on a bank's obligation. When considering the obligation, the Irish courts have often relied on relevant decisions of the courts in other common law jurisdictions, in particular, the decisions of the English courts. It should be noted, though, that decisions of English courts are not binding in Ireland, but may be of persuasive authority in Irish courts. Increasingly, the legislature and the judiciary have laid out significant exceptions to the duty of confidentiality.

Statutory duty

[17.2]   In addition to the common law duty of confidentiality, a statutory duty of confidentiality applies in certain instances.

Every officer and employee and every former officer and employee of the Central Bank and Financial Services Authority of Ireland (the 'central bank') or any constituent part, such as the banking regulator, namely the Irish Financial Services Regulatory Authority ('the financial regulator'), is precluded from disclosing any confidential information concerning (i) the business of any person or body which has come to his knowledge by virtue of his office or employment or (ii) any matter arising in connection with the performance of the functions of the central bank or the exercise of its powers if such disclosure is prohibited by the Treaty of Rome, the Statute of the European System of Central Banks or the Supervisory Directives.[1] At the time of his appointment, each officer and employee is required to acknowledge that he has been informed and understands his secrecy obligations.

However, the Central Bank and Financial Services Authority of Ireland Act 2003 amended the principal legislation by providing for a number of exceptions to this duty of confidentiality. Subject to the comments in the preceding paragraph, the central bank is required to report, as appropriate, to (i) the Garda Siochana or (ii) the

---

1 Central Bank Act 1942, s 33AK(1)(b).

Revenue Commissioners or (iii) the Director of Corporate Enforcement or (iv) the Competition Authority or (v) any other body, whether within Ireland or otherwise, charged with the detection or investigation of a criminal offence or (vi) any other body charged with the detection or investigation of a contravention of the Companies Acts or the Competition Act, any information relevant to that body that leads the central bank to suspect that a criminal offence may have been committed by a supervised entity or a supervised entity may have contravened a provision of the Companies Acts or the Competition Act.[2]

In relation to any licensed bank where the central bank identifies information (i) which it believes is or is likely to be material to an authority concerned with the enforcement of any law and (ii) which it believes it is unable to disclose to that authority and (iii) in respect of which it is not satisfied that the information has been disclosed to that authority by the directors of the licensed bank, then the central bank is required to issue to the directors or those responsible for the management of the licensed bank a document known as a 'disclosure issue notice' and the notice shall specify the name of the authority concerned and identify the information that the central bank has identified as causing it to issue the disclosure issue note.[3]

Subject to the first paragraph above, the central bank may disclose confidential information (i) required for the purposes of criminal proceedings or (ii) with the consent of the person to whom the information relates and, if the information was obtained from another person, that other person or (iii) where the central bank is or was the agent of a person or other persons, including an institution of the European Community, approved stock exchange, financial futures and options exchange, an inspector appointed under the Companies Act, a committee appointed under the Stock Exchange Act, to a liquidator, examiner, receiver or any other person involved in the liquidation or bankruptcy of a licensed bank, the Director of Corporate Enforcement and a series of other bodies.[4]

The implications of, and rationale for, the secrecy obligations of the central bank's officers and employees were highlighted in *Cully v Northern Bank Finance Corpn Ltd*,[5] where the High Court upheld the objections of the central bank to disclose information following the service of a subpoena. The court indicated:

> '... the provisions of s 31 of the Central Bank Act 1942 [now superseded by s 33AK as inserted by the Central Bank and Financial Services Authority of Ireland Act 2003] give rise to a claim of privilege on grounds of public policy from disclosure of any information of the type referred to in the oath of secrecy. Section 6(1) of the same Act provides that in relation to part, at least of the functions and duties of the central bank, "the constant and predominant aim shall be the welfare of the people as a whole". This gives some indication for the justification for granting an exceptional degree of protection to the confidentiality of the bank's transactions, as a matter of public interest.'

These non-disclosure requirements have been made subject to a number of exceptions as outlined in reg 19 of the European Communities (Licensing and Supervision of Credit Institutions) Regulations 1992,[6] reg 7 of the European

---

2 Central Bank Act 1942, s 33AK(3).
3 Central Bank Act 1942, s 33AK(4).
4 Central Bank Act 1942, s 33AK(5).
5 [1984] ILRM 683.
6 SI 395/1992.

Communities (Consolidated Supervision of Credit Institutions) Regulations 1992,[7] reg 28 of the European Communities (Deposit Guarantee Schemes) Regulations 1995[8] and s 49 of the Investment Intermediaries Act 1995.

Data protection

[17.3] The law relating to data protection regulates the collection, processing, keeping, use and disclosure of certain information relating to living individuals which is processed automatically. The Data Protection Act 1988 gave effect to the Council of Europe Convention for the Protection of Individuals with Regard to Automatic Processing of Personal Data, Strasbourg, 1981 (the 'Strasbourg Convention'). That Act was amended in part by the Data Protection (Amendment) Act 2003, which gave effect to Council Directive 95/46/EC of 24 October 1995.

The Data Protection Acts 1988 and 2003 (the 'Data Protection Acts')

[17.4] The Data Protection Acts require banks to register as data controllers with the Data Protection Commissioner. A registered data controller is prohibited from keeping or using personal data (mostly data relating to a living individual) for a purpose other than the purpose or purposes described in the registered entry and from disclosing personal data to a person who is not described in the entry (other than a person to whom disclosure is authorised under s 8 of the 1988 Act).

The Data Protection Acts require a data controller or data processor to protect the privacy of individuals with regard to personal data kept by it. These obligations include keeping the data accurate and up to date, not allowing personal data to be used or disclosed in any manner incompatible with the lawful purpose specified in the registration and taking appropriate security measures against unauthorised access, alteration, disclosure or destruction of the data.[9]

The Data Protection Acts provide that a data controller or data processor, so far as regards the collection of personal data or dealing with such data, owes a duty of care to the relevant subject of the data.[10] However, the Data Protection Acts disapply restrictions imposed under the Data Protection Acts in certain circumstances in relation to the disclosure of personal data by data controllers or data processors, including where the disclosure is required:

1   for the purpose of safeguarding the security of the state in the opinion of a senior police or army officer;
2   to prevent, detect or investigate offences, apprehend or prosecute offenders or assess or collect taxes or other moneys owed to the state, a local authority or a health board;
3   in the interests of protecting the international relations of the state;
4   by or under any enactment or by a rule of law or order of a court; and
5   for the purpose of obtaining legal advice or for the purpose of legal proceedings in which the person making the disclosure is a party or witness.[11]

---

7   SI 396/1992.
8   SI 168/1995.
9   Data Protection Act 1988, s 2.
10 Data Protection Act 1988, s 7.
11 Data Protection Act 1988, s 8.

The restrictions are also disapplied where the disclosure is made to the subject of the data or his agent, or where the disclosure is made at the request or with the consent of the subject of the data or a person acting on his behalf. In relation to the latter, standard bank documentation often contains provisions entitling the bank to make disclosures for the purposes of the Data Protection Acts.

A person authorised by the Data Protection Commissioner (an authorised officer) may, for the purpose of obtaining information necessary or expedient for the performance of the Data Protection Commissioner or of his functions, (i) enter premises of a data controller and inspect any data and inspect, examine, operate and test any data equipment, (ii) require the data controller or an employee to disclose any data and produce any data material, (iii) inspect and copy information for such data and (iv) require the data controller or any employee to gain further information.[12]

SCOPE OF BASIC POSITION

Common law duty

[17.5]   The starting point in considering a banker's duty of confidentiality is the English Court of Appeal's decision in *Tournier v National Provincial and Union Bank of England Ltd.*[13] This decision affirmed the common law duty of confidentiality which exists between a banker and its customer. Thus, confidentiality is an implied term in a contract in Ireland between a banker and its customer. This duty, though, is not absolute, but qualified. In *Chestvale Properties Ltd and Hoddle Investments Ltd v Glackin,*[14] the High Court stated: 'it is common case that the customary and contractual right of a client to confidentiality from his banker is and always has been subject to a very wide range of exceptions'.

Consent of the customer

[17.6]   The duty of confidentiality of a bank in respect of its customers' affairs may be disapplied where the customer consents to the disclosure in question. A consent for this purpose may be express or implied. In the case of implied consent, it is difficult to determine the scope of the exception and whether it applies will depend on the particular circumstances of each case. One circumstance in which implied consent to disclosure is usually inferred is where the customer provides a third party with the name of its bank for the purpose of the bank providing a reference in relation to the customer. The customer's implied consent will not protect the bank if it is negligent when providing information when giving a reference.

Some banks insert express provisions in their mandates and application forms permitting them to make, in relation to dealings with customers, intra-group disclosures, disclosures to regulators (including regulators outside of Ireland) and, in a few cases, disclosures to other third parties and a credit reference bureau.

Standard home loan mortgage documentation usually contains a consent by the customer to disclosure for the purpose of a securitisation by the lender. The new financial regulator, the Irish Financial Services Regulatory Authority, was established in 2004 in place of the Central Bank of Ireland, but has not yet published

---

12 Data Protection Act 1988, s 24.
13 [1924] 1 KB 461.
14 [1993] 3 IR 35.

a code of practice on consent. However, the code of practice issued by its predecessor for such transactions provides:

1   a loan secured by the mortgage of residential property may not be transferred without the written consent of the borrower. When seeking consent from either an existing or a new borrower, the lender must provide a statement containing sufficient information to enable the borrower to make an informed decision. This statement, which must be cleared in advance with the financial regulator, must include a clear explanation of the implications of a transfer and how the transfer might affect the borrower. The borrower must be approached on an individual basis and given reasonable time to give or decline to give his consent

2   when seeking a consent and where there is to be or where there may be an arrangement under which the original lender will service the mortgage as an agent of any transferee, the lender will confirm that the transferee's policy on the handling of arrears and in the setting of mortgage interest rates will be the same as that of the original lender and that the original lender will handle arrears as its agent;

3   where the lender in the ordinary course of business would no longer have control in relation to:
    (a) the setting of interest rates, and/or
    (b) determining the conduct of relations with borrowers whose mortgage payments are seriously in arrears,
    the lender must seek the borrower's consent to a transfer notwithstanding any previous consent which a borrower has given;

4   when seeking the borrower's consent to the transfer of his mortgage, as described in para 1 above, the lender will provide the borrower with the following information:
    (a) the name and address of the intended transferee and of any holding company, if applicable,
    (b) the relationship, if any, between the lender and the transferee,
    (c) a description of the intended transferee and its business, including details of how long it has been in operation and of its experience in the management of mortgages,
    (d) an explanation of the policy and procedures which will apply for the setting of the mortgage interest rate and for making repayments if the transfer takes place,
    (e) confirmation that, in the absence of a specific consent, the existing arrangements will continue to apply;

5   the terms of the transfer agreement shall require the transferee:
    (a) to allow transferred mortgages to be redeemed without charging a redemption fee (unless approved under s 28 of the Central Bank Act 1989),
    (b) to continue any existing mortgage protection insurance arrangements,
    (c) to allow the borrower to arrange his own house insurance,
    (d) to provide to the relevant authority the mortgage statistics previously provided by the original lender,
    (e) to comply with this code of practice in relation to any future transfer of these mortgages.

EXCEPTIONS, LIMITATIONS AND QUALIFICATIONS TO BASIC POSITION

[17.7] Statutory exceptions (under the Central Bank Act 1989, as amended) to the prohibition of disclosure by any constituent part of the central bank include:

1 disclosure required by a court in criminal proceedings;
2 disclosure made with the consent of the person to whom the information relates and of the person from whom the information was obtained;
3 disclosure to the principal where the central bank is acting as agent; and
4 disclosure where the central bank considers it necessary for the common good made to a person charged with the supervision of financial institutions.

An example of the third exception can be seen from the courts' decisions in *Desmond and Dedeir v Glackin, the Minister for Industry and Commerce of Ireland and the Attorney General.*[15] In that case, Glackin was appointed by the Minister for Industry and Commerce as an inspector for the purpose of investigating the affairs of two companies. The inspector requested the minister to obtain information from the central bank through the Minister for Finance concerning transactions of a related company. The central bank had relevant information arising out of its duties under the Exchange Control Act 1954. It was held in the High Court, and affirmed by the Supreme Court, that (i) as the central bank was acting as agent of the Minister for Finance in relation to its functions under the Exchange Control Act 1954, it was bound to divulge the relevant information to its principal, the Minister for Finance, (ii) the Minister for Finance was not bound by any duty of confidentiality under the Central Bank Act 1989 and (iii) the public interest required all the information which the inspector needed for the purposes of his investigation to be made available to him and that there was no countervailing public interest of equal or near equal weight in denying the inspector access to the information emanating from the central bank.

The public interest requirement referred to in the judgments and, indeed, the fourth 'common good' exception may mean that even where the financial regulator is acting as principal and not agent, as it does in its supervisory and licensing functions, it should disclose information to an inspector.

Each bank in Ireland is required to provide the financial regulator with 'such information and returns' concerning its business as the financial regulator may specify from time to time, or request in writing, being information and returns which the financial regulator considers to be necessary for the performance of its statutory functions.

The statutory function of the financial regulator includes the licensing and supervision of banks. Accordingly, a bank must comply with a request to provide information to the financial regulator, even where the bank's customer has obtained an injunction restraining disclosure. Since the legislation governing the functions of the financial regulator overrode the duty of confidence, it must also override inter-partes orders made on that basis, otherwise the financial regulator could not properly discharge its public duty of supervision.

The qualifications to the common law duty can be classified under the four heads as outlined in the *Tournier* decision:

1 where disclosure is required by law;
2 where there is a duty to the public to disclose;
3 where the interests of the bank require disclosure; and
4 where the disclosure is made by the express or implied consent of the customer (already covered above).

---

15 [1993] 3 IR 67.

Disclosure required by law

Legal proceedings

[17.8] The Bankers' Books Evidence Act 1879 provides that:

> 'On the application of any party to a legal proceeding a court or judge may order that such party be at liberty to inspect and take copies of any entries in a banker's book for any of the purposes of such proceedings.'

The expression 'banker's book', initially defined by s 9 of the 1879 Act, but amended by the Bankers' Book Evidence (Amendment) Act 1959 and subsequently expanded by the Central Bank Act 1989, now 'includes any records used in the ordinary business of a bank', including microfilm, magnetic tape and other records in any non-legible form capable of being reproduced in a permanent legible form. The expression 'used in the ordinary business of the bank' does not mean that the book must be in use each day, but a book which was used and now kept for reference purposes. It should be noted that the meaning of 'banker's book' as defined is not all inclusive and, following amendment by statute in 1989, it may include any record in a bank, however recorded, provided it is done so in the ordinary business of the bank.

The courts have adopted a cautious approach in permitting this Act to be used. In *L'Amie v Wilson*,[16] Andrews J stated:

> 'Such caution is requisite, even when the inspection applied for is of the account of a party to the action; but when the account is that of a third party, still greater caution is necessary; and before granting an inspection of a third party's account, the court or judge ought to be satisfied that there are good grounds for believing that there are entries in the account material to some issue to be tried in the action, and which would be evidence at the trial for the party applying for the inspection.'

In *Staunton v Counihan*,[17] Dixon J began his judgment by saying:

> 'The jurisdiction to order inspection of entries in a banking account conferred by s 7 of the Bankers' Books Evidence Act 1879 must be exercised with extreme caution even where it is the account of a party to the action.'

It should be noted, however, that the Bankers' Books Evidence Acts and the meaning of a banker's book do not limit the power of a court to order discovery or inspection of an item which may not be a banker's book.[18]

An example of the constraints of the application of s 7 can be seen from the decision in *Staunton v Counihan*.[19] In that case, the plaintiff sued the defendant as guarantor of a debt for £12,000 incurred by a company owned by the defendant's son, who was a co-guarantor. The plaintiff applied to inspect the company's account in a Dublin bank for the purpose of proving that the debt existed. In refusing the application, Dixon J approached the principles of the legislation on two grounds:

1   'the jurisdiction was intended really to extend only to accounts which were in form and substance those of a party to the action';

---

16 [1907] 2 IR 130.
17 (1957) 92 ILTR 32.
18 *Larkins v National Union of Mineworkers and Bank of Ireland Finance Ltd* [1985] IR 671.
19 (1957) 92 ILTR 32.

2   'the entries must be material to some issue in the action and, if they are so, must be admissible in evidence on behalf of the applicant'.

Dixon J found, on the first issue, that the account was not in any sense in form and substance the defendant's account, nor was it so closely connected with her that it could really be regarded as her account in another name and, on the second issue, the plaintiff's proof does not essentially depend on the entries in the company's bank account and therefore at this stage the entries were not clearly and necessarily admissible in evidence. These two grounds were applied by Carroll J in granting an order for inspection of bank accounts in Dublin.[20]

Where a bank is not a party to proceedings, notice of an application for inspection need not be served on the bank. In *Staunton v Counihan*, Dixon J considered notice on the party whose account was to be inspected was sufficient and in *Larkins v National Union of Mineworkers and Bank of Ireland Finance Ltd*,[21] an order for inspection was granted ex parte, but in *L'Amie v Wilson*,[22] Andrews J thought notice of the application should be given to the bank.

Discovery

[17.9]   The rules of discovery can be found in order 31 of the Rules of the Superior Courts 1986,[23] as amended by the Rules of the Superior Courts (No 2) 1993[24] and as further amended by the Rules of the Superior Courts (No 2) (Discovery) 1999.[25] Rule 12 provides:

> '(1)Any party may apply to the court by way of notice of motion for an order directing any other party to any cause or matter to make discovery on oath of the documents which are or have been in his or her possession or power, relating to any matter in question therein. Every such notice of motion shall specify the precise categories of documents in respect of which discovery is sought and shall be grounded upon the affidavit of the party seeking such an order of discovery which shall:
>
> (a)   verify that the discovery of documents sought is necessary for disposing fairly of the cause or matter or for savings costs;
>
> (b)   furnish the reasons why each category of documents is required to be discovered.
>
> (2) On the hearing of such application, the court may either refuse or adjourn the same, if satisfied that such discovery is necessary, or not necessary at that stage of the cause or matter ...
>
> (3) An order shall not be made under this rule if and insofar that the court shall be of the opinion that it is not necessary either for disposing fairly of the cause or matter or for saving costs.'

Rule 29 provides:

> 'Any person not a party to the cause or matter before the court who appears to the court to be likely to have or have had in his possession custody or power of any

---

20   See *Chemical Bank Ltd v McCormack* [1983] ILRM 350 where the order was not granted for foreign accounts.
21   [1985] IR 671.
22   [1907] 2 IR 130.
23   SI 15/1986.
24   SI 265/1993.
25   SI 233/1999.

documents which are relevant to an issue arising or likely to arise out of the cause or matter or is likely to be in a position to give evidence relevant to any such issue may by leave of the court upon the application of any party to the said cause or matter be directed by order of the court to answer such interrogatories or to make discovery of such documents or to permit inspection of such documents.'

The distinction between party and non-party discovery was explained and highlighted by the Chief Justice in *Allied Irish Banks plc and Allied Irish Banks (Holdings & Investments) Ltd v Ernst & Whinney and the Minister for Industry and Commerce*,[26] where the Chief Justice indicated:

1   that whereas an order for discovery under r 12 should only be refused or adjourned if the party resisting discovery discharged the onus of establishing that discovery was not necessary at all or at the time for disposing fairly of the cause or matter or for saving costs. By contrast, an order for discovery under r 29 should only be made where the applicant discharged the onus of establishing that the notice party was likely to have or to have had documents in his possession, custody or power relevant to an issue arising or likely to arise out of the cause or matter;

2   that whereas the court's discretion under r 12 was confined to its being satisfied that the order was not necessary. By contrast, under r 29, even assuming that the applicant has established the likelihood of the notice party having or having had relevant documents, the court had a further discretion which related to the oppression or prejudice which would be caused to the notice party and which would not be capable of being adequately compensated by the payment of the costs of making discovery;

3   that whereas an order for discovery under r 12 was sufficient if it directed discovery of a particular category of documents or of all documents relevant to the issues arising in the action, since the person making discovery would be a party to the action and would know the issues arising, By contrast, an order for discovery under r 29 was directed to a stranger to the action who would not have such knowledge and who could not reasonably be expected to investigate the pleadings or to engage a lawyer to do so for him, so that an order for discovery under r 29 should in some simple form, either by annexing of pleadings or by a schedule to the order, identify the issues, by reference to the pleadings, to which an alleged relevance occurred.

Similar orders for discovery may be made by tribunals of inquiry under the Tribunals of Inquiry (Evidence) Act 1921 and the Tribunals of Inquiry (Evidence) (Amendment) Act 1979 as applied by Geoghegan J in *Bailey, Bovale Developments Ltd and Bailey v Flood and Bank of Ireland*.[27]

An example of where the courts are willing to order discovery, even where the action does not directly affect the account holder, can be seen in the decision of *Flynn v RTE, Bird and Howard*.[28] In that case, the High Court ordered discovery of names of bank account holders in an action for defamation brought by a former employee of a bank who claimed the defendants defamed her in claiming she had induced customers to participate in a scheme aimed at evading tax.

---

26 [1993] 1 IR 375.
27 (Unreported, 15 May 1998), HC.
28 [2000] 3 IR 344.

The *Flynn v RTE* decision was cited with approval by the Supreme Court in *Von Gordon v Helaba Ruthin Landesbank Hessen-Thuringen International.*[29] However, the Supreme Court decided against ordering discovery of a lending transaction as it was the confidential business of a third party. Fennelly J stated: 'when considering whether to order discovery of such documents, the court will balance the interests of persons not party to the litigation'.

Where a mareva injunction is granted and the assets the subject of the injunction include moneys in a bank account, the court may, if it decides that the claimant is entitled to discovery of the balance in the account, exercise its powers under the Bankers' Books Evidence Act 1879 to order that the claimant may inspect and take copies of entries in the banker's books.

Subpoena

[17.10]   A bank which is compelled by subpoena to produce to a court bank statements will not breach its contractual duty of confidentiality by doing so without obtaining the customer's consent. This may pose problems for a bank in deciding whether or not it should inform its customer as it may be entitled, for its own protection or compelled by public duty, to refrain from informing its customer.

Consumer affairs

[17.11]   An authorised officer appointed by the Minister for Enterprise, Trade and Employment or by the Director of Consumer Affairs may for the purpose of obtaining information to enable the Director of Consumer Affairs to carry out her functions under the European Communities (Unfair Terms in Consumer Contracts) Regulations 1995:[30]

'(a) at all reasonable times enter premises at which any business or any activity in connection with a business is carried on . . .

(b) require any person who carries on such business or activity and any person employed in connection therewith to produce to the authorised officer any books, documents or records relating to such business or activity which are in that person's power or control and to give the officer information in regard to any entries in any books, documents and records,

(c) inspect and take copies from such books, documents and records,

(d) require any such person to give to the authorised officer any information the officer may require in regard to the persons carrying on such business or activity . . .

(e) require any such person to give to the officer any other information which the officer may reasonably require in regard to such business or activity.'

These powers are certainly intrusive, but it should be borne in mind that they are only to enable the Director of Consumer Affairs to carry out her functions under the regulations and therefore should not in the normal course involve opening accounts to the officer, but rather procedures adopted by banks in its dealings with consumer customers generally.

---

29 (Unreported, 17 December 2003).
30 SI 27/1995.

Company investigations

[17.12]   The Companies Act 1990 provides that in certain circumstances a company may have an inspector appointed to it to investigate its affairs. Subject to the court's approval, an inspector appointed to investigate the affairs of a company may also investigate the affairs of any other body corporate which is related to such company.

The Companies Act 1990 requires all officers and agents of a body corporate whose affairs are being investigated to produce to the inspectors all books and documents relating to the body corporate. Section 10(2) provides:

> 'If the inspectors consider that a person other than an officer or agent of the company or other body corporate is or may be in possession of any information concerning its affairs, they may require that person to produce to them any books or documents in his custody or power relating to the company or other body corporate, to attend before them and otherwise to give them all assistance in connection with the investigation which he is reasonably able to give; and it shall be the duty of that person to comply with the requirement.'

The problem that this statutory provision poses for banks was highlighted in the correspondence leading up to the application of *Chestvale Properties Ltd and Hoddle Investments Ltd v Glackin and Ansbacher Bankers Ltd, Noel Smyth and Partners and the Attorney General*.[31] Following the request to the bank from the inspector to deliver certain documents relating to the applicants, the applicants' solicitors wrote to the bank's solicitors stating:

> 'If your client [the bank] now complies with the demands and it is subsequently deemed that your client [the bank] was not obliged to do so, then our clients [the applicants] would have an appropriate remedy.'

The unenviable predicament for bankers was highlighted a month later by Murphy J in *Chestvale Properties Ltd and Hoddle Investments Ltd v Glackin*[32] when he said:

> 'Obviously, the bank and the solicitor are in an awkward position; if they neglect to produce books or documents which should properly have been produced, they expose themselves to the risk of penalties which might be imposed on them for contempt of court. On the other hand, if they hand over books or records which do not fall within the terms of the Act, they may be liable to their clients for damages for breach of contract.'

The impact of this predicament was felt by the bank a month later in *Chestvale Properties Ltd, Hoddle Investments Ltd and Glackin v Trustee Savings Bank and McInerney*.[33] When the bank was requested by the inspector to supply documents, it contended that, without their customer's consent or a High Court order, it could not comply with the inspector's request without breaching the duty of confidentiality which it owed to its customer. The court held that not only did the bank have to supply the documents, but also to pay the inspector his costs of the hearing.

When considering s 10 of the Companies Act 1990, the words of Costello J in *Chestvale Properties Ltd, Hoddle Investments Ltd and Glackin v Trustee Savings Bank and McInerney* should be heeded. He stated:

---

31 [1993] 3 IR 35.
32 (Unreported, 10 March 1992), HC.
33 [1993] 3 IR 55.

'It seems to me that the bank has misunderstood its statutory duty … It is a duty to give assistance if requested to do so under s 10(2) of the Act of 1990. It is not permitted to refuse assistance because of a contractual arrangement with a customer which may have involved a term of confidentiality.

The Oireachtas [Parliament] has made perfectly clear, to my mind, what people … are required to do. They are required to assist the inspector. They are not entitled to obstruct him and they must observe his requests. They are not entitled to ask their customer whether or not the customer objects. Whatever contractual arrangement there has been between the bank and the customer has been clearly overridden by the provisions put into this section by the Oireachtas and the manner in which it should comply with the request has been made clear by Murphy J. They are to give assistance to the inspector when requested to do so.'

The reference by Costello J to Murphy J was a reference to his decision in *Chestvale Properties Ltd and Hoddle Investments Ltd v Glackin*. Murphy J indicated in the course of his judgment that, under s 10 of the Companies Act 1990, there are two classes of obligation imposed on agents or former agents of a company whose affairs are being investigated, namely:

'First of all, an obligation to produce books and documents and, secondly, an obligation to attend and give *viva voce* evidence … Those words "all assistance in connection with the investigation" illuminate fully the nature of the obligation imposed upon an addressee with regard to not merely information, but also to the production of books and records. In my view, the nature of the obligation which is imposed upon officers or agents can indeed be expressed in terms comparable to that of the obligation imposed upon a person of whom discovery is sought … All the persons to whom the demand is addressed can do is to produce books and records which, in their honest opinion, may be of assistance to the inspector.'

Section 10 of the 1990 Act was challenged in a case involving the investigation of improper charging of interest and fees by a licensed bank on the grounds that it removed the privilege against self-incrimination. In *Re National Irish Bank Ltd (No 1)*,[34] the Supreme Court held (unanimously) that:

1   the right to silence was not absolute, but could in certain circumstances give way to the exigencies of the common good provided that the means used to curtail the right were proportionate to the public object to be achieved;
2   if there were grounds for believing that there was malpractice or illegality in the operation of the banking system, it was essential, in the public interest, that the public authority had the power to investigate the matter fully;
3   the powers given to the inspectors under s 10 of the 1990 Act were no greater than those which the public interest required; and
4   the interviewees were not entitled to refuse to answer questions put to them by the inspectors.

Dormant accounts

[17.13]   Under the Dormant Accounts Act 2001, the proceeds of accounts with banks which have been dormant for 15 years must, unless reactivated by the account

---

34   [1999] 3 IR 145.

holder following notification to it (at its last known address), be transferred to the Dormant Accounts Fund of the state. A bank which transfers money to the Fund is required not to refer to the account holder by name or in any manner by which the account holder could be identified.

Deposit interest retention tax

[17.14] The Finance Act 1986 introduced a concept commonly referred to as 'DIRT' – deposit interest retention tax. When making a payment of interest in respect of a deposit, a bank is required to deduct from that payment the standard rate of tax.[35] The bank is required to make a return to the Collector-General of the relevant interest paid by it and of the appropriate tax in relation to the payment of that interest (but it is not required that such return contains details of the recipients of the interest payments).[36]

Where the beneficial entitlement to interest on a deposit is held by a person who is not ordinarily resident in Ireland, tax is not to be deducted by the bank on the interest payable provided the beneficial owner declares, in such form as is prescribed by the Revenue Commissioners, that he is not ordinarily resident in Ireland. The declaration will include details of the name of the depositor, the address of his principal place of residence and the name of the country in which he is ordinarily resident. The declaration must be kept by the bank for six years or three years after the deposit is repaid, whichever is longer. The bank is required to make the declaration available to the inspector of taxes as and when required.[37]

Deduction of DIRT is not required in respect of interest on a deposit which is beneficially owned by a company within the charge to corporation tax, a pension scheme or charitable body. As a result of the Finance Act 2002, such bodies are required to provide banks paying deposit interest to them with their reference numbers. A bank is then required to return these numbers to the Revenue Commissioners, together with details of the names and addresses of such bodies to whom they have paid interest without deduction of DIRT.

A deposit account opened before 6 April 2001 may be designated by the bank holding the deposit as a 'special savings account' provided the depositor is an individual beneficially entitled to the interest who does not hold another special savings account and the amount of the deposit does not exceed 63,500 euros. The individual must make a declaration in such form as may be prescribed by the Revenue Commissioners. The declaration must include details of the name and address of the individual beneficially entitled to the interest. The bank is required to keep such declarations and make them available to the inspector of taxes as required.

Disclosure required by the Revenue Commissioners

[17.15] In recent years, the Revenue Commissioners have been given very extensive statutory powers to obtain information of a customer's account with its banker or indeed Irish-owned subsidiary banking institutions.[38]

---

35 Taxes Consolidation Act 1997, s 257.
36 Taxes Consolidation Act 1997, s 258.
37 Taxes Consolidation Act 1997, s 263.
38 Taxes Consolidation Act 1997, ss 899 to 912, as amended.

A bank may be required by the High Court to disclose details of a customer's account on the application of an inspector or other duly authorised officer of the Revenue Commissioners (this includes an account of a company which has been dissolved or an individual who has died). The High Court must be 'satisfied that there are reasonable grounds for the application being made'. The legislation provides that:[39]

> 'An authorised officer [of the Revenue Commissioners] may, subject to this section, make an application to a judge for an order requiring a financial institution to do either or both of the following, namely —
>
> (a) to make available for inspection by the authorised officer, such books, records or other documents as are in the financial institution's power, possession or procurement as contain or may (in the authorised officer's opinion formed on reasonable grounds) contain information relevant to a liability in relation to a taxpayer,
>
> (b) to furnish to the authorised officer such information, explanations and particulars as the authorised officer may reasonably require, being information, explanations and particulars that are relevant to any such liability and which are specified in the application.'

The Act enables the High Court to prohibit any transfer or dealing with any assets or moneys in the custody of the financial institution at the time the order is made. This provision was first introduced by s 18 of the Finance Act 1983. In the first reported decision on s 18,[40] Murphy J stated:

> 'Undoubtedly, any order made under the section would involve an invasion of the traditional bond of confidentiality between a banker and his customer.'

In the Supreme Court in the same case, the Chief Justice stated:

> 'Section 18 can be summarised with regard to its purpose and effect as giving to the High Court wide and entirely novel powers of forcing a bank to reveal the affairs of a customer and in addition, under certain circumstances, vests in the High Court a discretion to freeze the bank account of a taxpayer.'

Disclosure was granted under this section in *Liston v G O'C and A O'C*.[41] In that case, an inspector of taxes in the Investigation Branch of the Revenue Commissioners formed the view that the taxpayers maintained an account or accounts at specified branches of Allied Irish Banks and Bank of Ireland and that the books of both banks were likely to contain information regarding the taxpayers' financial affairs leading to the conclusion that returns of income made by them were false. Following an ex parte application by the inspector of taxes, an order was made by the High Court requiring the banks to furnish the inspector of taxes with particulars of all accounts held by the taxpayers at specified branches during a two-year period, as well as details of all lodgements and withdrawals into or out of the accounts for that period and any mandates or other instructions relating to the operation of the accounts. The High Court's decision was upheld by the Supreme Court. In giving the judgment of the court, Keane J explained the scope of the section:

---

39 Taxes Consolidation Act 1997, s 908(2), as amended by the Finance Act 1999, s 207(i).
40 *Re J B O'C v PCD and a Bank* [1985] IR 265.
41 [1996] 1 IR 501.

'The role of the inspector under the section is a purely investigative one. His belief that the information which he seeks from the bank will indicate that there have been significant omissions from the taxpayers' return of income may prove to be erroneous. The clear object of the provision is, however, to enable the Revenue Commissioners to obtain information of this nature in order to ensure that all taxpayers pay the tax which by law they are required to pay. That object would be seriously frustrated if an onus was imposed on the applicant to satisfy the court that the information sought would in fact disclose that false returns had been made. However, an order made under the section seriously abridges the right of confidentiality which every person dealing with a bank enjoys and it is for that reason that the Oireachtas not merely stipulated that the inspector must have reasonable grounds for his belief, but provided the additional and valuable safeguard that a High Court judge must be satisfied that such reasonable grounds exist before the institution concerned can be required to furnish the information sought.'

A further onus has been put on banks by the Finance Act 2002, in that where a bank is required by a court order to make documents available for inspection, the bank is required to 'afford the authorised officer reasonable assistance, including information, explanations and particulars, in relation to the use of all the electronic or other automatic means, if any, by which the books, records or other documents, in so far as they are in a non-legible form, are capable of being reproduced in a legible form and any data equipment or any associated apparatus or material'.[42] Thus, the bank is required to assist the Revenue Commissioners in investigating the details of its own customer's account.

A further Revenue power to breach the secrecy of a bank account was implemented in 1999. An authorised officer of the Revenue Commissioners may apply to the court and, provided the judge is satisfied that there are reasonable grounds for suspecting an offence is being, has been or is about to be committed, which would seriously prejudice the proper assessment or collection of tax, and a bank has material which is likely to be of substantial value to the investigation, the judge may authorise the authorising officer to inspect and take copies of any entries in books, records and other documents of the bank.[43]

Further powers were given to the Revenue Commissioners in 2004. Under the additional powers,[44] the Revenue Commissioners can investigate accounts not only of financial institutions, but institutions which are associated with the financial institutions. Essentially, these are foreign subsidiaries of Irish resident banks. It was not uncommon for persons to place funds in the Isle of Man, Cayman Islands and other locations outside Ireland. Many of those placing such funds preferred to place the funds in subsidiaries of Irish banks. The effect of these provisions and the court orders obtained by them by the Revenue Commissioners has caught many such a depositor who has been required to pay tax, interest and penalties on the interest earned from such deposits and in some cases tax, interest and penalties where the funds of the deposit constituted undeclared income.

---

42 Taxes Consolidation Act 1997, s 908 (6A) as inserted by the Finance Act 2002, s 132(1)(f).
43 Taxes Consolidation Act 1997, s 908A as inserted by the Finance Act 1999, s 207(j) and amended by the Finance Act 2004, s 88.
44 Taxes Consolidation Act 1997, s 908B as inserted by the Finance Act 2004, s 87.

Tax arrears

[17.16] A bank may be required to disclose to the Revenue Commissioners the amount standing to the credit of its customer in the event of the bank being informed by the Revenue Commissioners that the customer is in arrears of its tax payments. A bank will be obliged to make a disclosure where it has received written notification from the Revenue Commissioners (under s 1002 of the Taxes Consolidation Act 1997) that the bank's customer has defaulted, and not made good the default, 'in paying, remitting, or accounting for, any tax, interest on unpaid tax, or penalty to the Revenue Commissioners'.

The written notification (notice of attachment) will direct the bank:

1   to deliver to the Revenue Commissioners within ten days a written return specifying:
     (a) whether or not any debt is due by the bank to its customer, and
     (b) the amount of the debt or, where the debt is equal to or greater than the notified tax arrears, the amount of the so notified tax arrears; and
2   to pay to the Revenue Commissioners the lower of the amount of the debt or the amount of tax arrears notified.

Where the deposit is held in the bank by more than one party for their joint benefit, the bank must inform the depositors of the notice of attachment and that the deposit is deemed to be held for the benefit of the depositors equally unless evidence to the contrary is produced to the satisfaction of the bank within ten days. Unless such evidence is produced within ten days, the bank is required to pay to the Revenue Commissioners the amount of the deposit deemed to be held by the defaulting taxpayer (or, if lower, the amount stated in the notice of attachment). It can be seen that this requirement imposes on the bank a duty to disclose to one of its customers the fact that another customer has tax arrears of a specified amount.

Once a notice of attachment has been delivered to a bank, the bank is precluded from paying moneys to the depositor except to the extent that such moneys will not reduce the deposit below the amount specified in the notice. The legislation is silent as to whether a bank is still required to comply with an attachment notice where a security interest, whether by way of assignment or charge, is created over the depositor in favour of the bank itself or a third party. It is considered a bank will not be required to comply with an attachment notice in respect of a deposit over which there is a security assignment or over which it has a fixed charge (provided it is a blocked account). However, a floating charge over an account is unlikely to maintain priority over such a notice.

A further infringement of the relationship of confidentiality between a banker and customer arises on the service of a notice by the Revenue Commissioners on a bank under s 1001 of the 1997 Act. This provision, first introduced by s 115 of the Finance Act 1986, may affect any bank which has a fixed charge over the book debts of a company which has defaulted in its PAYE or VAT payments to the Revenue Commissioners. Following service of the notice, any subsequent moneys received by the bank from the company must be paid out to the Revenue Commissioners to discharge the outstanding tax.

Inheritance tax

[17.17] Where a sum of money exceeding 31,750 euros is lodged or deposited (other than in a current account) in Ireland with a bank in the joint names of two or more persons and one of such persons dies, the bank is not permitted to pay any part of the sum deposited to the survivor unless and until the bank receives a certificate from the Revenue Commissioners certifying there is no outstanding claim for inheritance tax (or the Revenue consent to such payment pending the ascertainment and payment of such tax).[45]

Thus, the death of the depositor will necessitate the Revenue Commissioners being informed of the account and its details before any further dealings may be made to the account.

EU Savings Tax Directive

[17.18]   The EU Council Directive (2003/48/EC of 3 June 2003) on the Taxation of Savings Income in the Form of Interest Payments and Related Matters was implemented into Irish law by the Finance Act 2004.[46] The legislation applies to all payments of interest made on or after 1 July 2005.

The purpose of the Directive is to ensure that interest payments made in one EU member state to an individual resident for tax purposes in another member state are taxed according to the law of the resident state. Thus, bank paying agents are obliged to establish the identity and residence of all individuals to whom they make interest payments. In addition, the paying agent is required to take reasonable steps to identify the beneficial owner if the paying agent has any information which suggests that an individual is not the beneficial owner of an interest payment. The paying agent is also required to report these details concerning the individuals, together with details of the interest payments, to the Revenue Commissioners.[47] The Revenue Commissioners are required to send this information to the relevant authorities in the appropriate member state. Similar arrangements have been put in place with some non-EU member states, namely Andorra, Liechtenstein, Monaco, San Marino and Switzerland.

Money laundering

[17.19]   The offence of money laundering may take any of the following forms:[48]

1   where a person conceals or disguises any property which is, or represents, his own proceeds of drug trafficking or other criminal activity for the purpose of avoiding prosecution for an offence or for the purpose of avoiding the making or enforcement of a confiscation order;
2   where a person converts or transfers property which is, or represents, his own proceeds of drug trafficking or other criminal activity or removes it from the state for the purpose of avoiding prosecution for an offence or for the purpose of avoiding the making or enforcement of a confiscation order;
3   where a person, knowing or believing that any property is, or represents, another person's proceeds of drug trafficking or other criminal activity, conceals or disguises that property for the purpose of assisting any person to avoid prosecution for an offence or for the purpose of assisting any person to avoid the making or enforcement of a confiscation order;

---

45 Capital Acquisitions Consolidation Act 2003, s 109(2).
46 Section 90 and Sch 4, as amended by the Finance Act 2005, s 144(1).
47 In July 2005, the Revenue Commissioners published detailed guidance notes for paying agents on the Irish legislation implementing the Savings Directive.
48 Criminal Justice Act 1994, s 31.

4   where a person, knowing or believing that any property is, or represents, another person's proceeds of drug trafficking or other criminal activity, converts or transfers that property or removes it from the state for the purpose of assisting any person to avoid the making or enforcement of a confiscation order;

5   where a person handles any property, knowing or believing that such property is, or represents, another person's proceeds of drug trafficking or other criminal activity.

On 1 March 2006, the Organisation for Economic Co-operation and Development announced that the Financial Action Task Force had completed an assessment of the implementation of its anti-money laundering and counter-terrorist financing standards in Ireland. Among its major findings were:

1   Ireland has a sound legal framework in place to combat money laundering, although the number of convictions for money laundering is somewhat low;

2   recent Irish legislation on combating terrorist financing is, on the whole, comprehensive, however, its effectiveness remains to be tested;

3   customer identification requirements are in place for financial institutions, however, these measures should be enhanced through the introduction of more comprehensive due diligence requirements;

4   as regards relevant non-financial businesses and professions, for example, accountants or real estate agents, certain measures have been put in place, but these need to be extended; and

5   preventive measures could be improved by providing the regulatory authorities with the power to apply an increased range of administrative sanctions directly for breaches of anti-money laundering and counter-terrorist financing obligations.

Under the Criminal Justice Act 1994 (as amended by the Criminal Justice (Terrorist Offences) Act 2005), every bank, including its directors, employees and officers, is required to report to the Garda Siochána where it 'suspects' that an offence of money laundering or financing terrorism in relation to the business of that bank has been or is being committed. A bank is also required to report to the Garda Siochána where it suspects that an offence in relation to drug trafficking, financing terrorism or other criminal activity has been or is being committed and that the services offered by the bank have been used to launder the proceeds of that offence or the bank holds funds in relation to any such activity. Furthermore, where the suspicion is that a transaction involves the proceeds of tax evasion, it should be reported.

A banker's difficulty in deciding whether to make a disclosure and run the risk of breaching its duty of confidentiality where it transpires there has been no offence is alleviated by the statutory provision that disclosure made in good faith in the course of making the report is not regarded as a breach of statutory or common law duty of confidentiality. Guidance notes for credit institutions have been issued by the Department of Finance with the approval of the Money Laundering Steering Committee. The guidance notes for anti-money laundering were last updated in May 2003. New guidance notes for the offence of financing terrorism were issued in March 2005. These guidance notes require banks to designate an officer at management level with responsibility for the bank's obligations in relation to the offences of money laundering and financing terrorism and to provide continuing training programmes for their employees. The role and duties of the money laundering reporting officer are set out in the guidance notes. Banks are required to have in place adequate arrangements and procedures to prevent and detect the commission of the offences of money laundering and financing terrorism.

There is a statutory obligation on all staff to report suspicions of money laundering. Directors, employees and officers of a bank are required to report to the Garda Siochána and the Revenue Commissioners where they suspect that an offence of money laundering has been or is being committed.[49] The guidance notes stipulate that some credit institutions may choose to require that unusual or suspicious transactions be drawn initially to the attention of the supervisory management to ensure that there are no facts that will negate the suspicion before further reporting to the money laundering reporting officer.

The Criminal Justice Act 1994 provides that a report may be made to the Garda Siochána and the Revenue Commissioners under the Act in accordance with an internal reporting procedure to be established by a bank for the purpose of facilitating the operation of the reporting obligation. Once an employee has reported his/her suspicion to another person in accordance with an established internal reporting procedure, he or she has satisfied the statutory obligation.[50] Thus, all banks have a clear obligation to ensure that each relevant employee knows to whom that employee should report any suspicions and that there is a clear reporting chain under which those suspicions will be passed without delay to the money laundering reporting officer. Failure to report a suspicious transaction carries monetary penalties and possible imprisonment for up to five years.[51]

Tipping off

[17.20] A bank (its directors, officers and employees) which discloses to its customer that it has made a report to the Garda Siochána in respect of funds in its customer's account will commit an offence under the 1994 Act if such disclosure 'is likely to prejudice any investigation arising from the report into whether an offence of money laundering or the financing of terrorism has been committed'. Thus, a bank is required to inform on its customer without alerting its customer to the fact. The 1994 Act has been amended in part by the Criminal Justice (Theft and Fraud Offences) Act 2001. This Act updates and expands the ambit of money laundering, as well as giving effect to provisions of the Convention of the European Communities' Financial Interests (Brussels, 26 July 1995) and the three Protocols to that Convention. The Act provides that the Minister for Justice may designate 'any state, or territorial unit within a state, that in his or her opinion has not in place adequate procedures for the detection of money laundering'. A bank (including any director, employee or officer) is required to report to the Garda Siochána any transaction with a state or territorial unit that has been so designated by the Minister for Justice. The Act specifically provides that a disclosure made in good faith shall not be treated as a breach of any restriction on the disclosure of information or involve the person making the disclosure in liability of any kind.

The 1994 Act was further amended by the Criminal Justice (Terrorist Offences) Act 2005. The purpose of this Act is to give effect to the European Union Framework Decision on Combating Terrorism, the International Convention Against the Taking of Hostages, the Convention on the Prevention and Punishment of Crimes Against Internationally Protected Persons, including Diplomatic Agents, the International Convention for the Suppression of Terrorist Bombings and the International Convention for the Suppression of the Financing of Terrorism. The Act also provides

---

49 Criminal Justice Act 1994, s 57(1).
50 Criminal Justice Act 1994, s 57(3)–(4).
51 Criminal Justice Act 1994, s 57(5).

additional measures concerning the financing of terrorism and terrorist groups for the purpose of complementing the Convention for the Suppression of the Financing of Terrorism.

Where a body corporate, such as a bank, commits an offence under the 2005 Act and the offence is attributable to neglect on the part of a director, manager, secretary or other officer of that body, that person is guilty of an offence and may be punished accordingly.[52]

Proceeds of crime

[17.21] The Proceeds of Crime Acts 1996 and 2005 enable a court to make an order[53] prohibiting a person from disposing of or otherwise dealing with property, including money, where the property constitutes, directly or indirectly, proceeds of crime or where the property was acquired in whole or in part with or in connection with property that, directly or indirectly, constitutes proceeds of crime.[54] To discharge the order, the applicant needs to show that the property does not constitute proceeds of crime or was not acquired with, or in connection with, property that constitutes proceeds of crime.

The Act specifically provides that no action or proceedings shall lie against a bank or any other person in any court in respect of any act or omission done or made in compliance with an order under the Act. Accordingly, a customer cannot in such circumstances have a remedy against its bank which has broken its duty of confidentiality in complying with a court order to make available details of its customer's account in compliance with a court order.

Criminal Assets Bureau

[17.22] The Criminal Assets Bureau Acts 1996 and 2005 established the Criminal Assets Bureau and set out its extensive functions and powers in relation to criminal and related activities. The broad objectives of the Bureau are:

1   the identification of assets, wherever situated, of persons which derive or are suspected to derive, directly or indirectly, from criminal activity;
2   the taking of appropriate action under the law to deprive or to deny those persons of the assets or the benefit of such assets; and
3   the pursuit of any investigation or the doing of any other preparatory work in relation to any proceedings arising from the objectives mentioned in paras 1 and 2 above.

The Acts allow a judge (on application by a Bureau member who is a Garda Siochána) to issue a search warrant for the search of any place or person in that place if the judge is satisfied that there are reasonable grounds for suspecting that evidence of or relating to assets or proceeds deriving from criminal activities, or to their identity or whereabouts, is to be found in that place. The Act provides that the court

---

52 Criminal Justice Act 1994, s 59 and the Criminal Justice (Terrorist Offences) Act 2005, s 45.
53 Following an ex parte application by a member of the Garda Siochána not below the rank of Chief Superintendent, an authorised officer of the Revenue Commissioners or a member of the Criminal Assets Bureau.
54 Such an order may be made for an interim period of 21 days. During this interim period, an interlocutory order may be sought extending the effect of the interim order.

order will have effect notwithstanding any other obligation as to secrecy or other restriction on disclosure of information imposed by statute or otherwise.[55]

Funds of an unlawful organisation

[17.23]   Under the Offences Against the State (Amendment) Act 1985, a bank is required, on receipt of a document 'purporting to be signed by the Minister for Justice', which states that, in the opinion of the minister, moneys described in the document and held by the bank are the property of an unlawful organisation, to pay the moneys so specified into the High Court. This statutory requirement runs for periods of three months and, if not renewed, lapses until renewed. The consequences of a bank failing to comply with such a requirement are heavy fines and/or imprisonment for the directors or officers of the bank, including the manager or other official of a branch of the bank.

As well as the bank being required to pay moneys into the High Court, it may be required by the court 'to produce and prove to the court all or specified documents that are relevant to the payment of the moneys or part of them into or out of the bank or to the opening, maintenance, operation or closing of any account at the bank in respect of the moneys or part of them'. Statutory protection is given to a bank which complies with a requirement of the minister.

A person claiming to be the owner of such moneys paid into the High Court may, within six months, apply to the court seeking an order that the moneys be returned with interest. The court will make the order if it is satisfied that the applicant is the owner of the moneys and the moneys do not belong to an unlawful organisation.

There was an unsuccessful constitutional challenge to this legislation following the transfer of funds to the High Court by the Bank of Ireland by an order from the Minister for Justice.[56] In that case, the bank was required to transfer to the High Court nearly £2 million held in the bank by the plaintiffs. The High Court held, however, that the legislation amounted to a permissible delimitation of property rights in the interests of the common good and the account holders, on proving that the funds did not belong to an unlawful organisation, were entitled to claim the funds in court.

Prosecution of criminal offences

[17.24]   Under s 299 of the Companies Act 1963,[57] if it appears to the liquidator in the course of a voluntary winding up that any past or present officer or member of the company has been guilty of any offence in relation to the company for which he is criminally liable, he shall report the matter to the Director of Public Prosecutions and the Director of Corporate Enforcement. In the event of a liquidator not making such a report, a person interested in the winding up may apply to the court seeking a court direction for such a report to be made. Similarly, in the case of a winding up of a company by the court, the court may direct the liquidator to refer any offence to the Director of Public Prosecutions and the Director of Corporate Enforcement.

Following such report, if the Director of Public Prosecutions or the Director of Corporate Enforcement institutes proceedings, it is the duty of every past and present

---

55   Criminal Assets Bureau Act 1996, s 14A(6).
56   *Clancy and McCarthy v Ireland and the Attorney General* [1989] ILRM 670.
57   As amended by the Company Law Enforcement Act 2001, s 51.

banker to the company 'to give all assistance in connection with the prosecution which he is reasonably able to give'.

Where it appears to the Irish stock exchange that a person has committed an offence under the insider dealing provisions of the Companies Act 1990, the exchange must make a report to the Director of Public Prosecutions. If the Director issues proceedings following such report, it is the duty of every person who appears to the Director to have relevant information 'to give all assistance in connection with the prosecution which he or they are reasonably able to give'. In applying the principles outlined by Costello J in *Chestvale Properties Ltd, Hoddle Investments Ltd and Glackin v Trustee Savings Bank and McInerney*,[58] a bank would be required to disclose details of such accounts as required by the Director of Public Prosecutions in the course of his proceedings for unlawful dealing.

Access to banker's book by Garda Síochána and Director of Corporate Enforcement

[17.25] The legislature has endeavoured to assist the Garda Síochána and, more recently, the Director of Corporate Enforcement in bringing to justice persons who may have committed a criminal offence by permitting them access to documentation held in a bank. The Bankers' Books Evidence Act 1879, as amended by the Central Bank Act 1989, the Disclosure of Certain Information for Taxation and Other Purposes Act 1996 and the Company Law Enforcement Act 2001, provides:

'If, on an application made by a member of the Garda Síochána not below the rank of Superintendent or the Director of Corporate Enforcement a court or judge is satisfied that there are reasonable grounds for believing—

(a) that an indictable offence has been committed; and
(b) that there is material in the possession of a bank specified in the application which is likely to be of substantial value (whether by itself or together with other material) to the investigation of the offence;

a court or judge may make an order that the applicant or another member of the Garda Síochána, or officer of the Director of Corporate Enforcement nominated by the Director, as the case may be, be at liberty to inspect and take copies of any entries in a banker's book, or inspect and take copies of any documentation associated with or relating to an entry in such book, for the purposes of investigation of the offence (the word "documentation" is deemed to include "information kept on microfilm, magnetic tape or in a non-legible form (by use of electronics or otherwise) which is capable of being reproduced in a permanent legible form").'

Duty to the public to disclose

[17.26] The second qualification to a banker's duty of confidentiality referred to in *Tournier v National Provincial and Union Bank of England*[59] is where there is a duty to the public to disclose. There had been a dearth of case law to illustrate this principle until the Supreme Court's decision in *National Irish Bank Ltd and National Irish Bank Financial Services Ltd v Radio Telefís Eireann*.[60] In that case, the

---

58 [1993] 3 IR 55.
59 [1924] 1 KB 461.
60 [1998] 2 IR 465.

defendants sought to publish information showing that certain named customers of the plaintiffs had, at the suggestion of the plaintiffs, used their moneys on deposit (with the plaintiffs) for the purpose of investing in an Isle of Man company, Clerical Medical Insurance, the result of which, the defendants alleged, enabled the return on such moneys to evade tax which would otherwise have been payable on the deposit accounts. Although it was not proved that the customers intended to evade tax and the plaintiffs denied it was the intention of the scheme to evade tax, the Supreme Court held by a three to two majority that the defendants could disclose to the public at large the information which they possessed, including the names of individual customers (albeit at the risk of a claim for defamation from the customers).

The principle of this exception to the duty of confidentiality was set out by Lynch J in his majority judgment, where he said:

'There is no doubt that there exists a duty and a right of confidentiality between banker and customer as also exists in many other relationships such as, for example, doctor and patient and lawyer and client. This duty of confidentiality extends to third parties into whose hands confidential information may come and such third parties can be injuncted to prohibit the disclosure of such confidential information. There is a public interest in the maintenance of such confidentiality for the benefit of society at large. On the other hand, there is also a public interest in defeating wrongdoing and where the publication of confidential information may be of assistance in defeating wrongdoing then the public interest in such publication may outweigh the public interest in the maintenance of confidentiality.'

In applying the principle in the case, Lynch J held:

'... the allegation which [the defendants] make is of serious tax evasion and this is a matter of genuine interest and importance to the general public and especially the vast majority who are law abiding taxpayers and I am satisfied that there is a public interest that the general public should be given this information.'

The lack of proof by the defendants of any wrongdoing, but simply an allegation of wrongdoing, made the majority decision somewhat surprising (although the editorial of the Irish Times at the time of the decision stated: 'perhaps we should not be unduly surprised. The Supreme Court has a proud and distinguished record of affirming individual rights and liberties'. No mention was made of the rights of customers to have their affairs kept confidential). In his dissenting judgment, Keane J (who succeeded Hamilton CJ as Chief Justice) with whom the then Chief Justice Hamilton concurred, pointed out that the details of the scheme were already the subject of inquiries by the Revenue Commissioners and the central bank. Keane J stated:

'The authorities ... made it clear that where someone is in possession of confidential information establishing that serious misconduct has taken place or is contemplated, the courts should not prevent disclosure to persons who have a proper interest in receiving the information. RTE, accordingly, should not be restrained in this case from disclosing to the Revenue Commissioners the confidential information in their possession which, they say, establishes that this scheme has been availed of in order to evade the payment of tax.'

Thus, according to the Supreme Court, disclosure to the public at large is in the public interest not just where there is wrongdoing, but also where there is a suspicion of wrongdoing.

The Supreme Court's decision was applied in *Minister for Enterprise, Trade and Employment v Ansbacher (Cayman) Ltd on the Application of the Revenue Commissioners.*[61] In that case, the High Court had appointed inspectors (pursuant to the Companies Act 1990) to investigate the affairs of Ansbacher (Cayman) Ltd. The report was presented to the court and the Revenue Commissioners were permitted access to the report. The Revenue Commissioners now sought access to further documents which the inspectors had acquired in the course of their investigation, but which were not included in the report. In granting the application (although limiting it somewhat), the president of the High Court stated:[62]

> 'In the circumstances of the present case, it is appropriate to have regard to the contractual duty of confidentiality which exists between a bank and its customer and to the constitutional right to privacy and to balance these rights against the interests sought to be vindicated by the applicant for an order. However, the public interest is paramount: see *National Irish Bank Ltd v Radio Telefis Eireann* ... limited disclosure such as disclosure of tax evasion to the Revenue Commissioners, the recipient of such disclosure having a particular interest as opposed to disclosure to the world at large, will almost inevitably result in the court finding the balance in favour of the disclosure.'

An interesting feature here is that the High Court president seems to have adopted the position of the dissenting judges in the *National Irish Bank* case in calling for limited disclosure to interested parties rather than the public at large. The High Court president held:[63]

> 'In making such order, I must have regard to the interests of the persons affected by the order sought and in particular to their contractual right of confidence in their dealings with their bank and their constitutional right to privacy. I must balance the interests of such persons against the public interest, in this case the effective functioning of the Revenue Commissioners. The disclosure sought is not to the public at large, but is limited to the applicant who has a special interest in obtaining the same ... The affairs of the company were conducted in a manner which disabled the applicant from assessing and collecting taxes. I am satisfied that the public interest in the assessment and collection of taxes outweighs the contractual right to confidentiality and the constitutional right to privacy of the individuals and companies mentioned in the report.'

Interest of the bank to disclose

[17.27] Where disclosure is justified under this exception, it must be restricted to that which is strictly necessary to protect the bank's interest. The classic example of this exception is where the bank discloses information in relation to its customer in order to enforce its rights against the customer by legal proceedings. The exception should also cover disclosure for the purpose of protecting the bank's business reputation in circumstances where it is brought into question by actions of the customer.

In relation to the relevance of this exception to disclosures between separate legal entities within a banking group, it would not be safe for a bank to assume such

---

61 [2004] 3 IR 193.
62 Ibid at 200 and 201.
63 Ibid at 203 and 204.

disclosures are permitted under this exemption. This intra-group disclosure issue was raised in *Kennedy v Allied Irish Banks plc*,[64] where disclosure between two members of an Irish banking group was at issue. The judge did not find it necessary to resolve the issue in the particular circumstances, but, in passing, stated that this is an 'interesting and important point for all banking groups'. The better view is that, as a general rule, express consent is necessary for such disclosure and the decision of the English Court of Appeal in *Bank of Tokyo Ltd v Karoon*[65] that each company in a group is to be regarded as a separate entity for disclosure purposes would probably be followed if the issue were to be considered by an Irish court. Some banks include in their standard documentation express consent of the customer to intra-group disclosures.

The question whether the bank's interest exception covers disclosure of information in relation to customers to credit bureaux has not been considered by the Irish courts. In the case of disclosure of information relating to customers who are not in default, it is unlikely that the exception would apply and the bank should have the consent of the customer before disclosing information in such circumstances. Standard documents used by some of the banks expressly provide for this.

SANCTIONS FOR CUSTOMERS

[17.28] A breach of the duty of confidentiality by a bank will result in damages being awarded to the relevant customer. There is a dearth of case law from the Irish courts. In assessing the level of damages, the courts would be likely to give effect to the rule in *Hadley v Baxendale*.[66] In that regard, the approach taken by the House of Lords in the recent English decision of *Jackson v Royal Bank of Scotland*[67] is likely to be followed in Ireland.

Powers of enforcement of the data protection legislation are conferred on the Data Protection Commissioner in relation to breaches of the Data Protection Acts by means of issuing enforcement notices. Non-compliance with an enforcement notice is a criminal offence. The Act enables the Commissioner to prohibit the transfer of personal data abroad where the Commissioner is of the opinion that the transfer is likely to lead to a contravention of the basic principles for data protection contained in the Strasbourg Convention.

CROSS-BORDER/EXTRA-TERRITORIAL ISSUES

Banks with foreign offices

[17.29] As already seen, s 7 of the Bankers' Books Evidence Act 1879 applies to records used in the ordinary business of a bank. Any bank which holds a banking licence from the financial regulator comes within the ambit of the Act. However, it has been decided that the records or other entries in a 'banker's book' should not apply to the books of a foreign branch of a licensed bank. In *Chemical Bank Ltd v McCormack*,[68] the High Court held:

---

64 (Unreported, 18 May 1995), HC, Murphy J.
65 [1986] 3 All ER 468.
66 (1854) 9 Excl 341.
67 [2005] 1 WLR 377.
68 [1983] ILRM 350.

'There are no clear words in the 1879 Act or the amending 1959 Act which would support the interpretation of an intention to have extra-territorial effect … *R v Grossman*[69] appears to be authority for the making of an order addressed to AIB as a company incorporated within the jurisdiction to make available for inspection in this country the account of the defendant … in the Park Avenue branch of the bank in New York. However, even if it is, I do not propose to make such an order in case there would be a conflict of jurisdiction, which should be avoided in the interest of the comity of courts.'

However, this restriction should be read subject to the powers of the Revenue Commissioners to access details of foreign accounts held by licensed banks and associated institutions.[70]

Foreign banks with offices in Ireland

[17.30]   It would seem that a bank with its head office outside Ireland would not be subject to the jurisdiction of the Irish courts so far as producing records which were kept outside the jurisdiction of Ireland, but only such records kept in Ireland relating to the bank's branch. In this regard, the courts are likely to follow the English decision of *MacKinnon v Donaldson Lufkin & Jenrette Securities Corpn.*[71]

Subpoenas from other jurisdictions

[17.31]   A foreign court may issue a subpoena on an international bank for the purpose of obtaining information in relation to an Irish branch. This raises issues of conflicts of law and respect for the comity of nations. Where the international bank has a branch or place of business in the jurisdiction where the subpoena is issued, the subpoena may be enforceable as a practical matter in that jurisdiction. However, where the revelation of information by a branch in Ireland in relation to dealings with its customers would be in breach of the bank's duty of confidentiality, the issue arises whether an Irish court would issue an injunction restraining the disclosure. There is no Irish case law directly on the point, but it is likely that an Irish court would follow the position taken by the English courts in *X Attorney General v A Bank*[72] and restrain such a disclosure, in particular, in circumstances where compliance with the injunction in Ireland would not result in the bank being in contempt of the foreign court which granted the subpoena. This conclusion is consistent with the approach taken by the High Court in *Chemical Bank Ltd v McCormack.*[73]

Obtaining evidence abroad for use in Irish proceedings

Subpoena

[17.32]   The usual means of securing the presence of a witness at a trial is by the service on him of a subpoena *ad testificandum*. To secure documents to be put in evidence, a subpoena *duces tecum* is served on the person in possession of them,

69 [1981] Crim LR 396.
70 See the Taxes Consolidation Act 1997, s 908 (referred to above).
71 [1988] 1 All ER 653.
72 [1983] 2 All ER 464.
73 [1983] ILRM 350.

requiring him to produce the documents in court. If the person on whom it is wished to serve the subpoena is out of the jurisdiction, no subpoena may be issued by the court. Where documents are held outside Ireland, but there is a person within Ireland in whose control they are, it would appear that there is power to compel that person to produce the documents. In *Chemical Bank Ltd v McCormack*,[74] the High Court held in relation to the Bankers' Books Evidence Act 1879 that while the court had an inherent jurisdiction to make an order compelling a bank incorporated in Ireland to produce an account maintained outside the jurisdiction for inspection, this should not be done as it would involve 'a conflict of jurisdiction, which should be avoided in the interest of the comity of courts'. It was also held that as the 1879 Act could not be interpreted as having extra-territorial effect, the High Court had no jurisdiction to order an inspection under the 1879 Act outside Ireland.

Evidence by commission

[17.33]   Where a person is abroad, but consents to give evidence or produce evidence, the High Court may permit the taking of evidence abroad by commission under an inherent jurisdiction which is recognised by the Rules of the Superior Courts and has been exercised for a long time.[75] The courts are reluctant to exercise this jurisdiction and will generally only do so in rare cases where it is necessary in the interests of justice.[76] Circumstances which have justified the use of the procedure on occasion include a witness not having sufficient financial resources to travel to Ireland.[77]

Letters of request

[17.34]   Letters of request may be issued in accordance with the Rules of the Superior Courts to a foreign court or judicial authority requesting the oral examination of a witness before the court or other competent authority in respect of the examination of witnesses. Where an order is made for the issue of a request to examine a witness in a foreign country with which a convention with Ireland exists, the procedure may be varied.

Obtaining information from banks in Ireland for use in foreign civil proceedings

Letters of request

[17.35]   Ireland has not yet ratified the 1968 Hague Convention on the Taking of Evidence Abroad in Civil and Commercial Matters (although the Law Reform Commission has recommended ratification). The position where letters of request are received in Ireland from a foreign court is covered by the Foreign Tribunals Evidence Act 1856, which provides that:

> 'Where, upon an application for this purpose, it is made to appear to any court or judge having authority under this Act that any court or tribunal of competent jurisdiction in a foreign country, before which any civil or commercial matter is

---

74 [1983] ILRM 350.
75 *Re Carbery Divorce Bill* [1920] 2 IR 345.
76 *Neil v Silcock* (1903) 38 ILTR 5.
77 *Keane v Hanley* [1938] Ir Jur Rep 16.

pending, is desirous of obtaining the testimony in relation to such matter of any witness or witnesses within the jurisdiction of such first-mentioned court, or of the court to which such judge belongs, or of such judge, it shall be lawful for such court or judge to order the examination upon oath, upon interrogatories or otherwise, before any person or persons named in such order, of such witness or witnesses accordingly; and it shall be lawful for the said court or judge, by the same order, of such court or judge, or any other judge having authority under this Act, by any subsequent order to command the attendance of any person to be named in such order, for the purpose of being examined, or the production of any writings or other documents to be mentioned in such order, and to give all such directions as to the time, place, and manner of such examination, and all other matters connected therewith, as may appear reasonable and just.'

The proceedings, which are the subject of the letters of request, must be civil or commercial. The 1856 Act provides that the giving of a certificate by a diplomatic agent or consul is evidence that the relevant matter pending before the foreign court is a civil or commercial matter. The letters of request must require testimony from named persons within Ireland. Any person duly authorised by the foreign court or tribunal may apply to the High Court to have evidence taken. There are two possible routes. Letters of request may be forwarded by a foreign embassy to the Department of Foreign Affairs. The Department transmits them to the Chief State Solicitor, who in turn makes an application to the High Court, which will normally direct the examination to take place before a District Court judge with questions put by counsel briefed by the Chief State Solicitor. The second procedure (and the one which may in practice be more expeditious) involves the sending of a letter of request to solicitors in Ireland who, acting as agents of the parties to the foreign proceedings, apply ex parte on affidavit to the High Court for an appropriate order directing that a specified witness attend to give evidence before an examiner, again, normally a District Court judge.

The court has a discretion in relation to the production of documents. In general, it must be satisfied that the documents are relevant to the proceedings. The witness's evidence is given under oath and the normal rules of evidence apply.

In *Re Chomutov Savings Bank*,[78] the Supreme Court reversed the High Court's decision and made an order requiring a witness to be examined notwithstanding the fact that the defendant to the foreign action had not yet been served with proceedings.

Obtaining information from banks in Ireland for use in foreign criminal proceedings

Request for assistance

[17.36] Under the Criminal Justice Act 1994, where the Minister for Justice receives 'a request for assistance' from a foreign court, tribunal or other authority in obtaining evidence in Ireland in connection with criminal proceedings in the foreign state and the minister is satisfied that an offence under the law of the foreign state has been committed (or that there are reasonable grounds for suspecting that such an offence has been committed) and that proceedings or an investigation into that offence are being carried out, he may nominate a judge of the District Court to

---

78 [1957] IR 355.

receive such of the evidence (including documents and other articles) to which the request relates as may appear to the judge to be appropriate to give effect to the request.

A typical summons would require a bank manager to attend the District Court to give evidence as to all bank accounts held legally and/or beneficially in the name of the person under investigation and any related accounts in the name of subsidiaries. The bank manager would typically be required to attend the court with:

1   copies of all bank statements and vouchers including ledgers, documents evidencing electronic fund transfers (for example, SWIFT transactions), pay cheques, debit advices, paying in slips and other credit advices for the account/accounts;
2   copies of all customer files, customer records cards, statement inquiry cards, account opening fees, records showing authorised signatory and all correspondence between either the bank and the account holder, the bank and third parties and internal bank correspondence and other records maintained by the bank relating to the monitoring of the accounts from the date of opening to the present time; and
3   copies of all documents held by the bank on computer or in hard copy in respect of the use of these accounts.

The summons typically provides that the provisions of the Bankers' Books Evidence Act 1879 must apply to the documents, namely, that the book or documents or microfilm was at the time of making the entry one of the ordinary books of the bank and that the entry was made in the usual and ordinary course of business of the bank and the books are in the custody or control of the bank.

Sequestration of bank deposits

Not applicable for enforcement of foreign penal law

[17.37]   The courts will not enforce a foreign sequestration order on the grounds that the courts will not be used to enforce a penal law of a foreign state as decided in *Buchanan Ltd v McVey*.[79] The reason for this approach is that the courts are not competent to arbitrate on the justice or injustice of the penal laws of foreign states. An example of the application of these principles arose in the case of *Larkins v National Union of Mineworkers and Bank of Ireland Finance Ltd*,[80] which attracted much publicity at the time (the principal officers of the union concerned, who were trustees of its funds, were Arthur Scargill, Michael McGahey and Ernest Heathfield). The English courts appointed the first four plaintiffs sequestrators following the failure of the first defendant (the union) to pay a fine. The sequestrators sought an interim order from the High Court claiming that the union had transferred funds of approximately £8 million from its account in the UK to bank accounts with the second defendant (the bank). The sequestrator claimed possession of the funds and they needed to establish the whereabouts of the funds with a view to preventing them from leaving the Irish jurisdiction. The Irish High Court made an interim order providing, inter alia, that:

1   the union, the bank, their servants and agents and 'any bank or financial institution' within the Irish jurisdiction be restrained from disposing of or

---

79   [1954] IR 89.
80   [1985] IR 671.

otherwise dealing in any manner with any moneys held in the union's account; and

2   the bank (or any financial institution or bank in Ireland served with notice of the order) produce for inspection 'the bankers' books, including correspondence or computer printouts from electronic recordings' relating to any account of the union held by the bank.

At the trial of the action (where it was held that the sequestrators were not entitled to the funds on deposit on the grounds that the court would not enforce a penal law or process of a foreign state), Barrington J gave his reasons for his 'very far-reaching order':

'In the normal course, a freezing order would have been sufficient to maintain the status quo and there would have been no justification for making an inspection order such as this ex parte. The necessity for the ex parte order arose from the fear that a portion of the funds had already been transferred to other financial institutions in Ireland, the identity of which was unknown to the sequestrators [as it transpired, funds had not been transferred to other financial institutions in Ireland, but to banks in New York, Luxembourg and Switzerland].'

Transfer of assets abroad

[17.38]   A further head under which the Revenue Commissioners may require disclosure arises under s 808 of the Taxes Consolidation Act 1997. Under this section, the Revenue Commissioners may require any person to furnish such particulars as they think necessary in connection with the transfer of assets abroad by persons ordinarily resident in Ireland. However, the banker–customer confidentiality relationship is respected by the exclusion of a bank from such disclosure requirement of 'any particulars of any ordinary banking transactions between the bank and a customer carried out in the ordinary course of banking business' save in limited circumstances.[81] Whether a transaction is one carried out in the ordinary course of banking business will depend upon the ordinary business of 'that type of banking institution' and not whether it is in the ordinary course of banking business generally.

This provision was first introduced by s 59 of the Finance Act 1974. In considering its application, it might be noted that the High Court in *Royal Trust Co (Ireland) Ltd and Whelan v The Revenue Commissioners*[82] applied the judgment of Megarry J in *Royal Bank of Canada v Inland Revenue Commissioners*.[83] This latter case involved the application of s 414(5) of the English Income Tax Act 1952, the relevant portion of which is identical to s 808(4) of the 1997 Act. In the course of his judgment, Megarry J stated:

'Questions as to the ambit of the term "ordinary banking transactions" are not made easier by the circumstances that at least on some views there are many different types of bank … A transaction that to one type of bank may be ordinary may to another type be exceptional … I certainly do not accept that every transaction lawfully carried out by a bank is a "banking transaction". Furthermore, even if they were "banking transactions", I cannot regard them as being "ordinary" banking transactions. I do not think it is for counsel for the

---

81 As specified in the Taxes Consolidation Act 1997, s 808(6).
82 [1982] ILRM 459.
83 [1972] 1 All ER 225.

Commissioners to establish that they were "unusual" or "extraordinary" or whatever is the appropriate antithesis to "ordinary"; it is for counsel for the bank to show that they were "ordinary" ... nothing will suffice him save a sufficient demonstration of ordinariness.'

In *Royal Trust Co (Ireland) Ltd and Whelan v The Revenue Commissioners*, the High Court held that one type of transaction came within the exclusion, but that the second type did not 'as there has not been what Megarry J described as "sufficient demonstration of ordinariness" with regard to them'.

REGULATION OF FINANCIAL MARKETS

Chinese Walls

[17.39] The financial regulator's Licensing and Supervisory Requirements and Standards for Credit Institutions set out non-statutory requirements of the financial regulator in relation to the licensing and supervision of banks and other financial institutions, under which each bank must satisfy the financial regulator with regard to resolution of conflicts of interest arising in the conduct of different types of activity under its control and that adequate arrangements have been made to protect the interest of its customers. The Requirements and Standards state that the financial regulator will require all banks to comply with codes of conduct which are issued by it.

The Code of Conduct for the Investment Business Services of Banks provides that a bank shall ensure that there are effective 'Chinese Walls' in place between the different business areas of the bank and between the bank and its connected parties in relation to information which could potentially give rise to a conflict of interest or be open to abuse. All procedures relating to the maintenance of Chinese Walls must be in writing and notified to all relevant officers and employees of the credit institution. Chinese Walls are defined as:

> 'An arrangement within the organisation of the credit institution, or between the credit institution and any associate of that credit institution, which requires information obtained by the credit institution or, as the case may be, associate, or a particular operating unit within the credit institution or associate in the course of carrying on one part of its business of any kind to be withheld in certain circumstances from other operating units or from persons with whom it deals in the course of carrying on another part of its business of any kind'.

CONCLUSION

[17.40] In the past decade, the common law duty of confidentiality has been increasingly eroded by the state in its attempt to hinder and prevent money laundering, drug dealing, terrorism and tax evasion. In respect of the first three areas of criminal activity, the state's measures have been generally in line with most other European states. The establishment of the Criminal Assets Bureau has been particularly successful in taking the assets of persons engaged in drug dealing.

The measures against tax evasion have been somewhat grounded on the results of a number of tribunals which have investigated the source of political donations. The Revenue Commissioners now have very extensive powers not only in accessing bank accounts in Ireland, but also offshore accounts in subsidiaries of Irish banks.

The current political climate of transparency was taken too far by the Supreme Court's majority decision in *National Irish Bank v RTE* (referred to in 'Duty to the Public to Disclose' above). The decision was an infringement of the right of individuals to conduct their affairs outside the glare of public curiosity. The interpretation by the president of the High Court (in *Minister for Enterprise, Trade and Employment v Ansbacher (Cayman) Ltd*) has brought the exception back to an appropriate level for curbing tax evasion. The High Court though is a lower court and the populist Supreme Court decision remains in place.

18 Italy

*Marcello Gioscia**
Giuseppe de Falco

SOURCES OF A BANK'S DUTY OF CONFIDENTIALITY

Introduction

[18.1] A bank's duty of confidence, that is the bank's duty not to reveal to third parties the existence and nature of its relationships with its clients (and that disclosed by those clients to it), has still not been expressly codified under Italian law, even if its existence has been recognised by the Italian Constitutional Court.[1] Therefore, given the recognised need for banks to maintain the confidentiality of transactions entered into with their clients, it is necessary to identify the legal sources which give rise to the banks' obligation to maintain such confidentiality.

Customary practice

[18.2] Some legal writers have maintained that the obligation of confidentiality in relation to banking transactions is based on art 47 of the Italian constitution, which provides that 'the Republic encourages and protects savings in any form'. The obligation to maintain confidentiality in banking transactions is, therefore, seen to constitute one of the elements essential for the encouragement and protection of savings. However, the Constitutional Court[2] has clarified that banks' customers have neither a constitutional right nor a personal right as the confidentiality relating to their bank accounts and transactions carried out by banks on their behalf remains subject to the security and proper functioning of the market and then to several exceptions.

The existence of an obligation to maintain confidentiality in banking transactions is undoubtedly implicitly supported by various provisions of Legislative Decree 385 of 1 September 1993 ('Banking Law'), as amended from time to time, which will be discussed in more detail below. Nevertheless, the legal source which more directly gives rise to the obligation of confidentiality in relation to banking transactions is generally considered by legal writers and judicial authority to be 'customary practice', which is a source of law consisting of the repetition of uniform behaviour

---

* The authors express their gratitude to Barbara Pansadoro for her valuable assistance.

1 Corte Costituzionale, 18 February 1992, n 51, which has defined bank secrecy as a duty of confidentiality upon banks in connection with the transactions, accounts and financial positions of their customers.
2 See Corte Costituzionale, 18 February 1992, n 51.

carried out in the belief that such behaviour is in compliance with the performance of legal obligations.[3]

Such customary practice, which imposes the obligation of confidentiality on banks, assumes importance in relationships between banks and their clients and assumes the nature of a contractual obligation owed by the banks to their clients by virtue of the fact that the banking contract is supplemented by various implied terms. In fact, art 1374 of the Civil Code requires the parties to a contract to act not only according to the terms of the contract, but also in accordance with the consequences that derive from law or, in the absence of law, common practice.

Obligations of fairness and good faith

[18.3]   According to some legal writers, the obligation owed by banks to maintain the confidentiality of banking transactions is based on legal rules embodying general principles of fairness and good faith. Therefore, the banks' obligation of confidentiality, rather than arising from individual contracts between banks and their clients, constitutes a specific application of the obligation – owed by a debtor and creditor in any given transaction – to act in accordance with rules of fairness,[4] with specific reference both to pre-contractual negotiations[5] and the subsequent performance of the contract.[6]

Banking Law

[18.4]   As mentioned above, the obligation to maintain the confidentiality of banking transactions is implicitly confirmed by various provisions of the Banking Law.

First, art 7 of the Banking Law – which replaces art 10 of Royal Decree 375 of 12 March 1936 ('Old Banking Law') – provides as follows:

'1   All notices, information and data in the possession of the Bank of Italy by virtue of its supervisory activities are covered by official secrecy and also in respect of public administrative bodies, except for the Minister of Economy and Finance as Chairman of the Credit Committee. Professional secrecy may not be invoked with respect to judicial authorities when the information requested is needed for investigations or proceedings involving breaches subject to criminal sanctions.

2   The officers and employees of the Bank of Italy, in exercising their supervisory functions, are public officers and are obliged to refer exclusively to the Governor all irregularities ascertained, even when such irregularities may constitute an offence.

3   Officers and employees of the Bank of Italy are bound by official secrecy.'

Although it has been argued that the secrecy obligation contained in art 10 of the Old Banking Law applies solely to the Bank of Italy and its personnel, it has also been argued, on the other hand, that this obligation constitutes a confirmation (albeit

---

3 Gianfelici *Il segreto Bancario*, Milan (1996) p 2; see Cass 18 July 1974, n 2147 in *Massimario* (1974) p 514.
4 Civil Code, art 1175.
5 Civil Code, art 1337.
6 Civil Code, art 1375.

indirect) of the existence of a general obligation owed by banks to maintain confidentiality of banking transactions.[7]

The above theory is founded primarily on two considerations, one of which is now superseded due to the repeal of art 2622 of the Civil Code. First, the obligation regards and covers all information concerning banks and neither provides for nor permits a distinction to be drawn between information relating to credit institutions and information relating to individual clients.

Secondly, art 135 of the Banking Law, which deals with corporate offences, provides that certain provisions of the Civil Code relating to corporate offences apply to those persons within a bank who perform functions of an administrative, managerial or supervisory nature. Among such provisions, the old version of art 2622 of the Civil Code[8] established that 'the directors, officers, statutory auditors and liquidators who, without just cause, for their own profit or for the profit of others, make use of or reveal information obtained by them by reason of their position, are punishable . . .' Since art 135 of the Banking Law expressly provides for the protection of information relating to banks, it is considered that the above-mentioned art 7 of the Banking Law cannot have as its sole and exclusive object such protection, but rather must be seen to establish the obligation to maintain confidentiality in relation to all information relating to both the bank and its individual clients. Such theory appears to remain sustainable, even now after the amendment to art 2622 of the Civil Code and art 622 of the Criminal Code, given that the sanction set out in art 622 of the Criminal Code will now apply irrespective of any reference made to it by the Banking Law (see 'Criminal Law' below).

Further, art 87, para 5 of the Banking Law (which replaces the last paragraph of art 78 of the Old Banking Law) regarding the protection of bank secrecy provides that the list of unsecured creditors – a summary of which must be produced by the receiver in proceedings for the compulsory winding up of a bank – 'is not to be made available', that is, it is not provided with the statement of creditors to be included in the court documents thereby avoiding the possibility that third parties may view it.

It is possible to infer from the above article (although indirectly in this case) further confirmation of the existence of the banker's duty to maintain confidentiality. Article 87, para 5 of the Banking Law has, on the one hand, strengthened the protection of bank confidentiality in relation to the specific bank's bankruptcy proceedings (*liquidazione coatta amministrativa*). On the other hand, it has eliminated any express reference to the principle of bank confidentiality (while art 78 of the Old Banking Law was clearly based on such principle).[9] In any case, the principle of the protection of bank confidentiality during compulsory administrative liquidation has been supported by the Italian Constitutional Court.[10]

---

7 Bricola *Commento sub art 10 lb* in AA VV *Codice commentato della Banca Milan* (1990) vol I, p 134ff.

8 Following the enactment of Law 366 of 3 October 2001, which provided for the repeal of art 2622 of the Civil Code (divulging of confidential information), art 2 of Legislative Decree 61 of 11 April 2002 added a para in art 622 of the Criminal Code (recently amended by art 15 of Law 262 of 28 December 2005), according to which the sanction provided for divulging a professional secret is increased 'if the fact is committed by directors, general managers, managers in charge of the drafting of corporate accounting documents, auditors or liquidators or by accounting firms'.

9 Galanti *Commento sub artt 87 e 88 Legge Bancaria* in *Commentario al Testo Unico delle leggi in materia bancaria e creditizia*, Padova (1994) p 87ff.

10 Corte Costituzionale, 14 January 1977, n 26 in *Giurisprudenza Costituzionale* (1977) I, p 80ff.

Criminal law

[18.5] There is an old judicial trend, now considered outdated, according to which the source of the banker's duty of confidentiality is also seen to be founded in criminal law. In particular, this trend relied on art 622 of the Criminal Code which punishes 'whoever, having knowledge of a secret by reason of his position, office or profession, reveals that secret, without just cause, or uses it for his own profit or the profit of others, if such behaviour can cause damage'.

Nevertheless, according to the majority of the more recent case law and legal theory, bank secrecy is not founded on criminal law principles. In particular, art 622 could not be applied to cases of breach of the banker's duty of confidentiality given that (i) the information provided to the bank by its clients is not a 'secret' of the type contemplated by art 622 and (ii) banking services – far from constituting individual professional services – are performed by corporate entities and are of a commercial nature.

However, following the insertion of para 2 in art 622 (see footnote 8) and the express extension of the prohibition of divulging professional secrets to directors, general managers, managers in charge of corporate accounting documents, auditors, liquidators and accounting firms, the explanation under point (ii) above no longer seems to be relevant.

Likewise, art 326 of the Criminal Code – which punishes public officials or persons entrusted with public service, who, in breach of the duties inherent in their position or service or in any way abuse their position, reveal official information which should remain secret or in any way facilitate such communication – cannot be applied to cases of the nature in question as information known by banks relating to their clients does not constitute a 'secret' as contemplated by this article.

EXCEPTIONS TO THE PRINCIPLE OF BANK SECRECY

Exceptions to bank secrecy in relation to the tax authorities

[18.6] With the coming into force of Part III of Law 413 of 30 December 1991 containing the 'provisions for transparency of relationships between tax authorities and taxpayers', bank secrecy, in relation to the tax authorities, was substantially reduced by means of modifications to numerous provisions contained in Decree of the President of the Republic ('DPR') 600 of 29 September 1973 (in relation to assessment of income tax) and DPR 633 of 26 October 1972 (in relation to VAT).[11]

In particular, the area in question is regulated by art 32 of DPR 600/1973 and art 51 of DPR 633/1972, as amended by art 18 of Law 413, subsequently by art 1, paras 402 and 403 of Law 311 of 30 December 2004 (the so-called '2005 Budget Law' containing rules on the annual and multi-annual accounts of the state) and more recently by art 2, para 9 of Decree 203 of 30 September 2005. These articles confer wide powers of audit on the tax authorities which may be exercised in requesting information and documentation (provided that it is relevant from a tax point of view) both directly from the person the subject of the tax audit and indirectly from third parties (including credit institutions, financial intermediaries, investment firms and

---

11 Gianfelici, n 3 above, p 16ff.

trust companies)[12] which have conducted relationships of an economic nature with that person.

With specific reference to the powers of the tax authorities to request information and documents from banks relating to their clients, it is necessary first to specify that the tax authorities may obtain from the banks not only copies of the accounts of the client under investigation, with details of all transactions connected with such accounts, but also all data, information and documents regarding any relationship or transaction carried out on behalf of the client irrespective of its connection with the accounts opened in the name of the client, including services rendered in favour of the client and guarantees granted in favour of the client by third parties. As a result, certain kinds of services (such as non-core services)[13] and transactions 'out of account' (such as the collection of a cheque at the counter or the request of a bank draft against payment in cash), which were covered by bank secrecy, can now be easily discovered and investigated by the tax authorities.

In this respect, art 1, para 332 of the 2005 Budget Law has imposed on banks the duty to identify all customers in relation to any transaction and irrespective of the value of the transaction (before the coming into force of the 2005 Budget Law, banks were only required to identify customers who carried out transactions 'out of account' if the value of the transaction was higher than 12,500 euros).

Once the requested documentation is obtained, the tax authorities may also request the bank to provide further information of a more specific nature by requesting them to respond to questionnaires.

There are no prerequisites provided for the exercise of this power. The relevant tax authorities make the request to the bank exclusively on the basis of their own discretional evaluation that such request is necessary, subject to authorisation by the regional director or area commander of the relevant tax authorities. As from 1 January 2007,[14] the requests and the relevant answers, even if negative, shall be made exclusively by electronic means.

If the tax authorities have not received the requested documentation from the bank within the time limit fixed by the tax authorities (which cannot, in any event, be under 30 days after the date of notification of the request to the bank and can be extended up to a further 20 days) or if the tax authorities have established reasons to doubt the correctness or the authenticity of the information received, they may,

---

12 It is worth noting that, as a result of the amendments introduced by the 2005 Budget Law, tax authorities can now request data, information and documents not only from banks and post offices, but also from financial intermediaries, investments firms, collective investment undertakings, Italian management companies and trust companies.

13 Pursuant to art 1, para 6 of Legislative Decree 58/1998 (the so-called 'Consolidated Law on Finance'), non-core services are:
1. safekeeping and administration of financial instruments;
2. safe custody services;
3. lending to investors to enable them to carry out transactions in financial instruments where the lender is involved in the transaction;
4. advice to undertakings on capital structure, industrial strategy and related matters and advice and services relating to mergers and the purchase of undertakings;
5. services related to the issue or placement of financial instruments, including the organisation and constitution of underwriting and placement syndicates;
6. investment advice concerning financial instruments;
7. foreign exchange trading where this is connected with the provision of investment services.

14 See the provision of the Tax Agency of 29 May 2006 published in the Official Gazette of the Republic of Italy no 126 of 1 June 2006.

subject to authorisation by the regional director or area commander, gain direct access to the bank's premises to obtain the relevant information in accordance with the procedures provided by a Decree of the Minister of Economy and Finance.

For the protection of the bank's client subject to the tax investigation, the bank is obliged to provide the client with immediate notice of the request for information received from the tax authorities and, further, all data and information collected by the tax authorities is covered by principles of secrecy, breach of which is punishable by specific administrative sanction (unless such breach constitutes a criminal offence and apart from any internal disciplinary actions).

Finally, it is necessary to note in this respect that art 3, paras 177 and 178 of Law 549 of 28 December 1995 (in relation to the rationalisation of public finance) helps to render the power of the tax authorities, referred to above, more effective providing that the tax authorities, in the performance of their duties, may request the person subject to the tax investigation to give a declaration containing the details of the nature of, and essential data relating to, their relationships with credit institutions, the post office, trust companies and all other domestic and foreign financial intermediaries.

Exceptions to bank secrecy in relation to the criminal judicial authorities

[18.7]   The extent of bank secrecy in respect of criminal judicial authorities is principally regulated by arts 248 and 255 of the new Criminal Procedure Code.[15]

Article 248, in relation to searches ordered by a criminal judicial authority, provides that, if the object of the search is to find a specific item, the judicial authority may ask the holder to deliver it, thereby avoiding the search (unless it is considered useful to proceed with the search for the completion of the investigation). Further, in order to locate the items to be seized or to ascertain other useful facts for the purposes of the investigation, the judicial authority or officers of the judicial police may examine documents and correspondence in the bank's possession (both Italian banks and foreign banks operating in Italy) and search such items in the event of a refusal by the bank.

Article 255, in relation to seizures from banks (Italian banks and foreign banks operating in Italy), grants to the judicial authority the power to seize documents, instruments, valuable goods, funds deposited in accounts and all other items, even if contained in a safe deposit box, when such authority has established reasons to consider that those items are pertinent to the offence, even if they do not belong to the accused and they are not registered in his name.

Based on art 248, the concerned bank does not have any right to refuse to comply with the judicial authority's request. Banks generally comply with informal requests from the criminal judicial authorities to receive specified information in order to avoid any personal intervention by the magistrate at the banks' offices for the retrieval of the relevant documentation. Such behaviour by the banks, at least in cases in which a direct response is given by letter by the banks to the criminal magistrate, on the one hand, appears to be consistent with a relatively common practice of co-operation between banks and criminal magistrates and, on the other, is

---

15 Conso-Grevi *Profili del nuovo codice di procedura penale*, Padova (1993) p 238.

considered by case law as lawful behaviour which does not constitute a breach of the duty of confidentiality.

In case the bank fails to observe the orders of the criminal judicial authority, criminal sanctions are applicable. In particular, reference is made to art 650 of the Criminal Code, which, in relation to a failure to observe the orders of the authority, expressly punishes those who do not observe an order made legally by the competent authority by reason of justice, public security, public order or hygiene. The provisions at issue are only applicable in cases not involving a more serious crime, in fact, a failure to observe a criminal magistrate's order by a bank may constitute a more serious offence – for example, aiding and abetting, receiving stolen goods or money laundering – with the consequent application of more severe criminal sanctions relating to such offence.

The bank is required to verify the authenticity of the order by the judicial authority, the adequacy of the relevant grounds or motives and the limits of any delegation of the judicial authority to the judicial police officers as such delegation cannot be of a generic nature, but must be precisely detailed both from a subjective and objective point of view. However, the bank does not have any power to challenge or question the legitimacy of an order by a criminal magistrate.

In relation to the issue of notifying the client of the investigation by the criminal authority, contrary to what is provided by the tax legislation in relation to tax investigations, the bank – from a civil point of view – is under no obligation to inform its client of the request for information made by the criminal magistrate and – from a criminal point of view – the bank may not reveal such information to the client, being under an obligation of criminal secrecy provided for by art 329 of the Criminal Procedure Code.

Nonetheless, if the request by the criminal magistrate does not relate to the bank–client relationship, documentation concerning the client or the production or seizure of documentation concerning the bank–client relationship, but rather the seizure of sums or assets held by the bank on an agency basis, the obligation on the bank not to notify the client of the request by the judicial authority no longer exists. In fact, such a seizure affects the right to deal with those assets and therefore the bank is obliged to notify the principal of the seizure.

Exceptions to bank secrecy in relation to the civil judicial authorities

[18.8]   A civil magistrate has the power to issue orders for the inspection of documents in the bank's possession or to require the bank to provide documents or information relevant to the outcome of civil proceedings pending between third parties.[16]

In particular, in accordance with art 118 of the Civil Procedure Code, a judge may order the parties to the civil proceedings or third parties to allow items in their possession to be inspected where it is essential for ascertaining the facts relating to the proceedings provided that this would not involve serious damage for the parties or for third parties.

---

16 Finocchiaro *Ispezione giudiziale (dir proc civ)* in *Enc Dir*, Milan (1972) p 948ff.

It is considered, however, that the bank may avoid the inspection of its clients' documents on the grounds that allowing the inspection and the consequent breach of the duty of confidentiality could involve damage to the bank arising from the loss of its clients' trust. Further, if the bank has doubts about the existence of the conditions for the admissibility of the evidence, it is under a duty to make a claim to the court objecting to the order for the inspection.

If the magistrate does not accept the bank's grounds for refusal or where the claim to the court is rejected, the bank must thereafter comply with the magistrate's order (according to art 118 of the Civil Procedure Code, a failure to comply may be considered by the judge in evaluating the behaviour of the party). On the other hand, such order exempts the bank from all civil liability in respect of its client as it would constitute just cause for the banker's disregard of the duty of confidentiality.

Further, in accordance with art 210 of the Civil Procedure Code, the civil judge, upon request by the counterparty, has the power to order the other party or a third party to produce in the proceedings documents or other items which he considers necessary for those proceedings within the same limits within which such documents may be ordered to be subject to inspection. In such a case, if the judge does not accept the justification of serious damage on which the bank's objection is based, the bank must comply with the civil magistrate's order, being exempt from all civil liabilities in respect of its client.

Regarding the relationship between the protection of bank secrecy and the obligation to testify, employees of the bank called to testify in civil proceedings may not fail to comply with the obligation to testify about facts and circumstances of which they have knowledge by reason of their employment since the right of abstention from giving testimony is accorded by law in exceptional cases, which this is not considered to be one.

Finally, a bank which has been notified of an act of seizure or attachment of items held by it on behalf of a client is obliged to make a third party declaration of seizure or attachment in accordance with art 547 of the Civil Procedure Code, according to which the third party (the holder of assets belonging to the party against whom the seizure or attachment has been ordered by the civil judge) must specify which items and sums are in its possession and when delivery must be made.

Exceptions to bank secrecy in relation to monetary regulations

[18.9] Following the coming into force of monetary regulations (DPR 148 of 31 March 1988, as amended), the movement of capital between Italian residents and residents of other EU member states was liberalised in accordance with the relevant regulations.[17]

Following this legislative initiative, the Italian Exchange Office ('UIC'), which was previously responsible for exchange control in the monopoly system, has only retained a supervisory role in respect of the credit institutions authorised to conduct exchange transactions and operate on the monetary market on their own behalf and in their own name.

---

17 Council Directive 88/361/EEC. See Gianfelici, n 3 above, p 151ff.

In its supervision of compliance with monetary regulations, the UIC has, amongst other things, the right to carry out inspections at the premises of banks and other locations where it has reason to believe that there are relevant documents on those premises and has the right to request the production of relevant account books, documents and correspondence (availing itself of the co-operation cf the tax authorities and the national institute for foreign trade). In respect of parties subject to the supervision of the Bank of Italy, the UIC may proceed to carry out the inspection directly using the inspection services of the Bank of Italy.

Further, the UIC – for survey and statistical purposes in relation to economic relationships with foreign entities – is also authorised to request that banks entitled to carry out transactions in foreign currency send information concerning foreign exchange transactions in which those banks are in any way involved (excluding, however, transactions for under 12,500 euros).

UIC officers and all other persons performing monetary supervisory functions are considered to be public officers and are bound by official secrecy in relation to information obtained in the performance of their duties.

Regarding the existing relationship between bank secrecy and monetary regulations, it is necessary to deal with the issue of so-called 'tax monitoring' introduced by Law 227 of 4 August 1990 containing the regulations for monitoring, for tax purposes, of transfers over a certain amount of cash, financial instruments and securities into and out of Italy.

In particular, art 1 of Law 227 of 1990, as amended from time to time, establishes that the banks authorised to carry out monetary transactions must maintain records of the transfer from or to a foreign entity of cash, instruments or securities greater than 12,500 euros[18] effected on behalf of or in favour of physical persons, non-commercial entities and certain other entities – expressly indicated in art 1 – which are resident in Italy. Such records, which have to contain the details of the transactions including name/business name, residence, tax code of the Italian resident on whose behalf or in favour of whom the transfer is effected and the identifying particulars of any accounts of destination, must be kept available to the tax authority for a period of five years and sent to the competent authority in accordance with specific terms and procedures established by Ministerial Decree.

These obligations are also applicable to the sale and purchase of foreign instruments and securities effected by the persons referred to above if an Italian authorised bank is involved in the transaction.

Exceptions to bank secrecy in relation to the Bank of Italy

[18.10] The Banking Law confers on the Bank of Italy wide powers to request information from banks for the performance of its supervisory functions. In particular, arts 51, 53 and 54 of the Banking Law govern the supervisory role which the Bank of Italy has in respect of banks subject to its supervision.[19]

---

18 This threshold has been fixed by Legislative Decree 290 of 17 October 2002 issued by the Ministry of the Economy and Finance and published in the Official Gazette of the Republic of Italy on 11 December 2002.

19 Berionne *Commento sub art 51* in *Commentario a cura di Capriglione*, p 262ff; Trequattrini *Vigilanza sulle banche* in *La nuova legge bancaria, Commentario a cura di Ferro-Luzzi e Castaldi*, Milan (1996) p 775ff.

With specific reference to the supervisory role, banks involved in an investigation conducted by the Bank of Italy are obliged to produce to the Bank of Italy's inspectors all documentation those inspectors consider appropriate.

It should be noted that, in accordance with art 7 of the Banking Law, all information obtained by the Bank of Italy through its supervisory activities is covered by official secrecy, including those in respect of public administrative bodies, except for the Minister of Economy and Finance, other than in cases provided for by law relating to the investigation of criminal breaches. Further, the employees of the Bank of Italy – in the performance of their supervisory duties – are considered to be public officers bound by official secrecy and they are obliged to refer all irregularities exclusively to the Governor of the Bank of Italy, even where there is an offence involved. The Governor must then refer information to the criminal judicial authority if the elements of a criminal offence can be made out in the facts referred to him by the inspectors.

Exceptions to bank secrecy in relation to the client's consent

[18.11]   Confidentiality in banking transactions is the contractual right of the bank's client and such right may be expressly or implicitly waived by the client.

Consequently, from a civil liability point of view (contractual and non-contractual), communication of client information to third parties (in particular, in relation to the solvency of the client) cannot be considered a breach of the duty of confidentiality if the client has requested the bank to make such communication in the interests of the client or where the client has otherwise authorised the communication of the information.

From a criminal law point of view, this conclusion is also valid even if there is an accusation of an offence under art 622 of the Criminal Code in relation to a breach of the duty of confidentiality. In fact, art 50 of the Criminal Code expressly excludes from punishment whoever prejudices or endangers a right with the consent of the person who may validly dispose of that right.

Exceptions to bank secrecy in relation to anti-money laundering regulations

[18.12]   With reference to the offence of money laundering, it should be noted that, in accordance with art 648 bis of the Criminal Code, whoever substitutes or transfers money, assets or other profits which are the proceeds of crime or performs other transactions in order to hinder the identification of criminal proceeds shall be punished with imprisonment between four and 12 years and a fine ranging from 1,032 to 15,494 euros. Further, such definition is complemented by art 648 (receiving of stolen goods)[20] and art 648 ter of the Criminal Code that punishes with the same sanctions whoever uses, in economic or financial activities, money, assets or other profits which are the proceeds of crime.

---

20 Article 648 of the Criminal Code punishes whoever, for the purpose of procuring a benefit for himself or others, acquires, receives or conceals money or property derived from any crime whatsoever or in any way participates in causing it to be acquired, received or concealed.

Among the provisions aimed at preventing the crime in question (so-called 'anti-money laundering regulations'), Law 197 of 5 July 1991 ('AML Law'), as amended from time to time and most recently by Legislative Decree 56 of 20 February 2004,[21] is of particular significance. Article 1 of the AML Law prohibits:

1   the transfer of money, cash or instruments to the bearer in euros or foreign currency when the value of the transfer is greater than 12,500 euros[22] (the transfer may only be performed through authorised intermediaries, including banks);
2   the issue of bank cheques and bank drafts in favour of third parties for amounts greater than 12,500 euros without including the details of the beneficiary and the non-assignment clause;
3   the issue of 'to the bearer' savings books for amounts greater than 12,500 euros.[23]

Article 2 of the AML Law provides that whoever performs transactions involving the transfer of money or other valuables of whatever nature which are greater than 12,500 euros with a bank or other expressly listed entity (such as the post office, e-money institutions, investment firms, insurance companies and financial intermediaries)[24] must be identified by the bank (or such other entity) and must indicate in writing its complete details or those of the party on whose behalf the transaction was undertaken. All the details of the transaction are archived and must be retained for a period of ten years. In addition, such identification shall also be made when, due to the nature and procedures of the transactions set up, it appears that several transactions effected at different times within a certain period of time, even if individually below the threshold amount, constitute parts of a single transaction.

In this respect, art 2 of Legislative Decree 56 has extended the list of entities that are subject to the duties of identification and record keeping to include accountants, auditors, labour consultants, lawyers and notary publics and delegated the Minister of Economy and Finance to list the transactions in respect of which such duties shall apply.

In addition, the list of entities subject to the duties of identification and record keeping has recently been extended by Law 29 of 26 January 2006 to include any person who provides services rendered by accountants, commercial experts and labour consultants without being enrolled in the relevant registers. In this respect, in opinion 99 of 21 April 2006, the Anti-Money Laundering Committee has clarified that such amendment was necessary to bring Italian anti-money laundering rules into line with EU provisions.

By Decree 141 of 3 February 2006, the Ministry of the Economy and Finance has established that the duties of identification and record keeping shall apply to lawyers, notary publics, accountants, labour consultants and accounting firms when on behalf of and for their clients, they execute any financial or real estate transaction and when

---

21 The implementation of Directive 2001/97/EC on the prevention of use of the financial system for the purposes of money laundering.
22 This threshold has been fixed by Ministerial Decree 25601 of 17 October 2002 issued by the Ministry of the Economy and Finance and published in the Official Gazette of the Republic of Italy no 290 of 11 December 2002.
23 Turone *Le tecniche di contrasto del riciclaggio* in *Cass pen mass amm* (1993) 1790, p 2692.
24 In this respect, see Decrees 142 and 143 of the Ministry of the Economy and Finance of 3 February 2006.

they assist in the planning or execution of transactions for their clients concerning the:

1   transfer, with any title, of real property or going concerns;
2   managing of money, securities or other assets;
3   opening and management of bank, saving or security accounts;
4   organisation of contributions necessary for the creation, operation or management of companies; and
5   creation, operation or management of trusts, companies or similar structures.

With direct reference to the issue of bank secrecy, art 3 of the AML Law provides that the person responsible for the branch office or other operational point of the authorised intermediary – amongst which are the banks – is under an obligation to notify to the responsible superior of that bank or other authorised intermediary every transaction that, by its nature or due to other circumstances, gives rise to a suspicion, based on the available facts, that the money, assets or profits the object of the transaction may derive from any of the types of criminal offences referred to in art 648 of the Criminal Code (receiving stolen goods).[25] Failure to make the report shall be punished by a pecuniary sanction ranging from 5–50% of the value of the transaction unless it constitutes a more serious crime (in which case, different sanctions would be applied depending on the criminal offence).

The responsible superior must examine such notice and, if he finds it to be founded, must transmit it without delay, electronically or by other means, to the UIC without any indication of the name of the person making the report. The UIC may exercise the powers conferred on it by the monetary regulations in order to examine the notification in further depth. In particular, the UIC can suspend the execution of a transaction for 48 hours.

Further, it is expressly provided that such notifications do not constitute breaches of the secrecy obligation and do not therefore involve liability of any kind. It is, in fact, expressly prohibited for those persons obliged to give notice, and anyone else having knowledge of such notice, to reveal the contents to parties other than those indicated above.

Finally, art 5 of the AML Law places authorised intermediaries under an obligation – which therefore also covers banks – to notify the Minister of the Economy and Finance within 30 days of becoming aware of any notification of a breach of the prohibitions contained in art 1 of the AML Law.

Still on the subject of money laundering, in November 1994, the Bank of Italy compiled and circulated their 'guidelines for the notification of suspect transactions', a manual addressed to bankers containing suggestions aimed at facilitating the work of the banking and finance system in the campaign against money laundering. Such guidelines provide, amongst other things, specific 'signs of anomaly' relating to transactions and conduct which could possibly involve breaches of the anti-money laundering regulations and to which authorised intermediaries – including banks – must have regard in the performance of their notification obligations referred to in art 3 of the AML Law.

---

25 Santacroce *La segnalazione di operazioni sospette dopo la legge 9 agosto 1993, n 328: Novità e prospettive di riforma in Banca, borsa e titoli di credito* (1995) I, p 165ff.

Anti-money laundering measures in compliance with the FATF recommendations

[18.13] Forty recommendations were drawn up by the Financial Action Task Force ('FATF')[26] in 1990 as an initiative to prevent the misuse of financial systems by persons laundering drug money and subsequently revised in 1996 and 2003 to ensure that they remain up to date and relevant to the evolving threat of money laundering.

As described under 'Exceptions to Bank Secrecy in Relation to Anti-Money Laundering Regulations' above, Italy has put in place a comprehensive anti-money laundering system ('AML system') which was initially set up in 1991, later updated a number of times and is still under reconsideration to reflect evolving money laundering typologies and compliance with the recommendations, even if there are still certain gaps which need to be filled, such as the application of a more effective sanctions regime (fines seem extremely low for a financial crime, which can generate considerable amounts of proceeds) and the identification of the ownership and control structure of a customer who is a legal person.

Recently, in line with the need to strengthen and constantly improve the AML system, Italy has ratified the Palermo Convention by means of Law 146 of 16 March 2006 in compliance with recommendations 2 and 35, according to which countries should become party to and implement the Vienna Convention[27] and the Palermo Convention[28] and ensure that the offence of money laundering is consistent with their standards. In particular, art 10 of Law 146 has introduced the administrative liability of legal persons with reference to the offence of money laundering.

In light of the scope of this article, compliance of the Italian AML rules with recommendations 1 (offence), 4 (financial institution secrecy or confidentiality), 13 (reporting of suspicious transactions and compliance) and 14 (protection against disclosure of information) is specifically analysed below. In addition, a brief overview of the recommendations and their compliance in Italy is set out in the table below. All recommendations 1, 4, 13 and 14 are fully observed.

In particular, as depicted under 'Exceptions to Bank Secrecy in Relation to Anti-Money Laundering Regulations' above, the definition of money laundering is set out in art 648 bis of the Criminal Code and complemented by two other provisions dealing with other aspects of the offence: art 648 (receiving stolen goods) and art 648 ter. Such definition is broad enough to cover all the situations referred to in the Vienna and Palermo Conventions and it complies with recommendation 1.

According to recommendation 4, 'countries should ensure that financial institution secrecy laws do not inhibit implementation of the FATF recommendations'. As described above, bank confidentiality is not provided for in Italian legislation. As a result, it cannot be invoked in criminal proceedings, nor before the supervisory

---

26 The FATF is an inter-governmental body created for the purpose of developing and promoting policies, both at national and international level, to combat money laundering and terrorist financing.
27 United Nations Convention against illicit trafficking in narcotic drugs and psychotropic substances (1988).
28 United Nations Convention against transnational organised crime (2000).

authorities (such as the Bank of Italy, the Italian Commission for Corporations and the Stock Exchange ('CONSOB') or the UIC) or the Financial Police (*Guardia di Finanza*) when conducting investigations. Furthermore, there are no restrictions on the sharing of information between financial institutions and art 14 of the Data Protection Code expressly limits the exercise of rights laid out in the law with regard to information collected on the basis of the AML Law.

Finally, with reference to the duty of reporting suspicious transactions provided by recommendations 13 and 14, as described in 'Exceptions to Bank Secrecy in Relation to Anti-Money Laundering Regulations' above, art 3 of the AML Law sets out the basis of the reporting requirements. In this respect, it is worth noting that, following enactment of three regulations by the Ministry of the Economy and Finance[29] and the relevant implementation of Directive 2001/97/EC, the reporting requirement has been extended to bureaux de change, post offices, stockbrokers, investment companies, trust companies, insurance companies and professions.

In February 2006, an assessment of the compliance of the Italian AML system with the FATF recommendations has been conducted by a team of staff of the International Monetary Fund ('IMF').[30] Overall, the IMF is of the opinion that the current Italian AML system 'is extensive and mature and achieves a high degree of compliance with most of the recommendations. The law enforcement efforts against money laundering have been quite successful' even if 'more effort needs to be devoted by supervisory authorities to ensure the legal framework is effectively implemented by reporting entities'.

A synthetic picture describing the compliance of the Italian AML system with the recommendations is given in the table below.

FATF recommendations	Content	Compliance in Italy
1	Scope of the criminal offence of money laundering	The recommendation is fully complied with
2	Liability of legal persons	The recommendation is complied with, but fines should be more proportionate and dissuasive
3	Provisional measures and confiscation	The recommendation is largely complied with. However: • the definition of assets subject to confiscation should include proceeds indirectly derived from the offence or assets intermingled with criminal proceeds; • provisions to render void dealings, transfer or disposal of assets should be provided by law
4	Financial institution secrecy or confidentiality	The recommendation is fully complied with

---

29 See Decrees 141, 142 and 143 of the Ministry of the Economy and Finance of 3 February 2006.
30 International Monetary Fund 'Italy: Financial Sector Assessment Programme – Detailed Assessment Report on Anti-Money Laundering and Combating the Financing of Terrorism', February 2006.

FATF recommendations	Content	Compliance in Italy
5	Customer due diligence and record keeping	The recommendation is partially complied with due to the: • absence of any requirement for the identification of customers with respect to occasional transactions that are wire transfers below a 12,500 euros threshold; • absence of any requirement for financial institutions to take reasonable measures to understand the ownership and control structure of a customer who is a legal person; • exemption from customer due diligence with respect to banks and branches abroad should be limited to those that are located in jurisdictions that effectively implement the recommendations
6	Politically exposed persons ('PEP')	The recommendation is not complied with due to the absence of specific requirements for the identification of PEP and senior management approval for establishing a business relationship with a PEP
7	Cross-border banking and similar relationships	The recommendation is not complied with due to the absence of specific requirements regarding procedures for the opening and operation of cross-border correspondent banking relationships
8	Non-face to face business relationships	The recommendation is fully complied with
9	Third parties and introduced business	The recommendation is partially complied with as: • there are not specific requirements for third parties to supply without delay copies of identification data and other relevant information relating to customer due diligence requirements to any requesting financial institutions; • it is not ensured that such third parties located abroad are regulated and supervised in accordance with the recommendations
10	Duty of record keeping upon financial institutions	The recommendation is fully complied with
11	Monitoring transactions and relationships	The recommendation is largely complied with. However, authorities should provide for effective enforceable requirements with respect to financial intermediaries that are not subject to prudential supervision

18.13   *Italy*

FATF recommendations	Content	Compliance in Italy
12	Duties upon non-financial businesses and professions	The recommendation is fully complied with
13	Reporting of suspicious transactions and compliance	The recommendation is fully complied with
14	Protection against disclosure of information	The recommendation is fully complied with
15	Programmes against money laundering	The recommendation is largely complied with. However, Italian law should provide for: • explicit requirements for screening procedures for hiring employees; • a guidance on how financial institutions, other than those prudentially supervised, should organise themselves to comply with AML requirements
16	Additional duties upon non-financial businesses and professions	The recommendation is fully complied with
17	Effective, proportionate and dissuasive sanctions	The recommendation is partially complied with: • the sanctions regime is not fully effective, proportionate and dissuasive (fines are too low for a crime of such nature); • legal persons are not subject to any sanction for failure to comply with the AML rules
18	Shell banks	The recommendation is partially complied with as financial institutions are not prohibited from: • entering or continuing banking relationships with shell banks; • establishing relations with foreign financial institutions that permit their accounts to be used by shell banks
19	Physical cross-border transportation of currency and bearable negotiable instruments	The recommendation is fully complied with
20	Development of secure techniques of money management	The recommendation is fully complied with
21	Measures to be taken with respect to countries that do not or insufficiently apply the recommendations	The recommendation is largely complied with. However, authorities should provide for adequate requirements with respect to business relationships and transactions with persons from countries which do not or insufficiently apply the FATF recommendations

FATF recommendations	Content	Compliance in Italy
22	Application of principles to branches and subsidiaries located abroad	The recommendation is partially complied with as there are no specific provisions that require the application of AML principles to foreign branches of financial institutions other than banks or foreign subsidiaries of Italian financial institutions
23	Regulatory and supervisory measures on financial institutions	The recommendation is partially complied with as there are inadequate supervision/on-site inspections with respect to securities and insurance sectors
24	Regulatory and supervisory measures on non-financial businesses and professions	The recommendation is not complied with as non-financial businesses and professions are not monitored for AML purposes
25	Guidelines from supervisory authorities	The recommendation is partially complied with as: • no feedback is provided to financial institutions; • no guidelines have been issued for non-financial businesses and professions
26	Establishment of financial intelligence units	The recommendation is largely complied with
27	Powers to the competent authorities	The recommendation is fully complied with
28	Obtaining of documents and information	The recommendation is fully complied with
29	Monitoring powers	The recommendation is largely complied with
30	Financial, human and technical resources	The recommendation is largely complied with
31	National co-operation	The recommendation is largely complied with
32	Statistics on matters	The recommendation is largely complied with
33	Transparency of legal persons	The recommendation is complied with
34	Information on trusts	The recommendation is largely complied with
35	International co-operation	The recommendation is fully complied with
36	Mutual legal assistance	The recommendation is fully complied with
37	Dual criminality	The recommendation is fully complied with
38	Co-ordinating procedures between foreign countries	The recommendation is fully complied with
39	Extradition	The recommendation is fully complied with
40	Other forms of co-operation	The recommendation is fully complied with

Exceptions to bank secrecy in relation to anti-terrorist regulations

[18.14]   A bank's duty of confidentiality is also derogated from the recent legislation issued in order to detect, prevent and fight the financing of terrorism and terrorist acts.

Considering the importance of taking action to fight the financing of terrorism and of the general rule set out under art 270 bis of the Criminal Code (as repealed by art 1, para 1 of Legislative Decree 374 of 18 October 2001), pursuant to which whoever finances, directly or indirectly, terrorist organisations shall be punished, Legislative Decree 369 of 12 October 2001 and the instructions of the Italian Exchange Office of 9 November 2001 imposed certain obligations on banks and other financial institutions subject to anti-money laundering provisions in order to counter terrorism.

In particular, banks and other financial institutions subject to anti-money laundering obligations are asked to take all relevant measures to freeze funds and other assets of terrorists whose personal data is on special lists made available by the Italian Exchange Office.

In addition, banks and other financial institutions shall report their adopted measures promptly to the Italian Exchange Office specifying the persons involved and the amount of the funds, as well as all the transactions and relationships which, according to the available information, can be considered linked or related, directly or indirectly, to the financing of terrorist acts or organisations.

Exceptions to bank secrecy in relation to anti-Mafia regulations

[18.15]   Law 575 of 31 May 1965, as subsequently modified and containing anti-Mafia provisions, is also of relevance in relation to bank secrecy as it confers on the criminal judicial authorities and the police the right to request from banks information and documentation considered useful for the purposes of Mafia investigations.[31]

In particular, art 2 bis, para 6 of Law 575 provides that the judicial authorities may request – either directly or through officials and agents of the judicial police – any officer of the public administration and any credit entity, including enterprises, corporations and other types of entity, to provide information and copies of documentation considered useful for the purposes of investigations of persons against whom preventive measures are proposed as there are reasons to suspect that those persons belong to a Mafia-style organisation.

Further, the judicial police officials, subject to authorisation by the criminal judicial authority, may seize from the banks documents considered relevant in accordance with the terms and procedures provided in arts 253, 254 and 255 of the Criminal Procedure Code.

Exceptions to bank secrecy in relation to foreign judicial authorities

[18.16]   Bank secrecy cannot be invoked in cases of specific decisions or requests for information made by a foreign criminal judge. Following such decisions and

---

31 Gianfelici, n 3 above, p 225ff.

requests, an Italian criminal judge may order a bank to testify or produce certain documents relating to the bank's relationship with its clients.

The European Convention on Judicial Assistance in Criminal Matters signed at Strasbourg on 20 April 1959 was ratified by Italy with Law 215 of 23 February 1961 and provides for the gathering of evidence by judicial authorities in one signatory state at the request of judicial authorities of another signatory state. In addition, the procedure applicable to international requests of this nature is specifically regulated by art 723 of the Criminal Procedure Code.

In relation to civil matters, any possible order by a civil magistrate requiring a bank to testify or produce certain documents in relation to its existing relationships with its clients is based, on the one hand, on the Hague Convention on Civil Procedure of 1 March 1954 and numerous bilateral agreements on civil procedure to which Italy is a signatory and, on the other, on art 64 of Law 218 of 31 May 1995 containing the reform of international private law (in particular, art 69 of that law governs the gathering of evidence by foreign judges).

INSIDER TRADING

[18.17]   Unauthorised use of inside information (insider trading), initially regulated by Law 157 of 17 May 1991, is mainly regulated by arts 180–187 septies (except for arts 185 and 187 ter) of Legislative Decree 58 of 24 February 1998. Such articles were recently replaced by art 9 of Law 62 of 18 April 2004 ('2004 Community Law'),[32] which made important amendments in respect of the persons to whom such provisions apply, the definition of inside information and the behaviour forbidden, as well as the investigation powers granted to the CONSOB.

In particular, it is worth noting that, by repealing the prohibition against insider trading set out in former art 180 of Legislative Decree 58, new art 184 of Legislative Decree 58 has clarified[33] that such prohibition shall apply to any member of the board of directors or of the management or supervisory bodies of an issuer and has decriminalised any conduct of tippees (namely, those who, having obtained, directly or indirectly, inside information from the insider, carry out any of the actions listed in points 1, 2 and 3 below).

In addition, art 187 quinquies of Legislative Decree 58 has introduced the liability of legal persons where the criminal offence of insider trading has been committed in its interest or to its advantage.[34]

---

32 The 2004 Community Law was published in the Official Gazette of the Republic of Italy no 96 of 27 April 2005 and came into force on 12 May 2005.

33 Before the introduction of such provision, legal scholars (see Musco *Diritto penale societario*, Milano (1999) p 315 and Ermetes *Abuso di infromazioni privilegiate e aggiotaggio su strumenti finanziari* in Rabitti-Bedogni (a cura di) *Il testo unico della intermediazione finanziaria*, Milano (1999) p 983) deemed that these persons fell within the category of insiders.

34 Pursuant to art 187 quinquies of Legislative Decree 58/1998, legal persons shall be liable for payment of a sum equal to the amount of the administrative sanction imposed for the offence of insider trading committed in their interest or to their advantage:
 'a) by persons performing representative, administrative or management functions in the entity or one of its organisational units having financial and functional autonomy and by persons who, de facto or otherwise, manage and control the entity;
 b) persons subject to the direction or supervision of a person referred to in subparagraph a),
 unless they demonstrate that such persons acted exclusively in their own interest or in the interest of third parties.'

Article 184, para 1 of Legislative Decree 58 punishes with imprisonment between one and six years and a fine ranging from 20,000 to 3 million euros[35] any person who, possessing inside information by virtue of being a member of the board of directors or of the management or supervisory bodies of an issuer, or of his holding in the capital of an issuer or of exercising his employment, profession, duties, including public duties, or position (so-called 'insiders'):

1   purchases, sells or carries out other transactions, directly or indirectly, for his own account or for the account of a third party, involving financial instruments using such information; or
2   discloses such information to others outside the normal exercise of his employment, profession, duties or position, without justified reason, or advises others, on such basis, to carry out any of the transactions referred to above;
3   recommends or induces others, on the basis of such information, to carry out any of the transactions referred to in point 1 above.

In addition, any person who, possessing inside information by virtue of the preparation or execution of criminal activities, carries out any of the actions listed under points 1, 2 or 3 above will be subject to the punishment referred to in art 184, para 1 of Legislative Decree 58.

From an analysis of the rule set out in art 184, para 1 of Legislative Decree 58, it appears that the actions forbidden to insiders are:

1   the carrying out of transactions on listed instruments (trading);
2   the communication of the inside information to third parties (tipping); and
3   the transmission of investment advice to third parties on the basis of the privileged information or encouraging third parties to trade (*tuyautage*).

As briefly pointed out above, the 2004 Community Law has decriminalised any conduct of tippees. As a result, any tippee cannot be punished with imprisonment, even if he committed the offence prior to the decriminalisation of the relevant rule (that is to say, 12 May 2005).[36] However, according to art 187 bis, para 4 of Legislative Decree 58, the conduct of tippees remains subject to pecuniary administrative sanctions ranging from 20,000 to 3 million euros.[37] In particular, art 187 bis, para 4 of Legislative Decree 58 establishes that the pecuniary administrative sanction applicable to insiders[38] shall also apply to 'any person who, possessing inside information and knowing or being capable of knowing through ordinary diligence its inside nature, carries out any of the actions' listed under points 1, 2 or 3 above.

Clearly, the offence is committed by virtue of the use of such particular information and not because of its simple possession. However, art 184 shall not apply to:

---

35 Pursuant to art 184, para 3 of Legislative Decree 58/1998, 'courts may increase the fine up to three times or up to the larger amount of ten times the product of the crime or the profit therefrom when, in view of the particular seriousness of the offence, the personal situation of the guilty party or the magnitude of the product of the crime or the profit therefrom, the fine appears inadequate even if the maximum fine is applied'.
36 See, in this respect, Court of Cassation, Fifth Criminal Section, judgment no 9391 of 17 March 2006.
37 According to para 5 of art 187 bis of Legislative Decree 58/1998, the 'pecuniary administrative sanctions referred to in paras 1, 2 and 4 shall be increased up to three times or up to the larger amount of ten times the product of the offence or the profit therefrom when, in view of the personal situation of the guilty party or the magnitude of the product of the offence or the profit therefrom, they appear inadequate even if the maximum sanctions are applied'.
38 The pecuniary administrative sanction set out in art 187 bis of Legislative Decree 58/1998 shall apply to insiders in addition to the sanctions set out under art 184 of Legislative Decree 58/1998.

1   transactions relating to monetary, exchange rate or public debt management policy concluded by the Italian state, another EU member state, the European System of Central Banks, a central bank of an EU member state or any other officially designated body or any person acting on their behalf;

2   trading in listed own shares, bonds or other financial instruments in buy-back programmes carried out by issuers or subsidiaries or affiliated companies or to transactions for the stabilisation of financial instruments that satisfy the conditions established by the CONSOB in a regulation.

Article 181 of Legislative Decree 58 provides for a general and very detailed definition of 'inside information' and a specific definition of 'inside information' in relation to derivatives on commodities[39] and for persons charged with the execution of orders concerning financial instruments.[40]

As a general rule, inside information means 'any information having a precise content that has not been made public relating, directly or indirectly, to one or more issuers of financial instruments or one or more financial instruments and that, if made public, would be likely to have a significant effect on the price of such instruments'.

In particular, para 3 of art 181 of Legislative Decree 58 specifies that information shall be deemed to be of a precise nature if:

1   it refers to a set of circumstances which exists or may reasonably be expected to come into existence or an event which has occurred or may reasonably be expected to occur; and

2   it is specific enough to enable a conclusion to be drawn as to the possible effect of the set of circumstances or events referred to in point 1 above on the prices of financial instruments.

In addition, the following para 4 clarifies that information which, if made public, would be likely to have a significant effect on the prices of financial instruments shall mean information a reasonable investor would be likely to use as part of the basis of his investment decisions.

As to the scope of application of the provision, art 182 of Legislative Decree 58 establishes that the offence is committed where the trading is carried out:

1   in Italy, in respect of financial instruments admitted, or for which an application has been made for admission, to trading on an Italian regulated market;

2   in Italy, in respect of financial instruments admitted to trading on an Italian regulated market, even if the instruments are traded in EU regulated markets; and

3   abroad, in respect of financial instruments traded in Italian regulated markets.

In addition, by virtue of para 4 of art 184 of Legislative Decree 58, which also includes in the definition of financial instruments non-listed financial instruments

---

39 Pursuant to art 181, para 2 of Legislative Decree 58/1998, 'in relation to derivatives on commodities, inside information shall mean information of a precise nature which has not been made public relating, directly or indirectly, to one or more such derivatives and which users of markets on which such derivatives are traded expect to receive in accordance with accepted market practice on those markets'.

40 Pursuant to art 181, para 5 of Legislative Decree 58/1998, 'for persons charged with the execution of orders concerning financial instruments, inside information shall also mean information conveyed by a client and related to the client's pending orders, which is of a precise nature, which relates directly or indirectly to one or more issuers of financial instruments or to one or more financial instruments and which, if made public, would be likely to have a significant effect on the prices of these financial instruments'.

whose value depends on a listed financial instrument, it seems that the criminal offence of insider trading has been extended to this type of non-listed financial instruments.

Legal scholars[41] deem that art 182 of Legislative Decree 58 makes reference both to the hypothesis pursuant to which the offence is committed abroad in respect of financial instruments traded in an Italian regulated market and to the hypothesis where the offence is committed abroad in respect of financial instruments traded in a foreign regulated market, provided that such instruments are also traded in an Italian regulated market (in particular, in this case, even if the activity is performed abroad by foreign persons on instruments belonging to foreign companies).

However, according to principle 3 set out in the 'guidelines on the information to the market' issued in June 2002 by the Italian Stock Exchange Authority ('Borsa Italiana SpA'), certain information, such as letters of intent and negotiations, are disclosed to the market where both the following events occur:

1   duties of confidentiality are not fulfilled by whoever has obtained such information; and
2   there are grounded reasons to deem that the relevant transactions, of which such information represents the initial step, will be carried out.

According to such guidelines, there is no breach of confidentiality duty if the issuers disclose inside information, by virtue of their office duty, to third parties legally or contractually bound to keep them confidential.

As to the CONSOB investigation powers, art 187 octies of Legislative Decree 58 sets out that the CONSOB shall investigate the breaches using the powers attributed to it with respect to the persons subject to its supervision by requiring information, data or documents from and hearing anyone who appears to be acquainted with the facts, establishing the time limits for the related communication, asking for existing telephone records and fixing the time limits for their receipt. In addition, the CONSOB can avail itself, amongst other things, of the co-operation of governmental bodies, have access to the information system of the taxpayer register, require the communication of personal data by way of derogation to the restrictions laid down in art 25(1) of the Data Protection Code and gain direct access, through a dedicated electronic connection, to the data contained in the Bank of Italy's Central Credit Register.

In this respect, it shall be noted that, pursuant to art 3.4.2 of the Regulation of the markets adopted on 21 December 2005 by Borsa Italiana SpA and approved by the CONSOB on 8 February 2006, where, in the course of market surveillance, the Borsa Italiana SpA acquires evidence suggesting that acts of insider trading may have been committed, it shall immediately report such evidence to the CONSOB.

According to some authoritative legal scholars,[42] the regulation of insider trading is additional to and separate from the regulation of bank secrecy. In fact, the regulation of bank secrecy places a limit on the communication of confidential information obtained by banks in order to protect the interests of third parties to whom such information refers; the banks, however, retain the freedom to use information for their own purposes subject to the duty of confidence.

---

41 Marchetti and Bianchi *La disciplina delle società quotate*, Milan (1999) vol II, p 2022; Cottino *La legge Draghi e le società quotate in borsa*, Turin (1999) p 418.
42 Buonuomo *Banca, Borsa e Titoli di Credito* (1995) I, p 137ff.

On the contrary, the regulation of insider trading censures the conduct of holders of information who use or divulge it or, on the basis of it, carry out the relevant transactions for their own benefit where the element which characterises the conduct as an offence is the active conduct of the insider/tippee who uses such information in order to realise an advantage.

As regards the general rule concerning information held by banks, it is useful to emphasise the difference between information requested from the bank by third parties and information which is exchanged between banks. In the first case, a specific authorisation is required from the concerned party, whilst in the second case it is generally considered permissible for banks to exchange information between themselves.

It has been stated that the practice of information exchange between banks may be considered permissible when it confirms the known position of the company, the subject of the information, but not when the information could be of interest to the bank with specific reference to a transaction in progress from which the bank could obtain an undue advantage.[43]

This is the natural consequence of the fact that, in the opinion of the majority of legal writers, insider trading constitutes a breach of a temporary secrecy, that is, confidential information is obtained and used by a person before the time in which the information is distributed and known, attempting in this way to anticipate the effect which in time would be produced by the spreading of the information.[44]

In the absence of case law on insider trading, some authors have even considered that unfavourable information transmitted by banks in relation to a certain party is spread so rapidly that a breach of temporary secrecy is not even conceivable.[45]

In conclusion, it has to be noted that Legislative Decree 58 imposes a series of detailed obligations on the issuer of securities to provide information in relation to the company's activities, which could affect the price of the shares or the financial situation of the issuer, in an attempt to reduce the level of concealed information which could be exploited by insiders.

CONFLICTS OF INTEREST

[18.18]   In considering bank secrecy and use of privileged information, one must necessarily consider the issue of conflict of interest, in which a bank could easily find itself involved. All financial information converges at the bank by virtue of its role as the centre of all monetary economic transactions.

By virtue of the varied activities of the bank, it may occur, for example, that the bank uses information, relating to a client, for the purposes of advising another client for an acquisition or the bank may exploit its knowledge of amounts held on deposit by its clients in order to advise other clients to invest or not invest in such clients.

The problem has arisen, in particular, as of the time when banks in Italy were authorised to operate as securities brokers in accordance with Law 1 of 2 January

43 Porzio *Insider Trading ed ordinamento bancario* in AA VV *Il dovere di riservatezza nel mercato finanziario: 'l'insider trading'*, p 321.
44 Carriero *Il problema dell'Insider trading* in *Foro Italiano* (1988) V, p 146.
45 Mazza *La repressione dell'Insider trading nel quadro della tutela del mercato azionario* in *Banca, Borsa e Titoli di Credito* (1988) I, p 673.

1991. Law 1 was abrogated by Legislative Decree 415 of 23 July 1996, which brought into effect Council Directive 93/22/EEC of 10 May 1993 relating to investment services in the securities sector, which in turn was repealed by Legislative Decree 58, whose provisions on intermediaries were implemented by CONSOB Regulation 11522 of 1 July 1998 ('Regulation on Intermediaries').

In particular, according to art 18 of Legislative Decree 58, the provision of investment services to the public on a professional basis is reserved for investment firms and banks.

Article 21 of Legislative Decree 58 states that banks (as well as all the authorised subjects) shall:

'(a) act diligently, correctly and transparently in the interests of customers and the integrity of the market;[46]
(b) acquire the necessary information from customers and operate in such a way that they are always adequately informed;
(c) organise themselves in such a way as to minimise the risk of conflicts of interest and, where such conflicts arise, act in such a way as to ensure transparency and the fair treatment of customers;
(d) have resources and procedures, including internal control mechanisms, likely to ensure the efficient provision of services; and
(e) conduct an independent, sound and prudent management and make appropriate arrangements for safeguarding the rights of customers in respect of the assets entrusted to them.'

As to the risk of conflict of interests provided for by (c) above, it should be noted that this was already regulated by art 16 of Law 1 and the Regulation of the Bank of Italy of 2 July 1991, which, in implementing art 16 and in order to guarantee the reduction of risk of conflict of interest, established the adoption of separation of accounting and organisation (Chinese Walls) thereby burdening the organisational structure of investment companies and banks.

The current formulation, confirming the wording of Legislative Decree 415, seems less concerned with providing the means for avoiding conflict of interest and more interested in reducing the risk of such conflict as far as possible.[47] In particular, from the analysis of art 21, it appears that the existence of conflict of interest is considered unavoidable in the performance of investment services, thus, such situations shall be regulated by making them transparent through adequate information to the client, a criterion which is already set out under art 1374 of the Civil Code.

Article 27, para 2 of the Regulation on Intermediaries specifies that transactions with or on behalf of the clients in conflict of interest can only be carried out where the banks have previously informed the investor in writing of the nature and extent of their interest in the transaction and the investor has expressly agreed in writing to

---

46 For this purpose, art 14 of Law 262 of 28 December 2005 has amended art 21a) by specifying that authorised intermediaries shall classify, on the basis of the minimum general criteria laid down by the CONSOB, the riskiness of financial products and individually managed investment portfolios and shall conform with the principle of the suitability of transactions recommended to investors or conducted on their account, in light of the profile of each client, determined on the basis of his experience in investing in financial products, financial situation, investment objectives and propensity to incur risks.

47 Miola and Piscitello *Commento sub art 17* in *Eurosim Commentario al D Lgs 23 luglio 1996*, n 415, a cura di Campobasso, p 117ff; Recine *Svolgimento dei servizi di investimento* in *Il Testo Unico dell'intermediazione finanziaria* a cura di Rabitti Bedogni C, Milan (1998) p 183ff.

such carrying out. Where the transaction is concluded by telephone, compliance with the foregoing information requirements and the issue of the related authorisation by the investor must be evidenced by a recording on magnetic tape or an equivalent medium.

As to the contract, art 23 of Legislative Decree 58 establishes that it shall be executed in writing and a copy given to customers. In case of a failure to comply with the prescribed form, the contract shall be null and void. However, certain types of contracts may or must be entered into in a different form due to justified technical reasons or the professional nature of the contracting parties. In this respect, by virtue of the power delegated to it by art 23 of Legislative Decree 58, the CONSOB has established in art 30, para 2 of the Regulation on Intermediaries that contracts relating to the supply of the following services need not be made in writing:

1   placement services, including door-to-door selling and distance marketing;
2   non-core services, except for those of financing investors and providing investment advice concerning financial instruments.

It is worth noting, in conclusion, the provisions of art 21(e) of Legislative Decree 58, according to which the banks (like all other investment enterprises) must conduct an 'independent, sound and prudent' management and adopt 'appropriate measures for safeguarding rights pertaining to deposited financial instruments and funds .

DATA PROTECTION CODE

[18.19]   Following the enactment of Legislative Decree 196 of 30 June 2003 ('Data Protection Code'), which has abrogated Law 675 of 30 December 1996, the regulation of the processing[48] of personal data[49] has been the object of a reform aimed at ensuring a high level of protection for the data subjects' rights and fundamental freedoms in compliance with the principles of simplification, harmonisation and effectiveness of the mechanisms by which data subjects can exercise their rights and the data controller can fulfil the relevant obligations.

The processing of personal data governed by the Data Protection Code includes data held abroad if the processing is performed by any entity established:

1   either in the state's territory; or
2   in a place that is under the state's sovereignty.

In addition, the Data Protection Code shall apply to the processing of personal data that is performed by an entity established in the territory of a country outside the EU, where such entity makes use in connection with the processing of equipment, whether electronic or otherwise, situated in the state's territory, unless such equipment is used solely for the purposes of transit through the territory of the EU.

The Data Protection Code amends the approach followed by Law 675 in respect of the notification of the processing of personal data to the *Garante* (the supervisory

---

48 Pursuant to art 4, para 1a) of the Data Protection Code, 'processing' shall mean any operation, or set of operations, carried out with or without the help of electronic or automated means, concerning the collection, recording, organisation, keeping, interrogation, elaboration, modification, selection, retrieval, comparison, utilisation, interconnection, blocking, communication, dissemination, erasure and destruction of data, whether the data is contained in a data bank or not.
49 Pursuant to art 4, para 1b) of the Data Protection Code, 'personal data' shall mean any information relating to natural or legal persons, bodies or associations that are or can be identified, even indirectly, by reference to any other information, including a personal identification number.

authority in respect of processing of personal data) by listing the few cases in which notification must be carried out, such as if the processing concerns genetic data, biometric data or data disclosing health and sex life where processed for the purpose of assisted reproduction.

The data controller, who is the person competent to determine the purposes and methods of the processing of personal data, can appoint a processor, who shall be a person having adequate knowledge, experience and reliability to ensure compliance with the provisions in force applying to the processing and shall abide by the instructions given by the controller in carrying out this processing and inform the data subject,[50] amongst others, of the purposes and use of the processing, the rights to access to his personal data and the entities or categories of entity to which the data may be communicated or which may get to know the data and the scope of dissemination of the data.

With regard to the right to access, art 7 of the Data Protection Code repeals the rule set out in art 13 of Law 675 and grants to the data subject a series of rights, including, by way of example, the right to obtain the cancellation of or block data dealt with in breach of the law, the updating or amendment of data, the right to object to the treatment of personal data for commercial or advertising purposes or to the sale of that data. The data subject exercises his rights by means of a request addressed to the data controller or processor. However, according to art 8 of the Data Protection Code, the data subject may not exercise the rights under art 7 by making a request to the data controller or processor if the personal data is processed in certain circumstances, such as pursuant to anti-money laundering provisions or during investigations.

In addition to the above duty of information vis-à-vis the data subject, art 23 of the Data Protection Code provides that, as a matter of principle, the express consent of the data subject is required, save that in the cases listed under art 24 of the Data Protection Code, such as, for example, where the processing is necessary to comply with an obligation imposed by a law, regulations or Community legislation, to fulfil a contractual obligation owed by the data subject, to pursue a legitimate interest of either the data controller or a third party recipient in the cases specified by the *Garante*, with regard to the activities of banking groups and subsidiaries or related companies or concerns data taken by public registers, lists, documents or records.

On this point, the Italian Banking Association clarified in circular LG/5499 of 14 August 1997 that there is a category of subjects which carry out an activity linked to the exercise of banking, to which personal data can be communicated, such as issuers of credit cards, companies which administer means of payment, etc.

In this respect, on 16 November 2004,[51] the *Garante* adopted a code of conduct and professional practice ('Code of Conduct') applying to information systems managed by private entities[52] with regard to consumer credit, reliability and timeliness in performing payments by virtue of the power delegated to it by arts 12 and 117 of the Data Protection Code. The Code of Conduct came into force on 1 January 2005 and clarifies that personal data contained in a credit information system may only be

---

50 See art 13 of the Data Protection Code.
51 See the provision of the *Garante* no 8 of 16 November 2004 published in the Official Gazette of the Republic of Italy no 300 of 23 December 2004.
52 The Code of Conduct does not apply to the information systems controlled by public bodies, in particular, it does not apply to the centralised risk service managed by the Bank of Italy.

processed by the manager[53] and participants (banks, financial brokers or any private entity that grants an extension for the payment related to the supply of goods and/or services) for the purpose of protecting credit and limiting relevant risks and, in particular, to assess data subjects' financial status and creditworthiness or their reliability and timeliness of payment.

The breach of these rights results in an obligation to pay compensation for damage which the controller must pay unless he is able to demonstrate that he has adopted all appropriate measures for avoiding any damage.[54]

The data subject may avail himself of his rights either before the ordinary judicial authority or before the 'authority for the protection of persons and other subjects in relation to the handling of personal data' established by the Data Protection Code.

CONCLUSION

[18.20]   Under Italian law, bank confidentiality is not, and never has been, a duty expressly codified, but simply recognised as a 'customary practice' aimed at safeguarding customers' privacy. As such, the banks' duty of confidentiality has been recognised and protected under the legal system to the extent that it does not become a tool to assist in the commission of a crime or tort. As a general principle, any right, including the right to secrecy, ends where a malevolent purpose begins or constitutional rights are breached.

Looking at the banks' duty of confidentiality from such perspective, it clearly appears the rationale behind the various exceptions to the banks' duty of confidentiality analysed above are mainly intended to ensure the full and absolute protection of constitutional rights. In particular, the banks' duty of confidentiality can neither thwart the fulfilment of social duties, such as the duty to contribute to public expenses by way of paying taxes, nor hinder the management of justice by impeding the investigation and prosecution of criminal offences. This is *le fil rouge* (common thread) which has led, and continuously leads, the Italian authorities to revise, amend and improve the relevant legal framework.

---

53 Pursuant to art 1 of the Code of Conduct, 'manager' shall mean the controller of the processing of the personal data recorded in a credit information system and managing the system by setting out the mechanism applying to its operation and use.

54 Article 2050 of the Civil Code.

19   Luxembourg

Pit Reckinger

INTRODUCTION

[19.1]   It is traditionally accepted that a banker receiving private information from or regarding his client owes his client a duty of confidence. Whereas in most jurisdictions this duty of confidence is merely a civil law obligation,[1] Luxembourg bank confidentiality originates from, and is based on, criminal law provisions. Together with Switzerland, Luxembourg therefore has the strongest bank confidentiality laws, constituting one of the pillars of its banking system.

Despite the lack of express legal provisions before 1981, the existence of a rule of confidence imposed on bankers has never been challenged in Luxembourg. Indeed, it is generally accepted that a democratic legal and political system must endeavour to protect the individual vis-à-vis his fellow citizens as a whole and preserve his intimacy and private life. Those are the objects, the *raison d'être*, of the duty of confidence.[2]

Discussions among authors and practitioners become more lively when they try to establish the legal basis and nature of bank secrecy in Luxembourg and when they try to set the limits of bank confidentiality. Torn between the conflict created by private interests (pursuant to which confidence must be safeguarded and discretion guaranteed) and public interests and the social order (which justify to a certain extent a transparency vis-à-vis the authorities), solutions are found on a case-by-case basis, each time further defining what is the scope of the duty of confidence of the banker.

Politically, in today's environment, bank confidentiality often has a negative connotation. Transparency to the contrary is a virtue. It is true that transparency is a necessity to combat crime and fight tax evasion. Transparency is also needed to detect market manipulations or insider dealing. It is, however, also true, and fundamental, that our society is not longing for the 'Brave New World' and that the right to privacy and the protection of freedom warrants that there are boundaries to transparency and bank confidentiality is one of them.

'Confidentiality' (*confidentialité*) is defined as 'what must remain secret'. 'Secrecy' itself does not need to be defined – every child knows what a secret is: anything most hidden, most intimate, shielded from other people's view or knowledge.[3] Swiss

---

1   Belgium: Com Namur (4 ch) 29 June 1995, JT 1996 p 328; England: see RNS Grandison in *Bank Confidentiality* (2nd edn, 1997) ch 8; France: Cassation Civ 1, 2 June 1993, Bull Civ I no 197.
2   R Hoffmann *Réflexions sur le fondement du secret professionnel*, Bull Droit et Banque, 1993, n 2, p 3ff.
3   Although there is a general tendency in Luxembourg to use the term 'bank secrecy', 'bank confidentiality' and 'bank secrecy' are interchangeable.

authors on bank secrecy[4] have used a descriptive definition of bank secrecy which is a useful start to an analysis of bank confidentiality laws in Luxembourg:

> 'Bank secrecy consists in the discretion which bankers have to apply to personal or financial information relating to their clients or third parties of which they have knowledge through the exercise of their profession.'

The last words of this definition 'through the exercise of their profession' introduce the concept of the banker being the 'necessary confident'[5] (*confident nécessaire*), such as a priest or a doctor. The banker is also considered in our society as a person with whom one ineluctably has to share intimate and confidential information. Basic principles of a right to privacy and protection of private life governing our systems must lead to making those confidents subject to a duty of confidence. By qualifying the banker as a 'necessary confident' in our society, we will later justify the criminal nature of the laws governing his duties of confidence.

From very early on, Luxembourg authors have insisted on the dual nature of bank confidentiality. It is not only the duty of confidence of the banker in respect of information which he receives, it is also the right of the client to the confidentiality of such information.[6]

Starting from this dual feature, authors, judges and practitioners try to establish the limits of bank confidentiality by determining when and by whom the banker may be authorised or forced to reveal secrets. The answer to those questions requires the prior analysis of the nature and origin of the basic rule of bank confidentiality.

NATURE AND ORIGIN OF THE DUTY OF CONFIDENCE

[19.2]   Under Luxembourg law, the duty of confidence of a banker, as well as of his supervisory authority, stems from art 458 of the Code Pénal:[7]

> 'Doctors, surgeons, health officers, pharmacists, midwives and all other persons who, through their function or profession, are entrusted with secrets and who, except in instances where they are called upon to testify in court and in instances where they are compelled by law to reveal such secrets, divulge such secrets, shall be punished by imprisonment from eight days to six months and to a fine from 500 to 5,000 euros.'

While the existence of bank confidentiality in the sense of a civil law obligation of the banker to such confidentiality was never challenged under Luxembourg law,[8] for a considerable time, authors have discussed the question whether a breach of the rule would be a criminal offence. The non-exhaustive list of art 458 of the Code Pénal does not explicitly mention the banker. This raised the question whether the banker

---

4 M Auber, PA Béguin, P Bernasconi, J Graziano-Von Burg, R Schwob and R Tréuillaud *Le secret bancaire suisse 'Ed Staempfli + Cie SA'* (3rd edn, 1995) p 43.
5 These words do equally transpire from the Code Pénal (art 458) which refers to the professional secrecy of the medical profession, but on which bank secrecy is based (see below).
6 A Dondelinger *Le Secret Bancaire*, Pasicrisie 23, p 1.
7 Code of Criminal Law.
8 C Schmit and A Dondelinger *Le Secret Bancaire dans la CEE et en Suisse* in *Le Secret Bancaire en Droit Luxembourgeois* (1973) p 140.

is one of those persons 'who, through their function or profession, are entrusted with secrets'.

Prominent doctrine traditionally insisted on the 'contractual basis' of bank secrecy (such as in England, where 'it is often an implied term of the contract between bank and customer, no more and no less'[9]) and thus concluded that a breach could not trigger criminal sanctions.[10]

Modern doctrine (adopted in particular by the banks' supervisory authority, then called the *Institut Monétaire Luxembourgeois* ('IML'), and the corporate association for banks in Luxembourg, *Association des Banques et Banquiers Luxembourgeois* ('ABBL')), however, emphasised the 'public role' of the banking profession and qualifies the banker as 'the necessary confident in the exercise of his profession'. Similarly, in France, eminent authors agree that the banker is the 'ineluctable confident'[11] of his client. Indeed, clients are in fact by contract or by law obliged to resort to the services offered by banks. The latter thus contribute to public service in the interests of the community, which establishes the public order feature of bank secrecy. The logical consequence was to include bankers in the non-exhaustive list of professions enumerated in art 458 of the Code Pénal.

In 1981, the Luxembourg legislator put an end to this now academic discussion. By the banking law of 23 April 1981, it was indirectly affirmed that a breach of the confidentiality rule under Luxembourg law was a criminal offence and that art 458 of the Code Pénal would apply to the banker upon such breach.[12]

The criminal nature of bank secrecy in Luxembourg was thereafter confirmed by the Luxembourg legislator through the banking law of 17 November 1984 and is currently governed by art 41 of the Law of 5 April 1993 on the financial sector (the 'Banking Law'). The Banking Law directly and expressly sets out the positive legal duty of confidence of banks, as well as settlement agents, central counterparties, clearing houses, foreign operators of systems designated as such in Luxembourg and all other professionals of the financial sector, ie any person professionally exercising an activity of the financial sector,[13] and provides that a breach is a criminal offence:

'(1) Directors, members of managerial and supervisory bodies, managers, employees and all other persons employed by credit institutions other professionals of the financial sector, settlement agents, central counterparties, clearing houses, and foreign operators of systems authorised in Luxembourg referred to in part I of the present law are obliged to keep secret all information entrusted to them in the course of

---

9 RNS Grandison, n 1 above, ch 8.
10 For a contractual basis, see T Biever and R Weber *Le secret professional des banques en droit luxembourgeois*, Feuilles de liaison de la Conference St Yves, 1959, Luxembourg; L Schaus *Le secret professionnel devant la loi*, conference given on 22 February 1938 for the Young Bar Association, Luxembourg St Paul, p 27. For a criminal law basis, see A Dondelinger, n 6 above; Association des Banques et Banquiers, Luxembourg (ABBL) *Avis au projet de loi portant réforme de l'impôt sur le revenu*, Doc parl nos 571–578, session ordinaire de la Chambre des Députés 1956–57.
11 C Gavalda and J Stoufflet *Le Secret Bancaire en France* colloque organised at the Sorbonne, October 1971, cited in Dondelinger, n 6 above.
12 J Guill and JN Schaus *La nouvelle loi bancaire luxembourgeoise du 23 avril 1981*, Feuilles de liaison de la Conférence St Yves, 1981, no 51, p 6.
13 The main professions concerned are financial advisers, brokers, commissioners, fund managers, distributors of investment funds, professional depositaries of securities, underwriters, market makers, etc.

their professional activities. The act of revealing such information shall be punished pursuant to art 458 of the Code Pénal.

(2) The obligation to secrecy ceases when the disclosure of information is authorised or imposed by or under the terms of a legal provision, even if the implementation of such legal provisions shall have preceded the present law.

(3) The obligation to secrecy shall not apply vis-à-vis national and foreign authorities in charge of prudential supervision acting within their powers and for the purpose of such supervision, and provided the information communicated is covered by the professional secrecy of the supervisory authority receiving it. The transmission of necessary information to a foreign authority for the purposes of prudential supervision must be made through the parent company or the shareholder or the member itself subject to such supervision.

(4) The obligation to secrecy shall not apply vis-à-vis shareholders or members, who themselves are a condition for the authorisation of the institution concerned, provided that the information communicated to these shareholders or members is necessary for the purposes of sound and prudent management and does not directly reveal the institution's commitments towards a customer other than a professional of the financial sector.

As a derogation to the preceding paragraph, the credit institution or the PSF [professional of the financial sector], being part of a financial group shall allow internal group control bodies access, when needed, to information relating to specified business relations to the extent necessary to the global management of legal risks and of reputation in respect of money laundering or terrorism in the sense of Luxembourg law.

(5) The obligation to secrecy shall not apply vis-à-vis professionals referred to in arts 29-1, 29-2 and 29-3, to the extent that the information which is communicated to these professionals are furnished as a part of a service contact relating to one of the activities governed by the legal provisions mentioned herebefore and subject to the condition that such information is indispensable to the execution of said service contact.

(6) Subject to the rules applicable pursuant to the Code Pénal, information referred to in paragraph (1), once revealed, shall only be used for the purposes for which the law permitted their disclosure.

(7) Anyone who is bound by the obligation to secrecy referred to in paragraph (1) who has legally revealed information covered by such an obligation shall not by the sole fact thereof have committed a civil or criminal offence.'

Turning to the dual feature of bank confidentiality as a duty of the banker and a right of the client, the criminal nature of bank confidentiality undoubtedly strengthens the legal view that the secrecy must be analysed first of all as an obligation of the banker. Furthermore, bank confidentiality belongs to the rules of public order to which only the law may grant exemptions.[14] Put differently, even though the rule of bank confidentiality is meant to protect the private interests of the client, the mere fact that

---

14 Doc parl no 3600, Commentaires des articles, p 8.

it is a criminal law rule, a breach of which entails criminal sanctions, must lead to the conclusion that the client and his bank could not, by private agreement, decide that this criminal law rule would not apply to their relationship.[15] On that basis, a large majority of accepted doctrine concludes that the duty of confidence is a matter of public order.[16]

To the extent that banks form part of public service and that bank secrecy is a rule of public order, the right of the client is limited and the power to trigger disclosure by the bank of information covered by bank secrecy may be at least partially withdrawn from the power of the client.[17] This is definitely the position which has been adopted by the banks' supervisory authority, today called the *Commission de Surveillance du Secteur Financier* ('CSSF')[18]. Despite doctrinal debates,[19] the public order character of Luxembourg bank secrecy was recently confirmed by the courts.[20]

The right and duty of confidence are not hard-and-fast rules, but are limited in scope pursuant to exemptions set up by art 458 of the Code Pénal and by art 41 of the Banking Law. It is therefore legitimate to raise[21] the question whether art 41 of the Banking Law creates a new duty of confidence, thus replacing the existing obligation firmly established on the basis of art 458 of the Code Pénal. In other words, is bank confidentiality today still one element of a single professional secrecy based on art 458 of the Code Pénal or has the Banking Law created a specific duty of confidence for banks to which the existing solutions derived from the application of art 458 of the Code Pénal may not be applied? Parliamentary documents which accompanied the introduction of the Banking Law firmly put aside any hesitations which one might have.[22] Doctrine adheres to this theory of continuity of the bank secrecy obligation in Luxembourg.[23] We may therefore conclude that art 41 of the Banking Law translates, incorporates and confirms the long-existing bank secrecy obligation based on art 458 of the Code Pénal, although it introduces certain additional exemptions.

---

15 A Hoffmann *La portée du secret bancaire*, Bull Droit et Banque, n 31, p 34.
16 J Guill *Transmission de données par un établissement de crédit à sa maison-mère ou à son siège social*, Bull Droit et Banque, 1983, n 2, p 17, Doc parl n 3600, Commentaires des articles; CSSF activities report 2003; A Hoffmann, n 15 above; C Liebertz and C Schmidt *Le secret bancaire luxembourgeois face au mandat dans la perspective du banquier*, ALJB Bull Droit et Banque, hors série, 2005; contra, see D Spielman *Le Secret Bancaire et l'Entraide Judiciaire Internationale Pénale au Grand-Duché de Luxembourg* (1999) 20 Les dossiers du Journal des Tribunaux at 36ff; A Serebriakoff *Le caractère d'ordre public du secret bancaire, conviction ou réalité?* in *Droit Bancaire et Financier à Luxembourg*, 2004, vol I, p 283 ff.
17 See 'Bankers and Clients' below.
18 As an appendix to its 2003 activities report, the CSSF has published the conclusions of its lawyers' committee which justifies and shares this conclusion.
19 See n 16 above.
20 Cour d'Appel, Saverys, *Struye de Swieland v Kredietbank Luxembourg SA*, 2 April 2003, no 26050 du rôle; Cour d'Appel, Hosdain, *Soupart v Kredietbank Luxembourg SA*, 2 April 2003, no 26256 du rôle.
21 J Schroeder *Le Secret Bancaire au Luxembourg* in *Le Secret Professionnel*, Conférence EFE 26/27 November 1996, Luxembourg.
22 Doc parl no 3600, Commentaires des articles, p 8, re art 41(1): '[art 41] recalls the obligation to professional secrecy'; and Doc parl no 3600–3601, avis IML, p 15, re art 41(1): 'there may currently no longer be any doubts on the continued existence of professional secrecy imposed on the professional of the financial sector'.
23 Inter alia, J Kauffman and A Steichen, cited in J Schroeder, n 21 above.

SANCTIONS TO A BREACH OF BANK CONFIDENTIALITY[24]

Criminal sanctions

[19.3] Article 41(1) of the Banking Law provides that disclosure of any information which is subject to bank confidentiality is punished by sanctions provided for in art 458 of the Code Pénal: imprisonment for up to six months or a fine (in current terms[25]) between 500 and 5,000 euros or both.

Pursuant to the general rules of Luxembourg criminal law, a breach of bank secrecy may only constitute a criminal offence if a 'material (tangible) element' and an 'intentional element' co-exist.

Tangible element

[19.4] The breach of secrecy must be duly evidenced. The banker must have revealed to another person or to the public in general secret information which he shares through, or by reason of, the exercise of his profession. The disclosure could be oral, written or derived from a positive or even negative (abstention) behaviour.

Intentional element

[19.5] The breach of secrecy must have been made 'intentionally'. Would mere negligence therefore not constitute a criminal offence if the breach were done without the banker being conscious that he was communicating information covered by secrecy?[26] The interpretation of what is 'intentional' at the time of disclosure is left to the courts and varies according to the different criminal offences existing under Luxembourg law. In terms of breaches of bank secrecy, the intention is sufficiently evidenced if the banker committed the breach of secrecy 'knowing that he was committing a criminal offence regardless of the intention or the goal for which the breach was committed'.[27] It is thus not necessary to commit a 'strictly speaking intentional' breach, but acting 'knowingly' (*en connaissance de cause*) will be sufficient to characterise the breach as a criminal offence. It should be noted that general provisions regarding criminal law, such as mitigating circumstances or excuses, may apply.

Criminal sanctions do not apply to corporate entities, but only to natural persons. To the extent that the person who has committed the breach and thus the offence has been identified, he will be personally subject to criminal sanctions. The problem is more delicate if the actual person within the corporate entity who committed the breach remains unidentified. According to authors and court cases, 'the managers of the corporate bodies must be actioned in court in their own name and be sentenced

---

24 For an in-depth study on sanctions of breaches of professional secrecy, see T Hoss *L'avocat et le réviseur d'entreprises: confidents nécessaires en droit luxembourgeois et en droit communautaire*, mémoire de DEA, 1 June 1996, Paris; and, in particular, on bank secrecy, see P Mousel and C Feipel *Les sanctions du secret bancaire*, Conférence EFE 26/27 November 1996, Luxembourg.
25 Following the enactment of various laws increasing the amounts of fines set out in the original Code Pénal of 1879.
26 T Hoss, n 24 above, nos 282 and 283.
27 JSG Nypels, cited in P Lambert *Le Secret Professionnel* (1985) p 133.

accordingly'.[28] It is therefore likely that in such cases managers of the bank or even the bank's managing director or directors would be subject to court action.[29]

Civil sanctions

[19.6] The obligation of confidence is also a civil law obligation. Disclosure of a secret may undoubtedly prejudice a client. Such prejudice gives rise to a liability action against the person who committed the breach and/or the bank (ie his employer). Vis-à-vis the person having committed the breach, it is an action in tort. Vis-à-vis the bank, the action will be based on the contractual relationship between the client and the banker. The Luxembourg Court of Appeal recently specified the regime applicable to the civil liability of bankers for breach of bank secrecy.[30] The motivation of these decisions, which may be criticised in various respects, is clear:

> 'The law grants to the person [the client] who has entered into a deposit agreement with a bank a right to secrecy from the bank. It is normal that the [client] information shared with the bank at the time of entering into the contract of deposit is kept secret. There is no particular hazard that this result, which is part of what the parties to the contract anticipated and what is protected by law through criminal sanctions, is not achieved. The secrecy obligation of the bank is therefore an obligation to achieve a result [*obligation de résultat*]. In case of breach of the obligation to achieve a result, the debtor of the obligation is presumed to be liable without need for any proof from the claimant of a fault or wrongdoing from the debtor.'

This recent court case first states that the secrecy obligation is an ancillary obligation to the deposit agreement entered into between the client and the bank. The content of such contractual confidentiality obligation will be the obligation to secrecy as set out under law.

The decision further concludes that such obligation is an obligation to achieve a result. In that, it conflicts with our prior understanding that the obligation to ensure confidentiality of the information transmitted to the banker was an obligation for the banker to do its best compared to a normally prudent professional (*obligation de moyens*), as opposed to an obligation to achieve a result. Indeed, the confidentiality obligation is part of the section of the Banking Law dealing with professional obligations of the bank, together with the 'know your customer' rules and rules of conduct. Such other obligations are all indisputably characterised as *obligations de moyens*. As a consequence of these court decisions, bankers may avoid their liability by evidencing that the breach of bank secrecy is due to a *force majeure* event or an action of a third party. They may no longer need to prove they have acted properly and thus avoid liability.

These decisions take a conservative view of the obligation of bank secrecy in line with the consistent characterisation that the obligation is a matter of public order.

The civil sanction to repair the damage caused clearly constitutes a remedy in monetary terms to any person who suffered from the breach. Under Luxembourg law, a court could not award penal (unless provided for by an agreement between the parties concerned), multiple or punitive damages.

---

28 S Stefani, G Levasseur and B Bouloc *Droit Pénal Général*, 14d Précis Dalloz no 311.
29 P Mousel and C Feipel, n 24 above.
30 Cour d'Appel, 2 April 2003, no 26050 and 26256 du rôle, Journal des tribunaux, 2003, p 316.

Disciplinary sanctions

[19.7]   Banks are subject to supervision by the CSSF. Following any breach of bank secrecy, the CSSF may issue injunctions against the bank concerned on the basis of art 59 of the Banking Law. To the extent that the bank does not follow any such injunction, its managers may be subject to suspension from the exercise of their functions. Any such injunction aimed at getting the bank to remedy an existing situation will, however, most certainly not be the sole measure taken by the CSSF. Indeed, at such time, a breach of law will have been committed and the prejudice caused. The CSSF will no doubt take additional measures directly aimed at the management of the bank concerned.

Article 7 of the Banking Law provides that the approval of the credit institution in Luxembourg is subject to the professional reputation of its management. If the managers have committed criminal offences, they would no longer qualify for the purposes of such condition of reputation and one of the conditions for approval of the credit institution concerned no longer exists. Such bank could therefore be subject to withdrawal of its banking licence.

In summary, the strength of Luxembourg bank secrecy rules results from the criminal sanctions attached to such a breach. The victim is generally less concerned by the fact that the person who committed the breach is made criminally liable. For bankers, the criminal sanction plays an essential, but moral, role.[31]; it will have an immediate effect on the exercise of their profession. It may also affect their bank by civil and disciplinary sanctions and, finally, it may affect their reputation.

SCOPE OF THE EXEMPTIONS TO BANK CONFIDENTIALITY

[19.8]   The purpose of this section is to determine the scope of exemptions to bank secrecy and thereby evidence the strength of Luxembourg bank secrecy which is, in principle, only lifted in the course of criminal investigations (including fiscal criminal investigations).

As indicated in the introduction, it is not possible to proceed by theoretical reasoning only. Solutions are found and limits are set on a case-by-case basis envisaging possible situations which a banker may face. For this reason, the following subsections will deal with the various situations where the banker is confronted with different entities, authorities and persons in day-to-day life on a national basis, while analysing the international situations in a separate and final section:

1   bankers and judges;
2   bankers and tax authorities;
3   bankers and shareholders;
4   bankers and supervisory authorities;
5   bankers and market abuse;
6   bankers and money laundering;
7   bankers and outsourcing;
8   bankers and clients;
9   bankers party to a court action;
10   bankers and international investigations.

---

31 A Bruyneel *Le Secret Bancaire en Belgique après l'arrêt du 24 octobre 1978*, observation sous Cass belge 25 October 1978 (1979) JT at 371, no 18, cited in Mousel and Feipel, n 24 above.

Bankers and judges

[19.9]   Unlike the section below which specifically deals with situations where the banker is a party to a court action, this section deals with situations where the banker as a 'third party' is confronted with judicial investigatory measures, including, in particular, where a banker is asked to testify or where the bank's premises are subject to an arrest or searches or seizures of documents relating to its clients and their accounts.

Civil law proceedings

The banker as a witness in civil courts

[19.10]   Article 41(2) of the Banking Law provides that the obligation to secrecy ceases when 'the disclosure of information is authorised or imposed by or under the terms of a legal provision, even if the implementation shall have preceded the present laws'. The first exemption to the duty of confidence is mentioned in art 458 of the Code Pénal which expressly lifts the prohibition to reveal secret information while testifying in court (see above). Pursuant to art 406 of the *Nouveau Code de Procédure Civile*, however, any person is obliged to testify under oath in a civil investigation unless he has a legitimate reason to refuse to testify.

Bank secrecy constitutes such a legitimate motive and may be opposed in response to a request to testify. Since 1957, court cases have decided that any person subject to professional secrecy may testify in court, but cannot be compelled to do so.[32] Whilst called as a witness, the banker may speak or remain silent at his discretion.[33]

Although a banker may also have received confidential information regarding third parties, he will most frequently be called to testify in a court case involving his client. Thus, he may receive the client's consent or even be under firm instructions from the client to testify. He will, however, never be bound to follow his client's request, but shall only be guided by his conscience.

Other civil law investigatory measures

[19.11]   Pursuant to the provisions of Luxembourg procedural law, a person may on the basis of a judgment or another authentic document of title or, pursuant to an authorisation granted by the president of the District Court in Luxembourg, put an arrest on bank accounts maintained with Luxembourg banks. In connection with any such procedure, the banker will be compelled to make a declaration (*déclaration affirmative*) setting out exactly what assets and rights are held for, or on behalf of, his client. Any such declaration has to be made only as and when the proceedings validating the arrest have been successfully concluded. In other words, the client must have been definitively ordered to a certain obligation and the arrest procedure must have been definitively validated. Then, but only then, will the banker have to disclose details of all assets and rights held by and for the person subject to the arrest. He may even have to disclose details of previous accounts held by the person concerned, which may have since been closed.[34]

Thus, the civil arrest procedure is an exemption to bank secrecy. Bank secrecy is safeguarded as the banker will only be obliged to disclose any information if the

---

32 Cour Supérieure de Justice (Cassation Criminelle), 21 March 1957, Pasicrisie 17, p 43.
33 L Schaus, n 10 above.

claim of the person instigating the arrest is adjudged to be justified by the court and the arrest is validated. In such case, the claimant has the right to receive information on the claim which he then 'owns' by judicial contract. From such point in time, the banker, as third party with whom the arrest was made, can be summoned by writ and only then can the banker deposit his declaration disclosing the client's position.[35]

In addition, the question has to be analysed whether a person could receive information from banks with the help of other investigatory measures available under civil procedural law. In particular, art 350 of the *Nouveau Code de Procédure Civile* is of interest and provides that:

> 'If there is a legitimate motive to preserve or establish before any judicial proceedings evidence of facts which may determine the solution of a dispute, investigatory measures, legally permitted, may be ordered at the request of an interested person in summary proceedings.'

For the same reasons as set out above, in civil matters, any such measure (which could include production of documents or testimonies) may only be authorised provided that bank secrecy would not be breached.[36] Similarly, art 284 of the *Nouveau Code de Procédure Civile* allows a judge to order a third party to disclose certain documents in the course of judicial proceedings. In respect of such a request, the Court of Appeal, however, specified that, even though bank secrecy was a legitimate motive to refuse the disclosure, it was not absolute. The disclosure had to occur where it is necessary to preserve the rights of defence, ie is absolutely required (*indispensable*) to discover the truth and there must not be other means for the claimant to obtain the document or information.[37]

Criminal law proceedings

The banker as a witness in criminal courts[38]

[19.12]   When called upon to testify in criminal proceedings, the question of exempting the banker from his obligation to secrecy no longer concerns private interests only, but also touches public interest. On this basis, some authors have concluded that a banker could not keep secret his knowledge of criminal offences.[39] Indeed, how could a banker call upon his conscience to keep criminal offences silent? On what grounds could he justify in his mind to keep a criminal unpunished?

Looking at medical secrecy, equally based on art 458 of the Code Pénal, judges have consistently ruled that doctors are free to reveal their secrets or bury them forever, even in front of the courts in relation to criminal offences.[40] The solution similarly applies to lawyers, the professional secrecy of whom is also based on the same legal provisions.[41]

---

34 Cour d'Appel, 5 February 1992, no 12949 du rôle, see also G Loesch and F Kremer *Le banquier face à la saisie-arrêt civile de droit commun* in ALJB Volume II, n 22-70.
35 For an in-depth analysis on the subject, see G Loesch and F Kremer, n 34 above.
36 For court cases confirming this principle, see Cour d'Appel (référé), 28 November 2000, no 19224 du rôle; ordonnance de référé, no 1157/97, 2 December 1997.
37 Cour d'Appel, 5 November 2003, n 26588.
38 For the money laundering offence where an obligation or denunciation exists, see 'Bankers and Money Laundering' below.
39 A Dondelinger *Le secret bancaire*, a speech given on 29 May 1972 on invitation of the Conference of the Young Bar.
40 Cour Supérieure de Justice (Appel Civil), 6 June 1961, 18 Pasicrisie at 351.
41 T Hoss, n 24 above, no 211.

From a strictly legal point of view, the same solution shall apply to the banker as the origin or basis of the professional secrecy is the same, ie art 458 of the Code Pénal.[42] It is therefore generally accepted that the legal solution applicable before the civil courts must be transposed into criminal law.[43]

In this respect, in a recent court case,[44] the Luxembourg courts had the occasion to recall the obligations of a Luxembourg banker vis-à-vis investigating magistrates. The terms used in the judgment seemed to imply that a banker is always under an obligation to furnish information to a judge. An author commenting on the decision has criticised it and confirms the position set out above that the banker remains free to decide to speak or remain silent.[45] This position has been expressly approved by a Court of Appeal decision of 30 March 2004 in the following terms: 'the banker can decide at his own discretion whether or not to testify in court'. The court further stated that the reference in art 77 of the *Code d'Instruction Criminelle* (Criminal Procedural Code) to art 458 of the Code Pénal only made sense if the option of the banker to testify or not to testify was fully maintained. A traditional author however, pointed to the limited interest of this strict legal position:

> 'In practice, banks have to measure the opportunity to testify in light of the right of search and of arrest or seizure of documents which is given to the investigating magistrate. As any information would have to be disclosed as part of such investigating powers of the investigating magistrate, it is difficult to imagine why and on what basis a banker could refuse to testify in front of the criminal courts.'

Other criminal law investigatory measures

[19.13]   While carrying out an investigation, the investigating magistrate may conduct searches on the premises of a bank or the domicile of bank employees, seize documents and put arrests on bank accounts with Luxembourg banks. Pursuant to art 88 of the *Code d'Instruction Criminelle*, in Luxembourg, a banker does not have the power to oppose any such proceedings and will have to disclose any information requested by the investigating magistrate. In the course of criminal investigations, there is no doubt that a banker does not have any possibility of opposing bank secrecy to those investigatory measures.

Bankers and tax authorities[46]

Direct taxes

[19.14]   In respect of direct taxes (mainly income tax), a grand-ducal decree of 24 March 1989[47] provides that the competent tax authorities in charge of income tax (*Administration des Contributions Directes*) 'are not authorised to request from credit institutions individual information on their clients'. This grand-ducal decree is to be regarded as a mere confirmation of a long-existing situation, ie that bank

---

42 L Schaus, n 10 above; J Kauffman, n 23 above.
43 A Schmitt and E Omes *La responsabilité du banquier en droit bancaire privé luxembourgeois, Les dossiers du Journal des Tribunaux*, n 55, p 69, n 109.
44 Tribunal d'Arrondissement, 8 June 2000, no 1326/2000.
45 A Hoffmann, Bull Droit et Banque, no 31, p 36.
46 For an in-depth study, see A Lutgen *Secret Bancaire, délit d'initié et fraude fiscale*, Conférence EFE, 27/28 November 1996 and A Steichen *Le secret bancaire face aux autorités publiques nationales et étrangères* (1995) Bull Droit et Banque no 24.
47 Mémorial A 1989, p 181.

secrecy is not to be levied vis-à-vis investigations by the income tax authorities in Luxembourg.[48] This principle, however, only applies in respect of the determination of taxation and no longer during the phase of recovery against taxpayers where the rights of the tax administration as a creditor are the same as any other ordinary creditor, in particular, in relation to arrests over bank accounts.[49]

Withholding taxes

[19.15] A law of 21 June 2005 implemented EU Council Directive 2003/48/EC dated 3 June 2003 on the taxation of savings income in the form of interest payments ('EU Savings Directive'). Pursuant to the EU Savings Directive, EU member states are required to provide to the fiscal authorities of other EU member states details of payments of interest or similar income made by paying agents within their jurisdiction to an individual resident in that other member state.

Existing bank confidentiality rules prohibit such provision of information to the tax authorities (see above) and a derogatory regime was therefore established whereby Luxembourg (together with Austria and Belgium) may, instead of a provision of information, operate a withholding tax system for a transitional period in relation to such payments unless clients otherwise elect the provision of information during such period. Where the withholding tax is applied, payment of interest and similar income is subject to withholding by the relevant paying agent in Luxembourg at the initial rate of 15% for a three-year period which started on 1 July 2005, at a rate of 20% for the subsequent three-year period and at a rate of 35% thereafter. Payment of the withholding tax (for which the Luxembourg bank/paying agent will be responsible) fully satisfies all obligations vis-à-vis the competent tax authorities. Instead of applying such withholding tax, the client may, however, opt for disclosure and direct his banker to transmit information on his interest income to his home tax authorities. Such an instruction constitutes one of the exemptions to bank confidentiality dealt with below under 'Bankers and Clients'.

Indirect taxes and inheritance taxes

[19.16] The law of 28 January 1948 on the correct and proper collection of taxes compels the banker to provide information and documents to the tax authorities in charge of indirect taxes (*Administration de l'Enregistrement et des Domaines*) in relation to assets and accounts held by a deceased resident, except in cases where no duties are payable in Luxembourg (such as direct succession to children). This law further grants a general right of investigation to the indirect tax administration in respect of any matter relating to taxes falling within the responsibility of the *Administration de l'Enregistrement* such as registration rights, inheritance taxes and mortgage duties (but excluding VAT) (art 30).

Any information so provided to the *Administration de l'Enregistrement et des Domaines* can in theory be used by the *Administration des Contributions Directes* (the authority responsible for direct income tax) in order to assess liability to income tax. Surprisingly, according to certain authors, the exchange of information does not occur[50]

---

48 According to explanatory notes to the draft decree, the decree is meant to 'clarify' the existence of bank secrecy vis-à-vis national tax administrations.
49 See Tribunal d'Arrondissement, no 554/99; A Schmitt and E Omes; n 43 above, n 102.
50 A Steichen, n 46 above, at 36.

or only takes place in cases of fiscal fraud.[51] Experience shows that this tends to be general practice and information circulates between those authorities, which has been recently confirmed by a declaration of the government announcing an intensified 'co-operation' between both tax authorities. The general prohibition applicable to direct taxes (above) thus seems partly circumvented through the exemption applicable to indirect taxes, even if their legality could be questioned and eventually challenged in court.[52]

Criminal fiscal law

[19.17] Luxembourg income tax laws[53] traditionally contained three types of offences in tax matters:

1   breach of fiscal regulation (*Steuerordnungswiedrigkeit*) (AO, para 413);
2   unintentional fiscal fraud (*Steuergefährdung*) (AO, para 402); and
3   intentional fiscal fraud (*Steuerhinterziehung*) (AO, para 396).

These offences, which are punishable by a fine, are, according to authoritative doctrine, deemed to be fiscal offences.[54] Thus, the banker may not divulge any information which might be requested by the tax authorities. The general position remains unchanged.

By a law of 22 December 1993, the Luxembourg legislator introduced a further degree of intentional fiscal fraud which involves (i) a fraud, (ii) over 'significant amounts', (iii) committed by 'systematic use of fraudulent manoeuvres', (iv) in order to hide pertinent evidence to the authorities or to convince it about untrue facts. This expanded offence of fiscal fraud is generally referred to as *escroquerie fiscale*.

The above criminal offence does not create a particular regime as regards bank secrecy in respect of criminal offences in general. Bank confidentiality rules do not apply in judicial investigations concerning *escroquerie fiscale*. It may give rise to testimonies, searches and arrest procedures under criminal law by the competent investigatory authorities. The subject will be of particular interest in international matters, which is dealt with below.[55]

Bankers and shareholders

[19.18] In the interests of the shareholders of a bank, an exemption to bank secrecy has been expressly introduced under Luxembourg law since 1981 vis-à-vis the main shareholders of a bank, ie 'those who directly or indirectly hold the majority of the shares or a participation allowing them to exercise a significant influence on the affairs of the bank concerned'. In such capacity, those shareholders are subject to authorisation by the CSSF. Their approval is one of the constituent elements of the issuance of a banking licence.

As those shareholders bear the ultimate risk of the management of the bank, it is normal that they are put in a position to obtain such information as is necessary

---

51 C Schmit and MP Weides-Schaeffer *Le Secret Bancaire en Droit Luxembourgeois* (1984) Cahiers de la BIL, no 5/84 at 36.
52 A Steichen, n 46 above, at 37.
53 The laws on indirect taxes mentioned above and the laws on value added tax contain other fiscal criminal offences.
54 A Steichen, n 46 above, at 46.
55 See 'Bankers and International Investigations' below.

properly to determine the measure of their liability. In principle, however, the Banking Law limits this exemption to the duty of confidence by excluding from the allowed disclosure any information which is privy to the assets of individual clients who are not professionals of the financial sector. In practice, this exemption allows, inter alia, the assessment of risks of a banking group at group level, while the Luxembourg entity may forward general information on its exposure without forwarding the names, identities and assets of individual clients.

By derogation to the principle that no specific client information may be transferred to shareholders, a further broadening of exemptions to the secrecy obligation was introduced by the law of 12 November 2004 on the fight against money laundering and financing of terrorism. Pursuant to that, information relating to specified business relations (including client information and specific transaction details) may be disclosed to internal group controllers 'to the extent necessary to the global management of legal risks and of reputation linked to money laundering or terrorism'. This exemption, which is justified by the need to combat crime, in fact allows the free transfer of client information to group internal auditors in such specific circumstances, it being noted that, due to the fact that the obligation of bank confidentiality is considered to be an obligation to achieve a result (see 'Sanctions to a Breach of Bank Confidentiality' above), it is up to such groups to take effective measures to avoid any leak resulting from such disclosure.

A particular situation arises where foreign banks have established a branch in Luxembourg, as opposed to a subsidiary. However, no distinction is made between a branch or a subsidiary. The same secrecy has to be observed by the branch in Luxembourg vis-à-vis its parent company as that observed by the subsidiary vis-à-vis its main shareholders. In this respect, it should be noted that although the branch will be subject to prudential supervision by a foreign authority, the CSSF retains a residual authority to supervise branches, in particular, in relation to banking secrecy.

Bankers and supervisory authorities

[19.19]   Being the second legal exemption provided for by the Banking Law, this exemption concerns requests for information originating from national and foreign authorities in charge of prudential supervision of a bank or another professional of the financial sector authorised in Luxembourg.

The CSSF is entrusted with the prudential supervision of banks, clearing systems, stock exchanges, investment funds and other professionals of the financial sector. Banks have an obligation to collaborate with the CSSF in its investigations, but any such investigation is only valid to the extent that the CSSF acts within the scope of its mission determined by the law of 23 December 1998 relating to the creation of the CSSF. The CSSF has general investigatory powers (art 53 of the Banking Law), but is itself subject to professional secrecy (art 44 of the Banking Law).

Information given to the CSSF may be forwarded to foreign authorities provided that:

1   the principle of reciprocity is observed – the foreign authority will only receive information to the extent that it also forwards information to the CSSF upon its own request;
2   the information is necessary for the purpose of prudential supervision; and
3   the information is covered by professional secrecy of the receiving foreign authority.

In respect of the last condition, it is interesting to note that there is no requirement regarding the stringency of the professional secrecy to which the foreign authority is subject and which varies from one country to another.

Upon requests from foreign supervisory authorities, the CSSF may either carry out the investigation itself and then forward it to the foreign authorities or authorise an intermediary or the foreign authority itself to proceed with the investigation.

A particular situation arises in connection with consolidated supervision where a subsidiary or a branch of a foreign bank is included in the consolidated supervision by a foreign authority. In such case, the investigations are made by the foreign authority in charge of supervision, but through the parent company, ie the foreign bank, which in turn has to request the relevant information from the Luxembourg subsidiary. Upon receipt of any information, the foreign authority is free to request confirmation of such information from the CSSF.

Bankers and market abuse

[19.20]   By a new law of 9 May 2006 (the 'Law on Market Abuse'), Luxemburg implemented EC Directive 2003/6 of 28 January 2006 on insider dealing and market manipulation, as amended (the 'Market Abuse Directive'), together with related directives and regulations.[56] The Law on Market Abuse covers the following two areas.

Insider dealing

[19.21]   The Law on Market Abuse replaces the existing law of 3 May 1991 on insider dealing (which itself was based on EC Directive 89/592 of 13 November 1989). The new law continues to prohibit certain persons who have knowledge of inside information to deal in financial instruments of the issuer concerned. Its scope is enlarged in the sense that (i) insiders comprise, in addition to shareholders, managers, directors, employees or advisers, any person having knowledge of inside information by virtue of his criminal activities, (ii) financial instruments include derivative instruments linked to financial instruments to which the inside information relates and (iii) the inside information, in addition to being precise and non-public, relates directly or indirectly to the issuer or the relevant financial instrument and is likely to have a significant effect on the price. It is important to stress that mere knowledge of inside information is not punishable, only its use is prohibited.

Market manipulation

[19.22]   The Law on Market Abuse introduces a new prohibition on the carrying out of transactions or the issuance of orders which give false or misleading signals as to

---

56 EC Directive 2003/124 of 22 December 2003 implementing Directive 2003/6/EC of the European Parliament and of the Council as regards the definition and public disclosure of inside information and the definition of market manipulation; EC Directive 2003/125 of 22 December 2003 implementing Directive 2003/6/EC of the European Parliament and of the Council as regards the fair presentation of investment recommendations and the disclosure of conflicts of interest and Regulation 2273/2003 of 22 December 2003 implementing Directive 2003/6/EC of the European Parliament and of the Council as regards exemptions for buy-back programmes and stabilisation of financial instrument.

the supply of demand for, or the price of, financial instruments. The prohibition includes any kind of fictitious proceedings or gross deception, except where such proceedings conform to market practice. In addition, the new law imposes obligations on the issuer in respect of inside information which such issuer must, pursuant to the new legal provisions, publish as soon as possible.

In respect of bank confidentiality, the Law on Market Abuse is innovative in two important respects. First, the CSSF (which is also the competent authority for ensuring observance of the Law on Market Abuse) is granted extensive investigatory powers with the right to conduct onsite inspections, as well as powers to issue sanctions, including fines (up to 125,000 euros (in addition to criminal sanctions which may apply)) and even temporary suspension of the professional activity of the person concerned. The specific investigatory powers granted to the CSSF do not change the situation for banks or other professionals of the financial sector because they already fall under its supervision on the basis of the Banking Law.

Secondly, the law creates a new exemption in the sense that – as is already the case in respect of money laundering – it obliges banks and other professionals of the financial sector, who have a suspicion that a transaction may constitute insider dealing or market manipulation, to inform the CSSF without delay. Where such a notification is made, it is forbidden for banks to inform any third party, in particular, the clients who initiated the transaction.

There are, however, fundamental differences between the denunciation obligation of a bank under the Law on Market Abuse, as opposed to the money laundering legislation:

1   the declaration under the Law on Market Abuse is made to the CSSF, not the prosecutor;
2   non-compliance with the obligation to declare suspicious transactions only gives rise to an administrative fine by the CSSF (up to 125,000 euros) and does not – as is the case for failure to declare suspect money laundering transactions – give rise to criminal sanctions for the banker;
3   the prohibition of tipping off under the Law on Market Abuse (opposite to the law on money laundering) only exists if a notification was made by the bank of a suspicious transaction, but, according to the wording of the Law on Market Abuse, it is not prohibited from informing the client if an investigation is started by the CSSF of which the bank is otherwise informed.

Finally, the Law on Market Abuse contains extended provisions on the power and duty of co-operation of the CSSF with foreign authorities in charge of market abuse. In the case of a request from a foreign authority from outside the EU, the CSSF must in addition make sure that the professional secrecy offers at least equivalent guarantees to the secrecy obligation to which the CSSF is a party.

Bankers and money laundering

[**19.23**]   Luxembourg has, over the years and even prior to the Banking Law, established legislation regarding money laundering.[57] Those rules, which initially

---

57 Law of 19 February 1973 regarding the sale of medical substances and the fight against drug addiction, as amended; arts 506-1–506-7 of the Code Pénal; law of 15 April 1993 regarding the financial sector; numerous circulars of the CSSF (see www.cssf.lu) and various international conventions such as the United Nations Convention of Vienna of 20 December 1988 against illegal drug trafficking and the summit creating the Financial Action Task Force on Money Laundering in June 1989.

aimed to prevent transactions which might involve drug money laundering, were extended and today cover laundering money derived from criminal offences relating to professional and organised crime in general (including, in particular, terrorism), as well as arms trafficking, prostitution, corruption and kidnapping of minors. The rules oblige banks to make thorough checks and controls in order to identify the origin of funds, the identity of their clients (including the beneficial owner) and suspect transactions and prohibit (through abstention) the banker from entering into certain transactions. In order to allow and oblige banks to denounce acts which might constitute money laundering, a legal exemption from bank secrecy was required and therefore introduced into the Banking Law and is today provided for in the law of 12 November 2004 relating to the fight against money laundering and financing of terrorism (the '2004 Money Laundering Law') which implemented EC Directive 2001/97. Since 2004, the bankers' obligations in relation to money laundering are no longer set out in the Banking Law, but are grouped in a separate law specifically dealing with money laundering aspects and which applies not only to banks and professionals of the financial sector, but also to other professions such as auditors, lawyers, notaries, estate agents and generally businesses selling high-value goods where a payment in cash is made for more than 15,000 euros.

Pursuant to the current obligations, these professionals (including bankers), their managers and employees must fully co-operate with the authorities in charge of the fight against money laundering and financing of terrorism. In this respect, each of them must:

1   of their own initiative, inform the public prosecutor of any fact which might be an indication of money laundering or of financing of terrorism, inter alia, by reason of the person concerned, the origin of the funds, the nature, the purpose or the proceedings of the transaction; and
2   furnish to the public prosecutor upon request all information necessary in accordance with the procedures established by the applicable legislation.

The transmission of information is done by the person designated within the bank's organisation responsible for reporting money laundering.

Professionals or their managers or employees may not communicate to the client concerned or to any third party that the information has been transmitted to the prosecutor or that an investigation has been started. However, one derogation to the prohibition of tipping off has been introduced allowing a branch or a subsidiary of a financial group to communicate to the internal group auditor that the information has been so transmitted, but then only under the express condition that prior authorisation from the public prosecutor was received.

In practice, banks are frequently faced with a situation where published information (for example, in newspaper articles) indicates that a client is to some extent involved in a criminal investigation abroad (with often only limited information or details), but where the bank's file on the client and the transactions which were carried out on his accounts have been duly justified and do not show any element which might indicate money laundering. The Luxembourg public prosecutor takes the view that in such case a banker would always be required to denounce his client.

If, however, it is later found that the information was wrong and that indeed the suspicion against the client was unfounded, a declaration by the banker to the prosecutor may have caused serious harm to the client. In order to avoid that, bankers are hesitant to comply with their denunciation obligation and the 2004 Money Laundering Law provides that a disclosure in good faith to the public prosecutor by a bank does not constitute a breach of bank secrecy and may not entail any liability on the part of the professional. Such provision is justified in particular in situations where the banker can have legitimate doubts about whether a fact is or is not an indication of money laundering, even though a mere indication of a suspicion of criminal activity published in a newspaper article cannot, in our opinion, by itself be an element which is sufficient for the denunciation obligation of the banker to come into existence. In a recent case, the courts have confirmed that such indication in a newspaper, having regard to the information available to the bank, was not in itself sufficient to trigger the requirement for a denunciation. The banker has thus become subject to an obligation of denunciation imposed by law and is, in this respect, exempted by law from bank secrecy vis-à-vis the public prosecutor.

Bankers and outsourcing

[19.24]   Banks more and more often outsource part of their business to outside professionals. The increased recourse to outsourcing is driven by globalisation, as well as by the requirement to reduce costs in a competitive environment. Bank secrecy has always been a handicap to implementing outsourcing solutions as client data could not be disclosed by Luxembourg bankers. Where Luxembourg banks or professionals of the financial sector took recourse to IT operating systems abroad (which has been an accepted practice within financial groups for many years), the CSSF insisted that any client data be made anonymous which required technically complicated and expensive solutions.

To remedy this situation, the Luxembourg legislator introduced three new categories of professionals of the financial sector by a law of 2 August 2003:

1   'client communication agents', ie professionals in charge of client reporting or of archiving;
2   'financial sector administrative agents', ie professionals who render administrative services to banks, other professionals and investment funds (mainly register and transfer activities, etc); and
3   'operators of financial sector information, technology systems and communication networks', ie professionals in charge of maintaining IT systems or communication networks of banks or professionals of the financial sector.

To the extent that information is communicated to any of these professionals as part of a service contract relating to the activities which are outsourced, the obligation to secrecy imposed by art 41 of the Banking Law does not apply. The exemption introduced in art 41(5) is justified because such professionals are subject to the same bank secrecy provisions, must have a proper organisation allowing compliance with the obligations to which they are subject and are also subject to the same supervisory authority.

Bankers and clients

[19.25]   In respect of a possible authorisation by, or instruction from, the client to disclose 'secret information', the 'public order character' inherent to Luxembourg bank confidentiality regains importance. Applied to private interests, the idea of 'public order' raises the question whether the client has the absolute right or power to relieve his bank of the obligation to secrecy. Is the client the 'master' of the secret?

The question of the public order character of bank secrecy has been, and continues to be, the subject of intensive debate. Dominant opinion endorses the theory that indeed banking secrecy is of public order.[58] For these authors, the fact that bank secrecy is subject to criminal sanctions and further because art 41(2) of the Banking Law implies that one could not derogate from bank secrecy unless such exemption is made by law must lead to this conclusion. Other authors insist on the fact that banking secrecy merely protects the private interests of the client who must be in a position to trigger disclosures. On that basis, they ineluctably conclude that banking secrecy cannot be of public order.[59]

As has been indicated above (see footnote 20), a recent court case, without however specifically setting out the grounds, confirmed the public order nature of bank secrecy. However, the public order nature may not have an adverse effect on the relationship between the banker and the client himself. In this context, one can point to a court case[60] which firmly stated that:

'Vis-à-vis himself [the client], the banker does not have an own right. He must follow instructions from the latter [the client]. Professional secrecy may not turn against interests of the clients. The banker may not be put in a position to judge what is, and what is not, in the interests of his client.'

While commenting on this decision, an author[61] recalls the context in which this decision was taken. A banker effectively refused to furnish certain documents to the heirs of a deceased client. It is a generally accepted principle that heirs 'continue the person' of the deceased client and therefore have the right to receive full information on the accounts of the client and request all documents in that respect. In this case, the position of the bank to refuse to deliver documents was clearly unjustified.

The question of the public order nature of bank secrecy was submitted to the 'committee of lawyers' set up within the CSSF which is composed of members of the CSSF and outside practitioners. The report insisted on the dual feature of the interest which is protected by bank secrecy rules: the personal/private interest of the client, together with the public/social interest of society referring (in this latter respect), in particular, to privacy rules by comparison to data protection regulation.

While confirming the dominant understanding that bank secrecy is of public order, the report demonstrates that a specific consent or instruction to disclosure from the client allows the bank to disclose information without there being a breach of its obligation to confidentiality provided such specific consent cannot be considered a total contractual waiver (which, as a result of the rules being of public order, would not be permitted).

The conclusion to which practitioners have therefore come is that bank secrecy is to be considered of public order which does not prevent disclosure upon specific instructions from the client: specific as to the contents of the information to be disclosed, specific as to the addressees of the information, specific as to the purpose and specific as to time. In other words, an authorisation to disclose information cannot be given on a general basis irrevocably for an undetermined duration.

In practice, the possibility for the client to grant specific disclosures is for banks to adapt to the needs of globalisation. Today, banks need to have recourse to specialised

---

58 See n 16 above.
59 See n 16 above.
60 Tribunal d'Arrondissement, 24 January 1991.
61 J Kauffman *Le Secret Bancaire en Droit Luxembourgeois – Aspects Actuels et Perspectives, Droit Bancaire et Financier au Grand-Duché de Luxembourg 10th anniversaire de l'Association Luxembourgeoise des Juristes de Banques*, vol 1, ed Larcier (1994) p 525.

professionals, in particular, in respect of IT (see 'Bankers and Outsourcing' above). Further, in order to allow a client to comply with its obligations vis-à-vis tax or anti-trust authorities, bankers may be asked to disclose specific information to the authorities.

Where a specific disclosure order has been given by the client, the banker is allowed to follow this instruction without breaching his confidentiality duty. In that context, recent authors,[62] while confirming the public order nature of bank secrecy, justify the possibility of specific disclosures through the legal theory of the mandate where the banker, following instructions from the client, is in fact deemed to act on a basis of a mandate on behalf of the client.

However, the banker is not under an obligation to provide negative confirmations that a person is not a client of the bank. Even if it can be argued that vis-à-vis such person who, by definition, is not a client, there cannot be any secrecy obligation and thus nothing should prevent a banker from answering such request. The banker may never undertake any action which is likely to put his confidentiality duty vis-à-vis the clients at risk. Precisely by giving 'negative confirmations', there may be situations where implicitly such negative confirmation entails confirmation on the circumstances of other clients of the bank which are thereby put at risk.

Bankers party to a court action

[19.26]   A different situation arises where the banker is one of the parties to a court case and would deem it to be in his own interest to reveal certain information for his defence which falls under his obligation to bank secrecy. Such a court case could involve his client or any third party. This question has been very clearly decided by the courts.

The legitimate interest of the banker permits disclosure of certain information.[63] Organising his own defence is most certainly a legitimate interest. Deciding the contrary would be highly prejudicial to the banker who would, in a court case, be prohibited from putting forward arguments for his own defence. Interestingly, in order to justify this exemption, the Luxembourg decision expressly refers to the famous *Tournier* case in England,[64] which constitutes the basis of bank confidentiality under common law.

Judges have, however, drawn limits on the scope of this exemption. Any such disclosure may only occur in cases involving 'financial interests' of the banker and with respect to information strictly necessary for the purposes of the defence. Where an action could only entail a 'moral prejudice' for the banker, disclosure would not be permitted. In practice, however, it will be extremely difficult to draw the line between cases only involving moral prejudice and those which also carry patrimonial interests.

An interesting problem has arisen in labour law matters. Luxembourg law obliges the employer who wishes to terminate an employment contract to set out very precisely the motives on which a dismissal of an employee is based. Regardless of the question whether the motives given by the employer justify the termination or not, if they are

---

62 C Liebertz and C Schmit, see n 16 above.
63 Tribunal d'Arrondissement, 26 June 1981, no 27163 du rôle.
64 *Tournier v National Provincial and Union Bank of England* [1924] 1 KB 461.

not indicated with sufficient precision in the letter to the employee, the dismissal will be declared to be abusive (irregular in form only) as the employee and the judge would not be in a position to determine on the basis of those imprecise motives whether the dismissal was justified. There is virtually no possibility to provide further evidence during the course of a possible court action.

Depending on the motives for the dismissal, the banker may, however, have to refer to precise files or precise clients where the employee purportedly acted wrongly. In fact, bank secrecy may prohibit him from revealing such details. Therefore, while having to observe his duty of confidence, court cases have held that the dismissal of an employee was abusive to the extent that the letter of termination did not give enough indications as to the motives for the dismissal,[65] for instance, by referring to the name of the customer and the details of the incriminating transactions.

To solve this paradox, it appears that only the legislator could introduce a solution by law.

Bankers and international investigations

[19.27] The next question concerns the obligation to bank secrecy at an international level already partly referred to above.

In Luxembourg, extra-territorial aspects mainly involve requests for assistance from foreign authorities to Luxembourg authorities or, more particularly, to Luxembourg courts in order to obtain information or documents or to arrest assets.

Luxembourg legal provisions basically deal with international co-operation at a judicial level. However, the situation of insider dealing and market manipulation has to be included and has been dealt with above.

Further, the duty of assistance has to be analysed under the double taxation treaties and, in particular, the European directives. In principle, double taxation treaties to which Luxembourg is a party contain provisions which cover the transmitting of information between the competent tax authorities. However, the traditional language to be found in the double taxation treaties contains reservations that none of the contracting parties is obliged to take any measures which (i) would be inconsistent with its administrative practice, or (ii) may not be obtained under its national financial legislation or, indeed, (iii) which may be contrary to applicable professional secrecy. Any direct request from foreign tax authorities to obtain information from Luxembourg banks would be barred by any of the three conditions.

There is also an EU Directive (Council Directive 77/799/EEC) providing for the transmission of information. A law of 15 March 1979 has introduced the obligations of this Directive into Luxembourg law. It again refers to the reservation that no tax administration is bound to make investigations or transmit information which law or practice do not empower the administration to do at a national level. Moreover, the express reservation of bank secrecy is again to be found in the law of 15 March 1979.

Finally, reference may be made to a Convention between member states of the EU which also attempts to eliminate double taxation between affiliated parties.[66] Information may be communicated to a commission which has to solve any issue of

---

65 *RNB v Goldstein*, Tribunal de Travail, 21 April 1997, no 2124197 du rôle.
66 Signed in Brussels on 23 July 1990.

double taxation. However, the members of such commission which comprise representatives of the various tax administrations concerned are bound by secrecy pursuant to art 9, para 6 of the Convention of 23 July 1990.

With respect to the judicial proceedings, it is necessary to distinguish between civil law and criminal law proceedings.

Civil law proceedings

Letters rogatory

[19.28]   Letters rogatory, or 'letters of request', involve a request for evidence made by a foreign court which is seeking information from the court in the place where records are maintained in order to obtain the information without directly or indirectly infringing the sovereignty of another country.[67] Similarly, as in England, the use of such letters rogatory is regulated in Luxembourg by the Hague Convention on the Taking of Evidence Abroad in Civil or Commercial Matters of 1970 (this Convention was approved in Luxembourg by a law of 19 March 1977) and by EC Regulation n 1206/2001 of 28 May 2001. The importance of this Convention and the Regulation for the purpose of investigations with a Luxembourg bank are extremely limited for two reasons.

Article 11 of the Convention provides that a letter rogatory is not executed to the extent that the person to whom it is addressed may invoke an exemption or a prohibition to testify. The same provisions are set out in art 14 of the Regulation. Bank secrecy constitutes a legal impeachment to testify. It is interesting to note that art 11 expressly refers to testimony and not to other investigation procedures such as arrests or searches. To the extent, however, that at a national level a banker may invoke secrecy in civil matters and refuse to hand over or produce documents, the same applies internationally. A report established by a commission comprised of representatives of the Ministry of Finance, the Ministry of Justice, the Ministry of Foreign Affairs and the ABBL very clearly states that it is the duty of the Luxembourg authorities to make sure that requests for taking evidence are only granted to the extent that they aim to search for and determine criminal offences. Article 14, para 2 of the Regulation indirectly permits to refuse any request on those motives.

More particularly, art 1 of the law of 19 March 1977 approving the Hague Convention of 1970 contains a reservation whereby Luxembourg declares that it will not continue any request under a letter rogatory in respect of 'pre-trial discovery of documents' in countries of common law.

Subpoena from other jurisdictions

[19.29]   Luxembourg banks receive subpoenas mainly issued by US courts whereby they are ordered to produce documents to be used in proceedings in a foreign country. In the absence of any particular convention, Luxembourg banks must oppose on the grounds of bank secrecy and are prevented from producing documents as requested.

---

67 RNS Grandison, n 1 above, p 197.

Criminal law proceedings[68]

Letters rogatory

[19.30]   International letters rogatory are governed by the law of 8 August 2000 on international judicial co-operation in criminal matters (the '2000 Law') and are generally based on the following conventions:

1   the European Convention regarding extradition of 13 December 1957 (the '1957 Convention');
2   the European Convention regarding judicial co-operation in criminal matters of 20 April 1959 (the '1959 Convention');
3   the Convention on extradition and judicial co-operation in criminal matters between the Benelux countries of 27 June 1962 (the '1962 Convention'); and
4   the Treaty regarding judicial co-operation in criminal matters between the Grand-Duchy of Luxembourg and the United States of America of 13 March 1997 (the '1997 US Treaty').

It is important to separate tax matters from other criminal law aspects.

Letters rogatory in fiscal matters

[19.31]   Until 1997, under both the 1959 Convention and the 1962 Convention, co-operation for criminal offences of a fiscal nature was not allowed. Although not expressly excluded by the text of these Conventions, authors unanimously concluded that the exclusion of fiscal matters is based on art 2(b) as a waiver of bank secrecy in this respect would be against 'public order or other essential interests of the country'.[69]

However, by a law of 27 August 1997, Luxembourg adopted an additional protocol (Protocol I) to the 1959 Convention. Pursuant to this law, international co-operation (at a judicial level only) pursuant to the 1959 Convention is granted for the criminal offence of expanded fiscal fraud (*escroquerie fiscale*) as defined by the law of 22 December 1993.[70] Luxembourg made express reservations to specify that co-operation will not be granted for so-called 'fiscal offences'[71] and that any information transmitted may only be used for the purpose of investigation of criminal offences (including *escroquerie fiscale*) for which judicial aid was requested (*principe de spécialité*).

The 2000 Law specifically confirms that, except as otherwise provided in international conventions, every request for co-operation will be refused for offences related to direct or indirect taxes applicable pursuant to Luxembourg law.

The situation under the 1997 US Treaty is specifically referred to in art 1, item 5 and follows the principle agreed upon in Protocol I.[72] The text of this 1997 US Treaty provides that judicial co-operation for fiscal offences will be granted in case the facts underlying the request allow the establishment of a 'reasonable presumption' that the criminal offence of expanded fiscal fraud exists. Discussions have arisen on the

---

68 For an in-depth study, see D Spielman, n 16 above.
69 A Steichen, n 46 above, at 24; J Kauffman, n 61 above, at 29.
70 See 'Bankers and Tax Authorities' above.
71 See 'Bankers and Tax Authorities' above.
72 In fact, the reason why it took two-and-a-half years to ratify the 1997 Treaty with the US was that this should be simultaneous to the same extension at European level.

wording of the 1997 US Treaty, combined with an exchange of letters between the US and Luxembourg, which could be deemed to soften the interpretation of what would constitute the offence of *escroquerie fiscale* for which co-operation is granted. Authors in Luxembourg agree, however, that the interpretation of the 1997 US Treaty must be such that co-operation will only be granted if the facts analysed constitute the criminal offence of expanded fiscal fraud as set out by Luxembourg law.[73]

Letters rogatory in general criminal matters

[19.32] In general criminal matters, co-operation will be granted if the following conditions are fulfilled: (i) the facts which give rise to the letter rogatory must constitute a criminal offence in both the requesting and requested state and (ii) the request will be refused when an offence is a political offence, is connected with a political offence or where the request is likely to prejudice the sovereignty, security, public order or other essential interests of the country.

Pursuant to the 1959 Convention, a letter rogatory is first transmitted through diplomatic channels to the Ministry of Justice, which has an overriding discretion to refuse to provide assistance. The most important duty of the Ministry of Justice is to ensure that any preliminary request in relation to a criminal offence would not be a façade for investigating other offences, mainly in fiscal matters. If authorised, the request passes to the public prosecutor, who again has the power to authorise the request or refuse it and then only transmit it to the investigating magistrate. On the basis of an order of the investigating magistrate, the letter rogatory will be executed.

It is only at that stage that the parties concerned receive knowledge of the letter rogatory. The parties concerned and any interested parties have ten days following the day the investigating measure is notified to the person where it is executed to appeal the decision of the investigating magistrate in Luxembourg. There is controversy in Luxembourg on the point whether for this purpose the bank which merely holds the accounts is an interested party and as such may itself exercise recourse against these decisions.

Testimonies

[19.33] If a banker is called upon to testify before the Luxembourg authorities (even on the basis of a foreign letter rogatory), the national situation explained above equally applies. The banker has a right to testify or may refuse to testify in civil as well as criminal matters invoking bank secrecy laws (see above).

The question of a banker being called upon to testify in a foreign court is extremely delicate. This raises the question of the extra-territorial effect of bank confidentiality laws. Article 41(2) of the Banking Law provides that the obligation to bank secrecy ceases where the disclosure of information is 'authorised or imposed by law'. Traditional doctrine held that the legislator could only have meant a 'Luxembourg' law. Indeed, Luxembourg law could not recognise the effect of a foreign law where it would be to release someone from criminal liability under Luxembourg law. Any other position would totally remove the efficiency of Luxembourg professional secrecy (and that would not only concern banks, but other professions such as the

---

73 P Santer *L'approbation du traité d'entraide judiciaire en matière pénale entre le Luxembourg et les Etats-Unis du 13 mars 1997* (2000) 14/2000 Codex at 359. Doc p 4599, pp 20 and 21.

medical and legal professions). Luxembourg would not accept the order of a foreign law which would not recognise those secrecy obligations.

This leaves the question as to whether the 'testimony exemption' also applies to foreign courts, ie whether there is an extra-territorial effect for the 'testimony exception'.

When art 458 of the Code Pénal was enacted (in 1879), that reference could only be understood as a reference to the Luxembourg courts. There have since been no court rulings on this subject. The question must, however, be raised if nowadays a different approach may have to be taken as a result of the evolution of the relationship between states and in particular the prevailing principle of courtesy between states. The 1959 Convention indeed allows a person from a requested state to be called as a witness in the requesting state. An interesting decision recently shed some light on this question.[74] A Dutch national residing in Luxembourg and employed by a Luxembourg bank was the subject of criminal proceedings in Belgium for certain actions carried out in Belgium and related to his activity as an employee of a Luxembourg bank. There is no evidence the employee concerned acted in breach of Luxembourg law. When the employee was interrogated by the Belgian judicial authorities on the matter, he approached clients and, on other aspects of services rendered for them in Belgium, he refused to answer and justified his refusal through his obligation to bank confidentiality in Luxembourg.

As part of a prejudicial question discussed before the European Court of First Instance in Luxembourg, the Luxembourg government set out its own interpretation on the effects of bank secrecy. The Luxembourg government first indicated that the Luxembourg laws on bank secrecy have indeed an extra-territorial effect in the sense that such laws would be ineffective if bankers were allowed to disclose any information outside Luxembourg. Conversely, according to the governmental position, exceptions to the bank secrecy laws equally have to be given an extended effect and the concept of judicial authorities contained in art 458 of the Code Pénal would not only cover Luxembourg judicial authorities, but also those of other member states. However, such exceptions must find their origin in the provisions of Luxembourg law. As a consequence, where art 458 of the Code Pénal provides that the bank secrecy obligation ceases when a person is called upon to testify before judicial authorities, this does not only cover Luxembourg judicial authorities, but also similar authorities of other countries. On that basis, and without further analysis, an unsuspecting reader of the government's position could come to the conclusion that, if a Luxembourg banker were called upon to testify before foreign courts, he would be authorised to disclose facts subject to bank confidentiality. If the banker talked, he would not be the subject of criminal proceedings in Luxembourg. That conclusion is, in our opinion, incorrect even on the assumption that the Luxembourg government's analysis on extra-territorial effect of the 'testimony exemption' were correct. In fact, the 'testimony exception' must be read together with the applicable provisions in Luxembourg civil procedure and criminal procedure laws.

As discussed above, in respect of the testimonies in Luxembourg civil and commercial courts, as well as in the criminal courts, the position has always been that those persons who are under a professional secrecy obligation can testify in court, but they cannot be forced to testify.[75] The 'testimony exception' must therefore be

---

74 Arrêt de la Cour CJCE, 10 December 2002.
75 See 'Bankers and Judges' above.

read in conjunction with the provisions of the Luxembourg civil procedure and criminal procedure codes, which, in both cases, allow the bearer of the secret to elect not to testify. If, therefore, the 'testimony exception' had extra-territorial effect and, in our opinion, this is by no means certain, it can only have that effect if at the same time the foreign court recognises the option of the holder of the secret to refuse to testify. In a jurisdiction where the right to refuse to testify is not granted, the 'testimony exception' should, in our opinion, not apply. This analysis is fully consistent with the aforementioned position of the Luxembourg government.

In addition, treaties applicable to international co-operation for the obtention of evidence in civil and commercial matters provide that the request to audition a person as a witness will not be given effect by the required state if that person has the right to refuse to testify under the law of the required state. This is the case not only under EC Regulation n 1206/2001 concerning the co-operation of the courts of member states in connection with the obtaining of evidence in civil and commercial matters (art 14), but also under the Hague Convention of 18 March 1970 on the obtaining abroad of evidence in civil and commercial matters (which is applicable between the United States and Luxembourg) (art 11). International treaties therefore recognise the right of persons subject to a secrecy obligation to refuse to testify. This is consistent with the analysis above concerning the extra-territorial effect.

CONCLUSION

[19.34] Outside Luxembourg, bank secrecy laws are envied by some, hated and vilified by others. Within Luxembourg, they constitute, together with all the other professional secrecies, an inherent element of the social and economic order of society. Over the years, men of law and men of finance have learned to live with bank secrecy. They modelled it on a case-by-case basis bearing in mind the basic principles of a democratic system and balancing public and private interests.

This chapter shows that bank secrecy in Luxembourg, although strongly protective of the private life and sphere of intimacy of individuals, is not a means to keep crimes undiscovered. Bank secrecy is lifted in order to 'do justice'.

With the implementation of new rules based on transparency (market abuse), but also meant to adapt to the necessities of globalisation (outsourcing), exemptions are introduced into the law allowing, where appropriate, disclosure of information. It will be important for future reforms not to lose sight of the fundamental justification of rules of confidentiality being the preservation of intimacy and private life as, without boundaries, democracy cannot be guaranteed.

20 Mexico

Thomas S Heather

INTRODUCTION

[20.1] Bank secrecy in Mexico has evolved from simply being a traditionally unregulated relationship of confidentiality between financial institutions and their clients to becoming a standard of banking practice within Mexican law. For many years, Mexican banking legislation simply made a broad reference to the obligation of banks to observe due confidentiality with regard to the accounts of their customers. This topic has earned particular attention in recent years as regulators have attempted to determine the corresponding responsibilities and obligations of financial institutions and their clients to bolster public confidence in the Mexican banking system on the one hand and to avoid certain criminal activities, such as money laundering and other white collar crimes, on the other.

In this chapter, the following topics will be reviewed: (i) the principles of bank secrecy, (ii) the general legal and conceptual framework, (iii) anti-money laundering and terrorism provisions, (iv) reporting criteria, requirements and confidentiality and (v) remedies against disclosure of bank secrets as they are applicable under Mexican banking law. Throughout the chapter, a particular focus will be taken on the applicability of bank secrecy to tax evasion and money laundering-related issues.

PRINCIPLES OF BANK SECRECY

[20.2] The principles which surround the concept of bank secrecy are found in both customary banking practices and existing law that regulates such practice. These principles, many of which derive from precepts of the political constitution of the United Mexican States, include:

1   the institution of private property itself and information gathered by financial entities;
2   the right to privacy (attributed to the individual client and arguably to the financial institution itself);
3   the professional obligation of a financial institution to maintain the secrecy of client information;
4   the contractual relationship between a bank and its client, whereby the dissemination of client information is prohibited; and
5   the legal consequences for disseminating a client's financial information without due cause, ie the extra-contractual responsibility under civil and criminal law.

The principles of bank secrecy have been cornerstones in promoting a basic confidence in financial institutions in Mexico since very early on in their inception and have become an inseparable element in promoting public trust in such financial services providers.

GENERAL LEGAL AND CONCEPTUAL FRAMEWORK

[20.3]   The legal framework of Mexican banking secrecy and confidentiality provisions are contained in:

1   the Credit Institutions Law (*Ley de Instituciones de Crédito*), published in the *Diario Oficial* ('DO') of 18 July 1990, and as subsequently amended (the 'Law');
2   the Anti-Money Laundering and Terrorist Financing Rules (the 'Rules'), published in the DO of 14 May 2005, defining certain rules to prevent money laundering and terrorist financing activities utilising banking services provided by Mexican financial institutions; and
3   the Credit Bureau Law (*Ley para Regular las Sociedades de Información Crediticia*), published in the DO of 15 January 2002 (the 'Credit Bureau Law').

The Law, the Rules and the Credit Bureau Law are collectively referred to here as the 'Bank Secrecy Statutes'. The Bank Secrecy Statutes work both to define which practices are basic for maintaining the institution of bank secrecy and provide the regulatory oversight functions concerning bank secrecy. The competent regulatory authorities are the Ministry of Finance and Public Credit (*Secretaría de Hacienda y Crédito Público*) ('SHCP') and the National Banking and Securities Commission ('CNBV'), a decentralised agency of the Ministry.

Pursuant to art 117 of the Law, confidential information is considered to be all information with respect to deposits, services or any other type of client transactions, as well as the relevant personal information for the client itself or its authorised signatories.

Financial institutions are prohibited from revealing confidential information to any person other than a party with a direct interest in the confidential information, such as the depositor or account holder or relevant beneficiary, including its legal representatives.

The exception to the foregoing arises when such information is requested by (i) a judicial authority pursuant to a resolution adopted in a legal procedure where the account holder or beneficiary is acting as a defendant, (ii) the Attorney General of the United Mexican States (*Procurador General de la República*), each state Attorney General and the military Attorney General (*Procurador General de Justicia Militar*) in connection with criminal offences, (iii) the federal tax authorities in respect of tax-related matters, (iv) the SHCP in connection with money laundering and terrorist activities, (v) the Federal Treasury (*Tesorería de la Federación*) in cases of official investigations, (vi) the Supreme Federal Auditor (*Auditoría Superior de la Federación*) in connection with accounts and agreements in which public resources are managed, deposited or transferred, (vii) the secretary or under secretaries of the Ministry of Public Services (*Secretaría de la Función Pública*) with regard to investigations of public employees or government officials and (viii) the Federal Electoral Institute (*Instituto Federal Electoral*) regarding investigations of campaign contributions. All of the above, except for (i), shall, in principle, file their request through the CNBV. Indeed, the exceptions have been significantly expanded to such an extent that, given the discretionary powers granted to the authorities under other laws, bank secrecy seems to have become relatively unprotected.

Additionally, the CNBV provides confidential information to foreign financial authorities if treaties of reciprocity and information sharing have been entered into. Likewise, financial institutions must reveal confidential information to the CNBV as a consequence of such agency's inspection and surveillance authority and to the National Bank (*Banco de México*), the Institute for the Protection of Banking Savings (*Instituto para la Protección al Ahorro Bancario*) and the Financial Services Users' Protection and Defence Commission (*Comisión para la Protección y Defensa de los Usuarios de Servicios Financieros*) in terms of their applicable laws and regulations. It is noted, however, that such other agencies are also subject to confidentiality requirements.

Mexican banks may reveal confidential information in connection with the sale of their portfolio to prospective purchasers. In such a case, the prospective purchasers must sign a confidentiality agreement undertaking not to reveal the confidential information. Additionally, as provided in the Credit Bureau Law, credit bureaux may release confidential information to other similar credit bureaux, financial institutions who have been designated as bureau service users and the proper administrative authorities, upon official request, as provided by regulatory jurisdictional powers without breaching the bank secrecy provisions of the Law.

ANTI-MONEY LAUNDERING AND TERRORISM PROVISIONS

[20.4] The topic of money laundering has been the focus of many discussions and recent legal reforms, first, to the Mexican Tax Code (*Codigo Fiscal de la Federación*) and later to the Criminal Code (*Código Penal Federal*). The Mexican Tax Code first considered the act of money laundering as a criminal felony in 1989. Such felony and provisions similar to those found in the Tax Code were incorporated into the Criminal Code in 1996. Additionally, in 1993, the then National Banking Commission (*Comisión Nacional Bancaria*) issued a basic guide to prevent money laundering through banks following the provisions issued by the Basle Commission, the 40 recommendations of the Financial Action Task Force ('FATF') on Money Laundering of the Organisation for Economic Development and the Model Regulation for money laundering of assets related to illicit drug trafficking of the Organisation of the American States. The purpose of the guide was to design a public–private partnership between the Mexican government and regulated financial institutions to combat both national and cross-border money laundering.

In May 1996, art 400 bis of the Federal Criminal Code (*Código Penal para el Distrito Federal en Materia de Fuero Común y para toda la República en Materia de Fuero Federal*) was amended to classify money laundering as a federal crime. The provisions were directed towards those individuals or corporate entities that participate in activities involving the acquisition, sale, administration, deposit, investment, transport or transfer within Mexico or abroad of funds of any nature with knowledge that such funds originate from an illegal activity and with the intent of disguising or falsifying the true origin of such funds.

The provisions in the Criminal Code also provide that those employees of financial institutions who aid or assist their clients engaged in such illicit activities may be guilty of the same crime if malicious intent is shown and therefore be subject to criminal prosecution on the same basis. Additionally, on 7 November 1996, the collaboration of individuals in money laundering activities was defined as typical of organised crime under the new Federal Law Against Organised Crime (*Ley Federal contra la Delincuencia Organisada*).

It was initially considered to make the act of financing terrorism a crime by amending art 139 of the Criminal Code which was aimed at individuals who, by means of violent acts against persons or property with the intent of causing fear or terror among the population, intend to reduce the authority of the Mexican state or pressurise it to adopt a specific policy or conduct. However, the act of financing terrorist activity has not been specified as a crime in Mexico and is only punishable as an ancillary offence to terrorism.

Article 115 of the Law was amended in 2004 to include, in addition to preventing, detecting and reporting money laundering, the obligation on financial institutions to enact measures and procedures to prevent and detect acts, omissions or operations in connection with terrorism and to report them to the SHCP through the CNBV. The CNBV guidelines are directed towards the prevention of activities related to the financing of terrorism through financial institutions in accordance with the eight recommendations of the FATF on terrorist financing. In the same year, the SHCP enacted certain administrative rules, which provide for specific provisions regarding (i) procedures and measures for the prevention and detection of money laundering and terrorist financing activities and (ii) reporting criteria related to such activities.

If money laundering and terrorism involves a financial institution, the SHCP, through the assistance of the relevant decentralised agencies (ie the CNBV), must file a prosecutorial complaint with the Federal Public Prosecutor (*Ministerio Público*). In practice, the applicable regulations have caused a noticeable increase in technical and administrative collaboration among Mexican banking and criminal authorities.

As a result of the above-mentioned amendments and enactments, the International Monetary Fund Country Report 05/436 issued in December 2005, which was prepared by the FATF, found Mexico to be in substantive compliance with most of the agency's recommendations, except for the recommendation to criminalise terrorist financing. It is noted that, in accordance with the political constitution of the United Mexican States (*Constitución Política de los Estados Unidos Mexicanos*), the Bank Secrecy Statutes prevail over the 40 recommendations of the FATF on money laundering and the eight recommendations of the FATF on terrorist financing.

REPORTING CRITERIA, REQUIREMENTS AND CONFIDENTIALITY

[20.5]   By issuing the Rules, regulators attempted to design reporting mechanisms that would not breach the concept of bank secrecy and confidentiality. As a result, the following financial institutions, as defined under the Law, must co-operate to combat money laundering and terrorist financing:

1   banks and credit institutions;
2   insurance and bonding companies;
3   general depositories;
4   financial leasing companies;
5   savings and loans institutions;
6   credit unions;
7   collection agencies;
8   broker–dealers and other stockmarket intermediaries;
9   currency exchangers;
10   special purpose financial institutions;
11   retirement fund administrators; and
12   any other financial intermediary.

Mexico's current money laundering and terrorist financing prevention regulations are comprised of three parts:

1 client identification provisions;
2 establishment of internal procedures and training programmes for the proper handling of transactions with a money laundering and/or terrorist financing potential; and
3 reporting requirements to assist the competent authorities in their monitoring of transactions with such potential.

Client identification and account opening

[20.6] Financial institutions must establish specific and strict client identification and 'know your customer' guidelines that must be included in their policy manuals. Prior to the opening of any account or to the execution of any agreement, financial institutions must open an identification file for the client (including the account owner, beneficiaries and co-owners) which must include the following information as a minimum.

Individuals

[20.7] In the case of Mexican individuals, the following information must be completed: full name, date of birth, nationality, Federal Tax Payer Registry *Registro Federal de Contribuyentes*) and Tax Payer Identification (*Cédula de Identificación Fiscal*) issued by the SHCP or Population Registry Code (*Clave única de Registro de Población*) issued by the Ministry of the Interior (*Secretaría de Gobernación*), profession, type of business or activity and personal domicile (number, street, city or location, postcode, telephone number and e-mail address, if applicable).

Companies or other legal entities

[20.8] In the case of Mexican legal entities, the following information must be completed: corporate name, domicile (number, street, city or location, postcode, telephone number and e-mail address, if applicable), nationality, name of the administrator, chief executive officer, officer or attorney-in-fact empowered to act on behalf of the legal entity, corporate business, activity or industry, Federal Tax Payer Registry (*Registro Federal de Contribuyentes*) and Tax Payer Identification (*Cédula de Identificación Fiscal*) issued by the SHCP, a copy of the company's or legal entity's public deed containing its articles of incorporation and byelaws duly registered and any other document evidencing its domicile, such as proof of payment of real estate tax, lease agreement and electricity, telephone or water services bills.

Foreign individuals and entities

[20.9] Foreign individuals and entities must comply with the equivalent requirements for Mexican entities or individuals and, additionally, must comply with the following: (i) individuals must present their passport and (ii) legal entities must show certified documents evidencing its legal incorporation and the formal powers of attorney of its legal representative and the passport of such legal representative.

Financial institutions must adopt guidelines in order to maintain and update the information and documents of their clients' identification file and, for that purpose, must verify and request the updated information and documents on a reasonable and continuing basis, especially when significant changes in the usual transactional patterns of a client are observed or whenever there are doubts about the accuracy as to such information or documentation.

The documents included in the client identification files must be kept by financial institutions during the tenure of the account or agreement and thereafter digitalised for at least ten years.

Internal procedures and training programmes

[20.10]   The internal procedure and training requirements are comprised of three parts: creating policy manuals and approval, training employees in detection, reporting and legal compliance in accordance with the policy manual and developing systems (electronic or manual) for meeting institutional reporting requirements.

The policy manual developed by financial institutions must include information pertaining to the detection of suspicious transactions for elevated reporting priority to the relevant authorities. Recommended criteria for consideration include the amount, frequency and type of transaction, the locations and regions in which the transactions are executed, the background and prior transactional history of the client, the types of monetary instruments used or requested, unusual amount or complexity of the transaction and apparent attempts to structure transactions so as to avoid triggering the US$10,000 value threshold and reporting requirements. An effective manual should also include information pertaining to reporting requirements, the governing rules, penalties for their breach and procedures for evaluating and verifying compliance, procedures for preventing illegal transactions and policies ensuring that training guidelines are met. The policy manual must be filed with, and approved by, the SHCP.

Training programmes should be instituted regularly and should cover matters included in the policy manual pertaining to the detection of suspicious transactions, proper reporting procedures, legal compliance and situation management, especially upon any change or modification of the rules material to any relevant subject.

Electronic or manual systems should be established to serve as a standard institutional method for the reporting of relevant transactions to the proper authorities on a regular basis. Penalties for non-compliance are strict; consequently, methods for ensuring proper functioning of surveillance systems must be implemented.

Reporting transactions

[20.11]   Three classes of transactions require subsequent notification to the competent authorities.

Reporting of relevant transactions

[20.12]   For the purposes of the Rules, a relevant transaction is a transaction for, or in excess of, US$10,000, its equivalent in pesos or in any other currency ('relevant transactions').

Financial institutions must deliver a quarterly report to the CNBV with the

470

information required in the relevant transaction's official reporting format issued by the SHCP no later than ten business days after the closing of the quarter. Such reporting must be made through electronic, magnetic or any other means, pursuant to the terms and conditions established by the SHCP.

Reporting of unusual transactions

[20.13] For the purposes of the Rules, an unusual transaction is any transaction, activity, conduct or behaviour that does not correspond with the history or activity known or declared by the client, or with his or her usual precedent of transactional behaviour, with respect to the amount, frequency, type or nature of a given transaction, without any reasonable explanation for such behaviour, or any transaction that, for any other reason, the financial institution considers the resources may lead to the support of, provide assistance to, help or co-operate in any way with the perpetration of money laundering and terrorism.

Financial institutions must send their reports of unusual transactions to the SHCP, through the CNBV, no later than 30 calendar days after the date on which the transaction is known whether by system, model, procedure or by an employee of the financial institutions, whichever occurs first.

In order to characterise an unusual transaction, financial institutions must consider, among others, the following principal circumstances, whether they arise separately or jointly:

1 types, amounts, frequency and nature of commonly carried out transactions in relation to their own background and the known commercial activities of the client;
2 unusual material amounts, complexity and non-frequent types of transactions carried out by clients and/or users of the financial institutions;
3 transactions carried out under an account in monetary instruments considered for the purposes of relevant transactions in multiple or fractioned amounts that, if added during five days, are equal to or the equivalent of US$10,000;
4 whenever clients or users attempt to bribe or threaten the financial institution's personnel in order to obtain co-operation to carry out unusual transactions against the Rules or any other manual or anti-money laundering provision;
5 whenever the transactions intended to be carried out by clients or users involve countries or jurisdictions that: (i) Mexican law considers apply preferred tax regimes or (ii) in the opinion of international organisations to which Mexico is a member, do not have measures to prevent, detect and stop transactions with illicit sources or the implementation of such measures is not efficient. In this respect, the SHCP provides periodical lists which include the countries and jurisdictions which are suspect; and
6 whenever it is believed or there are doubts with regard to a client as to whether he is a front for a third party.

In order to facilitate the process of identification of unusual transactions, the SHCP shall assist the financial institutions on a regular basis and shall provide guidelines, information and categories that allow recognition of transactions to be reported under the Rules.

In the event that a relevant transaction meets the characteristics of an unusual transaction, the financial institution must issue separate reports in connection with the same transaction.

Reporting of suspicious transactions

[20.14]   For the purposes of the Rules, a suspicious transaction is any transaction, activity or behaviour of directors, officers, employees or attorneys-in-fact of the financial institutions that may breach or contravene compliance with the Law or the Rules or any other transaction or activity that may be deemed as uncommon by the financial institutions ('suspicious transactions').

Financial institutions must send their reports of suspicious transactions to the SHCP, through the CNBV, no later than 30 calendar days after the date on which the transaction is known, whether by system, model, procedure or by the employee of the financial institution, whichever occurs first. Official forms issued by the SHCP, through electronic or any other means that complies with the terms and specifications set out by such Ministry, must be followed.

In order to characterise a suspicious transaction, financial institutions must take into account the following circumstances or possible events:

1   whenever it is observed that any executive, officer, employee or attorney-in-fact of the financial institution in question maintains a superior living standard than that corresponding to his income;
2   whenever, without due cause, any executive, officer, employee or attorney-in-fact of the financial institution has repeatedly participated in the performance of unusual transactions;
3   whenever there are suspicions that any executive, officer, employee or attorney-in-fact of the financial institution may have performed acts, may have failed to act or is involved in transactions that may support, provide assistance to, help or co-operate with the perpetration of money laundering and terrorism; and
4   whenever, without explanation, there is a lack of consistency between the duties entrusted to an executive, officer, employee or attorney-in-fact of a financial institution and the activities actually carried out.

In addition to the three types of transactions that require notification to the authorities mentioned above, financial institutions must, where possible, apply the Rules in their foreign branches and affiliates, specially those located in countries where no anti-money laundering regulations exist or where these types of regulations are not sufficiently enforced.

SANCTIONS

[20.15]   Financial institutions may not reveal confidential information, with the exception of information required by the competent authorities in the prosecution of felonies, ie tax evasion, terrorism or money laundering.

To safeguard confidential information, the Rules provide that officials of the SHCP and the CNBV, as well as the employees, officers, directors, statutory and external auditors of financial institutions, must maintain strict confidence with regard to any reports and information required to be delivered under the Rules and must abstain from releasing such privileged information to any third party other than the financial authorities.

Sanctions for failing to comply with Mexican regulations to counter money laundering may be imposed by means of civil or criminal penalties. At a civil level, failure effectively and in a timely manner to comply with client information gathering and file maintenance provisions, policy manual development and registration and/or the establishment of appropriate systems may subject a financial institution to a fine of up to the equivalent of approximately US$450,000.

At a criminal level, intentionally obstructing, failing to report, structuring or otherwise distorting transactions for the purposes of thwarting the reporting process with respect to one or more transactions may result in a prison term of five to 15 years and fines. If three or more persons are implicated as acting in concert to orchestrate such activities, they may face additional imprisonment for breaking organised crime statutes.

In connection with money laundering, the Federal Criminal Procedure Code (*Código Federal de Procedimientos Penales*) allows the Federal Public Prosecutor to confiscate assets related to such crime if all available judicial resources are exhausted.

CONCLUSIONS

[20.16]   Traditional practices in bank secrecy in Mexico have been sustained as a hallmark of financial institutions. Although new safeguards have arisen to detect illegal activities such as tax evasion, money laundering and terrorism, a developing legal framework continues to distinguish between relevant information for prosecution purposes and the right to maintain certain information confidential by financial institutions and the banking authorities. Although bank secrecy and confidentiality provisions have been increasingly regulated, globalisation and the economic integration of Mexico will undoubtedly continue to define and redefine the lines between public access and private domain of confidential information. Citizens and investors must be aware that the protection of bank secrecy in Mexico may not be a priority in our system.

21 The Netherlands

Victor P G de Serière[1]

INTRODUCTION

[21.1]   There is no statutory law in The Netherlands on the duty of confidentiality owed by banks to their customers. There are certain statutory rules which deal with aspects of bank secrecy:

1   article 10 of the constitution of The Netherlands lays down the principle of protection against disclosure of personal data;
2   article 64 of the Banking Act provides for the confidential treatment of data obtained by the Dutch central bank (*de Nederlandsche Bank NV*, often referred to as the 'DNB') in the course of its supervisory duties;
3   articles 31ff of the Securities Transactions Supervision Act contain similar provisions in respect of data available to the Financial Markets Authority (*de Autoriteit Financiële Markten*, 'AFM'), the governmental watchdog over financial markets and transactions in The Netherlands;
4   articles 63ff of the Financial Services Act contain provisions similar to those set out in arts 31ff of the Securities Transactions Supervision Act;
5   article 272 of the Criminal Code makes it a criminal offence to disclose data if confidentiality is required because of the nature of the function or profession of the person holding such data or on the basis of an express provision of the law;
6   the Act on the Protection of Personal Data provides for detailed regulations applicable in all cases where personal data relating to individuals is compiled and used.

These are examples of specific statutory provisions relating to certain instances of bank confidentiality. However, a general statutory rule on bank confidentiality does not exist; the duty of confidentiality which, under Dutch law, a bank generally owes its customer is based on the contractual relationship between the bank and its customers.

There is currently no discussion in The Netherlands on the question of whether such general statutory rules ought to be introduced. The arguments in favour of introducing legislation on this subject are:

1   the scope of the duty of confidentiality based on the contractual relationship between the customer and the bank is unclear;
2   there are numerous exceptions to the duty, which are not in any way co-ordinated and for this reason inconsistent with one another; and
3   there is uncertainty as to the territorial scope of the duty of confidentiality and on the effect of foreign law and judgments as constituting exceptions to the duty.

1 The author gratefully acknowledges the invaluable help given by Sandra Teerink of Allen & Overy in accomplishing the update of this chapter in the 4th edition of this book.

These arguments, which are in themselves convincing, have so far not led to any debate on the need for regulation of this subject matter in The Netherlands. The main reason for this is that the system, based on a general contractual duty to a certain measure eroded by various statutory disclosure obligations, is generally deemed to work satisfactorily both from the banks' and the customers' point of view. In addition, the drafting of a law on this subject will be a complex task requiring many existing statutory rules in different Acts to be amended; why embark on this if there is no certainty that the result will be any better than the current situation?

THE BANK'S DUTY OF CONFIDENTIALITY
The duty of confidentiality under civil law

[21.2] Under Dutch law, there undoubtedly exists a duty of banks to maintain confidentiality towards their customers. This duty is generally deemed to be based on the contractual relationship between the bank and its customers. This relationship, more often than not, is governed by the General Bank Conditions (*Algemene Bankvoorwaarden*) which have been developed by the Dutch Banking Association (*Nederlandse Vereniging van Banken*, 'NVB') in co-operation with its members and after consultation with consumer representative organisations. Banks in The Netherlands will invariably endeavour to ensure that these General Bank Conditions are part of the contractual relationship. The General Bank Conditions provide in art 2:

> 'The bank shall exercise due care in providing services. It will thereby, to the best of its ability, take into consideration the interests of the customer provided, however, that it is not required to use information which is available to it, but which is not in the public domain, including information which may affect quoted prices of securities.'

The phrases to 'exercise due care' and 'to the best of its ability, take into consideration the interests of the customer' are considered, inter alia, to contain the duty to maintain customer data confidentiality.

The proviso in art 2 that the bank is not required to use non-public information available to it is curious; essentially, it relates to the dilemma with which a bank may be confronted when the investment advisory departments of the bank are providing investment advice (or research reports) to its customers whilst, in other departments of the bank (for example, the credit department or corporate finance department), data is available which is confidential, but which is certainly relevant to the investment advice to be given or to the contents of research reports that the bank publishes. This problem will be addressed later in this chapter.

The duty of care and the duty to take into consideration the interests of customers would apply to the relationship between a bank and its customer even if they had not been expressed in the General Bank Conditions. These duties are generally considered applicable on the basis of the principle of reasonableness and fairness which is a cornerstone of the Dutch law of contract: see arts 6:2 and 6:248 of the Civil Code. The question arises whether the General Bank Conditions, by explicitly referring to this duty of care and this duty to take into consideration the interests of the customers, impose on banks obligations that are more far reaching than the obligations imposed by the principles of reasonableness and fairness of arts 6:2 and 6:248. In Dutch legal doctrine, it is argued that this is indeed the case, however, without specification as to what such extended duty may mean in practical terms.

The General Bank Conditions do not contain any specific provisions on the extent of the duty of confidentiality. Questions such as which data must be kept confidential and which data may, without the consent of the customer, be disclosed must be solved on an ad hoc basis, each time taking into account the specific circumstances in which the question arises. The General Bank Conditions likewise contain no provisions on exceptions to the general principle. Generally, the duty is thought to extend to all data that is not in the public domain. Obviously, where there is a legal duty to disclose (eg on the basis of a statute or by order of a court or supervisory authority), the duty to disclose would prevail. By and large, banks in The Netherlands are quite meticulous about maintaining the duty of confidentiality and will tend to seek customer consent whenever banks think this duty may arguably be breached.

Surprisingly perhaps, in The Netherlands there is virtually no case law on the extent of the duty of confidentiality based on art 2 of the General Bank Conditions. This absence of case law appears to indicate that, in practice, few occasions arise where there is a dispute between bank and customer in the application of the duty of confidentiality. A more down to earth reason for the absence of case law may be that the very reason why a customer is interested in a bank's strict adherence to rules of confidentiality often also constitutes a very good reason for that customer not to litigate on the issue.

There is one judgment of the District Court in Zwolle that perhaps deserves to be mentioned here.[2] In this case, the bank had advised a third party of the precarious financial condition of one of its customers. The third party was also doing business with this customer and providing it with financial facilities. Although it could be argued that it was logical and defensible for the bank to provide information to the third party, particularly given the context of discussions that had been conducted between all parties involved, the bank was nevertheless held liable. The judgment is of a lower court and therefore perhaps not too much weight should be given to it. Nevertheless, the judgment provides a clear warning that implied consent of a customer should not be easily assumed. Additionally, the judgment seems to indicate that also in (the early stages of) restructuring exercises, especially where lenders are not protected by commonly applicable disclosure provisions in the credit documentation, one should be careful about the exchange of information that is not specifically condoned by the borrower in distress.

What happens if the General Bank Conditions are not applicable? In certain contractual relations, for example, often in transactions between banks inter se and sometimes in transactions between banks and large corporate customers, the applicability of the General Bank Conditions is excluded. In addition, it is noted that the General Bank Conditions will not apply in relationships between customers and the foreign offices of a Dutch bank (see art 1 of the General Bank Conditions); in other words, applicability is territorially limited. Also, it is noted that the General Bank Conditions will only apply if expressly agreed upon by the customer. Implied acceptance of the General Bank Conditions is not easily assumed.

Where the General Bank Conditions do not apply, the duty of confidentiality would, in the present writer's view, still fully apply on the basis of the principles of

---

2 JOR 2000/130, dated 22 December 1999.

reasonableness and fairness discussed above (assuming, of course, that Dutch law applies). There is no logical justification for discriminating between these situations and those where art 2 applies, but where application is excluded for reasons of territoriality, a different approach must be taken: first, it must be determined, using the relevant conflicts of laws rules, which law applies to the contractual relationship concerned and whether a duty of confidentiality exists and what such duty entails must then be determined according to the applicable law.

The duty of confidentiality under criminal law

[21.3]   Article 272 of the Dutch Criminal Code provides:

> 'He who deliberately discloses a secret where he should know or reasonably be aware that because of his function or profession or a statutory provision, or because of his previous function or profession he is obliged not to disclose that secret, will be punished …'

Article 273 provides:

> '(1) He who deliberately discloses information relating to a trading or industrial or service enterprise with which he works or has worked, concerning which information a duty of secrecy has been imposed on him, or (2) he who discloses or uses non-public information which was obtained in the commission of a crime from automated data relating to a trading or industrial or service enterprise and such disclosure and use may damage such enterprise, will be punished …'

While art 272 addresses the breach of a general duty not to disclose confidential information acquired by a person in the performance of his function or profession, the scope of art 273(1) is rather more limited; it only relates to information concerning the enterprise where the person in question works or has worked. In other words, an employee of a bank would not necessarily be in breach of art 273(1) if he disclosed information about a customer rather than about the bank itself.

This chapter will not expand on the meaning of these provisions of criminal law, except to note the following. In its judgment of 18 December 1974,[3] the Amsterdam Court of Appeal determined, with respect to art 272, that the profession of a banker is not of such confidential nature that a duty of secrecy in relation to information which is obtained in the exercise of his profession may be considered to exist. This judgment is of course principally relevant in the criminal law context. The judgment has been criticised on the grounds that the underlying reasoning appeared to address the question of whether a banker could excuse himself from acting as a witness in legal proceedings (this relates to the privilege of refusal to testify, *verschoningsrecht*) rather than to answer the question of whether a duty of secrecy exists per se with respect to the profession of a banker even though there is no statutory basis for such duty of secrecy. The decision of the Court of Appeal was not submitted to the Supreme Court. Although the reasoning may be suspect, the decision itself is nevertheless approved in the legal doctrine; the nature of the profession of a banker is not such that a secrecy duty towards third parties should be deemed necessarily inherent in that profession. This duty to maintain secrecy thus denied to bankers is generally deemed to apply to, inter alia, notaries, lawyers, tax advisers, accountants, doctors and psychiatrists. It should be noted, with respect to these categories of professionals, that the fact that they are subject to a duty of secrecy pursuant to the

3 NJ 1975, 441.

provisions of art 272 does not necessarily mean that, for that reason, they have the privilege of refusal to testify in criminal proceedings pursuant to the provisions of arts 218 and 191 of the Code of Criminal Procedure; whether this privilege applies basically depends on whether a statutory basis for such privilege can be construed; this statutory basis must demonstrate that the legislator deemed the critical importance of confidentiality to outweigh the serious disadvantage of possible obstruction of justice. The exact boundaries of the privilege are thus unclear. For instance, it is now subject to debate in The Netherlands whether perhaps even a suspect's counsel could be made to testify in criminal proceedings against the suspect on issues where the traditional client–attorney privilege does not apply. Obviously, if that were permitted, this privilege is under serious threat and it is hoped that the Dutch courts will shortly set clear boundaries that remove this threat.

The duty of confidentiality pursuant to certain specific statutory provisions

[21.4] There are numerous statutes which provide for specific duties of confidentiality to be maintained. This chapter will not discuss all of these statutes, but will mention the following.

The Banking Act

[21.5] Article 64 of the Banking Act (*Wet toezicht kredietwezen* 1992) provides for the confidential treatment of data collected by the DNB in the course of its supervisory duties. These provisions enact the requirements on this subject imposed by the Second Banking Directive (Council Directive 89/646/EEC). The duty of confidentiality imposed on the DNB may, however, not prevent the DNB from using such data wherever necessary to perform its duties under the Banking Act. In this connection, one could think of the duty to assess whether an institution is subject to bank licence requirements, investigations as to the solvency or liquidity of a bank, the imposition of sanctions, the need for defence in cases of legal proceedings in which the DNB is involved, the exchange of information with the AFM or central bank authorities in other countries, etc. Article 64(5) of the Banking Act does allow the DNB to publish data acquired in the course of the exercise of its duties provided this data is anonymous (ie the identity of the financial institution involved cannot be deduced from the data published). The DNB and the AFM can publish a public warning regarding the fact that a certain entity is acting in breach of legislation, ie is active without a licence. Also, they can publish the fact that they have imposed a fine or a cease or desist penalty to a specific entity. The general view is that supervisory authorities should restrain themselves in publishing such facts. The current proposal for the Financial Supervision Act (*Wet op het financieel toezicht*), an Act which is intended to encompass, modernise and harmonise all existing Dutch laws on financial supervision and which is expected to be promulgated in 2007, contains a provision (art 1:81) to the effect that the supervisory authorities are in principle required to publish every fine or cease or desist penalty they have imposed on an entity. This leaves no room for consideration of the legitimate interests of the entity involved. This provision triggered severe criticism and it is as yet unclear whether it will be maintained in the final version of the Financial Supervision Act.

The Second Banking Directive leaves it to the domestic legislation of the member states to determine whether central bank officials have the privilege of refusal to testify in (criminal or civil) legal proceedings. Article 64 of the Dutch Banking Act provides that this privilege is not available in the case of criminal or civil proceedings. The privilege is, however, available to bank officials for those cases where they have been involved in an attempt at the financial restructuring of a bank: see art 64(4) of the Banking Act.

Finally, art 65 of the Banking Act provides for the disclosure of data to governmental agencies (both in The Netherlands and abroad). This disclosure is subject to restrictions and covenants which are not discussed here, but which are principally designed to prevent – to the extent practically feasible – the abuse of such data.

The securities laws

[21.6]   Article 31 of the Securities Transactions Supervision Act 1995 (*Wet toezicht effectenverkeer*, 'STSA') provides that data obtained by the AFM may not be published and is secret. The provisions of art 31 are clearly derived from those of art 64 of the Dutch Banking Act. With respect to the privilege of refusal to testify, the same system as described above applies. It is to be noted that art 31(5) allows the Minister of Finance to publish information provided such information cannot be attributed to individual enterprises or institutions. This provision corresponds with art 64(5) of the Banking Act described above. In addition, corresponding with art 65 of the Banking Act, art 33 allows the disclosure of data to governmental agencies both in The Netherlands and abroad, subject to basically the same restrictions and caveats mentioned above. Article 48 of the STSA allows for the disclosure to the public of certain data if disclosure enhances compliance with the STSA. This data includes refusals to grant licences, withdrawals of licences, the names and particulars of institutions that operate without a licence, etc. It is noted that there is no corresponding provision in the Banking Act.

The Financial Services Act

[21.7]   This Act (*Wet Financiele Dienstverlening*, 'WFD') came into force on 1 January 2006. It partially replaces the Act on Consumer Credit and mainly covers the provision of financial services to consumers. These services consist of advising, offering or brokering in credit transactions, mortgage loans, insurances, certain savings products, securities and certain other categories of investments. Article 63 of the WFD provides for similar provisions at those contained in the STSA described above. The supervisory authority for the implementation of the WFD is also the AFM.

The Act on the Protection of Personal Data

[21.8]   The Act on the Protection of Personal Data (*Wet bescherming persoonsgegevens*) aims to protect the right to privacy of individuals whose data is compiled in data systems. This Act serves to implement Council Directive 95/46/EC of 24 October 1995 and came into force on 1 September 2001. The Act imposes certain obligations on those who wish to compile and use personal data (the so-called 'controller'). These obligations include the following:

1   personal data may only be collected for specified, explicit and legitimate purposes;
2   personal data may only be processed if:
    (a) the subject has unambiguously given his consent or if this is necessary in the context of,

(b) the performance of a contract to which the individual concerned is a party,

(c) the fulfilment of statutory duties or public functions,

(d) vital interests of the data subject, or

(e) processing is necessary for the purposes of legitimate interests pursued by the controller, except where such interests are overridden by privacy interests;

3 data may only be used if this is done in a manner compatible with the purposes for which it was compiled;

4 if the purposes for which the data was compiled has been achieved, the data may, in principle, no longer be maintained in a manner where the identity of the individuals concerned may still be determined. There is an exception for continued maintenance of data for statistical and academic purposes;

5 it is prohibited to compile and use data relating to religion, race or ethnic origin, political opinions, health, sex life and membership of trade unions unless one of the statutory exemptions applies;

6 technical and organisational measures must be taken to protect personal data against accidental or unlawful destruction or accidental loss, alteration, unauthorised disclosure or access and the personal data must be accurate and kept up to date.

The Act contains elaborate statutory provisions requiring disclosure of the data to the individual concerned and protecting its legitimate interests. These statutory provisions will not be further described in this chapter.

The Act allows for a certain measure of self-regulation. Thus, in certain sectors of the economy, organisations of persons or entities that wish to set up data systems may develop and adopt codes of conduct. These codes of conduct can be submitted to the supervisory authority (*College bescherming persoonsgegevens*), which will then determine whether or not they comply with the requirements of the Act. It is clear that the Act applies to the data processing relating to customers maintained by banks in The Netherlands. The Privacy Code of Conduct for the Banking Industry was originally developed and issued by the NVB on 29 March 1989. It has since been revised. The supervisory authority has meanwhile confirmed that the revised Code is in line with the requirements of the Act.

THE EXCEPTIONS TO THE DUTY OF NON-DISCLOSURE

Express or implied consent of the customer

[21.9] An exception to the bank's duty of confidentiality exists if the customer consents to disclosure.

Express consent

[21.10] If the customer issues its express consent to the bank, the bank is discharged from its duty of confidentiality. The express consent can be provided once to cover all future communications and can be given in any form: in writing or verbally. Verbal consents may, in the event of subsequent disputes, give rise to evidentiary problems; banks are well advised to have consents properly documented. It is generally not advisable for banks to use a system whereby the bank requests consent on the condition that if the customer does not respond, consent will be deemed to have been given.

Implied consent

[21.11] A customer may issue an implied consent. If, for instance, a customer instructs or mandates a bank to carry out a certain transaction, it may generally be assumed that this instruction or mandate includes an authorisation for the bank to do all such things as are reasonably necessary or appropriate to implement such instruction or mandate, including disclosure of data concerning the customer concerned. Should it, however, be uncertain whether the customer understands or reasonably ought to understand that disclosure is necessary to carry out the instruction or mandate, it will be prudent for the bank to double check with the customer. The judgment of the Zwolle District Court,[4] discussed above, corroborates this.

Should a contract contain specific provisions to the effect that a bank is not required to keep client data confidential, a bank should still, when contemplating disclosure, consider whether, under the circumstances of the matter at hand, disclosure would be unduly harmful to the customer. The general principle of reasonableness and fairness requires this.

Consent directives

[21.12] With regard to the US practice of consent directives, the following comments from a Dutch law perspective are made. There is no doctrine or case law on this issue. However, if there is a consent directive signed by a customer on the basis of a US court order to sign, a bank in The Netherlands would, in the present author's view, in principle treat such consent as a valid consent to disclose. Whether a consent directive constitutes a valid consent should arguably be determined in accordance with principles of Dutch law which govern the relationship between bank and customer. If such consent is given under coercion (*bedreiging*: see art 3:44(2) of the Dutch Civil Code), the consent would be subject to nullification by the customer concerned, but a US court order cannot of itself constitute coercion under Dutch civil law. This is because coercion is, under Dutch law, only recognised if such coercion is 'illegal' (*onrechtmatig*) and, of course, a court order cannot by definition be illegal. The question arises whether by considering such consent directive a proper consent under Dutch law, The Netherlands would unjustifiably grant extra-territorial effect to a foreign judgment, which is not in itself enforceable in The Netherlands. The answer to this question must, in the present writer's view, be negative; if the fact that the consent is obtained by way of the threat of fines or imprisonment in the US does not in itself constitute coercion, the circumstance that a US court order underlies the consent directive should not be relevant from a Dutch law point of view.

Disclosure in the interests of the bank

[21.13] Disclosure in the interests of the bank is not under Dutch law specifically recognised as a valid exception to the rule of non-disclosure. However, when a bank is suing to recover from a customer overdue indebtedness, it goes without saying that such bank may make such disclosures as are necessary to protect its position. The

---

4 JOR 200/130, dated 22 December 1999.

same undoubtedly applies if a bank is a defendant in a suit brought by its customer. No one will argue that the defences of the bank would in such a case be curtailed by its duty of confidentiality.

This being said, the question arises as to what is the legal basis for this exception to the rule of confidentiality. Must the customer be deemed to have given an implied consent to the bank when the credit facility concerned was granted to him to disclose in case of his default? In the second instance, must the customer be deemed to have given his implied consent when he commenced litigation? This, it seems, can be convincingly argued. Furthermore, the argument could be made that the right of the customer to confidentiality in such cases must be deemed inferior to the more fundamental and therefore stronger right to substantiate one's position in legal proceedings.

The situation becomes somewhat more difficult, however, if the bank is involved in litigation with third parties where the bank would be better off if it could disclose details of transactions with other customers. In such a situation, could the bank make such disclosures without being exposed to liability towards such other customers? In these situations, the bank should generally not have the right to disclose without the customer's consent, but it appears arguable that the bank's fundamental right to substantiate its position in legal proceedings should also prevail in this case. There is no case law on this point.

The need to disclose customer data also arises in the context of takeovers of banks. The acquirer will wish to conduct extensive due diligence with respect to the target and this inevitably entails scrutiny of customer files. In these cases, it is impracticable to obtain customer consent or to anonymise data. Clearly, in these situations, the target cannot invoke any exception to his duty of confidentiality. One solution to this dilemma is to arrange for customer files to be scrutinised on a confidential basis by the acquirer's external accountants or legal advisers and that the data on customers in the due diligence reports is anonymous, but in case of 'problem files' where the target's exposure is significant, this approach is obviously inadequate. In that case, customer consent would probably have to be obtained.

A disclosure dilemma may also arise in the case of lending by bank syndicates. Here, the agency function is often entrusted to a relationship bank of the customer and there will usually be a significant disparity between the information available to the agent and that available to other syndicate banks. The credit documentation concerned normally does not address this issue and implied disclosure consent cannot always easily be construed. The dilemma may become even more acute where there are several layers of debt (senior, mezzanine, subordinated, high yield, etc) with different financial institutions acting as agents or trustees. Prudence would also suggest that in these instances customer consent should be obtained.

Disclosure within the banking group

[21.14]   A distinction must be made here between disclosure from one legal entity to another and disclosure by one department to the other within the same entity.

In so far as disclosure between one legal entity and another, both belonging to the same banking group, is concerned, the correct position must be that the legal concept of a group is not relevant in this context. A customer has a contractual relationship with one particular legal entity and that contractual relationship does not by implication or otherwise extend to other legal entities belonging to the same group.

In practical terms, of course, this position is rather difficult to implement. Consider the situation where a bank decides to discontinue extending credit to a customer because of the customer's threatened insolvency; if this customer then applies for a leasing transaction with a leasing subsidiary of the bank, may the bank inform its subsidiary of the increased credit risk or will a duty of confidentiality be breached by such action? The answer to this question is unclear. In Dutch banking practice, intra-group sharing of information is probably commonly done. The legal basis for this practice is likely to be implied customer consent.

In so far as disclosures between different departments within the same legal entity are concerned, there are no specific statutory or contractual restrictions to the flow of confidential information. There may be restrictions on the basis of Chinese Walls. The concept of Chinese Walls is discussed further at the end of the chapter.

Credit reference agencies

[**21.15**]   There are many credit reference agencies operating in The Netherlands. They are not subject to specific regulatory constraints. The banks are prevented, by virtue of their duty of confidentiality, to contribute to the data compiled by these agencies. There is no exception from this duty based on the general notion that disclosure is 'in the public interest' or on the basis that banks could, by disclosing credit risk to such agencies, legitimately protect their own positions. The banks are not statutorily restricted in using the data compiled by these agencies.

There is one agency, the Foundation for the Registration of Credit Data, better known as the 'BKR', which is a dominant force in this area. The BKR has been established by banks and financial institutions to prevent the occurrence of payment defaults, in particular, in relation to private loans to consumers. A bank or financial institution can become a participant by payment of an annual fee. Each participant is required to obtain information from the system if it intends to extend credit to a customer; this requirement is based on the provisions of the Consumer Credit Act (*Wet op het consumentenkrediet*) and the WFD. The system is very popular and is widely used for the purpose of checking credit data when extending loans or consumer credits to individual customers. More than 20,000 credit checks are routinely carried out daily. There are elaborate internal rules governing the provision of information to participants and third parties and providing for protection of the BKR's data banks. The operations of the BKR are subject to the detailed requirements of the Act on the Protection of Personal Data, discussed above.

Disclosure required by law

[**21.16**]   A distinction can be made between disclosures required by court judgments on the one hand and disclosures required by statutory provisions on the other.

Compulsion by court judgment

[**21.17**]   Here, a distinction could be made between various categories of court judgments and court orders. A much generalised attempt at such categorisation is made below (but note that the resulting scheme somewhat simplifies the issues):

1   a final domestic court judgment;
2   a domestic court judgment where a remedy is still available;

3   a domestic arbitral award; and
4   a domestic binding advice (*bindend advies*).

In 3 and 4, again, a distinction could be made between the situation where remedies are still available and the situation where this is not the case, but this will lead to an undesirable level of detail. A similar distinction could be made for foreign judgments, awards and advice:

1   a final foreign court judgment, order or subpoena not enforceable in The Netherlands;
2   a foreign court judgment where a remedy is still available, but not enforceable in The Netherlands;
3   a foreign court judgment that has become enforceable in The Netherlands;
4   a foreign arbitral award not enforceable in The Netherlands; and
5   a foreign arbitral award that has become enforceable in The Netherlands.

In the Dutch context, the question whether a judgment, order, subpoena or award will set aside the duty of confidentiality must always be considered from the viewpoint that this duty is a contractual one, which is not in any way specifically worked out in the contractual relationship between the bank and its customer. Thus, the answer to this question will very much depend on what should be considered reasonable and fair in the circumstances. This leads to an unfortunate uncertainty as to what the correct position in a given case would be. The Dutch banking community could, by promulgating rules on this subject (which could be made part of the General Bank Conditions or could be a separate code which the banks could, for instance, apply except where deviating contractual arrangements are made with customers), clarify their (and their customers') position, but no initiative has (yet) been taken to this end.

A final domestic court judgment

[21.18]   Here, there is no question that compliance with the judgment will be a justified exception to the duty of confidentiality. It is difficult to perceive any argument on the basis of which compliance with the court judgment could be denied. The only conceivable area of contention would be the interpretation of the meaning and extent of the court judgment.

A domestic court judgment where remedies are still available

[21.19]   In this situation, the question arises whether the judgment is enforceable from its rendition. If so, again, it would be difficult to construe any argument for non-compliance. Under certain circumstances, one could imagine that a bank could convincingly take the position that it ought to wait until the judgment has become final. This position would normally be the logical position to adopt if the judgment concerned is not immediately enforceable.

Domestic arbitral awards and advice

[21.20]   In these instances, there are no compelling reasons under Dutch law to take any other position than that described above with respect to judgments. With respect to binding advice, however, a bank may argue that it is entitled to refuse disclosure until the advice is confirmed by a court judgment to be enforceable.

Final foreign court judgments, orders or subpoenas not enforceable in The Netherlands

[21.21] Here, the position is difficult. There is no dependable case law. Could a bank reasonably argue that it may comply with such final court judgment even if it is not (yet) enforceable in The Netherlands? Is it, to put this question in a slightly different perspective, under all circumstances justified that the formality of obtaining an *exequatur* or a confirming domestic court judgment must first be taken care of? It is, at first sight, perfectly acceptable for a bank to take the position that it wishes to comply with a final foreign court judgment, even if it is not enforceable, but then, if the bank so complies, it effectively deprives its customer from the remedies which the customer might have if the claimant concerned were to seek recognition of its judgment in The Netherlands. It appears difficult to argue that a bank should be entitled to do this.

Foreign court judgments which are neither final nor enforceable

[21.22] Here, the bank would, under ordinary circumstances, be ill-advised to follow the foreign judgment. The argument that the bank, by doing this, will deprive the customer from (at least) two opportunities to employ remedies appears conclusive. The foregoing does not provide an answer for those cases where foreign courts serve a disclosure order or subpoena on the local branch office of a bank. In such cases, the bank is faced with the dilemma that a refusal to comply will expose it to sanctions in the foreign jurisdiction concerned, whilst compliance may entail a breach of its duty of confidentiality at home. In instances where there is doubt as to the correct position, a solution could be for the bank or the customer concerned to obtain a court order in The Netherlands in preliminary relief proceedings. The question will then arise, of course, of whether a Dutch judgment upholding the duty of confidence would constitute sufficient excuse for the foreign court concerned to allow non-compliance.

Foreign court judgments which have been made enforceable in The Netherlands

[21.23] The position is the same as discussed above with respect to final domestic court judgments.

Foreign arbitral awards

[21.24] With these, again, there are no compelling reasons to take any other position than as described above with respect to foreign court judgments.

The question how a court judgment becomes enforceable in The Netherlands will not be dealt with *in extenso* in this chapter, but, as stated above, the question is relevant for determining whether a bank is justified in complying with a judgment which is not enforceable in The Netherlands.

Generally, judgments will be enforced in accordance with Council Regulation 44/2001/EC of 22 December 2000 on Jurisdiction and Recognition and Enforcement of Judgments in Civil and Commercial Matters if such judgments are rendered in a country covered by the Regulation. It is to be noted that this Regulation only allows for extremely limited grounds on which enforcement of a foreign judgment can be denied: see arts 27 and 28 of the Regulation. A review of the merits of the case is not permitted under any circumstances: see art 29 of the Regulation.

Judgments obtained in countries that are not covered by the Regulation may become enforceable under the terms of the 1988 Lugano Convention on Jurisdiction and the Enforcement of Judgments in Civil and Commercial Matters (this is the Convention which aims to extend the original EU Convention that the Regulation has now replaced to EFTA member states). If neither the Regulation nor the Convention applies, there may be an applicable bilateral convention. The Netherlands does not have bilateral conventions with the US or Japan. If there is no bilateral convention, the claims in question must be re-litigated. In that case, if certain conditions are met, ie:

1   the foreign court in question has jurisdiction according to internationally accepted standards;
2   the judgment results from proceedings compatible with Dutch concepts of due process; and
3   the judgment does not contravene Dutch public policy;

then the foreign judgment will be recognised by the Dutch courts and they will give the same relief as the foreign judgment without re-litigation of the merits. The general description above as to the enforcement of judgments in The Netherlands is relevant to the extent that it demonstrates that, under certain (but generally quite limited) circumstances, the procedures which must be fulfilled to enforce a foreign judgment will give the defendant (or the bank's customer as intervening third party) an opportunity to oppose it. For banks which are inclined to conform to foreign judgments which are not enforceable in The Netherlands, this raises the question, discussed above, of whether they are authorised to deprive the defendant (or intervening customer) from such an opportunity.

Compulsion by statute

[21.25]   There are numerous statutory provisions requiring disclosure. This chapter will not attempt to deal with these exhaustively. However, statutory provisions that in practice appear to be the most important include the following.

Aspects relating to the collection of taxes

[21.26]   Articles 47ff of the General Act on State Taxes (*Algemene Wet Rijksbelastingen*) contain elaborate provisions on the duty to disclose data to the tax authorities. The Act provides in art 51 that no exception from this duty to disclose is allowed on the basis that the person concerned has a legal duty of secrecy. In other words, in principle, not only contractual, but also statutory duties not to disclose will be set aside for the purpose of tax collection. These duties not only relate to data on the basis of which the tax obligations of the disclosing party can be determined, but also those enabling the determination of tax obligations of third parties: see art 53. Where there is a duty to disclose information concerning third parties, only religious professionals, notaries, lawyers, doctors and pharmacists are entitled to invoke their duty of secrecy: see art 53A. Tax advisers and accountants are not legally entitled to a privilege of non-disclosure. However, pursuant to an announcement by the Ministry of Finance, tax advisers and accountants are not required to provide the tax inspector access to advice to, and correspondence with, a client within the scope of their practice (this is referred to as an informal privilege of non-disclosure).

As a consequence of these legal provisions, in principle, banks will need to disclose information on customers to the tax authorities. This obligation is also stated in art 10.8 of the Income Tax Act 2001 (*Wet op de inkomstenbelasting*) and art 22 of the Implementing Order Income Tax Act 2001 (*Uitvoeringsbesluit Wet op de inkomstenbelasting*). These oblige banks to provide information on their own accord relating to individual customers on, inter alia, savings balances, share deposits, interest and dividend receipts, annuities and endowment insurance.

The tax authorities themselves are only allowed to disclose information made available to them in the course of their duties to the extent that disclosure is necessary to implement the tax laws and to arrive at proper tax assessment or collection: see art 67(1). The Minister of Finance has the authority to grant dispensation from this duty of confidentiality. Article 67(1) does not in any way restrict the grounds on which such dispensation may be given; accordingly, there is some measure of discretion.

The judgment of the Supreme Court of 10 December 1974[5] in *Re Stad Rotterdam* may be of interest here. In an attempt to refuse to disclose information to a tax inspector (who had, for obvious reasons, asked an insurance company to disclose to him all the names of persons who had taken out insurance on pleasure boats), the insurance company, Stad Rotterdam, argued that the relevant provisions of the General Act on State Taxes are in breach of art 8 of the European Convention on Human Rights, which provides that each individual's private life, family life, home and correspondence should be respected. This argument was not accepted by the Supreme Court on the basis that art 8(2) of the Convention permits restrictions to the extent that they are 'necessary in a democratic society in the interests of the economic well being of the country'.

Inter alia, in consequence of the above Supreme Court judgment, the tax authorities and the Dutch banks deemed it necessary to clarify their mutual relationship in a Code of Conduct, which was the product of co-operation between the Ministry of Finance and an ad hoc committee representing the banks. The Code was established in 1984. The Code regulated the provision of information to the tax inspectorate relating to customers by banks in The Netherlands. The Code was replaced in 1998 by a resolution of the Director General of the Tax Administration and amended and restated by a resolution of 18 March 2002. The following features of this resolution are worth noting:

1   tax inspectors, when issuing a request for information, are not required to state the reasons for issuing such request other than to state that the information may be of interest in connection with tax assessments or tax collection against or from third parties. As a consequence, banks are, practically speaking, not in a position to argue in a given case that a request was unduly made;
2   tax inspectors should first try to obtain information from the taxpayers themselves before making requests for information to the banks. This rule aims to prevent unnecessary infringement of the duty of confidentiality which banks owe their customers. The rule does not apply if addressing the taxpayer will prejudice the position of the tax authorities;
3   information requests must be made in writing specifying the legal basis for the request;
4   banks have to comply with the request within a reasonable term, which is at most one month;

---

5 NJ 1975, 178.

5   tax inspectors are entitled to ask for non-individualised information relating to interest payments made by banks (whether as principal or intermediary), certain payments on bonds, dividend stripping activities and activities of subsidiaries of banks that engage in banking business;

6   in addition, certain other information may be requested on a non-individualised basis provided the Minister of Finance has explicitly authorised this. This authority, together with that described in 5 above, will, to a certain extent, allow 'fishing expeditions' by the tax inspectorate;

7   banks are not entitled to subject access to information to the prior consent of the customer concerned. Banks are not specifically prohibited from disclosing to their customers that an information request has been made by the tax authorities. Conversely, banks have no duty to make such disclosure and customers do not have the right to be informed by their bank or the tax authorities;

8   the tax authorities also have the right to obtain information from banks in The Netherlands in connection with foreign tax assessments or collections, but this right must be exercised pursuant to provisions of international conventions.

There is some doubt whether taxpayers can themselves invoke the benefit of the terms of this resolution. In a judgment of the Supreme Court of 23 May 1990,[6] a limited right to invoke the terms of the predecessor of this resolution, the Code of Conduct, was recognised and this was confirmed by a decision of the Dutch national Ombudsman of 21 March 2000.

In the area of tax collection in the international context, the provisions of the Act on the Provision of International Support for Tax Assessments 1986 (*Wet op de internationale bijstandverlening bij de heffing van belastingen*) are relevant. This Act was promulgated pursuant to the provisions of Council Directive 77/799/EEC of 19 December 1977 and has since been amended, inter alia, to implement EU Directive 2004/56/EU. It provides that the Minister of Finance will provide information to the competent authorities of another state (being an EU member state or another state with which a tax treaty has been conducted by The Netherlands) either at the request of such authorities or at the minister's own initiative: see arts 5, 6 and 7 of the Act. According to art 8 of the Act, the Minister of Finance may instruct an investigation to be conducted by tax officers. Such investigation could, for instance, be made in respect of books and records of banks. In the implementation of the provisions of the Act, the Dutch tax authorities are subject to the same duties of confidentiality which are imposed by art 67 of the General Act on State Taxes. On certain grounds set out in art 13 of this Act, the Minister of Finance may refuse to co-operate. These grounds include situations where considerations of Dutch 'public order' are at stake or where disclosure would lead to the revelation of commercial, industrial or professional secrets. In addition, the Act provides that the Minister of Finance may not provide information to the competent authorities of another country if there is no duty of confidentiality imposed on the tax authorities of such other country. This reciprocity principle is set out in art 14 of the Act. There is a fair amount of case law on the manner in which the provisions of this Act are implemented. This case law will not be discussed in this chapter.

Aspects relating to evidence in civil court proceedings

[21.27]   The duty of confidentiality of banks may be set aside on the basis of the rules of evidence in legal proceedings in civil matters. The rules of evidence under

---

6 BNB 1990/240.

Dutch law are set out in arts 149ff of the Code of Civil Procedure. It is important to note that there is no provision in Dutch procedural law for discovery or disclosure of documents either before or during court proceedings. An important means of proof is the examination of witnesses. This may be done during the court proceedings, at the initiative of one of the parties or at the initiative of the court itself (see art 166 of the Code of Civil Procedure) and also in preliminary hearings. These preliminary hearings (see arts 186ff) are permitted to be held according to special procedural rules designed to avoid unnecessary legal proceedings. The purpose is to extract information from counterparties unwilling to provide evidentiary documents or information voluntarily. Additionally, use is sometimes made of this procedural facility in the context of 'fishing expeditions'.

Article 165 of the Code of Civil Procedure provides that persons who are bound by a duty of secrecy in respect of information provided to them, in view of their function or profession, have the privilege of refusal to testify. This privilege applies both in testimonies taken during court proceedings and in preliminary hearings of witnesses. The privilege does not extend to employees of a bank. There are various (lower) court judgments confirming this. In the context of criminal proceedings, see the judgment of the Amsterdam Court of Appeal of 18 December 1974 discussed above.

In this context, reference should also be made to the Supreme Court judgment of 22 July 1986.[7] In that judgment, which related to the duty of secrecy imposed by statute (ie the Dutch Banking Act), the Supreme Court held the view that, in certain circumstances, the statutory duty of secrecy could be set aside depending on whether the fundamental principle that justice needs be done outweighs the requirement that secrecy be maintained; whether this is the case should be determined by the Dutch courts on an ad hoc basis. Legal writers have argued, on the basis of a Supreme Court judgment of 22 December 1989,[8] which will not be discussed in this chapter, that even in cases where there is no *statutory* duty, this determination must still take place.[9] It seems, in the present writer's opinion, that this view is only correct to the extent that the courts in taking witness testimonies should always consider whether questions put to a witness are relevant in the context of the evidence being sought.

Whenever testimonies are required to be taken abroad, this may be done by way of letters rogatory (*rogatoire commissies*) either on the basis of an applicable treaty (The Netherlands is a party to the Convention of 18 March 1970 on obtaining evidence in civil and commercial matters) or, in the absence of a treaty, on the basis of art 176 of the Code of Civil Procedure. The member states of this Convention include a number of European states and the US. Note that art 11 of the Convention deals with the question of the privilege of refusal to testify; it appears from this article that the Convention allows the privilege to be invoked not only if it is accorded by the law of the country which requests the testimony to be taken, but also if it is accorded by the law of the country where the testimony is to be taken, thus potentially expanding the legal basis for the refusal to testify. Note further that The Netherlands has declared under the Convention that it will not execute letters of request issued for the purpose of obtaining the type of pre-trial discovery of documents known in common law countries.

Finally on this subject, a brief word on civil law attachments. According to art 718 of the Code of Civil Procedure, attachments may be effected on goods and claims.

---

7 NJ 1986, 823.
8 NJ 1990, 779.
9 See, inter alia, P W Bartelings in 91/3 TVVS at 59.

Credit balances on bank current accounts and deposit accounts are 'claims' against the bank which may be attached. If attachment is made under a bank, the bank will need to make a declaration of the amount of the 'claims' which are the subject of the attachment within four weeks from the date of the attachment. The declaration must contain various details relating to the 'claims' as set out in art 476a of the Code of Civil Procedure. The bank, under which the attachment is made, is not entitled to invoke its duty of confidentiality towards the customer concerned. If the bank does not issue the required declaration, it may be forced to do so on penalty of payment of the amounts for which the attachment is effective: see art 477a(1). According to art 477a(2), the party who has effected the attachment has the right to contest the accuracy of the bank's declaration.

Aspects of the law of criminal procedure

[21.28] The Code of Criminal Procedure contains various provisions on the basis of which investigating authorities may seek information and data from banks. The following statutory provisions are mentioned without being exhaustive and without discussing these provisions in any detail.

Articles 94ff of the Code of Criminal Procedure permit the attachment of all assets which 'may serve to expose the truth or to demonstrate illegally obtained gains'. Assets which can be attached include financial assets held by suspects with banks. According to art 98, attachment may not be made on correspondence or other documents held by persons who have been granted the statutory privilege of refusal to testify. As discussed above, bank employees do not have this privilege.

Articles 126ff allow the conduct of a 'criminal financial investigation' in those cases where it is suspected that illegal financial gains are obtained in the course of the commitment of a crime in order to achieve dispossession. The principle of dispossession of illegally obtained gains is set out in art 36e of the Criminal Code. In this 'criminal financial investigation', banks may be required to disclose which assets (including moneys and securities) are held or have been held by it for the account of suspects. Assets so disclosed, including documents, may be attached. Banks and bank employees involved in this special type of investigation cannot refuse to co-operate on the basis of their duty of confidentiality towards customers.

Article 150 permits the public prosecutor, and art 192 permits the investigating judge (*rechter commissaris*), to enter premises and review items (including books and records). Although these provisions are designed principally to allow the inspection of the *locus delicti*, they may be employed in a broader context.

Article 213 provides for witnesses to be heard. Articles 217 and 218 contain provisions on the privilege of refusal to testify. As discussed above, bank employees have no right to invoke this privilege.

The Act on Identification when Providing Services

[21.29] The Act on the Determination of Identity when Providing Financial Services was promulgated on 19 May 1988 principally in an attempt to prevent tax fraud. Pursuant to Council Directive 91/308/EEC of 10 June 1991, this Act was replaced by the Act on Identification when Providing Financial Services 1993 (*Wet identificatie bij financiële dienstverlening*), which has the broader goal of also preventing money launderers from using banks and financial institutions on an anonymous basis. The 1993 Act was replaced by a new, broader Act, the Act on Identification when Providing Services 2002 (*Wet identificatie bij dienstverlening*), which has since been amended and is now also subject to further amendment. The Act imposes identification duties on 'financial institutions', which term is defined in the Act and its implementing regulations as including banks, brokers, investment funds, insurance companies, insurance brokers, securities houses and other categories of businesses designated from time to time as such by regulation. The term 'services' as used in the Act is widely defined. Accordingly, the Act does not only apply to banks and other financial institutions. The term 'services' includes, inter alia:

1   custody services for moneys, securities and other valuables;
2   opening of money and securities accounts, as well as accounts representing entitlements to precious metals and other valuables;
3   the letting of safe deposit boxes;
4   payment of coupons on bonds (and similar debt instruments);
5   conclusion of, and providing intermediary services in respect of, life insurance contracts if the premium to be paid exceeds a certain amount;
6   payments under life insurance contracts exceeding a certain amount;
7   provision of services in transactions which exceed a certain threshold;
8   the sale, or acting as intermediary in respect of a sale, of vehicles, ships, works of art, antiques, precious stones or metals or other valuable goods designated from time to time as such by implementing regulation against payment in whole or in part in cash; and
9   the provision of other services designated from time to time as such by implementing regulation.

The Act imposes a duty to determine the identity of a customer prior to providing services as described above. Accordingly, banks are prohibited from providing services to customers unless the identification procedures have been completed. Article 3 of the Act provides for the procedures to be followed for identification. If the (legal) person so identified is acting for a third party, such third party will also need to be identified in accordance with the provisions of the Act: see art 5(3). Banks are obliged to verify whether the person with whom it transacts is acting for a third party. The Act does not specify what is exactly meant by 'acting for a third party' and this omission may now and again lead to uncertainty.

There are certain exemptions from the above statutory requirements, which will not be discussed in this chapter. The data which financial institutions compile in the implementation of the Act must be properly filed and maintained for at least five years after termination of the relationship with the client. Non-compliance with the provisions of the Act constitutes a criminal offence.

The Act contains no specific provisions on making the data compiled available to the supervisory authorities. Neither does the Act contain any provisions by virtue of which the financial institutions concerned are to keep the data compiled confidential. For these matters, the legislator relies on the other laws discussed in this chapter.

There are a number of implementing regulations which provide for compliance with further procedural requirements. These include the Decision Designating Institutions and Services of 1 June 2003 (*Aanwijzingsbesluit instellingen en diensten Wet identificatie bij dienstverlening en Wet melding ongebruikelijke transacties*) and the Implementing Regulation most recently amended on 28 May 2003 (*Uitvoeringsbesluit Wet identificatie bij dienstverlening en Wet melding ongebruikelijke transacties*).

The Act on the Notification of Unusual Transactions

[21.30]   The Act on the Notification of Unusual Transactions (*Wet melding ongebruikelijke transacties*) came into force on 1 February 1994, again in the context of the implementation of Council Directive 91/308/EEC of 10 June 1991. It has been amended on several occasions, most recently on 1 January 2002. Essentially, the Act imposes a duty to notify a specific agency of all unusual transactions. The Act applies to whomsoever provides services in the conduct of a business or profession, including banking and insurance services, but also including other services that may be used to effect money laundering (such as transactions involving ships, cars, antiques, jewels, etc). As soon as an unusual transaction is proposed or effected, the financial institution involved is required to notify the agency set up to implement the Act (*Meldpunt ongebruikelijke transacties*). The notification includes:

1   the identity of the client;
2   the type and registration number of the identification papers of the client;
3   the nature, volume, time and place of the transaction;
4   the reason why the transaction is deemed unusual;
5   if applicable, a description of the assets involved; and
6   other data designated as such from time to time by regulation.

Whether a transaction is to be characterised as unusual must be determined according to guidelines (*indicatoren-lijst*) of the Minister of Finance. These guidelines are published regularly at no fewer than six-monthly intervals.

What happens after notification? The agency will register and analyse the transaction concerned and the data may be used for prosecution purposes. The agency is entitled to request the financial institution which has made a notification for additional information: see art 10 of the Act. The financial institution cannot invoke a duty of confidentiality.

The financial institution which makes a notification may not disclose this to the customer concerned: see art 19. The Act provides that all persons entrusted with duties in connection with its implementation are subject to a duty of non-disclosure, except to the extent disclosure is necessary to perform such duties: see art 18.

Naturally, banks and other financial institutions are concerned that they may incur civil liabilities towards third parties in connection with notifications made pursuant to the Act. For this reason, art 13 provides that notifying persons may not be held liable for notifications made unless it is proved that, given the circumstances of the case, notification should not reasonably have been made. The party who wishes to hold a notifying person liable is thus faced with a rather difficult burden of proof.

In addition to the civil law indemnity described above, financial institutions have the benefit of a criminal law indemnity: see art 12. Basically, the data which a financial institution provides on the basis of the Act may not be used for the prosecution of such a financial institution for fencing (*heling*). This perhaps requires some explanation. A bank which accepts moneys from a customer in the knowledge or reasonable suspicion that such moneys were obtained in the commission of a crime commits the criminal act of fencing (receiving stolen property). If the transfer of such moneys to the bank is notified in accordance with the requirements of the Act, the information thus supplied may not be used by the prosecution, but obviously this does not constitute a complete indemnity; the bank concerned may still be prosecuted on the basis of other evidence than that notified under the Act. Additionally, the provisions of art 12 only provide relief in the context of the criminal offence of fencing and not in case of other crimes. Accordingly, art 12 only provides a rather limited criminal law indemnity to banks and other financial institutions subject to the Act.

Most banks in The Netherlands have developed quite elaborate manuals in order to ensure compliance with the provisions of the Act (and of the Act on Identification when Providing Services) and have installed compliance officers who monitor, and can be consulted about, the implementation of the Act. Since the Act contains various provisions pursuant to which banks and other financial institutions have to use their own judgment as to whether or not to notify and as to the timing of a notification (and sometimes as to whether (and when) to notify subject to agreement with the agency as to how the matter will further be dealt with), there is an obvious need for such manuals.

Customer due diligence

[21.31] In 2001, the Basle Committee on Banking Supervision published the 'customer due diligence for banks' guidelines. According to these guidelines, 'all banks should be required to have in place adequate policies, practices and procedures that promote high ethical and professional standards and prevent the bank from being used, intentionally or unintentionally, by criminal elements'. Key elements that should be included in the customer due diligence procedures are customer acceptance policy, customer identification, ongoing monitoring of high-risk accounts and risk management. These guidelines have been made mandatory for Dutch banks by virtue of a separate Regulation CDD (*Regeling CDD kredietinstellingen en verzekeraars*) issued by the DNB on 23 December 2003. On 8 May 2003, the DNB, together with the NVB, also published a guideline for banks in relation to customer due diligence procedures to be maintained by banks. This guideline has meanwhile been elucidated upon by a DNB circular of April 2005 (*Nadere toelichting CDD Identificatie*). This circular, inter alia, provides guidelines as to how banks should identify and treat so-called 'politically exposed persons'. For this topic, see 'The Act on Identification when Providing Services' above.

A duty to disclose in the public interest

[21.32] Other than in Anglo-Saxon jurisdictions, which appear to recognise an exception to the duty of confidentiality in situations where a duty to disclose is in the public interest, for example, if there is knowledge of a crime being committed or fraud is deemed to exist, Dutch law does not explicitly recognise such exception. However, the principle that a statutory duty of confidentiality must give way to the overriding principle that justice must be done appears very similar in concept and effect: see the Supreme Court judgment of 22 July 1986 discussed above. Moreover, it can be convincingly argued that if there is knowledge or a strong indication of crime, the contractual duty of confidentiality will not prevent the bank from disclosing it because the principles of reasonableness and fairness would dictate that a customer cannot enforce his contractual rights vis-à-vis the bank in the context of a criminal cover up. The Act on the Notification of Unusual Transactions (discussed above) has obviously largely taken away the need to provide for a general statutory duty to disclose in the public interest.

REGULATION OF FINANCIAL MARKETS
Powers of regulatory bodies to require disclosure
Pursuant to the Banking Act

[21.33] The DNB has powers to require disclosure under arts 53ff of the Banking Act. Pursuant to art 53, the DNB is entitled to obtain information from institutions which it suspects are subject to bank licence requirements. Under art 54, the DNB has all the investigative powers required to fulfil its supervisory duties. These investigative powers extend to group companies of the bank concerned, as well as to all entities that, directly or indirectly, have an equity interest of 10% or more in the bank. Article 55 requires credit institutions to comply with elaborate periodic reporting obligations. Article 56 obliges credit institutions to make ad hoc reports if they no longer comply with the DNB's directives on solvency, liquidity or administrative organisation.

In addition to the above-described powers, arts 60 and 61 provide for procedures to be followed in cases where the DNB requires information to be verified from companies in other EU member states and vice versa if a central bank in another EU member state wishes the DNB to verify information concerning companies in The Netherlands.

All of the foregoing comprise investigative powers conferred on the DNB in the context of its supervisory duties under the Dutch Banking Act and there is nothing unusual about these powers.

Pursuant to the securities laws

[21.34] The AFM has similar investigative powers in the context of its supervisory functions in respect of stock exchanges and securities transactions. Under arts 29ff of the STSA, the AFM may obtain, or cause to be obtained, all the information which is reasonably necessary for the proper performance of the duties and responsibilities vested in the AFM under the STSA and in order to ascertain compliance with the statutory provisions. This information may be obtained, inter alia, from securities institutions (whether operating under a licence or a licence exemption), other group companies of securities institutions, entities that, directly or indirectly, have an equity interest of 10% or more in the institution concerned, stock exchanges, offerors of securities and generally from 'anyone that is reasonably suspected to be acting in breach of the STSA or its implementing regulations'.

There is uncertainty as to whether the AFM also has the right to inspect cash accounts of clients of a bank or documents which do not relate to broker–dealer activities or portfolio management activities of a bank. An interesting judgment was rendered in 1996 in a case brought before the president of the Council for Appeals for Business Enterprises (*College van Beroep voor het Bedrijfsleven*, 'CBB').[10] In this case, the STE (as the AFM was then called) had announced in a letter to ABN AMRO Bank NV that it would collect data and information at ABN AMRO in order to be able to ascertain whether the provisions of the STSA relating to insider trading had been complied with in a certain case. In its letter, the STE had asserted that the bank was under an obligation to extend to officials charged by the STE with supervisory duties every co-operation which they may reasonably require in the performance of their

10 CBB 15 October 1996, no 96/0033/113/226.

duties. At the request of the bank, the STE clarified that it also intended to inspect cash accounts of clients of ABN AMRO. The bank understandably objected vigorously to this extension by the STE of its investigative powers; these investigative powers were alleged by the STE to cover not only the securities business of the bank, but also its actual banking business. The president of the CBB considered that the position of the STE was incorrect to the extent that it also covered inspection by the STE of cash accounts other than those which directly related to the securities transactions effected by ABN AMRO to the order of the customer in respect of whom the suspicion had arisen. In other words, the president of the CBB did allow the investigative powers of the STE to extend to specific cash accounts, but did not allow these powers to be used in a more generalised manner.

Pursuant to the Act on the Supervision of Investment Undertakings

[21.35]   Article 19(1) of the Act on the Supervision of Investment Undertakings (*Wet toezicht beleggingsinstellingen*) provides that the DNB may seek information from, or conduct or cause to be conducted on its behalf, an investigation with, inter alia:

1 an applicant for a licence as fund manager of an investment institution;
2 an existing fund manager or investment institution (including fund managers and investment institutions operating from another EU member state under the UCITS Directive);
3 a custodian or depository company used by an investment institution; and
4 any entity that can reasonably be suspected to be acting in breach of the Act on the Supervision of Investment Undertakings or its Decree.

The term 'investment institutions' in the Act includes all sorts of open-end and closed-end type funds, whether or not incorporated. It also includes funds established abroad, participations or shares of which are offered for sale or traded in The Netherlands.

The investigation may be carried out to verify compliance with the requirements of the Act. The person from whom information is requested must furnish it within a period to be determined by the DNB. The person who is the object of an investigation must give the DNB access to all books and documents relating to the investment institution or, where applicable, the custodian or depository company and shall give all assistance necessary for the proper completion of the investigation.

Individualised information in respect of enterprises, institutions and depositaries obtained by the DNB may not be published and must be kept secret: see art 24(1) of the Act. In addition, according to art 24(2), data compiled by the DNB pursuant to the Act may not be disclosed or used other than for the purposes of the implementation of the Act.

Pursuant to the current draft of the Financial Supervision Act

[21.36]   While the current financial supervisory legislation provides that supervisory authorities may seek information from a limited number of persons and/or entities, the current proposal for the Financial Supervision Act provides that supervisory authorities may require information from 'any person': see art 1:57a of the draft Act. However, before the AFM can seek information from banks, it must first ask for this information from the DNB, since the DNB is the supervisory authority that granted the licence (and vice versa if the AFM is the licensing supervisory authority). Only if the DNB is not able to provide the requested information can the AFM request the information from another party. An exception to this rule can be made if it can be reasonably expected that the company in question acts in breach of legislation and the interests involved require immediate action.

The provisions of the STSA on insider trading

[21.37]   The provisions relating to insider trading were introduced in the Dutch Criminal Code on 16 February 1989 and were moved to the STSA with effect from 18 July 1992. The insider trading provisions were amended with effect from 1 October 2005 in the context of the implementation of the Market Abuse Directive. Because the Dutch insider trading rules are now rules implementing this Directive, the interpretation of the meaning of these rules is now ultimately the domain of the European Court rather than that of the Dutch national courts.

Article 46, para 1 of the STSA sets out the principal insider trading prohibitions and currently reads as follows:

> 'It is prohibited for any person ... to make use of prior knowledge by committing or bringing about any transaction
>
> a   in or from within The Netherlands or a state which is not a member state, in securities which are admitted to trading on a regulated market which is established or active in The Netherlands, or for which admission to trading on that market has been applied for;
> b   in or from within The Netherlands, in securities which are admitted to trading on a regulated market which is established or active in another member state or which are admitted to trading on an exchange established and formally admitted in a state which is not a member state, or in securities for which admission to trading on that market or exchange has been applied for; or
> c   in or from within The Netherlands or a state which is not a member state, in securities, not being securities as referred to under a or b of which the value is in whole or in part derived from the value of securities as described under a or b.'

While the insider trading prohibition that was in effect prior to 1 October 2005 did not contain any causal link requirement between the available prior knowledge and the transaction concerned, the current text does require that the prior knowledge is 'used' for the transaction concerned. This is not necessarily a causal link requirement *strictu sensu*, but it does mean that the availability of the prior knowledge was instrumental in the transaction. It remains to be seen to what extent the effective prosecution of insider trading cases in The Netherlands will be impeded by this requirement.

The persons who are subject to this prohibition are defined in paras 2 and 3 of art 46. A distinction is made between 'primary insiders' (para 2) and 'secondary insiders' (para 3). Primary insiders are persons or legal entities that are involved in the company concerned by holding senior management or supervisory positions or that hold equity positions and persons or legal entities that have obtained prior knowledge because of their involvement in criminal activities. Secondary insiders are all other persons or legal entities who know or ought reasonably to be aware that they have prior knowledge.

The term 'prior knowledge' is defined in para 4 as knowledge of non-public information that is concrete and that directly or indirectly pertains to the company concerned or to the trade in the securities concerned and that, if publicly disclosed, could have a significant effect on the quoted price of the securities concerned (or of derivatives related to such securities). Paragraph 5 contains a separate definition of 'prior knowledge' in relation to securities, the value of which is in whole or in part dependent on the value of commodities or raw materials. Prior knowledge of these types of securities (mainly commodity derivatives) is knowledge that investors may expect to be disclosed or that is required by applicable rules or regulations to be disclosed on the markets where these securities are traded.

There are certain exemptions to the insider trading prohibition. These are in part set out in para 7 of art 46. These exemptions relate to transactions where a prior legal obligation to enter into the transaction existed, transactions carried out in the context of share buy back programmes and stabilisation transactions. Exemptions are also set out in the Market Abuse Decree (*Besluit marktmisbruik*) of 14 September 2005. These exemptions relate, inter alia, to employee share and stock option plans, transactions in securities that were committed to in the context of (partial) public exchange offers, the issue of bonus stock and the carrying out of orders by brokers acting in good faith who possess prior knowledge about the trade in the securities concerned (and therefore this exemption does not apply to brokers who carry out orders where they possess prior knowledge about the company to which the securities in question relate). Of course, this latter exemption is very important to securities firms and banks.

Article 46(a) contains a prohibition to 'tip off'. There is an exemption for persons acting in the normal course of their function or duties. This exemption is of course important to securities firms and banks, but this exemption does not apply to investment recommendations. Banks may accordingly not give buy, sell or hold recommendations when possessing prior knowledge (but prior knowledge is attributed taking into account the existence of Chinese Walls), but the exemption does apply to persons who approach shareholders that hold significant equity stakes in targets in the context of a public bid if it is important that the commitment (or refusal to commit) of such shareholders is verified prior to launching a public bid.

Until 1999, the insider trading rules in The Netherlands did not include a duty for insiders to notify their transactions. As of 1999, this duty to notify is imposed on certain categories of insiders. This is currently provided in art 47(a) and (b) of the STSA. Notifications must be made to the AFM. The AFM maintains a public register of such notifications.

Article 47(c) of the STSA, newly introduced with the implementation of the Market Abuse Directive, provides that a securities institution which has a reasonable suspicion that a transaction is effected or a transaction order is given in breach of art 46 or 46(b) must report this suspicion forthwith to the AFM. Bank confidentiality no longer applies in these situations. Article 47(d) provides that if a securities institution reports such transaction in good faith, it is not liable for any damage a third party may suffer as a consequence of that report. A securities institution must keep the report confidential; it may not inform its client that it reported the transaction concerned.

Since 1987, the Amsterdam stock exchange required quoted companies to have a model code. With effect from 1 January 1999, there is a statutory duty for quoted companies to have an internal regulation set out in art 47(f) of the STSA. According to art 11 of the Decree to the STSA, the internal regulation must include the tasks and authorisations of the 'central officer', a compliance officer, if such officer is appointed, the obligations of directors, supervisory directors and senior management officers of quoted companies regarding the possession of, and transactions in securities related to, the company and, if applicable, the periods in which the aforementioned persons are not allowed to commit or bring about transactions in the securities, the so-called 'closed periods'. The AFM has published a model code which it considers to be appropriate. There is no statutory obligation to use this model code. The Association of Institutions that Issue Securities (*Vereniging van Effecten Uitgevende Instellingen*, the association that represents the interests of Dutch stock exchange quoted companies) has also published a model code, which is somewhat more elaborate than that of the AFM.

Pursuant to art 2 of the Economic Offences Act (*Wet economische delicten*, 'WED'), a breach of the insider trading prohibitions of the STSA constitutes a criminal offence (*misdrijf*). The Economic Surveillance Department (*Economische Controle Dienst*) is authorised to investigate possible breaches of art 46 of the STSA. The investigative powers based on the WED are more extensive than those based on the Dutch Criminal Procedure Code. It will be clear that banks cannot invoke any duty of secrecy in relation to these investigations. Furthermore, the AFM has also been granted extensive investigative powers pursuant to the STSA, as well as the authority to apply administrative sanctions and measures.

In furtherance of its powers and duties under the STSA, the STE (as the AFM was then called) promulgated a so-called 'Further Regulation' (*Nadere regeling gedragstoezicht effectenverkeer*) containing, inter alia, rules of conduct to be observed by securities institutions. The current version of the Further Regulation is dated 1 October 2005. Article 22 of the Further Regulation states that securities institutions must have an internal regulation containing a code of conduct for dealing with price-sensitive data. Article 23 of the Further Regulation, in addition, requires securities institutions to have a code of conduct for securities transactions carried out by employees for their own account. Each securities institution must have a supervisor (a compliance officer) who reviews compliance with the terms of these two codes.

Chinese Walls

[21.38]   The NVB has promulgated a specific code of conduct concerning Chinese Walls, to which banks in The Netherlands are expected to conform. This code is dated 8 November 1990. It has not since been modernised or adapted to current thinking on Chinese Walls.

The code prescribes that the institutions concerned must establish a procedural distinction between their credit business, underwriting business and brokerage business. The existence of these Chinese Walls must also be notified to customers. In addition, customers will need to be informed that if the institution concerned has price-sensitive information, such information will not be passed on to customers and will not be used in giving investment advice to clients. Banks and securities institutions are furthermore required to appoint within their organisation a so-called 'supervisor' (*toezichthouder*) whose function will be to effect compliance control. The code not only imposes obligations on the institutions, but also on the individual employees of such members. Employees must observe certain rules relating to the handling of price-sensitive information. They are prohibited from trading in securities or advising on investments in securities while they have inside information on such securities. This prohibition does not apply if the inside information relates to the 'trade in securities' (as opposed to inside information relating to the company to which the securities in question relate) and the members concerned act in good faith on the instructions of clients.

One of the principal aims of Chinese Walls is to ensure that sensitive knowledge available to one or more persons working on a particular matter is only legitimately used for that matter and is not divulged to others working in the same firm where such sensitive information may be used for other purposes. Is the establishment of an effective Chinese Wall sufficient to avoid the application of the insider trading prohibition of art 46 of the STSA? There is no case law on this issue and Dutch legal doctrine is not uniform in its answer to the question. The problem here is that grounds for disculpation will have to be found by the application of general principles of criminal law, which as such are ill suited to cope with questions of this kind. In relation to this, it is interesting to note that in the explanatory notes (*Memorie van toelichting*) relating to the 1999 amendments to the insider trading provisions in the STSA, the Minister of Finance made the comment that the mere existence of Chinese Walls would not be sufficient to exculpate a bank, but that it would need to be demonstrated that the Chinese Walls concerned actually work.[11]

The existence of Chinese Walls raises a number of legal questions, mainly in consequence of the fact that the above-mentioned code is insufficiently clear as to what a Chinese Wall actually is, for which purposes exactly it is being erected and in which instances information is nevertheless permitted to cross. The code, in the present writer's view, insufficiently recognises that, depending on which departments they are erected between, these Walls have different functions and purposes. It also does not effectively address the reality that most banks operate various banking and related activities through group companies. The Dutch Association of Banks would be well advised to amend the code to make it less abstract and more modern and practicable. The principles to be applied are quite clear. There are, however, two complex issues which need careful consideration: (i) the formulation of the exceptions to the principles and (ii) how to ensure that the rules, together with their exceptions, have the desired external effect (so that banks have an adequate measure of protection against third party civil liability).

Apart from this code of conduct, the DNB has enacted a regulation, the Regulation on Organisation and Control, which provides an elaborate set of rules as to how banks should be organised. These include rules on the maintenance of integrity that, implicitly rather than explicitly, require banks to install rigid Chinese Wall structures and rigorously to monitor their effectiveness.

The subject matter of Chinese Walls is a matter of both prudential supervision (ie the supervision of the DNB) and of the supervision of market conduct (ie the supervision of the AFM) and for this reason it is now also within the regulatory domain of the AFM. This supervisory authority has not promulgated specific rules on the imposition and maintenance of Chinese Walls by banks, but it has issued elaborate rules applicable to securities firms (and therefore also applicable to banks with a brokerage arm). These are contained in para 6 of the above-mentioned Further Regulation. Both the Regulation on Organisation and Control and the Further Regulation only contain abstract high-level rules that do not give specific guidance to banks and securities firms as to how to comply with these rules effectively. This is

---

11 See *Kamerstukken II* (1996–1997) 25095, p 3, n 6.

not to criticise the regulators, since this level of abstractness is probably largely inevitable, but it does mean, on the one hand, that banks and securities firms have little practical guidance on effective compliance and, on the other, that the regulators will be confronted with a wide variance in the way the rules are implemented in practice; this obviously does not make the supervisory task any easier in practical terms.

Further developments in relation to the enhancement of financial integrity and combating terrorist financing

[21.39] In consequence of the terrorist attacks in the US of 11 September 2001 and the ensuing actions of, amongst others, the Financial Action Task Force, on 16 November 2001, the Dutch Ministers of Finance and Justice issued a memorandum on the integrity of the financial sector and combating terrorism (*Nota integriteit financiële sector en terrorismebestrijding*). The memorandum contemplated further amendments to existing financial laws and regulations, which included stronger integrity requirements imposed on financial institutions that are subject to licence requirements, supervision of trust companies and finance companies (both categories of institutions had hitherto not been subject to specific supervision since they could effectively avail themselves of exemptions from the Dutch Banking Act and STSA licence requirements), the strengthening of the supervision of money transfers, widening the scope of the requirement to identify customers when providing financial services to them and the requirement to notify unusual transactions. A number of other areas of concern were noted in the memorandum: the need to counter the possible abuse of physical bearer securities (principally by moving towards complete dematerialisation of bearer securities), the need to make money laundering a separate criminal offence, the need to counter the abuse of corporate entities, the need to enhance the exchange of information between central banks and supervisory authorities, the need to enhance the investigative powers of the public prosecutors and the police (especially financial investigations), etc. A number of these concerns have, meanwhile, already led to amendment of the financial regulatory regime. Examples of this are the now more stringent provisions of the Act on Identification when Providing Services and the Act on the Notification of Unusual Transactions, both discussed above. On several other issues, new legislation is being prepared or has recently been adopted. The sense of urgency that some of these initiatives had in the immediate aftermath of 11 September 2001 has now to a certain degree been replaced by a more mature approach to the monumental task that the Dutch legislator has set itself.

A regulation that should be mentioned in this context is the Decree on Operational Integrity (*Besluit integere bedrijfsvoering kredietinstellingen en verzekeraars*) of 10 October 2003. Article 2 of this Decree provides that banks and insurance companies (financial institutions) should have adequate policies and organisational measures in place to prevent conflicts of interest. Article 3 provides that the management policies and procedures of a financial institution should prevent the institution from becoming involved in criminal activities or other activities that are generally deemed unacceptable in a manner that the reputation of the institution or financial markets generally is jeopardised. Article 6 provides that upon request of the supervisory authority (the DNB or the AFM) a financial institution will verify whether its books and records include data on persons that may jeopardise the reputation of the financial sector by virtue of their being related to terrorist or connected activities. This verification is to be reported to the supervisory authorities and evidently there is no confidentiality protection here for customers of financial institutions. Finally, we note the introduction, with effect from 6 January 2001, of provisions in the Dutch Criminal Code relating to money laundering. Article 420 bis of the Dutch Criminal Code makes money laundering a criminal offence. Money laundering is defined as (i) the hiding or disguising of the true nature, origin, disposal or removal of any asset of which the perpetrator knows or should reasonably suspect that that asset is directly or indirectly obtained by the commission of a crime or the hiding or disguising of the person entitled to such asset and (ii) acquiring, holding, using, converting or disposing of any such asset. The provisions cover assets of any nature, therefore, including money and securities in dematerialised form.

CONCLUSION

[21.40]   The duty of confidentially as part of the contractual relationship between banks and their customers is firmly entrenched in the Dutch system, even though there is no specific statutory basis for this duty. As discussed above, new laws and regulations have gradually eroded this duty. The present writer believes that this trend will continue and that even more transparency will be imposed in the continuing effort to combat money laundering and the financing of criminal activities and terrorism, but, going forward, this will be based on EU initiatives rather than unilateral action by the government.

22 Norway

Terje Sommer
Vibeke K Svendsby

THE BASIC POSITION

[22.1]   Bank confidentiality rules were introduced in Norwegian legislation as early as 1924 when the two first Banking Acts were passed by the *Stortinget* (the Norwegian Parliament). There was one Act for savings banks and another for commercial banks. Two new Acts were passed in 1961 and the scope of the confidentiality rules from 1924 was carried on into the new legislation and into a new Finance Activity Act 1988, which supplements the two Banking Acts.

The rules have always been aimed at protecting bank customers from the bank giving confidential information about them or their relationship with the bank to others. The obligation to keep customer information confidential is directed at the individual officer and employee of the bank, not at the bank itself. Any breach of the rules is a criminal offence. This model has been used for newer confidentiality rules in the Securities Trading Act 1997 with respect to investment firms, the Insurance Activity Act 1988 with respect to insurance companies and pension funds and the Stock Exchange Act 2000 with respect to exchanges and authorised marketplaces: see 'Other Financial Confidentiality Rules' below.

Although over time confidentiality provisions have been introduced in a number of pieces of financial legislation, the effect of the rules has at the same time been diluted by exemptions for the benefit of, inter alia, the tax authorities, the police, the competition authorities, the Financial Supervisory Authority in Norway ('FSAN', which supervises banks, insurance companies and investment firms), the stock exchange and even spouses under certain circumstances. Last, but not least, rules implementing the EC Money Laundering Directives[1] oblige individual officers and employees working within the financial community, as well as lawyers, auditors and other categories of professionals, to give confidential information of their own accord to the central prosecution authorities under certain circumstances.

The traditional Norwegian confidentiality provisions do not regulate how financial institutions shall collect and store information about customers. Such rules are laid down in the Personal Data Act 2000, which implemented the EC Personal Data Protection Directive.[2] In contrast to the confidentiality rules in the financial legislation, as a general rule, the Personal Data Act only applies to information about physical persons.

The current confidentiality provisions were made for a quite different society and today appear not to be well suited in all respects and there is therefore a need for

1 Council Directives 91/308/EC and 2001/97/EC.
2 Council Directive 95/46/EC.

modernising the rules. The FSAN has proposed an amendment of the rules, which the Ministry of Finance is presently reviewing: see 'Proposal for New Legislation' below.

Personal data rules

[22.2]   As mentioned above, the bank confidentiality rules in Norway are directed at the individual officer and employee of the bank and not at the bank itself. Bank confidentiality rules protect all customers, both physical persons and legal entities.

Although Norway is not a member of the EU, it has, as a party to the EEA agreement, undertaken to implement the various EU/EC directives.

The Personal Data Act implements Council Directive 95/46/EC. The Directive only protects physical persons and the Act regulates the collection and treatment of personal information and imposes restrictions on the disclosure of such information to others.

According to the Personal Data Act, financial institutions are, under certain conditions, allowed to collect and process personal data about customers who are physical persons. Disclosure of such information can only take place to the extent allowed under the Act. These restrictions come in addition to restrictions imposed in confidentiality rules elsewhere in the legislation, so that the strictest rule will always apply. Today, there is some inconsistency between the general rules in the Personal Data Act and the specific confidentiality rules elsewhere in the legislation. It is expected that the proposed new legislation will attempt to address this inconsistency.

SCOPE OF BASIC POSITION

[22.3]   The present confidentiality rules for banks can be found in the Commercial Bank Act 1961 and the Savings Bank Act 1961. Section 18 of the Commercial Bank Act (which is similar to the corresponding provision in the Savings Bank Act) reads as follows:

> 'Elected officers, employees and auditors of a commercial bank are obliged to treat as confidential any information which comes to their knowledge by virtue of their position concerning the bank or a customer thereof, or another bank or its customer, unless they are obliged to disclose information pursuant to this or any other Act. The duty of confidentiality does not apply to information, which the board of directors or anyone authorised by the board discloses on behalf of the bank to another bank.
>
> Notwithstanding this provision, the bank may carry on credit reference activity in accordance with the laws applying thereto.'

In principle, the confidentiality obligations apply to all matters which officers, employees and auditors receive knowledge of in their position in the bank. 'In connection' means that the person must have received the information in his capacity as employee, officer or auditor, irrespective of whether he actually received the information at the time when he was working. The duty of confidentiality only extends to information which was not publicly known or available at the time. The duty of confidentiality does not extend to matters which are public (other than through illegal disclosure by the bank employee or officer), for instance, through newspapers, television, radio, the Internet or because it is available upon a search of public registers.

The duty of confidentiality extends in principle to any disclosure of such information, including internally within the bank, except that information can be given on a 'need to know' basis. In particular, confidential information cannot freely be given to other legal entities within the same financial group: see 'Information Exchange Within the Group' below.

The confidentiality rules in the Banking Acts do not deal with the question of outsourcing or use of external consultants such as lawyers, etc. In practice, it has been accepted that confidential information can be disclosed to external consultants, but the FSAN stated in a circular of 17 April 2000 that they would regard such consultants as being directly subjected to the confidentiality rules in the Banking Acts. It will be the obligation of the outsourcing entity to ensure that such consultants undertake to keep information received confidential.

In late 2002, the *Stortinget* approved the government's proposal for new rules on securitisation. Under these rules, financial institutions wishing to assign a loan portfolio to a non-financial institution must notify the borrowers, who must object within a time of not less than three weeks. Under the Financial Contracts Act 1999, a financial institution may transfer a loan to another financial institution without the borrower's consent. The borrower must, however, be notified about the transfer. Neither of these sets of rules authorise the release of confidential information about the borrower(s) and specific consent must therefore be obtained. In the preparation documents for the new securitisation rules, the Ministry of Finance expressly states that when the seller is going to act as a service provider/manager of the sold loan portfolio, the seller may not disclose confidential customer information to the purchaser without customer consent, although it is acknowledged that the purchaser may have a legitimate interest in such information. The rules only apply to financial institutions.

A bank can of course disclose information about a customer to the customer. Under the Personal Data Act, a customer will also have a right to demand to see information registered on him. Norwegian banks (and other financial institutions) generally follow a strict practice when it comes to disclosing confidential information about customers to a person who purports to act on the customer's behalf. In many cases, for example, for companies, deceased persons and customers subject to bankruptcy proceedings, the relevant legislation will give the necessary directions. Problems may, however, arise when the customer is a non-resident of Norway: see the discussion starting at 'Cross-Border/Extra-Territorial Issues' below.

Other financial confidentiality rules

[22.4]   The most important other confidentiality rules in the financial legislation are the following:

1   the Finance Activity Act 1988, which contains a confidentiality rule for finance companies and mortgage institutions;
2   the Insurance Activity Act 1988, which contains rules for both life and non-life insurance companies, as well as pension funds;
3   the Securities Trading Act 1997 ('STA'), which regulates investment firms;
4   the Investment Fund Act 1981 ('IFA'), which regulates investment funds; and
5   the Stock Exchange Act 2000, which regulates exchanges and authorised marketplaces.

In broad terms, the provisions in these acts are similar to the rules in the Banking Acts.

The confidentiality rules in the STA and IFA go further than those in the Banking Acts and Insurance Activity Act. In the STA and IFA, 'neutral' customer information, such as name and address, is also covered by the confidentiality rules and an investment firm or investment fund manager may not disclose, even to other members of a group to which it belongs, that someone is a customer.

Information exchange within the group

[22.5] The wording of the confidentiality rules described above should, in principle, mean that customer information cannot be exchanged with other companies in the same financial group. In a circular of 17 April 2000, the FSAN has accepted that 'neutral' information about customers, such as name and address, is not confidential information within a group. Under these rules, a bank or insurance company may therefore disclose the name and address of a customer to other members within the group. Such information will, however, fall under the Personal Data Act and, for physical persons, a joint register would therefore need to be set up in accordance with the Personal Data Act and with the appropriate approval. Following strong objections from the Norwegian Financial Services Association to this interpretation, the FSAN accepted, in a letter of 27 April 2001, that general information about the customer relationship, such as the type of products provided to the customer, may also be exchanged within the group. More detailed information such as balances on accounts or loans will, however, be protected by the confidentiality rules and cannot be included in a 'group register' without an explicit consent of the customer.

Under the Banking Acts and the Finance Activity Act, finance institutions within a group must consolidate their exposure to customers. For this purpose, customer information must be exchanged.

It is important to note that if a financial group includes an investment firm or investment fund manager, even 'neutral' customer information will be protected and cannot be included in a group register without the explicit consent of the customer.

EXCEPTIONS, LIMITATIONS AND QUALIFICATIONS TO BASIC POSITION

Release of information by customer consent

[22.6] A customer may consent to disclosure of confidential information. Such consent should be informed and explicit. It will not suffice if a bank notifies its customers that, unless the customer objects, certain information will be disclosed to a third party. In particular, if the consent is of a general nature, this must be very clearly spelt out. Of course, in certain cases, consent must be regarded as implicit, typically when a customer asks his bank to transfer money to a third party or when he uses a bank card, since the bank then confirms that there are sufficient means for the payment in question.

In the letter of 27 April 2001 referred to above, the FSAN has accepted that a 'passive' consent is sufficient where a fund management company in a group wishes to inform other group members about the fact that a customer is a shareholder in a particular fund.

Disclosure to other financial institutions

[22.7] Under the Banking Acts and the Finance Activity Act, information can be disclosed to other finance institutions. Although the wording of the relevant paragraphs is quite wide, the right to disclose confidential customer information is probably limited to situations where a finance institution needs to discuss the customer with other finance institutions because of a special situation, for example, in circumstances where that institution is exposed to a loss. Under the Banking Acts and the Finance Activity Act, such disclosure shall be authorised by the board of directors.

To the extent that a bank can disclose information under this rule, the bank should also be allowed to share the information with foreign finance institutions, provided that such institutions themselves are subject to a high standard of confidentiality.

Money laundering rules

[22.8] Norwegian anti-money laundering regulations implement the First and Second EC Money Laundering Directives.[3] Norwegian anti-money laundering regulations also take into account the full obligations set out in the Financial Action Task Force ('FATF') recommendations (1996), but do not yet take into account the full obligations set out in the revised FATF recommendations (2003). With a few exceptions, Norway has fully implemented the elements of the United Nations Convention Against Illicit Traffic in Narcotic Drugs and Psychotic Substances 1988 (the Vienna Convention), the United Nations Convention Against Transnational Organised Crime 2000 (the Palermo Convention) and the United Nations Convention Against Financing of Terrorism 1999 (the Terrorist Financing Convention) that are relevant to the FATF recommendations. Money laundering is illegal in Norway under s 317 of the Penal Code. Charges can be brought for different types of money laundering, ranging in seriousness from drug-related money laundering to negligent money laundering.

The relevant Norwegian anti-money laundering rules can be found in the Anti-Money Laundering Act 2003. The Act applies to all the financial institutions that must be covered under the FATF recommendations. Under the money laundering rules, financial institutions must ensure that they know their customers and there are strict requirements regarding proof of identity for new customers.

In addition, as set out in the Anti-Money Laundering Act, under certain circumstances, certain categories of persons, including employees of a financial institution, are obliged to report suspicious transactions to a special agency – the National Authority for Investigation and Prosecution of Economic and Environmental Crime in Norway ('ØKOKRIM'). Such report must be made if there is a suspicion that a transaction is associated with the proceeds of crime or with offences covered by s 147a or 147b of the Penal Code and an internal investigation in the reporting entity fails to disprove the suspicion. Section 147a of the Penal Code covers various terrorist acts (a range of existing criminal offences committed with certain specific intentions) and s 147b of the Penal Code covers terrorist financing, implementing the Terrorist Financing Convention.

The Anti-Money Laundering Act states that reporting of suspicious transactions does not constitute a breach of the duty of secrecy and does not provide a basis for

---

3 Council Directives 91/308/EC and 2001/97/EC.

compensation or penalties. In addition, financial institutions may, notwithstanding the duty of secrecy, exchange necessary customer data when this is regarded as a necessary step in investigations of suspicions that a transaction is associated with the proceeds of crime or with offences covered by s 147a or 147b of the Penal Code.

The customer in question or an involved third party must not be informed about the report to the ØKOKRIM of a suspicious transaction. Norwegian law is in compliance with FATF recommendation 14 on this point.

A person or institution that wilfully does not comply with the above disclosure obligation is considered to be committing a criminal offence, which is punishable by a fine or imprisonment for up to one year.

The FATF performed an evaluation of the anti-money laundering measures in place in Norway in June 2005. The report concluded that Norway was non-compliant with respect to implementing anti-money laundering measures concerning the establishment of the customer relationship with politically exposed persons (FATF recommendation 6) and with respect to implementing anti-money laundering measures concerning the establishment of cross-border correspondent banking relationships (FATF recommendation 7). With respect to the remaining applicable recommendations, Norway was deemed to be compliant, largely compliant or partially compliant. With respect to the FATF's nine special recommendations, Norway's lack of implementation of SR VII Wire Transfer Rules and SR VIII Non-Profit Organisations was commented upon by the FATF. It is expected that the Norwegian anti-money laundering rules will be revised in connection with the implementation of the Third EC Money Laundering Directive.

Actions against terrorism

[22.9]   Norway has implemented the UN Convention Against the Financing of Terrorism of 9 December 1999 and UN Security Council Resolution 1373 of 28 September 2001 in a provisional decree of 2001.

If a bank or another financial institution is suspicious of a transaction being directly or indirectly connected with a terrorist act, the institution is obliged to report to the ØKOKRIM information about all circumstances which may indicate such a connection. This obligation is also imposed on the officers and employees of the institution.

A person or institution that wilfully does not comply with the above disclosure obligation is considered to be committing a criminal offence, which is punishable by a fine or imprisonment for up to one year.

Information to the police and prosecuting authorities

[22.10]   Previously, the confidentiality rules for employees of financial institutions would also apply to the police. On this basis, the police would have to obtain a court order to require information concerning a customer.

As from 25 June 2004, the Norwegian police can instruct employees of a financial institution to give a statement to them in connection with an investigation without having to obtain a court order.

The Prosecuting Authority of Norway may further instruct an employee of a financial institution to deliver documents or other items that are believed to be of importance as evidence to the police. The police may not request such delivery without a written order from the Prosecuting Authority.

Court proceedings

[22.11]   Both in criminal and civil cases, the courts can decide that employees of a financial institution shall give evidence of matters that would normally be subject to the confidentiality obligation.

Tax authorities

[22.12]   An important exception from the confidentiality rules is the right of the tax authorities to require detailed information about customers' accounts and Norwegian financial institutions must annually report electronically details about customers' accounts which, among other things, include balance and interest statements.

Financial Supervisory Authority Act

[22.13]   The FSAN carries out its activity in accordance with the Financial Supervisory Authority Act 1956 ('FSAN Act'). The Act gives the FSAN wide authority to require all kinds of information from financial institutions, insurance companies, investment firms and investment fund managers which is necessary for their supervision.

Stock Exchange Act

[22.14]   Under the Stock Exchange Act 2000, a Norwegian stock exchange has a right to require information about transactions from its members. The Act states that stock exchange members, unhindered by confidentiality rules, are obliged to give information that is necessary for the stock exchange to fulfil its legal obligations.

Competition Act

[22.15]   Under the Competition Act 2004, the competition authorities have the right to require information unhindered by the confidentiality rules.

Marriage Act

[22.16]   Under the Marriage Act 1991, spouses have the right to demand information about financial matters concerning each other from financial institutions and insurance companies unhindered by the confidentiality rules.

The above list does not purport to be exhaustive, but it seeks to deal with the main issues.

SANCTIONS FOR CUSTOMERS

[22.17]   Breach of the confidentiality rules in the Banking Acts is a criminal offence (when committed by negligence too) and is punishable by a fine or, in particularly aggravating circumstances, by imprisonment not exceeding three months.

Breach of the confidentiality rules in the Finance Activity Act, the Insurance Activity Act, the IFA and the STA is a criminal offence (when committed by negligence too) and is punishable by a fine or, in particularly aggravating circumstances, by imprisonment not exceeding one year.

CROSS-BORDER/EXTRA-TERRITORIAL ISSUES

Identifying the problems

[22.18] Separate problems concerning disclosure of information subject to the confidentiality rules arise when extra-territorial aspects are involved. If, for example, a US branch of a Norwegian bank is asked by a US court or regulator to supply information maintained with its head office in Oslo or a foreign bank's head office is requested by that country's courts or regulator to provide information regarding a customer's dealings with branches or subsidiaries in Norway, questions of sovereignty and confidentiality have to be addressed.

If a Norwegian bank or a branch or subsidiary of a foreign bank complies with the order of a foreign court or regulator, it may breach its duty of confidence to its customer. This may again give rise to legal action being commenced by the customer. On the other hand, failure to comply may leave the officers of the bank open to criminal charges, for instance, if a New York court finds the officer of the US bank in contempt of court because he cannot or will not provide information located in Norway.

There are a number of rules under Norwegian law that address such extra-territorial matters. However, not all problems are satisfactorily solved by these rules.

Law Courts Act

[22.19] The Law Courts Act 1915 contains general regulations, applicable both to civil and criminal matters, with respect to legal requests from foreign courts and similar requests from a Norwegian court to a foreign authority with respect to the taking of evidence.

Requests from foreign courts or other foreign authorities must be forwarded through the relevant Norwegian ministry (the Ministry of Justice or the Foreign Department, as the case may be) and will be passed on to the local city court. The court will initially resolve the matter of whether it has the competence to carry out the request or not. The request will be treated subject to Norwegian law.

Similarly, a Norwegian court may decide that a matter before it can be investigated abroad by requests for the hearing of evidence by foreign authorities and courts.

Treaties and conventions

[22.20] Norway is party to the Hague Conventions on the Taking of Evidence Abroad in Civil or Commercial Matters of 1 March 1954 (ratified by Norway and which came into force in 1958) and of 18 March 1970. Furthermore, Norway has ratified the Lugano Convention of 1988.

The incorporation of the Lugano Convention into Norwegian law is to be understood in such a manner that the regulations of the Convention, as *lex specialis*, supersede contradictory regulations, for example, in the Civil Procedures Act 1915 (a new Civil

Procedure Act was adopted on 17 June 2005 and will come into force on a date yet to be decided).

The Lugano Convention is concerned with civil matters and does not, for instance, include matters relating to tax or bankruptcy.

Norway entered into a treaty with the UK regarding civil procedures on 30 January 1931. The treaty has a separate section with regard to the taking of evidence. The treaty is no longer of any great importance, since the UK joined the Hague Convention on Taking Evidence Abroad in Civil or Commercial Matters of 18 March 1970 and the Convention on Service of Process of 15 November 1965, to which Norway is also a party.

Nordic Witness Act

[22.21]   Persons living in the Nordic countries, ie Denmark, Finland, Iceland, Sweden and Norway, are, according to the Nordic Witness Act 1975, obliged to give evidence before each respective national court where a matter is being treated.

A Norwegian court may summon Nordic persons and command them to appear as witnesses before the courts of Norway. The courts may only summon a witness when it is important that the witness gives his explanation in Norway and his explanation must be deemed to be important for the matter at hand. When making this evaluation, the court shall consider the importance of the case and whether the summons would greatly inconvenience the witness. Normal procedural regulations are followed with respect to the examination of the witness. This law has effect with respect to both civil and criminal matters.

Likewise, Norwegian citizens or persons having their domicile in Norway, Denmark, Finland, Iceland or Sweden have the same obligation to meet and give witness before the courts in these countries in accordance with the rules governing such procedures in each respective country and which in principle conform with the regulations in the 1975 Act.

OBTAINING INFORMATION FROM NORWEGIAN BANKS FOR USE IN FOREIGN CIVIL PROCEEDINGS

Introduction

[22.22]   A Norwegian court may issue an order for the obtaining of evidence in civil proceedings in courts of other countries upon request from that court, provided that the evidence requested relates to a matter which is being tried before the foreign court. The letter of request shall set out the nature of the matter and be accompanied by a list of the questions which are to be asked of the witness or contain precise instructions or information with respect to the matters about which the witness is to testify before the Norwegian court. The letter of request for a hearing before the Norwegian court can be denied if the courts of Norway find that the request would impair its sovereignty or security or is considered to be contrary to public interest.

Generally, it can be said that a person shall not be compelled to give any evidence which he could not be compelled to give in civil proceedings instituted under Norwegian law. The extent of disclosure to a foreign court shall not exceed that which would be available in Norwegian proceedings.

Subpoenas from other jurisdictions

[22.23] If a foreign court serves a subpoena on an international bank in order to obtain information relating to its overseas branches or subsidiaries and the bank makes a request or gives an order to its Norwegian branch to provide the same, the Norwegian officers of the bank may not obey such request without breaching their duty of confidence to customers and thus infringing the confidentiality laws of Norway where the information is maintained. Such information can only be made available through a decision made by the Norwegian courts as previously outlined.

The duty to appear before and give evidence to a Norwegian court

[22.24] Regulations with regard to the duty to give witness before the courts are regulated in the Civil Procedures Act 1915. Certain categories of people have no right to explain themselves to the court without permission from the person who has the right of confidence. This principle extends, for instance, to lawyers and defence lawyers in criminal cases.

Bank officers and employees do not fall under this category. However, a witness may refuse to answer questions if he cannot reply without disclosing a commercial or operative secret, or on the principle of self-incrimination. Disclosure of secrets means matters which are important to keep secret for competitive reasons. A legal duty of confidence with respect to other business matters does not exempt from the duty to appear as witness before the courts. In a case of disclosure of secrets, the court must evaluate each party's interest and it will be essential how important the explanation is as evidence in the case. The court will also take into account how important the matter is to the parties involved.

These evaluations will be made when a witness refuses to answer a question and the other party demands that he shall explain himself notwithstanding the principle stated above. In such cases, the court may oblige the witness to explain himself when, after an evaluation of the two parties' interests, it finds it is required. In such circumstances, the court may decide that the explanation only shall be given to the court and the parties in closed hearings and under order of confidentiality.

Generally, a Norwegian court will not be able to ask for information which would be in breach of a bank's duty of confidentiality in the foreign country, unless the court has the power and is willing to lift the duty of confidentiality.

OBTAINING EVIDENCE ABROAD FOR USE IN NORWEGIAN CIVIL PROCEEDINGS

Introduction

[22.25] In addition to the reverse situation of that described above, it may well be that a party that has brought proceedings in the Norwegian courts may wish to obtain evidence from, amongst others, foreign banks which are not a party to the proceedings. Where a claimant alleges that the defendant has misappropriated funds belonging to him and has transferred them through various banks in order to cover his tracks, the claimant may wish to obtain information of this nature. In such situations, Norwegian courts may at their discretion apply to the court in the country in which the relevant bank is situated for the requested information.

Letters of request

[22.26]   A Norwegian court can issue letters of request to obtain information from parties situated abroad. The success of such a request depends to a large extent on whether the country concerned is a party to a convention or treaty with Norway. As discussed above, Norway passed the Nordic Witness Act 1975 with regard to witnesses from the other Nordic countries and, in addition, bilateral treaties exist (among others) between Norway and the UK and Norway and Germany. In addition, Norway is a party to the Hague Convention on the Taking of Evidence Abroad in Civil and Commercial Matters 1970. Under the Hague Convention, a witness may be compelled to provide information in certain cases. Such information is not limited to oral evidence, but may require the witness to provide documentary evidence as well.

In relation to non-convention countries, a letter of request may still be issued by the Norwegian court, but whether the foreign court will assist or not is a matter of local law.

The Hague Convention 1970

[22.27]   Under the Hague Convention, when receiving a letter of request, the authority which executes a letter of request shall apply its own law as to the methods and procedures to be followed. However, it shall do its best to oblige the request as stated if this is not impossible because of that country's internal practice and procedures or declared contrary to public interest.

In a declaration to the Hague Convention, Norway has stated that it will not execute letters of request issued for the purpose of obtaining pre-trial discovery of documents as known in common law countries. Furthermore, a letter of request shall not be used to obtain evidence which is not intended for use in proceedings; commenced or contemplated.

In executing a letter of request, the requested authority shall apply the appropriate measures of compulsion to the same extent as are provided by its internal law for the execution of orders issued by the authorities of its own country or all requests made by parties in international proceedings.

The Lugano Convention

[22.28]   As mentioned above, Norway is a party to the Lugano Convention and there is nothing to prevent a claimant who has brought proceedings in Norway from bringing proceedings for disclosure of documents in the courts of the country in which the bank in question is based. Whether the foreign court will grant such an order will, of course, depend on local law.

OBTAINING EVIDENCE IN NORWAY FOR USE IN FOREIGN CRIMINAL PROCEEDINGS

[22.29]   Norway ratified the European Convention on Mutual Assistance in Criminal Matters 1959 in 1962. Norwegian authorities, when requested to do so by a rogatory letter from a foreign criminal court, may nominate a court in Norway to receive such of the evidence referred to in the request as appears to them to be appropriate, taking Norwegian law into account.

The Norwegian authorities must be satisfied that a criminal offence under the law of the country or territory in question has been committed or that there are reasonable grounds for suspecting that such an offence has been committed and proceedings in respect of that offence have been instituted in that country or an investigation into the offence is being carried out there.

OBTAINING EVIDENCE ABROAD FOR USE IN NORWEGIAN CRIMINAL PROCEEDINGS

[22.30] In a reverse situation to that described above, a Norwegian court may issue a rogatory letter requiring assistance from another government to obtain evidence outside Norway if an offence has been committed or there are reasonable grounds to suspect that an offence has been committed and proceedings in respect of that offence have been instituted or the offence is being investigated by the Norwegian courts upon request from either the police, the ØKOKRIM, the FSAN or any other appropriate authority.

When, for example, the ØKOKRIM is investigating a possible criminal act, it may ask the Norwegian courts to issue a rogatory letter to a court in another country and ask for investigation to be carried out before that court.

OTHER RELEVANT PROVISIONS
Money laundering rules

[22.31] The money laundering rules mentioned above also apply to Norwegian branches of foreign banks and financial institutions as regards services provided in Norway. These rules are based on the Second EC Money Laundering Directive,[4] but are on some points somewhat stricter than the Directive. It is assumed that the specific Norwegian rules do not apply if a bank or another financial institution in an EEA state outside Norway provides services directly from its main office.

Cross-border activities

[22.32] A foreign bank or other financial institution might provide services in Norway directly from its main office. If the institution is located in an EEA state, the Norwegian confidentiality rules shall apply according to a regulation of 1994 by the Ministry of Finance.[5] The Ministry has the authority to make exceptions to this provision and let the law of the foreign state prevail. As for foreign institutions outside the EEA, Norwegian rules and regulations apply in full.

Norwegian law does not have explicit rules of confidentiality for Norwegian banks or other financial institutions providing services directly in another country. It is assumed that the law of the foreign state applies in such cases, both inside and outside the EEA.

---

4 Council Directive 2001/97/EC.
5 Regulation 7 July 1994 as amended, most recently on 9 September 1998.

Financial Supervisory Authority Act

[22.33] The members and officers of the FSAN are bound by an obligation of confidentiality. According to the FSAN Act and regulations by the Ministry of Finance, the confidentiality rules do not, however, apply when it comes to supplying information to supervisory authorities that execute banking or other financial supervision regulations in other countries, both inside and outside the EEA. The FSAN has made agreements about information exchange with a number of foreign supervisory authorities, but such agreements are not sufficient in order to demand information from private institutions or persons.

Disclosure obligation upon stock exchange members

[22.34] As mentioned above, stock exchange members are obliged, unhindered by confidentiality rules, to give the stock exchange of which they are members information that is necessary to fulfil the legal obligations of the stock exchange. Firms with main offices outside Norway, but within the EEA, have the right to become stock exchange members, presupposing that they have the authority to provide investment services. The disclosure obligation also applies to foreign members, including banks and other financial institutions.

Foreign exchange regulations

[22.35] In accordance with the Foreign Currency Exchange Register Act 2004 and regulations given by the Ministry of Finance, banks and other financial institutions are obliged to report certain information to the Directorate of Customs and Excise relating to, among other matters, foreign exchange.

PROPOSAL FOR NEW LEGISLATION

[22.36] The FSAN has proposed new rules regarding exchange of customer information within the same group. The proposal is limited to financial groups as defined in the Finance Activity Act. The main element of the proposal is that companies within the group may freely exchange specified customer information, provided the receiving company is subject to confidentiality rules. The Ministry of Finance is at present reviewing the proposal. It is, at this point in time, not clear if the Ministry of Finance will promote the proposal from the FSAN or when revised legislation will be implemented.

CONCLUDING REMARKS

[22.37] In conclusion, it is fair to say that the obligation of bank confidentiality has been more or less eroded in several areas of national and international finance, both for control purposes and because of the internationalisation of the financial market. However, as has been shown in other areas, especially with regard to securities trading, the principle of confidentiality has been further enhanced in several aspects of such business. Furthermore, the basic principle and obligation of confidentiality between a bank and its customer is still in force, apart from those specific laws and regulations which have been enacted contrary to that principle.

23 Panama

Carlos Sucre Levy

INTRODUCTION: GENERAL PRINCIPLES AND EXISTING REGULATIONS

[23.1]   Panama's confidentiality principles are based on an individual's right to privacy found in the constitution, which have developed by the values that regulate trade and commercial transactions generally and banking and securities operations in particular.

These principles are regulated by the following legislation:

1   the constitution of the Republic of Panama: ss 17 (the authorities' obligation to 'protect the life, honour and property' of persons), 29 (the principle of the inviolability of private documents and communications) and 42 (an individual's right to have access to his or her personal information and protect it);
2   the Commerce Code: ss 88 and 89 set the foundations for privacy pertaining to the books of all businesses;
3   Law 18 of 1959: regulates numbered bank accounts;
4   the Criminal Code: s 170 sanctions breaches of professional secrecy;
5   Law 1 of 1984: regulates trusts and trustee services;
6   Decree Law 9 of 1998: the Banking Act;
7   Decree Law 1 of 1999: the Securities Act.

OVERVIEW OF BANK CONFIDENTIALITY

[23.2]   Bank operations in Panama are regulated through Decree Law 9 of 1998 (the 'Banking Act'), which also creates the Superintendancy of Banks, an independent government body with fiscal and regulatory powers over banks and their affiliates operating in Panama.

Chapter XIII ('bank confidentiality') of the Banking Act regulates a bank's obligation to maintain the confidentiality of its clients' information. Section 85 states:

> 'CONFIDENTIALITY OF BANKS. Banks may disclose information about their clients or about their transactions only with the consent of the clients, save in cases of formal requests from the competent authorities as prescribed by law.
>
> Banks may, at their discretion, disclose information about their clients to Credit Information Agencies.'

Therefore, banks are only allowed to disclose information about their clients or transactions if (i) the client duly consents to such disclosure or (ii) by the request of a competent authority in matters expressly permitted by law.

Although the Banking Act neither defines nor lists the competent authorities, current legislation recognises the following: (i) the Superintendancy of Banks, (ii) the National Securities Commission, (iii) the Financial Analysis Unit, (iv) the Attorney General's Office (*Ministerio Público*), (v) the courts, (vi) the General Comptroller's Office and (vii) the Bureau of Internal Revenue of the Ministry of Economy and Finance.

Additionally, Law 18 of 1959 on numbered accounts originally only authorised the criminal courts and the Attorney General's Office to request information on this type of account. Although later legislation has increased the number of authorities with access to information on this type of account, they still enjoy greater confidentiality than other bank accounts.

Moreover, s 84 of the Banking Law and other legislation that authorises public authorities to request and obtain information from banks obliges these authorities to keep confidential any information gathered from their investigations and prohibits them from sharing it with unauthorised parties or to use the information for purposes other than those of the original investigation.

COMPETENT AUTHORITIES
Superintendancy of Banks

[23.3]   The Superintendancy may only request general information on a bank's transactions, as well as specific information regarding credit facilities and loans provided by the bank. The Superintendancy is not authorised to request information on specific bank accounts (including numbered accounts) unless the account acts as collateral for a loan or credit operation.

National Securities Commission

[23.4]   See 'Regulation of Financial Markets' below.

Financial Analysis Unit

[23.5]   The Unit is in charge of analysing financial information obtained from public and private institutions to determine any possible links with money laundering activities. Banks must report any suspicious event, transaction or operation related to money laundering offences to the Unit.

Attorney General's Office

[23.6]   Within the summary proceedings of any criminal process, the Attorney General's Office, through the instruction of certain officials (the Attorney General, District Attorneys and other city officials), is authorised to request information from banks about their clients, including their numbered accounts. The information must be obtained through the legal mechanisms put in place by the agents of the Attorney General's Office who have the power to carry out the same proceedings executed by a civil court judge, including precautionary measures, judicial inspections, enquiries, exhibitory actions, testimonies, confessions, interviews, expert evidence, reconstructions, searches and seizures.

Courts

[23.7] Judges and magistrates from the criminal judiciary are authorised to request any information from banks, including numbered bank accounts. Judges and magistrates of the civil judiciary can request information through a discovery action, but the action cannot include numbered bank accounts.

General Comptroller's Office

[23.8] The General Comptroller is authorised to carry out inspections and investigations to determine the validity of operations affecting state funds and, whenever applicable, submit its findings to the Attorney General's Office. Throughout its investigation, it may request banks to provide information on particular accounts, including numbered accounts in certain (limited) instances in which the Comptroller's investigations: (i) are centred on criminal acts or related to state funds and (ii) are addressed to a specific person on which the investigation is centred.[1]

Bureau of Internal Revenue

[23.9] Although long recognised by the courts to be able to request bank records for tax investigations purposes, it was not until the tax reform in 2005 that a law (Law 6 of 2005) conferred the Bureau with powers to request information from banks, including information on numbered bank accounts, necessary to conduct tax evasion investigations.

LIABILITIES AND SANCTIONS FOR BREACHES OF BANK CONFIDENTIALITY

[23.10] Breaches of bank confidentiality result in the following criminal, civil, administrative and employment sanctions and liabilities:

1 criminal liability: s 170 of the Criminal Code provides for imprisonment ranging from ten months to two years and prohibits a person who reveals confidential information in breach of professional obligations from working in certain professions;

2 civil liability: a person may seek the payment of damages following the release of his or her information in breach of banking confidentiality obligations;

3 administrative liability: the Banking Act establishes several administrative penalties applicable to the breach of the banks' and authorities' confidentiality obligations:

(a) s 86 of the Banking Act stipulates fines of up to US$100,000 for banks and government officials who breach bank secrecy regulations,

(b) s 4 of Law 18 of 1959 (the Numbered Accounts Act) imposes fines on bank personnel ranging from US$1,000 to US$10,000 and imprisonment for up to six months on bank employees who provide information on numbered accounts to anyone other than the competent authorities;

---

1 *Deutsch Sudamerikanische Bank AG v General Comptroller's Office*, 27 January 1993. Ruling by the Administrative Court of the Supreme Court, Judiciary Registry, January 2003, pp 180–187.

4   employment liabilities: s 213.a.4 of the Labour Code allows an employer to lay off a worker who reveals information which may have a negative effect on the employer.

CROSS-BORDER/EXTRA-TERRITORIAL ISSUES

Superintendancy of Banks

[23.11]   As an international financial centre, Panamanian banking regulations subject foreign banks operating in Panama not only to the supervision of the Superintendancy of Banks, but also to the supervision of the country where their headquarters are located.

Foreign supervising entities can request information and carry out inspection visits in Panama to branches or subsidiaries of foreign banks for which they have supervision. Any information compiled must be strictly confidential and cannot be revealed by the foreign supervising entity without the authorisation of the Superintendancy of Banks. Moreover, the foreign supervising entity must provide the Superintendancy of Banks with a copy of any report or document drawn up during the inspection.

Foreign supervising entities wishing to inspect and obtain information from the Panamanian branch of banks headquartered in their country are required to sign a memorandum of understanding ('MOU') with the Superintendancy to 'ensure that relations among the parties are founded on principles of reciprocity and confidentiality and strictly adhere to the purpose of banking supervision' (s 31 of the Banking Act).

Currently, the Superintendancy has signed MOUs with Peru, El Salvador, Ecuador, Guatemala, Colombia, Brazil, Dominican Republic, Turks & Caicos, Montserrat, Bolivia, Nicaragua, Venezuela, Antigua, Honduras, Costa Rica, USA, Cayman Islands, Mexico, BVI and Canada.

Request for information issued by foreign courts

[23.12]   Banks and financial institutions must not provide information requested directly by a foreign court. Instead, the foreign court must issue a formal request through a 'letters rogatory' addressed to the Supreme Court of Panama or, in the event that a treaty for legal assistance exists, to the specially appointed authority. The Fourth Chamber of the Supreme Court (or the specially appointed authority) will review the merits of the request and will instruct the bank to provide the information to the foreign court if the request is duly substantiated and (for requests in criminal matters) the act is a criminal offence in Panama.

Currently, Panama has signed treaties for legal assistance on criminal matters with the following countries in order to expedite the exchange of information in criminal matters and investigations: Colombia, Mexico, Peru, Spain, Ukraine, United Kingdom and the United States of America.

International treaties

[23.13]   Panama is also signatory to the following international treaties affecting bank confidentiality.

Inter-American Convention Against Corruption

[23.14] By means of Law 42 of 1998, Panama adopted the Organisation of American States' Inter-American Convention Against Corruption. Article XVI of the Convention deals with the exchange of banking information among signatory countries:

'1. The Requested State shall not invoke bank secrecy as a basis for refusal to provide the assistance sought by the Requesting State. The Requested State shall apply this article in accordance with its domestic law, its procedural provisions, or bilateral or multilateral agreements with the Requesting State.

2. The Requesting State shall be obliged not to use any information received that is protected by bank secrecy for any purpose other than the proceeding for which that information was requested, unless authorised by the Requested State.'

It is clear that the text of the Convention in no way affects the long-standing Panamanian tradition regarding bank confidentiality since the Convention specifically conditions its enforcement to be in accordance with the applicable domestic laws of the state parties and the relevant treaties or other agreements that may be in force between or among them.

Central American Convention for the Prevention and Persecution of Laundering of Money and Assets Related to the Illegal Drug Trade

[23.15] Panama enacted this Convention through Law 51 of 1998. It is based on the premise that the laundering of money and assets related to the illegal drug trade and connected crimes are a social evil that must be forcefully resisted. It also recognises that moneys generated by these activities produce financial harm to the economies of each of the Central American nations and that the ultimate objective of money laundering is the legitimisation of illegally-obtained funds.

A provision reflecting modern 'know your customer' practices is included in art 11, where it is laid down that, in those state parties where numbered, anonymous or any other accounts operated by representatives are allowed, financial entities must know the real identity of their client in the event that such information is ever requested. Financial entities must use adequate means to verify the client's identity by means of a passport or any other valid identification. In the event that the financial entity, for any reason, has doubts that the person they regard as their client is not the beneficial owner of the account, they must determine the identity of the actual beneficial owner by any means at their disposal.

Article 12 of the Convention decrees that all entities involved in financial intermediation must comply with any information request submitted to them by the competent authorities.

Bank confidentiality principles remain unaltered by the provisions of this Convention since it is only applicable by the competent authorities acting on criminal investigation procedures. Article 19 states that no internal provisions of any of the state parties will be deemed as an impediment to comply with the Convention as long as the information is requested or shared by a competent authority in accordance with each party's laws.

REGULATION OF FINANCIAL MARKETS

[23.16] The Securities Act (Decree Law 1 of 1999), enacted a year after the Banking Act, follows the same competent authorities principles as the bank regulations. Therefore, broker–dealers, investment advisors and fund managers must keep their clients' information confidential unless (i) the client duly consents to such disclosure or (ii) a competent authority requests the information. The authorities competent to request banking information are also authorised to request information on securities transactions. However, the Securities Act does not allow foreign authorities to supervise or inspect the Panamanian branches of securities intermediaries headquartered in their country.

Conflicts of interest

[23.17] Sections 39 and 40 of the Securities Act require that all broker–dealers and financial advisors treat their clients fairly and only give advice regarding a security transaction where there is reasonable cause that such advice is adequate for that particular client, based on the information provided by the client on his or her investment objectives, financial circumstances and particular needs.

The National Securities Commission issued Accord 5-2003 to govern conduct and ethics standards for stockmarkets, broker–dealers and financial advisors and mandates them to approve a Code of Conduct. Under the Accord, these entities must inform their clients at least each quarter of any conflict of interest that may arise while providing their services, including:[2] (i) any investments made in securities issued by the entity or an affiliated company, (ii) any investments made in securities where the entity or an affiliated company acts as insurer or underwriter and (iii) any relationship with an issuer of securities for which the entity supplies economic and financial data that may derive from an investment recommendation.

CONCLUSIONS

[23.18] Banks are only authorised to provide information regarding their operations to the Superintendancy of Banks, foreign bank supervisory entities where their headquarters are located (for branches of foreign banks), the National Securities Commission if they have a licence to act as broker–dealer, financial advisor or fund manager, the Bureau of Internal Revenue of the Ministry of Economy and Finance, but only for tax investigation purposes, the Financial Analysis Unit regarding transactions suspected of being connected to money laundering operations or the General Comptroller's Office for investigations regarding the use of state funds.

Banks may not reveal or provide information regarding their clients' transactions unless:

1   the client expressly authorises it;
2   the bank receives a written order by one of the competent authorities mentioned above and only for the information requested in such an order;
3   regarding numbered accounts, the information is requested as part of a criminal investigation for an act punishable in Panama and the request has been issued by the Attorney General's Office, a criminal judge, the Financial Analysis Unit or the General Comptroller's Office.

2 Section 20, Accord 5-2003, National Securities Commission, Official Gazette, no 25,109, 5 August 2004.

24   Poland

Tomasz Wardyński CBE
Michał Steinhagen
Katarzyna Petruczenko

INTRODUCTION

[24.1]   The transformation of the Polish economy which started in 1989 and the attendant increasing number of commercial entities and the rapid development of their activities has meant that information possessed by banks about their customers has become very useful to a number of bodies who, therefore, have expressed a need for it. Criminal investigative authorities, judicial bodies, tax authorities, banking supervisory bodies and common commercial entities have also been attempting to convince banks that they should have access to information about bank customers.

At the same time as the restrictions imposed on commercial activity by the previous regime were being eased, a number of spectacular financial dealings of a dubious, if not fraudulent, nature surfaced indicating, quite clearly, the absence of a well-developed system of controls of the marketplace and, of course, banking such as may be expected in a developed market economy.

The provisions of the Banking Act of 31 January 1989 did not regulate bank confidentiality adequately and precisely and those matters were not satisfactorily clarified until 1997.

Poland's accession to the European Union required Polish legislation and practice to be adjusted accordingly. On 1 February 1994, the Europe Agreement, establishing an association between the European Communities and their member states, on the one part, and the Republic of Poland, on the other, came into force which, by arts 69 and 83, obliged Poland to approximate, among other things, its banking legislation to European standards. On 1 May 2004, Poland became a member of the EU. Now, two years after accession to the EU, the process of transposition of *acquis communautaire* is close to an end. Poland was one of the countries which requested postponement for the transposition of provisions on co-operative credit institutions until the end of 2007 (Financial Conglomerates Directive 2002/87/EEC).

Moreover, it must be stressed that the obligation to keep banking details confidential falls under art 8, clause 1 of the European Convention on Human Rights concerning the right to privacy.

THE RULE OF CONFIDENTIALITY UNDER POLISH LAW

Source and scope

[24.2] The concept of bank confidentiality arises from art 104 of the Banking Act, dated 29 August 1997. The provisions of that article significantly improved the regulations under the previous banking law of 1989 and reflect art 16 of the Second Banking Directive[1] of 15 December 1989 on the co-ordination of the laws, regulations and administrative provisions relating to the taking up and pursuit of the business of credit institutions and amending Council Directive 77/780/EEC.[2] After several amendments, the provisions of this article are now in conformity with art 30 of Directive 2000/12/EC of the European Parliament and of the Council of 20 March 2000 (the Codification Directive). The transposition included the two directives dealing with money laundering, ie 91/308/EEC and 2001/97/EC.

Article 104 defines banking confidentiality in three dimensions: persons who are responsible for maintaining banking confidentiality, the ambit of information which is subject to the rule and the time within which information is to be kept confidential. Banks are subject to the requirement of confidentiality and art 104 also extends that obligation directly to bank employees and the persons entrusted with implementing actions by banks.

The provision applies to the following information:

1   any information concerning banking operations obtained in the course of negotiations and during the performance and conclusion of the contract on the basis of which the bank performs the operations;
2   information concerning the provision of information to the police under the conditions specified in art 20, paras 4 to 10 of the Police Act of 6 April 1990 and concerning the notification referred to in art 20, para 13 of that Act. The duty to preserve secrecy applies in respect of parties to the contract, other persons whom the information concerns and third parties (art 104, para 4).

The obligation to preserve bank confidentiality does not apply to cases in which:

1   without disclosure of the information covered by bank confidentiality – due to the essence and nature of the banking operation or due to the provisions in force – it is impossible properly to carry out the contract on the basis of which the banking operation is performed or properly to perform the acts connected with the performance and conclusion of this contract;
2   the information covered by bank confidentiality is disclosed to domestic or foreign entrepreneurs whom the bank, pursuant to art 6a to d, entrusted with the performance, permanent or temporary, of operations connected with carrying on banking activity to the extent necessary properly to perform such operations;
3   the information covered by bank confidentiality is provided to advocates or legal counsel in connection with the provision of legal assistance to the bank;
4   the provision of the information covered by bank confidentiality is necessary in order to carry out and conclude contracts of sale of receivable debts classified pursuant to separate provisions in the category of lost receivable debts;

---

1 Council Directive 89/646/EEC.
2 Currently, it is art 30 of the Banking Directive 2000/12/EC on the taking up and pursuit of the business of credit institutions.

5   the provision of the information covered by bank confidentiality is necessary in order to carry out and conclude contracts of sale of receivable debts and contracts of subparticipation referred to in art 92a, para 1 and contracts of provision of investment rating of securitised receivable debts and insurance against the insolvency risk of debtors of securitised receivable debts connected with them;

6   the provision of the information covered by bank confidentiality is necessary in order to carry out and conclude contracts with subjects referred to in art 92a, para 3 and in the case where the subjects concluded with the bank from which they acquired receivable debts contracts for servicing these securitised receivable debts.

A literal interpretation of art 104, para 1 of the Banking Act suggests that bank confidentiality does not cover the information on persons who have not concluded an agreement (with the bank). Legal opinion, however, rejects that interpretation, arguing that bank confidentiality arises at the time when the bank is provided with the information covered by the scope of the article, regardless of whether an agreement is concluded or not. It seems a judicial ruling is required finally to decide the matter.

Information which falls within the scope of the list above is to be kept confidential indefinitely.

The subjects and persons employed in the bank who were provided with information covered by bank confidentiality or to whom such information was disclosed, according to the provision of (para 2) subparagraphs 1, 2 and 4 to 6, may only use the information for the purpose of carrying out and concluding the contracts referred to in these paragraphs. Accordingly, the same rule applies to advocates or legal counsel provided with information covered by bank confidentiality in connection with the provision of legal assistance to the bank.

Apart from the exceptions mentioned above, the law only allows disclosure in two situations: upon the request of institutions or persons specified by law or with the written consent of the person whose information is covered by the provision. Such consent has to specify the information and a person to whom the information can be disclosed.[3]

Criminal and civil liability

[24.3]   Disclosure of confidential banking information constitutes a criminal offence in Poland.

Article 171, para 5 of the Banking Act states that anyone who, being obliged to keep banking information confidential, discloses or uses such information in breach of the authorisation specified in the legislation shall be punishable by a fine of up to PLN 1 million and imprisonment for up to three years. The criminal sanctions cover both bank employees and persons entrusted to carry out actions by the bank, who are mentioned in art 104, para 1 of the Banking Act, as well as persons to whom such information is disclosed, upon their request, under art 105, para 1 of the Banking Act, which is discussed further below.

Provisions of the Banking Act also regulate some aspects of civil liability for breach of the rule of bank confidentiality.

3 Banking Act, art 104, para 2.

Article 105, para 5 indicates who is to be liable and make good the loss resulting from breach of the rule. By that article, the bank is liable for the loss resulting from disclosure and inappropriate use of such information. Article 105, para 5 is not a separate legal basis for bank liability and needs to be read in conjunction with arts 415 or 471 of the Civil Code, depending on whether the claim for loss is based on liability for breach of an obligation (statutory or contractual) or in tort.

Bank liability is excluded if the loss results from disclosure by the persons or institutions authorised by legislation to require banks to provide them with information which is otherwise confidential.[4]

Remedies for breach of the duty of confidentiality

[24.4]   Article 104, para 1 of the Banking Act imposes a statutory obligation on the bank, bank employees and the persons entrusted to carry out actions by the bank to keep information confidential concerning persons being a party to an agreement (with a bank) and persons who are not parties to such agreements, but who performed certain actions in connection with the conclusion of such agreements.

When the duty of confidentiality arises from an obligation (statutory or contractual), the person whose information is to be kept confidential may claim damages from a bank for breach of the obligation, unless the disclosure of the information is a consequence of circumstances for which the bank, its employees and the persons entrusted to carry out actions on behalf of the bank are not responsible.[5] The burden of proof that such disclosure is due to such circumstances lies with the bank.

The civil liability of a bank for breach of the obligation not to reveal confidential banking information can be limited by a contract concluded between a bank and a customer. Under art 473, para 1 of the Civil Code, a bank cannot, however, exclude liability for loss caused to a customer intentionally. A limitation of bank civil liability to a customer for disclosing confidential information does not release a bank, bank employees and the persons entrusted to carry out actions by the bank from the criminal liability specified in art 171, para 5 of the Banking Act.

A person whose information is to be kept confidential by the bank can also seek damages from a bank under the rule of liability for illicit acts as stipulated in art 415 of the Civil Code (rule of tort). However, the person needs to prove that the disclosure was caused by the negligence of a bank, its employees or the persons entrusted to carry out actions by the bank, that losses were incurred and that a causal link exists between the two.

If it is decided by a court that bank confidentiality only covers persons who conclude an agreement with a bank, then those who provide a bank with information which is covered by art 104, para 1 of the Banking Act, but who do not conclude an agreement, can seek damages from the bank for disclosure of the information under the rule of liability for dishonest contractual acts (doctrine of *culpa in contrahendo*). In order to succeed in seeking such claims, the person needs to satisfy the above conditions of art 415 of the Civil Code. A claim for damages for disclosure of confidential information by an institution or a person authorised by legislation to request that the banks provide them with confidential information can be based,

---

4 Banking Act, art 104, para 6.
5 Article 105 of the Banking Act, read in conjunction with art 471 of the Civil Code and art 104, para 1 of the Banking Act.

depending on the circumstances, on one of the legal bases mentioned above, ie liability for breach of an obligation, tort or *culpa in contrahendo*.

Although it is not possible under Polish law to apply for an injunction to restrain a bank from disclosing confidential information on the basis of showing a mere intent to do so, an interim injunction may be possible when disclosure has already occurred and further disclosure is intended by a bank. In order to obtain security of the claim in the form of an interim injunction, the claimant needs to show to the court that (i) grounds for the claim already exist, (ii) the claim is credible and (iii) the absence of the security could make it impossible to satisfy the claim. Security in the form of an interim injunction is only temporary relief and, therefore, a court will oblige a successful claimant to instigate proceedings against a bank for satisfaction of a secured claim within a specified period of time, which cannot be longer than two weeks.

Under art 18 of the Act on Combating Unfair Competition of 16 April 1993, which sets out the civil remedies for an act of unfair competition,[6] a customer (ie someone engaged in commercial activity)[7] whose interest has been threatened or infringed may demand that the bank:

1   ceases to disclose the customer's business secrets;
2   eliminates the effects of the disclosure of such secrets;
3   issues or publishes one or more statements with appropriate content and in a defined form;
4   redresses any losses by paying damages under general legal principles (ie arts 415 or 471 of the Civil Code);
5   surrenders unjustified benefits to the customer under general legal principles. This demand is based on arts 405 to 414 of the Civil Code, by which any party who, without legal grounds, has gained a material benefit at the expense of another shall be obliged to surrender that benefit (to the latter party) in kind and, if that is impossible, to surrender an equivalent monetary value. The duty to surrender the benefit includes not only any benefit gained directly, but also anything which, in the case of sale, loss or damage, has been gained in exchange for that benefit or as a redress of such loss or damage. This provision could be of particular use for benefits gained by the bank as a result of the use of confidential information concerning a customer for cross-selling;
6   pays an appropriate amount of money to a specified social purpose connected with supporting Polish culture or the protection of national heritage if an act of unfair competition was committed.

It is also possible to argue that banking information is a personal asset and, as such, is protected by the provisions of arts 23 and 24 of the Civil Code in the same way as personal correspondence, creative and scientific works and inventions. On that basis, it could be possible to seek an injunction because, in certain circumstances, revealing banking details could be detrimental to a person's social or commercial position and situation and could lead to the disclosure of other matters. Moreover, a customer can require a bank which has divulged confidential information, which constitutes a

---

6 An act of unfair competition is defined as activity contrary to law or good behaviour if it constitutes a threat or infringes the interest of another undertaking or customer (Act on Combating Unfair Competition, art 3, para 1). An act of unfair competition is, among other things, the delivery, disclosure or making use of the secret information of a person engaged in commercial activity or its purchase from a non-authorised person (Act on Combating Unfair Competition, art 11, para 1).
7 Act on Combating Unfair Competition, art 2.

personal asset, to perform acts necessary to remedy the effects of such disclosure and, in particular, make or publish a statement with appropriate content and in a defined form. Irrespective of a customer's right to seek damages, under the general rules of the Civil Code, a customer can demand pecuniary damages for intangible harm inflicted (*krzywda* – this can include, for example, the psychological distress suffered or damage to the reputation of an individual or commercial entity). The amount of damages is set by the court.

EXCEPTIONS TO THE RULE OF BANK CONFIDENTIALITY

[24.5]   Article 105 of the Banking Act constitutes an exception to the principle of non-disclosure to third persons. It provides for a wide range of persons or institutions which have *ex lege* access to confidential information. Banks, state bodies and persons to whom confidential bank information has been disclosed are obliged to use such information exclusively within the limits of the authorisation specified in para 1 of art 105.[8] This means that confidential information received from a bank under art 105, paras 1 or 2 of the Banking Act cannot be disclosed further to other persons or institutions, including those listed in that article, unless provisions of law provide otherwise.

Information exchanged between banks and provided to the National Bank of Poland

[24.6]   Article 105, para 1, points 1), 1a) and 1b) of the Banking Act state that a bank shall be obliged to disclose information subject to bank secrecy exclusively to:

1   other banks and credit institutions to the extent that this information is necessary in connection with carrying out banking operations and with acquiring and transferring receivable debts;
2   subject to reciprocity – to other institutions authorised by statutory law to grant credits – about receivable debts and about bank accounts, turnover and positions to the extent that such information is necessary in connection with granting credits, loans, bank guarantees and suretyships;
3   other banks, credit institutions or financial institutions to the extent necessary for the implementing of the applicable provisions concerning consolidated supervision, including, in particular, for the preparation of consolidated financial statements or for managing large exposure risk.

A bank shall also disclose to the National Bank of Poland confidential information needed for the control and collection of data necessary to prepare a balance of payments, foreign debt and foreign obligations of the state, as well as to other banks which are authorised to act as an agent in the execution of transfer of money abroad by residents and to make settlements in the country with non-residents within the scope specified in the Act of 27 July 2002 on Foreign Exchange Law.[9]

---

8 Banking Act, art 105, para 3.
9 Banking Act, art 105, para 1, point 3).

Information disclosed to the Commission for Banking Supervision

[24.7]   A bank is also obliged to disclose confidential information at the request of the Commission for Banking Supervision within the scope of supervision exercised under the Banking Act and the Act on the National Bank of Poland of 29 August 1997, inspectors of banking supervision, who are referred to in art 139, para 1, point 2 of the Banking Act, and persons authorised by a resolution of the Commission for Banking Supervision within the scope specified in such authorisation[10] (art 105, para 1, point 2) a) of the Banking Act).

The obligation to disclose confidential information to the above-mentioned persons is directly connected with the statutory supervisory tasks imposed on the Commission for Banking Supervision under art 25, para 2 of the Act on the National Bank of Poland and art 133 of the Banking Act.

In order for the Commission for Banking Supervision to fulfil such tasks, it is vested with wide control over banks. For instance, art 139, para 1, point 2) of the Banking Act states that banks, as well as branches and agencies of foreign banks in Poland, shall be obliged to enable authorised persons to perform supervisory tasks specified in art 133, para 2 and, in particular, to make books, balance sheets, registers, plans, reports and other documents accessible to them and enable them, upon a written request, to make copies of such documents and other carriers of information and provide them with any explanations requested by such persons.

Information disclosed to the courts, public prosecutors and court executive officers

[24.8]   Confidential information is to be disclosed, if requested, by:

1   a court or public prosecutor in connection with proceedings pending in a case of offence or fiscal offence:
   (a)   against a natural person being a party to a contract made with the bank, to the extent that the information concerns the natural person,
   (b)   committed in connection with the activities of a legal person or organisational unit without legal personality, to the extent that the information concerns this legal person or organisational unit;[11]
2   a court or public prosecutor in connection with carrying out an application for legal assistance made by a foreign state entitled to request the provision of information covered by bank secrecy under a ratified international agreement binding Poland;[12]

---

10 The following persons can be authorised on the basis of a resolution of the Commission for Banking Supervision to request a bank to provide them with confidential information: (i) an auditor who examines a bank upon an order issued directly by the Commission for Banking Supervision (Banking Act, art 135, para 2), (ii) persons authorised in connection with the performance of consolidated supervision to perform on-the-spot checks in undertakings (ie among others things, banks) to which a bank, which is referred to in art 141f, para 1, point 1, is a dominant undertaking or which has close links with that bank and in the undertakings which are a part of holding companies referred to in art 141f, para 1, points 2 to 3 (Banking Act, art 141h) and (iii) other persons authorised to perform the activities of banking supervision specified in art 133, para 2 of the Banking Act and tasks of the Commission for Banking Supervision specified in art 25, para 2 of the Act on the National Bank of Poland.
11 Banking Act, art 105, para 1, point 2 b).
12 Banking Act, art 105, para 1, point 2 c).

3   a court in connection with inheritance proceedings or proceedings for division of marital property or lawsuit for maintenance or alimony pension pending against a natural person being a party to a contract;[13]

4   a court executive officer in connection with pending execution proceedings.[14]

Information disclosed to the directors of customs offices

[24.9]   Article 105, para 1, point 2) e) of the Banking Act states that a director of customs offices shall be provided with confidential information, upon request, if it is in connection with:

1   a criminal case or fiscal penal case pending against a natural person, being a party to a contract concluded with a bank;

2   a criminal case or fiscal penal case pending concerning an offence committed within the scope of activity of legal persons or organisational units having no legal personality who are holders of an account.

Information disclosed to the president of the Supreme Chamber of Control

[24.10]   Article 105, para 1, point 2) f) of the Banking Act states that the President of the Supreme Chamber of Control shall be provided, upon his request, with confidential information (by the bank) to the extent necessary to carry out control proceedings specified in the Act of 23 December 1994 on the Supreme Chamber of Control.

The Supreme Chamber of Control is authorised, among other things, to control the activity of the state and municipal legal persons, as well as the activity of other organisational units and entities carrying out commercial activity within the scope that they use state or municipal assets or resources and fulfil their financial obligations to the state.[15]

Banks covered by art 2 of the Supreme Chamber of Control Act are obliged, upon the request of the Supreme Chamber of Control, to deliver all or any documents and materials which are necessary to prepare and conduct such control, subject to the provisions on confidential information protected by legislation.[16] Authorised representatives of the Supreme Chamber of Control are entitled, among other things:

1   to have access to all or any documents connected with the activity of the controlled entity and collect and secure the documents and other evidence, subject to the provisions on secret information protected by legislation;[17]

2   to demand delivery of written and oral explanations from the employees of an entity being inspected.[18]

---

13 Banking Act, art 105, para 1, point 2 d).
14 Banking Act, art 105, para 1, point 2 l).
15 Act on Supreme Chamber of Control, art 2.
16 Act on Supreme Chamber of Control, art 29, point 1).
17 Act on Supreme Chamber of Control, art 29, point 2) b).
18 Act on Supreme Chamber of Control, art 29, point 2) e).

Information disclosed to the chairman of the Securities and Exchange Commission

[24.11] Confidential information shall be delivered to the chairman of the Securities and Exchange Commission, upon request, by a bank within the scope necessary to exercise supervision, including the conduct of explanatory proceedings, by virtue of the Act referred to in art 4, para 1, subparagraph 8 and the Act of 27 May 2004 on Investment Funds.[19]

The Securities and Exchange Commission shall, among other things, supervise the observance of the rules of fair trading and competition in public trading in securities and supervise the provision of public access to reliable information on the securities market.

In connection with the performance of supervision tasks, the chairman of the Commission, its authorised representatives and the employees of the Commission's Office, shall have access to:

1 confidential information within the meaning of art 154 of the Act on Trading in Financial Instruments;
2 other information, including information subject to professional secrecy, referred to in art 19 para 1, being in possession of natural persons or other entities, in particular, mentioned in arts 20, 21 and 23, as well as art 150 of the Act on Trading in Financial Instruments. This information and the information obtained by the Commission under arts 20, 21 and 23 may only, unless otherwise provided by the provisions of other acts, be used for the purpose of performing supervision tasks. In particular, they can constitute evidence in administrative proceedings conducted by the Commission.[20]

Information disclosed to the president of the board of management of the Banking Guarantee Fund

[24.12] The president of the board of management of the Banking Guarantee Fund is entitled to receive confidential information from a bank, to the extent specified in the Act of 14 December 1994 on the Banking Guarantee Fund.[21]

Under art 38, para 6 of the Act on the Banking Guarantee Fund, banks which are covered by an obligatory deposit guarantee scheme are obliged to provide the Banking Guarantee Fund with all information, other than that provided to the National Bank of Poland, which is necessary to fulfil the Fund's tasks. The scope of such information is specified by the president of the National Bank of Poland, upon the motion of the Banking Guarantee Fund.[22]

The tasks of the Fund are listed in art 4 of the Act on the Banking Guarantee Fund. They cover, among other things:

1 analysis of the information about entities covered by the deposit guarantee scheme;[23]

---

19 Banking Law, art 105, para 1, point 2) g).
20 Act on Supervision over Capital Markets, art 24.
21 Banking Law, art 105, para 1, point 2) h).
22 Act on Banking Guarantee Fund, art 38, para 7.
23 Act on Banking Guarantee Fund, art 4, para 1, point 3).

2   control of appropriate use of the repayable financial assistance given to entities covered by the deposit guarantee scheme in case of a danger of insolvency or for the purpose of purchasing shares in the banks.[24]

Information disclosed to auditors

[24.13]   A bank is obliged to provide confidential information to a certified auditor, upon request, authorised to examine the financial statements of a bank under a contract concluded with a bank.[25]

Information disclosed to the Commission for Supervision over Insurance and Retirement Pension Funds

[24.14]   Confidential information is to be delivered by a bank, upon request, to the Commission for Supervision over Insurance and Retirement Pension Funds for supervision of the performance of a bank as a depositary under the Act of 28 August 1997 on Organisation and Operation of Retirement Pension Funds.[26]

Article 204a, para 2, point 2) of the Act provides that the person authorised by the supervisory body (ie the Retirement Pension Funds Supervisory Office) is entitled to have access to the premises of a depositary to check whether activity connected with holding the assets of the funds complies with the law and the agreement on holding assets of the fund. The person carrying out the inspection has the right, among other things, to (i) check all books, documents and other sources of information, (ii) demand preparation and delivery of copies of such documents and sources of information and (iii) require information from the members of the executive bodies and employees of the controlled entity.[27]

Information disclosed to the trustee and his deputy

[24.15]   According to art 105, para 2 of the Banking Act, confidential information is also to be disclosed to a trustee and his deputy within the scope and according to the rules specified in the Act of 29 August 1997 on the Lien's Letters and the Mortgage Banks. Lien's letters (mortgage bonds) are securities issued by mortgage banks on the basis of receivables of those banks secured with a mortgage.

A trustee and his deputy are appointed for each mortgage bank by the Commission for Banking Supervision. They cannot be employees of a bank and their obligation is to control a mortgage bank[28] within the scope provided for in art 30 of the Act. According to art 30, the trustee is obliged to verify whether:

24 Act on Banking Guarantee Fund, art 4, para 2, point 2), read in conjunction with point 1).
25 Banking Act, art 105, para 1, point 2) i).
26 Banking Act, art 105, para 1, point 2) j).
27 Act on Organisation and Operation of Retirement Pension Funds, art 204a, para 3, points 1) to 3).
28 The activity of a mortgage bank covers, among other things:
   1   granting credits secured by a mortgage;
   2   granting credits not secured by a mortgage which are referred to in art 3, para 2 (ie credits which are granted to or which are partly secured by the National Bank of Poland, the governments or central banks of member states of the EU, OECD and local authorities);
   3   purchase of the receivables of other banks deriving from credits granted by those banks which are secured by a mortgage and receivables deriving from credits not secured by a mortgage which are referred to in point 2;

1 the obligations deriving from lien's letters being in circulation are secured by a mortgage bank in accordance with the provisions of the Act;
2 a bank mortgage value of a real estate adopted by a mortgage bank has been established in accordance with byelaws which are mentioned in art 22, para 2 of the Act;
3 a mortgage bank complies with the limits specified in art 18 of the Act (ie a total amount of nominal values of the mortgage lien's letters being in circulation);
4 the manner in which a mortgage bank runs a register for security of the lien's letters complies with the conditions of this Act;
5 a mortgage bank provides, in accordance with this Act, a security for planned emission of the lien's letters and control and whether the appropriate records have been made to the register for security of the lien's letters.

In order to fulfil his tasks, which are referred to in art 30 of the Act, a trustee is entitled to check the accounting books, registers, plans and other documents of a bank at any time.[29] The bank is obliged to provide a trustee and his deputy, in connection with the performance of their duties and within the scope specified in para 1, with confidential bank information.[30] Under art 32, para 1b of the Act, a trustee and his deputy are obliged not to disclose the information they receive during the performance of their duties.

Information disclosed to the Social Insurance Institution

[**24.16**]   Banks are obliged, upon written request from the Social Insurance Institution, to prepare and deliver information concerning numbers of the bank accounts of payers of insurance premiums and to deliver details which allow identification of the holders of such bank accounts.[31]

Information disclosed to institutions authorised to collect and provide information to banks and other institutions authorised to grant credit

[**24.17**]   Under art 105, para 4 of the Banking Act, banks are entitled, jointly with bank commercial associations, to establish institutions authorised to collect, process and provide secret banking information:

1 to banks, to the extent that such information is needed in connection with the performance of banking operations;

---

4 emission of the mortgage lien's letters, the basis of which constitutes the receivables of a mortgage bank:
  (a) deriving from granted credits secured by a mortgage, and
  (b) deriving from purchased receivables of other banks to which those banks are entitled due to credits which were granted by those banks and secured by a mortgage;
5 emission of the public lien's letter, the basis of which constitutes:
  (a) receivables of a mortgage bank deriving from credits which are not secured by a mortgage which are referred to in point 2,
  (b) receivables of other banks purchased by a mortgage bank deriving from credits granted by those banks and not secured by a mortgage which are referred to in point 2 (Act on the Lien's Letters and the Mortgage Banks, art 12).
29 Act on the Lien's Letters and the Mortgage Banks, art 32, para 1.
30 Act on the Lien's Letters and the Mortgage Banks, art 32, para 1a.
31 Banking Act, art 105, para 2a.

2   to other institutions authorised by statutory law to grant credit information on receivable debts, turnover and bank account balances, to the extent that such information is necessary in connection with granting credits, loans, bank guarantees and suretyships.

Information disclosed to the Commercial Information Office

[24.18] The Act of 14 February 2003 on Making Accessible Commercial Information provides principles and procedures for commercial information to be made available on the repayment credibility of undertakings and consumers, in particular, information on delays in the performance of pecuniary obligations to third parties who or which are not specified at the moment this information is made available.[32]

Under art 105, para 4a) of the Banking Act, institutions established on the basis of art 105, para 4 of the Banking Act are entitled to provide the Commercial Information Office, operating on the basis of the Act on Making Accessible Commercial Information, with information within the scope and upon the conditions defined in that Act. Banks are entitled to provide offices, which are mentioned in art 105, para 4a) of the Banking Act, with information on obligations arising from contracts connected with the performance of banking acts if such contracts include a clause allowing for the provision of such information.[33]

Under art 2 of the Act, 'commercial information' means information:

1   *in relation to a legal person or organisational unit having no legal personality*: firm name, registered office and address, number under which the undertaking is registered in the appropriate register and indication of a register court, tax identification number, REGON number (ie statistical number), first names and surnames of the persons being members of the executive bodies, proxies of the undertaking or unit and main subject of the commercial activity;
2   *in relation to a natural person*: first name and surname, nationality, residence, identification number, information concerning identity card or other document confirming the identity of a person, date of birth and, additionally, in relation to a natural person engaged in commercial activity, firm name, registered office and address, tax identification number, REGON number, number under which the undertaking is registered in the appropriate register and indication of a register court, first names and surnames of proxies, if any, and main subject of the commercial activity;
3   *on pecuniary obligation*: legal title, amount and currency, due amount, date of arising of amount due, state of proceedings concerning obligation, including information on court decisions, information on questioning by a debtor of the obligation in whole or in part, date of sending of a call for payment, including warning of intention to provide information to the office and a firm and registered office of such office, and other information delivered in the course and on the conditions specified in art 10 of the Act.

Under art 14, para 4 of the Act on Making Accessible Commercial Information, the office shall only disclose the commercial information of a consumer's obligations to

---

32 Act on Making Accessible Commercial Information, art 1.
33 Banking Act, art 105, para 4b.

(i) the undertaking which has concluded a contract with the office on making such information accessible, (ii) other offices or institutions established on the basis of art 105, para 4 of the Banking Act to comply with the motions requesting disclosure of such information and (iii) entities specified in art 16, para 1 of the Act, ie the National Prosecutor, Main Chief of Police, Chief of the Government Security Office, General Inspector of Fiscal Control, General Inspector of Financial Information, directors of the fiscal offices, directors of the fiscal control offices, General Inspector of Banking Supervision, president of the Supreme Chamber of Control, the courts and the directors of customs offices.

An undertaking, which concluded a contract on making commercial information accessible and has been authorised by the consumer to request such information, is entitled to request that commercial information on that consumer's obligations be disclosed to it within 30 days from a day such authorisation has been granted.[34] If a consumer refuses to grant such authorisation, an undertaking is entitled to refuse to conclude a contract on consumer credit or conclude such contract on conditions less favourable for the consumer.[35]

A person or organisational unit which receives commercial information from the office is obliged to erase it within 90 days from the day it was received. A person or organisational unit receiving the commercial information concerning a consumer is not permitted to disclose it to other persons. These obligations do not apply to the entities listed in art 16, para 1 of the Act on Making Available Commercial Information.[36]

Information disclosed to the state security services and the police

[24.19]   Under art 105, para 1, point 2) k) and l) of the Banking Act, a bank, upon request, is obliged to deliver confidential information to:

1   the state security services, the Intelligence Agency, the police, the military police, the Frontier Guard, the Prison Service and their officials or soldiers, holding written authorisations, within the scope necessary for conducting verification proceedings pursuant to the provision for protecting private information; and
2   the police, if it is necessary for effective crime prevention, detection or for determining offenders and obtaining evidence under the rules and procedure referred to in art 20 of the Police Act of 6 April 1990. Under art 20, para 3, in conjunction with para 5 of the Police Act, the police are entitled to use information processed by the banks, which is subject to bank secrecy, upon the consent granted by a relevant district court.

Information disclosed to the issuers of electronic payment instruments

[24.20]   Under art 105, para 1, point 2) m), a bank is obliged to provide confidential information to the issuers of electronic payment instruments, which are not banks,

---

34 Act on Making Accessible Commercial Information, art 15, para 1.
35 Act on Making Accessible Commercial Information, art 15, para 2.
36 Act on Making Accessible Commercial Information, art 17.

within the scope specified by the Act on the Instruments of Electronic Payments of 12 September 2002.

The issuers of electronic payment instruments are, among other things, (i) the issuers of payment cards and (ii) banks and electronic money institutions issuing electronic monetary instruments (ie an electronic device on which money is stored electronically, in particular, an electronic card loaded to a specified amount).[37]

Banks and electronic money institutions which have concluded a contract on electronic money instruments are obliged to guarantee safety within the scope of transferring electronic money by implementing measures which make the collection by non-authorised persons of information on actions and settlements carried out with a holder impossible[38] (ie a natural person, legal person or any other person who or which, on the basis of a contract on electronic payment instruments, executes on his behalf and account the operations specified in a contract).[39]

Issuers of electronic payment instruments are entitled to exchange information on holders who or which improperly perform their obligations deriving from a contract on electronic payment instruments. Such information covers (i) for natural persons: name and surname, PESEL record number, residence and description of the improper performance of a contract and (ii) for non-natural persons: name (firm), registered office and address, tax identification number and description of the improper performance of a contract.[40] This information can also be collected and disclosed to the issuers by institutions referred to in art 105, para 4 of the Banking Act.[41]

Under art 10, para 3 of the Act on the Instruments of Electronic Payments, the obligation not to disclose information concerning a holder or user to a non-authorised person was also imposed on a settlement agent (ie a bank or other legal person which had concluded a contract with an acceptor on the acceptance of a payment made by use of the electronic payment instrument).

Processing by banks and other institutions of information constituting bank secrecy

[**24.21**]   Pursuant to art 105a of the Banking Law, the processing by banks, other institutions authorised by statutory law to grant credits and institutions established under art 105, para 4 of information constituting bank secrecy, to the extent that it refers to natural persons (consumers), may be performed, subject to arts 104, 105 and 106 to 106c, for the purposes of the assessment of creditworthiness and credit risk analysis.

Subject to para 3, institutions referred to in para 1 may process information constituting bank secrecy, to the extent that it refers to natural persons (consumers), after the obligation under a contract with a bank or any other institution authorised by statutory law to grant credits ceases to exist and provided the written consent of the person whom the information concerns has been obtained. Such consent may be withdrawn at any time.

---

37 Act on the Instruments of Electronic Payments, art 2, point 6.
38 Act on the Instruments of Electronic Payments, art 2, point 62, para 1.
39 Act on the Instruments of Electronic Payments, art 2, point 11.
40 Act on the Instruments of Electronic Payments, art 68, paras 1 to 3.
41 Act on the Instruments of Electronic Payments, art 68, para 4.

Institutions referred to in para 1 may process information constituting bank secrecy and the information referred to in art 105, para 4, subparagraph 2, to the extent that it refers to natural persons (consumers), after an obligation under a contract with a bank or any other institution authorised by statutory law to grant credits ceases to exist without the consent of the person whom the information concerns if both of the following conditions are fulfilled:

1   the person is in default or delay in excess of 60 days in rendering performance under a contract with a bank or any other institution authorised by statutory law to grant credits;
2   following the occurrence of circumstances referred to in para 1, at least 30 days have elapsed since that person's notification by the bank or any other institution authorised by statutory law to grant credits of its intention to process information concerning that person which constitutes bank secrecy without that person's consent.

Information constituting bank secrecy may be processed in the cases referred to in para 3 for a period not exceeding five years from the date the obligation ceases to exist.

The minister competent for financial institutions, having invited the opinion of the relevant supervision authorities, shall specify, by a regulation, the scope of the processed information referred to in para 3 and the procedure for such removal taking account of the proper protection of the rights of persons whom the information concerns, as well as the necessity to ensure the security of moneys accumulated in banks and other institutions authorised by statutory law to grant credits.

Money laundering and counteracting the financing of terrorism

[24.22]   Provisions aimed at the prevention of money laundering and financing of terrorism are also an exception to the rule of bank confidentiality.

Article 105, para 2 of the Banking Act states that the scope of, and the rules concerning, disclosure of information held by banks which is to be disclosed to the General Inspector of Financial Information is to be regulated by separate legislation. The relevant provisions are included in the Act of 16 November 2000 on Counteracting the Introduction to the Financial Circulation of Assets Coming from Illegal or Undisclosed Sources and on Counteracting the Financing of Terrorism.

On the basis of art 8, para 1 of the Act of 16 November 2000, the 'obliged institutions' (ie banks, branches of banks, banks carrying out brokerage activities, etc) performing transactions upon the order of a client which exceeds 15,000 euros, whether the transactions comprise one or more operations, are obliged to register such transactions if the circumstances indicate they are connected with each other.

Entities running casinos within the meaning of the Act of 29 July 1992 on Games and Spread Betting are obliged to register transactions where the purchase or sale of tokens exceeds a value equal to 1,000 euros.[42]

In the case of contracts of life insurance, the obligation is excluded if the sum of periodic premiums to be paid in a particular year will not exceed 1,000 euros or a single premium will not exceed 2,500 euros.[43]

---

42 Act of 16 November 2000, art 8, para 1a.
43 Act of 16 November 2000, art 8, para 1c.

The above obligations also apply if the circumstances indicate that the money may come from an illegal or undisclosed source regardless of the value and type of the transaction.[44]

In order to fulfil the registration obligations, banks are to identify customers each time a disposition or order is made to perform a transaction on the basis of documents presented or upon conclusion of an agreement.[45] The identification includes the personal details of a customer such as name, surname (firm), citizenship, residential address (address of a registered office seat of a legal person or organisational unit having no legal personality), details of a document on the basis of which identity of a person was confirmed (extract from the court register, other document indicating organisational form of a legal person, identity card or passport of a natural person), organisational form of a legal person or organisational unit having no legal personality and document confirming authorisation to act on behalf of the legal person or an organisational unit having no legal personality.[46] Identification also includes the beneficiaries of the transaction and covers the establishment and record of their identity (name, surname and firm) and address.[47]

Information on a registered transaction is to be passed to the General Inspector of Financial Information.[48] Such information is to include:

1   date and place of execution of the transaction;
2   name, surname, citizenship, address, PESEL record number or code of a country and features of the document on the basis of which the person executing the transaction was identified;
3   amount, currency and type of the transaction;
4   number of the bank account used to execute the transaction and information concerning the owner or person who uses that bank account;
5   information concerning a natural person, legal person or organisational unit having no legal personality on behalf of which the transaction was made;
6   name, surname or firm and address of the beneficiary of the transaction and, if such address cannot be established, name (firm) of his bank;
7   justification of the registration of transactions which is referred to in art 8, para 3 of the Act.[49]

The information listed in points 1 to 6 is to be delivered to the General Inspector of Financial Control by a bank where it was given a disposition or order to perform a transaction or is to perform a transaction, in relation to which a reasonable suspicion exists that such order may be connected with an offence stipulated in art 299 of the Penal Code.[50]

Under art 16a, para 2 of the Act of 16 November 2000, a bank is obliged immediately to inform the General Inspector of Financial Control of a bank account for a client of whom a reasonable suspicion exists that he or it is connected with the commitment of a terrorist act and each transaction to which such a client is a party.

A bank is also obliged immediately to make accessible information concerning transactions covered by the provisions of the Act upon the written request of the

---

44 Act of 16 November 2000, art 8, para 3.
45 Act of 16 November 2000, art 9, para 1.
46 Act of 16 November 2000, art 9, para 2.
47 Act of 16 November 2000, art 9, para 3.
48 Act of 16 November 2000, art 11, para 1.
49 Act of 16 November 2000, art 12, para 1.
50 Act of 16 November 2000, art 16, para 1.

General Inspector of Financial Information. This includes the following: providing information on the parties to the transaction, content of the documents, including balance and turnover of the bank account, and delivery of certified copies of such documents or making appropriate documents available to the authorised employees of the appropriate unit of the Ministry of Finance to make notes on, or copies of, such documents.[51]

Fulfilment of the obligations imposed by the Act of 16 November 2000 is supervised by the General Inspector of Financial Control.[52] Control is performed by inspectors – employees of the appropriate unit of the Ministry of Finance who are authorised by the General Inspector.[53] Upon the request of an inspector, a bank is obliged to provide him with all the documents and materials necessary to carry on the inspection, which is referred to in art 21, para 1 of the Act, with the exception of documents and materials (including information) covered by state secrecy.[54]

Control, which is referred to in para 1, is also performed, within the scope of supervision or control, in the course of, and on the basis of, rules specified in other provisions by:

1   the Commission for Banking Supervision in relation to banks and branches of foreign banks;
2   the Securities and Exchange Commission in relation to banks conducting brokerage activity and banks running securities accounts.[55]

All the financial information collected and passed on by such organs under the Act is subject to the protection specified in the provisions of separate Acts.[56]

Provisions preventing money laundering are also included in art 106 of the Banking Act. Under art 106, para 1, a bank is to counteract the abuse of its activity for any purposes connected with offences referred to in art 299 of the Penal Code or with the intention of concealing criminal activity.

It should be noted that, under art 108, a bank shall not be responsible for damage which may result from performing, in good faith, the duties specified in art 106, para 1. In this case, where the circumstances referred to in art 106, para 1 have not been connected with an offence or concealing criminal actions, the responsibility for any damage resulting from the suspension of banking operations shall be borne by the Treasury.

Sanctions for failure to report suspicious transactions

[24.23]   As indicated above, in general, obliged institutions performing transactions upon the order of a client which exceed 15,000 euros, both where the transaction comprises one or more operations, are obliged to register such transaction if the circumstances indicate that they are connected with each other. The above obligation also applies if the circumstances indicate that the money may come from an illegal or undisclosed source regardless of the value and type of the transaction.[57] This regulation conforms to Financial Action Task Force ('FATF') recommendation 13.

---

51 Act of 16 November 2000, art 13a, para1.
52 Act of 16 November 2000, art 21, para 1.
53 Act of 16 November 2000, art 21, para 2.
54 Act of 16 November 2000, art 22, para 1.
55 Act of 16 November 2000, art 21, para 3.
56 Act of 16 November 2000, art 30.
57 Act of 16 November 2000, art 8, para 3.

Article 107 of the Banking Act states that a bank employee who, in breach of his duties, fails to report the circumstances specified in art 106, para 1 shall bear personal responsibility, which may include criminal liability. Criminal liability for such failure is provided for by the Act of 16 November 2000. Article 35, para 1 of the Act of 16 November 2000 stipulates sanctions for anyone who, acting in the name or on behalf of the obliged institution, contrary to the provisions of the Act of 16 November 2000, fails to fulfil the obligation to:

1   register transactions or to keep registers of transactions and documents concerning transactions;
2   identify the customer under the relevant procedures or keep information relating to the identification;
3   notify the financial information authority about a transaction or about keeping an account for an entity referred to in art 16a, para 1;
4   withhold a transaction or block the account.

These offences are punishable by up to three years' imprisonment. Pursuant to art 35, para 2 of the Act of 16 November 2000, the same sanction applies to revealing information gathered under the Act to unauthorised persons, account owners, the persons concerned with the transaction or using the information in a way contrary to the Act.

Pursuant to art 36 of the Act of 16 November 2000, refusal to provide relevant information or documents to the General Inspector, concealing information or providing false information is punishable by imprisonment from three months to five years. If these actions cause serious damage, the sanction varies from six months to eight years' imprisonment.

Criminal offences connected with money laundering

[24.24]   As required by FATF recommendation 1, criminal offences connected with money laundering are punishable by Polish law. This is provided for by art 299 of the Polish Penal Code. Pursuant to art 299, para 1, anyone who accepts, transfers or takes abroad or helps to transfer property rights or possession or undertakes other actions which may conceal the criminal origin of legal tenders, securities or foreign currency, property rights or movable or immovable property originating from profits connected with committing an offence is subject to imprisonment from six months to eight years.

The same sanction is provided for an employee of a bank, financial or credit institution or other entity upon which an obligation to register transactions is imposed by law, who accepts cash or foreign currency, transfers or converts it or accepts it in any other circumstances where suspicions may be aroused that it may constitute the gains of an offence referred to in para 1 or provides other services to conceal its criminal origin or secure it from sequestration.[58] If the action referred to in paras 1 and 2 is undertaken in agreement with other persons or is connected with significant profits, the punishment increases from one to ten years' imprisonment.[59]

A person responsible in a bank, financial or credit institution for notifying the management board or financial supervision body about a financial transaction, who does not perform his duties immediately in a form required by law, despite

---

58 Penal Code, art 299, para 2.
59 Penal Code, art 299, paras 5 and 6.

suspicious circumstances of the transaction, is punishable by up to three years' imprisonment.[60] The same sanction applies to a person responsible for appointing someone authorised to receive the information referred to in para 3 or to pass this information to the authorised person who does not satisfy the legal requirements.[61]

In sentencing the persons guilty of the offences indicated above in paras 1 and 2, the court will also order the forfeiture of goods originating from the offence or their equivalent unless they are returned to the owner.[62]

Information disclosed in connection with counteracting other criminal actions

[24.25]   Pursuant to art 106a, para 1 of the Banking Act, where there is a justified suspicion that a bank's activity is being used for the purpose of concealing criminal actions, for purposes connected with offences other than the offence referred to in art 299 of the Penal Code or an act of terrorism, the bank shall notify the public prosecutor. The public prosecutor who receives this notification may demand supplementary information in addition to the course of actions taken pursuant to art 307 of the Act of 6 June 1997 (Code of Criminal Procedure).[63]

Article 106b, para 1 of the Banking Act states that, except for the cases specified in arts 105 and 106a, the public prosecutor conducting proceedings for an offence or fiscal offence may only demand that the bank, persons employed by the bank or persons through whom the bank performs banking operations provide confidential information on the basis of a ruling issued upon his motion by the locally competent regional court.

The motion referred to in para 1 shall include:

1   the number of the case;
2   a description of the offence being the subject matter of the preparatory proceedings, together with its legal qualification;
3   the circumstances justifying the need to make the information available;
4   an indication of the person or organisational unit concerning the information;
5   the subject obliged to make the information and data available;
6   the type and scope of the information.[64]

Having examined the motion, the court shall, by a ruling, express consent for the information to be made available, specifying its type and scope and the person or organisational unit that it concerns, as well as the subject obliged to make it available, or it shall refuse to grant consent for the information to be made available.[65]

The public prosecutor authorised by the court shall inform in writing the subject obliged to make the information available about the contents of the court's ruling, the person or unit that the information is to concern and the type and scope of such information.[66]

---

60 Penal Code, art 299, para 3.
61 Penal Code, art 299, para 4.
62 Penal Code, art 299, para 7.
63 Banking Act, art 106a, para 2.
64 Banking Act, art 106b, para 2.
65 Banking Act, art 106b, para 3.
66 Banking Act, art 106b, para 5.

According to art 106c of the Banking Act, the public prosecutor conducting the proceedings in the cases specified in art 105, para 1, subpara 2, letters b) and c) may, on the basis of a ruling issued upon his motion by the locally competent regional court, request the provision of information protected by bank confidentiality by the subjects to which the bank disclosed such information. The provisions of art 106b, paras 2 to 5 shall apply accordingly.

Fiscal incursions into bank confidentiality

[24.26]   The wide scope of information, including that of a confidential nature, which is in the banks' possession also has to be disclosed to the tax authorities and fiscal control authorities.

Article 105, para 2 of the Banking Act states that the scope of, and the rules concerning, disclosure of information held by banks which is to be disclosed to the tax authorities or fiscal control authorities is regulated by separate legislation. These Acts are the Tax Ordinance Act of 29 August 1997 and the Fiscal Control Act of 28 September 1991. Under these Acts, in certain circumstances, the tax and fiscal control authorities were given almost unlimited access to information possessed by banks about their customers.

Under art 82, para 2 of the Tax Ordinance Act, banks are to prepare and provide to the revenue monthly information concerning opened and closed bank accounts of undertakings engaged in commercial activity. The information covers the number of the bank account, particulars enabling identification of the holders of such account and the date when the account has been opened or closed.

Banks are also subject to tax inspections by the tax authorities. The inspectors, to the extent authorised, are entitled, in particular, to request access to records, account books and all documents connected with the purpose of the inspection and to make copies, extracts, notes, printouts and download data in electronic form.[67]

Under arts 33 and 33a of the Fiscal Control Act, banks are obliged to supply the confidential details of customer accounts upon the written request of the General Inspector of Fiscal Control or a Director of a Fiscal Control Office, but only in the following circumstances:

1   in connection with the preparatory proceedings initiated in a penal case and offence, a fiscal penal case or fiscal offence;[68]
2   in connection with an inspection (initiated by an inspector under issued authorisation) after the prior summons of a taxpayer by the inspector to provide such information or to authorise the financial institutions to pass on the information, but only where a taxpayer:
    (a) has not given consent to the information being disclosed,
    (b) has not authorised the Fiscal Control Office to apply to the financial institution for the information to be passed on, or
    (c) has not, within the time limit specified by the Fiscal Control Office, provided information or authorisation mentioned above, or
    (d) has not delivered the information which is required to be completed or compared with information provided by a financial institution.[69]

---

67 Tax Ordinance Act, art 286, para 1, point 4).
68 Fiscal Control Act, art 33, para 1.
69 Fiscal Control Act, art 33a, para 1.

The General Inspector of Fiscal Control or a Director of a Fiscal Control Office can request the following information concerning the suspect customer:

1   bank or savings accounts and the amount in such accounts, as well as their turnover and balance;
2   pecuniary or securities accounts and amount in such accounts, as well as their turnover and balance;
3   credit contracts or loan contracts concluded, as well as deposit contracts;
4   state treasury shares or state treasury bonds acquired through banks, as well as trading in these securities;
5   trading in deposit certificates issued by banks or in other securities.[70]

In the course of the penal or offence proceedings and fiscal penal or offence proceedings by an inspector, control proceedings by a Director of a Fiscal Control Office or General Inspector of Fiscal Control, access to the information referred to in art 33 is to be given exclusively to the inspector conducting the proceedings, his superior and appropriate organs of fiscal control. The information has to be kept duly secured at the premises in compliance with the provisions on the protection of confidential information and, upon completion of the proceedings, removed from the case files and lodged in a safe.[71] The information collected and processed in the course of fiscal control constitutes a fiscal secret.

The following persons are obliged to observe a fiscal secret: (i) inspectors and employees of Fiscal Control Offices, (ii) persons who are referred to in art 13, para 4, ie those authorised on the basis of international agreements ratified by Poland and, in case of control of means provided to Poland by EU institutions, representatives of EU bodies, (iii) the General Inspector of Fiscal Control, inspectors and employees in the appropriate office for public finances and (iv) persons who, on the basis of separate provisions, undertake professional traineeship in the Fiscal Control Offices.[72]

Files containing such confidential details are only accessible to:

1   the minister responsible for public finances and the General Inspector of Fiscal Control in the course of tax proceedings or fiscal penal and fiscal offence proceedings;
2   the General Inspector of Financial Information under the provisions on counteracting the involvement in financial dealings of assets originating from illegal or undisclosed sources;
3   the tax authorities or other fiscal control authorities in connection with tax proceedings initiated under a previous decision, in connection with initiated control proceedings or penal and offence, fiscal penal or fiscal offence proceedings;
4   the administration court where a party has filed a complaint;
5   the Citizens' Rights Ombudsman in connection with his participation in the proceedings held before an administrative court;
6   the General Public Prosecutor on the motion of a competent public prosecutor:
    (a) in the cases specified in section IV of the Code of Administrative Procedure,
    (b) in connection with the participation of a public prosecutor in proceedings held before an administrative court;

---

70 Fiscal Control Act, art 33, para 1
71 Fiscal Control Act, art 33b, paras 1 to 3.
72 Fiscal Control Act, art 34, paras 1 and 2.

7   the state security services and its authorised officers or soldiers within the scope necessary to perform control proceedings on the basis of provisions on the protection of confidential information.[73]

Provisions of the Tax Ordinance Act and Fiscal Control Act introduced a concept of fiscal confidentiality which concerns, inter alia, information obtained by the tax authorities or fiscal control authorities from banks and indicates those authorities and officials obliged to maintain such confidentiality, whilst providing criminal penalties for any breach as such information is characterised as an official secret by the Penal Code.

The Citizens' Rights Ombudsman found that these provisions infringed the right to privacy and confidentiality of correspondence provided in the Polish constitution and subsequently asked the Constitutional Tribunal to adjudicate upon the conformity of these regulations with the constitution. On 24 June 1997, the Constitutional Tribunal held that the rights of fiscal authorities to demand information from banks were in conformity with the constitution.[74]

Exceptions to the rule of confidentiality other than those in the Banking Act

[24.27]   The list included in art 105 of the Banking Act does not include all the exceptions to the principle that confidential information should not be revealed to third persons. Other exceptions can be found in art 144, para 2 of the Banking Act and art 27 of the Banking Guarantee Fund Act.

Access to confidential information is granted to a supervisor for simplification of the recovery programme by a bank.[75] Under art 144, para 2 of the Banking Act, the supervisor shall have a right to participate in the work of the bank's bodies and obtain any information necessary to perform his duties.

Information possessed by a bank shall also be accessible to the general receiver and trustee in bankruptcy proceedings who, within 30 days from the day the bank was declared bankrupt, shall, among other things, establish a list of depositors on the basis of the bank's records and provide in writing to the Bank Guarantee Fund the guaranteed amounts due to each depositor prepared in accordance with a sample specified by the Bank Guarantee Fund Act.[76]

The customer's consent

[24.28]   Consent of the customer to disclosure of information constitutes an exception to the rule of confidentiality under the principle of *volenti non fit injuria*.

The rule of confidentiality can be modified without restricition by the person whose information should be kept confidential by the bank. The consent of the customer can

---

73 Fiscal Control Act, art 34a, para 1.
74 Constitutional Tribunal, SK 21/96.
75 Under the Banking Act, art 142, para 1, if a bank incurs a balance sheet loss or there is a threat of such loss or a risk of insolvency by a bank, the management board of the bank is obliged immediately to notify the Commission for Banking Supervision and present to it a recovery programme for the bank with confirmation of its implementation. The Commission for Banking Supervision may adopt a decision on the appointment of a supervisor for the implementation of the recovery programme by the bank: Banking Act, art 144, para 1.
76 Act on Bank Guarantee Fund, art 27, para 1, point 1).

be of a general nature and release the bank from all obligations deriving from art 104, para 1 of the Banking Act. It can also be restricted to the particular person(s), information and/or time within which the confidential information is to be kept secret.

The consent of a customer to a bank revealing wholly or in part confidential information is to be given in writing to the bank and to indicate precisely the scope of such release. Article 104, para 3 of the Banking Act states that the information is not to be disclosed to third parties (by the bank), with the exception of those cases specified in arts 105, 106a and 106b of the Banking Act and also where a person, being a party to the contract, authorises the bank in writing to disclose certain information to a person or organisational unit indicated by that party.

ACCESS TO INFORMATION BY FOREIGN AUTHORITIES

[24.29]   Foreign state institutions, such as the courts and prosecuting or fiscal authorities, may also, in certain circumstances, request legal assistance and the delivery of information which is normally protected by bank confidentiality. There are several instances in which a foreign institution or state can request legal assistance and the delivery of information from an institution or bank in Poland.

In the case of a crime or an offence or civil matter handled by a foreign court, confidential banking information can be revealed to foreign courts or prosecuting authorities if there is an international treaty concerning legal assistance in criminal or civil cases, but only where reciprocity exists. Poland has concluded bilateral treaties concerning legal assistance in criminal and civil cases with a number of countries. Poland is also a signatory to the following treaties concerning legal assistance in civil cases:

1   the Hague Convention on Civil Procedure of 17 July 1905;
2   the Hague Convention on Civil Procedure of 17 March 1954.

Obviously, the respective EU rules regarding provision of information and assistance in criminal and civil matters are also applicable. However, for Polish investigatory authorities to require the disclosure of such confidential information, a legal basis must exist under the Banking Act. This cannot simply be done on the basis of a request from abroad. Such legal basis is provided by art 105, para 1, point 2) c) of the Banking Act, which states that a bank shall be obliged to disclose information subject to bank secrecy to, and at the request of, a court or prosecutor in connection with an application for legal aid made by a foreign country entitled to request information which is a bank secret under an international agreement ratified by Poland. In addition, one can envisage a certain informal and unofficial exchange of information between the investigative authorities of countries on a quid pro quo basis, especially in cases of organised crime, drug trafficking, etc.

In the absence of an international treaty concerning legal assistance, a court or other institution of a foreign country may seek legal assistance from a Polish court in accordance with the procedures provided in the Civil Procedure Code and Penal Procedure Code. In principle, foreign courts and institutions need to communicate with the Polish courts and institutions through the Ministry of Justice.

Under art 1131, para 2 of the Civil Procedure Code, the courts will refuse to render legal assistance if:

1   the action requested would be contrary to the basic principles of legal order in Poland or would infringe the country's sovereignty;
2   carrying out the requested activity is not within the jurisdiction of a Polish court;
3   the state which files the application refuses legal assistance to the Polish courts.

Under art 588, paras 2 to 3 of the Penal Procedure Code, the Polish courts and prosecutor are also entitled to refuse legal assistance if:

1   the requested action would be contrary to the basic principles of legal order in Poland or would infringe the country's sovereignty;
2   performance of a requested action does not fall within the scope of the court's or prosecutor's activity under Polish law;
3   the state which filed the motion requiring legal assistance does not guarantee reciprocity in this respect;
4   the motion requiring legal assistance concerns an act which is not an offence under Polish law.

This area of information interchange relates to the treaties on the prevention of double taxation and tax evasion. All these treaties anticipate this interchange and it is possible that the tax authorities authorised to acquire information for their own purposes could pass on such information. In addition, the minister responsible for public finances or his authorised representative is authorised to demand confidential information from the banks if such a request is submitted by foreign tax authorities within the scope of, and according to the rules provided in, the treaties on the prevention of double taxation and tax evasion and other international agreements ratified by Poland.[77]

TRACING OF FUNDS

[24.30]   All the measures and procedures described above may in principle be applied to tracing funds held in banks.

Access to funds in local banks

[24.31]   Funds kept in bank accounts are the most available assets for creditors if a debtor defaults. It is possible for a creditor to obtain an interim injunction securing a claim by way of sequestrating assets held in an account. Polish law obliges trading entities to quote their bank account numbers on their business stationery. The main difficulty, however, is the fact that a creditor does not have access to any information concerning the balance held in the debtor's account and, therefore, the creditor's efforts may well be in vain as accounts that are frozen may be empty.

As mentioned above, a bank is under an obligation to disclose to a court executive officer bearing enforcement title confidential information concerning a debtor. Such information may cover a debtor's bank accounts and their turnover, as well as the balance of the accounts. This obviously assists enforcement proceedings. However, a court executive officer is able to freeze financial resources held by a party in a given bank without even indicating the number of the account. This is effected by a simple notice served by the court executive officer in accordance with art 889 of the Civil Procedure Code.

---

[77] Tax Ordinance Act, art 82, para 3.

In the case of claims pertaining to foreigners, Polish courts have jurisdiction if the debtor's assets comprise financial resources kept in bank accounts in Poland. Thus, foreign entities may act as claimants and, as such, enjoy all rights granted by the Civil Procedure Code. Consequently, when granted an executory title, they may, by using a Polish court executive officer, seize the debtor's funds.

Subpoena from foreign courts

[24.32]   Any subpoenas ordering disclosure of information by Polish banks or foreign banks situated in Poland can be enforced in Poland under Regulation 44/2001 where they originate from an EU member state.

In case of subpoenas issued in other countries, they can only be enforced after the requirements of the Civil Procedure Code are fulfilled. The enforceability of subpoenas and the execution of judgments of a foreign court in Poland would be subject to the provisions of art 1150 of the Civil Procedure Code. This provides that judgments of a foreign court issued in civil cases, which are subject to court proceedings in Poland and which are enforceable through execution proceedings, constitute executory titles and are enforceable in Poland on condition of reciprocity, provided that such judgments are enforceable in the country of issue and subject to additional requirements as defined in art 1146, para 1 of the Civil Procedure Code.

Those conditions are the following:

1   the judgment must be final in the country of its origin;
2   the subject matter of the judgment must not belong to the exclusive jurisdiction of the Polish courts or the court of the other country;
3   a party must not have been deprived of the possibility of his defence and, in cases where he does not enjoy an ability to take personal action before the court, appropriate representation;
4   the judgment must not be inconsistent with the basic principles of Polish legal order;
5   there must not have been prior final judgment rendered by a Polish court;
6   there must not have been any court proceedings launched in Poland before the judgment of the foreign court became final and if, in rendering a judgment, Polish law should have been applied, then such law is actually applied unless the foreign law applied in the case does not materially differ from the applicable Polish law.

Tracing of funds abroad

[24.33]   Once funds have been transferred to a foreign bank, the chances of tracing such funds depend on the policy on banking confidentiality in the jurisdiction in which the bank is situated. Even on the assumption that one was aware to which bank the funds were transferred and had obtained an injunction or other form of judgment in Poland, enforceability would depend entirely upon whether such an injunction or judgment is recognised in that jurisdiction.

MISCELLANEOUS
Insider trading

[24.34]   Insider trading is an offence under the Act on Trading in Financial Instruments of 29 July 2005 and punishable by six months' to five years' imprisonment, a fine up to PLN 5 million (approximately US$1.5 million) or both.[78] The Securities and Exchange Commission can submit applications to a prosecutor that an investigation be conducted, who, in turn, can require that stockbrokers and banks divulge details of relevant transactions.

This is possible under the provisions of art 105, para 1, point 2) b) or c) of the Banking Act that enable the prosecutor to require information in relation to criminal proceedings pending against an account holder. As in any jurisdiction, such offences are difficult to detect and prove. However, under criminal law, the penal provisions of the Act on Trading in Financial Instruments are unusually draconian and the absence of jurisprudence could lead to their improper application. It must be stressed that inside information is any information which is not publicly known and which could significantly affect the value of securities.

Criminal investigatory bodies must also be given access to bank details whenever bank accounts are being used for the preparation of crimes or the concealment of ill-gotten gains.

Personal Data Protection Act

[24.35]   The Personal Data Protection Act of 29 August 1997 defines the rights and responsibilities of persons and institutions maintaining databases and the rights of persons whose personal details are kept in them.

The Act guarantees the protection of the rights of individuals and their freedoms. Under the provisions, the processing of personal data should not infringe the rights of the person to whom they pertain and persons whose details are being processed have the right to know where such data is held, by whom and for what purpose. Supervisory rights within the scope of processing personal details in accordance with the provisions of the Personal Data Protection Act have been vested in the General Inspector for the Protection of Personal Data.

The provisions of the Personal Data Protection Act constitute a separate legal basis for the protection of personal data of customers (being natural persons) which has been collected by a bank. Disclosure of the data under the Act may only be effected in accordance with the conditions specified in it. Personal data can be processed (ie among other things, disclosed) by banks in the situations specified in art 23, para 1 of the Personal Data Protection Act, subject to the provisions of art 104 of the Banking Act:

1   a person gives his consent unless the processing actions are aimed at removing his details;
2   it is necessary to fulfil a right or obligation deriving from provisions of law;
3   it is necessary to fulfil obligations deriving from an agreement if a person to whom the data relates is a party to such agreement or if it is necessary to take action before the agreement is concluded on demand of a person whose data it concerns;
4   it is necessary to perform tasks specified by law which are performed for the public good;
5   it is necessary to fulfil the legally justified purposes of the administrators or receivers of data and the processing of data does not infringe the rights and freedoms of the person to whom such data relates.

---

78 Act on Trading in Financial Instruments, art 181, para 1, in connection with art 156, para 1.

In order to secure the safety of the personal details processed by the administrator of such data, the administrator is obliged, under art 36 of the Personal Data Protection Act, to apply technical and organisational measures which guarantee the protection of processed personal data. In particular, he needs to secure such data from being disclosed to or taken by an unauthorised person, processed in breach of the Act, amended, lost, damaged or destroyed.

Cross-selling

[24.36]   So-called 'cross-selling', which involves the divulging of any confidential information by a bank, is prohibited. In the light of arts 104 and 105 of the Banking Act, the fact that an account of a particular person is held at a particular bank will only be disclosed to a party that has a justifiable legal right to know. Cross-selling is not a practice that has become a problem in Poland in relation to banks, which treat confidentiality seriously.

Conflict of interest

[24.37]   It is a general rule in Polish civil and commercial law that a person or entity taking care of the affairs of another cannot act to the detriment of such a party. Therefore, if a bank conducts the financial affairs of a customer in a manner which could affect the interest of another customer, it would become essential for the bank to construct a so-called 'Chinese Wall' otherwise the bank might expose itself to liability for damages vis-à-vis both of its customers and evidence would have to be produced to prove that access given to information concerning the interests of both customers was not used to the detriment of either. In practice, if ever such a conflict of interests is identified, both customers need to be advised of the fact.

CONCLUSION

[24.38]   The evolution of laws aimed at limiting bank confidentiality is, increasingly, becoming an intrusion into the personal privacy of citizens. Attempts have been made to justify this on the basis of the necessity to protect the fiscal interests of the state. Bearing in mind the lack of clarity of Polish tax laws and the aptitude of the tax authorities to interpret these provisions by only taking into account the interests of the state, one has to say that the area of abuse is becoming greater than ever.

25 Portugal

Manuel P Barrocas
Teresa Baptista

INTRODUCTION

[25.1] Article 26 of the Portuguese constitution[1] makes provision for the protection of privacy.[2] It is generally understood that bank confidentiality obligations fall within the scope of this constitutional protection.[3]

In addition, the bank confidentiality legal regime is established in several statutory provisions, as follows:

1 the Banking Law (more specifically, the 'Legal Regime for Credit Institutions' as laid down in Decree Law 298/92, dated 31 December, amended by Decree Law 201/02, dated 26 September, the last amendment being made on 17 October 2003). This Law sets out a detailed regime in relation to bank confidentiality obligations which forms part of the rules relating to the conduct of banks, their directors and employees. In addition, the conflict of interests between the activity of banks vis-à-vis the public and particularly their customers and their private interests is covered by this Law;

2 the Criminal Code (Decree Law 48/95, dated 15 March) and other criminal law legislation, including the Criminal Procedure Code;

3 the Civil Code (Decree Law 47344, dated 25 November 1966);

4 data protection legislation (Law 67/98, dated 26 October);

5 other legislation (namely Decree Law 15/93, dated 22 January; Decree Law 313/93, dated 15 September, Law 11/2004, dated 27 March and Law 30-G/2000, dated 29 December).

LEGAL REGIME OF BANK CONFIDENTIALITY OBLIGATIONS

Bank confidentiality and the legal system and a summary of some major issues

[25.2] Bank confidentiality is, in short, defined by law as the secrecy which banks, their directors, employees and other people working or providing services to a bank

---

1 The Portuguese constitution is dated 2 April 1976 and was last revised in January 1997.
2 The text of this provision is as follows: 'everyone is entitled to their personal identity, civil capacity, citizenship, good name and reputation, image, free expression and privacy'.
3 Only a small number of tax law commentators have held the opinion that the need for the tax authorities to obtain information for tax purposes does not allow the constitutional protection of the bank confidentiality obligation. However, this is not only a minority view, but also a highly controversial one.

551

must keep in relation to their customers' business or activity, ie the economic, financial and personal data concerning customers which has been acquired by virtue of their banking activity.

One of the first references to bank confidentiality in Portuguese law dates back to the nineteenth century, more particularly, to the Law of 1881 ruling the activities of the Bank of Portugal. Since then, the principle of bank confidentiality has been covered under Portuguese law. The purpose of the law has always been the protection of a customer's investments and savings, thereby accomplishing the public economic interest of creating a climate of confidence. Bearing in mind that a customer's right to bank confidentiality is connected to the constitutional protection of the right to privacy, it has always been understood that the customer is not only someone who enters into a particular transaction with a bank, but also someone who has initiated contacts with the bank with a view to entering into a possible transaction. Therefore, any information and personal data about a prospective customer of the bank who, with a view to entering into a transaction, has supplied the bank with personal data without, however, reaching a final agreement is also covered by bank confidentiality. Therefore, the matter of bank confidentiality may be relevant within the scope of pre-contractual liability. Bank confidentiality, however, takes on a special importance during a transaction with the bank and after it has been concluded.

A classic question in bank confidentiality concerns the limits of bank confidentiality vis-à-vis the interests of a criminal investigation. Until 1994, banks, the police and the criminal courts faced this problem and invariably the banks refused to provide information on their customers to the police or criminal courts. However, Act 36/94, dated 29 September, on measures against corruption, economic and financial crimes, amended by Law 5/02, dated 11 January 2002, implemented new legislation obliging banks to provide confidential information whenever the criminal investigation relates to bribery and certain defined financial and economic crimes (generally, the so-called 'white collar' crimes), as well as, since the latest amendment, terrorism and certain forms of trafficking. Bearing in mind the importance of this Law, special reference is made to this below.

Recently, another Law has been adopted (Law 11/04) which strengthens the principles provided for by Law 5/02, dated 11 January 2002. This new Law imposes obligations on banks (and other financial institutions subject to professional privilege/secrecy) to override privilege in cases where the banks may suspect they are dealing with money from illicit activities (such as the exploitation of prostitution, child abuse, drug trafficking and gun running). It also imposes significant penalties in cases where they fail to comply with these obligations.

In practice, and as a consequence of this new Law, strict obligations are imposed on banks and other financial institutions: (i) the obligation to demand identification from their clients and attorneys, (ii) the requirement to refuse certain financial operations without identification of the participants and to abstain from participating in them, (iii) the obligation to retain documents used during the making of those transactions, (iv) the obligation to audit those transactions, (v) the duty to communicate any irregularity to the Attorney General, (vi) the obligation to create appropriate control mechanisms and provide proper instructions to their employees and (vii) the duty to co-operate with any relevant authority. Non-compliance with these obligations is punishable by a fine ranging from 1,000 to 2,500,000 euros.

The authority responsible for supervising compliance by the banks and financial institutions with these obligations is the Bank of Portugal, which is required to notify the Attorney General when these have been breached.

It is clear, however, that in the cases described above, banks or other institutions involved are not subject to penalties for breaching the principle of secrecy. This is by virtue of the fact that the law also provides that this kind of information does not fall within the notion of secrecy; therefore, no liability arises where it has been provided in good faith (the 'bona fide principle').

The Banking Law and the scope of bank confidentiality

[25.3]   One of the major purposes of the Banking Law is to define and keep banking activity within appropriate codes of professional conduct and to consider the customer as a consumer of services.

Banking legislation applies to:

1   banks;
2   investment companies, leasing, factoring and hire-purchase companies and electronic currency institutions; and
3   any other entities which the law considers to be similar to banks for certain specific purposes, which are generally referred to here as 'banks' even though, technically, the entities indicated at 2 and 3 are not, strictly speaking, banks.

This broad application of the Banking Law to all those entities is an important factor in the protection of customer rights. As indicated above, the supervision of all banking activities in Portugal is conducted by the Bank of Portugal.

The first relevant provision of the Banking Law (art 78) on the confidentiality obligation provides as follows:

'1 Members of the board of directors and the supervisory board of credit institutions, its employees, proxies and all other people who provide them with services, whether permanently or not, shall not disclose or use information on facts relating to the activity of the institution or its relations with customers obtained exclusively during the performance of their functions or the provision of services.
2   Bank confidentiality covers, amongst other things, customer names, deposit accounts and all other banking operations.
3   The confidentiality obligation does not end on the termination of contractual relations.'

Consequently, the following persons are, within and in addition to the banks, obliged to maintain confidentiality and abide by the bank confidentiality legislation:

1   members of the board of directors and supervisory board of banks;
2   bank employees and proxies; and
3   any other person or entity providing services to a bank on a permanent or occasional basis.

The confidentiality obligation includes (i) the duty not to disclose and (ii) the duty not to make use of any information on facts or data concerning banking activity relating to customers, provided that this information was acquired during the course of exercising their business responsibilities. These duties of confidentiality do not end with the termination of their responsibilities or employment with the bank.

Infringement of these duties is a criminal offence.

Exceptions to the bank confidentiality obligation

[25.4]   The exceptions are laid down both in the Banking Law and other legislation.

Article 79 of the Banking Law provides that:

'1   The facts concerning the relationship between the customer and the bank may be disclosed in the event of the customer giving consent.
2   Beyond this case, facts covered by the confidentiality obligation may only be disclosed:
   a)   to the Bank of Portugal;
   b)   to the Securities Board;
   c)   to the Guarantor of Deposit Funds and the System of Indemnities to Investors;
   d)   under the provisions of criminal law;
   e)   where there is another legal provision that expressly provides for a limitation to the confidentiality obligation.'

Exceptions provided for in the Banking Law

Customer's consent

[25.5]   To understand better what is included within the notion of customer consent, it is useful to point out that a customer's consent is not required for information which has become known by the public and so lost its secret nature. On the other hand, certain persons are authorised by the customer or by law to have access to confidential information kept by the bank. Such is the case for, inter alia:

1   the guarantors of certain commercial papers in the possession of a bank, such as bills of exchange, who need to know the information covered by confidentiality concerning those documents in order to exercise their rights or duties;
2   proxies;
3   third parties representing the bank's customer by operation of law (for instance, a representative of a minor, etc); and
4   bankruptcy/insolvency trustees.

Although there is no legal requirement that the customer's consent should be given in writing, in practice, this is the most advisable way of communicating with the bank.

Information provided to certain entities authorised by law

[25.6]   In addition to the entities to whom the customer's affairs may be disclosed under the paragraphs above, the following entities may also be entitled to receive confidential information in certain limited circumstances:[4]

1   the Bank of Portugal (as the central bank), for instance, in connection with the sanctions to be applied to the issuing of dishonoured cheques, which constitutes a crime;
2   the Securities Board in connection with its function of supervising the securities market;
3   the Guarantor of Deposit Funds; and

---

4 The Banking Law does not set out a duty of co-operation between banks and tax entities as an exception to bank confidentiality.

4   entities authorised to have access to bank data under certain special legislation mentioned below.

Exceptions provided for in other legislation

The Criminal Code

[25.7]   Article 195 of the Criminal Code provides that:

'whoever, without permission, discloses confidential information relating to a third party obtained by virtue of his profession, status or employment is subject to a one-year imprisonment penalty or, alternatively, to a pecuniary fine calculated on a daily basis and up to a maximum of 240 days as established by the court.'[5]

In addition, art 196 establishes that:

'whoever, without permission, takes advantage or benefits from confidential information concerning the commercial, industrial, professional or artistic activity of a third party by virtue of his profession, status or employment is subject to a one-year imprisonment penalty or, alternatively, to a pecuniary fine calculated on a daily basis up to a maximum of 240 days.'

The Criminal Code considers that criminal liability may be excluded on the grounds of protecting or satisfying an interest which is clearly more important than the interest protected by the bank confidentiality rules, which may, therefore, be overridden.

Moreover, the Criminal Code establishes an exception based on necessity (art 34):

'An act is not considered illegal where it is an adequate way to remove a threat to the legitimate interests of someone or of a third party, provided that (cumulatively):

(I)   the threat has not been voluntarily created by it;
(II)   the interest can be considered reasonably superior to the interest which may be offended by the threat; and
(III)   it is reasonable to impose upon the third party the loss or damage of its interest taking into consideration the nature or the greater importance attributed to the interest threatened.'

As a consequence, in criminal law matters, other interests may prevail over bank secrecy.

Following the adoption of Law 11/2004 implementing Directive 2001/97/CE, which amended Directive 91/308/EEC, the Criminal Code has also been amended to include new provisions on the prohibition of money laundering, thereby establishing more stringent measures intended to override bank (and other financial institution) confidentiality where a suspicion of money laundering exists.

This new Law has resulted in several modifications to the Portuguese legal regime: for the first time, money laundering has been made an offence even though there is no requirement to demonstrate the illicit origin of the funds. The new provisions make the acceptance of the possibility that the funds originate from an illicit source enough to secure a conviction.

---

5 Under art 47 of the Criminal Code, the amount of a criminal fine calculated on the basis of days is fixed by the judge on a case-by-case basis between 1 and 498.80 euros per day.

In addition, provision 368-A of the Criminal Code relates to the prohibition on concealing or assisting in the concealment of all moneys originating from an illicit nature, for example, the exploitation of prostitution, child abuse, extortion, drug trafficking, gun running, trafficking in human tissue, organs and protected species, tax fraud, corruption, etc.

Any person converting these moneys, transferring them or facilitating any operation of conversion or transfer with the intention of concealing their illicit origin or for the purposes of protecting the owner or a participant in those infractions from being punished faces a prison sentence of between two to 12 years. In addition, any person concealing the true nature, origin, location, disposition, transaction or ownership of the moneys, or the rights relating to them, may be punished with the same custodial sentence. In practice, only one criminal regime for all possible forms of the crime exists, which means that anyone implied in an illicit operation is punishable with the same penalty.

In a case of money laundering, where a criminal procedure complaint is lodged, the complaint may only be made by the injured party and within the procedural time limits.

The Criminal Procedure Code

[25.8]   This provides that credit institutions may invoke bank confidentiality to avoid having to make depositions or statements in criminal investigation procedures. However, where the judge has doubts regarding the confidential nature of the information required from a bank, he will only reach a decision on the disclosure obligations after consulting the relevant professional or banking association which represents the persons owing the disclosure duty.

Article 135 of the Code provides:

> '1   Priests, lawyers, doctors, journalists and members of credit institutions and other people permitted or obliged by law to keep professional confidentiality may refuse to make any statements or provide information covered by the confidentiality duty.
> 2   If the court has reasonable doubts on the validity of the refusal, it may take all necessary measures to resolve the doubt. If the court concludes that the refusal is not legally valid, it may order that the statement be produced.'

In the latter case, the entity representing the professional involved (union, association, etc) is also likely to be heard in order to help the court to decide whether the confidentiality obligation should be overridden.

In addition, art 182 of the Criminal Procedure Code regulates the presentation to the court of documents or other items which the above professionals and credit institutions have in their possession. According to this legal provision, the credit institutions must provide the criminal authorities, at their request, with any documents or other items held by them which may be seized. The credit institution may refuse to do so in writing and then it will be for the criminal authority to decide whether the protection is to be accepted or not. As noted above, the criminal authority may override the confidentiality obligation where it is considered necessary to assure the protection of interests of greater importance.

Furthermore, art 181 of the Criminal Procedure Code also permits the seizure of money, documents or other items deposited with a credit institution (even in a bank's private safe) if they are connected with the commission of a crime and are of great importance in helping the investigation. There is no requirement that the documents or other items be owned by a suspect involved in a criminal investigation.

Article 181.2 establishes that the criminal investigating judge may inspect any correspondence in the possession of banks or other banking documentation with a view to deciding which assets are to be seized. The judge and all persons who have co-operated with him are subject to a strict duty of confidentiality in relation to the information obtained under these conditions.

Any inspections and searches carried out at credit institutions should be preceded by an express court decision, in respect of which a prior copy must be provided to the bank, except in special cases, for instance, the suspicion of terrorism, violent crime and others offences where the inspection or search may be conducted by the police before an authorisation is granted. In any event, the court should later confirm the legitimacy of these investigations.

Other legislation

DECREE LAW 15/93, DATED 22 JANUARY, ON CRIMINAL INVESTIGATIONS CONCERNING THE PRODUCTION, PREPARATION OR TRADING IN NARCOTICS AND FUNDS CONNECTED WITH THIS ACTIVITY

[25.9] Bribery and certain crimes of a financial and economic nature (the so-called 'white collar' crimes) have specific legislation allowing the police, duly authorised by a criminal investigation judge, to have access to confidential bank information.

In addition, an important bill on criminal investigation concerning the production, preparation or trading of narcotics and funds connected with this activity (Decree Law 15/93, dated 22 January, as amended by several bills, the most relevant being Law 45/96, dated 3 September) authorises access to information covered by bank confidentiality and outlines the duty of credit institutions to provide such information to the authorities.

Under art 60, this bill establishes, on the grounds of criminal authority investigations and requirements, that a competent court may request any information, as well as the presentation of documents relating to assets or bank deposits, inter alia, which belong to individuals suspected or accused of having committed crimes relating to the production, preparation or trading of narcotics. In cases where these requests relate to banking, financial or equivalent entities, the request may be addressed by the Bank of Portugal. The entities in question, both public (including the tax authorities) and private (including all credit institutions), cannot refuse to provide the authorities with the information or documents requested.

THE USE OF CREDIT INSTITUTIONS TO LAUNDER MONEY

[25.10] The use of credit institutions to launder money also has a special legal regime following Council Directive 91/308/EEC, dated 10 June 1991. The implementation of that Directive resulted in the promulgation of new legislation (Decree Law 313/93, dated 15 September) which provides that:

1 credit institutions are obliged to inform the criminal authorities whenever they suspect funds or transactions are connected with money laundering. The information provided by such credit institutions may only be used in the investigation and punishment of those crimes. The criminal authorities who

receive the information requested must guarantee the anonymity of the credit institution. On the other hand, the credit institutions cannot disclose to their customers or third parties that they have provided the criminal authorities with the information, not even when a criminal proceeding or investigation is taking place;

2   credit institutions are obliged not to follow or give effect to any customer instruction whenever they suspect it may be connected or related to money laundering and must immediately inform the criminal authorities. If it is impossible for the credit institution to refuse execution of the instruction given by the customer or if the refusal is likely to prejudice the criminal authority investigation, the bank is permitted to execute the customer's instruction, but must immediately thereafter inform the criminal authorities.

This Directive has been amended by Directive 2001/97/EC of the European Parliament and Council, which has introduced important modifications to the previous Directive, at that time reflected in Law 11/2004, dated 27 March.

Whereas the previous Directive reflected best international practice in this area, the new Directive attempts to set a higher standard of financial sector protection from illicit activities which may have potentially harmful consequences. In practice, it appeared that this sector was being used to launder the proceeds arising from all manner of illicit activities, such as drug trafficking, organised crime and others. In this sense, it has established real duties and obligations for credit institutions, particularly banks, including, inter alia, obligations to identify customers, keep records and report suspicious transactions which could lead to criminal proceedings. Failure to comply with these obligations will result in the direct liability of, and sanctions against, the banks concerned. This consolidates an improvement introduced by the new Directive reflected in the above-mentioned Law 11/2004.

Tax legislation

[25.11]   Exceptions concerning tax matters are also established by law. They may be summarised by the following powers given to the tax authorities, inter alia:

1   banks are obliged to give access to private safety deposit boxes and inform the tax authorities of their contents in connection with inheritance tax;
2   where a taxpayer has tried to pay tax by using cheques which have not been honoured, this gives the tax authorities power to make inquiries of banks concerning such accounts; and
3   information on funds which have not been drawn upon for 15 years under certain conditions.

As briefly mentioned above, certain tax law commentators hold the view that the above-mentioned constitutional provision relating to the protection of citizen privacy does not always cover information falling within the scope of bank confidentiality. Their view is based on the fact that the relevant provision of the constitution only refers to basic rights of citizens connected with human dignity and spiritual values such as philosophical and religious convictions or sexual inclinations. Therefore, the financial circumstances of individuals would fall outside the scope of protection given by the constitution. Consequently, under this point of view, where the information kept by banks relates to the above basic rights, bank confidentiality is effective. If this is not the case, it may be overridden for tax purposes, particularly with a view to obtaining information on the financial circumstances of bank customers.

Moreover, the same commentators have stated that the duty relating to the public interest in obtaining tax information is of greater importance than the interests protected by bank confidentiality. Therefore, banks should provide information covered by the bank confidentiality obligation to give the tax authorities information on the real income of companies, given that the principle of taxing accurate and true income is also laid down as a taxpayer's right in the constitution.[6] In addition, according to the same legal commentators, bank customers will not be affected by these measures since the tax authorities are subject to the duty of tax confidentiality which covers precisely the information obtained on the financial circumstances of taxpayers.[7] However, the majority of legal commentators have argued against this on the ground that this position would, in fact, jeopardise the value of bank confidentiality. Indeed, it was almost consensually understood that this confidentiality obligation fell within the constitutional protection and that there was no exception in favour of the tax authorities. Furthermore, other authors, who have disagreed with the opinion of these tax commentators, have pointed out that the activities of the tax authorities, when carrying out an investigation into the financial circumstances of individuals, may even be punishable under criminal law. As regards the duties of tax authority employees, the amendment provided by Law 5/02, dated 11 January, on measures against corruption and economic and financial crimes should be noted as detailed below.

An amendment to the tax procedural code by Law 30-G/2000 has finally given the tax authorities power to access banking documents directly without the prior need to obtain a court order where authorisation for the presentation or inspection by the tax authorities has been refused. Where a taxpayer refuses to provide or give consent to the inspection of documents which relate to tax benefits, favourable tax regimes or dormant account records of individuals subject to income tax, the current position is that the tax authorities may access these without obtaining a prior court order. In practice, this legislation provides the tax authorities with powers to access all bank documents, but only in the situations prescribed by law, such as where an individual's declared income for taxation purposes is considerably different from his lifestyle. This provision does not apply to documents which relate to information on the use of credit.

This is, of course, an exceptional measure and may be appealed by a special procedure through the tax courts. However, it is believed that new legal measures are soon to be considered empowering the authorities to have clear access to bank data, even where a tax-related offence is not suspected. This legislation is considered to be justified on the grounds of an ongoing auditing process relating to tax evasion and fraud being undertaken by the Portuguese government, which has led to positive initial results.

Other legal provisions

[25.12]　There are further exceptions to the bank confidentiality rule including, inter alia:

6　This principle is set out in art 104, para 2 of the constitution, which states that 'taxation of companies shall be applied on their real income'.

7　Notwithstanding this, even those commentators agree that a search made by the tax authorities at the home or premises of the taxpayer, particularly companies, as set out in art 125 of the Corporate Income Tax Code, can only be made with the previous authorisation of a court if the taxpayer does not agree to it voluntarily.

1   the right of the civil courts to receive information from banks. This includes:
    (a)   information concerning funds or assets owned by debtors (bank customers) in civil actions for money in the possession of banks,
    (b)   in connection with the enforcement of letters of request addressed by foreign authorities or foreign courts to Portuguese civil courts under international conventions, and
    (c)   for obtaining legal aid;
2   in certain cases, the parliamentary committee for investigations, a committee with investigatory powers which reports on breaches of the constitution by parliamentary members, may request information from private entities;
3   a bank customer's spouse may request information from the bank in cases where:
    (a)   the customer is unable to manage the bank account as a result of its whereabouts being unknown and provided that no power of attorney has been granted to anyone else, or
    (b)   the customer provides the spouse with a general proxy for the administration of assets;
4   in addition, as seen further below regarding relevant case law, the supervisory department of a bank may inspect the accounts of its employees suspected of having been involved in irregular or dishonest transactions.

As mentioned above, the supervising authorities are also subject to a duty (art 80 of the Banking Law) as follows:

'1.   Everyone carrying out or who has carried out functions in the Bank of Portugal, or who renders or has rendered services, both on a permanent or occasional basis, is subject to the confidentiality obligation in respect of facts which have come to their knowledge exclusively by virtue of the exercise of their functions or services and they may not disclose or use the information so obtained.'

The facts covered by the confidentiality obligation may only be disclosed in the following cases:

1   through the customer's consent given to the Bank of Portugal;
2   in pursuance of the provisions of criminal law or criminal procedure law;
3   in connection with court proceedings relating to the bankruptcy or winding up of companies under certain conditions; and
4   the disclosure of certain data is allowed for statistical purposes provided that it does not include the identification of individuals or institutions.

Co-operation with regulatory entities and other entities

[25.13]   Pursuant to art 81 of the Banking Law, the Bank of Portugal may exchange information with other entities as indicated below, although they should keep this confidential:

1   the Securities Board under certain limited conditions;
2   the Insurance Institute (the regulatory and supervisory entity of insurance activity) and the Central Institute for Credit to Agriculture;
3   other banking supervisory authorities of the EU member states in compliance with EC directives; and

4   co-operation agreements entered into with supervising authorities of credit institutions with a registered seat in Portugal and of institutions of an equivalent nature with a registered seat abroad. This information may be supplied on an individual or consolidated basis.

Co-operation agreements with countries outside the EU, as set out in art 82 of the Banking Law, may only be executed where such countries provide a guarantee of confidentiality at least equivalent to the one granted by the Portuguese Banking Law.

Under art 83 of the Banking Law, credit institutions are permitted under the bank confidentiality rules to establish a system whereby they exchange and maintain a central register of information on banking business risks.

Remedies for breach of the bank confidentiality obligation

[25.14] Article 84 relates to the remedy for infringement of the bank confidentiality obligation. This provision states that:

> 'Without prejudice to other penalties which may be applicable, the infringement of bank confidentiality is subject to the Criminal Code.'

Therefore, the possibility of both civil and criminal liability exists. Civil liability, particularly in contract for breach of the confidentiality obligation, is governed by the general regime of civil liability. The law does not specify the form of damages which can be claimed. Thus, damages which may be claimed are those which, under the general regime of civil liability, could have been caused by any unlawful act.

Special reference to the Data Protection Act

[25.15]   Data protection legislation is covered by Law 67/98, dated 26 October, implementing Council Directive 95/46/EC of 24 October 1995 relating to the protection of individuals in relation to the treatment of personal data and the free circulation of such data. Therefore, this law incorporates the EU regime on the transfer of personal data within the EU and third countries. The national supervising entity, which may also issue opinions, is the National Commission for Data Protection, an independent administrative entity.

The scope of this law covers the handling of personal data by totally or partially electronic means, as well as the non-electronic handling of personal data contained in manual files or destined to be stored in such files (except dealings made by individuals of their exclusive personal or domestic activities) either (i) within the scope of activities of the establishment responsible for the handling of this data located in the Portuguese territory, (ii) outside the national territory in a place where Portuguese law is applicable by virtue of international law or (iii) where the responsibility for the handling of the data is not established in the EU, but has recourse to means, whether electronically or otherwise, located in the Portuguese territory, save if such means are only used to traffic data throughout the EU

Article 3 of Law 67/98 provides for several definitions, amongst which are the following:

1   'personal data' is defined as 'any information of whatever nature irrespective of its medium including sound and image, relating to an individual identified or

identifiable ("the owner of the personal data")'. An individual is considered identifiable where they may be identified directly or indirectly, namely by means of a reference to an identification number or to one or more specific elements of their physical, physiological, psychological, economic, cultural or social identity;

2   'treatment/handling of data' is defined as 'any operation or aggregate of operations of personal data, made with or without recourse to electronic means, such as the collection, registration, organisation, conservation, adjustment or alteration, the recovery of, consulting, use, communication through transmission, broadcast or any other form of making available, with comparison or interconnection, as well as the blockage, erasure or destruction';

3   'consent of the owner of personal data' is defined as any free, specific and informed expression of intention, under which the owner accepts that its personal data is to be treated or handled.

Beyond regulating the manner in which such data is handled and the principles which must be complied with, this law establishes, at art 6, the conditions under which the treatment of data is lawful. Such treatment is only permitted if the respective owner of the data has clearly provided its consent or if the treatment is necessary for:

1   the execution of contracts to which the owner of the data is a party or was involved in previous applications regarding the formation of the contract or declaration of intent to contract made at its request;

2   the compliance with a legal obligation in respect of which the responsibility for the treatment is subject;

3   the protection of vital interests of the owner of data if the latter is physically or legally incapable of providing consent;

4   the execution of a task of public interest or in the activities of public authorities in which capacity the party responsible for the treatment is acting or a third recipient of such data; or

5   the pursuit of lawful interests by the party responsible for treatment of the data or a third party recipient of the data, provided that the rights, freedom or guarantees of the owner of the data do not prevail.

Article 7 governs the treatment of sensitive data prohibiting the treatment of personal data referring to philosophical, political or religious beliefs and private, racial or ethnic issues, as well as health and sexual issues, including genetic information. If the National Commission for Data Protection grants permission on the grounds of public interest, the handling of this data may be carried out where necessary for the exercise of statutory functions by the party responsible for the data or where the owner of data has provided its express consent to such treatment (both cases requiring compliance with certain rules).

The treatment of this kind of data is also allowed where:

1   it is necessary to protect vital interests of the owner of data or of another person and the owner is physically or legally prevented from expressing its consent;

2   it is carried out with the consent of the owner provided to certain non-profitable entities of a political or ideological nature, within certain limitations;

3   it relates to data clearly made public by its owner, provided that it may lawfully be concluded from its declarations that consent is being given in relation to such treatment; or

4   it is necessary for the declaration, exercise or defence of a right in a court procedure and is made exclusively for that purpose.

According to art 17 of Law 67/98, the entities responsible for the treatment of personal data, as well as those who, in connection with the exercise of their functions, become aware of the personal data, are obliged to maintain professional secrecy even after the termination of their functions. This does not exclude the duty to supply compulsory information required by law, except where this relates to information for statistical purposes.

Law 67/98 also contains provisions on the treatment of data and the organisation of files made by the competent authorities in connection with the suspicion of illegal activities.

Special reference to the bona fide principle

[25.16]   The Civil Code is strongly influenced, as far as contractual relations are concerned, by the bona fide principle.[8] This principle is laid down in art 227 of the Civil Code in relation to the concept of fault in the formation of contracts generally and provides as follows:

> '1   Whoever negotiates with a third party for the completion of a contract
>   must, both in the preliminary stages and in the formation of the contract,
>   act according to the principle of bona fide (good faith), otherwise such a
>   person, if at fault, shall be held liable for any damage caused to the other
>   party.'

In this provision, there is a reference to the distinction between the two stages precedent to the contract: (i) the so-called 'negotiation stage', consisting of the preparation of the contents of the agreement and (ii) the so-called 'decision stage', where each of the parties issue a declaration to contract, more precisely, the proposal and its acceptance.

Throughout the Portuguese legal system, there are various applications of this principle in several areas of the law. Consequently, whenever there is no specific rule concerning any particular point of bank confidentiality, the banks, in performing their functions or discharging their contractual duties vis-à-vis their customers, must act in the protection of the customers' interests using loyalty and due diligence, including informing the customers on any matters affecting their interests.

Notwithstanding this, the duty of confidentiality does not authorise the bank to use any information concerning a customer to protect another customer in a conflict of interest situation. The bona fide principle is, however, useful in controlling the attitude of banks towards their customers and in limiting their use of information contrary to their duty to protect customers' interests, including any customer faced with a conflict of interest situation with another customer of the same bank. It is the application of this principle that art 74 of the Banking Law reflects:

> 'the bank directors and employees must proceed diligently in their relations with
> customers, being loyal and discrete and dealing conscientiously with the interests
> of the customers that have been entrusted to them.'

It is therefore important to note that, where conflicts of interest are concerned, both the law and banking practice in Portugal do not require banks to provide their

---

8 A large number of legal articles have been written on the principle of bona fides, eg António Meneses Cordeiro *Da Boa Fé no Direito Civil* in Coimbra (ed) (1985) vols I and II; António Meneses Cordeiro *Banca, Bolsa e Crédito* in Almedina (ed) *Estatutos de Direito Comercial e de Direito da Economia* (1990) vol I.

customers with advice which may result in the infringement of bank confidentiality obligations relating to another customer or any protected data held by a bank. In other words, banks are not permitted to provide this information to any customer, even where they are engaged in advising them on a business matter, where this infringes the confidentiality obligation owed to another customer. The principle of bona fide is also reflected in Law 67/98, dated 26 October (see above), as a general principle on the treatment of such data (art 5, 1.a) of this Law).

A special reference to legislation on measures against corruption, economic and financial crimes, terrorism and certain types of trafficking offences

[25.17] Act 36/94, dated 29 September, on measures against corruption, economic and financial crimes was amended by Law 5/02, dated 11 January. The scope of application of this Law, dealing with breaches of secrecy (as well as a special regime for the collection of evidence and goods by the state), is, according to art 1 of Law 5/02, as follows:

1   trafficking of narcotics;
2   terrorism and terrorist organisations;
3   gun running;
4   certain forms of corruption and embezzlement;
5   money laundering;
6   criminal association;
7   illegal commerce (contraband);
8   trafficking and illegal alteration of stolen vehicles;
9   trafficking of minors and certain connected crimes; and
10 counterfeiting of currency and items equivalent to currency.

Article 2, no 1 of Law 5/02 on the breach of secrecy states:

'In the stages of enquiry, production of evidence and procedural trials relating to the crimes outlined at art 1, the professional secrecy of members of corporate bodies of credit institutions and financial companies, and of their employees and persons who render services to such institutions, as well as the secrecy of tax authority employees, shall cease if there are reasons to believe that the respective information is of interest in finding the truth.'

The extension of the scope of Law 5/02 to breaches by employees of the tax authorities was an important amendment not included in Law 36/94 given that the list of offences has also been expanded.

In addition, art 2 contains the following provisions of importance which should be noted:

'2   For the purposes of this law, the regime laid down above depends only on the decision, with reasons, of a competent court.
3   The decision referred to in the previous paragraph must identify the persons covered by the measure and should specify the information to be provided and documents to be requested; such decision may be general in its terms to each of the addressees where further particulars are not possible.
4   If the person or people who own the accounts or the participants to the transactions are not known, the identification of the accounts and

transactions in relation to which information is required is considered sufficient.

5   In the case of information relating to a person accused in criminal proceedings or a collective entity, the decision referred to in number 2 above shall be general in nature and include:

   a)   tax information;
   b)   information relating to bank accounts in the name of the accused or the collective entity and their respective transactions, or in relation to which such person or the collective entity has the power to effect transactions;
   c)   information relating to banking and financial transactions where the accused or the collective entity is a participant;
   d)   identification of the other participants in the operations referred to at items b) and c);
   e)   supporting documents in respect of the information referred to in the previous numbers.

6   In order to comply with the provisions contained in the previous paragraphs, the courts and the police responsible for the investigation have access to the database of the tax authorities.'

On the other hand, art 3 of Law 5/02 regulates the procedure, establishing the steps outlined in art 2 referred to above, applicable to credit institutions or financial companies. In short, it provides that a request may be made either by a court or – by delegation of the latter – a criminal authority responsible for the investigation to the credit institutions or financial companies for all information and supporting documents considered relevant. Such entities are obliged to provide the authorities with the requested documents within certain deadlines, established in Law 5/02, failing which (or if the authorities suspect that certain documents or information have been withheld) the court can order the production of such documents. If the credit institutions or financial companies mentioned above are not known, the court can request that the Bank of Portugal divulges the request for documents and information.

Article 4 of the same legislation governs the 'control of bank accounts' as follows:

1   the credit institution is under an obligation to inform the court or the police of information on any transfers relating to the bank account within 24 hours;
2   the control of the bank account may be either authorised or imposed, depending upon the circumstances of the case, by a court order where this procedure is important in uncovering the facts. This court order shall identify:
   (a) the bank account(s) covered by the measure,
   (b) the respective duration period, and
   (c) the court or police body responsible for the control of the bank account;
3   the court decision may also order the suspension of any transfers or transactions specified where this is necessary to prevent money laundering.

It should be noted that the persons referred to in art 2, no 1, ie the members of corporate bodies of credit institutions and financial companies, their employees and those who render services, as well as tax authority employees, are bound by a judicial secrecy obligation in relation to the above-mentioned proceedings, in the event that they have knowledge of them. They are not permitted to disclose any knowledge relating to these proceedings to the persons whose accounts are controlled or in respect of which there has been a request for the provision of documents and information.

If any of these people fail to comply with the provisions on producing information and documents without just cause or supply false information or documents, penalties of imprisonment from six months to three years or a corresponding fine of not less than 60 days can be applied (art 13 of Law 5/02).

CASE LAW
Criminal law cases

[25.18] The case law on bank confidentiality has mainly focused on criminal, civil and labour cases and a reasonably large amount of case law has been adjudicated. Most cases concern the classic issue relating to the protection of bank confidentiality in the face of an order or request from the criminal authorities to the bank requiring the latter to disclose private information for the purposes of helping in the investigation of a crime.

Even when the law was less clear on the limits of bank confidentiality, the Court of Appeal held that bank confidentiality can be overridden by the higher interests of a criminal investigation and criminal justice.[9] This position has also been followed in other judgments, for instance, by the Courts of Appeal of Coimbra (dated 31 October 1990, 6 July 1994 and 17 April 1996) and Évora (dated 5 November and 12 May 1992) as discussed in further detail below.

In the judgment of the Court of Appeal of Coimbra, dated 31 October 1990, the court considered the Criminal Code in force at the time on the duty of disclosure of information relating to a person suspected of having stolen and used valuables belonging to a third party. The court based its judgment on the principle that the 'interest of the good administration of justice is clearly of higher value than the interest of obtaining and maintaining a climate of confidence of bank clients', despite this also being an important concern. The court therefore decided that the bank should disclose the information requested by the criminal authorities where such disclosure ensured justice was done.

The principle stated by the court in this judgment, which has been followed in other similar cases, provides a clear option on the conflict of interests in question, that is, the conflict between the interest of bank customers continuing to have trust in the banking system and the interests of the community at large in preserving criminal justice.

The same understanding was held in the following judgments:

1 the judgment of the Court of Appeal of Coimbra, dated 31 January 1990, which also concerned a theft of valuables. The court decided that the bank should disclose the identity of the person who received them;
2 in the judgment of the Court of Appeal of Évora, dated 5 November 1991, the court had in mind that, in the context of a criminal investigation, any relevant information should be disclosed by the bank where the criminal authorities consider that the requested information is 'necessary and adequate for the purpose of accomplishing the public interest';
3 in the judgment of the Court of Appeal of Évora, dated 12 May 1992, also dealing with the investigations in a criminal case, the court decided that 'the purpose of investigating the facts is clearly higher than the ground on which the

---

9 Eg the judgment of the Court of Appeal of Oporto, dated 11 November 1991.

bank confidentiality obligation is based; in the event of a conflict between the public interest of the state in acting against anyone who breaks criminal laws and the right to privacy of the citizens, the former should prevail over the latter'.

Moreover, in the judgment of the Supreme Court of Justice, dated 12 November 1986, it was held that the Public Prosecutor should commence criminal proceedings even where the facts forming the basis of the crime brought to his knowledge occurred through a breach of the bank confidentiality obligation.

In the decisions of the Court of Appeal of Coimbra, dated 6 July 1994, the Supreme Court of Justice, dated 4 November 1981, and the Court of Appeal of Évora dated 11 October 1994, judgment in the first two cases was given in the context of a criminal investigation of dishonoured cheques; the third related to joint bank accounts. All judgments concluded that the interests of conducting criminal investigations should override the duty of bank confidentiality. The Supreme Court of Justice decided that 'in the case of unpaid cheques, bank secrecy cannot prevail over the right of the court to order the production of necessary documents in collating evidence of the crime'.

In the judgment of the Court of Appeal of Coimbra, dated 17 April 1996, the court reinforced former decisions when it said: 'it is legal to override the bank confidentiality obligation when this is necessary for the purposes of a criminal investigation'. This judgment, therefore, established on a strict basis (ie not depending on the particular circumstances of the case) the priority of one interest over the other.

This priority does not apply where the purpose of the investigation is not the defence of a public interest or where such investigation does not necessarily require disclosure. Where no matter of public interest is at stake, bank confidentiality may not be overridden without a specific legal provision permitting it. This was established, for instance, in the judgment of the Supreme Court of Justice, dated 21 May 1980. The court held that:

> 'If there is no specific legal provision which authorises banks to disclose information to the criminal authorities in respect of certain client data, the bank confidentiality obligation should be upheld and the bank has the right to refuse any request for disclosure under these conditions.'

Similarly, the judgment of the Supreme Court of Justice, dated 20 October 1988, concluded that the bank confidentiality obligation promotes the creation of a climate of confidence with banks and may only be overridden when the law allows derogation.

Additionally, in the judgment of the Court of Oporto, dated 9 January 2002, the court concluded that the directors and employees of the tax administration are bound to keep secret facts relating to the tax position of taxpayers. However, such a duty ceases under the applicable provisions of the Penal Code and Criminal Procedure Code.

Civil law cases

[25.19] As with the above cases where the priority of the interests of criminal investigations prevailed over bank confidentiality, the civil courts have handed down decisions acknowledging that certain private interests must also prevail over bank confidentiality. This has been the position on the attachment of funds. In these actions, the court may require bank co-operation to obtain information facilitating the identification of funds to be attached. The courts have decided that in these cases it is not just that, based on bank confidentiality rules, a party may avoid the attachment of their own funds available for the payment of an undisputed debt.[10]

Specifically, in the judgment of the Court of Appeal of Lisbon, dated 22 June 1995, the court decided that all banks are obliged to execute a court order relating to the attachment of funds and, moreover, the bank must inform the court where the amount of money in the customer's account is less than the amount which the court has ordered be attached.

More recent cases, for example, the judgment of the Court of Lisbon, dated 20 January 2000, focused on the breach of bank confidentiality in cases of attachment of accounts subsequent to a court claim filed by the creditor with limited knowledge on the identification of bank accounts.

However, in other cases where 'a party has a mere interest in proving a fact in a lawsuit based on bank information', the courts have not agreed to set aside the bank confidentiality obligation. For example, the Supreme Court of Justice delivered a judgment, dated 10 April 1980, in a civil matter, according to which it considered that, as a general rule, anyone, even someone who is not a party to an action, is under a duty to co-operate in the pursuit of justice. However, refusing to co-operate is legitimate if the co-operation results in a breach of the bank confidentiality obligation which binds all directors and employees of banks.

In addition, the bank confidentiality obligation was not overridden in the judgment of the Supreme Court of Justice, dated 8 February 1990. The court concluded in this case that a court may not override the confidentiality obligation of a bank by ordering a bank inspection with a view to investigating accounts for tax purposes where this is not expressly permitted by law. This judgment is particularly interesting as it challenges the public interest issues of the payment of taxes and bank confidentiality.

The factual background may be summarised as follows: in a judicial action for the distribution of an inheritance estate, the Public Prosecutor sued the heirs on the ground of failure to file a complete list of the entire estate with the tax authorities. According to the Public Prosecutor, this was an attempt to avoid the payment of tax under the inheritance tax rules. The heirs maintained that, in fact, there were bank accounts forming part of the estate, which were not identified. The tax authorities notified the bank, which refused to identify the accounts. The heirs also failed to identify the accounts. The Public Prosecutor then requested the court to dispatch an agent to the bank's premises to review in person the documents necessary to identify the bank accounts. The bank maintained its refusal to co-operate.

The first instance court accepted the position of the heirs based on the bank confidentiality obligation. The Court of Appeal, however, decided in favour of the Public Prosecutor, considering that, since there was a lack of information provided by the heirs to allow the proper determination of the values on which inheritance tax would be applied, the inspection at the premises of the bank was necessary. Moreover, the court held that an order made by a court should always be executed either by public or by private entities and this included banks.

The heirs filed an appeal with the Supreme Court of Justice and maintained that bank confidentiality could only be overridden if there is a specific legal provision

10 Judgments of the Court of Appeal of Coimbra, dated 7 November 1989, the Court of Appeal of Lisbon, dated 22 June 1995 and 8 October 1996, the Court of Appeal of Oporto, dated 12 June 1995 and the Court of Appeal of Évora, dated 18 June 1996.

permitting such an exception to the duty of confidentiality, which was not the case here. The Court of Justice held in favour of the heirs. It pointed out that, although there was a conflict between two public interests, that is, the payment of taxes and preserving bank confidentiality, the latter should be protected and should prevail over the former whenever there is no legal provision permitting an exception to the confidentiality obligation. The court concluded that the bank was entitled to refuse the disclosure of information and considered that the bank confidentiality obligation in this case was a lawful limit to the duty of banks to co-operate with the authorities in the pursuit of justice.

This was also the conclusion of a judgment of the Court of Appeal of Oporto, dated 21 October 1996, on an employment law matter. This appeal was filed by an employee against his employer after the employee claimed he had been unfairly dismissed. During the production of evidence in the court of first instance, an issue was raised concerning the conflict between bank confidentiality and the necessity of disclosing information kept by banks. This issue was relevant in support of the employee's defence. The Court of Appeal of Oporto decided:

> 'In labour matters, bank confidentiality must prevail over the general duty to co-operate with the courts in order to provide evidence which may be relevant to settle the dispute.'

In another context, the judgment of the Court of Appeal of Lisbon, dated 5 July 1989, also on an employment law matter, decided that there was no breach of bank confidentiality in a case where the Internal Inspection Department of a bank investigated the accounts of its employees who were suspected of having made irregular or dishonest transactions.

Similarly, the Supreme Court of Justice delivered a judgment of 29 May 1991, according to which:

> 'the bank is entitled to make all necessary investigations in the defence of its interests, including examining the bank account of an employee who is suspected of having committed irregular acts. For this purpose, the employee does not qualify as a bank customer where irregular acts have been committed by him.'

The judgment of the Court of Oporto, dated 21 May 2001, decided that, within the scope of bank confidentiality, bank secrecy is not breached by the right of an employee to request from its employer bank the disclosure to the court of internal audits made at the bank (since, in this case, the employee needed to extract from these documents evidence to support a particular claim against the employer), provided that the names of clients and identification of the accounts are not disclosed.

More recently, the Court of Lisbon handed down judgments on 14 November 2000 and 28 February 2002 stating that the right of a bank account holder to obtain information on account transactions is transmissible to the respective heirs who, therefore, become the beneficiaries of the duty of bank confidentiality. Consequently, a bank cannot refuse such information to the heirs (after evidence is produced on the death of the owner) on the basis of bank confidentiality.

CONCLUSIONS

[25.20] Bank confidentiality is governed in Portugal by several legal provisions, including the Banking Law, which assures bank customers (as well as those providing information to banks with a view to becoming customers) that their affairs will not be disclosed to third parties, except in limited circumstances as provided by statute.

Bank confidentiality is legally considered a professional duty and, therefore, more than merely a contractual obligation. As a consequence, its infringement is punishable as a crime and may give rise to imprisonment and civil liability for bank directors, employees and suppliers of services to banks. The criminal sanction is expressly laid down by law, both in the Banking Law and the Criminal Code. Civil liability is governed by the Civil Code. Banking law does not establish any limitation on the amount of damages which can be claimed from a bank in such cases.

The most significant exception to the bank confidentiality rule relates to criminal investigations. The pursuit of justice in a criminal action has a higher value than bank confidentiality. However, it is necessary for the criminal investigation judge to make a prior and express order that banks disclose the information protected by the confidentiality rules.

Some civil case law has also established that banks must co-operate with the courts on the attachment of funds belonging to a bank customer owing money to a third party where the latter has applied to the court for the attachment of such funds.

In contrast and in civil matters of a different nature, including employment matters, the breach of the bank confidentiality obligation should only be allowed by a court in exceptional and duly justified circumstances.

The data protection legislation is particularly detailed and follows the EU regime. Banks may, under international conventions, be obliged to co-operate with other foreign banks, criminal authorities and others in supplying information about their clients. The service of a judicial claim document in connection with actions pending in foreign courts and addressed to a national court for service on a bank, for instance, to request the disclosure of information is governed both by domestic law and international conventions.

Of special importance in this respect is legislation on measures against organised crime and economic and financial crimes, which cover money laundering, the unlawful production of and trafficking in narcotics, 'white collar' crime and, given the latest and most recent amendment, terrorism, terrorist organisations and certain types of trafficking, including that of minors and firearms. This recent amendment takes on particular importance since it has expanded (i) the scope of offences where breach of the secrecy duty is required and (ii) the scope of the breach of secrecy, since it now also covers the professional secrecy of tax authority employees, thus permitting a more effective response in international and EU actions against these kinds of crimes.

26 Singapore

Alvin Yeo
Joy Tan

INTRODUCTION

Singapore as a financial centre of international importance

[26.1] Over the past couple of decades, Singapore has developed into an international financial centre rivalling, and in some sectors even surpassing, more traditionally renowned financial hubs like Tokyo and Hong Kong. In the *Global Competitiveness Report* (2005–2006), compiled by the Swiss-based World Economic Forum, Singapore was ranked as the sixth most competitive nation, ahead of the United Kingdom (ranked 13th) and New Zealand (ranked 16th). In the *World Competitiveness Yearbook* (2005), compiled by the International Institute for Management Development, Singapore was ranked in third place, after the United States and Hong Kong.

Certainly, within the South-East Asian region, Singapore is the pre-eminent financial centre with 108 commercial banks (five of which are local) as at February 2006, 47 merchant banks, 42 representative offices of banks and nine international money brokers. Of special importance is the emergence and growth of the Asian dollar market, centred in Singapore, which, at the end of 2003, consisted of a pool of assets of some US$509.1 billion.

Singapore's success as a financial centre has been achieved partly through building on its position at the crossroads of international trade. So, for instance, one writer opined that Singapore's strategic location on traditional international trade routes has resulted in her present importance to international trade, transportation and finance.[1]

This success has also been achieved partly by design, in that the government has identified financial services as an integral part of the economy and promulgated various measures to help the sector grow. As one senior government leader described this at the second reading of the Banking (Amendment) Bill of January 1984:

> 'Since the introduction of the Banking Act in 1971, Singapore has developed into a financial centre of international importance. This is indicated by the presence of a large number of financial institutions of international standing and reputation, the advent of new financial instruments, the rapid development of the Asian dollar market, the extensive nature of the financial transactions entered into and the numerous financial services that are now being provided.'[2]

---

1 Dennis Campbell *International Bank Secrecy* (1992) p 578.
2 Parliamentary debates, 17 January 1994, at the second reading of the Banking (Amendment) Bill by the then First Deputy Prime Minister Goh Keng Swee.

Singapore's financial sector is regulated by the Monetary Authority of Singapore ('MAS'), which is regarded as the de facto central bank.

Banker–customer relationship under the 2003 statutory regime

[26.2]   In the Singapore chapter in the previous edition of this book, the writers discussed the new statutory regime introduced by way of the Banking (Amendment) Bill 2001 ('the 2001 amendments'). Although a revised edition of the Banking Act (Cap 19) was published in 2003, no substantive changes were made to the law, the material amendment being a renumbering of various provisions in the Act.

We previously examined the axiomatic principle arising from the landmark English case of *Tournier v National Provincial and Union Bank of England*,[3] that is, a bank would be under a contractual duty not to divulge information concerning its customer's account to third parties, which duty is implied by virtue of the banker–customer relationship. Within Singapore's legal framework, under the Banking Act (Cap 19), the bank would also be under a statutory obligation not to make unauthorised disclosure.

It was concluded therefore that, in Singapore, the duty of bank confidentiality stemmed from two sources:

1   the English common law contractual duty of confidentiality as received in Singapore; and
2   a statutory duty imposed by s 47 of the Banking Act ('s 47').

We adopted the view that this *general* position – that the contractual duty owed at common law runs parallel with the statutory duty enforced by statute – has not changed despite the material and far-reaching amendments to the Banking Act in 2001. However, as the 2001 amendments substantially revised the structure of the s 47 bank confidentiality provisions and did away with the exceptions to bank confidentiality owed at common law, in the chapter in the previous edition, we considered that the 2001 amendments could be viewed as qualifying and, to some extent, a codification of, the common law.

In this chapter, we will embark on a similar discussion, primarily focusing on the statutory regime introduced by the 2001 amendments, as well as highlight any other developments in this area of law in the past few years.

The reception of English common law in Singapore

[26.3]   As will be discussed in detail below, the statutory regime introduced by the 2001 amendments raises questions as to the extent to which the English common law position (and, in particular, the common law exceptions to the duty of confidentiality) continues to apply in Singapore. Nevertheless, a brief outline of the manner in which English common law is received in Singapore is still relevant as a starting point to this discussion.

The reception of English law in Singapore was effected by the Letters Patent issued on 27 November 1826. This is more commonly referred to as the Second Charter of Justice that established the Court of the Judicature of the Prince of Wales, Singapore

3 [1924] 1 KB 461.

and Malacca (the Straits Settlements). Thereafter, English law and equity, as it stood in England in 1826, became part of the law of the Straits Settlements.[4] Section 5 of the Civil Law Act was later enacted providing that, in relation to commercial issues not governed by any Singapore statute, the relevant law applicable in England (covering both common law and statute) would apply.

In 1993, to overcome the difficulties in applying s 5 of the Civil Law Act, the Singapore Parliament passed the Application of English Law Act 1993 ('AELA') which provided, inter alia, for the continuing reception of the English common law in Singapore in so far as:

1   it was part of the law of Singapore immediately before the commencement of this Act; and
2   it is applicable to the circumstances of Singapore and its inhabitants and is subject to such modifications as those circumstances may require.[5]

The AELA also lists the specific English statutes which are deemed to be part of Singapore law, save where provided otherwise by Singapore statutes.

BASIC RULE OF CONFIDENTIALITY PRIOR TO THE 2001 AMENDMENTS

Nature of the banker's obligation

[26.4]   Prior to the 2001 amendments to the Banking Act, it was generally accepted that the common law duty of confidentiality applies to civil liability, while s 47 creates a statutory obligation, the breach of which would constitute a criminal offence.[6]

The English contractual duty under *Tournier*

[26.5]   The landmark English case of *Tournier v National Provincial and Union Bank of England*[7] laid down the principle that the banker's obligation to keep particulars of a customer's account confidential is an implied term that arises out of the banker–customer contractual relationship.

As there was no other provision made by any law having force in Singapore imposing a contractual duty of secrecy and since this was treated as part of the law of Singapore immediately before the commencement of the AELA, this common law principle continued to be in force in Singapore, at least until the 2001 amendments.

The scope of this common law contractual duty under *Tournier* has been extensively covered in Chapter 11, England. In brief, under the duty, the bank is obliged under an implied term of the contract between itself and its customer not to divulge information as to the state of the customer's account, any of the customer's transactions with the bank or any information relating to the customer acquired through the keeping of this account to third parties.

---

4 Campbell, n 1 above, pp 580–581. See also Walter Woon *The Singapore Legal Systems* (1989).
5 Section 3 of the Application of English Law Act. This Act repeals the previous s 5 of the Civil Law Act, which was the relevant law that had provided for the continuing reception of the common law.
6 Poh Chu Chai *Law of Banker and Customer* (4th edn, 1999) p 572.
7 [1924] 1 KB 461.

This is, however, a qualified obligation. The bank may release the above-stated information when:

1   an order of court compels the bank to disclose;
2   the disclosure is necessitated by a duty to the public;
3   the protection of the bank's interests requires disclosure; or
4   there is an express or implied consent of the customer.

Since the AELA, English authorities are now not strictly binding on Singapore courts, but nevertheless considered highly persuasive.

The former statutory duty of confidentiality: comparison with contractual duty

[26.6]   In Singapore, the former statutory duty of confidentiality, imposed by the old s 47, provided for a general prohibition against disclosure of the affairs of the customer's account, which was then qualified by various exceptions. The general prohibition against disclosure was contained in the old s 47(3). This duty was not merely imposed on bank 'officials',[8] but also covered any person who has any means of access to the records of the bank by reason of his capacity or office and any person in a 'professional relationship' with the bank (for example, wide enough to cover solicitors and accountants who were engaged by the bank). The old s 47(4) provided for certain exceptions to this general prohibition.

Before the 2001 amendments, the differences between the two regimes lay not so much in the general rule of confidentiality, but rather in the exceptions to the general rule and there was some uncertainty arising from the overlap between the local statute then prevailing and the common law which stemmed from Singapore's legacy as a former English law jurisdiction.

Similarities and differences in the exceptions under the old regime

[26.7]   It would appear that some of the defences available to a bank at common law were different from those under the former s 47. In theory, this would mean that the banks would be able to rely on the common law exceptions as defences in civil actions brought against them by their customers, whereas, if prosecuted, they and their employees would be confined to the statutory exceptions under s 47.

The first exception to the contractual duty, whereby the disclosure may be made under compulsion of law, found a parallel of sorts under the old s 47(4)(d) and (e). The second exception to the contractual duty, whereby a disclosure may be made under a duty to the public, had no corresponding provision under the statutory duty. The third exception under the contractual duty of confidentiality is to allow disclosure to be made in the interests of the bank. This was mirrored in the old s 47(4)(b) and (c). Finally, the exception that disclosure may be made under the express or implied consent of the customer does not find an exact parallel enacted under the statutory duty of confidentiality – the former s 47(4)(a) provided that nothing less than a *written* consent by the customer or his personal representatives would suffice to lift the prohibition.

---

8 The former s 47(11) defined 'official' of the bank to include a director and an employee of the bank.

The differences in the exceptions raised the issue of whether the public interest and implied consent exceptions apply under the statutory regimes. It was argued by one writer that the then s 47 was not exhaustive since this would result in a narrow interpretation.[9] The prevalent view at the time was that the common law duty and statutory duty supplemented each other and s 47 was not exhaustive as it would not be in keeping with the legislative intent if the common law exceptions, which would constitute a valid defence to civil liability, were not also available as a defence in respect of the more onerous criminal liability. The issue had then yet to be resolved by the Singapore courts.

It would appear, however, that the legislature had seen fit to take up the resolution of the issue themselves with the enactment of the 2001 amendments. It now seems clear, under the new statutory regime, that the exceptions to the statutory duty stated in the Banking Act are intended to be *exhaustive* and the common law exceptions are not to apply.

THE 2001 AMENDMENTS: THE NEW STATUTORY DUTY OF CONFIDENTIALITY

[26.8] As we have mentioned in the previous edition of this chapter, on 16 May 2001, the Singapore government introduced in Parliament the Banking (Amendment) Bill, which revised various provisions of the Banking Act. Focusing on prudential oversight issues, the Bill was expressed to reflect the MAS' new risk-focused supervisory approach that enhanced its oversight on banks without increasing their cost of regulatory compliance. In the words of the (then) Deputy Prime Minister (and concurrent chairman of the MAS) in moving the Bill:

> '[MAS'] objective of ensuring financial stability is unchanged, but in order to have a more dynamic and vibrant financial sector, we have shifted emphasis from regulation to supervision. We have moved away from one-size-fits-all laws and regulations towards tailored supervision of individual institutions according to each institution's financial strength, risk management capability and risk profile.'[10]

In line with this policy, s 47 was amended to provide for a revised banking secrecy regime whereby banks would be given greater operational flexibility in handling customer information while still being subject to sufficient safeguards to ensure that the confidentiality of customer information is not compromised.

The then Deputy Prime Minister described this as follows:

> 'Tight banking secrecy is important to maintaining the confidence of customers in our banking system. However, our present banking secrecy provisions have impeded banks wanting to take advantage of potential operational benefits and savings. For example, banks find it difficult to securitise mortgage loans or to outsource data processing to third parties ... We have considered both the

---

9 Myint Soe 'Changes in the Law Relating to Banking Secrecy, the Banking (Amendment) Act 1983' [1983] 25 Mal LR 387.
10 Parliamentary debates, 16 May 2001, at the second reading of the Banking (Amendment) Bill, col 1684. (An example of this policy is the enactment of the new s 9A, which reduces the paid-up capital requirement for banking subsidiaries of local banks which have met the former $1.5 billion capital requirement to $100 million. This was to facilitate the setting up of banking subsidiaries that adopt new business models such as Internet banking.)

operational requirements of the banks and the need to preserve customer confidentiality. The measures set out in s 47 strike a careful balance between these two sets of considerations.'[11]

In 2003, certain minor revisions were made to the Banking Act, but s 47 remained in the same form as that pursuant to the 2001 amendments.

Overview of the current s 47 and exceptions

[26.9]   The current s 47 enacts a more extensive set of circumstances under which banks can disclose customer information and the terms of such disclosure are now set out separately in the Third Schedule to the 2003 revised edition of the Banking Act (the Third Schedule was previously known as the Sixth Schedule). The Third Schedule contains two parts – Pt I, which contains many of the old exceptions in existence under the previous statutory regime, and Pt II, which contains most of the new exceptions.

Both Schedules contain a first, second and third column, which contain, in relation to each exception, the purpose of the permitted disclosure (lawful purpose), the person or class of persons to which that disclosure may be made (lawful recipient) and certain conditions which must be complied with in relation to that disclosure (conditions), respectively.

Section 47(2) provides that a bank may, for a lawful purpose, disclose customer information to the corresponding lawful recipient and in compliance with any applicable conditions (primary disclosure).

In relation to the exceptions in Pt I, the lawful recipient of information, not just the bank itself, is permitted to make further disclosure of the information (secondary disclosure) without penalty. However, under s 47(5), the lawful recipient of information furnished pursuant to any of the exceptions in Pt II is not permitted to make secondary disclosure, except as authorised under the Third Schedule or if required to do so by an order of court. A breach of this section would constitute an offence.

Section 47 applies not only to banks, but to merchant (and investment) banks, subject to the notifications set out in the Third Schedule to the Banking Regulations (2004 Rev Ed). The Merchant Bank Directive 12 on Banking Secrecy, issued under the former regime, has been revoked.

Subject matter of the statutory duty: customer information

[26.10]   Section 47(1) prohibits a bank in Singapore ('the bank') or any of its officers from disclosing customer information except as expressly provided in the Act.

Under s 40A, 'customer information' (in relation to the bank) means:

'(a) any information relating to, or any particulars of, an account of a customer of the bank, whether the account is in respect of a loan, investment or any other type of transaction, but does not include any information that is not referable to any named customer or group of named customers; or

---

11 Parliamentary debates, n 10 above, col 1689.

(b) deposit information, which means any information relating to:
  (i) any deposit of a customer of the bank;
  (ii) funds of a customer under management by the bank; or
  (iii) any safe deposit box maintained by, or any safe custody arrangements made by, a customer with the bank,

but does not include any information that is not referable to any named customer or group of named customers.'

Under the former s 47(3), the statutory duty of confidentiality only applied to 'information regarding the money or other relevant particulars of the account of [the] customer'. The subject matter of the common law duty is wider than this, for instance, in *Tournier*,[12] the bank had made disclosure to a third party of the fact that the customer had diverted the proceeds of a cheque to a bookmaker, which information neither related to the money in the customer's account nor is it a particular of his account. This was seen to be an anomaly and it had been suggested that the narrower scope of the duty as per the statute should apply on the principle of statutory interpretation that a penal statute be narrowly construed. The current definition of 'customer information', therefore, brings the statutory duty of confidentiality more in line with the *Tournier* common law position and does away with the anomaly.

It should be noted that this position is also consistent with the position in Malaysia, where the equivalent provision prohibits the disclosure of 'any information or document whatsoever relating to the affairs or account' of a customer.

The new ss 40 and 47 of the Banking Act are set out in the Appendix to this chapter.

The issue of what constituted customer information was addressed in the local case of *PSA Corpn v Korea Exchange Bank*.[13] In that case, PSA commenced action against Korea Bank for payment under two guarantees of a contractor, CY Singapore. Korea Bank's main defence was that PSA did not open an account with CY Singapore as required under the contract, but with its Korean affiliate, CY Korea. PSA sought discovery of account opening documents between Korea Bank and non-parties, CY Singapore and CY Korea. Korea Bank admitted the documents sought were relevant, but said it was precluded by s 47 of the Act from giving discovery.

PSA's main argument regarding confidentiality was that the documents did not contain protected 'account information' and that the old definition of protected information under the former s 47 was unchanged by the 2001 amendments.

Rejecting PSA's argument, the High Court held that the new, wider definition of customer information under s 47 protected the documents and refused to make the discovery order sought against Korea Bank.[14]

The current exceptions

[26.11] Much of the attention generated by the 2001 amendments centred on the new exceptions to the general rule on bank secrecy (which are largely to be found in Pt II of the Third Schedule), which did not exist under the original regime. These new exceptions were by and large welcomed as necessary developments in the law to

---

12 *Tournier v National Provincial and Union Bank of England* [1924] 1 KB 461.
13 [2002] 3 SLR 37.
14 [2002] 3 SLR 37 at 43.

reflect the current practice and needs of banks in the climate of internationalisation, specialisation and competition in the new millennium.

Part I of the Third Schedule mainly contains the exceptions set out in the old s 47(4). These will be briefly discussed before turning to the Pt II exceptions.

Parts I and II of the Third Schedule are set out in the Appendix to this chapter.

Part I, items 3 and 4: proceedings in camera under s 47(3)

[26.12]   Items 3 and 4 relate to disclosure made in connection with the bankruptcy/winding up of the customer and with proceedings between the bank and customer(s) (with the exception of item 4(c), which is dealt with below). It is to be noted that under s 47(3), in cases involving such disclosure, a court is empowered to direct that the proceedings be held in camera and make other orders necessary to ensure confidentiality of the customer information.

The High Court opined obiter in *PSA Corpn v Korea Exchange Bank* that the current s 47(3) was too narrow and should not be confined to items 3 and 4. This was because there are other exceptions which may require the court's assistance to ensure confidentiality, for example, items 6 and 7 of Pt I of the Third Schedule, which pertain to garnishee proceedings and a court order pursuant to Pt IV of the Evidence Act (Cap 97).[15]

Part I, item 4: disclosure in connection with conduct of proceedings over property of the bank

[26.13]   The previous exception under s 47(4)(c) was where disclosure was made with a view to instituting or conducting civil proceedings between the bank and its customer or guarantor relating to the customer's banking transaction or in an interpleader situation. Item 4 substitutes 'guarantor' with the more encompassing 'surety', dispenses with the qualification 'civil', thus arguably expanding the exception to arbitration proceedings, and adds the following situation:

> '(c) between the bank and one or more parties in respect of property, whether movable or immovable, in or over which some right or interest has been conferred or alleged to have been conferred on the bank by the customer or his surety.'

This exception permits the bank to rely on customer information in order to prove its title or right to property, which property is the subject of litigation between the bank and third parties (who may not be the customer), as distinct from the interpleader situation. Conversely, this also permits the third parties to obtain discovery against the bank in order to challenge such title. This is a welcome addition to the limited 'litigation' exceptions under the former regime.

However, we consider that these exceptions should have even wider scope than that currently provided for, as was also noted in *PSA Corpn v Korea Exchange Bank*. The High Court, in holding that a court could not order disclosure from a bank if none of the Third Schedule exceptions applied, had the following comments:

> 'It may well be that the present case calls for further amendments to be made to the Act to include an exception which allows disclosure in litigation between a bank and the beneficiary of an instrument issued by the bank. Indeed, there are

---

15   [2002] 3 SLR 37 at 44.

many instances of banks issuing instruments like guarantees, performance bonds and letters of credit. It seems to be incongruous that where there is litigation between, say, a bank and a surety relating to the banking transaction of a customer, discovery of relevant documents pertaining to "customer information" is allowed, but yet where a beneficiary sues a bank on any of the instruments I have mentioned, such disclosure is not allowed. Since the dispute between the beneficiary and the bank relates to an instrument which must have been issued at the request of the customer, the customer should not be in a position to complain if information relating to his account is disclosed so long as it satisfies the test of relevance in the litigation. In addition, the current s 47(3) can be expanded to allow the court to make such directions and orders it thinks fit to ensure confidentiality where this exception, if available, applies.

However, it is for Parliament to decide whether any further exception to banking secrecy or confidentiality is required and whether the current s 47(3) should be expanded.'[16]

It remains to be seen if Parliament does act to expand the 'litigation' exceptions to bank secrecy.

Part I, item 7: disclosure pursuant to Pt IV of the Evidence Act

[26.14]   Under Pt I of the Third Schedule, the exception under item 7 permits primary disclosure in order to comply with an order of court pursuant to the powers conferred under Pt IV of the Evidence Act – relieving banks from the necessity of attending and producing their books in court.

This is not strictly a new exception – under the former s 47(4)(d), banking secrecy obligations would not apply to the officials of any bank who, by compulsion of any written law in force in Singapore (including Pt IV of the Evidence Act), are required to give information to the police or a public officer who is duly authorised under that law to obtain that information or to a court in the investigation or prosecution of a criminal offence under any such law. However, s 47(4)(d) addressed entirely criminal matters and did not cover the situation of disclosure orders made by the court under Pt IV of the Evidence Act in civil cases. This was a loophole in the drafting that was addressed by the 2001 amendments.

The main section in Pt IV of the Evidence Act is s 175(1), which provides that:

'On the application of any party to a legal proceeding, the court or a judge may order that such party be at liberty to inspect and take copies of any entries in a banker's book for any of the purposes of such proceedings.'

'Bankers' book' is defined in s 170 of the Evidence Act as follows:

'"Bankers' books" includes ledgers, day books, cash books, account books and all other books used in the ordinary business of the bank.'

The unreported High Court case of *Anthony Wee Soon Kim v UBS AG*[17] clarifies that the exception under item 7 *only* applies to orders made under Pt IV of the Evidence Act and, if disclosure of confidential banking documents is being ordered via some other means, an order under Pt IV of the Evidence Act would have to be sought as

---

16 [2002] 3 SLR 37 at 43–44.
17 Suit no 834 of 2001, SIC no 1595 of 2002.

well. In the *Anthony Wee* decision, defendants who had applied for and obtained *subpoena duces tecum* against other banks to produce banking documents relating to the plaintiff were ordered to take out an application under s 175 of the Evidence Act to enable the banks to make the disclosure pursuant to the subpoena. It seems clear from this decision that a disclosure order under s 175 would be necessary before a bank would be exempted under this item from its duty of confidentiality, notwithstanding that an order under some other provision for disclosure had already been obtained.

This does, however, create a problem as an additional 'exempting' application under s 175 might be difficult to obtain in relation to disclosure orders to trace funds of fraudsters under the principle set out in *Bankers Trust v Shapira*[18] – the scope of such orders are often wider than the orders for inspection of bankers' books pursuant to s 175.

Further, s 175 contemplates an existing legal proceeding and an 'exempting' application cannot be brought in a pre-action situation, for instance, in relation to disclosure pursuant to a *Norwich Pharmacal*[19] order or even pre-action Mareva injunction orders.

Formerly, despite this, banks would, as a matter of practice, comply with such disclosure orders rather than risk being in contempt of court. (Previously, the wider *Tournier* exception of disclosure pursuant to compulsion of law might have applied to this situation.) It remains to be seen, after the *Anthony Wee* decision, how this lacuna will be addressed in practice by banks, especially now that the s 47 exceptions would appear to be exhaustive. Although the *Anthony Wee* decision has been appealed against and the Court of Appeal has rendered its decision,[20] this lacuna was not addressed by the court.

On an interesting note, the court expounded on the definition of 'bankers' books' in s 170 of the Evidence Act. In the first place, to constitute 'record' or 'books' within the meaning of 'bankers' books', the documents must be properly sorted and filed. The appellant did not raise any contention as to this point, but argued that correspondence and facility letters are not 'bankers' books'. The court disagreed and held that the expression 'other books' in the definition of 'bankers' books' in s 170 included any form of permanent record maintained by a bank in relation to the transactions of a customer. Chao JA (as he then was) opined:

> '[I]n interpreting the expression "other books" in the definition, we should take a purposive approach and recognise the changes effected in the practices of bankers. Any form of a permanent record maintained by a bank in relation to the *transactions* of a customer should be viewed as falling within the scope of that expression. Correspondence between a bank and a customer which records a transaction clearly formed an integral part of the account of that customer and there is no good reason why it should be excluded. Otherwise, the object behind the enactment of Pt IV of the Act would be undermined and banks would be troubled to have to come to court with the documents, including correspondence, relating to the account(s) of each customer. Thus, we agree with the approach taken in *Williams v Williams*. However, such records should be contrasted with notes taken by bank officers of meetings with customers and such notes cannot be

---

18 [1980] 3 All ER 353.
19 *Norwich Pharmacal Co v Customs & Excise Commissioners* [1974] AC 133.
20 *Wee Soon Kim Anthony v UBS AG* [2003] 2 SLR 91.

regarded as entries in books kept by the bank for the purpose of its ordinary business within the meaning of "bankers' books" (*Re Howglen Ltd* [2001] 1 All ER 376).'

Part I, item 9: disclosure pursuant to compliance with the Banking Act, the Deposit Insurance Act 2005 and notices and directives issued by the MAS

[26.15] A deposit insurance scheme which provides an explicit, limited guarantee to insured depositors that they will be compensated, up to a specified amount, in the event of a failure of a full bank or a finance company in Singapore was established by the Deposit Insurance Act 2005, which has come into force with effect from 1 April 2006. Accordingly, item 9 has been amended to permit disclosure to lawful recipients for the purposes of complying with the provisions of the Deposit Insurance Act 2005.

Part II, item 1: disclosure in connection with performance of duty

[26.16] As a matter of practice in Singapore, as well as elsewhere, bank officers already often disclose customer information to their colleagues in Singapore, as well as in overseas branches and to their professional advisers. Item 1 has formally recognised this practice as an exception to the duty of bank secrecy.

The scope of the exception is as follows. A bank officer may disclose customer information to his fellow bank officer in Singapore, or to an officer designated in writing by the head office overseas, in connection with the performance of duty on the part of both parties. The lawful recipient in this case does not, however, include bank officers from overseas branches and subsidiaries (who have not been so designated by the head office).

Another lawful recipient of such information would be the bank's auditor, lawyer, consultant or other professional adviser appointed or engaged by the bank under a contract of service.

Part II, item 2: conduct of internal audit and risk management

[26.17] Pursuant to this exception, in connection with the conduct of internal audit or risk management, a foreign bank in Singapore may now disclose customer information to (i) its head office or parent bank, (ii) an overseas branch designated by the head office and (iii) a designated 'related corporation' (ie its subsidiaries or affiliates). A local bank may disclose to its parent bank or any related designated corporation.

Several writers[21] have mentioned the lacuna in the old regime where disclosure is permitted under the previous s 47(4)(f) to a bank's head office (of information relating to credit/foreign exchange details), under s 47(4)(k) to a bank's local parent bank (of information relating to credit facilities) and s 47(4)(l) to a bank's head office and branch (for the purposes of collating and processing information). It appeared

---

21 Eg Tan Sin Liang 'Banking secrecy – legal implications for banks in Singapore under the Banking (Amendment) Act 2001' [2001] Straits Lawyer, August, at 28.

that while disclosure could be made to a branch of a bank and a parent bank, no disclosure could be made to a subsidiary. Now, at least for the purpose of this exception, a subsidiary can finally be made (by designation) a lawful recipient of customer information.

Part II, item 3: outsourcing operational functions

[26.18] This is a particularly welcome exception which allows a bank to outsource its operational functions and thereby disclose customer information to 'any person including the head office of the bank or any branch thereof outside Singapore' who is engaged to perform the functions.

It has become increasingly more commercially expedient for banks in Singapore to outsource many of their operational functions, such as the processing of credit cards to third parties, who might enjoy greater economies of scale in that particular function than the banks themselves. This enabled banks to focus on their core banking business in the value chain. However, such activities were not strictly authorised under the former banking secrecy regime – instead, approval from the MAS on a case-by-case basis under the old s 47(12) was necessary before such outsourcing activities could take place. This has now been addressed by the exception in item 3.

The exception draws a distinction between local and domestic outsourcing. If the outsourced function is to be performed outside Singapore, the MAS has sought to impose conditions on the outsourcing contracts, as compared with domestic outsourcing, where no such conditions are imposed. This appears from the parliamentary debate at the second reading of the Banking (Amendment) Bill 2001 to have been done to safeguard against the foreign lawful recipient wrongfully disclosing customer information. However, the deterrent effect against foreign service providers committing an offence under s 47(5) would be open to question, given that the penalties would be difficult to enforce extra-territorially. For that reason, before it will permit a bank in Singapore to disclose customer information overseas, the MAS therefore stipulates a certain level of standing in proposed foreign outsource service providers and in the legal and regulative framework of its home jurisdiction.[22]

In furtherance of these concerns, if any outsourced function is to be performed outside Singapore, reference must be made to the MAS Notice to Banks entitled 'Banking Secrecy – Conditions for Outsourcing' ('MAS 634'). One of the key stipulations of MAS 634 requires banks to notify the MAS of all outsourcing arrangements involving the disclosure and protection of customer information upon entering into the relevant outsourcing agreement outside the jurisdiction.

Part II, item 4: mergers and acquisitions

[26.19] This exception permits a bank to disclose customer information in connection with a merger/acquisition, or proposed merger/acquisition, of the bank or its financial holding company to any person participating or otherwise involved in the merger/acquisition or proposed merger/acquisition (including his lawyers and other advisers), whether or not the merger/acquisition is subsequently entered into or completed.

---

22 Parliamentary debates, n 10 above, cols 1709–1710, per the Deputy Prime Minister BG Lee Hsien Loong.

Obviously, one of the big challenges in the merger/acquisition of a bank is in overcoming the banking secrecy issue. Since not all banks would have provided for a consent to such disclosure in their account opening forms in anticipation of a merger/acquisition, a bank may have to undertake the onerous and commercially inexpedient task of corresponding with its million (or more) customers to obtain their consents prior to making disclosure.

It is to be noted that contemporaneously with the coming into effect of this exception in July 2001, there was a rash of merger and acquisition activity in the banking sector in 2001. This exception no doubt facilitated such activity as the banks involved were able to share and exchange information freely in negotiations and due diligence exercises without having to engage in the time-consuming exercise of obtaining customer consents.

Part II, item 5: restructuring, transfer and sale of credit facilities

[26.20] This exception permits a bank to disclose customer information in connection with the restructure, transfer or sale (or proposed restructure, transfer or sale) of credit facilities of the bank to any transferee, purchaser or person participating or otherwise involved (including his lawyers and other advisers), whether or not the restructure/transfer/sale is subsequently entered into or completed. There is a caveat that only information relating to the relevant credit facilities may be disclosed (and not deposit information relating to funds in the customer's account).

This exception was enacted to make it easier for banks to take advantage of potential benefits in dealing with existing credit facilities, in particular, with regard to securitising mortgage loans and engaging in asset securitisation generally. Prior to this, there was obvious difficulty for a bank to engage in transactions for the transfer or sale of its credit facilities when the identity of the borrowers could not be disclosed without being in breach of bank secrecy. Now, a bank would be entitled to disclose customer information in connection with transfers or assignments of its loans, for instance, via novation agreements, participation agreements and assignment agreements, as well as in asset securitisation and loan mortgage securitisation. Further, customer information may be disclosed in connection with restructuring of credit facilities – although this term is not defined, this would in all likelihood include rescheduling of loans and private 'work outs'.

Part II, item 7: credit bureau

[26.21] This exception has resulted in the establishment of a Consumer Credit Bureau ('the Bureau') in Singapore, which would allow banks to obtain credit evaluations regarding certain customers and obtain information about 'delinquent' customers they would wish to avoid. The exception permits the sharing of certain customer information between a member bank and the Bureau and between fellow members of the Bureau.

Under item 7, a Bureau member bank can disclose certain customer information to the Bureau and to fellow members for the purpose of 'assessing the creditworthiness of the customers of banks'. This is subject to two caveats. First, no deposit information is to be disclosed and, secondly, secondary disclosure to one member by the Bureau of information disclosed by another member is to be regulated by the MAS.

The Bureau has been formally constituted and has been in operation since the end of 2002. The preliminary feedback from the consumer public regarding the Bureau has been mixed – while many acknowledge the benefit to the banking sector, most appear concerned about the risks to privacy and potential inroads into the confidentiality of their bank information. To cater for this, the access to such information is governed by a Code of Conduct, which lays down strict privacy principles by which all members must abide. For instance, all members must take all necessary precautions to ensure that information provided by the Bureau is properly and accurately recorded, maintained and protected against loss, unauthorised access, use, modification and disclosure.

Part II, item 9: cross-marketing

[26.22]   This exception facilitates the extension of cross-marketing capability to promote financial products and services in Singapore of any local financial institution which is licensed or regulated by the MAS to customers of the bank. As banks in Singapore may not be experts across the entire spectrum of financial products, cross-marketing was seen as desirable to help broaden consumer choice.

In the parliamentary debates during the second reading of the Banking (Amendment) Bill 2001, the issue of increased customer demand for rapid Internet processing and e-payments was mentioned, together with the examples of Citigroup's successful use of the MSN portal and the emergence of PayPal in competition with credit card companies.[23] Cross-marketing was seen to cater for perceived growing customer demand, both for new products which may not be offered by more traditional banks and a one-stop 'banking-cum-services' centre. Additionally, in the face of increased competition, banks were under pressure to enter into mutual alliances and tie ups with other financial institutions to cross-market their own products and services and to provide a one stop financial centre.

To address the concern about the potential invasion of customers' privacy regarding unsolicited approaches by allied third party institutions, such as insurance providers and credit card companies, banks are only permitted to disclose the customer's name, identity, address and contact numbers. No deposit information or credit or investment information, for example, the amount of funds in a customer's account and his investment profile, which might be very useful for the cross-marketing party, may be disclosed. Further, cross-marketing of non-financial products and services, cross-marketing with a party who is not an MAS-regulated financial institution and cross-marketing of financial products and services outside Singapore would not come within the exception.

APPLICABILITY OF, AND COMPARISON WITH, COMMON LAW UNDER THE CURRENT STATUTORY REGIME

Status of the exceptions

[26.23]   As mentioned above, it was previously considered, under the old bank secrecy regime, that the common law duty of confidentiality and the *Tournier*[24]

23 Parliamentary debates, n 10 above, col 1699.
24 *Tournier v National Provincial and Union Bank of England* [1924] 1 KB 461.

exceptions would still be implied in the Singapore civil law context, notwithstanding the 'co-existing' statutory regime under s 47. It was then pertinent to consider the differences between the two regimes (for instance, 'negative' consent is an exception under *Tournier*, but s 47 requires actual written consent).

Under the statutory regime pursuant to the 2001 amendments, the amended s 47(1) provided as follows:

> 'Customer information shall not, in any way, be disclosed by a bank in Singapore or any of its officers to any other person *except as expressly provided in this Act*' (emphasis added).

Therefore, it appeared that there was little scope for arguing that the common law exceptions can be implied in the Singapore context. So while the common law regarding the existence of an implied contractual duty of confidentiality should still subsist save as qualified by the statute, it is now unlikely that the *Tournier* common law exceptions would still apply even as defences to a civil action for breach of contract by the customer, since that would lead to the anomalous situation that an exception might be a good defence at civil law, but not under criminal law.

This approach seems to be consistent with the High Court's decision in *PSA Corpn v Korea Exchange Bank*,[25] discussed above. Woo JC (as he then was) concluded his judgment with the strong statement that s 47 sets out the general prohibition against disclosure and the (only) exceptions to this are to be found in the Third Schedule (and, implicitly, not under the common law).[26]

Of further note is the current s 47(8), which states that nothing in s 47 shall prevent a bank from entering into an express agreement with a customer for a *higher* standard of confidentiality than that contemplated by the new statutory regime. There was no corresponding provision in the former s 47.

It is submitted that the existence of this section does recognise (if by implication only) that the common law contractual duty of 'civil' confidentiality exists side by side with the statutory 'criminal' duty. Further, the section would seem to clarify that the statute, to a certain extent, operates to codify the common law, such that the common law position is (now) the same as the statutory position (ie under common law, the terms that will be implied into the banker–customer contract would be *the same provisions* under s 47), *save where* the statutory provisions are modified to impose a higher standard by an express term of the banker–customer contract.

Contractual obligation on the bank versus criminal liability on bank officials

[26.24]   As noted above, the common law duty imposes a contractual obligation on the bank itself. Previously, the former s 47 imposed a statutory prohibition on the bank's *officials* and any other person with access to the bank's records, the breach of which would result in the commission of a criminal offence, and not strictly by the bank itself. This distinction was criticised and one writer[27] pointed out that the prohibitions set out in s 47 would, in practice, apply equally to the bank just as much as to its officials.

---

25 [2002] 3 SLR 37.
26 [2002] 3 SLR 37 at 43.
27 Chai, n 6 above, pp 578–579.

Further, the scope of the former s 47 was very wide, also covering 'any person who by reason of his capacity or office has any means of access to the records'. Thus, it was not restricted to a person rendering professional services to the bank, but could in theory include the junior clerk or messenger boy who may have means of access to the bank's records.

Both these aspects have now been amended in the current s 47(1), which now clarifies that the duty of confidentiality (and criminal penalties for breach) lies on the bank as well as its officers. ('Officers' is defined in s 2 of the Banking Act and includes a director, secretary, employee, receiver, manager and liquidator of the bank and, although it does not expressly say so, would seem to exclude the junior clerk or messengers of the bank.)

Further, the s 47(1) primary duty is not now extended to any person other than the bank and its officers (for example, the bank's professional or other advisers) in the first instance. Instead, where customer information was disclosed to lawful recipients, under an exception in the Third Schedule which does not permit secondary disclosure, only then is a secondary duty not to disclose further imposed on those lawful recipients under s 47(5).

These provisions bring the statutory duty of confidentiality in line with the position at common law.

The respective remedies/penalties for breach of confidentiality

[26.25]   As stated earlier, it is generally accepted that if a bank, its officers and any lawful recipient under a Pt II exception breach their duty of confidentiality, they will find themselves faced with both a civil claim by the customer and a prosecution by the state for the commission of a criminal offence.

Under the contractual duty of confidentiality, the customer can avail himself of two remedies:

1   *injunction*: it is generally accepted that when a customer discovers that his bank intends to or has breached its duty of confidentiality without his consent, he can apply to the court for an order to restrain the bank from breaching or further breaching its duty. The grant of an injunction will be according to the general principles in the leading case of *American Cyanamid Co v Ethicon Ltd*;[28]
2   *damages*: the customer has the option of withdrawing his mandate by closing his account with the bank and then suing the bank for damages for breach of contract. Damages will be assessed in accordance with the general rules relating to measurement of damages under contract law.

In practice, the damage is done when the disclosure is made and would be difficult to quantify in monetary terms, which means that the injunction (if the customer is aware of the proposed disclosure in time) remains the most effective remedy.

Under the statutory duty of confidentiality, s 47(6) provides that an individual may be punished with a fine not exceeding $125,000 or imprisonment for a term not exceeding three years or both. In the case of a corporation, a fine not exceeding $250,000 may be imposed.

It is further provided in s 66 of the Banking Act that any director, managing director

28   [1975] AC 396.

or manager of the bank who had wilfully failed to take any reasonable steps to secure compliance with the provisions of the Banking Act shall be liable to a fine of up to $125,000 or imprisonment for a term of up to three years or to both. This means that the senior management in the bank cannot simply avoid liability by a subordinate breaching the duty of confidentiality, but must show that they had taken reasonable steps to ensure such compliance.

Duration of the duty of confidentiality

Contractual duty

[26.26]   The English Court of Appeal in *Tournier* were of the view that the duty of secrecy commenced once the contractual relationship has been entered into and that it continued even after the termination of the banker–customer relationship, whereby the customer closed his account with the bank.

Statutory duty

[26.27]   Under the former regime, the stated persons were prohibited from disclosure during employment by, or professional relationship with, the bank or after the termination of such employment or relationship. This position is preserved in the current s 47(7)(b). Nothing is said about the status of the *customer's* relationship with the banks. In the circumstances, it is arguable from a literal reading of the section that there is no duty to preserve the confidentiality of someone who used to be a customer *after* he has closed his account with the bank.

Although 'bank' and 'banking business' are defined in the Banking Act, there is no definition of a 'customer'. *Halsbury's Laws of England* defines a customer as 'someone who has an account with a bank or who is in such relationship with the bank that the relationship of banker–customer exists, even though at this stage he has no account'.[29]

It is submitted that the statutory duty should continue even after the cessation of the banker–customer relationship. As pointed out by one writer,[30] this interpretation would be consistent with the contractual duty of confidentiality and in the interests of any customer. A further argument canvassed by the same writer is that although the statutory provision does not deal with the customer's rights in themselves, it prohibits the disclosure by the stipulated persons even after the termination of their employment by, or professional relationship with, the bank. Seen in this light, the legislative intent must have been that the customer's right of confidentiality be protected perpetually.

CONFIDENTIALITY IN THE REGULATION OF FINANCIAL MARKETS

Powers of regulators

[26.28]   The MAS regulates the conduct of banks and financial institutions pursuant to the MAS Act and the Banking Act and, in particular, may inspect, obtain and use

---

29 3(1) *Halsbury's Laws* (4th edn, reissue) para 148.
30 Cheong May Fong 'Banking Secrecy in Malaysia' (1993) 20 JMCL 157 at 166, in relation to the Malaysian provisions on secrecy, which is similarly silent on the issue.

customer information pursuant to Pt VII of the Banking Act under conditions of secrecy.

If the MAS considers that a bank is carrying on its business in a manner likely to be detrimental to the interests of its depositors and other creditors or has insufficient assets to cover its liabilities to the public, it may initiate a special investigation of the bank's books and, if the bank is incorporated outside Singapore, may disclose the information obtained to its parent supervisory authority as long as:

1   the customer information does not contain deposit information;
2   the customer information is required by the parent supervisory authority for the sole purpose of carrying out its supervisory functions; and
3   the parent supervisory authority:
   (a) is prohibited by the laws applicable to the parent supervisory authority from disclosing the customer information obtained by it to any other person, or
   (b) has given to the authority such written undertaking as to the confidentiality of the information obtained as the authority may determine.

Such parent supervisory authority is empowered by Pt VII of the Banking Act to conduct a similar inspection within Singapore of the bank's books for the sole purpose of carrying out its supervisory functions and with the consent of the MAS provided that it is prevented from disclosing information obtained by it in the course of the inspection to any other person or has given to the MAS a written undertaking as to the confidentiality of the information obtained. Information obtained pursuant to these powers is to be kept strictly confidential and s 47 of the Banking Act applies to the parent supervisory authority.

Insider dealing

[26.29]   Related to the issue of confidentiality in financial market regulation is that concerning insider dealing and market abuse. The Securities Industry Act, which previously governed Singapore's insider dealing laws, was repealed with effect from 1 October 2002 and the relevant provisions relating to insider dealing were reformulated in Pt XII (market conduct) of the Securities and Futures Act (Cap 289, 2006 Rev Ed) ('SFA').

Under the previous law, for an insider dealing offence to be made, it had to be proved that the insider acquired the information by virtue of his position in the company or through his relationship with a person who held such a position. Subsequently, this test was considered overly focused on a connection with the relevant company, as opposed to a connection with undisclosed market-sensitive information (irrespective of the insider's connection with the company). The law was thus amended to adopt the latter test in order properly to reflect the true nature of the insider dealing offence.

In March 2000, the MAS also introduced the concept of civil actions (with a six-year limitation period) for insider dealing. Apart from being a criminal offence, insider dealing can give rise to two distinct civil remedies, namely, a fine imposed by the MAS and a claim for damages by investors who had traded contemporaneously with the insider. This resolved the past problems of enforcement being limited to criminal proceedings, which was further made difficult by the higher burden of proof of 'beyond a reasonable doubt'. The MAS successfully took its first civil penalty action against three individuals for breaches of the insider trading provisions of the SFA in October 2004.

The SFA further provides for the extra-territorial application of its insider dealing laws, for example, to activities that occur outside of Singapore relating to securities which are listed on the exchange or securities of companies incorporated in Singapore.

ANTI-MONEY LAUNDERING INITIATIVES

Overview

[26.30] Since 1991, Singapore has been a member of the Financial Action Task Force ('FATF') and participated in various FATF initiatives, including the revision of the FATF recommendations. Singapore is also a member of the Asia Pacific Group on Money Laundering ('APG') that was formed in 1997 to prevent and detect money laundering in the area. In June 2005, Singapore hosted the inaugural joint plenary meeting between the FATF and the APG to discuss challenges in anti-money laundering ('AML') and combating the financing of terrorism ('CFT') that were germane to the region.

By 1999, in the Review of FATF Anti-Money Laundering Systems and Mutual Evaluation Procedures 1992–1999, Singapore was observed to have complied with most of the FATF recommendations, significantly in its criminalisation of drug money laundering, as well as laundering of the proceeds of other serious crimes. Singapore was highlighted as an example of a tightly regulated system for the banking, insurance and securities sectors where both off and onsite examinations are conducted by the financial supervisor and institutions are further required to conduct internal and external audits of their accounts and controls. On the other hand, the Review opined that secrecy obligations for banks and most other financial records inhibited Singapore's co-operation in cross-border mutual legal assistance.

By 8 August 2003, in the IMF Country Report No 04/104 dated 26 April 2004 on Singapore, it was remarked that:

> 'Singapore now has in place a sound and comprehensive legal, institutional and policy and supervisory framework for AML/CFT and the authorities have demonstrated a strong commitment to its effective implementation. Though some steps have been taken with the enactment of a domestic mutual assistance law and ongoing negotiations for several bilateral treaties, the effectiveness of cross-border mutual legal assistance needs to be improved as it relates to compulsory assistance at international request, including the provision of bank records… Some aspects of best practice for customer due diligence need to be specified more clearly and in greater detail, though implementation was observed in individual institutions.'

Consistent with the international efforts against money laundering and terrorist financing, the following legislation has been enacted in Singapore:

1   the Corruption, Drug Trafficking and Other Serious Crimes (Confiscation of Benefits) Act (Cap 65A, 2000 Rev Ed) ('the CBA');
2   the Terrorism (Suppression of Financing) Act (Cap 325, 2003 Rev Ed) ('the TSFA');
3   the United Nations Act (Cap 339, 2002 Rev Ed) ('the UN Act'); and
4   the Mutual Assistance in Criminal Matters Act (Cap 190A, 2001 Rev Ed) ('the MACMA').

In addition, the MAS has also issued various directions to banks, finance companies, money changing and remittance licencees, capital markets services licencees, financial advisers, insurers and approved trustees concerning the prevention of money laundering and terrorist financing. These directions, the leading instrument being MAS Notice No 626 issued to banks (latest edition of 11 November 2002), have legal effect and contravention of these directions may result in various sanctions (see ss 27 and 27A of the Monetary Authority of Singapore Act (Cap 186, 1999 Rev Ed)). The MAS also carries out regular offsite reviews and onsite inspections of financial institutions as part of ensuring compliance with these directions.

Further, the MAS released a consultation paper on the proposed revision to Notice 626 ('draft MAS Notice 626'). These amendments seek not only to reflect the prevailing international standards (such as the revised FATF recommendations), but also to address some of the perceived insufficiencies in the current system. The contents of this paper will be discussed in detail later.

In terms of the implementation and enforcement of AML/CFT legislation in Singapore, the MAS works closely with the Suspicious Transaction Reporting Office ('STRO'), one of the three branches of the Financial Investigation Division ('FID') set up within the Commercial Affairs Department (which is part of the Singapore Police Force). The STRO is the chief agency that analyses suspicious transactions reported by banks and financial institutions.

The FID was set up with the particular purpose of combating money laundering and terrorism financing activities. Other than the STRO, the other two branches of the FID are the Financial Investigation Branch ('FIB') and Proceeds of Crime Unit ('PCU'). The FIB is primarily in charge of the investigation of offences under the CBA and TSFA, including fraud against banks. It also renders assistance to overseas enforcement agencies. As for the PCU, it investigates and traces property that represents the proceeds of criminal conduct and seizes and manages assets in custody for their eventual disposal or confiscation in accordance with the CBA.

Although the AML/CFT regime in Singapore is relatively new, the awareness among financial institutions, non-financial institutions and especially individuals of the offences of money laundering and terrorist financing is steadily growing. We will now further elaborate on the more pertinent aspects of the AML/CFT regime.

Types of criminal conduct which give rise to money laundering offences

[**26.31**]   Money laundering predicate offences extend beyond drug trafficking to cover other serious crimes, as well as the conspiracy, incitement and abetment of these offences (s 2, First/Second Schedule of the CBA). Singapore adopts a 'list' approach to predicate crimes. The list includes various crimes that are serious in nature (for example, hijacking and kidnapping), but excludes those that cannot be linked to money laundering.

It should be noted that, under the CBA, criminal conduct is not confined to conduct which would constitute a serious offence in Singapore, but also includes conduct which would constitute a serious foreign offence, defined as an offence (other than a foreign drug trafficking offence) against the laws of a foreign country and which would, if that foreign offence had occurred in Singapore, have constituted a serious offence pursuant to the list set out in the Second Schedule of the CBA.

Any person, including a bank, will be guilty of a money laundering offence punishable with a maximum penalty of imprisonment of seven years and/or a fine of $200,000 if he:

1   enters into or is otherwise concerned, whether in Singapore or elsewhere, in an arrangement knowing or having reasonable grounds to believe that, by that arrangement, (i) it will facilitate the retention or control of benefits of drug trafficking or criminal conduct by/on behalf of or (ii) the benefits of drug trafficking or criminal conduct are used to secure funds or acquire property (by way of investment or otherwise) for another person (whom the bank knows or has reasonable grounds to believe has been/is involved in, or has benefited from, drug trafficking or criminal conduct);

2   conceals, disguises or converts, transfers or removes from the jurisdiction any property which, in whole or in part, directly or indirectly represents another person's benefits of drug trafficking or criminal conduct (for the purpose of assisting any person to avoid prosecution for a drug trafficking offence, foreign drug trafficking offence, serious offence or serious foreign offence or the enforcement of a confiscation order issued under the CBA); or

3   acquires any property for no or inadequate consideration knowing, or having reasonable grounds to believe, that the property, in whole or in part, directly or indirectly represents another person's benefits of drug trafficking or criminal conduct.

Circumstances which give rise to reporting of suspicious transactions

[26.32]   The reporting of suspicious transactions is a key source of intelligence for the enforcement authorities. As such, the duty on the part of financial institutions (as well as non-financial institutions) to report suspicious transactions is mandatory, as provided for in the CBA and referred to in MAS Notice 626.

Where a person in the course of his professional duties comes to know or has reasonable grounds to suspect that any property represents the proceeds of drug trafficking or criminal conduct, he is obliged to disclose the knowledge or suspicion to the authorities. If he fails to do so, the maximum penalty shall be a fine of $10,000. Such disclosure is not to be treated as a breach of any restriction upon the disclosure imposed by law, contract or rules of professional conduct. In other words, it will not be considered a breach of a bank's confidentiality obligations (s 39 of the CBA and clause 6.8 of MAS Notice 626).

Under clause 6 of the current MAS Notice 626, banks are also to 'exercise due diligence by implementing adequate systems for identifying and detecting suspicious transactions'. Identification of any transaction listed as examples of suspicious transactions should prompt initial enquiries and further investigations as to the source of funds. Such transactions are broadly categorised as those not making economic sense, relating to investments, involving large amounts of cash, bank accounts, transfers abroad and unidentified parties (see the Appendix at the end of this chapter for the provisions of suspicious transactions as set out in MAS Notice 626).

Each bank shall have a proper reporting system (which reports back to the STRO) so as to facilitate the discharge of an employee's obligation to report. If the employee has actual knowledge of the customer having engaged in drug trafficking or criminal conduct, the matter must be reported promptly to the relevant officer who must in turn immediately report it to the STRO. If the employee has reasonable grounds to suspect these activities, the bank officer must promptly evaluate whether there are reasonable grounds for such belief and immediately report the case to the STRO. If the bank officer takes the contrary view, there is no need to report to the STRO, but this opinion must be properly recorded. Care must also be taken to ensure that the customer whose name has been brought to the attention of the STRO does not become aware of this.

Further, pursuant to s 48 of the CBA, it is an offence for a person who knows or has reasonable grounds to suspect a money laundering investigation is being or about to be conducted to tip off another person with information which is likely to prejudice the investigation. The maximum penalty will be imprisonment of three years and/or a fine of $30,000.

FATF/IMF evaluations of Singapore

[26.33]   As referred to above, in April 2004, the IMF released a Country Report No 04/104 on Singapore. This is the product of the IMF's Financial Sector Assessment Programme, through which the Report on the Observance of Standards and Codes ('ROSC') is generated. The ROSC summarises the level of Singapore's observance of international standards relating to various aspects, including AML/CFT, and the key summary on the level of Singapore's compliance has been set out earlier.

It was observed that, in addition to Singapore's sound and comprehensive legal, institutional, policy and supervisory framework for AML/CFT, she possessed a well-regarded legal system, efficient judiciary, low crime rate and intolerance for corruption. There was a strong framework for the prevention and detection of money laundering and financing of terrorism in accordance with the FATF recommendations, together with a culture of compliance and well-monitored and effective implementation measures, backed up with proper statistical recording. The CBA had not only criminalised money laundering for a range of serious offences beyond drug trafficking, it also mandated a duty on all persons to report suspicious transactions and lowered the standard for criminal intent for money laundering to that of 'reasonable grounds', consistent with the international standard. Measures have also been adopted to implement UN resolutions (the UN Act) and the financing of terrorism has been criminalised (the TSFA). Besides, legally-binding MAS Notices with their sector-specific requirements in the areas of customer due diligence, internal controls and training significantly strengthened the legal framework. As to the money laundering typology, it was observed that white-collar crime was most common, as the known incidence of drug trafficking, corruption and other serious crimes was comparatively low.

However, there were a few key areas that the FATF highlighted for improvement:

1   lack of specific provisions addressing the tracing and identification of proceeds;
2   lack of detailed, firm and explicit guidelines in the MAS Notices so as to assist financial institutions in the practical implementation of requirements;
3   lack of customer identification measures for wire transfers;
4   limitations on mutual legal assistance in the areas of providing bank records, restraining proceeds, enforcing confiscation orders, extradition and the scope of the MACMA; and
5   non-ratification of the Palermo Convention Against Transnational Crime.

In response, the Singapore authorities have already begun their efforts in strengthening the AML/CFT regime. As alluded to earlier, the MAS has released draft MAS Notice 626 that includes guidelines pertaining to terrorist financing, a more comprehensive regime of customer due diligence ('CDD') that is risk based and customer identification measures for cross-border wire transfers. In effect, draft MAS Notice 626 does address and implement most of the recommendations put forward in the IMF's Country Report No 04/104 on Singapore.

Under draft MAS Notice 626, banks must comply with more detailed CDD requirements before establishing business relations with their customers unless it is essential not to interrupt the normal conduct of business and the risks of money laundering and terrorist financing have been effectively managed. These measures include customer identification, verification of a customer's identity and beneficial ownership and obtaining information on the purpose and intended nature of business relations. Customer information must also be reviewed periodically. Depending on the circumstances, banks may either adopt simplified or enhanced CDD measures. For instance, where there is a higher risk of money laundering and terrorist financing (when the bank is dealing with private banking customers, non-resident customers and politically exposed persons), enhanced CDD measures should be employed.

Further, in line with the FATF's Special Recommendation VII on Wire Transfers, draft MAS Notice 626 obliges banks to identify and record information, including the name of the originator, the originator's account number and address in a cross-border wire transfer, if the amount to be transferred exceeds a certain threshold. This threshold amount has yet to be determined and remains the subject of future discussions.

Challenges to the AML/CFT regime

[26.34] As outlined above, one of the main challenges faced by Singapore is its restricted involvement in mutual legal assistance in AML/CFT. In 2006, the MACMA was amended to remove certain rigidities of the legislation so that Singapore can play a more active role in mutual legal assistance and provide timely assistance to a non-treaty country in order to prosecute a terrorist or major international criminal.

In the past, the assistance of a mutual legal existence treaty was a pre-condition to certain forms of assistance that involve coercive measures (for example, search warrants in aid of a criminal prosecution in a foreign country). Now, in the absence of such a treaty, assistance can still be rendered on a case-by-case basis provided that the requesting country affords such reciprocal treatment. Further, the local courts now have the discretion to enforce a foreign confiscation order from a country notwithstanding the absence of a treaty.

The newly enacted UN Act further seeks to ensure that the legislation is adequate to overcome any lacuna that would prevent Singapore from effectively fulfilling her international obligations. The government will have the power to pass such necessary regulations so as to give effect to the decisions of the UN Security Council. With the amendment of the MAS Act, s 27A(1)(b) also grants the MAS the power to make regulations to give effect to such resolutions, for example, the MAS (Anti-Terrorism Measures) Regulations 2002, the MAS (Freezing of Assets of Former President of Liberia and Connected Persons) Regulations 2004 and the MAS (Freezing of Assets of Persons – Democratic Republic of the Congo) Regulations 2006.

On the enforcement front, investigation and prosecution efforts have similarly been smooth and effective. Between 1999 and 2004, the PCU has seized close to $100 million in assets. The STRO has positively reported that the number of suspicious transaction reporting has risen steadily, indicating a strong AML/CFT regime.

The above demonstrates Singapore's commitment to dealing with the challenges to the AML/CFT regime on all fronts and staying abreast of continuing international development in this regard.

Safeguards in terms of local rules for banking/financial secrecy; cross-border issues

[26.35]   Notwithstanding the need to strengthen the AML/CFT regime, this should not adversely affect the operations of the financial institutions and it is necessary to balance legitimate measures to be taken to address AML/CFT globally on the one hand with the protection of customer privacy and confidentiality on the other.

Accordingly, apart from such enabling legislation as discussed in the previous section, the standard bank secrecy obligations under s 47 of the Banking Act would continue to apply. As such, if a local bank wished to transmit information about their customers from Singapore to another jurisdiction, it would only be permitted to do so if the circumstances fell within one of the Third Schedule exceptions (for instance, pursuant to an internal audit or outsourcing and only to lawful recipients such as the bank's head office or parent bank) and if it does so pursuant to a Pt II exception, further disclosure would be prohibited.

This can give rise to difficulties where requests for customer information initiated overseas are received by local banks. Such requests cannot be automatically acceded to without encountering difficulties under s 47 of the Banking Act. Part I, items 8 and 9 of the Third Schedule permit disclosure as would be necessary for compliance with a request by the MAS or any of its directives or, in the case of a bank incorporated outside Singapore, the bank's parent supervisory authority. However, compliance with other requests not covered by the Third Schedule (including a request by a supervisory authority of the bank or branch in a major commercial jurisdiction, albeit not its parent supervisory authority) would put a local bank in technical breach of s 47. The safest route would be to require the requesting authority to seek assistance from the MAS or the relevant enforcement authorities or to apply to a Singapore court for authorisation pursuant to various legislative routes such as under the CBA or the MACMA. Such safeguards may give rise to administrative difficulties, but may be necessary to balance the interests of foreign parties/regulatory authorities with the need to protect the privacy of Singapore's banking business.

For instance, s 31 of the CBA requires authorities investigating a drug trafficking or serious offence to apply to the Singapore High Court for a production order of relevant material/information against a financial institution and the Singapore High Court must be satisfied that:

1   there are reasonable grounds for suspecting that a specified person has carried on or has benefited from drug trafficking or criminal conduct, as the case may be;
2   there are reasonable grounds for believing that the material to which the application relates:
    (a)   is likely to be of substantial value (whether by itself or together with other material) to the investigation for the purpose of which the application is made, and

(b) does not consist of or include items subject to legal privilege; and

3 there are reasonable grounds for believing that it is in the public interest to produce the material to which the application relates.

To protect customer information from being further disseminated, applications for a production order are to be heard in camera.

A financial institution which complies with a production order shall not be treated as being in breach of bank confidentiality restrictions and no action shall lie against a financial institution which in good faith produces materials or gives access to materials relating to the account of its customer pursuant to such compliance with a production order (s 31(4), (5) of the CBA).

There are also safeguards within various statutes to prevent unnecessary intrusion into the privacy of Singapore's businesses and individuals. For example, under s 41 of the CBA, any authorised officer is not permitted to disclose information to a corresponding authority of another country unless:

1 there exists an arrangement under which the corresponding authority of the foreign country has agreed to communicate to Singapore, upon Singapore's request, information received by the corresponding authority; and

2 the corresponding authority has given appropriate undertakings:
   (a) for protecting the confidentiality of anything communicated to it, and
   (b) for controlling the use that will be made of it, including an undertaking that it will not be used as evidence in any proceedings.

It is otherwise a criminal offence for any authorised officer who receives information in the performance of his duties under the CBA to disclose any such information, save where lawfully required to do so by any court or under the provisions of any written law.

Also, under the MACMA, if it is not in the public interest to provide assistance, the authorities have a general power to decline the request. Assistance will also be declined if the foreign authority is seeking information without due basis or there are substantial grounds to believe that the accused is being targetted by the foreign country on account of his race, religion, sex, ethnic origin, nationality or political opinions.

CONCLUSION

[26.36]   It can be seen that the duty of confidentiality in Singapore is an onerous one because the banks owe a contractual duty to their customers and, at the same time, they are also subject to a strict statutory duty of confidentiality which carries with it a criminal liability.

The confidentiality provisions in the Banking Act have undergone considerable amendments since the 1971 legislation, the most recent substantive change being the 2001 amendments, followed by the publication of a revised edition in 2003. This is a commendable effort on the part of the legislature in ensuring that there is sufficient supervision of the banks by the MAS, yet at the same time in seeking to address the public interest of pursuing criminal and civil remedies and the private concerns of commercial and lay persons that the banks should not be over-regulated to the extent of practical unworkability. This ongoing effort to strike the right balance is particularly conspicuous in the area of bank confidentiality.

To deal with the current concerns in the arena of money laundering and terrorist financing, Singapore has implemented an effective and comprehensive legal, institutional and supervisory AML/CTF framework. This robust approach is likely to enhance Singapore's reputation as a well-regulated financial centre.

APPENDIX

Banking Act (Cap 19)

Interpretation of this Part

[26.37]   40A. In this Part—

'customer', in relation to a bank, includes the Authority or any monetary authority or central bank of any other country or territory, but does not include any company which carries on banking business or such other financial institution as may be designated by the Authority by notice in writing;

'customer information', in relation to a bank, means—

(a) any information relating to, or any particulars of, an account of a customer of the bank, whether the account is in respect of a loan, investment or any other type of transaction, but does not include any information that is not referable to any named customer or group of named customers; or

(b) deposit information;

'deposit information', in relation to a bank, means any information relating to—

(a) any deposit of a customer of the bank;

(b) funds of a customer under management by the bank; or

(c) any safe deposit box maintained by, or any safe custody arrangements made by, a customer with the bank,

but does not include any information that is not referable to any named person or group of named persons;

'funds of a customer under management' means any funds or assets of a customer (whether of the bank or any financial institution) placed with that bank for the purpose of management or investment;

'parent bank', in relation to a bank, means a financial institution which is able to exercise a significant influence over the direction and management of the bank or which has a controlling interest in the bank;

'parent supervisory authority', in relation to a bank incorporated outside Singapore, means the supervisory authority which is responsible, under the laws of the country or territory where the bank or its parent bank is incorporated, formed or established, for supervising the bank or its parent bank, as the case may be.

Banking secrecy

[26.38]   47.—(1) Customer information shall not, in any way, be disclosed by a bank in Singapore or any of its officers to any other person except as expressly provided in this Act.

(2) A bank in Singapore or any of its officers may, for such purpose as may be specified in the first column of the Third Schedule, disclose customer information to

such persons or class of persons as may be specified in the second column of that Schedule, and in compliance with such conditions as may be specified in the third column of that Schedule.

(3) Where customer information is likely to be disclosed in any proceedings referred to in item 3 or 4 of Part I of the Third Schedule, the court may, either of its own motion, or on the application of any party to the proceedings or the customer to which the customer information relates —

(a) direct that the proceedings be held in camera; and
(b) make such further orders as it may consider necessary to ensure the confidentiality of the customer information.

(4) Where an order has been made by a court under subsection (3), any person who, contrary to such an order, publishes any information that is likely to lead to the identification of any party to the proceedings shall be guilty of an offence and shall be liable on conviction to a fine not exceeding $125,000.

(5) Any person (including, where the person is a body corporate, an officer of the body corporate) who receives customer information referred to in Pt II of the Third Schedule shall not, at any time, disclose the customer information or any part thereof to any other person, except as authorised under that Schedule or if required to do so by an order of court.

(6) Any person who contravenes subsection (1) or (5) shall be guilty of an offence and shall be liable on conviction —

(a) in the case of an individual, to a fine not exceeding $125,000 or to imprisonment for a term not exceeding 3 years or to both; or
(b) in any other case, to a fine not exceeding $250,000.

(7) In this section and in the Third Schedule, unless the context otherwise requires —

(a) where disclosure of customer information is authorised under the Third Schedule to be made to any person which is a body corporate, customer information may be disclosed to such officers of the body corporate as may be necessary for the purpose for which the disclosure is authorised under that Schedule; and
(b) the obligation of any officer or other person who receives customer information referred to in Pt II of the Third Schedule shall continue after the termination or cessation of his appointment, employment, engagement or other capacity or office in which he had received customer information.

(8) For the avoidance of doubt, nothing in this section shall be construed to prevent a bank from entering into an express agreement with a customer of that bank for a higher degree of confidentiality than that prescribed in this section and in the Third Schedule.

(9) Where, in the course of an inspection under s 43 or an investigation under s 44 or the carrying out of the Authority's function of supervising the financial condition of any bank, the Authority incidentally obtains customer information and such information is not necessary for the supervision or regulation of the bank by the Authority, then, such information shall be treated as secret by the Authority.

(10) This section and the Third Schedule shall apply, with such modifications as may be prescribed by the Authority, to a merchant bank approved as a financial institution under s 28 of the Monetary Authority of Singapore Act (Cap 186) as if the reference to a bank in this section were a reference to such merchant bank.

Third Schedule

Part I Further disclosure not prohibited

[26.39]

First column	Second column	Third column
Purpose for which customer information may be disclosed	**Persons to whom information may be disclosed**	**Conditions**
1. Disclosure is permitted in writing by the customer or, if he is deceased, his appointed personal representative.	Any person as permitted by the customer or, if he is deceased, his appointed personal representative.	
2. Disclosure is solely in connection with an application for a grant of probate or letters of administration in respect of a deceased customer's estate.	Any person whom the bank in good faith believes is entitled to the grant of probate or letters of administration.	
3. Disclosure is solely in connection with— (a) where the customer is an individual, the bankruptcy of the customer; or (b) where the customer is a body corporate, the winding up of the customer.	All persons to whom the disclosure is necessary for the purpose specified in the first column.	*Note: Court may order the proceedings to be held in camera [see s 47 (3) and (4)].*
4. Disclosure is solely with a view to the institution of, or solely in connection with, the conduct of the proceedings— (a) between the bank and the customer or his surety relating to the banking transaction of the customer; (b) between the bank and 2 or more parties making adverse claims to money in an account of the customer where the bank seeks relief by way of interpleader; or (c) between the bank and one or more parties in respect of property, whether movable or immovable, in or over which some right or interest has been conferred or alleged to have been conferred on the bank by the customer or his surety.	All persons to whom the disclosure is necessary for the purpose specified in the first column.	*Note: Court may order the proceedings to be held in camera [see s 47 (3)and (4)].*

First column	*Second column*	*Third column*
Purpose for which customer information may be disclosed	**Persons to whom information may be disclosed**	**Conditions**
5. Disclosure is necessary for— (a) compliance with an order or request made under any specified written law to furnish information, for the purposes of an investigation or prosecution, of an offence alleged or suspected to have been committed under any written law; or (b) the making of a complaint or report under any specified written law for an offence alleged or suspected to have been committed under any written law.	Any police officer or public officer duly authorised under the specified written law to carry out the investigation or prosecution or to receive the complaint or report, or any court.	
6. Disclosure is necessary for compliance with a garnishee order served on the bank attaching moneys in the account of the customer.	All persons to whom the disclosure is required to be made under the garnishee order.	
7. Disclosure is necessary for compliance with an order of the Supreme Court or a Judge thereof pursuant to the powers conferred under Pt IV of the Evidence Act (Cap 97).	All persons to whom the disclosure is required to be made under the court order.	
8. Where the bank is a bank incorporated outside Singapore, the disclosure is strictly necessary for compliance with a request made by its parent supervisory authority solely in connection with the supervision of the bank.	The parent supervisory authority of the bank incorporated outside Singapore.	(a) No deposit information shall be disclosed to the parent supervisory authority. (b) The parent supervisory authority is prohibited by the laws applicable to it from disclosing the customer information obtained by it to any person unless compelled to do so by the laws or courts of the country or territory where it is established.
9. Disclosure is in compliance with the provisions of this Act, the Deposit Insurance Act 2005 or any notice or directive issued by the Authority to banks.	The Authority or any person authorised or appointed by the Authority.	

Part II Further disclosure prohibited

[26.40]

First column	Second column	Third column
Purpose for which customer information may be disclosed	**Persons to whom information may be disclosed**	**Conditions**
1. Disclosure is solely in connection with the performance of duties as an officer, or a professional adviser of the bank.	Any— (a) officer of the bank in Singapore; (b) officer designated in writing by the head office of the bank; or (c) auditor, lawyer, consultant or other professional adviser appointed or engaged by the bank under a contract for service.	
2. Disclosure is solely in connection with the conduct of internal audit of the bank or the performance of risk management.	In the case of— (a) a bank incorporated outside Singapore— (i) the head office or parent bank of the bank; (ii) any branch of the bank outside Singapore designated in writing by the head office of the bank; or (iii) any related corporation of the bank designated in writing by the head office of the bank; or (b) a bank incorporated in Singapore— (i) the parent bank; or (ii) any related corporation of the bank designated in writing by the head office of the bank.	
3. Disclosure is solely in connection with the performance of operational functions of the bank where such operational functions have been outsourced.	Any person including the head office of the bank or any branch thereof outside Singapore which is engaged by the bank to perform the outsourced functions.	If any outsourced function is to be performed outside Singapore, the disclosure shall be subject to such conditions as may be specified in a notice issued by the Authority or otherwise imposed by the Authority.
4. Disclosure is solely in connection with— (a) the merger or proposed merger of the bank or its financial holding company with another company; or	Any person participating or otherwise involved in the merger, acquisition or issue, or proposed merger, acquisition or issue, including any of his lawyers or other	

First column	*Second column*	*Third column*
Purpose for which customer information may be disclosed	**Persons to whom information may be disclosed**	**Conditions**
(b) any acquisition or issue, or proposed acquisition or issue, of any part of the share capital of the bank or its financial holding company, whether or not the merger or acquisition is subsequently entered into or completed.	professional advisers (whether or not the merger or acquisition is subsequently entered into or completed).	
5. Disclosure is solely in connection with the restructure, transfer or sale, or proposed restructure, transfer or sale, of credit facilities (whether or not the restructure, transfer or sale is completed).	Any transferee, purchaser or any other person participating or otherwise involved in the restructure, transfer or sale, or proposed restructure, transfer or sale, including any of his lawyers or other professional advisers (whether or not the restructure, transfer or sale is subsequently entered into or completed).	No customer information, other than information relating to the relevant credit facilities, shall be disclosed.
6. In the case of a customer who has been issued with a credit or charge card by a bank in Singapore, disclosure is strictly necessary for notification of the suspension or cancellation of the card by the bank by reason of the customer's default in payment to the bank.	Any financial institution in Singapore which issues credit or charge cards.	No customer information, other than information relating to the following, may be disclosed: (a) the customer's name and identity; (b) the amount of the debt outstanding on the customer's credit or charge card; (c) the date of suspension or cancellation of the customer's credit or charge card, as the case may be.
7. Disclosure is strictly necessary— (a) for the collation, synthesis or processing of customer information by the credit bureau for the purposes of the assessment of the creditworthiness of the customers of banks; or (b) for the assessment, by other members of the credit bureau specified in the second column, of the creditworthiness of the customers of banks.	Any— (a) credit bureau of which the bank is a member; (b) other member of the credit bureau that is— (i) a bank or merchant bank; (ii) a person, or a person belonging to a class of persons, recognised by the Authority, by notification published in the *Gazette*, as authorised to receive the information, where that member receives such information from the credit bureau.	(a) No deposit information shall be disclosed. (b) The disclosure by any credit bureau to any person referred to in paragraph (b) of the second column shall be subject to such conditions as may be specified in a notice issued by the Authority or otherwise imposed by the Authority.

First column	Second column	Third column
Purpose for which customer information may be disclosed	**Persons to whom information may be disclosed**	**Conditions**
8. Disclosure is strictly necessary for the assessment of the creditworthiness of the customer in connection with or relating to a bona fide commercial transaction.	Any other bank or merchant bank in Singapore.	No customer information, other than information of a prospective commercial general nature and not related to the details of the customer's account with the bank, shall be disclosed.
9. Disclosure is solely in connection with the promotion, to customers of the bank in Singapore, of financial products and services made available in Singapore by any financial institution specified in the second column.	Any financial institution in Singapore which is licensed or otherwise regulated by the Authority.	No customer information, other than the customer's name, identity, address, and contact number shall be disclosed.
10. Disclosure is solely in connection with the payment of compensation to insured depositors under the Deposit Insurance Act 2005.	(a) The deposit insurance agency; or (b) any person authorised or appointed by the deposit insurance agency to perform its functions under the Deposit Insurance Act 2005.	(a) The disclosure by the deposit insurance agency to any person referred to in paragraph (b) of the second column shall be subject to such conditions as may be specified in a notice issued by the Authority or otherwise imposed by the Authority. (b) The disclosure by any person referred to in paragraph (b) of the second column to any other person referred to in the same paragraph shall be subject to such conditions as may be specified in a notice issued by the Authority or otherwise imposed by the Authority.

Part III Interpretation

[26.41]   In this Schedule, unless the context otherwise requires—

'appointed personal representative', in relation to a deceased person, means a person appointed as executor or administrator of the estate of the deceased person;
'credit bureau' means a credit bureau recognised as such by the Authority by notification in the *Gazette* for the purposes of this Schedule;
'deposit insurance agency' has the same meaning as in s 2 (1) of the Deposit Insurance Act 2005;
'insured depositor' has the same meaning as in s 2 (1) of the Deposit Insurance Act 2005;

'lawyer' means an advocate and solicitor of the Supreme Court of Singapore, or any person who is duly authorised or registered to practise law in a country or territory other than Singapore by a foreign authority having the function conferred by law of authorising or registering persons to practise law in that country or territory;

'merchant bank' means a merchant bank approved as a financial institution under s 28 of the Monetary Authority of Singapore Act (Cap 186);

'public officer' includes any officer of a statutory board;

'specified written law' means the Companies Act (Cap 50), the Criminal Procedure Code (Cap 68), the Goods and Services Tax Act (Cap 117A), the Income Tax Act (Cap 134), the Internal Security Act (Cap 143), the Kidnapping Act (Cap 151) and the Prevention of Corruption Act (Cap 241);

'surety', in relation to a customer of a bank, includes any person who has given the bank security for the liability of the customer by way of a mortgage or a charge.

MAS Notice 626 Appendix II – examples of suspicious transactions

1 General comments

[26.42] The list of situations given below is intended mainly as a means of highlighting the basic ways in which money may be laundered. While each individual situation may not be sufficient to suggest that money laundering is taking place, a combination of such situations may be indicative of such a transaction. Further, the list is by no means complete, and will require constant updating and adaptation to changing circumstances and new methods of laundering money. The list is intended solely as an aid, and must not be applied as a routine instrument in place of common sense.

A customer's declarations regarding the background of such transactions should be checked for plausibility. Not every explanation offered by the customer can be accepted without scrutiny.

It is justifiable to suspect any customer who is reluctant to provide normal information and documents required routinely by the bank in the course of the business relationship. Banks should pay attention to customers who provide minimal, false or misleading information or, when applying to open an account, provide information that is difficult or expensive for the bank to verify.

2 Transactions which do not make economic sense

[26.43]

i)   a customer relationship with the bank that does not appear to make economic sense, for example, a customer having a large number of accounts with the same bank, frequent transfers between different accounts or exaggeratedly high liquidity;

ii)   transactions in which assets are withdrawn immediately after being deposited, unless the customer's business activities furnish a plausible reason for immediate withdrawal;

iii) transactions that cannot be reconciled with the usual activities of the customer, for example, the use of letters of credit and other methods of trade finance to move money between countries where such trade is not consistent with the customer's usual business;

iv) transactions which, without plausible reason, result in the intensive use of what was previously a relatively inactive account, such as a customer's account which shows virtually no normal personal or business related activities but is used to receive or disburse unusually large sums which have no obvious purpose or relationship to the customer and/or his business;

v) provision of bank guarantees or indemnities as collateral for loans between third parties that are not in conformity with market conditions;

vi) unexpected repayment of an overdue credit without any plausible explanation;

vii) back-to-back loans without any identifiable and legally admissible purpose.

3 Transactions involving large amounts of cash

[26.44]

i) exchanging an unusually large amount of small-denominated notes for those of higher denomination;

ii) purchasing or selling of foreign currencies in substantial amounts by cash settlement despite the customer having an account with the bank;

iii) frequent withdrawal of large amounts by means of cheques, including travellers' cheques;

iv) frequent withdrawal of large cash amounts that do not appear to be justified by the customer's business activity;

v) large cash withdrawals from a previously dormant/inactive account, or from an account which has just received an unexpected large credit from abroad;

vi) company transactions, both deposits and withdrawals, that are denominated by unusually large amounts of cash, rather than by way of debits and credits normally associated with the normal commercial operations of the company, eg cheques, letters of credit, bills of exchange, etc;

vii) depositing cash by means of numerous credit slips by a customer such that the amount of each deposit is not substantial, but the total of which is substantial;

viii) the deposit of unusually large amounts of cash by a customer to cover requests for bankers' drafts, money transfers or other negotiable and readily marketable money instruments;

ix) customers whose deposits contain counterfeit notes or forged instruments;

x) large cash deposits using night safe facilities, thereby avoiding direct contact with the bank;

xi) customers making large and frequent cash deposits but cheques drawn on the accounts are mostly to individuals and firms not normally associated with their business;

xii) customers who together, and simultaneously, use separate tellers to conduct large cash transactions or foreign exchange transactions.

4 Transactions involving bank accounts

[26.45]

i) matching of payments out with credits paid in by cash on the same or previous day;

ii) paying in large third party cheques endorsed in favour of the customer;

iii) substantial increases in deposits of cash or negotiable instruments by a professional firm or company, using client accounts or in-house company or trust accounts, especially if the deposits are promptly transferred between other client company and trust accounts;

iv) high velocity of funds through an account, ie low beginning and ending daily balances, which do not reflect the large volume of funds flowing through an account;

v) multiple depositors using a single bank account;

vi) an account opened in the name of a money changer that receives structured deposits;

vii) an account operated in the name of an offshore company with structured movement of funds.

5 Transactions involving transfers abroad

[26.46]

i) transfer of money abroad by an interim customer in the absence of any legitimate reason;

ii) a customer which appears to have accounts with several banks in the same locality, especially when the bank is aware of a regular consolidated process from such accounts prior to a request for onward transmission of the funds elsewhere;

iii) repeated transfers of large amounts of money abroad accompanied by the instruction to pay the beneficiary in cash;

iv) large and regular payments that cannot be clearly identified as bona fide transactions, from and to countries associated with (i) the production, processing or marketing of narcotics or other illegal drugs or (ii) criminal conduct;

v) substantial increase in cash deposits by a customer without apparent cause, especially if such deposits are subsequently transferred within a short period out of the account and/or to a destination not normally associated with the customer;

vi) building up large balances, not consistent with the known turnover of the customer's business, and subsequent transfer to account(s) held overseas;

vii) cash payments remitted to a single account by a large number of different persons without an adequate explanation.

6 Investment-related transactions

[26.47]

i) purchasing of securities to be held by the bank in safe custody, where this does not appear appropriate given the customer's apparent standing;

ii) requests by a customer for investment management services where the source of funds is unclear or not consistent with the customer's apparent standing;

iii) larger or unusual settlements of securities transactions in cash form;

iv) buying and selling of a security with no discernible purpose or in circumstances which appear unusual.

7 Transactions involving unidentified parties

[26.48]

i) provision of collateral by way of pledge or guarantee without any discernible plausible reason by third parties unknown to the bank and who have no identifiable close relationship with the customer;

ii) transfer of money to another bank without indication of the beneficiary;

iii) payment orders with inaccurate information concerning the person placing the orders;

iv) use of pseudonyms or numbered accounts for effecting commercial transactions by enterprises active in trade and industry;

v) holding in trust of shares in an unlisted company whose activities cannot be ascertained by the bank;

vi) customers who wish to maintain a number of trustee or clients' accounts that do not appear consistent with their type of business, including transactions that involve nominee names.

8 Miscellaneous transactions

[26.49]

i) purchase or sale of large amounts of precious metals by an interim customer;

ii) purchase of bank cheques on a large scale by an interim customer;

iii) extensive or increased use of safe deposit facilities that do not appear to be justified by the customer's personal or business activities.

27   South Africa

Angela Itzikowitz

BANKER–CUSTOMER RELATIONSHIP

[27.1]   This chapter examines the legal aspects of the relationship between a bank and its customer and, in particular, the banker's duty of secrecy to his client under South African law.

The relationship between a bank and a customer is based on contract and is one of debtor and creditor in terms of which the bank becomes owner of the money deposited in the customer's current account and is obliged to pay cheques drawn on it by the customer.[1] The contract founding this relationship is neither one of agency nor of the Roman law of *depositum* or *mutuum* since not all its consequences can be explained under these contracts of loan. Because of the complexity of the relationship, it has been classified as one *sui generis*.[2]

In so far as the contract between the bank and the customer obliges the bank to render certain services, the so-called *services de caisse*, to the customer on his instructions, it has been classified as a contract of *mandatum*. The bank–customer relationship is based on a comprehensive mandate in terms of which the customer lends money to the bank on his current account, the bank undertakes to repay it on demand by honouring cheques drawn on it and to perform certain other services for the customer, such as the collection of cheques and other instruments, and the keeping and accounting of his current account. The fact that the customer lends money to the bank or the bank, in the case of an overdraft, to the customer, does not determine the nature of the contract between them; these loans facilitate the execution of the comprehensive mandate between the parties.[3]

THE DUTY OF SECRECY

[27.2]   There is perhaps no more hallowed a custom than that of a banker to preserve confidentiality or privacy in regard to his customers' affairs.[4]

---

1 See *London Joint Stock Bank Ltd v McMillan and Arthur* [1918] AC 777, HL; *Standard Bank of South Africa Ltd v Oneanate Investments (Pty) Ltd* 1995 4 SA 510 (C) at 530ff; *G S George Consultants and Investments (Pty) Ltd v Datasys (Pty) Ltd* 1988 3 SA 726 (W); and *ABSA Bank Ltd v Standard Bank of South Africa Ltd* [1997] 4 All SA 693, SCA.
2 A contract *sui generis* is a contract of its own kind. *G S George Consultants and Investments (Pty) Ltd v Datasys (Pty) Ltd* 1988 3 SA 726 (W) at 735–736; and *Comr of Customs and Excise v Bank of Lisbon International Ltd* 1994 1 SA 205 (N) at 213–214. See, generally, F R Malan and J T Pretorius *Malan on Bills of Exchange, Cheques and Promissory Notes* (4th edn, 2002) chapter 16 ('Malan') on which I have relied heavily.
3 Malan, n 2 above, p 336.
4 C Smith 'The Banker's Duty of Secrecy' (1979) Modern Business Law 24.

Notwithstanding this confidential relationship between the bank and its customer, there has never evolved in South African banking law a legal privilege such as that which exists between an attorney and his client.[5] It has, however, been argued that a bank has a limited privilege under s 236(4) of the Criminal Procedure Act 1977[6] in so far as this section entitles the bank to withhold disclosure unless expressly ordered by a court. A similar provision is contained in s 31 of the Civil Proceedings Evidence Act 1965.[7]

The duty of secrecy was first recognised in *Abrahams v Burns*[8] and has subsequently been recognised in a number of decisions.[9] Banking secrecy is founded on legislation, contract and the protection of privacy. Several legislative enactments apply to bank secrecy and expressly or impliedly give recognition to it. Examples of such statutes are set out below.

The Promotion of Access to Information Act 2002[10] gives effect to the constitutional right of access to information held by the state and any information that is held by another person and that is required for the exercise or protection of any rights. In terms of s 64(1) of the Act, access to certain information is limited. The head of a private body, for example, a bank, must refuse a request for access to a record of the body if the record contains, amongst other things, financial, commercial, scientific or technical information, a disclosure of which would be likely to cause harm to the commercial or financial interest of the customer. Section 65 provides that the head of a private body, such as a bank, must refuse a request for access to a record of that body if its disclosure would constitute an action for breach of duty of confidence owed to a third party in terms of an agreement. Such information could only be procured by a subpoena (writ) served on the bank to disclose.

Section 33 of the Reserve Bank Act 1989[11] provides that no director, officer or employee of the bank may disclose to any person, except to the minister, the Director General: Finance or for the purpose of the performance of his duties or functions or when required to do so before a court of law or under any law, any information relating to the affairs of the bank, a shareholder or client of the bank acquired in the performance of his duties or functions or other information pertaining to the activities of the bank.

Where the information relates to the client of the bank, it may only be disclosed with the written consent of the minister and the governor after consultation with the client concerned.

Section 87(2) of the Banks Act 1990[12] prohibits the husband of a depositor with a banking institution from obtaining, save with her written consent, any particulars concerning any deposit she has with that institution.

---

5 Smith, n 4 above.
6 Act 51 of 1977.
7 Act 25 of 1965. See W G Schulze 'Big Sister is Watching You: Banking Confidentiality and Secrecy Under Siege' (2001) 13 SA Merc LJ 601.
8 1914 CPD 452.
9 *G S George Consultants and Investments (Pty) Ltd v Datasys (Pty) Ltd* 1988 3 SA 726 (W); *Sasfin (Pty) Ltd v Beukes* 1989 1 SA 1 (A); *Cywilnat (Pty) Ltd v Densam (Pty) Ltd* 1989 3 SA 59 (W) and *Densam (Pty) Ltd v Cywilnat (Pty) Ltd* 1991 1 SA 100 (A).
10 Act 2 of 2002.
11 Act 90 of 1989.
12 Act 94 of 1990.

These statutes proceed from the assumption that a bank is under a duty to keep its clients' information confidential without indicating what the basis of that duty is.[13] Generally, bank secrecy is said to have a contractual foundation and a bank's duty to keep its customers' information confidential is seen as an express or implied term of the banker–customer contract.[14] In so far as this contract can be classified as one of mandate, the bank's duty of secrecy can be characterised as an example of a mandatary's duty to perform his mandate in good faith.[15] In this sense, banking secrecy is not a peculiar institution, but is similar to the duty of secrecy resting on other professionals.

However, in so far as a bank is obliged to keep all information concerning a customer confidential, including the fact that he was a customer,[16] contract alone does not provide the foundation of banking secrecy.

The Code of Banking Practice,[17] a self-regulatory mechanism which sets guidelines relating to the relationship between banks and their customers, deals, among other things, with issues of confidentiality. Section 4 provides that the bank will treat the customer's personal information (such as his name and address) as private and confidential even when the customer ceases to be a customer. It states further that no information about the customer's account will be disclosed to anyone, including other companies within the banking group, other than in circumstances permitted by law.

Moreover, banks are obliged to keep all confidential information secret whether it relates to a customer or to any other person. A bank is under a duty to respect the financial and personal privacy of its customers and other members of the public and not to harm their creditworthiness or personal integrity by disclosing confidential information.[18]

This duty is, however, not absolute and there are circumstances justifying disclosure. In South African law, as in English law, the oft-cited *Tournier v National Provincial and Union Bank of England* forms the cornerstone of bank secrecy.[19] *Tournier* recognised four qualifications to this duty:

1   where disclosure is under compulsion of law;
2   where there is a duty to the public to disclose;
3   where the interests of the bank require disclosure; and
4   where the disclosure is made with the express or implied consent of the customer.

THE QUALIFICATIONS TO THE DUTY
Where disclosure is under compulsion of law

[27.3]   This exception arises where a bank has to give evidence in a court of law or is obliged by a court order or statute to disclose information. At the time of the

---

13 Malan, n 2 above, p 378 and see n 245.
14 1991 1 SA 100 (A).
15 Malan, n 2 above, p 379 and see nn 250–252.
16 *Tournier v National Provincial and Union Bank of England* [1924] 1 KB 461 at 485.
17 The Code, which has no force of law, is to a large extent based on the Banking Code (3rd edn, March 1997) of the British Bankers' Association. The Code became effective on 3 April 2000.
18 Malan, n 2 above, p 380.
19 For a discussion of the facts, see chapter 11, England.

Tournier judgment,[20] compulsion by law on banks to release confidential information about their customers was unusual. Besides the Bankers' Books Evidence Act 1897 cited by Banks LJ in *Tournier*, the only other instance was under s 5 of the Extradition Act 1873. The picture today under both English and South African law is very different. In South Africa, the last decade has seen the promulgation of a plethora of statutes obliging or permitting banks to disclose confidential information.

Income Tax Act 1962

[27.4] Sections 74 and 74A of the Income Tax Act 1962[21] provide that the Commissioner for Inland Revenue may, for the purposes of the administration of the Act in relation to any taxpayer, require such taxpayer or *any other person* to furnish to the Commissioner such information, documents or items as he may require. For the purposes of an inquiry contemplated in s 74C, any person may, by written notice issued by the presiding officer, be required to appear before him in order to be questioned under oath or solemn declaration.

The question that arises in this regard is whether the Commissioner will be able to rely on s 74A to obtain information from banks about their customers without a court order compelling it to do so. It has been argued that in so far as s 74A does not expressly authorise or compel banks to disclose information about their customers, they would not be permitted to do so. It is a well-established rule of the interpretation of statutes, so the argument goes, that there is a presumption that the legislature does not intend to alter the common law any more than is necessary.[22] Any legislative provision that aims at infringing a common law fiduciary relationship should therefore state so unambiguously. If ss 74 and 74A were to be interpreted in such a way so as to allow banks to disclose information to the Commissioner, the Commissioner could effectively go on 'fishing expeditions' relating to the financial affairs of the bank's customers. The argument to the contrary is that in so far as a bank is *any person*, these provisions also apply to it.[23]

National Prosecuting Authority Act 1998

[27.5] Section 28(1) of the National Prosecuting Authority Act 1998[24] provides that if the investigating director has reason to suspect that an offence has been or is being committed or that an attempt has been made to commit an offence, he may hold an inquiry. The investigating director may, for purposes of the inquiry, summon *any person* he believes is able to furnish any information on the subject to appear before him and be questioned by him. The director may also summon *any person* who is believed to have any book, document or other object relating to the subject of inquiry to be questioned or to produce such book, document or object. The question which has yet to be answered by the courts is whether this provision would permit a bank to disclose information relating to the affairs of its customer. In so far as a bank is *any person*, it would seem to apply to a bank (see s 74 of the Income Tax Act 1962 discussed above). There is, however, an argument that the bank would be able to rely

---

20 *Tournier v National Provincial and Union Bank of England* [1924] 1 KB 461.
21 Act 58 of 1962.
22 Schulze, n 7 above, at 611.
23 Malan, n 2 above, p 379.
24 Act 32 of 1998.

on s 236(4) of the Criminal Procedure Act 1977 and withhold disclosure of any document, book or object unless production is ordered by a court.[25]

Criminal Procedure Act 1977

[27.6] In terms of s 236(4) of the Criminal Procedure Act 1977, no bank shall be compelled to produce any books of account (including any ledger, daybook or cashbook) at any criminal proceedings unless the court concerned orders that such book be produced. Section 31 of the Civil Proceedings Evidence Act 1963 contains a similar provision. Information obtained under compulsion of a court order is always subject to an implied (and sometimes express) undertaking that it will only be used for the purposes of the action. The undertaking applies to all documents disclosed under specific orders, as well as documents produced under discovery.

Attorneys Act 1979

[27.7] Section 78(13) of the Attorneys Act 1979[26] obliges a bank to furnish to the Council of the Law Society a certificate indicating the balance of an attorney's trust, savings or other interest bearing account if the Council requires it.

Usury Act 1968

[27.8] Section 10(2) of the Usury Act 1968[27] provides that, on a written demand by a borrower or credit receiver, the money lender or credit grantor shall furnish to the borrower or credit receiver, among other things, the amount of the principal debt, the finance charges levied, the annual finance charges payable and the total amount paid off in respect of the principal debt. The court in *Varvarigos v Fidelity Bank Ltd*,[28] relying on *Ideal Finance Corpn v Coetzee*,[29] a decision of the Court of Appeal, held that the surety of a debtor was entitled to claim a statement of information from the creditor in terms of s 10(2) of the Usury Act despite the fact that the definition of a surety is not incorporated in the definition of borrower in the Usury Act. The National Credit Act 2005[30] will repeal the Usury Act in due course and the finding of the court in *Varvarigos* was concerned specifically with the Usury Act.

Money laundering legislation

[27.9] The statutes regulating money laundering are the Prevention of Organised Crime Act 1998[31] ('POCA') and the Financial Intelligence Centre Act 2001[32] ('FICA'). Regulations promulgated under these Acts clarify and amplify the various obligations and provide for certain exemptions.[33] In the main, the POCA contains the substantive money laundering provisions, while the FICA provides the

---

25 Schulze, n 7 above, at 612.
26 Act 53 of 1979.
27 Usury Act 73 of 1968.
28 1989 4 SA 384 (W).
29 1970 3 SA 1 (A) and see also *Goldberg v Grosvenor Finance & Trust Co* 1950 4 SA 154 (W).
30 National Credit Act 34 of 2005.
31 Act 121 of 1998.
32 Act 38 of 2001.
33 GN R416 of 1 April 1999, GN R850 of 1 September 2000 and GN 24176 of 20 December 2002.

administrative framework.[34] In addition, regs 47 and 48 promulgated under the Banks Act 1990 require banks to establish independent compliance functions as part of their risk management process and to implement and maintain policies and procedures to guard against the bank being used for purposes of market abuse, including money laundering.

Prevention of Organised Crime Act 1998

[27.10] The POCA applies to proceeds of unlawful activity, which is far wider than proceeds of crime. 'Proceeds of unlawful activity' is defined in s 1 of the POCA to mean:

> 'Any property or any service, advantage, benefit or reward which was derived, received or retained, directly or indirectly, in the Republic or elsewhere, at any time before or after the commencement of this Act, in connection with or as a result of any unlawful activity carried on by any person, and includes any property representing property so derived.'

Property is widely defined in s 1(1) to include money.

'Unlawful activity' means 'any conduct which constitutes a crime or which contravenes any law whether such conduct occurred before or after the commencement of the Act and whether such conduct occurred in the Republic or elsewhere'.

Section 2 of the Interpretation Act 1957[35] defines the term 'law' as meaning 'any law, proclamation, ordinance, Act of Parliament or other enactment having the force of law'. 'Unlawful activity', as defined, would thus include the commission of common law crimes, contraventions of statutes, regulations and possibly even unlawful contracts.

Both definitions provide for retrospectivety and extra-territoriality. In other words, the proceeds were and will continue to be proceeds of unlawful activities no matter when or where they were received or retained. It should be pointed out, however, that it is the definitions and not the Act itself that operate retrospectively. In *National Director of Public Prosecutions v Basson*,[36] the Court of Appeal held that in South African law there is a presumption against the operation of a statute retrospectively. The court further held that a statute that operates retrospectively will breach s 35(3)(l) and (n) of the Constitution Act 1996.[37]

Furthermore, s 1(1)(xv) of the POCA makes the connection between the 'proceeds' and the 'unlawful activity' a fairly loose one (not necessarily restricted by the element of causation as was the position prior to the amendment of this section) by including any property or benefit which was 'derived, received or retained … in connection with or as a result of any unlawful activity'. As a result, the definition of 'proceeds of unlawful activity' is very wide ranging.

On the assumption that the money is retained in connection with unlawful activity, the Act restricts the definitions of the offences relating to proceeds of unlawful

---

34 The FICA and the regulations enable the Financial Intelligence Centre to issue guidance notes to accountable institutions.
35 Act 33 of 1957.
36 [2002] 2 All SA 247.
37 Act 108 of 1996.

activities to situations where the person 'knows or ought reasonably to have known' or, in the case of s 29 of the FICA, suspects or knows or ought reasonably to have known that the property is the proceeds of unlawful activities. Unless the requisite state of mind is present on the part of the accused, he cannot be successfully prosecuted under the relevant laundering offences.

For the purposes of the Act, a person has knowledge of a fact if he actually knew or if the court is satisfied that he believed there to be a reasonable possibility of the existence of that fact and then failed to obtain information to confirm the existence of that fact.[38] Furthermore, a person who negligently fails to appreciate the criminal nature of the money or property and engages in a transaction involving such money or property commits an offence under the POCA.

Negligence is defined in s 1(3) of the Act as follows:

'[f]or purposes of this Act a person ought reasonably to have known or suspected a fact, if the conclusions that he ought to have reached are those which would have been reached by a reasonably diligent and vigilant person having both –

(a) the general knowledge, skill, training and experience that may reasonably be expected of a person in his or her position; and
(b) the general knowledge, skill, training and experience that he in fact has.'

Section 1(3) goes further than the common law test for negligence in that it directs the court to examine both the actual and the expected general knowledge, skill, training and experience of a person in the accused's position, as opposed to the common law where the court only goes beyond the accused's actual circumstances when the accused professes to have a certain skill or holds a position which indicates that the person has such a skill.

Section 4 of the POCA deals with the offence of money laundering, s 5 with assisting another to launder the proceeds of unlawful activity and s 6 with the acquisition, use or possession of proceeds of unlawful activities.

Financial Intelligence Centre Act 2001

[27.11] The FICA applies to 'accountable institutions' (defined in Sch 1), supervisory bodies (set out in Sch 2), reporting institutions (defined in Sch 3) and persons. Different obligations are imposed on the different institutions, bodies or persons with the most onerous of these imposed on accountable institutions. The list of accountable institutions covers most of the players in the financial services or financial market arena. Among others, banks, long-term insurers, investment advisors, dealers in foreign exchange and money remitters are listed as accountable institutions. The Minister of Finance, in consultation with the Money Laundering Advisory Council (constituted in terms of the Act), is empowered by notice in the Government Gazette to add to or delete from this list of accountable institutions and to exempt an institution from compliance with all or some of the provisions on conditions for the period determined in the notice.[39]

Money laundering control measures applicable to accountable institutions are as follows.

---

38 POCA, s 1(2).
39 FICA, ss 73 and 74.

IDENTIFICATION

[27.12]   In terms of s 21(1) of the FICA, an accountable institution may not establish a business relationship or conclude a single transaction with a client or prospective client unless it has taken the prescribed steps to establish and verify the identity of the client or prospective client, as the case may be. Identification of the 'principal' and 'agent' and proof of authority are required where the client is acting on behalf of another or someone is acting on his behalf.

An accountable institution that enters into a transaction or conducts a business relationship, either new or existing, without identifying the person will be guilty of an offence.[40] A 'business relationship' is defined in the FICA to mean '… an arrangement between a client and an accountable institution for the purpose of concluding transactions on a regular basis'. Until one ascribes a meaning to 'transaction', this definition is meaningless. 'Transaction' is defined in s 1 of the FICA as 'a transaction concluded between a client and an accountable institution in accordance with the type of business carried on by that institution'. This definition is largely circuitous and, insofar as it includes the word 'transaction', has only a limiting effect: first, it is limited to a transaction concluded between a client and an accountable institution and, secondly, it is limited to transactions 'in accordance with the type of business carried on by that institution'.

A 'transaction' is usually regarded as a voluntary act (see, in this regard, *Colonial Treasurer v Rand Water Board*)[41] and certain activities would fall outside the ambit of the FICA for identification and verification purposes if they do not involve any voluntary co-operation of the client.

In June 2004, the Financial Intelligence Centre ('the Centre'), established in terms of the FICA, issued a guidance note entitled 'Guidance to Financial Services Industries Regulated by the Financial Services Board Concerning the Meaning of the Word "Transaction"'.[42]

Of 'transaction', the guidance note states the following:

> 'While this definition does not attribute a particular meaning to the term "transaction", it conveys the concept that the term may have different meanings depending on the type of business undertaken by different accountable institutions and would be applied differently among them. In short, the term must be applied in each instance in accordance with the nature of the business carried on by the accountable institutions in question … Transactions are concluded on the basis of agreements between the parties to a transaction. Following the definition of the term "transaction" in the Act, as well as the dictionary meaning of the term, these agreements must be aimed at a piece of business done between an accountable institution and a client, in accordance with the nature of the business carried on by the institution concerned. A basic guideline, which can be inferred from this, is that any instructions or request by a client to an accountable institution to perform some act to give effect to the business relationship between them can be regarded as a transaction.'

The guidance note then proceeds to state that, for the purposes of the identification and verification obligation, 'transaction' is understood to be more limited in its scope:

---

40 FICA, s 46.
41 1907 TS 479 at 482.
42 GN 735 26469 (18 June 2004). This guidance note was issued via the Registrar of Banks.

'For the purpose of the obligation to establish and verify clients' identities as referred to in this guidance note, the term "transaction" is not understood to include activities which happen automatically, or which an intermediary will perform automatically, without instructions from the client. These consequences include, for example, periodic contractual payments by clients to institutions and periodic automatic increases in such payments, as well as further business that accountable institutions may do with others in the course of giving effect to the clients' original mandate.'

The guidance note concludes by listing examples of what might be regarded as 'transactions' for the purposes of client identification in respect of the relevant accountable institutions. However, it states emphatically that the list is not exhaustive, but merely provides examples of the types of activities that might be regarded as transactions in relation to certain accountable institutions. The main impact of the guidance note does not, however, lie in the lists of examples of transactions that are provided, but rather in its exclusion of certain acts from the ambit of 'transaction'. The guidance note restricts the meaning of 'transaction' to acts that require the voluntary co-operation of the client.

Furthermore, accountable institutions are required to take reasonable steps to maintain the correctness of its client identification information. Information such as addresses and surnames is likely to change and accountable institutions are obliged to take reasonable steps to ensure that their records remain correct and up to date.[43]

South Africa adopts a risk-based approach in respect of the verification of certain particulars of clients, which in essence allows for the degree of due diligence performed on a client to be aligned to the level of the money laundering risk posed by that client. A risk-based approach is advocated by the Centre[44] and reg 21 specifically requires accountable institutions to obtain additional information in respect of its clients' business relationships and transactions where there is a high risk of money laundering. This information should include particulars concerning the client source of income and the source of income involved in a particular transaction or business relationship.[45]

South Africa joined the Financial Action Task Force ('FATF') in 2003. During the 2003 FATF evaluation of the South African legislation, the FATF voiced concern in its report about 'the large number of exemptions from the customer identification and record keeping requirement, some of which seemed [to it] unduly to limit the effectiveness of the law'. The FATF advised that these exemptions should be amended or their number decreased. In response, the legislature was, at least initially, reluctant to create further exemptions.

RECORD KEEPING

[27.13] The duty to keep records will arise when an accountable institution establishes a business relationship or concludes a single transaction with a client.[46] Records must be kept in respect of the following: the identity of the client, of the person on whose behalf the client is acting and of any person acting on behalf of the

---

43 Regulation 19.
44 The Centre issued a guidance note concerning identification of clients on 19 April 2004 published in Government Gazette 26278 of 30 April 2004.
45 Regulation 21.
46 FICA, s 22.

client, the authority to act where a 'principal and agent' relationship is involved, the manner in which the identity of the relevant person was established, the nature of the business relationship or transaction, the amounts involved and the parties to the transaction, as well as all accounts at the institution that are involved in the transaction or business relationship. The name of the person who obtained the information must also be recorded. Records relating to the establishment of a business relationship must be kept for a period of at least five years from the date on which the business relationship was terminated and, in the case of a single transaction, five years from the date on which the transaction was concluded.[47] These records may be kept in electronic form, stored centrally or contracted out to a third party.[48]

The Centre can access records kept by or on behalf of the accountable institution and, where these records are not by nature public records, access can be obtained by a warrant issued in chambers.[49]

REPORTING

[27.14] In terms of s 27 of the FICA, the Centre may request a bank (or any other accountable institution) to state whether a specified person is or was a client of the bank or whether a specified person is acting or has acted on behalf of any client of the bank.

The FICA provides for a hybrid reporting system – a combination of threshold and suspicion-based reporting. Accountable institutions will, within a prescribed period, have to report cash transactions paid out and received above a limit to be prescribed by the Centre.[50] The threshold will be prescribed by regulation and different thresholds may be prescribed for different institutions (at the time of writing, no thresholds have been prescribed).

Section 28A provides that an accountable institution which has in its possession or under its control any property owned or controlled by any entity which has committed or attempted to commit or facilitate any terrorist related offence as defined in the Protection of Constitutional Democracy Against Terrorist and Related Activities Act 2004[51] ('POCDATARA') must, within the prescribed period, report that fact and any other prescribed particulars to the Centre. Similarly, reports must be made if the institution has in its possession or under its control property owned or controlled by a specific entity identified in a notice issued by the President in terms of the POCDATARA. The Director of the Centre may direct an accountable institution that has made a report to report at such intervals as may be determined, whether the institution is still in possession or control of such property and any change in the circumstances concerning the accountable institution's possession or control of that property.

The duty to report suspicious and unusual transactions is more widely cast. It applies not only to accountable institutions, but to any person who carries on business.

---

47 FICA, s 23.
48 FICA, s 24.
49 FICA, s 26.
50 FICA, s 28.
51 Protection of Constitutional Democracy Against Terrorist and Related Activities Act 33 of 2004.

Section 29(1) provides:

'A person who carries on a business or is in charge of or manages a business or who is employed by a business and who knows or ought reasonably to have known or suspected that –

(a) the business has received or is about to receive the proceeds of unlawful activities; or property which is connected to an offence relating to the financing of terrorist and related activities;

(b) a transaction or series of transactions to which the business is a party –
  (i)   facilitated or is likely to facilitate the transfer of the proceeds of unlawful activities; or property which is connected to an offence relating to the financing of terrorist and related activities;
  (ii) has no apparent business or lawful purpose;
  (iii) is conducted for the purpose of avoiding giving rise to a reporting duty under this Act; or
  (iv) may be relevant to the investigation of an evasion or attempted evasion of a duty to pay any tax, duty or levy imposed by legislation administered by the Commissioner for the South African Revenue Service; or
  (v)   relates to an offence relating to the financing of terrorist and related activities; or

(c) the business has been used or is about to be used in any way for money laundering purposes or to facilitate the commission of an offence relating to the financing of terrorist and related activities,

must, within the prescribed period after the knowledge was acquired or the suspicion arose, report to the Centre the grounds for the knowledge or suspicion and the prescribed particulars concerning the transaction or series of transactions.'[52]

Terrorist and related activities are widely defined in the POCDATARA and 'money laundering' or 'money laundering activity' is defined to mean:

'An activity which has or is likely to have the effect of concealing or disguising the nature, source, location, disposition or movement of the proceeds of unlawful activities or any interest which anyone has in such proceeds, and includes any activity which constitutes an offence in terms of s 64 of this Act or ss 4, 5 or 6 [POCA].'

Transactions in respect of which inquiries were made, but which were not concluded, must also be reported if they may have caused any of the consequences set out in s 29(1) above.[53]

No person who has made or must make a report in terms of s 29 may disclose that fact or any information regarding the report to any other person, including the person in respect of whom the report is or must be made.[54] To do so would constitute tipping off, which is criminalised in terms of the Act.[55] Similarly, no person who knows or suspects that the report has been made may disclose that knowledge or suspicion or any information regarding the contents or suspected contents to any person,

---

52 See reg 23, as amended.
53 FICA, s 29(2).
54 Section 29(3).
55 Section 68(1). The penalty is imprisonment for a period not exceeding 15 years or a fine not exceeding R10,000.

including the person in respect of whom the report is or is to be made, otherwise than in defined circumstances.[56]

Any person, accountable institution or reporting institution required to report under the Act[57] may continue with that transaction unless directed otherwise by the Centre.[58]

The duty to report overrides any duty of secrecy or confidentiality or any other restriction on the disclosure of information save for the common law right to professional privilege between an attorney and the attorney's client.[59]

Failure to comply with the reporting obligation, to keep records and to identify and verify clients constitutes an offence for which a person is liable to a fine not exceeding R10 million or to imprisonment for a period not exceeding 15 years.[60]

No action, whether criminal or civil, will lie against a person (including a bank) who reports in good faith as required by the Act.[61] The immunity granted seems to be a general one in so far it contains no qualification that it applies exclusively to crimes established under the FICA. To hold otherwise would expose the person who has reported in good faith to the risk of prosecution under other statutes such as the Income Tax Act 1962 or the Exchange Control Regulations promulgated in terms of the Currency and Exchanges Act 1933.[62] Thus, provided that the defence is related to information contained in a report to the Centre, such person would be protected from prosecution under the FICA and any other statute. If the immunity is a limited one confined only to the FICA, this provision (s 38) and the reporting provision (s 29) would be subject to a constitutional challenge on the basis that they unjustifiably breach the right against self-incrimination in s 35(3)(j) of the constitution.

A person who reports will be a competent, but not a compellable, witness. Unless the person testifies at the criminal proceedings, no evidence concerning his identity is admissible.[63]

The Centre must be informed if an accountable institution, through electronic transfer, sends money into or out of South Africa above a limit to be prescribed, where the institution is acting on behalf or on the instruction of another person.[64]

INTERNAL COMPLIANCE

[27.15]   Accountable institutions are obliged to formulate and implement internal rules concerning the establishment and verification of the identity of persons who must be identified and of the records to be kept.[65]

An accountable institution must provide training to employees and must appoint a person responsible for compliance by the employees with the provisions of the FICA and internal rules.[66]

---

56 Section 29(4).
57 FICA, ss 28 and 29.
58 FICA, s 33.
59 FICA, s 37.
60 FICA, s 68(1).
61 FICA, s 38(1).
62 Act 9 of 1933.
63 FICA, s 38(2).
64 FICA, s 31.
65 FICA, s 42.
66 FICA, s 43.

Failure to formulate and implement internal rules and to provide training or appoint a compliance officer will constitute an offence. On conviction, a person will be liable to imprisonment not exceeding five years or to a fine not exceeding R1 million.[67]

THE FINANCIAL INTELLIGENCE CENTRE

[27.16] All reports must be made to the Centre. The Centre is a juristic person outside the public service, but within the public administration as envisaged by s 195 of the constitution and is accountable to the Minister of Finance.[68]

Functions of the Centre include the collection, analysis and interpretation of all information disclosed to it.[69] The Centre will also disseminate information to the relevant investigating authorities, intelligence and the South African Revenue Services and provide advice and assistance to such authorities. Information may also be exchanged with international bodies which have functions similar to those performed by the Centre.[70] The Centre does not, however, have investigative powers.

The next hurdle is, of course, the successful implementation of the legislation. While property suspected of being the proceeds or instrumentalities of unlawful activities has been attached and forfeited in terms of Chapter 5 of the POCA, there has to date been no successful conviction of any person under any of the money laundering offences. Creating a culture of compliance within the financial services industry will not be easy and the questioning of customers' legitimacy and integrity conflicts with established practice. The effectiveness of costly and burdensome requirements imposed on accountable institutions must be routinely reviewed by the financial industry, the enforcement authorities, politicians and the legislature to ensure that they continue to be justified in deterring money launderers.

Duty to the public to disclose

[27.17] An explanation of this qualification was given by Banks LJ in *Tournier*[71] as follows:

> 'Many instances of this [exception] might be given. They may be summed up in the language of Lord Finlay in *Weld-Blundell v Stephens*[72] where he speaks of cases where there is a higher duty than the private duty involved, as where "danger to state or public duty may supersede the duty of the agent to its principal".'[73]

The scope of this duty remains undefined by South African case law and is probably the most difficult of the exceptions, the dividing line between a state or public duty and a private duty being hard to define. It is for this reason that the view has been

---

67 FICA, s 68(1).
68 FICA, s 2.
69 FICA, s 3.
70 FICA, s 4.
71 *Tournier v National Provincial and Union Bank of England* [1924] 1 KB 461.
72 [1920] AC 956 at 965.
73 [1924] 1 KB 461 at 473, per Bankes LJ, referred to in a paper by R Grady 'Privacy Law Issues Reform Proposals and their Impact on the Financial Industry' presented at the 14th Annual Banking Law and Practice Conference, 22 May 1997.

advanced that the licence to disclose by reason of such a duty should not be too highly assumed.[74]

It is interesting to note in passing that when the South African government appointed a Commission of Enquiry into the Rapid Depreciation of the Rand (the Myburgh Commission), banks would not disclose information to the Commission without a subpoena first having been issued compelling disclosure, thereby bringing it within the exception 'disclosure under compulsion of law'. Arguably, the documents could have been disclosed without a subpoena under the exception 'duty to the public to disclose', but the banks were not willing to take this risk.[75]

Disclosure in the bank's interest

[27.18]   This exception would come into play where there is litigation between the bank and its customer or if a bank brings an action against a guarantor or surety. Details of the amount will obviously be disclosed in the summons and, when a guarantor is sued, details of the guaranteed account must be disclosed. If there is no litigation considered or pending, the question arises whether a surety or guarantor would be entitled to disclosure of information relating to the guaranteed account or the principal debt. To the extent that such disclosure is permitted, it would not be under this qualification, but rather on the basis of implied consent or under compulsion of law (see 'Where Disclosure is Under Compulsion of Law' above).

In *G S George Consultants of Investments (Pty) Ltd v Datasys (Pty) Ltd*,[76] the court had to consider whether a bank could cede[77] (transfer) its claim against its customer to a third party. The bank purported to cede to the respondent its rights against the applicants arising from the granting of overdraft facilities to the latter. The applicants argued that the rights were not cedable since such a cession would constitute a breach of the bank's duty of secrecy. The court accepted this argument and concluded that a banker cannot cede or, by necessary implication, pledge his personal rights against his customers. Stegman J held that in the absence of agreement to the contrary, the contract of a banker and customer obliges the banker to guard information relating to his customer's business with the banker as confidential, subject to certain exceptions, none of which, in his opinion, was relevant. The court held further that such duty of secrecy imports the element of *delectus personae* into the contract and that the banker's claims against his customer were not cedable without the consent of the customer.[78]

At first blush, the judgment seems correct. However, a disclosure of information which necessarily flows from the exercise of its rights by the bank, even though it is an indirect exercise of this right, involving a sale and a cession is justified. The existence of a duty of secrecy does not therefore provide sufficient reason for finding that the bank's rights were not cedable.[79]

---

74 M Megrah, F R Ryder and A Bueno *Paget's Law of Banking* (9th edn, 1982) p 54, cited by P Latmer 'Liability in Defamation and Negligence Following Breach of Banking Secrecy' (2000) 8 J Financial Crime 2 at 150. See, in this regard, *Libyan Arab Foreign Bank v Bankers Trust Co* [1989] QB 728, referred to in chapter 11, England.
75 See, in this regard, *Price Waterhouse v BCCI Holdings (Luxembourg) SA* [1992] BCLC 583, referred to in chapter 11, England.
76 1988 3 SA 726 (W).
77 In South African law, the terms 'cede' and 'cession' are used to denote a transfer of rights. Unlike English law, the term 'assignment' denotes a transfer of rights and obligations.
78 1988 3 SA 726 (W) at 737E–F and 739D–E.
79 See *Sasfin v Beukes* 1989 1 SA 1 (A) where Van Heerden JA, in his minority judgment, expressed doubt as to the correctness of the *G S George* judgment.

In *Cywilnat (Pty) Ltd v Densam (Pty) Ltd*,[80] Goldstein J rejected the *G & George* judgment and stated that 'if a bank wishes to sue its customers for an overdraft, it may do so revealing the amount of the overdraft to the world. I cannot see why the interposition of a cessionary should change the principle'. In *Densam (Pty) Ltd v Cywilnat (Pty) Ltd*,[81] the Court of Appeal confirmed the decision of the trial court that a banker could validly cede monetary claims owed to it by its customer. Botha JA was of the view that it was reasonable and proper for a bank to further its own interests in regard to collecting an overdraft by ceding its claim to a third party.[82] In response to the appellant's suggestion that a bank may want to cede its claim for an ulterior purpose unrelated to the furtherance of its own interest, Botha JA stated that the mere fact that a bank has ceded its claim would raise a prima facie inference, if nothing appeared to the contrary, that the bank had decided to dispose of its claim to realise and liquidate its own interest,[83] but the court did not consider it necessary to pursue this point any further. Consequently, the court held that the application of principles laid down in *Tournier* to the facts of the case before it led to the conclusion that the bank was not precluded from ceding its claim against the appellant to the respondent.[84]

Botha JA also disagreed with Stegman J's view that the duty of secrecy which a banker owes its customer imports the element of *delectus personae* into the contract. He stated that Stegman J had only based his view with regard to the element of *delectus personae* on the banker's obligation to maintain confidentiality; the nature of the customer's obligation to pay the amount of the banker's claim had not been mentioned. This approach was, in Botha JA's view, contrary to principle and authority. The question whether a claim was not cedable on the basis that a contract involved a *delectus personae* fell to be answered with reference not to the nature of the cedent's obligations vis-à-vis the debtor, which remained unaffected by the cession, but rather to the nature of the debtor's obligations vis-à-vis the cedent, which was the counterpart of the cedent's right, the subject matter of the transfer comprising the cession.[85]

Applying the principle that, unless the contract is so personal in its character that it can make any reasonable or substantial difference to the other party whether the cedent or cessionary is entitled to enforce the performance of the obligation, the right of action can be freely ceded, the court found that it would make no difference at all to the appellant whether it was the bank or the respondent who exercised the right to enforce payment.[86] Accordingly, the court held that the bank's claim against the appellant had been cedable.

Parties can, of course, stipulate that the rights cannot be ceded by the inclusion of a so-called *pactum de non cedendo* into the contract.

Disclosure to other companies within the group[87]

[27.19]   An area of concern is the growing perception that banks can release confidential information about their customers, without their consent, to other

---

80 1989 3 SA 59 (W).
81 1991 1 SA 100 (A).
82 1991 1 SA 100 (A) at 110–111.
83 1991 1 SA 100 (A) at 111B–C.
84 1991 1 SA 100 (A) at 111E–F.
85 1991 1 SA 100 (A) at 112A–B.
86 See S Scott 'Can a Banker Cede his Claims Against his Customers?' (1989) 1 SA Merc LJ 248.
87 'Group' is defined in s 6.7 of the Code as 'a holding company as defined in the Companies Act 61 of 1973 and its wholly-owned subsidiaries'.

companies – both banking and non-banking entities – within the group. Banks argue that such an exchange of information is in their interest and is necessary to protect the group. This information may, however, be released not only for the protection of the bank's interest, but also for marketing purposes, particularly in the light of the diversification of banks' business interests. In practice, banks usually rely on the implied consent of their customers for disclosure 'in the interests of the bank'. There is thus an evident connection between disclosure 'in the bank's interest' and disclosure 'with the express or implied consent of the customer'. The giving of information to other companies within the group cannot, however, without more, be said to be with 'the implied consent of the customer' as a customer may not be aware of the practice. A customer intends to bank with a bank, not a group, and the contract, where the duty of secrecy is a *naturalia* of such contract, is with a particular bank and not the banking group.

It is interesting to note that s 4 of the Code of Banking Practice provides that 'the bank's interest will not be used to disclose information about a customer (including the customer's name and address) to any other company in the group for marketing purposes'.

The marketing of services is dealt with in s 2.8 of the Code. It provides that the bank may give certain information about existing customers to other subsidiaries within the banking group for marketing purposes where it informs the customers of its intention. While the customer may withhold his consent to the dissemination of such information, the Code provides that if the customer does not withhold consent, it will presume that the customer has agreed to the bank continuing the practice. Quiescence will be taken to amount to consent in this case. Whether the banks can assume implied consent in this way is doubtful, but the issue has not yet been pertinently raised. As far as new customers are concerned, express consent to the dissemination of such information is required.

Credit reference agencies[88]

[27.20]   Another area of concern relates to the disclosure by banks to credit reference agencies. It is not clear under which of the *Tournier* exceptions this practice would fall – 'in the interests of the bank', 'duty to the public to disclose' or whether disclosure in these circumstances can be justified at all. As credit default is on the increase and customers will, as result, have to pay higher charges, it may well fall under a 'duty to the public to disclose'. In so far as the giving of this information is associated with disclosure within a banking group, it may be better housed under the qualification 'in the interests of the bank'.

Section 4.2 of the Banking Code deals with credit reference agencies. It provides that information about a customer's debts owed to the bank may be disclosed to credit reference agencies under the following circumstances:

1   where the customer has fallen behind with his payments and has not made proposals satisfactory to the bank for repayment following formal demand and the customer has been given at least 28 days' notice of the bank's intention to disclose;
2   where the customer has given the bank written consent;

---

88   A credit reference agency is defined in s 6.4 of the Code as 'an organisation which holds information which is of relevance to lenders'.

3   where the customer has a cheque referred to the drawer, the information is placed on a cheque verification service; or

4   where the amount owed or arrears amount is in dispute, the fact (but not the amount) of this dispute will also be disclosed.

The bank will not give any other information about the customer to credit reference agencies without the customer's prior written consent.

Disclosure with express or implied consent

[27.21]   Express consent occasions no difficulty – the customer will have expressly consented to disclosure. Where a customer refers a creditor to his bank for a credit report, for example, no difficulty will arise.[89] A more complex issue is where a bank seeks to rely on disclosure with the customer's implied consent. As a matter of practice, a customer's consent is implied where disclosure is made to a guarantor or prospective guarantor regarding a guaranteed account.

Status opinions/bankers' references

[27.22]   As a service to customers, a bank often obtains status opinions on the creditworthiness of third parties by addressing a request to the bank of the third party. While the perennial question in this regard is whether the express consent of the customer is required (and a court has yet to decide this issue), the better view seems to be that it is not necessary provided certain general requirements are met. These requirements are, among others, that the information given be in general terms, is correct and given to another bank or made known to a customer of the supplying bank.[90] Generally, the practices in South Africa are regulated by the 'agency agreement' adhered to by all clearing banks and may fall within the scope of banking business with the practice being regarded as impliedly authorised by the customer, a view alluded to by Atkin LJ in *Tournier*.

A further issue concerns the potential delictual liability (tort) of the bank giving the reference to third parties. In *Standard Chartered Bank of Canada v Nedperm Bank Ltd*,[91] the court had to decide whether and under what circumstances a bank incurred liability for a banker's reference or status opinion concerning a customer. The plaintiff sued the defendant for damages allegedly suffered as a result of a negligent misstatement made by the defendant. That liability for negligent misstatement or negligent misrepresentation is part of our law is accepted.[92] On appeal, the court found that the report provided was inaccurate and misleading as the company concerned was not trading normally and was heavily dependent on borrowings from the defendant bank. On the question of negligence, the court had no difficulty in holding that, given the comprehensive and intimate knowledge of the defendant's officials of the affairs of the company, a skilled banker, acting reasonably, would not have given the report in question. As Corbett CJ said, 'it seems to me, therefore, that the bank had either to give a true report [that is, a report which truly reflected its knowledge of the position] or decline to give a report'. The court held, further, that the case was not of the kind that 'raises the spectre of limitless liability or places an

89 Smith, n 4 above.
90 Malan, n 2 above, p 382.
91 WLD 12673/89, 19 March 1992, overruled on appeal in 1994 4 SA 747 (A).
92 *Administrateur, Natal v Trust Bank van Africa Bpk* 1979 3 SA 824 (A); *Bayer SA (Pty) Ltd v Frost* 1991 4 SA 559 (A) at 568. See Malan, n 2 above, p 382ff.

undue or unfair burden upon the bank'; the defendant could have refused to give the report or it could have disclaimed liability for negligence.

CROSS-BORDER/EXTRA-TERRITORIAL ISSUES

Obtaining evidence in South Africa for use in foreign civil proceedings

[27.23]   South Africa has been a party to the Convention on the Taking of Evidence Abroad in Civil or Commercial Matters of 1970 ('the Convention') since 1997. The Convention has not been incorporated into South African domestic law and as a result, until its incorporation by Parliament, individuals in South Africa cannot claim any direct rights under it.

In addition, it must be noted that, by appending certain reservations to the Convention on accession, South Africa has eschewed the option of obtaining evidence through a special commission appointed by the requesting state, even once the Convention has been incorporated into domestic law. Until such incorporation into domestic law, the obtaining of evidence in South Africa for use in foreign civil proceedings is governed by various statutes which are outlined below.

Section 3 of the Foreign Courts Evidence Act 1962[93] provides that if a foreign party or court wishes to obtain evidence from witnesses in South Africa, an application must be lodged with a judge of the High Court.

In terms of the Supreme Court Act 1959,[94] evidence may be obtained without resorting to the lodging of an application. Section 33 provides that when a letter of request in connection with civil proceedings is received from any state, territory or court outside South Africa and is sent by the Director General of Justice to the registrar of a South African court with the intimation that the minister considers such request desirable, the registrar must submit the letter of request to a judge in chambers to give effect to it.

Similarly, the Magistrates' Courts Act 1944[95] provides that a magistrate may appoint a person to act as a commissioner for the purposes of taking evidence from witnesses outside South Africa provided that it is expedient and consistent with the interests of justice.

However, in terms of the Protection of Businesses Act 1978,[96] when complying with a letter of request in connection with civil proceedings, no person shall, in complying with any letter of request, furnish any information as to any business without the permission of the Minister of Economic Affairs.

Obtaining evidence in South Africa for use in foreign criminal proceedings

[27.24]   The International Co-operation in Criminal Matters Act 1996[97] provides that on the submission to the Director General of a request by a foreign court or

---

93 Foreign Courts Evidence Act 80 of 1962.
94 Supreme Court Act 59 of 1959.
95 Magistrates' Courts Act 32 of 1944.
96 Protection of Businesses Act 99 of 1978.
97 International Co-operation in Criminal Matters Act 75 of 1996.

appropriate foreign government body for assistance in obtaining evidence in the Republic, the Director General, provided he is satisfied that proceedings have been instituted in a court exercising jurisdiction in the requesting state, that there are reasonable grounds for believing that an offence has been committed or that it is necessary to determine whether an offence has been so committed and that an investigation in that respect is being conducted in the requesting state, shall submit the request for assistance to the minister for his approval. On notification of the minister's approval, the Director General must forward the request to the magistrate within whose area of jurisdiction the witness resides for execution.

With specific reference to the identification of the proceeds of unlawful activities and the combating of money laundering activities and the financing of terrorist and related activities, the FICA provides for the exchange of information with similar bodies in other countries regarding money laundering activities and similar offences.

In terms of s 40 of the FICA, an entity or investigating authority outside South Africa which performs similar functions to those of the Centre, may, at the initiative of the Centre or on written request, obtain information which the Centre reasonably believes is relevant to the identification of the proceeds of unlawful activities, the combating of money laundering or financing of terrorist and related activities or similar offences in the country in which that entity is established. Information held by the Centre may only be provided to an entity referred to above pursuant to a written agreement between the Centre and such entity or the authority, which is responsible for that entity, regulating the exchange of information between the Centre and such entity. The agreement does not take effect until the minister has approved it in writing.

Obtaining evidence abroad for use in South African civil proceedings

[27.25]   Traditionally, evidence in a foreign state was obtained by means of a letter of request or evidentiary commissions executed by South African diplomatic and consular officials under art 5(j) of the Vienna Convention on Consular Relations 1963. However, according to common law tradition, witnesses need to be present in court so they can be fully cross-examined under oath. As outlined above, while South Africa has been a party to the Convention on the Taking of Evidence Abroad in Civil or Commercial Matters of 1970 since 1997, the Convention has not been incorporated into domestic law.

Obtaining evidence abroad for use in South African criminal proceedings

[27.26]   Section 2 of the International Co-operation in Criminal Matters Act 1996 provides that if it is in the interests of justice that evidence is obtained from a person who is in a foreign state, a court may issue a letter of request for assistance from that foreign state to obtain evidence for use in the proceedings. A judge in chambers or a magistrate may, on application, issue a letter of request if he is satisfied that there are:

> 'Reasonable grounds for believing that an offence has been committed in the Republic or that it is necessary to determine whether an offence has been committed; that an investigation in respect thereof is being conducted; and that for

purposes of the investigation it is necessary in the interests of justice that information be obtained from a person or authority in a foreign state.'

Once the letter of request is issued, it is sent to the Director General for transmission to the specified court or to the appropriate government body in the requested state. In cases of urgency, a letter of request may be sent directly to the court exercising jurisdiction or to the appropriate government body in the place where the evidence is to be obtained. In these instances, the Director General must be provided with a copy of the letter of request.

CONCLUSION

[27.27]   In South Africa, as elsewhere, banks will continuously have to balance the duty of confidentiality they owe to their clients with their heightened obligations to disclose confidential information. As increased disclosure is called for by statute and in the wake of terrorism, it is doubtful whether the duty of secrecy as upheld in *Tournier*[98] will endure and secrecy may be defined more by the exceptions to it than the duty itself.

---

98 *Tournier v National Provincial and Union Bank of England* [1924] 1 KB 461.

28 Spain

Carlos Paredes

INTRODUCTION

[28.1] The principle of bank secrecy and the corresponding duty of credit institutions to maintain confidential information obtained in respect of clients was traditionally rendered as a commercial usage of widespread compliance and part of the Spanish banking system. It was widely accepted that the principle was inspired by, and based upon, the special nature of the relationship between the banker and his client that involves a special degree of confidence placed by the client on his financial adviser and credit provider.

Since the enactment of the Spanish constitution of 1978, the principle of bank secrecy has been closely linked to the right of citizens to their privacy and to the obligation of professionals to keep confidential matters concerning their clients. At the same time, and whilst the principle was gaining explicit constitutional support, Spanish legislation eroded its scope by introducing limits in areas such as tax, supervision of credit entities by regulators and avoidance of money laundering activities. The principle of bank secrecy has only recently been explicitly acknowledged and regulated by positive legislation: Law 44/2002 of 22 November on the reform of the financial system recognises the existence of banking secrecy by adding a new additional provision to Law 26/1988 of 29 July on discipline and supervision of credit entities.

In this chapter, we will analyse the current legal status of the principle of bank secrecy in Spain. For this purpose, the text is divided into five different sections:

1 legal basis of the principle of bank secrecy;
2 scope of the principle;
3 remedies available under Spanish law in case of breach of the duty of bank secrecy;
4 limits to the general principle set out by Spanish legislation; and
5 a special reference to related obligations of confidentiality as regards the Spanish securities market.

LEGAL BASIS OF THE PRINCIPLE OF BANK SECRECY

[28.2] Before the enactment of the Spanish constitution of 27 December 1978, there was a great deal of controversy in academic circles as to the legal basis of the principle of bank secrecy. For a number of scholars, the principle was an implied term of contracts entered into between clients and banking institutions.[1] The general

---

1 See eg J M Otero Novas *El Secreto Bancario. Vigencia y Alcance*, Revista de Derecho Bancario y Bursátil 1985, pp 736 and 737.

principle contained in art 57 of the Spanish Commercial Code and art 1.258 of the Civil Code, by virtue of which contracting parties are obliged to comply not only with the terms of what has been expressly agreed in the contract, but also with those conditions deriving from good faith, usage and the law, supported this conclusion.

Others took into consideration existing legal provisions creating a duty of confidentiality in specific circumstances and in respect of particular entities, so as to extend its scope to cover the relationship between banking institutions and their clients.[2] These legal provisions were as follows:

1   art 23 of the Statutes of the Bank of Spain approved by Decree of 24 July 1947, which, under the heading 'bank secrecy', prohibited the Spanish Central Bank from passing on to third parties any information in relation to funds deposited in current accounts opened by an identified person or entity, with the exception of information released to the interested party, its representative or the Spanish courts. A judgment of the Supreme Court of 28 November 1928 had given the application of the Statutes of the Bank of Spain to private banks in the absence of any other applicable regulation;

2   art 16 of Decree Law of Nationalisation of the Bank of Spain of 7 June 1962, which created a central credit risk information-gathering service available to all private banks and obliged these entities to send periodical information to the Bank of Spain in respect of the concession of credits to third party clients. Banks were allowed to request information from the Bank of Spain, but had to adhere to a special duty of secrecy as to the information obtained.

Another important sector of Spanish scholars understood that the legal basis of the principle of bank secrecy lay in a commercial usage borne from banking practice due to the special relationship of confidence between a banker and his clients.[3] (The existence of a commercial usage in respect of bank secrecy could still be sustained today, provided that no specific legislation had been enacted, since the principle meets the two main requirements to be considered a commercial usage and therefore part of Spanish law: it has been a widespread practice for a long time in the Spanish banking sector and there is a conviction that the duty of secrecy binds all credit institutions. In fact, all credit entities have accepted this special duty as part of the provision of banking-related services to clients.)

The enactment of the Spanish constitution in 1978 provided a further element to reinforce and substantiate the legal basis of the principle binding banking institutions, as eventually confirmed by the judgment of the Spanish Constitutional Court of 26 November 1984. In essence, the court understood that the principle of bank secrecy was one of the rights, and a corresponding obligation, created under the constitution deserving protection and of mandatory compliance, as follows:

1   from the point of view of clients, the Spanish Constitutional Court understood that bank secrecy was part of, and an expression of, the right of Spanish citizens to have their privacy guaranteed as provided by art 18 of the constitution. In this respect, movements of current accounts and the information that in general may be gathered by a credit institution regarding its clients would form part of clients' privacy and, therefore, would merit the protection of the Spanish constitution and its enforcement in case of breach;

2 See eg L M Cazorla *El secreto bancario*, Madrid 1978, p 78 and R Jiménez de Parga *El secreto bancario en el Derecho español*, Revista de Derecho Mercantil 1969, p 399.

3 See eg Garrigues *Contratos Bancarios*, Madrid 1958, p 52 and M J Guillén Ferrer *El secreto bancario. Sus límites legales*, Valencia 1997, p 79.

2   from the point of view of financial entities, the Spanish Constitutional Court established a constitutional support for their obligation of confidentiaity in art 20 of the Spanish constitution that regulates professional secrecy. The general principle of professional secrecy could be invoked by credit entities so as to protect, with certain limits as described below, information gathered from clients in the course of their relationship.

However, the Constitutional Court did not grant an unlimited protection to the principle of bank confidentiality. In the case at hand, the court limited it by the application of a further principle contained in the Spanish constitution obliging Spanish citizens to collaborate in sustaining public expenditure through a tax system. This principle should allow the Spanish tax authorities to investigate and seek information from credit institutions as regards their clients, subject to procedures and requisites established by law that should, to the extent these were followed, preserve the privacy of the client subject to investigation. As the Constitutional Court established, the right to privacy should prohibit an illegal and arbitrary investigation into the private affairs of individuals and entities (including current account movements) if this was not carried out following the requisites and conditions set out by law.

A subsequent Constitutional Court ruling in the form of a summons of 23 July 1986 reaffirmed the doctrine contained in the 1984 judgment by stating that the principle of bank secrecy formed part of the economic privacy of entities and individuals which was only limited when other constitutional rights deserved protection and the law established the procedure and necessary requisites to balance both principles.

During the following years, additional legislation explicitly acknowledged the principle of bank confidentiality and its enforceability under Spanish law in the field of the Spanish securities markets and with respect to the Bank of Spain.

As regards the Spanish securities market, Law 24/1988 of 28 July has provided in art 81 the overall obligation of entities and individuals, that in carrying out their profession or functions or due to any other reasons, should they obtain information in relation to the securities markets, they must keep it confidential and safeguard it from any unlawful or improper use, without prejudice to reporting and co-operation duties to judicial and administrative bodies. Any such individual or entity shall adopt appropriate measures to avoid any abusive or unfair use of the information and, if it cannot be avoided, to remedy the consequences arising from such abusive or unfair use.

In more detail, Royal Decree 629/1993 of 3 May has established a general code of conduct applicable to all entities and individuals performing activities within the Spanish securities market. According to the code, which is mandatory even on entities merely providing advisory services, all the information that entities active in the securities markets may obtain from clients in order to identify them and gather their financial situation, investment expertise and purpose of the investment will be confidential and will not be used for the market member's own benefit or that of a different party. Royal Decree 629/1993 also provides that these entities and individuals must have an internal code of conduct to regulate the activities of their officers, employees and representatives.

Law 3/1994 of 14 April, implementing the Second Banking Co-ordination Directive[4] in Spain and amending Royal Legislative Decree 1298/1986 of 28 June, has imposed

---

4 Council Directive 89/646/EEC.

on the Bank of Spain a special duty of confidentiality and secrecy in respect of any information and documentary materials obtained in the course of its prudential supervisory role on credit institutions. The same obligation applies to all officials that perform or have carried out activities with the Bank of Spain. These individuals are precluded from making any declaration, testifying, publishing or exhibiting any data or reserved document even after leaving their position with the Bank of Spain. As exceptions to the overall obligation to keep the above information confidential, Royal Legislative Decree 1298/1986 sets out the following:

1 when the affected party has expressly agreed to such disclosure;
2 the data has been aggregated with other information for mere statistical purposes;
3 the information has been requested from a criminal court, in connection with a bankruptcy/insolvency proceeding (provided the information does not relate to third parties involved in the relaunching of the relevant entity) or in respect of disciplinary proceedings initiated against credit entities;
4 information released to other regulatory and supervisory bodies in Spain so that these may perform their duties, including auditors;
5 information submitted by the Bank of Spain to the European Central Bank or central banks, members of the system of European Central Banks or any other authority supervising payment and clearance systems;
6 information released by the Bank of Spain to supervisory entities of foreign countries, provided that reciprocity exists and rules of secrecy are similar to those applicable in Spain;
7 information provided by the Bank of Spain to Spanish settlement and clearing systems, provided it is aimed at allowing the correct operation of any such systems;
8 information that may be needed to prevent money laundering activities;
9 information released with the prior authorisation of the Ministry of Economy to the tax authorities in accordance with, and subject to, the conditions set out in art 93 of the General Tax Law (Law 58/2003 of 17 December);
10 information provided by the Bank of Spain to the Ministry of Economy or to the Spanish regional governments; and
11 information requested by a parliamentary investigation committee.

This special duty of secrecy of employees and officials of the Bank of Spain has been further recognised by Law 13/1994 of 1 June, on the Autonomy of the Bank of Spain and in the Internal Regulation of the Central Bank of 14 November 1996. We will refer to this legislation in the course of this chapter.

Notwithstanding the above, it was not until the enactment of Law 44/2002 of 22 November on the reform of the financial system that banking secrecy was specifically recognised by legislation in connection with pure commercial banking activities. The Seventeenth Additional Provision of Law 44/2002 added a new additional provision to Law 26/1988 of 29 July on discipline and supervision of credit entities establishing the duty of credit entities operating in Spain to maintain bank confidentiality.

This legislation sets out that entities and any other persons subject to the supervision of credit entities (ie managers and directors of credit entities and significant shareholders and their managers and directors) are obliged to safeguard and keep strictly confidential (without communication to third parties) all information relating to balances, operations and any other clients' transactions. As general exceptions to this duty of confidentiality, Law 44/2002 mentions all information (i) which the client or applicable law has allowed communication to third parties or (ii) in respect of which an obligation to communicate to the supervisory authorities exists or a request in connection has been made by the supervisory authorities. In these exceptional cases, the delivery of confidential data must comply with the instructions of the client or with those provided by applicable law.

An additional exception to the duty to keep confidential clients' information is that sharing confidential information among credit entities belonging to the same consolidated group is not subject to the restrictions imposed by Law 44/2002.

Law 44/2002 finally states that any breach of the aforementioned regulations will be deemed a serious offence, which will be punished according to the ordinary sanctions procedure provided under Law 26/1988 (see below for a description of the sanctions regime).

SCOPE OF THE PRINCIPLE OF BANK SECRECY

[28.3]   Before the enactment of Law 44/2002, since Spain lacked a specific legal regime applicable to the principle of bank secrecy (especially for commercial banking activities), its scope needed to be determined in conjunction with the rules, referred to above, that had been the legal basis of its binding nature for many years under Spanish law.

Today, the new regulations have confirmed that the obligation to maintain confidentiality refers to all information relating to balances, operations and any other client transactions. Although these new regulations have not explained in more detail what the scope of the principle is, it can be argued, based on the new rules enacted and on the fact that bank secrecy had previously been considered by a majority of scholars as a commercial usage binding upon a credit institution in its dealings with clients, that the principle of bank secrecy must be construed as having a broad scope that covers all the information obtained by credit entities from clients, since it derives from the special relationship created based on confidence and trust. Confidentiality will therefore cover the following information:

1   all that gathered by the bank whilst entering into particular and usual banking transactions (ie deposit taking, credit accounts or lending), thus including balance sheet details, turnover, volume of sales, identity of clients and the specific terms and conditions and purpose of the relevant banking operation; and
2   all that factual information and opinions surpassing the economic terms of the particular transaction entered into or service provided to the client and that may be of a personal or economic nature and that must be deemed to have been released by the client to their banker in the context of their professional relationship.

This broad conclusion has been supported since 1978 by the constitutional basis of the principle of bank secrecy. To the extent that the duty of bank confidentiality is connected with the right of privacy of clients as protected by the Spanish constitution, such right (and the corresponding obligation on the provider of banking services) must be interpreted broadly and may only be limited to the extent that it enters into conflict, or needs to be interpreted in conjunction, with another right protected by the Spanish constitution and such limits as set out in law. In light of the Constitutional Court's judgment of 26 November 1984, we will analyse the scope of the principle of bank secrecy and in relation to the particular facts subject to revision, namely, the level of information that credit entities are obliged to provide to the tax authorities as regards movements of bank accounts held by clients.

28.3 *Spain*

Another specific area of concern is the reports prepared by credit institutions regarding the economic situation of their clients. Although a number of scholars have understood in the past that the principle of secrecy should only cover details regarding particular and usual banking transactions, it seems, taking into consideration the nature of the principle of bank secrecy as a long-standing commercial usage before the enactment of the new legislation and the recognition granted to the principle by the Spanish Constitutional Court as part of the right of Spanish citizens to their privacy, that the release of any report that may serve to identify the client or/and a particular transaction entered into with a credit institution and/or the economic or financial position of the client requires the prior approval of that client. This conclusion is further supported by the fact that the Law 44/2002 regulations that recognise the existence of a duty to keep confidential information regarding clients of a credit entity refer to 'the information relating to balances, operations and any other clients' transactions'.

As regards additional legislation, it is worth mentioning that Royal Legislative Decree 1298/1986 and the Internal Regulations of the Bank of Spain consider privileged information subject to the duty of secrecy to be all the data, documents and information gathered by the Bank of Spain in the performance of the functions vested upon it by existing legislation. Thus, all such information gathered as agent bank to the Spanish Treasury, currency exchange provider and supervisor of the banking system, including, in particular, credit entities, will be subject to the duty of confidentiality.

In the securities market, all information obtained by market participants, including credit entities, in respect of investors, issues and transactions in the market must be kept confidential and safeguarded from improper use as provided for in art 81 of Law 24/1988. In this context, it is important to determine the level of activities and services that credit entities established in Spain (including branches of foreign institutions and EU-based entities under the Second Banking Co-ordination Directive,[5] as implemented in Spain by Law 3/1994) may provide to clients, since information obtained in the provision of those services will be affected by the duty of confidentiality and proper use. In essence, credit entities may perform in Spain all the activities restricted to duly authorised professionals in the securities market (ie investment services companies, namely, securities companies, agencies and portfolio management companies). These include, inter alia:

1 the receipt of orders from clients and their execution or providing for their execution;
2 the intermediation in the placement of securities on the account of issuers and their underwriting;
3 the negotiation of securities on their own account;
4 the provision of credit to the market; and
5 the provision of deposit and discretionary portfolio management services to clients.

In addition, it is provided in the code of conduct contained in Royal Decree 629/1993 that the information obtained from clients by market participants, including credit entities, in compliance with their obligation to 'know your customer' (financial position, market knowledge, purpose of the investment, etc) in order to provide a proper and professional service and to verify the identity of a customer for anti-money laundering purposes will be covered by the principle of secrecy.

5 Council Directive 89/646/EEC.

Below, we will analyse the limits applicable to the principle of bank secrecy affecting its scope. These limits refer, essentially, to the powers of the administrative and judicial authorities to obtain information from credit entities. It is also natural to understand that the scope of the principle of bank secrecy must be limited and constrained by the will of the person or entity protected by it. Thus, if the bank has obtained permission to release any information from the person to whom the information relates, such disclosure must not be deemed in breach of the principle of bank secrecy. This conclusion is contained in Law 44/2002, which, as explained above, exempts from the duty of confidentiality not only the information which must be disclosed by mandate of law or regulatory authority as provided by law, but also the dissemination of information to which the client has consented.

The approval by the affected client as a limit to the principle of bank secrecy was already considered in Royal Legislative Decree 1298/1986. This Decree exempts from the obligation of confidentiality vested on officials of the Bank of Spain that information released with the consent of the affected party. Circular 3/1995 of 25 September of the Bank of Spain, which regulates the central credit risk information-gathering system of the Central Bank, has allowed for information in respect of an individual to be made available to a credit institution with which such client has no contractual relationship, although the client may exercise his/her right to amend or cancel the relevant information should the data be inaccurate or not pertinent. Similarly, the regulations aimed at protecting personal data (specially Organic Law 15/1999 of 13 December on the protection of personal data) provide, when referring to the activity of companies who provide information about the financial position of third parties, that any personal data used in that regard must be obtained from public sources or with the consent of the affected party. In the field of personal data, Organic Law 15/1999 sets out the general rules applicable to the management of data, including communication and storage regulations and rights vested on the holders of the data. In particular, these regulations limit the rendering of outsourcing services to companies which administer personal data by requiring certain minimum contents in the relevant outsourcing agreement aimed at protecting the confidentiality of the data. Additionally, Organic Law 15/1999 limits transfers of personal data to persons or companies located in countries not providing an equivalent protection level to that achieved in Spain, subject to certain exceptions.

The issue of bank confidentiality is also linked to the provision of Internet services by credit entities. The duty to keep confidential all personal data regarding the client is also applicable to these transactions. In this connection, Law 34/2002 of 11 July on information services and electronic commerce, which develops Council Directive 2000/31/EC, sets out the general rules applicable to providers of Internet services located in Spain (information to be displayed on the website, prohibition of unsolicited commercial e-mails, validity of electronic agreements and resolution of disputes, inter alia). This Law will also be generally applicable to providers of Internet services located within the EEA or EU provided that the services relate to specific subjects (such as intellectual property, direct insurance, contracts with natural persons qualifying as consumers, etc).

Finally, it is worth mentioning whether the bank may limit claims for breach of confidentiality. This issue has to be considered from the standpoint of general liability rules. In that regard, exoneration of liability can only be admitted, if agreed to, in the case of negligence, but not in the case of wilful misconduct; likewise, limitation of liability is generally accepted if agreed to between the parties. However, these general rules are restricted in the event that one of the parties (ie the client of the bank) is a consumer; should this be the case, a clause exonerating or limiting the bank's liability for breach of confidentiality included in a set of general terms and conditions not discussed by the parties could be deemed abusive and, thus, null and void.

REMEDIES

[28.4] Due to the existence of a variety of rights and principles serving as the legal basis to the principle of bank secrecy under Spanish law, there are also an important number of remedies available or that, arguably, could be used in the case of a breach by a credit entity of its obligation to keep confidential information gathered from its clients. For the purpose of this section, we have analysed the following possible actions or claims that may be brought by a client against the credit entity which has infringed its obligation of bank secrecy.

A claim based on the protection granted by the Spanish constitution over the right to privacy

[28.5] As we have already mentioned above, the Spanish Constitutional Court has established that the principle of bank secrecy is an expression of the right to privacy contained in art 18 of the Spanish constitution.[6] In this respect, Organic Law 1/1982 of 5 May has developed art 18 of the constitution, allowing for a claim to be brought before the courts for an alleged breach of privacy and empowering the courts to take the necessary measures and steps to put an end to the breach and to reinstate the injured party in the lawful exercise of his rights. Organic Law 1/1982 also envisages the possible adoption of measures by the courts to prevent any further unlawful breach of the right of privacy and the right of the affected party to be compensated for damages suffered. Such damages will be measured taking into consideration the use that may have been made of the information obtained and the benefit obtained by the entity or person in breach. The statute of limitation for any legal action taken pursuant to a breach of art 18 of the Spanish constitution is four years from the time such action could have been taken by the damaged party. Law 62/1978 of 26 December further develops the judicial protection of constitutional rights (including those deriving from art 18 of the constitution) and allows for an especially quick summary procedure to be used before the courts in a claim based on a breach of the right of privacy contained in art 18 of the Spanish constitution.

A criminal claim due to the breach of the duty of professional secrecy binding credit entities

[28.6] The judgment of the Spanish Constitutional Court of 26 November 1984 declared the close connection between the principle of bank secrecy and the duty of professional confidentiality owed by professionals to third parties contained in art 20 of the constitution. This has served as the basis for a number of Spanish scholars to defend the possible initiation of a criminal claim in the case of a breach of the obligation of secrecy owed by a banker to his client[7] (the Spanish Supreme Court

---

6 Constitutional Court judgment of 26 November 1984.
7 See eg A Jorge Barreiro *El delito de revelación de secretos (profesionales y laborales)*, Revista La Ley, 1996-3, p 1.298 and F Morales Prats *Comentarios al Nuevo Código Penal (Dir: G Quintero Olivares)*, 1997, p 996.

also seemed to sustain this position in its judgment of 24 September 1968 in which it ruled that a criminal offence had been committed by employees of a non-banking business entity that had divulged details and information from clients to third parties). Article 199.2 of the Spanish Criminal Code approved by Organic Law 10/1995 of 23 November imposes on a professional that has breached a duty of confidentiality by divulging information obtained in the course of the profession a penalty of imprisonment of between one and four years, a fine of up to 216,367.20 euros and a prohibition against performing his past professional activities for a period ranging between two and six years. Under Spanish law, a criminal action may only be initiated against individuals and not legal entities. In accordance with art 31 of the Spanish Criminal Code, however, the administrator or person acting on behalf of a legal entity meeting the requisites and conditions of a criminal action will be deemed criminally responsible for such conduct. The statute of limitation for this type of offence is established by the Criminal Code as five years from the last date in which the offence was committed.

A claim based on the breach of a duty vested on the credit entity with respect to its banking relationships

[28.7] As already mentioned, before the enactment of Law 44/2002, a majority of Spanish scholars have understood the legal basis of bank secrecy to lie, in addition to the 1978 constitution, on a commercial usage created through the widespread perception in the banking sector of the existence of that principle and its mandatory nature. This commercial usage would allow a third party client that has entered into a particular contractual arrangement with a credit institution (ie a loan, credit or opening of account) to claim a breach of an implied term of its contract if the banker discloses information delivered to it without the client's consent. This conclusion has been supported (and continues to be supported following the enactment of Law 44/2002) by the terms of art 1258 of the Spanish Civil Code that oblige contracting parties to comply not only with the conditions expressly contained in the relevant contract, but also with all other terms that may derive not only from good faith and usage, but also from applicable law. The remedies available to the client will therefore include those provided by the Spanish Commercial and Civil Codes for a breach of contract: the right to be indemnified for damages suffered. In this case, the statute of limitation will be 15 years from the date any such claim for breach of contract could have been exercised.

On the other hand, if the disclosure of the confidential information by a credit institution were made outside a specific contractual relationship, including in respect of information gathered from preliminary contacts not deriving from a contract or in respect of advisory services not provided in the context of a contractual relationship, the client would need to rely on the general principles of the Spanish law on tort. Under art 1902 of the Spanish Civil Code, any individual or entity causing damage to a third party due to actions taken or conduct performed knowingly or negligently is liable to indemnify such third party for the damage. Accordingly, the client would be allowed to be indemnified for the damage suffered due to the disclosure by the credit institution, in breach of its duty of professional diligence, of the information gathered. In this case, the statute of limitation will be one year from the date when the injured party became aware of the damage.

An administrative action by the Bank of Spain based on the disciplinary regime of Law 26/1988, as amended by Law 44/2002

[28.8] Protection of bank confidentiality through disciplinary measures has been developed by Law 44/2002. As mentioned above, Law 44/2002 has specified that the breach of the obligation of safeguarding confidential information will be deemed a serious offence under Law 26/1988. Pursuant to Law 26/1988, a serious offence may lead to the imposition of the following sanctions:

1   to the credit entity:
   (a) a public admonition published in the Spanish Official Gazette, and/or
   (b) a fine of up to 0.5% of its equity or up to 150,000 euros, whichever is higher;
2   to the responsible managers or members of the board:
   (a) a private admonition,
   (b) a public admonition,
   (c) a fine of up to 90,000 euros to each of the responsible managers or directors, or
   (d) a prohibition to act as managers or directors of a credit or financial entity, including, as the case may be, a temporary suspension from their respective offices not exceeding one year (this sanction can be imposed together with the aforementioned fine).

Law 26/1988 sets out several criteria to determine the actual sanction to be imposed from those capable of being chosen. Additionally, this law states that members of the board of a credit entity will be liable for serious offences except where (i) they have a justified reason for not attending the relevant meeting or voted against the relevant resolution from which the offence originated or (ii) the relevant offence is exclusively attributed to delegated bodies, general managers or other persons with powers in the credit entity.

A claim before the recently-created Commissioner for the Defence of Banking Services' Clients and the Commissioner for the Defence of the Investor

[28.9]   Law 44/2002 has also created the Commissioner for the Defence of Banking Services' Clients and the Commissioner for the Defence of the Investor, dependent, respectively, upon the Bank of Spain and the National Securities Market Commission. (An additional commissioner has been appointed for the insurance industry.) Royal Decree 303/2004 has implemented the provisions of Law 44/2002 by establishing the regulations governing these commissioners who are entrusted with the duty to protect the rights of consumers of financial services. They (i) consider any complaints made by consumers and users of financial services and forward them to the relevant supervisory bodies within the Bank of Spain or the National Securities Market Commission where a possible breach of transparency or client protection duties may exist and (ii) advise consumers and users of banking services on their rights in connection with transparency and client protection regulations. As a prerequisite for having access to the commissioners, the client must first file a claim before the clients' complaints desk that all credit entities and investment services companies are obliged to have or, as the case may be, before the clients' Ombudsman that any entity or group of entities may appoint.

Commissioners are appointed from persons with renowned prestige within the financial services industry who have at least ten years' professional experience. They are bodies that do not have executive functions and their decisions cannot be appealed.

Where a credit or investment services entity decides to appoint a clients' Ombudsman, the resolutions issued by the Ombudsman against the relevant entity will be binding. Law 44/2002 authorised the Ministry of Economy to develop the regulation on complaints desks and Ombudsman, which was implemented by Order ECO/734/2004 of 11 March on customer services and departments and the Ombudsman of credit entities.

An administrative action by the securities market regulator or Bank of Spain for breach of a provision protecting clients' interests

[28.10]　Finally, as stated above, securities market regulations in Spain impose on market participants – including credit institutions providing such services – an overall duty of confidentiality and the obligation to safeguard the information obtained in the course of providing those services. Regulations further impose on credit entities active in the securities market the obligation to abide by a code of conduct that includes the duty to maintain confidential details obtained from clients as to their financial situation, knowledge or expertise in investments and the purpose of the investment so as to comply with the obligation imposed on market participants to 'know your customer'. Failure by a credit institution to meet these obligations may qualify as a 'serious offence' or a 'less serious offence' punishable from a private caution up to a fine equal to 2% of the aggregate amount of share capital plus reserves of the entity, including suspension or limitation on activities in the market for a period of up to one year. Members of the board of the entity convicted of a 'serious offence' may receive a punishment themselves, varying from a public caution to a suspension from their post for a period of up to one year.

LIMITS

[28.11]　The principle of bank secrecy has been acknowledged and recognised by the Spanish courts, with an unquestionable legal and constitutional basis, a long time before its express recognition regarding pure banking activities pursuant to Law 44/2002.

Notwithstanding this, and as provided by the Spanish Constitutional Court and now recognised by Law 44/2002, it is not a right or principle without legal boundaries. In this section, we analyse the main limits to the principle of bank secrecy introduced by Spanish legislation. Law 44/2002 does not specify the limits of the principle of bank secrecy; on the contrary, it merely provides that these limits are those set out in law or by the consent of the affected client. Apart from the consent of the affected party, we may distinguish the following limits.

Limits deriving from the Spanish constitution

[28.12]　The Spanish Constitutional Court ruling of 26 November 1984, whilst confirming the right of clients to bank secrecy as part of their right to privacy, concluded that this was not an unlimited right, especially if it conflicted with another right deserving protection under the Spanish constitution. In the case at hand, the Constitutional Court ruled that the right of privacy was limited by the obligation of Spanish entities and individuals to support the general expenditure of the state by contributing to the tax system (art 31 of the Spanish constitution). The disclosure of bank account movements and transactions could thus be justified with the need to secure compliance with the obligation contained in art 31 of the constitution, provided that the appropriate legal measures were complied with so as to avoid any arbitrary and discretionary interference in the privacy of the individual. The summary decision of the Constitutional Court of 23 July 1986 confirmed the status of the principle of bank secrecy as part of the right of individuals and entities to their privacy with special constraints as regards the Spanish tax system.

Organic Law 1/1982 of 5 May also contemplated the existence of limits to the rights and principles contained in the Spanish constitution. In a general sense, it established that the rights protected by the constitution could be limited by laws and social custom. Thus, no illegal breach of the principle of privacy could be deemed to exist when an exception was contained in a law safeguarding the basic elements of the right and avoiding any possible discretionary or abusive use of the exception. In addition, the Organic Law included, as a further exception, the possibility that the beneficiary of the right consented to the interference in his privacy; if granted, this consent could be revoked at any time.

Tax-related limits

[28.13]   The scope of the principle of bank secrecy has been especially eroded when it has conflicted with Spanish tax legislation. In the ruling of 26 November 1984, the Constitutional Court admitted the right of the Spanish tax authorities to investigate bank accounts and their movements (with certain restrictions as explained below) provided the relevant conditions set out in law were complied with and such investigation was approved by the appropriate authorities.

Subsequent to the ruling of the Constitutional Court, the former General Tax Law 230/1963 of 28 December was modified by Law 10/1985 of 26 April. The amended art 111 of the former General Tax Law introduced the following new regulation:

1   a general principle under which credit entities could not rely on the principle of bank secrecy to deny compliance with a request for information duly submitted by the tax authorities; and
2   the following conditions having to be met by the tax authorities' request for information regarding account movements, deposit and credit accounts operations and, in general, banking transactions:
    (a)   the request would need to be authorised by the General Directorate of Tax or the territorial Delegate of the Treasury,
    (b)   the solicitation would need to determine the transaction subject to investigation,
    (c)   it would also need to identify the affected taxpayer, and
    (d)   set out the period of time to which the duty of disclosure applied.

Article 111 of the former General Tax Law was further amended by Law 31/1991 of 30 December to clarify and eventually extend the level of detail that the Spanish tax authorities could seek to obtain from Spanish credit institutions. In essence, the amendment included the possibility that the authorities could request the disclosure of payment orders and issue of cheques and, more importantly, information regarding the origin and destination of account movements, payment orders and cheques issued.

The new terms of art 111 of the former General Tax Law soon received criticism from scholars[8] because it granted power to the tax authorities to request information regarding the origin and destination of movements.

As a consequence, the Spanish Supreme Court, in a summons dated 30 September 1992, requested a ruling from the Constitutional Court on the latest amendment to art 111 arguing a possible breach of the doctrine established by the Constitutional Court's judgment of 26 November 1984. The Supreme Court stated that the breach would have been committed in defining the level of information that could be gathered from clients when reviewing bank statements and account movements.

According to the Constitutional Court's ruling of 26 November 1984, although conditions and requirements would need to be introduced by law to ensure that the tax authorities did not conduct discretionary interferences with individuals' privacy, the disclosure by credit entities of bank statements would not breach the right to privacy under the constitution since those statements would only provide generic information of the underlying transactions, not the particular details of such transactions, including their motives or considerations.

Based on this ruling, the Supreme Court hinted at the possibility that the obligation contained in the revised art 111 to disclose the origin and destination of account movements and payment orders could be considered an obligation to release not only generic information about transactions, but their particular details and underlying motives as well, information that could be protected by the Spanish constitutional right to privacy.

Unfortunately, the Constitutional Court's judgment of 28 June 1994 did not clarify this important issue. It did, however, declare unconstitutional the last amendment introduced in art 111 of the former General Tax Law based on a formal rather than substantive defect: the inappropriateness of an annual budget law (such as Law 31/1991 for the annual budget of 1992) permanently to regulate issues with effect beyond the state incomes and expenses of the fiscal year in question.

Notwithstanding the above, the Spanish legislator took into consideration the concerns of the Spanish Supreme Court and those of scholars who had argued against the revised text of art 111 of the former General Tax Law. The last amendment to the former General Tax Law introduced by Law 25/1995 of 20 July clarified that the requests for information regarding the 'origin' and 'destination' of account movements and payment orders should only cover the identity of the persons or accounts being the origin and destination of such movements or payments. In this regard, the most recent General Tax Law (Law 58/2003 of 17 December), which abrogates the former General Tax Law and was enacted in 2003, has confirmed the approach of the aforementioned amendment in its new art 93.

Within the tax field, the obligation to keep confidential information obtained by the authorities and public officials and servants in connection with the management of taxes (subject to the limits stated by law) has also been recognised by Law 1/1998 of

---

8 See eg P M Herrera Molina and A de Prada García *Los preceptos de la LGT modificados por leyes de presupuestos: ¿una bomba de relojería jurídica? (Comentario a la cuestión de inconstitucionalidad sobre los arts 111.3 y 128.5 de la LGT)*, Revista de Derecho Financiero y Hacienda Pública, no 227, p 823 ff.

26 February, which regulates the rights of taxpayers. Furthermore, Law 1/1998 establishes a general duty vested on officials or civil servants to keep absolutely secret confidential data concerning taxpayers, subject only to exceptions provided by law.

The duty to provide information to the Spanish courts

[28.14]   The principle of bank secrecy has been further restricted by the obligation imposed in art 18 of Organic Law 6/1985 of 1 July on the judicial power upon public and private entities or persons to provide assistance, in the manner provided by law, to the judiciary in the development of judicial functions.

Therefore, banking entities will be subject to the general requirements contained in the Spanish courts' procedural rules to assist the civil and criminal courts in their activities. As regards the Bank of Spain specifically, notwithstanding the fact that Royal Legislative Decree 1298/1986 of 28 June, as amended by Law 3/1994 of 14 April, only obliges the Bank of Spain to comply with requests for information from the civil courts in connection with insolvency and bankruptcy proceedings (see above), it seems clear that the Central Bank will be equally obliged to assist the civil courts in all other types of proceedings.

Similarly, as regards the securities markets and services provided by credit entities in their connection, art 81 of Law 24/1988 has expressly provided that entities active in the market shall be exempt from their duty of confidentiality in respect of the information requested by the administrative authorities or the judiciary in accordance with the law.

In respect of the assistance due to the civil courts, art 330 of the Civil Procedural Law establishes the obligation on third party entities (including credit entities) that are not party to a civil litigation to disclose private documents when, at the request of one of the litigants, the court understands the disclosure of such documentation to be relevant in order to render its judgment. The court shall hear the affected credit entity holding the relevant information and issue a summary ruling in that connection. The party requested by the court can claim that the documents are not removed so that they may be disclosed to, and inspected by, the secretary of the court in the place where they are deposited. If, on the other hand, the credit institution is a party to the litigation, the documents will need to be disclosed and the proceedings referred to above will not apply.

As regards criminal proceedings, Spanish law establishes the obligation without limitation of third parties to disclose any information requested from a criminal court. The court will, however, be obliged to take the necessary measures to protect the secrecy and privacy of the requested third party if the data held by such party was eventually not of interest for the relevant criminal investigation. Organic Law 6/1985 sets out the general principles for international judicial co-operation in Spain when no international treaty is applicable. According to art 276, Spanish courts will obtain judicial assistance from foreign courts through a formal request addressed to the Justice Ministry that will forward it, via the Foreign Affairs Ministry and the relevant Spanish Embassy, to the competent authorities. Articles 277 and 278 oblige the Spanish courts to assist foreign judicial authorities, provided that the following conditions are met:

1   Spanish courts benefit from the same assistance in the jurisdiction making the request;

2   the proceedings or the subject matter of the request do not fall within the exclusive jurisdiction of the Spanish courts;

3   the contents of the activity to be carried out fall within the competence of the relevant Spanish court (if this is not the case, the latter will forward the request to the competent court and inform the requesting foreign judicial authority);

4   the request meets all the necessary prerequisites of authenticity; and

5   the request is not contrary to Spanish public policy.

As regards international treaties and in respect of civil matters, Spain is a party to the Hague Convention on the Taking of Evidence Abroad in Civil or Commercial Matters 1970 and the Convention of the Interamerican Conference on Rogatory Letters 1975. On matters of criminal proceedings, Spain is a party to the European Convention on Judicial Assistance on Criminal Matters 1954.

In connection with injunctions issued by the courts, arts 590 and 591 of the Civil Procedural Law allow the courts to request from financial institutions information about the assets of a litigating party so that these may be subject to a freezing order before the final outcome of court proceedings. Certain case law has determined the obligation of the courts, prior to issuing any injunction, to determine the identity, exact nature and details of the accounts opened by the affected litigant and the amounts that must be subject to the relevant freezing order.[9] Nevertheless, Spanish courts have in the past issued all-embracing injunction orders affecting all accounts (and their sums) opened by the relevant litigant in all and every branch of the credit entity affected (there have been cases in which the courts have delivered injunction orders to the Bankers' Association for them to have effect on all associated credit entities).

The supervision of the Bank of Spain and the securities market regulator (National Securities Market Commission)

[28.15]   The principle of bank secrecy has been further restricted by the prudential supervision exercised over credit institutions by the Bank of Spain and, as regards services provided in connection with the securities markets, the National Securities Market Commission ('CNMV'). Law 26/1988 of 29 July has granted the Bank of Spain overall responsibility for the supervision and inspection of credit entities established in Spain and branches of foreign credit entities opened in the Spanish territory (with limits as regards branches of EU credit entities).

Law 26/1988 and its developing secondary legislation have set out the disclosure and information requirements regarding accountancy that credit entities must provide to the Bank of Spain on a periodical basis so that it may carry out its supervisory functions. Circular 4/2004 of 22 December of the Bank of Spain has detailed the procedures, principles and level of information that credit entities will need to comply with as regards the keeping of their accounts. Article 4 of the Circular sets out the information that must be sent periodically to Bank of Spain, art 72 establishes the obligation of credit entities to have those procedures and information available to

---

9 See eg resolution of the first instance judge no 7 of Palma de Mallorca of 16 June 1998. This resolution was subsequently overturned by the Provincial Court of the Balearic Islands on 3 February 1999, which ruled that all-embracing injunction orders affecting all accounts in a relevant credit entity could be issued without identifying the details of the accounts.

the Bank of Spain for its supervision and inspection and the First Additional Provision of the Circular further empowers the Bank of Spain to request from credit entities any information additional to the periodical data submitted by credit entities that is deemed necessary to clarify or detail the information received or for any other purpose connected to the prudential supervision of credit entities.

In addition to the terms of Law 26/1988 and as part of the supervisory role of the Bank of Spain, Law 13/1992 of 1 June and its developing secondary legislation have detailed the solvency and capital requirements that credit entities in Spain, on a consolidated basis, will need to comply with in line with the requirements of Council Directives 89/299/EEC, 89/646/EEC, 89/647/EEC and 92/30/EEC. This legislation, which has been further complemented by Law 5/2005 of 22 April on supervision of financial conglomerates and Royal Decree 1332/2005 of 11 November, also determines the level of information to be provided periodically to the Bank of Spain so that it can supervise compliance with capital adequacy ratios and investment limits as regards large risks that can be taken by a consolidated group of credit entities.

Failure by credit entities to comply with the above disclosure obligations towards the Bank of Spain may be considered, depending on the importance of the information not delivered and the particular circumstances of each case, a 'very serious offence' or a 'serious offence' punishable by a public caution to the imposition of a fine up to 1% of the equity or even the loss of the licence to operate as a credit entity. Members of the board of the affected entity will also be deemed responsible if they acted with knowledge or negligence and could be penalised with a wide variety of punishments ranging from a fine of up to 150,000 euros to a prohibition to act as a director or manager of a credit entity for a period of up to ten years.

It has been debated by scholars whether the seemingly all-embracing obligation of disclosure contained in Law 26/1988, Law 13/1992, Law 5/2005 and Royal Decree 1332/2005 should include the particularities of transactions entered into by credit entities with third party clients.[10] In this context, scholars have argued against the duty of full disclosure based on the terms of the old, but still in force, art 49 of the Banking Law of 31 December 1946, which obliged banks to collaborate with the Central Bank in its supervisory functions without having to disclose details of particular transactions and operations. It seems, in the present writer's opinion, that art 49 of the Banking Law should not serve today as a limit to the extensive powers of investigation and supervision vested in the Bank of Spain by the aforementioned regulations. The prudential supervision of the Bank of Spain, especially as regards the solvency of credit entities, is a key element to safeguard the interests of end consumers in the banking sector and constitutes the basis of the principle of recognition of other EU member state resident entities.

As regards protection of personal data, the recently enacted Law 44/2002 has amended the legal regime applicable to the central credit risk information gathering service of the Bank of Spain adapting its regime to the general rules contained in Organic Law 15/1999 of 13 December on protection of personal data. Based on the new regulation, the declaring entities (mainly credit entities and the Bank of Spain) are obliged to communicate to the Bank of Spain all data necessary to identify the persons with whom credit risks exist and the characteristics of these persons and risks. In turn, all declaring entities have the right to request and obtain from the Bank

---

10 See eg M J Guillén Ferrer *El secreto bancario. Sus límites legales*, Valencia 1997, p 237.

of Spain reports on any given person, provided that this person (i) has some kind of risk with the requesting entity, (ii) has requested a loan or a similar transaction or (iii) is a guarantor or main debtor in any payment document or obligation which the relevant entity is considering to acquire. The declaring entities are obliged to keep confidential all information obtained from the Bank of Spain, which must be solely used for the purposes of evaluating risks or granting credits. In addition, the communication of risk information by the declaring entities to third parties (other than the Bank of Spain) is prohibited, except if (i) made with the express consent of the affected party or (ii) if the relevant data refers to legal entities and is communicated to a financial entity pertaining to the same consolidated group as the declaring entity or (iii) if the data referring to an individual or natural physical persons is necessary to be communicated to any other financial entity pertaining to the same consolidated group for purposes of compliance with risk concentration and equity ratios regulations. The Bank of Spain also has a duty to ensure the confidentiality of its recorded data. However, communication of this data by the Bank of Spain to other foreign supervisory bodies is permitted, provided that similar protections to those granted by Spanish regulations exist in the receiving countries.

In the securities markets, credit entities are allowed by virtue of Law 24/1988 of 28 July to perform all activities that securities companies and agencies are capable of performing as duly licensed entities to operate in the Spanish securities markets (see above). In this respect, and as provided by art 84 of Law 24/1988, credit entities will be subject to the supervision of the CNMV in the course of carrying out activities and providing services in the securities markets. Thus, banks, savings banks, branches of foreign entities and credit entities providing services in Spain without a permanent establishment will need to abide by the rules of conduct contained in Law 24/1988 as developed by secondary legislation and will be subject to the supervision of the CNMV. Article 85 of Law 24/1988 empowers the CNMV to request all information deemed necessary from market participants obliging them to make available to the CNMV and even giving publicity, if so requested, to registers, documents and books. The CNMV is further empowered to carry out inspections considered necessary over entities active in the securities market subject to its supervision. In turn, art 90 of Law 24/1988 sets out that all information collected by the CNMV as regards their supervision and inspection functions will be subject to professional secrecy and safeguarded. However, there are certain exceptions to this general obligation of secrecy:

1 when the affected party has expressly agreed to such disclosure;
2 when the data has been aggregated with other information for mere statistical purposes;
3 when the information has been requested from a criminal or civil court (although in the latter case, supervisory requirements of the relevant investment services company must be kept secret);
4 information requested by the judicial authorities in connection with a bankruptcy/insolvency proceeding of an investment services company (provided the information does not relate to third parties involved in the relaunching of the bankrupt or insolvent company);
5 information requested by a court or administrative authority in respect of disciplinary proceedings;
6 information released to the Spanish regional governments, the Bank of Spain and other regulatory and supervisory bodies in Spain for them to perform their duties, including auditors;
7 information that may be needed to prevent money laundering activities;

8   information requested by a parliamentary investigation committee;

9   information released by the CNMV to supervisory bodies of foreign countries, provided that reciprocity exists and rules of secrecy are similar to those applicable in Spain;

10   information provided by the CNMV to Spanish settlement and clearing systems, provided it is aimed at allowing the correct operation of any such systems;

11   information released with the prior authorisation of the Ministry of Economy to the tax authorities in accordance with, and subject to, the conditions set out in art 93 of the General Tax Law (Law 58/2003 of 17 December); and

12   information provided by the CNMV to the Ministry of Economy or Spanish regional governments.

Restrictions contained in provisions aimed at avoiding money laundering

[28.16]   Law 19/1993 of 28 December (as amended by Law 19/2003 of 4 July) implemented Council Directives 91/308/EEC and 2001/97/EC on the prevention of money laundering in Spain. This Law also reflects the recommendations set out by the Financial Action Task Force on Money Laundering, of which Spain has been a member since 1994. According to the Law and Royal Decree 925/1995 of 9 June, as amended by Royal Decree 54/2005 of 21 January, credit entities are obliged to disclose to the Executive Service of the Commission for the Prevention of Money Laundering information in respect of:

1   any transaction where there are indications or certainty that it is connected with any crime punishable by more than three years' imprisonment;

2   any transaction that points to an obvious lack of correspondence with the nature, turnover or operational background of the clients, provided there is no apparent reason;

3   any transaction involving physical cash movements or cheques issued by credit entities exceeding 30,000 euros;

4   any transactions exceeding the above amount with counterparties resident in territories or countries designated for these purposes by an Order of the Ministry of Economy and the Treasury, as well as any transactions to or from such territories or countries regardless of the place of residence of the parties involved; and

5   any transactions listed in the applicable provisions of this regulation upon the proposal of the Commission on Prevention of Money Laundering and Financial Crime. No applicable provisions implementing this regulation have yet been enacted, but they could see the light of day in the future.

In principle, the information delivered to the Executive Service will need to include the identity of the parties to the transaction (including the beneficial participants), the known business activity of the persons involved in the transaction and the correlation between the activity and the transaction, the nature, amounts, dates and place of performance of the operation, the activities performed by the reporters in order to investigate the reported transactions, any indicative circumstances of the illegal origin or that points to a lack of economic, professional or business justification for the activities and any other relevant data as determined by the Executive Service.

Failure to report is considered a very serious offence. Article 9 of Law 19/1993 provides that the following sanctions may be imposed when very serious offences are committed:

1   a public warning;
2   a fine, the minimum amount being 90,151.82 euros and the maximum being the higher of 5% of the equity capital of the institution, twice the monetary value of the operation or 1,502,530.26 euros;
3   in the case of entities subject to administrative authorisation for their operation, the revocation of such authorisation.

The sanction provided for in subparagraph 2, which is mandatory in every case, will be imposed, together with one of those provided for in subparagraphs 1 and 3.

In addition to the sanction imposed on the entity for the commission of very serious offences, one or more of the following sanctions may be imposed on the persons who, holding posts of administration or management in the entity, were responsible for the offence:

1   a fine for each person of between 60,101.21 and 601,012.10 euros;
2   dismissal from their position and barred from holding posts of administration or management in the same entity for a maximum period of five years;
3   dismissal from their position and barred from holding posts of administration or management in any entity subject to this Law for a maximum period of ten years.

The sanction provided for in subparagraph 1, which is mandatory in every case, may be applied, together with one of those provided for in subparagraphs 2 and 3.

Law 19/1993 also provides a prohibition against 'tipping off', which means that financial institutions, their directors, officers and employees are prohibited from disclosing either to the customer or to third persons that information has been transmitted to the Executive Service or that a transaction is being investigated for a possible link to money laundering. Failure to comply with this obligation is considered a very serious offence.

The statute of limitations in respect of very serious offences is five years.

Law 19/1993 specifically exempts credit entities from any liability towards clients for any breach of their duty of confidentiality deriving from a contract or otherwise at the time of making, in good faith, the relevant disclosures provided in the Law. With regard to terrorism, Spain is also a party to the International Convention for the Suppression of the Financing of Terrorism enacted in New York in 1999, which refers to rules similar to those set out in Law 19/1993 already in force; a similar regulation is also contained in Law 12/2003 of 21 May on the prevention and blocking of terrorist financing.

Royal Decree 338/1990 of 9 March, which regulates the tax identity number, sets out certain limits to the confidentiality of banking transactions establishing that credit entities must request the tax identity number of persons requesting cash payment of bank drafts issued by a credit entity or any third party (provided, in the last case, that the amount cashed exceeds €3,005 euros). Credit entities are also obliged to communicate to the tax authorities all drafts issued against cash, goods or securities, except those issued against a bank account.

Limits deriving from auditing regulations

[28.17]   As regards limits deriving from auditing regulations, Law 19/1988 of 12 July on auditing states that companies subject to audits are obliged to provide any and all information required by the auditor to perform the audit of their financial statements. Having taken into account that, pursuant to law, credit entities must audit their financial statements, in certain circumstances, the obligation vested on audited credit entities to comply with the requests made by the external auditor may be considered an exception to the duty of secrecy.

Restrictions set out in connection with parliamentary investigation committees

[28.18]   The regulation governing parliamentary investigation committees also imposes certain limits on the principle of bank secrecy stating that financial entities, as well as the tax authorities, must submit any data or information requested by a parliamentary investigation committee, provided that:

1   the data refers to persons holding or having held an office as senior officials in the government, public administration, public entities or companies controlled by the public administration;
2   the investigation is related to the duties performed by the relevant person; and
3   the committee understands that it would not be possible to complete the investigation without such data and information.

Restrictions contained in the regulations for the defence of competition

[28.19]   Finally, it is worth mentioning the wide scope of the powers of inspection vested by Law 16/1989 of 17 July on the Service for the Defence of Competition, the administrative body entrusted with the investigation of concentrations of a significant size and conduct that may limit or restrict competition in the Spanish market or constitute an abuse of dominant position. In the course of investigations, officers of the Service may also request an oral explanation in situ. According to art 33 of Law 16/1989, officers of the Service are empowered to investigate, obtain copies and even retain, for a maximum period of ten days, documents, books and records, in whatever medium, that are deemed necessary for the due application of the Law. Legal entities and individuals are obliged to collaborate with the Service making the requested documents and data available to that administrative body. Obstructing the investigation may lead to the imposition of fines up to 1% of the turnover of the immediately preceding financial year.

SPECIAL REFERENCE TO THE SECURITIES MARKET REGULATIONS

[28.20]   We have already mentioned the obligation contained in art 81 of Law 24/1988 on participants in the Spanish securities market to maintain the confidentiality of, and safeguard, information gathered whilst providing services so that it cannot be improperly used by third parties, without prejudice to reporting to and fulfilling their co-operation duties with the judicial and administrative bodies. Any such individual or entity shall adopt appropriate measures to avoid any abusive or unfair use of the information and, if it cannot be avoided, to remedy the consequences arising from such abusive or unfair use.

In addition to the above, art 81 of Law 24/1988 has implemented in Spain Council Directive 89/592/EEC and prohibited the abusive use of so-called 'inside information'.

Subject to certain exceptions, art 81 generally precludes any party or person having inside information (and who acknowledges or who, at least, should have acknowledged the special nature of such information) from carrying out the following activities, directly or indirectly, on their own behalf or on behalf of a third party:

1   to prepare or enter into a transaction in the market regarding the securities to which the information refers or financial instruments or contracts related to these securities (subject to certain exceptions, such as the design of the transaction which constitutes the inside information or any other transactions made pursuant to the applicable regulations);

2   to communicate such information to third parties except in the ordinary course of their employment, profession, post or duties;

3   to recommend to a third party to purchase or dispose of such securities, financial instruments or contracts or to encourage that any other third party purchases or disposes of such securities, financial instruments or contracts based on such information.

Article 81 of Law 24/1988 defines 'inside information' as any information that, being specific and referring to one or various issuers of securities, financial instruments or contracts or to one or various securities, financial instruments or contracts, is not public and, had it been made public, could have influenced an investor's decision and hence the price in the market (or organised trading system) of the relevant security or securities, financial instruments or contracts in any significant manner. This definition also applies to negotiable securities or other financial instruments for which the listing in an organised market or trading system has been requested.

Article 99 of Law 24/1988 considers any breach of the prohibition contained in art 81 as a 'very serious offence'. In addition, Organic Law 10/1995 introduced for the first time a criminal offence regarding the use of inside information. According to art 285, any individual with confidential information that may be relevant for the quoted price of a listed security to which he may have had access in the course of a professional or business activity is precluded from using it or disclosing it to a third party with the intention of obtaining a benefit or causing a loss of 450,759 euros or more. The offence is punishable with imprisonment of one to six years and a fine of up to three times the benefit obtained or ranging between 432 and 215,367.20 euros.

Finally, Law 24/1988 considers the problem of information gathered by professionals providing a variety of services in the securities market and the possibility that such information be released or be available through different departments where conflicts of interest could arise. In this regard, art 83 of Law 24/1988, as amended by Law 44/2002, obliges market participants, including those merely providing investment advisory services, to ensure that information gathered through the performance of an activity is not accessible directly or indirectly by the staff of the same entity employed in another activity, thus eliminating possible conflicts of interest.

Furthermore, in order to prevent any leaking of inside information and to safeguard all confidential information before it is disclosed to the public, art 83 bis of Law 24/1988, introduced by Law 44/2002, imposes certain duties on the issuers of securities during the phase of study and decision on the structure of any transaction, including, inter alia, (i) limiting the number of persons dealing with the inside information, (ii) setting up measures to preserve the security of the information flow,

(iii) maintaining updated records of the persons having had access to the inside information or (iv) informing these persons of their confidentiality duties.

These provisions supplemented those previously established by Royal Decree 629/1993 defining a general code of conduct which is mandatory on entities acting in the securities markets, including credit entities, by virtue of which the appropriate 'Chinese Walls' in respect of different departments providing different services in the securities markets need to be introduced to ensure that no flow of information between departments is possible and, thus, ensuring that final investment decisions are taken by each department separately.

CONCLUSION

[28.21]   Although in the past banking secrecy has been recognised by scholars and the Spanish courts with unquestionable legal and constitutional basis, it was not until the enactment of Law 44/2002 that banking secrecy was specifically recognised by positive legislation.

Although it is not expressly provided for in the applicable legislation, it is commonly understood that the principle of bank secrecy covers the following information:

1   everything gathered by the bank whilst entering into particular and usual banking transactions, including balances, operations and any other clients' transactions; and
2   all factual information and opinions surpassing the economic terms of the particular transaction entered into or service provided to the client that may be of a personal or economic nature and that must be deemed to have been released by the clients to their banker in the context of their professional relationship.

However, this right of banking secrecy, connected to the right to privacy as protected by the Spanish constitution, is not unlimited. The most evident of these limits is the will of the affected client, who may in any case allow for the secrecy to be lifted. In addition, the law provides for additional limitations to banking secrecy; among those, we may highlight the limits derived from the Spanish constitution, the tax regulations, the duty to co-operate with the Spanish courts and regulatory authorities and, more recently, from the regulations aimed at preventing money laundering.

29   Sweden

André Andersson
Daniel Jönsson

INTRODUCTION

[29.1]   Bank confidentiality has a long tradition in Sweden dating back to the seventeenth century. Its main purpose is to protect customers who have a need for confidentiality, primarily regarding trade secrets, but also regarding personal circumstances.

However, not only customers gain from bank confidentiality. Trust and mutual confidence between banks and their customers are essential to banking business and confidentiality is a necessary condition. Bank confidentiality thus serves an important purpose in banking business and thereby supports not only the interests of the customers, but also the interests of the banks, the business community and the public at large.

Bank confidentiality may, however, be misused in order to conceal criminal behaviour. The public thus also has an interest in limiting bank confidentiality and therefore Swedish rules have been provided with several exceptions. The current rules on bank confidentiality attempt to balance the duty of loyalty to customers to keep information about them confidential on the one hand and the interest of the public to disclose criminal behaviour on the other.

THE NATURE AND EXTENT OF BANK CONFIDENTIALITY

The general rule on bank confidentiality

[29.2]   Swedish bank confidentiality is partly founded on a contractual basis and partly stipulated by law. The general statutory rule is found in the Banking and Financing Business Act (*Lag* (2004:297) *om Bank-och Finansieringsrörelse*, 'BFBA'), Ch 1, s 10: 'the relations of individuals to a bank may not be disclosed without legal cause'.

There is no further legislation regarding bank confidentiality and there are very few precedents. Legal literature contains only a few works in this area.

The rule is only applicable to the private sector. Confidentiality in the public sector is governed by the Secrecy Act (*Sekretesslagen* (1980:100)), which, however, will not be discussed in this chapter.

Many issues regarding confidentiality are solved internally in the banks and it should be noted that Swedish banks in general have a good reputation for following the rules on confidentiality. The banks are supervised by the Swedish Financial Supervisory Authority (*Finansinspektionen*, 'FSA').

A customer of the bank

[29.3]   The expression 'the relations of individuals to a bank' refers to the relations of individual persons and entities in the bank's capacity as a bank. The individuals and entities referred to shall be customers of the bank's banking business. Thus, information relating to, for example, the bank's employees, landlords and lawyers does not fall within the scope of bank confidentiality.

The bank is prevented from disclosing the relations between the bank and its customers. The bank is also prevented from disclosing the fact that an individual is a customer of the bank. If an individual ceases to be a customer of the bank, the bank still has an obligation to keep the information confidential. A person who negotiates or has been negotiating with the bank about becoming a customer shall, as regards bank confidentiality, be treated as a person who is or has been a customer of the bank.

Information covered by confidentiality

[29.4]   Information is covered by bank confidentiality if the individual typically may have a reason to consider it as confidential and may wish to keep it confidential. The rule is vague and it is often hard to establish whether certain information should be treated as confidential. If there is uncertainty, the bank should consider the information as confidential.

Confidentiality covers the relations between the individual and the bank. However, the word 'between' should not be interpreted narrowly; confidentiality covers all information concerning the relationship. The information covered by bank confidentiality is normally of an economic or financial character. However, information of a more personal nature is also covered.

Information which an officer of the bank receives from the customer in his capacity as an employee of the bank is naturally covered by the confidentiality. In addition, the confidentiality covers information which the officer has learned about in a way other than in his capacity as an employee of the bank. The confidentiality also covers information not expressly given by the customer to the bank, but which the bank has been able to obtain through observations or conclusions. The rules on confidentiality thus apply regardless of how the bank has obtained the information.

Information known to the general public

[29.5]   Bank confidentiality does not cover information already known to the general public or known to a substantial number of persons, nor does the confidentiality cover information which anyone is able to obtain easily.

Disclosure or use of the information

[29.6]   According to the wording of the statutory rule on bank confidentiality, the bank may not disclose relations between the bank and an individual. However, it is also clear that the bank may not use the information in any other way if such use may be in conflict with the customer's interests. If the bank unlawfully uses the information, the bank is liable for any damage the customer suffers, regardless of whether the information is also disclosed to a third party.

Bank confidentiality prohibits all possible kinds of disclosures, such as the handing out of documents, as well as giving oral information.

THE REMEDIES AVAILABLE

Generally on available remedies

[29.7]   The obligation to keep certain information confidential is civil. Thus, a breach of the obligation is not a criminal offence. The main remedy is a liability for damages imposed on the bank and its officers. It should also be noted that the bank may take disciplinary action under Swedish labour law against an employee if the employee breaches the rules on bank confidentiality.

The bank's liability for damages

[29.8]   The wording of the rule in the BFBA does not state who has the obligation to keep certain information confidential. However, it is absolutely clear that the bank has this obligation. This means that the bank is primarily liable for economic damage resulting from a breach of confidentiality committed by any of the bank's bodies (for example, the board of directors or senior management). The bank is also vicariously liable for damage resulting from breaches committed by another person if the bank is responsible for such person's actions. This includes employees assisting customers (such as employees in the securities brokerage business) and employees who in their employment learn about the customers' relations with the bank in any other way. Normally, the bank is also liable if a person commits a breach of the confidentiality after he has left his employment with the bank. However, the bank is not liable for damage if the shareholders or auditors disclose confidential information.

In most cases, liability for damage presupposes wilfulness or negligence. However, it has been debated in legal literature whether the bank should be liable even if it has not caused the damage wilfully or by negligence, ie that the liability should be strict. There are no precedents and the extent of the banks' liability is therefore unclear.

Other parties' liability for damages

[29.9]   In addition to the bank, a number of other persons have an obligation to keep certain information confidential. Among these are founders, trustees, members of the board of directors, delegates, liquidators and auditors. All members of the board of directors have this liability (including employee representatives and board members appointed by the government). The chief executive officer is liable either as a member of the board or as a delegate. In addition, the shareholders have an obligation to keep information confidential.

All of the aforementioned persons have a legal obligation to keep certain information confidential. However, only some of them also have a liability for damages to a third party if they breach the obligation. The rules on liability for damages to customers of a bank are found in the Savings Bank Act (*Sparbankslag* (1987:619)) and the Act on Membership Banks (*Lag* (1995:1570) *om medlemsbanker*) and are only applicable in relation to savings banks and membership banks. As regards banks which are incorporated as limited liability companies, which is the case for the majority of banks in Sweden, there are no rules on damages to customers payable by the different directors and representatives of a bank for breaches of the rules on bank confidentiality. It is thus not possible for a customer who has suffered damage resulting from a breach of bank confidentiality by a bank incorporated as a limited liability company to claim for damages from anyone else but the bank.

The liability of a founder, member of the board of directors, chief executive officer or delegate of a savings bank arises if they wilfully or negligently contravene the Savings Bank Act or the BFBA (including the rule on bank confidentiality) and thereby cause damage to a customer. The same applies in a membership bank where a member of the board or a delegate is liable for damage if they wilfully or negligently contravene the Act on Membership Banks or the BFBA (including the rule on bank confidentiality).

The auditors of a membership bank or savings bank are liable for damage caused by them through a wilful or negligent contravention of the BFBA (including the rule on bank confidentiality). Where an accounting firm is auditor, both the firm and the auditor principally responsible for the audit shall be liable for such damage.

As is the case for the directors and other representatives of banks which are incorporated as limited liability companies, it is not possible for a customer of such bank to receive damages from a bank auditor should the auditor disclose information covered by bank confidentiality.

A member of a membership bank or a person who is entitled to vote without being a member of the membership bank has a liability for damage caused by him through a wilful or grossly negligent contravention of, among other statutes, the BFBA (including the rule on bank confidentiality). However, members rarely obtain information covered by confidentiality. It should be noted that if information becomes widespread among a large number of members (for example, at a general meeting), the information will lose its confidential character:

> 'A member of a membership bank or a person entitled to vote without being a member is liable for the damage which he, wilfully or by gross negligence, causes the membership bank, another member or any other person by being an accessory to a contravention of this Act, the Capital Adequacy Act (*Lag* (1994:2004) *om kapitaltäckning och stora exponeringar för kreditinstitut och värdepappersbolag*), the applicable act on annual accounts, the BFBA or the statutes.'[1]

Shareholders of banks, which are incorporated as limited liability companies, do not have any liability to pay damages to customers should the shareholders disclose information covered by bank confidentiality.

Naturally, other employees and officers of the bank also have an obligation to keep information confidential. Normally, however, they do not have a liability for damage towards the customers if they breach the obligation.

Third parties do not have any obligation to keep information confidential.

Reduction of awarded damages

[29.10] The liability to pay damages under the Savings Bank Act or the Act on Membership Banks described above may under certain circumstances be reduced

---

1 Act on Membership Banks, Ch 11, s 3.

having regard to the nature of the action, the extent of the damage caused and other circumstances.

Joint and several liability for damages

[29.11] The liability to pay damages under the Savings Bank Act or the Act on Membership Banks is joint and several if more than one person is liable for the damage according to the rules described above. If someone, due to a joint and several liability for the damage, pays more than his share of the damages, he is entitled to reasonable reimbursement from the other liable persons.

EXCEPTIONS
General

[29.12] The main purpose of bank confidentiality is to protect the interests of the individual customers and the banks. However, these interests are to an increasing extent being balanced by the risk that the confidentiality may be used to conceal illegal behaviour. The public interest to prevent this has therefore resulted in a large number of exceptions to the obligation to keep information confidential.

According to the general rule on bank confidentiality, information may not be disclosed without legal cause. There are a large number of situations when 'legal cause' must be considered to exist. These exceptions cover, first, where there is an obligation for the bank to disclose certain information and, secondly, where the bank has a right to disclose information, even though there is no obligation to do so.

Consent from the customer

[29.13] Bank confidentiality mainly exists in order to protect the customers and the bank may disclose information if the customer gives his consent. A consent may be withdrawn at any time.

If a bank's obligation to maintain confidentiality had been based merely on a contractual relationship, the banks could have been able to disregard the confidentiality obligation wholly through agreements with their customers. However, bank confidentiality also exists on a statutory basis and not all kinds of 'consents' or agreements may set the obligation of confidentiality aside. For instance, a bank may not in advance, through clauses in standard forms or in general terms, remove itself from the obligation of confidentiality. Such 'consents' would probably not be considered valid. However, a customer may in a specific case give his consent for the bank to disclose certain information, for example, Internet banking.

Information handled internally within the bank

[29.14] A bank has to handle information (including confidential information) internally in order to carry out its ordinary business. This is not in conflict with the obligation of confidentiality as long as it is done in the bank's duty of loyalty. This could involve disclosure of information by officers to the management, within the management or by the bank to its auditor.

However, if the information were to be distributed generally within the bank, the information would lose its confidential character. Such distribution is in conflict with

653

the obligation of confidentiality and it is therefore necessary to keep confidential information within a limited group of persons in the bank.

Information exchanged between a parent bank and a subsidiary may be handled in the same way as information distributed within the bank.

Information provided by a bank to an outsourced part of its business is subject to the general rule and may not be disclosed without legal cause, which is assessed on a case-by-case basis, taking into consideration the obligation for the entity, to which certain services are outsourced, to keep the information confidential and whether the relevant entity is conducting any other business and the possibility for such entity to abuse the information.

The Financial Supervisory Authority

[29.15] The FSA promotes stability and efficiency in the Swedish financial market. The FSA supervises banks and other financial institutions and monitors, for example, the banks' compliance with applicable legislation. The FSA may, when carrying out its supervisory functions, request the banks to provide the FSA with necessary information. The banks must, if requested to do so, disclose the information regardless of bank confidentiality.

A bank authorised in another jurisdiction is primarily supervised by the competent authority in the bank's home jurisdiction. However, the FSA also supervises Swedish branches of foreign banks and banks that conduct cross-border activities in Sweden in co-operation with the competent authorities in such banks' home jurisdictions. Swedish banks may in a similar way also be supervised by the competent authorities in other jurisdictions, even if the primary responsibility rests with the FSA. Swedish bank confidentiality does not prevent banks from providing the FSA and/or other competent authorities with requested information.

If a bank is part of a group, the other companies of the group shall also disclose information, regardless of bank confidentiality, if requested to do so by the FSA. The same applies when part of a bank's business has been outsourced and the company, to which the business has been outsourced, is requested by the FSA to disclose information. The information obtained shall, as a general rule, be kept confidential by the FSA. The FSA may, however, provide the competent authorities in other states in the EEA with information, regardless of this confidentiality.

Information to the tax authorities

[29.16] The tax authorities have been given extensive powers to obtain information from banks in order to make it possible for the tax authorities to perform their work and to make tax control more efficient.

The Swedish system for simplified tax returns is based on the fact that the banks, among others, provide the tax authorities with information. This has resulted in extensive obligations for the banks to provide the tax authorities with information regarding interest, capital balance and nominee shares. In addition, the tax authorities can request a bank to provide them with information regarding the legal relations between the bank and an individual. The tax authorities do not have to suspect any illegal behaviour, nor is it a prerequisite for the request that the interest of the tax authorities to obtain information in any objective way is considered to outweigh the customer's interest of confidentiality. These obligations also apply to foreign banks and other foreign companies conducting financing and insurance activities in Sweden through a branch or another permanent establishment:

> 'The tax authority may order anyone, who is or may be required to maintain accounting records ... to give a statement of a transaction between him and someone else or disclose a document or submit a copy of a document which concerns the transaction.'[2]

The obligation to give the above-described information is also applicable to foreign banks and other foreign companies conducting financing and insurance business cross-border into Sweden. Such companies are obliged to submit a written document to the FSA stating that they undertake to report to the tax authorities the information required pursuant to the Act on Simplified Tax Returns and Statement of Earnings and Tax Deduction before they start doing business in Sweden:

> 'Foreign companies that conduct banking activities ... in Sweden without establishing a branch or a corresponding establishment here, must before the business activities are initiated submit a written undertaking to the Financial Supervisory Authority that they will submit statement of earnings and tax deductions in accordance with this statute.'[3]

Testimonies and production of documents to a court

[29.17] Swedish law contains a civil duty to testify in court. In certain cases, this duty is limited by reason of secrecy. However, bank confidentiality does not restrict or limit the obligation to testify and bank officers have to disclose information when testifying, regardless of the fact that the information is normally covered by bank confidentiality. Among those who may be obliged to testify are the bank management, other employees of a bank and a bank's auditors. A witness may not disclose information which has no relevance to the case in which he is heard. However, a witness may refuse to testify regarding circumstances which are considered to be trade secrets, unless there are extraordinary reasons. This covers not only the witness's own trade secrets, but also other trade secrets which are to be kept confidential by the witness.

Trade secrets include information regarding a business enterprise or its operations which are kept secret and which, if disclosed, would typically result in damage to the entity's ability to compete. The definition implies that it has to be information used in the operation of a business; personal knowledge of an employee in itself is not protected. The information also has to be secret, meaning, first, on a subjective level, that the entity has an intention to keep the information secret and, secondly, on an objective level, that the entity has taken measures in order to protect the information and prohibit access to it by unauthorised parties. From how the business is conducted, it should be clear to the employees that the information should be kept secret. The group of persons with access to the information must in some sense be limited, but the information can be protected even if known by several people. The disclosure should also typically result in damage to the entity's ability to compete.

Bank officers may have information constituting trade secrets of the bank, as well as information of a customer's trade secrets. As stated above, a witness may refuse to

---

2 Act on Simplified Tax Returns and Statement of Earnings and Tax Deduction (*Lag* (2001:1227) *om självdeklarationer och kontrolluppgifter*), Ch 17, s 4, para 1.
3 Act on Simplified Tax Returns and Statement of Earnings and Tax Deduction, Ch 13, s 1.

testify. However, because of the rules on bank confidentiality, a bank officer must use this possibility to refuse to give testimonies regarding customers' trade secrets.

A Swedish bank which is a party to, or an officer of a Swedish bank who testifies in, legal proceedings in a foreign country shall follow the Swedish rules on bank confidentiality.

Swedish law contains an obligation to produce documents to a court which may be of importance as evidence in proceedings. A bank may be ordered by a court to produce documents which are normally covered by bank confidentiality, even if the bank is not a party to the proceedings. However, the limitation regarding trade secrets when testifying also applies to the obligation to produce documents.

Foreign courts can ask for evidence to be obtained before a Swedish court. Basically, the rules regarding testimonies and production of documents described above shall also apply in these cases.

Information to prosecutors and the police

[29.18]   An individual's dealings with a bank may be of interest to prosecutors or the police when they investigate crimes. There are two formal ways for the prosecutors or the police to obtain information from banks: (i) through a search of premises or (ii) through seizure.

A search of premises may be conducted concerning a person suspected of a crime in order to find material which has been seized or in order to gather information of importance for the investigation of a crime. A search of premises may also be conducted at a bank in order to achieve the above-mentioned purposes if the crime has been committed in the bank, if the suspect has been arrested in the bank or if there is a particular reason to believe that material which has been seized or other information of importance will be found. A bank has no obligation to disclose information to the prosecutor or the police in other cases.

In addition, a bank may disclose information normally covered by bank confidentiality in order to provide the prosecutor or the police with information of importance for an investigation without a seizure or search of premises:

> 'A credit institution shall disclose information regarding the relation between individuals and the institution, if it is requested to do so by the investigator in charge in an investigation conducted in accordance with the provisions on preliminary criminal investigations or if it is requested by a prosecution, in a case of legal assistance raised by another state or an international court.'[4]

Provided the bank is very cautious, it can be reasonably helpful towards the prosecutors or the police. A seizure or a search of premises is not normally needed for the bank to be able to do this.

It should be noted that the above-mentioned circumstances concern the situation when the bank itself has no reason to suspect the customer of a crime. If the bank knows or has reason to suspect that a customer has committed a crime, the bank should not use bank confidentiality in order to protect the suspect/criminal. If the bank learns or suspects that a crime has been committed, the bank has a right to disclose the information in question, regardless of requests from the prosecutor/police.

4 BFBA, Ch 1, s 11.

Foreign courts may also request coercive measures. Property may be seized at the request of a foreign court if it could reasonably have importance for an investigation of a crime or if the object of the seizure has been the subject of a crime. A search of premises may be used to locate such property.

Information to the enforcement service authorities

[29.19] According to the Enforcement Code (*Utsökningsbalk* (1981:774)), banks (and other third parties) are obliged to provide the enforcement service authorities with information that may be of importance when the authorities judge whether a seizure or restraint may be obtained. The information that may be disclosed, regardless of the confidentiality, shall concern a customer's claims on the bank or other 'dealings' with the bank. The bank shall disclose the information to the extent that the information may be of importance in order to determine whether the debtor has any possessions that may be restrained. The bank is allowed (but has no obligation) to inform the customer of the measures taken by the enforcement service authorities.

Disclosure in the interest of the bank

[29.20] Another important exception to the obligation of confidentiality is the bank's right to protect itself and its interests towards its customers and others. In doing this, for example, in legal proceedings or when taking coercive measures, the bank may disclose information normally covered by bank confidentiality. However, a bank may not disclose information in litigation against a customer if the customer's damage from the disclosure is substantially greater than the gain for the bank.

Information to the Central Bank of Sweden

[29.21] The Central Bank of Sweden (*Riksbanken*) works to maintain price stability and to promote a safe and efficient payment system. Swedish banks have an obligation to provide the Central Bank of Sweden with certain information. This obligation must be fulfilled regardless of bank confidentiality.

Information to other public authorities

[29.22] In principle, bank confidentiality must also be kept in relation to public authorities. The bank is only obliged to disclose information when it is a statutory requirement. The most important and extensive exceptions have been discussed above. There are many additional exceptions, such as the obligation to disclose information to the Data Inspection Board, to chief guardians and to the supervisory authorities for bankruptcies.

In addition to the obligations to disclose information, the banks are entitled to disclose information in other situations. If there is a significant public interest for disclosure of information and there is no duty of loyalty to the customers preventing the disclosure, information may be disclosed. In doubtful cases, the information should be kept confidential.

Information to foreign courts and authorities

[29.23] Foreign authorities may be involved in legal proceedings in Sweden, in which case the rules described above will be applicable. As a general rule, Swedish

657

courts are not available for public law claims by foreign authorities, for example, regarding tax or crime. However, in some situations, there may be a legal requirement for Swedish authorities to assist foreign authorities, for example, pursuant to Swedish international treaties.

Information to other third parties

[29.24] As stated above, an individual may be given access to information covered by bank confidentiality in legal proceedings (through a testimony or a directive to produce documents) or in connection with enforcement by the enforcement service authorities. As a general rule, bank confidentiality shall be maintained in other cases. However, there are also statutory exceptions to this rule and, for example, the following persons have a right to information in certain situations: the shareholders in the bank, liquidators, guardians, the estate of a deceased person, auditors and spouses.

A bank may sometimes also be allowed to give information to other banks, for instance, when a loan is being moved, when a loan has been granted by a syndicate or in relation to a second ranking security (see below regarding credit information). However, the general rule is that banks shall not be treated differently from other third parties and that bank confidentiality shall be kept between banks.

There are also situations where a guarantor of a person is entitled to receive information from the bank regarding the customer of the bank whose obligations the guarantor is guaranteeing.

OTHER REGULATIONS RELATING TO BANK CONFIDENTIALITY

[29.25] In addition to the general rules on bank confidentiality, other rules exist regarding how and when banks may disclose or use information, including the following statutory regulations.

The Personal Data Act

[29.26] The EC Directive of 1995 on the protection of individuals with regard to the processing of personal data and on the free movement of such data[5] was implemented in Sweden by the Personal Data Act (*Personuppgiftslagen* (1998:204)), which contains regulations for registers and data regarding private individuals stored using electronic data processing ('EDP'). The Personal Data Act provides rules regarding how data concerning private individuals should be kept, handled and made available in order to prevent improper encroachment on the integrity of registered individuals.

The Personal Data Act prohibits the disclosure of information that may be used in conflict with the Act. These restrictions apply together with the rules on bank confidentiality. It is difficult to establish which rules are the most far reaching. The conclusion must be that a bank should be extra cautious when disclosing information relating to private individuals if the information is stored on EDP systems.

---

5 Council Directive 95/46/EC.

The Credit Information Act

[29.27] The Credit Information Act (*Kreditupplysningslag* (1973:1173)) regulates the professional provision of credit information. The Act includes rules cn which information may be stored and provided. It prohibits the storage and provision of information regarding political or religious beliefs, race, criminal record, health and poor credit history, unless a person has been declared bankrupt by a court or similar authority.

Although information may be provided according to the Credit Information Act, the rule on bank confidentiality still takes precedence if there is a conflict between the two, for example, information regarding a customer's creditworthiness can be based on the customer's relationship with the bank. The fact that this information can be disclosed under the Credit Information Act does not mean that disclosure is permitted according to the rule on bank confidentiality.

Pursuant to the Act, information regarding loans, their misuse or failure to pay may be disclosed if the details are disclosed for the purposes of credit information and the company receiving the information holds a permit from the Data Inspection Board. This also applies, in certain cases, to foreign banks and other credit institutions domiciled within the EEA.

Apart from the situations described above, a bank may, in certain circumstances, disclose credit information without being in conflict with the rules on bank confidentiality. Information may be disclosed when it includes a positive judgment on the customer's creditworthiness as, in these cases, the customer is supposed not to have any objections against a disclosure. It is harder to decide whether a bank may disclose unfavourable credit information without the customer's consent. As stated above, a bank may disclose information regarding customers if the reasons for the disclosure are significant enough. Since accurate and fairly extensive credit information is of great importance to the business community as a whole, a bank may in principle give credit information. However, great care should be taken in order not to breach the rule on bank confidentiality. The credit information should be very general in nature and not include specific details regarding the customer's relationship with the bank.

Through changes in the Credit Information Act, the rules also apply to information given between banks from 1 July 1997.

The sanctions against breaches of the Act are penal in nature and an offender may be sentenced to prison for up to a year if the offence is considered serious.

The Market Abuse Act

[29.28] Insider trading and improper market influence is prohibited under the Market Abuse Act (*Lag* (2005:377) *om straff för marknadsmissbruk vid handel med finansiella instrument*).

A person who has received private information which is likely to have a material influence on the price of financial instruments is prohibited from trading in such instruments on his own behalf or on behalf of another person/entity, nor may he cause or induce any other person/entity to trade in such financial instruments. The prohibition applies to all persons who possess inside information regardless of their position. Banks and bank officers are not excluded from these regulations and bank officers are among those who typically may have inside information. The sanctions against insider trading are penal in nature and an offender can be sentenced to up to four years' imprisonment if the offence is considered serious. Any gains from insider trading may be forfeited if this is deemed reasonable.

A person is also prohibited from acting improperly in a way which affects the price or other conditions for the trade of financial instruments or in a way which is misleading to buyers or sellers of such instruments. The sanctions are penal and a person can be sentenced to up to two years' imprisonment.

A bank has a duty to report to the FSA if a transaction constitutes or is connected with insider trading or improper market influence and the bank will not be held responsible for disclosing such information. Any person who wilfully or negligently disregards this duty to report can be fined. The same applies if the bank discloses to the customer or any third party that a report has been filed.

The Money Laundering Act

[29.29] The EC Money Laundering Directive 1991[6] was implemented in Sweden in 1993 by the Money Laundering Act (*Lag* (1993:768) *om åtgärder mot penningtvätt*, 'MLA'), which was last revised in July 2005, together with the Money Laundering Regulation (*Förordning* (2002:552) *om åtgärder mot penningtvätt och finansiering av särskild allvarlig brottslighet i vissa fall*). The purpose of the MLA is to make it more difficult to legitimise funds which have been obtained through crime. To accomplish this, the MLA contains a provision obliging a bank to investigate all transactions which the bank suspects concern funds obtained through crime and the bank shall inform the National Police Board about all circumstances which indicate money laundering. Bank confidentiality does not prevent the disclosure of such information.

The offences of money laundering and aiding and abetting certain specified money laundering activities are each punishable by up to six years' imprisonment, a fine or both. Wilful or grossly negligent failure to examine potential, or to report specified, money laundering activities is punishable by a fine. The same applies to disclosing to the customer or any third party that an examination has been performed, that a report has been filed or that the police are investigating.

The most recent assessment of the implementation of anti-money laundering and counter-terrorist financing standards in Sweden took place in February 2006. According to this assessment, the Swedish legal structures in place to combat money laundering are generally sound, but their level of effectiveness has yet to be fully tested. Customer identification requirements are in place for financial institutions, however, these measures could be further enhanced through a more comprehensive due diligence framework.

The Terrorism Suppression Act

[29.30] The UN Convention for the Suppression of the Financing of Terrorism of 9 December 1999 (54/109) has been implemented in Sweden by the Terrorism Suppression Act (*Lag* (2002:444) *om straff för finansiering av särskild allvarlig brottslighet i vissa fall*). This Act contains a provision obliging a bank to investigate and disclose information about certain crimes listed in the Act. The crimes that fall

---

6 Council Directive 91/308/EEC.

under the provisions of the Act are particularly serious crimes typically linked to terrorism.

The offence of not investigating or disclosing information with regard to these crimes is punishable by a fine. The same applies if the bank discloses to the customer or any third party that an examination has been performed, that a report has been filed or that the police are investigating.

SUMMARY

[29.31]   Swedish bank confidentiality is civil in nature and the basic rule is that 'the relations of individuals to a bank may not be disclosed without legal cause'. The confidentiality is sanctioned through liability in damages for the bank and, in respect of savings banks and membership banks, for certain persons, for example, members of the board of directors and the members themselves.

There are extensive exceptions to the rule on confidentiality, mainly in the interests of the public. The most important exception may be the right for the tax authorities to obtain information from banks. Other important exceptions deal with the disclosure after consent from the customer, information handled internally within the bank and information given to prosecutors and the police. In addition, other legislation may be of importance for a bank when handling information, for example, the Personal Data Act and the Market Abuse Act.

30   Switzerland

Stefan Breitenstein

INTRODUCTION

[30.1]   Swiss banking secrecy, or bank confidentiality, is by no means as absolute as some people outside Switzerland tend to believe. It is, however, also not going to be abolished as many foreign commentators predict. Rather, it will continue to adapt over time to the changing legal, commercial and political environment. Conceptually, Swiss banking secrecy has remained unchanged since its introduction in 1934. However, its application and scope have evolved substantially over the last 20 years. The definition of the scope of banking secrecy by the Swiss legislators has always required a balance between the protection of the privacy of bank customers and law enforcement by the states inside and outside their boundaries. The increased globalisation of the previously national economies and the substantial harmonisation of financial laws have lead to an increased co-operation in international law enforcement. As a result, the balance of interest has gradually shifted from the protection of bank customers' privacy to international co-operation in law enforcement. The changes to Swiss banking secrecy clearly reflect this development. As described in more detail below, Swiss banking secrecy gradually eroded over time in matters of criminal legal assistance, enforcement of financial market regulations (insider trading), consolidated supervision of internationally active banking groups, money laundering and, most recently, terrorist financing. The only major area where the protection of privacy of bank customers still prevails over law enforcement is international tax enforcement. In this area, banking secrecy continues to be upheld, except where tax fraud is involved. In this connection, it should be noted that Switzerland applies a very narrow definition of tax fraud and normally requires intentional deceit by means of false documents or documents containing untrue information.

NATURE AND EXTENT OF THE BANKER'S DUTY OF CONFIDENCE

Nature

Non-contractual

[30.2]   The Swiss Civil Code ('CC')[1] protects the privacy rights of any legal or physical person in general by art 28. Long before Switzerland had a banking law, the Swiss Federal Supreme Court recognised that the privacy rights of a person included

---

1 CC 10 December 1907, RS 210.

information relating to his financial affairs.[2] It is therefore generally recognised in Swiss law that confidential information obtained by a bank concerning its customers and their financial affairs is protected by the privacy rights of the CC.[3]

An intrusion into the privacy rights in breach of art 28 of the CC also qualifies as a tort within the meaning of art 41 of the Swiss Code of Obligations ('CO').[4] Accordingly, a breach of banking secrecy could, depending on the circumstances, lead to civil law sanctions even if the bank's confidential information is not covered by a contractual relationship, but concerns third parties. Possible sanctions include court injunctions and the award of damages. Tort claims for breach of bank confidentiality are, however, rare, since in most cases there exists a contractual basis for an action which is normally the preferred basis for such claims.

An ordinary action under art 28a of the CC may take some time, which normally frustrates the claimant who is seeking quick relief. A claimant who can make a prima facie case evidencing that (i) his privacy rights have been illegally breached or the breach is imminent and (ii) the breach will cause damage which cannot be easily recovered is entitled to provisional measures under art 28a of the CC, such as temporary injunctions or restraint orders. Swiss law does not, however, grant a court the power to award punitive damages. In this connection, it is important to note that the payment of taxes which the claimant is obliged to pay under the applicable law may not be considered damage within the meaning of Swiss law. Penalties payable by the claimant for the avoidance of taxes or for breach of exchange control provisions may be attributed to the claimant's own fault and compensation may therefore not be awarded.

Contractual

[30.3]   The relationship between a bank and its customers is generally contractual in nature and governed by a number of provisions of the CO. The qualification of the relationship between the bank and its customers largely depends on the services requested by the individual customer. It is, however, clear that most customer relationships contain some elements of a mandate.[5] The key provision for mandate contracts provides that the agent has to execute a mandate faithfully and diligently (art 398 of the CO). The bank has to treat as confidential all information the customer requests the bank to keep secret. The customer is considered the master of the 'secret'. Bank confidentiality is therefore a right of the customer and a duty of the bank. It is not a right of the bank.

Certain contractual relationships between the bank and the customer may not be qualified as mandates, but rather as a loan agreement or other non-mandate types of agreement, in which case the question arises whether the bank is under a duty of

---

2 Decision of the Federal Tribunal ('BGE') 64 (1938) II 162 (169).

3 B Kleiner, R Schwob and Ch Winzeler in Bodmer, Kleiner and Lutz *Kommentar zum Schweizerischen Bankengesetz* (16th edn, 2005) BkL, art 47, n 5; D Guggenheim *Die Verträge der Schweizerischen Bankpraxis* (3rd edn, 1986) p 24; P Honegger and Th Frick *Das Bankengeheimnis im Konzern und bei Übernahmen* in Swiss Review of Business Law (1996) pp 1–10; P Bernasconi *Le secret bancaire suisse entre deux feux: procédures pénales et fiscales* in Bernasconi *Les nouveaux défis au secret bancaire suisse* (1996) pp 9–22.

4 CO 30 March 1911, RS 220; Kleiner, Schwob and Winzeler, n 3 above, BkL art 47, nn 3 and 5; Guggenheim, n 3 above, p 24; Stratenwerth, Günter in Watter/Vogt/Bauer/Winzeler (Hrsg) *Basler Kommentar, Bankengesetz*, Basle/Genf/München, art 47, n 1.

5 M Aubert, P A Béguin, P Bernasconi, J G Burg, R Schwob and R Treuilland *Le secret bancaire suisse* (3rd edn, 1995) pp 480–502.

confidentiality. Most Swiss legal scholars take the view that the confidentiality covenant is customary and is at least implied in all banking agreements, unless disclosure is clearly required by the nature of the business transaction in question.[6] This is supported by the fact that art 47 of the Swiss Federal Banking Law ('BkL')[7] clearly establishes a duty of confidentiality to the bank, even though not in a civil law context. Unauthorised disclosure of confidential facts by the bank, therefore, constitutes a breach of contract. Consequently, the contractual duty of confidentiality and the protection of a customer's privacy rights guaranteed in art 28 of the CC form the basis for the banking secret protected by art 47 of the BkL.

The Swiss Federal Act on Exchanges and Securities Trading ('SESTA')[8] provides, among others, for legal standards of professional conduct for securities dealers. Such standards include the duty to act faithfully and diligently.[9] As a result, securities dealers have to safeguard their customer's interest and keep customer information confidential if asked implicitly or explicitly by the customer, even if the contractual relationship between the customer and the securities dealer does not in all respects qualify as a mandatory contract.[10] Cross-border transactions of foreign securities dealers providing their services in Switzerland are only subject to the Swiss confidentiality standards if the foreign securities dealers have an office with permanent employees in the form of a branch or representative office in Switzerland or if they are members of the Swiss exchange. Without such presence in Switzerland, foreign securities dealers are not subject to the Swiss confidentiality standards.[11]

The remedies for breach of contract under Swiss law are either specific performance, which may mean an injunction prohibiting the disclosure of confidential information, or damages. Again, losses attributable to the customer's own fault cannot be claimed as damages or will at least result in a reduction of the compensation awarded. This applies in particular to taxes and penalties which become payable as a result of an unauthorised disclosure of confidential information.

Criminal

[30.4] It is a particularity of Swiss law that bank confidentiality is not only protected by civil and contract law, but also by criminal law. Article 47 of the BkL makes breach of bank confidentiality a crime. This provision was included in 1934 in the BkL at a time when countries in the vicinity of Switzerland introduced legislation that attempted to gain control over the foreign assets of its nationals or discriminated against people for the mere reason of their race, religion or political belief. As these objectives were pursued by all kinds of intelligence and espionage, it was deemed necessary to enact a criminal provision protecting bank customers and as a defence against the intrusion of Swiss sovereignty.

The present wording of art 47 of the BkL reads as follows:

'1 Whoever divulges a secret entrusted to him or of which he has become aware in his capacity as officer, employee, mandatory liquidator or

---

6 Kleiner, Schwob and Winzeler, n 3 above, BkL, art 47, n 4; Aubert et al, n 5 above, pp 50–51.
7 BkL 8 November 1934, as amended, RS 952.0.
8 SESTA 24 March 1995, RS 954.1.
9 SESTA, art 11.
10 SESTA, art 11 sets a (contractually motivated) professional standard for faithful and diligent execution of client orders; cf G Hertig and U Schuppisser *Kommentar zum Schweizerischen Kapitalmarktrecht* (1999) SESTA, art 11, n 7ss.
11 Hertig and Schuppisser, n 10 above, SESTA, art 11, n 19s.

commissioner of a bank, as representative of the Banking Commission, officer or employee of a recognised auditing company and whoever tries to induce others to breach professional secrecy, shall be punished by imprisonment for not more than six months or by a fine of not more than SFr50,000.

2 If the act has been committed by negligence, the penalty shall be a fine not exceeding SFr30,000.

3 The breach of professional secrecy remains punishable even after termination of the official or employment relationship or the exercise of the profession.

4 Federal and cantonal regulations concerning the obligation to testify and furnish information to a government authority shall apply.'

It must be noted that two types of information are subject to the provision: (i) confidential information entrusted to the bank by its customers and (ii) confidential information which came to the attention of the bank in the course of executing the customer agreement. Secrets related to the bank's own business are not covered by art 47 of the BkL, but may constitute business secrets protected by art 162 of the Swiss Penal Code ('PC').[12]

Article 47 of the BkL is clearly criminal in nature and its enforcement is not dependent upon complaint of the damaged party, but must be prosecuted *ex officio*. Even negligent breach of banking secrecy can be punished. This indicates the historic importance the Swiss legislator attributed to banking secrecy as compared, for instance, with attorney–client privilege, a breach of which will only be prosecuted upon complaint of the client and only if the breach was wilful.

In line with this provision of the BkL, art 43 of the SESTA provides for an equivalent provision incriminating the breach of professional secrecy of securities dealers or members of an exchange. The wording of art 43 of the SESTA is materially the same as art 47 of the BkL. Article 43 has, however, a somewhat wider scope of application since it not only protects the relationship between customer and securities dealer, but also information a stock exchange receives when executing orders. Accordingly, the SESTA adds an additional layer of protection of customers who execute exchange transactions through banks or securities dealers.

Data protection

[30.5] In 1992, Switzerland enacted a Federal Law on Data Protection ('LDP')[13] which is designed to protect the individual's right to control the use of private data related to him. Since the scope of application comprises private data and includes information relating to the financial situation of a customer, the LDP is not strengthening the level of protection already provided by art 47 of the BkL and art 43 of the SESTA. These provisions constitute a *lex specialis* relative to the LDP. The rules set out in the LDP on the processing, storing and transferring of data have no direct impact on bank confidentiality and do not extend the duties of a bank or securities dealer to safeguard its customers' confidentiality.[14]

In a case where a multinational banking group intends to transfer data abroad in order to centralise the data processing, special requirements of the LDP must, however, be

---

12 PC 21 December 1937, RS 311.0.
13 LDP 19 June 1992, RS 235.1.
14 Kleiner, Schwob and Winzeler, n 3 above, BkL, art 47, nn 14 and 403ss.

observed. Under the LDP, a data transfer is, in principle, only permissible to countries with data protection laws that are substantially equivalent to Swiss laws. If this is not the case, special agreements must be entered into in order to provide for the required data protection level. Further, the data transfer abroad must be notified to the Federal Officer for Data Protection if customer consent is not obtained. The data processing abroad of banks is governed by a special circular of the Federal Banking Commission which is discussed in 'Recent Developments' below.

Administrative

[30.6]   Article 23 ter of the BkL and art 35, para 3 of the SESTA stipulate that the Federal Banking Commission may take such measures as it deems appropriate to remedy irregularities in the conduct of a bank or securities dealer. Breach of banking secrecy, as provided in art 47 of the BkL or breach of professional secrecy as provided in art 43 of the SESTA, may constitute such an irregularity and entail administrative sanctions. These sanctions may range from a warning addressed to the bank or securities dealer to the effect that the persons who breached banking or professional secrecy be dismissed to the withdrawal of the banking or securities dealer licence.

Extent

In time

[30.7]   A bank's confidentiality obligation continues for as long as the customer whose secrets are involved has a reasonable interest to keep them confidential, even if the contractual relationship between the customer and the bank or the securities dealer has been terminated.

Territorial reach

[30.8]   All banks or securities dealers licensed to do business in Switzerland, either as Swiss legal entities or branches or representative offices of foreign banks or securities dealers or as members of the Swiss exchange, are subject to the banking or professional secrecy obligation with respect to business activities in Switzerland.

Customer relationships of foreign branches of Swiss banks or securities dealers are, however, not protected by the criminal law provision of art 47 of the BkL and art 43 of the SESTA.[15]

Swiss legal scholars do not have a uniform opinion on whether a breach of Swiss banking secrecy by an act that occurs outside Switzerland is punishable under art 47 of the BkL.[16] As the provision on criminal protection of banking or professional secrecy would make little sense if anyone could cross the Swiss border and divulge protected information with impunity, the divulging of confidential information outside Switzerland should also be subject to criminal sanction. The enforcement of such criminal sanction may, however, not be possible.

---

15 Kleiner, Schwob and Winzeler, n 3 above, BkL, art 47, n 366.
16 Affirmative Kleiner, Schwob and Winzeler, n 3 above, BkL, art 47, n 373; Aubert et al, n 5 above, pp 100–102 outlines the different positions and its repercussions.

Persons bound by banking and professional secrecy

[30.9] Persons bound by the secrecy obligation are those who, in the course of discharging their duties and legal obligations, obtain access to confidential customer information.

Public servants such as the members and officers of the Federal Banking Commission, officers of the Swiss National Bank, tax inspectors, etc are bound by special confidentiality rules governing their respective offices, which involve criminal sanctions as well.[17]

EXCEPTIONS

Customer consent

General

[30.10] Bank confidentiality[18] is not only for the benefit of bank customers in the strict sense, but also for the benefit of third persons who had contacts with customers or about whom the bank obtained confidential information in the ordinary course of its banking business. In order to simplify matters, all those persons are referred to here as 'customers'.

Express or implied consent

[30.11] As the customer is the master of the privileged information, his express or implied consent releases the bank from its confidentiality duty. Since such release must be legally valid, the bank may be in a difficult situation if it has reason to believe that the consent of the customer may not have been given voluntarily, but under material duress originating from a third party, including foreign public authorities. Under the CO, consents given under material duress may be subsequently voided by the customer. Under these circumstances, banks will usually try to obtain clear evidence that the consent expresses the customer's actual intent, for example, by means of prior written consent. Like any communication between the parties to a contract, such a consent will have to be construed in accordance with the 'principle of good faith' established by Swiss jurisprudence. This means communication with the client has to be understood as a reasonable person would have understood it under the given circumstances in good faith.[19] Given the fact that bank confidentiality not only protects a contractual right of the customer, but also his privacy, the test becomes particularly delicate in respect of court-ordered waivers.

Persons acting in lieu of the customer

[30.12] The consent does not need to be given by the customer himself, but may be given by any person authorised under the applicable law to act on behalf of the customer. Thus, consent may also be given by agents or proxies appointed by the customer, legal representatives such as parents, spouses (if applicable), tutors, officers and directors of a legal entity or successors, heirs and assignees or executors

---

17 Cf PC, art 320.
18 In the following sections, the terms 'bank confidentiality' or 'secrecy' and 'bank' also include 'professional secrecy' and 'securities dealer'.
19 Cf BGE 111 (1985) II 276 (279).

of the customer's will.[20] However, such consent may not be effective if information concerning the customer is of a strictly personal nature. The situation becomes particularly difficult for the bank when the customer is no longer available to clarify inconsistent or partial consent.

Litigation involving the customer

If the customer sues the bank

[30.13]   Article 47 of the BkL does not contain an express exception referring to an action by the customer against the bank. However, a customer who sues the bank, but insists that the bank abstains from disclosing facts covered by bank confidentiality when defending its position, acts against the general principle of good faith. Accordingly, banks are entitled to disclose confidential information to the courts to the extent necessary or useful for their defence without breaching their duty of confidentiality.

If the bank sues the customer

[30.14]   Bank confidentiality does not prevent customers from being sued by Swiss banks. The customer may not invoke bank confidentiality as a defence in an action by the bank for breach of contract.

The bank as third party claimant/defendant

[30.15]   Frequently, Swiss banks are involved in litigation between a customer and a third party because they hold assets which form the subject of the dispute and which may be subject to civil or criminal attachment orders. In these cases, banks are entitled to protect their own interests by claiming preferential rights such as liens, rights to set-off or other security rights which they may have.[21] According to Swiss jurisprudence, banks must disclose their interests in time otherwise their rights are forfeited.[22] The exercising of such preferential rights does not constitute a breach of bank confidentiality.[23]

Compulsion by law

Civil proceedings

[30.16]   Article 47, para 4 of the BkL expressly reserves federal and cantonal provisions on the duty to testify or disclose information to the public authorities. With respect to civil proceedings, three different systems have been adopted by the federal and cantonal legislatures.[24]

The first system expressly waives testimony by all persons bound by a professional secret, which is generally deemed to include bank confidentiality.[25] The second

---

20 Aubert et al, n 5 above, pp 299–351.
21 Kleiner, Schwob and Winzeler, n 3 above, BkL, art 47, n 92.
22 BGE 109 (1983) III 22, 111 (1985) III 21, 112 (1986) III 59, 113 (1987) III 104 and 117 (1991) III 74.
23 BGE 109 (1983) III 22.
24 Cf also Guggenheim, n 3 above, pp 26–28; Aubert et al, n 5 above, pp 133–210.
25 This applies to Berne, Geneva, Glarus, Neuchâtel, Jura and Vaud.

system mentions all professions entitled to refuse testimony without, however, mentioning banks, which means bank officers are obliged to testify.[26] The third system requires the judge to balance the interests involved in each single case and thereafter decide whether a bank officer has to testify.[27]

Usually, the obligation of banks to submit documents is subject to the same rules.[28] Where bank confidentiality is protected, courts may take various measures in order to prevent protected information from being disclosed, such as limiting the access of the parties to the file, excluding the public from hearings, covering certain parts of documents, sealing of documents and examination by the judge in the absence of the parties in order to determine whether they should be excluded. In addition, the courts may appoint an expert who himself is bound by banking secrecy.[29]

Such protective measures raise difficult questions of due process and require a careful balancing of the interests involved in each single case. Irrespective of the applicable cantonal system, a bank must provide a court with otherwise protected information in marital disputes if one spouse requests information on the financial situation of the other.[30]

Arbitration

[30.17]   Arbitration courts do not have the power to compel testimony or subpoena documents.[31] Moreover, an arbitration court cannot release a bank from its secrecy obligation without the consent of the customer as master of the secret, since art 47, para 4 of the BkL only reserves federal and cantonal procedural law, but not arbitral rules.[32] However, by taking recourse to the ordinary courts, arbitrators may gain access to privileged information and indirectly force banks to give evidence under the applicable local procedural rules.[33]

International judicial assistance in civil matters

[30.18]   Switzerland grants judicial assistance in civil proceedings to members of the Treaty on the Law of Civil Procedure signed in The Hague on 1 March 1954 (the '1954 Convention').[34] According to art 11 of the 1954 Convention, the same coercive measures apply in judicial assistance procedures as in domestic civil procedures. This means that the applicable cantonal rules of civil procedure decide the scope of

---

26 This applies to Appenzell (AI), Basle (city and country), Obwalden, Solothurn, Schaffhausen, Schwyz and Thurgau.
27 This applies to Aargau, Appenzell (AR), Fribourg, Grisons, Lucerne, Nidwalden, St Gallen, Ticino, Uri, Valais, Zug and Zurich and also to procedures governed by the Federal Code of Civil Procedure (4 December 1947, RS 273).
28 Kleiner, Schwob and Winzeler, n 3 above, BkL, art 47, n 100; Aubert et al, n 5 above, p 139.
29 Cf arts 38, 51, 52, 55 and 56 of the Federal Code on Civil Procedure.
30 Cf CC, art 170, para 2.
31 Kleiner, Schwob and Winzeler, n 3 above, BkL, art 47, n 99.
32 Aubert et al, n 5 above, pp 141–142.
33 Cf art 184 of the Swiss Statute on Private International Law ('PIL Statute') (18 December 1987, RS 291) and art 27 of the Concordat on Arbitration (27 March 1969, RS 279). Article 27, para 2 of the Concordat expressly reserves the right of the arbitration court, if necessary, to refer to the cantonal court where the arbitration court is seated and request the respective evidence proceedings to overcome the limits set by bank confidentiality. The same applies for international arbitration courts in Switzerland (art 184, para 2 of the PIL Statute); cf Aubert et al, n 5 above, pp 141–143.
34 RS 0.274.12.

the protection of bank confidentiality.[35] With respect to countries that are not members of the 1954 Convention, Switzerland will only act upon letters rogatory as a matter of comity and leave it to the cantons to decide whether they want to apply coercive measures with regard to depositions of witnesses and submission of documents.

The canton of Zurich and most other cantons exclude judicial assistance in fiscal, military and political matters or if judicial assistance is contrary to Swiss public policy and reserve the power to refuse judicial assistance completely if the foreign country does not grant reciprocity. Upon request by the foreign authority and if the parties agree, evidence can be taken in accordance with foreign procedural rules; however, coercive measures will always remain subject to the applicable cantonal rules.[36]

This autonomy of cantonal rules of civil procedures with regard to the protection of bank confidentiality was not modified by the adoption of the Hague Convention on the Taking of Evidence Abroad in Civil or Commercial Matters of 18 March 1970[37] (the '1970 Convention') in force since 1 January 1995. Pursuant to art 11 of the 1970 Convention, a person has the right to withhold testimony, provided the laws of the requested state allow for such a right. Accordingly, an evidence request pursuant to the 1970 Convention will be executed pursuant to the procedural rules of the cantonal *lex loci*.[38] Whether bank confidentiality remains protected is, therefore, still subject to the federal and cantonal rules of civil procedures as described above. The 1970 Convention does not have a substantive impact on these procedural rules.

Collection of debt and bankruptcy

[30.19] Proceedings concerning forced execution of debt and bankruptcy are governed by the revised Federal Law on Debt Enforcement and Bankruptcy with effect from 1 January 1997.[39] Once the execution officer has seized a bank account, the bank cannot refuse information by invoking bank confidentiality.[40] Banks are therefore obliged to provide customer information at a relatively early stage of the enforcement proceedings, otherwise they risk prosecution.[41] This also applies to civil attachments which are granted as provisional measures upon summary proceedings without strict proof of a claim, provided the attachment is based on an enforceable title.[42]

In bankruptcy proceedings, the trustee of a bankrupt customer is entitled to full disclosure of account information.[43] In the bank's own bankruptcy, the trustee or officially appointed liquidator has full access to all information concerning the banking relationship. Foreign bankruptcy trustees may, however, have to resort to a Swiss ancillary bankruptcy proceeding pursuant to art 166ss of the Swiss Private

---

35 J Schwarz *Das Bankgeheimnis bei Rechtshilfe gemäss dem Haager Übereinkommen vom 18. März 1970 über die Beweisaufnahme im Ausland in Zivil- oder Handelssachen* in Swiss Journal of Jurisprudence (1995) pp 284–286.
36 Cf PIL Statute, art 11 and Zurich Statute on Organisation of the Judiciary, arts 116 and 117.
37 RS 0.274.132.
38 Cf Aubert et al, n 5 above, pp 602–608; Schwarz, n 35 above, p 285; Bernasconi, n 3 above, pp 12–14.
39 SchKG, RS 281.1.
40 BGE 112 (1986) III 98, 102 (1974) III 6 and leading case BGE 75 (1949) III 106 (109).
41 PC, art 324, para 5.
42 Cf Kleiner, Schwob and Winzeler, n 3 above, BkL, art 47, n 91; BGE 109 (1983) III 22 (24).
43 Kleiner, Schwob and Winzeler, n 3 above, BkL, art 47, n 82.

International Law Statute of 18 December 1987, under which the Swiss trustee is given full access to the account information. The provisions of arts 25ss and 33ss of the BkL regarding the restructuring and liquidation of banks may apply.[44]

Consolidated supervision of international banking groups

[30.20] In the past, bank confidentiality could substantially interfere with internal information supervision needs in internationally active banking groups. It has been correctly argued that the obvious need for consolidated risk assessment and supervision to maintain the safety and soundness of the banking institution outweighs the single customer's interest in unrestricted bank confidentiality.[45] As of 1 February 1995, the BkL expressly provides for a provision regulating the upstream information flow in internationally active banking groups. Article 4 quinquies of the BkL authorised Swiss subsidiaries to forward to their foreign parent companies, which are themselves supervised by a banking or financial market supervisory authority, customer information or documents not publicly available which are necessary for the purpose of consolidated supervision, provided, however:

1   such information is used exclusively for internal control or direct supervision of banks or other financial intermediaries subject to a respective licence;
2   the parent company and its supervisory authority responsible for consolidated supervision are bound by official or professional secrecy standards; and
3   such information may not be transmitted to third parties without prior consent of the subsidiary bank or without a general authorisation in a treaty.[46]

It is now generally recognised that a Swiss banking subsidiary of an internationally active banking group may, under the above conditions, transfer customer-related information to the parent company without breaching bank confidentiality.[47] Such information flow primarily affects bank customers who borrow money from the Swiss banking subsidiary or have credit lines outstanding.

It is noteworthy that the SESTA does not provide an analogous provision to art 4 quinquies of the BkL. Although the supervisory regimes in the BkL and SESTA are virtually identical and there are good reasons to permit the upstream flow of information,[48] a limitation on confidentiality of securities dealers would require a statutory basis. The lack of such statutory basis has, in practice, not caused problems, since internationally active securities dealers normally also hold a banking licence in Switzerland, thus allowing the application of art 4 quinquies of the BkL.

On-site inspections in Switzerland

[30.21] Since 1 October 1999, Switzerland has permitted limited on-site inspections with Swiss banking subsidiaries and branch offices by foreign bank supervisors as part of the consolidated supervision of internationally active banking

---

44 Kleiner, Schwob and Winzeler, n 3 above, BkL, art 47, n 337.
45 Cf Kleiner, Schwob and Winzeler, n 3 above, BkL, art 47, n 341; Aubert et al, n 5 above, pp 410–411; Honegger and Frick, n 3 above, pp 4–7; W de Capitani *Das Bankgeheimnis im Konzern* in Swiss Review of Business Law (1997) pp 76–81.
46 Cf language of art 4 quinquies of the BkL.
47 Cf Honegger and Frick, n 3 above, p 5; Kleiner, Schwob and Winzeler, n 3 above, BkL, art 47, n 342ss; Aubert et al, n 5 above, pp 426–427.
48 Cf R Watter and R Malacrida *Das Börsengesetz im internationalen Kontext* in Meier-Schatz *Das neue Börsengesetz der Schweiz* (1996) p 162.

groups. Such on-site inspections require, however, the prior approval of the Federal Banking Commission, which is granted if the following requirements are met:

1 the requesting foreign authority is responsible for consolidated supervision in accordance with their home country rules;
2 the information received is exclusively used for banking supervision;
3 the foreign authority is bound by official or professional secrecy; and
4 the foreign authority is not transmitting the information received, without prior approval of the Federal Banking Commission, to other authorities that are entrusted with supervisory duties in the public interest. The transmission of information to penal authorities is not permitted whenever legal assistance in criminal matters would be excluded.

The scope of the permissible on-site inspections includes the adequate organisation, risk monitoring and assessment, compliance with equity and risk diversification requirements and reporting obligations of Swiss subsidiaries. In case the foreign authorities wish to review assets and deposits of individual customers, such review is effected by the staff of the Federal Banking Commission and the transmission of subsequent reports of the Federal Banking Commission to the foreign authorities is subject to judicial review. This procedure adequately protects the bank confidentiality of private clients. The bank confidentiality of commercial clients is, however, waived due to prevailing interests in the consolidated supervision of internationally active banking groups.

Criminal proceedings

[30.22] With regard to Swiss criminal proceedings, the situation is relatively straightforward.[49] During the stage of mere preliminary investigations by the police, bank confidentiality remains protected. However, based on art 47, para 4 of the BkL, the Federal Code of Criminal Procedure,[50] as well as all cantonal rules on criminal procedure, can require banks to testify before official prosecutors and the criminal courts.[51] When testifying, bank officers have to draw the attention of the judge to the fact that answers to questions may involve disclosure of banking secrets. It is then up to the judge or prosecuting officer to determine whether the information is relevant and necessary for the purpose of the prosecution.

If a judge freezes an account by a blocking order in connection with a criminal investigation against a customer, the bank may inform its customer about such freeze unless the judge orders the bank to desist from doing so. Such a freeze and desist order may put the bank in a difficult position if the customer requests the execution of certain transactions from the blocked account or if the customer tries to withdraw money from his account. In co-operation with the chief magistrates of the cantonal justice and police authorities, the Swiss Bankers' Association has issued recommendations on how to deal with such blocking order.[52] The recommendations

49 Cf Kleiner, Schwob and Winzeler, n 3 above, BkL, art 47, n 94ss; Aubert et al, n 5 above pp 144–155; Bernasconi, n 3 above, pp 14–17; Ch Baer *Revision des Rechtshilfegesetzes und des Bundesgesetzes zum Rechtshilfevertrag mit den Vereinigten Staaten von Amerika* in Swiss Review of Business Law (1995) pp 80–84.
50 Federal Code of Criminal Procedure, 15 June 1934, RS 312.0.
51 BGE 95 (1969) I 439 (444), 96 (1970) I 737 (749), 104 (1978) IV 125 (129).
52 Cf recommendation of the Swiss Bankers' Association addressed to the cantonal prosecuting authorities on blocking and cease and desist orders dated 17 March 1997 (*Empfehlung an die kantonalen Strafverfolgungsbehörden betreffend Kontosperren und Schweigepflicht der Bank*, circular no 1286D).

set out the circumstances in which the bank may inform the customer about the blocking order.

Delicate problems arise for banks if disclosure of documents and information is requested with regard to third parties not involved in the alleged offence. Generally, Swiss rules on criminal procedures are governed by the principle of appropriateness. Accordingly, the means used by the government in enforcing the laws must be appropriate to the objectives pursued. This requires a balancing of interests between the public interest in the enforcement of the laws and the interests of protecting the privacy of the parties involved.[53] The federal and cantonal rules on criminal procedure provide for several protective measures, among which are the sealing of documents seized until a judge decides in a formal procedure whether the information is relevant for the criminal investigation and should serve as evidence. Documents may also be partially admitted by blanking out sections containing protected information.[54] As it is not admissible to have 'secret files' in Swiss criminal procedure, the possibility of making certain documents only accessible to the judge, but not to the other parties, does not exist and would be contrary to the principles of due process.

International legal assistance in criminal matters

[30.23] International legal assistance in criminal matters by the Swiss authorities has become more important in recent years due to the international integration of the financial markets.[55] Pursuant to the Federal Statute on International Judicial Assistance in Criminal Matters dated 20 March 1981 (the 'Criminal Assistance Statute'),[56] the Treaty with the United States dated 25 May 1973 (the 'US Treaty'),[57] the respective federal statute dated 3 October 1973[58] and the European Convention on Judicial Assistance in Criminal Matters dated 20 April 1959 (the 'European Convention'),[59] banks can be compelled to testify and submit documents before the courts of the requesting countries. This legislation was subject to a substantial revision which has been implemented with effect from 1 February 1997.[60]

The following text summarises the most important features of Swiss legal assistance in criminal matters.

Whether legal assistance is granted by Switzerland is determined primarily by the applicable treaty provisions. If no treaty applies or if a request goes beyond Switzerland's treaty obligations, assistance may be granted under the Criminal Assistance Statute. This does not impose a legally enforceable obligation on Switzerland to grant assistance to the requesting country.[61] However, the Swiss

---

53 See BGE 98 (1972) Ia 418.
54 Cf art 69, para 3 of the Federal Code of Criminal Procedure.
55 Reportedly, approximately 400 judgments were given between 1990 and 1994 by the Swiss Federal Supreme Court relative to requests for mutual assistance in criminal matters: cf Bernasconi, n 3 above, p 14.
56 RS 351.1.
57 RS 0.351.933.6.
58 RS 351.93.
59 RS 0.351.1.
60 Cf *Botschaft betreffend die Änderung des Rechtshilfegesetzes und des Bundesgesetzes zum Staatsvertrag mit den USA über gegenseitige Rechtshilfe in Strafsachen sowie den Bundesbeschluss über einen Vorbehalt zum Europäischen Übereinkommen über die Rechtshilfe in Strafsachen* dated 29 March 1995, BBI 1995 III, pp 1–59; R Wyss *Die Revision der Gesetzgebung über die internationale Rechtshilfe in Strafsachen* in Swiss Journal of Jurisprudence (1997) pp 33–43.
61 Criminal Assistance Statute, art 1, para 4.

authorities are bound by the provisions of the Criminal Assistance Statute and therefore a refusal of assistance is only possible on grounds set out in the applicable treaty or the Criminal Assistance Statute.[62]

First, it has to be reviewed whether the request concerns a proceeding in criminal matters. As such, a term is defined broadly. The Federal Supreme Court has, for example, held that legal assistance would be justified in a matter being investigated by the *Commission des Operations de Bourse* ('COB'), the French securities industry supervisory authority, although the COB is not a judicial authority. The court held that the preliminary investigations of the COB were likely to develop into a criminal procedure and therefore approved the legal assistance request.[63]

In the absence of a treaty, Switzerland may refuse legal assistance if the requesting country does not grant reciprocity, except where a particularly serious offence, national interests or the interest of the incriminated person or a Swiss victim demands otherwise.[64] Assistance may also be refused when it is contrary to essential Swiss national interests.[65]

No legal assistance will be granted if the foreign procedure does not adequately provide for protection of human and civil rights or otherwise suffers from grave defects.[66] Furthermore, assistance is generally excluded for military offences and those of a predominantly political character,[67] ie if they were committed in a fight for or against political power or have a close connection with such fight,[68] except in some particularly serious cases such as genocide or if extreme means were used (for example, hijacking or taking of hostages).[69] The term 'political crime' is narrowly construed.[70] In addition, no assistance will be granted if the offence was aimed at reducing fiscal charges or taxes (except with respect to gambling and trafficking in drugs, weapons and explosives,[71] evading currency regulations or economic policy).[72]

Legal assistance is only given in lifting bank confidentiality if coercive measures can be applied by the Swiss authorities. Under the Criminal Assistance Statute, as well as under the European Convention and the US Treaty, coercive measures are generally only admissible if the offence being prosecuted contains the elements (other than intent or negligence) of an offence punishable under Swiss law (the requirement of dual criminality).[73]

The US Treaty also requires that the incriminated offence be one listed in its annex.[74] If the request concerns other crimes, Switzerland may only grant assistance and apply coercive measures under the Criminal Assistance Statute. However, neither the requirement of dual criminality nor the annex are applicable with respect to certain

---

62 Kleiner, Schwob and Winzeler, n 3 above, BkL, art 47, n 142.
63 See BGE 118 (1992) Ib 457; cf also BGE 109 (1983) Ib 47.
64 Criminal Assistance Statute, art 8; BGE 110 (1984) Ib 173 (176).
65 Criminal Assistance Statute, art 1a, para 2; US Treaty, art 3, para 1(a).
66 Criminal Assistance Statute, art 2.
67 Criminal Assistance Statute, art 3, para 1; US Treaty, art 2, para 1(c).
68 BGE 113 (1987) Ib 175, 109 (1983) Ib 71, 106 (1980) Ib 309.
69 Criminal Assistance Statute, art 3, para 2.
70 BGE 113 Ib 175 (180).
71 US Treaty, art 2, para 1(c).
72 Criminal Assistance Statute, art 3, para 3; US Treaty, art 2, para 1(c).
73 Criminal Assistance Statute, art 64, para 1; reservation by Switzerland made under the European Convention, art 5, para 1(a); US Treaty, art 4, para 2(a).
74 US Treaty, art 4, para 2(a).

cases of organised crime, in which Switzerland will grant legal assistance even in tax matters if exponents of organised crime are involved and such assistance is necessary for effective law enforcement.[75] This means that, in cases of organised crime, it is possible to grant legal assistance to the US with respect to offences against tax, anti-trust and securities laws.

As Switzerland endeavours to prevent misuse of information furnished by way of legal assistance, it will request the foreign authority not to use such information for the prosecution of any offence for which Switzerland would not grant judicial assistance if it were made the object of a separate request (the requirement of speciality).[76] In practice, the Swiss authorities require an express confirmation by the requesting country in the absence of a treaty.[77] Consequently, any further use of information requires the approval of the Swiss authorities unless the offence for which legal assistance was sought is being requalified by the requesting country in light of the information provided and the requalified offence would continue to be eligible for mutual assistance or the information is used against perpetrators otherwise involved in the prosecuted offence.[78]

Switzerland refuses coercive measures for forcing a witness to appear in proceedings held abroad. Therefore, a Swiss bank officer summoned to appear in foreign proceedings must not do so if this would jeopardise bank confidentiality.[79]

The Criminal Assistance Statute, as well as the US Treaty, provide for a certain degree of participation by foreign authorities and the application of certain procedural rules in the execution of the request for judicial assistance. Thus, foreign judges or prosecutors and similar officers may be present when depositions are taken and when documents are seized. However, even under the US Treaty and the Criminal Assistance Statute, performance of the legal assistance requested is primarily the task of the cantonal authorities who, as far as coercive measures are concerned, apply their own cantonal procedural rules[80] and foreign officers must take a passive role, except where federal law determines otherwise.[81]

In practice, a Swiss magistrate is often unable to determine which documents or information are relevant to a complex case. He will be tempted to consult his foreign colleague when screening documents and questioning witnesses. Therefore, the danger exists that the foreign officer may obtain access to confidential information before the right to such access has been determined in judicial proceedings.[82] The Swiss Federal Supreme Court held that when in doubt the Swiss magistrate must exclude the presence of foreign representatives.[83] This rule has not changed, even though the new art 65a of the Criminal Assistance Statute now provides that the presence of foreign officials during the execution of the request may be requested.[84]

Measures to protect confidential information, where admissible, are the same as provided by the laws on federal and cantonal criminal procedure unless a treaty

---

75 US Treaty, arts 6 and 7.
76 Criminal Assistance Statute, art 67; US Treaty, art 5.
77 BGE 110 (1984) Ib 173 (177), 107 (1981) Ib 264 (271).
78 Criminal Assistance Statute, art 67, para 2.
79 Criminal Assistance Statute, art 69; US Treaty, art 23ss; European Convention, art 8ss.
80 Criminal Assistance Statute, arts 16ss and 64; US Treaty, art 37, para 2.
81 BGE 113 (1987) Ib 157 (169), 106 (1980) Ib 260 (261), 103 (1977) Ia 206 (214); cf also European Convention, art 3, para 1.
82 Cf also Bernasconi, n 3 above, pp 16–17.
83 BGE 113 (1987) Ib 157 (169).
84 Cf Criminal Assistance Statute, art 65a, para 1.

contains specific rules.[85] For example, the US Treaty provides for an exclusion of US representatives until it has been determined whether or not the relevant information can be disclosed.

The determination whether Switzerland grants legal assistance is made in a special procedure in which the persons concerned, including banks, who are asked to provide information, may challenge the legal assistance and appeal to the cantonal courts and the Federal Supreme Court.[86]

Administrative assistance

[30.24] Swiss banks and securities dealers and Swiss branches of foreign banks and securities dealers are subject to supervision by the Federal Banking Commission, to which they must fully disclose all information required for effective supervision.[87] Officers and staff of the Federal Banking Commission are strictly bound by their own secrecy obligation.[88]

Since customer relationships of a Swiss bank's foreign branch are not covered by art 47 of the BkL, disclosure of the relevant information to the competent foreign authorities is not subject to criminal sanctions by Switzerland. The disclosure of confidential customer information by the staff of the foreign branch will normally be governed by the relevant foreign law.[89]

Parallel to the ever-increasing globalisation of the players in the financial markets, cross-border co-operation among banking and securities supervisory agencies has been continuously expanded in the past few years. Accordingly, the BkL provides for administrative assistance in favour of foreign supervisory authorities to implement international co-operation among supervisory agencies. The relevant provision became effective on 1 February 1997 and was materially amended with effect from 1 February 2006.[90] Pursuant to art 23 sexies of the BkL and art 38 of the SESTA, the Federal Banking Commission may, on the one hand, request information or documents from a foreign bank and financial market supervisory authorities in order to assure its consolidated supervision of internationally active banking groups under the home country rule.[91] On the other hand, the Federal Banking Commission may assist foreign supervisory agencies. It may forward confidential information and documents related to the matter for which assistance is requested to a foreign supervisory authority provided the following requirements are met:

1   the transmitted information will be used exclusively for the direct supervision of banks, exchanges, broker–dealers and other financial intermediaries subject to a licensing requirement or is forwarded to other authorities or courts for such purpose;

---

85 US Treaty, art 12, para 3(d) and (e).
86 Cf Wyss, n 60 above, pp 35–37.
87 BkL, art 23 bis, para 2; SESTA, art 35, para 2.
88 PC, art 320; cf Ch Breining-Kaufmann, B Kleiner and D Zobl in Bodmer, Kleiner and Lutz *Kommentar zum Schweizerischen Bankengesetz* (16th edn, 2005) BkL, art 23, n 37.
89 Kleiner, Schwob and Winzeler, n 3 above, BkL, art 47, n 366.
90 BkL, art 23 sexies and SESTA, art 38; cf B Kleiner in Bodmer, Kleiner and Lutz *Kommentar zum Schweizerischen Bankengesetz* (16th edn, 2005), n 3 above, BkL, art 23 sexies, nn 1–21; U Zulauf *Rechtshilfe-Amtshilfe, Zur Zusammenarbeit der Eidgenössischen Bankenkommission mit ausländischen Aufsichtsbehörden im Rahmen der neuen Banken-, Börsen- und Anlagefondsgesetzgebung des Bundes* in Swiss Review of Business Law (1995) pp 50–62; Ph Jacquemond *Revision der internationalen Amtshilfe gemäss dem Gesetz über die Börsen und den Effektenhandel (BEHG)* in Swiss Review of Business Law (2005), p 221.
91 BkL, art 23 sexies, para 1; SESTA, art 38, para 1.

2   the foreign supervisory agency is bound by official or professional secrecy provided that the rules regarding the publicity of proceedings and information of the public are reserved.

The Federal Banking Commission may, after consultation with the Federal Office for Legal Affairs, authorise the transmission of information to the criminal authorities for other purposes than the supervision of financial institutions, unless criminal assistance would be excluded, ie there exist grounds that would exclude criminal assistance in the matter concerned.

These provisions are designed to provide bank-related and customer-related data to foreign supervisory authorities. The transfer of customer-related data is, however, subject to judicial review allowing a review of whether the interests of a foreign supervisory authority prevail over the protection of bank confidentiality.[92] The amendments that became effective on 1 February 2006 substantially changed the previous restrictive practice and are based on the principle that bank customers who deal in foreign securities markets implicitly accept the rules of these foreign securities markets and have therefore waived Swiss bank confidentiality in connection with the enforcement of the applicable rules of these foreign securities markets.

Administrative assistance is currently mainly used for cross-border insider dealing investigations. Until 2004, the Federal Banking Commission issued 157 assistance orders, more than half of which were challenged before the Swiss Federal Supreme Court.[93] A substantial body of case law has developed in the meantime. Following the Swiss Federal Supreme Court decisions, administrative assistance with the US Securities and Exchange Commission ('SEC') and the Italian CONSOB was on hold until 1 February 2006. With respect to the SEC, the Federal Supreme Court held that the requirements for administrative assistance are not met as the litigation releases of the SEC are not consistent with the obligation not to pass received information to other authorities without prior approval by the Federal Banking Commission. The conceptual difference between the Swiss and US supervisory system caused this unsatisfactory situation which led to the amendments that became effective on 1 February 2006. Under the newly-amended provisions, administrative assistance in favour of the SEC is now possible.

Tax authorities

[30.25]   Swiss banks, including branches of foreign institutions, have to account for stamp duties on the purchase and sale of securities, including transactions made for the account of customers, and for withholding taxes on dividends paid to shareholders and interest paid to their customers. The Swiss Federal Tax Authority is entitled to inspect the relevant files and therefore has access to customer data. The federal laws on stamp duties and withholding taxes prohibit, however, the use of customer data for any purpose other than enforcement of the respective taxes.[94] The information may not even be used for assessing other federal taxes, such as federal income tax. In line with this disclosure duty, banks have to testify in criminal proceedings regarding evasion of Swiss stamp duties and withholding taxes by their customers.[95]

---

92 BkL, art 23 sexies, para 3; SESTA, art 38, para 6.
93 Federal Banking Commission Annual Report (2004) p 92.
94 Article 37, para 5 of the Federal Law on Stamp Tax, 27 June 1973, RS 641.10; art 40, para 5 of the Federal Law on Withholding Tax, 13 October 1965, RS 642.21.
95 BGE 104 (1978) IV 125.

With respect to the bank's own income taxes, the bank has to disclose the same information to the tax authorities as any other taxpayer. However, the tax authorities have no power to compel disclosure of any information protected by bank confidentiality.[96] If such information is directly relevant to the assessment of the bank's taxes, for example, reserves for bad debts, compensation for damages paid to customers, etc, the bank has to exhaust other means, such as submission of certificates by independent auditors or an independent expert, before disclosing the information to the authorities.

A similar situation exists under the Swiss Federal Law on Value Added Tax.[97] Whereas ordinary banking transactions are not subject to VAT, certain services of a bank, such as asset management and fiduciary transactions, are nevertheless taxable if the services are provided to persons domiciled in Switzerland. Services provided to persons domiciled outside Switzerland are exempt from VAT. In order to receive such an exemption, the Swiss federal tax authorities request proof that the recipient of the services is domiciled abroad. According to the tax authorities, a bank may submit all relevant documents containing the identity and foreign domicile of the customer. The bank cannot invoke bank confidentiality. However, the tax authorities are only allowed to use the customer information for the purposes of assessing VAT and are bound to preserve bank confidentiality.[98]

With regard to income and wealth taxes of the bank's customers, both cantonal and federal tax law require the bank to certify the relevant information to the customer only. Thus, the bank cannot be compelled to submit documents or information directly to the tax authorities for the purpose of tax assessment or tax audit of its customers.[99] Nevertheless, in criminal proceedings for tax fraud, the bank has to testify as in any other criminal procedure.[100] Tax fraud is defined as 'an intentional deceit of the tax authorities by means of documents containing untrue information for the purpose of obtaining an illegal tax advantage . . .' (compare BGE 96 (1970) I 337ss). However, the definition has been subsequently broadened and brought into line with the notion of fraud as defined in art 146 of the PC to include other types of malicious deceit such as a 'conspiracy with third persons', 'special machinations, tricks or a construction of lies' or even mere silence if it can be foreseen that the victim will not double check given a particular relationship of trust.[101] The latter will hardly ever exist vis-à-vis the tax authorities, whereas the other terms of malicious deceit may extend the term 'tax fraud'. The traditional definition still applies with respect to direct federal taxes.[102]

The consequence of this development in domestic Swiss law may be less interesting than the effect in the area of international legal assistance. Though, in the same case in which the Federal Supreme Court seemed to announce a broader definition of 'tax fraud', it tightened the conditions for granting legal assistance (to Germany under the European Convention) by requesting that in tax fraud cases the request must present a prima facie case and sufficient facts to support a reasonable suspicion. This is

96 Cf Aubert et al, n 5 above, pp 242–243; X Oberson *Questions actuelles concernant le secret bancaire dans la procedure fiscale* in Bernasconi *Les nouveaux défis au secret bancaire suisse* (1996) pp 61–62.
97 VAT Law 2 September 1999, RS 641.20.
98 VAT Law, art 62, para 3 and *Broschüre Nr 14 Finanzbereich der ESTV*, art 2.1.3.2.
99 Kleiner, Schwob and Winzeler, n 3 above, BkL, art 47, n 105ss.
100 BGE 108 (1982) Ib 231 (236).
101 BGE 111 (1985) Ib 242 (248).
102 Article 186 of the Federal Law on Direct Tax, 14 December 1990, RS 642.11.

contrary to the principle adhered to in other cases of legal assistance, according to which the facts as presented in the request will be generally accepted by the Swiss authorities without examination of the merits.[103]

Normal tax evasion by means of failing to declare certain income items or assets is not considered a serious crime in Switzerland, but only a misdemeanour and, therefore, the bank cannot be compelled to testify in the relevant enforcement proceedings or to disclose customer data. However, this rule does not apply to withholding tax and stamp duties.[104]

Based on the treaties ratified by Switzerland concerning avoidance of double taxation, bank confidentiality remains protected.[105] This continues to be true even after the agreement between the EU and Switzerland regarding a new withholding tax on interest for bonds held by EU residents.

Other administrative authorities

[30.26] Unless expressly provided by law, banks have no duty to disclose privileged information in administrative proceedings. A notable exception concerns the acquisition of interests in Swiss real estate by foreigners, which is strictly regulated.[106]

Insider dealing

[30.27] Since 1 July 1988, insider dealing is a crime. Under art 161 of the PC, any director, manager, auditor, attorney or agent of a company or co-operative, or an entity controlling it or controlled by it, and any member of a governmental body or agency or a public servant or any auxiliary person may be considered an insider. Persons directly or indirectly informed by an insider are considered 'tippees' if they know or should have known that the information is illegally disclosed by the insider.

Disclosure and use of inside information is punished if it relates to shares, participation certificates, bonds, debentures, other negotiable instruments or rights issued by Swiss or foreign companies listed on an official exchange or an official secondary market in Switzerland, or if it concerns options for the purchase or sale of such securities. Securities traded merely 'over the counter' are not included. Information is considered to be inside information if it is confidential and concerns a planned rights issue, a merger or a similar occurrence of comparable importance if it can be foreseen that its disclosure to the public will substantially affect the price of the securities. Under the case law of the Swiss Federal Supreme Court, a change in profit forecasts does not constitute inside information within the meaning of the PC. Apart from disclosure to third persons for the purpose of obtaining a profit, the insider also breaches the law if he uses the information to obtain a profit for himself or a third person. The penalties range from a fine to imprisonment of up to three years.

As a consequence of art 161 of the PC, bank confidentiality can be lifted in domestic insider dealing cases (pursuant to the respective cantonal and federal statutes on

---

103 BGE 111 (1985) Ib 242, 114 (1988) Ib 56, 115 Ib 68, 116 Ib 96; cf also Criminal Assistance Statute, art 3, para 3.
104 Kleiner, Schwob and Winzeler, n 3 above, BkL, art 47, n 118.
105 Kleiner, Schwob and Winzeler, n 3 above, BkL, art 47, n 300.
106 Cf the respective Federal Law dated 16 December 1983, RS 211.412.41, arts 22, para 3 and 31.

criminal procedure, banks are required to testify before prosecutors and the criminal courts), as well as in international legal and administrative assistance proceedings with respect to foreign insider dealing cases. The same holds for the recently-introduced criminal provision on market manipulation (art 161 bis of the PC).

Under the US Treaty, the two governments signed a Memorandum of Understanding dated 10 November 1987, by which Switzerland also agreed to grant assistance in so-called 'civil proceedings' relative to insider dealing conducted by the SEC.

The administrative assistance procedure has developed into an efficient tool to prosecute cross-border insider dealing cases. Under the case law of the Swiss Federal Supreme Court and the practice of the Federal Banking Commission, the interest of an efficient cross-border insider dealing prosecution outweighs the interest of the bank's customer in protecting his privacy. Administrative assistance is routinely granted by the Federal Banking Commission which is, among others, the result of case law that places a very low threshold on the suspicion that insider dealing has occurred. It is sufficient for foreign authorities to state that immediately prior to the public disclosure of the insider information trading volume increased and prices changed. The Federal Banking Commission does not have to review such statements made by the foreign authorities.[107]

Money laundering

[30.28] The Swiss legislation against money laundering rests on four mutually reinforcing pillars and constitutes a combination of administrative law, industry self-regulation and criminal provisions. The first and main pillar consists of the Federal Law Against Money Laundering in the Financial Sector dated 10 October 1997 ('Money Laundering Act').[108] The second pillar consists of the new Federal Banking Commission Ordinance on Money Laundering dated 17 January 2003 ('FBC Money Laundering Ordinance') specifying banks' duties under the Money Laundering Act, as well as with regard to terrorist financing.[109] The third pillar consists of the self-regulatory system put in place by the Swiss Bankers' Association in the form of the Swiss Banks' Code of Conduct with Regard to the Exercise of Due Diligence, as amended ('CDB 03'), which embodies the 'know your customer' rules of the Swiss banks. Finally, the fourth pillar consists of the criminal provision regarding money laundering contained in arts 305 bis and 305 ter of the PC. All four pillars directly affect bank confidentiality.

The Money Laundering Act

[30.29] The Money Laundering Act came into force on 1 April 1998 and aims to prevent money laundering within the meaning of art 305 bis of the PC. The Money Laundering Act applies to all financial intermediaries, which not only includes banks and securities dealers, but also financial intermediaries such as investment advisors, so far not under supervision by any regulatory agency. The Money Laundering Act sets out a number of due diligence obligations, as well as obligations to act in the event of suspicion of money laundering and puts in place a system of supervision through self-regulating bodies of the financial industry.

---

107 BGE 125 (1999) II 65 and 126 (2000) II 406; see also the Federal Banking Commission Annual Report (2001) p 39.
108 RS 955.0
109 See the website of the Federal Banking Commission at www.cfb.admin.ch.

The due diligence obligations include, first, the verification of the identity of the bank customer upon entering into a business relationship. Such verification includes, in particular, the identification of the beneficial owner of the funds. In this regard, banks have to require the customer to provide a written declaration disclosing the identity of the beneficial owner if (i) the customer is not the beneficial owner or the beneficial ownership is in doubt, (ii) the customer is a domiciliary company and (iii) a cash transaction is effected for a large sum, ie SFr25,000 or more. A further verification of the identity of the customer and the beneficial owner is required in the course of the business relationship if doubts arise as to the identity of the customer or the beneficial owner of the funds. In cases where a transaction or the business relationship appears to be unusual (except where it is manifestly legal) or there is reason to believe that the assets are the proceeds of a crime or that a criminal organisation has the power to dispose of them, the bank is under the duty to investigate the economic background and purpose of the transaction and the business relationship. Such special investigation must be documented in writing. The Money Laundering Act requires a bank to draw up its documentation regarding the transactions effected and its due diligence investigations in such a manner that qualified third parties can accurately understand the transactions and business relationship and verify compliance with the Money Laundering Act. The documentation must be retained in a form that enables the bank, within a reasonable time period, to comply with information requests or freezing orders by the authorities. After the termination of the business relationship or the completion of the transaction, documents and records must be kept for at least ten years. Finally, banks must ensure that their staff are adequately trained to ensure full compliance with the Money Laundering Act.

If a bank knows or presumes, on the basis of founded suspicion, that assets involved in the business relationship are related to money laundering, that they are the proceeds of a crime or that a criminal organisation has power over the assets, it shall without delay notify the reporting office for money laundering. Further, the bank immediately has to freeze the assets it holds for the customer to the extent they are related to the reporting obligation. The freezing of the assets shall continue to be effective until the receipt of a decision by the competent prosecuting authorities about a freezing order, but for a maximum of five working days after the notification. As long as the assets are frozen, the bank shall not notify the customer or any third party concerned about such report.

The duty to report and freeze assets in cases of suspicion of money laundering conflicts with bank confidentiality. For this reason, art 11 of the Money Laundering Act explicitly confirms that a bank which reports a suspicion under the Money Laundering Act and freezes funds concerned cannot be prosecuted for breach of bank confidentiality and also cannot be held liable for breach of contract provided it can show that it applied the due diligence required by the circumstances. The Money Laundering Act does not specify the meaning of 'due diligence required by the circumstances'. In any case, there exists, so far, no published court decision as to breach of bank confidentiality or possible related breach of contract under this provision.

For the purpose of the Money Laundering Act, banks are supervised by the Federal Banking Commission.

The FBC Money Laundering Ordinance

[30.30]   The FBC Money Laundering Ordinance became effective on 1 July 2003 and contains detailed rules regarding the fight against money laundering. It establishes a number of principles, sets out organisational measures to be implemented by banks and establishes principles of due diligence that have to be observed by banks to prevent money laundering. The principles set out in the FBC Money Laundering Ordinance include the prohibition of accepting assets which the bank knows or should have known originate from a crime committed in Switzerland or abroad. This, in particular, also includes the bribing of foreign officials. Further, a bank is not allowed to maintain a business relationship with companies or persons which the bank knows or should have known are part of a terrorist or criminal organisation or support or finance such organisations. The banks are also not allowed to maintain business relationships with other banks that do not maintain a physical presence (offshore banks) in the country of incorporation unless they are part of an adequately supervised banking group.

The FBC Money Laundering Ordinance requires banks to put in place an electronic transaction supervising scheme that allows the identification of transactions with an increased risk profile. Such transactions have to be defined by the banks on the basis of criteria such as the inflow and outflow of money, material deviation with regard to transaction type, volume and sequence compared with the ordinary course of the business relationship and material deviation with regard to transaction type, volume and sequence compared with similar business relationships. In any case, transactions with an increased risk profile include cash deposits of more than SFr100,000 at the beginning of the business relationship and any founded suspicion of money laundering. In order to enable banks to establish founded suspicions of money laundering, the Ordinance contains an extensive annex that lists specific types of transactions.

For the 'know your customer' rules, the Ordinance explicitly refers to the CDB 03. With respect to payments made abroad, Swiss banks are now obliged to indicate the name, account number and domicile of the payee in order to allow the tracking of money trails. In connection with customers or transactions with an increased risk profile, Swiss banks have to undertake reasonable inquiries regarding the background of the customer and transaction. These inquiries have to be documented. Business relationships with politically exposed persons[110] can only be entered into with the approval of the management of the bank, who have to review annually the continuation of the business relationship.

The Swiss Banks' Code of Conduct

[30.31] In an attempt to preserve the international reputation of the Swiss banking community, to establish rules ensuring the 'know your customer rules' and a business conduct that is beyond reproach when accepting funds from new customers, the Swiss Bankers' Association promulgated a code of conduct on a self-regulatory basis as early as 1977. This code of conduct has regularly been amended and is currently defined as the CDB 03, with effect from 1 July 2003. All Swiss banks which are party to the CDB 03 undertake:

---

110 Section a, art 1 of the FBC Money Laundering Ordinance defines politically exposed persons as those with prominent public functions abroad: (i) head of state or head of government, high politicians at national level, high functionaries in administration, justice, military and political parties at national level, high officers of companies of national importance controlled by the state and (ii) any company or person that evidently has a close family, personal or business relationship with any of the persons named above.

1   to identify the client when establishing a business relationship and, if in doubt, request confirmation from the client as to who beneficially owns the deposited amounts;
2   not to support capital flight actively; and
3   not to aid and abet tax evasion actively by providing misleading representations.[111]

The CDB 03 contains specific guidance as to the identification of individuals and legal entities residing or domiciled in Switzerland or abroad.

A bank is further obliged to ascertain that the customer is the beneficial owner of the assets to be deposited by means of a written statement to be signed by the customer if it has any doubt that the customer does not beneficially own the assets. Normally, the bank may assume that its client is also the beneficial owner. The CDB 03, however, provides for guidance when a bank should have doubts, in particular, when a power of attorney is conferred on someone who clearly would not have sufficiently close links to the customer, or the financial standing of someone requesting to carry out a transaction is known to the bank and the assets deposited or about to be deposited are disproportionate to that individual's financial circumstances. In these cases, the bank must require a written confirmation by the customer that he beneficially owns the assets, on the so-called 'Form A'.

Interestingly, if the beneficial owner of the assets is not identical to the customer, ie if the beneficial owner has no contractual relationship with the bank, the bank may neither accept instructions from him nor forward information to him, otherwise it would risk being in breach of bank confidentiality. Moreover, the Federal Supreme Court has held that the beneficial owner of assets has no standing to challenge an order against the contractual counterparty of the bank in legal assistance procedures.[112]

Failure to comply with the CDB 03 may lead to an investigation by the independent supervisory board for the CDB and eventually to sanctions against the bank, such as a fine of up to SFr10 million. Further, breaches of the CDB 03 may jeopardise a bank's licence as its proper business conduct is then in doubt.

Criminal provisions

[30.32]   The criminal provisions with respect to money laundering include arts 305 bis and 305 ter of the PC.

Art 305 bis, para 1 of the PC holds, in essence, that whoever commits an act which is likely to jeopardise the investigation of the source or location of assets or their confiscation which he knows or must assume originates from a crime shall be punished by imprisonment or a fine. The offence is aimed at preventing the investigation of the origin, discovery or confiscation of assets. Since straightforward financial transactions, such as the acceptance of deposits, could qualify as money laundering activities, the Federal Banking Commission takes the view that banks should refrain from certain activities, such as labelling accounts with pseudonyms rather than real names.

Pursuant to art 305 ter, para 1 of the PC, a person who accepts and holds deposits or manages investments must establish with all due diligence the identity of the

---

111 CDB 03, art 1.
112 BGE 121 (1995) II 459 (462).

beneficial owner. The standards for establishing such identity are set out in the CDB 03. Accordingly, if a bank complies in form and substance with these standards, it will exclude the risk of committing a criminal act within the meaning of art 305 ter, para 1 of the PC.

Art 305 ter, para 2 of the PC establishes the right of banks to inform the Swiss criminal authorities if they recognise circumstances indicating money laundering activities. While this notification right of banks still exists, it has, in practice, been superseded by the notification duty contained in the Money Laundering Act.

Recent developments

Dormant accounts

[30.33] The core issue of the now settled dispute on Holocaust-related claims was the treatment of dormant accounts by Swiss banks. The CC and art 47 of the BkL regarding bank confidentiality put very high standards of proof upon heirs of deceased bank customers for locating bank accounts and being recognised as the new legitimate owner of such accounts. Due to a lack of available proper inheritance documentation, most Holocaust victims and their heirs were not in a position to meet these strict standards of proof and be recognised by Swiss banks as the legitimate owners of bank accounts. As part of the settlement of the dispute on Holocaust-related claims, Swiss banks were required to publish dormant account details, which seems at the outset incompatible with bank confidentiality. The solution adopted was a pragmatic one. The Federal Banking Commission took the view that where there is no master of the secret anymore, there cannot be banking secrecy. Therefore, the banks have to act in the best interests of the heirs of former bank customers, which is to learn about their entitlements.

Currently, a new federal law on dormant assets is in preparation which will provide for a statutory duty of banks to avoid the breaking up of customer relationships by organisational means. After a dormancy period of ten years, assets have to be reported to a newly created contact office. Such contact office will maintain a list of dormant assets. Persons who have established prima facie evidence of a claim are granted access to such list. After a dormancy period of 50 years, unclaimed assets accrue to the Swiss Confederation, provided, however, that five years prior to accrual the list of dormant assets is published.

US backup withholding tax

[30.34] In 2001, the US introduced a new backup withholding tax on dividends and interest paid on US securities. In connection with this new tax scheme, Swiss banks have entered into qualified intermediary agreements with the Internal Revenue Service ('IRS'). In order to protect bank confidentiality, these agreements provide that compliance with the qualified intermediary agreement is reviewed by external auditors which, in most cases, are the same firms auditing the Swiss bank for statutory and banking purposes. Such audit firms are instructed by the IRS and report directly to them. Such reports shall, however, not contain the name of customers and the identity of the beneficial owners. This scheme allows the maintenance of bank confidentiality and assures compliance with US tax laws. Some authors have, however, raised concerns about certain reporting requirements with regard to non-US persons. As a result of the uncertainties, a number of non-US private clients have decided to discontinue investing in US securities.

685

EU withholding tax

[30.35] With effect from 1 July 2005, Switzerland entered into a bilateral treaty with the European Union regarding withholding tax on interest income. Under this treaty, Switzerland levies a special withholding tax on interest income of physical persons domiciled in the EU who maintain a bank account with a Swiss bank. The withholding tax is progressively increased to 35% and only applies to interest income, but not to dividend income or capital gains on shares. 75% of the proceeds of this special withholding tax are remitted to the EU. The EU resident may escape the withholding tax by authorising the Swiss bank to disclose the interest income to the tax authorities of his EU country of residence. This special withholding tax gives the EU resident bank customer the option to remain protected by bank confidentiality.

Outsourcing

[30.36] In recent years, many Swiss banks have resorted to the outsourcing of certain functions, in particular, data processing. In response to this development, the Federal Banking Commission issued a circular on 26 August 1999 setting out the principles governing outsourcing. The circular was amended on 22 August 2002 and its aims are to ensure the proper organisation of banks and the protection of bank confidentiality. The principles include the duty of the bank to secure bank confidentiality with adequate technical and organisational measures. Bank customers have to be informed about the outsourcing. Such information may be contained in the bank's general business conditions if the outsourcing is made within Switzerland. In the case of outsourcing involving the transfer of customer data abroad, the bank customer must be informed in detail in a separate document beforehand. The bank customer must be given the opportunity to terminate the banking relationship without financial consequences. These rules ensure that the bank customer has been given a choice before limitations on the protection of bank confidentiality are put in place.

Securitisation and bank confidentiality

[30.37] Under Swiss law, a valid assignment of claims requires that the assignor discloses at least the name of the debtor and the amount of the assigned debt to the assignee. Accordingly, securitisation conflicts with bank confidentiality as the name of the bank customer and the amount of his debt owed to the bank are protected by bank confidentiality. Securitisation of customer receivables by Swiss banks therefore requires a waiver of bank confidentiality by the bank customer concerned. Without such waiver, securitisation would constitute a breach of bank confidentiality, which could not only lead to civil damage claims, but also to criminal sanctions and withdrawal of the banking licence. Some authors have even argued that an assignment in breach of bank confidentiality is void. The Swiss legislator does not consider it necessary to change bank confidentiality in order to facilitate asset securitisation.

Internet banking and bank confidentiality

[30.38] Internet banks and Internet banking are not governed by special banking laws, but rather have to comply with normal banking law, including, in particular, bank confidentiality. Since information transmitted on the Internet is not protected, banks that use Internet communication with their customers risk breaching bank confidentiality. Therefore, all banks engaging in Internet banking require Internet banking customers to sign an appropriate waiver of bank confidentiality.

Terrorist financing

[30.39] Article 5 of the new FBC Money Laundering Ordinance prohibits Swiss banks from maintaining any business relationships with organisations or persons which the bank knows or should know is a criminal or terrorist organisation or a person who is part of such an organisation or supports or finances such an organisation. Further, banks are not allowed to finance such persons or otherwise support them.

Even before the coming into force of the FBC Money Laundering Ordinance, the fight against terrorism and terrorist financing has been seamlessly included in the anti-money laundering legislation. The 'Bush' lists published by the US government were communicated to all Swiss banks, with either the request immediately to notify any assets of listed persons or organisations to the notification office and freeze their assets or, depending on the requirements of the 'Bush' lists, conduct a special inquiry in accordance with art 6 of the Money Laundering Act to clarify the economic background of the account holder. These measures lead to the freezing of a number of accounts. In accordance with the Money Laundering Act, such freeze is, however, temporary and will only last until criminal or criminal assistance proceedings have been completed.

31 United States

Danforth Newcomb*

INTRODUCTION

[31.1] US law requiring financial institutions to treat customer information confidentially reflects the nature of general law in the United States. Financial privacy law can be found both in federal law and the law of individual states. It is found in court decisions, statutes, administrative regulations and even in informal guidance published by bank regulatory agencies. To understand the US law of financial privacy, one must examine both the sources of that law and the historical context in which it arose.

Until recent years, US financial privacy law dealt mostly with the proper reach of domestic government access to bank records. There has been little concern until recently about access to financial information by either private parties or governments from outside the United States, a theme that is important in many other nations such as Switzerland, Luxembourg and Uruguay.

Financial privacy law in the United States has its origins in various state court decisions. In more recent years, federal statutes have dominated the scene and largely supplanted the state case law. This is best seen in the imbalance in the United States between privacy concerns and anti-money laundering provisions. Finally, with the advent of computers and the marketing of electronic data, the United States, like Europe and elsewhere, has seen a rise in concerns about financial data used for commercial purposes and a corresponding legislative response. The picture that will emerge shows a dynamic and multi-layered legal structure that only provides limited financial privacy in the United States.

THE BASIC POSITION

[31.2] The US law of financial privacy is a patchwork of cases and federal statutes that do not provide a comprehensive or coherent regime to protect financial information. Financial privacy law in the United States first developed as common, or judge-made, law and arose out of bank customer claims that their bank had breached an implied contract or tort duty of confidentiality when the bank provided account information to government investigators. In almost all cases, the law

* The author wishes to acknowledge the substantial assistance of his partners Bradley K Sabel, for the first draft of the discussion of insider trading and ethical walls, and Patrick Robbins, for the first draft of the discussion of specified unlawful activities in the discussion of money laundering statutes. E Alexandra Dosman and Matthew J Reynolds provided much needed editorial and cite checking assistance which is gratefully acknowledged.

689

developed as a reaction to perceived excesses that invaded a loosely defined zone of privacy found in the law of torts or implied contract. Far more comprehensive, coherent and explicit are the duties to collect and retain information about customers and their transactions placed on financial institutions by anti-money laundering laws and regulations. These cases and later statutes reflect an evolving balancing act between financial privacy and legitimate investigation methods. That balance was repeatedly struck to bar investigators from scanning financial data of large numbers of customers looking for investigative leads or suspicious conduct, but permitting broad access to bank records in pursuit of identified investigations of actual offences. In other words, 'fishing expeditions' to find previously undetected breaches are generally prohibited, but searches to find leads and evidence for investigation of known or suspected breaches are permitted.

SCOPE OF THE BASIC POSITION

[31.3] To understand how the basic position is actually applied, one must understand US common law, federal and some state statutes and administrative regulations under the federal statutes.

The development of US case law of financial privacy

[31.4] Somewhat surprisingly, a bank customer's right to privacy of account information is not frequently litigated in the United States. While US laws and regulations governing banks are found both at the state and federal levels, the rights of bank customers were historically found in the laws of the individual states. Prior to the 1960s, there was no substantial case law that articulated a duty of financial privacy owed by a bank to its customers. An article published in the Harvard Law Review in 1890 by Louis Brandeis (who was not yet a US Supreme Court Justice) and Professor Samuel Warren presented an early argument for the right of privacy.[1] A leading scholar of the law of torts, Professor William L Prosser, published an article entitled 'Privacy' in the California Law Review some 70 years later.[2] However, neither article seems to have engendered significant judicial adherence as applied to the rights of bank customers. Cases that have attempted to determine the scope of financial privacy arose from what was perceived to have been an excess of investigative zeal by police authorities.

An early, but isolated, case in New Jersey

[31.5] An early example is *Brex v Smith* from 1929.[3] In this action, the members of the Newark city police force sought to enjoin the state prosecutor from reviewing the bank accounts of each of the city's police officers. The only stated reason for the review was to 'assist him in some investigation he is making'.[4] It is notable that this action was brought in a court of equity in the days before the unification of equity courts and law courts. Generally, the equity courts were far more willing to develop creative solutions for situations which appeared to be novel or not otherwise previously decided by the law courts. The decision in this case is not a model of

---

1 Louis D Brandeis and Samuel D Warren 'The Right to Privacy' (1890) 4 Harv L Rev 193.
2 William L Prosser 'Privacy'(1960) 48 Cal LR 383.
3 146 A 34 (NJ Ch 1929).
4 Ibid at 35.

clarity, weaving together both concepts of implied contract and an apparent tort theory of a right of personal privacy. The court seems to have been most concerned by the fact that the prosecutor failed to follow the usual procedures for an investigation by empanelling a grand jury and issuing subpoenas. Accordingly, the judge issued an injunction barring the prosecutor from his sweeping inquiry of the banks concerning the accounts of all the policemen. This decision seems to have had little effect on the US jurisprudence of financial privacy for more than 30 years.

The first thoughtful analysis from Idaho

[31.6] The first case carefully to consider the relationship between a bank and its depositors was decided by the Supreme Court of Idaho in December 1961: *Peterson v Idaho First National Bank*.[5] Mr Peterson's employer requested information regarding his account from the bank which the bank voluntarily disclosed. Peterson then filed a complaint against the bank to recover damages for alleged breaches of his right to privacy. The trial court dismissed the claim on the grounds that it failed to state a claim upon which relief could be granted. The Idaho Supreme Court, speaking through its chief justice, reversed that dismissal. In doing so, the court first considered the scholarly treatises on the right to privacy by Professors Prosser and Warren and Justice Brandeis. The court also considered the Restatement of Torts, s 867 which defined the right of privacy as prohibiting unreasonable and serious interference with another's interest in not having his affairs known to others.[6] The court also noted that the State of California has a constitutional provision which guarantees the right to privacy and concluded that a majority of the states recognised such a right.[7] The court concluded, however, that Peterson's right to privacy had not been damaged as there had been no communication to the public of the information (beyond his employer) which was an essential element of the tort of invasion of privacy.

Rather than stopping at that point, the court then considered whether the plaintiff was entitled to relief on some other ground. The court began this analysis by positing that the relationship between a bank and its depositor, at least in certain circumstances, is one of an implied contract of agency. Accordingly, an agent is subject to a duty to its principal not to use or communicate confidential information. The court found no cases directly on the point, including *Brex v Smith*, the New Jersey Chancery Court case. The court concluded by negative inference from other cases relating to a bank's obligations to comply with lawful subpoenas and other investigative process that 'inviolate secrecy is one of the inherent and fundamental precepts of the relationship of the bank and its customers or depositors'.[8] On the basis that it is implicit in the contract of the bank with its customer that no information may be disclosed by the bank unless authorised by law or by the customer, the court concluded that the bank must be liable for breach of such an implied contract. This decision was the first American decision to analyse carefully the basis for a claim of financial privacy by a bank customer and has been subsequently cited as the seminal case in this area.

---

5 367 P 2d 284 (Idaho 1961).
6 Restatement (First) of Torts § 867 (1939). See also the Restatement (Second) of Torts §§ 867, 652A–652I (1979).
7 Cal Const art I, § 1 (1972).
8 367 P 2d at 291.

Florida considers contract and tort theories

[31.7]   Eight years later, the intermediate appellate court of Florida clearly faced the choice between a contract and a tort theory of financial privacy. In *Milohnich v First National Bank of Miami Springs*, a depositor alleged damage arising from disclosure of confidential information by the bank to private third parties.[9] The majority opinion concluded that a bank had an implied contractual duty to maintain the confidentiality of its customers' information. In doing so, the court relied on *Peterson v Idaho First National Bank* and the English precedent of *Tournier v National Provincial and Union Bank of England*.[10]

New York case law unclear

[31.8]   It is somewhat surprising that the courts of New York have not had more jurisprudence concerning a bank's obligations of confidentiality given New York's prominent position in the banking community in the United States. It was not until 1978 that a New York intermediate appellate court considered the question indirectly. In *Graney Development Corpn v Taksen*, the court considered the nature of the confidential relationship between a bank and its borrowers.[11] In doing so, it assumed that there was a duty of confidentiality between a bank and its depositors based on a common law right of privacy. The court refused, however, to extend that duty to a borrowing relationship. Accordingly, the court's assumption about the duty of confidentiality is mere dicta and not binding precedent.

Ten years after the *Graney* decision, the federal appellate court sitting in New York was faced with the question of whether New York law had recognised a duty of confidentiality for depositors.[12] The case arose when a New York bank became suspicious of deposits made by a Bermudian couple and reported those suspicions to the Attorney General in Bermuda who conducted an investigation and, as a result, the couple pleaded guilty to breaches of Bermuda's currency restrictions. The two Bermudians then came to New York and brought an action in the federal courts of New York under the diversity jurisdiction against the New York bank.

Among other claims, the plaintiffs sought recovery on a common law theory under the law of the State of New York. The federal Court of Appeals examined the state law claims at great length reviewing the development of state law theories in various jurisdictions outside of New York and considered carefully both the case law in New York and the state legislation relating to privacy generally. The federal appellate court in the end concluded that the State of New York had not yet recognised a financial privacy for bank depositors and went on to conclude that the issue was sufficiently significant that it would be a mistake for a federal court to attempt to predict the outcome of that issue in the courts of the State of New York. Accordingly, the court abstained from ruling on the matter and dismissed the state law claim with an express reservation that the plaintiffs could refile their claim in the New York state courts.

The plaintiffs accepted the court's invitation to refile their claim in the state court and did so in a matter entitled *Young v Chemical Bank*.[13] Justice Baer, sitting in the trial

---

9 224 So 2d 759 (Fla Dist Ct App 1969).
10 [1924] 1 KB 461.
11 400 NYS 2d 717 (Sup Ct Monroe County 1978), affd 411 NYS 2d 756 (1st Dept 1978).
12 *Young v Chemical Bank*, 882 F 2d 633 (2nd Cir 1989), cert denied, 493 US 1072 (1990).
13 *Young v Chemical Bank*, 208 NY LJ 21 (1992).

courts of New York County, concluded that no prior New York court had recognised a duty of confidentiality imposed upon a bank with respect to customer information. However, the court went on to conclude that such a duty existed based on the quasi-fiduciary relationship between a bank and its depositors which the court noted was akin to the attorney–client relationship or the doctor and patient relationship. The court also looked at the exceptions to that duty concluding that there was an exception where the bank, acting in good faith, had a reasonable basis for a belief that a crime was being committed. In that circumstance, the bank was privileged to initiate contact with law enforcement authorities concerning its suspicions. Since this decision was at a motion to dismiss stage before factual evidence had been gathered, the court suggested that additional fact finding would be needed to resolve whether there had been a breach of the duty of confidentiality.

Shortly after issuing this decision, Justice Baer retired from the state courts (to take up a position as a judge in the federal courts of New York) and the case was reassigned to Justice Myriam Altman. Justice Altman granted a motion for reargument of the case and dismissed the case finding that all of the damages the plaintiffs sought were barred under New York precedent.[14] This decision may have been influenced by recently enacted federal anti-money laundering legislation which will be discussed later in this chapter.[15] Justice Altman's decision rested on a proposition that the plaintiffs may not profit from their own criminal conduct. While Justice Baer had been sufficiently concerned about this doctrine to limit the extent of the recovery in his decision, Justice Altman concluded that the plaintiffs' admission of criminal conduct in Bermuda as a result of their guilty plea barred any recovery by them for the conduct of Chemical Bank in reporting its suspicions about the depositors' activities. Justice Altman's decision mooted the prior ruling that for the first time had found a duty of confidentiality in New York law. Effectively, Justice Altman's decision leaves for another day the question as to whether New York courts will find a common law duty for a bank to keep information of its depositors confidential.

California cases balance privacy and investigation

[31.9]   In the mid-1970s, cases arose in California that addressed the extent of exceptions to banks' duties of confidentiality to customers. These cases clearly showed the shift from judge-made case precedent to new federal legislation that has become the predominant source of confidentiality obligations and exceptions today. In *Burrows v Superior Court*, the California Supreme Court addressed California's constitutional provision against unreasonable searches and seizures which is similar to the provision of the US federal constitution.[16] In *Burrows*, a police detective, having obtained information about various bank accounts, contacted several banks and requested that they provide copies of bank statements and other materials relating to a depositor's transactions. At least one bank voluntarily provided bank statements to the officer without the benefit of any legal process being served on the bank. The court, in analysing the duties of the bank, harkened back to the original *Brex* concern about unfettered access by police authorities to financial records. In *Burrows*, the court concluded that voluntary unregulated disclosure to police authorities without the benefit of the procedures inherent in issuing a subpoena

---

14 *Young v Chemical Bank*, No 2211/89 (Sup Ct NY County, 15 April 1993).
15 31 USC § 5318(g)(3) (1992).
16 529 P 2d 590 (Cal 1974).

exceeded the expectations of privacy that citizens legitimately had on the basis of both the California constitution and the Fourth Amendment to the federal constitution and, accordingly, ruled that the evidence obtained from the bank without the benefit of the subpoena was not admissible in the trial of this depositor.

Federal statutes become the primary source of law

[31.10] In weighing the balance between legitimate inquiry by investigative authorities and an expectation of privacy as to financial records, the California court analysed these issues as formulated by the federal legislature. So, we should turn to the enactment of federal legislation which becomes, after 1970, the dominant source of jurisprudence with respect to a bank's obligations of confidentiality to its customers.

The Third Party Record Keepers Act creates a narrow and limited protection in tax investigations

[31.11] In reaction to a US Supreme Court decision, *United States v Miller*,[17] holding that depositors had no constitutionally created protection from investigation for their bank records, Congress adopted an amendment to the Internal Revenue Code, as part of the Tax Reform Act 1976, known as the Third Party Record Keepers Act.[18] Congress passed this amendment in reaction to the court's holding that there was no expectation of privacy with respect to financial records kept at banks.[19] The Third Party Record Keepers Act requires that, whenever the Internal Revenue Service issues a summons for a production of records of any person other than the person who receives the summons, the target of the summons shall be notified and provided an opportunity to intervene in any proceedings for the enforcement of the summons, as well as an opportunity to stay compliance with the summons pursuant to the Internal Revenue Code. The definition of a third party record keeper includes a broad range of financial institutions, consumer reporting agencies, brokers, attorneys, accountants and, under an amendment in 1982, barter exchanges. While the Third Party Record Keepers Act was first limited to summonses issued under the administrative authority of the Internal Revenue Code, Congress soon moved to apply broader restrictions on federal information gathering again in reaction to the Supreme Court holding in *United States v Miller*.

The Right to Financial Privacy Act creates some limitation on federal investigations

[31.12] The broader reaction by Congress to the Supreme Court's decision in *United States v Miller* came in 1978 with the enactment of the Right to Financial Privacy Act.[20] This statute limits federal (but not state or local) governmental access to information, but contains significant exceptions and limitations. The Act covers information of individuals and small partnerships of up to five individuals, but does

---

17 *United States v Miller*, 425 US 435 (1976).
18 Those provisions are codified in 26 USC § 7609(a) (2002).
19 Pub L No 94-455, 90 Stat 1520, 1976 USCCAN 3797 n 8. The same legislation limited use of 'John Doe' summons to 'fish' for information.
20 12 USC §§ 3401–22 (2002).

not protect corporate customers' or other legal entities' information. Broadly, the statute prohibits financial institutions in the United States from disclosing customer information to the federal government unless proper procedures are followed to gain access and the customer is notified. Rarely are customers able to prevent the financial institution from providing the information required by the government. The principal practical effect, however, is that the previous practices of either enormously broad subpoenas or informal requests for information and unsupervised scanning of the files of a financial institution by a federal agent have been stopped.

A federal statute creates restrictions on disclosure to third parties

[31.13]   Until 1999, federal statutes did not restrict access of private litigants or state or local officials to information held by financial institutions with the limited exception that suspicious activity reports are not discoverable in private litigation. In other words, federal statutes provide no restrictions on private litigants or non-federal governments and only limited restrictions on the federal government's ability to access most of the information required to be retained under federal anti-money laundering laws. This gap in US privacy law was remedied in 1999 as a by-product of new federal legislation that primarily addressed the commercial use of consumer financial information. The Gramm-Leach-Bliley Act ('GLBA')[21] is the first US statute that deals with the disclosure of non-public personal information of private individual consumers. In summary, the GLBA prohibits a financial institution from

---

21 The Gramm-Leach-Bliley Act 1999 ('GLBA'), Pub L No 106-102, 106th Congress, lst Sess (12 November 1999), 113 Stat 1338–1481 (1999), amended the Bank Holding Company Act 956, 12 USC §§ 1841–1850 (2000) and other statutes. The relevant sections of the GLBA are codified in 15 USC §§ 6801–6809 and 6821–6827 (2000). In May 2000, the Office of the Comptroller of the Currency ('OCC'), the Board of Governors of the Federal Reserve System ('Board'), the Federal Deposit Insurance Corporation ('FDIC') and the Office of Thrift Supervision ('OTS') published substantially identical regulations relating to privacy of consumer financial information. 12 CFR pt 40 (2006) (OCC); 12 CFR pt 216 (Regulation P) (2003) (Board); 12 CFR pt 332 (2006) (FDIC); 12 CFR pt 573 (2006) (OTS). See the joint release accompanying the regulations, 65 Fed Reg 35, 162–236 (1 June 2000). See also the proposed regulation, 65 Fed Reg 8,788–8,816 (22 February 2000) and the accompanying joint release, 65 Fed Reg 8,770–8,816 (22 February 2000). Since the regulations are identical, this chapter only refers to Regulation P of the Board. See also 16 CFR pt 313 (2006) (Regulation of the Federal Trade Commission ('FTC') carrying out the financial privacy rules of the GLBA for financial institutions subject to the FTC's enforcement authority pursuant to 15 USC § 6805(a)(7) (2000)); 17 CFR pt 248 (2002) (Regulation S-P of the Securities and Exchange Commission carrying out the financial privacy rules of the GLBA for brokers, dealers and investment companies pursuant to 15 USC § 6805(a)(3), (4) and (5) (2000)).

See Charles M Horn 'Financial Services Privacy at the Start of the 21st Century: Conceptual Perspective'(2001) 5 NC Banking Inst 89; Neal R Pandozzi 'Beware of Banks Bearing Gifts: Gramm-Leach-Bliley and the Constitutionality of Federal Financial Privacy Legislation' (2001) 55 U Miami L Rev 163; Michael A Benoit and Nicole F Munro 'Recent Federal Privacy Initiatives Affecting the Electronic Delivery of Financial Services'(2001) 56 Bus Law 1143.

15 USC §§ 6821–6827 (2000) prohibit pretext calling or 'customer identity theft' to obtain personal financial information through false or fraudulent means. See 'Interagency Guidelines Establishing Standards for Safeguarding Customer Information Rule of the Department of the Treasury', the OCC, the OTS, the Board and the FDIC, 66 Fed Reg 8616–8641 (1 February 2001). For the proposed rule, see 65 Fed Reg 39,471–489 (26 June 2000).

The enactment of the bank secrecy provisions of the GLBA was spurred by the alleged misuse of account information by US Bancorp to telemarketers and the debiting of customer accounts for transactions with third party vendors without customer authorisation. See *Hatch v US Bank National Association*, DN Civil Action No 99-872 (D Minn 4 October 1999) (action by the Attorney General of Minnesota). See Stephen F Ambrose Jr and Joseph W Gelb 'Consumer Privacy Regulation and Litigation' (2001) 56 Bus Law 1157 at 1158–59 for a discussion of the case.

disclosing non-public personal information about a consumer to non-affiliated third parties unless the institution satisfies various notice and opt-out requirements and the consumer has not elected to opt out of the disclosure.[22] The opt-out requirement operates in effect as a consent by the consumer to disclosure.[23]

The GLBA only protects non-public personal information regarding consumers, a 'consumer' being 'an individual who obtains, from a financial institution, financial products or services which are to be used primarily for personal, family, or household purposes ...'[24]

The GLBA applies to financial institutions. The GLBA defines 'financial institution' as 'any institution the business of which is engaging in financial activities as described in s 4(k) of the Bank Holding Company Act'.[25] Financial activities are the activities set out in the Regulation.[26] It follows that the definition of financial institution goes far beyond those institutions that are customarily considered to be financial institutions.[27]

'Non-public personal information' means (i) personally identifiable financial information and (ii) any list, description or other grouping of consumers (and publicly available information pertaining to them) that is derived using any personally identifiable information that is not publicly available.[28] 'Personally identifiable financial information' means any information (i) a consumer provides to a financial institution to obtain a financial product or service from the institution, (ii) about a consumer resulting from any transaction involving a financial product or service between a financial institution and a consumer or (iii) the financial institution otherwise obtains about a consumer in connection with providing a financial product or service to that consumer.[29] The term does not include publicly available information.[30]

The GLBA requires a financial institution to establish a policy regarding its practices for the protection and disclosure of non-public personal information.[31] The financial institution must notify[32] each consumer who has a customer relationship with the

---

22 See 12 CFR § 216.10(a)(1) (2002); 15 USC § 6802(a), (b)(1) (2000).
23 The financial institution must have given the consumer a reasonable opportunity to opt out of the disclosure and the consumer does not opt out. 12 CFR § 216.10(a)(1)(iii), (iv) (2002).
24 GLBA § 509(9) (1999).
25 15 USC § 6809(3)(A) (2000). See 12 CFR § 216.3(k); 12 USC § 1843(k) (2000).
26 12 CFR § 225.86 (2002) (Regulation Y).
27 Insofar as the OCC, the FDIC, the Board and the OTS have jurisdiction, 'financial institution' means state member banks, bank holding companies and certain of their non-bank subsidiaries or affiliates, state uninsured branches and agencies of foreign banks, commercial lending companies owned or controlled by foreign banks, Edge Act or Agreement corporations (12 CFR § 216.1(b)(1) (2002)), banks insured with the FDIC (other than state member banks), insured state branches of foreign banks and certain subsidiaries of such entities (12 CFR § 332.1(b)(1) (2002)), FDIC insured savings associations and certain of their subsidiaries (12 CFR § 573.1(b)(1) (2002)).
28 12 CFR § 216.3(n) (2002). See 15 USC § 6809(4) (2000).
29 12 CFR § 216.3(o) (2002).
30 12 CFR § 216.3(n)(2) and (p) (2002) ('publicly available information' means any information that a financial institution has a reasonable basis to believe is lawfully made available to the general public from government records, widely distributed media or disclosures to the general public that are required to be made by federal, state or local law).
31 See 15 USC § 6803(a) (2000); 12 CFR § 216.6(a)(8) (2002). The disclosure must also address disclosure to affiliates. Ibid.
32 The financial institution must provide 'a clear and conspicuous notice that accurately reflects [its] privacy policies and practices'. 12 CFR § 216.4(a) (2002). 'Clear and conspicuous' is defined in 12 CFR § 216.3(b) (2002). See 15 USC § 6803(a) (2000).

bank (a customer)[33] about this policy at the beginning of the customer relationship and thereafter once a year.[34] The information must include the financial institution's policies and practices regarding the disclosure of non-public personal information relating to customers and former customers to non-affiliated third parties, as well as to the financial institution's affiliates and, in general, regarding the protection of non-public personal information about consumers.[35] The notice must inform customers as to what non-public personal information is collected from them, how this information is maintained and used and with whom this information is shared.[36]

The progress in financial institution secrecy made by the GLBA lies in the fact that, after having received this information, the customer/consumer has a right to opt out, ie he may direct the financial institution not to disclose his non-public personal information to non-affiliated third parties. By exercising this right, the consumer prevents the external use of his data.

Even if a consumer has not made use of his possibility to opt out, the financial institution may not disclose to a non-affiliated third party, except to a consumer reporting agency, any information that gives access to a customer's account for the purpose of telemarketing, direct mail marketing or other marketing through electronic mail to the customer.

If the consumer has not opted out of the disclosure of his non-public personal information to non-affiliated third parties, a non-affiliated third party that receives non-public personal information from a financial institution is itself under an obligation not to disclose such information to any other person that is a non-affiliated third party (ie there is a limit on the reuse of information).[37]

A few state statutes also provide limited protection

[31.14]   Nineteen of the 50 states have adopted legislation that protects a customer's financial information to some degree. Generally, there is an express exception to that protection for various forms of authorised access by investigators. Several of these statutes also require notice to the customer when the institution 'receives' or 'is served' process to gain access to the customer's information. These statutes are generally more comprehensive than the Right to Financial Privacy Act

---

33   The notice must be given to (i) an individual who becomes the financial institution's *customer* (ie a consumer who has a customer relationship with the financial institution, 12 CFR § 216.3(i) and (i) (2002)) not later than when the financial institution establishes a customer relationship and (ii) a *consumer* before the financial institution discloses any non-public information about the consumer to any non-affiliated third party. 12 CFR § 216.4(a)(1), (2) (2002).

34   12 CFR § 216.5 (2002); 15 USC § 6803(a) (2000).

35   The notice must include, among other things, (i) the categories of non-public personal information that the financial institution collects, (ii) the categories of non-public personal information that the financial institution discloses, (iii) the categories of affiliates and non-affiliated third parties to whom the financial institution discloses non-public personal information, (iv) the same information about the financial institution's former customers and (v) an explanation of the consumer's rights to opt out of the disclosure. 12 CFR § 216.6(a) (2002). See 15 USC § 6803(b) (2000). If a financial institution does not disclose, and does not wish to reserve the right to disclose, non-public personal information about customers or former customers to affiliates or non-affiliated third parties, the financial institution may simply state that fact, in addition to certain required information (simplified notice). 12 CFR § 216.6(c)(5) (2002).

36   See 15 USC § 6803 (2000).

37   15 USC § 6802(c) (2000). See 12 CFR § 216.11 (2002). This prohibition on reuse of information does not apply if the disclosure to another third party would be lawful if made directly to such other third party by the financial institution. 15 USC § 6802(c) (2000).

creating a general protection for the financial information and then authorising procedures for permitted access. However, most states do not have such statutes and some that do have them limit the protection to electronic fund transfer information or other narrow classes of information.[38] So, while privacy statutes in the few states where they exist provide more comprehensive protection for financial information than do the federal statutes, there is only a minority of states with such protection. Even in states where such protection exists, it does not pose much of an obstacle to the access of such information by either government investigators or private litigants.

EXCEPTIONS, LIMITATIONS AND QUALIFICATIONS TO THE BASIC POSITION

[31.15] Each of the sources of financial privacy law in the United States contains its own exceptions, limitations and qualifications. The largest class of exceptions, limitations and qualifications arises from the development of anti-money laundering statutes which have dramatically increased the customer information available to investigators and required financial institutions to report certain types of transactions as suspicious. This shift to requiring the private sector to alert law enforcement authorities to suspect activity is a fundamental shift in the US law of financial privacy.

The exception for suspicious activity in the common law

[31.16] In *Suburban Trust v Waller*, the Maryland intermediate appellate court considered the obligations and duties of a bank when it was suspicious of a customer's transactions and reported those suspicions to the police.[39] The court started its analysis by recognising that the relationship between a bank and its customers is one of a debtor and creditor or a contractual relationship. In following the implied contractual theory, the court examined the *Tournier* precedent carefully and then considered the discussion in *Peterson v Idaho First National Bank*, as well as the decision in *Brex v Smith*. The court then considered the circumstances under which a bank's obligations of confidentiality are released or the circumstances under which a bank has a public duty of disclosure. Again referencing the *Tournier*, *Brex* and *Peterson* cases, the court concluded that a customer in Maryland has a right to expect confidentiality of all information regarding his account in the absence of compulsion by law. In reaching that conclusion, the court's decision was buttressed by the adoption by the Maryland general assembly three years earlier of a statute that

---

38 Ala Code § 5-5A-43 (2002); Alaska Stat § 06.05.175 (2002); Cal Gov't Code § 7460 (2002); Conn Gen Stat Ann § 36-9j (West 2002); Conn Gen Stat Ann § 36a-41 (West 2002); Conn Gen Stat Ann § 36a-42 (West 2002); Conn Gen Stat Ann § 36a-43 (West 2002); Conn Gen Stat Ann § 36a-45 (West 2002); Fla Stat Ann § 655.059 (West 2002); Fla Stat Ann § 659.062 (West 2002); 205 Ill Comp Stat Ann 5/48.1 (West 2002); Iowa Code Ann § 527.10 (West 2002); La Rev Stat Ann § 9:3571 (West 2002); Md Code Ann Fin Inst § 1-302 (West 2002); Mass Gen Laws Ann ch 167B, § 7 (West 2002); Mass Gen Laws Ann ch 167B, § 16 (West 2002); Me Rev Stat Ann tit 9-B, § 161 (West 2001); Minn Stat Ann § 13B.06 (2002); N Rev Stat Ann § 359-C (2002); NC Gen Stat § 53B-1 (2002); ND Cent Code § 6-08.103 (2001); Okla Stat Ann tit 6 § 2201–2206 (2002); Or Rev Stat § 192.550 (2001); Utah Code Ann § 7-14-1 (2002); 8 Vt Stat Ann tit 8 § 10203 (2005).
39 408 A 2d 758 (Md Ct Spec App 1979).

explicitly created a duty of confidentiality between fiduciary institutions and their customers.[40] Accordingly, the Maryland court upheld the verdict against the bank for voluntarily disclosing its suspicions concerning the nature of the depositor's transactions. As will be discussed in the next section, this decision came just a few years before a federal requirement for reporting of suspicious activity was imposed.

An Indiana case finds broader exceptions to privacy

[31.17] In 1985, the Indiana intermediate appellate court considered what limitations or exceptions existed in the law of implied contract between a bank and its depositor as to confidentiality.[41] At trial, a jury had returned a verdict in favour of a bank customer who claimed to have been injured by the disclosure by the bank of information to a police officer conducting an arson investigation. After the customer's acquittal on the arson charges, he sued the bank on a number of theories. The Indiana court found that, while the right of privacy exists, a bank customer had no legitimate expectation that bank records were within its zone of protection. The court also found that the verdict as to slander was erroneous as the bank had a qualified privilege based on its duty to provide information in connection with a proper police investigation. As to the verdicts with respect to a breach of an implied contract between the depositor and the bank, the court concluded that, while there is an implied duty of confidentiality on a bank, the exceptions noted in the *Tournier* case and in the Indiana law of slander and privacy permit a bank to give information to law enforcement officers without a subpoena or search warrant. The presiding judge in a dissenting opinion concluded that a bank's disclosure of information without legal compulsion constitutes a breach of a contractual duty between the bank and its customer. The dissent found the reasoning in the Maryland case, *Suburban Trust Co v Waller*, to be persuasive and accordingly concluded that the court should recognise that a bank's duty of confidentiality to its customers does not end upon a policeman's informal oral request for information.

The divergent results in these two common law cases as to when public policy overrides financial privacy can also be seen in the federal Right to Financial Privacy Act.

Federal statute exceptions and limitations

[31.18] There are important exceptions and limitations in the Right to Financial Privacy Act. The most important exception is an appropriate means of access such as an administrative summons or subpoena, a search warrant, judicial subpoena or consent by the customer to disclosure. In certain circumstances, a so-called 'formal written request' may also meet the requirements of the statute. In addition to a requirement of the appropriate 'means of access' to obtain the information, the customer must first be notified by the government. The government must also certify to the financial institutions that such notice has been provided to the customer and that an appropriate waiting period has elapsed. This affords the customer rights similar to those under the Third Party Record Keepers Act to challenge the issuance of the means of access. It is also important to note that access by one agency in compliance with the Right to Financial Privacy Act may result in that agency transferring its information to other authorities in the government that it believes are

---

40 Md Code Ann Fin Inst, § 1-302 (West 2002).
41 *Indiana National Bank v Chapman*, 482 NE 2d 474 (Ind Ct App 1985).

seized of jurisdiction to address matters found in the documents received from the financial institutions. However, there is a requirement that the transmittal be accompanied by a certification, after the fact, describing the nature of the inquiry. These broad exceptions to the statute's protection effectively make this statute a minor procedural impediment for a federal government investigator in obtaining a customer's financial information. The broad authority of federal investigators to issue subpoenas and like process makes the statute's protection of privacy an insubstantial obstacle in an investigation.

Anti-money laundering and anti-terrorist financing legislation

[31.19]   Even more significant limitations on financial privacy in the United States can be found in evolving duties of financial institutions under anti-money laundering legislation.

The Bank Secrecy Act was the first federal law

[31.20]   In 1970, the federal government enacted anti-money laundering legislation under the title of the Bank Secrecy Act ('BSA').[42] That title was something of a misnomer since the primary provision of the Act required banks to retain for a period of five years copies of records relating to most significant banking transactions. This legislation arose from a concern by regulators that, as modern records storage methods and the volume of transactions proliferated, there would not be sufficient records available to trace financial transactions without a uniform requirement for a retention.[43] In addition to the retention requirements, the statute provides that banks are required to report on two broad categories of transactions that do not generate records, namely, the receipt of currency and other monetary instruments from outside the United States and domestic cash transactions in excess of $10,000. Neither of these types of transactions inherently creates an audit trail. The regulations promulgated pursuant to this legislation require that banks file two reports with the government: a so-called 'currency transaction report' (form 4789) and a 'currency and monetary instrument report' (form 4790).[44] The cash reporting requirements imposed on banks by the BSA are subject to certain exemptions for transactions from other domestic financial institutions and, under certain fairly carefully controlled circumstances, commercial enterprises. Parenthetically, it is worth noting that a similar requirement has been imposed on commercial enterprises pursuant to the Internal Revenue Code.[45] This Code requires taxpayers to file a form 8300 for cash payments in excess of $10,000 received in a trade or business.

The BSA itself imposes no penalty for breaches by banks, but rather delegates to the Secretary of the Treasury authority to issue regulations, the breaches of which are subject to both civil and criminal penalties. While many of the statute's requirements and the implementing regulations simply codify practices that banks have had for years in retaining records and in some cases reporting certain kinds of transactions, the BSA was a significant development in the law of customer confidentiality. For the first time, there was a uniform national standard for record retention. The BSA also

---

42   12 USC § 1951 (2002).
43   12 USC § 1951 (2002).
44   31 CFR § 103.22, 103.23 (2002).
45   26 USC § 6501 (2002).

furnished the basis for a developing requirement for reporting suspicious transactions to the federal government.

Suspicious transaction reporting

[31.21] The initial BSA regulations adopted a presumption that transactions in cash in excess of $10,000 were sufficiently likely to be suspicious as to be worthy of reporting to the government. The evolution of that presumption is one of the most interesting aspects of American anti-money laundering policy because, almost as soon as the regulation established the rigid $10,000 threshold, a practice known as 'smurfing' developed. Street-level money launderers would deposit or withdraw funds just below the threshold amount to avoid the report and do so with such frequency as to permit substantial volumes of funds to be transferred without any report being required. This cat and mouse game evolved over the years until the development of a requirement that 'suspicious activity' be reported with only the broadest attempt at a regulatory definition of what exactly amounts to suspicion.

A suspicious activity report is required for any transaction of $5,000 or more where the institution knows, suspects or has reasons to suspect that the transaction:

1   involves funds derived from illegal activity;
2   is designed to evade the requirements of the reporting regulations; or
3   has no business or apparent lawful purpose and is not of the sort in which the particular customer would normally be expected to engage and the institution knows of no reasonable explanation for the transaction after examining the available facts, including the background and possible purposes of the transaction.[46]

Under these conditions, the institution must file a suspicious activity report.

Under the regulations, as promulgated since 1996, banks are required to report any transaction which has no business or apparent lawful purpose and is not the sort in which the particular customer would normally be expected to engage. The institution is permitted to inquire as to whether there is a reasonable explanation for the transactions after examining all of the facts, including the background and possible purposes for the transactions. Nevertheless, this very subjective standard is a dramatic departure from the initial presumption of suspicion inherent in the first regulations promulgated under the BSA. While initially only applicable to banks, the requirement to file suspicious activity reports now applies to most financial institutions, including broker–dealers, casinos and money transmitters. Financial institutions and their employees benefit from a safe harbour that provides unqualified protection from customer claims arising from filing a report. At the same time, financial institutions may not disclose to any person involved in the reported transaction that a report has been filed. In recent years, the volume of reports has increased both as regulators have questioned financial institutions about transactions that the regulator believes should have been reported and as a result of several high-profile enforcement actions against financial institutions for failing to file required reports.

The Supreme Court upholds the BSA

[31.22] Shortly after the Secretary of the Treasury issued the initial BSA regulations in April 1972, a constitutional challenge to the Act and its regulations

---

46 31 CFR § 103.18 (2002).

was mounted by the California Bankers' Association in the federal courts of California.[47] The principal basis for the challenge was that the Act and its regulations breached the Fourth Amendment to the federal constitution's guarantee against unreasonable searches and seizures. That proposition rests on a citizen's legitimate expectations as to privacy which later courts considered determinative and was the subject of subsequent US Supreme Court decisions.[48]

Under an expedited procedure for challenging the constitutionality of statutes, the matter was argued in January 1974 before the US Supreme Court and decided four months later.[49] The court concluded that depositors had no reasonable expectation of privacy with respect to their financial records maintained at banks and as required by the BSA regulations to be available for government investigators. Similarly, the cash reporting requirements, both domestic and foreign, did not contravene the provision of the Fourth Amendment restrictions on searches and seizures. The decision reserved the question of whether the record retention requirements, when coupled with a subpoena, would breach the Fourth Amendment as there was no factual basis for such a matter to be considered in that decision.

In a decision two years later, *United States v Miller*, the question of the power to subpoena bank records in aid of a criminal prosecution was resolved by the court which again concluded that the Fourth Amendment did not restrict the ability of Congress and the Secretary of the Treasury to require the retention of bank records.[50] The court made a careful distinction between private records maintained in an individual's home and records of his transactions held outside his home at financial institutions. In effect, these decisions put to rest a carefully crafted challenge to the federal government's anti-money laundering legislation.

Post-9/11 legislation

[**31.23**] From the somewhat modest privacy heights that federal legislation reached with the enactments of the Third Party Record Keepers Act and the Right to Financial Privacy Act, the pendulum of federal legislation again swung back in succeeding years, particularly since 11 September 2001, toward greater disclosure on the part of financial institutions. The original anti-money laundering provisions that emanated from the Bank Secrecy Act 1970 received significant expansions and enhancements in two pieces of legislation, the Anunzio Wiley Anti-Money Laundering Act ('Anunzio Wiley') and the so-called 'USA Patriot' Act 2001 ('Patriot Act').[51]

For the first time, a crime of money laundering was created by Anunzio Wiley and imposes up to 20 years' imprisonment for money laundering. The section prohibits a person from engaging in a financial transaction with property that involves the proceeds of 'specified unlawful activity'. The person must also conduct the financial transaction (i) with intent to promote the carrying on of specified unlawful activity or (ii) knowing that the transaction is designed to conceal the ownership of the proceeds of specified unlawful activity.[52] 'Specified unlawful activity' is defined[53] and includes the following crimes.

---

47 *Stark v Connally*, 347 F Supp 1242 (ND Cal 1972); affd in part and revd in part sub nom *California Bankers Association v Shultz*, 416 US 21 (1974).
48 See, eg, *United States v Miller*, 425 US 435 (1976).
49 *Shultz*, 416 US 21.
50 *Miller*, 425 US 435.
51 31 USC §§ 5311–5331 (2002).
52 18 USC § 1956 (2003).
53 18 USC § 1956(c)(7) (2003).

All 'racketeering activity' under the Racketeer Influenced and Corrupt Organisations statute,[54] which includes:

1   any act or threat involving murder, kidnapping, gambling, arson, robbery, bribery, extortion, obscenity or dealing in narcotics that is a felony under state law;
2   bribery of a public official;[55]
3   bribery in connection with a sporting event;[56]
4   counterfeiting;[57]
5   theft from interstate shipments;[58]
6   embezzlement from pension and welfare funds;[59]
7   extortionate credit transactions;[60]
8   identification fraud;[61]
9   credit card fraud;[62]
10   interstate transmission of gambling information;[63]
11   mail and wire fraud;[64]
12   bank fraud;[65]
13   unlawful procurement of citizenship/naturalisation;[66]
14   reproduction of citizenship or naturalisation papers;[67]
15   obscenity;[68]
16   obstruction of justice and witness tampering;[69]
17   passport and visa fraud/misuse;[70]
18   human trafficking;[71]
19   Hobbs Act (interference with interstate commerce);[72]
20   interstate travel in aid of racketeering and interstate transportation of gambling paraphernalia;[73]
21   bribery in connection with an employee benefit plan;[74]
22   gambling;[75]
23   money laundering;[76]
24   murder-for-hire;[77]
25   sexual exploitation of a minor;[78]

54   18 USC § 1961(1) (2003).
55   18 USC § 201 (2003).
56   18 USC § 224 (2003).
57   18 USC §§ 471–473 (2003).
58   18 USC § 659 (2003).
59   18 USC § 664 (2003).
60   18 USC §§ 891–894 (2003).
61   18 USC § 1028 (2003).
62   18 USC § 1029 (2003).
63   18 USC § 1084 (2003).
64   18 USC §§ 1341, 1343 (2003).
65   18 USC § 1344 (2003).
66   18 USC § 1425 (2003).
67   18 USC § 1436 (2003).
68   18 USC §§ 1461–1465 (2003).
69   18 USC §§ 1503, 1505, 1511–13 (2003).
70   18 USC §§ 1542, 1546 (2003).
71   18 USC §§ 1581–1591, 2321–2424 (2003).
72   18 USC § 1951 (2003).
73   18 USC §§ 1952–1953 (2003).
74   18 USC § 1954 (2003).
75   18 USC § 1955 (2003).
76   18 USC §§ 1956–1957 (2003).
77   18 USC § 1958 (2003).
78   18 USC §§ 2251–2252, 2260 (2003).

26 interstate transportation of stolen property;[79]
27 trafficking in counterfeit copyrighted materials and criminal infringement;[80]
28 trafficking in counterfeit cigarettes;[81]
29 use or trafficking in weapons of mass destruction;[82]
30 certain union breaches;[83]
31 bankruptcy fraud;[84]
32 securities fraud;[85]
33 felony narcotics breaches;[86]
34 the Bank Secrecy Act;[87]
35 Immigration and Nationality Act breaches (if for personal gain);[88] and
36 terrorism.[89]

If the financial transaction occurred in whole or in part within the US, an offence against a foreign nation involving:

1 narcotics breaches;
2 murder, kidnapping, robbery, extortion, arson or crimes of violence;
3 fraud by or against a foreign bank;
4 bribery of a public official or embezzlement of public funds by or for a public official;
5 smuggling of a controlled item under the Arms Export Control Act or Export Administration Regulations;
6 an extraditable offence under any multilateral treaty to which the US is a party (eg a war crime); and
7 any act constituting a 'continuing criminal enterprise'.[90]

Other federal offences:

1 destruction of aircraft;[91]
2 violence at international airports;[92]
3 influencing, impeding or retaliating against a federal official by threatening or injuring a family member;[93]
4 concealment of assets, false oaths and claims in bankruptcy;
5 bribery;[94]
6 commissions or gifts for procuring loans;[95]
7 assassination of a congressional or Cabinet officer;[96]
8 counterfeiting;[97]

---

79 18 USC §§ 2312–2313, 2314 (2003).
80 18 USC §§ 2318–2321 (2003).
81 18 USC §§ 2341–2346 (2003).
82 18 USC §§ 175–178, 229, 831 (2003).
83 29 USC §§ 186, 501(c) (2003).
84 11 USC chs 1–13 (2003).
85 15 USC chs 1–100 and 18 USC § 1518 (2003).
86 21 USC chs 1–24 (2003).
87 31 USC §§ 5311–5330 and 12 USC §§ 1818, 1829 (2003).
88 8 USC chs 1–15 (2003).
89 18 USC § 2332b(g)(5)(B) (2003).
90 21 USC § 848 (2003).
91 18 USC § 32 (2003).
92 18 USC § 37 (2003).
93 18 USC § 115 (2003).
94 18 USC § 152 (2003).
95 18 USC § 215 (2003).
96 18 USC § 351 (2003).
97 18 USC §§ 500–503 (2003).

9   counterfeit securities from states and private entities;[98]
10 smuggling or customs breaches;[99]
11 embezzlement of public money;[100]
12 embezzlement by a bank or insurance officer or of farm credit agency property;[101]
13 theft or bribery from federal programmes;[102]
14 espionage;[103]
15 trafficking in nuclear material;[104]
16 explosives breaches;[105]
17 extortionate demand/kidnapping;[106]
18 firearms trafficking;[107]
19 conspiracy to kill, kidnap, maim or injure property in a foreign country;[108]
20 making fraudulent bank entries and loan and receivership fraud;[109]
21 computer fraud;[110]
22 murder (on federal property or of a law enforcement or foreign official);[111]
23 kidnapping;[112]
24 injury to government property;[113]
25 presidential assassination;[114]
26 bank and postal robbery;[115]
27 violence against maritime navigation;[116]
28 copyright infringement;[117]
29 trafficking in counterfeit goods;[118]
30 terrorism;[119]
31 use of weapons of mass destruction;[120]
32 breach of the Chemical Diversion and Trafficking Act 1988;
33 aviation smuggling;[121]
34 transportation of drug smuggling (s 422 of the Controlled Substances Act);
35 breach of the Arms Export Control Act;
36 breach of the Export Administration Act 1979;
37 breach of the International Emergency Economic Powers Act;
38 breach of the Trading with the Enemy Act;

98 18 USC § 513 (2003).
99 18 USC §§ 541–542, 545, 549 (2003).
100 18 USC § 641 (2003).
101 18 USC §§ 656–658 (2003).
102 18 USC § 666 (2003).
103 18 USC §§ 793–794, 798 (2003).
104 18 USC § 831 (2003).
105 18 USC § 844(f)(i) (2003).
106 18 USC § 875 (2003).
107 18 USC §§ 922, 924 (2003).
108 18 USC § 956 (2003).
109 18 USC §§ 1005–1007, 1014, 1032 (2003).
110 18 USC § 1030 (2003).
111 18 USC §§ 1111, 1114, 1116 (2003).
112 18 USC §§ 1201–1203 (2003).
113 18 USC §§ 1361–1363 (2003).
114 18 USC § 1751 (2003).
115 18 USC §§ 2113–2114 (2003).
116 18 USC §§ 2280–2281 (2003).
117 18 USC § 2319 (2003).
118 18 USC § 2320 (2003).
119 18 USC §§ 2332a, 2332b, 2332g, 2332h, 2339A–B (2003); 49 USC § 46502 (2003).
120 18 USC § 2332b (2003).
121 19 USC § 1590 (2003).

39   breach of the Food Stamp Act 1977 (of $5,000 or more);
40   breach of the Housing Act 1949;
41   breach of the Foreign Agents Registration Act 1938;
42   breach of the Foreign Corrupt Practices Act;
43   breach of the Atomic Energy Act 1954;
44   any act constituting an offence involving a federal health care offence; and
45   a felony breach of:
   (a)   the Federal Water Pollution Control Act,[122]
   (b)   the Ocean Dumping Act,[123]
   (c)   the Act to Prevent Pollution from Ships,[124]
   (d)   the Safe Drinking Water Act,[125]or
   (e)   the Resources Conservation and Recovery Act.[126]

Anunzio Wiley also broadly enhanced the obligations of banks affirmatively to participate in anti-money laundering efforts by adoption of specific policies, including an express requirement that suspicious activities be reported. The Patriot Act, enacted after the terrorist attacks of 11 September 2001, expanded that regime to cover many other financial institutions beyond banks, including securities firms, insurance companies, money transmitters and mutual funds. In March 2006, the Patriot Act was re-authorised by Congress.

The Patriot Act combines anti-money laundering and anti-terrorist financing provisions

[31.24]   The Patriot Act, somewhat like the original Bank Secrecy Act, simply laid out broad goals and left to the implementing regulators the detailed requirement applicable to financial institutions. The regulations promulgated pursuant to the Patriot Act have been slow to be issued. These regulations reflect the difficulties of applying anti-money laundering procedures developed for the banking industry to other financial institutions. The Patriot Act requirement that all US financial institutions have anti-money laundering programmes has engendered a great deal of institutional uncertainty among many segments of the financial industry. This has been particularly difficult in those parts of the market which have segmented operations such as the mutual fund business. In that business, the ultimate account holder may have little to do with the investment advisor or custodian institution that holds his account. Accordingly, in the mutual fund industry, the regulations currently permit the delegation or subcontracting of certain anti-money laundering requirements to those institutions that deal directly with the beneficial owners.[127] Nevertheless, the overall effect of the two statutes has been to broaden the anti-money laundering requirements and, accordingly, the obligation of financial institutions both to identify customers and retain information concerning transaction histories. The Patriot Act also reinforces prior requirements to check customers against government lists of terrorist and prohibited persons.

---

122   33 USC ch 26 (2003).
123   33 USC ch 27 (2003).
124   33 USC ch 33 (2003).
125   42 USC ch 6A, sub-ch XII (2003).
126   42 USC ch 82 (2003).
127   FinCEN, 67 Fed Reg 21117 (29 April 2002) (codified at 31 CFR § 103).

Suspicious activity reports are now widely required

[31.25] One of the most significant developments is the expansion of the number of institutions required to file suspicious activity reports. The Patriot Act required not only banks but also broker–dealers and money service businesses to file such reports.[128] There are indications that this requirement will be further expanded to include institutions such as mutual funds.[129]

The triggering events for filing a report were not changed by the Patriot Act. However, the application to non-banking financial institutions of this requirement, which until the adoption of the Patriot Act had been used primarily for banking institutions, has proved to be difficult for many financial institutions that do not record a customer's transactions in the same way that banks do. In many cases, such institutions do not deal directly with the customer, but provide bulk services to other segments of their industry, so they have difficulty in detecting conduct that requires a report.

Accounts for shell banks are prohibited

[31.26] A second aspect of the Patriot Act which has had a significant influence on financial privacy in the United States is its prohibition on US financial institutions maintaining correspondent accounts with foreign institutions that do not have a physical presence in any jurisdiction and that are not affiliated with another bank, so-called 'shell banks'.[130] The Patriot Act's definition of 'correspondent account' is far broader than the traditional use of that term, so many additional relationships have been caught up in this regulation.[131] The shell bank provisions have a safe harbour that permits correspondent accounts at covered financial institutions that have obtained an appropriate certificate from the foreign financial institution. This provision and the provisions with respect to delegation by mutual funds of certain obligations have led to an initial flurry of contractual certifications and assurances being exchanged among financial institutions, particularly those in the United States, and those that have accounts with institutions in the United States as to the foreign institution's compliance with various anti-money laundering regimes. Until the regulations under the Patriot Act have weathered the test of time and the industry has adapted to those regulations, it can be expected that there will be a fair amount of uncertainty in this area.

Private banking due diligence is mandated

[31.27] The Patriot Act also requires enhanced due diligence with respect to private bank accounts, which are defined as having a minimum aggregate deposit or assets of not less than $1 million and as having been established on behalf of one or more individuals.[132] Such an enhanced due diligence programme must include steps to ascertain the identity of all nominal and beneficial holders of the account and to obtain information about the lines of business and sources of wealth of such persons,

---

128 1 CFR §§ 103.18–103.21 (2002).
129 'A Report to Congress in Accordance with § 356(c) of the USA Patriot Act' submitted by the Secretary of the Treasury, the Board of Governors of the Federal Reserve System and the Securities and Exchange Commission, at 37 (31 December 2002).
130 USA Patriot Act § 313; 31 CFR § 103.135 (2002).
131 31 USC § 5318A (e)(1)(B) (2002).
132 USA Patriot Act § 312; 31 USC § 5318(i)(4)(B)(i) (2002).

as well as the sources of funds deposited in the account. In addition, banks are required to determine whether any of the individuals are so-called 'covered persons'.[133] In such a case, the institution must have procedures that are designed to detect and report transactions that may involve the proceeds of foreign corruption and the due diligence programme should assess the risk factors that would require specific transaction monitoring in such cases.

'Know your customer'

[31.28] These provisions for transaction monitoring and enhanced due diligence of certain customers are a substantially diluted version of an earlier 'know your customer' practice and transaction profiling originally promulgated by bank regulators in 1998. Those proposals were subsequently withdrawn after a storm of protest, largely from non-banking centre legislators and rural constituents who found such profiling of all customer accounts to be intrusive and offensive to their sense of privacy.[134]

Information sharing finds statutory protection

[31.29] Another outgrowth of the Patriot Act has been the adoption of provisions for anti-terrorist and anti-money laundering information sharing among financial institutions.[135] The regulations provide that information sharing can be used for no purpose other than to identify and report activities relating to terrorism or money laundering and that the information can only be used in connection with the decision to close or maintain an account or engage in a transaction.

The broad provisions of the Patriot Act, which permit regulatory adjustments to suit the goals articulated in the legislation, are likely to result in a relatively stable environment for financial institutions on the legislative front accompanied by adjustments in the regulatory structure that were similar to the initial history of the Bank Secrecy Act after its adoption in 1970. The most likely course will be a series of revisions in the initial regulations after sufficient experience has developed in the financial community so as to persuade the regulators, particularly the Department of the Treasury, that there are either less burdensome or more effective procedures. This trend can best be illustrated in the shift from the Bank Secrecy Act's initial reliance

---

133 USA Patriot Act § 312(a)(i)(3)(B); 31 USC § 5318(i)(3)(B) (2002); 31 CFR § 103 (2002). A 'covered person' is a person identified in the course of normal account opening, maintenance or compliance procedures to be a 'senior foreign political figure', any member of a senior foreign political figure's 'immediate family' and any 'close associate' of a senior foreign political figure.

A 'senior foreign political figure' is a senior official in the executive, legislative, administrative, military or judicial branches of a foreign government (whether elected or not), a senior official of a major foreign political party or a senior executive of a foreign government-owned corporation. In addition, a 'senior foreign political figure' includes any corporation, business or other entity that has been formed by, or for the benefit of, a senior foreign political figure.

The 'immediate family' of a senior foreign political figure typically includes the figure's parents, siblings, spouse, children and in-laws.

A 'close associate' of a senior foreign political figure is a person who is widely and publicly known to maintain an unusually close relationship with the senior foreign political figure and includes a person who is in a position to conduct substantial domestic and international financial transactions on behalf of the senior foreign political figure.

'Guidance on Enhanced Scrutiny for Transactions' issued by the bank regulators and found at www.federalreserve.gov/BOARDDOCS/SRLetters/2001/sr0103.htm

134 'Daily Report for Executive No 43', 63 Fed Reg 67516, 67524, 67529 and 67536 (5 March 1999).

135 USA Patriot Act § 314(b); 31 USC § 5318(h) (2002), 31 CFR § 103.110 (2002).

on the presumed suspicious activity of $10,000 in currency being used for a banking transaction or being transmitted across boundaries to the much greater reliance now on the use of suspicious activity reports as a far more targetted method for identifying transactions in the financial flows of the US economy which warrant investigative attention.

The Patriot Act is the latest statute in US federal anti-money laundering laws which started in 1970 with the Bank Secrecy Act. Whether there will be a reaction to perceived excesses of the Patriot Act in the next few years, as there was in the late 1970s with the Third Party Record Keepers Act and the Right to Financial Privacy Act, is yet to be seen. What is clear today is that the current federal law requires financial institutions to collect and retain customer identity and transaction information and report suspicious activity. Privacy restrictions on government access to this information are minimal. Federal statutes provide customers with only the most fundamental protections and grant access for governmental investigations with only limited procedural restrictions.

Limitations and exceptions in the Gramm-Leach-Bliley Act

[31.30] There are numerous exceptions to the privacy protection of the GLBA, the most important being as follows.

Business customers

[31.31] The GLBA does not cover the privacy of bank customers that are companies[136] or individuals who obtain financial products or services for business, commercial or agricultural purposes.[137] These non-protected customers only have recourse to the protection provided by common law.

Affiliates

[31.32] The consumer cannot elect that non-public personal information not be disclosed to the financial institution's affiliates, an affiliate being any company that controls, is controlled by, or is under common control with, the financial institution. This exception is especially noteworthy when considering the combination of banks, insurance companies and securities companies in one financial holding company group permitted by the GLBA. Thus, for instance, an insurance company may provide customer information to its bank affiliate.[138]

Outsourcing and third party providers; joint marketing

[31.33] A financial institution is always allowed to forward data, even to a non-affiliated third party, to perform services for or functions on behalf of the financial

---

136 'Company' is defined in 12 CFR § 216.3(d) (2002).
137 See the definition of 'consumer' in 12 CFR § 216.3(e) (2002).
138 Note, however, that the privacy notice must contain information on the categories of affiliates to whom the financial institution discloses non-public personal information, 12 CFR § 216.6(a)(3) (2002), and that the simplified notice is only available if the financial institution does not disclose, and does not wish to reserve the right to disclose, non-public personal information about customers and former customers to affiliates or non-affiliated third parties. 12 CFR § 216.6(c)(5) (2002). Since third party providers and servicers of a financial institution are non-affiliated parties, a financial institution's disclosure policy must address disclosure to such providers and servicers. 12 CFR §§ 116.6(a)(5) and 116.13 (2002).

institution, for instance, to carry out marketing tasks or where the financial institution wants to outsource some activity. However, in this case, the financial institution is required to enter into a confidentiality agreement with the third party that prohibits the third party from disclosing or using the information other than to carry out the purposes for which the financial institution disclosed the information. The services that a non-affiliated party performs for the financial institution may include marketing of the financial institution's own products or services or marketing of financial products or services offered jointly by several financial institutions.

Processing and servicing of transactions

[31.34] A financial institution is always allowed to disclose non-public personal information when this is necessary to effect, administer or enforce a transaction[139] that a consumer requests or authorises or in connection with (i) servicing or processing a financial product or service that a consumer requests or authorises, (ii) maintaining or servicing the consumer's account with the financial institution or with another entity as part of a private label credit card programme or other extension of credit on behalf of such entity or (iii) a proposed or actual securitisation, secondary market sale (including sales of servicing rights) or similar transactions related to a transaction of the consumer.

Governmental authorities

[31.35] The GLBA only addresses the disclosure of information to private third parties. The GLBA does not apply to disclosures to governmental authorities in accordance with the Right to Financial Privacy Act and other federal reporting statutes[140] or to state insurance authorities,[141] disclosures made to comply with federal, state or local laws or rules, disclosures made to comply with an investigation or a subpoena or summons by federal, state or local authorities or disclosures made to respond to judicial process or government regulatory authorities having jurisdiction over the financial institution.[142]

Consumer reporting agency

[31.36] The GLBA does not prohibit disclosure to a consumer reporting agency in connection with the Fair Credit Reporting Act.[143]

Sale or merger

[31.37] The GLBA does not prohibit disclosure in connection with a proposed or actual sale, merger, transfer or exchange of all or a portion of a business or operating unit of the financial institution if the disclosure of non-public personal information solely concerns consumers of such business or unit.[144]

---

139 'Necessary to effect, administer or enforce a transaction' is defined in 12 CFR § 216.14(b) (2002).
140 15 USC § 6802(e)(5) (2000); 12 CFR § 216.15(a)(4) (2002). See, eg, 12 USC §§ 3401–22 (2000) (Right to Financial Privacy Act 1978); 31 USC ch 53, sub-ch II (2000) (Records and Reports on Monetary Instruments and Transactions) and 12 USC ch 21 (2000) (Financial Record Keeping).
141 15 USC § 6802(e)(5) (2000); 12 CFR § 216.15(a)(4) (2002).
142 15 USC § 6802(e)(8) (2000); 12 CFR § 216.15(a)(7) (2002).
143 15 USC § 6802(e)(6) (2000); 12 CFR § 216.15(a)(5) (2002). See 15 USC §§ 1681–1681v (2000) (Fair Credit Reporting Act).
144 15 USC § 6802(e)(7) (2000); 12 CFR § 216.15(a)(6) (2002).

Rating agencies

[31.38]   The GLBA does not prohibit disclosure of information to rating agencies of the financial institution and the financial institution's attorneys, accountants and auditors.[145]

Miscellaneous

[31.39]   The GLBA does not prohibit disclosure of information (i) to protect the confidentiality or security of the financial institution's records pertaining to the consumer, the service, product or transaction, (ii) to protect against or prevent actual or potential fraud, unauthorised transactions, claims or other liability, (iii) for required institutional risk control or for resolving consumer disputes or inquiries, (iv) to persons holding a legal or beneficial interest relating to the consumer or (v) to persons acting in a fiduciary or representative capacity on behalf of the consumer.[146]

A consumer can, of course, always authorise an individual disclosure of non-public personal information even if such consumer has generally opted out of disclosure.[147]

The financial privacy provisions of the GLBA do not supersede state law, except to the extent that state law is inconsistent, and then only to the extent of such inconsistency.[148] State law is not inconsistent if it affords greater protection than the privacy provisions of the GLBA.[149] This provision will cause much uncertainty.

Federal statutory summary and trends

[31.40]   Federal statutory law with respect to financial privacy can be seen to follow somewhat the same pattern as the case law development. The federal legislature, like the judges deciding the cases, has sought to set a balance between unfettered freedom for government investigators and restrictions on such investigations that would impede what Congress believed to be legitimate law enforcement objectives. The initial Bank Secrecy Act legislation of the 1970s was a modest requirement compared to the provisions adopted in the most recent Patriot Act when the judicial interpretations supporting the Bank Secrecy Act, particularly *United States v Miller*, concluded that there were no protections in the federal constitution with respect to financial records. Congress reacted by adopting both the Third Party Record Keepers Act and the Right to Financial Privacy Act. While both statutes have broad exceptions for legitimate law enforcement procedures, their prohibitions on unfettered investigative discretion and private co-operation between the financial institutions and the investigative agencies have continued since the enactment of the statutes in the late 1970s.

The second important trend in this statutory development has been the increased requirement since the Bank Secrecy Act 1970 for financial institutions to keep records and, in certain circumstances, call the government's attention to transactions and other information about customers where there appears to be reasonable basis for suspecting criminal conduct. Once again, even in this area, a balance has been struck. On the one hand, the Patriot Act requires identity information be obtained, but, on the

---

145 15 USC § 6802(e)(4) (2000); 12 CFR § 216.15(a)(3) (2002).
146 15 USC § 6802(e)(3) (2000); 12 CFR § 216.15(a)(2) (2002).
147 15 USC § 6802(e)(2) (2000); 12 CFR § 216.15(a)(1) (2002).
148 15 USC § 6807(a) (2000).
149 15 USC § 6807(b) (2000).

other, the 1999 regulatory efforts to require transaction profiles for every customer were withdrawn after substantial public outcry against the keeping of such information for all customers across the board. The later and more limited efforts in the Patriot Act to collect additional information about so-called 'private' bank customers with accounts in excess of $1 million or belonging to foreign political figures reflect a practical political compromise that Congress could reasonably argue was a subset of depositors that should be subject to heightened due diligence.

SANCTIONS FOR CUSTOMERS

[31.41]   Perhaps because of the narrow protection financial institutions' customers in the United States have for their financial records, there are few cases where customers have prevailed for a breach of that protection. The majority of the common law cases consider whether the customer has any legal protection for his records and never reach the question of the proper remedy. In the few cases that reach the question, the proper remedy for a breach of common law duty has been either an injunction against the improper investigation, as in *Brex*,[150] or money damages. The *Brex* court recognised that money damages for such a breach are often hard to measure and are an inadequate remedy after information is disclosed. The *Burrows* court also issued an order to surpass evidence derived from the disclosed information rather than damages.[151]

Justice Baer, in his subsequently moot opinion in *Young v Chemical Bank*, discussed the proper measure of damages against a bank for breach of its duty of confidentiality. Young had sought damages as a consequence of her money laundering criminal conviction in Bermuda based upon information the bank disclosed. She claimed damages for the criminal fine she paid, legal expenses of the criminal money laundering case, business damages and emotional distress. Justice Baer denied her those damages as contrary to New York public policy and too remote from the bank's breach of duty. He limited damages to those 'flowing from the breach of duty itself'.[152] He left open whether there were in fact any such damages. Justice Altman dismissed the case finding that New York public policy barred any recovery by Young. The court in *Suburban Trust* reached a similar conclusion as to the measure of damages. It denied damages for lost reputation as too speculative and not proved with reasonable certainty and sent the case back for a new trial on that issue.[153] A Florida court also briefly referred to the proper damages in *Milohnech*. In a concurring opinion, one judge argued that the complaint did not adequately allege a contractual relationship, but did allege that the bank committed a business tort and that, accordingly, the proper measure of damages was based upon a tort theory of damages rather than a contractual one.[154] So, the type and extent of a common law remedy is at best unclear, but appears to favour pre-disclosure restraints over speculative damages.

The drafters of the Right to Financial Privacy Act reach a similar conclusion. That statute, through its notice to customers and delayed disclosure mechanism, affords the opportunity for the customer to challenge any disclosure before it is made.[155] If

---

150   146 A 34 (NJ Ch 1929).
151   529 P 2d 590 (Cal 1974).
152   *Young v Chemical Bank*, 882 F 2d 633 (2nd Cir 1989), cert denied, 493 US 1072 (1990).
153   408 A 2d 758 (Md Ct Spec App 1979).
154   224 So 2d 759 (Fla Dist Ct App 1969).
155   12 USC § 3417 (2003).

the Act has been breached, there is a statutory civil penalty against the government of $100. The Act also allows actual damages, attorney's fees and, for wilful or intentional breaches, punitive damages against the government. If a financial institution disclosed customer information in good faith reliance on a government certificate of compliance with the Act, it is not liable to the customer for such disclosure.[156] The statutory remedies are exclusive, so a customer may not prevent his bank records from being admitted into evidence in proceedings even if those records are obtained in breach of the Act.[157]

The Third Party Record Keepers Act has a notice provision similar to that of the broader federal statute. The only remedy in this statute for a taxpayer is to challenge the Internal Revenue Service summons served on the financial institution. This statute also has a safe harbour provision for financial institutions that rely in good faith on an Internal Revenue Service certificate of compliance.[158]

Under both the common law and the federal statutes, the best and most effective remedy is to challenge disclosure before it happens. Post-disclosure remedies are rarely used and of questionable value. Financial institutions generally enjoy a safe harbour from customers' claims if they make a good faith disclosure to the government in apparent compliance with the statute.

CROSS-BORDER ISSUES

[31.42]   Given the relative paucity of financial privacy jurisprudence in the United States and the broad exceptions to any such restrictions available for legitimate domestic investigation by government and private litigants, it comes as little surprise that much of the US jurisprudence on financial privacy relates to the intersection between the efforts of US civil and criminal investigations to obtain information and the restrictions found in the laws of other nations on the disclosure of such information. Once again, as in the domestic arena, this law started with the development of individual cases, but in recent years has largely shifted to government-to-government arrangements which obviate the need for individual judicial determinations of conflicts of jurisdiction.

Interhandel is the leading case

[31.43]   The starting point for consideration of US procedures to obtain information protected by foreign financial privacy laws is the so-called *Interhandel* case.[159] A Swiss holding company sought the return of certain assets held during the Second World War by the United States government's economic sanctions programme. The claim was dismissed when the Swiss company was unable to comply fully with the civil discovery requirements in the New York case because of Swiss financial privacy provisions. In that case, the Supreme Court concluded that 'fear of criminal prosecution constitutes a weighty excuse for non-production'.[160] The Supreme Court

---

156 12 USC § 3417 (2003).
157 12 USC § 3417(d) (2003), *US v Davis*, 953 F 2d 1482 (10th Cir 1992), cert denied, 504 US 945 (1992).
158 26 USC § 7609 (2002).
159 *Societe Internationale pour Participations Industrielles et Commerciales SA v Rogers*, 357 US 197 (1958).
160 Ibid at 211.

reversed the dismissal of the claim and sent the case back to the trial court for further proceedings.[161]

It is ironic that, in the *Interhandel* case, a private foreign plaintiff is suing the United States government over foreign policy matters. This case falls somewhere in the middle of a continuum between a civil action between two private plaintiffs and a criminal investigation by the United States government. That continuum is important to understanding when reviewing the subsequent cases that address whether foreign privacy laws present an effective obstacle to US investigations and civil discovery.

The Restatement summarises the case law

[31.44]   The American Law Institute's Restatement (Third) of the Law of the Foreign Relations of the United States has attempted to codify the myriad of cases that have addressed this continuum. The Restatement attempts to set out where courts should come down on the question of foreign discovery. The Restatement's formulation of the rule is that in deciding whether to order production of information located abroad, a US court should take into account:

1   the importance to the investigation or litigation of the documents or information requested;
2   the degree or specificity of the request;
3   whether the information originated in the United States;
4   the availability of alternative means of securing the information; and
5   the extent to which non-compliance with the request would undermine important interests of the United States or compliance with a request would undermine important interests of the state where the information is located.[162]

A practical view of discovery case law

[31.45]   While many courts have applied the Restatement's test to the facts of a particular case, the practical distillation of those cases would appear to be that criminal investigations are generally successful in compelling production of foreign information.[163] Conversely, where the parties are private parties engaged in a civil dispute, the courts are often reluctant to enforce cross-border subpoenas.[164] Even with respect to civil discovery between private parties, there is a significant difference in the outcome depending upon whether the holder of the information is a party to the action. Generally, if the holder of the information is a party in the case, the courts will impose sanctions for non-production which penalised that party's continued involvement in the case similar to the procedures followed in the *Interhandel* case. So, if a financial institution is a non-party custodian of records and receives a subpoena in a civil action between two other private parties for records protected by non-US financial privacy laws and located outside the United States, there is some prospect that the institution will be successful in defending on the basis of the non-US financial privacy law. Conversely, in criminal cases, even where the financial institution is an uninvolved custodian of records, the *Bank of Nova Scotia*

---

161 Ibid.
162 Restatement (Third) of the Foreign Relations Law of the United States § 442 (1998).
163 See *Re Grand Jury Proceedings (Bank of Nova Scotia)*, 740 F 2d 817 (11th Cir 1984), cert denied, 469 US 1106 (1985), but see *Re Sealed Case*, 832 F 2d 1268 (DC Cir 1987).
164 See *Ings v Ferguson*, 282 F 2d 149 (2nd Cir 1960); *Laker Airways Ltd v Pan Am World Airways*, 607 F Supp 324 (SDNY 1985).

case[165] is authority for the use of cross-border subpoenas for the production of information despite the existence of foreign financial privacy laws.

The Hague Convention as an alternative method

[31.46]   In addition to the use of subpoenas, there are a variety of alternative means that are available for the gathering of information from outside of the United States. Most common are letters rogatory either on the basis of international comity or pursuant to the Hague Convention on the Taking of Evidence.[166] It is important to note, however, the US Supreme Court decision in the *Aerospatiale* case, which made it clear that the Hague Convention, as a treaty, is the supreme law of the land, but it is not the only means for gathering foreign evidence in the civil cases.[167] Accordingly, financial institutions may find themselves subject to attempts to reach financial information outside the United States through subpoenas despite the availability of the Hague Convention.[168] There is authority, at least in New York, that post-judgment subpoenas to financial institutions for information about accounts of customers outside the State of New York are not enforceable when such subpoenas are in aid of execution of a judgment that would not be enforceable outside that state.[169]

Compelled consents raise conflict of jurisdiction

[31.47]   There are also cases in the United States in which the bank customer is a party to the action where the courts have required the customer to sign a waiver or authorisation under the foreign financial privacy law authorising disclosure of his account information.[170] The court enforces its order in civil matters by imposing coercive sanctions within the litigation or in criminal matters by using its contempt authority to impose sanctions. In reaction to this practice, courts of the jurisdiction where the information is located have ruled that such waivers are not effective under their law.[171]

Multilateral co-operation is the most frequently used method

[31.48]   In gathering information in criminal investigations, the federal government's experience in litigating cases, such as the *Bank of Nova Scotia* case and the compelled consent cases, had the practical effect of forcing a careful review of the expenditure of resources necessary to gather foreign information through the use of unilateral means. As a consequence of that evaluation, today it is relatively

---

165 See *Bank of Nova Scotia*, 740 F 2d at 817.
166 Hague Convention on the Taking of Evidence Abroad in Civil or Commercial Matters, opened for signature on 18 March 1970, 23 UST 2555, TIAS No 7444, 847 UNTS 231.
167 *Societe Nationale Industrielle Aerospatiale v United States District Court*, 482 US 522 (1987).
168 See, eg, *Dietrich v Bauer*, No 95 Civ 7051, 2000 WL 1171132 (SDNY 16 August 2000), but see *Intercontinental Credit Corpn v Roth*, 595 NYS 2d (Sup Ct NY County 1991) which held that, at least in New York, a judgment creditor seeking information about foreign bank accounts is required to pursue the Hague Convention where such procedures are available.
169 *Walsh v Bustos*, 46 NYS 2d 240 (NYC City Ct NY County 1943).
170 The leading case that popularised this procedure is *United States v Ghidoni*, 732 F 2d 814 (11th Cir 1984). The procedure was subsequently validated by the Supreme Court in *Doe v United States*, 487 US 201 (1988).
171 *Re ABC Ltd* [1984] CILR 130 (Grand Court of Cayman Islands).

rare that such techniques are used when there are viable alternatives available.[172] The emphasis in recent years by the federal government has been on expanding the alternative co-operative means of information gathering so as not to be forced to resort to cross-border subpoenas.

Financial intelligence units institutionalise co-operation

[31.49]   The most frequently used tool is informal co-operation among enforcement authorities. In recent years, this has led to the development of so-called 'financial intelligence units' ('FIUs') under the auspices of the OECD's Financial Action Task Force.[173] The Egmont Group is a network dedicated to the enhancement and development of informal co-operation through FIUs. More than 100 countries have joined the Egmont Group and established FIUs. The Financial Crimes Enforcement Network ('FinCEN') is the United States' FIU and a member of the Egmont Group. This group issued 'Principles for Information Exchange' in 2001 and 'Best Practices for Exchange of Information' in 2004.

Mutual legal assistance treaties create legal obligations

[31.50]   The United States also has a network of more than 40 bilateral mutual legal assistance treaties with an ever increasing number of countries.[174] These treaties are supplemented by a network of executive agreements in which an agency of the United States government enters into specific co-operation agreements with its counterpart in another nation.[175] These executive agreements are particularly prevalent among the securities regulating agencies and the anti-trust regulators. There is no centralised repository in which the executive agreements can be found or are publicly available, however, the US Department of State website indicates which countries are currently party to mutual legal assistance treaties with the United States.[176] Another form of treaty that has particular relevance with respect to taxation matters is the so-called 'Tax Information Exchange Agreements'.[177] The United States has recently negotiated a number of treaties to facilitate the exchange of tax information between the United States and other nations. Finally, both as a matter of bank regulation and pursuant to the Patriot Act, bank regulatory agencies have recently placed significant requirements on US banks with foreign branches and foreign banks with US branches for access to information relevant to customer accounts that have connections to the United States.[178] These provisions are contained in regulations which usually require mechanisms by which information can be made promptly available in the United States concerning the identity and transactions of any accounts having connections to the US banking system.[179]

---

172 US Department of Justice, US Attorney's Manual § 9–13.525 (1997).
173 The Hague, 'Statement of Purpose of the Egmont Group', 13 June 2001, at
     www1.oecd.org/fatf/Ctry-orgpages/org-egmont_en.htm.
174 See http://travel.state.gov/mlat.html.
175 Ibid.
176 Ibid.
177 26 USC § 927 (2002).
178 USA Patriot Act § 319(b); 31 USC § 5318(k)(2)–(3) (2002).
179 Ibid.

The practical upshot of these alternative means of accessing non-US financial information is that, in most cases, the outcome of the case turns on the specific facts and the range of available alternatives in that case. Cross-border subpoenas, while available and often threatened, can frequently be dealt with by early intervention and negotiation accompanied by use of alternative methods. The key is usually representation by a US counsel with substantial practical experience in these matters.

REGULATION OF FINANCIAL MARKETS

[31.51] The regulation of financial markets in the United States is spread over a large number of federal and state agencies. For example, banks may have a charter granted either by the federal government or any of the 50 states. If the bank takes consumer deposits, it will also be subject to the Federal Deposit Insurance Corporation regulations.

In addition to the various bank regulations, nearly each of the financial sectors has its own distinct regulation at both the federal and state levels. Securities markets are regulated by the federal Securities and Exchange Commission ('SEC') and 50 state securities regulators. In addition, the New York Stock Exchange and National Association of Securities Dealers also regulate certain aspects of the securities business.

Each of these regulators and many others have authority to issue subpoenas and other investigative processes to obtain customer records from financial institutions. Since the development of anti-money laundering laws, mostly at the federal level, there have been some efforts to co-ordinate and harmonise these regulations. FinCEN has become the central source for anti-money laundering and anti-terrorism regulations. Similarly, the federal bank regulators formed the Federal Financial Institution's Examination Council to promulgate a single bank examination manual for the Bank Secrecy Act and anti-money laundering matters.

Regulators generally have broad authority to investigate suspected breaches of the statutes they administer. The tools for a financial institution's regulators to conduct such investigations generally include the ability to conduct onsite examinations of financial institutions and the power to issue subpoenas for both documents and testimony. If the regulator complies with the generally simple procedural requirements to issue such subpoena and the subpoena is directed with only a modest degree of particularity to obtain information or at least facially relates to activities subject to the regulator's grant of authority, then a financial institution's duty of customer confidentiality is no impediment to the subpoena. In short, in the United States, regulators of financial institutions may obtain information from such institutions with little or no practical restrictions so long as it is broadly related to the regulators' area of regulation. In fact, as was discussed previously, most financial institutions must review customer transactions and report to the regulator any suspicious transaction even before the regulator has started an investigation.

Once a regulator has obtained information from a financial institution, the regulator is generally restricted from disclosing such information except pursuant to authorised procedures or protocol. For example, agencies may generally not disclose information to the press or other persons, except in connection with the proper performance of their activities.

The international nature of money laundering and terrorism has led to increased co-operation among domestic and international regulators, particularly in the sharing of investigative information. See the discussion above on FIUs and the Egmont Group.

The SEC routinely shares information with domestic and international regulators. Through its Office of International Affairs, it uses over 30 bilateral information exchange arrangements with securities regulators in other nations. In addition, the SEC is a participant with 27 other nations' regulators in a multilateral Memorandum of Understanding for information sharing among securities regulators.

The criminal division of the US Department of Justice has a similar office of International Affairs to facilitate international information sharing under bilateral and multilateral treaties. See the discussion above on mutual legal assistance treaties. The Department also has extensive domestic protocols for information sharing with federal and state regulators.

With the enactment of the Patriot Act, information sharing procedures were enhanced in two ways. First, FinCEN has a new procedure under s 314(a) of the Act to alert more than 27,000 financial institutions of law enforcement interest in specific people in order to locate accounts and transactions of those people. More than 480 such requests have been processed by 1 March 2006. These resulted in nearly 2,000 accounts being identified and nearly $15 million being located.

The second procedure under s 314(b) provides a safe harbour for financial institutions that register and meet minimal procedural safeguards to share information of suspected money laundering activity by their customers with other financial institutions.

Many of these procedures for sharing information find their origins in the SEC's investigation of insider trading breaches. Starting in the early 1980s, the SEC started to develop many of the domestic and international information sharing tools in use today. Insider trading investigations require information from three separate sources. First, information from stockbrokers about who traded the security, secondly, from the source of the inside information, often the company issuing the security, who knew the information and, thirdly, where the proceeds of the securities transaction are if the proceeds have moved out of the account in which the transaction was conducted. Obtaining information from these three sources and collating it to show an abuse of the market is now routine because of the ease with which such information is shared.

Insider trading

[31.52] Many financial institutions participate in commercial lending activities which may give their officers or employees access to non-public material information about potential commercial borrowers. The institution or an affiliate may also participate in proprietary trading activities which may include trading in the securities of such commercial borrowers. Some of the same officers or employees of the institution may participate in both the commercial lending activities of the institution and the proprietary trading activities of the institution or the affiliate.

Under US law, even if officers or employees of the institution do not actually use the material non-public information, it is required to demonstrate to the applicable regulatory authorities that it has adequate controls in place to prevent an officer or employee possessing material non-public information which has been obtained in connection with its commercial lending activities from using it for personal gain or for the institution's gain in its proprietary trading activities or in the affiliate's trading activities.[180] This subject is also the topic of a short discussion in the Trading Activities Manual published by the Federal Reserve Board's Division of Banking Supervision and Regulation, 'Part V – Supervisory Issues' (March 1994).

The reason for preventing the flow of such information is to prevent 'insider trading' – a term of art which refers to the use of material non-public information in securities trading activities. Generally, insider trading laws prohibit anyone who has acquired material non-public information about an issuer from buying or selling securities of such issuer or from communicating (often referred to as 'tipping') such information to another person who might be expected to buy or sell the issuer's securities unless and until the information is made public. The purpose of this prohibition is to protect the integrity of securities markets.[181]

The penalties for breaching insider trading laws are significant. Individuals who engage in insider trading activities may be subject to (i) civil penalties of up to three times the profit gained or loss avoided in connection with such activities, (ii) a criminal penalty of up to $1 million and (iii) a jail term of up to ten years. The penalties for a company (as well as possibly certain supervisory persons) that failed to take appropriate steps to prevent insider trading include (i) a civil penalty of up to $1 million or three times the gain or loss avoided, whichever is greater and (ii) a criminal penalty of up to $2.5 million. The seriousness of these penalties reflects the gravity with which such breaches are perceived. It should be noted that insider trading laws continue to evolve both in the legislature and in the courts, which are continuously interpreting the rather broad, vague statutes currently in effect.

Traditionally, insider trading law concepts only applied to corporate 'insiders', generally directors, officers or employees of an issuer who had access to material non-public information regarding that issuer. However, insider trading law has evolved to include not only corporate insiders, but virtually anyone who has access

---

180 Both the Comptroller of the Currency and the Federal Reserve Board have directed banks under their supervision to establish ethical wall-type policies and procedures with respect to the investment activities of their trust departments to ensure that information does not flow out of the commercial lending department. The Comptroller of the Currency has stated that:
  'Every national bank exercising fiduciary powers shall adopt written policies and procedures to ensure that the federal securities laws are complied with in connection with any decision or recommendation to purchase or sell any security. Such policies and procedures, in particular, shall ensure the national bank trust departments shall not use material inside information in connection with any decision or recommendation to purchase or sell any security.'
  12 CFR § 9.7(d) (1995); 'Policy Statement Concerning Use of Inside Information' 43 Fed Reg 12755 (17 March 1978), codified as Fed Res Reg Serv § 3-1550 (declaring use of inside information to be an unsound banking practice, but giving member banks flexibility in devising procedures to prevent breaches).
181 The primary underlying federal statutory sources of insider trading prohibitions are found in ss 10(b) and 14(e) of the Securities Exchange Act 1934, as amended ('Exchange Act') and s 17(a) of the Securities Act 1933, as amended. 15 USC §§ 78j, 78n and 77q (2004). These provisions do not specifically mention 'insider trading'. Their application to insider trading activities has evolved through judicial interpretation of the statutes, as well as through rulemaking by the SEC, specifically rules 10b-5 and 14e-3. 17 CFR § 240 10b-5, 14e-3 (2005). In addition, the following additional federal securities laws were enacted in the wake of the insider trading scandals of the 1980s: the Insider Trading Sanctions Act 1984, Pub L 98-376, 98 Stat 1264 (1984) (codified as amended at 15 USC § 78c–78ff (2003)); the Insider Trading and Securities Fraud Enforcement Act 1988, Pub L 100-704, 102 Stat 4677 (1988) (codified as amended in scattered sections of 15 USC) and the Securities Enforcement Remedies and Penny Stock Reform Act 1990, Pub L 101-429, 104 Stat 931 (1990) (codified as amended in scattered sections of 15 USC).

to an issuer's material non-public information.[182] As a result of this wider scope of the interpretation of the term 'insider', directors, officers or employees of the institution or its affiliate who gain access to material non-public information as a result of the institution's commercial lending activities would be subject to prohibitions against using such information or tipping such information to others, as more fully described below.

The standard of materiality

[31.53]   The seminal case setting out the standard for materiality is the Supreme Court's 1976 decision in *TSC Industries Inc v Northway Inc*[183] in which the court stated that '[a]n omitted fact is material if there is a substantial likelihood that a reasonable shareholder would consider it important in deciding how to vote'.[184] This language has formed the basis for the position that material information is any information that a reasonable investor would be likely to consider important in a decision to buy, hold or sell securities. This standard is commonly translated into the following economic terms: material information is any information which could reasonably affect the price of the securities. This practical restatement of the definition of material information highlights one of the difficulties associated with the determination of whether information is 'material' or not.

A regulator or aggrieved plaintiff makes this determination in hindsight when it is obvious how the information ultimately affected the market for the securities. As a result, it is imperative that any securities transaction which could be viewed as one based on material non-public information be carefully reviewed and documented to form the basis for a position that the trade was not based on such material non-public information.

Common examples of information which may be regarded as material include (i) projections of future earnings or losses, (ii) financial liquidity problems, (iii) major marketing changes, (iv) news of a pending or proposed joint venture, (v) merger, acquisition or tender offer, (vi) news of a significant sale of assets or the disposition

---

182 For example, members of creditors' committees in bankruptcy proceedings have been considered insiders for these purposes. See *Re Federated Department Stores Inc*, No 1-90-00130, 1992 Bankr LEXIS 392 (Bankr SD Ohio 20 November 1992) (discussed below).

In the bankruptcy reorganisation proceedings involving the retailers Allied Stores Corpn and Federated Department Stores Inc ('debtors'), the United States Trustee for the District of Ohio argued that members of the pre-merger bondholders committee ('committee') would be breaching their fiduciary obligations as committee members by trading in the securities of the debtors or their affiliates. The United States Bankruptcy Court for the Southern District of Ohio requested comments from the SEC in response to a motion made by committee member Fidelity Management and Research Co ('Fidelity'). Fidelity's motion proposed an information blocking device which was reasonably designed to prevent Fidelity trading personnel from receiving any non-public information through Fidelity's committee personnel and to prevent Fidelity's committee personnel from receiving information regarding Fidelity's trading in securities of the debtors or their affiliates in advance of such trades. The SEC supported Fidelity's motion.

183 426 US 438, 444–450 (1976).

184 Furthermore, the court stated (ibid at 450) that:

'The issue of materiality may be characterised as a mixed question of law and fact, involving as it does the application of a legal standard to a particular set of facts … The determination requires delicate assessments of the inferences a "reasonable shareholder" would draw from a given set of facts and the significance of those inferences to him, and these assessments are peculiarly ones for the trier of fact. Only if the established omissions are "so obviously important to an investor that reasonable minds cannot differ on the question of materiality" is the ultimate issue of materiality appropriately resolved "as a matter of law" by summary judgment.'

of a subsidiary, (vii) changes in dividend policies or the declaration of a stock split or the offering of additional securities, (viii) changes in management, (ix) major personnel changes, (x) significant new products or discoveries, (xi) significant litigation or government investigations or (xii) the gain or loss of a substantial customer or supplier. This information becomes material non-public information when it has not been publicly disclosed.

When is information non-public?

[31.54]   When material information is no longer non-public is as ambiguous as the determination of materiality. 'Non-public' information is any information which has not been generally disclosed to the marketplace. Again, the determination of whether particular information is public is often made with the benefit of hindsight. With this in mind, there are a few general rules which may be helpful in avoiding the characterisation of particular information as non-public.

If the institution suspects it may be in possession of material non-public information relating to an issuer, it would be advisable for it or its affiliate to refrain from trading in such entity's securities for a specific number of days before a public filing relating to such issuer is released. It may also be prudent to refrain from trading in the issuer's securities until at least one full business day after the public filing has been released. The institution should be able to point to some fact that demonstrates that the information has been publicly disclosed. Examples would be the announcement of the information in a newspaper with widespread publication such as the Wall Street Journal, its disclosure on the Dow Jones broad tape or other major news wire service such as Reuters or its public filing with the SEC. Mere rumours printed in a trade press or an announcement by a client or government agency may not be enough. Care should be taken to gather reasonable evidence that the information was no longer non-public if the transaction were to be scrutinised at a later time.

In the context of s 16 of the Exchange Act,[185] the SEC has identified 'window periods' which are specific time periods when there should be the least amount of inside information available about an issuer that is unavailable to the investing public. Some issuers adopt blackout periods during which no employee can trade in the issuer's stock. An example of such a blackout period would be a prohibition against trading in the issuer's stock for a period commencing on the first day of the month in which the quarterly earnings of such issuer are scheduled to be released to the public until the third business day after the public release of the quarterly earnings. The purpose of such blackout periods is to help prevent inadvertent breaches of insider trading laws, as well as to avoid even the appearance of an improper transaction when material information has not yet been disclosed to the public. Even during window periods, many issuers require that employees obtain

---

185 Section 16 of the Exchange Act is designed to discourage corporate insiders from taking advantage of their access to information by engaging in short-term trading in the company's securities. Section 16(a) requires every person who beneficially owns more than 10% of a class of equity securities registered under s 12 of the Exchange Act and every officer and director of every company that has a class of equity securities registered under that section to file certain reports with the SEC detailing such persons' purchases and sales of equity securities of such company. Section 16 only reaches specified combinations of transactions by specific classes of people. It would not apply to the institution's facts unless the institution owned more than 10% of the equity securities of one of its commercial borrowers and such borrowers were registered pursuant to s 12 of the Exchange Act. Nonetheless, the guidelines set out above which are borrowed from the s 16 context may also be useful to the institution's efforts to prevent breaches of applicable insider trading laws.

pre-clearance from the general counsel's office or compliance department before a transaction may be made in such issuer's securities.

Attribution of material non-public information

[31.55]   Financial institutions face a difficult problem with respect to material non-public information because the entire institution may be deemed to have access to any material non-public information in the possession of any one individual or department. Even if an employee trades in securities on behalf of the institution without knowledge of any material non-public information, if an employee in another department possesses material non-public information about the issuer, the second employee's knowledge may be imputed to the financial institution as a whole, including the first employee. If the second employee's knowledge of the inside information is attributed to the financial institution, then it is likely that most tests for insider trading have been met. An ethical wall allows the financial institution to demonstrate that material non-public information from elsewhere in the company did not come into the possession of the employee who made the trading decision on the company's behalf.

The economic benefit of having an effective ethical wall is that it grants a financial institution the opportunity to continue to trade in an issuer's securities notwithstanding the fact that particular individuals associated with the financial institution may possess material non-public information about such issuer. If it is not possible to create and implement an effective ethical wall, it may be necessary for the financial institution to employ an alternative method of avoiding insider trading liability, such as restricting or ceasing its trading activities in the securities of the issuers about which the financial institution as a whole (the institution or the affiliate) may have material non-public information. As explained in greater detail below, many financial institutions protect themselves against insider trading claims through the use of both an ethical wall and the use of restricted and watch lists.

Ethical walls

[31.56]   Financial institutions have adopted a number of procedures to avoid the misuse of material non-public information. The use of ethical walls and restricted lists with varying levels of restrictions have become common. In some rare cases, banks have taken the drastic measure of divestiture of investment activities when participating in banking activities which could or would potentially bring the bank into the possession of material non-public information.

Ethical walls generally

[31.57]   Without employing an effective set of carefully constructed procedures, if an institution, or its affiliate which shares employees with the institution, were to trade in the securities of the commercial borrowers, it would subject itself to a very high risk of being deemed to be in breach of applicable insider trading laws. Ethical walls are a series of procedures which create informational barriers. Constructed and implemented effectively, ethical walls limit and control the flow of material non-public information relating to issuers.

A properly structured and implemented ethical wall may serve as a defence in a lawsuit alleging that an entity used material non-public information in breach of insider trading laws or that an entity breached a fiduciary duty in *failing* to use such material non-public information to benefit the accounts over which a fiduciary duty is exercised.[186]

An ethical wall is created through the adoption and implementation of a series of policies and procedures designed to prevent the flow of material non-public information from one department to another. Generally, the starting point of an effective ethical wall is a detailed policy statement distributed to all relevant personnel stating the company's position with respect to the use of material non-public information and clearly stating that those found breaching the policy will be dismissed from the company or otherwise severely disciplined. Such a policy statement is often supplemented by educational programmes which teach employees how to safeguard confidential information, including an awareness of discussions in public places and preserving the confidentiality of documents.

Routinely, part of the policy is a statement to the effect that confidential information is only shared on a 'need to know basis'. Accordingly, no individual with access to such information would discuss it with an individual who participated in trading decisions unless that person was deemed to need to know such information and, once the information was communicated, such person would be considered to be 'over the wall'. Once an individual has access to confidential information which may be characterised as material non-public information, that person is over the wall and is no longer able to engage in trading activities which might include trading in the securities of the entity about which the company possesses material non-public information. Companies should have and observe established guidelines for bringing individuals over an ethical wall and maintain detailed records as to the names of such individuals and the date on which they were brought over the wall.

An effective ethical wall commonly relies upon physical barriers between trading departments and departments which might come into possession of material non-public information. Such physical barriers may include separate, locked offices, locked cabinets containing sensitive information and segregation of administrative personnel (such as secretaries, word processors, clerical employees and messengers) and restricted computer access. Some companies employ code words or names when discussing confidential information and a minority of companies may include periodic security checks of telephone lines as part of their surveillance reviews.

The SEC has publicly stated that it has not mandated any particular set of informational blocking devices and procedures because the type and formality of such devices and procedures necessarily varies with the size and type of activities of the entity using them. However, the SEC has favourably cited a report published by the Division of Market Regulation specifying minimum elements which should be contained in any effective information blocking device procedure at multi-service broker–dealer firms. According to the report, such procedures should include, at a minimum, (i) substantial control (preferably by the compliance department) of relevant interdepartmental communications, (ii) the review of employee trading through the effective maintenance of some combination of watch, restricted and rumour lists, (iii) memorialisation of ethical wall procedures and documentation of actions taken pursuant to those procedures and (iv) review or restriction of

---

186   SEC rule 10b5-1 provides an affirmative defence to claims of insider trading if the company has an ethical wall. 17 CFR § 240, 10b5-1 (2005).

proprietary trading while the firm is in possession of material non-public information.[187]

The burden of ensuring that such procedures are adequate rests on the company asserting that its ethical wall is effective in insulating its trading activities from the activities through which the company has gained access to material non-public information. It is the responsibility of the company to monitor the effectiveness of its ethical wall and create and maintain sufficient documentation to permit review of both the procedures and the adequacy of monitoring such procedures by the SEC or the self-regulatory organisation responsible for the company.

Small institutions face a particularly difficult task in constructing an effective ethical wall because personnel in the commercial department may also function in the department in which investment decisions are made. Alternatively, the personnel in each department may be in unavoidably close proximity to one another. Such circumstances would be likely to make it impossible to isolate inside information from the commercial lending department to the trading department. The only solution for such institutions is to educate personnel about the prohibitions on the use of inside information until it has been disclosed to the public and refrain from trading in the securities of companies about which anyone within the institution possesses material non-public information. The institution's legal or compliance department should issue a policy statement regarding the prohibition on the use of inside information and ensure that employees sign a statement that they have read and understand the bank's policies in that respect. The effect of this type of policy would be to suspend trading in the securities of a publicly traded company about which inside information is known until such information is disclosed to the public. This is the same result which would arise through the use of a restricted list.

Restricted and watch lists

[31.58]   Restricted and watch lists are additional tools which companies use to prevent breaches of insider trading laws. Generally speaking, a restricted list is a current list of securities in which proprietary, employee and certain solicited customer transactions are restricted or prohibited. A watch list is a current list of securities that generally do not carry trading restrictions, but whose trading is subject to close scrutiny by a company's compliance and/or legal department. Although the dissemination of a watch list is generally limited, a restricted list is usually distributed periodically throughout the company to make employees aware of those securities that they are restricted or prohibited from recommending and/or trading.

A company's procedures should explain why, when and how a security should be placed on and deleted from a restricted or watch list and which activities are prohibited or restricted when a security is on either list. According to the National Association of Securities Dealers, a self-regulatory organisation with oversight responsibility for broker–dealers, the minimum documentation for the use of restricted and watch lists is as follows:

1   reasonable written standards or criteria for placing a security on and deleting a
     security from such lists must be established;

---

187 'Report by the Division of Market Regulation, Securities and Exchange Commission,
    Broker–Dealer Policies and Procedures Designed to Segment the Flow and Prevent the Misuse of
    Material Non-public Information' (1990).

2   restricted list documentation must include the date and time the security was added to and deleted from the list. It should also include the name of each contact person (such as the involved investment banker or research analyst) who was responsible for the addition or deletion and can answer specific questions concerning the timing and circumstances of the addition or deletion;

3   watch list records must include the date the security was added to and deleted from the list. They should also include the name of each contact person (such as the involved investment banker or research analyst) who was responsible for the addition or deletion and can answer specific questions concerning the timing and circumstances of the addition or deletion;

4   the company's rationale for additions to and deletions from the watch and restricted lists need not be recorded as long as the name of the contact person is recorded. This person should know the rationale if questioned by the SEC or a self-regulatory organisation.

The institution's procedures must adequately address how it will monitor employee trading outside the company for transactions in a watch or restricted list security. If the company permits an employee to maintain a securities account with a non-affiliated broker–dealer, it must require the employee to have duplicate confirmations and account statements sent to it as an employer with supervisory responsibility.

The institution's procedures should specify the time period covered and frequency of any review of proprietary and employee trading and the department or person responsible for the review. The procedures should also impose a requirement that the reviewer initial or sign a record reflecting the completion of the review.[188]

Finally, it should be noted that ethical walls and restricted lists may not be a defence to breaches of the US securities laws on underwriting of securities. While there are complex and changing rules about which financial institutions in the United States may participate in this activity, the so-called 'due diligence defence' may not protect an institution if one part of that institution has non-public information that should have been, but was not, disclosed in connection with the offering of a security. The reasons behind this is that rule 10b5-1, which sanctions ethical walls, was not promulgated under the statute governing securities offerings so it is widely believed not to offer a defence to breaches of the securities offering laws.

CONCLUSION

[31.59]   Financial privacy in the United States is found in a patchwork of cases and federal statutes. It is subsumed by the government's powers of investigation and the anti-money laundering laws. Like most matters of US law, financial privacy is fact-specific and multi-layered and requires careful analysis in each instance.

---

188 National Association of Securities Dealers 'Notice to Members No 91-45', National Association of Securities Dealers/New York Stock Exchange 'Joint Memo on Chinese Wall Policies and Procedures' (1991).

32 International Anti-Money Laundering Initiatives

Chris McNeil
Stephen Revell

INTRODUCTION

[32.1]   The current international co-operative effort against money laundering has been unprecedented; the collective will of the worldwide community of nations is being marshalled to combat the US$1.5 trillion laundered annually.[1]

Geo-political issues arising from serious crime, terrorism, drug-related activities and major 'conventional' crime, such as electronic fraud, have produced both national and international initiatives to combat money laundering. The fight against money laundering and terrorist financing has been accepted as a bona fide exception to bank confidentiality. This chapter provides an overview and a discussion of these important exceptions.

INTERNATIONAL INITIATIVES
Background

[32.2]   The proliferation of international crime during the 1990s was fuelled by the growth in international trade, the international transfer of goods, products and services and the reliance on electronic transfers. These free market activities caused financial crime to accelerate exponentially, so much so that, in order to combat money laundering, a high level of cross-border organisation and international co-operation was necessary.

Supranational organisations such as the Financial Action Task Force ('FATF'), the United Nations, the World Bank and the International Monetary Fund co-ordinated an international and high-level response. These institutions and the high-level policy determinants they instituted have shaped national and international anti-money laundering strategies, including the existing strategy of the European Union.

United Nations
Vienna and Palermo Conventions

[32.3]   The first major international initiative was developed by the United Nations and was the UN Convention against Illicit Traffic in Narcotics, Drugs and

---

1 Foreign and Commonwealth Office of the United Kingdom's estimate found at:
  http://www.fco.gov.uk/servlet/Front?pagename=OpenMarket/Xcelerate/ShowPage&c=Page&cid=104
  4901623023.

Psychotropic Substances 1988 ('the Vienna Convention'). The Vienna Convention stipulated that UN member states should criminalise property derived from the sale of narcotic or psychotropic substances.[2]

This initial convention had the weakness of having too narrow a focus with its emphasis on drug-related money laundering. The exposure of high-level political corruption scandals and the occurrence of high levels of criminality undertaken by organised crime galvanised collective international pressure against a range of predicate (ie underlying) criminality. The result of this international pressure culminated in the instrument which became known as the 'Palermo Convention' – the United Nations Convention Against Transnational Organised Crime 2000.

The Palermo Convention expanded the scope of the criminal conduct constituting a predicate offence to money laundering and focused on the criminalisation of money laundering itself. A range of criminal offences, other than simply drug trafficking, were considered as predicate offences to money laundering.

The International Convention for the Suppression of the Financing of Terrorism

[32.4] Ongoing terrorism caused the UN to develop the International Convention for the Suppression for the Financing of Terrorism in December 1999. To attempt to stop terrorist financing, art 2 identifies the collection of funds for a terrorist act as an offence which should be established as criminal under local law.[3] Under art 8, each state is to take measures to identify, detect and seize assets associated with terrorist financing. Again, in order to emphasise that bank confidentiality is not absolute, all states were directed by art 12(2) that the existence of bank secrecy is not of itself sufficient grounds to refuse a request for mutual legal assistance from another member state.

The Convention Against Corruption

[32.5] The existence of large-scale corruption and consequential money laundering scandals compelled the UN to prepare the UN Convention Against Corruption which was adopted by the General Assembly on 31 October 2003. The convention criminalises a number of corrupt acts and requires each UN member state to adopt legislative measures to criminalise the proceeds of crime emanating from corrupt, predicate criminality.[4] Further, under art 40, in an effort to codify the principle that bank confidence is not absolute, each UN member state must ensure that where there are domestic criminal investigations, there exist mechanisms within the legal system to overcome obstacles arising from bank secrecy laws.

The Basle Group of Banking Supervisors

[32.6] As long ago as August 1981, the Basle Group of Banking Supervisors indicated that 'co-operation cannot be complete unless effective arrangements exist for the exchange of information between supervisory authorities about banking activities within their own jurisdictions on a confidential basis'.[5] The view taken by

2 Article 3(1)(b).
3 Article 4(a).
4 Article 23.
5 Basle Committee: banking secrecy and international co-operation in banking supervision.

the Basle Committee was that professional banking secrecy impeded the flow of information from banks to regulators and among regulators themselves. Although money laundering was not the focus of the paper, the banking secrecy impediment to anti-money laundering has been identified and subsequently addressed by FATF recommendation 4.

In December 1988, the Basle Committee prepared a statement of ethical principles described as the 'Prevention of Criminal Use of the Banking System for the Purpose of Money Laundering'. Although the principles were not binding in law, they were to be encouraged and were the expected standards of conduct. In the preamble, the Committee state that 'all members of the Committee firmly believe that supervisors cannot be indifferent to the use of banks by criminals'.

Under its fourth ethical principle, the Basle Committee proposed that it is a necessity for banks to co-operate with law enforcement authorities to the 'extent permitted by specific local regulations relating to customer confidentiality'. The ethical statements suggest that the banker–client relationship is not sacrosanct and therefore it is necessary to consider and have the ability to freeze suspicious clients' accounts, deny assistance to clients and sever client relationships where these actions are consistent with local laws.

THE FATF
Background

[32.7]   The FATF has been the most instrumental organ in developing anti-money laundering principles and applying pressure to encourage legislative reform at a national level. It was established in 1989 in Paris by the Group of Seven ('G-7') nations. It has become the focus of multilateral, anti-money laundering efforts.[6] The heads of state of the G-7, the members of the European Commission and eight other countries originally constituted the task force. The FATF now has 31 member states and two observers.[7]

The FATF 40 recommendations on anti-money laundering and nine special recommendations concerning terrorist financing

[32.8]   The FATF was charged with examining international money laundering techniques and trends and, in 1990, it developed 40 recommendations for combating money laundering. These recommendations were reviewed for the first time six years later in 1996 due to the evolution of money laundering typologies. After the terrorist attacks in September 2001, the scope and mandate of the recommendations expanded and, in 2003, eight special recommendations were developed for implementation. There has since been one further recommendation which was added in October 2004.

---

6 The G-7 consists of France, United States of America, United Kingdom, Germany, Japan, Italy and Canada.

7 The FATF members are Argentina, Australia, Austria, Belgium, Brazil, Canada, Denmark, Finland, France, Germany, Greece, Hong Kong (China), Iceland, Ireland, Italy, Japan, Luxembourg, Mexico, the Netherlands, New Zealand, Norway, Portugal, the Russian Federation, Singapore, South Africa, Spain, Sweden, Switzerland, Turkey, the United Kingdom and the United States of America. Observers are: the Gulf Co-operation Council and the People's Republic of China.

The recommendations are recognised by the World Bank and the International Monetary Fund as being the international standards for anti-money laundering and the FATF is proactive in promoting the recommendations as the best practice standard with which all members must comply. Even unaffiliated, non-member countries must work toward equivalence with the recommendations if they are not to be deemed as being 'non-co-operative'. For example, at the moment, the two countries which are the remaining 'non-co-operative' jurisdictions are Myanmar and Nigeria.

Recommendation 1 concerning predicate criminality

[32.9] FATF recommendation 1 suggests that countries should consider the criminalisation of money laundering in line with the Vienna and Palermo conventions. Additionally, recommendation 1 proposes that countries should consider which underlying offences give rise to a money laundering offence.

Recommendation 1 advocates that countries 'should include all serious offences with a view to including the widest range of predicate (underlying) offences'.

There are five options put forward by the FATF for countries to consider as the basis for determining which offences should constitute a predicate or underlying offence to money laundering, being:

1 all criminal offences; or
2 to a threshold linked to a category of serious offences; or
3 to a threshold linked to a penalty of imprisonment applicable to the predicate offence; or
4 a defined list of predicate offences; or
5 a combination of any of the above approaches.

Notwithstanding the approach that is taken, the FATF suggests countries should include a range of serious offences within the designated categories of offences.[8]

Recommendation 13 concerning reporting suspicious transactions

[32.10] The test proposed for the obligation to report suspicious transactions falls under recommendation 13. Under this provision, it is recommended that where a bank has 'reasonable grounds to suspect' that funds are the proceeds of criminality, the financial institution should be required to report the suspicion to the financial intelligence unit.[9] This recommendation therefore suggests that suspicious transaction reports should be made upon a reasonable suspicion only, not a basis in fact which is far less than what would be required to establish a criminal offence in most jurisdictions. Recommendation 13 impliedly provides that suspicious reporting is an exception to bank confidence, but the test should be based on perceived, rather than proven, criminality.

---

8 Participation in an organised criminal group and racketeering, terrorism including terrorist financing, trafficking human beings and migrant smuggling, sexual exploitation including children, illicit trafficking in narcotic drugs and psychotropic substances, illicit arms trafficking, illicit trafficking in stolen or other goods, corruption and bribery, fraud, counterfeiting currency, piracy of products, environmental crime, murder, grievous bodily injury, kidnapping, illegal restraint and hostage taking, robbery and theft, smuggling, extortion, forgery, piracy, insider dealing and market manipulation.
9 The scope of the recommendation is wider and covers not only banks, but other financial institutions.

By way of further clarity concerning the conflict between bank confidence and reporting requirements, recommendation 4 stipulates that 'countries should ensure that financial institution secrecy laws do not inhibit the implementation of the 40 recommendations'.

Recommendation 14 concerning confidence

[32.11] As a further measure which requires derogation from banking confidentiality, recommendation 14(a) requires that legal provisions should be implemented to protect employees of banks who make suspicious transaction reports from any civil or criminal liability where the report is made in good faith. This protection from liability is recommended to include circumstances where the officers did not comprehend the nature of the predicate criminality or know whether or not it occurred. This recommendation therefore proposes a safe harbour for banks from any proceedings for breach of confidentiality where a suspicious report has been made.

Pursuant to recommendation 14(b), a bank's officers, employees and directors are required to be prohibited by law to divulge to the customer that a suspicious transaction report has been made to the financial intelligence unit. There is no suggestion that the prohibition against 'tipping off' ought to carry criminal penalties as has occurred in some jurisdictions. This further explains the assured acceptance of these qualifications to bank confidentiality.

FATF membership and non-co-operative territories

[32.12] The right to FATF membership is governed by the Organisation for Economic Co-operation and Development. Membership of the task force will only be considered for 'strategically important' countries.[10] This fact has been voiced as a criticism, as it is evidence of the political nature of the FATF and the pervading influence on the task force by the Organisation for Economic Co-operation and Development.

Countries or groups of countries may, however, be admitted as observers. The most recent notable addition was China in February 2005 and it is envisaged that, after evaluation of its anti-money laundering and terrorist financing system, China will be eligible for full membership.[11]

The mutual evaluation process is a centrepiece of FATF membership. Each country voluntarily submits to an assessment of its compliance with the recommendations by other members. The evaluation involves a review of the member's anti-money laundering legislation, systems and controls.

Membership is a considerable privilege. Unfortunately, however, the path to FATF membership and the consequential rights and dispensations it entails is not achieved solely by compliance with the task force's recommendations. The members of the FATF, for example, afford a reduction of client verification requirements for their own regulated entities. This reduction in due diligence requirements is not extended to non-aligned offshore financial centres and consequentially their banks have been significantly affected by the burden of verification requirements imposed on them

---

10 FATF annual report 2003–2004.
11 FATF annual report 2004–2005.

and their clients by FATF members. Some non-member countries have even higher levels of compliance with the recommendations than members.

Another device the task force has used to distance themselves from other countries is to deem a country as being a 'non-co-operative country'. As evidence of the geo-political power and effect of the FATF, by deeming countries 'non-co-operative', the FATF has been able to enforce anti-money laundering legislative development in those countries. In the first non-co-operative territory review in 2000, there were 15 countries designated as being non-co-operative, but this has now been reduced to only Myanmar and Nigeria.[12] The FATF has also issued countermeasures against two countries: Nauru in 2001 and Ukraine in 2002. These countermeasures entailed enhanced monitoring of transactions and stringent client verification requirements, warning that transactions with entities based in the domicile might run the risk of money laundering.[13]

FATF-style regional bodies

[32.13] Following the lead of the FATF, there has been a proliferation of other international groups and collectives which monitor money laundering and co-exist and communicate with the FATF. These groups work principally to ensure that the high-level recommendations are implemented in their regional countries. For the Asia Pacific region, the Asia Pacific Group on Money Laundering was created in 1997. Other regional groups are the Caribbean Financial Action Task Force, the Financial Action Task Force of South America, the Middle East and North Africa Financial Action Task Force, the Eurasian Group, the Select Committee of Experts on the Evaluation of Anti-Money Laundering Measures and the Eastern and South African Anti-Money Laundering Group.

The Wolfsberg Group

[32.14] The Wolfsberg Group was established by 12 private banks in 2000. The group responded to the threat of international money laundering by developing principles, known as the 'Wolfsberg principles', as guidance for private banks in pursuing sound business conduct.[14] These guidelines are comprehensive and the commitment of members of the group to the guidelines provides tremendous leverage in the fight against money laundering.

The World Bank and International Monetary Fund

[32.15] The World Bank has intensified efforts in recent times to prevent crime and terrorism. Funding the activities of criminals and terrorists by money laundering causes incalculable economic and social harm. In recent times, the World Bank has been proactive in fighting financial crime, corruption and curbing money laundering. Large-scale serious international crime is insidious and difficult to control at a

---

12 The original 15 non-co-operative territories being Bahamas, Cayman Islands, Cook Islands, Dominica, Israel, Lebanon, Liechtenstein, Marshall Islands, Nauru, Niue, Panama, Philippines, Russia, St Kitts and Nevis, St Vincent and the Grenadines.

13 Http://www.fatf-gafi.org/dataoecd/45/30/33693959.pdf.

14 The Wolfsberg Group banks are ABN AMRO Group NV, Bank of Tokyo-Mitsubishi Ltd, Barclays Bank, Citigroup, Credit Suisse Group, Deutsche Bank AG, Goldman Sachs, HSBC, JP Morgan Private Bank, Santander Central Hispano, Societe Generale and UBS AG.

national level. Therefore, international organisations such as the World Bank are well placed to train, comment upon, develop and enhance national governance, fraud and corruption strategies.

In this way, the World Bank and International Monetary Fund have jointly, through a 12-month pilot programme commenced in 2003, begun to undertake regular assessments of anti-money laundering and terrorist financing. The process for reviewing a country's anti-money laundering compliance was incorporated into the Financial Sector Assessment Programme. The pilot programme was reassessed in March 2004 and the executive board voted to expand assessment to encompass all of the FATF recommendations and provide technical assistance to countries and regulators.

A review evidenced that the International Monetary Fund and the World Bank were having a positive impact on international anti-money laundering compliance and countries, post review, have responded by developing and improving anti-money laundering standards.

THE INITIAL EUROPEAN RESPONSE – THE FIRST AND SECOND EUROPEAN ANTI-MONEY LAUNDERING DIRECTIVES

[32.16] In response to the international anti-money laundering initiatives, the European Commission announced that it would implement anti-money laundering legislation. The first working of the legislation was aimed at integrating the FATF recommendations and the Vienna Convention into workable legislation to criminalise money laundering throughout the EU. The legislation is known as the 'First Directive'.[15]

First European Money Laundering Directive 91/308/EEC (the 'First Directive')

[32.17] The Council of Economic and Finance Ministers adopted this Directive on 10 June 1991 primarily as a response to the FATF recommendations. It was proposed as a means of protecting financial institutions and markets from being abused by drug trafficking criminals. Member states were to prohibit, but not necessarily criminalise, money laundering.

The scope of the First Directive covered banks and other financial intermediaries[16] and it focused, to its detriment, on the placement stage of money laundering, which is the entry of criminal cash into the financial system. The aim of targeting drug trafficking money launderers also proved to be a weakness as there was a sole focus on money laundering derived from drug-related underlying predicate criminality. In recital 9, however, the Commission did recommend that member states prohibit the laundering of assets of serious organised crime and terrorism.

---

15 91/308/EEC.
16 The first Money Laundering Directive (91/308/EEC) defines credit and financial institutions on the basis of the activities they carry out. The width of the directive was such that it covered almost all financial intermediaries.

The First Directive imposed obligations of:

1   customer verification;
2   suspicious transaction reporting;
3   obligatory training of employees in anti-money laundering matters; and
4   the implementation of anti-money laundering compliance procedures.

With regard to bank confidentiality, arts 5 and 6 of the First Directive require banks to examine suspicious transactions and inform the authorities of any circumstances they discover concerning money laundering. This is therefore mandatory suspicious reporting. Article 9 of the First Directive provides that disclosures made in 'good faith' do not breach any restriction on the disclosure of information or involve liability of any kind. Therefore, reporting suspicious transactions is a clear exception at directive level to bank confidence.[17] Additionally, 'tipping off' or disclosing to any person or third party that a suspicious transaction report has been made to the authorities is prohibited under art 8.[18]

Second European Money Laundering Directive 2001/97/EC (the 'Second Directive')

[32.18]   The Second Directive was an amending directive implemented to address two principal matters. The weakness of the First Directive, in that it focused on drug-related laundering, was realised. Money laundering is not only related to the proceeds of drug trafficking, but also other social evils such as human trafficking, fraud, corruption, gun running, theft, robbery and other serious criminal offences warranting a long term of imprisonment. Therefore, the range of criminal offences was expanded to include all serious crime.

The second matter compelling the amendment was the vulnerability of non-financial professionals to abuse by money launderers. The sector regulated by anti-money laundering legislation was widened to include a range of the professions and high-value dealers: lawyers, notaries, tax advisors and accountants, real estate agents, casinos and dealers in high-value assets, for example, car sellers, jewellers and art dealers.

The failure of the EU to harmonise the approach of the Second Directive within Europe

[32.19]   The distillation of the FATF recommendations by bodies such as the European Commission and finally transposition into national regulations by member states has meant that although the regulations are derived from the same source, various countries have implemented widely different standards.

Within the European Union, the transposition of the Second Directive into enabling legislation within the member states has been fragmented. This patchy adoption has led to 'regulatory arbitrage' where jurisdictions with less stringent anti-money laundering measures, supervision and due diligence requirements have benefited. The legislation is perceived, somewhat unfortunately, as 'red tape' and inhibiting business.

---

17 See recital 15 of the first Money Laundering Directive (91/308/EEC).
18 Article 8 91/308/EEC.

The Commission envisages that there will be a difference in anti-money laundering regulatory requirements between member states. Significantly for international businesses, the consequences of these national differences have been extremely burdensome. The primary concern is the failure to enable mutual recognition within member states for equivalence of anti-money laundering regulations. The result is that compliance processes, especially concerning verification of the identity of customers, are tedious and even where multi-jurisdictional relationships for those same customers exist, verification can be repetitious.

To the detriment of a pan-European approach, not all European Union member states have implemented the Second Directive and, due to non-compliance, infraction proceedings have been commenced against France and Greece.

As the amendments to the First Directive by the Second Directive were foreshadowed prior to the terrorist attacks of 11 September 2001, the additional nine FATF special recommendations concerning terrorist financing were not included in the amendments and this has necessitated a Third Directive which is outlined below.[19]

THIRD EUROPEAN MONEY LAUNDERING DIRECTIVE 2005/60/EC (THE 'THIRD DIRECTIVE')

Rationale for replacing the Second Directive

[32.20]   The Third Directive was published in the Official Journal on 25 October 2005. The Third Directive is substantially different from the two preceding directives and therefore it cannot really be considered to be an amending directive. The changes were comprehensive enough to mean that the new directive will render the preceding directives redundant, although it is looked upon as an ongoing revision.

The necessity for the Third Directive was to incorporate the amendments to the FATF 40 recommendations which took place during 2003 and to include the measures outlined in the additional nine special recommendations concerning terrorist financing. The revision amalgamated anti-money laundering methodology and a framework for the suppression of terrorism.

It is yet to be seen how the latest directive will be transposed nationally. Certainly, criticism has been extended to the implementing measures which enable countries to legislate beyond the scope of the Third Directive. As a consequence for pan-European business, it is likely that there will be different interpretations of the articles during the transposition process leading to assorted and unequal national legislation amongst the member states. The practical effect on business will be detrimental as the positive aspects of the Third Directive, such as the ability for banks to determine their own risk-based approach, will be inhibited by national legislation. The ability for member states to go beyond the articles of the Third Directive means that it can only be considered to be a minimum harmonisation directive.

Suspicious reporting

[32.21]   By obtaining confidential information, businesses, banks and other members of the regulated sector have an obligation to report, under art 22(1)(a),

---

19 2005/60/EC.

where the information gives rise to 'reasonable grounds to suspect that money laundering or terrorist financing' has occurred. Therefore, the confidentiality obligations banks have to their customers are subordinate to suspicious reporting obligations. Therefore, the incriminating information must be reported by the supervised institution to the financial intelligence unit without compunction and of its own volition.

It is not necessary to prove the existence of a predicate criminal offence, simply a reasonable suspicion that predicate criminality has occurred leading to money laundering or terrorist financing compels a suspicious transaction report to be made by the bank.

There are exemption provisions to the mandatory obligation to report suspicious transactions found in art 23(2), principally for notaries, lawyers, auditors, external accountants and tax advisors. The exemptions arise where the information that leads to the suspicion comes in the course of assisting or advising the client in ascertaining its legal position in privileged circumstances. There are no parallel provisions for banks and other financial institutions.

Of considerable importance to confidentiality is art 26 whereby the suspicious transaction disclosures that have been made pursuant to arts 22(1) or 23 shall not be regarded as giving rise to liability in contract or for any legislative, regulatory or administrative provision. Therefore, banks and other members of the regulated sector are protected from any action for breach of confidentiality for a disclosure made in good faith to the financial intelligence unit.

Tipping off

[32.22]   Members of the regulated sector and their employees are prohibited by art 28 from disclosing that a suspicious report has been made either to the customer or a third party. This prohibition is generally known as the prohibition against 'tipping off'. The tipping off provision does not apply to informing the competent authorities or between member states or peculiarly to third countries provided that those third countries meet the criteria defined in art 28(3).[20]

In addition, art 28(4) provides that the prohibition does not apply to individuals within the same legal person or 'network'. A network is defined as a larger structure having common management, ownership or compliance control. Therefore, multinational banking institutions could have the ability to report intra-group suspicious reports and their nature to a central control function internationally without fear of contravening the tipping off provision in the Third Directive.

Further, art 28(5) states that it is permissible for members of the regulated sector, in cases related to the same customer and the same transaction from differing member states or even third countries, to exchange information for the prevention of money laundering or terrorist financing, provided the parties are subject to the same obligations regarding professional secrecy and data protection.

It is not a tipping off offence under art 28(1) where a member of the regulated sector endeavours to dissuade a customer from committing a money laundering offence. This is useful as the 'gatekeepers' are frequently faced with this scenario.

---

20 Third countries belonging to the same group as defined by art 2(12) of Directive 2002/87/EC dated 16 December 2002 on the supplementary supervision of credit institutions, insurance undertakings and investment forms in a financial conglomerate.

Interestingly, member states are to 'inform' one another and the Commission of third countries that they have determined have met the equivalent provisions laid down in art 28(3), (4) and (5). The mechanism for this is not considered and there must be, having regard to the lack of co-ordination of the First and Second Directives, a fair degree of scepticism as to how this will work in practice. Members of the regulated sector should consider carefully the ramifications of the transmission of information to third parties. The Commission may, under the implementing measures of art 40(4), designate that a third country does not meet equivalent conditions and therefore, under art 29, the Commission may prohibit disclosure between members covered by the directive and members from that third country. There were no designations as at 30 April 2006.

Serious crimes

[32.23]   The Third Directive has made some effort in art 3(5) to provide a definition of a serious crime. It is defined as the illegal trafficking of narcotics, activities of criminal organisations, serious fraud, corruption, all offences punishable by the deprivation of liberty for a maximum of more than one year and, in states where there are minimum thresholds, offences punishable by more than six months' imprisonment and any of the serious acts described in arts 1 to 4 of the Framework Decision, for example, gun running, child pornography and people trafficking.[21]

Risk-based approach

[32.24]   One of the central precepts of the Third Directive is the newly-introduced principle that the regulators should give consideration to banks and other members of the regulated sector adopting their own risk assessment and controls to inhibit money laundering and terrorist financing. The development of this principle can be considered as a reaction to the criticism by the regulated sector of the inflexibility of the anti-money laundering regime under the Second Directive, particularly in taking into consideration low-risk circumstances and attributes.

Whilst the adoption of a risk-based approach has merits, there are consequences for both the national regulators and the regulated sector. Regulators, in order for industry to develop the methodology necessary to make the risk assessments, must give guidance and examples of both high and low-risk money laundering typologies, whilst the regulated sector will have to be directly concerned with evaluating and assessing its own risks.

For banks and other businesses within the regulated sector, it will be necessary to risk assess and grade their clients. Whereas a document gathering exercise has proliferated in order to meet the verification requirements of the Second Directive, the risk-based considerations of the Third Directive will be likely to cause greater investment and expenditure in risk methodology and techniques and possibly a reduction of the 'box ticking', paper creating, client approval process engendered by the Second Directive.

Beneficial ownership

[32.25]   According to art 9(1) of the Third Directive, banks should verify the beneficial owners of clients with which they deal prior to the establishment of a

21 2002/475/JHA.

business relationship. There are numerous difficulties with endeavouring to pierce the 'veil of incorporation' prior to the establishment of a business relationship. There will be privacy considerations for the beneficial owners and in some circumstances there may not be an association or relationship between the management and beneficial owners. The verification of the identity of the beneficial owner will require inspecting the original documents for corporate entities, otherwise any real launderer may easily utilise fraud or, if the documents are not inspected, misrepresent to disguise the true beneficiary. Additionally, there are some structures which distinguish the legal and beneficial ownership, for example, trusts and foundations.

Political exposure

[32.26] The existence of political exposure in a transaction is a heightened anti-money laundering scenario enshrined in the Third Directive. Neither of the two preceding anti-money laundering directives addressed the obligation to determine elements of political exposure within a transaction. However, as with the UN Convention Against Corruption, there is clearly an international appetite to ensure that public officials are monitored so that they do not benefit corruptly from their public position.

Pursuant to s 3, art 14(4) of the Third Directive, it will be necessary to have risk-based measures in place to determine whether a customer is a politically exposed person. Additionally, senior management approval of the relationship must occur, as well as determination of the source of wealth and ongoing monitoring of that relationship will also be required. These provisions are almost an exact reproduction of FATF recommendation 6.

The obligation to determine whether there is a politically exposed element to the relationship under art 13(4) does not arise within the 'home jurisdiction', but only, however, for other member states or third countries.[22] This is a weakness; it may therefore be possible in such circumstances for politically exposed persons to transact within their own country without detection and subsequent monitoring.

If risk-based measures are used, it will be crucial to establish whether a relationship is politically exposed and that the beneficial owners of corporate structures are ascertained. Other risk-based measures that can be used are to establish the domicile of the commercial structure or of the individual clients and assess this against perceived corruption within that domicile or secrecy of the commercial structure which may afford anonymity.

The two most pressing issues concerning political exposure are its duration, for example, is it envisaged to continue after the public official has left office and to what extent family members may also be regarded as politically exposed. Neither of these issues is considered in the Third Directive and will either require extensive guidance from regulators or unambiguous policies and procedures from those of the regulated sector, including banks.

Members of the regulated sector have lobbied the European Commission concerning the implementing measures of the Third Directive to consider producing a definitive list identifying politically exposed individuals. The cost and maintenance of such a

---

22 The FATF interpretive notes to the 40 recommendations (2003) suggest that 'countries are encouraged to extend the requirements of recommendation 6 (concerning identification and monitoring of PEPs) to individuals who hold prominent public functions in their own country'.

list by the European Union is regarded as prohibitive, however, it is undoubtedly much more inexpensive than the identification of politically exposed individuals being undertaken singularly and in isolation throughout the thousands of regulated sector businesses within the member states.

Implementing measures

[32.27]   There is also a process for further measures to be implemented by the Commission. This enables the Commission to develop further enabling provisions for a defined period of four years after the publication of the directive in the Official Journal.

The implementing measures are to be in respect of:

1   clarification of the technical definitions (for a six-month period);
2   technical criteria for low and high-risk circumstances; and
3   an assessment for persons carrying out occasional defined business.

This procedure may mean that further codification takes place subsequent to national transposition of the Third Directive.

The challenge for both the European Commission and its member states is to transpose the Third Directive so that all of the members of the regulated sector are encompassed evenly without prejudicing either countries or industry sectors. The failure to do so will impact on the competitiveness of members of the regulated sector within the Union and will significantly inhibit both intra-European business and extra-national European business.

THE EFFECT OF INTERNATIONAL ANTI-MONEY LAUNDERING INITIATIVES ON BANK CONFIDENTIALITY

[32.28]   Participation in criminality by banks is illegal, as it should be in most jurisdictions. In recent times, the high-level, international anti-money laundering initiatives have eroded bank confidentiality to such an extent that anti-money laundering considerations are a bona fide exception to banking confidentiality. This is stated no more unequivocally than in FATF recommendation 4, discussed earlier in this chapter, whereby 'countries should ensure that financial institution secrecy laws do not inhibit the implementation of the recommendations'. This is a wide-ranging suggestion and principally covers a bank's suspicious reporting obligations.

The practical effect and impact of the high-level principles and recommendations is, however, only felt under the transposed national legislation. It is the national legislation which determines the reporting thresholds, for example, FATF recommendation 13 suggests that where a financial institution has 'reasonable grounds to suspect' that funds are the proceeds of criminal activity or terrorist financing, there ought to be a compulsion by law or regulation to report these suspicions to that country's financial intelligence unit. This is an objective threshold and the high-level recommendations do not suggest the practicalities, such as whether countries should impose criminal or civil sanctions for a failure to report a suspicious transaction.

By way of further diminution, according to recommendation 14, financial institutions and their officers and employees ought to be protected by legal provisions from any civil or criminal liability arising from a breach of confidence where a suspicion was reported in good faith to the financial intelligence unit. It is suggested that this protection should extend to whether or not the reporter knew the underlying predicate criminal conduct or whether illegal activity occurred. Indeed, banks within the Wolfsberg Group agree that where suspicious activity is noticed it may be appropriate for the controlled function (reporting officer) to report the business relationship to the authorities, therefore, where the local law allows it, bank confidence in such a circumstance is secondary to suspicious reporting obligations.

THE FUTURE OF ANTI-MONEY LAUNDERING THOUGHT, REGULATION AND THE DEVELOPMENT OF ANTI-MONEY LAUNDERING PRACTICES

[32.29]   Money laundering, terrorist financing and the threat of serious organised crime is such that international efforts have been, and will continue to be, made to counter them. International organised crime and money laundering is like a matrix correlating with banking and financial services. Because it traverses national boundaries, a weakness exists for policing which criminals have exploited. Therefore, international bodies such as the FATF, the United Nations, the IMF and the World Bank will continue to collaborate to ensure that anti-money laundering is promulgated and considered as a serious matter by the world community.

The intersection of geo-political forces and national interests can hardly be more acute than for terrorist financing. In recent times, entire sovereign nations have been labelled the 'central bankers of world terrorism'.[23] Clearly, the recent terrorist atrocities have pushed terrorist financing to the forefront of regulatory compliance.

Whether it is by money laundering or terrorist financing, the FATF recommendations clearly indicate that secrecy and banking confidentiality should not protect the criminal or terrorist. It is therefore a matter for each country to legislate the threshold required for a suspicious transaction report to be made. However, it is recommended that the threshold be on 'reasonable grounds' in order to bring as many matters to the attention of the authorities as possible.

Unequivocally, anti-money laundering compliance will be an ongoing reputation and regulatory consideration for business internationally. It is a constantly evolving regulatory discipline. The combination of international pressure and the catchphrase of 'taking the profit out of crime' give politicians fertile ground for developing further codes. Notwithstanding, there has been a growing chorus of professionals who, while supporting broadly the FATF initiatives, are less than satisfied with some of the disproportionate regulation, especially for low-risk situations.

With there being no respite from the constant regulatory burden of anti-money laundering initiatives, business will have to accede to these high-level principles and ensure that, by lobbying effectively, the more serious criminal and money laundering offences constitute the focus of resources.

---

23 Condoleeza Rice, speaking before the US Senate on 16 February 2006, described Iran as 'the central banker for terrorism'.

Index